Programme for International Student Assessment
Programme international pour le suivi des acquis des élèves

# PISA™ 2006

## Volume 2: Data / *Données*

OECD

ORGANISATION FOR ECONOMIC CO-OPERATION AND DEVELOPMENT
ORGANISATION DE COOPÉRATION ET DE DÉVELOPPEMENT ÉCONOMIQUES

## ORGANISATION FOR ECONOMIC CO-OPERATION AND DEVELOPMENT

The OECD is a unique forum where the governments of 30 democracies work together to address the economic, social and environmental challenges of globalisation. The OECD is also at the forefront of efforts to understand and to help governments respond to new developments and concerns, such as corporate governance, the information economy and the challenges of an ageing population. The Organisation provides a setting where governments can compare policy experiences, seek answers to common problems, identify good practice and work to co-ordinate domestic and international policies.

The OECD member countries are: Australia, Austria, Belgium, Canada, the Czech Republic, Denmark, Finland, France, Germany, Greece, Hungary, Iceland, Ireland, Italy, Japan, Korea, Luxembourg, Mexico, the Netherlands, New Zealand, Norway, Poland, Portugal, the Slovak Republic, Spain, Sweden, Switzerland, Turkey, the United Kingdom and the United States. The Commission of the European Communities takes part in the work of the OECD.

OECD Publishing disseminates widely the results of the Organisation's statistics gathering and research on economic, social and environmental issues, as well as the conventions, guidelines and standards agreed by its members.

> *This work is published on the responsibility of the Secretary-General of the OECD. The opinions expressed and arguments employed herein do not necessarily reflect the official views of the Organisation or of the governments of its member countries.*

Corrigenda to OECD publications may be found on line at: *www.oecd.org/publishing/corrigenda.*

*PISA™, OECD/PISA™ and the PISA logo are trademarks of the Organisation for Economic Co-operation and Development (OECD). All use of OECD trademarks is prohibited without written permission from the OECD.*

© OECD 2007

## ORGANISATION DE COOPÉRATION ET DE DÉVELOPPEMENT ÉCONOMIQUES

L'OCDE est un forum unique en son genre où les gouvernements de 30 démocraties œuvrent ensemble pour relever les défis économiques, sociaux et environnementaux que pose la mondialisation. L'OCDE est aussi à l'avant-garde des efforts entrepris pour comprendre les évolutions du monde actuel et les préoccupations qu'elles font naître. Elle aide les gouvernements à faire face à des situations nouvelles en examinant des thèmes tels que le gouvernement d'entreprise, l'économie de l'information et les défis posés par le vieillissement de la population. L'Organisation offre aux gouvernements un cadre leur permettant de comparer leurs expériences en matière de politiques, de chercher des réponses à des problèmes communs, d'identifier les bonnes pratiques et de travailler à la coordination des politiques nationales et internationales.

Les pays membres de l'OCDE sont : l'Allemagne, l'Australie, l'Autriche, la Belgique, le Canada, la Corée, le Danemark, l'Espagne, les États-Unis, la Finlande, la France, la Grèce, la Hongrie, l'Irlande, l'Islande, l'Italie, le Japon, le Luxembourg, le Mexique, la Norvège, la Nouvelle-Zélande, les Pays-Bas, la Pologne, le Portugal, la République slovaque, la République tchèque, le Royaume-Uni, la Suède, la Suisse et la Turquie. La Commission des Communautés européennes participe aux travaux de l'OCDE.

Les Éditions OCDE assurent une large diffusion aux travaux de l'Organisation. Ces derniers comprennent les résultats de l'activité de collecte de statistiques, les travaux de recherche menés sur des questions économiques, sociales et environnementales, ainsi que les conventions, les principes directeurs et les modèles développés par les pays membres.

> *Cet ouvrage est publié sous la responsabilité du Secrétaire général de l'OCDE. Les opinions et les interprétations exprimées ne reflètent pas nécessairement les vues de l'OCDE ou des gouvernements de ses pays membres.*

Les corrigenda des publications de l'OCDE sont disponibles sur : *www.oecd.org/editions/corrigenda.*

*PISA™, OECD/PISA™ et le logo de PISA sont des marques de l'Organisation de coopération et de développement économiques (OCDE). Toute utilisation de ces marques doit faire l'objet d'une autorisation écrite de l'OCDE.*

© OCDE 2007

# Foreword

In today's global economy, the prosperity of countries now derives to a large extent from their human capital, and to succeed in a rapidly changing world, individuals need to advance their knowledge and skills throughout their lives. Education systems need to lay strong foundations for this, by fostering learning and strengthening the capacity and motivation of young adults to continue learning beyond school. Parents, students, those who teach and who run education systems, and the general public alike therefore need good information on how well their schools prepare students for life. Many countries monitor students' learning in order to provide answers to this question. Comparative international assessments can extend and enrich the national picture by providing a larger context within which to interpret national performance.

In response to this need for cross-nationally comparable evidence on student performance, the Organisation for Economic Co-operation and Development (OECD) launched the OECD Programme for International Student Assessment (PISA™) in 1997. PISA represents a commitment by governments to monitor the outcomes of education systems in terms of student achievement on a regular basis and within an internationally agreed common framework. PISA has now become the most comprehensive and rigorous international programme to assess student performance and to collect data on the student, family and institutional factors that can help to explain differences in performance. The countries participating in PISA together make up close to 90% of the world economy.

*PISA 2006: Science Competencies for Tomorrow's World* presents first results from the most recent PISA survey, which focused on science and also assessed mathematics and reading. It is divided into two volumes. This volume presents the data underlying the analysis that is reported in Volume 1. Volume 1 gives the most comprehensive international picture of science learning today, exploring not only how well students perform, but also their interests in science and their awareness of the opportunities that science competencies bring as well as the environment that schools offer for science learning. Volume 1 places the performance of students, schools and countries in the context of their socio-economic background and identifies important educational policies and practices that are associated with educational success.

Both volumes, as well as the PISA database and sample test questions from the PISA surveys, are available on line at *www.pisa.oecd.org*.

The report is the product of a collaborative effort between the countries participating in PISA, the experts and institutions working within the framework of the PISA Consortium, and the OECD. A full list of those people who contributed to this publication is available in Volume 1 of this report. The report is published on the responsibility of the Secretary-General of the OECD.

**Ryo Watanabe**
*Chair of the PISA Governing Board*

**Barbara Ischinger**
*Director for Education, OECD*

# Avant-propos

Au sein de l'économie mondialisée d'aujourd'hui, la prospérité des nations dépend dans une large mesure de leur capital humain et, pour réussir dans un monde qui évolue rapidement, les individus doivent continuer à étoffer leurs connaissances et compétences tout au long de la vie. Pour ce faire, les systèmes éducatifs ont la responsabilité de poser les bases de cet apprentissage, notamment en équipant les individus de connaissances indispensables et en renforçant la capacité et la volonté des jeunes adultes de continuer à apprendre au-delà de leur formation initiale. Toutes les parties prenantes – les élèves, les parents, les enseignants et les gestionnaires du système éducatif, ainsi que le grand public – doivent être tenues informées de l'efficacité avec laquelle l'école prépare les élèves à la vie d'adulte. De nombreux pays suivent l'évolution de l'apprentissage des élèves afin de mieux appréhender ces enjeux. Les analyses comparatives internationales peuvent étoffer et enrichir les états des lieux réalisés à l'échelon national en offrant un contexte plus large dans lequel interpréter les résultats nationaux.

L'Organisation de coopération et de développement économiques (OCDE) a lancé le Programme international pour le suivi des acquis des élèves (PISA™) en 1997 pour répondre au besoin de données sur la performance des élèves qui soient comparables au niveau international. L'enquête PISA est une nouvelle expression de la volonté des gouvernements des pays de l'OCDE d'étudier, de façon suivie et à l'intérieur d'un cadre conceptuel approuvé par tous, les résultats des systèmes éducatifs en termes d'acquis des élèves. Il s'agit aujourd'hui du programme international le plus complet et le plus rigoureux dans le domaine de l'évaluation des compétences des élèves et la collecte de données sur des facteurs relatifs aux élèves, aux familles et aux établissements en vue d'expliquer les différences de performance d'un pays à l'autre. Les pays prenant part à l'enquête PISA représentent près de 90 % de l'économie mondiale.

*PISA 2006 : Les compétences en sciences, un atout pour réussir* présente les premiers résultats du cycle d'enquête PISA le plus récent, dont le domaine d'évaluation majeur était la culture scientifique mais qui s'est également penché sur les mathématiques et la compréhension de l'écrit. Ce rapport est divisé en deux volumes, le second mettant en avant les données qui sous-tendent les analyses figurant dans le premier. Le Volume 1 fournit la vue d'ensemble internationale sur l'apprentissage des sciences la plus complète à l'heure actuelle, explorant non seulement les performances des élèves mais aussi leur intérêt envers les sciences, leur conscience des débouchés pour l'avenir que peuvent apporter de solides compétences en sciences, ainsi que le cadre proposé par les établissements pour l'enseignement des sciences. Il replace les performances des élèves, des établissements et des pays dans leur contexte socioéconomique et identifie les politiques et pratiques d'éducation importantes qui sont gage de succès éducatif.

Les deux volumes, ainsi que la base de données PISA et des exemples de questionnaires PISA, sont disponibles en ligne à l'adresse *www.pisa.oecd.org*.

Cet ouvrage est le fruit des efforts concertés des pays participant à l'enquête PISA, des experts et des institutions qui œuvrent au sein du consortium PISA et de l'OCDE. La liste complète des personnes ayant contribué à cette publication est disponible dans le Volume 1 du présent rapport. Le présent rapport est publié sous la responsabilité du Secrétaire général de l'OCDE.

**Ryo Watanabe**
*Président du Conseil des pays participants du PISA*

**Barbara Ischinger**
*Directeur, Direction de l'éducation de l'OCDE*

# Table of contents
## Table des matières

7

11

13

17

# Reader's Guide

## Data underlying the figures

This volume presents the data referred to in Chapters 2 to 6 of Volume 1. The data are also available, with additional detail, on the PISA website (*www.pisa.oecd.org*). Five symbols are used to denote missing data:

a   The category does not apply in the country concerned. Data are therefore missing.

c   There are too few observations to provide reliable estimates (*i.e.* there are fewer than 30 students or less than 3 % of students for this cell or too few schools for valid inferences).

m   Data are not available. These data were collected but subsequently removed from the publication for technical reasons.

w   Data have been withdrawn at the request of the country concerned.

x   Data are included in another category or column of the table.

## Calculation of international averages

An OECD average was calculated for most indicators presented in this report. In the case of some indicators, a total representing the OECD area as a whole was also calculated:

▪ The OECD average takes the OECD countries as a single entity, to which each country contributes with equal weight. For statistics such as percentages or mean scores, the OECD average corresponds to the arithmetic mean of the respective country statistics.

▪ The OECD total takes the OECD countries as a single entity, to which each country contributes in proportion to the number of 15-year-olds enrolled in its schools (see Annex A3 for data). It illustrates how a country compares with the OECD area as a whole.

In this publication, the OECD total is generally used when references are made to the overall situation in the OECD area. Where the focus is on comparing performance across education systems, the OECD average is used. In the case of some countries, data may not be available for specific indicators, or specific categories may not apply. Readers should, therefore, keep in mind that the terms OECD average and OECD total refer to the OECD countries included in the respective comparisons.

## Rounding of figures

Because of rounding, some figures in tables may not exactly add up to the totals. Totals, differences and averages are always calculated on the basis of exact numbers and are rounded only after calculation.

All standard errors in this publication have been rounded to two decimal places. Where the value 0.00 is shown, this does not imply that the standard error is zero, but that it is smaller than 0.005.

### Reporting of student data

The report uses "15-year-olds" as shorthand for the PISA target population. PISA covers students who are aged between 15 years 3 months and 16 years 2 months at the time of the assessment and who have completed at least 6 years of formal schooling, regardless of the type of institution in which they are enrolled and of whether they are in full-time or part-time education, of whether they attend academic or vocational programmes, and of whether they attend public or private schools or foreign schools within the country.

### Reporting of school data

The principals of the schools in which students were assessed provided information on their schools' characteristics by completing a school questionnaire. Where responses from school principals are presented in this publication, they are weighted so that they are proportionate to the number of 15-year-olds enrolled in the school.

### Abbreviations used in this report

The following abbreviations are used in this report:

GDP     Gross Domestic Product
ISCED   International Standard Classification of Education
PPP     Purchasing power parity
S.D.    Standard deviation
S.E.    Standard error

### Further documentation

For further information on the PISA assessment instruments and the methods used in PISA, see the *PISA 2006 Technical Report* (OECD, forthcoming) and the PISA website (*www.pisa.oecd.org*).

This report uses the OECD's StatLinks service. Below each table and chart is a url leading to a corresponding Excel workbook containing the underlying data. These urls are stable and will remain unchanged over time. In addition, readers of the *PISA 2006: Science Competencies for Tomorrow's World* e-book will be able to click directly on these links and the workbook will open in a separate window.

# Guide du lecteur

### *Données des figures*

Ce volume présente les données auxquelles il est fait référence dans les Chapitres 2 à 6 du Volume 1. Des détails supplémentaires sont disponibles sur le site Web de l'enquête PISA (*www.pisa.oecd.org*). Les cinq symboles suivants indiquent que des données sont manquantes :

a   la catégorie ne s'applique pas au pays concerné, les données sont donc manquantes ;

c   les observations sont trop peu nombreuses pour calculer des estimations fiables (par exemple, les données portent sur moins de 30 élèves ou 3 % des élèves ou les établissements ne sont pas suffisamment nombreux pour faire des déductions valides) ;

m   les données ne sont pas disponibles. Elles ont été collectées mais ont ensuite été exclues de la publication par des raisons techniques ;

w   les données ont été exclues à la demande du pays concerné ;

x   les données sont incluses dans une autre catégorie ou dans une autre colonne du tableau.

### *Calcul des moyennes internationales*

La moyenne de l'OCDE est calculée pour la plupart des indicateurs présentés dans ce rapport. La valeur totale, calculée à l'échelle de l'OCDE tous pays confondus, est également ajoutée dans certains indicateurs :

- la moyenne de l'OCDE est calculée selon l'hypothèse que les pays membres de l'OCDE constituent une seule entité à laquelle chaque pays contribue dans la même mesure. Dans les statistiques telles que les proportions et les valeurs moyennes, la moyenne de l'OCDE est la moyenne arithmétique des valeurs de tous les pays de l'OCDE ;

- le total de l'OCDE est calculé selon l'hypothèse que les pays de l'OCDE constituent une seule entité à laquelle chaque pays contribue dans une mesure proportionnelle au nombre d'élèves de 15 ans inscrits dans ses établissements d'enseignement (voir l'annexe A3 pour des données chiffrées). Le total de l'OCDE permet de comparer les pays par rapport à la situation générale dans tous les pays de l'OCDE.

Dans ce rapport, le total de l'OCDE est la valeur utilisée lorsqu'il est fait référence à la situation dans l'ensemble des pays de l'OCDE, alors que la moyenne de l'OCDE est la variable employée lorsqu'il s'agit de comparer les performances des systèmes d'éducation entre eux. Par ailleurs, il arrive que les données de certains pays ne soient pas disponibles pour des indicateurs spécifiques ou que des catégories particulières de données ne soient pas applicables. Le lecteur doit garder présent à l'esprit le fait que les termes « moyenne de l'OCDE » et « total de l'OCDE » font référence aux pays inclus dans les comparaisons.

### Arrondis

Dans certains tableaux, il arrive que la somme des chiffres ne corresponde pas exactement au total mentionné en raison des ajustements d'arrondi. Les totaux, les différences et les moyennes sont systématiquement calculés à partir des chiffres exacts. Ils ne sont arrondis qu'une fois calculés.

Toutes les erreurs types présentées dans ce rapport sont arrondies à la deuxième décimale. Si « 0.00 » est indiqué, cela ne signifie pas que l'erreur type est nulle, mais qu'elle est inférieure à 0.005.

### Présentation des données relatives aux élèves

Le rapport désigne la population cible de l'enquête PISA par l'expression générique « les jeunes de 15 ans ». En pratique, il fait référence aux élèves qui avaient entre 15 ans et 3 mois accomplis et 16 ans et 2 mois accomplis au moment de l'évaluation et qui avaient suivi au moins 6 années d'enseignement formel, quels que soient le mode de scolarisation (à temps plein ou à temps partiel), la filière d'enseignement (générale ou professionnelle), ou le type d'établissement (établissement privé, public, ou étranger situé au sein du pays).

### Présentation des données relatives aux établissements

Les chefs d'établissement des élèves soumis à l'évaluation ont été priés de remplir un questionnaire portant sur les caractéristiques de leur établissement. Les réponses des chefs d'établissement présentées dans ce rapport sont pondérées en fonction des effectifs d'élèves de 15 ans inscrits dans leur établissement.

### Abréviations

Les abréviations suivantes sont employées dans ce rapport :

GDP     Produit intérieur brut (PIB)
ISCED   Classification internationale type de l'éducation (CITE)
PPP     Parités de pouvoir d'achat (PPA)
S.D.    Écart type (Éc. T.)
S.E.    Erreur type (Er. T.)

### Autres références

Pour plus d'informations sur les instruments d'évaluation et la méthodologie de l'enquête PISA, il y a lieu de consulter le rapport technique sur le cycle PISA 2006 (*PISA 2006 Technical Report*, OCDE, à paraître) et le site Web de l'enquête PISA (*www.pisa.oecd.org*).

Ce rapport applique le système « StatLinks » de l'OCDE : tous les tableaux et figures sont accompagnés d'un lien hypertexte (URL) qui donne accès à un classeur au format Excel contenant les données de référence. Ces liens sont stables et ne seront pas modifiés à l'avenir. De plus, il suffit aux lecteurs de la version électronique de *PISA 2006 : Les compétences en sciences, un atout pour réussir* de cliquer sur ces liens pour ouvrir les classeurs correspondants dans une autre fenêtre.

# I. Data / *Données*

[Part 1/1]

**Table 2.1a** **Percentage of students at each proficiency level on the science scale**

Tableau 2.1a Pourcentage d'élèves à chaque niveau de compétence sur l'échelle de culture scientifique

| | Proficiency levels | | | | | | | | | | | | |
|---|---|---|---|---|---|---|---|---|---|---|---|---|---|
| | Below Level 1 (below 334.94 score points) | | Level 1 (from 334.94 to 409.54 score points) | | Level 2 (from 409.54 to 484.14 score points) | | Level 3 (from 484.14 to 558.73 score points) | | Level 4 (from 558.73 to 633.33 score points) | | Level 5 (from 633.33 to 707.93 score points) | | Level 6 (above 707.93 score points) | |
| | % | S.E. | % | S.E. | % | S.E. | % | S.E. | % | S.E. | % | S.E. | % | S.E. |
| **OECD** | | | | | | | | | | | | | | |
| Australia | 3.0 | (0.3) | 9.8 | (0.5) | 20.2 | (0.6) | 27.7 | (0.5) | 24.6 | (0.5) | 11.8 | (0.5) | 2.8 | (0.3) |
| Austria | 4.3 | (0.9) | 12.0 | (1.0) | 21.8 | (1.0) | 28.3 | (1.0) | 23.6 | (1.1) | 8.8 | (0.7) | 1.2 | (0.2) |
| Belgium | 4.8 | (0.7) | 12.2 | (0.6) | 20.8 | (0.8) | 27.6 | (0.8) | 24.5 | (0.8) | 9.1 | (0.5) | 1.0 | (0.2) |
| Canada | 2.2 | (0.3) | 7.8 | (0.5) | 19.1 | (0.6) | 28.8 | (0.6) | 27.7 | (0.6) | 12.0 | (0.5) | 2.4 | (0.2) |
| Czech Republic | 3.5 | (0.6) | 12.1 | (0.8) | 23.4 | (1.2) | 27.8 | (1.1) | 21.7 | (0.9) | 9.8 | (0.9) | 1.8 | (0.3) |
| Denmark | 4.3 | (0.6) | 14.1 | (0.8) | 26.0 | (1.1) | 29.3 | (1.0) | 19.5 | (0.9) | 6.1 | (0.7) | 0.7 | (0.2) |
| Finland | 0.5 | (0.1) | 3.6 | (0.4) | 13.6 | (0.7) | 29.1 | (1.1) | 32.2 | (0.9) | 17.0 | (0.7) | 3.9 | (0.3) |
| France | 6.6 | (0.7) | 14.5 | (1.0) | 22.8 | (1.1) | 27.2 | (1.1) | 20.9 | (1.0) | 7.2 | (0.6) | 0.8 | (0.2) |
| Germany | 4.1 | (0.7) | 11.3 | (1.0) | 21.4 | (1.1) | 27.9 | (1.1) | 23.6 | (0.9) | 10.0 | (0.6) | 1.8 | (0.2) |
| Greece | 7.2 | (0.9) | 16.9 | (0.9) | 28.9 | (1.2) | 29.4 | (1.0) | 14.2 | (0.8) | 3.2 | (0.3) | 0.2 | (0.1) |
| Hungary | 2.7 | (0.3) | 12.3 | (0.8) | 26.0 | (1.2) | 31.1 | (1.1) | 21.0 | (0.9) | 6.2 | (0.6) | 0.6 | (0.2) |
| Iceland | 5.8 | (0.5) | 14.7 | (0.8) | 25.9 | (0.7) | 28.3 | (0.9) | 19.0 | (0.7) | 5.6 | (0.5) | 0.7 | (0.2) |
| Ireland | 3.5 | (0.5) | 12.0 | (0.8) | 24.0 | (0.9) | 29.7 | (1.0) | 21.4 | (0.9) | 8.3 | (0.6) | 1.1 | (0.2) |
| Italy | 7.3 | (0.5) | 18.0 | (0.6) | 27.6 | (0.8) | 27.4 | (0.6) | 15.1 | (0.6) | 4.2 | (0.3) | 0.4 | (0.1) |
| Japan | 3.2 | (0.4) | 8.9 | (0.7) | 18.5 | (0.9) | 27.5 | (0.9) | 27.0 | (1.1) | 12.4 | (0.6) | 2.6 | (0.3) |
| Korea | 2.5 | (0.5) | 8.7 | (0.8) | 21.2 | (1.0) | 31.8 | (1.2) | 25.5 | (0.9) | 9.2 | (0.8) | 1.1 | (0.3) |
| Luxembourg | 6.5 | (0.4) | 15.6 | (0.7) | 25.4 | (0.7) | 28.6 | (0.9) | 18.1 | (0.7) | 5.4 | (0.3) | 0.5 | (0.1) |
| Mexico | 18.2 | (1.2) | 32.8 | (0.9) | 30.8 | (1.2) | 14.8 | (0.7) | 3.2 | (0.3) | 0.3 | (0.1) | 0.0 | a |
| Netherlands | 2.3 | (0.4) | 10.7 | (0.9) | 21.1 | (1.0) | 26.9 | (0.9) | 25.8 | (1.0) | 11.5 | (0.8) | 1.7 | (0.2) |
| New Zealand | 4.0 | (0.4) | 9.7 | (0.6) | 19.7 | (0.8) | 25.1 | (0.7) | 23.9 | (0.8) | 13.6 | (0.7) | 4.0 | (0.4) |
| Norway | 5.9 | (0.8) | 15.2 | (0.8) | 27.3 | (0.8) | 28.5 | (1.0) | 17.1 | (0.7) | 5.5 | (0.4) | 0.6 | (0.1) |
| Poland | 3.2 | (0.4) | 13.8 | (0.6) | 27.5 | (0.9) | 29.4 | (1.0) | 19.3 | (0.8) | 6.1 | (0.4) | 0.7 | (0.1) |
| Portugal | 5.8 | (0.8) | 18.7 | (1.0) | 28.8 | (0.9) | 28.8 | (1.2) | 14.7 | (0.9) | 3.0 | (0.4) | 0.1 | (0.1) |
| Slovak Republic | 5.2 | (0.6) | 15.0 | (0.9) | 28.0 | (1.0) | 28.1 | (1.0) | 17.9 | (1.0) | 5.2 | (0.5) | 0.6 | (0.1) |
| Spain | 4.7 | (0.4) | 14.9 | (0.7) | 27.4 | (0.8) | 30.2 | (0.7) | 17.9 | (0.8) | 4.5 | (0.4) | 0.3 | (0.1) |
| Sweden | 3.8 | (0.4) | 12.6 | (0.6) | 25.2 | (0.9) | 29.5 | (0.9) | 21.1 | (0.9) | 6.8 | (0.5) | 1.1 | (0.2) |
| Switzerland | 4.5 | (0.5) | 11.6 | (0.6) | 21.8 | (0.9) | 28.2 | (0.8) | 23.5 | (1.1) | 9.1 | (0.8) | 1.4 | (0.3) |
| Turkey | 12.9 | (0.8) | 33.7 | (1.3) | 31.3 | (1.4) | 15.1 | (1.1) | 6.2 | (1.2) | 0.9 | (0.3) | 0.0 | a |
| United Kingdom | 4.8 | (0.5) | 11.9 | (0.6) | 21.8 | (0.7) | 25.9 | (0.7) | 21.8 | (0.6) | 10.9 | (0.5) | 2.9 | (0.3) |
| United States | 7.6 | (0.9) | 16.8 | (0.9) | 24.2 | (0.9) | 24.0 | (0.8) | 18.3 | (1.0) | 7.5 | (0.6) | 1.5 | (0.2) |
| **OECD total** | 6.9 | (0.3) | 16.3 | (0.3) | 24.2 | (0.4) | 25.1 | (0.3) | 18.7 | (0.3) | 7.4 | (0.2) | 1.4 | (0.1) |
| **OECD average** | 5.2 | (0.1) | 14.1 | (0.1) | 24.0 | (0.2) | 27.4 | (0.2) | 20.3 | (0.1) | 7.7 | (0.1) | 1.3 | (0.0) |
| **Partners** | | | | | | | | | | | | | | |
| Argentina | 28.3 | (2.3) | 27.9 | (1.4) | 25.6 | (1.3) | 13.6 | (1.3) | 4.1 | (0.6) | 0.4 | (0.1) | 0.0 | a |
| Azerbaijan | 19.4 | (1.5) | 53.1 | (1.6) | 22.4 | (1.4) | 4.7 | (0.9) | 0.4 | (0.2) | 0.0 | a | a | a |
| Brazil | 27.9 | (1.0) | 33.1 | (1.0) | 23.8 | (0.9) | 11.3 | (0.9) | 3.4 | (0.4) | 0.5 | (0.2) | 0.0 | (0.0) |
| Bulgaria | 18.3 | (1.7) | 24.3 | (1.3) | 25.2 | (1.2) | 18.8 | (1.1) | 10.3 | (1.1) | 2.6 | (0.5) | 0.4 | (0.2) |
| Chile | 13.1 | (1.1) | 26.7 | (1.5) | 29.9 | (1.2) | 20.1 | (1.4) | 8.4 | (1.0) | 1.8 | (0.3) | 0.1 | (0.1) |
| Colombia | 26.2 | (1.7) | 34.0 | (1.6) | 27.2 | (1.5) | 10.6 | (1.0) | 1.9 | (0.3) | 0.2 | (0.1) | 0.0 | a |
| Croatia | 3.0 | (0.4) | 14.0 | (0.7) | 29.3 | (0.9) | 31.0 | (1.0) | 17.7 | (0.9) | 4.6 | (0.4) | 0.5 | (0.1) |
| Estonia | 1.0 | (0.2) | 6.7 | (0.6) | 21.0 | (0.9) | 33.7 | (1.0) | 26.2 | (0.9) | 10.1 | (0.7) | 1.4 | (0.3) |
| Hong Kong-China | 1.7 | (0.4) | 7.0 | (0.7) | 16.9 | (0.8) | 28.7 | (0.9) | 29.7 | (1.0) | 13.9 | (0.8) | 2.1 | (0.3) |
| Indonesia | 20.3 | (1.7) | 41.3 | (2.2) | 27.5 | (1.5) | 9.5 | (2.0) | 1.4 | (0.5) | 0.0 | a | a | a |
| Israel | 14.9 | (1.2) | 21.2 | (1.0) | 24.0 | (0.9) | 20.8 | (1.0) | 13.8 | (0.8) | 4.4 | (0.5) | 0.8 | (0.2) |
| Jordan | 16.2 | (0.9) | 28.2 | (0.9) | 30.8 | (0.8) | 18.7 | (0.8) | 5.6 | (0.7) | 0.6 | (0.2) | 0.0 | a |
| Kyrgyzstan | 58.2 | (1.6) | 28.2 | (1.1) | 10.0 | (0.8) | 2.9 | (0.4) | 0.7 | (0.2) | 0.0 | a | a | a |
| Latvia | 3.6 | (0.5) | 13.8 | (1.0) | 29.0 | (1.2) | 32.9 | (0.9) | 16.6 | (1.0) | 3.8 | (0.4) | 0.3 | (0.1) |
| Liechtenstein | 2.6 | (1.0) | 10.3 | (2.1) | 21.0 | (2.8) | 28.7 | (2.6) | 25.2 | (2.5) | 10.0 | (1.8) | 2.2 | (0.8) |
| Lithuania | 4.3 | (0.4) | 16.0 | (0.8) | 27.4 | (0.9) | 29.8 | (0.9) | 17.5 | (0.8) | 4.5 | (0.6) | 0.4 | (0.2) |
| Macao-China | 1.4 | (0.2) | 8.9 | (0.5) | 26.0 | (1.0) | 35.7 | (1.1) | 22.8 | (0.7) | 5.0 | (0.3) | 0.3 | (0.1) |
| Montenegro | 17.3 | (0.8) | 33.0 | (1.2) | 31.0 | (0.9) | 14.9 | (0.7) | 3.6 | (0.4) | 0.3 | (0.1) | 0.0 | a |
| Qatar | 47.6 | (0.6) | 31.5 | (0.6) | 13.9 | (0.5) | 5.0 | (0.4) | 1.6 | (0.1) | 0.3 | (0.1) | 0.0 | (0.0) |
| Romania | 16.0 | (1.5) | 30.9 | (1.6) | 31.8 | (1.6) | 16.6 | (1.2) | 4.2 | (0.8) | 0.5 | (0.1) | 0.0 | a |
| Russian Federation | 5.2 | (0.7) | 17.0 | (1.1) | 30.2 | (0.9) | 28.3 | (1.3) | 15.1 | (1.1) | 3.7 | (0.5) | 0.5 | (0.1) |
| Serbia | 11.9 | (0.9) | 26.6 | (1.2) | 32.3 | (1.3) | 21.8 | (1.2) | 6.6 | (0.6) | 0.8 | (0.2) | 0.0 | a |
| Slovenia | 2.8 | (0.3) | 11.1 | (0.7) | 23.1 | (0.7) | 27.6 | (1.1) | 22.5 | (1.1) | 10.7 | (0.6) | 2.2 | (0.3) |
| Chinese Taipei | 1.9 | (0.3) | 9.7 | (0.8) | 18.6 | (0.9) | 27.3 | (0.8) | 27.9 | (1.0) | 12.9 | (0.8) | 1.7 | (0.2) |
| Thailand | 12.6 | (0.8) | 33.5 | (1.0) | 33.2 | (0.9) | 16.3 | (0.8) | 4.0 | (0.4) | 0.4 | (0.1) | 0.0 | a |
| Tunisia | 27.7 | (1.1) | 35.1 | (0.9) | 25.0 | (1.0) | 10.2 | (1.0) | 1.9 | (0.4) | 0.1 | (0.1) | 0.0 | a |
| Uruguay | 16.7 | (1.2) | 25.4 | (1.1) | 29.8 | (1.5) | 19.7 | (1.1) | 6.9 | (0.5) | 1.3 | (0.2) | 0.1 | (0.1) |

StatLink ⟲⟲⟲ http://dx.doi.org/10.1787/142056138443

Pour consulter la version française intégrale de ce tableau, suivre ce lien :
StatLink ⟲⟲⟲ http://dx.doi.org/10.1787/152610887346

[Part 1/2]

**Table 2.1b** Percentage of students at each proficiency level on the science scale, by gender

Tableau 2.1b  Pourcentage d'élèves à chaque niveau de compétence sur l'échelle de culture scientifique, selon le sexe

| | Males – Proficiency levels | | | | | | | | | | | | | |
|---|---|---|---|---|---|---|---|---|---|---|---|---|---|---|
| | Below Level 1 (below 334.94 score points) | | Level 1 (from 334.94 to 409.54 score points) | | Level 2 (from 409.54 to 484.14 score points) | | Level 3 (from 484.14 to 558.73 score points) | | Level 4 (from 558.73 to 633.33 score points) | | Level 5 (from 633.33 to 707.93 score points) | | Level 6 (above 707.93 score points) | |
| | % | S.E. | % | S.E. | % | S.E. | % | S.E. | % | S.E. | % | S.E. | % | S.E. |
| **OECD** | | | | | | | | | | | | | | |
| Australia | 3.6 | (0.4) | 10.3 | (0.6) | 19.7 | (0.9) | 26.6 | (0.9) | 24.2 | (0.7) | 12.3 | (0.7) | 3.3 | (0.4) |
| Austria | 3.6 | (0.8) | 11.6 | (1.3) | 22.7 | (1.6) | 27.5 | (1.3) | 23.3 | (1.4) | 9.7 | (1.0) | 1.6 | (0.3) |
| Belgium | 5.0 | (1.0) | 12.9 | (1.0) | 20.8 | (1.0) | 25.6 | (0.9) | 24.5 | (0.9) | 9.9 | (0.7) | 1.3 | (0.2) |
| Canada | 2.4 | (0.4) | 8.1 | (0.7) | 18.1 | (0.7) | 27.5 | (0.7) | 28.1 | (0.9) | 12.9 | (0.6) | 2.8 | (0.3) |
| Czech Republic | 2.6 | (0.5) | 11.7 | (1.0) | 24.5 | (1.6) | 28.0 | (1.4) | 21.4 | (1.4) | 9.9 | (1.0) | 2.0 | (0.4) |
| Denmark | 4.2 | (0.7) | 13.6 | (1.0) | 24.8 | (1.2) | 28.6 | (1.2) | 21.0 | (1.2) | 7.0 | (0.9) | 0.8 | (0.3) |
| Finland | 0.6 | (0.2) | 4.3 | (0.6) | 14.6 | (0.8) | 28.0 | (1.3) | 30.8 | (1.1) | 17.0 | (1.0) | 4.6 | (0.5) |
| France | 7.5 | (1.0) | 14.5 | (1.2) | 22.2 | (1.4) | 25.3 | (1.5) | 20.9 | (1.3) | 8.5 | (0.8) | 1.1 | (0.3) |
| Germany | 4.4 | (0.8) | 10.5 | (1.1) | 21.6 | (1.2) | 25.9 | (1.2) | 23.8 | (1.4) | 11.5 | (1.0) | 2.2 | (0.4) |
| Greece | 9.3 | (1.3) | 18.9 | (1.3) | 27.2 | (1.2) | 26.4 | (1.4) | 14.2 | (1.1) | 3.7 | (0.5) | 0.3 | (0.1) |
| Hungary | 2.8 | (0.5) | 12.8 | (1.1) | 25.2 | (1.5) | 28.7 | (1.3) | 22.0 | (1.1) | 7.6 | (0.9) | 0.8 | (0.2) |
| Iceland | 6.9 | (0.7) | 15.5 | (1.0) | 25.8 | (1.4) | 26.0 | (1.6) | 19.2 | (1.1) | 5.8 | (0.7) | 0.8 | (0.2) |
| Ireland | 4.1 | (0.7) | 12.5 | (1.3) | 23.2 | (1.2) | 28.8 | (1.2) | 21.1 | (1.1) | 8.9 | (0.9) | 1.4 | (0.3) |
| Italy | 8.0 | (0.7) | 17.5 | (0.9) | 25.9 | (1.0) | 27.4 | (0.9) | 15.8 | (0.7) | 4.9 | (0.4) | 0.6 | (0.1) |
| Japan | 3.6 | (0.6) | 9.2 | (1.0) | 18.1 | (1.1) | 25.8 | (1.1) | 26.5 | (1.5) | 13.7 | (0.9) | 3.3 | (0.5) |
| Korea | 3.2 | (0.7) | 9.2 | (1.0) | 20.8 | (1.6) | 30.2 | (1.4) | 25.5 | (1.3) | 9.9 | (1.1) | 1.3 | (0.4) |
| Luxembourg | 7.0 | (0.6) | 15.1 | (1.0) | 23.8 | (1.2) | 27.2 | (1.3) | 19.6 | (1.1) | 6.6 | (0.6) | 0.8 | (0.2) |
| Mexico | 17.4 | (1.5) | 32.1 | (1.3) | 30.5 | (1.4) | 15.8 | (0.9) | 3.8 | (0.4) | 0.3 | (0.1) | 0.0 | a |
| Netherlands | 2.4 | (0.5) | 9.9 | (1.0) | 20.7 | (1.4) | 27.3 | (1.2) | 24.9 | (1.3) | 13.0 | (1.1) | 2.0 | (0.4) |
| New Zealand | 5.0 | (0.7) | 10.3 | (0.8) | 19.4 | (1.2) | 24.1 | (1.2) | 22.8 | (1.1) | 14.0 | (1.0) | 4.4 | (0.7) |
| Norway | 7.3 | (1.2) | 15.1 | (0.9) | 26.5 | (1.1) | 27.7 | (1.1) | 16.7 | (1.2) | 6.0 | (0.7) | 0.7 | (0.2) |
| Poland | 3.7 | (0.5) | 13.6 | (0.8) | 26.9 | (1.5) | 28.6 | (1.4) | 19.1 | (1.1) | 7.2 | (0.7) | 0.9 | (0.3) |
| Portugal | 5.9 | (0.9) | 18.3 | (1.5) | 28.3 | (1.2) | 27.9 | (1.5) | 15.5 | (1.0) | 3.9 | (0.6) | 0.1 | (0.1) |
| Slovak Republic | 5.5 | (0.9) | 14.6 | (1.1) | 27.0 | (1.5) | 27.4 | (1.4) | 18.8 | (1.4) | 6.0 | (0.8) | 0.8 | (0.3) |
| Spain | 5.2 | (0.5) | 14.4 | (0.9) | 26.4 | (1.0) | 29.7 | (1.0) | 18.7 | (1.0) | 5.1 | (0.5) | 0.5 | (0.2) |
| Sweden | 4.1 | (0.6) | 13.1 | (0.9) | 24.0 | (1.1) | 28.6 | (1.4) | 21.5 | (1.1) | 7.3 | (0.7) | 1.2 | (0.3) |
| Switzerland | 4.6 | (0.6) | 10.9 | (0.6) | 20.8 | (1.1) | 28.5 | (1.1) | 24.0 | (1.2) | 9.7 | (0.9) | 1.4 | (0.3) |
| Turkey | 15.2 | (1.2) | 35.0 | (1.6) | 29.0 | (1.6) | 13.8 | (1.2) | 6.2 | (1.3) | 0.9 | (0.4) | 0.0 | a |
| United Kingdom | 5.3 | (0.7) | 11.4 | (0.9) | 20.5 | (0.8) | 24.1 | (0.9) | 22.5 | (0.8) | 12.3 | (0.8) | 3.7 | (0.5) |
| United States | 8.3 | (1.2) | 17.4 | (1.3) | 22.3 | (1.2) | 23.4 | (1.1) | 18.6 | (1.3) | 8.4 | (0.8) | 1.6 | (0.4) |
| **OECD total** | 7.4 | (0.4) | 16.5 | (0.4) | 23.2 | (0.5) | 24.2 | (0.4) | 18.9 | (0.5) | 8.2 | (0.3) | 1.6 | (0.1) |
| **OECD average** | 5.6 | (0.1) | 14.1 | (0.2) | 23.4 | (0.2) | 26.4 | (0.2) | 20.5 | (0.2) | 8.5 | (0.1) | 1.5 | (0.1) |
| **Partners** | | | | | | | | | | | | | | |
| Argentina | 30.7 | (2.7) | 28.1 | (1.7) | 25.1 | (1.6) | 12.2 | (1.3) | 3.4 | (0.6) | 0.4 | (0.2) | 0.0 | a |
| Azerbaijan | 22.4 | (1.8) | 52.2 | (1.8) | 20.2 | (1.6) | 4.7 | (1.0) | 0.4 | (0.2) | 0.0 | a | a | a |
| Brazil | 26.8 | (1.2) | 31.6 | (1.2) | 24.9 | (1.2) | 11.9 | (1.2) | 4.0 | (0.5) | 0.7 | (0.3) | 0.1 | (0.1) |
| Bulgaria | 21.2 | (2.1) | 25.5 | (1.6) | 23.4 | (1.6) | 17.3 | (1.3) | 9.2 | (1.2) | 2.8 | (0.6) | 0.5 | (0.2) |
| Chile | 10.8 | (1.2) | 25.0 | (1.9) | 29.7 | (1.5) | 22.2 | (1.5) | 9.9 | (1.3) | 2.3 | (0.5) | 0.1 | (0.1) |
| Colombia | 25.2 | (1.9) | 32.2 | (1.4) | 27.6 | (2.0) | 12.3 | (1.5) | 2.5 | (0.5) | 0.2 | (0.1) | 0.0 | a |
| Croatia | 3.4 | (0.7) | 14.8 | (1.0) | 28.8 | (1.2) | 29.7 | (1.2) | 17.9 | (1.0) | 4.7 | (0.5) | 0.7 | (0.2) |
| Estonia | 1.2 | (0.4) | 7.4 | (0.8) | 21.0 | (1.1) | 33.2 | (1.2) | 25.4 | (1.4) | 10.2 | (0.9) | 1.6 | (0.3) |
| Hong Kong-China | 1.9 | (0.5) | 7.3 | (0.8) | 15.9 | (1.1) | 26.8 | (1.1) | 30.4 | (1.3) | 14.7 | (1.1) | 2.8 | (0.5) |
| Indonesia | 18.7 | (2.2) | 39.9 | (3.1) | 28.0 | (2.0) | 11.5 | (3.0) | 1.8 | (0.8) | 0.0 | a | a | a |
| Israel | 16.0 | (1.6) | 21.3 | (1.3) | 21.7 | (1.1) | 19.6 | (1.1) | 14.7 | (1.2) | 5.4 | (0.8) | 1.3 | (0.3) |
| Jordan | 21.6 | (1.4) | 29.2 | (1.4) | 27.8 | (1.2) | 16.2 | (1.2) | 4.6 | (0.9) | 0.6 | (0.3) | 0.0 | a |
| Kyrgyzstan | 60.0 | (1.8) | 26.2 | (1.3) | 9.7 | (1.0) | 3.2 | (0.6) | 1.0 | (0.3) | 0.0 | a | | a |
| Latvia | 4.0 | (0.6) | 15.1 | (1.1) | 29.3 | (1.6) | 31.9 | (1.5) | 15.4 | (1.2) | 4.0 | (0.6) | 0.3 | (0.1) |
| Liechtenstein | 3.0 | (1.7) | 10.2 | (3.9) | 22.8 | (4.6) | 31.0 | (4.4) | 20.8 | (4.1) | 10.6 | (2.8) | 1.5 | (1.2) |
| Lithuania | 4.9 | (0.5) | 17.2 | (1.0) | 27.9 | (1.2) | 28.5 | (1.2) | 16.9 | (1.1) | 4.1 | (0.6) | 0.4 | (0.2) |
| Macao-China | 1.8 | (0.3) | 9.5 | (0.7) | 24.2 | (1.0) | 34.4 | (1.5) | 23.5 | (1.6) | 6.2 | (0.6) | 0.3 | (0.2) |
| Montenegro | 17.7 | (1.0) | 33.1 | (1.5) | 30.4 | (1.4) | 15.0 | (0.9) | 3.5 | (0.5) | 0.3 | (0.2) | a | a |
| Qatar | 57.7 | (1.0) | 26.2 | (1.0) | 9.5 | (0.7) | 4.3 | (0.4) | 1.9 | (0.2) | 0.4 | (0.1) | 0.0 | (0.0) |
| Romania | 17.6 | (1.6) | 30.7 | (1.7) | 29.4 | (1.6) | 16.9 | (1.6) | 4.6 | (0.8) | 0.7 | (0.2) | 0.0 | a |
| Russian Federation | 5.6 | (0.8) | 17.0 | (1.1) | 29.3 | (1.3) | 27.5 | (2.0) | 15.6 | (1.4) | 4.4 | (0.7) | 0.7 | (0.2) |
| Serbia | 12.9 | (1.1) | 27.9 | (1.4) | 31.0 | (1.6) | 20.6 | (1.5) | 6.5 | (0.7) | 1.0 | (0.3) | 0.0 | a |
| Slovenia | 3.2 | (0.4) | 12.1 | (1.0) | 24.0 | (1.1) | 26.6 | (1.6) | 21.5 | (1.5) | 10.2 | (1.0) | 2.4 | (0.5) |
| Chinese Taipei | 2.0 | (0.4) | 9.7 | (1.0) | 17.4 | (0.9) | 26.4 | (1.2) | 28.8 | (1.2) | 13.8 | (1.1) | 2.0 | (0.4) |
| Thailand | 17.1 | (1.6) | 34.7 | (1.4) | 29.1 | (1.2) | 14.9 | (1.0) | 3.8 | (0.6) | 0.5 | (0.2) | 0.0 | a |
| Tunisia | 29.3 | (1.4) | 34.2 | (1.3) | 24.5 | (1.2) | 9.8 | (1.2) | 2.0 | (0.5) | 0.1 | (0.1) | 0.0 | a |
| Uruguay | 18.2 | (1.8) | 25.8 | (1.9) | 27.8 | (1.9) | 18.9 | (1.5) | 7.3 | (0.7) | 1.7 | (0.4) | 0.2 | (0.1) |

StatLink ⚓ http://dx.doi.org/10.1787/142056138443

Pour consulter la version française intégrale de ce tableau, suivre ce lien :
StatLink ⚓ http://dx.doi.org/10.1787/152610887346

[Part 2/2]

**Table 2.1b** Percentage of students at each proficiency level on the science scale, by gender

Tableau 2.1b Pourcentage d'élèves à chaque niveau de compétence sur l'échelle de culture scientifique, selon le sexe

| | Below Level 1 (below 334.94 score points) | | Level 1 (from 334.94 to 409.54 score points) | | Level 2 (from 409.54 to 484.14 score points) | | Level 3 (from 484.14 to 558.73 score points) | | Level 4 (from 558.73 to 633.33 score points) | | Level 5 (from 633.33 to 707.93 score points) | | Level 6 (above 707.93 score points) | |
|---|---|---|---|---|---|---|---|---|---|---|---|---|---|---|
| | % | S.E. | % | S.E. | % | S.E. | % | S.E. | % | S.E. | % | S.E. | % | S.E. |
| Australia | 2.5 | (0.3) | 9.3 | (0.6) | 20.8 | (0.8) | 28.9 | (0.6) | 25.0 | (0.7) | 11.2 | (0.7) | 2.4 | (0.3) |
| Austria | 5.0 | (1.3) | 12.5 | (1.2) | 20.8 | (1.5) | 29.0 | (1.5) | 24.1 | (1.6) | 7.9 | (0.9) | 0.8 | (0.2) |
| Belgium | 4.6 | (0.7) | 11.4 | (0.8) | 20.8 | (1.1) | 29.9 | (1.4) | 24.4 | (1.2) | 8.3 | (0.7) | 0.6 | (0.2) |
| Canada | 1.9 | (0.3) | 7.5 | (0.7) | 20.0 | (0.9) | 30.2 | (0.9) | 27.2 | (0.9) | 11.2 | (0.8) | 2.0 | (0.3) |
| Czech Republic | 4.7 | (0.9) | 12.5 | (1.2) | 22.0 | (1.4) | 27.5 | (1.4) | 22.2 | (1.3) | 9.6 | (1.1) | 1.6 | (0.3) |
| Denmark | 4.5 | (0.8) | 14.5 | (1.0) | 27.1 | (1.3) | 30.0 | (1.3) | 18.1 | (1.1) | 5.2 | (0.7) | 0.6 | (0.3) |
| Finland | 0.4 | (0.2) | 2.8 | (0.5) | 12.6 | (0.9) | 30.3 | (1.3) | 33.7 | (1.3) | 16.9 | (1.0) | 3.3 | (0.5) |
| France | 5.8 | (0.7) | 14.6 | (1.2) | 23.4 | (1.4) | 28.9 | (1.3) | 20.8 | (1.3) | 6.0 | (0.8) | 0.5 | (0.2) |
| Germany | 3.7 | (0.7) | 12.1 | (1.2) | 21.1 | (1.3) | 29.9 | (1.5) | 23.3 | (1.1) | 8.4 | (0.7) | 1.4 | (0.4) |
| Greece | 5.1 | (0.8) | 14.9 | (1.0) | 30.7 | (1.8) | 32.5 | (1.5) | 14.1 | (1.1) | 2.7 | (0.5) | 0.1 | (0.1) |
| Hungary | 2.6 | (0.5) | 11.9 | (1.2) | 26.9 | (1.6) | 33.6 | (1.7) | 19.8 | (1.3) | 4.8 | (0.7) | 0.4 | (0.2) |
| Iceland | 4.7 | (0.7) | 14.0 | (1.1) | 25.9 | (1.2) | 30.5 | (1.5) | 18.8 | (1.0) | 5.4 | (0.8) | 0.7 | (0.3) |
| Ireland | 3.0 | (0.5) | 11.5 | (0.9) | 24.8 | (1.7) | 30.6 | (1.6) | 21.6 | (1.2) | 7.6 | (0.8) | 0.9 | (0.3) |
| Italy | 6.5 | (0.5) | 18.5 | (0.8) | 29.3 | (1.0) | 27.4 | (0.9) | 14.4 | (0.7) | 3.6 | (0.4) | 0.3 | (0.1) |
| Japan | 2.8 | (0.7) | 8.5 | (1.0) | 18.8 | (1.2) | 29.2 | (1.3) | 27.5 | (1.6) | 11.2 | (0.9) | 2.0 | (0.4) |
| Korea | 1.8 | (0.4) | 8.3 | (1.1) | 21.5 | (1.1) | 33.3 | (1.4) | 25.5 | (1.3) | 8.6 | (0.9) | 0.9 | (0.3) |
| Luxembourg | 6.1 | (0.6) | 16.1 | (1.0) | 27.0 | (1.1) | 29.9 | (1.1) | 16.5 | (0.9) | 4.1 | (0.5) | 0.3 | (0.2) |
| Mexico | 18.9 | (1.3) | 33.4 | (1.1) | 31.0 | (1.1) | 13.9 | (0.8) | 2.6 | (0.4) | 0.2 | (0.1) | 0.0 | a |
| Netherlands | 2.2 | (0.5) | 11.5 | (1.2) | 21.6 | (1.2) | 26.6 | (1.3) | 26.8 | (1.3) | 9.9 | (0.8) | 1.3 | (0.3) |
| New Zealand | 3.1 | (0.4) | 9.1 | (0.8) | 20.0 | (1.2) | 26.0 | (1.0) | 24.9 | (1.1) | 13.3 | (1.1) | 3.6 | (0.5) |
| Norway | 4.3 | (0.7) | 15.3 | (1.1) | 28.1 | (1.1) | 29.4 | (1.6) | 17.5 | (1.2) | 4.9 | (0.7) | 0.5 | (0.2) |
| Poland | 2.7 | (0.4) | 13.9 | (0.8) | 28.1 | (1.0) | 30.3 | (1.2) | 19.5 | (1.1) | 5.0 | (0.6) | 0.5 | (0.2) |
| Portugal | 5.6 | (0.9) | 19.0 | (1.1) | 29.3 | (1.2) | 29.8 | (1.5) | 14.0 | (1.2) | 2.2 | (0.3) | 0.0 | (0.0) |
| Slovak Republic | 4.8 | (0.7) | 15.5 | (1.3) | 29.2 | (1.2) | 28.8 | (1.3) | 17.0 | (1.3) | 4.4 | (0.5) | 0.4 | (0.2) |
| Spain | 4.3 | (0.5) | 15.4 | (1.0) | 28.3 | (1.2) | 30.7 | (0.9) | 17.1 | (0.9) | 4.0 | (0.4) | 0.2 | (0.1) |
| Sweden | 3.4 | (0.5) | 12.0 | (0.9) | 26.4 | (1.6) | 30.4 | (1.4) | 20.6 | (1.3) | 6.2 | (0.7) | 1.0 | (0.3) |
| Switzerland | 4.4 | (0.5) | 12.2 | (0.8) | 22.8 | (1.1) | 27.8 | (1.0) | 23.0 | (1.3) | 8.4 | (1.0) | 1.4 | (0.4) |
| Turkey | 10.1 | (1.1) | 32.2 | (1.8) | 34.1 | (1.9) | 16.6 | (1.4) | 6.1 | (1.2) | 0.9 | (0.4) | 0.0 | a |
| United Kingdom | 4.3 | (0.5) | 12.4 | (0.9) | 23.0 | (1.0) | 27.7 | (1.0) | 21.1 | (1.0) | 9.4 | (0.7) | 2.1 | (0.4) |
| United States | 6.8 | (0.4) | 16.2 | (1.1) | 26.2 | (1.2) | 24.6 | (1.0) | 18.0 | (1.0) | 6.7 | (0.8) | 1.5 | (0.4) |
| **OECD total** | **6.3** | **(0.3)** | **16.2** | **(0.3)** | **25.3** | **(0.4)** | **26.1** | **(0.4)** | **18.5** | **(0.3)** | **6.5** | **(0.2)** | **1.1** | **(0.1)** |
| **OECD average** | **4.7** | **(0.1)** | **14.0** | **(0.2)** | **24.7** | **(0.2)** | **28.5** | **(0.2)** | **20.2** | **(0.2)** | **6.9** | **(0.1)** | **1.0** | **(0.1)** |
| Argentina | 26.2 | (2.5) | 27.8 | (1.7) | 26.0 | (1.5) | 14.9 | (1.7) | 4.6 | (0.9) | 0.5 | (0.2) | a | a |
| Azerbaijan | 16.1 | (1.7) | 54.1 | (1.8) | 24.8 | (1.8) | 4.7 | (0.9) | 0.4 | (0.2) | a | a | a | a |
| Brazil | 28.9 | (1.2) | 34.4 | (1.1) | 22.8 | (1.2) | 10.7 | (0.9) | 2.8 | (0.5) | 0.4 | (0.2) | 0.0 | a |
| Bulgaria | 15.2 | (1.8) | 23.1 | (1.9) | 27.0 | (1.8) | 20.5 | (1.6) | 11.4 | (1.5) | 2.4 | (0.5) | 0.4 | (0.2) |
| Chile | 15.7 | (1.4) | 28.6 | (1.5) | 30.1 | (1.5) | 17.6 | (1.6) | 6.6 | (1.0) | 1.2 | (0.4) | 0.1 | (0.1) |
| Colombia | 27.0 | (2.0) | 35.5 | (2.1) | 26.9 | (2.0) | 9.1 | (1.2) | 1.4 | (0.4) | 0.1 | (0.1) | a | a |
| Croatia | 2.6 | (0.5) | 13.1 | (1.2) | 29.7 | (1.5) | 32.3 | (1.4) | 17.5 | (1.2) | 4.4 | (0.6) | 0.4 | (0.1) |
| Estonia | 0.7 | (0.2) | 6.0 | (0.7) | 21.0 | (1.2) | 34.2 | (1.5) | 27.0 | (1.3) | 10.0 | (1.0) | 1.2 | (0.3) |
| Hong Kong-China | 1.5 | (0.3) | 6.7 | (0.8) | 17.9 | (1.1) | 30.5 | (1.6) | 29.1 | (1.3) | 13.0 | (1.2) | 1.3 | (0.3) |
| Indonesia | 22.0 | (1.6) | 42.7 | (1.9) | 27.0 | (1.7) | 7.3 | (1.2) | 1.0 | (0.4) | 0.0 | a | a | a |
| Israel | 13.8 | (1.4) | 21.1 | (1.1) | 26.3 | (1.4) | 22.0 | (1.4) | 12.9 | (1.0) | 3.5 | (0.5) | 0.3 | (0.2) |
| Jordan | 10.8 | (1.0) | 27.1 | (1.2) | 33.7 | (1.0) | 21.2 | (1.3) | 6.5 | (0.7) | 0.7 | (0.2) | 0.0 | a |
| Kyrgyzstan | 56.6 | (1.7) | 29.9 | (1.3) | 10.4 | (0.9) | 2.6 | (0.4) | 0.5 | (0.2) | 0.0 | a | a | a |
| Latvia | 3.2 | (0.6) | 12.7 | (1.2) | 28.7 | (1.5) | 33.9 | (1.3) | 17.7 | (1.2) | 3.7 | (0.5) | 0.2 | (0.1) |
| Liechtenstein | 2.3 | (1.2) | 10.3 | (2.6) | 19.4 | (3.6) | 26.7 | (3.3) | 29.0 | (3.7) | 9.5 | (2.3) | 2.8 | (1.3) |
| Lithuania | 3.8 | (0.6) | 14.8 | (1.3) | 26.8 | (1.4) | 31.1 | (1.2) | 18.1 | (1.2) | 5.0 | (0.8) | 0.4 | (0.2) |
| Macao-China | 1.0 | (0.3) | 8.2 | (0.7) | 27.8 | (1.4) | 36.9 | (1.5) | 22.0 | (1.1) | 3.8 | (0.6) | 0.2 | (0.1) |
| Montenegro | 16.8 | (1.1) | 32.8 | (1.8) | 31.6 | (1.1) | 14.8 | (0.9) | 3.8 | (0.5) | 0.2 | (0.2) | 0.0 | a |
| Qatar | 37.3 | (0.9) | 36.9 | (1.0) | 18.3 | (0.9) | 5.9 | (0.6) | 1.4 | (0.2) | 0.2 | (0.1) | 0.0 | a |
| Romania | 14.3 | (1.9) | 31.2 | (2.0) | 34.2 | (2.5) | 16.2 | (1.5) | 3.9 | (1.0) | 0.2 | (0.1) | a | a |
| Russian Federation | 4.9 | (0.7) | 16.9 | (1.4) | 31.1 | (1.1) | 29.1 | (1.3) | 14.6 | (1.1) | 3.0 | (0.4) | 0.3 | (0.2) |
| Serbia | 10.9 | (1.2) | 25.3 | (1.5) | 33.5 | (1.5) | 23.1 | (1.4) | 6.6 | (0.7) | 0.6 | (0.2) | a | a |
| Slovenia | 2.4 | (0.5) | 10.1 | (0.7) | 22.3 | (0.9) | 28.6 | (1.1) | 23.5 | (1.4) | 11.2 | (1.0) | 1.9 | (0.4) |
| Chinese Taipei | 1.9 | (0.4) | 9.7 | (1.1) | 19.9 | (1.4) | 28.3 | (1.1) | 26.9 | (1.5) | 12.0 | (1.1) | 1.4 | (0.3) |
| Thailand | 9.3 | (0.9) | 32.6 | (1.2) | 36.3 | (1.2) | 17.3 | (1.1) | 4.1 | (0.5) | 0.4 | (0.1) | 0.0 | a |
| Tunisia | 26.2 | (1.4) | 35.9 | (1.4) | 25.4 | (1.3) | 10.6 | (1.3) | 1.8 | (0.6) | 0.1 | (0.1) | a | a |
| Uruguay | 15.3 | (1.3) | 25.0 | (1.2) | 31.7 | (1.9) | 20.5 | (1.5) | 6.5 | (0.7) | 0.9 | (0.3) | 0.1 | (0.1) |

*Females – Proficiency levels*

OECD · Partners

StatLink ▒▒▒▒ http://dx.doi.org/10.1787/142056138443

Pour consulter la version française intégrale de ce tableau, suivre ce lien :
StatLink ▒▒▒▒ http://dx.doi.org/10.1787/152610887346

[Part 1/2]

**Table 2.1c** **Mean score, variation and gender differences in student performance on the science scale**

Tableau 2.1c Score moyen, différences de score selon le sexe et répartition des scores sur l'échelle de culture scientifique

| | All students | | | | Gender differences | | | | | |
| | Mean score | | Standard deviation | | Males | | Females | | Difference (M - F) | |
| | Mean | S.E. | S.D. | S.E. | Mean score | S.E. | Mean score | S.E. | Score dif. | S.E. |
|---|---|---|---|---|---|---|---|---|---|---|
| **OECD** | | | | | | | | | | |
| Australia | 527 | (2.3) | 100 | (1.0) | 527 | (3.2) | 527 | (2.7) | 0 | (3.8) |
| Austria | 511 | (3.9) | 98 | (2.4) | 515 | (4.2) | 507 | (4.9) | 8 | (4.9) |
| Belgium | 510 | (2.5) | 100 | (2.0) | 511 | (3.3) | 510 | (3.2) | 1 | (4.1) |
| Canada | 534 | (2.0) | 94 | (1.1) | 536 | (2.5) | 532 | (2.1) | 4 | (2.2) |
| Czech Republic | 513 | (3.5) | 98 | (2.0) | 515 | (4.2) | 510 | (4.8) | 5 | (5.6) |
| Denmark | 496 | (3.1) | 93 | (1.4) | 500 | (3.6) | 491 | (3.4) | **9** | (3.2) |
| Finland | 563 | (2.0) | 86 | (1.0) | 562 | (2.6) | 565 | (2.4) | -3 | (2.9) |
| France | 495 | (3.4) | 102 | (2.1) | 497 | (4.3) | 494 | (3.6) | 3 | (4.0) |
| Germany | 516 | (3.8) | 100 | (2.0) | 519 | (4.6) | 512 | (3.8) | 7 | (3.7) |
| Greece | 473 | (3.2) | 92 | (2.0) | 468 | (4.5) | 479 | (3.4) | **-11** | (4.7) |
| Hungary | 504 | (2.7) | 88 | (1.6) | 507 | (3.3) | 501 | (3.5) | 6 | (4.2) |
| Iceland | 491 | (1.6) | 97 | (1.2) | 488 | (2.6) | 494 | (2.1) | -6 | (3.4) |
| Ireland | 508 | (3.2) | 94 | (1.5) | 508 | (4.3) | 509 | (3.3) | 0 | (4.3) |
| Italy | 475 | (2.0) | 96 | (1.3) | 477 | (2.8) | 474 | (2.5) | 3 | (3.5) |
| Japan | 531 | (3.4) | 100 | (2.0) | 533 | (4.9) | 530 | (5.1) | 3 | (7.4) |
| Korea | 522 | (3.4) | 90 | (2.4) | 521 | (4.8) | 523 | (3.9) | -2 | (5.5) |
| Luxembourg | 486 | (1.1) | 97 | (0.9) | 491 | (1.8) | 482 | (1.8) | **9** | (2.9) |
| Mexico | 410 | (2.7) | 81 | (1.5) | 413 | (3.2) | 406 | (2.6) | 7 | (2.2) |
| Netherlands | 525 | (2.7) | 96 | (1.6) | 528 | (3.2) | 521 | (3.1) | 7 | (3.0) |
| New Zealand | 530 | (2.7) | 107 | (1.4) | 528 | (3.9) | 532 | (3.6) | -4 | (5.2) |
| Norway | 487 | (3.1) | 96 | (2.0) | 484 | (3.8) | 489 | (3.2) | -4 | (3.4) |
| Poland | 498 | (2.3) | 90 | (1.1) | 500 | (2.7) | 496 | (2.6) | 3 | (2.5) |
| Portugal | 474 | (3.0) | 89 | (1.7) | 477 | (3.7) | 472 | (3.2) | 5 | (3.3) |
| Slovak Republic | 488 | (2.6) | 93 | (1.8) | 491 | (3.9) | 485 | (3.0) | 6 | (4.7) |
| Spain | 488 | (2.6) | 91 | (1.0) | 491 | (2.9) | 486 | (2.7) | 4 | (2.4) |
| Sweden | 503 | (2.4) | 94 | (1.4) | 504 | (2.7) | 503 | (2.9) | 1 | (3.0) |
| Switzerland | 512 | (3.2) | 99 | (1.7) | 514 | (3.3) | 509 | (3.6) | **6** | (2.7) |
| Turkey | 424 | (3.8) | 83 | (3.2) | 418 | (4.6) | 430 | (4.1) | **-12** | (4.1) |
| United Kingdom | 515 | (2.3) | 107 | (1.5) | 520 | (3.0) | 510 | (2.8) | **10** | (3.4) |
| United States | 489 | (4.2) | 106 | (1.7) | 489 | (5.1) | 489 | (4.0) | 1 | (3.5) |
| **OECD total** | 491 | (1.2) | 104 | (0.6) | 492 | (1.4) | 490 | (1.3) | 3 | (1.3) |
| **OECD average** | 500 | (0.5) | 95 | (0.3) | 501 | (0.7) | 499 | (0.6) | 2 | (0.7) |
| **Partners** | | | | | | | | | | |
| Argentina | 391 | (6.1) | 101 | (2.6) | 384 | (6.5) | 397 | (6.8) | **-13** | (5.6) |
| Azerbaijan | 382 | (2.8) | 56 | (1.9) | 379 | (3.1) | 386 | (2.7) | **-8** | (2.0) |
| Brazil | 390 | (2.8) | 89 | (1.9) | 395 | (3.2) | 386 | (2.9) | **9** | (2.3) |
| Bulgaria | 434 | (6.1) | 107 | (3.2) | 426 | (6.6) | 443 | (6.9) | **-17** | (5.8) |
| Chile | 438 | (4.3) | 92 | (1.8) | 448 | (5.4) | 426 | (4.4) | **22** | (4.8) |
| Colombia | 388 | (3.4) | 85 | (1.8) | 393 | (4.1) | 384 | (4.1) | 9 | (4.6) |
| Croatia | 493 | (2.4) | 86 | (1.4) | 492 | (3.3) | 494 | (3.1) | -2 | (4.1) |
| Estonia | 531 | (2.5) | 84 | (1.1) | 530 | (3.1) | 533 | (2.9) | -4 | (3.1) |
| Hong Kong-China | 542 | (2.5) | 92 | (1.9) | 546 | (3.5) | 539 | (3.5) | 7 | (4.9) |
| Indonesia | 393 | (5.7) | 70 | (3.3) | 399 | (8.2) | 387 | (3.7) | 12 | (6.3) |
| Israel | 454 | (3.7) | 111 | (2.0) | 456 | (5.6) | 452 | (4.2) | 3 | (6.5) |
| Jordan | 422 | (2.8) | 90 | (1.9) | 408 | (4.5) | 436 | (3.3) | **-29** | (5.3) |
| Kyrgyzstan | 322 | (2.9) | 84 | (2.0) | 319 | (3.6) | 325 | (3.0) | **-6** | (3.0) |
| Latvia | 490 | (3.0) | 84 | (1.3) | 486 | (3.5) | 493 | (3.2) | -7 | (3.1) |
| Liechtenstein | 522 | (4.1) | 97 | (3.1) | 516 | (7.6) | 527 | (6.3) | -11 | (11.1) |
| Lithuania | 488 | (2.8) | 90 | (1.4) | 483 | (3.1) | 493 | (3.1) | **-9** | (2.8) |
| Macao-China | 511 | (1.1) | 78 | (0.8) | 513 | (1.8) | 509 | (1.6) | 4 | (2.7) |
| Montenegro | 412 | (1.1) | 80 | (0.9) | 411 | (1.7) | 413 | (1.7) | -2 | (2.6) |
| Qatar | 349 | (0.9) | 84 | (0.8) | 334 | (1.2) | 365 | (1.3) | **-32** | (1.9) |
| Romania | 418 | (4.2) | 81 | (2.4) | 417 | (4.1) | 419 | (4.8) | -2 | (3.3) |
| Russian Federation | 479 | (3.7) | 90 | (1.4) | 481 | (4.1) | 478 | (3.7) | 3 | (2.7) |
| Serbia | 436 | (3.0) | 85 | (1.6) | 433 | (3.3) | 438 | (3.8) | -5 | (3.8) |
| Slovenia | 519 | (1.1) | 98 | (1.0) | 515 | (2.0) | 523 | (1.9) | **-8** | (3.2) |
| Chinese Taipei | 532 | (3.6) | 94 | (1.6) | 536 | (4.3) | 529 | (5.1) | 7 | (6.0) |
| Thailand | 421 | (2.1) | 77 | (1.5) | 411 | (3.4) | 428 | (2.5) | **-17** | (3.9) |
| Tunisia | 386 | (3.0) | 82 | (2.0) | 383 | (3.2) | 388 | (3.5) | -5 | (3.4) |
| Uruguay | 428 | (2.7) | 94 | (1.8) | 427 | (4.0) | 430 | (2.7) | -3 | (4.0) |

Note: Values that are statistically significant are indicated in bold (see Annex A3).
*StatLink* http://dx.doi.org/10.1787/142056138443

Pour consulter la version française intégrale de ce tableau, suivre ce lien :
*StatLink* http://dx.doi.org/10.1787/152610887346

[Part 2/2]

**Table 2.1c** Mean score, variation and gender differences in student performance on the science scale

Tableau 2.1c  Score moyen, différences de score selon le sexe et répartition des scores sur l'échelle de culture scientifique

| | | 5th | | 10th | | 25th | | 75th | | 90th | | 95th | |
|---|---|---|---|---|---|---|---|---|---|---|---|---|---|
| | | Score | S.E. | Score | S.E. | Score | S.E. | Score | S.E. | Score | S.E. | Score | S.E. |
| OECD | Australia | 358 | (3.5) | 395 | (3.4) | 459 | (2.6) | 598 | (2.5) | 653 | (2.9) | 685 | (3.4) |
| | Austria | 341 | (9.3) | 378 | (6.2) | 443 | (5.4) | 582 | (4.1) | 633 | (3.6) | 663 | (4.1) |
| | Belgium | 336 | (7.3) | 374 | (5.4) | 442 | (3.8) | 584 | (2.4) | 634 | (2.3) | 660 | (2.7) |
| | Canada | 372 | (4.7) | 410 | (3.7) | 472 | (2.5) | 601 | (2.2) | 651 | (2.4) | 681 | (2.8) |
| | Czech Republic | 350 | (6.0) | 385 | (5.2) | 443 | (4.6) | 583 | (3.9) | 641 | (4.3) | 672 | (4.7) |
| | Denmark | 341 | (5.9) | 373 | (4.8) | 432 | (4.3) | 562 | (2.9) | 615 | (3.7) | 646 | (4.3) |
| | Finland | 419 | (4.4) | 453 | (3.3) | 506 | (2.9) | 622 | (2.5) | 673 | (2.9) | 700 | (3.1) |
| | France | 320 | (6.3) | 359 | (5.5) | 424 | (5.3) | 570 | (4.0) | 623 | (4.0) | 653 | (3.8) |
| | Germany | 345 | (8.1) | 381 | (7.0) | 447 | (5.3) | 587 | (3.6) | 642 | (3.2) | 672 | (3.6) |
| | Greece | 317 | (7.3) | 353 | (5.4) | 413 | (4.4) | 537 | (3.3) | 589 | (4.1) | 619 | (3.8) |
| | Hungary | 358 | (4.4) | 388 | (4.2) | 442 | (3.5) | 566 | (3.3) | 617 | (3.1) | 646 | (4.2) |
| | Iceland | 328 | (4.9) | 364 | (3.1) | 424 | (2.6) | 560 | (2.3) | 614 | (2.9) | 644 | (3.4) |
| | Ireland | 351 | (5.8) | 385 | (4.4) | 444 | (4.6) | 575 | (3.4) | 630 | (3.7) | 660 | (4.9) |
| | Italy | 318 | (3.1) | 351 | (2.8) | 409 | (3.0) | 543 | (2.4) | 598 | (2.6) | 630 | (2.8) |
| | Japan | 356 | (6.1) | 396 | (6.2) | 465 | (5.1) | 603 | (3.1) | 654 | (3.1) | 685 | (3.6) |
| | Korea | 367 | (8.4) | 403 | (5.7) | 462 | (4.1) | 586 | (3.8) | 635 | (4.7) | 662 | (5.9) |
| | Luxembourg | 322 | (3.9) | 358 | (2.8) | 419 | (2.0) | 556 | (2.4) | 609 | (2.8) | 640 | (2.6) |
| | Mexico | 281 | (4.4) | 306 | (4.2) | 354 | (3.6) | 465 | (2.9) | 516 | (3.0) | 544 | (3.5) |
| | Netherlands | 362 | (5.9) | 395 | (5.4) | 456 | (4.7) | 596 | (2.6) | 646 | (3.4) | 675 | (3.6) |
| | New Zealand | 347 | (5.2) | 389 | (4.5) | 455 | (3.6) | 608 | (2.9) | 667 | (3.3) | 699 | (3.1) |
| | Norway | 328 | (7.8) | 365 | (5.6) | 422 | (3.9) | 553 | (3.0) | 610 | (3.5) | 641 | (3.4) |
| | Poland | 352 | (3.8) | 381 | (2.9) | 434 | (2.7) | 562 | (3.1) | 615 | (3.3) | 645 | (3.3) |
| | Portugal | 329 | (5.4) | 357 | (4.8) | 411 | (4.2) | 539 | (3.0) | 588 | (2.9) | 617 | (3.2) |
| | Slovak Republic | 334 | (5.6) | 368 | (3.7) | 426 | (3.2) | 555 | (4.0) | 609 | (4.1) | 638 | (3.9) |
| | Spain | 338 | (4.1) | 370 | (3.7) | 427 | (3.0) | 552 | (3.1) | 604 | (3.0) | 633 | (3.1) |
| | Sweden | 347 | (3.8) | 381 | (4.0) | 439 | (3.3) | 569 | (2.8) | 622 | (2.6) | 654 | (3.4) |
| | Switzerland | 340 | (5.0) | 378 | (4.9) | 445 | (3.9) | 584 | (3.5) | 636 | (3.8) | 665 | (4.6) |
| | Turkey | 301 | (2.8) | 325 | (3.2) | 366 | (2.6) | 475 | (5.8) | 540 | (9.7) | 575 | (9.8) |
| | United Kingdom | 337 | (5.4) | 376 | (4.3) | 441 | (3.2) | 590 | (3.1) | 652 | (2.9) | 685 | (3.5) |
| | United States | 318 | (4.5) | 349 | (5.9) | 412 | (5.4) | 567 | (4.6) | 628 | (4.3) | 662 | (4.8) |
| | **OECD total** | 321 | (1.8) | 354 | (1.9) | 416 | (1.6) | 567 | (1.3) | 626 | (1.3) | 659 | (1.5) |
| | **OECD average** | 340 | (1.0) | 375 | (0.9) | 434 | (0.7) | 568 | (0.6) | 622 | (0.7) | 652 | (0.8) |
| Partners | Argentina | 218 | (9.9) | 259 | (9.0) | 324 | (7.2) | 461 | (6.6) | 520 | (6.5) | 555 | (6.6) |
| | Azerbaijan | 300 | (3.1) | 316 | (2.4) | 344 | (2.6) | 414 | (3.5) | 456 | (6.4) | 485 | (7.3) |
| | Brazil | 254 | (4.5) | 281 | (3.2) | 328 | (2.3) | 447 | (4.5) | 510 | (5.6) | 549 | (5.3) |
| | Bulgaria | 266 | (8.1) | 300 | (7.1) | 358 | (6.4) | 509 | (7.8) | 577 | (8.2) | 612 | (8.3) |
| | Chile | 295 | (4.8) | 323 | (4.1) | 374 | (4.0) | 501 | (5.9) | 560 | (6.5) | 595 | (6.1) |
| | Colombia | 247 | (6.3) | 280 | (4.5) | 332 | (4.8) | 445 | (4.7) | 496 | (4.6) | 528 | (4.7) |
| | Croatia | 354 | (4.5) | 383 | (3.8) | 433 | (3.1) | 553 | (2.7) | 604 | (3.2) | 634 | (3.5) |
| | Estonia | 392 | (4.7) | 422 | (3.8) | 474 | (3.2) | 589 | (3.1) | 640 | (3.3) | 668 | (3.7) |
| | Hong Kong-China | 380 | (6.2) | 418 | (6.1) | 482 | (3.6) | 609 | (2.8) | 655 | (3.5) | 682 | (3.1) |
| | Indonesia | 286 | (4.1) | 307 | (3.5) | 345 | (4.2) | 438 | (8.0) | 488 | (11.8) | 518 | (11.7) |
| | Israel | 275 | (5.7) | 310 | (5.2) | 374 | (4.8) | 535 | (4.6) | 601 | (4.5) | 636 | (5.5) |
| | Jordan | 276 | (5.2) | 309 | (4.0) | 362 | (2.8) | 484 | (3.5) | 537 | (4.5) | 568 | (5.4) |
| | Kyrgyzstan | 191 | (4.9) | 220 | (3.8) | 267 | (3.2) | 372 | (3.3) | 428 | (5.0) | 468 | (6.7) |
| | Latvia | 348 | (5.2) | 380 | (4.2) | 432 | (3.7) | 547 | (3.5) | 597 | (3.5) | 627 | (3.1) |
| | Liechtenstein | 358 | (11.2) | 393 | (12.8) | 457 | (7.3) | 591 | (7.1) | 643 | (9.4) | 675 | (13.4) |
| | Lithuania | 340 | (3.8) | 370 | (3.2) | 425 | (3.3) | 551 | (3.5) | 604 | (4.2) | 633 | (5.5) |
| | Macao-China | 378 | (3.6) | 409 | (2.5) | 458 | (1.9) | 566 | (1.8) | 611 | (1.8) | 635 | (2.6) |
| | Montenegro | 286 | (2.7) | 312 | (2.1) | 355 | (2.2) | 466 | (2.2) | 517 | (3.0) | 549 | (3.7) |
| | Qatar | 229 | (2.1) | 253 | (1.4) | 292 | (1.8) | 396 | (1.4) | 462 | (2.6) | 505 | (4.1) |
| | Romania | 291 | (4.5) | 314 | (5.0) | 361 | (5.2) | 473 | (5.7) | 526 | (5.7) | 557 | (8.2) |
| | Russian Federation | 333 | (5.6) | 364 | (5.4) | 418 | (4.4) | 541 | (4.2) | 596 | (3.9) | 627 | (4.2) |
| | Serbia | 297 | (4.9) | 327 | (4.0) | 377 | (3.8) | 495 | (3.9) | 545 | (4.4) | 576 | (4.0) |
| | Slovenia | 358 | (3.8) | 391 | (2.8) | 449 | (2.7) | 589 | (2.1) | 647 | (3.3) | 680 | (3.0) |
| | Chinese Taipei | 369 | (4.5) | 402 | (5.0) | 466 | (5.3) | 602 | (3.4) | 651 | (2.7) | 676 | (3.4) |
| | Thailand | 300 | (4.0) | 325 | (3.4) | 368 | (2.8) | 471 | (3.3) | 524 | (3.8) | 554 | (4.2) |
| | Tunisia | 254 | (4.2) | 283 | (3.4) | 328 | (2.9) | 440 | (4.2) | 495 | (6.0) | 527 | (6.9) |
| | Uruguay | 274 | (4.7) | 306 | (4.4) | 363 | (4.1) | 493 | (3.3) | 550 | (3.6) | 583 | (4.2) |

Note: Values that are statistically significant are indicated in bold (see Annex A3).
StatLink ━━━ http://dx.doi.org/10.1787/142056138443

Pour consulter la version française intégrale de ce tableau, suivre ce lien :
StatLink ━━━ http://dx.doi.org/10.1787/152610887346

[Part 1/1]

**Table 2.2a** **Percentage of students at each proficiency level on the *identifying scientific issues* scale**

Tableau 2.2a Pourcentage d'élèves à chaque niveau de compétence sur l'échelle d'*identification des questions d'ordre scientifique*

| | Proficiency levels | | | | | | | | | | | | |
|---|---|---|---|---|---|---|---|---|---|---|---|---|---|
| | Below Level 1 (below 334.94 score points) | | Level 1 (from 334.94 to 409.54 score points) | | Level 2 (from 409.54 to 484.14 score points) | | Level 3 (from 484.14 to 558.73 score points) | | Level 4 (from 558.73 to 633.33 score points) | | Level 5 (from 633.33 to 707.93 score points) | | Level 6 (above 707.93 score points) | |
| | % | S.E. | % | S.E. | % | S.E. | % | S.E. | % | S.E. | % | S.E. | % | S.E. |
| **OECD** | | | | | | | | | | | | | | |
| Australia | 2.5 | (0.2) | 8.1 | (0.4) | 18.7 | (0.6) | 28.5 | (0.6) | 26.6 | (0.6) | 12.6 | (0.5) | 3.1 | (0.4) |
| Austria | 3.3 | (0.6) | 12.2 | (0.9) | 23.9 | (1.2) | 30.7 | (1.2) | 23.1 | (1.1) | 6.4 | (0.8) | 0.3 | (0.1) |
| Belgium | 4.5 | (0.8) | 10.5 | (0.6) | 21.2 | (0.8) | 28.5 | (0.8) | 24.0 | (0.7) | 9.7 | (0.5) | 1.5 | (0.2) |
| Canada | 2.9 | (0.3) | 8.0 | (0.5) | 18.9 | (0.6) | 29.3 | (0.6) | 26.6 | (0.7) | 11.6 | (0.6) | 2.7 | (0.3) |
| Czech Republic | 4.4 | (0.8) | 13.4 | (0.9) | 24.9 | (1.2) | 28.4 | (1.2) | 20.5 | (1.0) | 7.3 | (0.7) | 1.2 | (0.3) |
| Denmark | 4.4 | (0.5) | 13.7 | (0.9) | 26.3 | (1.0) | 31.5 | (0.9) | 18.6 | (0.8) | 5.1 | (0.6) | 0.4 | (0.2) |
| Finland | 0.9 | (0.2) | 4.0 | (0.4) | 14.5 | (0.7) | 30.6 | (0.9) | 32.9 | (1.1) | 14.5 | (0.7) | 2.6 | (0.3) |
| France | 6.7 | (0.7) | 13.7 | (0.9) | 21.9 | (1.0) | 27.2 | (1.2) | 21.4 | (1.0) | 7.9 | (0.7) | 1.2 | (0.3) |
| Germany | 4.5 | (0.8) | 11.3 | (0.8) | 22.2 | (0.8) | 29.2 | (1.0) | 23.6 | (1.0) | 7.9 | (0.6) | 1.3 | (0.2) |
| Greece | 8.1 | (0.8) | 16.5 | (0.8) | 29.3 | (0.9) | 30.0 | (0.9) | 13.7 | (0.8) | 2.2 | (0.3) | 0.1 | (0.1) |
| Hungary | 3.9 | (0.6) | 14.2 | (0.8) | 31.1 | (1.0) | 33.6 | (1.0) | 14.8 | (0.8) | 2.3 | (0.4) | 0.1 | (0.1) |
| Iceland | 6.6 | (0.6) | 14.0 | (0.8) | 24.7 | (0.9) | 27.1 | (0.8) | 19.2 | (0.7) | 7.3 | (0.5) | 1.1 | (0.2) |
| Ireland | 3.0 | (0.4) | 10.7 | (0.8) | 23.2 | (1.1) | 29.2 | (0.8) | 22.9 | (0.9) | 9.2 | (0.7) | 1.8 | (0.3) |
| Italy | 8.2 | (0.5) | 17.0 | (0.6) | 27.9 | (0.7) | 26.8 | (0.7) | 15.3 | (0.7) | 4.4 | (0.4) | 0.5 | (0.1) |
| Japan | 4.8 | (0.8) | 9.7 | (0.7) | 19.4 | (0.9) | 27.0 | (1.0) | 24.9 | (1.0) | 11.5 | (0.7) | 2.5 | (0.3) |
| Korea | 3.0 | (0.5) | 8.8 | (0.8) | 21.3 | (0.9) | 32.2 | (1.1) | 25.4 | (1.1) | 8.2 | (0.8) | 1.1 | (0.3) |
| Luxembourg | 5.8 | (0.4) | 15.8 | (0.6) | 27.6 | (0.8) | 29.5 | (0.9) | 16.9 | (0.8) | 4.1 | (0.3) | 0.3 | (0.1) |
| Mexico | 15.1 | (1.0) | 29.0 | (0.9) | 32.8 | (0.9) | 18.0 | (0.7) | 4.5 | (0.4) | 0.5 | (0.1) | 0.0 | (0.0) |
| Netherlands | 3.2 | (0.6) | 9.0 | (0.8) | 19.4 | (1.1) | 26.0 | (1.3) | 25.3 | (1.1) | 13.6 | (0.8) | 3.5 | (0.4) |
| New Zealand | 3.4 | (0.4) | 8.9 | (0.6) | 18.5 | (0.7) | 25.5 | (0.9) | 25.1 | (1.0) | 14.2 | (0.8) | 4.3 | (0.4) |
| Norway | 5.3 | (0.8) | 14.5 | (0.8) | 27.2 | (0.9) | 29.5 | (1.0) | 17.7 | (0.9) | 5.2 | (0.6) | 0.6 | (0.2) |
| Poland | 4.0 | (0.4) | 15.7 | (0.9) | 30.4 | (0.8) | 30.8 | (0.9) | 15.7 | (0.8) | 3.1 | (0.4) | 0.2 | (0.1) |
| Portugal | 4.8 | (0.6) | 15.7 | (0.9) | 27.7 | (1.0) | 29.4 | (1.1) | 17.6 | (1.0) | 4.5 | (0.5) | 0.3 | (0.1) |
| Slovak Republic | 7.0 | (0.8) | 15.8 | (1.1) | 29.5 | (1.2) | 28.9 | (1.1) | 15.2 | (1.2) | 3.5 | (0.4) | 0.2 | (0.1) |
| Spain | 4.5 | (0.3) | 13.8 | (0.7) | 27.9 | (0.7) | 32.1 | (0.6) | 17.5 | (0.7) | 3.9 | (0.4) | 0.3 | (0.1) |
| Sweden | 4.7 | (0.4) | 13.1 | (0.8) | 25.4 | (1.1) | 29.7 | (1.1) | 19.7 | (0.9) | 6.5 | (0.5) | 1.0 | (0.2) |
| Switzerland | 3.7 | (0.4) | 10.6 | (0.6) | 21.4 | (0.9) | 29.9 | (0.8) | 24.4 | (1.0) | 9.0 | (0.7) | 1.0 | (0.2) |
| Turkey | 11.2 | (0.9) | 31.2 | (1.2) | 34.2 | (1.3) | 18.1 | (1.2) | 4.9 | (0.9) | 0.5 | (0.2) | a | a |
| United Kingdom | 4.8 | (0.5) | 11.3 | (0.4) | 22.5 | (0.6) | 26.6 | (0.8) | 22.0 | (0.7) | 10.1 | (0.5) | 2.7 | (0.3) |
| United States | 5.6 | (0.7) | 16.0 | (1.1) | 25.2 | (0.9) | 26.7 | (0.9) | 18.4 | (0.9) | 6.9 | (0.6) | 1.2 | (0.3) |
| **OECD total** | 6.3 | (0.2) | 15.6 | (0.3) | 25.1 | (0.3) | 26.6 | (0.3) | 18.5 | (0.3) | 6.7 | (0.2) | 1.2 | (0.1) |
| **OECD average** | 5.2 | (0.1) | 13.5 | (0.1) | 24.6 | (0.2) | 28.3 | (0.2) | 20.0 | (0.2) | 7.1 | (0.1) | 1.3 | (0.0) |
| **Partners** | | | | | | | | | | | | | | |
| Argentina | 25.3 | (2.0) | 28.6 | (1.1) | 27.7 | (1.3) | 14.1 | (1.2) | 4.0 | (0.6) | 0.4 | (0.2) | 0.0 | a |
| Azerbaijan | 38.9 | (2.1) | 42.8 | (1.6) | 15.8 | (1.2) | 2.4 | (0.4) | 0.2 | (0.1) | 0.0 | a | a | a |
| Brazil | 25.3 | (1.1) | 30.1 | (1.3) | 27.1 | (1.2) | 12.9 | (0.9) | 4.0 | (0.5) | 0.6 | (0.2) | 0.0 | (0.0) |
| Bulgaria | 20.8 | (2.0) | 23.9 | (1.2) | 24.5 | (1.2) | 18.7 | (1.2) | 9.3 | (1.0) | 2.5 | (0.6) | 0.3 | (0.1) |
| Chile | 11.2 | (0.9) | 24.3 | (1.2) | 32.2 | (0.9) | 22.0 | (1.1) | 8.7 | (0.9) | 1.6 | (0.4) | 0.1 | (0.1) |
| Colombia | 22.4 | (1.4) | 28.1 | (1.2) | 30.3 | (1.2) | 15.1 | (1.0) | 3.6 | (0.5) | 0.5 | (0.2) | 0.0 | a |
| Croatia | 3.1 | (0.5) | 13.5 | (0.8) | 29.2 | (0.9) | 31.5 | (1.0) | 17.7 | (0.8) | 4.5 | (0.5) | 0.6 | (0.1) |
| Estonia | 1.1 | (0.2) | 7.8 | (0.7) | 24.6 | (0.9) | 36.9 | (0.9) | 23.9 | (1.0) | 5.5 | (0.6) | 0.3 | (0.1) |
| Hong Kong-China | 3.7 | (0.5) | 9.2 | (0.6) | 18.6 | (0.8) | 28.3 | (1.0) | 25.7 | (0.9) | 12.0 | (0.8) | 2.5 | (0.4) |
| Indonesia | 22.3 | (1.7) | 37.0 | (1.7) | 28.5 | (1.3) | 10.5 | (1.7) | 1.5 | (0.5) | 0.2 | (0.2) | a | a |
| Israel | 14.8 | (1.0) | 20.0 | (0.7) | 24.2 | (0.8) | 21.4 | (0.9) | 13.8 | (0.9) | 4.6 | (0.5) | 1.1 | (0.2) |
| Jordan | 19.7 | (0.9) | 29.6 | (1.2) | 30.6 | (1.2) | 16.1 | (0.9) | 3.7 | (0.5) | 0.3 | (0.1) | a | a |
| Kyrgyzstan | 55.3 | (1.5) | 28.6 | (1.1) | 12.1 | (0.8) | 3.3 | (0.5) | 0.6 | (0.2) | 0.1 | (0.0) | 0.0 | a |
| Latvia | 3.9 | (0.6) | 13.6 | (1.0) | 29.1 | (1.0) | 33.0 | (1.2) | 17.1 | (1.1) | 3.1 | (0.4) | 0.2 | (0.1) |
| Liechtenstein | 2.7 | (0.8) | 7.8 | (1.6) | 23.2 | (2.6) | 30.4 | (2.7) | 25.6 | (3.1) | 8.7 | (1.9) | 1.6 | (0.8) |
| Lithuania | 4.9 | (0.5) | 17.0 | (1.0) | 30.6 | (1.0) | 31.1 | (1.0) | 14.0 | (0.9) | 2.3 | (0.3) | 0.1 | (0.1) |
| Macao-China | 2.8 | (0.3) | 13.0 | (0.8) | 30.4 | (0.9) | 33.9 | (0.9) | 17.1 | (0.7) | 2.6 | (0.4) | 0.1 | (0.1) |
| Montenegro | 21.5 | (0.8) | 32.6 | (1.1) | 29.2 | (0.9) | 13.9 | (0.7) | 2.6 | (0.4) | 0.2 | (0.1) | a | a |
| Qatar | 43.8 | (0.6) | 35.3 | (1.1) | 14.8 | (0.7) | 4.6 | (0.3) | 1.2 | (0.2) | 0.2 | (0.1) | 0.0 | a |
| Romania | 16.7 | (1.4) | 33.8 | (1.6) | 32.7 | (1.4) | 14.1 | (1.4) | 2.6 | (0.6) | 0.1 | (0.1) | a | a |
| Russian Federation | 7.6 | (0.8) | 19.9 | (1.2) | 31.4 | (0.8) | 26.8 | (1.1) | 11.8 | (1.0) | 2.3 | (0.3) | 0.2 | (0.1) |
| Serbia | 12.6 | (1.0) | 25.7 | (1.0) | 35.4 | (1.0) | 21.1 | (1.2) | 5.0 | (0.5) | 0.3 | (0.1) | a | a |
| Slovenia | 2.0 | (0.2) | 9.5 | (0.7) | 23.5 | (0.7) | 31.8 | (1.0) | 24.7 | (1.1) | 7.6 | (0.6) | 0.9 | (0.2) |
| Chinese Taipei | 4.1 | (0.6) | 12.2 | (0.9) | 21.9 | (0.8) | 29.5 | (1.0) | 23.5 | (0.9) | 7.9 | (0.6) | 0.9 | (0.2) |
| Thailand | 17.1 | (0.9) | 31.4 | (1.0) | 31.6 | (1.0) | 15.8 | (0.9) | 3.7 | (0.5) | 0.3 | (0.1) | 0.0 | a |
| Tunisia | 28.9 | (1.5) | 33.6 | (1.2) | 24.6 | (0.9) | 10.3 | (0.9) | 2.4 | (0.5) | 0.2 | (0.1) | 0.0 | a |
| Uruguay | 15.9 | (1.2) | 26.4 | (1.0) | 29.4 | (1.1) | 19.6 | (0.9) | 7.4 | (0.6) | 1.2 | (0.3) | 0.1 | (0.1) |

*StatLink* ᗧᕕᒿ http://dx.doi.org/10.1787/142056138443

Pour consulter la version française intégrale de ce tableau, suivre ce lien :
*StatLink* ᗧᕕᒿ http://dx.doi.org/10.1787/152610887346

[Part 1/2]

**Table 2.2b** **Percentage of students at each proficiency level on the *identifying scientific issues* scale, by gender**

Tableau 2.2b  Pourcentage d'élèves à chaque niveau de compétence sur l'échelle d'*identification des questions d'ordre scientifique*, selon le sexe

| | | Males – Proficiency levels | | | | | | | | | | | | |
|---|---|---|---|---|---|---|---|---|---|---|---|---|---|---|
| | | Below Level 1 (below 334.94 score points) | | Level 1 (from 334.94 to 409.54 score points) | | Level 2 (from 409.54 to 484.14 score points) | | Level 3 (from 484.14 to 558.73 score points) | | Level 4 (from 558.73 to 633.33 score points) | | Level 5 (from 633.33 to 707.93 score points) | | Level 6 (above 707.93 score points) | |
| | | % | S.E. | % | S.E. | % | S.E. | % | S.E. | % | S.E. | % | S.E. | % | S.E. |
| OECD | Australia | 3.6 | (0.4) | 9.6 | (0.6) | 20.2 | (0.7) | 27.7 | (0.9) | 25.1 | (0.8) | 11.1 | (0.7) | 2.7 | (0.5) |
| | Austria | 3.8 | (0.7) | 14.2 | (1.1) | 26.8 | (1.7) | 29.8 | (1.6) | 19.8 | (1.4) | 5.2 | (0.7) | 0.3 | (0.2) |
| | Belgium | 5.5 | (1.2) | 11.9 | (1.0) | 21.9 | (1.2) | 27.0 | (0.9) | 23.3 | (0.9) | 8.8 | (0.7) | 1.6 | (0.3) |
| | Canada | 3.8 | (0.5) | 9.1 | (0.6) | 19.2 | (0.7) | 29.0 | (0.9) | 25.8 | (0.9) | 10.8 | (0.8) | 2.3 | (0.3) |
| | Czech Republic | 4.8 | (0.9) | 14.9 | (1.2) | 27.1 | (1.6) | 27.6 | (1.6) | 18.4 | (1.3) | 6.2 | (0.7) | 1.0 | (0.3) |
| | Denmark | 5.1 | (0.8) | 15.6 | (1.1) | 25.9 | (1.2) | 30.3 | (1.3) | 18.1 | (1.1) | 4.5 | (0.8) | 0.3 | (0.2) |
| | Finland | 1.3 | (0.3) | 5.8 | (0.6) | 17.2 | (1.0) | 31.7 | (1.0) | 29.7 | (1.1) | 12.1 | (0.9) | 2.1 | (0.3) |
| | France | 8.4 | (1.1) | 15.1 | (1.3) | 22.7 | (1.5) | 24.7 | (1.4) | 19.8 | (1.2) | 8.0 | (0.8) | 1.2 | (0.3) |
| | Germany | 5.5 | (1.0) | 12.6 | (1.0) | 23.1 | (1.1) | 28.3 | (1.2) | 22.3 | (1.2) | 6.9 | (0.7) | 1.3 | (0.3) |
| | Greece | 11.5 | (1.1) | 19.7 | (1.4) | 29.4 | (1.2) | 25.9 | (1.2) | 11.6 | (1.0) | 1.7 | (0.4) | 0.1 | (0.1) |
| | Hungary | 4.8 | (0.9) | 16.7 | (1.2) | 30.6 | (1.3) | 31.2 | (1.3) | 14.5 | (1.1) | 2.2 | (0.6) | 0.1 | a |
| | Iceland | 9.0 | (0.9) | 16.6 | (1.4) | 25.4 | (1.3) | 25.1 | (1.3) | 17.0 | (1.0) | 6.0 | (0.7) | 0.8 | (0.3) |
| | Ireland | 4.1 | (0.6) | 12.2 | (1.0) | 24.1 | (1.3) | 28.6 | (1.2) | 20.8 | (1.1) | 8.6 | (1.0) | 1.7 | (0.4) |
| | Italy | 10.4 | (0.8) | 18.7 | (0.8) | 27.0 | (1.0) | 25.0 | (1.0) | 14.2 | (0.8) | 4.3 | (0.4) | 0.5 | (0.1) |
| | Japan | 5.8 | (0.9) | 11.3 | (1.0) | 20.5 | (1.1) | 26.3 | (1.2) | 23.1 | (1.2) | 10.7 | (1.1) | 2.3 | (0.4) |
| | Korea | 4.3 | (0.7) | 10.5 | (1.0) | 22.3 | (1.3) | 32.0 | (1.4) | 22.9 | (1.6) | 7.0 | (0.9) | 0.9 | (0.3) |
| | Luxembourg | 7.4 | (0.5) | 16.6 | (0.9) | 27.3 | (1.3) | 28.3 | (1.3) | 16.2 | (1.2) | 3.9 | (0.5) | 0.3 | (0.1) |
| | Mexico | 16.3 | (1.4) | 30.1 | (1.4) | 31.4 | (1.2) | 17.4 | (0.9) | 4.3 | (0.4) | 0.5 | (0.1) | 0.0 | (0.0) |
| | Netherlands | 3.6 | (0.7) | 9.7 | (1.1) | 20.2 | (1.3) | 26.9 | (1.5) | 24.0 | (1.2) | 12.6 | (1.1) | 3.0 | (0.6) |
| | New Zealand | 4.4 | (0.6) | 11.1 | (0.8) | 19.9 | (1.1) | 24.9 | (1.5) | 23.0 | (1.2) | 13.0 | (1.4) | 3.7 | (0.5) |
| | Norway | 7.4 | (1.1) | 16.8 | (1.1) | 27.3 | (1.3) | 27.7 | (1.2) | 15.5 | (1.1) | 4.9 | (0.7) | 0.4 | (0.3) |
| | Poland | 5.3 | (0.6) | 17.6 | (1.1) | 30.2 | (1.2) | 28.9 | (1.1) | 14.6 | (0.8) | 3.1 | (0.5) | 0.2 | (0.1) |
| | Portugal | 6.0 | (0.9) | 17.2 | (1.2) | 28.1 | (1.2) | 28.0 | (1.3) | 16.3 | (1.1) | 4.2 | (0.7) | 0.3 | (0.2) |
| | Slovak Republic | 8.8 | (1.2) | 17.8 | (1.4) | 29.9 | (1.4) | 27.1 | (1.6) | 13.3 | (1.2) | 2.9 | (0.4) | 0.2 | (0.1) |
| | Spain | 6.0 | (0.5) | 14.9 | (1.0) | 28.7 | (1.0) | 30.1 | (1.0) | 16.3 | (0.9) | 3.8 | (0.4) | 0.3 | (0.1) |
| | Sweden | 5.7 | (0.6) | 15.0 | (1.0) | 26.0 | (1.4) | 28.1 | (1.4) | 18.4 | (1.2) | 6.0 | (0.5) | 0.8 | (0.3) |
| | Switzerland | 4.1 | (0.5) | 11.4 | (0.8) | 21.9 | (1.0) | 30.3 | (1.0) | 23.3 | (1.0) | 8.0 | (0.8) | 0.9 | (0.2) |
| | Turkey | 15.2 | (1.4) | 34.5 | (1.7) | 31.5 | (1.7) | 14.8 | (1.5) | 3.9 | (1.0) | 0.2 | (0.1) | a | a |
| | United Kingdom | 5.8 | (0.7) | 12.3 | (0.8) | 21.9 | (0.9) | 25.8 | (1.2) | 21.1 | (1.2) | 10.3 | (0.8) | 2.8 | (0.4) |
| | United States | 7.3 | (0.9) | 18.1 | (1.6) | 24.2 | (1.4) | 25.0 | (1.4) | 17.9 | (1.2) | 6.6 | (0.7) | 0.9 | (0.2) |
| | **OECD total** | 7.7 | (0.3) | 17.3 | (0.4) | 24.9 | (0.4) | 25.3 | (0.4) | 17.4 | (0.3) | 6.3 | (0.2) | 1.1 | (0.1) |
| | **OECD average** | 6.5 | (0.2) | 15.3 | (0.2) | 25.1 | (0.2) | 27.1 | (0.2) | 18.5 | (0.2) | 6.5 | (0.1) | 1.1 | (0.1) |
| Partners | Argentina | 29.9 | (2.3) | 29.9 | (1.4) | 25.4 | (1.6) | 11.7 | (1.3) | 2.7 | (0.7) | 0.3 | (0.2) | 0.0 | a |
| | Azerbaijan | 41.6 | (2.3) | 41.9 | (1.9) | 14.0 | (1.2) | 2.4 | (0.6) | 0.2 | (0.1) | 0.0 | a | a | a |
| | Brazil | 27.3 | (1.3) | 29.9 | (1.6) | 25.9 | (1.8) | 12.3 | (1.1) | 3.8 | (0.7) | 0.7 | (0.3) | 0.1 | a |
| | Bulgaria | 25.9 | (2.4) | 25.4 | (1.4) | 22.9 | (1.7) | 15.7 | (1.3) | 7.9 | (0.9) | 1.9 | (0.5) | 0.2 | (0.1) |
| | Chile | 11.0 | (1.1) | 23.9 | (1.6) | 31.9 | (1.2) | 22.6 | (1.3) | 8.9 | (1.1) | 1.6 | (0.4) | 0.1 | (0.1) |
| | Colombia | 23.1 | (1.8) | 28.7 | (1.7) | 28.6 | (1.6) | 15.0 | (1.3) | 4.0 | (0.6) | 0.6 | (0.2) | a | a |
| | Croatia | 4.5 | (0.7) | 16.4 | (1.4) | 30.8 | (1.3) | 30.0 | (1.3) | 14.6 | (1.0) | 3.2 | (0.4) | 0.4 | (0.1) |
| | Estonia | 1.6 | (0.4) | 10.6 | (1.0) | 27.1 | (1.4) | 35.9 | (1.3) | 20.3 | (1.2) | 4.1 | (0.7) | 0.2 | (0.1) |
| | Hong Kong-China | 4.6 | (0.8) | 10.1 | (1.1) | 19.9 | (1.3) | 27.5 | (1.3) | 25.2 | (1.3) | 10.5 | (1.0) | 2.1 | (0.4) |
| | Indonesia | 21.2 | (2.2) | 36.1 | (2.3) | 28.7 | (1.6) | 12.1 | (2.8) | 1.6 | (0.8) | 0.4 | (0.4) | a | a |
| | Israel | 17.3 | (1.6) | 21.2 | (1.3) | 22.5 | (1.3) | 19.2 | (1.2) | 13.5 | (1.1) | 5.0 | (0.7) | 1.4 | (0.3) |
| | Jordan | 25.9 | (1.6) | 30.3 | (1.4) | 27.6 | (1.4) | 13.0 | (1.5) | 2.9 | (0.7) | 0.2 | (0.1) | a | a |
| | Kyrgyzstan | 60.8 | (1.8) | 25.5 | (1.4) | 9.8 | (0.9) | 3.1 | (0.6) | 0.7 | (0.2) | 0.1 | (0.1) | 0.0 | a |
| | Latvia | 5.5 | (0.8) | 17.5 | (1.4) | 31.4 | (1.4) | 30.0 | (1.7) | 13.5 | (1.3) | 2.0 | (0.5) | 0.2 | (0.1) |
| | Liechtenstein | 4.0 | (1.6) | 8.8 | (3.7) | 25.1 | (5.6) | 32.5 | (4.1) | 22.2 | (4.6) | 6.8 | (2.7) | 0.5 | a |
| | Lithuania | 6.4 | (0.7) | 19.8 | (1.1) | 32.4 | (1.3) | 28.5 | (1.2) | 11.1 | (1.2) | 1.6 | (0.4) | 0.1 | (0.1) |
| | Macao-China | 4.0 | (0.5) | 15.1 | (1.0) | 30.8 | (1.6) | 31.3 | (1.4) | 16.4 | (1.1) | 2.3 | (0.5) | 0.1 | (0.1) |
| | Montenegro | 24.3 | (1.1) | 34.4 | (1.3) | 26.6 | (1.3) | 12.7 | (1.1) | 2.0 | (0.5) | 0.1 | a | a | a |
| | Qatar | 55.1 | (1.2) | 29.8 | (1.5) | 9.9 | (0.8) | 3.8 | (0.4) | 1.2 | (0.2) | 0.2 | (0.1) | 0.0 | a |
| | Romania | 20.5 | (1.7) | 34.8 | (2.2) | 29.9 | (1.9) | 12.3 | (1.4) | 2.3 | (0.6) | 0.2 | (0.2) | a | a |
| | Russian Federation | 9.8 | (1.2) | 22.3 | (1.6) | 31.0 | (1.2) | 24.2 | (1.2) | 10.3 | (1.2) | 2.2 | (0.4) | 0.1 | (0.1) |
| | Serbia | 15.5 | (1.2) | 28.5 | (1.2) | 33.5 | (1.4) | 18.1 | (1.2) | 4.2 | (0.5) | 0.3 | (0.1) | a | a |
| | Slovenia | 3.0 | (0.4) | 11.9 | (0.8) | 26.1 | (1.0) | 31.0 | (1.6) | 21.3 | (1.7) | 6.0 | (0.6) | 0.7 | (0.2) |
| | Chinese Taipei | 4.9 | (0.8) | 12.6 | (1.0) | 21.7 | (1.0) | 29.3 | (1.4) | 23.1 | (1.1) | 7.7 | (0.8) | 0.8 | (0.3) |
| | Thailand | 25.0 | (1.6) | 33.6 | (1.6) | 25.8 | (1.4) | 12.4 | (1.5) | 3.0 | (0.6) | 0.1 | (0.1) | a | a |
| | Tunisia | 33.2 | (1.8) | 33.9 | (1.4) | 22.3 | (1.2) | 8.6 | (0.9) | 1.9 | (0.6) | 0.1 | (0.1) | a | a |
| | Uruguay | 19.6 | (1.9) | 27.9 | (1.9) | 27.4 | (2.0) | 17.4 | (1.3) | 6.3 | (0.7) | 1.2 | (0.4) | 0.1 | a |

*StatLink* ᵇᵖ http://dx.doi.org/10.1787/142056138443

Pour consulter la version française intégrale de ce tableau, suivre ce lien :
*StatLink* ᵇᵖ http://dx.doi.org/10.1787/152610887346

[Part 2/2]

**Table 2.2b** Percentage of students at each proficiency level on the *identifying scientific issues* scale, by gender

Tableau 2.2b Pourcentage d'élèves à chaque niveau de compétence sur l'échelle d'*identification des questions d'ordre scientifique*, selon le sexe

| | | Females – Proficiency levels | | | | | | | | | | | | | |
|---|---|---|---|---|---|---|---|---|---|---|---|---|---|---|---|
| | | Below Level 1 (below 334.94 score points) | | Level 1 (from 334.94 to 409.54 score points) | | Level 2 (from 409.54 to 484.14 score points) | | Level 3 (from 484.14 to 558.73 score points) | | Level 4 (from 558.73 to 633.33 score points) | | Level 5 (from 633.33 to 707.93 score points) | | Level 6 (above 707.93 score points) | |
| | | % | S.E. | % | S.E. | % | S.E. | % | S.E. | % | S.E. | % | S.E. | % | S.E. |
| OECD | Australia | 1.5 | (0.2) | 6.4 | (0.5) | 17.0 | (0.8) | 29.3 | (0.7) | 28.2 | (0.8) | 14.2 | (0.7) | 3.5 | (0.4) |
| | Austria | 2.8 | (0.9) | 10.2 | (1.2) | 20.8 | (1.5) | 31.5 | (1.5) | 26.6 | (1.4) | 7.7 | (1.0) | 0.4 | (0.1) |
| | Belgium | 3.5 | (0.6) | 9.0 | (0.7) | 20.4 | (0.9) | 30.2 | (1.1) | 24.6 | (1.0) | 10.7 | (0.7) | 1.5 | (0.3) |
| | Canada | 1.9 | (0.3) | 6.9 | (0.6) | 18.5 | (0.8) | 29.6 | (1.1) | 27.5 | (1.3) | 12.4 | (0.7) | 3.1 | (0.4) |
| | Czech Republic | 3.9 | (1.0) | 11.4 | (1.3) | 22.1 | (1.7) | 29.3 | (1.7) | 23.2 | (1.5) | 8.7 | (1.2) | 1.4 | (0.4) |
| | Denmark | 3.7 | (0.5) | 11.8 | (1.0) | 26.6 | (1.4) | 32.6 | (1.4) | 19.1 | (1.1) | 5.7 | (0.7) | 0.4 | (0.2) |
| | Finland | 0.4 | (0.1) | 2.2 | (0.4) | 11.9 | (1.0) | 29.4 | (1.7) | 36.0 | (1.6) | 17.0 | (1.0) | 3.1 | (0.4) |
| | France | 5.1 | (0.7) | 12.3 | (1.0) | 21.2 | (1.2) | 29.5 | (1.5) | 22.8 | (1.2) | 7.9 | (1.2) | 1.2 | (0.4) |
| | Germany | 3.3 | (0.7) | 9.9 | (1.0) | 21.2 | (1.2) | 30.3 | (1.3) | 25.1 | (1.3) | 8.9 | (0.8) | 1.3 | (0.3) |
| | Greece | 4.7 | (0.8) | 13.2 | (0.9) | 29.3 | (1.3) | 34.0 | (1.2) | 15.9 | (1.0) | 2.8 | (0.4) | 0.2 | (0.1) |
| | Hungary | 2.9 | (0.5) | 11.5 | (0.9) | 31.7 | (1.3) | 36.2 | (1.4) | 15.1 | (1.1) | 2.3 | (0.5) | 0.3 | (0.2) |
| | Iceland | 4.2 | (0.6) | 11.3 | (0.9) | 23.9 | (1.7) | 29.0 | (1.1) | 21.5 | (1.1) | 8.6 | (0.8) | 1.4 | (0.3) |
| | Ireland | 2.0 | (0.4) | 9.2 | (0.9) | 22.3 | (1.4) | 29.9 | (1.2) | 25.0 | (1.3) | 9.9 | (0.8) | 1.8 | (0.4) |
| | Italy | 5.9 | (0.6) | 15.4 | (0.7) | 28.7 | (0.9) | 28.6 | (0.9) | 16.4 | (0.9) | 4.4 | (0.5) | 0.4 | (0.1) |
| | Japan | 3.9 | (1.2) | 8.2 | (0.9) | 18.4 | (1.3) | 27.7 | (1.4) | 26.8 | (1.6) | 12.3 | (1.1) | 2.8 | (0.4) |
| | Korea | 1.7 | (0.5) | 7.1 | (1.0) | 20.1 | (1.1) | 32.4 | (1.4) | 28.1 | (1.3) | 9.4 | (1.0) | 1.2 | (0.4) |
| | Luxembourg | 4.2 | (0.5) | 15.0 | (0.8) | 28.0 | (1.0) | 30.7 | (1.3) | 17.7 | (1.0) | 4.2 | (0.4) | 0.3 | (0.2) |
| | Mexico | 14.0 | (1.1) | 28.0 | (1.0) | 34.1 | (1.0) | 18.6 | (0.8) | 4.7 | (0.5) | 0.5 | (0.2) | 0.0 | (0.1) |
| | Netherlands | 2.8 | (0.7) | 8.3 | (0.9) | 18.6 | (1.4) | 25.1 | (1.7) | 26.6 | (1.6) | 14.6 | (1.5) | 3.9 | (0.6) |
| | New Zealand | 2.5 | (0.4) | 6.8 | (0.9) | 17.3 | (1.3) | 26.1 | (1.6) | 27.1 | (1.4) | 15.4 | (1.0) | 4.8 | (0.6) |
| | Norway | 3.0 | (0.6) | 12.1 | (1.0) | 27.0 | (1.1) | 31.4 | (1.7) | 20.0 | (1.1) | 5.6 | (0.9) | 0.9 | (0.3) |
| | Poland | 2.7 | (0.4) | 13.9 | (1.1) | 30.7 | (1.5) | 32.6 | (1.4) | 16.7 | (1.0) | 3.2 | (0.5) | 0.2 | (0.1) |
| | Portugal | 3.8 | (0.6) | 14.3 | (1.1) | 27.3 | (1.3) | 30.7 | (1.7) | 18.9 | (1.3) | 4.8 | (0.6) | 0.3 | (0.1) |
| | Slovak Republic | 5.1 | (0.8) | 13.7 | (1.3) | 29.1 | (1.7) | 30.7 | (1.6) | 17.2 | (1.6) | 4.0 | (0.7) | 0.2 | (0.1) |
| | Spain | 2.9 | (0.4) | 12.6 | (0.8) | 27.2 | (0.9) | 34.2 | (0.8) | 18.7 | (0.8) | 4.1 | (0.5) | 0.3 | (0.1) |
| | Sweden | 3.7 | (0.6) | 11.1 | (1.0) | 24.7 | (1.3) | 31.4 | (1.3) | 21.0 | (1.1) | 7.1 | (0.9) | 1.1 | (0.4) |
| | Switzerland | 3.2 | (0.5) | 9.7 | (0.7) | 20.9 | (1.2) | 29.4 | (1.1) | 25.6 | (1.2) | 9.9 | (0.8) | 1.2 | (0.3) |
| | Turkey | 6.3 | (0.9) | 27.3 | (1.4) | 37.6 | (1.6) | 22.0 | (1.4) | 6.1 | (1.0) | 0.8 | (0.4) | a | a |
| | United Kingdom | 3.8 | (0.6) | 10.3 | (0.8) | 23.1 | (0.9) | 27.5 | (1.0) | 22.8 | (0.9) | 9.9 | (0.8) | 2.6 | (0.4) |
| | United States | 4.0 | (0.7) | 13.9 | (1.4) | 26.3 | (1.4) | 28.3 | (1.1) | 19.0 | (1.0) | 7.1 | (0.8) | 1.4 | (0.5) |
| | **OECD total** | 4.8 | (0.3) | 13.8 | (0.4) | 25.4 | (0.5) | 28.0 | (0.4) | 19.6 | (0.3) | 7.1 | (0.2) | 1.3 | (0.1) |
| | **OECD average** | 3.8 | (0.1) | 11.8 | (0.2) | 24.2 | (0.2) | 29.6 | (0.2) | 21.5 | (0.2) | 7.8 | (0.1) | 1.4 | (0.1) |
| Partners | Argentina | 21.3 | (2.2) | 27.3 | (1.6) | 29.6 | (1.6) | 16.2 | (1.6) | 5.1 | (1.0) | 0.4 | (0.3) | 0.0 | a |
| | Azerbaijan | 36.0 | (2.4) | 43.7 | (2.1) | 17.7 | (1.4) | 2.4 | (0.5) | 0.2 | (0.1) | 0.0 | a | a | a |
| | Brazil | 23.6 | (1.4) | 30.3 | (1.6) | 28.0 | (1.3) | 13.4 | (1.0) | 4.1 | (0.5) | 0.5 | (0.2) | 0.0 | a |
| | Bulgaria | 15.3 | (2.0) | 22.2 | (1.6) | 26.2 | (1.3) | 21.9 | (1.6) | 10.9 | (1.3) | 3.1 | (0.8) | 0.4 | (0.2) |
| | Chile | 11.4 | (1.1) | 24.9 | (1.3) | 32.5 | (1.3) | 21.2 | (1.2) | 8.4 | (1.2) | 1.5 | (0.5) | 0.1 | (0.1) |
| | Colombia | 21.9 | (1.4) | 27.6 | (1.6) | 31.8 | (1.7) | 15.1 | (1.2) | 3.3 | (0.7) | 0.4 | (0.3) | 0.0 | a |
| | Croatia | 1.7 | (0.4) | 10.5 | (0.8) | 27.5 | (1.2) | 33.1 | (1.3) | 20.8 | (1.3) | 5.7 | (0.7) | 0.7 | (0.2) |
| | Estonia | 0.6 | (0.3) | 4.8 | (0.8) | 21.9 | (1.2) | 37.9 | (1.6) | 27.5 | (1.2) | 7.0 | (0.8) | 0.4 | (0.2) |
| | Hong Kong-China | 2.9 | (0.6) | 8.4 | (1.0) | 17.4 | (1.2) | 29.1 | (1.6) | 26.1 | (1.2) | 13.3 | (1.3) | 2.8 | (0.6) |
| | Indonesia | 23.4 | (1.5) | 38.0 | (1.7) | 28.3 | (1.5) | 8.8 | (1.0) | 1.4 | (0.5) | 0.0 | a | a | a |
| | Israel | 12.5 | (1.2) | 18.8 | (1.2) | 26.0 | (1.5) | 23.6 | (1.5) | 14.1 | (1.1) | 4.3 | (0.6) | 0.9 | (0.3) |
| | Jordan | 13.6 | (1.0) | 28.9 | (1.3) | 33.6 | (1.6) | 19.0 | (1.1) | 4.4 | (0.6) | 0.4 | (0.2) | a | a |
| | Kyrgyzstan | 50.6 | (1.8) | 31.4 | (1.8) | 14.0 | (1.0) | 3.4 | (0.6) | 0.5 | (0.2) | 0.1 | (0.0) | a | a |
| | Latvia | 2.3 | (0.7) | 9.9 | (1.1) | 27.0 | (1.6) | 35.9 | (1.8) | 20.5 | (1.2) | 4.2 | (0.7) | 0.2 | (0.1) |
| | Liechtenstein | 1.6 | (1.1) | 6.9 | (2.4) | 21.6 | (3.6) | 28.6 | (3.8) | 28.5 | (3.9) | 10.3 | (2.7) | 2.5 | (1.4) |
| | Lithuania | 3.4 | (0.6) | 14.1 | (1.2) | 28.6 | (1.3) | 33.8 | (1.2) | 17.0 | (1.2) | 3.1 | (0.5) | 0.1 | (0.1) |
| | Macao-China | 1.5 | (0.3) | 10.9 | (1.1) | 29.9 | (1.1) | 36.7 | (1.2) | 17.9 | (0.9) | 3.0 | (0.5) | 0.1 | (0.1) |
| | Montenegro | 18.6 | (1.1) | 30.7 | (1.8) | 32.0 | (1.2) | 15.2 | (1.2) | 3.2 | (0.5) | 0.2 | (0.1) | a | a |
| | Qatar | 32.3 | (0.8) | 41.0 | (1.0) | 19.8 | (0.9) | 5.5 | (0.4) | 1.1 | (0.3) | 0.3 | (0.1) | 0.0 | a |
| | Romania | 13.0 | (1.5) | 32.8 | (2.1) | 35.4 | (1.8) | 15.8 | (2.1) | 2.9 | (0.7) | 0.1 | a | a | a |
| | Russian Federation | 5.6 | (0.7) | 17.7 | (1.3) | 31.8 | (1.1) | 29.2 | (1.3) | 13.1 | (1.0) | 2.4 | (0.4) | 0.2 | (0.1) |
| | Serbia | 9.6 | (1.1) | 22.8 | (1.4) | 37.3 | (1.8) | 24.3 | (1.6) | 5.7 | (0.7) | 0.3 | (0.1) | a | a |
| | Slovenia | 1.0 | (0.3) | 7.1 | (1.0) | 20.8 | (1.0) | 32.6 | (1.1) | 28.1 | (1.3) | 9.2 | (0.9) | 1.2 | (0.3) |
| | Chinese Taipei | 3.3 | (0.6) | 11.8 | (1.3) | 22.1 | (1.2) | 29.7 | (1.4) | 24.0 | (1.4) | 8.1 | (0.9) | 1.0 | (0.3) |
| | Thailand | 11.3 | (0.9) | 29.8 | (1.2) | 36.0 | (1.2) | 18.2 | (1.0) | 4.3 | (0.6) | 0.4 | (0.2) | 0.0 | a |
| | Tunisia | 25.0 | (1.6) | 33.3 | (1.4) | 26.7 | (1.1) | 11.8 | (1.2) | 2.9 | (0.7) | 0.3 | (0.2) | 0.0 | a |
| | Uruguay | 12.5 | (0.9) | 24.9 | (1.4) | 31.3 | (1.4) | 21.7 | (1.0) | 8.4 | (0.8) | 1.2 | (0.3) | 0.0 | (0.0) |

*StatLink* ⌦ http://dx.doi.org/10.1787/142056138443

Pour consulter la version française intégrale de ce tableau, suivre ce lien :
*StatLink* ⌦ http://dx.doi.org/10.1787/152610887346

[Part 1/2]

**Table 2.2c**  Mean score, variation and gender differences in student performance on the *identifying scientific issues* scale

*Tableau 2.2c*  Score moyen, différences de score selon le sexe et répartition des scores sur l'échelle d'*identification des questions d'ordre scientifique*

| | | All students | | | | Gender differences | | | | | |
|---|---|---|---|---|---|---|---|---|---|---|---|
| | | Mean score | | Standard deviation | | Males | | Females | | Difference (M - F) | |
| | | Mean | S.E. | S.D. | S.E. | Mean score | S.E. | Mean score | S.E. | Score dif. | S.E. |
| **OECD** | Australia | 535 | (2.3) | 98 | (1.2) | 525 | (3.2) | 546 | (2.6) | **-21** | (3.6) |
| | Austria | 505 | (3.7) | 90 | (2.2) | 495 | (4.2) | 516 | (4.7) | **-22** | (4.6) |
| | Belgium | 515 | (2.7) | 100 | (2.3) | 508 | (3.8) | 523 | (3.1) | **-14** | (4.3) |
| | Canada | 532 | (2.3) | 97 | (1.3) | 525 | (2.7) | 539 | (2.4) | **-14** | (2.4) |
| | Czech Republic | 500 | (4.2) | 99 | (3.4) | 492 | (4.8) | 511 | (5.3) | **-19** | (5.7) |
| | Denmark | 493 | (3.0) | 90 | (1.4) | 488 | (3.5) | 499 | (3.2) | **-11** | (3.2) |
| | Finland | 555 | (2.3) | 84 | (1.1) | 542 | (2.7) | 568 | (2.6) | **-26** | (2.8) |
| | France | 499 | (3.5) | 104 | (2.4) | 491 | (4.6) | 507 | (3.7) | **-16** | (4.7) |
| | Germany | 510 | (3.8) | 98 | (2.4) | 502 | (4.5) | 518 | (3.9) | **-16** | (3.4) |
| | Greece | 469 | (3.0) | 92 | (2.1) | 453 | (4.1) | 485 | (3.1) | **-31** | (4.3) |
| | Hungary | 483 | (2.6) | 81 | (1.8) | 477 | (3.4) | 489 | (3.3) | **-13** | (4.1) |
| | Iceland | 494 | (1.7) | 103 | (1.4) | 479 | (2.9) | 509 | (2.4) | **-30** | (4.1) |
| | Ireland | 516 | (3.3) | 95 | (1.7) | 508 | (4.4) | 524 | (3.5) | **-16** | (4.6) |
| | Italy | 474 | (2.2) | 99 | (1.5) | 466 | (2.9) | 483 | (2.5) | **-17** | (3.4) |
| | Japan | 522 | (4.0) | 106 | (2.5) | 513 | (5.1) | 531 | (6.6) | **-18** | (8.5) |
| | Korea | 519 | (3.7) | 91 | (2.4) | 508 | (4.9) | 530 | (4.2) | **-22** | (5.7) |
| | Luxembourg | 483 | (1.1) | 92 | (0.9) | 477 | (1.7) | 489 | (1.8) | **-11** | (2.8) |
| | Mexico | 421 | (2.6) | 85 | (1.6) | 418 | (2.9) | 425 | (2.8) | **-7** | (2.2) |
| | Netherlands | 533 | (3.3) | 103 | (2.9) | 527 | (3.8) | 539 | (3.5) | **-12** | (3.2) |
| | New Zealand | 536 | (2.9) | 106 | (1.6) | 525 | (3.7) | 547 | (3.7) | **-22** | (4.9) |
| | Norway | 489 | (3.1) | 94 | (2.0) | 478 | (3.9) | 501 | (3.3) | **-24** | (3.7) |
| | Poland | 483 | (2.5) | 84 | (1.1) | 476 | (2.8) | 490 | (2.7) | **-13** | (2.5) |
| | Portugal | 486 | (3.1) | 91 | (1.9) | 480 | (3.6) | 493 | (3.4) | **-13** | (3.1) |
| | Slovak Republic | 475 | (3.2) | 96 | (3.6) | 465 | (4.5) | 485 | (3.6) | **-20** | (5.1) |
| | Spain | 489 | (2.4) | 89 | (1.1) | 482 | (2.7) | 496 | (2.6) | **-15** | (2.1) |
| | Sweden | 499 | (2.6) | 96 | (1.4) | 491 | (2.9) | 507 | (3.1) | **-16** | (3.0) |
| | Switzerland | 515 | (3.0) | 95 | (1.4) | 510 | (3.1) | 520 | (3.3) | **-10** | (2.4) |
| | Turkey | 427 | (3.4) | 79 | (2.7) | 414 | (4.1) | 443 | (3.6) | **-29** | (3.8) |
| | United Kingdom | 514 | (2.3) | 106 | (1.5) | 510 | (2.9) | 517 | (2.8) | **-7** | (3.2) |
| | United States | 492 | (3.8) | 100 | (1.7) | 484 | (4.6) | 500 | (3.8) | **-16** | (3.6) |
| | **OECD total** | **491** | **(1.1)** | **102** | **(0.6)** | **483** | **(1.3)** | **499** | **(1.2)** | **-16** | **(1.4)** |
| | **OECD average** | **499** | **(0.5)** | **95** | **(0.4)** | **490** | **(0.7)** | **508** | **(0.6)** | **-17** | **(0.7)** |
| **Partners** | Argentina | 395 | (5.7) | 100 | (3.1) | 381 | (5.8) | 408 | (6.4) | **-27** | (5.2) |
| | Azerbaijan | 353 | (3.1) | 66 | (2.6) | 349 | (3.3) | 357 | (3.3) | **-8** | (2.3) |
| | Brazil | 398 | (2.8) | 93 | (1.9) | 394 | (3.2) | 402 | (3.0) | **-7** | (2.5) |
| | Bulgaria | 427 | (6.3) | 109 | (3.3) | 411 | (6.6) | 445 | (7.1) | **-34** | (5.6) |
| | Chile | 444 | (4.1) | 89 | (1.7) | 445 | (5.0) | 443 | (4.1) | 3 | (4.5) |
| | Colombia | 402 | (3.4) | 96 | (2.4) | 401 | (4.4) | 404 | (4.0) | -3 | (4.8) |
| | Croatia | 494 | (2.6) | 86 | (1.6) | 480 | (3.5) | 507 | (3.1) | **-27** | (4.1) |
| | Estonia | 516 | (2.6) | 77 | (1.3) | 504 | (3.1) | 528 | (2.6) | **-25** | (2.8) |
| | Hong Kong-China | 528 | (3.2) | 101 | (2.2) | 520 | (4.1) | 535 | (4.5) | **-15** | (5.9) |
| | Indonesia | 393 | (5.6) | 77 | (2.7) | 397 | (8.0) | 389 | (3.6) | 8 | (6.0) |
| | Israel | 457 | (3.9) | 114 | (2.0) | 451 | (5.9) | 463 | (4.0) | **-12** | (6.6) |
| | Jordan | 409 | (2.8) | 89 | (1.8) | 393 | (4.6) | 425 | (2.8) | **-32** | (5.1) |
| | Kyrgyzstan | 321 | (3.2) | 93 | (2.0) | 311 | (3.6) | 330 | (3.3) | **-20** | (2.9) |
| | Latvia | 489 | (3.3) | 83 | (1.5) | 473 | (3.7) | 504 | (3.5) | **-31** | (3.1) |
| | Liechtenstein | 522 | (3.7) | 91 | (3.1) | 508 | (7.0) | 534 | (5.7) | **-26** | (10.3) |
| | Lithuania | 476 | (2.7) | 84 | (1.4) | 463 | (2.9) | 489 | (3.0) | **-26** | (2.7) |
| | Macao-China | 490 | (1.2) | 79 | (1.0) | 483 | (1.9) | 498 | (1.6) | **-15** | (2.6) |
| | Montenegro | 401 | (1.2) | 83 | (1.1) | 393 | (2.0) | 409 | (1.8) | **-16** | (2.9) |
| | Qatar | 352 | (0.8) | 79 | (0.8) | 334 | (1.2) | 371 | (1.3) | **-37** | (2.1) |
| | Romania | 409 | (3.6) | 77 | (2.7) | 401 | (3.6) | 418 | (4.4) | **-17** | (3.5) |
| | Russian Federation | 463 | (4.2) | 89 | (1.3) | 453 | (4.6) | 472 | (4.1) | **-20** | (2.6) |
| | Serbia | 431 | (3.0) | 83 | (1.8) | 420 | (3.3) | 441 | (3.6) | **-21** | (3.7) |
| | Slovenia | 517 | (1.4) | 87 | (0.8) | 504 | (2.0) | 530 | (2.0) | **-27** | (2.8) |
| | Chinese Taipei | 509 | (3.7) | 95 | (1.9) | 506 | (4.4) | 512 | (5.0) | -6 | (5.8) |
| | Thailand | 413 | (2.5) | 83 | (1.5) | 394 | (3.7) | 427 | (2.8) | **-33** | (4.1) |
| | Tunisia | 384 | (3.8) | 88 | (2.2) | 373 | (3.9) | 394 | (4.2) | **-21** | (3.4) |
| | Uruguay | 429 | (3.0) | 95 | (2.0) | 418 | (4.2) | 439 | (2.8) | **-21** | (3.9) |

Note: Values that are statistically significant are indicated in bold (see Annex A3).
*StatLink* http://dx.doi.org/10.1787/142056138443

Pour consulter la version française intégrale de ce tableau, suivre ce lien :
*StatLink* http://dx.doi.org/10.1787/152610887346

[Part 2/2]

**Table 2.2c** **Mean score, variation and gender differences in student performance on the *identifying scientific issues* scale**

Tableau 2.2c  Score moyen, différences de score selon le sexe et répartition des scores sur l'échelle de l'*identification des questions d'ordre scientifique*

| | | Percentiles | | | | | | | | | | |
|---|---|---|---|---|---|---|---|---|---|---|---|---|
| | | 5th | | 10th | | 25th | | 75th | | 90th | | 95th | |
| | | Score | S.E. | Score | S.E. | Score | S.E. | Score | S.E. | Score | S.E. | Score | S.E. |
| OECD | Australia | 368 | (4.3) | 406 | (3.1) | 471 | (2.7) | 604 | (2.8) | 658 | (3.2) | 689 | (3.6) |
| | Austria | 351 | (6.8) | 383 | (6.7) | 443 | (4.8) | 571 | (3.8) | 618 | (4.1) | 644 | (4.0) |
| | Belgium | 340 | (8.6) | 382 | (6.6) | 449 | (3.7) | 587 | (2.9) | 639 | (2.9) | 668 | (3.5) |
| | Canada | 363 | (4.9) | 404 | (4.1) | 469 | (2.9) | 599 | (2.3) | 652 | (2.5) | 683 | (2.9) |
| | Czech Republic | 341 | (8.2) | 376 | (5.9) | 434 | (4.7) | 570 | (4.5) | 625 | (5.2) | 656 | (5.2) |
| | Denmark | 341 | (5.5) | 375 | (4.5) | 432 | (4.0) | 556 | (3.2) | 607 | (3.2) | 637 | (4.4) |
| | Finland | 411 | (4.0) | 446 | (3.5) | 501 | (3.1) | 612 | (2.9) | 659 | (2.8) | 686 | (3.2) |
| | France | 319 | (7.0) | 358 | (5.9) | 427 | (5.5) | 576 | (3.5) | 629 | (3.7) | 659 | (4.5) |
| | Germany | 341 | (8.3) | 381 | (6.6) | 444 | (5.0) | 579 | (3.4) | 630 | (3.5) | 660 | (4.0) |
| | Greece | 309 | (6.1) | 347 | (5.3) | 411 | (4.4) | 533 | (2.9) | 581 | (3.4) | 608 | (3.2) |
| | Hungary | 347 | (5.7) | 378 | (4.4) | 430 | (3.6) | 539 | (3.3) | 583 | (3.6) | 610 | (4.4) |
| | Iceland | 318 | (5.0) | 358 | (4.8) | 426 | (2.5) | 566 | (2.2) | 625 | (3.1) | 656 | (3.7) |
| | Ireland | 357 | (5.7) | 391 | (4.9) | 450 | (4.0) | 584 | (3.3) | 638 | (3.4) | 668 | (4.4) |
| | Italy | 310 | (4.7) | 347 | (3.5) | 409 | (3.0) | 543 | (2.8) | 600 | (2.7) | 632 | (3.4) |
| | Japan | 337 | (8.2) | 381 | (6.9) | 453 | (5.6) | 597 | (3.9) | 652 | (4.0) | 682 | (4.0) |
| | Korea | 361 | (7.6) | 400 | (6.0) | 461 | (4.4) | 583 | (4.1) | 630 | (4.1) | 657 | (5.0) |
| | Luxembourg | 329 | (2.9) | 362 | (2.3) | 421 | (2.0) | 548 | (2.3) | 600 | (2.4) | 628 | (2.5) |
| | Mexico | 280 | (6.1) | 312 | (4.7) | 365 | (3.4) | 479 | (2.8) | 529 | (3.0) | 559 | (3.9) |
| | Netherlands | 360 | (7.3) | 397 | (5.7) | 462 | (4.5) | 606 | (3.5) | 662 | (4.0) | 694 | (4.5) |
| | New Zealand | 356 | (4.8) | 396 | (4.8) | 465 | (4.3) | 612 | (3.0) | 668 | (3.0) | 701 | (3.5) |
| | Norway | 333 | (7.6) | 368 | (5.7) | 426 | (3.6) | 555 | (3.1) | 608 | (4.0) | 640 | (4.1) |
| | Poland | 344 | (3.9) | 374 | (3.2) | 425 | (3.0) | 542 | (3.2) | 591 | (2.7) | 619 | (3.7) |
| | Portugal | 336 | (5.4) | 367 | (4.3) | 423 | (4.1) | 551 | (3.4) | 603 | (3.7) | 632 | (4.9) |
| | Slovak Republic | 315 | (8.5) | 356 | (4.9) | 416 | (3.6) | 541 | (3.6) | 592 | (3.6) | 622 | (3.7) |
| | Spain | 341 | (4.1) | 374 | (3.2) | 431 | (2.7) | 550 | (2.4) | 599 | (2.7) | 627 | (3.1) |
| | Sweden | 338 | (4.5) | 374 | (4.2) | 435 | (3.2) | 566 | (3.2) | 619 | (3.1) | 653 | (3.3) |
| | Switzerland | 350 | (4.9) | 387 | (4.4) | 452 | (3.9) | 583 | (3.1) | 633 | (3.7) | 661 | (4.6) |
| | Turkey | 304 | (5.1) | 330 | (3.8) | 374 | (3.2) | 480 | (4.7) | 531 | (6.7) | 561 | (8.5) |
| | United Kingdom | 337 | (6.1) | 377 | (4.3) | 443 | (2.9) | 587 | (2.8) | 648 | (2.8) | 682 | (3.2) |
| | United States | 330 | (5.8) | 362 | (5.3) | 420 | (4.7) | 563 | (4.2) | 621 | (4.9) | 654 | (5.2) |
| | **OECD total** | **324** | **(2.0)** | **359** | **(1.6)** | **420** | **(1.4)** | **563** | **(1.1)** | **621** | **(1.5)** | **655** | **(1.6)** |
| | **OECD average** | **339** | **(1.1)** | **375** | **(0.9)** | **436** | **(0.7)** | **565** | **(0.6)** | **618** | **(0.7)** | **648** | **(0.8)** |
| Partners | Argentina | 219 | (13.2) | 263 | (10.2) | 334 | (6.9) | 464 | (5.4) | 518 | (6.0) | 552 | (7.3) |
| | Azerbaijan | 247 | (4.5) | 271 | (4.1) | 310 | (3.5) | 395 | (3.3) | 435 | (4.3) | 461 | (5.0) |
| | Brazil | 249 | (4.6) | 281 | (2.8) | 334 | (3.1) | 459 | (3.8) | 520 | (5.5) | 555 | (5.5) |
| | Bulgaria | 251 | (8.2) | 289 | (8.7) | 350 | (7.3) | 504 | (7.6) | 571 | (7.4) | 607 | (8.4) |
| | Chile | 300 | (6.1) | 330 | (3.9) | 383 | (4.1) | 505 | (5.0) | 561 | (5.4) | 594 | (6.8) |
| | Colombia | 234 | (8.6) | 274 | (6.9) | 343 | (4.7) | 468 | (4.1) | 519 | (4.7) | 551 | (5.1) |
| | Croatia | 354 | (5.2) | 384 | (4.1) | 435 | (3.2) | 552 | (2.8) | 604 | (3.5) | 634 | (4.9) |
| | Estonia | 387 | (5.3) | 415 | (4.0) | 464 | (3.7) | 570 | (2.9) | 613 | (2.9) | 639 | (3.5) |
| | Hong Kong-China | 352 | (6.6) | 393 | (5.4) | 461 | (4.4) | 599 | (3.8) | 652 | (4.5) | 683 | (4.4) |
| | Indonesia | 269 | (5.2) | 297 | (3.9) | 342 | (4.2) | 444 | (7.1) | 495 | (10.5) | 522 | (9.2) |
| | Israel | 272 | (6.4) | 311 | (5.5) | 378 | (4.2) | 538 | (4.7) | 604 | (5.4) | 641 | (5.6) |
| | Jordan | 262 | (5.3) | 297 | (3.6) | 351 | (3.0) | 470 | (3.5) | 522 | (3.5) | 550 | (4.0) |
| | Kyrgyzstan | 167 | (6.2) | 203 | (4.4) | 263 | (4.4) | 382 | (3.3) | 436 | (4.2) | 473 | (5.8) |
| | Latvia | 346 | (6.1) | 377 | (5.2) | 434 | (4.2) | 547 | (3.4) | 594 | (3.5) | 621 | (4.1) |
| | Liechtenstein | 366 | (11.2) | 405 | (11.7) | 461 | (6.6) | 589 | (7.1) | 634 | (12.1) | 667 | (9.1) |
| | Lithuania | 336 | (4.5) | 366 | (3.2) | 419 | (3.4) | 535 | (3.4) | 583 | (3.5) | 609 | (4.5) |
| | Macao-China | 358 | (3.5) | 388 | (2.5) | 437 | (2.4) | 545 | (2.0) | 591 | (2.5) | 615 | (3.1) |
| | Montenegro | 263 | (3.1) | 294 | (2.1) | 344 | (2.0) | 460 | (1.9) | 508 | (2.5) | 537 | (3.4) |
| | Qatar | 234 | (2.5) | 258 | (1.8) | 300 | (1.6) | 398 | (2.2) | 453 | (2.6) | 495 | (2.7) |
| | Romania | 284 | (6.2) | 311 | (5.1) | 357 | (4.2) | 461 | (4.9) | 510 | (6.4) | 539 | (6.4) |
| | Russian Federation | 315 | (5.8) | 348 | (5.7) | 402 | (4.6) | 524 | (4.7) | 576 | (4.9) | 607 | (4.5) |
| | Serbia | 289 | (6.9) | 323 | (4.9) | 377 | (3.6) | 487 | (3.0) | 533 | (3.4) | 560 | (3.4) |
| | Slovenia | 372 | (3.1) | 402 | (4.0) | 457 | (2.3) | 579 | (1.9) | 627 | (2.6) | 655 | (3.3) |
| | Chinese Taipei | 344 | (5.7) | 379 | (5.9) | 444 | (5.5) | 578 | (3.2) | 628 | (3.7) | 655 | (3.8) |
| | Thailand | 276 | (4.6) | 307 | (3.7) | 358 | (3.4) | 469 | (3.4) | 520 | (4.2) | 551 | (4.6) |
| | Tunisia | 240 | (6.0) | 271 | (3.7) | 324 | (4.2) | 442 | (4.7) | 499 | (7.1) | 532 | (8.2) |
| | Uruguay | 271 | (7.9) | 308 | (5.2) | 365 | (4.2) | 494 | (3.2) | 552 | (3.7) | 584 | (5.1) |

Note: Values that are statistically significant are indicated in bold (see Annex A3).
StatLink ᵍ http://dx.doi.org/10.1787/142056138443

Pour consulter la version française intégrale de ce tableau, suivre ce lien :
StatLink ᵍ http://dx.doi.org/10.1787/152610887346

[Part 1/1]

**Table 2.3a** Percentage of students at each proficiency level on the *explaining phenomena scientifically* scale

Tableau 2.3a Pourcentage d'élèves à chaque niveau de compétence sur l'échelle d'*explication scientifique de phénomènes*

| | | Proficiency levels | | | | | | | | | | | | |
|---|---|---|---|---|---|---|---|---|---|---|---|---|---|---|
| | | Below Level 1 (below 334.94 score points) | | Level 1 (from 334.94 to 409.54 score points) | | Level 2 (from 409.54 to 484.14 score points) | | Level 3 (from 484.14 to 558.73 score points) | | Level 4 (from 558.73 to 633.33 score points) | | Level 5 (from 633.33 to 707.93 score points) | | Level 6 (above 707.93 score points) | |
| | | % | S.E. | % | S.E. | % | S.E. | % | S.E. | % | S.E. | % | S.E. | % | S.E. |
| **OECD** | Australia | 3.5 | (0.3) | 10.7 | (0.4) | 21.8 | (0.5) | 27.7 | (0.6) | 22.9 | (0.7) | 10.7 | (0.8) | 2.7 | (0.3) |
| | Austria | 4.1 | (0.7) | 11.0 | (0.9) | 21.5 | (1.0) | 27.6 | (1.0) | 23.9 | (1.0) | 10.2 | (0.8) | 1.8 | (0.3) |
| | Belgium | 5.8 | (0.8) | 13.6 | (0.7) | 22.0 | (0.7) | 27.2 | (0.7) | 21.8 | (0.7) | 8.4 | (0.4) | 1.2 | (0.2) |
| | Canada | 2.8 | (0.3) | 8.9 | (0.5) | 19.9 | (0.7) | 27.9 | (0.7) | 25.3 | (0.8) | 12.1 | (0.6) | 3.1 | (0.2) |
| | Czech Republic | 2.8 | (0.5) | 10.2 | (0.8) | 20.9 | (1.0) | 27.5 | (1.0) | 23.1 | (1.1) | 12.0 | (0.9) | 3.5 | (0.4) |
| | Denmark | 4.2 | (0.5) | 13.4 | (0.8) | 25.3 | (0.8) | 28.9 | (1.0) | 19.4 | (0.8) | 7.5 | (0.7) | 1.3 | (0.3) |
| | Finland | 0.5 | (0.1) | 3.5 | (0.3) | 13.9 | (0.6) | 28.1 | (0.9) | 31.4 | (0.9) | 17.5 | (0.8) | 5.1 | (0.5) |
| | France | 7.7 | (0.7) | 16.6 | (1.0) | 25.5 | (0.9) | 27.3 | (0.9) | 16.9 | (0.8) | 5.3 | (0.5) | 0.6 | (0.2) |
| | Germany | 3.9 | (0.6) | 11.5 | (0.9) | 20.6 | (0.9) | 27.6 | (1.0) | 22.5 | (1.0) | 11.1 | (0.9) | 2.7 | (0.3) |
| | Greece | 6.7 | (0.8) | 17.1 | (1.0) | 28.8 | (1.0) | 28.3 | (1.1) | 15.0 | (0.9) | 3.6 | (0.4) | 0.5 | (0.1) |
| | Hungary | 2.5 | (0.3) | 10.0 | (1.1) | 23.6 | (1.1) | 30.2 | (0.9) | 22.6 | (1.0) | 9.0 | (0.6) | 2.1 | (0.3) |
| | Iceland | 5.0 | (0.5) | 15.0 | (0.8) | 27.6 | (0.9) | 29.6 | (0.8) | 17.4 | (0.7) | 4.9 | (0.5) | 0.5 | (0.1) |
| | Ireland | 4.5 | (0.5) | 12.6 | (0.7) | 24.6 | (1.0) | 28.0 | (1.2) | 19.9 | (0.9) | 8.5 | (0.7) | 1.8 | (0.3) |
| | Italy | 7.5 | (0.5) | 16.9 | (0.6) | 27.0 | (0.7) | 26.9 | (0.6) | 15.7 | (0.6) | 5.2 | (0.3) | 0.8 | (0.1) |
| | Japan | 2.8 | (0.4) | 9.0 | (0.7) | 20.5 | (1.0) | 28.5 | (0.8) | 25.8 | (1.0) | 11.0 | (0.9) | 2.4 | (0.3) |
| | Korea | 2.7 | (0.5) | 10.9 | (0.7) | 24.1 | (0.9) | 30.9 | (1.3) | 22.7 | (0.8) | 7.6 | (0.9) | 1.2 | (0.4) |
| | Luxembourg | 6.8 | (0.4) | 16.4 | (0.7) | 26.3 | (1.0) | 27.7 | (0.9) | 17.2 | (0.7) | 5.0 | (0.4) | 0.6 | (0.2) |
| | Mexico | 19.5 | (1.2) | 33.3 | (0.8) | 29.7 | (0.9) | 13.9 | (0.7) | 3.2 | (0.4) | 0.4 | (0.1) | 0.0 | (0.0) |
| | Netherlands | 2.6 | (0.4) | 10.5 | (0.8) | 21.3 | (1.0) | 28.6 | (1.2) | 24.9 | (0.9) | 10.3 | (0.6) | 1.8 | (0.3) |
| | New Zealand | 4.7 | (0.5) | 11.4 | (0.7) | 21.0 | (0.8) | 24.7 | (1.0) | 21.9 | (0.9) | 12.1 | (0.6) | 4.2 | (0.4) |
| | Norway | 5.8 | (0.7) | 13.8 | (0.7) | 25.4 | (0.9) | 27.9 | (0.8) | 18.8 | (0.9) | 7.1 | (0.6) | 1.2 | (0.2) |
| | Poland | 3.2 | (0.4) | 13.0 | (0.8) | 25.6 | (1.0) | 28.9 | (1.0) | 19.9 | (0.8) | 7.9 | (0.5) | 1.6 | (0.3) |
| | Portugal | 5.8 | (0.7) | 19.5 | (1.1) | 31.0 | (0.8) | 27.9 | (1.1) | 13.1 | (0.7) | 2.5 | (0.3) | 0.1 | (0.1) |
| | Slovak Republic | 4.2 | (0.5) | 13.0 | (0.8) | 26.1 | (1.3) | 28.7 | (0.9) | 19.5 | (0.9) | 7.2 | (0.7) | 1.4 | (0.3) |
| | Spain | 5.6 | (0.5) | 15.2 | (0.7) | 26.1 | (0.7) | 28.2 | (0.7) | 17.8 | (0.7) | 6.1 | (0.4) | 0.9 | (0.1) |
| | Sweden | 4.0 | (0.6) | 11.6 | (0.8) | 23.4 | (1.0) | 29.3 | (0.9) | 21.2 | (0.8) | 8.6 | (0.6) | 1.8 | (0.3) |
| | Switzerland | 5.2 | (0.6) | 12.2 | (0.6) | 21.9 | (0.9) | 28.0 | (0.9) | 22.4 | (0.8) | 8.5 | (0.6) | 1.8 | (0.3) |
| | Turkey | 14.3 | (0.9) | 33.4 | (1.2) | 29.8 | (1.3) | 14.9 | (1.0) | 6.1 | (1.1) | 1.4 | (0.5) | 0.1 | (0.0) |
| | United Kingdom | 4.6 | (0.4) | 12.7 | (0.6) | 21.7 | (0.7) | 25.2 | (0.7) | 20.7 | (0.6) | 11.4 | (0.6) | 3.8 | (0.3) |
| | United States | 8.4 | (0.9) | 18.0 | (1.1) | 23.6 | (0.9) | 23.4 | (0.9) | 16.9 | (0.9) | 7.8 | (0.6) | 2.0 | (0.3) |
| | **OECD total** | 7.4 | (0.3) | 16.9 | (0.3) | 24.1 | (0.3) | 24.7 | (0.3) | 17.7 | (0.3) | 7.5 | (0.2) | 1.7 | (0.1) |
| | **OECD average** | 5.4 | (0.1) | 14.2 | (0.1) | 24.0 | (0.2) | 27.0 | (0.2) | 19.7 | (0.2) | 8.0 | (0.1) | 1.8 | (0.0) |
| **Partners** | Argentina | 29.9 | (2.1) | 28.1 | (1.1) | 24.5 | (1.3) | 13.2 | (1.2) | 3.8 | (0.6) | 0.5 | (0.2) | 0.0 | a |
| | Azerbaijan | 10.5 | (1.0) | 39.9 | (1.6) | 37.0 | (1.8) | 10.7 | (1.1) | 1.8 | (0.5) | 0.1 | (0.1) | a | a |
| | Brazil | 28.0 | (1.0) | 33.3 | (0.9) | 23.6 | (0.8) | 10.9 | (0.8) | 3.5 | (0.4) | 0.7 | (0.2) | 0.1 | (0.1) |
| | Bulgaria | 15.0 | (1.5) | 23.4 | (1.3) | 26.3 | (1.3) | 20.8 | (1.2) | 10.8 | (1.1) | 3.1 | (0.6) | 0.6 | (0.3) |
| | Chile | 14.8 | (1.0) | 27.9 | (1.3) | 28.9 | (0.9) | 18.2 | (1.1) | 8.1 | (0.8) | 1.9 | (0.4) | 0.1 | (0.1) |
| | Colombia | 30.8 | (1.7) | 33.1 | (1.3) | 24.1 | (1.4) | 9.9 | (0.8) | 1.9 | (0.3) | 0.2 | (0.1) | a | a |
| | Croatia | 3.2 | (0.4) | 14.4 | (0.8) | 29.5 | (1.1) | 30.1 | (1.3) | 17.3 | (0.9) | 4.8 | (0.4) | 0.7 | (0.1) |
| | Estonia | 1.0 | (0.2) | 6.5 | (0.6) | 20.2 | (0.9) | 29.5 | (1.2) | 27.1 | (1.1) | 12.9 | (0.8) | 2.9 | (0.3) |
| | Hong Kong-China | 1.5 | (0.4) | 6.3 | (0.6) | 16.1 | (0.8) | 28.2 | (0.9) | 29.0 | (0.8) | 15.5 | (0.8) | 3.4 | (0.4) |
| | Indonesia | 20.3 | (1.4) | 40.5 | (2.3) | 27.3 | (1.5) | 10.3 | (2.0) | 1.5 | (0.5) | 0.0 | a | 0.0 | a |
| | Israel | 16.3 | (1.1) | 23.3 | (0.8) | 24.7 | (1.0) | 20.1 | (0.9) | 11.4 | (0.8) | 3.6 | (0.3) | 0.6 | (0.2) |
| | Jordan | 14.4 | (0.8) | 24.3 | (0.9) | 29.1 | (0.9) | 21.2 | (0.8) | 8.9 | (0.8) | 1.8 | (0.4) | 0.2 | (0.1) |
| | Kyrgyzstan | 51.3 | (1.6) | 31.9 | (1.2) | 12.7 | (0.8) | 3.3 | (0.4) | 0.8 | (0.2) | 0.1 | (0.1) | a | a |
| | Latvia | 4.3 | (0.6) | 15.0 | (0.9) | 29.5 | (1.1) | 30.6 | (0.9) | 16.0 | (0.9) | 4.2 | (0.4) | 0.5 | (0.1) |
| | Liechtenstein | 3.3 | (1.0) | 11.0 | (1.9) | 22.6 | (3.5) | 28.9 | (4.2) | 23.2 | (3.2) | 9.2 | (1.8) | 1.8 | (0.9) |
| | Lithuania | 4.6 | (0.5) | 15.0 | (0.8) | 26.2 | (0.9) | 28.3 | (1.0) | 18.6 | (0.8) | 6.1 | (0.6) | 1.2 | (0.3) |
| | Macao-China | 1.5 | (0.3) | 8.0 | (0.5) | 23.4 | (0.9) | 34.0 | (0.9) | 24.9 | (0.9) | 7.5 | (0.6) | 0.7 | (0.2) |
| | Montenegro | 16.0 | (0.6) | 32.2 | (0.8) | 31.1 | (0.8) | 15.6 | (0.8) | 4.6 | (0.5) | 0.4 | (0.1) | a | a |
| | Qatar | 43.6 | (0.6) | 32.4 | (0.7) | 15.8 | (0.5) | 5.9 | (0.4) | 1.8 | (0.3) | 0.5 | (0.1) | 0.1 | (0.0) |
| | Romania | 13.8 | (1.5) | 30.0 | (1.5) | 32.5 | (1.3) | 17.6 | (1.2) | 5.3 | (0.8) | 0.8 | (0.2) | 0.0 | (0.0) |
| | Russian Federation | 5.0 | (0.6) | 15.9 | (0.9) | 29.6 | (0.9) | 29.1 | (1.1) | 15.3 | (0.9) | 4.5 | (0.4) | 0.6 | (0.1) |
| | Serbia | 11.9 | (0.9) | 25.2 | (1.0) | 31.3 | (1.0) | 21.9 | (1.1) | 8.1 | (0.6) | 1.5 | (0.2) | 0.1 | (0.0) |
| | Slovenia | 3.5 | (0.3) | 10.7 | (0.6) | 22.0 | (1.0) | 27.0 | (0.9) | 21.4 | (0.7) | 11.5 | (0.7) | 3.9 | (0.4) |
| | Chinese Taipei | 1.7 | (0.3) | 8.7 | (0.7) | 17.1 | (0.9) | 25.4 | (0.8) | 26.7 | (1.0) | 16.1 | (0.9) | 4.2 | (0.4) |
| | Thailand | 12.3 | (0.9) | 34.7 | (1.3) | 33.8 | (1.1) | 15.0 | (0.9) | 3.7 | (0.4) | 0.4 | (0.1) | 0.0 | (0.0) |
| | Tunisia | 28.3 | (1.3) | 35.4 | (1.0) | 25.0 | (1.0) | 9.0 | (0.8) | 2.1 | (0.5) | 0.1 | (0.1) | 0.0 | a |
| | Uruguay | 18.8 | (1.1) | 26.4 | (1.0) | 27.9 | (1.2) | 18.3 | (0.8) | 6.9 | (0.5) | 1.5 | (0.3) | 0.2 | (0.1) |

*StatLink* ᎏᎏ▊ http://dx.doi.org/10.1787/142056138443

Pour consulter la version française intégrale de ce tableau, suivre ce lien :
*StatLink* ᎏᎏ▊ http://dx.doi.org/10.1787/152610887346

[Part 1/2]

**Table 2.3b Percentage of students at each proficiency level on the *explaining phenomena scientifically* scale, by gender**

Tableau 2.3b Pourcentage d'élèves à chaque niveau de compétence sur l'échelle d'*explication scientifique de phénomènes*, selon le sexe

| | | Males – Proficiency levels | | | | | | | | | | | | | |
|---|---|---|---|---|---|---|---|---|---|---|---|---|---|---|---|
| | | Below Level 1 (below 334.94 score points) | | Level 1 (from 334.94 to 409.54 score points) | | Level 2 (from 409.54 to 484.14 score points) | | Level 3 (from 484.14 to 558.73 score points) | | Level 4 (from 558.73 to 633.33 score points) | | Level 5 (from 633.33 to 707.93 score points) | | Level 6 (above 707.93 score points) | |
| | | % | S.E. | % | S.E. | % | S.E. | % | S.E. | % | S.E. | % | S.E. | % | S.E. |
| OECD | Australia | 3.5 | (0.4) | 10.4 | (0.6) | 20.1 | (0.7) | 26.7 | (0.7) | 23.5 | (0.8) | 12.3 | (0.8) | 3.5 | (0.5) |
| | Austria | 3.4 | (0.8) | 9.6 | (1.1) | 21.0 | (1.2) | 26.6 | (1.2) | 25.2 | (1.3) | 11.7 | (0.9) | 2.6 | (0.4) |
| | Belgium | 5.5 | (1.0) | 13.3 | (0.9) | 20.6 | (0.9) | 25.7 | (1.0) | 22.7 | (1.2) | 10.3 | (0.7) | 1.9 | (0.2) |
| | Canada | 2.6 | (0.4) | 8.6 | (0.6) | 17.6 | (0.9) | 26.5 | (0.9) | 27.0 | (1.0) | 13.8 | (0.7) | 3.9 | (0.3) |
| | Czech Republic | 1.8 | (0.5) | 8.7 | (1.0) | 20.6 | (1.4) | 27.7 | (1.3) | 23.8 | (1.4) | 13.2 | (1.1) | 4.2 | (0.5) |
| | Denmark | 3.4 | (0.6) | 12.0 | (1.1) | 23.4 | (1.1) | 28.9 | (1.2) | 21.5 | (1.0) | 9.1 | (1.0) | 1.8 | (0.4) |
| | Finland | 0.5 | (0.2) | 3.8 | (0.5) | 13.4 | (0.9) | 26.1 | (1.3) | 30.9 | (1.1) | 18.6 | (1.0) | 6.6 | (0.6) |
| | France | 7.5 | (0.9) | 16.0 | (1.2) | 23.3 | (1.2) | 26.4 | (1.5) | 18.8 | (1.4) | 7.1 | (0.8) | 0.9 | (0.3) |
| | Germany | 3.6 | (0.8) | 10.1 | (0.9) | 19.2 | (1.1) | 26.4 | (1.5) | 23.7 | (1.3) | 13.4 | (1.1) | 3.6 | (0.5) |
| | Greece | 7.8 | (1.1) | 17.1 | (1.2) | 27.0 | (1.2) | 26.8 | (1.6) | 15.9 | (1.2) | 4.6 | (0.6) | 0.8 | (0.2) |
| | Hungary | 2.4 | (0.5) | 9.1 | (1.4) | 21.5 | (1.6) | 28.3 | (1.4) | 24.3 | (1.3) | 11.5 | (0.9) | 3.0 | (0.5) |
| | Iceland | 5.4 | (0.6) | 14.8 | (1.0) | 26.2 | (1.1) | 28.5 | (1.2) | 18.6 | (1.0) | 5.9 | (0.8) | 0.6 | (0.3) |
| | Ireland | 4.7 | (0.7) | 12.1 | (1.0) | 23.3 | (1.3) | 27.7 | (1.5) | 20.0 | (1.2) | 9.7 | (1.0) | 2.5 | (0.5) |
| | Italy | 7.4 | (0.6) | 15.5 | (0.9) | 25.1 | (1.0) | 26.8 | (0.9) | 17.6 | (0.8) | 6.5 | (0.5) | 1.2 | (0.1) |
| | Japan | 3.1 | (0.7) | 8.3 | (1.1) | 18.9 | (1.2) | 26.0 | (1.1) | 26.8 | (1.3) | 13.5 | (1.2) | 3.3 | (0.5) |
| | Korea | 3.0 | (0.6) | 10.4 | (1.1) | 22.1 | (1.2) | 30.2 | (1.6) | 23.9 | (1.4) | 8.9 | (1.0) | 1.5 | (0.5) |
| | Luxembourg | 6.1 | (0.6) | 14.9 | (1.2) | 23.3 | (1.3) | 27.4 | (1.1) | 20.3 | (1.0) | 6.9 | (0.6) | 1.0 | (0.3) |
| | Mexico | 16.9 | (1.4) | 31.7 | (1.0) | 30.5 | (1.3) | 16.0 | (1.1) | 4.4 | (0.5) | 0.5 | (0.1) | 0.0 | a |
| | Netherlands | 2.3 | (0.4) | 9.1 | (0.9) | 20.0 | (1.2) | 28.4 | (1.8) | 25.2 | (1.3) | 12.5 | (0.9) | 2.6 | (0.4) |
| | New Zealand | 5.0 | (0.7) | 11.1 | (0.9) | 19.9 | (1.2) | 22.9 | (1.2) | 22.3 | (1.1) | 13.4 | (1.0) | 5.4 | (0.6) |
| | Norway | 6.7 | (1.0) | 13.2 | (0.8) | 23.5 | (1.2) | 27.7 | (1.2) | 19.1 | (1.2) | 8.3 | (0.9) | 1.5 | (0.3) |
| | Poland | 2.9 | (0.5) | 11.9 | (0.8) | 24.3 | (1.7) | 27.9 | (1.5) | 21.0 | (1.0) | 9.8 | (0.8) | 2.3 | (0.4) |
| | Portugal | 5.1 | (0.8) | 17.6 | (1.3) | 30.0 | (1.3) | 28.5 | (1.5) | 15.1 | (1.1) | 3.5 | (0.6) | 0.2 | (0.1) |
| | Slovak Republic | 3.8 | (0.7) | 11.3 | (0.9) | 24.2 | (1.4) | 28.3 | (1.5) | 21.0 | (1.3) | 9.2 | (0.9) | 2.1 | (0.5) |
| | Spain | 5.2 | (0.7) | 13.3 | (0.9) | 24.9 | (1.0) | 28.5 | (1.0) | 19.2 | (0.9) | 7.5 | (0.6) | 1.4 | (0.3) |
| | Sweden | 4.1 | (0.8) | 11.0 | (0.9) | 21.8 | (1.2) | 28.5 | (1.0) | 22.3 | (0.9) | 9.9 | (0.8) | 2.3 | (0.4) |
| | Switzerland | 4.4 | (0.7) | 10.8 | (0.7) | 20.3 | (1.1) | 28.6 | (1.3) | 23.7 | (1.2) | 9.9 | (0.8) | 2.2 | (0.4) |
| | Turkey | 14.3 | (1.2) | 33.9 | (1.9) | 29.3 | (1.5) | 14.4 | (1.2) | 6.6 | (1.3) | 1.5 | (0.5) | 0.1 | a |
| | United Kingdom | 4.5 | (0.6) | 11.3 | (0.7) | 20.0 | (0.8) | 23.8 | (1.0) | 21.4 | (1.0) | 13.8 | (0.7) | 5.2 | (0.5) |
| | United States | 8.7 | (1.1) | 16.8 | (1.2) | 21.9 | (1.3) | 22.3 | (1.2) | 18.4 | (1.2) | 9.6 | (0.9) | 2.3 | (0.4) |
| | **OECD total** | 7.1 | (0.3) | 15.9 | (0.4) | 22.8 | (0.4) | 24.0 | (0.4) | 18.9 | (0.4) | 9.1 | (0.3) | 2.2 | (0.1) |
| | **OECD average** | 5.2 | (0.1) | 13.3 | (0.2) | 22.6 | (0.2) | 26.3 | (0.2) | 20.8 | (0.2) | 9.5 | (0.2) | 2.3 | (0.1) |
| Partners | Argentina | 30.1 | (2.5) | 27.7 | (1.6) | 24.4 | (1.5) | 13.4 | (1.5) | 3.7 | (0.7) | 0.6 | (0.2) | 0.0 | a |
| | Azerbaijan | 12.8 | (1.2) | 40.4 | (1.9) | 35.1 | (2.0) | 9.8 | (1.2) | 1.9 | (0.5) | 0.1 | (0.1) | a | a |
| | Brazil | 24.7 | (1.1) | 32.0 | (1.2) | 25.2 | (1.2) | 12.5 | (1.1) | 4.4 | (0.7) | 1.0 | (0.3) | 0.1 | (0.1) |
| | Bulgaria | 16.4 | (1.9) | 24.3 | (1.6) | 24.6 | (1.8) | 19.7 | (1.5) | 11.1 | (1.2) | 3.2 | (0.7) | 0.8 | (0.4) |
| | Chile | 11.0 | (1.3) | 25.2 | (1.7) | 30.2 | (1.3) | 20.5 | (1.3) | 10.3 | (1.1) | 2.6 | (0.6) | 0.2 | (0.1) |
| | Colombia | 27.7 | (2.1) | 31.7 | (1.5) | 25.4 | (1.7) | 11.9 | (1.3) | 2.8 | (0.5) | 0.4 | (0.2) | a | a |
| | Croatia | 3.0 | (0.5) | 13.8 | (1.0) | 28.2 | (1.5) | 29.7 | (1.6) | 18.5 | (1.2) | 5.8 | (0.7) | 1.0 | (0.2) |
| | Estonia | 1.1 | (0.3) | 6.4 | (0.7) | 19.0 | (1.3) | 29.1 | (1.7) | 27.4 | (1.7) | 13.2 | (1.0) | 3.7 | (0.5) |
| | Hong Kong-China | 1.6 | (0.5) | 5.7 | (0.7) | 14.4 | (1.0) | 25.2 | (1.1) | 29.9 | (1.2) | 18.0 | (1.2) | 5.2 | (0.7) |
| | Indonesia | 17.1 | (1.6) | 39.7 | (3.2) | 28.5 | (1.9) | 12.7 | (3.0) | 2.0 | (0.8) | 0.0 | a | 0.0 | a |
| | Israel | 16.1 | (1.7) | 22.5 | (1.2) | 22.5 | (1.6) | 20.0 | (1.5) | 13.1 | (1.2) | 4.9 | (0.5) | 1.0 | (0.3) |
| | Jordan | 18.4 | (1.3) | 24.9 | (1.4) | 26.5 | (1.1) | 19.9 | (1.2) | 8.3 | (1.2) | 1.7 | (0.6) | 0.2 | (0.1) |
| | Kyrgyzstan | 51.3 | (2.0) | 30.5 | (1.5) | 13.1 | (1.1) | 3.8 | (0.5) | 1.1 | (0.3) | 0.2 | (0.1) | a | a |
| | Latvia | 4.1 | (0.7) | 14.2 | (1.4) | 28.3 | (1.5) | 30.5 | (1.3) | 16.9 | (1.3) | 5.2 | (0.7) | 0.7 | (0.2) |
| | Liechtenstein | 3.4 | (1.8) | 9.6 | (3.2) | 21.4 | (4.9) | 29.6 | (5.4) | 23.6 | (4.5) | 10.7 | (2.9) | 1.7 | (1.2) |
| | Lithuania | 4.3 | (0.6) | 14.1 | (0.9) | 26.0 | (1.2) | 27.9 | (1.4) | 19.5 | (1.1) | 6.8 | (0.7) | 1.4 | (0.4) |
| | Macao-China | 1.7 | (0.3) | 7.6 | (0.7) | 21.0 | (1.0) | 32.0 | (1.5) | 27.2 | (1.3) | 9.3 | (0.9) | 1.1 | (0.3) |
| | Montenegro | 14.9 | (1.1) | 31.4 | (1.3) | 31.2 | (1.4) | 16.4 | (1.0) | 5.4 | (0.8) | 0.6 | (0.3) | a | a |
| | Qatar | 52.0 | (0.9) | 29.0 | (1.0) | 11.3 | (0.8) | 4.9 | (0.4) | 2.0 | (0.3) | 0.6 | (0.2) | 0.1 | a |
| | Romania | 14.2 | (1.6) | 28.5 | (1.8) | 30.5 | (1.8) | 18.8 | (1.8) | 6.7 | (1.0) | 1.2 | (0.3) | 0.1 | (0.1) |
| | Russian Federation | 4.3 | (0.8) | 14.4 | (1.1) | 27.7 | (1.2) | 29.0 | (1.2) | 17.4 | (1.3) | 6.3 | (0.8) | 0.9 | (0.2) |
| | Serbia | 11.8 | (1.1) | 24.9 | (1.2) | 30.8 | (1.2) | 21.5 | (1.3) | 8.9 | (0.8) | 2.1 | (0.4) | 0.2 | (0.1) |
| | Slovenia | 3.4 | (0.4) | 10.5 | (0.7) | 21.2 | (1.1) | 26.3 | (1.1) | 21.0 | (1.0) | 12.7 | (0.9) | 4.8 | (0.6) |
| | Chinese Taipei | 1.5 | (0.3) | 7.6 | (0.7) | 15.9 | (1.0) | 24.4 | (1.2) | 27.0 | (1.1) | 18.3 | (1.3) | 5.3 | (0.8) |
| | Thailand | 14.1 | (1.3) | 34.2 | (1.5) | 31.2 | (1.4) | 15.6 | (1.2) | 4.3 | (0.7) | 0.5 | (0.2) | 0.0 | a |
| | Tunisia | 27.1 | (1.5) | 35.1 | (1.3) | 25.6 | (1.4) | 9.5 | (0.9) | 2.5 | (0.7) | 0.2 | (0.1) | a | a |
| | Uruguay | 18.0 | (1.6) | 25.7 | (1.6) | 26.7 | (2.2) | 19.2 | (1.2) | 7.9 | (0.9) | 2.1 | (0.4) | 0.4 | (0.2) |

StatLink http://dx.doi.org/10.1787/142056138443

Pour consulter la version française intégrale de ce tableau, suivre ce lien :
StatLink http://dx.doi.org/10.1787/152610887346

[Part 2/2]

**Table 2.3b** **Percentage of students at each proficiency level on the** *explaining phenomena scientifically* **scale, by gender**

Tableau 2.3b  Pourcentage d'élèves à chaque niveau de compétence sur l'échelle d'*explication scientifique de phénomènes*, selon le sexe

| | | Females – Proficiency levels | | | | | | | | | | | | |
|---|---|---|---|---|---|---|---|---|---|---|---|---|---|---|
| | | Below Level 1 (below 334.94 score points) | | Level 1 (from 334.94 to 409.54 score points) | | Level 2 (from 409.54 to 484.14 score points) | | Level 3 (from 484.14 to 558.73 score points) | | Level 4 (from 558.73 to 633.33 score points) | | Level 5 (from 633.33 to 707.93 score points) | | Level 6 (above 707.93 score points) | |
| | | % | S.E. | % | S.E. | % | S.E. | % | S.E. | % | S.E. | % | S.E. | % | S.E. |
| OECD | Australia | 3.5 | (0.3) | 11.1 | (0.6) | 23.6 | (0.8) | 28.7 | (0.9) | 22.1 | (1.0) | 9.0 | (0.6) | 2.0 | (0.3) |
| | Austria | 4.8 | (1.0) | 12.6 | (1.2) | 21.9 | (1.4) | 28.6 | (1.5) | 22.5 | (1.3) | 8.6 | (1.0) | 0.9 | (0.2) |
| | Belgium | 6.2 | (0.8) | 13.9 | (0.9) | 23.5 | (1.1) | 28.9 | (1.1) | 20.7 | (1.0) | 6.3 | (0.5) | 0.4 | (0.2) |
| | Canada | 2.9 | (0.4) | 9.3 | (0.7) | 22.1 | (0.8) | 29.4 | (1.0) | 23.6 | (1.0) | 10.4 | (0.7) | 2.2 | (0.3) |
| | Czech Republic | 4.1 | (0.8) | 12.2 | (1.1) | 21.3 | (1.4) | 27.2 | (1.2) | 22.1 | (1.5) | 10.5 | (1.3) | 2.5 | (0.4) |
| | Denmark | 4.9 | (0.7) | 14.9 | (1.0) | 27.2 | (1.3) | 28.9 | (1.3) | 17.4 | (1.1) | 5.9 | (0.8) | 0.8 | (0.2) |
| | Finland | 0.5 | (0.2) | 3.2 | (0.5) | 14.4 | (0.9) | 30.1 | (1.2) | 32.0 | (1.5) | 16.3 | (1.1) | 3.6 | (0.5) |
| | France | 7.9 | (0.8) | 17.2 | (1.2) | 27.5 | (1.2) | 28.2 | (1.3) | 15.1 | (1.0) | 3.7 | (0.6) | 0.3 | (0.2) |
| | Germany | 4.2 | (0.6) | 13.0 | (1.2) | 22.1 | (1.4) | 29.0 | (1.4) | 21.1 | (1.3) | 8.7 | (0.9) | 1.8 | (0.3) |
| | Greece | 5.5 | (0.9) | 17.1 | (1.3) | 30.7 | (1.4) | 29.8 | (1.3) | 14.1 | (1.0) | 2.6 | (0.4) | 0.2 | (0.1) |
| | Hungary | 2.7 | (0.5) | 11.0 | (1.2) | 25.9 | (1.2) | 32.2 | (1.6) | 20.8 | (1.3) | 6.2 | (0.9) | 1.2 | (0.3) |
| | Iceland | 4.6 | (0.7) | 15.3 | (1.1) | 29.0 | (1.3) | 30.7 | (1.1) | 16.2 | (1.0) | 3.8 | (0.5) | 0.3 | (0.2) |
| | Ireland | 4.4 | (0.6) | 13.0 | (1.0) | 25.9 | (1.6) | 28.3 | (1.5) | 19.8 | (1.4) | 7.3 | (0.8) | 1.2 | (0.3) |
| | Italy | 7.7 | (0.6) | 18.3 | (0.8) | 28.9 | (1.1) | 27.0 | (0.8) | 13.8 | (0.8) | 3.9 | (0.4) | 0.4 | (0.1) |
| | Japan | 2.5 | (0.5) | 9.6 | (1.1) | 22.1 | (1.4) | 30.9 | (1.2) | 24.8 | (1.4) | 8.4 | (0.9) | 1.6 | (0.3) |
| | Korea | 2.5 | (0.6) | 11.4 | (1.0) | 26.1 | (1.5) | 31.6 | (1.5) | 21.5 | (1.1) | 6.2 | (0.9) | 0.8 | (0.4) |
| | Luxembourg | 7.5 | (0.6) | 17.9 | (1.1) | 29.4 | (1.5) | 27.9 | (1.4) | 14.0 | (0.9) | 3.1 | (0.5) | 0.2 | (0.2) |
| | Mexico | 21.9 | (1.3) | 34.7 | (1.1) | 28.8 | (1.1) | 12.1 | (0.7) | 2.1 | (0.3) | 0.3 | (0.1) | 0.0 | a |
| | Netherlands | 3.0 | (0.6) | 11.9 | (1.2) | 22.6 | (1.3) | 28.9 | (1.3) | 24.5 | (1.1) | 8.0 | (0.6) | 1.1 | (0.3) |
| | New Zealand | 4.4 | (0.6) | 11.6 | (0.9) | 22.0 | (1.1) | 26.4 | (1.5) | 21.6 | (1.2) | 10.9 | (1.0) | 3.1 | (0.6) |
| | Norway | 4.8 | (0.7) | 14.4 | (1.0) | 27.4 | (1.1) | 28.3 | (1.4) | 18.5 | (1.1) | 5.8 | (0.7) | 0.9 | (0.3) |
| | Poland | 3.5 | (0.5) | 14.1 | (1.1) | 26.9 | (1.0) | 29.8 | (1.1) | 18.9 | (1.2) | 6.0 | (0.7) | 0.9 | (0.3) |
| | Portugal | 6.4 | (0.8) | 21.3 | (1.3) | 31.8 | (1.2) | 27.4 | (1.3) | 11.3 | (0.8) | 1.7 | (0.3) | 0.0 | (0.1) |
| | Slovak Republic | 4.6 | (0.7) | 14.7 | (1.2) | 28.1 | (1.9) | 29.1 | (1.4) | 17.8 | (1.1) | 5.1 | (0.7) | 0.6 | (0.2) |
| | Spain | 6.1 | (0.6) | 17.1 | (0.8) | 27.3 | (1.0) | 28.0 | (0.9) | 16.3 | (0.8) | 4.7 | (0.5) | 0.5 | (0.1) |
| | Sweden | 3.9 | (0.6) | 12.2 | (1.0) | 25.1 | (1.3) | 30.2 | (1.2) | 20.1 | (1.2) | 7.3 | (0.8) | 1.2 | (0.3) |
| | Switzerland | 6.0 | (0.6) | 13.7 | (0.8) | 23.6 | (1.1) | 27.3 | (1.1) | 21.1 | (1.0) | 7.0 | (0.9) | 1.4 | (0.3) |
| | Turkey | 14.3 | (1.3) | 32.9 | (1.9) | 30.4 | (1.8) | 15.4 | (1.2) | 5.5 | (1.1) | 1.3 | (0.5) | 0.0 | a |
| | United Kingdom | 4.7 | (0.5) | 14.0 | (0.9) | 23.4 | (1.1) | 26.5 | (0.8) | 20.0 | (0.7) | 9.0 | (0.8) | 2.4 | (0.4) |
| | United States | 8.1 | (0.9) | 19.2 | (1.2) | 25.2 | (1.0) | 24.5 | (1.1) | 15.4 | (1.0) | 5.9 | (0.7) | 1.7 | (0.4) |
| | **OECD total** | **7.6** | **(0.3)** | **17.9** | **(0.5)** | **25.5** | **(0.4)** | **25.5** | **(0.4)** | **16.4** | **(0.3)** | **5.8** | **(0.2)** | **1.2** | **(0.1)** |
| | **OECD average** | **5.6** | **(0.1)** | **15.1** | **(0.2)** | **25.5** | **(0.2)** | **27.7** | **(0.2)** | **18.5** | **(0.2)** | **6.5** | **(0.1)** | **1.1** | **(0.1)** |
| Partners | Argentina | 29.7 | (2.5) | 28.4 | (1.4) | 24.6 | (1.7) | 13.0 | (1.6) | 3.8 | (0.7) | 0.4 | (0.3) | a | a |
| | Azerbaijan | 8.1 | (1.1) | 39.2 | (2.0) | 39.1 | (1.9) | 11.7 | (1.2) | 1.7 | (0.5) | 0.1 | a | a | a |
| | Brazil | 30.8 | (1.4) | 34.3 | (1.2) | 22.2 | (1.0) | 9.5 | (0.9) | 2.7 | (0.5) | 0.5 | (0.2) | 0.0 | a |
| | Bulgaria | 13.5 | (1.6) | 22.5 | (1.7) | 28.3 | (1.4) | 21.9 | (1.5) | 10.5 | (1.3) | 3.0 | (0.6) | 0.4 | (0.2) |
| | Chile | 19.3 | (1.3) | 31.1 | (1.5) | 27.5 | (1.2) | 15.5 | (1.3) | 5.4 | (0.8) | 1.1 | (0.4) | 0.1 | (0.1) |
| | Colombia | 33.4 | (2.0) | 34.3 | (2.1) | 23.0 | (2.0) | 8.2 | (1.1) | 1.1 | (0.3) | 0.1 | a | a | a |
| | Croatia | 3.4 | (0.6) | 15.0 | (1.2) | 30.9 | (1.4) | 30.4 | (1.4) | 16.1 | (1.2) | 3.8 | (0.6) | 0.4 | (0.2) |
| | Estonia | 0.9 | (0.2) | 6.6 | (0.8) | 21.4 | (1.2) | 29.8 | (1.6) | 26.8 | (1.3) | 12.6 | (1.0) | 2.0 | (0.4) |
| | Hong Kong-China | 1.4 | (0.4) | 6.9 | (0.7) | 17.7 | (1.2) | 31.1 | (1.5) | 28.1 | (1.1) | 13.0 | (1.0) | 1.7 | (0.3) |
| | Indonesia | 23.7 | (1.7) | 41.4 | (2.0) | 26.0 | (1.5) | 7.8 | (1.3) | 1.0 | (0.4) | 0.0 | a | a | a |
| | Israel | 16.5 | (1.6) | 24.2 | (1.2) | 26.9 | (1.4) | 20.2 | (1.6) | 9.8 | (1.2) | 2.3 | (0.4) | 0.2 | (0.1) |
| | Jordan | 10.5 | (1.0) | 23.7 | (1.3) | 31.6 | (1.2) | 22.5 | (1.2) | 9.5 | (0.9) | 2.0 | (0.5) | 0.2 | (0.1) |
| | Kyrgyzstan | 51.2 | (1.6) | 33.1 | (1.4) | 12.4 | (1.0) | 2.7 | (0.4) | 0.6 | (0.2) | 0.0 | a | a | a |
| | Latvia | 4.5 | (0.8) | 15.8 | (1.1) | 30.5 | (1.3) | 30.6 | (1.3) | 15.0 | (0.9) | 3.3 | (0.4) | 0.4 | (0.1) |
| | Liechtenstein | 3.2 | (1.3) | 12.1 | (2.6) | 23.7 | (4.5) | 28.3 | (4.9) | 22.8 | (3.6) | 8.0 | (2.1) | 2.0 | (1.1) |
| | Lithuania | 4.8 | (0.6) | 15.9 | (1.1) | 26.4 | (1.1) | 28.8 | (1.3) | 17.7 | (1.1) | 5.4 | (0.8) | 0.9 | (0.3) |
| | Macao-China | 1.3 | (0.3) | 8.4 | (0.7) | 25.9 | (1.4) | 36.0 | (1.4) | 22.5 | (1.5) | 5.6 | (0.7) | 0.4 | (0.2) |
| | Montenegro | 17.2 | (1.0) | 33.0 | (1.1) | 31.0 | (1.6) | 14.7 | (1.1) | 3.9 | (0.6) | 0.2 | (0.2) | a | a |
| | Qatar | 35.0 | (1.1) | 35.9 | (0.9) | 20.3 | (0.9) | 6.8 | (0.6) | 1.6 | (0.3) | 0.3 | (0.1) | 0.0 | a |
| | Romania | 13.5 | (2.0) | 31.5 | (1.9) | 34.4 | (1.8) | 16.4 | (1.7) | 3.8 | (0.9) | 0.4 | (0.2) | 0.0 | a |
| | Russian Federation | 5.6 | (0.7) | 17.2 | (1.1) | 31.5 | (1.2) | 29.2 | (1.3) | 13.3 | (1.0) | 2.9 | (0.4) | 0.4 | (0.2) |
| | Serbia | 12.0 | (1.2) | 25.5 | (1.3) | 31.8 | (1.6) | 22.4 | (1.7) | 7.3 | (0.9) | 1.0 | (0.2) | 0.0 | a |
| | Slovenia | 3.6 | (0.5) | 10.9 | (0.9) | 22.8 | (1.7) | 27.7 | (1.4) | 21.8 | (1.2) | 10.2 | (1.0) | 2.9 | (0.5) |
| | Chinese Taipei | 2.0 | (0.4) | 10.0 | (1.1) | 18.5 | (1.3) | 26.5 | (1.2) | 26.3 | (1.5) | 13.7 | (1.2) | 3.1 | (0.6) |
| | Thailand | 10.9 | (0.9) | 35.0 | (1.6) | 35.8 | (1.6) | 14.6 | (1.1) | 3.3 | (0.5) | 0.4 | (0.1) | 0.0 | (0.0) |
| | Tunisia | 29.4 | (1.5) | 35.7 | (1.4) | 24.4 | (1.4) | 8.7 | (1.1) | 1.7 | (0.6) | 0.1 | a | 0.0 | a |
| | Uruguay | 19.6 | (1.3) | 27.0 | (1.3) | 29.0 | (1.3) | 17.4 | (0.9) | 5.9 | (0.6) | 1.0 | (0.3) | 0.1 | a |

StatLink ᵃ᎔ᔕ http://dx.doi.org/10.1787/142056138443

Pour consulter la version française intégrale de ce tableau, suivre ce lien :
StatLink ᵃ᎔ᔕ http://dx.doi.org/10.1787/152610887346

[Part 1/2]

**Table 2.3c** Mean score, variation and gender differences in student performance on the *explaining phenomena scientifically* scale

Tableau 2.3c Score moyen, différences de score selon le sexe et répartition des scores sur l'échelle d'*explication scientifique de phénomènes*

| | | All students | | | | Gender differences | | | | | |
|---|---|---|---|---|---|---|---|---|---|---|---|
| | | Mean score | | Standard deviation | | Males | | Females | | Difference (M - F) | |
| | | Mean | S.E. | S.D. | S.E. | Mean score | S.E. | Mean score | S.E. | Score dif. | S.E. |
| OECD | Australia | 520 | (2.3) | 102 | (1.0) | 527 | (3.1) | 513 | (2.7) | **13** | (3.6) |
| | Austria | 516 | (4.0) | 100 | (2.1) | 526 | (4.4) | 507 | (4.7) | **19** | (4.8) |
| | Belgium | 503 | (2.5) | 102 | (1.9) | 510 | (3.4) | 494 | (3.1) | **16** | (4.1) |
| | Canada | 531 | (2.1) | 100 | (1.2) | 539 | (2.6) | 522 | (2.3) | **17** | (2.5) |
| | Czech Republic | 527 | (3.5) | 102 | (1.8) | 537 | (4.3) | 516 | (4.6) | **21** | (5.7) |
| | Denmark | 501 | (3.3) | 96 | (1.4) | 512 | (3.8) | 491 | (3.7) | **21** | (3.4) |
| | Finland | 566 | (2.0) | 88 | (1.1) | 571 | (2.5) | 562 | (2.5) | **9** | (3.0) |
| | France | 481 | (3.2) | 100 | (1.8) | 489 | (4.2) | 474 | (3.4) | **15** | (4.1) |
| | Germany | 519 | (3.7) | 103 | (2.0) | 529 | (4.5) | 508 | (3.7) | **21** | (3.7) |
| | Greece | 476 | (3.0) | 93 | (1.9) | 478 | (4.3) | 475 | (3.0) | 3 | (4.2) |
| | Hungary | 518 | (2.6) | 94 | (1.5) | 529 | (3.2) | 507 | (3.6) | **22** | (4.4) |
| | Iceland | 488 | (1.5) | 92 | (1.2) | 491 | (2.6) | 485 | (2.1) | 6 | (3.7) |
| | Ireland | 505 | (3.2) | 100 | (1.6) | 510 | (4.4) | 501 | (3.5) | **9** | (4.6) |
| | Italy | 480 | (2.0) | 100 | (1.3) | 487 | (2.8) | 472 | (2.5) | **15** | (3.4) |
| | Japan | 527 | (3.1) | 97 | (1.8) | 535 | (4.6) | 519 | (4.4) | **16** | (6.6) |
| | Korea | 512 | (3.3) | 91 | (2.3) | 517 | (4.8) | 506 | (4.0) | 11 | (5.7) |
| | Luxembourg | 483 | (1.1) | 97 | (0.9) | 495 | (1.8) | 471 | (2.0) | **25** | (3.0) |
| | Mexico | 406 | (2.7) | 83 | (1.6) | 415 | (3.3) | 398 | (2.6) | **18** | (2.3) |
| | Netherlands | 522 | (2.7) | 95 | (1.7) | 531 | (3.1) | 512 | (3.1) | **18** | (3.0) |
| | New Zealand | 522 | (2.8) | 111 | (1.5) | 528 | (4.0) | 517 | (3.6) | **11** | (5.2) |
| | Norway | 495 | (3.0) | 101 | (1.7) | 498 | (3.9) | 492 | (3.2) | 6 | (3.9) |
| | Poland | 506 | (2.5) | 95 | (1.2) | 514 | (2.9) | 498 | (2.8) | **17** | (2.7) |
| | Portugal | 469 | (2.9) | 87 | (1.7) | 477 | (3.6) | 462 | (3.0) | **16** | (3.2) |
| | Slovak Republic | 501 | (2.7) | 97 | (1.9) | 512 | (4.0) | 490 | (3.0) | **22** | (4.7) |
| | Spain | 490 | (2.4) | 98 | (1.0) | 499 | (2.8) | 481 | (2.7) | **18** | (2.6) |
| | Sweden | 510 | (2.9) | 99 | (1.8) | 516 | (3.0) | 504 | (3.5) | **12** | (3.1) |
| | Switzerland | 508 | (3.3) | 102 | (1.8) | 517 | (3.4) | 498 | (3.9) | **18** | (2.8) |
| | Turkey | 423 | (4.1) | 86 | (3.5) | 423 | (4.7) | 423 | (4.5) | 1 | (4.1) |
| | United Kingdom | 517 | (2.3) | 110 | (1.4) | 527 | (3.0) | 506 | (2.7) | **21** | (3.5) |
| | United States | 486 | (4.3) | 110 | (1.5) | 492 | (5.3) | 480 | (4.0) | **13** | (3.6) |
| | **OECD total** | 489 | (1.2) | 107 | (0.6) | 497 | (1.4) | 481 | (1.3) | **15** | (1.2) |
| | **OECD average** | 500 | (0.5) | 98 | (0.3) | 508 | (0.7) | 493 | (0.6) | **15** | (0.7) |
| Partners | Argentina | 386 | (6.0) | 104 | (2.8) | 387 | (6.4) | 386 | (7.0) | 0 | (5.8) |
| | Azerbaijan | 412 | (3.0) | 63 | (2.0) | 408 | (3.3) | 417 | (3.0) | **-9** | (1.9) |
| | Brazil | 390 | (2.7) | 91 | (2.0) | 400 | (3.0) | 382 | (2.9) | **19** | (2.4) |
| | Bulgaria | 444 | (5.8) | 105 | (3.4) | 442 | (6.5) | 447 | (6.5) | -5 | (5.8) |
| | Chile | 432 | (4.1) | 94 | (1.8) | 448 | (5.1) | 414 | (4.1) | **34** | (4.6) |
| | Colombia | 379 | (3.4) | 90 | (1.6) | 388 | (4.3) | 371 | (4.3) | **18** | (4.8) |
| | Croatia | 492 | (2.5) | 87 | (1.4) | 498 | (3.2) | 487 | (3.3) | **11** | (4.1) |
| | Estonia | 541 | (2.6) | 91 | (1.3) | 544 | (3.2) | 537 | (3.0) | 6 | (3.3) |
| | Hong Kong-China | 549 | (2.5) | 94 | (2.1) | 560 | (3.5) | 539 | (3.3) | **21** | (4.6) |
| | Indonesia | 395 | (5.1) | 72 | (2.9) | 403 | (7.0) | 386 | (3.8) | 17 | (5.7) |
| | Israel | 443 | (3.6) | 109 | (2.0) | 451 | (5.4) | 436 | (4.0) | **16** | (6.4) |
| | Jordan | 438 | (3.1) | 98 | (1.9) | 427 | (4.6) | 448 | (4.1) | **-21** | (6.0) |
| | Kyrgyzstan | 334 | (3.1) | 85 | (1.8) | 335 | (3.9) | 333 | (2.9) | 2 | (3.0) |
| | Latvia | 486 | (2.9) | 88 | (1.3) | 491 | (3.6) | 481 | (3.2) | **10** | (3.3) |
| | Liechtenstein | 516 | (4.1) | 97 | (3.0) | 519 | (7.5) | 513 | (6.4) | 6 | (11.1) |
| | Lithuania | 494 | (3.0) | 96 | (1.8) | 499 | (3.3) | 490 | (3.4) | **9** | (3.1) |
| | Macao-China | 520 | (1.2) | 83 | (1.2) | 527 | (2.0) | 513 | (1.6) | **14** | (2.7) |
| | Montenegro | 417 | (1.1) | 82 | (0.9) | 421 | (1.8) | 412 | (1.7) | **9** | (2.7) |
| | Qatar | 356 | (1.0) | 88 | (0.9) | 342 | (1.4) | 371 | (1.6) | **-29** | (2.3) |
| | Romania | 426 | (4.0) | 83 | (2.4) | 431 | (4.3) | 421 | (4.5) | 10 | (3.6) |
| | Russian Federation | 483 | (3.4) | 90 | (1.3) | 493 | (4.0) | 474 | (3.4) | **19** | (2.6) |
| | Serbia | 441 | (3.1) | 90 | (1.6) | 444 | (3.7) | 438 | (3.8) | 6 | (4.1) |
| | Slovenia | 523 | (1.5) | 105 | (1.1) | 528 | (2.3) | 518 | (2.2) | **10** | (3.3) |
| | Chinese Taipei | 545 | (3.7) | 101 | (1.7) | 554 | (4.3) | 535 | (5.3) | **19** | (6.1) |
| | Thailand | 420 | (2.1) | 75 | (1.3) | 418 | (3.4) | 421 | (2.2) | -3 | (3.6) |
| | Tunisia | 383 | (2.9) | 83 | (2.4) | 386 | (3.1) | 381 | (3.5) | 5 | (3.1) |
| | Uruguay | 423 | (2.9) | 99 | (1.8) | 429 | (4.0) | 418 | (3.1) | **11** | (4.0) |

Note: Values that are statistically significant are indicated in bold (see Annex A3).
*StatLink* ᴍᴬᴾ http://dx.doi.org/10.1787/142056138443

Pour consulter la version française intégrale de ce tableau, suivre ce lien :
*StatLink* ᴍᴬᴾ http://dx.doi.org/10.1787/152610887346

[Part 2/2]

**Table 2.3c** **Mean score, variation and gender differences in student performance on the *explaining phenomena scientifically* scale**

Tableau 2.3c  Score moyen, différences de score selon le sexe et répartition des scores sur l'échelle d'*explication scientifique de phénomènes*

| | | \multicolumn{12}{c}{Percentiles} |
| | | 5th | | 10th | | 25th | | 75th | | 90th | | 95th | |
| | | Score | S.E. | Score | S.E. | Score | S.E. | Score | S.E. | Score | S.E. | Score | S.E. |
|---|---|---|---|---|---|---|---|---|---|---|---|---|---|
| OECD | Australia | 351 | (3.2) | 388 | (3.0) | 450 | (2.7) | 592 | (2.8) | 650 | (3.1) | 683 | (3.1) |
| | Austria | 343 | (7.5) | 382 | (7.3) | 447 | (4.9) | 590 | (4.0) | 642 | (3.5) | 672 | (3.9) |
| | Belgium | 328 | (6.5) | 365 | (5.8) | 432 | (4.0) | 578 | (2.3) | 632 | (2.4) | 661 | (2.5) |
| | Canada | 362 | (4.4) | 400 | (3.4) | 464 | (2.8) | 601 | (2.5) | 657 | (2.4) | 689 | (2.6) |
| | Czech Republic | 360 | (6.3) | 395 | (5.1) | 456 | (4.5) | 598 | (3.8) | 659 | (4.6) | 694 | (4.7) |
| | Denmark | 342 | (5.1) | 376 | (5.0) | 435 | (4.0) | 568 | (3.6) | 627 | (3.8) | 658 | (4.2) |
| | Finland | 420 | (4.8) | 452 | (3.3) | 506 | (2.6) | 626 | (2.5) | 679 | (2.8) | 709 | (4.0) |
| | France | 313 | (5.6) | 349 | (5.5) | 412 | (4.7) | 552 | (3.3) | 609 | (3.9) | 640 | (3.6) |
| | Germany | 345 | (6.8) | 381 | (6.2) | 448 | (5.5) | 592 | (3.8) | 651 | (3.6) | 684 | (4.6) |
| | Greece | 321 | (6.5) | 356 | (5.4) | 413 | (4.1) | 541 | (3.6) | 596 | (3.5) | 626 | (4.2) |
| | Hungary | 365 | (3.8) | 398 | (4.0) | 453 | (3.2) | 583 | (3.4) | 639 | (4.3) | 674 | (5.5) |
| | Iceland | 335 | (4.3) | 369 | (3.3) | 425 | (2.3) | 553 | (2.4) | 606 | (2.9) | 636 | (4.3) |
| | Ireland | 340 | (6.1) | 377 | (5.0) | 436 | (4.1) | 575 | (3.9) | 635 | (3.9) | 668 | (4.4) |
| | Italy | 315 | (3.7) | 350 | (3.2) | 411 | (2.8) | 548 | (2.6) | 608 | (2.6) | 642 | (2.6) |
| | Japan | 362 | (6.5) | 399 | (5.3) | 462 | (4.2) | 595 | (2.9) | 649 | (3.6) | 680 | (3.9) |
| | Korea | 359 | (6.3) | 392 | (5.0) | 450 | (3.9) | 576 | (4.1) | 627 | (5.1) | 656 | (5.9) |
| | Luxembourg | 321 | (2.9) | 357 | (2.5) | 416 | (2.2) | 552 | (1.8) | 608 | (2.4) | 639 | (4.2) |
| | Mexico | 274 | (4.8) | 301 | (3.7) | 349 | (3.2) | 462 | (2.9) | 514 | (3.5) | 545 | (4.1) |
| | Netherlands | 360 | (5.3) | 394 | (5.6) | 455 | (4.7) | 589 | (2.7) | 643 | (3.3) | 673 | (3.5) |
| | New Zealand | 339 | (5.9) | 378 | (4.3) | 445 | (3.6) | 601 | (3.2) | 664 | (3.1) | 700 | (4.1) |
| | Norway | 327 | (8.2) | 366 | (5.1) | 427 | (3.6) | 565 | (3.2) | 624 | (3.3) | 656 | (4.0) |
| | Poland | 353 | (4.4) | 384 | (3.8) | 438 | (2.8) | 572 | (3.3) | 630 | (3.2) | 664 | (3.8) |
| | Portugal | 329 | (4.7) | 357 | (4.5) | 409 | (3.8) | 530 | (2.7) | 581 | (2.9) | 610 | (3.7) |
| | Slovak Republic | 342 | (4.5) | 377 | (5.5) | 435 | (3.0) | 568 | (3.6) | 626 | (3.8) | 660 | (5.1) |
| | Spain | 329 | (4.0) | 364 | (3.2) | 423 | (2.7) | 558 | (3.1) | 616 | (2.6) | 649 | (2.9) |
| | Sweden | 346 | (7.2) | 382 | (5.6) | 443 | (3.6) | 578 | (3.3) | 636 | (3.6) | 669 | (3.4) |
| | Switzerland | 333 | (5.3) | 373 | (4.6) | 438 | (4.1) | 580 | (3.4) | 635 | (4.8) | 667 | (4.7) |
| | Turkey | 297 | (3.8) | 321 | (2.9) | 363 | (2.7) | 475 | (6.5) | 542 | (11.2) | 584 | (12.5) |
| | United Kingdom | 340 | (4.5) | 375 | (3.4) | 439 | (3.0) | 594 | (2.9) | 660 | (3.4) | 696 | (3.9) |
| | United States | 311 | (5.5) | 345 | (5.2) | 404 | (5.5) | 565 | (4.8) | 632 | (4.6) | 670 | (6.0) |
| | **OECD total** | 317 | (2.0) | 351 | (1.6) | 412 | (1.6) | 565 | (1.3) | 629 | (1.5) | 664 | (2.2) |
| | **OECD average** | 339 | (1.0) | 373 | (0.9) | 433 | (0.7) | 569 | (0.6) | 626 | (0.7) | 658 | (0.9) |
| Partners | Argentina | 207 | (12.8) | 252 | (8.4) | 320 | (6.3) | 459 | (6.6) | 516 | (5.5) | 552 | (6.9) |
| | Azerbaijan | 314 | (2.8) | 334 | (2.9) | 368 | (2.9) | 452 | (3.6) | 494 | (5.3) | 523 | (8.1) |
| | Brazil | 252 | (4.5) | 280 | (3.1) | 328 | (2.5) | 447 | (4.2) | 512 | (5.4) | 551 | (6.5) |
| | Bulgaria | 276 | (9.4) | 312 | (6.1) | 370 | (5.6) | 516 | (6.9) | 583 | (8.0) | 618 | (8.8) |
| | Chile | 284 | (4.3) | 314 | (4.0) | 366 | (4.0) | 495 | (5.7) | 560 | (6.1) | 597 | (6.7) |
| | Colombia | 230 | (5.8) | 264 | (5.2) | 319 | (4.5) | 439 | (4.5) | 495 | (4.6) | 528 | (4.1) |
| | Croatia | 351 | (4.1) | 380 | (3.8) | 432 | (3.5) | 552 | (3.3) | 606 | (3.8) | 638 | (4.1) |
| | Estonia | 393 | (5.1) | 422 | (3.1) | 477 | (3.2) | 604 | (3.2) | 658 | (3.5) | 688 | (3.7) |
| | Hong Kong-China | 387 | (7.0) | 423 | (5.0) | 488 | (3.4) | 615 | (2.7) | 667 | (3.3) | 695 | (3.9) |
| | Indonesia | 284 | (4.1) | 307 | (4.1) | 345 | (3.2) | 440 | (7.7) | 492 | (9.9) | 521 | (9.5) |
| | Israel | 269 | (6.0) | 304 | (5.6) | 366 | (4.2) | 520 | (4.7) | 587 | (4.2) | 625 | (4.2) |
| | Jordan | 278 | (4.9) | 314 | (3.7) | 371 | (3.5) | 505 | (4.1) | 563 | (5.3) | 597 | (5.9) |
| | Kyrgyzstan | 199 | (5.2) | 228 | (4.2) | 279 | (3.3) | 386 | (3.4) | 438 | (5.0) | 475 | (5.5) |
| | Latvia | 340 | (4.8) | 373 | (3.8) | 427 | (3.6) | 546 | (4.0) | 599 | (3.7) | 631 | (4.1) |
| | Liechtenstein | 357 | (10.1) | 390 | (10.5) | 450 | (7.3) | 586 | (7.2) | 640 | (8.7) | 670 | (12.2) |
| | Lithuania | 338 | (4.3) | 370 | (4.1) | 428 | (3.5) | 561 | (3.8) | 617 | (5.1) | 651 | (6.3) |
| | Macao-China | 381 | (4.3) | 413 | (3.1) | 464 | (2.0) | 578 | (2.3) | 626 | (2.5) | 652 | (2.8) |
| | Montenegro | 289 | (2.3) | 314 | (2.2) | 359 | (2.0) | 471 | (1.8) | 526 | (2.7) | 559 | (4.6) |
| | Qatar | 226 | (2.5) | 252 | (1.8) | 296 | (2.2) | 406 | (1.8) | 472 | (2.5) | 515 | (2.5) |
| | Romania | 297 | (5.7) | 321 | (5.3) | 367 | (6.0) | 481 | (4.8) | 535 | (7.2) | 567 | (7.2) |
| | Russian Federation | 335 | (5.1) | 367 | (4.3) | 422 | (4.5) | 544 | (3.8) | 600 | (4.2) | 634 | (4.3) |
| | Serbia | 295 | (5.6) | 326 | (4.7) | 380 | (3.6) | 502 | (3.9) | 557 | (3.8) | 589 | (4.2) |
| | Slovenia | 353 | (4.7) | 388 | (3.9) | 449 | (2.0) | 595 | (2.6) | 661 | (3.3) | 698 | (5.4) |
| | Chinese Taipei | 373 | (4.5) | 407 | (5.0) | 474 | (5.7) | 619 | (3.9) | 673 | (3.4) | 702 | (3.4) |
| | Thailand | 304 | (3.8) | 327 | (2.7) | 368 | (2.5) | 468 | (2.7) | 519 | (4.0) | 551 | (4.2) |
| | Tunisia | 253 | (3.4) | 281 | (3.0) | 327 | (3.1) | 437 | (3.8) | 491 | (6.8) | 526 | (9.5) |
| | Uruguay | 260 | (7.0) | 295 | (4.9) | 357 | (4.2) | 490 | (3.3) | 550 | (3.8) | 586 | (5.4) |

Note: Values that are statistically significant are indicated in bold (see Annex A3).
*StatLink* http://dx.doi.org/10.1787/142056138443

Pour consulter la version française intégrale de ce tableau, suivre ce lien :
*StatLink* http://dx.doi.org/10.1787/152610887346

**PISA 2006: Vol. 2 Data/*Données***

[Part 1/1]

**Table 2.4a** Percentage of students at each proficiency level on the *using scientific evidence* scale

Tableau 2.4a Pourcentage d'élèves à chaque niveau de compétence sur l'échelle d'*utilisation de faits scientifiques*

| | Proficiency levels | | | | | | | | | | | | | |
|---|---|---|---|---|---|---|---|---|---|---|---|---|---|---|
| | Below Level 1 (below 334.94 score points) | | Level 1 (from 334.94 to 409.54 score points) | | Level 2 (from 409.54 to 484.14 score points) | | Level 3 (from 484.14 to 558.73 score points) | | Level 4 (from 558.73 to 633.33 score points) | | Level 5 (from 633.33 to 707.93 score points) | | Level 6 (above 707.93 score points) | |
| | % | S.E. | % | S.E. | % | S.E. | % | S.E. | % | S.E. | % | S.E. | % | S.E. |
| **OECD** | | | | | | | | | | | | | | |
| Australia | 3.9 | (0.3) | 9.4 | (0.5) | 18.8 | (0.6) | 26.2 | (0.6) | 24.4 | (0.6) | 13.3 | (0.5) | 3.9 | (0.4) |
| Austria | 8.1 | (1.2) | 12.5 | (1.1) | 20.4 | (1.0) | 24.0 | (0.9) | 21.8 | (0.9) | 10.6 | (0.8) | 2.4 | (0.4) |
| Belgium | 7.1 | (0.8) | 10.8 | (0.6) | 18.1 | (0.7) | 24.6 | (0.8) | 24.7 | (0.7) | 12.6 | (0.6) | 2.1 | (0.3) |
| Canada | 2.5 | (0.3) | 7.7 | (0.5) | 17.2 | (0.7) | 27.0 | (0.8) | 27.9 | (0.7) | 14.2 | (0.6) | 3.6 | (0.3) |
| Czech Republic | 7.5 | (0.9) | 13.6 | (0.9) | 22.3 | (1.1) | 24.9 | (1.1) | 19.7 | (0.9) | 9.3 | (0.8) | 2.8 | (0.4) |
| Denmark | 7.8 | (0.7) | 15.4 | (0.7) | 23.9 | (0.9) | 26.2 | (1.0) | 18.2 | (0.8) | 7.1 | (0.6) | 1.4 | (0.3) |
| Finland | 1.0 | (0.2) | 4.4 | (0.4) | 13.9 | (0.7) | 26.0 | (0.7) | 29.6 | (0.8) | 18.3 | (0.7) | 6.7 | (0.5) |
| France | 7.2 | (0.8) | 12.6 | (0.8) | 19.5 | (1.0) | 23.5 | (1.0) | 22.7 | (1.0) | 12.0 | (0.8) | 2.6 | (0.5) |
| Germany | 6.7 | (1.0) | 11.5 | (0.9) | 18.9 | (0.8) | 25.4 | (0.9) | 22.7 | (1.0) | 11.5 | (0.8) | 3.3 | (0.4) |
| Greece | 11.3 | (1.1) | 16.7 | (0.9) | 26.3 | (1.1) | 27.1 | (1.1) | 14.0 | (0.9) | 4.0 | (0.5) | 0.5 | (0.1) |
| Hungary | 6.0 | (0.7) | 13.8 | (0.9) | 24.3 | (1.1) | 28.0 | (1.1) | 18.8 | (0.9) | 7.7 | (0.7) | 1.4 | (0.2) |
| Iceland | 8.6 | (0.6) | 15.0 | (0.7) | 22.4 | (0.8) | 25.6 | (1.0) | 18.7 | (0.7) | 7.8 | (0.6) | 1.9 | (0.3) |
| Ireland | 5.4 | (0.6) | 12.5 | (0.7) | 22.6 | (0.8) | 27.6 | (1.0) | 21.5 | (1.1) | 8.8 | (0.7) | 1.6 | (0.3) |
| Italy | 11.9 | (0.6) | 17.7 | (0.7) | 25.0 | (0.6) | 24.6 | (0.6) | 14.9 | (0.6) | 5.2 | (0.4) | 0.8 | (0.1) |
| Japan | 4.6 | (0.6) | 8.7 | (0.7) | 15.5 | (0.8) | 22.8 | (0.8) | 25.4 | (1.0) | 16.7 | (0.9) | 6.2 | (0.5) |
| Korea | 3.1 | (0.6) | 8.0 | (0.8) | 17.1 | (0.7) | 27.3 | (1.2) | 26.7 | (1.0) | 14.4 | (1.0) | 3.4 | (0.5) |
| Luxembourg | 9.2 | (0.4) | 14.4 | (0.7) | 21.7 | (0.7) | 25.4 | (0.6) | 19.0 | (0.7) | 8.4 | (0.6) | 1.8 | (0.3) |
| Mexico | 23.7 | (1.3) | 29.1 | (0.9) | 27.5 | (0.9) | 15.2 | (0.7) | 4.0 | (0.4) | 0.5 | (0.1) | 0.0 | (0.0) |
| Netherlands | 3.8 | (0.6) | 12.1 | (1.0) | 19.5 | (0.8) | 23.9 | (1.2) | 23.9 | (1.4) | 13.7 | (1.0) | 3.2 | (0.3) |
| New Zealand | 5.4 | (0.6) | 10.0 | (0.7) | 17.7 | (0.7) | 22.0 | (0.8) | 22.5 | (0.8) | 15.5 | (0.8) | 6.9 | (0.5) |
| Norway | 10.2 | (0.9) | 18.4 | (0.9) | 25.5 | (1.0) | 23.8 | (1.2) | 15.5 | (0.9) | 5.5 | (0.5) | 1.2 | (0.2) |
| Poland | 5.6 | (0.6) | 14.9 | (0.8) | 25.5 | (0.7) | 27.7 | (0.9) | 18.8 | (0.9) | 6.6 | (0.6) | 1.0 | (0.3) |
| Portugal | 9.7 | (0.9) | 17.8 | (0.9) | 25.5 | (1.0) | 25.7 | (1.1) | 16.2 | (0.9) | 4.6 | (0.4) | 0.5 | (0.2) |
| Slovak Republic | 9.8 | (0.9) | 16.1 | (1.1) | 25.3 | (1.2) | 25.2 | (1.0) | 16.7 | (0.9) | 6.0 | (0.6) | 0.9 | (0.2) |
| Spain | 7.2 | (0.5) | 15.3 | (0.7) | 25.5 | (0.6) | 28.0 | (0.6) | 18.0 | (0.7) | 5.2 | (0.4) | 0.7 | (0.1) |
| Sweden | 6.7 | (0.6) | 14.1 | (0.8) | 23.3 | (1.1) | 27.1 | (0.8) | 19.5 | (0.8) | 7.7 | (0.5) | 1.6 | (0.2) |
| Switzerland | 5.9 | (0.6) | 11.0 | (0.5) | 19.2 | (0.8) | 25.7 | (0.7) | 23.3 | (0.8) | 11.4 | (0.6) | 3.4 | (0.4) |
| Turkey | 19.1 | (1.1) | 30.3 | (1.4) | 27.0 | (1.3) | 15.2 | (1.0) | 6.8 | (1.0) | 1.6 | (0.5) | 0.1 | (0.1) |
| United Kingdom | 6.8 | (0.5) | 12.5 | (0.6) | 20.1 | (0.6) | 23.8 | (0.8) | 21.1 | (0.8) | 11.7 | (0.5) | 4.0 | (0.4) |
| United States | 10.0 | (1.5) | 16.1 | (0.8) | 22.1 | (1.1) | 22.8 | (0.9) | 17.8 | (0.8) | 8.7 | (0.8) | 2.5 | (0.4) |
| **OECD total** | 9.5 | (0.4) | 15.6 | (0.3) | 21.7 | (0.3) | 23.1 | (0.3) | 18.5 | (0.3) | 9.1 | (0.2) | 2.5 | (0.1) |
| **OECD average** | 7.9 | (0.1) | 14.1 | (0.1) | 21.7 | (0.2) | 24.7 | (0.2) | 19.8 | (0.2) | 9.4 | (0.1) | 2.4 | (0.1) |
| **Partners** | | | | | | | | | | | | | | |
| Argentina | 31.9 | (2.4) | 24.6 | (1.2) | 23.4 | (1.2) | 13.8 | (1.1) | 5.4 | (0.7) | 0.9 | (0.3) | 0.1 | (0.1) |
| Azerbaijan | 48.0 | (2.1) | 33.2 | (1.3) | 13.9 | (1.2) | 4.1 | (0.8) | 0.7 | (0.2) | 0.0 | (0.0) | a | a |
| Brazil | 35.0 | (1.3) | 28.3 | (1.1) | 20.9 | (0.9) | 11.0 | (0.8) | 4.0 | (0.4) | 0.8 | (0.3) | 0.1 | (0.1) |
| Bulgaria | 27.7 | (2.3) | 20.7 | (1.2) | 21.0 | (1.2) | 16.6 | (1.2) | 9.9 | (1.0) | 3.2 | (0.7) | 0.9 | (0.3) |
| Chile | 16.0 | (1.3) | 23.9 | (1.3) | 26.9 | (1.2) | 20.0 | (1.3) | 10.0 | (0.9) | 2.8 | (0.5) | 0.3 | (0.1) |
| Colombia | 29.0 | (2.0) | 32.0 | (1.4) | 26.0 | (1.4) | 10.5 | (0.9) | 2.3 | (0.3) | 0.2 | (0.1) | 0.0 | a |
| Croatia | 5.2 | (0.6) | 15.1 | (0.8) | 26.8 | (1.0) | 28.4 | (1.0) | 17.8 | (0.9) | 5.8 | (0.5) | 0.9 | (0.2) |
| Estonia | 1.9 | (0.3) | 8.2 | (0.6) | 20.3 | (0.8) | 30.7 | (1.2) | 25.2 | (1.2) | 11.6 | (0.7) | 2.2 | (0.3) |
| Hong Kong-China | 2.7 | (0.4) | 7.6 | (0.7) | 16.1 | (0.7) | 26.8 | (1.0) | 28.9 | (0.9) | 14.9 | (0.8) | 3.0 | (0.3) |
| Indonesia | 28.1 | (2.6) | 35.0 | (1.7) | 24.2 | (1.5) | 10.2 | (1.9) | 2.4 | (1.0) | 0.1 | (0.1) | a | a |
| Israel | 18.3 | (1.3) | 18.0 | (0.9) | 20.3 | (0.8) | 18.5 | (0.8) | 14.6 | (0.9) | 7.7 | (0.6) | 2.6 | (0.3) |
| Jordan | 23.6 | (1.2) | 27.3 | (1.2) | 27.4 | (1.2) | 15.7 | (0.9) | 5.1 | (0.6) | 0.8 | (0.3) | 0.0 | a |
| Kyrgyzstan | 69.8 | (1.3) | 18.1 | (0.8) | 7.8 | (0.6) | 3.0 | (0.5) | 1.1 | (0.3) | 0.1 | (0.1) | 0.0 | a |
| Latvia | 5.2 | (0.7) | 14.1 | (0.9) | 26.2 | (1.0) | 30.9 | (1.0) | 18.3 | (1.0) | 5.0 | (0.5) | 0.4 | (0.1) |
| Liechtenstein | 3.9 | (1.1) | 9.7 | (1.8) | 19.4 | (3.0) | 24.3 | (2.4) | 22.0 | (2.7) | 15.4 | (2.0) | 5.3 | (1.4) |
| Lithuania | 6.7 | (0.6) | 15.8 | (0.9) | 25.3 | (0.9) | 28.0 | (0.9) | 18.0 | (0.9) | 5.6 | (0.6) | 0.8 | (0.2) |
| Macao-China | 2.4 | (0.3) | 9.4 | (0.5) | 24.8 | (0.8) | 33.5 | (0.9) | 23.0 | (1.0) | 6.4 | (0.5) | 0.5 | (0.2) |
| Montenegro | 22.8 | (0.6) | 29.5 | (0.9) | 27.2 | (0.8) | 14.9 | (0.7) | 4.9 | (0.5) | 0.7 | (0.2) | 0.0 | a |
| Qatar | 59.3 | (0.6) | 22.4 | (0.6) | 10.8 | (0.6) | 4.8 | (0.3) | 1.9 | (0.2) | 0.6 | (0.1) | 0.1 | (0.1) |
| Romania | 25.1 | (2.4) | 25.5 | (1.4) | 25.7 | (1.8) | 16.6 | (1.8) | 5.8 | (0.8) | 1.2 | (0.3) | 0.1 | (0.1) |
| Russian Federation | 7.7 | (0.8) | 16.4 | (0.9) | 27.2 | (1.0) | 26.3 | (0.8) | 15.9 | (1.0) | 5.4 | (0.5) | 1.1 | (0.2) |
| Serbia | 18.7 | (1.2) | 25.4 | (1.0) | 27.4 | (1.1) | 19.4 | (1.2) | 7.5 | (0.7) | 1.4 | (0.3) | 0.1 | (0.1) |
| Slovenia | 3.5 | (0.3) | 11.6 | (0.5) | 22.7 | (0.7) | 27.5 | (0.7) | 22.3 | (0.7) | 10.2 | (0.5) | 2.2 | (0.4) |
| Chinese Taipei | 3.1 | (0.5) | 9.9 | (0.8) | 17.5 | (0.8) | 26.6 | (0.9) | 27.1 | (1.1) | 13.5 | (0.7) | 2.3 | (0.3) |
| Thailand | 16.3 | (0.9) | 29.2 | (1.0) | 29.9 | (0.9) | 16.8 | (0.7) | 6.4 | (0.7) | 1.1 | (0.2) | 0.1 | (0.1) |
| Tunisia | 31.7 | (1.4) | 29.8 | (1.1) | 24.0 | (1.1) | 11.2 | (0.8) | 3.0 | (0.6) | 0.3 | (0.1) | 0.0 | a |
| Uruguay | 19.8 | (1.1) | 22.3 | (1.0) | 26.3 | (0.9) | 20.1 | (0.9) | 9.1 | (0.6) | 2.1 | (0.4) | 0.3 | (0.1) |

StatLink http://dx.doi.org/10.1787/142056138443

Pour consulter la version française intégrale de ce tableau, suivre ce lien :
StatLink http://dx.doi.org/10.1787/152610887346

[Part 1/2]

**Table 2.4b**   **Percentage of students at each proficiency level on the *using scientific evidence* scale, by gender**

Tableau 2.4b   Pourcentage d'élèves à chaque niveau de compétence sur l'échelle d'*utilisation de faits scientifiques*, selon le sexe

| | | Males – Proficiency levels | | | | | | | | | | | | |
|---|---|---|---|---|---|---|---|---|---|---|---|---|---|---|
| | | Below Level 1 (below 334.94 score points) | | Level 1 (from 334.94 to 409.54 score points) | | Level 2 (from 409.54 to 484.14 score points) | | Level 3 (from 484.14 to 558.73 score points) | | Level 4 (from 558.73 to 633.33 score points) | | Level 5 (from 633.33 to 707.93 score points) | | Level 6 (above 707.93 score points) | |
| | | % | S.E. | % | S.E. | % | S.E. | % | S.E. | % | S.E. | % | S.E. | % | S.E. |
| **OECD** | Australia | 4.5 | (0.5) | 10.0 | (0.8) | 18.7 | (0.9) | 24.8 | (0.9) | 24.3 | (0.7) | 13.4 | (0.7) | 4.3 | (0.6) |
| | Austria | 7.1 | (0.9) | 12.5 | (1.2) | 21.6 | (1.4) | 23.0 | (1.2) | 21.5 | (1.1) | 11.4 | (1.0) | 2.9 | (0.5) |
| | Belgium | 8.0 | (1.0) | 11.7 | (0.9) | 18.4 | (1.1) | 23.6 | (0.9) | 23.6 | (0.9) | 12.3 | (0.7) | 2.4 | (0.3) |
| | Canada | 2.9 | (0.4) | 8.2 | (0.7) | 16.6 | (1.0) | 26.2 | (1.2) | 27.6 | (1.0) | 14.5 | (0.7) | 4.0 | (0.5) |
| | Czech Republic | 6.7 | (0.8) | 14.0 | (1.2) | 23.4 | (1.6) | 24.7 | (1.4) | 19.0 | (1.2) | 9.2 | (0.9) | 3.0 | (0.5) |
| | Denmark | 8.1 | (0.9) | 15.3 | (1.3) | 23.4 | (1.4) | 25.3 | (1.1) | 18.9 | (1.0) | 7.4 | (0.8) | 1.6 | (0.4) |
| | Finland | 1.2 | (0.3) | 5.3 | (0.6) | 15.0 | (1.2) | 25.4 | (1.1) | 28.2 | (1.0) | 17.8 | (1.0) | 7.1 | (0.7) |
| | France | 8.3 | (1.1) | 13.1 | (1.1) | 19.2 | (1.2) | 22.1 | (1.4) | 21.5 | (1.1) | 12.6 | (1.2) | 3.2 | (0.6) |
| | Germany | 7.0 | (1.1) | 11.1 | (1.0) | 19.1 | (1.3) | 24.0 | (1.3) | 22.4 | (1.2) | 12.5 | (1.0) | 3.8 | (0.5) |
| | Greece | 14.4 | (1.7) | 18.4 | (1.1) | 24.9 | (1.4) | 23.8 | (1.4) | 13.5 | (1.1) | 4.2 | (0.6) | 0.7 | (0.2) |
| | Hungary | 6.9 | (1.0) | 14.2 | (1.0) | 23.6 | (1.4) | 26.2 | (1.4) | 19.1 | (1.2) | 8.3 | (1.1) | 1.7 | (0.4) |
| | Iceland | 10.0 | (0.8) | 15.3 | (1.1) | 22.2 | (1.1) | 24.4 | (1.1) | 18.2 | (1.0) | 7.9 | (0.8) | 2.1 | (0.4) |
| | Ireland | 6.6 | (0.8) | 13.3 | (1.2) | 22.0 | (1.2) | 26.7 | (1.0) | 20.6 | (1.2) | 9.1 | (0.8) | 1.7 | (0.5) |
| | Italy | 13.2 | (0.9) | 16.9 | (0.8) | 24.3 | (0.8) | 24.1 | (0.9) | 15.2 | (0.8) | 5.5 | (0.4) | 0.9 | (0.1) |
| | Japan | 5.0 | (0.8) | 9.3 | (1.0) | 15.5 | (1.2) | 22.1 | (1.1) | 24.3 | (1.4) | 17.0 | (1.2) | 6.8 | (0.7) |
| | Korea | 4.2 | (0.8) | 8.5 | (0.9) | 17.4 | (1.0) | 26.0 | (1.5) | 26.1 | (1.3) | 14.3 | (1.4) | 3.5 | (0.7) |
| | Luxembourg | 10.3 | (0.6) | 14.0 | (1.0) | 20.4 | (1.1) | 24.7 | (0.9) | 19.0 | (0.9) | 9.5 | (0.6) | 2.2 | (0.4) |
| | Mexico | 23.8 | (1.6) | 28.3 | (1.1) | 27.4 | (1.1) | 15.6 | (0.9) | 4.4 | (0.4) | 0.6 | (0.2) | 0.0 | (0.0) |
| | Netherlands | 3.5 | (0.7) | 12.0 | (1.4) | 19.7 | (1.2) | 24.5 | (1.6) | 22.8 | (1.5) | 13.8 | (0.9) | 3.7 | (0.4) |
| | New Zealand | 6.6 | (1.0) | 10.9 | (1.4) | 17.8 | (1.0) | 21.1 | (1.1) | 21.7 | (1.0) | 14.8 | (1.1) | 7.1 | (0.8) |
| | Norway | 11.9 | (1.2) | 18.3 | (1.2) | 25.0 | (1.2) | 22.3 | (1.5) | 15.1 | (1.1) | 6.1 | (0.7) | 1.2 | (0.3) |
| | Poland | 6.7 | (0.8) | 15.3 | (1.0) | 25.0 | (1.0) | 26.2 | (1.1) | 18.5 | (1.2) | 7.2 | (0.8) | 1.2 | (0.4) |
| | Portugal | 10.3 | (1.2) | 17.6 | (1.2) | 25.3 | (1.4) | 24.6 | (1.4) | 15.9 | (1.2) | 5.6 | (0.8) | 0.7 | (0.3) |
| | Slovak Republic | 10.6 | (1.2) | 16.3 | (1.5) | 24.5 | (1.5) | 24.2 | (1.3) | 16.4 | (1.2) | 6.8 | (0.8) | 1.2 | (0.4) |
| | Spain | 8.1 | (0.7) | 15.1 | (0.8) | 25.1 | (0.9) | 27.1 | (0.9) | 17.8 | (0.8) | 6.0 | (0.6) | 0.9 | (0.2) |
| | Sweden | 7.8 | (0.9) | 14.3 | (1.0) | 22.6 | (1.3) | 26.6 | (1.0) | 19.1 | (1.1) | 7.8 | (0.7) | 1.7 | (0.5) |
| | Switzerland | 6.1 | (0.8) | 10.7 | (0.8) | 18.8 | (1.0) | 26.1 | (0.9) | 23.3 | (1.0) | 11.6 | (0.7) | 3.6 | (0.5) |
| | Turkey | 22.1 | (1.6) | 31.2 | (1.6) | 24.6 | (1.7) | 13.9 | (1.1) | 6.5 | (1.1) | 1.6 | (0.6) | 0.1 | (0.1) |
| | United Kingdom | 7.4 | (0.8) | 12.0 | (0.8) | 19.1 | (0.8) | 22.9 | (1.1) | 20.9 | (1.1) | 13.1 | (0.7) | 4.7 | (0.6) |
| | United States | 11.5 | (1.8) | 16.5 | (1.0) | 20.8 | (1.3) | 21.7 | (1.1) | 17.8 | (1.1) | 9.2 | (0.9) | 2.6 | (0.4) |
| | **OECD total** | 10.5 | (0.5) | 15.8 | (0.3) | 21.0 | (0.4) | 22.1 | (0.4) | 18.2 | (0.3) | 9.5 | (0.3) | 2.8 | (0.2) |
| | **OECD average** | 8.7 | (0.2) | 14.3 | (0.2) | 21.4 | (0.2) | 23.8 | (0.2) | 19.4 | (0.2) | 9.7 | (0.2) | 2.7 | (0.1) |
| **Partners** | Argentina | 35.6 | (2.7) | 24.8 | (1.4) | 22.5 | (1.5) | 11.9 | (1.3) | 4.4 | (0.8) | 0.7 | (0.3) | 0.1 | (0.1) |
| | Azerbaijan | 50.1 | (2.4) | 31.3 | (1.6) | 13.6 | (1.3) | 4.1 | (0.8) | 0.8 | (0.2) | 0.0 | (0.0) | a | a |
| | Brazil | 34.4 | (1.6) | 27.5 | (1.5) | 21.5 | (1.1) | 10.8 | (0.9) | 4.6 | (0.6) | 1.0 | (0.3) | 0.1 | a |
| | Bulgaria | 31.9 | (2.7) | 21.6 | (1.6) | 19.1 | (1.3) | 14.8 | (1.3) | 8.8 | (1.0) | 2.8 | (0.7) | 1.1 | (0.4) |
| | Chile | 14.2 | (1.5) | 22.7 | (1.4) | 27.3 | (1.5) | 20.7 | (1.3) | 11.3 | (1.2) | 3.4 | (0.7) | 0.4 | (0.2) |
| | Colombia | 29.1 | (2.5) | 31.1 | (1.9) | 25.6 | (1.7) | 11.3 | (1.3) | 2.7 | (0.5) | 0.2 | (0.1) | 0.0 | a |
| | Croatia | 6.0 | (0.9) | 16.1 | (1.1) | 26.5 | (1.3) | 26.8 | (1.3) | 17.6 | (1.2) | 6.0 | (0.7) | 1.0 | (0.2) |
| | Estonia | 2.4 | (0.4) | 9.5 | (1.0) | 20.0 | (1.3) | 29.5 | (1.7) | 24.5 | (1.7) | 11.6 | (0.8) | 2.6 | (0.4) |
| | Hong Kong-China | 3.2 | (0.6) | 8.1 | (0.9) | 15.1 | (1.0) | 25.3 | (1.5) | 29.1 | (1.4) | 15.8 | (1.1) | 3.4 | (0.5) |
| | Indonesia | 28.2 | (3.3) | 33.7 | (2.2) | 23.7 | (1.8) | 11.3 | (2.7) | 3.0 | (1.6) | 0.1 | (0.1) | a | a |
| | Israel | 20.6 | (1.9) | 18.4 | (1.5) | 18.5 | (1.1) | 17.0 | (1.0) | 14.0 | (1.1) | 8.2 | (0.9) | 3.3 | (0.5) |
| | Jordan | 30.9 | (1.8) | 27.3 | (1.4) | 24.0 | (1.4) | 12.8 | (1.3) | 4.3 | (0.9) | 0.7 | (0.4) | 0.0 | a |
| | Kyrgyzstan | 71.9 | (1.6) | 16.0 | (1.0) | 7.5 | (0.8) | 3.2 | (0.5) | 1.3 | (0.4) | 0.1 | (0.1) | 0.0 | a |
| | Latvia | 6.3 | (0.9) | 15.9 | (1.2) | 26.4 | (1.6) | 29.4 | (1.5) | 16.6 | (1.2) | 5.0 | (0.7) | 0.4 | (0.2) |
| | Liechtenstein | 4.3 | (1.7) | 10.3 | (3.2) | 22.2 | (6.1) | 24.3 | (4.7) | 22.2 | (3.5) | 12.3 | (3.0) | 4.4 | (1.7) |
| | Lithuania | 7.9 | (0.9) | 17.3 | (1.1) | 26.5 | (1.2) | 26.0 | (1.3) | 16.5 | (1.4) | 5.1 | (0.7) | 0.7 | (0.3) |
| | Macao-China | 3.1 | (0.4) | 9.8 | (0.7) | 24.1 | (1.0) | 31.7 | (1.3) | 23.2 | (1.1) | 7.5 | (0.9) | 0.6 | (0.2) |
| | Montenegro | 24.3 | (1.2) | 30.0 | (1.3) | 25.7 | (1.3) | 14.9 | (1.0) | 4.5 | (0.8) | 0.6 | (0.3) | a | a |
| | Qatar | 67.0 | (0.9) | 18.1 | (0.8) | 8.0 | (0.6) | 4.1 | (0.4) | 2.0 | (0.3) | 0.8 | (0.2) | 0.1 | (0.1) |
| | Romania | 27.9 | (2.5) | 25.3 | (1.7) | 23.3 | (1.7) | 15.7 | (1.5) | 6.2 | (1.0) | 1.4 | (0.3) | 0.2 | (0.1) |
| | Russian Federation | 8.8 | (1.2) | 16.9 | (1.2) | 26.6 | (1.4) | 25.1 | (1.5) | 15.3 | (1.3) | 6.0 | (0.6) | 1.3 | (0.3) |
| | Serbia | 20.7 | (1.3) | 26.2 | (1.1) | 26.8 | (1.3) | 17.4 | (1.4) | 7.2 | (0.7) | 1.6 | (0.4) | 0.2 | (0.1) |
| | Slovenia | 4.0 | (0.4) | 12.9 | (0.8) | 23.9 | (1.1) | 26.8 | (1.1) | 20.6 | (1.0) | 9.5 | (0.8) | 2.3 | (0.6) |
| | Chinese Taipei | 3.6 | (0.6) | 10.2 | (0.9) | 16.6 | (1.0) | 26.1 | (1.3) | 27.1 | (1.3) | 13.8 | (1.0) | 2.5 | (0.4) |
| | Thailand | 22.3 | (1.5) | 29.8 | (1.4) | 26.3 | (1.4) | 14.9 | (1.3) | 5.6 | (0.9) | 1.1 | (0.3) | 0.1 | (0.1) |
| | Tunisia | 34.2 | (1.8) | 29.2 | (1.5) | 22.8 | (1.5) | 10.6 | (1.1) | 3.0 | (0.6) | 0.2 | (0.1) | a | a |
| | Uruguay | 21.8 | (1.5) | 23.3 | (1.6) | 23.9 | (1.6) | 18.8 | (1.3) | 9.5 | (0.8) | 2.3 | (0.4) | 0.4 | (0.2) |

StatLink ⟨🔗⟩ http://dx.doi.org/10.1787/142056138443

Pour consulter la version française intégrale de ce tableau, suivre ce lien :
StatLink ⟨🔗⟩ http://dx.doi.org/10.1787/152610887346

[Part 2/2]

**Table 2.4b** Percentage of students at each proficiency level on the *using scientific evidence* scale, by gender

Tableau 2.4b Pourcentage d'élèves à chaque niveau de compétence sur l'échelle d'*utilisation de faits scientifiques*, selon le sexe

| | | **Females – Proficiency levels** | | | | | | | | | | | | |
|---|---|---|---|---|---|---|---|---|---|---|---|---|---|---|
| | | **Below Level 1 (below 334.94 score points)** | | **Level 1 (from 334.94 to 409.54 score points)** | | **Level 2 (from 409.54 to 484.14 score points)** | | **Level 3 (from 484.14 to 558.73 score points)** | | **Level 4 (from 558.73 to 633.33 score points)** | | **Level 5 (from 633.33 to 707.93 score points)** | | **Level 6 (above 707.93 score points)** | |
| | | % | S.E. | % | S.E. | % | S.E. | % | S.E. | % | S.E. | % | S.E. | % | S.E. |
| OECD | Australia | 3.3 | (0.4) | 8.8 | (0.5) | 18.9 | (0.8) | 27.6 | (0.8) | 24.6 | (0.8) | 13.2 | (0.7) | 3.6 | (0.4) |
| | Austria | 9.1 | (1.9) | 12.6 | (1.3) | 19.2 | (1.4) | 25.1 | (1.4) | 22.1 | (1.3) | 9.9 | (1.1) | 1.9 | (0.5) |
| | Belgium | 6.1 | (0.8) | 9.9 | (0.9) | 17.7 | (1.0) | 25.8 | (1.0) | 25.9 | (1.0) | 12.8 | (0.8) | 1.8 | (0.4) |
| | Canada | 2.1 | (0.3) | 7.1 | (0.6) | 17.8 | (0.7) | 27.8 | (0.8) | 28.2 | (1.0) | 13.9 | (0.7) | 3.3 | (0.3) |
| | Czech Republic | 8.4 | (1.4) | 13.1 | (1.2) | 20.9 | (1.3) | 25.1 | (1.4) | 20.6 | (1.3) | 9.4 | (1.2) | 2.5 | (0.5) |
| | Denmark | 7.6 | (0.9) | 15.5 | (1.0) | 24.4 | (1.2) | 27.1 | (1.5) | 17.5 | (1.1) | 6.8 | (0.8) | 1.2 | (0.3) |
| | Finland | 0.8 | (0.2) | 3.6 | (0.6) | 12.9 | (0.9) | 26.6 | (1.0) | 31.1 | (1.2) | 18.8 | (1.0) | 6.3 | (0.7) |
| | France | 6.1 | (0.8) | 12.1 | (1.1) | 19.8 | (1.2) | 24.8 | (1.4) | 23.8 | (1.2) | 11.4 | (0.9) | 2.0 | (0.4) |
| | Germany | 6.5 | (1.0) | 11.9 | (1.3) | 18.5 | (1.1) | 26.9 | (1.4) | 23.1 | (1.5) | 10.4 | (1.1) | 2.7 | (0.4) |
| | Greece | 8.2 | (0.8) | 14.9 | (1.1) | 27.7 | (1.4) | 30.5 | (1.5) | 14.6 | (1.1) | 3.9 | (0.6) | 0.3 | (0.2) |
| | Hungary | 5.1 | (0.8) | 13.3 | (1.2) | 24.9 | (1.3) | 30.0 | (1.5) | 18.5 | (1.2) | 7.1 | (0.8) | 1.0 | (0.3) |
| | Iceland | 7.1 | (0.7) | 14.8 | (0.9) | 22.6 | (1.4) | 26.9 | (1.6) | 19.2 | (1.1) | 7.8 | (0.7) | 1.7 | (0.4) |
| | Ireland | 4.4 | (0.6) | 11.7 | (1.0) | 23.1 | (1.2) | 28.4 | (1.4) | 22.5 | (1.6) | 8.5 | (1.1) | 1.4 | (0.3) |
| | Italy | 10.7 | (0.8) | 18.4 | (0.9) | 25.7 | (0.8) | 25.0 | (0.9) | 14.7 | (0.7) | 4.8 | (0.5) | 0.7 | (0.2) |
| | Japan | 4.2 | (1.0) | 8.1 | (1.0) | 15.5 | (1.1) | 23.6 | (1.1) | 26.6 | (1.4) | 16.5 | (1.2) | 5.6 | (0.7) |
| | Korea | 2.0 | (0.5) | 7.5 | (1.0) | 16.8 | (1.1) | 28.6 | (1.4) | 27.4 | (1.4) | 14.4 | (1.2) | 3.3 | (0.6) |
| | Luxembourg | 8.2 | (0.7) | 14.9 | (0.8) | 23.1 | (0.9) | 26.1 | (0.9) | 18.9 | (0.9) | 7.4 | (0.8) | 1.4 | (0.3) |
| | Mexico | 23.6 | (1.4) | 29.9 | (1.1) | 27.7 | (1.0) | 14.8 | (0.9) | 3.6 | (0.4) | 0.4 | (0.1) | 0.0 | (0.0) |
| | Netherlands | 4.1 | (0.7) | 12.1 | (1.1) | 19.4 | (1.4) | 23.3 | (1.4) | 24.9 | (1.7) | 13.6 | (1.4) | 2.6 | (0.4) |
| | New Zealand | 4.3 | (0.6) | 9.3 | (0.8) | 17.6 | (1.0) | 22.9 | (1.1) | 23.2 | (1.2) | 16.1 | (1.2) | 6.7 | (0.7) |
| | Norway | 8.2 | (0.8) | 18.5 | (1.1) | 26.0 | (1.2) | 25.3 | (1.4) | 15.8 | (1.2) | 5.0 | (0.7) | 1.2 | (0.3) |
| | Poland | 4.5 | (0.6) | 14.5 | (0.8) | 25.9 | (1.2) | 29.2 | (1.4) | 19.1 | (1.0) | 6.0 | (0.7) | 0.9 | (0.2) |
| | Portugal | 9.1 | (1.1) | 18.0 | (1.1) | 25.7 | (1.2) | 26.7 | (1.3) | 16.6 | (1.3) | 3.6 | (0.5) | 0.3 | (0.2) |
| | Slovak Republic | 9.0 | (1.1) | 15.8 | (1.4) | 26.2 | (1.4) | 26.2 | (1.3) | 17.1 | (1.0) | 5.2 | (0.7) | 0.5 | (0.2) |
| | Spain | 6.3 | (0.6) | 15.6 | (0.9) | 25.9 | (1.1) | 28.9 | (0.8) | 18.3 | (0.9) | 4.5 | (0.4) | 0.5 | (0.2) |
| | Sweden | 5.4 | (0.7) | 14.0 | (1.1) | 24.1 | (1.5) | 27.6 | (1.0) | 19.9 | (1.2) | 7.6 | (0.8) | 1.4 | (0.3) |
| | Switzerland | 5.8 | (0.7) | 11.4 | (0.8) | 19.7 | (1.0) | 25.3 | (1.1) | 23.3 | (1.1) | 11.3 | (0.8) | 3.2 | (0.5) |
| | Turkey | 15.3 | (1.5) | 29.3 | (1.9) | 29.9 | (1.6) | 16.8 | (1.4) | 7.0 | (1.1) | 1.5 | (0.5) | 0.1 | (0.1) |
| | United Kingdom | 6.1 | (0.6) | 12.9 | (0.9) | 21.1 | (1.0) | 24.8 | (1.1) | 21.3 | (1.0) | 10.4 | (0.7) | 3.3 | (0.4) |
| | United States | 8.5 | (1.3) | 15.7 | (1.2) | 23.4 | (1.3) | 23.9 | (1.1) | 17.9 | (0.9) | 8.1 | (0.9) | 2.4 | (0.5) |
| | **OECD total** | 8.6 | (0.4) | 15.5 | (0.5) | 22.3 | (0.4) | 24.0 | (0.4) | 18.8 | (0.3) | 8.6 | (0.3) | 2.3 | (0.2) |
| | **OECD average** | 7.0 | (0.2) | 13.8 | (0.2) | 22.1 | (0.2) | 25.7 | (0.2) | 20.2 | (0.2) | 9.0 | (0.2) | 2.1 | (0.1) |
| Partners | Argentina | 28.6 | (2.5) | 24.3 | (1.6) | 24.2 | (1.7) | 15.5 | (1.5) | 6.3 | (0.9) | 1.1 | (0.5) | 0.1 | a |
| | Azerbaijan | 45.6 | (2.1) | 35.3 | (1.5) | 14.3 | (1.4) | 4.1 | (0.8) | 0.5 | (0.3) | 0.0 | a | a | a |
| | Brazil | 35.5 | (1.5) | 28.9 | (1.2) | 20.4 | (1.1) | 11.1 | (1.1) | 3.5 | (0.5) | 0.7 | (0.2) | 0.0 | (0.0) |
| | Bulgaria | 23.3 | (2.3) | 19.7 | (1.5) | 23.0 | (1.6) | 18.5 | (1.4) | 11.1 | (1.4) | 3.7 | (0.8) | 0.8 | (0.3) |
| | Chile | 18.1 | (1.6) | 25.3 | (1.9) | 26.3 | (1.5) | 19.3 | (1.7) | 8.6 | (1.1) | 2.1 | (0.4) | 0.3 | (0.2) |
| | Colombia | 29.0 | (2.1) | 32.8 | (1.6) | 26.4 | (1.6) | 9.8 | (1.1) | 1.9 | (0.4) | 0.1 | (0.2) | a | a |
| | Croatia | 4.5 | (0.7) | 14.1 | (1.1) | 27.1 | (1.3) | 30.0 | (1.2) | 17.9 | (1.3) | 5.6 | (0.6) | 0.7 | (0.2) |
| | Estonia | 1.4 | (0.3) | 6.7 | (0.8) | 20.5 | (1.1) | 31.9 | (1.5) | 25.8 | (1.4) | 11.7 | (1.0) | 1.9 | (0.3) |
| | Hong Kong-China | 2.2 | (0.4) | 7.2 | (0.8) | 17.1 | (1.2) | 28.4 | (1.4) | 28.6 | (1.4) | 14.0 | (1.2) | 2.6 | (0.4) |
| | Indonesia | 27.9 | (2.3) | 36.5 | (1.6) | 24.8 | (1.6) | 9.0 | (1.4) | 1.7 | (0.6) | 0.1 | (0.1) | a | a |
| | Israel | 16.0 | (1.6) | 17.8 | (1.0) | 22.1 | (1.4) | 20.1 | (1.1) | 15.1 | (1.2) | 7.1 | (0.7) | 1.9 | (0.4) |
| | Jordan | 16.4 | (1.4) | 27.4 | (1.7) | 30.9 | (1.4) | 18.6 | (1.2) | 5.9 | (0.6) | 0.9 | (0.3) | 0.0 | a |
| | Kyrgyzstan | 68.0 | (1.5) | 20.0 | (1.2) | 8.1 | (0.7) | 2.9 | (0.5) | 1.0 | (0.3) | 0.1 | (0.1) | 0.0 | a |
| | Latvia | 4.3 | (0.7) | 12.3 | (1.1) | 25.9 | (1.1) | 32.3 | (1.7) | 20.0 | (1.3) | 4.9 | (0.7) | 0.4 | (0.2) |
| | Liechtenstein | 3.6 | (1.5) | 9.1 | (2.3) | 17.0 | (3.1) | 24.3 | (3.6) | 21.8 | (3.9) | 18.1 | (3.4) | 6.1 | (2.3) |
| | Lithuania | 5.4 | (0.6) | 14.2 | (1.0) | 23.9 | (1.1) | 30.0 | (1.5) | 19.6 | (1.4) | 6.0 | (0.7) | 0.8 | (0.3) |
| | Macao-China | 1.7 | (0.3) | 9.0 | (0.9) | 25.4 | (1.2) | 35.4 | (1.4) | 22.8 | (1.4) | 5.4 | (0.5) | 0.4 | (0.2) |
| | Montenegro | 21.2 | (1.2) | 29.0 | (1.6) | 28.7 | (1.2) | 15.0 | (1.0) | 5.3 | (0.6) | 0.7 | (0.3) | 0.0 | a |
| | Qatar | 51.4 | (1.1) | 26.9 | (1.0) | 13.7 | (1.0) | 5.6 | (0.4) | 1.9 | (0.3) | 0.5 | (0.1) | 0.1 | (0.1) |
| | Romania | 22.4 | (2.8) | 25.8 | (1.7) | 28.0 | (2.4) | 17.4 | (2.7) | 5.4 | (1.1) | 1.0 | (0.4) | 0.0 | a |
| | Russian Federation | 6.6 | (0.9) | 15.8 | (1.2) | 27.8 | (1.2) | 27.4 | (1.1) | 16.4 | (1.3) | 4.9 | (0.6) | 1.0 | (0.3) |
| | Serbia | 16.6 | (1.6) | 24.7 | (1.4) | 28.0 | (1.4) | 21.5 | (1.6) | 7.9 | (0.9) | 1.3 | (0.3) | 0.0 | a |
| | Slovenia | 3.0 | (0.5) | 10.3 | (0.8) | 21.5 | (1.1) | 28.2 | (1.2) | 24.0 | (1.0) | 10.8 | (0.8) | 2.2 | (0.5) |
| | Chinese Taipei | 2.6 | (0.6) | 9.5 | (1.0) | 18.5 | (1.3) | 27.2 | (1.2) | 27.1 | (1.4) | 13.0 | (1.1) | 2.1 | (0.4) |
| | Thailand | 11.9 | (0.8) | 28.8 | (1.2) | 32.7 | (1.0) | 18.3 | (1.0) | 7.1 | (0.8) | 1.1 | (0.3) | 0.1 | (0.1) |
| | Tunisia | 29.5 | (1.5) | 30.3 | (1.4) | 25.1 | (1.8) | 11.8 | (1.1) | 3.0 | (0.7) | 0.3 | (0.2) | 0.0 | a |
| | Uruguay | 17.9 | (1.4) | 21.4 | (1.2) | 28.7 | (1.2) | 21.3 | (1.4) | 8.8 | (0.9) | 1.9 | (0.5) | 0.1 | (0.1) |

StatLink ▯▯▯ http://dx.doi.org/10.1787/142056138443

Pour consulter la version française intégrale de ce tableau, suivre ce lien :
StatLink ▯▯▯ http://dx.doi.org/10.1787/152610887346

[Part 1/2]

**Table 2.4c  Mean score, variation and gender differences in student performance on the *using scientific evidence* scale**

Tableau 2.4c  Score moyen, différences de score selon le sexe et répartition des scores sur l'échelle d'*utilisation de faits scientifiques*

| | | All students | | | | Gender differences | | | | | |
|---|---|---|---|---|---|---|---|---|---|---|---|
| | | Mean score | | Standard deviation | | Males | | Females | | Difference (M - F) | |
| | | Mean | S.E. | S.D. | S.E. | Mean score | S.E. | Mean score | S.E. | Score dif. | S.E. |
| *OECD* | Australia | 531 | (2.4) | 107 | (1.1) | 530 | (3.4) | 533 | (3.0) | -3 | (4.2) |
| | Austria | 505 | (4.7) | 116 | (3.4) | 509 | (4.9) | 500 | (6.2) | 9 | (6.1) |
| | Belgium | 516 | (3.0) | 113 | (2.4) | 512 | (3.8) | 521 | (3.8) | -9 | (4.7) |
| | Canada | 542 | (2.2) | 99 | (1.3) | 541 | (2.7) | 542 | (2.3) | -1 | (2.3) |
| | Czech Republic | 501 | (4.1) | 113 | (2.4) | 501 | (5.0) | 500 | (5.4) | 1 | (6.5) |
| | Denmark | 489 | (3.6) | 107 | (1.7) | 490 | (4.1) | 487 | (4.0) | 3 | (3.8) |
| | Finland | 567 | (2.3) | 96 | (1.2) | 564 | (3.0) | 571 | (2.7) | **-7** | (3.3) |
| | France | 511 | (3.9) | 114 | (2.6) | 509 | (5.0) | 513 | (4.2) | -4 | (4.7) |
| | Germany | 515 | (4.6) | 115 | (3.3) | 517 | (5.6) | 513 | (4.5) | 4 | (4.3) |
| | Greece | 465 | (4.0) | 107 | (3.2) | 456 | (5.6) | 475 | (3.7) | **-20** | (5.4) |
| | Hungary | 497 | (3.4) | 102 | (2.1) | 497 | (4.1) | 498 | (4.5) | -1 | (5.2) |
| | Iceland | 491 | (1.7) | 111 | (1.4) | 487 | (3.1) | 495 | (2.5) | -7 | (4.4) |
| | Ireland | 506 | (3.4) | 102 | (1.6) | 503 | (4.8) | 509 | (3.5) | -7 | (4.8) |
| | Italy | 467 | (2.3) | 111 | (1.6) | 466 | (3.2) | 468 | (3.1) | -2 | (4.2) |
| | Japan | 544 | (4.2) | 116 | (2.5) | 543 | (5.8) | 545 | (6.4) | -2 | (8.9) |
| | Korea | 538 | (3.7) | 102 | (2.9) | 535 | (5.2) | 542 | (4.5) | -8 | (6.4) |
| | Luxembourg | 492 | (1.1) | 113 | (1.1) | 493 | (2.0) | 490 | (2.2) | 3 | (3.5) |
| | Mexico | 402 | (3.1) | 94 | (1.8) | 404 | (3.7) | 401 | (3.0) | 3 | (2.7) |
| | Netherlands | 526 | (3.3) | 106 | (2.0) | 527 | (3.8) | 524 | (3.7) | 3 | (3.5) |
| | New Zealand | 537 | (3.3) | 121 | (1.7) | 532 | (4.4) | 541 | (4.3) | -10 | (5.8) |
| | Norway | 473 | (3.6) | 109 | (1.9) | 469 | (4.2) | 476 | (3.9) | -7 | (3.8) |
| | Poland | 494 | (2.7) | 98 | (1.4) | 492 | (3.0) | 495 | (3.0) | -3 | (2.8) |
| | Portugal | 472 | (3.6) | 103 | (1.9) | 473 | (4.2) | 471 | (4.0) | 2 | (3.8) |
| | Slovak Republic | 478 | (3.3) | 108 | (2.5) | 478 | (4.8) | 478 | (3.6) | 0 | (5.6) |
| | Spain | 485 | (3.0) | 101 | (1.2) | 484 | (3.4) | 485 | (3.1) | -1 | (2.5) |
| | Sweden | 496 | (2.6) | 106 | (1.5) | 494 | (3.1) | 499 | (3.2) | -5 | (3.4) |
| | Switzerland | 519 | (3.4) | 111 | (1.9) | 520 | (3.6) | 517 | (3.9) | 2 | (2.9) |
| | Turkey | 417 | (4.3) | 97 | (3.2) | 410 | (5.2) | 426 | (4.6) | **-16** | (4.7) |
| | United Kingdom | 514 | (2.5) | 117 | (1.7) | 517 | (3.1) | 510 | (3.1) | 6 | (3.8) |
| | United States | 489 | (5.0) | 116 | (2.5) | 486 | (6.1) | 491 | (4.6) | -5 | (4.1) |
| | **OECD total** | **492** | **(1.5)** | **117** | **(0.9)** | **490** | **(1.7)** | **493** | **(1.6)** | **-2** | **(1.5)** |
| | **OECD average** | **499** | **(0.6)** | **108** | **(0.4)** | **498** | **(0.8)** | **501** | **(0.7)** | **-3** | **(0.8)** |
| *Partners* | Argentina | 385 | (7.0) | 117 | (3.6) | 374 | (7.4) | 396 | (7.7) | **-23** | (6.2) |
| | Azerbaijan | 344 | (4.0) | 77 | (2.4) | 342 | (4.5) | 347 | (3.9) | **-6** | (2.4) |
| | Brazil | 378 | (3.6) | 105 | (2.7) | 382 | (3.9) | 375 | (3.8) | **6** | (2.7) |
| | Bulgaria | 417 | (7.5) | 127 | (3.7) | 404 | (8.0) | 430 | (8.2) | **-26** | (6.7) |
| | Chile | 440 | (5.1) | 103 | (1.9) | 447 | (6.2) | 431 | (5.2) | **16** | (5.3) |
| | Colombia | 383 | (3.9) | 91 | (2.4) | 386 | (4.5) | 381 | (4.8) | 5 | (4.9) |
| | Croatia | 490 | (3.0) | 96 | (1.9) | 488 | (4.1) | 493 | (3.5) | -5 | (4.8) |
| | Estonia | 531 | (2.7) | 93 | (1.3) | 529 | (3.2) | 533 | (3.0) | -5 | (3.3) |
| | Hong Kong-China | 542 | (2.7) | 99 | (1.8) | 544 | (3.8) | 541 | (4.0) | 2 | (5.5) |
| | Indonesia | 386 | (7.3) | 83 | (3.4) | 388 | (10.2) | 383 | (5.0) | 5 | (7.3) |
| | Israel | 460 | (4.7) | 133 | (2.3) | 456 | (6.7) | 464 | (5.4) | -8 | (7.6) |
| | Jordan | 405 | (3.3) | 101 | (2.3) | 385 | (5.5) | 424 | (3.6) | **-39** | (6.3) |
| | Kyrgyzstan | 288 | (3.8) | 105 | (2.5) | 280 | (4.7) | 295 | (3.9) | **-15** | (3.7) |
| | Latvia | 491 | (3.4) | 92 | (1.8) | 484 | (4.1) | 497 | (3.6) | **-13** | (3.6) |
| | Liechtenstein | 535 | (4.3) | 111 | (3.6) | 524 | (8.2) | 544 | (6.8) | -20 | (12.2) |
| | Lithuania | 487 | (3.1) | 99 | (1.8) | 478 | (3.7) | 495 | (3.3) | **-17** | (3.0) |
| | Macao-China | 512 | (1.2) | 84 | (1.0) | 512 | (2.0) | 511 | (1.6) | 0 | (2.7) |
| | Montenegro | 407 | (1.3) | 93 | (1.1) | 403 | (2.0) | 411 | (2.0) | **-8** | (3.1) |
| | Qatar | 324 | (1.2) | 103 | (1.0) | 307 | (1.5) | 341 | (1.9) | **-35** | (2.5) |
| | Romania | 407 | (6.0) | 104 | (3.1) | 403 | (6.0) | 412 | (6.7) | -9 | (4.6) |
| | Russian Federation | 481 | (4.2) | 102 | (1.6) | 478 | (4.5) | 483 | (4.4) | -5 | (3.1) |
| | Serbia | 425 | (3.7) | 100 | (1.9) | 419 | (4.0) | 431 | (4.8) | **-11** | (4.9) |
| | Slovenia | 516 | (1.3) | 100 | (1.0) | 510 | (2.3) | 522 | (2.0) | **-12** | (3.4) |
| | Chinese Taipei | 532 | (3.7) | 100 | (1.8) | 532 | (4.5) | 532 | (5.1) | 0 | (6.0) |
| | Thailand | 423 | (2.6) | 91 | (1.8) | 409 | (4.2) | 433 | (2.7) | **-24** | (4.5) |
| | Tunisia | 382 | (3.7) | 95 | (2.4) | 377 | (4.1) | 387 | (4.3) | **-10** | (3.9) |
| | Uruguay | 429 | (3.1) | 107 | (1.9) | 425 | (4.0) | 433 | (3.5) | -8 | (4.1) |

Note: Values that are statistically significant are indicated in bold (see Annex A3).
StatLink ⟶ http://dx.doi.org/10.1787/142056138443

Pour consulter la version française intégrale de ce tableau, suivre ce lien :
StatLink ⟶ http://dx.doi.org/10.1787/152610887346

[Part 2/2]

**Table 2.4c** **Mean score, variation and gender differences in student performance on the *using scientific evidence* scale**

Tableau 2.4c   Score moyen, différences de score selon le sexe et répartition des scores sur l'échelle d'*utilisation de faits scientifiques*

| | | Percentiles | | | | | | | | | | |
|---|---|---|---|---|---|---|---|---|---|---|---|---|
| | | 5th | | 10th | | 25th | | 75th | | 90th | | 95th | |
| | | Score | S.E. | Score | S.E. | Score | S.E. | Score | S.E. | Score | S.E. | Score | S.E. |
| OECD | Australia | 348 | (3.8) | 390 | (3.3) | 459 | (2.8) | 607 | (2.7) | 665 | (2.7) | 698 | (3.5) |
| | Austria | 305 | (11.2) | 350 | (9.0) | 428 | (6.2) | 589 | (4.6) | 649 | (4.7) | 680 | (4.7) |
| | Belgium | 312 | (9.8) | 360 | (7.2) | 442 | (4.5) | 599 | (2.4) | 652 | (2.6) | 680 | (3.3) |
| | Canada | 370 | (4.3) | 408 | (4.3) | 477 | (2.9) | 612 | (2.2) | 664 | (2.5) | 695 | (3.1) |
| | Czech Republic | 312 | (8.6) | 353 | (6.6) | 423 | (5.1) | 581 | (4.7) | 644 | (5.4) | 681 | (5.9) |
| | Denmark | 310 | (6.6) | 349 | (4.8) | 416 | (4.3) | 564 | (3.9) | 624 | (4.6) | 658 | (5.3) |
| | Finland | 406 | (5.4) | 442 | (4.0) | 504 | (2.9) | 633 | (2.7) | 690 | (2.9) | 722 | (3.9) |
| | France | 311 | (7.9) | 359 | (6.7) | 432 | (5.9) | 595 | (4.2) | 654 | (4.1) | 685 | (4.3) |
| | Germany | 317 | (11.2) | 361 | (8.1) | 440 | (6.8) | 597 | (3.9) | 658 | (4.2) | 691 | (4.4) |
| | Greece | 279 | (9.9) | 325 | (7.9) | 399 | (5.8) | 539 | (3.8) | 596 | (4.3) | 630 | (4.3) |
| | Hungary | 325 | (7.6) | 362 | (6.3) | 429 | (4.2) | 568 | (4.4) | 628 | (4.8) | 661 | (4.4) |
| | Iceland | 303 | (5.3) | 345 | (4.1) | 414 | (3.1) | 570 | (2.4) | 632 | (3.3) | 666 | (3.3) |
| | Ireland | 331 | (5.4) | 370 | (5.0) | 437 | (4.5) | 579 | (3.1) | 635 | (3.8) | 666 | (4.5) |
| | Italy | 279 | (5.0) | 323 | (3.5) | 393 | (3.0) | 545 | (2.8) | 606 | (2.8) | 642 | (2.9) |
| | Japan | 340 | (8.6) | 388 | (7.9) | 468 | (5.9) | 627 | (3.6) | 685 | (3.4) | 719 | (4.8) |
| | Korea | 359 | (9.1) | 402 | (7.6) | 473 | (5.4) | 611 | (4.1) | 664 | (4.3) | 694 | (5.0) |
| | Luxembourg | 296 | (4.3) | 341 | (3.1) | 415 | (2.5) | 572 | (1.9) | 635 | (2.8) | 668 | (3.0) |
| | Mexico | 248 | (6.0) | 280 | (5.4) | 339 | (3.8) | 467 | (3.3) | 523 | (3.0) | 554 | (3.6) |
| | Netherlands | 346 | (6.5) | 382 | (6.5) | 446 | (5.3) | 606 | (3.4) | 662 | (2.9) | 691 | (3.0) |
| | New Zealand | 331 | (7.1) | 377 | (5.2) | 453 | (4.4) | 624 | (3.4) | 687 | (4.5) | 725 | (4.9) |
| | Norway | 294 | (7.9) | 334 | (5.8) | 398 | (4.5) | 549 | (3.8) | 613 | (3.4) | 649 | (4.7) |
| | Poland | 330 | (4.7) | 365 | (3.7) | 425 | (3.4) | 563 | (3.5) | 621 | (3.5) | 652 | (4.0) |
| | Portugal | 297 | (6.9) | 337 | (6.0) | 401 | (5.2) | 547 | (3.4) | 602 | (3.5) | 634 | (4.3) |
| | Slovak Republic | 294 | (8.1) | 336 | (5.8) | 407 | (4.6) | 554 | (4.2) | 615 | (4.1) | 647 | (4.1) |
| | Spain | 315 | (5.5) | 355 | (3.6) | 418 | (3.6) | 556 | (3.2) | 610 | (3.2) | 641 | (3.8) |
| | Sweden | 318 | (6.4) | 359 | (4.9) | 425 | (3.5) | 570 | (3.0) | 630 | (3.3) | 664 | (3.2) |
| | Switzerland | 325 | (6.4) | 368 | (5.0) | 445 | (4.4) | 597 | (3.5) | 656 | (4.5) | 691 | (5.5) |
| | Turkey | 271 | (4.6) | 302 | (3.7) | 352 | (3.3) | 479 | (6.9) | 548 | (9.2) | 589 | (10.5) |
| | United Kingdom | 316 | (6.2) | 361 | (4.3) | 434 | (3.6) | 597 | (2.9) | 661 | (3.2) | 699 | (3.8) |
| | United States | 296 | (10.1) | 335 | (8.8) | 405 | (7.0) | 573 | (5.1) | 640 | (5.2) | 677 | (5.9) |
| | **OECD total** | 297 | (2.8) | 338 | (2.8) | 409 | (2.0) | 577 | (1.5) | 642 | (1.7) | 679 | (1.9) |
| | **OECD average** | 316 | (1.3) | 357 | (1.1) | 427 | (0.8) | 576 | (0.7) | 635 | (0.7) | 668 | (0.8) |
| Partners | Argentina | 181 | (12.3) | 229 | (12.3) | 311 | (8.2) | 467 | (6.4) | 533 | (6.9) | 571 | (6.9) |
| | Azerbaijan | 226 | (5.3) | 250 | (4.6) | 292 | (4.2) | 391 | (5.2) | 446 | (7.2) | 483 | (8.2) |
| | Brazil | 215 | (7.5) | 250 | (5.2) | 307 | (3.3) | 446 | (4.6) | 518 | (6.0) | 557 | (7.0) |
| | Bulgaria | 216 | (10.2) | 256 | (8.8) | 325 | (8.1) | 506 | (8.7) | 585 | (9.3) | 624 | (8.7) |
| | Chile | 275 | (5.2) | 309 | (5.3) | 367 | (5.4) | 511 | (6.7) | 576 | (5.9) | 613 | (6.5) |
| | Colombia | 233 | (8.2) | 266 | (6.3) | 324 | (5.1) | 445 | (4.7) | 497 | (4.3) | 529 | (4.4) |
| | Croatia | 333 | (5.8) | 367 | (4.3) | 424 | (3.8) | 557 | (3.5) | 614 | (3.8) | 645 | (3.4) |
| | Estonia | 374 | (5.3) | 409 | (3.9) | 468 | (3.3) | 595 | (3.2) | 650 | (3.4) | 681 | (3.8) |
| | Hong Kong-China | 367 | (6.0) | 408 | (4.7) | 479 | (4.4) | 613 | (3.1) | 663 | (3.2) | 691 | (3.3) |
| | Indonesia | 255 | (6.5) | 282 | (5.8) | 328 | (5.9) | 440 | (9.1) | 498 | (14.3) | 532 | (13.8) |
| | Israel | 241 | (7.4) | 286 | (6.5) | 366 | (6.0) | 558 | (5.5) | 635 | (4.6) | 676 | (5.2) |
| | Jordan | 235 | (6.6) | 277 | (4.4) | 339 | (3.6) | 474 | (4.2) | 532 | (5.1) | 566 | (5.8) |
| | Kyrgyzstan | 125 | (6.7) | 160 | (4.9) | 218 | (4.3) | 352 | (4.0) | 424 | (6.8) | 473 | (9.1) |
| | Latvia | 332 | (6.7) | 370 | (5.5) | 429 | (4.5) | 555 | (3.5) | 606 | (3.4) | 636 | (3.2) |
| | Liechtenstein | 354 | (19.1) | 388 | (11.3) | 458 | (10.1) | 619 | (7.6) | 681 | (12.4) | 710 | (12.4) |
| | Lithuania | 321 | (5.2) | 357 | (3.8) | 418 | (4.0) | 557 | (3.9) | 612 | (4.3) | 643 | (4.9) |
| | Macao-China | 367 | (3.8) | 401 | (2.9) | 456 | (1.7) | 571 | (2.0) | 618 | (2.4) | 645 | (3.4) |
| | Montenegro | 258 | (2.7) | 288 | (3.1) | 342 | (1.9) | 469 | (2.4) | 529 | (3.0) | 565 | (4.3) |
| | Qatar | 174 | (2.8) | 203 | (2.4) | 254 | (1.9) | 382 | (1.8) | 462 | (2.8) | 515 | (3.0) |
| | Romania | 239 | (7.5) | 273 | (6.8) | 335 | (7.9) | 480 | (6.8) | 541 | (7.0) | 576 | (8.2) |
| | Russian Federation | 311 | (6.5) | 350 | (5.6) | 413 | (4.9) | 551 | (4.7) | 611 | (5.1) | 647 | (4.7) |
| | Serbia | 260 | (5.4) | 295 | (5.4) | 357 | (4.8) | 495 | (4.6) | 554 | (4.4) | 589 | (4.8) |
| | Slovenia | 351 | (4.3) | 386 | (3.1) | 447 | (2.0) | 586 | (2.6) | 647 | (3.2) | 679 | (3.1) |
| | Chinese Taipei | 356 | (5.8) | 393 | (5.9) | 464 | (6.0) | 605 | (3.3) | 656 | (3.5) | 683 | (3.2) |
| | Thailand | 280 | (4.5) | 309 | (4.1) | 361 | (3.2) | 483 | (3.7) | 544 | (4.9) | 581 | (5.1) |
| | Tunisia | 227 | (4.9) | 260 | (5.1) | 317 | (3.9) | 447 | (4.9) | 506 | (6.4) | 541 | (7.7) |
| | Uruguay | 249 | (5.2) | 287 | (5.1) | 355 | (4.6) | 504 | (2.9) | 566 | (3.8) | 602 | (4.0) |

Note: Values that are statistically significant are indicated in bold (see Annex A3).
StatLink ▊▊▊ http://dx.doi.org/10.1787/142056138443

Pour consulter la version française intégrale de ce tableau, suivre ce lien :
StatLink ▊▊▊ http://dx.doi.org/10.1787/152610887346

43

[Part 1/1]
### Table 2.5 Gender differences in performance on the science scale after taking student programmes into account
Tableau 2.5 Différences de scores selon le sexe sur l'échelle de culture scientifique, après contrôle du niveau et de la filière d'enseignement

| | | Gender differences in science performance (M - F) | | | | | |
|---|---|---|---|---|---|---|---|
| | | Overall | | Within school | | After accounting for the programme level and programme destination in which students are enrolled[1] | |
| | | Score difference | S.E. | Score difference | S.E. | Score difference | S.E. |
| OECD | Australia | 0 | (3.8) | -2 | (2.2) | -1 | (2.2) |
| | Austria | 8 | (4.9) | **16** | (2.9) | **18** | (2.8) |
| | Belgium | 1 | (4.1) | **15** | (2.0) | **15** | (1.7) |
| | Canada | 4 | (2.2) | **6** | (2.1) | **7** | (2.0) |
| | Czech Republic | 5 | (5.6) | **18** | (3.0) | **19** | (3.0) |
| | Denmark | **9** | (3.2) | **9** | (2.8) | **10** | (2.8) |
| | Finland | -3 | (2.9) | -3 | (2.9) | -3 | (2.8) |
| | France | 3 | (4.0) | **20** | (2.1) | **21** | (2.0) |
| | Germany | 7 | (3.7) | **17** | (2.4) | **17** | (2.4) |
| | Greece | **-11** | (4.7) | **7** | (3.0) | **7** | (3.0) |
| | Hungary | 6 | (4.2) | **27** | (2.4) | **27** | (2.4) |
| | Iceland | -6 | (3.4) | -6 | (3.3) | -5 | (3.3) |
| | Ireland | 0 | (4.3) | 2 | (3.7) | 4 | (3.6) |
| | Italy | 3 | (3.5) | **13** | (2.0) | **13** | (1.9) |
| | Japan | 3 | (7.4) | 2 | (2.6) | 2 | (2.6) |
| | Korea | -2 | (5.5) | 1 | (3.8) | 1 | (3.4) |
| | Luxembourg | **9** | (2.9) | **11** | (3.0) | **17** | (2.7) |
| | Mexico | **7** | (2.2) | **14** | (1.5) | **15** | (1.5) |
| | Netherlands | **7** | (3.0) | **15** | (2.1) | **16** | (1.7) |
| | New Zealand | -4 | (5.2) | 2 | (4.0) | 3 | (4.0) |
| | Norway | -4 | (3.4) | -4 | (3.6) | -4 | (3.6) |
| | Poland | 3 | (2.5) | **5** | (2.4) | **5** | (2.4) |
| | Portugal | 5 | (3.3) | **10** | (2.8) | **18** | (2.4) |
| | Slovak Republic | 6 | (4.7) | **17** | (2.8) | **18** | (2.8) |
| | Spain | 4 | (2.4) | **6** | (2.1) | **6** | (2.1) |
| | Sweden | 1 | (3.0) | 3 | (2.7) | 3 | (2.7) |
| | Switzerland | **6** | (2.7) | **15** | (2.3) | **15** | (2.2) |
| | Turkey | **-12** | (4.1) | -2 | (2.6) | -2 | (2.6) |
| | United Kingdom | **10** | (3.4) | **10** | (2.5) | **11** | (2.5) |
| | United States | 1 | (3.5) | 3 | (2.6) | 6 | (2.4) |
| | **OECD average** | **2** | (0.7) | **8** | (0.5) | **9** | (0.5) |
| Partners | Argentina | **-13** | (5.6) | 0 | (3.5) | 4 | (3.4) |
| | Azerbaijan | **-8** | (2.0) | **-8** | (1.5) | **-8** | (1.5) |
| | Brazil | **9** | (2.3) | **10** | (2.3) | **15** | (2.3) |
| | Bulgaria | **-17** | (5.8) | 4 | (3.2) | 5 | (3.2) |
| | Chile | **22** | (4.8) | **18** | (3.0) | **18** | (2.9) |
| | Colombia | 9 | (4.6) | 13 | (3.8) | 16 | (3.7) |
| | Croatia | -2 | (4.1) | **16** | (2.3) | **22** | (2.1) |
| | Estonia | -4 | (3.1) | 0 | (2.5) | 1 | (2.5) |
| | Hong Kong-China | 7 | (4.9) | **19** | (2.7) | **21** | (2.5) |
| | Indonesia | 12 | (6.3) | **8** | (1.5) | **8** | (1.6) |
| | Israel | 3 | (6.5) | 3 | (4.3) | 4 | (4.3) |
| | Jordan | **-29** | (5.3) | **-16** | (5.0) | **-16** | (5.0) |
| | Kyrgyzstan | **-6** | (3.0) | **-7** | (2.4) | **-6** | (2.4) |
| | Latvia | **-7** | (3.1) | -4 | (2.8) | -2 | (2.7) |
| | Liechtenstein | -11 | (11.1) | 6 | (6.8) | 5 | (6.5) |
| | Lithuania | **-9** | (2.8) | -2 | (2.6) | -2 | (2.5) |
| | Macao-China | 4 | (2.7) | **16** | (3.0) | **19** | (2.6) |
| | Montenegro | -2 | (2.6) | **10** | (2.3) | **12** | (2.3) |
| | Qatar | **-32** | (1.9) | **-13** | (6.8) | **-12** | (6.4) |
| | Romania | -2 | (3.3) | **16** | (2.4) | **16** | (2.4) |
| | Russian Federation | 3 | (2.7) | **8** | (2.3) | **12** | (2.3) |
| | Serbia | -5 | (3.8) | **15** | (2.1) | **19** | (2.0) |
| | Slovenia | **-8** | (3.2) | **21** | (2.6) | **22** | (2.5) |
| | Chinese Taipei | 7 | (6.0) | **9** | (2.2) | **9** | (2.2) |
| | Thailand | **-17** | (3.9) | **-9** | (2.5) | **-6** | (2.5) |
| | Tunisia | -5 | (3.4) | **8** | (2.5) | **9** | (2.4) |
| | Uruguay | -3 | (4.0) | **8** | (3.0) | **12** | (2.8) |

Note: Values that are statistically significant are indicated in bold (see Annex A3).
1. The programme level indicates whether the student is in a lower (ISCED Level 2) or upper (ISCED Level 3) secondary programme. The programme designation indicates the destination of the study programme: A, B or C (see Annex A1).
StatLink 🖳 http://dx.doi.org/10.1787/142056138443

Pour consulter la version française intégrale de ce tableau, suivre ce lien :
StatLink 🖳 http://dx.doi.org/10.1787/152610887346

[Part 1/1]

**Table 2.6**  Socio-economic indicators[1] and the relationship with performance in science

Tableau 2.6  Les indicateurs socioéconomiques et le rapport avec la performance des élèves en sciences

| | Mean performance on the science scale | Socio-economic indicators | | | |
|---|---|---|---|---|---|
| | | GDP per capita (In equivalent USD using purchasing power parities) | Percentage of the population in the age group 35-44 years that has attained at least upper secondary education | Mean PISA index of economic social and cultural status (ESCS) | Cumulative expenditure per student between 6 and 15 years (In equivalent USD using purchasing power parities) |
| Australia | 527 | 34 238 | 66 | 0.21 | 63 675 |
| Austria | 511 | 34 409 | 84 | 0.20 | 86 473 |
| Belgium | 510 | 33 028 | 72 | 0.17 | 70 818 |
| Canada | 534 | 34 052 | 88 | 0.37 | m |
| Czech Republic | 513 | 20 727 | 93 | 0.03 | 37 822 |
| Denmark | 496 | 34 090 | 83 | 0.31 | 78 479 |
| Finland | 563 | 30 923 | 87 | 0.26 | 64 519 |
| France | 495 | 30 352 | 71 | -0.09 | 66 640 |
| Germany | 516 | 30 826 | 85 | 0.29 | 56 283 |
| Greece[2] | 473 | 29 564 | 65 | -0.15 | 48 423 |
| Hungary[3] | 504 | 17 506 | 81 | -0.09 | 37 295 |
| Iceland | 491 | 36 499 | 67 | 0.77 | 83 893 |
| Ireland | 508 | 38 844 | 70 | -0.02 | 57 263 |
| Italy[2, 3] | 475 | 28 168 | 54 | -0.07 | 75 864 |
| Japan | 531 | 30 773 | m | -0.01 | 69 165 |
| Korea | 522 | 22 277 | 88 | -0.01 | 52 598 |
| Luxembourg | 486 | m | m | 0.09 | m |
| Mexico | 410 | 10 767 | 23 | -0.99 | 17 535 |
| Netherlands | 525 | 35 365 | 76 | 0.25 | 67 302 |
| New Zealand[2] | 530 | 26 070 | 82 | 0.10 | 52 475 |
| Norway[2] | 487 | 35 853 | 78 | 0.42 | 88 157 |
| Poland[2, 3] | 498 | 13 951 | 50 | -0.30 | 31 295 |
| Portugal[3] | 474 | 20 043 | 26 | -0.62 | 53 126 |
| Slovak Republic | 488 | 15 983 | 92 | -0.15 | 23 392 |
| Spain | 488 | 27 507 | 54 | -0.31 | 56 591 |
| Sweden | 503 | 32 111 | 90 | 0.24 | 72 743 |
| Switzerland[2, 3] | 512 | 36 276 | 85 | 0.09 | 94 377 |
| Turkey[2, 3] | 424 | 7 709 | 25 | -1.28 | 12 576 |
| United Kingdom | 515 | 32 890 | 67 | 0.19 | 64 007 |
| United States | 489 | 41 674 | 88 | 0.14 | 91 770 |

| | Adjusted performance on the science scale | | | | Change in expenditure per student in primary and secondary education (1995=100, 2004 constant prices) | | |
|---|---|---|---|---|---|---|---|
| | Science performance adjusted by GDP per capita | Science performance adjusted by GDP per capita and the percentage of the age group 35-44 years with upper secondary attainment | Science performance adjusted by the mean PISA index of economic social and cultural status | Science performance adjusted by cumulative expenditure per student between 6 and 15 years | 1995-2000 | 2000-2004 | 1995-2004 |
| Australia | 516 | 528 | 516 | 525 | 125 | 114 | 138 |
| Austria | 499 | 494 | 500 | 494 | m | 100 | m |
| Belgium | 502 | 506 | 501 | 504 | m | m | m |
| Canada | 524 | 514 | 514 | m | m | m | m |
| Czech Republic | 527 | 497 | 511 | 526 | 92 | 131 | 124 |
| Denmark | 485 | 480 | 479 | 484 | 114 | 107 | 121 |
| Finland | 558 | 546 | 549 | 560 | 108 | 116 | 122 |
| France | 491 | 494 | 500 | 491 | 113 | m | m |
| Germany | 511 | 500 | 500 | 518 | m | m | 105 |
| Greece[2] | 471 | 478 | 482 | 480 | 156 | 131 | 192 |
| Hungary[3] | 524 | 502 | 508 | 518 | 105 | 149 | 157 |
| Iceland | 475 | 489 | 449 | 476 | m | m | m |
| Ireland | 489 | 502 | 509 | 510 | 129 | 150 | 181 |
| Italy[2, 3] | 476 | 492 | 479 | 466 | 96 | 109 | 105 |
| Japan | 527 | m | 532 | 526 | 116 | 109 | 127 |
| Korea | 534 | 510 | 522 | 527 | m | m | m |
| Luxembourg | m | m | m | m | m | m | m |
| Mexico | 443 | 468 | 463 | 436 | 115 | 117 | 130 |
| Netherlands | 512 | 515 | 511 | 520 | 116 | 120 | 136 |
| New Zealand[2] | 535 | 521 | 525 | 535 | m | m | m |
| Norway[2] | 472 | 474 | 464 | 469 | 93 | 118 | 109 |
| Poland[2, 3] | 525 | 528 | 514 | 515 | 147 | 128 | 183 |
| Portugal[3] | 490 | 524 | 508 | 478 | 146 | 106 | 154 |
| Slovak Republic | 512 | 477 | 496 | 511 | 111 | 141 | 155 |
| Spain | 490 | 506 | 505 | 490 | 121 | 112 | 136 |
| Sweden | 496 | 483 | 490 | 495 | 104 | 116 | 117 |
| Switzerland[2, 3] | 497 | 493 | 507 | 490 | 94 | 111 | 105 |
| Turkey[2, 3] | 463 | 483 | 493 | 453 | 158 | 161 | 211 |
| United Kingdom | 506 | 516 | 504 | 512 | 99 | 124 | 120 |
| United States | 464 | 463 | 481 | 469 | 118 | 114 | 130 |

1. Source: Education at a Glance (OECD, 2007).
2. Public expenditure only.
3. Public institutions only.
StatLink http://dx.doi.org/10.1787/142056138443

Pour consulter la version française intégrale de ce tableau, suivre ce lien :
StatLink http://dx.doi.org/10.1787/152610887346

45

[Part 1/2]

**Table 2.7**  Mean score, variation and gender differences in student performance on the *knowledge about science* scale

Tableau 2.7  Score moyen, différences de score selon le sexe et répartition des scores sur l'échelle de *connaissances à propos des sciences*

| | | All students | | | | Gender differences | | | | | |
|---|---|---|---|---|---|---|---|---|---|---|---|
| | | Mean score | | Standard deviation | | Males | | Females | | Difference (M - F) | |
| | | Mean | S.E. | S.D. | S.E. | Mean score | S.E. | Mean score | S.E. | Score dif. | S.E. |
| **OECD** | Australia | 533 | (1.9) | 100 | (0.9) | 529 | (2.6) | 538 | (2.3) | **-10** | (3.3) |
| | Austria | 504 | (3.3) | 99 | (1.8) | 500 | (3.8) | 507 | (4.2) | -7 | (4.6) |
| | Belgium | 519 | (2.3) | 103 | (1.5) | 513 | (3.1) | 525 | (2.8) | **-11** | (3.8) |
| | Canada | 537 | (2.0) | 97 | (1.0) | 534 | (2.5) | 541 | (2.1) | **-7** | (2.3) |
| | Czech Republic | 499 | (2.9) | 100 | (1.4) | 496 | (3.8) | 503 | (4.1) | -7 | (5.2) |
| | Denmark | 493 | (2.6) | 94 | (1.2) | 490 | (3.1) | 495 | (2.9) | -6 | (3.1) |
| | Finland | 558 | (1.7) | 89 | (1.2) | 550 | (2.3) | 566 | (2.2) | **-16** | (2.9) |
| | France | 507 | (3.1) | 112 | (1.7) | 503 | (4.2) | 512 | (3.9) | -9 | (5.3) |
| | Germany | 512 | (3.1) | 101 | (1.7) | 509 | (4.1) | 515 | (3.2) | -6 | (3.8) |
| | Greece | 471 | (2.8) | 97 | (1.5) | 459 | (3.9) | 483 | (2.9) | **-24** | (4.2) |
| | Hungary | 492 | (2.2) | 86 | (1.4) | 490 | (2.8) | 495 | (3.1) | -5 | (3.9) |
| | Iceland | 493 | (1.8) | 101 | (1.4) | 483 | (2.7) | 502 | (2.5) | **-20** | (3.6) |
| | Ireland | 513 | (2.7) | 93 | (1.3) | 508 | (3.7) | 517 | (2.8) | **-9** | (3.8) |
| | Italy | 472 | (1.8) | 99 | (1.1) | 468 | (2.5) | 476 | (2.4) | **-8** | (3.4) |
| | Japan | 532 | (3.2) | 108 | (1.7) | 528 | (4.5) | 535 | (4.9) | -8 | (7.0) |
| | Korea | 527 | (3.0) | 92 | (1.8) | 520 | (4.2) | 533 | (3.3) | **-14** | (4.8) |
| | Luxembourg | 488 | (1.3) | 100 | (1.1) | 486 | (2.0) | 490 | (2.1) | -4 | (3.2) |
| | Mexico | 413 | (2.1) | 83 | (1.0) | 412 | (2.7) | 414 | (2.2) | -1 | (2.5) |
| | Netherlands | 530 | (2.6) | 101 | (1.5) | 528 | (3.3) | 532 | (3.2) | -4 | (3.7) |
| | New Zealand | 539 | (2.5) | 108 | (1.2) | 532 | (3.5) | 546 | (3.5) | **-14** | (5.1) |
| | Norway | 480 | (2.7) | 100 | (1.7) | 471 | (3.6) | 490 | (3.2) | **-18** | (4.2) |
| | Poland | 491 | (2.1) | 90 | (1.3) | 486 | (2.4) | 495 | (2.5) | **-9** | (2.6) |
| | Portugal | 481 | (2.7) | 93 | (1.8) | 478 | (3.3) | 484 | (3.1) | -6 | (3.6) |
| | Slovak Republic | 478 | (2.3) | 95 | (1.5) | 473 | (3.7) | 484 | (2.8) | **-10** | (4.5) |
| | Spain | 489 | (2.0) | 90 | (0.8) | 485 | (2.4) | 492 | (2.2) | **-7** | (2.4) |
| | Sweden | 498 | (2.2) | 98 | (1.3) | 494 | (2.6) | 502 | (2.9) | -7 | (3.2) |
| | Switzerland | 514 | (2.7) | 100 | (1.2) | 511 | (3.0) | 518 | (3.2) | **-6** | (3.0) |
| | Turkey | 425 | (3.1) | 83 | (1.8) | 415 | (3.9) | 437 | (3.5) | **-22** | (4.1) |
| | United Kingdom | 517 | (1.9) | 106 | (1.4) | 517 | (2.5) | 516 | (2.6) | 0 | (3.3) |
| | United States | 492 | (3.7) | 104 | (1.6) | 487 | (4.5) | 497 | (3.6) | **-10** | (3.3) |
| | **OECD total** | 492 | (1.1) | 105 | (0.5) | 488 | (1.3) | 497 | (1.2) | **-8** | (1.2) |
| | **OECD average** | 500 | (0.5) | 97 | (0.3) | 495 | (0.6) | 505 | (0.6) | **-10** | (0.7) |
| **Partners** | Argentina | 397 | (4.8) | 100 | (1.6) | 384 | (4.9) | 408 | (5.7) | **-24** | (4.9) |
| | Azerbaijan | 355 | (2.1) | 62 | (1.2) | 352 | (2.4) | 358 | (2.3) | **-6** | (2.1) |
| | Brazil | 394 | (2.5) | 95 | (1.5) | 393 | (3.0) | 394 | (2.7) | -1 | (2.8) |
| | Bulgaria | 426 | (5.5) | 113 | (2.5) | 411 | (6.0) | 441 | (6.1) | **-30** | (5.6) |
| | Chile | 443 | (3.7) | 96 | (1.4) | 447 | (4.7) | 437 | (3.9) | 10 | (4.6) |
| | Colombia | 396 | (2.9) | 92 | (1.6) | 397 | (3.8) | 396 | (3.5) | 1 | (4.5) |
| | Croatia | 494 | (2.1) | 88 | (1.2) | 486 | (3.0) | 502 | (2.7) | **-16** | (3.8) |
| | Estonia | 523 | (2.1) | 82 | (1.1) | 516 | (2.5) | 531 | (2.5) | **-15** | (2.9) |
| | Hong Kong-China | 542 | (2.5) | 98 | (1.4) | 540 | (3.4) | 543 | (3.5) | -3 | (4.8) |
| | Indonesia | 387 | (2.8) | 73 | (1.3) | 387 | (3.7) | 387 | (2.8) | 0 | (3.5) |
| | Israel | 466 | (3.4) | 122 | (1.8) | 463 | (5.0) | 469 | (4.0) | -6 | (6.1) |
| | Jordan | 409 | (2.5) | 87 | (1.7) | 393 | (3.8) | 424 | (2.8) | **-32** | (4.4) |
| | Kyrgyzstan | 309 | (2.5) | 96 | (1.6) | 302 | (3.4) | 315 | (2.6) | **-13** | (3.2) |
| | Latvia | 491 | (2.6) | 84 | (1.1) | 480 | (3.3) | 502 | (2.8) | **-21** | (3.3) |
| | Liechtenstein | 526 | (4.2) | 98 | (4.8) | 517 | (8.8) | 535 | (6.6) | -18 | (12.9) |
| | Lithuania | 482 | (2.1) | 88 | (1.0) | 472 | (2.7) | 493 | (2.8) | **-22** | (3.4) |
| | Macao-China | 505 | (1.2) | 82 | (1.3) | 502 | (1.7) | 508 | (1.9) | -5 | (2.7) |
| | Montenegro | 407 | (1.6) | 83 | (1.1) | 400 | (2.0) | 414 | (2.4) | **-14** | (3.0) |
| | Qatar | 343 | (1.0) | 88 | (1.0) | 328 | (1.4) | 359 | (1.7) | **-31** | (2.5) |
| | Romania | 413 | (3.6) | 86 | (2.3) | 405 | (3.7) | 420 | (4.0) | **-15** | (3.2) |
| | Russian Federation | 475 | (3.3) | 94 | (1.5) | 469 | (3.7) | 481 | (3.4) | **-11** | (2.9) |
| | Serbia | 431 | (2.6) | 86 | (1.1) | 422 | (3.1) | 439 | (3.2) | **-18** | (3.6) |
| | Slovenia | 510 | (1.6) | 98 | (1.1) | 498 | (2.0) | 522 | (2.8) | **-25** | (3.5) |
| | Chinese Taipei | 525 | (3.0) | 95 | (1.2) | 523 | (3.5) | 528 | (3.5) | -4 | (5.0) |
| | Thailand | 421 | (1.8) | 85 | (1.3) | 405 | (2.9) | 433 | (2.2) | **-28** | (3.6) |
| | Tunisia | 389 | (2.6) | 89 | (1.6) | 381 | (2.8) | 397 | (3.3) | **-15** | (3.2) |
| | Uruguay | 431 | (2.4) | 102 | (1.4) | 425 | (3.5) | 438 | (2.6) | **-13** | (4.0) |

Note: Values that are statistically significant are indicated in bold (see Annex A3).
StatLink http://dx.doi.org/10.1787/142056138443

Pour consulter la version française intégrale de ce tableau, suivre ce lien :
StatLink http://dx.doi.org/10.1787/152610887346

[Part 2/2]

**Table 2.7** Mean score, variation and gender differences in student performance on the *knowledge about science* scale

Tableau 2.7 Score moyen, différences de score selon le sexe et répartition des scores sur l'échelle de *connaissances à propos des sciences*

| | | Percentiles | | | | | | | | | | |
|---|---|---|---|---|---|---|---|---|---|---|---|---|
| | | 5th | | 10th | | 25th | | 75th | | 90th | | 95th | |
| | | Score | S.E. | Score | S.E. | Score | S.E. | Score | S.E. | Score | S.E. | Score | S.E. |
| **OECD** | Australia | 362 | (3.5) | 407 | (3.0) | 468 | (3.1) | 602 | (2.5) | 658 | (2.5) | 691 | (4.1) |
| | Austria | 339 | (5.5) | 369 | (6.4) | 436 | (4.6) | 574 | (4.2) | 630 | (4.3) | 662 | (4.0) |
| | Belgium | 342 | (5.2) | 379 | (4.7) | 450 | (4.0) | 591 | (1.9) | 649 | (3.6) | 681 | (4.6) |
| | Canada | 372 | (3.6) | 410 | (3.2) | 475 | (2.4) | 605 | (2.0) | 657 | (2.1) | 689 | (3.8) |
| | Czech Republic | 340 | (4.0) | 369 | (3.9) | 427 | (4.5) | 570 | (2.8) | 630 | (4.9) | 662 | (4.6) |
| | Denmark | 339 | (6.8) | 371 | (3.6) | 428 | (3.9) | 557 | (3.5) | 612 | (2.8) | 643 | (3.8) |
| | Finland | 408 | (6.3) | 443 | (3.5) | 499 | (2.9) | 620 | (2.2) | 671 | (2.5) | 698 | (2.0) |
| | France | 316 | (7.8) | 360 | (5.1) | 432 | (4.6) | 588 | (3.9) | 648 | (2.9) | 683 | (5.6) |
| | Germany | 336 | (8.9) | 374 | (4.9) | 445 | (3.8) | 583 | (2.8) | 638 | (3.8) | 673 | (2.7) |
| | Greece | 311 | (6.2) | 346 | (4.1) | 407 | (3.6) | 539 | (3.3) | 593 | (3.2) | 623 | (4.5) |
| | Hungary | 352 | (4.2) | 378 | (3.3) | 431 | (3.3) | 552 | (3.9) | 604 | (3.5) | 632 | (3.7) |
| | Iceland | 321 | (5.0) | 360 | (2.8) | 425 | (2.8) | 565 | (2.8) | 620 | (3.8) | 653 | (3.3) |
| | Ireland | 353 | (4.8) | 391 | (3.6) | 449 | (3.2) | 578 | (2.9) | 632 | (3.3) | 663 | (4.3) |
| | Italy | 307 | (2.8) | 343 | (2.6) | 403 | (2.7) | 540 | (2.4) | 599 | (2.6) | 633 | (2.9) |
| | Japan | 348 | (6.6) | 390 | (7.3) | 460 | (5.5) | 609 | (3.4) | 665 | (3.9) | 698 | (2.8) |
| | Korea | 370 | (6.5) | 402 | (4.9) | 466 | (4.2) | 591 | (3.5) | 643 | (4.0) | 672 | (5.1) |
| | Luxembourg | 320 | (6.0) | 356 | (3.4) | 421 | (2.4) | 560 | (2.9) | 616 | (2.4) | 650 | (3.0) |
| | Mexico | 281 | (3.7) | 310 | (2.9) | 356 | (3.0) | 469 | (2.6) | 520 | (2.4) | 548 | (2.7) |
| | Netherlands | 359 | (5.6) | 396 | (4.5) | 462 | (4.2) | 601 | (3.2) | 660 | (3.1) | 693 | (3.1) |
| | New Zealand | 354 | (5.6) | 397 | (4.2) | 464 | (5.1) | 615 | (3.0) | 678 | (3.2) | 706 | (3.9) |
| | Norway | 313 | (7.9) | 351 | (4.4) | 413 | (4.4) | 550 | (2.9) | 606 | (4.1) | 639 | (3.7) |
| | Poland | 343 | (3.9) | 371 | (3.2) | 428 | (2.8) | 555 | (3.7) | 606 | (3.5) | 639 | (4.0) |
| | Portugal | 331 | (3.8) | 361 | (3.4) | 416 | (4.0) | 548 | (3.0) | 603 | (3.4) | 629 | (3.7) |
| | Slovak Republic | 318 | (4.5) | 350 | (5.3) | 416 | (2.7) | 543 | (3.6) | 603 | (4.2) | 634 | (4.1) |
| | Spain | 338 | (4.2) | 370 | (3.2) | 428 | (2.5) | 552 | (2.5) | 605 | (3.1) | 634 | (2.7) |
| | Sweden | 333 | (5.1) | 369 | (4.2) | 431 | (2.6) | 567 | (2.3) | 624 | (3.9) | 657 | (4.3) |
| | Switzerland | 346 | (4.4) | 377 | (3.3) | 448 | (3.5) | 586 | (3.5) | 644 | (4.1) | 672 | (4.0) |
| | Turkey | 293 | (4.4) | 324 | (3.0) | 368 | (3.2) | 481 | (5.1) | 536 | (5.7) | 572 | (6.5) |
| | United Kingdom | 336 | (2.6) | 382 | (3.9) | 446 | (3.1) | 590 | (2.2) | 650 | (1.8) | 681 | (3.8) |
| | United States | 321 | (6.5) | 354 | (5.2) | 419 | (5.8) | 567 | (4.0) | 628 | (4.5) | 664 | (4.9) |
| | **OECD total** | 320 | (2.1) | 355 | (1.6) | 418 | (1.6) | 567 | (1.5) | 630 | (1.4) | 664 | (1.7) |
| | **OECD average** | 337 | (1.0) | 372 | (0.8) | 434 | (0.7) | 568 | (0.6) | 624 | (0.6) | 656 | (0.7) |
| **Partners** | Argentina | 228 | (9.2) | 265 | (6.9) | 329 | (5.3) | 466 | (5.6) | 524 | (5.2) | 560 | (4.7) |
| | Azerbaijan | 256 | (3.4) | 276 | (2.4) | 313 | (2.4) | 394 | (2.7) | 436 | (5.1) | 463 | (5.1) |
| | Brazil | 235 | (4.4) | 273 | (3.0) | 334 | (4.1) | 455 | (3.5) | 520 | (4.8) | 557 | (4.1) |
| | Bulgaria | 247 | (6.8) | 283 | (6.2) | 347 | (5.4) | 503 | (7.1) | 576 | (7.5) | 615 | (7.5) |
| | Chile | 289 | (4.4) | 326 | (3.9) | 379 | (4.2) | 507 | (4.5) | 572 | (4.3) | 606 | (6.4) |
| | Colombia | 238 | (6.1) | 277 | (4.1) | 338 | (4.6) | 458 | (3.5) | 513 | (3.5) | 546 | (4.2) |
| | Croatia | 351 | (4.4) | 379 | (3.4) | 435 | (3.0) | 555 | (2.3) | 607 | (3.0) | 641 | (3.4) |
| | Estonia | 390 | (4.2) | 417 | (2.9) | 468 | (2.9) | 580 | (3.1) | 628 | (3.6) | 656 | (4.3) |
| | Hong Kong-China | 372 | (6.0) | 411 | (5.1) | 478 | (4.0) | 611 | (3.4) | 664 | (2.6) | 693 | (3.2) |
| | Indonesia | 268 | (2.8) | 292 | (2.9) | 338 | (3.4) | 434 | (3.1) | 482 | (4.6) | 511 | (6.2) |
| | Israel | 267 | (7.2) | 311 | (4.8) | 382 | (5.0) | 554 | (4.9) | 623 | (4.2) | 665 | (6.0) |
| | Jordan | 266 | (3.9) | 295 | (3.2) | 350 | (2.7) | 468 | (3.5) | 522 | (4.3) | 548 | (4.0) |
| | Kyrgyzstan | 147 | (6.0) | 188 | (3.9) | 246 | (3.7) | 372 | (3.5) | 428 | (3.8) | 463 | (4.9) |
| | Latvia | 350 | (4.9) | 378 | (4.6) | 434 | (3.5) | 550 | (3.3) | 598 | (3.1) | 628 | (4.6) |
| | Liechtenstein | 361 | (12.1) | 394 | (14.7) | 457 | (11.6) | 598 | (7.7) | 649 | (9.2) | 682 | (12.7) |
| | Lithuania | 338 | (3.3) | 365 | (2.7) | 420 | (3.2) | 544 | (2.5) | 596 | (2.6) | 624 | (4.1) |
| | Macao-China | 364 | (3.2) | 396 | (3.3) | 451 | (2.7) | 562 | (2.3) | 611 | (3.5) | 639 | (5.0) |
| | Montenegro | 269 | (3.1) | 299 | (4.3) | 352 | (2.4) | 465 | (2.5) | 516 | (3.9) | 544 | (3.8) |
| | Qatar | 203 | (3.8) | 234 | (4.0) | 286 | (1.8) | 397 | (1.9) | 460 | (2.8) | 499 | (3.2) |
| | Romania | 278 | (5.2) | 306 | (5.3) | 353 | (4.3) | 469 | (5.8) | 528 | (5.6) | 558 | (6.0) |
| | Russian Federation | 321 | (4.6) | 350 | (4.5) | 414 | (4.1) | 541 | (4.0) | 599 | (5.0) | 630 | (3.0) |
| | Serbia | 290 | (3.6) | 318 | (3.4) | 372 | (3.5) | 490 | (3.5) | 542 | (3.1) | 573 | (3.4) |
| | Slovenia | 348 | (3.3) | 382 | (3.1) | 442 | (2.6) | 579 | (3.1) | 638 | (2.7) | 671 | (3.5) |
| | Chinese Taipei | 358 | (5.4) | 400 | (4.7) | 462 | (5.0) | 593 | (3.2) | 644 | (3.4) | 673 | (3.3) |
| | Thailand | 280 | (3.9) | 312 | (4.2) | 365 | (2.2) | 478 | (2.7) | 533 | (3.6) | 564 | (2.7) |
| | Tunisia | 242 | (3.4) | 274 | (3.1) | 332 | (2.6) | 449 | (3.7) | 509 | (5.7) | 537 | (5.1) |
| | Uruguay | 266 | (6.5) | 302 | (2.9) | 363 | (4.1) | 503 | (3.5) | 562 | (2.6) | 596 | (5.3) |

Note: Values that are statistically significant are indicated in bold (see Annex A3).
StatLink ◉◢◤ http://dx.doi.org/10.1787/142056138443

Pour consulter la version française intégrale de ce tableau, suivre ce lien :
StatLink ◉◢◤ http://dx.doi.org/10.1787/152610887346

47

[Part 1/2]

**Table 2.8** **Mean score, variation and gender differences in student performance on the "Earth and space systems" scale**

Tableau 2.8 Score moyen, différences de score selon le sexe et répartition des scores sur l'échelle « systèmes de la Terre et de l'univers »

| | All students | | | | Gender differences | | | | | |
| | Mean score | | Standard deviation | | Males | | Females | | Difference (M - F) | |
| | Mean | S.E. | S.D. | S.E. | Mean score | S.E. | Mean score | S.E. | Score dif. | S.E. |
|---|---|---|---|---|---|---|---|---|---|---|
| *OECD* Australia | 530 | (1.9) | 98 | (0.8) | 538 | (2.6) | 522 | (2.4) | 16 | (3.2) |
| Austria | 503 | (3.6) | 105 | (2.1) | 511 | (4.1) | 493 | (4.4) | 18 | (4.8) |
| Belgium | 496 | (2.4) | 114 | (1.6) | 507 | (3.3) | 485 | (3.1) | 22 | (4.2) |
| Canada | 540 | (1.8) | 98 | (0.9) | 549 | (2.4) | 531 | (1.9) | 18 | (2.3) |
| Czech Republic | 526 | (3.6) | 119 | (1.7) | 539 | (4.5) | 509 | (4.8) | 29 | (6.2) |
| Denmark | 487 | (2.8) | 98 | (1.5) | 500 | (3.5) | 474 | (3.0) | 26 | (3.4) |
| Finland | 554 | (1.8) | 100 | (1.2) | 562 | (2.4) | 547 | (2.5) | 14 | (3.2) |
| France | 463 | (2.8) | 103 | (1.6) | 473 | (3.8) | 453 | (3.2) | 19 | (4.3) |
| Germany | 510 | (3.6) | 118 | (1.7) | 516 | (4.9) | 505 | (3.6) | 11 | (4.9) |
| Greece | 477 | (2.9) | 107 | (1.7) | 480 | (4.1) | 475 | (3.2) | 5 | (4.5) |
| Hungary | 512 | (2.7) | 106 | (2.0) | 516 | (3.5) | 508 | (3.6) | 8 | (4.6) |
| Iceland | 503 | (1.6) | 96 | (1.7) | 507 | (2.7) | 499 | (2.3) | 7 | (3.8) |
| Ireland | 508 | (2.8) | 102 | (1.6) | 515 | (3.9) | 501 | (3.2) | 14 | (4.2) |
| Italy | 474 | (2.0) | 113 | (1.2) | 481 | (3.1) | 467 | (2.5) | 15 | (3.9) |
| Japan | 530 | (3.0) | 99 | (1.4) | 544 | (4.0) | 517 | (4.2) | 26 | (5.9) |
| Korea | 533 | (3.0) | 98 | (1.8) | 540 | (4.4) | 526 | (3.6) | 14 | (5.2) |
| Luxembourg | 471 | (1.6) | 101 | (1.1) | 484 | (2.2) | 457 | (2.1) | 27 | (3.1) |
| Mexico | 412 | (2.4) | 99 | (1.4) | 420 | (3.2) | 404 | (2.4) | 16 | (2.9) |
| Netherlands | 518 | (2.7) | 106 | (1.5) | 530 | (3.3) | 505 | (3.5) | 25 | (4.0) |
| New Zealand | 530 | (2.4) | 107 | (1.1) | 536 | (3.3) | 524 | (3.4) | 12 | (4.5) |
| Norway | 497 | (2.8) | 102 | (1.7) | 501 | (3.8) | 493 | (3.1) | 8 | (4.0) |
| Poland | 501 | (2.4) | 104 | (1.6) | 510 | (2.8) | 493 | (2.9) | 17 | (3.1) |
| Portugal | 479 | (2.7) | 93 | (1.7) | 488 | (3.3) | 472 | (3.3) | 16 | (3.7) |
| Slovak Republic | 503 | (2.6) | 105 | (2.1) | 512 | (4.1) | 495 | (3.0) | 17 | (5.1) |
| Spain | 493 | (2.3) | 108 | (1.1) | 503 | (2.8) | 484 | (2.7) | 19 | (3.1) |
| Sweden | 498 | (2.3) | 103 | (1.3) | 508 | (3.0) | 488 | (3.0) | 20 | (3.8) |
| Switzerland | 502 | (2.9) | 108 | (1.3) | 515 | (3.4) | 489 | (3.4) | 26 | (3.4) |
| Turkey | 425 | (3.6) | 101 | (2.0) | 427 | (4.4) | 423 | (4.0) | 4 | (4.3) |
| United Kingdom | 505 | (1.9) | 106 | (1.3) | 515 | (2.6) | 494 | (2.6) | 21 | (3.4) |
| United States | 504 | (4.0) | 116 | (1.8) | 508 | (4.8) | 500 | (4.1) | 7 | (3.9) |
| **OECD total** | **493** | **(1.1)** | **114** | **(0.6)** | **500** | **(1.3)** | **486** | **(1.3)** | **15** | **(1.4)** |
| **OECD average** | **500** | **(0.5)** | **104** | **(0.3)** | **508** | **(0.6)** | **491** | **(0.6)** | **17** | **(0.8)** |
| *Partners* Argentina | 384 | (5.4) | 113 | (2.1) | 388 | (5.6) | 380 | (6.6) | 7 | (5.8) |
| Azerbaijan | 400 | (2.5) | 77 | (1.3) | 396 | (2.9) | 404 | (2.8) | -8 | (2.7) |
| Brazil | 375 | (2.5) | 101 | (1.7) | 387 | (3.2) | 364 | (2.8) | 23 | (3.1) |
| Bulgaria | 443 | (5.5) | 117 | (2.5) | 445 | (6.1) | 441 | (6.3) | 4 | (5.7) |
| Chile | 428 | (3.4) | 95 | (1.3) | 444 | (4.3) | 410 | (3.4) | 35 | (4.0) |
| Colombia | 370 | (2.9) | 105 | (1.8) | 384 | (4.6) | 359 | (4.0) | 26 | (6.1) |
| Croatia | 497 | (2.4) | 97 | (1.2) | 502 | (3.2) | 493 | (3.1) | 9 | (4.1) |
| Estonia | 540 | (2.4) | 98 | (1.3) | 545 | (3.2) | 535 | (2.9) | 10 | (3.7) |
| Hong Kong-China | 525 | (2.4) | 96 | (1.4) | 533 | (3.6) | 518 | (3.2) | 15 | (4.9) |
| Indonesia | 402 | (2.9) | 85 | (1.2) | 406 | (4.1) | 397 | (3.0) | 9 | (4.0) |
| Israel | 417 | (3.2) | 113 | (1.7) | 430 | (4.9) | 404 | (3.5) | 25 | (5.7) |
| Jordan | 421 | (2.9) | 107 | (1.6) | 413 | (4.5) | 429 | (3.5) | -16 | (5.4) |
| Kyrgyzstan | 315 | (2.6) | 101 | (1.5) | 316 | (3.9) | 314 | (3.1) | 1 | (4.7) |
| Latvia | 494 | (3.3) | 105 | (1.4) | 501 | (4.1) | 487 | (3.6) | 13 | (3.8) |
| Liechtenstein | 513 | (4.8) | 103 | (4.3) | 521 | (9.4) | 506 | (7.6) | 14 | (14.1) |
| Lithuania | 487 | (2.5) | 108 | (1.4) | 492 | (3.1) | 481 | (3.2) | 12 | (3.7) |
| Macao-China | 506 | (1.4) | 86 | (1.7) | 513 | (2.0) | 499 | (2.2) | 14 | (3.2) |
| Montenegro | 411 | (1.8) | 99 | (1.2) | 419 | (2.4) | 404 | (2.7) | 15 | (3.6) |
| Qatar | 350 | (1.1) | 104 | (1.1) | 330 | (1.8) | 369 | (2.2) | -39 | (3.2) |
| Romania | 407 | (4.0) | 94 | (2.1) | 409 | (4.3) | 405 | (4.6) | 4 | (3.6) |
| Russian Federation | 482 | (3.4) | 105 | (1.4) | 491 | (4.2) | 473 | (3.6) | 18 | (3.6) |
| Serbia | 441 | (2.7) | 99 | (1.7) | 447 | (3.2) | 434 | (3.6) | 12 | (4.1) |
| Slovenia | 534 | (1.7) | 119 | (1.4) | 537 | (2.4) | 530 | (3.4) | 7 | (4.8) |
| Chinese Taipei | 529 | (3.0) | 95 | (1.3) | 537 | (3.5) | 520 | (4.3) | 17 | (5.0) |
| Thailand | 430 | (1.7) | 84 | (1.3) | 430 | (2.8) | 430 | (2.1) | -1 | (3.5) |
| Tunisia | 352 | (2.6) | 96 | (1.6) | 354 | (2.8) | 350 | (3.8) | 4 | (4.3) |
| Uruguay | 397 | (2.6) | 114 | (2.1) | 410 | (4.0) | 385 | (3.2) | 25 | (4.8) |

Note: Values that are statistically significant are indicated in bold (see Annex A3).
*StatLink* http://dx.doi.org/10.1787/142056138443

Pour consulter la version française intégrale de ce tableau, suivre ce lien :
*StatLink* http://dx.doi.org/10.1787/152610887346

[Part 2/2]

**Table 2.8** **Mean score, variation and gender differences in student performance on the "Earth and space systems" scale**

Tableau 2.8 Score moyen, différences de score selon le sexe et répartition des scores sur l'échelle « systèmes de la Terre et de l'univers »

| | | 5th | | 10th | | 25th | | 75th | | 90th | | 95th | |
|---|---|---|---|---|---|---|---|---|---|---|---|---|---|
| | | Score | S.E. | Score | S.E. | Score | S.E. | Score | S.E. | Score | S.E. | Score | S.E. |
| **OECD** | Australia | 370 | (1.8) | 402 | (2.6) | 463 | (2.5) | 599 | (2.2) | 652 | (2.1) | 686 | (3.3) |
| | Austria | 325 | (8.1) | 364 | (5.8) | 432 | (4.3) | 574 | (3.3) | 639 | (4.4) | 669 | (4.5) |
| | Belgium | 301 | (5.3) | 345 | (4.6) | 420 | (3.1) | 576 | (2.9) | 642 | (3.0) | 678 | (2.4) |
| | Canada | 373 | (3.1) | 409 | (3.5) | 477 | (2.8) | 608 | (2.0) | 664 | (2.4) | 696 | (3.7) |
| | Czech Republic | 336 | (6.9) | 372 | (6.1) | 441 | (4.7) | 612 | (3.3) | 680 | (4.6) | 723 | (6.2) |
| | Denmark | 326 | (4.5) | 360 | (4.3) | 421 | (4.0) | 556 | (2.9) | 612 | (3.4) | 643 | (5.0) |
| | Finland | 387 | (4.9) | 425 | (5.1) | 488 | (3.5) | 624 | (2.6) | 684 | (3.7) | 715 | (3.6) |
| | France | 295 | (4.8) | 329 | (4.7) | 393 | (4.6) | 534 | (3.7) | 595 | (3.9) | 626 | (4.1) |
| | Germany | 313 | (8.1) | 356 | (5.4) | 429 | (5.1) | 591 | (3.1) | 662 | (4.3) | 704 | (4.6) |
| | Greece | 297 | (5.3) | 340 | (4.6) | 407 | (4.0) | 551 | (3.4) | 616 | (4.5) | 650 | (4.6) |
| | Hungary | 337 | (5.3) | 374 | (5.7) | 440 | (3.5) | 585 | (4.6) | 653 | (5.4) | 689 | (4.3) |
| | Iceland | 341 | (5.0) | 378 | (2.7) | 438 | (2.7) | 568 | (2.3) | 625 | (4.6) | 656 | (4.3) |
| | Ireland | 330 | (5.7) | 371 | (5.7) | 440 | (4.1) | 580 | (3.3) | 639 | (4.1) | 672 | (4.1) |
| | Italy | 290 | (4.2) | 328 | (3.5) | 397 | (2.7) | 553 | (2.9) | 621 | (3.1) | 659 | (4.0) |
| | Japan | 361 | (4.8) | 403 | (5.7) | 463 | (3.7) | 600 | (3.3) | 656 | (3.6) | 687 | (2.7) |
| | Korea | 366 | (4.8) | 405 | (5.8) | 467 | (3.6) | 599 | (3.4) | 658 | (3.5) | 686 | (4.5) |
| | Luxembourg | 304 | (4.3) | 339 | (3.7) | 400 | (2.5) | 540 | (2.8) | 604 | (2.9) | 639 | (3.1) |
| | Mexico | 249 | (4.4) | 286 | (3.3) | 346 | (3.3) | 480 | (3.4) | 540 | (4.0) | 572 | (3.0) |
| | Netherlands | 340 | (7.2) | 378 | (6.3) | 444 | (4.5) | 591 | (3.1) | 657 | (4.4) | 689 | (2.9) |
| | New Zealand | 356 | (4.4) | 393 | (3.8) | 456 | (3.3) | 607 | (3.3) | 667 | (4.0) | 699 | (4.1) |
| | Norway | 327 | (6.1) | 368 | (4.9) | 430 | (3.5) | 570 | (3.1) | 627 | (3.5) | 659 | (3.2) |
| | Poland | 329 | (4.7) | 365 | (3.8) | 427 | (4.1) | 573 | (3.6) | 639 | (3.5) | 673 | (5.6) |
| | Portugal | 327 | (5.8) | 361 | (5.3) | 415 | (3.5) | 546 | (3.1) | 602 | (3.7) | 632 | (4.8) |
| | Slovak Republic | 329 | (6.5) | 368 | (3.5) | 431 | (4.1) | 575 | (3.8) | 642 | (3.9) | 678 | (5.9) |
| | Spain | 314 | (4.9) | 355 | (4.1) | 420 | (3.3) | 566 | (2.9) | 635 | (3.3) | 673 | (2.9) |
| | Sweden | 328 | (4.9) | 365 | (3.4) | 427 | (3.5) | 567 | (3.1) | 630 | (2.8) | 670 | (4.1) |
| | Switzerland | 316 | (4.5) | 359 | (4.4) | 431 | (3.3) | 579 | (3.0) | 641 | (4.6) | 675 | (4.8) |
| | Turkey | 264 | (5.4) | 300 | (4.7) | 358 | (3.7) | 494 | (5.3) | 559 | (6.4) | 592 | (7.9) |
| | United Kingdom | 333 | (4.6) | 368 | (3.0) | 432 | (2.7) | 581 | (2.5) | 640 | (2.3) | 672 | (3.2) |
| | United States | 314 | (6.2) | 355 | (6.2) | 421 | (6.0) | 584 | (4.4) | 660 | (5.1) | 697 | (5.2) |
| | **OECD total** | 306 | (2.4) | 346 | (1.6) | 414 | (1.8) | 573 | (1.5) | 641 | (1.9) | 678 | (2.4) |
| | **OECD average** | 326 | (1.0) | 364 | (0.9) | 428 | (0.7) | 572 | (0.6) | 635 | (0.7) | 669 | (0.8) |
| **Partners** | Argentina | 197 | (6.5) | 238 | (6.4) | 307 | (6.9) | 463 | (7.0) | 527 | (6.9) | 566 | (7.8) |
| | Azerbaijan | 273 | (5.2) | 301 | (2.9) | 349 | (3.1) | 450 | (3.6) | 502 | (4.7) | 530 | (4.8) |
| | Brazil | 212 | (5.0) | 249 | (3.6) | 307 | (2.6) | 441 | (3.7) | 508 | (6.0) | 548 | (4.2) |
| | Bulgaria | 258 | (10.8) | 298 | (6.6) | 364 | (6.0) | 523 | (6.1) | 596 | (6.2) | 640 | (7.5) |
| | Chile | 279 | (3.2) | 309 | (3.9) | 362 | (3.9) | 494 | (4.7) | 554 | (5.7) | 587 | (6.7) |
| | Colombia | 194 | (7.5) | 238 | (4.8) | 301 | (3.8) | 442 | (3.6) | 505 | (5.9) | 545 | (5.4) |
| | Croatia | 339 | (3.9) | 376 | (4.0) | 430 | (3.6) | 562 | (3.0) | 624 | (2.7) | 661 | (3.8) |
| | Estonia | 378 | (6.6) | 415 | (3.6) | 476 | (3.0) | 609 | (2.8) | 666 | (4.3) | 697 | (2.5) |
| | Hong Kong-China | 359 | (6.1) | 400 | (4.8) | 460 | (3.0) | 592 | (3.2) | 647 | (3.5) | 678 | (4.4) |
| | Indonesia | 257 | (3.8) | 288 | (4.3) | 347 | (3.3) | 461 | (3.2) | 512 | (5.0) | 542 | (6.0) |
| | Israel | 233 | (5.5) | 274 | (4.8) | 340 | (4.7) | 494 | (3.3) | 565 | (4.5) | 600 | (6.1) |
| | Jordan | 242 | (7.0) | 284 | (4.6) | 350 | (3.3) | 497 | (3.7) | 560 | (3.8) | 593 | (4.8) |
| | Kyrgyzstan | 145 | (5.5) | 186 | (3.9) | 250 | (4.3) | 383 | (3.4) | 441 | (3.5) | 475 | (5.5) |
| | Latvia | 316 | (7.2) | 357 | (5.5) | 424 | (4.5) | 565 | (4.9) | 631 | (6.5) | 667 | (3.6) |
| | Liechtenstein | 336 | (18.7) | 377 | (10.0) | 443 | (7.8) | 585 | (8.3) | 643 | (12.4) | 676 | (11.6) |
| | Lithuania | 302 | (4.7) | 343 | (3.5) | 416 | (4.2) | 558 | (4.2) | 630 | (4.7) | 664 | (3.8) |
| | Macao-China | 364 | (4.8) | 394 | (2.9) | 446 | (2.9) | 567 | (2.1) | 617 | (3.9) | 644 | (3.6) |
| | Montenegro | 251 | (4.2) | 286 | (3.9) | 344 | (2.6) | 477 | (2.6) | 543 | (3.9) | 581 | (4.9) |
| | Qatar | 186 | (4.4) | 221 | (3.5) | 281 | (1.2) | 416 | (2.9) | 488 | (3.2) | 532 | (3.0) |
| | Romania | 255 | (4.9) | 285 | (5.2) | 344 | (2.9) | 471 | (5.4) | 533 | (7.0) | 562 | (5.4) |
| | Russian Federation | 311 | (5.8) | 349 | (4.2) | 409 | (5.2) | 553 | (3.9) | 621 | (4.0) | 660 | (3.7) |
| | Serbia | 275 | (4.5) | 312 | (4.6) | 373 | (4.3) | 509 | (3.7) | 570 | (4.1) | 606 | (5.2) |
| | Slovenia | 339 | (3.6) | 378 | (3.9) | 450 | (3.3) | 615 | (3.4) | 687 | (4.5) | 732 | (4.0) |
| | Chinese Taipei | 364 | (4.2) | 402 | (4.9) | 466 | (4.0) | 596 | (2.4) | 648 | (2.7) | 681 | (3.3) |
| | Thailand | 293 | (5.1) | 324 | (2.8) | 371 | (2.7) | 487 | (2.1) | 540 | (4.6) | 575 | (4.4) |
| | Tunisia | 193 | (4.7) | 231 | (3.6) | 288 | (2.4) | 419 | (3.6) | 482 | (5.5) | 517 | (6.1) |
| | Uruguay | 210 | (8.4) | 251 | (5.1) | 322 | (3.5) | 475 | (3.4) | 546 | (3.1) | 583 | (4.6) |

Note: Values that are statistically significant are indicated in bold (see Annex A3).
StatLink ☜☞ http://dx.doi.org/10.1787/142056138443

Pour consulter la version française intégrale de ce tableau, suivre ce lien :
StatLink ☜☞ http://dx.doi.org/10.1787/152610887346

[Part 1/2]

**Table 2.9** Mean score, variation and gender differences in student performance on the "Living systems" scale

Tableau 2.9 Score moyen, différences de score selon le sexe et répartition des scores sur l'échelle « systèmes vivants »

| | All students | | | | Gender differences | | | | | |
|---|---|---|---|---|---|---|---|---|---|---|
| | Mean score | | Standard deviation | | Males | | Females | | Difference (M - F) | |
| | Mean | S.E. | S.D. | S.E. | Mean score | S.E. | Mean score | S.E. | Score dif. | S.E. |
| Australia | 522 | (2.1) | 108 | (1.1) | 522 | (2.9) | 521 | (2.6) | 1 | (3.6) |
| Austria | 522 | (3.4) | 102 | (2.1) | 524 | (4.2) | 521 | (4.3) | 3 | (5.1) |
| Belgium | 502 | (2.2) | 104 | (1.5) | 503 | (3.0) | 501 | (2.9) | 2 | (3.9) |
| Canada | 530 | (2.1) | 106 | (1.0) | 534 | (2.6) | 527 | (2.3) | **8** | (2.5) |
| Czech Republic | 525 | (2.8) | 94 | (1.4) | 528 | (3.5) | 521 | (3.9) | 7 | (4.9) |
| Denmark | 505 | (2.9) | 104 | (1.3) | 510 | (3.5) | 499 | (3.2) | **11** | (3.6) |
| Finland | 574 | (1.8) | 93 | (1.4) | 569 | (2.4) | 579 | (2.5) | **-10** | (3.2) |
| France | 490 | (3.0) | 107 | (1.6) | 494 | (3.8) | 486 | (3.7) | 7 | (4.4) |
| Germany | 524 | (3.0) | 99 | (1.5) | 526 | (4.0) | 522 | (3.1) | 4 | (4.0) |
| Greece | 475 | (2.7) | 97 | (1.5) | 469 | (3.8) | 481 | (2.8) | **-12** | (4.0) |
| Hungary | 509 | (2.4) | 98 | (1.5) | 515 | (3.2) | 503 | (3.3) | **12** | (4.3) |
| Iceland | 481 | (1.6) | 94 | (1.4) | 479 | (2.5) | 484 | (2.3) | -5 | (3.5) |
| Ireland | 506 | (3.0) | 104 | (1.3) | 505 | (4.0) | 506 | (3.4) | -2 | (4.6) |
| Italy | 488 | (1.7) | 99 | (1.0) | 489 | (2.5) | 486 | (2.3) | 3 | (3.3) |
| Japan | 526 | (2.7) | 93 | (1.4) | 529 | (3.9) | 523 | (4.1) | 6 | (5.9) |
| Korea | 498 | (2.8) | 90 | (1.7) | 501 | (4.1) | 495 | (3.2) | 6 | (4.7) |
| Luxembourg | 499 | (1.4) | 106 | (1.2) | 504 | (2.3) | 493 | (2.2) | **11** | (3.4) |
| Mexico | 402 | (2.2) | 85 | (1.0) | 409 | (2.8) | 396 | (2.2) | **13** | (2.5) |
| Netherlands | 509 | (2.4) | 92 | (1.3) | 512 | (3.0) | 507 | (2.8) | 5 | (3.3) |
| New Zealand | 528 | (2.7) | 119 | (1.4) | 529 | (3.7) | 527 | (4.0) | 2 | (5.6) |
| Norway | 496 | (2.8) | 106 | (1.8) | 495 | (3.6) | 498 | (3.2) | -3 | (3.8) |
| Poland | 509 | (2.1) | 98 | (1.4) | 510 | (2.5) | 508 | (2.7) | 2 | (2.9) |
| Portugal | 475 | (2.4) | 86 | (1.5) | 480 | (3.1) | 470 | (2.9) | **9** | (3.5) |
| Slovak Republic | 500 | (2.3) | 96 | (1.8) | 505 | (3.6) | 494 | (3.0) | **11** | (4.8) |
| Spain | 498 | (2.2) | 102 | (0.9) | 502 | (2.6) | 493 | (2.5) | **8** | (2.7) |
| Sweden | 512 | (2.2) | 98 | (1.3) | 513 | (2.9) | 511 | (2.8) | 2 | (3.6) |
| Switzerland | 512 | (2.8) | 103 | (1.3) | 514 | (3.2) | 510 | (3.1) | 4 | (3.0) |
| Turkey | 425 | (3.6) | 95 | (2.2) | 422 | (4.4) | 429 | (4.0) | -7 | (4.3) |
| United Kingdom | 525 | (2.2) | 116 | (1.5) | 530 | (2.8) | 521 | (3.0) | **9** | (3.9) |
| United States | 487 | (4.1) | 117 | (1.6) | 491 | (5.0) | 482 | (4.1) | **9** | (3.8) |
| **OECD total** | 490 | (1.2) | 110 | (0.6) | 493 | (1.3) | 487 | (1.3) | **6** | (1.2) |
| **OECD average** | 502 | (0.5) | 100 | (0.3) | 504 | (0.6) | 500 | (0.6) | **4** | (0.7) |
| Argentina | 391 | (5.2) | 108 | (1.8) | 386 | (5.2) | 395 | (6.2) | -9 | (5.4) |
| Azerbaijan | 398 | (2.6) | 70 | (1.3) | 392 | (3.1) | 403 | (2.8) | **-11** | (2.6) |
| Brazil | 403 | (2.5) | 97 | (1.6) | 409 | (3.2) | 398 | (2.8) | **11** | (3.5) |
| Bulgaria | 445 | (5.3) | 111 | (2.5) | 436 | (6.0) | 455 | (5.9) | **-19** | (5.6) |
| Chile | 434 | (3.7) | 101 | (1.5) | 447 | (4.8) | 420 | (3.8) | **27** | (4.6) |
| Colombia | 384 | (2.8) | 91 | (1.5) | 391 | (3.7) | 377 | (3.6) | **13** | (4.5) |
| Croatia | 498 | (2.1) | 90 | (1.2) | 495 | (3.0) | 500 | (2.7) | -5 | (3.9) |
| Estonia | 540 | (2.4) | 97 | (1.4) | 534 | (3.0) | 546 | (2.9) | **-12** | (3.3) |
| Hong Kong-China | 558 | (2.3) | 95 | (1.4) | 564 | (3.2) | 552 | (3.4) | **12** | (4.8) |
| Indonesia | 391 | (2.8) | 72 | (1.3) | 394 | (3.6) | 388 | (3.0) | 5 | (3.4) |
| Israel | 458 | (3.0) | 113 | (1.5) | 460 | (4.5) | 457 | (3.6) | 2 | (5.5) |
| Jordan | 450 | (2.9) | 105 | (1.7) | 435 | (4.6) | 465 | (3.3) | **-31** | (5.4) |
| Kyrgyzstan | 330 | (2.3) | 91 | (1.4) | 330 | (3.1) | 330 | (2.5) | 0 | (3.3) |
| Latvia | 481 | (2.8) | 90 | (1.3) | 480 | (3.4) | 483 | (3.0) | -3 | (3.3) |
| Liechtenstein | 524 | (4.4) | 100 | (5.3) | 521 | (9.1) | 526 | (6.2) | -5 | (12.5) |
| Lithuania | 503 | (2.5) | 105 | (1.2) | 500 | (3.1) | 506 | (3.2) | -6 | (3.7) |
| Macao-China | 525 | (1.3) | 81 | (1.7) | 528 | (2.0) | 522 | (1.9) | 7 | (3.1) |
| Montenegro | 430 | (1.5) | 83 | (1.2) | 427 | (1.9) | 433 | (2.3) | -6 | (2.9) |
| Qatar | 361 | (0.9) | 77 | (0.8) | 343 | (1.3) | 380 | (1.7) | **-37** | (2.4) |
| Romania | 426 | (3.5) | 90 | (2.2) | 429 | (4.0) | 423 | (4.0) | 6 | (3.6) |
| Russian Federation | 490 | (3.2) | 95 | (1.0) | 495 | (3.9) | 485 | (3.2) | **9** | (3.0) |
| Serbia | 449 | (2.6) | 90 | (1.3) | 444 | (3.0) | 455 | (3.3) | **-11** | (3.5) |
| Slovenia | 517 | (1.6) | 104 | (1.4) | 515 | (2.4) | 519 | (2.8) | -4 | (4.1) |
| Chinese Taipei | 549 | (3.3) | 102 | (1.4) | 556 | (3.7) | 542 | (4.7) | 15 | (5.3) |
| Thailand | 432 | (1.8) | 79 | (1.3) | 425 | (2.8) | 437 | (2.1) | **-13** | (3.3) |
| Tunisia | 392 | (2.6) | 89 | (1.7) | 392 | (3.0) | 392 | (3.3) | 0 | (3.6) |
| Uruguay | 433 | (2.3) | 104 | (1.7) | 434 | (3.6) | 432 | (2.7) | 2 | (4.3) |

Note: Values that are statistically significant are indicated in bold (see Annex A3).
StatLink http://dx.doi.org/10.1787/142056138443

Pour consulter la version française intégrale de ce tableau, suivre ce lien :
StatLink http://dx.doi.org/10.1787/152610887346

[Part 2/2]

**Table 2.9** Mean score, variation and gender differences in student performance on the "Living systems" scale

Tableau 2.9 Score moyen, différences de score selon le sexe et répartition des scores sur l'échelle « systèmes vivants »

| | | Percentiles | | | | | | | | | | |
|---|---|---|---|---|---|---|---|---|---|---|---|---|
| | | 5th | | 10th | | 25th | | 75th | | 90th | | 95th | |
| | | Score | S.E. | Score | S.E. | Score | S.E. | Score | S.E. | Score | S.E. | Score | S.E. |
| OECD | Australia | 341 | (2.2) | 383 | (2.8) | 449 | (2.7) | 601 | (2.2) | 656 | (3.2) | 692 | (3.9) |
| | Austria | 352 | (6.0) | 389 | (4.4) | 451 | (4.1) | 594 | (3.8) | 652 | (5.2) | 686 | (6.3) |
| | Belgium | 324 | (8.6) | 362 | (4.3) | 434 | (3.7) | 576 | (2.5) | 631 | (2.7) | 664 | (2.6) |
| | Canada | 349 | (5.5) | 391 | (4.4) | 460 | (3.0) | 603 | (2.7) | 664 | (2.2) | 698 | (2.7) |
| | Czech Republic | 372 | (3.8) | 403 | (3.5) | 457 | (3.7) | 592 | (3.5) | 648 | (4.3) | 680 | (4.3) |
| | Denmark | 333 | (5.2) | 372 | (5.0) | 434 | (3.8) | 577 | (3.5) | 638 | (3.7) | 669 | (4.3) |
| | Finland | 418 | (5.1) | 455 | (2.9) | 511 | (2.6) | 637 | (2.2) | 688 | (3.2) | 724 | (3.5) |
| | France | 311 | (7.0) | 354 | (3.8) | 418 | (5.4) | 565 | (4.2) | 626 | (3.5) | 659 | (4.5) |
| | Germany | 355 | (7.8) | 390 | (4.2) | 457 | (3.9) | 593 | (3.2) | 649 | (3.5) | 682 | (2.0) |
| | Greece | 313 | (5.3) | 351 | (4.8) | 410 | (4.9) | 541 | (3.9) | 595 | (3.0) | 629 | (3.8) |
| | Hungary | 350 | (6.2) | 381 | (2.4) | 442 | (3.7) | 577 | (4.7) | 636 | (2.7) | 667 | (3.2) |
| | Iceland | 324 | (6.1) | 361 | (3.2) | 419 | (3.1) | 546 | (2.9) | 601 | (2.4) | 631 | (3.1) |
| | Ireland | 333 | (5.8) | 369 | (3.7) | 434 | (3.3) | 576 | (2.8) | 641 | (3.3) | 673 | (4.3) |
| | Italy | 326 | (3.4) | 358 | (2.6) | 419 | (2.8) | 556 | (2.5) | 615 | (2.8) | 652 | (2.9) |
| | Japan | 369 | (7.4) | 405 | (4.4) | 465 | (4.8) | 590 | (3.5) | 639 | (2.3) | 671 | (4.0) |
| | Korea | 350 | (8.1) | 384 | (4.6) | 436 | (2.6) | 562 | (3.2) | 611 | (3.3) | 641 | (3.8) |
| | Luxembourg | 321 | (4.8) | 358 | (2.9) | 426 | (3.0) | 573 | (3.0) | 635 | (2.3) | 670 | (5.2) |
| | Mexico | 262 | (3.7) | 295 | (2.8) | 345 | (3.2) | 460 | (2.7) | 511 | (2.7) | 542 | (3.3) |
| | Netherlands | 357 | (5.0) | 385 | (3.6) | 446 | (4.2) | 576 | (2.6) | 627 | (3.6) | 659 | (3.2) |
| | New Zealand | 334 | (3.7) | 372 | (3.8) | 446 | (5.2) | 611 | (4.0) | 679 | (3.6) | 720 | (5.2) |
| | Norway | 316 | (7.1) | 361 | (7.3) | 426 | (4.0) | 571 | (3.6) | 628 | (3.7) | 663 | (4.2) |
| | Poland | 351 | (6.0) | 382 | (3.5) | 443 | (2.4) | 577 | (3.1) | 639 | (3.0) | 670 | (3.0) |
| | Portugal | 334 | (4.9) | 365 | (4.2) | 415 | (3.1) | 535 | (2.6) | 587 | (3.1) | 615 | (3.3) |
| | Slovak Republic | 341 | (3.2) | 374 | (3.5) | 435 | (3.5) | 565 | (3.8) | 626 | (3.2) | 657 | (5.6) |
| | Spain | 330 | (3.8) | 364 | (2.8) | 428 | (2.8) | 568 | (3.0) | 629 | (3.8) | 665 | (3.0) |
| | Sweden | 350 | (5.9) | 382 | (4.0) | 446 | (3.5) | 579 | (3.3) | 638 | (3.2) | 670 | (3.3) |
| | Switzerland | 338 | (5.7) | 376 | (3.4) | 442 | (3.0) | 583 | (3.3) | 642 | (3.1) | 681 | (5.7) |
| | Turkey | 272 | (3.1) | 307 | (3.7) | 359 | (2.7) | 488 | (6.0) | 549 | (7.5) | 590 | (6.5) |
| | United Kingdom | 330 | (5.1) | 380 | (3.4) | 449 | (2.9) | 608 | (3.1) | 670 | (3.3) | 708 | (3.9) |
| | United States | 300 | (5.3) | 332 | (5.1) | 403 | (5.2) | 570 | (4.3) | 639 | (5.2) | 680 | (4.5) |
| | **OECD total** | 311 | (2.3) | 346 | (2.5) | 413 | (1.8) | 568 | (1.5) | 632 | (1.5) | 669 | (1.6) |
| | **OECD average** | 335 | (1.0) | 371 | (0.7) | 433 | (0.7) | 572 | (0.6) | 630 | (0.7) | 664 | (0.7) |
| Partners | Argentina | 207 | (8.4) | 250 | (6.0) | 317 | (6.4) | 466 | (5.0) | 528 | (6.2) | 566 | (5.7) |
| | Azerbaijan | 283 | (3.7) | 308 | (3.9) | 351 | (2.6) | 442 | (3.3) | 487 | (4.5) | 515 | (4.9) |
| | Brazil | 245 | (4.9) | 279 | (3.6) | 338 | (3.0) | 465 | (3.8) | 529 | (5.2) | 568 | (6.9) |
| | Bulgaria | 269 | (7.6) | 303 | (6.2) | 369 | (5.5) | 521 | (6.2) | 591 | (8.6) | 631 | (6.7) |
| | Chile | 272 | (4.9) | 309 | (4.2) | 366 | (4.1) | 502 | (5.8) | 569 | (5.0) | 606 | (6.3) |
| | Colombia | 229 | (5.0) | 265 | (5.4) | 325 | (3.8) | 444 | (4.4) | 498 | (3.5) | 531 | (5.1) |
| | Croatia | 354 | (2.7) | 383 | (3.6) | 436 | (3.0) | 558 | (2.6) | 616 | (2.8) | 650 | (4.3) |
| | Estonia | 376 | (5.9) | 415 | (4.4) | 474 | (3.2) | 608 | (3.8) | 664 | (5.5) | 696 | (3.8) |
| | Hong Kong-China | 398 | (6.9) | 432 | (4.2) | 496 | (4.2) | 625 | (2.1) | 676 | (2.9) | 706 | (4.5) |
| | Indonesia | 274 | (2.8) | 299 | (2.6) | 343 | (3.0) | 439 | (3.1) | 487 | (5.3) | 513 | (5.7) |
| | Israel | 276 | (6.2) | 317 | (3.3) | 382 | (5.7) | 538 | (5.2) | 604 | (4.4) | 645 | (3.6) |
| | Jordan | 277 | (6.1) | 316 | (4.0) | 381 | (2.8) | 522 | (2.9) | 585 | (3.9) | 622 | (6.5) |
| | Kyrgyzstan | 177 | (3.8) | 214 | (5.1) | 273 | (3.9) | 388 | (2.8) | 441 | (4.2) | 478 | (3.3) |
| | Latvia | 331 | (6.0) | 361 | (4.1) | 420 | (4.5) | 543 | (3.6) | 598 | (4.2) | 628 | (5.1) |
| | Liechtenstein | 359 | (12.3) | 397 | (15.5) | 453 | (8.7) | 595 | (10.8) | 646 | (9.7) | 682 | (19.4) |
| | Lithuania | 331 | (4.0) | 365 | (3.9) | 431 | (3.7) | 573 | (3.7) | 638 | (3.9) | 673 | (5.6) |
| | Macao-China | 389 | (4.5) | 416 | (3.2) | 472 | (2.2) | 581 | (2.3) | 631 | (3.4) | 656 | (3.3) |
| | Montenegro | 294 | (3.8) | 323 | (2.7) | 374 | (2.1) | 483 | (2.3) | 539 | (4.3) | 570 | (4.7) |
| | Qatar | 240 | (3.1) | 266 | (1.7) | 309 | (2.0) | 410 | (1.6) | 463 | (2.8) | 496 | (2.8) |
| | Romania | 283 | (4.8) | 316 | (5.0) | 364 | (3.6) | 485 | (4.0) | 547 | (5.8) | 578 | (8.1) |
| | Russian Federation | 336 | (4.0) | 366 | (4.1) | 426 | (3.9) | 554 | (3.8) | 613 | (4.1) | 645 | (2.4) |
| | Serbia | 304 | (3.0) | 332 | (3.6) | 388 | (4.0) | 510 | (2.9) | 570 | (3.9) | 597 | (3.4) |
| | Slovenia | 348 | (3.7) | 381 | (2.9) | 445 | (2.9) | 592 | (2.7) | 653 | (2.7) | 685 | (5.6) |
| | Chinese Taipei | 375 | (5.4) | 412 | (4.2) | 479 | (4.2) | 621 | (3.5) | 676 | (3.0) | 710 | (4.1) |
| | Thailand | 302 | (4.1) | 329 | (3.0) | 379 | (2.4) | 484 | (2.7) | 533 | (4.2) | 562 | (3.8) |
| | Tunisia | 247 | (4.2) | 277 | (3.0) | 330 | (1.9) | 449 | (3.9) | 508 | (6.5) | 540 | (7.4) |
| | Uruguay | 263 | (7.1) | 300 | (4.3) | 363 | (4.1) | 502 | (3.5) | 563 | (3.4) | 604 | (3.9) |

Note: Values that are statistically significant are indicated in bold (see Annex A3).
StatLink ☞ http://dx.doi.org/10.1787/142056138443

Pour consulter la version française intégrale de ce tableau, suivre ce lien :
StatLink ☞ http://dx.doi.org/10.1787/152610887346

[Part 1/2]

**Table 2.10** **Mean score, variation and gender differences in student performance on the "Physical systems" scale**

Tableau 2.10 Score moyen, différences de score selon le sexe et répartition des scores sur l'échelle « systèmes physiques »

| | All students | | | | Gender differences | | | | | |
|---|---|---|---|---|---|---|---|---|---|---|
| | Mean score | | Standard deviation | | Males | | Females | | Difference (M - F) | |
| | Mean | S.E. | S.D. | S.E. | Mean score | S.E. | Mean score | S.E. | Score dif. | S.E. |
| Australia | 515 | (1.9) | 101 | (1.0) | 528 | (2.6) | 502 | (2.3) | 26 | (3.2) |
| Austria | 518 | (3.7) | 105 | (2.1) | 540 | (4.0) | 495 | (4.1) | 45 | (4.6) |
| Belgium | 507 | (2.1) | 103 | (1.3) | 519 | (2.9) | 494 | (2.8) | 25 | (3.8) |
| Canada | 529 | (1.9) | 99 | (1.0) | 543 | (2.4) | 514 | (2.0) | 29 | (2.4) |
| Czech Republic | 534 | (3.3) | 108 | (1.6) | 551 | (3.9) | 512 | (4.3) | 39 | (5.4) |
| Denmark | 502 | (2.8) | 101 | (1.4) | 517 | (3.3) | 488 | (3.3) | 29 | (3.5) |
| Finland | 560 | (1.7) | 93 | (1.0) | 576 | (2.4) | 544 | (2.2) | 32 | (3.0) |
| France | 482 | (2.7) | 97 | (1.4) | 494 | (3.4) | 472 | (3.5) | 22 | (4.2) |
| Germany | 516 | (3.1) | 105 | (1.4) | 526 | (4.1) | 506 | (3.2) | 20 | (4.1) |
| Greece | 474 | (2.8) | 101 | (1.7) | 482 | (3.8) | 467 | (3.2) | 15 | (4.1) |
| Hungary | 533 | (2.5) | 97 | (1.4) | 550 | (3.2) | 514 | (3.2) | 36 | (4.1) |
| Iceland | 493 | (1.6) | 96 | (1.2) | 501 | (2.5) | 486 | (2.5) | 15 | (3.8) |
| Ireland | 504 | (2.6) | 96 | (1.2) | 516 | (3.7) | 493 | (3.0) | 23 | (4.0) |
| Italy | 472 | (1.7) | 99 | (1.0) | 485 | (2.5) | 460 | (2.4) | 25 | (3.5) |
| Japan | 530 | (3.2) | 107 | (1.5) | 541 | (4.4) | 519 | (4.5) | 22 | (6.4) |
| Korea | 530 | (3.0) | 99 | (1.8) | 537 | (4.5) | 522 | (3.6) | 15 | (5.4) |
| Luxembourg | 474 | (1.1) | 92 | (1.4) | 493 | (2.1) | 455 | (1.9) | 38 | (3.3) |
| Mexico | 414 | (2.1) | 84 | (1.0) | 423 | (2.8) | 406 | (2.1) | 18 | (2.6) |
| Netherlands | 531 | (2.5) | 96 | (1.4) | 547 | (3.3) | 515 | (2.9) | 32 | (3.6) |
| New Zealand | 516 | (2.4) | 110 | (1.2) | 529 | (3.4) | 503 | (3.5) | 26 | (5.0) |
| Norway | 491 | (2.7) | 102 | (1.7) | 500 | (3.5) | 482 | (3.0) | 18 | (3.6) |
| Poland | 497 | (2.1) | 95 | (1.1) | 512 | (2.4) | 482 | (2.6) | 30 | (2.8) |
| Portugal | 462 | (2.4) | 87 | (1.6) | 476 | (3.0) | 449 | (2.8) | 27 | (3.2) |
| Slovak Republic | 504 | (2.5) | 103 | (1.6) | 520 | (3.8) | 486 | (2.8) | 35 | (4.6) |
| Spain | 477 | (1.8) | 90 | (0.7) | 488 | (2.2) | 465 | (2.1) | 23 | (2.3) |
| Sweden | 517 | (2.2) | 102 | (1.5) | 526 | (2.6) | 507 | (2.9) | 19 | (3.3) |
| Switzerland | 506 | (2.6) | 99 | (1.1) | 522 | (3.2) | 490 | (3.1) | 32 | (3.2) |
| Turkey | 416 | (3.1) | 85 | (1.9) | 417 | (3.8) | 415 | (3.5) | 2 | (3.9) |
| United Kingdom | 508 | (2.0) | 109 | (1.3) | 526 | (2.7) | 492 | (2.5) | 34 | (3.4) |
| United States | 485 | (3.8) | 109 | (1.3) | 495 | (4.8) | 475 | (3.8) | 20 | (4.1) |
| **OECD total** | **489** | **(1.1)** | **107** | **(0.5)** | **500** | **(1.3)** | **478** | **(1.2)** | **22** | **(1.3)** |
| **OECD average** | **500** | **(0.5)** | **99** | **(0.3)** | **513** | **(0.6)** | **487** | **(0.6)** | **26** | **(0.7)** |
| Argentina | 383 | (4.7) | 102 | (1.8) | 385 | (4.8) | 382 | (5.7) | 2 | (4.9) |
| Azerbaijan | 433 | (2.1) | 64 | (1.2) | 429 | (2.5) | 436 | (2.4) | -7 | (2.5) |
| Brazil | 385 | (2.6) | 99 | (1.6) | 398 | (3.3) | 374 | (2.7) | 24 | (3.0) |
| Bulgaria | 436 | (4.6) | 98 | (2.2) | 437 | (5.2) | 435 | (5.3) | 2 | (5.1) |
| Chile | 433 | (3.6) | 99 | (1.4) | 452 | (4.6) | 411 | (3.6) | 40 | (4.3) |
| Colombia | 378 | (2.7) | 93 | (1.5) | 389 | (3.5) | 369 | (3.7) | 20 | (4.6) |
| Croatia | 493 | (2.2) | 89 | (1.3) | 508 | (3.0) | 478 | (2.7) | 30 | (3.9) |
| Estonia | 535 | (2.0) | 87 | (1.2) | 547 | (2.7) | 522 | (2.4) | 25 | (3.1) |
| Hong Kong-China | 546 | (2.4) | 98 | (1.4) | 563 | (3.4) | 529 | (3.4) | 34 | (4.8) |
| Indonesia | 386 | (3.0) | 74 | (1.2) | 393 | (4.2) | 378 | (3.1) | 15 | (4.1) |
| Israel | 443 | (3.1) | 110 | (1.4) | 453 | (4.5) | 433 | (3.9) | 20 | (5.7) |
| Jordan | 433 | (2.6) | 95 | (1.4) | 427 | (4.1) | 439 | (2.9) | -13 | (4.9) |
| Kyrgyzstan | 349 | (2.2) | 87 | (1.4) | 352 | (3.0) | 347 | (2.4) | 5 | (3.0) |
| Latvia | 495 | (2.4) | 83 | (1.2) | 507 | (3.1) | 483 | (2.8) | 24 | (3.1) |
| Liechtenstein | 515 | (4.1) | 97 | (4.2) | 527 | (8.3) | 505 | (6.1) | 22 | (11.8) |
| Lithuania | 490 | (2.2) | 89 | (1.2) | 499 | (2.6) | 481 | (2.6) | 18 | (2.8) |
| Macao-China | 518 | (1.6) | 93 | (1.4) | 527 | (2.0) | 508 | (2.6) | 19 | (3.5) |
| Montenegro | 407 | (1.5) | 78 | (1.2) | 414 | (1.9) | 400 | (2.1) | 14 | (2.7) |
| Qatar | 358 | (1.0) | 100 | (1.1) | 345 | (2.0) | 370 | (2.0) | -25 | (3.5) |
| Romania | 429 | (3.2) | 76 | (1.9) | 435 | (3.6) | 422 | (3.5) | 13 | (2.9) |
| Russian Federation | 479 | (2.9) | 93 | (1.3) | 495 | (3.6) | 465 | (3.1) | 30 | (3.2) |
| Serbia | 435 | (2.7) | 90 | (1.1) | 442 | (3.4) | 428 | (3.3) | 14 | (3.6) |
| Slovenia | 531 | (1.5) | 104 | (1.4) | 546 | (2.3) | 516 | (2.3) | 31 | (3.5) |
| Chinese Taipei | 545 | (3.1) | 100 | (1.4) | 558 | (3.6) | 532 | (4.5) | 25 | (5.1) |
| Thailand | 407 | (1.8) | 80 | (1.2) | 411 | (2.9) | 405 | (2.1) | 6 | (3.4) |
| Tunisia | 393 | (2.2) | 79 | (1.4) | 399 | (2.5) | 387 | (2.7) | 12 | (2.9) |
| Uruguay | 421 | (2.4) | 97 | (1.3) | 428 | (3.5) | 415 | (2.9) | 14 | (4.2) |

Note: Values that are statistically significant are indicated in bold (see Annex A3).
*StatLink* ᕯᕯᕯᕯ http://dx.doi.org/10.1787/142056138443

Pour consulter la version française intégrale de ce tableau, suivre ce lien :
*StatLink* ᕯᕯᕯᕯ http://dx.doi.org/10.1787/152610887346

[Part 2/2]

**Table 2.10** | **Mean score, variation and gender differences in student performance on the "Physical systems" scale**

Tableau 2.10 | Score moyen, différences de score selon le sexe et répartition des scores sur l'échelle « systèmes physiques »

| | | 5th | | 10th | | 25th | | 75th | | 90th | | 95th | |
|---|---|---|---|---|---|---|---|---|---|---|---|---|---|
| | | Score | S.E. | Score | S.E. | Score | S.E. | Score | S.E. | Score | S.E. | Score | S.E. |
| OECD | Australia | 350 | (4.1) | 387 | (3.2) | 447 | (2.4) | 586 | (1.9) | 641 | (3.0) | 676 | (3.8) |
| | Austria | 342 | (6.6) | 380 | (6.9) | 446 | (4.5) | 590 | (4.1) | 651 | (5.3) | 690 | (4.7) |
| | Belgium | 337 | (4.5) | 372 | (4.1) | 437 | (3.4) | 579 | (2.2) | 639 | (2.7) | 674 | (3.3) |
| | Canada | 361 | (4.5) | 399 | (3.5) | 465 | (2.6) | 597 | (2.5) | 652 | (2.3) | 687 | (3.1) |
| | Czech Republic | 359 | (7.0) | 393 | (4.8) | 459 | (4.5) | 608 | (4.3) | 675 | (4.7) | 711 | (4.4) |
| | Denmark | 333 | (5.3) | 372 | (4.9) | 434 | (4.1) | 573 | (3.7) | 631 | (3.5) | 667 | (5.3) |
| | Finland | 406 | (3.6) | 439 | (3.6) | 497 | (3.3) | 624 | (2.2) | 680 | (2.4) | 709 | (3.5) |
| | France | 317 | (6.3) | 356 | (4.7) | 418 | (4.1) | 548 | (2.9) | 605 | (4.1) | 635 | (4.3) |
| | Germany | 339 | (4.6) | 376 | (4.8) | 443 | (4.0) | 588 | (3.5) | 650 | (4.4) | 690 | (6.6) |
| | Greece | 306 | (6.7) | 343 | (3.3) | 406 | (3.5) | 545 | (4.9) | 605 | (3.7) | 638 | (3.4) |
| | Hungary | 376 | (6.0) | 407 | (2.8) | 465 | (3.0) | 601 | (4.0) | 663 | (3.9) | 692 | (5.0) |
| | Iceland | 331 | (5.5) | 369 | (3.0) | 428 | (3.3) | 558 | (1.8) | 617 | (3.1) | 647 | (3.4) |
| | Ireland | 347 | (3.9) | 380 | (4.9) | 439 | (4.3) | 570 | (3.1) | 630 | (3.5) | 664 | (4.4) |
| | Italy | 311 | (2.6) | 343 | (2.9) | 403 | (2.8) | 541 | (2.3) | 602 | (2.8) | 636 | (2.6) |
| | Japan | 344 | (6.0) | 390 | (5.4) | 460 | (4.9) | 603 | (2.8) | 664 | (3.7) | 697 | (2.9) |
| | Korea | 361 | (7.6) | 401 | (5.1) | 464 | (4.5) | 598 | (3.2) | 655 | (3.6) | 689 | (4.2) |
| | Luxembourg | 325 | (3.9) | 353 | (2.8) | 409 | (2.8) | 538 | (2.0) | 594 | (3.2) | 628 | (3.5) |
| | Mexico | 276 | (3.5) | 307 | (2.9) | 358 | (2.8) | 472 | (3.1) | 524 | (3.1) | 553 | (3.3) |
| | Netherlands | 373 | (6.1) | 403 | (4.4) | 463 | (4.2) | 599 | (2.4) | 653 | (2.9) | 687 | (3.4) |
| | New Zealand | 332 | (4.8) | 374 | (4.3) | 440 | (3.7) | 593 | (2.6) | 657 | (3.9) | 692 | (3.4) |
| | Norway | 322 | (5.3) | 361 | (4.5) | 423 | (4.6) | 562 | (3.1) | 621 | (3.5) | 654 | (3.7) |
| | Poland | 346 | (3.9) | 373 | (3.3) | 430 | (3.0) | 563 | (3.0) | 620 | (4.1) | 654 | (3.6) |
| | Portugal | 320 | (5.7) | 351 | (3.6) | 402 | (3.4) | 521 | (3.4) | 573 | (4.2) | 605 | (3.4) |
| | Slovak Republic | 337 | (4.9) | 370 | (4.1) | 431 | (3.1) | 573 | (4.2) | 639 | (5.4) | 674 | (4.4) |
| | Spain | 329 | (3.2) | 358 | (2.8) | 413 | (2.7) | 539 | (2.4) | 595 | (2.8) | 627 | (2.9) |
| | Sweden | 351 | (3.7) | 383 | (2.9) | 446 | (2.7) | 587 | (2.9) | 647 | (5.7) | 685 | (4.7) |
| | Switzerland | 344 | (4.2) | 380 | (3.3) | 439 | (3.1) | 574 | (3.3) | 632 | (5.0) | 667 | (4.3) |
| | Turkey | 283 | (3.1) | 310 | (3.5) | 358 | (2.9) | 473 | (5.0) | 528 | (4.8) | 560 | (6.5) |
| | United Kingdom | 332 | (5.1) | 370 | (4.0) | 435 | (2.2) | 585 | (2.5) | 647 | (2.6) | 683 | (2.8) |
| | United States | 312 | (4.4) | 344 | (5.3) | 403 | (5.2) | 561 | (4.2) | 630 | (3.6) | 664 | (4.1) |
| | **OECD total** | **315** | **(1.6)** | **350** | **(1.5)** | **412** | **(2.0)** | **563** | **(1.8)** | **629** | **(1.4)** | **665** | **(1.6)** |
| | **OECD average** | **337** | **(0.9)** | **371** | **(0.7)** | **432** | **(0.7)** | **568** | **(0.6)** | **627** | **(0.7)** | **661** | **(0.7)** |
| Partners | Argentina | 213 | (8.6) | 251 | (7.0) | 317 | (5.8) | 450 | (5.9) | 513 | (5.1) | 548 | (7.1) |
| | Azerbaijan | 329 | (3.7) | 352 | (3.1) | 389 | (2.9) | 474 | (3.2) | 517 | (4.3) | 542 | (3.6) |
| | Brazil | 225 | (2.6) | 257 | (3.6) | 319 | (2.6) | 448 | (3.1) | 512 | (4.7) | 555 | (6.8) |
| | Bulgaria | 279 | (4.9) | 315 | (5.8) | 368 | (4.9) | 501 | (5.1) | 562 | (5.9) | 601 | (7.0) |
| | Chile | 281 | (4.8) | 310 | (3.6) | 366 | (4.0) | 500 | (4.5) | 563 | (4.6) | 600 | (4.3) |
| | Colombia | 221 | (4.3) | 255 | (5.5) | 316 | (4.3) | 440 | (3.6) | 495 | (4.2) | 528 | (4.9) |
| | Croatia | 351 | (4.2) | 381 | (2.8) | 430 | (3.4) | 552 | (2.8) | 609 | (3.0) | 641 | (3.0) |
| | Estonia | 390 | (5.3) | 422 | (4.1) | 476 | (2.8) | 596 | (3.8) | 648 | (3.6) | 677 | (2.6) |
| | Hong Kong-China | 377 | (4.9) | 414 | (3.8) | 481 | (3.7) | 614 | (3.3) | 670 | (2.9) | 700 | (3.6) |
| | Indonesia | 266 | (4.6) | 291 | (2.5) | 334 | (3.6) | 436 | (4.1) | 485 | (5.3) | 512 | (6.0) |
| | Israel | 262 | (5.9) | 303 | (4.6) | 366 | (3.3) | 517 | (3.9) | 587 | (4.2) | 620 | (4.9) |
| | Jordan | 275 | (4.3) | 312 | (4.2) | 369 | (3.5) | 499 | (4.1) | 555 | (4.3) | 588 | (5.5) |
| | Kyrgyzstan | 204 | (5.2) | 238 | (3.3) | 293 | (3.6) | 407 | (2.9) | 459 | (3.6) | 488 | (3.5) |
| | Latvia | 359 | (4.2) | 387 | (3.0) | 436 | (4.0) | 551 | (3.2) | 603 | (4.8) | 633 | (4.0) |
| | Liechtenstein | 360 | (13.0) | 390 | (11.0) | 447 | (7.3) | 584 | (8.0) | 640 | (11.4) | 675 | (15.7) |
| | Lithuania | 343 | (4.4) | 373 | (2.4) | 428 | (3.0) | 551 | (3.5) | 608 | (3.5) | 637 | (3.4) |
| | Macao-China | 366 | (4.6) | 394 | (2.9) | 453 | (3.2) | 582 | (2.9) | 637 | (4.1) | 669 | (3.6) |
| | Montenegro | 281 | (3.8) | 306 | (3.3) | 354 | (2.9) | 459 | (2.6) | 510 | (3.3) | 542 | (5.3) |
| | Qatar | 204 | (3.8) | 236 | (3.5) | 291 | (2.5) | 418 | (2.1) | 489 | (3.4) | 531 | (3.5) |
| | Romania | 307 | (4.2) | 332 | (3.8) | 376 | (3.3) | 479 | (4.2) | 529 | (5.4) | 561 | (7.7) |
| | Russian Federation | 329 | (3.7) | 359 | (3.9) | 415 | (4.5) | 541 | (3.0) | 602 | (2.7) | 634 | (4.3) |
| | Serbia | 289 | (4.5) | 318 | (3.0) | 372 | (4.7) | 496 | (3.1) | 555 | (4.1) | 587 | (4.7) |
| | Slovenia | 359 | (3.2) | 396 | (3.2) | 455 | (2.3) | 605 | (2.8) | 666 | (5.3) | 704 | (4.8) |
| | Chinese Taipei | 375 | (4.7) | 410 | (4.2) | 479 | (4.8) | 616 | (2.5) | 671 | (3.2) | 702 | (3.2) |
| | Thailand | 280 | (2.7) | 303 | (3.7) | 353 | (2.5) | 460 | (2.6) | 513 | (3.7) | 545 | (3.1) |
| | Tunisia | 264 | (3.8) | 290 | (3.2) | 339 | (2.4) | 445 | (3.4) | 499 | (4.6) | 526 | (5.5) |
| | Uruguay | 259 | (4.4) | 298 | (6.0) | 357 | (3.2) | 489 | (4.6) | 547 | (4.9) | 581 | (4.1) |

Note: Values that are statistically significant are indicated in bold (see Annex A3).
StatLink http://dx.doi.org/10.1787/142056138443

Pour consulter la version française intégrale de ce tableau, suivre ce lien :
StatLink http://dx.doi.org/10.1787/152610887346

[Part 1/2]

**Table 3.1**  Mean score, variation and gender differences on the *interest in learning science topics* scale

**Tableau 3.1**  Score moyen, différences de score selon le sexe et répartition des scores sur l'échelle *intérêt pour l'acquisition de nouveaux savoirs et savoir-faire en sciences*

| | | All students | | | | Gender differences | | | | | |
|---|---|---|---|---|---|---|---|---|---|---|---|
| | | Mean score | | Standard deviation | | Males | | Females | | Difference (M - F) | |
| | | Mean | S.E. | S.D. | S.E. | Mean score | S.E. | Mean score | S.E. | Score dif. | S.E. |
| *OECD* | Australia | 465 | (1.3) | 97 | (0.9) | 467 | (1.8) | 463 | (1.9) | 4 | (2.6) |
| | Austria | 507 | (1.9) | 87 | (1.1) | 508 | (2.6) | 505 | (2.7) | 4 | (3.6) |
| | Belgium | 503 | (1.4) | 92 | (1.1) | 506 | (1.9) | 499 | (2.0) | **6** | (2.6) |
| | Canada | 469 | (1.5) | 104 | (1.3) | 471 | (1.9) | 467 | (1.8) | 4 | (2.3) |
| | Czech Republic | 489 | (2.0) | 91 | (1.5) | 482 | (2.5) | 499 | (2.4) | **-17** | (2.9) |
| | Denmark | 463 | (1.8) | 92 | (1.2) | 455 | (2.6) | 471 | (2.3) | **-17** | (3.3) |
| | Finland | 448 | (2.1) | 92 | (1.2) | 445 | (2.6) | 451 | (2.4) | **-7** | (2.8) |
| | France | 520 | (2.4) | 96 | (1.4) | 522 | (3.1) | 518 | (2.5) | 4 | (3.0) |
| | Germany | 513 | (1.8) | 88 | (1.2) | 514 | (2.5) | 512 | (2.1) | 2 | (2.9) |
| | Greece | 549 | (1.7) | 91 | (1.3) | 546 | (2.2) | 552 | (2.4) | **-6** | (3.1) |
| | Hungary | 522 | (1.9) | 82 | (1.5) | 518 | (2.5) | 526 | (2.3) | **-9** | (3.1) |
| | Iceland | 466 | (2.1) | 108 | (1.9) | 464 | (3.1) | 468 | (2.5) | -3 | (3.8) |
| | Ireland | 481 | (1.9) | 89 | (1.4) | 484 | (2.3) | 478 | (2.7) | 6 | (3.4) |
| | Italy | 529 | (1.3) | 78 | (0.8) | 533 | (2.0) | 525 | (1.5) | **8** | (2.3) |
| | Japan | 512 | (2.1) | 104 | (1.5) | 518 | (3.0) | 505 | (2.5) | **13** | (3.6) |
| | Korea | 486 | (2.1) | 94 | (1.7) | 491 | (2.8) | 480 | (2.7) | **11** | (3.6) |
| | Luxembourg | 515 | (1.4) | 93 | (1.3) | 515 | (2.0) | 514 | (2.1) | 0 | (3.0) |
| | Mexico | 611 | (1.7) | 87 | (1.0) | 607 | (2.3) | 614 | (2.0) | **-7** | (2.4) |
| | Netherlands | 452 | (2.0) | 88 | (1.4) | 458 | (2.4) | 445 | (2.4) | **13** | (2.7) |
| | New Zealand | 461 | (2.0) | 100 | (1.6) | 464 | (2.8) | 459 | (2.7) | 5 | (3.9) |
| | Norway | 472 | (2.2) | 103 | (1.4) | 470 | (2.9) | 475 | (2.9) | -5 | (3.8) |
| | Poland | 501 | (1.8) | 83 | (1.2) | 502 | (2.2) | 499 | (2.2) | 3 | (2.5) |
| | Portugal | 571 | (1.8) | 79 | (1.1) | 570 | (2.4) | 571 | (2.0) | -1 | (2.6) |
| | Slovak Republic | 522 | (1.9) | 84 | (1.4) | 526 | (2.5) | 517 | (2.6) | **10** | (3.2) |
| | Spain | 534 | (1.6) | 89 | (0.8) | 535 | (2.2) | 533 | (1.9) | 2 | (2.7) |
| | Sweden | 454 | (2.3) | 91 | (1.7) | 447 | (3.4) | 462 | (2.2) | **-15** | (3.6) |
| | Switzerland | 504 | (1.5) | 88 | (1.0) | 506 | (2.0) | 501 | (2.0) | 5 | (2.7) |
| | Turkey | 540 | (2.6) | 103 | (1.5) | 545 | (3.2) | 534 | (3.1) | **11** | (3.5) |
| | United Kingdom | 464 | (1.7) | 96 | (1.2) | 465 | (2.2) | 462 | (2.5) | 3 | (3.2) |
| | United States | 480 | (2.8) | 104 | (1.5) | 489 | (3.1) | 470 | (3.2) | **19** | (2.9) |
| | **OECD total** | **507** | **(0.9)** | **105** | **(0.5)** | **510** | **(1.0)** | **503** | **(1.1)** | **7** | **(1.1)** |
| | **OECD average** | **500** | **(0.3)** | **92** | **(0.2)** | **501** | **(0.5)** | **499** | **(0.4)** | **2** | **(0.6)** |
| *Partners* | Argentina | 567 | (3.0) | 89 | (1.3) | 562 | (3.8) | 572 | (3.0) | **-10** | (3.3) |
| | Azerbaijan | 612 | (2.3) | 74 | (1.2) | 609 | (2.6) | 615 | (2.9) | **-6** | (3.0) |
| | Brazil | 592 | (2.2) | 92 | (1.1) | 588 | (2.8) | 596 | (2.5) | **-8** | (3.0) |
| | Bulgaria | 523 | (2.4) | 113 | (1.9) | 516 | (2.8) | 530 | (3.2) | **-13** | (3.6) |
| | Chile | 591 | (3.3) | 99 | (1.4) | 588 | (3.9) | 595 | (4.1) | -7 | (4.5) |
| | Colombia | 644 | (3.5) | 103 | (1.7) | 633 | (4.5) | 652 | (3.5) | **-19** | (3.9) |
| | Croatia | 535 | (1.9) | 88 | (1.1) | 534 | (2.6) | 537 | (2.4) | -4 | (3.2) |
| | Estonia | 502 | (1.5) | 76 | (1.2) | 500 | (2.2) | 504 | (1.9) | -4 | (2.8) |
| | Hong Kong-China | 536 | (2.1) | 104 | (1.7) | 547 | (3.0) | 525 | (2.6) | **22** | (3.6) |
| | Indonesia | 608 | (2.1) | 76 | (1.0) | 600 | (2.4) | 616 | (2.5) | **-16** | (3.0) |
| | Israel | 509 | (2.6) | 114 | (2.1) | 512 | (3.5) | 506 | (3.4) | 6 | (4.6) |
| | Jordan | 609 | (1.9) | 83 | (1.3) | 602 | (2.7) | 617 | (2.5) | **-15** | (3.6) |
| | Kyrgyzstan | 580 | (1.8) | 81 | (1.1) | 571 | (2.3) | 588 | (2.1) | **-17** | (2.5) |
| | Latvia | 504 | (1.9) | 71 | (1.2) | 503 | (2.4) | 504 | (2.3) | -1 | (2.8) |
| | Liechtenstein | 504 | (5.5) | 86 | (5.2) | 502 | (8.5) | 506 | (6.9) | -5 | (10.8) |
| | Lithuania | 544 | (1.9) | 85 | (1.3) | 537 | (2.5) | 552 | (2.2) | **-14** | (2.9) |
| | Macao-China | 524 | (1.8) | 94 | (1.3) | 527 | (2.6) | 520 | (2.0) | **8** | (3.1) |
| | Montenegro | 561 | (1.6) | 97 | (1.4) | 551 | (2.1) | 571 | (2.4) | **-20** | (3.1) |
| | Qatar | 565 | (1.3) | 106 | (1.3) | 568 | (1.9) | 562 | (2.1) | 6 | (3.2) |
| | Romania | 591 | (2.3) | 83 | (1.6) | 588 | (3.5) | 594 | (2.3) | -6 | (3.8) |
| | Russian Federation | 541 | (2.1) | 76 | (1.1) | 538 | (2.5) | 544 | (2.4) | **-6** | (2.7) |
| | Serbia | 523 | (2.0) | 90 | (1.4) | 523 | (2.9) | 522 | (2.3) | 1 | (3.3) |
| | Slovenia | 505 | (1.4) | 96 | (1.2) | 511 | (1.8) | 499 | (2.2) | **12** | (3.0) |
| | Chinese Taipei | 533 | (2.0) | 105 | (1.5) | 542 | (2.9) | 524 | (2.3) | **18** | (3.1) |
| | Thailand | 642 | (1.9) | 81 | (1.1) | 630 | (2.6) | 651 | (2.3) | **-20** | (3.2) |
| | Tunisia | 590 | (1.9) | 85 | (1.2) | 588 | (2.4) | 593 | (2.4) | -5 | (3.0) |
| | Uruguay | 567 | (2.2) | 92 | (1.4) | 566 | (3.0) | 568 | (2.5) | -1 | (3.4) |

Note: Values that are statistically significant are indicated in bold (see Annex A3).
*StatLink* http://dx.doi.org/10.1787/142102278412

Pour consulter la version française intégrale de ce tableau, suivre ce lien :
*StatLink* http://dx.doi.org/10.1787/152630454851

[Part 2/2]

**Table 3.1** **Mean score, variation and gender differences on the *interest in learning science topics* scale**

**Tableau 3.1** Score moyen, différences de score selon le sexe et répartition des scores sur l'échelle *intérêt pour l'acquisition de nouveaux savoirs et savoir-faire en sciences*

| | | Percentiles | | | | | | | | | | |
|---|---|---|---|---|---|---|---|---|---|---|---|---|
| | | 5th | | 10th | | 25th | | 75th | | 90th | | 95th | |
| | | Score | S.E. | Score | S.E. | Score | S.E. | Score | S.E. | Score | S.E. | Score | S.E. |
| **OECD** | Australia | 292 | (3.6) | 343 | (2.6) | 411 | (1.7) | 527 | (1.3) | 579 | (2.2) | 614 | (2.7) |
| | Austria | 359 | (4.3) | 398 | (3.5) | 453 | (2.5) | 563 | (2.2) | 613 | (3.0) | 644 | (3.7) |
| | Belgium | 349 | (3.8) | 390 | (2.5) | 446 | (2.0) | 562 | (2.0) | 615 | (2.3) | 648 | (2.7) |
| | Canada | 288 | (4.0) | 340 | (3.1) | 411 | (1.9) | 534 | (1.6) | 590 | (2.5) | 629 | (3.3) |
| | Czech Republic | 331 | (5.7) | 376 | (4.6) | 435 | (2.6) | 548 | (1.9) | 599 | (3.1) | 628 | (3.7) |
| | Denmark | 300 | (6.3) | 343 | (4.9) | 410 | (2.9) | 523 | (2.2) | 573 | (2.5) | 602 | (3.0) |
| | Finland | 290 | (4.6) | 330 | (4.0) | 392 | (2.8) | 509 | (2.4) | 559 | (2.7) | 590 | (3.1) |
| | France | 363 | (5.5) | 405 | (3.6) | 462 | (2.9) | 581 | (2.8) | 635 | (3.4) | 671 | (4.1) |
| | Germany | 365 | (5.4) | 404 | (3.4) | 460 | (2.3) | 570 | (2.2) | 619 | (2.6) | 650 | (3.9) |
| | Greece | 399 | (4.6) | 436 | (2.9) | 492 | (2.2) | 606 | (2.3) | 660 | (3.1) | 697 | (4.7) |
| | Hungary | 384 | (4.6) | 420 | (3.6) | 472 | (2.4) | 576 | (2.4) | 621 | (3.5) | 649 | (3.9) |
| | Iceland | 267 | (7.9) | 328 | (5.6) | 407 | (2.9) | 535 | (2.7) | 590 | (2.8) | 627 | (4.7) |
| | Ireland | 329 | (4.8) | 370 | (3.7) | 428 | (2.4) | 539 | (2.4) | 589 | (2.9) | 621 | (4.2) |
| | Italy | 407 | (2.3) | 437 | (1.8) | 480 | (1.5) | 577 | (1.7) | 625 | (2.2) | 658 | (2.8) |
| | Japan | 332 | (5.6) | 386 | (4.7) | 455 | (2.5) | 575 | (2.1) | 632 | (3.2) | 670 | (5.0) |
| | Korea | 323 | (6.2) | 373 | (3.9) | 434 | (2.3) | 540 | (2.3) | 593 | (3.3) | 631 | (5.4) |
| | Luxembourg | 357 | (4.3) | 398 | (3.3) | 458 | (1.9) | 575 | (1.8) | 627 | (2.8) | 661 | (3.5) |
| | Mexico | 472 | (3.1) | 503 | (2.1) | 554 | (2.0) | 667 | (2.4) | 721 | (3.0) | 757 | (3.9) |
| | Netherlands | 296 | (4.4) | 341 | (3.4) | 401 | (2.0) | 507 | (2.3) | 557 | (3.5) | 590 | (5.1) |
| | New Zealand | 285 | (5.5) | 334 | (3.8) | 404 | (2.5) | 524 | (2.3) | 579 | (3.3) | 615 | (4.2) |
| | Norway | 287 | (6.8) | 345 | (5.4) | 416 | (2.7) | 537 | (2.5) | 592 | (2.6) | 627 | (3.8) |
| | Poland | 364 | (4.5) | 400 | (2.9) | 450 | (2.2) | 553 | (2.3) | 601 | (2.9) | 635 | (4.2) |
| | Portugal | 446 | (3.1) | 474 | (2.7) | 520 | (1.9) | 619 | (2.3) | 669 | (2.8) | 704 | (4.2) |
| | Slovak Republic | 382 | (4.3) | 417 | (3.3) | 468 | (2.1) | 575 | (2.3) | 625 | (3.1) | 659 | (4.0) |
| | Spain | 390 | (2.7) | 426 | (2.3) | 478 | (1.7) | 591 | (2.0) | 644 | (2.9) | 680 | (3.5) |
| | Sweden | 291 | (7.8) | 339 | (5.5) | 405 | (3.4) | 510 | (2.6) | 559 | (3.2) | 593 | (4.0) |
| | Switzerland | 354 | (4.0) | 393 | (3.0) | 450 | (2.5) | 561 | (1.9) | 611 | (2.7) | 643 | (2.7) |
| | Turkey | 372 | (5.6) | 413 | (3.7) | 473 | (3.3) | 606 | (3.4) | 669 | (4.5) | 710 | (6.6) |
| | United Kingdom | 295 | (4.7) | 341 | (3.7) | 408 | (2.4) | 525 | (2.1) | 579 | (2.8) | 613 | (3.7) |
| | United States | 300 | (6.1) | 351 | (4.7) | 418 | (3.1) | 545 | (3.7) | 606 | (5.5) | 644 | (6.5) |
| | **OECD total** | **332** | **(2.4)** | **380** | **(1.5)** | **444** | **(1.0)** | **573** | **(1.2)** | **635** | **(1.3)** | **675** | **(1.4)** |
| | **OECD average** | **342** | **(0.9)** | **385** | **(0.7)** | **445** | **(0.4)** | **559** | **(0.4)** | **611** | **(0.6)** | **645** | **(0.8)** |
| **Partners** | Argentina | 423 | (5.8) | 457 | (3.4) | 510 | (3.3) | 626 | (3.6) | 680 | (4.1) | 712 | (5.5) |
| | Azerbaijan | 497 | (3.2) | 522 | (2.5) | 562 | (2.4) | 656 | (3.3) | 707 | (4.7) | 739 | (5.0) |
| | Brazil | 446 | (4.6) | 478 | (3.2) | 530 | (2.8) | 651 | (2.6) | 710 | (2.8) | 748 | (3.5) |
| | Bulgaria | 339 | (4.9) | 386 | (4.0) | 452 | (3.1) | 592 | (3.6) | 659 | (4.7) | 703 | (5.9) |
| | Chile | 432 | (5.7) | 469 | (3.5) | 526 | (3.6) | 654 | (4.0) | 716 | (5.7) | 756 | (5.5) |
| | Colombia | 478 | (4.7) | 516 | (4.6) | 573 | (3.7) | 710 | (4.9) | 780 | (7.7) | 823 | (6.9) |
| | Croatia | 390 | (3.9) | 427 | (3.7) | 481 | (2.4) | 591 | (2.5) | 644 | (3.0) | 677 | (3.5) |
| | Estonia | 379 | (4.4) | 411 | (3.2) | 457 | (2.3) | 550 | (2.2) | 596 | (2.9) | 624 | (3.0) |
| | Hong Kong-China | 365 | (6.2) | 412 | (4.0) | 476 | (2.7) | 599 | (2.5) | 660 | (3.3) | 703 | (5.7) |
| | Indonesia | 492 | (2.9) | 515 | (2.8) | 556 | (2.7) | 657 | (2.8) | 707 | (3.2) | 739 | (3.8) |
| | Israel | 318 | (7.3) | 370 | (5.5) | 442 | (2.8) | 578 | (3.4) | 650 | (6.3) | 699 | (6.6) |
| | Jordan | 480 | (3.9) | 508 | (3.0) | 556 | (2.2) | 662 | (2.4) | 714 | (2.7) | 747 | (3.5) |
| | Kyrgyzstan | 453 | (3.1) | 481 | (2.4) | 526 | (2.0) | 631 | (2.3) | 685 | (3.4) | 720 | (4.2) |
| | Latvia | 388 | (4.0) | 416 | (2.6) | 459 | (2.4) | 548 | (2.3) | 591 | (3.1) | 619 | (4.3) |
| | Liechtenstein | 371 | (14.4) | 398 | (12.4) | 450 | (10.0) | 557 | (9.9) | 609 | (11.8) | 637 | (20.4) |
| | Lithuania | 409 | (4.7) | 440 | (3.2) | 491 | (2.4) | 599 | (2.8) | 651 | (2.8) | 685 | (4.5) |
| | Macao-China | 370 | (5.6) | 410 | (3.0) | 468 | (2.1) | 582 | (2.3) | 637 | (3.4) | 674 | (5.7) |
| | Montenegro | 402 | (5.2) | 442 | (3.4) | 501 | (2.7) | 622 | (2.0) | 679 | (3.1) | 720 | (4.1) |
| | Qatar | 400 | (4.8) | 444 | (2.8) | 502 | (1.9) | 627 | (2.3) | 698 | (2.9) | 748 | (4.5) |
| | Romania | 460 | (4.8) | 491 | (4.7) | 539 | (4.1) | 641 | (2.7) | 696 | (3.2) | 733 | (5.2) |
| | Russian Federation | 422 | (3.4) | 450 | (2.7) | 492 | (2.5) | 588 | (2.3) | 636 | (2.9) | 667 | (3.6) |
| | Serbia | 376 | (4.9) | 413 | (2.7) | 466 | (2.3) | 580 | (2.5) | 633 | (3.2) | 669 | (4.4) |
| | Slovenia | 346 | (4.5) | 385 | (2.8) | 448 | (1.9) | 565 | (2.1) | 621 | (3.2) | 658 | (5.3) |
| | Chinese Taipei | 357 | (6.0) | 407 | (3.7) | 472 | (2.6) | 598 | (2.6) | 659 | (3.4) | 700 | (4.5) |
| | Thailand | 516 | (3.2) | 543 | (2.7) | 587 | (2.0) | 693 | (3.0) | 747 | (2.9) | 784 | (3.7) |
| | Tunisia | 461 | (4.8) | 488 | (2.9) | 533 | (2.2) | 643 | (2.5) | 699 | (4.4) | 738 | (4.6) |
| | Uruguay | 416 | (4.5) | 453 | (3.5) | 509 | (3.1) | 625 | (2.6) | 681 | (3.4) | 717 | (4.8) |

Note: Values that are statistically significant are indicated in bold (see Annex A3).
*StatLink* http://dx.doi.org/10.1787/142102278412

Pour consulter la version française intégrale de ce tableau, suivre ce lien :
*StatLink* http://dx.doi.org/10.1787/152630454851

[Part 1/2]

**Table 3.2** **Mean score, variation and gender differences on the *support for scientific enquiry* scale**

Tableau 3.2 Score moyen, différences de score selon le sexe et répartition des scores sur l'échelle *valeur accordée à la démarche scientifique*

| | | All students | | | Gender differences | | | | | |
| | | Mean score | | Standard deviation | | Males | | Females | | Difference (M - F) | |
| | | Mean | S.E. | S.D. | S.E. | Mean score | S.E. | Mean score | S.E. | Score dif. | S.E. |
|---|---|---|---|---|---|---|---|---|---|---|---|
| OECD | Australia | 487 | (1.6) | 98 | (0.9) | 488 | (2.4) | 486 | (1.8) | 2 | (2.8) |
| | Austria | 515 | (2.4) | 112 | (2.0) | 515 | (3.3) | 515 | (3.0) | 0 | (4.1) |
| | Belgium | 492 | (1.7) | 88 | (1.2) | 492 | (2.3) | 492 | (2.0) | 0 | (2.7) |
| | Canada | 501 | (1.9) | 105 | (1.1) | 497 | (2.5) | 504 | (2.0) | -7 | (2.5) |
| | Czech Republic | 485 | (2.4) | 80 | (1.6) | 484 | (2.8) | 485 | (3.0) | -1 | (3.4) |
| | Denmark | 483 | (2.6) | 85 | (1.5) | 484 | (3.2) | 482 | (2.9) | 2 | (3.2) |
| | Finland | 479 | (2.0) | 86 | (1.4) | 471 | (2.7) | 487 | (2.3) | -16 | (2.9) |
| | France | 507 | (2.5) | 94 | (1.6) | 513 | (3.6) | 501 | (2.7) | 12 | (3.8) |
| | Germany | 518 | (2.7) | 113 | (1.5) | 517 | (3.5) | 519 | (3.0) | -2 | (3.5) |
| | Greece | 533 | (2.4) | 95 | (1.4) | 525 | (2.9) | 540 | (3.1) | -15 | (3.8) |
| | Hungary | 512 | (2.0) | 87 | (1.7) | 506 | (3.2) | 517 | (2.2) | -11 | (3.7) |
| | Iceland | 491 | (2.2) | 112 | (1.9) | 484 | (3.0) | 498 | (2.8) | -14 | (3.7) |
| | Ireland | 484 | (1.9) | 86 | (1.1) | 488 | (2.3) | 481 | (2.6) | 7 | (3.0) |
| | Italy | 511 | (1.6) | 90 | (1.1) | 508 | (2.1) | 513 | (2.1) | -5 | (2.6) |
| | Japan | 468 | (2.3) | 111 | (1.8) | 475 | (3.5) | 460 | (3.1) | 16 | (4.7) |
| | Korea | 495 | (2.4) | 99 | (1.9) | 501 | (3.3) | 490 | (3.3) | 11 | (4.2) |
| | Luxembourg | 522 | (1.9) | 117 | (1.5) | 523 | (2.9) | 520 | (2.6) | 3 | (3.9) |
| | Mexico | 536 | (2.0) | 90 | (1.2) | 538 | (2.5) | 534 | (2.0) | 5 | (2.2) |
| | Netherlands | 447 | (1.7) | 69 | (1.0) | 450 | (1.9) | 444 | (2.2) | 6 | (2.3) |
| | New Zealand | 470 | (1.8) | 89 | (1.3) | 471 | (2.6) | 469 | (2.6) | 2 | (3.7) |
| | Norway | 485 | (2.5) | 111 | (1.6) | 482 | (3.3) | 489 | (3.3) | -7 | (4.3) |
| | Poland | 513 | (2.2) | 89 | (1.3) | 510 | (2.5) | 516 | (2.6) | -6 | (2.7) |
| | Portugal | 538 | (2.0) | 88 | (1.3) | 541 | (2.5) | 535 | (2.6) | 7 | (3.2) |
| | Slovak Republic | 497 | (2.0) | 76 | (1.1) | 502 | (2.7) | 492 | (2.5) | 10 | (3.5) |
| | Spain | 529 | (1.7) | 91 | (1.0) | 532 | (2.5) | 526 | (1.9) | 6 | (2.8) |
| | Sweden | 471 | (3.0) | 100 | (1.8) | 469 | (3.9) | 473 | (2.9) | -4 | (3.6) |
| | Switzerland | 510 | (2.0) | 103 | (1.1) | 511 | (2.5) | 510 | (2.5) | 1 | (3.0) |
| | Turkey | 563 | (3.3) | 126 | (2.0) | 549 | (3.8) | 579 | (3.7) | -30 | (3.9) |
| | United Kingdom | 470 | (1.8) | 89 | (1.0) | 476 | (2.2) | 464 | (2.5) | 12 | (3.0) |
| | United States | 490 | (2.5) | 99 | (1.4) | 491 | (3.1) | 490 | (2.8) | 2 | (3.2) |
| | **OECD total** | 501 | (0.8) | 103 | (0.5) | 503 | (1.0) | 500 | (0.9) | 2 | (1.1) |
| | **OECD average** | 500 | (0.4) | 96 | (0.3) | 500 | (0.5) | 500 | (0.5) | -1 | (0.6) |
| Partners | Argentina | 506 | (2.9) | 89 | (1.8) | 503 | (4.0) | 509 | (3.1) | -6 | (4.0) |
| | Azerbaijan | 542 | (2.8) | 98 | (1.4) | 538 | (3.3) | 545 | (3.4) | -7 | (3.6) |
| | Brazil | 519 | (1.8) | 92 | (1.4) | 520 | (2.8) | 518 | (2.1) | 2 | (3.3) |
| | Bulgaria | 527 | (3.9) | 112 | (2.2) | 515 | (4.8) | 539 | (4.1) | -24 | (4.8) |
| | Chile | 564 | (3.0) | 108 | (1.6) | 567 | (3.2) | 561 | (4.2) | 6 | (4.4) |
| | Colombia | 546 | (2.6) | 92 | (1.6) | 549 | (3.7) | 543 | (3.0) | 6 | (4.1) |
| | Croatia | 514 | (1.8) | 83 | (1.2) | 519 | (2.6) | 510 | (2.3) | 9 | (3.2) |
| | Estonia | 497 | (1.8) | 80 | (1.4) | 495 | (2.3) | 499 | (2.5) | -4 | (3.1) |
| | Hong Kong-China | 529 | (2.3) | 100 | (1.4) | 540 | (3.2) | 519 | (2.7) | 21 | (3.6) |
| | Indonesia | 521 | (2.8) | 90 | (1.3) | 516 | (3.3) | 527 | (3.3) | -11 | (3.3) |
| | Israel | 512 | (3.1) | 121 | (2.1) | 509 | (4.2) | 514 | (4.0) | -6 | (5.3) |
| | Jordan | 555 | (3.0) | 110 | (1.9) | 543 | (4.5) | 567 | (3.9) | -23 | (6.1) |
| | Kyrgyzstan | 502 | (2.5) | 105 | (1.3) | 489 | (3.6) | 513 | (3.0) | -23 | (4.3) |
| | Latvia | 494 | (2.1) | 76 | (1.1) | 490 | (2.7) | 497 | (2.5) | -8 | (3.0) |
| | Liechtenstein | 524 | (5.8) | 104 | (5.2) | 516 | (10.3) | 531 | (7.8) | -15 | (14.0) |
| | Lithuania | 541 | (2.4) | 95 | (1.7) | 532 | (2.8) | 549 | (2.9) | -17 | (3.1) |
| | Macao-China | 521 | (1.5) | 85 | (1.1) | 524 | (2.2) | 518 | (2.1) | 6 | (3.1) |
| | Montenegro | 529 | (1.7) | 97 | (1.3) | 526 | (2.5) | 532 | (2.6) | -6 | (3.7) |
| | Qatar | 520 | (1.7) | 146 | (1.5) | 505 | (2.7) | 535 | (2.4) | -30 | (4.0) |
| | Romania | 540 | (3.2) | 102 | (2.0) | 540 | (4.5) | 540 | (3.8) | 0 | (5.2) |
| | Russian Federation | 508 | (2.6) | 83 | (1.1) | 507 | (3.2) | 509 | (2.7) | -3 | (2.9) |
| | Serbia | 520 | (2.2) | 94 | (1.6) | 523 | (2.8) | 517 | (2.6) | 6 | (3.1) |
| | Slovenia | 502 | (1.5) | 96 | (1.5) | 499 | (2.1) | 504 | (2.1) | -5 | (3.0) |
| | Chinese Taipei | 546 | (2.2) | 104 | (1.3) | 552 | (2.7) | 538 | (2.6) | 14 | (2.9) |
| | Thailand | 569 | (2.3) | 102 | (1.5) | 559 | (3.7) | 575 | (2.9) | -16 | (4.7) |
| | Tunisia | 534 | (2.6) | 111 | (1.3) | 530 | (3.6) | 538 | (3.0) | -8 | (4.0) |
| | Uruguay | 510 | (1.9) | 84 | (1.4) | 516 | (2.3) | 505 | (2.5) | 11 | (2.8) |

Note: Values that are statistically significant are indicated in bold (see Annex A3).
StatLink ᏤᎶᏏ http://dx.doi.org/10.1787/142102278412

Pour consulter la version française intégrale de ce tableau, suivre ce lien :
StatLink ᏤᎶᏏ http://dx.doi.org/10.1787/152630454851

[Part 2/2]

**Table 3.2** **Mean score, variation and gender differences on the *support for scientific enquiry* scale**

Tableau 3.2 Score moyen, différences de score selon le sexe et répartition des scores sur l'échelle *valeur accordée à la démarche scientifique*

| | | \multicolumn{12}{c}{Percentiles} |
|---|---|---|---|---|---|---|---|---|---|---|---|---|
| | | \multicolumn{2}{c}{5th} | \multicolumn{2}{c}{10th} | \multicolumn{2}{c}{25th} | \multicolumn{2}{c}{75th} | \multicolumn{2}{c}{90th} | \multicolumn{2}{c}{95th} |
| | | Score | S.E. | Score | S.E. | Score | S.E. | Score | S.E. | Score | S.E. | Score | S.E. |
| **OECD** | Australia | 335 | (2.9) | 369 | (2.4) | 422 | (2.0) | 550 | (2.0) | 614 | (2.7) | 653 | (3.0) |
| | Austria | 336 | (6.6) | 375 | (4.8) | 441 | (3.2) | 590 | (3.4) | 656 | (3.8) | 695 | (5.1) |
| | Belgium | 354 | (4.2) | 386 | (3.1) | 434 | (1.9) | 549 | (2.1) | 605 | (3.0) | 639 | (2.5) |
| | Canada | 338 | (3.5) | 375 | (2.5) | 433 | (2.3) | 567 | (2.2) | 635 | (2.6) | 678 | (4.2) |
| | Czech Republic | 360 | (5.2) | 388 | (2.7) | 433 | (2.7) | 535 | (2.9) | 587 | (3.5) | 618 | (3.5) |
| | Denmark | 348 | (4.7) | 381 | (3.5) | 428 | (2.6) | 536 | (3.2) | 591 | (5.0) | 626 | (5.5) |
| | Finland | 347 | (5.0) | 377 | (2.7) | 423 | (2.2) | 534 | (2.6) | 590 | (3.1) | 624 | (3.8) |
| | France | 356 | (5.4) | 392 | (3.4) | 447 | (3.4) | 567 | (2.9) | 625 | (4.1) | 661 | (4.1) |
| | Germany | 336 | (5.4) | 379 | (3.8) | 445 | (3.1) | 593 | (3.5) | 661 | (4.4) | 702 | (5.1) |
| | Greece | 380 | (3.4) | 415 | (4.0) | 470 | (2.8) | 595 | (2.9) | 654 | (3.8) | 690 | (5.2) |
| | Hungary | 374 | (4.5) | 405 | (3.0) | 457 | (2.5) | 568 | (2.8) | 620 | (4.0) | 650 | (4.7) |
| | Iceland | 311 | (7.4) | 359 | (4.0) | 422 | (2.8) | 562 | (2.8) | 634 | (4.4) | 674 | (5.5) |
| | Ireland | 347 | (4.0) | 378 | (2.8) | 427 | (2.4) | 540 | (2.3) | 595 | (3.0) | 629 | (4.2) |
| | Italy | 368 | (3.2) | 402 | (2.5) | 453 | (1.9) | 568 | (1.9) | 623 | (2.6) | 657 | (2.6) |
| | Japan | 289 | (5.5) | 336 | (4.0) | 401 | (2.9) | 538 | (2.8) | 605 | (3.5) | 646 | (3.9) |
| | Korea | 342 | (4.1) | 376 | (3.5) | 431 | (2.5) | 558 | (3.0) | 622 | (4.5) | 660 | (5.7) |
| | Luxembourg | 334 | (4.6) | 377 | (4.1) | 445 | (3.0) | 599 | (2.5) | 670 | (4.4) | 711 | (5.1) |
| | Mexico | 393 | (3.5) | 423 | (3.3) | 474 | (2.9) | 595 | (1.9) | 652 | (3.1) | 687 | (2.9) |
| | Netherlands | 336 | (3.9) | 362 | (2.6) | 402 | (2.1) | 491 | (1.9) | 534 | (2.7) | 562 | (3.6) |
| | New Zealand | 331 | (4.6) | 365 | (3.2) | 412 | (2.0) | 526 | (2.8) | 586 | (3.7) | 622 | (4.4) |
| | Norway | 305 | (6.2) | 352 | (4.0) | 415 | (3.5) | 556 | (3.3) | 625 | (3.6) | 667 | (5.8) |
| | Poland | 375 | (3.5) | 405 | (2.8) | 453 | (2.5) | 569 | (3.2) | 629 | (3.5) | 666 | (4.4) |
| | Portugal | 402 | (4.0) | 431 | (3.0) | 478 | (2.5) | 594 | (3.0) | 652 | (4.1) | 689 | (5.0) |
| | Slovak Republic | 379 | (4.0) | 404 | (2.6) | 446 | (2.5) | 544 | (2.4) | 596 | (2.6) | 629 | (4.9) |
| | Spain | 388 | (3.3) | 419 | (2.1) | 470 | (2.1) | 587 | (2.5) | 646 | (3.0) | 681 | (3.5) |
| | Sweden | 312 | (6.3) | 353 | (4.8) | 410 | (3.0) | 536 | (3.6) | 596 | (4.4) | 632 | (4.9) |
| | Switzerland | 344 | (3.9) | 382 | (3.7) | 443 | (2.5) | 578 | (2.5) | 643 | (2.9) | 680 | (3.5) |
| | Turkey | 363 | (6.6) | 407 | (4.1) | 476 | (4.2) | 648 | (4.4) | 729 | (6.0) | 779 | (6.0) |
| | United Kingdom | 332 | (3.4) | 362 | (2.4) | 411 | (2.0) | 526 | (2.6) | 585 | (3.1) | 621 | (4.0) |
| | United States | 339 | (4.3) | 373 | (3.5) | 425 | (2.7) | 553 | (3.1) | 619 | (4.7) | 660 | (4.5) |
| | **OECD total** | 343 | (1.5) | 379 | (1.2) | 434 | (1.0) | 566 | (1.0) | 632 | (1.3) | 674 | (1.4) |
| | **OECD average** | 349 | (0.9) | 384 | (0.6) | 437 | (0.5) | 562 | (0.5) | 623 | (0.7) | 660 | (0.8) |
| **Partners** | Argentina | 364 | (7.9) | 395 | (5.1) | 448 | (3.9) | 564 | (3.5) | 619 | (4.9) | 654 | (5.2) |
| | Azerbaijan | 390 | (3.7) | 421 | (3.4) | 475 | (2.7) | 604 | (3.8) | 670 | (4.8) | 712 | (5.9) |
| | Brazil | 375 | (3.4) | 404 | (3.1) | 456 | (2.0) | 578 | (2.6) | 638 | (3.3) | 676 | (3.7) |
| | Bulgaria | 352 | (8.1) | 391 | (5.3) | 451 | (4.1) | 600 | (4.1) | 670 | (5.4) | 716 | (7.0) |
| | Chile | 389 | (5.3) | 426 | (5.2) | 491 | (3.1) | 636 | (3.7) | 702 | (4.4) | 742 | (5.2) |
| | Colombia | 401 | (5.7) | 431 | (4.9) | 482 | (4.2) | 606 | (3.4) | 664 | (5.3) | 701 | (6.0) |
| | Croatia | 386 | (4.4) | 413 | (2.6) | 459 | (1.9) | 567 | (2.5) | 621 | (2.7) | 654 | (3.3) |
| | Estonia | 373 | (2.9) | 397 | (3.3) | 443 | (2.6) | 549 | (2.3) | 599 | (2.8) | 631 | (3.7) |
| | Hong Kong-China | 377 | (4.2) | 408 | (3.8) | 460 | (3.3) | 593 | (3.2) | 660 | (4.8) | 700 | (4.0) |
| | Indonesia | 382 | (4.4) | 411 | (3.7) | 458 | (3.2) | 580 | (3.6) | 638 | (4.0) | 676 | (5.4) |
| | Israel | 322 | (5.6) | 364 | (4.2) | 433 | (3.7) | 588 | (3.5) | 663 | (5.2) | 716 | (5.9) |
| | Jordan | 374 | (6.9) | 417 | (4.8) | 484 | (3.8) | 628 | (3.4) | 692 | (3.4) | 735 | (4.5) |
| | Kyrgyzstan | 338 | (3.1) | 370 | (2.7) | 429 | (3.1) | 569 | (3.3) | 640 | (4.4) | 682 | (5.1) |
| | Latvia | 374 | (3.7) | 399 | (2.4) | 442 | (3.0) | 543 | (3.2) | 590 | (3.3) | 621 | (4.6) |
| | Liechtenstein | 360 | (12.9) | 395 | (10.8) | 456 | (10.4) | 592 | (7.4) | 658 | (14.7) | 695 | (10.9) |
| | Lithuania | 391 | (4.9) | 422 | (3.9) | 476 | (2.8) | 604 | (3.3) | 661 | (3.9) | 698 | (4.8) |
| | Macao-China | 387 | (3.2) | 415 | (2.6) | 463 | (2.0) | 577 | (2.1) | 632 | (2.9) | 666 | (4.4) |
| | Montenegro | 378 | (4.0) | 412 | (2.7) | 464 | (2.2) | 591 | (2.3) | 652 | (4.1) | 691 | (5.4) |
| | Qatar | 299 | (3.4) | 341 | (2.8) | 416 | (2.8) | 614 | (3.5) | 711 | (3.7) | 770 | (5.9) |
| | Romania | 377 | (8.2) | 413 | (5.4) | 472 | (4.1) | 606 | (3.7) | 669 | (4.6) | 711 | (5.7) |
| | Russian Federation | 381 | (3.8) | 407 | (2.6) | 451 | (2.5) | 561 | (3.0) | 616 | (4.0) | 649 | (4.6) |
| | Serbia | 374 | (4.8) | 406 | (3.2) | 457 | (3.1) | 580 | (3.3) | 639 | (3.9) | 678 | (4.1) |
| | Slovenia | 350 | (3.4) | 388 | (2.6) | 443 | (1.9) | 561 | (2.2) | 621 | (2.8) | 658 | (5.0) |
| | Chinese Taipei | 385 | (3.7) | 418 | (3.1) | 475 | (3.0) | 613 | (2.9) | 681 | (4.2) | 722 | (4.7) |
| | Thailand | 409 | (4.1) | 441 | (3.4) | 498 | (3.4) | 636 | (2.9) | 702 | (3.6) | 745 | (5.5) |
| | Tunisia | 356 | (3.4) | 395 | (3.5) | 460 | (3.5) | 606 | (3.7) | 678 | (3.9) | 724 | (5.4) |
| | Uruguay | 377 | (3.4) | 405 | (3.7) | 453 | (2.7) | 565 | (2.2) | 617 | (3.8) | 652 | (4.8) |

Note: Values that are statistically significant are indicated in bold (see Annex A3).
StatLink http://dx.doi.org/10.1787/142102278412

Pour consulter la version française intégrale de ce tableau, suivre ce lien :
StatLink http://dx.doi.org/10.1787/152630454851

[Part 1/2]
**Table 3.3  Index of self-efficacy in science and performance on the science scale, by quarters of the index[1]**

Tableau 3.3  Indice de perception des capacités personnelles en sciences et scores sur l'échelle de culture scientifique, par quartile de l'indice

| | Index of self-efficacy in science | | | | | | | | | | | | | | | |
|---|---|---|---|---|---|---|---|---|---|---|---|---|---|---|---|---|
| | All students | | Males | | Females | | Gender difference (M - F) | | Bottom quarter | | Second quarter | | Third quarter | | Top quarter | |
| | Mean index | S.E. | Mean index | S.E. | Mean index | S.E. | Dif. | S.E. | Mean index | S.E. | Mean index | S.E. | Mean index | S.E. | Mean index | S.E. |
| Australia | 0.12 | (0.01) | 0.19 | (0.03) | 0.04 | (0.02) | **0.14** | (0.04) | -1.18 | (0.01) | -0.21 | (0.00) | 0.38 | (0.00) | 1.47 | (0.02) |
| Austria | -0.11 | (0.02) | -0.10 | (0.03) | -0.12 | (0.03) | 0.02 | (0.04) | -1.26 | (0.03) | -0.40 | (0.00) | 0.15 | (0.01) | 1.08 | (0.02) |
| Belgium | -0.07 | (0.02) | -0.02 | (0.03) | -0.13 | (0.02) | **0.11** | (0.03) | -1.29 | (0.02) | -0.34 | (0.00) | 0.22 | (0.00) | 1.13 | (0.01) |
| Canada | 0.21 | (0.01) | 0.30 | (0.02) | 0.13 | (0.02) | **0.17** | (0.02) | -1.05 | (0.02) | -0.12 | (0.00) | 0.47 | (0.00) | 1.55 | (0.02) |
| Czech Republic | 0.14 | (0.02) | 0.17 | (0.02) | 0.11 | (0.02) | **0.07** | (0.03) | -0.91 | (0.02) | -0.15 | (0.00) | 0.37 | (0.01) | 1.27 | (0.02) |
| Denmark | -0.08 | (0.02) | 0.04 | (0.03) | -0.20 | (0.03) | **0.24** | (0.03) | -1.34 | (0.02) | -0.40 | (0.01) | 0.21 | (0.01) | 1.20 | (0.02) |
| Finland | 0.02 | (0.02) | 0.08 | (0.02) | -0.03 | (0.02) | **0.10** | (0.03) | -1.06 | (0.02) | -0.27 | (0.00) | 0.26 | (0.01) | 1.18 | (0.02) |
| France | -0.06 | (0.02) | 0.08 | (0.03) | -0.18 | (0.02) | **0.26** | (0.03) | -1.19 | (0.02) | -0.34 | (0.00) | 0.21 | (0.01) | 1.09 | (0.02) |
| Germany | 0.06 | (0.02) | 0.13 | (0.03) | -0.01 | (0.02) | **0.14** | (0.03) | -1.10 | (0.03) | -0.23 | (0.00) | 0.33 | (0.00) | 1.25 | (0.02) |
| Greece | -0.13 | (0.02) | -0.05 | (0.03) | -0.20 | (0.02) | **0.15** | (0.03) | -1.24 | (0.02) | -0.43 | (0.01) | 0.10 | (0.01) | 1.06 | (0.02) |
| Hungary | -0.06 | (0.01) | -0.01 | (0.02) | -0.11 | (0.02) | **0.11** | (0.03) | -1.05 | (0.02) | -0.34 | (0.00) | 0.14 | (0.00) | 1.02 | (0.02) |
| Iceland | 0.14 | (0.02) | 0.31 | (0.02) | -0.03 | (0.02) | **0.34** | (0.04) | -1.30 | (0.03) | -0.16 | (0.01) | 0.49 | (0.01) | 1.52 | (0.02) |
| Ireland | 0.01 | (0.02) | 0.08 | (0.03) | -0.06 | (0.03) | **0.14** | (0.04) | -1.26 | (0.03) | -0.29 | (0.01) | 0.30 | (0.01) | 1.28 | (0.02) |
| Italy | -0.20 | (0.01) | -0.15 | (0.01) | -0.26 | (0.01) | **0.11** | (0.02) | -1.12 | (0.01) | -0.41 | (0.00) | -0.02 | (0.00) | 0.74 | (0.01) |
| Japan | -0.53 | (0.02) | -0.49 | (0.02) | -0.58 | (0.02) | **0.09** | (0.03) | -1.72 | (0.03) | -0.71 | (0.00) | -0.26 | (0.00) | 0.56 | (0.02) |
| Korea | -0.21 | (0.02) | -0.20 | (0.03) | -0.23 | (0.02) | 0.04 | (0.04) | -1.26 | (0.03) | -0.45 | (0.00) | 0.01 | (0.00) | 0.83 | (0.02) |
| Luxembourg | -0.13 | (0.02) | -0.05 | (0.02) | -0.22 | (0.02) | **0.16** | (0.03) | -1.36 | (0.02) | -0.41 | (0.00) | 0.14 | (0.01) | 1.10 | (0.02) |
| Mexico | 0.09 | (0.02) | 0.07 | (0.02) | 0.12 | (0.02) | **-0.05** | (0.02) | -0.97 | (0.01) | -0.21 | (0.00) | 0.34 | (0.00) | 1.21 | (0.01) |
| Netherlands | 0.03 | (0.02) | 0.09 | (0.02) | -0.03 | (0.02) | **0.11** | (0.03) | -1.16 | (0.03) | -0.24 | (0.00) | 0.30 | (0.00) | 1.22 | (0.02) |
| New Zealand | -0.02 | (0.02) | 0.05 | (0.03) | -0.09 | (0.03) | **0.14** | (0.04) | -1.27 | (0.02) | -0.35 | (0.00) | 0.25 | (0.01) | 1.28 | (0.02) |
| Norway | 0.12 | (0.02) | 0.21 | (0.02) | 0.03 | (0.02) | **0.18** | (0.03) | -1.11 | (0.03) | -0.11 | (0.01) | 0.37 | (0.00) | 1.35 | (0.02) |
| Poland | 0.26 | (0.02) | 0.24 | (0.02) | 0.28 | (0.02) | -0.04 | (0.03) | -0.82 | (0.02) | -0.06 | (0.00) | 0.47 | (0.00) | 1.44 | (0.02) |
| Portugal | 0.21 | (0.02) | 0.23 | (0.02) | 0.19 | (0.02) | 0.04 | (0.03) | -0.91 | (0.02) | -0.11 | (0.01) | 0.47 | (0.01) | 1.37 | (0.02) |
| Slovak Republic | 0.11 | (0.02) | 0.16 | (0.03) | 0.05 | (0.03) | **0.10** | (0.03) | -0.91 | (0.02) | -0.19 | (0.00) | 0.32 | (0.01) | 1.21 | (0.02) |
| Spain | -0.07 | (0.02) | -0.03 | (0.03) | -0.10 | (0.03) | **0.07** | (0.03) | -1.38 | (0.02) | -0.36 | (0.00) | 0.25 | (0.00) | 1.22 | (0.01) |
| Sweden | -0.07 | (0.03) | 0.04 | (0.03) | -0.18 | (0.03) | **0.21** | (0.03) | -1.30 | (0.04) | -0.32 | (0.01) | 0.22 | (0.01) | 1.14 | (0.02) |
| Switzerland | -0.19 | (0.02) | -0.11 | (0.02) | -0.27 | (0.02) | **0.16** | (0.03) | -1.33 | (0.02) | -0.46 | (0.00) | 0.07 | (0.00) | 0.96 | (0.02) |
| Turkey | 0.02 | (0.03) | -0.03 | (0.03) | 0.07 | (0.03) | **-0.10** | (0.04) | -1.23 | (0.03) | -0.28 | (0.01) | 0.30 | (0.00) | 1.27 | (0.02) |
| United Kingdom | 0.19 | (0.02) | 0.32 | (0.02) | 0.05 | (0.02) | **0.27** | (0.03) | -1.04 | (0.02) | -0.17 | (0.00) | 0.43 | (0.01) | 1.52 | (0.02) |
| United States | 0.22 | (0.02) | 0.32 | (0.03) | 0.12 | (0.03) | **0.20** | (0.03) | -1.11 | (0.02) | -0.13 | (0.01) | 0.48 | (0.00) | 1.65 | (0.02) |
| **OECD total** | **0.03** | **(0.01)** | **0.09** | **(0.01)** | **-0.03** | **(0.01)** | **0.12** | **(0.01)** | **-1.18** | **(0.01)** | **-0.28** | **(0.00)** | **0.29** | **(0.00)** | **1.32** | **(0.01)** |
| **OECD average** | **0.00** | **(0.00)** | **0.06** | **(0.00)** | **-0.06** | **(0.00)** | **0.12** | **(0.01)** | **-1.17** | **(0.00)** | **-0.29** | **(0.00)** | **0.26** | **(0.00)** | **1.21** | **(0.00)** |
| Argentina | -0.05 | (0.02) | -0.06 | (0.03) | -0.04 | (0.03) | -0.03 | (0.04) | -1.16 | (0.02) | -0.33 | (0.01) | 0.21 | (0.01) | 1.09 | (0.02) |
| Azerbaijan | -0.46 | (0.03) | -0.42 | (0.04) | -0.49 | (0.03) | 0.07 | (0.04) | -1.88 | (0.03) | -0.75 | (0.01) | -0.13 | (0.01) | 0.94 | (0.02) |
| Brazil | -0.05 | (0.02) | -0.10 | (0.02) | -0.01 | (0.02) | **-0.08** | (0.03) | -1.20 | (0.02) | -0.34 | (0.01) | 0.21 | (0.01) | 1.12 | (0.02) |
| Bulgaria | -0.05 | (0.03) | -0.10 | (0.03) | 0.01 | (0.03) | **-0.11** | (0.04) | -1.28 | (0.03) | -0.36 | (0.01) | 0.21 | (0.01) | 1.25 | (0.03) |
| Chile | 0.06 | (0.02) | 0.08 | (0.03) | 0.05 | (0.03) | 0.03 | (0.04) | -1.08 | (0.02) | -0.25 | (0.00) | 0.33 | (0.01) | 1.25 | (0.02) |
| Colombia | 0.09 | (0.02) | 0.09 | (0.03) | 0.09 | (0.03) | 0.00 | (0.03) | -1.00 | (0.02) | -0.21 | (0.01) | 0.33 | (0.00) | 1.24 | (0.02) |
| Croatia | 0.14 | (0.02) | 0.12 | (0.02) | 0.16 | (0.02) | -0.04 | (0.03) | -0.96 | (0.02) | -0.11 | (0.00) | 0.40 | (0.00) | 1.25 | (0.01) |
| Estonia | 0.03 | (0.02) | 0.01 | (0.02) | 0.04 | (0.02) | -0.03 | (0.03) | -0.98 | (0.01) | -0.28 | (0.00) | 0.24 | (0.01) | 1.13 | (0.02) |
| Hong Kong-China | 0.06 | (0.02) | 0.15 | (0.03) | -0.02 | (0.02) | **0.17** | (0.04) | -1.07 | (0.02) | -0.21 | (0.00) | 0.30 | (0.00) | 1.23 | (0.02) |
| Indonesia | -0.70 | (0.02) | -0.70 | (0.02) | -0.70 | (0.03) | -0.01 | (0.03) | -1.68 | (0.02) | -0.93 | (0.00) | -0.47 | (0.00) | 0.28 | (0.01) |
| Israel | 0.03 | (0.03) | 0.11 | (0.04) | -0.05 | (0.03) | **0.16** | (0.05) | -1.33 | (0.03) | -0.28 | (0.01) | 0.30 | (0.01) | 1.42 | (0.02) |
| Jordan | 0.21 | (0.02) | 0.12 | (0.03) | 0.31 | (0.03) | **-0.19** | (0.04) | -0.99 | (0.02) | -0.12 | (0.01) | 0.48 | (0.01) | 1.48 | (0.02) |
| Kyrgyzstan | -0.15 | (0.02) | -0.16 | (0.03) | -0.14 | (0.02) | -0.02 | (0.03) | -1.38 | (0.02) | -0.46 | (0.01) | 0.16 | (0.01) | 1.09 | (0.02) |
| Latvia | -0.02 | (0.02) | -0.05 | (0.03) | 0.01 | (0.03) | -0.06 | (0.03) | -0.97 | (0.02) | -0.30 | (0.01) | 0.17 | (0.01) | 1.03 | (0.02) |
| Liechtenstein | -0.12 | (0.06) | 0.05 | (0.10) | -0.26 | (0.06) | **0.31** | (0.12) | -1.32 | (0.09) | -0.42 | (0.01) | 0.11 | (0.02) | 1.18 | (0.08) |
| Lithuania | 0.01 | (0.02) | -0.01 | (0.02) | 0.03 | (0.02) | -0.03 | (0.03) | -0.96 | (0.02) | -0.23 | (0.00) | 0.24 | (0.00) | 0.99 | (0.02) |
| Macao-China | -0.11 | (0.02) | -0.04 | (0.02) | -0.17 | (0.02) | **0.13** | (0.03) | -1.22 | (0.02) | -0.40 | (0.00) | 0.14 | (0.00) | 1.06 | (0.02) |
| Montenegro | -0.02 | (0.02) | -0.06 | (0.02) | 0.01 | (0.02) | -0.07 | (0.04) | -1.25 | (0.02) | -0.33 | (0.01) | 0.24 | (0.01) | 1.25 | (0.02) |
| Qatar | -0.09 | (0.02) | 0.01 | (0.03) | -0.19 | (0.02) | **0.19** | (0.04) | -1.65 | (0.02) | -0.38 | (0.00) | 0.23 | (0.01) | 1.45 | (0.02) |
| Romania | -0.35 | (0.02) | -0.34 | (0.03) | -0.35 | (0.03) | 0.01 | (0.04) | -1.57 | (0.04) | -0.63 | (0.01) | -0.08 | (0.01) | 0.90 | (0.02) |
| Russian Federation | -0.01 | (0.03) | -0.04 | (0.04) | 0.02 | (0.03) | -0.06 | (0.03) | -1.22 | (0.04) | -0.31 | (0.01) | 0.28 | (0.01) | 1.22 | (0.02) |
| Serbia | 0.05 | (0.02) | 0.03 | (0.03) | 0.08 | (0.03) | -0.06 | (0.04) | -1.09 | (0.02) | -0.27 | (0.01) | 0.28 | (0.01) | 1.30 | (0.03) |
| Slovenia | -0.10 | (0.01) | -0.06 | (0.02) | -0.15 | (0.02) | **0.09** | (0.03) | -1.20 | (0.01) | -0.40 | (0.01) | 0.15 | (0.00) | 1.04 | (0.02) |
| Chinese Taipei | 0.18 | (0.02) | 0.20 | (0.02) | 0.16 | (0.02) | 0.04 | (0.03) | -1.02 | (0.02) | -0.13 | (0.01) | 0.45 | (0.00) | 1.42 | (0.01) |
| Thailand | 0.06 | (0.02) | 0.00 | (0.02) | 0.11 | (0.02) | **-0.11** | (0.03) | -0.85 | (0.01) | -0.14 | (0.00) | 0.30 | (0.00) | 0.94 | (0.02) |
| Tunisia | -0.11 | (0.02) | -0.08 | (0.02) | -0.13 | (0.02) | 0.05 | (0.03) | -1.04 | (0.01) | -0.40 | (0.00) | 0.06 | (0.01) | 0.94 | (0.02) |
| Uruguay | 0.13 | (0.02) | 0.11 | (0.02) | 0.14 | (0.03) | -0.03 | (0.04) | -1.01 | (0.02) | -0.15 | (0.01) | 0.39 | (0.01) | 1.28 | (0.02) |

Note: Values that are statistically significant are indicated in bold (see Annex A3).
1. Results based on students' self-reports.
*StatLink* http://dx.doi.org/10.1787/142102278412

Pour consulter la version française intégrale de ce tableau, suivre ce lien :
*StatLink* http://dx.doi.org/10.1787/152630454851

[Part 2/2]

**Table 3.3**   Index of self-efficacy in science and performance on the science scale, by quarters of the index[1]

*Tableau 3.3*   *Indice de perception des capacités personnelles en sciences et scores sur l'échelle de culture scientifique, par quartile de l'indice*

| | Performance on the science scale, by quarters of this index | | | | | | | Change in the science score per unit of this index | | Increased likelihood of students in the bottom quarter of this index scoring in the bottom quarter of the science performance distribution | | Explained variance in student performance (r-squared x 100) | |
| | Bottom quarter | | Second quarter | | Third quarter | | Top quarter | | | | | | | |
| | Mean score | S.E. | Mean score | S.E. | Mean score | S.E. | Mean score | S.E | Effect | S.E. | Ratio | S.E. | Percentage | S.E. |
|---|---|---|---|---|---|---|---|---|---|---|---|---|---|---|
| **Australia** | **464** | (2.1) | 511 | (2.5) | 540 | (2.5) | **595** | (2.9) | **44.3** | (0.94) | **2.7** | (0.10) | 23.6 | (0.96) |
| Austria | 458 | (4.8) | 493 | (4.6) | 530 | (3.7) | 569 | (4.6) | 44.3 | (2.03) | 2.4 | (0.14) | 19.4 | (1.56) |
| **Belgium** | **462** | (3.7) | 507 | (2.6) | 525 | (3.3) | **568** | (2.9) | **39.2** | (1.25) | **2.3** | (0.11) | 16.2 | (1.03) |
| Canada | 481 | (2.8) | 523 | (2.7) | 551 | (2.5) | 589 | (3.0) | 39.0 | (1.11) | 2.5 | (0.12) | 19.6 | (1.07) |
| **Czech Republic** | **474** | (4.0) | 507 | (4.7) | 533 | (3.7) | **560** | (4.0) | **36.6** | (1.82) | **2.0** | (0.12) | 12.1 | (1.01) |
| Denmark | 444 | (3.4) | 479 | (3.6) | 508 | (3.8) | 557 | (3.6) | 41.4 | (1.48) | 2.4 | (0.15) | 20.8 | (1.36) |
| **Finland** | **514** | (2.5) | 547 | (2.6) | 579 | (3.0) | **613** | (3.2) | **41.0** | (1.61) | **2.5** | (0.14) | 19.6 | (1.46) |
| France | 443 | (4.3) | 482 | (3.9) | 512 | (4.6) | 550 | (4.6) | 44.6 | (1.85) | 2.2 | (0.14) | 17.3 | (1.37) |
| **Germany** | **466** | (5.5) | 511 | (3.8) | 536 | (3.7) | **579** | (3.8) | **44.1** | (1.87) | **2.4** | (0.15) | 20.2 | (1.49) |
| Greece | 438 | (3.3) | 461 | (4.2) | 482 | (4.2) | 515 | (4.0) | 30.3 | (1.68) | 1.7 | (0.11) | 9.7 | (1.04) |
| **Hungary** | **469** | (3.7) | 497 | (3.8) | 510 | (3.5) | **541** | (3.6) | **32.1** | (2.34) | **1.9** | (0.12) | 9.7 | (1.34) |
| Iceland | 434 | (3.0) | 478 | (3.0) | 505 | (3.0) | 551 | (3.5) | 38.0 | (1.50) | 2.5 | (0.15) | 21.1 | (1.47) |
| **Ireland** | **455** | (3.8) | 493 | (3.2) | 526 | (3.6) | **565** | (4.1) | **40.3** | (1.26) | **2.4** | (0.16) | 19.9 | (1.15) |
| Italy | 439 | (2.3) | 469 | (3.0) | 490 | (2.6) | 505 | (3.1) | 34.6 | (1.71) | 1.8 | (0.08) | 8.0 | (0.78) |
| Japan | 483 | (4.7) | 530 | (3.8) | 550 | (3.4) | 564 | (3.7) | 32.8 | (1.72) | 2.2 | (0.12) | 10.5 | (0.98) |
| Korea | 477 | (4.6) | 513 | (3.8) | 536 | (3.2) | 563 | (5.0) | 38.0 | (2.11) | 2.2 | (0.13) | 14.2 | (1.38) |
| **Luxembourg** | **442** | (2.7) | 477 | (2.6) | 496 | (3.1) | **533** | (2.6) | **31.8** | (1.41) | **2.0** | (0.10) | 11.9 | (0.97) |
| Mexico | 386 | (3.2) | 406 | (2.8) | 413 | (3.1) | 436 | (3.9) | 21.0 | (1.62) | 1.5 | (0.10) | 5.2 | (0.76) |
| **Netherlands** | **487** | (3.6) | 523 | (4.1) | 540 | (3.5) | **568** | (4.8) | **31.4** | (1.66) | **2.0** | (0.14) | 11.2 | (1.22) |
| New Zealand | 464 | (3.4) | 503 | (3.9) | 549 | (3.9) | 612 | (3.1) | 53.2 | (1.47) | 2.5 | (0.14) | 27.3 | (1.26) |
| **Norway** | **440** | (3.5) | 482 | (3.6) | 496 | (4.0) | **541** | (3.5) | **32.9** | (1.55) | **2.3** | (0.17) | 14.1 | (1.09) |
| Poland | 445 | (2.7) | 483 | (3.1) | 512 | (3.2) | 553 | (2.9) | 42.7 | (1.59) | 2.5 | (0.13) | 19.5 | (1.17) |
| **Portugal** | **434** | (3.6) | 469 | (3.4) | 477 | (4.3) | **517** | (3.9) | **31.7** | (1.87) | **1.9** | (0.11) | 10.9 | (1.16) |
| Slovak Republic | 452 | (3.4) | 480 | (3.9) | 501 | (3.6) | 529 | (3.9) | 33.5 | (2.17) | 1.9 | (0.10) | 9.8 | (1.27) |
| **Spain** | **441** | (3.0) | 479 | (2.7) | 499 | (2.8) | **536** | (2.9) | **34.6** | (1.31) | **2.2** | (0.12) | 16.4 | (0.99) |
| Sweden | 452 | (3.1) | 492 | (3.0) | 515 | (3.5) | 561 | (3.2) | 37.8 | (1.57) | 2.4 | (0.14) | 17.4 | (1.30) |
| **Switzerland** | **457** | (3.5) | 498 | (3.1) | 525 | (3.6) | **567** | (4.2) | **43.2** | (1.79) | **2.4** | (0.11) | 17.3 | (1.37) |
| Turkey | 387 | (2.7) | 415 | (3.3) | 430 | (4.5) | 467 | (6.7) | 28.6 | (2.39) | 2.0 | (0.12) | 12.5 | (1.38) |
| **United Kingdom** | **443** | (3.1) | 497 | (2.4) | 532 | (3.2) | **592** | (2.7) | **52.6** | (1.23) | **2.8** | (0.14) | 26.8 | (1.07) |
| United States | 436 | (3.2) | 477 | (4.1) | 499 | (5.8) | 547 | (6.6) | 36.0 | (1.89) | 1.9 | (0.17) | 15.0 | (1.78) |
| **OECD total** | **449** | (1.1) | 482 | (1.1) | 498 | (1.9) | **540** | (2.1) | **33.1** | (0.74) | **1.8** | (0.05) | 11.0 | (0.53) |
| **OECD average** | **452** | (0.6) | 489 | (0.6) | 513 | (0.7) | **551** | (0.7) | **37.7** | (0.31) | **2.2** | (0.02) | 15.9 | (0.22) |
| **Argentina** | **364** | (7.4) | 386 | (6.1) | 399 | (7.1) | **428** | (6.6) | **26.2** | (2.56) | **1.6** | (0.14) | 5.8 | (1.18) |
| Azerbaijan | 370 | (3.2) | 382 | (3.7) | 387 | (3.3) | 394 | (3.3) | 7.4 | (1.30) | 1.4 | (0.11) | 2.3 | (0.84) |
| **Brazil** | **358** | (2.9) | 379 | (3.4) | 400 | (3.5) | **427** | (4.6) | **27.3** | (1.84) | **1.6** | (0.11) | 8.4 | (0.92) |
| Bulgaria | 383 | (5.4) | 429 | (5.4) | 451 | (6.4) | 485 | (7.9) | 31.6 | (2.65) | 2.1 | (0.17) | 9.8 | (1.22) |
| **Chile** | **404** | (3.9) | 429 | (4.6) | 443 | (4.9) | **477** | (6.4) | **29.5** | (2.23) | **1.7** | (0.13) | 9.2 | (1.19) |
| Colombia | 361 | (4.0) | 387 | (4.2) | 390 | (4.4) | 416 | (4.4) | 21.7 | (1.94) | 1.6 | (0.16) | 5.3 | (0.90) |
| **Croatia** | **448** | (2.6) | 482 | (2.8) | 502 | (3.1) | **542** | (3.4) | **40.2** | (1.45) | **2.2** | (0.12) | 17.8 | (1.12) |
| Estonia | 486 | (2.9) | 518 | (3.0) | 544 | (3.3) | 578 | (4.0) | 41.9 | (1.88) | 2.4 | (0.16) | 18.2 | (1.52) |
| **Hong Kong-China** | **498** | (3.3) | 534 | (2.7) | 549 | (4.1) | **588** | (3.4) | **35.7** | (1.55) | **2.1** | (0.12) | 13.8 | (1.14) |
| Indonesia | 376 | (5.0) | 392 | (6.2) | 401 | (7.0) | 404 | (5.7) | 12.5 | (2.41) | 1.4 | (0.11) | 2.0 | (0.83) |
| **Israel** | **431** | (4.8) | 451 | (5.4) | 468 | (4.8) | **489** | (5.2) | **19.4** | (2.17) | **1.4** | (0.12) | 4.1 | (0.92) |
| Jordan | 396 | (3.1) | 419 | (3.4) | 432 | (3.5) | 447 | (4.4) | 17.5 | (1.67) | 1.5 | (0.09) | 4.0 | (0.71) |
| **Kyrgyzstan** | **317** | (4.7) | 325 | (3.4) | 322 | (3.3) | **330** | (4.1) | **4.9** | (1.89) | **1.1** | (0.08) | 0.4 | (0.27) |
| Latvia | 456 | (4.1) | 482 | (3.6) | 494 | (4.3) | 528 | (4.3) | 34.6 | (2.16) | 1.8 | (0.15) | 11.4 | (1.41) |
| **Liechtenstein** | **472** | (9.6) | 502 | (9.2) | 538 | (11.2) | **577** | (9.4) | **33.8** | (5.84) | **2.2** | (0.42) | 13.4 | (3.47) |
| Lithuania | 447 | (3.8) | 479 | (3.8) | 498 | (3.7) | 528 | (4.0) | 38.3 | (1.89) | 2.0 | (0.13) | 11.9 | (1.02) |
| **Macao-China** | **479** | (2.8) | 502 | (2.5) | 520 | (2.5) | **542** | (2.6) | **26.8** | (1.32) | **1.9** | (0.12) | 10.1 | (1.02) |
| Montenegro | 373 | (2.0) | 402 | (2.6) | 426 | (2.6) | 451 | (2.7) | 28.3 | (1.24) | 2.2 | (0.14) | 13.5 | (1.10) |
| **Qatar** | **331** | (2.1) | 344 | (2.2) | 356 | (2.3) | **376** | (2.3) | **11.5** | (0.94) | **1.3** | (0.09) | 3.1 | (0.50) |
| Romania | 384 | (4.9) | 422 | (4.8) | 425 | (5.1) | 444 | (5.5) | 21.2 | (2.00) | 1.8 | (0.15) | 7.1 | (1.24) |
| **Russian Federation** | **440** | (4.0) | 473 | (3.6) | 492 | (4.7) | **513** | (5.7) | **29.4** | (1.87) | **2.0** | (0.15) | 10.5 | (1.43) |
| Serbia | 396 | (3.4) | 431 | (3.2) | 447 | (3.5) | 471 | (4.1) | 26.8 | (1.71) | 2.0 | (0.13) | 9.7 | (1.17) |
| **Slovenia** | **471** | (2.7) | 508 | (2.9) | 534 | (3.1) | **571** | (3.2) | **39.6** | (2.33) | **2.1** | (0.11) | 13.9 | (1.46) |
| Chinese Taipei | 483 | (3.9) | 528 | (4.1) | 544 | (3.8) | 576 | (3.6) | 35.0 | (1.45) | 2.4 | (0.13) | 14.1 | (1.02) |
| **Thailand** | **404** | (2.8) | 420 | (3.2) | 419 | (3.4) | **441** | (3.2) | **18.0** | (2.00) | **1.3** | (0.11) | 3.0 | (0.62) |
| Tunisia | 366 | (2.6) | 380 | (4.1) | 388 | (3.9) | 410 | (5.2) | 19.3 | (2.29) | 1.4 | (0.10) | 3.7 | (0.76) |
| **Uruguay** | **398** | (3.5) | 419 | (3.5) | 437 | (4.5) | **465** | (3.7) | **29.3** | (1.80) | **1.7** | (0.10) | 8.5 | (1.06) |

*OECD* / *Partners*

Note: Values that are statistically significant are indicated in bold (see Annex A3).
1. Results based on students' self-reports.
*StatLink* http://dx.doi.org/10.1787/142102278412

Pour consulter la version française intégrale de ce tableau, suivre ce lien :
*StatLink* http://dx.doi.org/10.1787/152630454851

[Part 1/2]

**Table 3.4   Index of self-concept in science and performance on the science scale, by quarters of the index[1]**

Tableau 3.4   Indice de perception de soi en sciences et scores sur l'échelle de culture scientifique, par quartile de l'indice

| | Index of self-concept in science | | | | | | | | | | | | | | |
| | All students | | Males | | Females | | Gender difference (M - F) | | Bottom quarter | | Second quarter | | Third quarter | | Top quarter | |
| | Mean index | S.E. | Mean index | S.E. | Mean index | S.E. | Dif. | S.E. | Mean index | S.E. | Mean index | S.E. | Mean index | S.E. | Mean index | S.E. |
|---|---|---|---|---|---|---|---|---|---|---|---|---|---|---|---|---|
| **OECD** | | | | | | | | | | | | | | | | |
| Australia | -0.03 | (0.01) | 0.07 | (0.02) | -0.14 | (0.02) | **0.22** | (0.03) | -1.29 | (0.01) | -0.31 | (0.00) | 0.30 | (0.00) | 1.17 | (0.01) |
| Austria | 0.09 | (0.02) | 0.20 | (0.03) | -0.03 | (0.04) | **0.23** | (0.04) | -1.30 | (0.02) | -0.26 | (0.01) | 0.40 | (0.01) | 1.51 | (0.01) |
| Belgium | -0.14 | (0.02) | -0.01 | (0.03) | -0.27 | (0.02) | **0.26** | (0.03) | -1.39 | (0.02) | -0.37 | (0.01) | 0.14 | (0.00) | 1.06 | (0.01) |
| Canada | 0.27 | (0.02) | 0.42 | (0.02) | 0.12 | (0.02) | **0.30** | (0.03) | -1.15 | (0.02) | -0.05 | (0.01) | 0.59 | (0.00) | 1.68 | (0.01) |
| Czech Republic | -0.03 | (0.02) | 0.01 | (0.03) | -0.09 | (0.02) | **0.10** | (0.04) | -1.02 | (0.02) | -0.28 | (0.00) | 0.18 | (0.00) | 0.98 | (0.02) |
| Denmark | -0.08 | (0.02) | 0.13 | (0.03) | -0.29 | (0.03) | **0.41** | (0.03) | -1.33 | (0.02) | -0.36 | (0.01) | 0.23 | (0.01) | 1.13 | (0.02) |
| Finland | 0.06 | (0.02) | 0.17 | (0.02) | -0.04 | (0.02) | **0.20** | (0.03) | -0.96 | (0.02) | -0.22 | (0.01) | 0.37 | (0.01) | 1.07 | (0.02) |
| France | -0.11 | (0.02) | 0.10 | (0.02) | -0.30 | (0.02) | **0.40** | (0.02) | -1.36 | (0.02) | -0.39 | (0.01) | 0.15 | (0.01) | 1.17 | (0.01) |
| Germany | 0.26 | (0.02) | 0.44 | (0.03) | 0.07 | (0.02) | **0.37** | (0.03) | -0.95 | (0.02) | -0.12 | (0.00) | 0.53 | (0.01) | 1.57 | (0.01) |
| Greece | 0.04 | (0.02) | 0.21 | (0.02) | -0.14 | (0.02) | **0.35** | (0.03) | -1.19 | (0.02) | -0.28 | (0.00) | 0.31 | (0.01) | 1.30 | (0.02) |
| Hungary | -0.21 | (0.02) | -0.09 | (0.02) | -0.35 | (0.02) | **0.26** | (0.03) | -1.28 | (0.02) | -0.51 | (0.01) | 0.01 | (0.01) | 0.93 | (0.02) |
| Iceland | 0.10 | (0.02) | 0.32 | (0.02) | -0.11 | (0.03) | **0.43** | (0.04) | -1.32 | (0.02) | -0.20 | (0.01) | 0.49 | (0.01) | 1.45 | (0.02) |
| Ireland | -0.13 | (0.02) | -0.09 | (0.03) | -0.16 | (0.03) | **0.07** | (0.03) | -1.42 | (0.02) | -0.42 | (0.01) | 0.15 | (0.01) | 1.20 | (0.02) |
| Italy | 0.16 | (0.01) | 0.28 | (0.02) | 0.03 | (0.02) | **0.25** | (0.03) | -0.90 | (0.01) | -0.14 | (0.00) | 0.43 | (0.00) | 1.26 | (0.01) |
| Japan | -0.87 | (0.02) | -0.64 | (0.03) | -1.11 | (0.02) | **0.47** | (0.03) | -2.13 | (0.01) | -1.10 | (0.01) | -0.61 | (0.00) | 0.36 | (0.02) |
| Korea | -0.71 | (0.02) | -0.58 | (0.03) | -0.85 | (0.02) | **0.28** | (0.03) | -1.93 | (0.01) | -0.92 | (0.00) | -0.47 | (0.01) | 0.48 | (0.02) |
| Luxembourg | 0.24 | (0.02) | 0.33 | (0.02) | 0.14 | (0.02) | **0.19** | (0.03) | -1.10 | (0.02) | -0.10 | (0.01) | 0.57 | (0.01) | 1.59 | (0.01) |
| Mexico | 0.53 | (0.01) | 0.54 | (0.02) | 0.52 | (0.01) | 0.02 | (0.02) | -0.45 | (0.01) | 0.30 | (0.00) | 0.74 | (0.00) | 1.54 | (0.01) |
| Netherlands | -0.33 | (0.02) | -0.14 | (0.02) | -0.54 | (0.01) | **0.40** | (0.03) | -1.51 | (0.02) | -0.58 | (0.01) | -0.03 | (0.01) | 0.80 | (0.02) |
| New Zealand | -0.06 | (0.02) | 0.06 | (0.02) | -0.17 | (0.03) | **0.22** | (0.04) | -1.25 | (0.02) | -0.33 | (0.01) | 0.25 | (0.01) | 1.09 | (0.02) |
| Norway | 0.05 | (0.02) | 0.27 | (0.02) | -0.17 | (0.02) | **0.44** | (0.03) | -1.18 | (0.02) | -0.27 | (0.01) | 0.36 | (0.01) | 1.29 | (0.02) |
| Poland | 0.08 | (0.02) | 0.13 | (0.02) | 0.04 | (0.02) | **0.09** | (0.03) | -0.90 | (0.02) | -0.21 | (0.01) | 0.34 | (0.01) | 1.11 | (0.01) |
| Portugal | 0.31 | (0.02) | 0.36 | (0.02) | 0.25 | (0.02) | **0.10** | (0.03) | -0.73 | (0.02) | 0.11 | (0.01) | 0.56 | (0.01) | 1.28 | (0.02) |
| Slovak Republic | 0.15 | (0.02) | 0.22 | (0.02) | 0.08 | (0.02) | **0.14** | (0.03) | -0.83 | (0.02) | -0.11 | (0.00) | 0.36 | (0.01) | 1.17 | (0.01) |
| Spain | -0.01 | (0.01) | 0.11 | (0.02) | -0.13 | (0.02) | **0.24** | (0.03) | -1.25 | (0.01) | -0.32 | (0.00) | 0.31 | (0.01) | 1.22 | (0.01) |
| Sweden | 0.01 | (0.02) | 0.17 | (0.03) | -0.15 | (0.02) | **0.32** | (0.03) | -1.27 | (0.02) | -0.32 | (0.01) | 0.35 | (0.01) | 1.29 | (0.02) |
| Switzerland | 0.10 | (0.01) | 0.26 | (0.02) | -0.07 | (0.02) | **0.34** | (0.02) | -1.11 | (0.01) | -0.22 | (0.01) | 0.40 | (0.01) | 1.32 | (0.01) |
| Turkey | 0.15 | (0.03) | 0.19 | (0.04) | 0.11 | (0.03) | 0.07 | (0.04) | -1.15 | (0.02) | -0.12 | (0.01) | 0.54 | (0.00) | 1.34 | (0.02) |
| United Kingdom | 0.02 | (0.01) | 0.20 | (0.02) | -0.15 | (0.02) | **0.35** | (0.02) | -1.07 | (0.01) | -0.24 | (0.01) | 0.27 | (0.01) | 1.12 | (0.01) |
| United States | 0.20 | (0.02) | 0.36 | (0.03) | 0.05 | (0.03) | **0.31** | (0.03) | -1.10 | (0.02) | -0.13 | (0.00) | 0.54 | (0.00) | 1.51 | (0.02) |
| **OECD total** | **0.03** | **(0.01)** | **0.16** | **(0.01)** | **-0.11** | **(0.01)** | **0.27** | **(0.01)** | **-1.29** | **(0.01)** | **-0.29** | **(0.00)** | **0.37** | **(0.00)** | **1.31** | **(0.01)** |
| **OECD average** | **0.00** | **(0.00)** | **0.13** | **(0.00)** | **-0.13** | **(0.00)** | **0.26** | **(0.01)** | **-1.19** | **(0.00)** | **-0.28** | **(0.00)** | **0.29** | **(0.00)** | **1.20** | **(0.00)** |
| **Partners** | | | | | | | | | | | | | | | | |
| Argentina | 0.26 | (0.03) | 0.31 | (0.03) | 0.22 | (0.03) | **0.09** | (0.03) | -0.84 | (0.03) | -0.04 | (0.01) | 0.55 | (0.01) | 1.40 | (0.02) |
| Azerbaijan | 0.65 | (0.03) | 0.64 | (0.04) | 0.65 | (0.03) | -0.01 | (0.03) | -0.55 | (0.02) | 0.45 | (0.01) | 0.92 | (0.01) | 1.76 | (0.02) |
| Brazil | 0.36 | (0.02) | 0.43 | (0.02) | 0.31 | (0.02) | **0.12** | (0.03) | -0.63 | (0.01) | 0.04 | (0.00) | 0.58 | (0.00) | 1.47 | (0.01) |
| Bulgaria | 0.37 | (0.02) | 0.41 | (0.02) | 0.32 | (0.02) | **0.10** | (0.02) | -0.69 | (0.02) | 0.08 | (0.01) | 0.62 | (0.00) | 1.45 | (0.01) |
| Chile | 0.18 | (0.02) | 0.28 | (0.02) | 0.08 | (0.02) | **0.20** | (0.03) | -0.91 | (0.02) | -0.15 | (0.00) | 0.44 | (0.01) | 1.35 | (0.02) |
| Colombia | 0.75 | (0.02) | 0.77 | (0.03) | 0.73 | (0.02) | 0.04 | (0.03) | -0.21 | (0.01) | 0.54 | (0.01) | 0.94 | (0.01) | 1.73 | (0.01) |
| Croatia | -0.03 | (0.02) | 0.03 | (0.02) | -0.08 | (0.02) | **0.11** | (0.03) | -1.09 | (0.02) | -0.28 | (0.00) | 0.20 | (0.01) | 1.07 | (0.01) |
| Estonia | 0.11 | (0.02) | 0.17 | (0.02) | 0.05 | (0.02) | **0.12** | (0.03) | -0.85 | (0.01) | -0.14 | (0.00) | 0.29 | (0.01) | 1.15 | (0.02) |
| Hong Kong-China | -0.25 | (0.02) | -0.03 | (0.02) | -0.47 | (0.03) | **0.44** | (0.04) | -1.41 | (0.02) | -0.58 | (0.01) | 0.03 | (0.01) | 0.95 | (0.02) |
| Indonesia | 0.16 | (0.03) | 0.20 | (0.05) | 0.13 | (0.03) | 0.07 | (0.04) | -0.73 | (0.01) | -0.14 | (0.00) | 0.39 | (0.01) | 1.13 | (0.01) |
| Israel | 0.27 | (0.02) | 0.35 | (0.04) | 0.19 | (0.03) | **0.15** | (0.05) | -1.20 | (0.03) | -0.04 | (0.01) | 0.65 | (0.01) | 1.68 | (0.02) |
| Jordan | 0.74 | (0.02) | 0.77 | (0.02) | 0.72 | (0.03) | 0.05 | (0.03) | -0.37 | (0.02) | 0.52 | (0.01) | 1.07 | (0.01) | 1.75 | (0.01) |
| Kyrgyzstan | 0.69 | (0.02) | 0.72 | (0.02) | 0.67 | (0.02) | **0.05** | (0.02) | -0.30 | (0.01) | 0.45 | (0.01) | 0.94 | (0.01) | 1.68 | (0.01) |
| Latvia | 0.03 | (0.02) | 0.11 | (0.02) | -0.05 | (0.02) | **0.16** | (0.02) | -0.78 | (0.01) | -0.21 | (0.00) | 0.17 | (0.00) | 0.94 | (0.02) |
| Liechtenstein | 0.09 | (0.05) | 0.30 | (0.09) | -0.10 | (0.07) | **0.39** | (0.12) | -1.23 | (0.07) | -0.25 | (0.02) | 0.37 | (0.03) | 1.47 | (0.06) |
| Lithuania | -0.24 | (0.02) | -0.15 | (0.02) | -0.33 | (0.02) | **0.18** | (0.02) | -1.13 | (0.01) | -0.50 | (0.01) | -0.12 | (0.00) | 0.79 | (0.02) |
| Macao-China | -0.11 | (0.02) | 0.10 | (0.02) | -0.36 | (0.03) | **0.45** | (0.04) | -1.20 | (0.02) | -0.45 | (0.00) | 0.15 | (0.00) | 1.05 | (0.03) |
| Montenegro | 0.49 | (0.01) | 0.51 | (0.02) | 0.47 | (0.02) | 0.04 | (0.03) | -0.60 | (0.02) | 0.21 | (0.01) | 0.74 | (0.00) | 1.62 | (0.01) |
| Qatar | 0.59 | (0.01) | 0.66 | (0.02) | 0.52 | (0.02) | **0.14** | (0.03) | -0.76 | (0.02) | 0.33 | (0.01) | 0.93 | (0.01) | 1.84 | (0.01) |
| Romania | 0.34 | (0.02) | 0.38 | (0.03) | 0.31 | (0.02) | **0.07** | (0.03) | -0.63 | (0.02) | 0.05 | (0.01) | 0.58 | (0.01) | 1.37 | (0.02) |
| Russian Federation | 0.16 | (0.02) | 0.20 | (0.02) | 0.13 | (0.02) | **0.07** | (0.02) | -0.70 | (0.02) | -0.12 | (0.00) | 0.36 | (0.00) | 1.11 | (0.02) |
| Serbia | 0.24 | (0.02) | 0.28 | (0.03) | 0.20 | (0.02) | **0.07** | (0.03) | -0.93 | (0.02) | -0.04 | (0.01) | 0.54 | (0.00) | 1.40 | (0.01) |
| Chinese Taipei | -0.40 | (0.02) | -0.17 | (0.02) | -0.66 | (0.02) | **0.50** | (0.02) | -1.57 | (0.02) | -0.73 | (0.00) | -0.17 | (0.00) | 0.86 | (0.01) |
| Slovenia | 0.22 | (0.01) | 0.33 | (0.02) | 0.12 | (0.02) | **0.22** | (0.03) | -0.82 | (0.02) | -0.09 | (0.00) | 0.48 | (0.01) | 1.32 | (0.02) |
| Thailand | 0.69 | (0.01) | 0.73 | (0.02) | 0.66 | (0.02) | **0.07** | (0.02) | -0.28 | (0.01) | 0.57 | (0.00) | 0.83 | (0.01) | 1.64 | (0.02) |
| Tunisia | 0.64 | (0.02) | 0.71 | (0.02) | 0.57 | (0.03) | **0.13** | (0.03) | -0.46 | (0.02) | 0.34 | (0.01) | 0.97 | (0.01) | 1.70 | (0.01) |
| Uruguay | 0.35 | (0.02) | 0.34 | (0.02) | 0.36 | (0.02) | -0.03 | (0.03) | -0.75 | (0.02) | 0.09 | (0.00) | 0.61 | (0.00) | 1.46 | (0.02) |

Note: Values that are statistically significant are indicated in bold (see Annex A3).
1. Results based on students' self-reports.
*StatLink* ꞏꞏꞏꞏ http://dx.doi.org/10.1787/142102278412

Pour consulter la version française intégrale de ce tableau, suivre ce lien :
*StatLink* ꞏꞏꞏꞏ http://dx.doi.org/10.1787/152630454851

[Part 2/2]

**Table 3.4  Index of self-concept in science and performance on the science scale, by quarters of the index[1]**

Tableau 3.4  Indice de perception de soi en sciences et scores sur l'échelle de culture scientifique, par quartile de l'indice

| | | Performance on the science scale, by quarters of this index | | | | | | | Change in the science score per unit of this index | | Increased likelihood of students in the bottom quarter of this index scoring in the bottom quarter of the science performance distribution | | Explained variance in student performance (r-squared x 100) | |
| | | Bottom quarter | | Second quarter | | Third quarter | | Top quarter | | | | | | | |
| | | Mean score | S.E. | Mean score | S.E. | Mean score | S.E. | Mean score | S.E | Effect | S.E. | Ratio | S.E. | Percentage | S.E. |
|---|---|---|---|---|---|---|---|---|---|---|---|---|---|---|---|
| OECD | Australia | **478** | (2.5) | 519 | (2.5) | 552 | (2.8) | **589** | (3.6) | **42.9** | (1.27) | **2.4** | (0.10) | 18.4 | (1.05) |
| | Austria | **479** | (4.6) | 508 | (5.6) | 530 | (5.4) | **544** | (5.6) | **23.4** | (1.68) | **1.6** | (0.12) | 6.7 | (1.06) |
| | Belgium | **490** | (3.9) | 520 | (3.2) | 536 | (3.5) | **550** | (3.9) | **25.7** | (1.94) | **1.6** | (0.09) | 6.7 | (0.95) |
| | Canada | **494** | (3.0) | 519 | (2.9) | 554 | (2.9) | **592** | (2.9) | **34.3** | (1.04) | **2.1** | (0.10) | 16.0 | (0.88) |
| | Czech Republic | **502** | (5.0) | 519 | (4.5) | 527 | (4.0) | **527** | (5.0) | **11.9** | (2.28) | **1.3** | (0.10) | 1.0 | (0.41) |
| | Denmark | **456** | (3.6) | 483 | (3.5) | 511 | (4.1) | **545** | (4.1) | **32.8** | (1.45) | **1.9** | (0.11) | 12.5 | (1.07) |
| | Finland | **524** | (2.8) | 548 | (3.1) | 577 | (3.0) | **608** | (3.2) | **41.3** | (1.58) | **2.0** | (0.12) | 16.7 | (1.29) |
| | France | **469** | (3.9) | 482 | (3.8) | 509 | (4.4) | **539** | (5.0) | **27.8** | (1.65) | **1.4** | (0.09) | 7.8 | (0.98) |
| | Germany | **494** | (4.1) | 513 | (4.3) | 531 | (4.9) | **556** | (5.2) | **24.9** | (1.54) | **1.5** | (0.11) | 6.6 | (0.86) |
| | Greece | **459** | (3.3) | 464 | (3.8) | 481 | (4.5) | **494** | (4.7) | **15.6** | (1.55) | **1.2** | (0.09) | 2.9 | (0.58) |
| | Hungary | **495** | (3.8) | 500 | (3.1) | 506 | (3.5) | **520** | (5.1) | **10.3** | (2.70) | **1.1** | (0.09) | 1.1 | (0.57) |
| | Iceland | **437** | (3.3) | 476 | (3.4) | 516 | (3.3) | **551** | (3.4) | **40.3** | (1.58) | **2.6** | (0.18) | 21.5 | (1.52) |
| | Ireland | **471** | (3.7) | 500 | (4.5) | 525 | (4.3) | **566** | (4.3) | **35.0** | (1.59) | **2.0** | (0.14) | 15.4 | (1.31) |
| | Italy | **462** | (2.4) | 467 | (2.9) | 479 | (2.8) | **490** | (3.8) | **14.7** | (1.66) | **1.1** | (0.05) | 1.9 | (0.43) |
| | Japan | **492** | (4.3) | 533 | (3.8) | 545 | (4.0) | **559** | (3.9) | **25.2** | (1.73) | **1.9** | (0.11) | 6.2 | (0.85) |
| | Korea | **487** | (3.8) | 504 | (4.1) | 529 | (3.9) | **569** | (4.9) | **33.6** | (1.75) | **1.8** | (0.10) | 12.6 | (1.25) |
| | Luxembourg | **457** | (2.4) | 481 | (3.1) | 495 | (2.9) | **521** | (3.2) | **23.4** | (1.26) | **1.6** | (0.10) | 6.7 | (0.73) |
| | Mexico | **406** | (2.7) | 413 | (3.4) | 415 | (3.5) | **415** | (4.3) | **6.1** | (1.66) | 1.1 | (0.06) | 0.4 | (0.20) |
| | Netherlands | **502** | (3.5) | 518 | (3.7) | 538 | (4.0) | **561** | (6.2) | **25.2** | (2.51) | **1.5** | (0.11) | 6.2 | (1.29) |
| | New Zealand | **492** | (3.1) | 517 | (3.8) | 548 | (3.9) | **593** | (4.6) | **41.2** | (1.98) | **1.8** | (0.11) | 13.6 | (1.28) |
| | Norway | **448** | (3.4) | 475 | (3.6) | 505 | (3.7) | **535** | (3.5) | **34.3** | (1.51) | **1.9** | (0.11) | 13.5 | (1.07) |
| | Poland | **477** | (3.1) | 489 | (3.5) | 506 | (3.8) | **522** | (3.5) | **22.2** | (1.72) | **1.3** | (0.10) | 4.2 | (0.62) |
| | Portugal | **442** | (3.9) | 471 | (3.7) | 478 | (4.1) | **496** | (5.4) | **25.7** | (2.22) | **1.5** | (0.11) | 5.5 | (1.03) |
| | Slovak Republic | **473** | (3.7) | 485 | (4.4) | 493 | (4.4) | **510** | (4.4) | **18.3** | (2.14) | **1.3** | (0.10) | 2.7 | (0.60) |
| | Spain | **458** | (2.4) | 475 | (3.1) | 504 | (3.2) | **524** | (3.4) | **27.6** | (1.21) | **1.6** | (0.09) | 9.4 | (0.72) |
| | Sweden | **458** | (3.3) | 491 | (3.1) | 520 | (3.3) | **559** | (4.0) | **38.2** | (1.49) | **2.3** | (0.13) | 18.2 | (1.29) |
| | Switzerland | **478** | (4.1) | 506 | (3.4) | 528 | (4.0) | **552** | (4.6) | **30.8** | (1.59) | **1.8** | (0.10) | 9.0 | (0.97) |
| | Turkey | **410** | (3.7) | 427 | (4.4) | 432 | (4.8) | **437** | (6.2) | **11.0** | (1.99) | 1.2 | (0.10) | 1.8 | (0.58) |
| | United Kingdom | **475** | (3.1) | 502 | (3.0) | 529 | (3.6) | **563** | (3.9) | **38.9** | (1.69) | **1.6** | (0.09) | 10.9 | (0.92) |
| | United States | **455** | (2.9) | 475 | (4.6) | 504 | (5.5) | **528** | (6.9) | **28.8** | (2.25) | **1.4** | (0.11) | 8.0 | (1.35) |
| | **OECD total** | **477** | (1.2) | 485 | (1.2) | 499 | (1.6) | **511** | (2.4) | **14.9** | (0.79) | **1.1** | (0.03) | 2.2 | (0.25) |
| | **OECD average** | **471** | (0.6) | 493 | (0.7) | 513 | (0.7) | **537** | (0.8) | **27.0** | (0.32) | **1.6** | (0.02) | 8.8 | (0.18) |
| Partners | Argentina | 396 | (7.5) | 404 | (5.8) | 408 | (7.2) | 397 | (7.3) | 4.0 | (3.09) | 1.1 | (0.10) | 0.1 | (0.22) |
| | Azerbaijan | 382 | (4.1) | 387 | (3.7) | 387 | (3.4) | 383 | (3.3) | 1.1 | (1.68) | 1.2 | (0.12) | 0.0 | (0.12) |
| | Brazil | 393 | (4.0) | 397 | (4.4) | 393 | (3.4) | 394 | (4.4) | 1.9 | (2.23) | 1.0 | (0.08) | 0.0 | (0.09) |
| | Bulgaria | 431 | (6.1) | 443 | (6.5) | 434 | (6.9) | 450 | (7.6) | 8.6 | (2.83) | 1.1 | (0.10) | 0.5 | (0.32) |
| | Chile | 419 | (3.9) | 433 | (4.5) | 453 | (5.6) | 461 | (6.4) | 19.3 | (2.05) | 1.4 | (0.10) | 3.6 | (0.73) |
| | Colombia | 385 | (4.1) | 397 | (4.9) | 392 | (5.4) | 391 | (5.1) | 3.2 | (2.99) | 1.0 | (0.09) | 0.1 | (0.17) |
| | Croatia | **480** | (3.2) | 496 | (3.6) | 511 | (3.9) | **508** | (4.3) | **13.9** | (2.06) | **1.3** | (0.11) | 2.0 | (0.58) |
| | Estonia | **503** | (3.0) | 523 | (3.4) | 542 | (3.9) | **559** | (4.1) | **27.9** | (1.89) | **1.5** | (0.12) | 7.3 | (0.97) |
| | Hong Kong-China | **525** | (3.5) | 550 | (4.0) | 569 | (4.6) | **578** | (4.3) | **22.1** | (1.82) | **1.5** | (0.14) | 5.6 | (0.93) |
| | Indonesia | **417** | (9.8) | 405 | (6.0) | 387 | (3.9) | **371** | (3.7) | **-24.4** | (3.84) | **0.6** | (0.07) | 6.9 | (1.79) |
| | Israel | **423** | (4.5) | 452 | (4.9) | 476 | (4.5) | **492** | (5.8) | **25.3** | (1.88) | **1.6** | (0.11) | 6.7 | (0.97) |
| | Jordan | **401** | (3.4) | 419 | (3.3) | 429 | (3.4) | **448** | (4.5) | **21.3** | (2.11) | **1.4** | (0.11) | 4.1 | (0.74) |
| | Kyrgyzstan | **357** | (4.3) | 334 | (3.7) | 315 | (3.8) | **307** | (3.7) | **-23.8** | (2.24) | **0.5** | (0.05) | 5.1 | (0.83) |
| | Latvia | **478** | (4.0) | 483 | (3.3) | 500 | (3.6) | **501** | (5.1) | **14.1** | (2.45) | 1.1 | (0.09) | 1.4 | (0.47) |
| | Liechtenstein | **506** | (11.1) | 507 | (10.1) | 528 | (11.4) | **553** | (10.8) | **19.6** | (4.99) | 1.3 | (0.32) | 4.7 | (2.40) |
| | Lithuania | **467** | (4.0) | 479 | (3.3) | 497 | (4.0) | **511** | (3.9) | **22.4** | (1.83) | **1.3** | (0.10) | 3.8 | (0.62) |
| | Macao-China | **491** | (3.0) | 503 | (3.5) | 519 | (3.7) | **520** | (3.6) | **13.6** | (1.84) | **1.3** | (0.12) | 2.3 | (0.62) |
| | Montenegro | 410 | (2.8) | 418 | (2.4) | 412 | (2.5) | 416 | (2.9) | 1.9 | (1.79) | 1.0 | (0.10) | 0.1 | (0.10) |
| | Qatar | **339** | (2.3) | 354 | (2.2) | 360 | (2.1) | **357** | (2.4) | **7.8** | (1.07) | **1.3** | (0.07) | 0.9 | (0.26) |
| | Romania | 416 | (5.4) | 422 | (4.8) | 418 | (5.4) | 419 | (6.1) | 1.9 | (2.78) | 0.9 | (0.11) | 0.0 | (0.12) |
| | Russian Federation | **467** | (3.3) | 475 | (4.2) | 491 | (4.2) | **490** | (6.4) | **13.8** | (2.70) | **1.2** | (0.09) | 1.3 | (0.53) |
| | Serbia | **427** | (3.4) | 440 | (3.3) | 435 | (4.0) | **443** | (4.8) | **6.5** | (1.69) | 1.1 | (0.08) | 0.5 | (0.28) |
| | Slovenia | **518** | (2.7) | 517 | (3.2) | 524 | (4.1) | **536** | (4.0) | **10.5** | (1.86) | 1.0 | (0.07) | 0.9 | (0.31) |
| | Chinese Taipei | **517** | (3.3) | 522 | (4.2) | 544 | (4.4) | **548** | (5.6) | **13.9** | (1.74) | **1.2** | (0.08) | 2.1 | (0.54) |
| | Thailand | **424** | (3.4) | 421 | (3.2) | 421 | (3.1) | **417** | (3.7) | **-4.1** | (2.13) | 0.9 | (0.07) | 0.2 | (0.16) |
| | Tunisia | **381** | (3.3) | 385 | (4.4) | 393 | (4.4) | **396** | (4.0) | **7.5** | (2.01) | 1.0 | (0.07) | 0.6 | (0.33) |
| | Uruguay | **417** | (3.7) | 436 | (4.6) | 441 | (4.6) | **441** | (4.9) | **12.7** | (2.39) | **1.2** | (0.10) | 1.5 | (0.56) |

Note: Values that are statistically significant are indicated in bold (see Annex A3).
1. Results based on students' self-reports.
StatLink ⇱ http://dx.doi.org/10.1787/142102278412

Pour consulter la version française intégrale de ce tableau, suivre ce lien :
StatLink ⇱ http://dx.doi.org/10.1787/152630454851

[Part 1/2]

**Table 3.5   Index of general value of science and performance on the science scale, by quarters of the index[1]**

Tableau 3.5   Indice de valorisation générale des sciences et scores sur l'échelle de culture scientifique, par quartile de l'indice

| | Index of general value of science | | | | | | | | | | | | | | | |
| | All students | | Males | | Females | | Gender difference (M - F) | | Bottom quarter | | Second quarter | | Third quarter | | Top quarter | |
| | Mean index | S.E. | Mean index | S.E. | Mean index | S.E. | Dif. | S.E. | Mean index | S.E. | Mean index | S.E. | Mean index | S.E. | Mean index | S.E. |
|---|---|---|---|---|---|---|---|---|---|---|---|---|---|---|---|---|
| **OECD** | | | | | | | | | | | | | | | | |
| Australia | -0.05 | (0.01) | 0.00 | (0.02) | -0.11 | (0.02) | **0.12** | (0.03) | -1.22 | (0.01) | -0.45 | (0.00) | 0.14 | (0.01) | 1.31 | (0.01) |
| Austria | -0.12 | (0.02) | -0.02 | (0.03) | -0.22 | (0.03) | **0.20** | (0.03) | -1.42 | (0.02) | -0.51 | (0.01) | 0.24 | (0.01) | 1.20 | (0.01) |
| Belgium | -0.16 | (0.02) | -0.10 | (0.03) | -0.23 | (0.02) | **0.14** | (0.03) | -1.23 | (0.02) | -0.49 | (0.00) | 0.05 | (0.01) | 1.01 | (0.01) |
| Canada | 0.14 | (0.01) | 0.21 | (0.02) | 0.07 | (0.01) | **0.14** | (0.02) | -1.06 | (0.01) | -0.28 | (0.00) | 0.40 | (0.01) | 1.51 | (0.01) |
| Czech Republic | -0.12 | (0.02) | -0.08 | (0.02) | -0.19 | (0.02) | **0.11** | (0.03) | -1.12 | (0.02) | -0.43 | (0.01) | 0.03 | (0.01) | 1.03 | (0.02) |
| Denmark | -0.27 | (0.01) | -0.22 | (0.02) | -0.32 | (0.02) | **0.11** | (0.03) | -1.22 | (0.01) | -0.58 | (0.01) | -0.14 | (0.01) | 0.86 | (0.02) |
| Finland | 0.07 | (0.02) | 0.09 | (0.02) | 0.04 | (0.02) | **0.06** | (0.03) | -0.90 | (0.02) | -0.34 | (0.00) | 0.24 | (0.01) | 1.26 | (0.02) |
| France | -0.17 | (0.02) | -0.13 | (0.03) | -0.21 | (0.02) | **0.09** | (0.03) | -1.28 | (0.02) | -0.53 | (0.01) | 0.09 | (0.01) | 1.04 | (0.02) |
| Germany | -0.10 | (0.02) | 0.02 | (0.03) | -0.22 | (0.03) | **0.25** | (0.04) | -1.41 | (0.02) | -0.46 | (0.01) | 0.26 | (0.01) | 1.23 | (0.02) |
| Greece | -0.04 | (0.02) | -0.01 | (0.03) | -0.07 | (0.02) | 0.06 | (0.02) | -1.14 | (0.02) | -0.38 | (0.01) | 0.24 | (0.01) | 1.12 | (0.02) |
| Hungary | -0.04 | (0.02) | 0.02 | (0.03) | -0.10 | (0.02) | **0.12** | (0.03) | -1.12 | (0.02) | -0.35 | (0.00) | 0.22 | (0.01) | 1.09 | (0.02) |
| Iceland | -0.19 | (0.02) | -0.12 | (0.02) | -0.27 | (0.02) | **0.15** | (0.03) | -1.40 | (0.02) | -0.58 | (0.01) | 0.01 | (0.01) | 1.19 | (0.02) |
| Ireland | 0.02 | (0.02) | 0.07 | (0.02) | -0.02 | (0.03) | **0.09** | (0.03) | -1.19 | (0.02) | -0.39 | (0.01) | 0.28 | (0.01) | 1.38 | (0.02) |
| Italy | -0.01 | (0.01) | 0.07 | (0.02) | -0.09 | (0.01) | **0.16** | (0.02) | -1.08 | (0.01) | -0.35 | (0.01) | 0.24 | (0.00) | 1.17 | (0.01) |
| Japan | -0.18 | (0.02) | -0.03 | (0.02) | -0.33 | (0.03) | **0.30** | (0.03) | -1.42 | (0.02) | -0.53 | (0.01) | -0.02 | (0.01) | 1.26 | (0.02) |
| Korea | 0.27 | (0.02) | 0.31 | (0.03) | 0.22 | (0.02) | **0.08** | (0.03) | -0.81 | (0.02) | -0.19 | (0.01) | 0.49 | (0.01) | 1.57 | (0.02) |
| Luxembourg | -0.02 | (0.02) | 0.04 | (0.03) | -0.09 | (0.02) | **0.13** | (0.04) | -1.41 | (0.02) | -0.39 | (0.01) | 0.31 | (0.01) | 1.40 | (0.02) |
| Mexico | 0.37 | (0.02) | 0.39 | (0.02) | 0.34 | (0.02) | **0.05** | (0.02) | -0.81 | (0.02) | 0.01 | (0.01) | 0.67 | (0.01) | 1.60 | (0.01) |
| Netherlands | -0.21 | (0.02) | -0.09 | (0.02) | -0.34 | (0.02) | **0.25** | (0.03) | -1.25 | (0.02) | -0.46 | (0.01) | -0.12 | (0.01) | 0.99 | (0.02) |
| New Zealand | -0.13 | (0.02) | -0.08 | (0.02) | -0.19 | (0.03) | **0.11** | (0.04) | -1.25 | (0.02) | -0.49 | (0.01) | 0.03 | (0.01) | 1.19 | (0.02) |
| Norway | -0.14 | (0.02) | -0.06 | (0.03) | -0.22 | (0.02) | **0.16** | (0.04) | -1.38 | (0.03) | -0.49 | (0.01) | 0.06 | (0.01) | 1.25 | (0.02) |
| Poland | 0.22 | (0.02) | 0.22 | (0.02) | 0.23 | (0.02) | -0.01 | (0.03) | -0.78 | (0.01) | -0.21 | (0.01) | 0.42 | (0.01) | 1.47 | (0.02) |
| Portugal | 0.37 | (0.01) | 0.42 | (0.02) | 0.32 | (0.02) | **0.10** | (0.02) | -0.67 | (0.01) | -0.04 | (0.01) | 0.63 | (0.01) | 1.56 | (0.02) |
| Slovak Republic | 0.03 | (0.02) | 0.09 | (0.03) | -0.04 | (0.03) | **0.13** | (0.04) | -0.96 | (0.01) | -0.34 | (0.00) | 0.22 | (0.01) | 1.19 | (0.02) |
| Spain | 0.29 | (0.01) | 0.36 | (0.02) | 0.22 | (0.02) | **0.14** | (0.02) | -0.90 | (0.01) | -0.11 | (0.01) | 0.61 | (0.00) | 1.57 | (0.01) |
| Sweden | -0.19 | (0.02) | -0.13 | (0.03) | -0.24 | (0.03) | **0.11** | (0.04) | -1.37 | (0.02) | -0.53 | (0.01) | 0.01 | (0.01) | 1.14 | (0.02) |
| Switzerland | -0.11 | (0.01) | -0.03 | (0.02) | -0.19 | (0.02) | **0.16** | (0.02) | -1.31 | (0.02) | -0.47 | (0.00) | 0.22 | (0.00) | 1.12 | (0.01) |
| Turkey | 0.46 | (0.03) | 0.37 | (0.04) | 0.57 | (0.02) | **-0.20** | (0.03) | -0.88 | (0.03) | 0.01 | (0.01) | 0.82 | (0.01) | 1.89 | (0.01) |
| United Kingdom | -0.16 | (0.01) | -0.03 | (0.02) | -0.28 | (0.02) | **0.26** | (0.03) | -1.26 | (0.01) | -0.54 | (0.01) | 0.00 | (0.01) | 1.17 | (0.01) |
| United States | 0.15 | (0.02) | 0.22 | (0.03) | 0.07 | (0.03) | **0.15** | (0.04) | -1.12 | (0.02) | -0.31 | (0.00) | 0.41 | (0.01) | 1.61 | (0.01) |
| **OECD total** | **0.08** | **(0.01)** | **0.15** | **(0.01)** | **0.01** | **(0.01)** | **0.13** | **(0.01)** | **-1.16** | **(0.01)** | **-0.32** | **(0.00)** | **0.34** | **(0.00)** | **1.46** | **(0.01)** |
| **OECD average** | **0.00** | **(0.00)** | **0.06** | **(0.00)** | **-0.06** | **(0.00)** | **0.12** | **(0.01)** | **-1.15** | **(0.00)** | **-0.37** | **(0.00)** | **0.24** | **(0.00)** | **1.28** | **(0.00)** |
| **Partners** | | | | | | | | | | | | | | | | |
| Argentina | 0.05 | (0.02) | 0.09 | (0.03) | 0.01 | (0.03) | **0.09** | (0.04) | -1.16 | (0.02) | -0.29 | (0.01) | 0.33 | (0.01) | 1.31 | (0.02) |
| Azerbaijan | 0.53 | (0.02) | 0.49 | (0.03) | 0.58 | (0.03) | -0.09 | (0.04) | -0.73 | (0.02) | 0.22 | (0.01) | 0.82 | (0.01) | 1.81 | (0.01) |
| Brazil | 0.26 | (0.02) | 0.30 | (0.02) | 0.22 | (0.02) | **0.08** | (0.03) | -0.89 | (0.01) | -0.13 | (0.01) | 0.53 | (0.01) | 1.52 | (0.02) |
| Bulgaria | 0.26 | (0.02) | 0.20 | (0.03) | 0.32 | (0.02) | **-0.12** | (0.04) | -0.91 | (0.02) | -0.17 | (0.01) | 0.55 | (0.01) | 1.56 | (0.02) |
| Chile | 0.58 | (0.02) | 0.66 | (0.02) | 0.48 | (0.03) | **0.19** | (0.04) | -0.73 | (0.02) | 0.26 | (0.01) | 0.92 | (0.01) | 1.87 | (0.01) |
| Colombia | 0.47 | (0.02) | 0.49 | (0.03) | 0.45 | (0.02) | 0.04 | (0.04) | -0.67 | (0.01) | 0.16 | (0.01) | 0.72 | (0.01) | 1.66 | (0.02) |
| Croatia | 0.15 | (0.01) | 0.19 | (0.02) | 0.11 | (0.02) | **0.07** | (0.03) | -0.90 | (0.01) | -0.20 | (0.01) | 0.35 | (0.01) | 1.34 | (0.01) |
| Estonia | 0.14 | (0.01) | 0.18 | (0.02) | 0.11 | (0.02) | **0.07** | (0.03) | -0.92 | (0.01) | -0.19 | (0.01) | 0.37 | (0.01) | 1.31 | (0.01) |
| Hong Kong-China | 0.55 | (0.02) | 0.60 | (0.03) | 0.49 | (0.02) | **0.10** | (0.03) | -0.61 | (0.01) | 0.03 | (0.01) | 0.82 | (0.01) | 1.95 | (0.01) |
| Indonesia | 0.31 | (0.02) | 0.30 | (0.03) | 0.33 | (0.02) | -0.04 | (0.03) | -0.70 | (0.01) | -0.03 | (0.01) | 0.57 | (0.01) | 1.42 | (0.02) |
| Israel | 0.24 | (0.03) | 0.26 | (0.04) | 0.22 | (0.04) | 0.05 | (0.06) | -1.27 | (0.02) | -0.15 | (0.01) | 0.64 | (0.01) | 1.75 | (0.01) |
| Jordan | 0.60 | (0.02) | 0.49 | (0.03) | 0.70 | (0.03) | **-0.21** | (0.04) | -0.74 | (0.02) | 0.30 | (0.01) | 0.96 | (0.01) | 1.87 | (0.02) |
| Kyrgyzstan | 0.41 | (0.02) | 0.32 | (0.02) | 0.49 | (0.02) | **-0.17** | (0.03) | -0.82 | (0.01) | 0.09 | (0.01) | 0.72 | (0.01) | 1.65 | (0.02) |
| Latvia | 0.01 | (0.02) | 0.03 | (0.02) | 0.00 | (0.02) | 0.03 | (0.03) | -0.98 | (0.01) | -0.31 | (0.00) | 0.23 | (0.01) | 1.11 | (0.02) |
| Liechtenstein | -0.14 | (0.05) | -0.05 | (0.09) | -0.21 | (0.07) | 0.16 | (0.13) | -1.37 | (0.07) | -0.49 | (0.02) | 0.16 | (0.03) | 1.16 | (0.06) |
| Lithuania | 0.15 | (0.02) | 0.10 | (0.02) | 0.21 | (0.02) | **-0.12** | (0.03) | -0.89 | (0.02) | -0.20 | (0.01) | 0.36 | (0.01) | 1.35 | (0.02) |
| Macao-China | 0.54 | (0.01) | 0.50 | (0.02) | 0.58 | (0.02) | **-0.08** | (0.03) | -0.58 | (0.02) | 0.17 | (0.01) | 0.76 | (0.01) | 1.81 | (0.02) |
| Montenegro | 0.24 | (0.02) | 0.26 | (0.02) | 0.22 | (0.02) | 0.04 | (0.03) | -0.93 | (0.02) | -0.12 | (0.01) | 0.53 | (0.01) | 1.50 | (0.02) |
| Qatar | 0.41 | (0.02) | 0.34 | (0.03) | 0.48 | (0.02) | **-0.14** | (0.03) | -1.22 | (0.02) | 0.02 | (0.01) | 0.89 | (0.01) | 1.95 | (0.01) |
| Romania | 0.22 | (0.03) | 0.22 | (0.04) | 0.22 | (0.03) | 0.00 | (0.04) | -0.91 | (0.03) | -0.15 | (0.01) | 0.49 | (0.01) | 1.44 | (0.02) |
| Russian Federation | 0.02 | (0.01) | 0.07 | (0.02) | -0.02 | (0.02) | **0.09** | (0.02) | -1.00 | (0.01) | -0.30 | (0.00) | 0.25 | (0.01) | 1.14 | (0.02) |
| Serbia | 0.07 | (0.02) | 0.12 | (0.02) | 0.02 | (0.02) | **0.10** | (0.03) | -1.09 | (0.01) | -0.28 | (0.01) | 0.30 | (0.01) | 1.35 | (0.02) |
| Slovenia | 0.02 | (0.01) | 0.03 | (0.02) | 0.01 | (0.02) | 0.02 | (0.03) | -1.04 | (0.01) | -0.35 | (0.00) | 0.23 | (0.01) | 1.24 | (0.02) |
| Chinese Taipei | 0.72 | (0.02) | 0.80 | (0.02) | 0.63 | (0.02) | **0.17** | (0.03) | -0.60 | (0.01) | 0.19 | (0.01) | 1.12 | (0.01) | 2.16 | (0.00) |
| Thailand | 0.77 | (0.02) | 0.66 | (0.02) | 0.86 | (0.02) | **-0.20** | (0.02) | -0.40 | (0.01) | 0.44 | (0.01) | 1.10 | (0.01) | 1.96 | (0.01) |
| Tunisia | 0.70 | (0.02) | 0.66 | (0.04) | 0.75 | (0.03) | **-0.09** | (0.04) | -0.59 | (0.02) | 0.41 | (0.01) | 1.07 | (0.01) | 1.93 | (0.01) |
| Uruguay | -0.10 | (0.02) | -0.11 | (0.03) | -0.08 | (0.02) | -0.03 | (0.03) | -1.16 | (0.02) | -0.45 | (0.01) | 0.16 | (0.01) | 1.07 | (0.02) |

Note: Values that are statistically significant are indicated in bold (see Annex A3).
1. Results based on students' self-reports.
StatLink ᵐˢᵖ http://dx.doi.org/10.1787/142102278412

Pour consulter la version française intégrale de ce tableau, suivre ce lien :
StatLink ᵐˢᵖ http://dx.doi.org/10.1787/152630454851

[Part 2/2]

**Table 3.5** Index of general value of science and performance on the science scale, by quarters of the index[1]

Tableau 3.5  Indice de valorisation générale des sciences et scores sur l'échelle de culture scientifique, par quartile de l'indice

| | | Performance on the science scale, by quarters of this index | | | | | | | Change in the science score per unit of this index | | Increased likelihood of students in the bottom quarter of this index scoring in the bottom quarter of the science performance distribution | | Explained variance in student performance (r-squared x 100) | |
| | | Bottom quarter | | Second quarter | | Third quarter | | Top quarter | | | | | | | |
| | | Mean score | S.E. | Mean score | S.E. | Mean score | S.E. | Mean score | S.E | Effect | S.E. | Ratio | S.E. | Percentage | S.E. |
|---|---|---|---|---|---|---|---|---|---|---|---|---|---|---|---|
| OECD | Australia | **476** | (2.9) | 516 | (2.53) | 546 | (2.92) | 573 | (2.8) | **36.9** | (1.08) | **2.3** | (0.09) | 14.3 | (0.76) |
| | Austria | **475** | (4.9) | 508 | (4.34) | 532 | (4.60) | 536 | (4.7) | **23.9** | (1.88) | **1.9** | (0.15) | 6.6 | (1.00) |
| | Belgium | **486** | (4.2) | 513 | (3.20) | 523 | (3.44) | 539 | (3.1) | **23.6** | (2.18) | **1.7** | (0.09) | 4.9 | (0.87) |
| | Canada | **502** | (3.0) | 527 | (2.85) | 551 | (2.63) | 566 | (2.7) | **25.3** | (1.11) | **1.8** | (0.09) | 7.7 | (0.66) |
| | Czech Republic | **480** | (4.9) | 516 | (4.60) | 528 | (3.89) | 548 | (4.5) | **28.8** | (1.80) | **2.0** | (0.12) | 7.1 | (0.91) |
| | Denmark | **472** | (3.6) | 484 | (4.42) | 500 | (4.72) | 530 | (3.9) | **27.7** | (1.81) | **1.5** | (0.09) | 6.3 | (0.79) |
| | Finland | **526** | (3.8) | 555 | (3.57) | 577 | (2.77) | 596 | (2.8) | **31.5** | (1.54) | **2.1** | (0.13) | 10.7 | (1.03) |
| | France | **463** | (4.8) | 491 | (4.74) | 509 | (4.21) | 524 | (4.3) | **26.6** | (1.92) | **1.7** | (0.09) | 6.2 | (0.83) |
| | Germany | **483** | (6.0) | 519 | (4.38) | 539 | (3.36) | 550 | (4.9) | **26.9** | (1.49) | **2.0** | (0.13) | 8.8 | (0.90) |
| | Greece | **442** | (4.2) | 469 | (4.16) | 489 | (3.96) | 496 | (3.9) | **24.1** | (1.69) | **1.7** | (0.10) | 5.8 | (0.77) |
| | Hungary | **475** | (3.8) | 501 | (3.96) | 515 | (3.68) | 526 | (4.1) | **23.4** | (1.78) | **1.7** | (0.14) | 5.7 | (0.85) |
| | Iceland | **445** | (3.7) | 484 | (3.92) | 505 | (3.32) | 536 | (3.3) | **33.0** | (1.76) | **2.3** | (0.15) | 13.1 | (1.29) |
| | Ireland | **465** | (4.8) | 502 | (3.86) | 526 | (3.59) | 546 | (3.3) | **30.9** | (1.19) | **2.2** | (0.16) | 11.2 | (0.84) |
| | Italy | **441** | (2.4) | 469 | (2.57) | 487 | (2.50) | 507 | (3.1) | **28.8** | (1.25) | **1.8** | (0.08) | 7.4 | (0.66) |
| | Japan | **486** | (5.1) | 532 | (3.52) | 546 | (4.04) | 562 | (3.3) | **27.5** | (1.76) | **2.2** | (0.13) | 8.9 | (1.01) |
| | Korea | **494** | (5.1) | 520 | (4.41) | 533 | (3.35) | 543 | (4.9) | **22.3** | (2.20) | **1.7** | (0.12) | 5.8 | (1.09) |
| | Luxembourg | **450** | (2.8) | 479 | (3.13) | 500 | (2.51) | 519 | (2.9) | **24.6** | (1.41) | **1.9** | (0.11) | 8.2 | (0.93) |
| | Mexico | **390** | (4.0) | 406 | (3.17) | 416 | (3.37) | 430 | (3.5) | **17.7** | (1.61) | **1.5** | (0.09) | 4.5 | (0.79) |
| | Netherlands | **484** | (4.2) | 526 | (3.78) | 544 | (3.47) | 564 | (4.4) | **33.8** | (1.53) | **2.4** | (0.14) | 11.1 | (0.98) |
| | New Zealand | **485** | (4.1) | 519 | (3.75) | 551 | (4.17) | 574 | (3.6) | **35.4** | (1.74) | **2.0** | (0.15) | 10.8 | (1.06) |
| | Norway | **445** | (4.2) | 483 | (4.16) | 503 | (3.06) | 529 | (3.7) | **30.8** | (1.39) | **2.1** | (0.12) | 12.6 | (1.15) |
| | Poland | **464** | (3.3) | 487 | (3.39) | 513 | (3.23) | 529 | (3.0) | **27.6** | (1.42) | **1.9** | (0.11) | 8.0 | (0.78) |
| | Portugal | **443** | (4.3) | 464 | (4.20) | 485 | (3.64) | 506 | (3.7) | **28.1** | (1.78) | **1.8** | (0.15) | 8.3 | (0.97) |
| | Slovak Republic | **452** | (4.2) | 485 | (3.70) | 501 | (3.74) | 522 | (4.1) | **30.4** | (2.26) | **2.0** | (0.15) | 8.3 | (1.12) |
| | Spain | **455** | (4.0) | 490 | (3.55) | 499 | (3.17) | 511 | (3.4) | **22.3** | (1.27) | **1.9** | (0.10) | 6.0 | (0.68) |
| | Sweden | **464** | (4.1) | 495 | (3.25) | 515 | (3.29) | 546 | (3.8) | **31.4** | (1.76) | **2.1** | (0.13) | 11.8 | (1.35) |
| | Switzerland | **474** | (4.2) | 509 | (3.50) | 528 | (4.27) | 536 | (3.6) | **26.0** | (1.31) | **1.9** | (0.09) | 6.6 | (0.71) |
| | Turkey | **386** | (3.5) | 416 | (4.54) | 436 | (4.31) | 459 | (5.5) | **26.1** | (1.81) | **2.1** | (0.16) | 12.0 | (1.20) |
| | United Kingdom | **463** | (3.4) | 507 | (2.85) | 531 | (3.44) | 563 | (3.1) | **39.2** | (1.43) | **2.2** | (0.11) | 13.0 | (0.87) |
| | United States | **449** | (4.4) | 476 | (4.93) | 507 | (4.87) | 529 | (4.5) | **29.9** | (1.38) | **1.9** | (0.11) | 9.5 | (0.80) |
| | **OECD total** | **461** | (1.4) | **487** | (1.47) | **504** | (1.45) | **517** | (1.5) | **21.8** | (0.50) | **1.6** | (0.03) | **4.8** | (0.22) |
| | **OECD average** | **464** | (0.8) | **495** | (0.70) | **514** | (0.66) | **533** | (0.7) | **28.1** | (0.30) | **1.9** | (0.02) | **8.7** | (0.17) |
| Partners | Argentina | **379** | (6.9) | 398 | (6.64) | 395 | (6.39) | 403 | (7.3) | **9.6** | (2.33) | **1.3** | (0.12) | 0.9 | (0.44) |
| | Azerbaijan | **371** | (3.2) | 384 | (3.27) | 388 | (3.59) | 392 | (3.4) | **8.6** | (1.26) | **1.5** | (0.13) | 2.3 | (0.68) |
| | Brazil | **366** | (3.4) | 386 | (3.80) | 402 | (4.19) | 411 | (3.8) | **19.0** | (1.52) | **1.6** | (0.13) | 4.2 | (0.64) |
| | Bulgaria | **406** | (6.8) | 430 | (6.69) | 451 | (7.40) | 460 | (7.3) | **20.5** | (2.37) | **1.6** | (0.14) | 3.8 | (0.83) |
| | Chile | **414** | (4.7) | 434 | (5.36) | 443 | (5.82) | 462 | (5.4) | **17.9** | (1.58) | **1.5** | (0.11) | 3.9 | (0.62) |
| | Colombia | **374** | (4.1) | 391 | (5.33) | 391 | (4.81) | 398 | (4.2) | **10.6** | (1.62) | **1.3** | (0.10) | 1.3 | (0.41) |
| | Croatia | **467** | (3.0) | 488 | (3.47) | 505 | (3.10) | 515 | (3.3) | **20.6** | (1.38) | **1.7** | (0.09) | 4.7 | (0.63) |
| | Estonia | **492** | (3.1) | 525 | (3.16) | 545 | (3.62) | 564 | (3.7) | **31.6** | (1.50) | **2.2** | (0.10) | 11.1 | (0.95) |
| | Hong Kong-China | **511** | (4.2) | 539 | (4.04) | 556 | (4.19) | 564 | (3.8) | **21.0** | (1.90) | **1.8** | (0.14) | 5.4 | (0.86) |
| | Indonesia | **380** | (5.8) | 391 | (6.99) | 399 | (5.97) | 404 | (4.9) | **11.8** | (1.83) | **1.3** | (0.09) | 2.1 | (0.70) |
| | Israel | **420** | (5.2) | 457 | (4.49) | 474 | (4.79) | 486 | (4.5) | **22.0** | (1.76) | **1.8** | (0.11) | 5.6 | (0.86) |
| | Jordan | **384** | (3.8) | 423 | (3.58) | 436 | (4.04) | 450 | (3.6) | **24.6** | (1.49) | **2.1** | (0.13) | 8.1 | (0.84) |
| | Kyrgyzstan | **309** | (3.9) | 326 | (3.79) | 330 | (3.49) | 333 | (4.0) | **10.9** | (1.58) | **1.4** | (0.08) | 1.6 | (0.48) |
| | Latvia | **460** | (4.2) | 486 | (3.56) | 503 | (4.08) | 512 | (4.1) | **23.6** | (1.85) | **1.8** | (0.14) | 5.6 | (0.87) |
| | Liechtenstein | **495** | (11.3) | 511 | (10.73) | 538 | (11.18) | 549 | (9.4) | **19.6** | (4.61) | **1.6** | (0.33) | 4.5 | (1.98) |
| | Lithuania | **452** | (3.5) | 479 | (3.80) | 506 | (3.10) | 517 | (3.6) | **28.6** | (1.53) | **1.9** | (0.12) | 8.1 | (0.75) |
| | Macao-China | **491** | (2.5) | 511 | (2.68) | 517 | (2.56) | 525 | (2.5) | **14.0** | (1.28) | **1.6** | (0.11) | 2.8 | (0.51) |
| | Montenegro | **393** | (2.5) | 411 | (2.51) | 422 | (2.70) | 426 | (2.5) | **12.9** | (1.35) | **1.5** | (0.12) | 2.6 | (0.54) |
| | Qatar | **319** | (2.3) | 353 | (3.10) | 366 | (3.31) | 369 | (3.2) | **15.9** | (0.84) | **1.9** | (0.11) | 5.8 | (0.60) |
| | Romania | **387** | (4.8) | 415 | (5.21) | 432 | (4.92) | 441 | (5.1) | **23.2** | (1.73) | **1.8** | (0.12) | 7.4 | (1.00) |
| | Russian Federation | **458** | (4.5) | 478 | (4.25) | 485 | (4.29) | 497 | (4.6) | **17.6** | (1.63) | **1.5** | (0.11) | 2.9 | (0.53) |
| | Serbia | **419** | (3.4) | 431 | (4.07) | 444 | (3.82) | 451 | (4.3) | **11.5** | (1.52) | **1.3** | (0.09) | 1.7 | (0.45) |
| | Slovenia | **484** | (2.9) | 511 | (3.36) | 538 | (3.53) | 551 | (3.1) | **28.2** | (1.93) | **1.8** | (0.10) | 7.3 | (0.98) |
| | Chinese Taipei | **502** | (5.1) | 532 | (3.95) | 545 | (3.26) | 550 | (4.0) | **17.8** | (1.26) | **1.8** | (0.09) | 4.1 | (0.55) |
| | Thailand | **393** | (3.1) | 416 | (2.81) | 430 | (2.94) | 445 | (3.1) | **22.2** | (1.28) | **1.8** | (0.12) | 7.0 | (0.78) |
| | Tunisia | **357** | (3.7) | 381 | (3.97) | 394 | (3.99) | 412 | (3.6) | **21.7** | (1.43) | **1.8** | (0.11) | 6.9 | (0.88) |
| | Uruguay | **414** | (4.3) | 429 | (3.45) | 435 | (4.60) | 441 | (3.8) | **11.6** | (1.99) | **1.2** | (0.08) | 1.2 | (0.43) |

Note: Values that are statistically significant are indicated in bold (see Annex A3).
1. Results based on students' self-reports.
*StatLink*  http://dx.doi.org/10.1787/142102278412

Pour consulter la version française intégrale de ce tableau, suivre ce lien :
*StatLink* http://dx.doi.org/10.1787/152630454851

[Part 1/2]

**Table 3.6 Index of personal value of science and performance on the science scale, by quarters of the index[1]**

Tableau 3.6 Indice de valorisation personnelle des sciences et scores sur l'échelle de culture scientifique, par quartile de l'indice

| | Index of personal value of science | | | | | | | | | | | | | | | |
| | All students | | Males | | Females | | Gender difference (M - F) | | Bottom quarter | | Second quarter | | Third quarter | | Top quarter | |
| | Mean index | S.E. | Mean index | S.E. | Mean index | S.E. | Dif. | S.E. | Mean index | S.E. | Mean index | S.E. | Mean index | S.E. | Mean index | S.E. |
|---|---|---|---|---|---|---|---|---|---|---|---|---|---|---|---|---|
| **OECD** | | | | | | | | | | | | | | | | |
| Australia | 0.02 | (0.01) | 0.06 | (0.02) | -0.04 | (0.02) | **0.10** | (0.03) | -1.29 | (0.01) | -0.35 | (0.00) | 0.30 | (0.00) | 1.41 | (0.01) |
| Austria | -0.36 | (0.02) | -0.27 | (0.03) | -0.45 | (0.03) | **0.18** | (0.03) | -1.66 | (0.02) | -0.74 | (0.01) | -0.05 | (0.01) | 1.01 | (0.02) |
| Belgium | -0.15 | (0.01) | -0.08 | (0.02) | -0.23 | (0.02) | **0.15** | (0.03) | -1.27 | (0.02) | -0.45 | (0.00) | 0.13 | (0.00) | 0.99 | (0.01) |
| Canada | 0.20 | (0.01) | 0.23 | (0.02) | 0.16 | (0.02) | 0.07 | (0.02) | -1.11 | (0.01) | -0.16 | (0.00) | 0.49 | (0.00) | 1.57 | (0.01) |
| Czech Republic | -0.15 | (0.02) | -0.21 | (0.03) | -0.08 | (0.03) | **-0.13** | (0.03) | -1.21 | (0.02) | -0.44 | (0.00) | 0.10 | (0.00) | 0.94 | (0.02) |
| Denmark | -0.18 | (0.02) | -0.17 | (0.02) | -0.18 | (0.03) | 0.01 | (0.03) | -1.37 | (0.02) | -0.55 | (0.01) | 0.12 | (0.01) | 1.10 | (0.02) |
| Finland | -0.09 | (0.02) | -0.14 | (0.02) | -0.05 | (0.02) | **-0.09** | (0.02) | -1.15 | (0.02) | -0.41 | (0.01) | 0.19 | (0.01) | 0.99 | (0.02) |
| France | -0.14 | (0.02) | -0.06 | (0.03) | -0.22 | (0.02) | **0.16** | (0.03) | -1.40 | (0.02) | -0.47 | (0.01) | 0.16 | (0.01) | 1.13 | (0.02) |
| Germany | -0.23 | (0.02) | -0.14 | (0.02) | -0.34 | (0.03) | **0.20** | (0.04) | -1.54 | (0.02) | -0.60 | (0.01) | 0.07 | (0.01) | 1.14 | (0.02) |
| Greece | -0.08 | (0.02) | -0.01 | (0.02) | -0.15 | (0.02) | **0.14** | (0.02) | -1.19 | (0.01) | -0.41 | (0.01) | 0.18 | (0.01) | 1.12 | (0.02) |
| Hungary | 0.01 | (0.02) | 0.00 | (0.02) | 0.02 | (0.02) | -0.02 | (0.03) | -1.09 | (0.02) | -0.30 | (0.01) | 0.26 | (0.01) | 1.16 | (0.02) |
| Iceland | -0.15 | (0.02) | -0.02 | (0.03) | -0.27 | (0.03) | **0.25** | (0.04) | -1.57 | (0.02) | -0.53 | (0.01) | 0.19 | (0.01) | 1.33 | (0.02) |
| Ireland | 0.00 | (0.02) | -0.04 | (0.03) | 0.04 | (0.03) | **-0.08** | (0.04) | -1.33 | (0.02) | -0.35 | (0.01) | 0.30 | (0.01) | 1.37 | (0.02) |
| Italy | 0.16 | (0.01) | 0.22 | (0.02) | 0.09 | (0.01) | **0.13** | (0.02) | -0.84 | (0.01) | -0.10 | (0.01) | 0.38 | (0.00) | 1.18 | (0.01) |
| Japan | -0.23 | (0.02) | -0.08 | (0.02) | -0.38 | (0.02) | **0.30** | (0.02) | -1.32 | (0.02) | -0.52 | (0.01) | 0.00 | (0.01) | 0.93 | (0.02) |
| Korea | -0.06 | (0.02) | 0.03 | (0.03) | -0.15 | (0.02) | **0.18** | (0.03) | -1.07 | (0.02) | -0.37 | (0.00) | 0.17 | (0.00) | 1.03 | (0.02) |
| Luxembourg | -0.10 | (0.02) | -0.06 | (0.03) | -0.14 | (0.02) | **0.08** | (0.04) | -1.46 | (0.02) | -0.49 | (0.01) | 0.22 | (0.01) | 1.33 | (0.02) |
| Mexico | 0.69 | (0.01) | 0.69 | (0.01) | 0.69 | (0.01) | 0.00 | (0.02) | -0.30 | (0.01) | 0.41 | (0.00) | 0.90 | (0.00) | 1.76 | (0.02) |
| Netherlands | -0.21 | (0.01) | -0.08 | (0.02) | -0.35 | (0.02) | **0.27** | (0.03) | -1.24 | (0.01) | -0.49 | (0.01) | 0.02 | (0.00) | 0.85 | (0.02) |
| New Zealand | 0.04 | (0.02) | 0.07 | (0.02) | 0.02 | (0.03) | 0.05 | (0.04) | -1.22 | (0.02) | -0.28 | (0.01) | 0.31 | (0.01) | 1.37 | (0.02) |
| Norway | -0.11 | (0.02) | -0.04 | (0.03) | -0.19 | (0.03) | **0.16** | (0.04) | -1.37 | (0.02) | -0.44 | (0.01) | 0.19 | (0.01) | 1.17 | (0.02) |
| Poland | 0.32 | (0.01) | 0.26 | (0.02) | 0.39 | (0.02) | **-0.13** | (0.03) | -0.72 | (0.01) | 0.06 | (0.01) | 0.50 | (0.00) | 1.46 | (0.02) |
| Portugal | 0.47 | (0.01) | 0.48 | (0.02) | 0.46 | (0.02) | 0.02 | (0.02) | -0.56 | (0.02) | 0.25 | (0.01) | 0.66 | (0.01) | 1.53 | (0.02) |
| Slovak Republic | -0.04 | (0.02) | -0.02 | (0.03) | -0.07 | (0.03) | 0.05 | (0.03) | -1.04 | (0.02) | -0.35 | (0.00) | 0.21 | (0.01) | 1.01 | (0.02) |
| Spain | 0.05 | (0.01) | 0.09 | (0.02) | 0.01 | (0.02) | **0.08** | (0.02) | -1.11 | (0.01) | -0.25 | (0.01) | 0.30 | (0.00) | 1.26 | (0.01) |
| Sweden | -0.10 | (0.02) | -0.08 | (0.02) | -0.13 | (0.03) | 0.05 | (0.03) | -1.34 | (0.02) | -0.43 | (0.01) | 0.20 | (0.01) | 1.16 | (0.02) |
| Switzerland | -0.22 | (0.02) | -0.14 | (0.02) | -0.30 | (0.02) | **0.16** | (0.02) | -1.42 | (0.01) | -0.56 | (0.00) | 0.06 | (0.01) | 1.04 | (0.01) |
| Turkey | 0.30 | (0.03) | 0.27 | (0.04) | 0.35 | (0.03) | **-0.08** | (0.03) | -0.97 | (0.02) | -0.01 | (0.01) | 0.57 | (0.01) | 1.63 | (0.02) |
| United Kingdom | 0.04 | (0.01) | 0.12 | (0.02) | -0.05 | (0.02) | **0.18** | (0.03) | -1.14 | (0.01) | -0.31 | (0.01) | 0.27 | (0.00) | 1.33 | (0.01) |
| United States | 0.29 | (0.02) | 0.34 | (0.03) | 0.24 | (0.02) | **0.09** | (0.03) | -0.98 | (0.02) | -0.01 | (0.01) | 0.51 | (0.01) | 1.64 | (0.01) |
| **OECD total** | 0.13 | (0.01) | 0.18 | (0.01) | 0.08 | (0.01) | **0.10** | (0.01) | -1.10 | (0.01) | -0.20 | (0.00) | 0.41 | (0.00) | 1.42 | (0.01) |
| **OECD average** | 0.00 | (0.00) | 0.04 | (0.00) | -0.04 | (0.00) | **0.08** | (0.01) | -1.18 | (0.00) | -0.32 | (0.00) | 0.26 | (0.00) | 1.23 | (0.00) |
| **Partners** | | | | | | | | | | | | | | | | |
| Argentina | 0.35 | (0.02) | 0.36 | (0.03) | 0.34 | (0.02) | 0.01 | (0.03) | -0.78 | (0.02) | 0.09 | (0.01) | 0.58 | (0.01) | 1.51 | (0.02) |
| Azerbaijan | 0.75 | (0.02) | 0.69 | (0.02) | 0.82 | (0.02) | **-0.14** | (0.02) | -0.35 | (0.02) | 0.50 | (0.01) | 1.01 | (0.01) | 1.85 | (0.02) |
| Brazil | 0.48 | (0.02) | 0.43 | (0.02) | 0.52 | (0.02) | **-0.09** | (0.03) | -0.64 | (0.02) | 0.20 | (0.01) | 0.72 | (0.01) | 1.64 | (0.01) |
| Bulgaria | 0.39 | (0.02) | 0.33 | (0.02) | 0.45 | (0.02) | **-0.12** | (0.03) | -0.73 | (0.02) | 0.14 | (0.01) | 0.58 | (0.01) | 1.55 | (0.02) |
| Chile | 0.52 | (0.02) | 0.55 | (0.03) | 0.49 | (0.03) | 0.06 | (0.04) | -0.66 | (0.02) | 0.22 | (0.01) | 0.80 | (0.01) | 1.73 | (0.01) |
| Colombia | 0.88 | (0.02) | 0.83 | (0.03) | 0.93 | (0.03) | **-0.10** | (0.03) | -0.12 | (0.02) | 0.57 | (0.00) | 1.14 | (0.01) | 1.96 | (0.02) |
| Croatia | 0.19 | (0.02) | 0.20 | (0.02) | 0.17 | (0.02) | 0.03 | (0.03) | -0.88 | (0.02) | -0.08 | (0.00) | 0.43 | (0.00) | 1.27 | (0.02) |
| Estonia | 0.14 | (0.01) | 0.11 | (0.02) | 0.16 | (0.02) | -0.05 | (0.03) | -0.86 | (0.01) | -0.15 | (0.01) | 0.33 | (0.01) | 1.23 | (0.02) |
| Hong Kong-China | 0.52 | (0.01) | 0.60 | (0.02) | 0.44 | (0.02) | **0.16** | (0.03) | -0.54 | (0.01) | 0.23 | (0.01) | 0.69 | (0.01) | 1.69 | (0.02) |
| Indonesia | 0.51 | (0.02) | 0.51 | (0.03) | 0.51 | (0.02) | -0.01 | (0.03) | -0.36 | (0.01) | 0.28 | (0.00) | 0.66 | (0.01) | 1.46 | (0.01) |
| Israel | 0.23 | (0.02) | 0.30 | (0.03) | 0.16 | (0.03) | **0.14** | (0.05) | -1.17 | (0.02) | -0.16 | (0.01) | 0.55 | (0.01) | 1.70 | (0.02) |
| Jordan | 0.74 | (0.02) | 0.71 | (0.03) | 0.77 | (0.02) | -0.06 | (0.03) | -0.39 | (0.02) | 0.50 | (0.00) | 1.01 | (0.01) | 1.84 | (0.02) |
| Kyrgyzstan | 0.73 | (0.02) | 0.66 | (0.02) | 0.78 | (0.02) | **-0.12** | (0.02) | -0.36 | (0.01) | 0.45 | (0.00) | 0.97 | (0.01) | 1.84 | (0.01) |
| Latvia | 0.13 | (0.02) | 0.11 | (0.02) | 0.15 | (0.02) | -0.04 | (0.03) | -0.81 | (0.01) | -0.10 | (0.01) | 0.32 | (0.00) | 1.10 | (0.02) |
| Liechtenstein | -0.26 | (0.05) | -0.12 | (0.08) | -0.37 | (0.07) | **0.25** | (0.12) | -1.54 | (0.07) | -0.66 | (0.02) | 0.08 | (0.03) | 1.11 | (0.06) |
| Lithuania | 0.25 | (0.01) | 0.18 | (0.02) | 0.33 | (0.02) | **-0.15** | (0.03) | -0.71 | (0.01) | -0.04 | (0.00) | 0.48 | (0.00) | 1.29 | (0.02) |
| Macao-China | 0.34 | (0.01) | 0.38 | (0.02) | 0.30 | (0.02) | **0.08** | (0.03) | -0.61 | (0.01) | 0.08 | (0.01) | 0.54 | (0.01) | 1.36 | (0.02) |
| Montenegro | 0.48 | (0.02) | 0.47 | (0.02) | 0.49 | (0.02) | -0.02 | (0.03) | -0.73 | (0.02) | 0.23 | (0.01) | 0.74 | (0.01) | 1.69 | (0.02) |
| Qatar | 0.50 | (0.01) | 0.51 | (0.02) | 0.48 | (0.02) | 0.03 | (0.03) | -1.00 | (0.02) | 0.18 | (0.01) | 0.84 | (0.01) | 1.97 | (0.01) |
| Romania | 0.48 | (0.01) | 0.47 | (0.02) | 0.49 | (0.02) | -0.02 | (0.04) | -0.53 | (0.02) | 0.24 | (0.01) | 0.66 | (0.01) | 1.56 | (0.02) |
| Russian Federation | 0.16 | (0.02) | 0.15 | (0.02) | 0.17 | (0.02) | -0.02 | (0.02) | -0.86 | (0.01) | -0.13 | (0.00) | 0.40 | (0.00) | 1.22 | (0.01) |
| Serbia | 0.29 | (0.02) | 0.31 | (0.02) | 0.26 | (0.02) | 0.04 | (0.03) | -0.83 | (0.02) | 0.00 | (0.01) | 0.51 | (0.01) | 1.46 | (0.02) |
| Slovenia | 0.14 | (0.01) | 0.12 | (0.02) | 0.16 | (0.02) | -0.04 | (0.03) | -1.04 | (0.02) | -0.15 | (0.01) | 0.41 | (0.01) | 1.33 | (0.02) |
| Chinese Taipei | 0.60 | (0.01) | 0.74 | (0.02) | 0.44 | (0.02) | **0.30** | (0.02) | -0.51 | (0.01) | 0.27 | (0.00) | 0.78 | (0.01) | 1.85 | (0.01) |
| Thailand | 0.79 | (0.02) | 0.73 | (0.02) | 0.83 | (0.02) | **-0.10** | (0.02) | -0.03 | (0.01) | 0.49 | (0.01) | 0.93 | (0.00) | 1.77 | (0.02) |
| Tunisia | 0.71 | (0.02) | 0.68 | (0.03) | 0.75 | (0.02) | -0.07 | (0.04) | -0.42 | (0.02) | 0.45 | (0.01) | 0.99 | (0.01) | 1.84 | (0.01) |
| Uruguay | 0.22 | (0.02) | 0.15 | (0.03) | 0.29 | (0.02) | **-0.15** | (0.03) | -0.94 | (0.02) | -0.06 | (0.01) | 0.49 | (0.01) | 1.39 | (0.02) |

Note: Values that are statistically significant are indicated in bold (see Annex A3).
1. Results based on students' self-reports.
StatLink http://dx.doi.org/10.1787/142102278412

Pour consulter la version française intégrale de ce tableau, suivre ce lien :
StatLink http://dx.doi.org/10.1787/152630454851

[Part 2/2]

**Table 3.6** Index of personal value of science and performance on the science scale, by quarters of the index[1]

Tableau 3.6 Indice de valorisation personnelle des sciences et scores sur l'échelle de culture scientifique, par quartile de l'indice

| | | Performance on the science scale, by quarters of this index | | | | | | | Change in the science score per unit of this index | | Increased likelihood of students in the bottom quarter of this index scoring in the bottom quarter of the science performance distribution | | Explained variance in student performance (r-squared x 100) | |
| | Bottom quarter | | Second quarter | | Third quarter | | Top quarter | | | | | | | |
| | Mean score | S.E. | Mean score | S.E. | Mean score | S.E. | Mean score | S.E | Effect | S.E. | Ratio | S.E. | Percentage | S.E. |
|---|---|---|---|---|---|---|---|---|---|---|---|---|---|---|
| **Australia** | **484** | (2.5) | 511 | (2.6) | 538 | (2.6) | **578** | (2.9) | **33.2** | (0.93) | **2.0** | (0.07) | 12.9 | (0.68) |
| Austria | **497** | (3.8) | 512 | (4.1) | 516 | (5.8) | **525** | (5.9) | **10.1** | (1.99) | **1.2** | (0.08) | 1.2 | (0.50) |
| Belgium | **486** | (3.8) | 512 | (2.9) | 525 | (2.7) | **538** | (3.6) | **23.1** | (1.85) | **1.6** | (0.08) | 4.7 | (0.73) |
| Canada | **504** | (2.6) | 528 | (2.4) | 539 | (2.9) | **575** | (2.9) | **24.8** | (1.04) | **1.6** | (0.07) | 8.0 | (0.67) |
| Czech Republic | **510** | (3.9) | 514 | (4.7) | 523 | (4.9) | **524** | (5.2) | **8.0** | (2.32) | **1.1** | (0.10) | 0.5 | (0.33) |
| Denmark | **474** | (3.6) | 486 | (3.7) | 499 | (3.9) | **529** | (4.7) | **22.0** | (1.54) | **1.3** | (0.10) | 5.7 | (0.79) |
| Finland | **532** | (2.9) | 555 | (3.1) | 571 | (3.1) | **596** | (2.8) | **29.0** | (1.37) | **1.8** | (0.11) | 8.9 | (0.85) |
| France | **466** | (4.1) | 484 | (3.7) | 507 | (4.3) | **531** | (5.3) | **25.0** | (2.02) | **1.6** | (0.10) | 6.4 | (1.02) |
| Germany | **500** | (5.1) | 517 | (4.3) | 531 | (4.3) | **544** | (5.0) | **17.9** | (1.53) | **1.4** | (0.09) | 4.0 | (0.64) |
| Greece | **452** | (3.8) | 467 | (4.2) | 479 | (4.5) | **499** | (4.1) | **19.7** | (1.81) | **1.4** | (0.09) | 4.0 | (0.71) |
| Hungary | 502 | (4.3) | 502 | (3.4) | 501 | (3.7) | 512 | (4.5) | **5.7** | (2.12) | 1.0 | (0.09) | 0.3 | (0.25) |
| Iceland | **449** | (3.1) | 481 | (3.3) | 500 | (3.4) | **541** | (3.7) | **29.9** | (1.55) | **2.0** | (0.12) | 12.9 | (1.23) |
| Ireland | **466** | (3.8) | 501 | (4.1) | 518 | (3.9) | **553** | (3.7) | **29.6** | (1.29) | **2.1** | (0.12) | 11.6 | (0.95) |
| Italy | **460** | (3.0) | 479 | (2.7) | 475 | (3.0) | **489** | (3.1) | **13.1** | (1.59) | **1.2** | (0.07) | 1.3 | (0.31) |
| Japan | **499** | (4.8) | 529 | (3.9) | 543 | (4.0) | **555** | (4.1) | **25.4** | (1.86) | **1.7** | (0.09) | 5.6 | (0.77) |
| Korea | **490** | (4.4) | 517 | (4.0) | 530 | (3.6) | **553** | (5.5) | **28.3** | (2.64) | **1.7** | (0.11) | 7.5 | (1.32) |
| Luxembourg | **470** | (2.4) | 484 | (2.5) | 490 | (2.8) | **504** | (2.9) | **12.6** | (1.41) | **1.2** | (0.08) | 2.1 | (0.47) |
| Mexico | **411** | (3.2) | 409 | (3.3) | 412 | (2.7) | 413 | (3.5) | **3.2** | (1.48) | 1.0 | (0.06) | 0.1 | (0.10) |
| Netherlands | **507** | (3.5) | 523 | (4.0) | 537 | (4.1) | **552** | (4.8) | **22.1** | (1.74) | **1.4** | (0.07) | 4.2 | (0.68) |
| New Zealand | **492** | (3.3) | 520 | (3.5) | 534 | (4.0) | **583** | (3.9) | **32.3** | (1.57) | **1.6** | (0.11) | 9.9 | (0.96) |
| Norway | **457** | (3.3) | 484 | (3.3) | 497 | (4.4) | **523** | (3.5) | **24.6** | (1.36) | **1.6** | (0.09) | 7.6 | (0.80) |
| Poland | **495** | (3.9) | 497 | (3.2) | 492 | (3.3) | 509 | (2.9) | **5.2** | (1.48) | 1.0 | (0.07) | 0.3 | (0.14) |
| Portugal | **452** | (3.7) | 470 | (4.1) | 478 | (4.1) | **498** | (4.4) | **20.7** | (1.90) | **1.4** | (0.09) | 3.9 | (0.71) |
| Slovak Republic | 485 | (4.2) | 489 | (4.3) | 493 | (3.6) | 493 | (4.9) | **3.4** | (3.05) | 1.0 | (0.08) | 0.1 | (0.17) |
| Spain | **461** | (2.9) | 485 | (3.2) | 496 | (3.5) | **514** | (3.3) | **21.4** | (1.27) | **1.5** | (0.07) | 5.2 | (0.59) |
| Sweden | **469** | (3.3) | 499 | (3.2) | 512 | (4.6) | **539** | (4.2) | **26.6** | (1.65) | **1.8** | (0.11) | 8.4 | (1.00) |
| Switzerland | **488** | (3.8) | 505 | (3.7) | 519 | (3.7) | **535** | (4.6) | **19.9** | (1.55) | **1.4** | (0.07) | 4.0 | (0.62) |
| Turkey | **403** | (3.0) | 415 | (4.3) | 423 | (4.7) | **457** | (6.7) | **20.2** | (2.08) | **1.3** | (0.12) | 6.4 | (1.06) |
| United Kingdom | **480** | (3.4) | 500 | (3.2) | 521 | (3.1) | **563** | (3.2) | **32.4** | (1.42) | **1.6** | (0.07) | 9.1 | (0.77) |
| United States | **459** | (4.0) | 482 | (5.2) | 490 | (5.3) | **528** | (6.2) | **25.0** | (1.69) | **1.4** | (0.08) | 6.1 | (0.85) |
| **OECD total** | **478** | (1.2) | **493** | (1.4) | **490** | (1.5) | **508** | (2.1) | **12.6** | (0.65) | **1.1** | (0.02) | 1.5 | (0.16) |
| **OECD average** | **477** | (0.7) | **495** | (0.7) | **506** | (0.7) | **528** | (0.8) | **20.5** | (0.32) | **1.5** | (0.02) | 5.4 | (0.14) |
| Argentina | **402** | (6.3) | 398 | (6.6) | 390 | (6.9) | **387** | (7.6) | **-5.1** | (2.40) | **0.8** | (0.08) | 0.2 | (0.23) |
| Azerbaijan | 382 | (4.2) | 385 | (3.2) | 382 | (3.2) | 386 | (3.4) | 1.9 | (1.69) | 1.1 | (0.13) | 0.1 | (0.19) |
| Brazil | **395** | (4.5) | 394 | (3.6) | 388 | (3.6) | 388 | (3.6) | **-2.6** | (1.78) | **0.9** | (0.06) | 0.1 | (0.10) |
| Bulgaria | 437 | (6.4) | 435 | (7.4) | 436 | (7.1) | 441 | (7.0) | 1.9 | (1.98) | 1.0 | (0.07) | 0.0 | (0.06) |
| Chile | **429** | (4.1) | 434 | (5.1) | 440 | (4.9) | **451** | (6.5) | **8.4** | (2.12) | **1.1** | (0.08) | 0.7 | (0.37) |
| Colombia | **392** | (5.0) | 396 | (5.1) | 385 | (4.8) | **382** | (4.5) | **-6.4** | (2.20) | 0.9 | (0.09) | 0.4 | (0.27) |
| Croatia | **487** | (3.1) | 496 | (3.2) | 494 | (3.6) | **499** | (3.8) | **4.5** | (1.69) | 1.1 | (0.07) | 0.2 | (0.17) |
| Estonia | **512** | (3.5) | 527 | (3.5) | 535 | (3.4) | **553** | (3.6) | **19.2** | (1.51) | **1.4** | (0.09) | 3.7 | (0.57) |
| Hong Kong-China | **519** | (3.9) | 530 | (3.9) | 549 | (3.9) | **570** | (3.6) | **22.1** | (1.45) | **1.5** | (0.08) | 4.6 | (0.55) |
| Indonesia | 397 | (8.5) | 394 | (6.7) | 393 | (5.3) | 390 | (3.7) | -4.4 | (3.78) | 0.9 | (0.06) | 0.2 | (0.36) |
| Israel | **432** | (5.1) | 457 | (5.4) | 470 | (4.9) | **479** | (4.9) | **15.8** | (1.81) | **1.4** | (0.11) | 2.7 | (0.62) |
| Jordan | **403** | (4.0) | 423 | (3.7) | 430 | (3.7) | **437** | (4.1) | **15.8** | (2.07) | **1.5** | (0.09) | 2.5 | (0.61) |
| Kyrgyzstan | **339** | (4.6) | 327 | (4.3) | 323 | (3.4) | **311** | (3.8) | **-11.5** | (2.06) | 0.9 | (0.07) | 1.5 | (0.50) |
| Latvia | **480** | (3.8) | 487 | (3.7) | 494 | (4.3) | **499** | (4.5) | **10.2** | (2.21) | **1.2** | (0.08) | 0.9 | (0.38) |
| Liechtenstein | 506 | (9.5) | 529 | (11.8) | 523 | (15.0) | 536 | (12.3) | **11.6** | (5.16) | 1.2 | (0.30) | 1.7 | (1.51) |
| Lithuania | **471** | (3.8) | 483 | (4.2) | 492 | (4.1) | **507** | (4.1) | **17.3** | (1.82) | **1.4** | (0.09) | 2.5 | (0.48) |
| Macao-China | **503** | (2.3) | 510 | (2.9) | 510 | (2.4) | **521** | (2.9) | **7.9** | (1.59) | 1.1 | (0.09) | 0.6 | (0.26) |
| Montenegro | **419** | (2.3) | 416 | (2.6) | 412 | (3.1) | **406** | (3.1) | **-4.0** | (1.62) | **0.8** | (0.07) | 0.3 | (0.21) |
| Qatar | **329** | (2.1) | 352 | (1.9) | 363 | (2.1) | **363** | (2.1) | **11.2** | (0.92) | **1.5** | (0.09) | 2.5 | (0.40) |
| Romania | 411 | (4.5) | 419 | (5.1) | 424 | (5.2) | 421 | (5.6) | **5.0** | (2.14) | 1.1 | (0.10) | 0.3 | (0.23) |
| Russian Federation | 482 | (4.4) | 477 | (3.9) | 481 | (4.3) | 479 | (4.7) | 1.1 | (1.84) | 0.9 | (0.07) | 0.0 | (0.06) |
| Serbia | **445** | (3.6) | 444 | (3.8) | 430 | (4.2) | **428** | (4.2) | **-7.9** | (1.70) | **0.8** | (0.07) | 0.7 | (0.32) |
| Slovenia | **507** | (3.2) | 515 | (3.2) | 521 | (3.6) | **542** | (3.7) | **13.7** | (2.24) | **1.3** | (0.08) | 1.8 | (0.60) |
| Chinese Taipei | **517** | (4.3) | 524 | (4.4) | 539 | (4.1) | **549** | (3.9) | **13.2** | (1.21) | **1.3** | (0.06) | 1.7 | (0.31) |
| Thailand | **408** | (3.1) | 414 | (3.0) | 424 | (3.5) | **438** | (3.6) | **16.6** | (1.81) | **1.3** | (0.09) | 2.5 | (0.55) |
| Tunisia | **363** | (3.1) | 382 | (4.0) | 393 | (3.7) | **407** | (4.1) | **18.5** | (1.61) | **1.6** | (0.09) | 4.1 | (0.66) |
| Uruguay | **439** | (3.8) | 430 | (3.5) | 427 | (3.7) | **423** | (4.7) | **-4.5** | (2.24) | **0.7** | (0.06) | 0.2 | (0.19) |

Note: Values that are statistically significant are indicated in bold (see Annex A3).
1. Results based on students' self-reports.
*StatLink*  http://dx.doi.org/10.1787/142102278412

Pour consulter la version française intégrale de ce tableau, suivre ce lien :
*StatLink* http://dx.doi.org/10.1787/152630454851

[Part 1/1]

**Table 3.7**   **The importance of doing well in science, reading and mathematics at school[1]**

Tableau 3.7   Importance attachée à l'obtention de bons résultats en sciences, en compréhension de l'écrit et en mathématiques

| | | Percentage of students reporting that doing well in the subject area is important or very important | | | | | | | | | | | | | | | |
| | | All students | | | | | | Males | | | | | | Females | | | | | | |
| | | Science | | Reading | | Mathematics | | Science | | Reading | | Mathematics | | Science | | Reading | | Mathematics | |
| | | % | S.E. | % | S.E. | % | S.E. | % | S.E. | % | S.E. | % | S.E. | % | S.E. | % | S.E. | % | S.E. |
|---|---|---|---|---|---|---|---|---|---|---|---|---|---|---|---|---|---|---|---|
| OECD | Australia | 72.0 | (0.6) | 94.5 | (0.2) | 93.7 | (0.3) | 71.0 | (0.8) | 91.9 | (0.4) | 94.9 | (0.4) | 73.1 | (0.8) | 97.2 | (0.3) | 92.6 | (0.4) |
| | Austria | 65.4 | (1.2) | 88.5 | (0.8) | 91.2 | (0.5) | 65.8 | (1.5) | 82.0 | (1.2) | 91.6 | (0.7) | 64.9 | (1.4) | 95.2 | (0.5) | 90.7 | (0.6) |
| | Belgium | 64.4 | (0.8) | 82.2 | (0.6) | 90.0 | (0.6) | 63.8 | (1.2) | 75.3 | (1.0) | 90.0 | (0.9) | 65.2 | (1.0) | 89.4 | (0.5) | 90.0 | (0.6) |
| | Canada | 83.4 | (0.5) | 90.2 | (0.3) | 95.3 | (0.3) | 81.7 | (0.7) | 85.6 | (0.5) | 95.3 | (0.4) | 85.1 | (0.7) | 94.7 | (0.3) | 95.4 | (0.4) |
| | Czech Republic | 53.7 | (1.3) | 88.7 | (0.7) | 89.3 | (0.7) | 48.6 | (1.5) | 84.3 | (1.1) | 91.3 | (0.8) | 60.4 | (2.0) | 94.3 | (0.5) | 86.8 | (1.0) |
| | Denmark | 69.5 | (0.7) | 96.4 | (0.3) | 96.8 | (0.3) | 69.4 | (1.0) | 94.4 | (0.5) | 97.0 | (0.4) | 69.6 | (1.0) | 98.3 | (0.3) | 96.7 | (0.4) |
| | Finland | 61.8 | (0.8) | 79.4 | (0.7) | 86.0 | (0.6) | 57.6 | (1.1) | 67.7 | (1.2) | 87.1 | (0.8) | 66.0 | (1.1) | 90.9 | (0.7) | 84.9 | (0.7) |
| | France | 64.1 | (1.1) | 83.4 | (0.7) | 89.7 | (0.5) | 65.6 | (1.5) | 77.4 | (1.1) | 91.5 | (0.7) | 62.8 | (1.1) | 89.1 | (0.7) | 88.0 | (0.7) |
| | Germany | 75.8 | (0.8) | 92.2 | (0.5) | 94.5 | (0.3) | 77.7 | (1.0) | 88.3 | (0.9) | 94.6 | (0.5) | 73.9 | (1.1) | 96.2 | (0.5) | 94.4 | (0.5) |
| | Greece | 74.1 | (0.7) | 79.9 | (0.8) | 86.2 | (0.6) | 77.9 | (1.1) | 72.3 | (1.2) | 88.3 | (0.9) | 70.4 | (1.1) | 87.4 | (0.8) | 84.1 | (0.9) |
| | Hungary | 65.9 | (0.9) | 82.6 | (0.7) | 83.4 | (0.7) | 65.0 | (1.2) | 75.0 | (1.0) | 82.7 | (1.0) | 66.9 | (1.3) | 90.6 | (0.7) | 84.2 | (1.0) |
| | Iceland | 68.0 | (0.8) | 91.7 | (0.4) | 97.8 | (0.2) | 68.3 | (1.4) | 87.9 | (0.7) | 97.2 | (0.4) | 67.7 | (1.1) | 95.5 | (0.5) | 98.3 | (0.3) |
| | Ireland | 74.8 | (0.9) | 92.9 | (0.5) | 95.8 | (0.4) | 71.0 | (1.3) | 90.6 | (0.7) | 96.1 | (0.5) | 78.7 | (1.0) | 95.1 | (0.5) | 95.6 | (0.5) |
| | Italy | 81.9 | (0.6) | 92.8 | (0.3) | 90.5 | (0.4) | 83.0 | (0.8) | 88.8 | (0.4) | 90.7 | (0.6) | 80.8 | (0.7) | 97.0 | (0.3) | 90.4 | (0.5) |
| | Japan | 68.0 | (0.8) | 88.0 | (0.6) | 87.2 | (0.6) | 70.2 | (1.0) | 83.9 | (0.8) | 87.4 | (0.8) | 65.7 | (1.1) | 92.2 | (0.6) | 87.1 | (0.8) |
| | Korea | 75.2 | (0.7) | 92.4 | (0.5) | 87.8 | (0.6) | 77.3 | (1.0) | 89.9 | (0.7) | 87.9 | (0.9) | 73.0 | (1.0) | 95.0 | (0.5) | 87.7 | (0.8) |
| | Luxembourg | 66.8 | (0.7) | 86.1 | (0.5) | 84.8 | (0.6) | 63.4 | (1.0) | 81.8 | (0.7) | 88.4 | (0.7) | 70.2 | (1.0) | 90.5 | (0.6) | 81.3 | (0.9) |
| | Mexico | 88.8 | (0.4) | 96.3 | (0.3) | 97.4 | (0.3) | 86.9 | (0.7) | 95.0 | (0.4) | 97.0 | (0.5) | 90.5 | (0.5) | 97.4 | (0.3) | 97.8 | (0.2) |
| | Netherlands | 72.5 | (0.9) | 86.5 | (0.6) | 89.5 | (0.5) | 72.0 | (1.4) | 81.0 | (0.9) | 91.4 | (0.7) | 73.0 | (1.2) | 92.4 | (0.6) | 87.4 | (0.8) |
| | New Zealand | 75.6 | (0.8) | 93.2 | (0.4) | 95.1 | (0.3) | 74.4 | (1.2) | 90.8 | (0.7) | 95.3 | (0.5) | 76.6 | (1.1) | 95.3 | (0.5) | 94.9 | (0.5) |
| | Norway | 77.4 | (0.8) | 83.8 | (0.7) | 91.0 | (0.4) | 76.3 | (1.0) | 76.5 | (1.0) | 91.2 | (0.6) | 78.6 | (1.1) | 91.4 | (0.7) | 90.8 | (0.7) |
| | Poland | 77.1 | (0.7) | 88.4 | (0.5) | 86.4 | (0.6) | 73.5 | (1.0) | 82.5 | (0.9) | 85.6 | (0.7) | 80.7 | (0.8) | 94.1 | (0.5) | 87.2 | (0.8) |
| | Portugal | 83.0 | (0.7) | 87.9 | (0.6) | 89.9 | (0.6) | 80.7 | (0.9) | 85.1 | (0.8) | 89.3 | (0.9) | 85.5 | (0.9) | 90.9 | (0.7) | 90.4 | (0.7) |
| | Slovak Republic | 60.5 | (1.4) | 91.1 | (0.5) | 87.7 | (0.8) | 56.9 | (1.6) | 87.2 | (0.8) | 89.1 | (0.8) | 64.1 | (1.6) | 95.1 | (0.5) | 86.2 | (1.1) |
| | Spain | 73.6 | (0.6) | 84.4 | (0.4) | 88.8 | (0.5) | 73.4 | (0.9) | 79.0 | (0.6) | 87.7 | (0.7) | 73.9 | (0.9) | 89.9 | (0.5) | 89.8 | (0.5) |
| | Sweden | 72.9 | (0.8) | 94.1 | (0.4) | 94.9 | (0.4) | 72.6 | (1.1) | 90.3 | (0.8) | 93.8 | (0.7) | 73.2 | (1.1) | 98.0 | (0.3) | 96.0 | (0.5) |
| | Switzerland | 62.0 | (0.9) | 90.1 | (0.5) | 92.3 | (0.5) | 61.4 | (1.2) | 85.2 | (0.9) | 94.8 | (0.5) | 62.7 | (1.1) | 95.2 | (0.4) | 89.7 | (0.7) |
| | Turkey | 80.7 | (0.9) | 93.6 | (0.6) | 93.0 | (0.5) | 80.4 | (1.2) | 91.9 | (0.9) | 91.8 | (0.7) | 81.1 | (1.1) | 95.7 | (0.5) | 94.4 | (0.6) |
| | United Kingdom | 83.6 | (0.6) | 95.3 | (0.3) | 96.1 | (0.2) | 84.7 | (0.7) | 93.2 | (0.5) | 96.2 | (0.3) | 82.7 | (0.9) | 97.3 | (0.4) | 95.9 | (0.4) |
| | United States | 82.3 | (0.6) | m | m | 93.9 | (0.4) | 80.5 | (1.0) | m | m | 93.6 | (0.6) | 84.1 | (0.8) | m | m | 94.2 | (0.5) |
| | **OECD total** | 77.7 | (0.2) | 90.4 | (0.2) | 92.3 | (0.1) | 77.2 | (0.3) | 86.5 | (0.3) | 92.2 | (0.2) | 78.2 | (0.3) | 94.3 | (0.2) | 92.3 | (0.2) |
| | **OECD average** | 72.5 | (0.2) | 89.2 | (0.1) | 91.2 | (0.1) | 71.7 | (0.2) | 84.7 | (0.2) | 91.6 | (0.1) | 73.4 | (0.2) | 93.8 | (0.1) | 90.8 | (0.1) |
| Partners | Argentina | 85.1 | (0.8) | 88.3 | (0.8) | 91.9 | (0.5) | 83.7 | (1.1) | 85.3 | (1.1) | 90.4 | (0.8) | 86.4 | (0.9) | 90.9 | (0.9) | 93.2 | (0.6) |
| | Azerbaijan | 88.3 | (0.7) | 92.3 | (0.7) | 88.5 | (0.6) | 88.7 | (0.9) | 89.7 | (0.9) | 90.3 | (0.7) | 88.0 | (0.9) | 95.2 | (0.8) | 86.6 | (0.9) |
| | Brazil | 88.4 | (0.6) | 95.3 | (0.3) | 93.9 | (0.4) | 87.8 | (0.7) | 92.9 | (0.6) | 94.0 | (0.5) | 88.9 | (0.7) | 97.2 | (0.3) | 93.8 | (0.5) |
| | Bulgaria | 82.6 | (0.8) | 93.0 | (0.7) | 91.8 | (0.6) | 80.1 | (1.1) | 89.7 | (1.1) | 89.9 | (0.9) | 85.3 | (0.8) | 96.6 | (0.5) | 93.8 | (0.8) |
| | Chile | 89.1 | (0.6) | 94.3 | (0.4) | 96.6 | (0.3) | 87.9 | (0.9) | 92.9 | (0.5) | 96.4 | (0.4) | 90.5 | (0.7) | 96.0 | (0.4) | 96.9 | (0.4) |
| | Colombia | 91.2 | (0.7) | 94.1 | (0.5) | 95.5 | (0.4) | 89.2 | (1.1) | 92.2 | (0.6) | 95.7 | (0.8) | 92.9 | (0.7) | 95.8 | (0.7) | 95.4 | (0.5) |
| | Croatia | 63.0 | (1.1) | 83.8 | (0.8) | 80.8 | (0.9) | 63.1 | (1.2) | 76.7 | (1.0) | 83.7 | (1.0) | 63.0 | (1.5) | 90.4 | (0.9) | 78.1 | (1.5) |
| | Estonia | 81.9 | (0.6) | 91.9 | (0.4) | 92.7 | (0.4) | 80.4 | (0.8) | 87.4 | (0.7) | 91.2 | (0.7) | 83.4 | (0.9) | 96.4 | (0.4) | 94.3 | (0.5) |
| | Hong Kong-China | 71.5 | (1.0) | 91.0 | (0.6) | 92.3 | (0.5) | 76.9 | (1.1) | 87.3 | (1.0) | 92.6 | (0.8) | 66.4 | (1.3) | 94.5 | (0.5) | 92.0 | (0.7) |
| | Indonesia | 89.9 | (0.7) | 95.8 | (0.5) | 96.3 | (0.3) | 88.3 | (0.9) | 95.2 | (0.7) | 96.1 | (0.4) | 91.6 | (0.8) | 96.4 | (0.5) | 96.5 | (0.3) |
| | Israel | 68.4 | (1.0) | 84.7 | (0.6) | 93.1 | (0.6) | 69.8 | (1.2) | 79.1 | (1.0) | 91.0 | (0.9) | 67.0 | (1.5) | 90.1 | (0.7) | 95.1 | (0.8) |
| | Jordan | 93.0 | (0.5) | 87.3 | (0.8) | 89.9 | (0.6) | 92.3 | (0.8) | 82.6 | (1.3) | 88.1 | (0.9) | 93.8 | (0.6) | 91.7 | (0.6) | 91.5 | (0.7) |
| | Kyrgyzstan | 90.2 | (0.6) | 94.0 | (0.4) | 93.5 | (0.4) | 89.1 | (0.8) | 92.8 | (0.6) | 93.2 | (0.6) | 91.0 | (0.7) | 94.9 | (0.5) | 93.8 | (0.5) |
| | Latvia | 71.4 | (0.9) | 91.1 | (0.6) | 94.0 | (0.5) | 67.8 | (1.2) | 87.1 | (1.0) | 94.0 | (0.6) | 74.8 | (1.1) | 94.9 | (0.5) | 93.9 | (0.7) |
| | Liechtenstein | 64.8 | (2.1) | 87.3 | (1.9) | 92.7 | (1.5) | 64.5 | (3.9) | 77.7 | (3.6) | 92.7 | (2.6) | 65.1 | (3.3) | 95.5 | (1.6) | 92.7 | (1.7) |
| | Lithuania | 84.0 | (0.6) | 93.6 | (0.5) | 93.9 | (0.4) | 82.1 | (1.0) | 90.1 | (0.7) | 93.1 | (0.5) | 86.0 | (0.8) | 97.1 | (0.5) | 94.8 | (0.5) |
| | Macao-China | 78.7 | (0.7) | 93.2 | (0.5) | 86.1 | (0.7) | 79.5 | (1.0) | 89.9 | (0.8) | 87.2 | (1.0) | 77.7 | (1.2) | 97.1 | (0.5) | 84.8 | (1.1) |
| | Montenegro | 76.5 | (0.7) | 86.6 | (0.5) | 76.3 | (0.7) | 75.6 | (1.1) | 81.1 | (0.9) | 79.2 | (0.9) | 77.4 | (1.0) | 92.3 | (0.8) | 73.3 | (1.0) |
| | Qatar | 82.9 | (0.5) | 76.6 | (0.5) | 81.4 | (0.5) | 85.0 | (0.8) | 74.7 | (0.9) | 82.0 | (0.8) | 80.9 | (0.6) | 78.3 | (0.7) | 80.8 | (0.7) |
| | Romania | 78.0 | (1.1) | 93.2 | (0.7) | 89.7 | (0.7) | 75.7 | (1.5) | 90.1 | (0.8) | 88.8 | (0.9) | 80.1 | (1.2) | 96.1 | (0.6) | 90.4 | (0.8) |
| | Russian Federation | 75.3 | (0.7) | 92.6 | (0.5) | 91.9 | (0.5) | 75.2 | (1.1) | 89.7 | (0.7) | 92.6 | (0.6) | 75.3 | (0.9) | 95.2 | (0.6) | 91.3 | (0.7) |
| | Serbia | 65.1 | (1.0) | 85.1 | (0.6) | 75.2 | (0.9) | 62.6 | (1.3) | 79.3 | (0.9) | 76.9 | (1.0) | 67.7 | (1.2) | 91.0 | (0.7) | 73.5 | (1.2) |
| | Slovenia | 71.9 | (0.8) | 87.0 | (0.5) | 89.0 | (0.5) | 71.7 | (1.1) | 82.0 | (0.8) | 89.4 | (0.6) | 72.2 | (1.3) | 91.8 | (0.6) | 88.7 | (0.7) |
| | Chinese Taipei | 77.6 | (0.7) | 87.9 | (0.4) | 83.4 | (0.6) | 81.9 | (0.7) | 82.7 | (0.7) | 85.4 | (0.7) | 72.8 | (0.9) | 93.6 | (0.4) | 81.2 | (1.0) |
| | Thailand | 97.4 | (0.3) | 95.8 | (0.4) | 98.1 | (0.2) | 95.8 | (0.5) | 94.0 | (0.7) | 97.0 | (0.4) | 98.6 | (0.2) | 97.1 | (0.3) | 98.8 | (0.2) |
| | Tunisia | 89.9 | (0.6) | 74.3 | (1.1) | 85.6 | (0.7) | 89.5 | (0.9) | 71.0 | (1.3) | 86.7 | (0.8) | 90.3 | (0.7) | 77.4 | (1.2) | 84.7 | (0.9) |
| | Uruguay | 83.1 | (0.8) | 84.4 | (0.6) | 92.0 | (0.5) | 80.0 | (1.1) | 80.1 | (1.0) | 91.9 | (0.7) | 86.0 | (0.9) | 88.3 | (0.8) | 92.1 | (0.7) |

1. Results based on students' self-reports.
*StatLink* http://dx.doi.org/10.1787/142102278412

Pour consulter la version française intégrale de ce tableau, suivre ce lien :
*StatLink* http://dx.doi.org/10.1787/152630454851

[Part 1/2]

**Table 3.8** Index of general interest in science and performance on the science scale, by quarters of the index[1]

Tableau 3.8 Indice d'intérêt général pour les sciences et scores sur l'échelle de culture scientifique, par quartile de l'indice

| | | Index of general interest in science | | | | | | | | | | | | | |
| | All students | | Males | | Females | | Gender difference (M - F) | | Bottom quarter | | Second quarter | | Third quarter | | Top quarter | |
| | Mean index | S.E. | Mean index | S.E. | Mean index | S.E. | Dif. | S.E. | Mean index | S.E. | Mean index | S.E. | Mean index | S.E. | Mean index | S.E. |
|---|---|---|---|---|---|---|---|---|---|---|---|---|---|---|---|---|
| **OECD** | | | | | | | | | | | | | | | | |
| Australia | -0.22 | (0.01) | -0.23 | (0.02) | -0.21 | (0.02) | -0.02 | (0.02) | -1.66 | (0.02) | -0.33 | (0.00) | 0.17 | (0.00) | 0.94 | (0.01) |
| Austria | 0.05 | (0.02) | 0.08 | (0.02) | 0.03 | (0.02) | 0.05 | (0.03) | -1.07 | (0.02) | -0.13 | (0.00) | 0.34 | (0.00) | 1.07 | (0.01) |
| Belgium | 0.02 | (0.02) | 0.00 | (0.03) | 0.06 | (0.02) | -0.06 | (0.03) | -1.31 | (0.03) | -0.14 | (0.00) | 0.39 | (0.00) | 1.16 | (0.01) |
| Canada | 0.11 | (0.01) | 0.10 | (0.02) | 0.12 | (0.01) | -0.02 | (0.02) | -1.11 | (0.02) | -0.07 | (0.00) | 0.44 | (0.00) | 1.17 | (0.01) |
| Czech Republic | -0.03 | (0.02) | -0.05 | (0.03) | -0.02 | (0.02) | -0.03 | (0.03) | -1.08 | (0.03) | -0.20 | (0.00) | 0.23 | (0.00) | 0.91 | (0.02) |
| Denmark | -0.17 | (0.02) | -0.17 | (0.03) | -0.18 | (0.03) | 0.01 | (0.04) | -1.52 | (0.03) | -0.37 | (0.00) | 0.17 | (0.01) | 1.03 | (0.02) |
| Finland | -0.25 | (0.02) | -0.24 | (0.03) | -0.25 | (0.02) | 0.01 | (0.03) | -1.45 | (0.02) | -0.44 | (0.00) | 0.05 | (0.00) | 0.86 | (0.02) |
| France | 0.20 | (0.02) | 0.23 | (0.03) | 0.18 | (0.02) | 0.05 | (0.03) | -1.04 | (0.02) | -0.02 | (0.00) | 0.53 | (0.00) | 1.33 | (0.01) |
| Germany | 0.19 | (0.02) | 0.22 | (0.02) | 0.15 | (0.02) | **0.07** | (0.03) | -0.94 | (0.03) | 0.01 | (0.01) | 0.48 | (0.00) | 1.19 | (0.02) |
| Greece | 0.19 | (0.02) | 0.19 | (0.03) | 0.20 | (0.02) | -0.01 | (0.04) | -1.06 | (0.02) | -0.02 | (0.00) | 0.51 | (0.00) | 1.35 | (0.02) |
| Hungary | -0.07 | (0.01) | -0.07 | (0.02) | -0.08 | (0.02) | 0.02 | (0.03) | -1.10 | (0.02) | -0.26 | (0.00) | 0.18 | (0.00) | 0.89 | (0.02) |
| Iceland | -0.15 | (0.02) | -0.09 | (0.03) | -0.21 | (0.03) | **0.12** | (0.04) | -1.68 | (0.03) | -0.31 | (0.01) | 0.25 | (0.00) | 1.16 | (0.02) |
| Ireland | -0.14 | (0.02) | -0.19 | (0.03) | -0.10 | (0.03) | **-0.09** | (0.04) | -1.59 | (0.02) | -0.25 | (0.01) | 0.26 | (0.00) | 1.00 | (0.01) |
| Italy | 0.18 | (0.01) | 0.18 | (0.02) | 0.18 | (0.01) | 0.00 | (0.02) | -0.82 | (0.01) | -0.01 | (0.00) | 0.42 | (0.00) | 1.13 | (0.01) |
| Japan | -0.13 | (0.02) | -0.04 | (0.03) | -0.22 | (0.03) | **0.18** | (0.04) | -1.44 | (0.03) | -0.26 | (0.00) | 0.22 | (0.00) | 0.96 | (0.01) |
| Korea | -0.24 | (0.02) | -0.22 | (0.03) | -0.27 | (0.02) | 0.06 | (0.04) | -1.48 | (0.02) | -0.35 | (0.00) | 0.08 | (0.00) | 0.77 | (0.01) |
| Luxembourg | 0.14 | (0.02) | 0.12 | (0.02) | 0.15 | (0.02) | -0.03 | (0.03) | -1.12 | (0.03) | -0.04 | (0.00) | 0.46 | (0.00) | 1.25 | (0.02) |
| Mexico | 0.76 | (0.01) | 0.74 | (0.02) | 0.78 | (0.02) | **-0.04** | (0.02) | -0.28 | (0.01) | 0.50 | (0.00) | 1.01 | (0.00) | 1.81 | (0.01) |
| Netherlands | -0.35 | (0.02) | -0.33 | (0.02) | -0.36 | (0.02) | 0.04 | (0.03) | -1.68 | (0.03) | -0.45 | (0.00) | -0.02 | (0.00) | 0.77 | (0.01) |
| New Zealand | -0.10 | (0.02) | -0.13 | (0.03) | -0.07 | (0.03) | -0.06 | (0.04) | -1.42 | (0.03) | -0.23 | (0.00) | 0.25 | (0.00) | 1.00 | (0.02) |
| Norway | -0.03 | (0.03) | 0.02 | (0.03) | -0.09 | (0.03) | **0.10** | (0.04) | -1.51 | (0.04) | -0.18 | (0.01) | 0.35 | (0.01) | 1.21 | (0.02) |
| Poland | 0.06 | (0.02) | 0.04 | (0.02) | 0.07 | (0.02) | -0.03 | (0.02) | -0.92 | (0.02) | -0.12 | (0.00) | 0.28 | (0.00) | 0.98 | (0.01) |
| Portugal | 0.16 | (0.02) | 0.16 | (0.02) | 0.16 | (0.02) | -0.01 | (0.02) | -0.90 | (0.02) | -0.03 | (0.00) | 0.43 | (0.00) | 1.15 | (0.02) |
| Slovak Republic | -0.11 | (0.02) | -0.09 | (0.03) | -0.13 | (0.02) | 0.05 | (0.03) | -1.22 | (0.03) | -0.28 | (0.00) | 0.19 | (0.00) | 0.88 | (0.01) |
| Spain | -0.18 | (0.01) | -0.20 | (0.02) | -0.16 | (0.02) | -0.04 | (0.02) | -1.37 | (0.02) | -0.32 | (0.00) | 0.10 | (0.00) | 0.86 | (0.01) |
| Sweden | -0.13 | (0.03) | -0.15 | (0.04) | -0.12 | (0.03) | -0.03 | (0.04) | -1.47 | (0.04) | -0.27 | (0.01) | 0.22 | (0.00) | 1.00 | (0.02) |
| Switzerland | 0.00 | (0.02) | 0.02 | (0.02) | -0.01 | (0.02) | 0.03 | (0.02) | -1.20 | (0.02) | -0.15 | (0.00) | 0.32 | (0.00) | 1.05 | (0.01) |
| Turkey | 0.22 | (0.02) | 0.22 | (0.03) | 0.24 | (0.03) | -0.02 | (0.03) | -0.99 | (0.02) | -0.03 | (0.01) | 0.53 | (0.01) | 1.38 | (0.02) |
| United Kingdom | -0.01 | (0.02) | 0.06 | (0.02) | -0.08 | (0.02) | **0.13** | (0.02) | -1.19 | (0.02) | -0.17 | (0.00) | 0.30 | (0.00) | 1.02 | (0.01) |
| United States | 0.03 | (0.02) | 0.05 | (0.02) | 0.01 | (0.03) | 0.04 | (0.03) | -1.29 | (0.03) | -0.16 | (0.00) | 0.37 | (0.00) | 1.20 | (0.02) |
| **OECD total** | 0.09 | (0.01) | 0.10 | (0.01) | 0.07 | (0.01) | **0.03** | (0.01) | -1.16 | (0.01) | -0.12 | (0.00) | 0.41 | (0.00) | 1.22 | (0.01) |
| **OECD average** | 0.00 | (0.00) | 0.01 | (0.00) | -0.01 | (0.00) | 0.02 | (0.01) | -1.23 | (0.00) | -0.17 | (0.00) | 0.32 | (0.00) | 1.08 | (0.00) |
| **Partners** | | | | | | | | | | | | | | | | |
| Argentina | 0.22 | (0.02) | 0.14 | (0.03) | 0.30 | (0.03) | **-0.16** | (0.04) | -1.02 | (0.02) | -0.04 | (0.01) | 0.52 | (0.00) | 1.43 | (0.03) |
| Azerbaijan | 0.60 | (0.02) | 0.58 | (0.03) | 0.63 | (0.03) | -0.06 | (0.03) | -0.58 | (0.02) | 0.32 | (0.00) | 0.83 | (0.01) | 1.84 | (0.02) |
| Brazil | 0.51 | (0.02) | 0.44 | (0.03) | 0.58 | (0.02) | **-0.14** | (0.03) | -0.73 | (0.02) | 0.22 | (0.00) | 0.79 | (0.00) | 1.77 | (0.02) |
| Bulgaria | 0.18 | (0.02) | 0.12 | (0.03) | 0.25 | (0.02) | **-0.14** | (0.03) | -1.05 | (0.03) | -0.03 | (0.01) | 0.49 | (0.01) | 1.32 | (0.02) |
| Chile | 0.36 | (0.02) | 0.31 | (0.02) | 0.41 | (0.03) | **-0.11** | (0.04) | -0.80 | (0.02) | 0.11 | (0.01) | 0.65 | (0.00) | 1.47 | (0.02) |
| Colombia | 1.15 | (0.02) | 1.11 | (0.03) | 1.18 | (0.03) | -0.07 | (0.03) | 0.04 | (0.02) | 0.84 | (0.01) | 1.35 | (0.01) | 2.36 | (0.03) |
| Croatia | 0.17 | (0.02) | 0.12 | (0.02) | 0.22 | (0.02) | **-0.10** | (0.03) | -0.92 | (0.02) | -0.02 | (0.00) | 0.46 | (0.00) | 1.17 | (0.01) |
| Estonia | 0.19 | (0.01) | 0.19 | (0.02) | 0.19 | (0.02) | 0.00 | (0.02) | -0.72 | (0.02) | 0.01 | (0.00) | 0.40 | (0.00) | 1.06 | (0.02) |
| Hong Kong-China | 0.19 | (0.01) | 0.33 | (0.02) | 0.06 | (0.03) | **0.27** | (0.04) | -1.03 | (0.03) | 0.00 | (0.01) | 0.51 | (0.00) | 1.30 | (0.02) |
| Indonesia | 0.56 | (0.02) | 0.55 | (0.02) | 0.56 | (0.02) | -0.01 | (0.02) | -0.18 | (0.01) | 0.32 | (0.00) | 0.69 | (0.00) | 1.40 | (0.01) |
| Israel | -0.21 | (0.03) | -0.17 | (0.04) | -0.25 | (0.04) | 0.08 | (0.05) | -1.92 | (0.03) | -0.43 | (0.01) | 0.22 | (0.01) | 1.28 | (0.03) |
| Jordan | 0.68 | (0.02) | 0.64 | (0.03) | 0.71 | (0.03) | -0.07 | (0.04) | -0.47 | (0.03) | 0.43 | (0.00) | 0.93 | (0.00) | 1.81 | (0.02) |
| Kyrgyzstan | 0.91 | (0.01) | 0.88 | (0.02) | 0.92 | (0.02) | -0.04 | (0.02) | -0.05 | (0.01) | 0.62 | (0.00) | 1.09 | (0.00) | 1.97 | (0.02) |
| Latvia | 0.16 | (0.02) | 0.18 | (0.03) | 0.15 | (0.02) | 0.03 | (0.03) | -0.64 | (0.02) | -0.01 | (0.00) | 0.34 | (0.00) | 0.97 | (0.02) |
| Liechtenstein | -0.06 | (0.05) | -0.09 | (0.08) | -0.04 | (0.06) | -0.05 | (0.10) | -1.45 | (0.10) | -0.18 | (0.02) | 0.32 | (0.02) | 1.09 | (0.06) |
| Lithuania | 0.35 | (0.01) | 0.32 | (0.02) | 0.37 | (0.02) | **-0.05** | (0.03) | -0.51 | (0.02) | 0.13 | (0.00) | 0.55 | (0.00) | 1.22 | (0.01) |
| Macao-China | 0.10 | (0.01) | 0.20 | (0.02) | 0.00 | (0.02) | **0.21** | (0.03) | -0.92 | (0.02) | -0.10 | (0.00) | 0.34 | (0.00) | 1.08 | (0.02) |
| Montenegro | 0.42 | (0.02) | 0.34 | (0.03) | 0.50 | (0.02) | **-0.16** | (0.04) | -0.86 | (0.03) | 0.21 | (0.01) | 0.73 | (0.01) | 1.59 | (0.02) |
| Qatar | 0.28 | (0.02) | 0.38 | (0.03) | 0.20 | (0.02) | **0.18** | (0.04) | -1.38 | (0.03) | 0.04 | (0.01) | 0.66 | (0.00) | 1.81 | (0.02) |
| Romania | 0.38 | (0.02) | 0.36 | (0.02) | 0.41 | (0.02) | -0.05 | (0.03) | -0.67 | (0.02) | 0.13 | (0.01) | 0.58 | (0.01) | 1.50 | (0.03) |
| Russian Federation | 0.28 | (0.02) | 0.23 | (0.02) | 0.33 | (0.02) | **-0.10** | (0.02) | -0.59 | (0.02) | 0.08 | (0.00) | 0.49 | (0.00) | 1.14 | (0.02) |
| Serbia | 0.26 | (0.02) | 0.20 | (0.03) | 0.32 | (0.02) | **-0.12** | (0.03) | -0.85 | (0.02) | 0.05 | (0.00) | 0.53 | (0.00) | 1.30 | (0.02) |
| Slovenia | 0.03 | (0.02) | 0.10 | (0.02) | -0.03 | (0.02) | **0.12** | (0.03) | -1.14 | (0.02) | -0.14 | (0.00) | 0.35 | (0.00) | 1.07 | (0.01) |
| Chinese Taipei | 0.09 | (0.02) | 0.23 | (0.02) | -0.07 | (0.02) | **0.29** | (0.03) | -1.20 | (0.02) | -0.08 | (0.00) | 0.45 | (0.00) | 1.18 | (0.01) |
| Thailand | 0.79 | (0.02) | 0.68 | (0.02) | 0.88 | (0.02) | **-0.20** | (0.03) | -0.14 | (0.02) | 0.57 | (0.00) | 0.98 | (0.00) | 1.76 | (0.02) |
| Tunisia | 0.77 | (0.02) | 0.74 | (0.03) | 0.80 | (0.02) | **-0.06** | (0.03) | -0.26 | (0.02) | 0.51 | (0.00) | 0.99 | (0.01) | 1.87 | (0.02) |
| Uruguay | 0.25 | (0.02) | 0.22 | (0.03) | 0.27 | (0.02) | -0.05 | (0.03) | -0.94 | (0.03) | 0.03 | (0.01) | 0.56 | (0.01) | 1.35 | (0.02) |

Note: Values that are statistically significant are indicated in bold (see Annex A3).
1. Results based on students' self-reports.
StatLink ⟜ http://dx.doi.org/10.1787/142102278412

Pour consulter la version française intégrale de ce tableau, suivre ce lien :
StatLink ⟜ http://dx.doi.org/10.1787/152630454851

[Part 2/2]
**Table 3.8 Index of general interest in science and performance on the science scale, by quarters of the index[1]**

Tableau 3.8 Indice d'intérêt général pour les sciences et scores sur l'échelle de culture scientifique, par quartile de l'indice

| | | Performance on the science scale, by quarters of this index | | | | | | | Change in the science score per unit of this index | | Increased likelihood of students in the bottom quarter of this index scoring in the bottom quarter of the science performance distribution | | Explained variance in student performance (r-squared x 100) | |
| | | Bottom quarter | | Second quarter | | Third quarter | | Top quarter | | | | | | | |
| | | Mean score | S.E. | Mean score | S.E. | Mean score | S.E. | Mean score | S.E | Effect | S.E. | Ratio | S.E. | Percentage | S.E. |
|---|---|---|---|---|---|---|---|---|---|---|---|---|---|---|---|
| OECD | Australia | **491** | (2.5) | 511 | (3.0) | 544 | (2.8) | **564** | (3.3) | **27.4** | (1.01) | **1.7** | (0.08) | 9.0 | (0.66) |
| | Austria | **477** | (5.5) | 508 | (4.3) | 521 | (5.0) | **538** | (4.9) | **26.0** | (2.19) | **1.8** | (0.13) | 5.6 | (0.80) |
| | Belgium | **466** | (4.2) | 507 | (2.9) | 532 | (2.8) | **540** | (3.6) | **28.9** | (1.77) | **2.1** | (0.11) | 9.2 | (1.13) |
| | Canada | **502** | (2.8) | 531 | (2.5) | 550 | (3.0) | **561** | (3.3) | **23.6** | (1.12) | **1.7** | (0.08) | 6.1 | (0.60) |
| | Czech Republic | **489** | (4.8) | 510 | (4.3) | 526 | (4.3) | **527** | (4.9) | **19.9** | (2.55) | **1.5** | (0.10) | 2.8 | (0.78) |
| | Denmark | **458** | (3.8) | 488 | (4.2) | 507 | (3.6) | **532** | (4.2) | **26.9** | (1.56) | **1.8** | (0.12) | 9.4 | (0.99) |
| | Finland | **525** | (3.1) | 555 | (3.0) | 573 | (2.8) | **602** | (3.3) | **31.5** | (1.74) | **2.1** | (0.12) | 12.0 | (1.21) |
| | France | **446** | (3.8) | 491 | (4.2) | 516 | (3.7) | **536** | (4.4) | **34.7** | (1.80) | **2.2** | (0.15) | 11.6 | (1.01) |
| | Germany | **478** | (4.9) | 520 | (3.9) | 529 | (4.2) | **545** | (4.7) | **28.5** | (2.38) | **1.9** | (0.12) | 6.7 | (1.08) |
| | Greece | **444** | (3.9) | 468 | (4.1) | 481 | (4.1) | **503** | (4.0) | **21.9** | (1.91) | **1.7** | (0.11) | 5.8 | (1.02) |
| | Hungary | **480** | (4.0) | 499 | (3.3) | 514 | (3.7) | **525** | (4.2) | **20.4** | (2.42) | **1.5** | (0.11) | 3.7 | (0.82) |
| | Iceland | **448** | (3.2) | 480 | (3.7) | 509 | (3.1) | **532** | (3.6) | **27.9** | (1.36) | **2.0** | (0.13) | 11.7 | (1.03) |
| | Ireland | **468** | (4.2) | 500 | (3.7) | 529 | (3.7) | **542** | (3.9) | **29.1** | (1.29) | **2.0** | (0.12) | 11.4 | (0.96) |
| | Italy | **449** | (2.5) | 468 | (2.8) | 488 | (2.6) | **500** | (3.0) | **22.7** | (1.51) | **1.6** | (0.07) | 4.0 | (0.51) |
| | Japan | **480** | (4.8) | 523 | (3.7) | 556 | (3.1) | **568** | (4.0) | **34.4** | (1.71) | **2.4** | (0.12) | 12.6 | (1.05) |
| | Korea | **482** | (4.8) | 505 | (4.0) | 536 | (3.3) | **567** | (4.5) | **33.8** | (2.04) | **1.9** | (0.11) | 13.0 | (1.22) |
| | Luxembourg | **453** | (2.7) | 486 | (2.5) | 497 | (2.8) | **512** | (3.2) | **21.3** | (1.61) | **1.8** | (0.11) | 4.9 | (0.72) |
| | Mexico | **400** | (3.9) | 410 | (3.8) | 420 | (2.5) | **411** | (3.7) | **5.6** | (1.81) | **1.3** | (0.07) | 0.4 | (0.23) |
| | Netherlands | **494** | (3.6) | 515 | (3.2) | 535 | (3.2) | **557** | (6.5) | **24.5** | (2.16) | **1.6** | (0.11) | 6.8 | (1.27) |
| | New Zealand | **493** | (3.1) | 528 | (3.8) | 547 | (4.1) | **560** | (4.5) | **26.2** | (1.69) | **1.7** | (0.10) | 6.3 | (0.84) |
| | Norway | **441** | (3.3) | 487 | (3.6) | 506 | (4.0) | **525** | (3.3) | **26.9** | (1.32) | **2.3** | (0.16) | 11.3 | (1.09) |
| | Poland | **478** | (3.7) | 488 | (2.9) | 504 | (3.7) | **523** | (3.0) | **18.9** | (1.63) | **1.3** | (0.08) | 2.9 | (0.47) |
| | Portugal | **449** | (3.8) | 462 | (4.0) | 486 | (4.6) | **502** | (4.0) | **22.1** | (2.02) | **1.5** | (0.11) | 4.8 | (0.95) |
| | Slovak Republic | **462** | (4.0) | 487 | (3.6) | 498 | (4.1) | **509** | (4.1) | **23.1** | (2.63) | **1.5** | (0.09) | 4.7 | (1.04) |
| | Spain | **459** | (3.1) | 477 | (3.9) | 501 | (3.2) | **520** | (3.3) | **24.9** | (1.23) | **1.7** | (0.10) | 6.9 | (0.64) |
| | Sweden | **465** | (3.2) | 494 | (3.5) | 521 | (3.5) | **539** | (3.8) | **27.4** | (1.45) | **1.9** | (0.15) | 9.7 | (1.05) |
| | Switzerland | **462** | (3.5) | 511 | (3.5) | 532 | (3.8) | **543** | (3.6) | **32.5** | (1.53) | **2.2** | (0.10) | 9.7 | (0.88) |
| | Turkey | **396** | (3.7) | 419 | (4.3) | 434 | (4.8) | **450** | (5.8) | **20.1** | (1.89) | **1.6** | (0.13) | 5.5 | (0.85) |
| | United Kingdom | **478** | (3.6) | 508 | (3.2) | 536 | (3.4) | **542** | (3.8) | **27.8** | (1.47) | **1.7** | (0.09) | 6.2 | (0.65) |
| | United States | **465** | (3.5) | 494 | (4.6) | 503 | (5.9) | **498** | (7.3) | **13.3** | (2.47) | **1.3** | (0.11) | 1.8 | (0.72) |
| | **OECD total** | **466** | (1.3) | 495 | (1.2) | 505 | (1.8) | **500** | (2.0) | **13.0** | (0.79) | **1.4** | (0.04) | 1.6 | (0.21) |
| | **OECD average** | **466** | (0.7) | 494 | (0.7) | 514 | (0.7) | **529** | (0.8) | **25.1** | (0.33) | **1.8** | (0.02) | 7.2 | (0.17) |
| Partners | Argentina | 390 | (7.7) | 392 | (7.2) | 404 | (6.4) | 388 | (6.7) | -1.5 | (2.28) | 1.0 | (0.11) | 0.0 | (0.08) |
| | Azerbaijan | 368 | (3.0) | 385 | (3.8) | 390 | (3.5) | 390 | (3.2) | 7.3 | (1.24) | 1.6 | (0.13) | 1.7 | (0.62) |
| | Brazil | 387 | (4.1) | 394 | (4.4) | 397 | (3.8) | 386 | (3.6) | 0.1 | (1.38) | 1.0 | (0.07) | 0.0 | (0.03) |
| | Bulgaria | 411 | (5.4) | 439 | (6.4) | 451 | (7.0) | 447 | (7.5) | 11.5 | (2.31) | 1.4 | (0.11) | 1.2 | (0.47) |
| | Chile | 429 | (4.3) | 440 | (5.3) | 444 | (4.5) | 440 | (6.4) | 4.7 | (1.73) | 1.1 | (0.08) | 0.2 | (0.17) |
| | Colombia | 393 | (4.8) | 395 | (5.0) | 392 | (4.3) | 373 | (4.7) | -8.2 | (1.95) | 1.0 | (0.10) | 0.8 | (0.39) |
| | Croatia | 470 | (3.2) | 488 | (3.1) | 503 | (3.4) | 512 | (3.5) | 19.5 | (1.83) | 1.6 | (0.09) | 3.9 | (0.73) |
| | Estonia | 509 | (3.5) | 531 | (3.2) | 541 | (3.8) | 546 | (3.7) | 17.4 | (1.95) | 1.5 | (0.11) | 2.5 | (0.54) |
| | Hong Kong-China | 499 | (3.3) | 537 | (4.0) | 560 | (3.1) | 573 | (3.3) | 28.9 | (1.41) | 2.0 | (0.14) | 9.7 | (0.88) |
| | Indonesia | 378 | (7.3) | 393 | (7.2) | 399 | (5.7) | 405 | (4.9) | 13.9 | (3.07) | 1.5 | (0.08) | 1.7 | (0.89) |
| | Israel | 427 | (5.8) | 461 | (4.6) | 477 | (4.6) | 468 | (5.4) | 14.0 | (2.02) | 1.5 | (0.14) | 2.7 | (0.78) |
| | Jordan | 397 | (3.5) | 418 | (3.8) | 436 | (4.2) | 441 | (3.5) | 16.6 | (1.72) | 1.6 | (0.10) | 3.2 | (0.66) |
| | Kyrgyzstan | 336 | (5.1) | 323 | (3.4) | 323 | (3.4) | 314 | (3.6) | -9.6 | (2.21) | 0.9 | (0.08) | 0.9 | (0.42) |
| | Latvia | 483 | (4.1) | 489 | (3.7) | 491 | (4.2) | 497 | (4.4) | 7.7 | (2.81) | 1.1 | (0.08) | 0.4 | (0.29) |
| | Liechtenstein | 487 | (9.6) | 517 | (10.3) | 540 | (11.1) | 545 | (11.4) | 19.8 | (4.77) | 1.8 | (0.35) | 4.9 | (2.30) |
| | Lithuania | 462 | (3.8) | 481 | (3.8) | 500 | (3.9) | 509 | (3.8) | 23.7 | (2.34) | 1.5 | (0.09) | 3.6 | (0.66) |
| | Macao-China | 486 | (2.2) | 501 | (2.9) | 521 | (2.4) | 536 | (2.6) | 23.4 | (1.63) | 1.7 | (0.13) | 6.4 | (0.85) |
| | Montenegro | 395 | (2.9) | 409 | (3.0) | 414 | (2.6) | 432 | (2.9) | 12.4 | (1.40) | 1.5 | (0.12) | 2.5 | (0.57) |
| | Qatar | 333 | (1.8) | 355 | (2.1) | 364 | (2.4) | 355 | (2.6) | 4.8 | (0.84) | 1.3 | (0.08) | 0.6 | (0.20) |
| | Romania | 392 | (4.8) | 421 | (4.9) | 434 | (5.2) | 427 | (4.8) | 11.4 | (2.28) | 1.7 | (0.14) | 1.6 | (0.59) |
| | Russian Federation | 472 | (4.4) | 481 | (4.1) | 479 | (4.5) | 487 | (4.9) | 8.0 | (2.52) | 1.2 | (0.11) | 0.4 | (0.27) |
| | Serbia | 419 | (4.0) | 439 | (3.5) | 443 | (4.0) | 443 | (4.1) | 7.3 | (1.68) | 1.4 | (0.09) | 0.6 | (0.28) |
| | Slovenia | 489 | (2.8) | 516 | (3.7) | 528 | (3.4) | 544 | (3.4) | 24.1 | (2.02) | 1.6 | (0.08) | 5.0 | (0.83) |
| | Chinese Taipei | 489 | (4.3) | 525 | (4.1) | 550 | (3.7) | 566 | (4.0) | 28.1 | (1.32) | 2.2 | (0.12) | 9.1 | (0.80) |
| | Thailand | 403 | (3.0) | 413 | (3.0) | 429 | (3.5) | 439 | (3.2) | 17.8 | (1.96) | 1.5 | (0.09) | 3.3 | (0.73) |
| | Tunisia | 365 | (3.2) | 379 | (4.0) | 395 | (4.2) | 406 | (4.7) | 16.6 | (1.76) | 1.4 | (0.13) | 3.2 | (0.60) |
| | Uruguay | 426 | (3.7) | 435 | (3.7) | 431 | (4.3) | 426 | (4.4) | 0.7 | (2.01) | 1.0 | (0.08) | 0.0 | (0.05) |

Note: Values that are statistically significant are indicated in bold (see Annex A3).
1. Results based on students' self-reports.
*StatLink* ᵐˢᵖ http://dx.doi.org/10.1787/142102278412

Pour consulter la version française intégrale de ce tableau, suivre ce lien :
*StatLink* ᵐˢᵖ http://dx.doi.org/10.1787/152630454851

[Part 1/2]

**Table 3.9   Index of enjoyment of science and performance on the science scale, by quarters of the index[1]**

Tableau 3.9   Indice du plaisir apporté par les sciences et scores sur l'échelle de culture scientifique, par quartile de l'indice

| | | All students | | Males | | Females | | Gender difference (M - F) | | Bottom quarter | | Second quarter | | Third quarter | | Top quarter | |
|---|---|---|---|---|---|---|---|---|---|---|---|---|---|---|---|---|---|
| | | Mean index | S.E. | Mean index | S.E. | Mean index | S.E. | Dif. | S.E. | Mean index | S.E. | Mean index | S.E. | Mean index | S.E. | Mean index | S.E. |
| OECD | Australia | -0.08 | (0.02) | -0.03 | (0.02) | -0.12 | (0.02) | **0.09** | (0.03) | -1.39 | (0.01) | -0.39 | (0.00) | 0.29 | (0.00) | 1.19 | (0.01) |
| | Austria | -0.21 | (0.03) | -0.19 | (0.03) | -0.24 | (0.03) | 0.04 | (0.04) | -1.57 | (0.01) | -0.65 | (0.01) | 0.08 | (0.01) | 1.28 | (0.01) |
| | Belgium | -0.01 | (0.02) | 0.03 | (0.03) | -0.05 | (0.03) | **0.08** | (0.03) | -1.25 | (0.02) | -0.31 | (0.00) | 0.29 | (0.00) | 1.22 | (0.01) |
| | Canada | 0.17 | (0.01) | 0.22 | (0.02) | 0.13 | (0.02) | **0.09** | (0.02) | -1.17 | (0.01) | -0.11 | (0.00) | 0.47 | (0.00) | 1.50 | (0.01) |
| | Czech Republic | -0.06 | (0.02) | -0.15 | (0.02) | 0.06 | (0.03) | **-0.21** | (0.03) | -1.13 | (0.02) | -0.35 | (0.01) | 0.17 | (0.01) | 1.07 | (0.02) |
| | Denmark | -0.07 | (0.02) | -0.07 | (0.03) | -0.08 | (0.02) | 0.01 | (0.03) | -1.26 | (0.02) | -0.43 | (0.01) | 0.20 | (0.01) | 1.19 | (0.01) |
| | Finland | 0.11 | (0.02) | 0.02 | (0.02) | 0.20 | (0.02) | **-0.18** | (0.03) | -1.03 | (0.01) | -0.13 | (0.01) | 0.45 | (0.00) | 1.16 | (0.02) |
| | France | 0.14 | (0.02) | 0.22 | (0.03) | 0.06 | (0.03) | **0.16** | (0.03) | -1.12 | (0.02) | -0.15 | (0.00) | 0.43 | (0.01) | 1.41 | (0.01) |
| | Germany | -0.09 | (0.02) | -0.01 | (0.03) | -0.17 | (0.02) | **0.15** | (0.04) | -1.42 | (0.02) | -0.52 | (0.01) | 0.21 | (0.01) | 1.39 | (0.01) |
| | Greece | 0.08 | (0.02) | 0.18 | (0.03) | -0.02 | (0.03) | **0.20** | (0.04) | -1.22 | (0.02) | -0.23 | (0.01) | 0.38 | (0.01) | 1.39 | (0.02) |
| | Hungary | 0.19 | (0.02) | 0.14 | (0.02) | 0.25 | (0.02) | **-0.10** | (0.03) | -0.95 | (0.01) | -0.08 | (0.01) | 0.46 | (0.01) | 1.35 | (0.01) |
| | Iceland | -0.03 | (0.02) | 0.07 | (0.02) | -0.13 | (0.03) | **0.20** | (0.04) | -1.46 | (0.02) | -0.43 | (0.01) | 0.36 | (0.01) | 1.43 | (0.02) |
| | Ireland | -0.18 | (0.02) | -0.21 | (0.03) | -0.15 | (0.03) | -0.06 | (0.04) | -1.50 | (0.02) | -0.47 | (0.01) | 0.17 | (0.01) | 1.09 | (0.02) |
| | Italy | 0.12 | (0.01) | 0.16 | (0.02) | 0.08 | (0.02) | **0.08** | (0.02) | -0.97 | (0.01) | -0.13 | (0.00) | 0.41 | (0.00) | 1.16 | (0.01) |
| | Japan | -0.26 | (0.02) | -0.01 | (0.03) | -0.51 | (0.03) | **0.50** | (0.03) | -1.50 | (0.02) | -0.67 | (0.00) | -0.01 | (0.01) | 1.13 | (0.01) |
| | Korea | -0.17 | (0.02) | -0.04 | (0.03) | -0.30 | (0.03) | **0.26** | (0.04) | -1.36 | (0.01) | -0.56 | (0.00) | 0.08 | (0.01) | 1.16 | (0.02) |
| | Luxembourg | -0.04 | (0.02) | -0.07 | (0.02) | -0.01 | (0.03) | -0.06 | (0.03) | -1.43 | (0.01) | -0.43 | (0.01) | 0.30 | (0.01) | 1.42 | (0.01) |
| | Mexico | 0.64 | (0.01) | 0.62 | (0.02) | 0.65 | (0.02) | -0.03 | (0.02) | -0.29 | (0.01) | 0.40 | (0.00) | 0.92 | (0.00) | 1.53 | (0.01) |
| | Netherlands | -0.32 | (0.02) | -0.19 | (0.02) | -0.46 | (0.02) | **0.27** | (0.03) | -1.43 | (0.01) | -0.68 | (0.00) | -0.06 | (0.01) | 0.88 | (0.01) |
| | New Zealand | -0.01 | (0.02) | 0.04 | (0.03) | -0.05 | (0.03) | **0.10** | (0.04) | -1.26 | (0.02) | -0.29 | (0.01) | 0.34 | (0.01) | 1.19 | (0.02) |
| | Norway | -0.01 | (0.02) | 0.11 | (0.03) | -0.13 | (0.03) | **0.24** | (0.04) | -1.39 | (0.02) | -0.33 | (0.01) | 0.36 | (0.01) | 1.34 | (0.02) |
| | Poland | -0.25 | (0.02) | -0.31 | (0.02) | -0.19 | (0.02) | **-0.12** | (0.03) | -1.33 | (0.02) | -0.62 | (0.01) | -0.01 | (0.01) | 0.96 | (0.02) |
| | Portugal | 0.31 | (0.02) | 0.30 | (0.02) | 0.33 | (0.02) | -0.03 | (0.02) | -0.66 | (0.02) | 0.05 | (0.00) | 0.55 | (0.00) | 1.31 | (0.01) |
| | Slovak Republic | -0.01 | (0.02) | 0.00 | (0.02) | -0.02 | (0.03) | 0.02 | (0.03) | -1.00 | (0.01) | -0.30 | (0.01) | 0.20 | (0.01) | 1.07 | (0.02) |
| | Spain | -0.14 | (0.02) | -0.15 | (0.02) | -0.12 | (0.02) | -0.03 | (0.03) | -1.34 | (0.01) | -0.43 | (0.01) | 0.14 | (0.01) | 1.09 | (0.01) |
| | Sweden | -0.10 | (0.02) | -0.10 | (0.04) | -0.10 | (0.02) | 0.01 | (0.05) | -1.36 | (0.02) | -0.50 | (0.01) | 0.24 | (0.01) | 1.22 | (0.02) |
| | Switzerland | -0.06 | (0.02) | -0.02 | (0.03) | -0.10 | (0.02) | **0.07** | (0.03) | -1.31 | (0.01) | -0.44 | (0.01) | 0.22 | (0.01) | 1.29 | (0.01) |
| | Turkey | 0.41 | (0.02) | 0.40 | (0.03) | 0.43 | (0.03) | -0.03 | (0.03) | -0.87 | (0.02) | 0.15 | (0.01) | 0.73 | (0.01) | 1.65 | (0.01) |
| | United Kingdom | -0.08 | (0.02) | 0.03 | (0.02) | -0.19 | (0.02) | **0.22** | (0.03) | -1.24 | (0.01) | -0.34 | (0.00) | 0.22 | (0.01) | 1.03 | (0.01) |
| | United States | -0.03 | (0.02) | 0.06 | (0.03) | -0.12 | (0.02) | **0.19** | (0.03) | -1.29 | (0.02) | -0.34 | (0.01) | 0.28 | (0.01) | 1.23 | (0.02) |
| | **OECD total** | 0.03 | (0.01) | 0.10 | (0.01) | -0.04 | (0.01) | **0.14** | (0.01) | -1.24 | (0.01) | -0.30 | (0.00) | 0.35 | (0.00) | 1.31 | (0.00) |
| | **OECD average** | 0.00 | (0.00) | 0.03 | (0.00) | -0.04 | (0.00) | **0.07** | (0.01) | -1.22 | (0.00) | -0.32 | (0.00) | 0.30 | (0.00) | 1.24 | (0.00) |
| Partners | Argentina | 0.02 | (0.02) | -0.07 | (0.04) | 0.10 | (0.02) | **-0.17** | (0.04) | -1.21 | (0.02) | -0.25 | (0.01) | 0.34 | (0.01) | 1.21 | (0.02) |
| | Azerbaijan | 0.76 | (0.02) | 0.70 | (0.03) | 0.81 | (0.03) | **-0.11** | (0.03) | -0.40 | (0.02) | 0.57 | (0.00) | 1.11 | (0.01) | 1.74 | (0.01) |
| | Brazil | 0.39 | (0.02) | 0.32 | (0.02) | 0.44 | (0.02) | **-0.12** | (0.03) | -0.64 | (0.01) | 0.07 | (0.00) | 0.68 | (0.00) | 1.45 | (0.01) |
| | Bulgaria | 0.39 | (0.02) | 0.32 | (0.03) | 0.46 | (0.02) | **-0.14** | (0.03) | -0.63 | (0.02) | 0.17 | (0.01) | 0.63 | (0.00) | 1.40 | (0.01) |
| | Chile | 0.26 | (0.02) | 0.26 | (0.03) | 0.25 | (0.03) | 0.01 | (0.03) | -0.92 | (0.02) | -0.08 | (0.01) | 0.56 | (0.01) | 1.46 | (0.01) |
| | Colombia | 0.81 | (0.02) | 0.78 | (0.03) | 0.82 | (0.03) | -0.04 | (0.03) | -0.22 | (0.02) | 0.60 | (0.01) | 1.09 | (0.01) | 1.75 | (0.01) |
| | Croatia | 0.10 | (0.02) | 0.05 | (0.02) | 0.15 | (0.02) | **-0.09** | (0.03) | -1.03 | (0.02) | -0.17 | (0.00) | 0.35 | (0.01) | 1.24 | (0.01) |
| | Estonia | 0.02 | (0.02) | -0.04 | (0.03) | 0.08 | (0.02) | **-0.12** | (0.03) | -1.02 | (0.01) | -0.27 | (0.01) | 0.25 | (0.01) | 1.12 | (0.02) |
| | Hong Kong-China | 0.38 | (0.01) | 0.54 | (0.02) | 0.21 | (0.02) | **0.33** | (0.03) | -0.77 | (0.01) | 0.14 | (0.01) | 0.62 | (0.00) | 1.53 | (0.01) |
| | Indonesia | 0.77 | (0.02) | 0.75 | (0.03) | 0.79 | (0.03) | -0.04 | (0.03) | -0.09 | (0.01) | 0.55 | (0.00) | 0.98 | (0.00) | 1.64 | (0.01) |
| | Israel | -0.04 | (0.03) | -0.03 | (0.04) | -0.05 | (0.04) | 0.02 | (0.05) | -1.61 | (0.02) | -0.44 | (0.00) | 0.38 | (0.01) | 1.52 | (0.01) |
| | Jordan | 0.80 | (0.02) | 0.83 | (0.02) | 0.77 | (0.03) | 0.05 | (0.04) | -0.37 | (0.02) | 0.60 | (0.01) | 1.16 | (0.00) | 1.81 | (0.01) |
| | Kyrgyzstan | 0.94 | (0.01) | 0.87 | (0.02) | 1.01 | (0.02) | **-0.14** | (0.02) | -0.06 | (0.01) | 0.76 | (0.01) | 1.25 | (0.00) | 1.83 | (0.01) |
| | Latvia | 0.00 | (0.02) | -0.05 | (0.02) | 0.04 | (0.02) | **-0.09** | (0.03) | -0.85 | (0.01) | -0.20 | (0.00) | 0.17 | (0.00) | 0.87 | (0.01) |
| | Liechtenstein | -0.22 | (0.05) | -0.18 | (0.09) | -0.25 | (0.07) | 0.07 | (0.13) | -1.51 | (0.04) | -0.70 | (0.02) | 0.09 | (0.04) | 1.27 | (0.06) |
| | Lithuania | 0.21 | (0.02) | 0.12 | (0.02) | 0.29 | (0.02) | **-0.17** | (0.03) | -0.80 | (0.02) | -0.04 | (0.01) | 0.41 | (0.00) | 1.26 | (0.01) |
| | Macao-China | 0.41 | (0.01) | 0.52 | (0.02) | 0.31 | (0.02) | **0.21** | (0.03) | -0.64 | (0.02) | 0.21 | (0.01) | 0.64 | (0.01) | 1.45 | (0.01) |
| | Montenegro | 0.27 | (0.01) | 0.22 | (0.02) | 0.32 | (0.02) | **-0.10** | (0.03) | -0.97 | (0.02) | 0.01 | (0.01) | 0.64 | (0.00) | 1.38 | (0.01) |
| | Qatar | 0.37 | (0.01) | 0.47 | (0.02) | 0.28 | (0.02) | **0.20** | (0.03) | -1.11 | (0.02) | 0.13 | (0.01) | 0.78 | (0.01) | 1.70 | (0.01) |
| | Romania | 0.45 | (0.02) | 0.43 | (0.02) | 0.48 | (0.02) | -0.05 | (0.03) | -0.56 | (0.02) | 0.24 | (0.01) | 0.69 | (0.01) | 1.45 | (0.02) |
| | Russian Federation | 0.13 | (0.02) | 0.09 | (0.03) | 0.16 | (0.02) | **-0.07** | (0.03) | -0.82 | (0.01) | -0.16 | (0.00) | 0.38 | (0.00) | 1.11 | (0.01) |
| | Serbia | 0.08 | (0.02) | 0.09 | (0.03) | 0.06 | (0.02) | 0.03 | (0.03) | -1.05 | (0.01) | -0.19 | (0.00) | 0.34 | (0.01) | 1.21 | (0.01) |
| | Slovenia | -0.13 | (0.01) | -0.16 | (0.02) | -0.10 | (0.02) | -0.06 | (0.03) | -1.34 | (0.01) | -0.47 | (0.01) | 0.19 | (0.01) | 1.10 | (0.02) |
| | Chinese Taipei | 0.17 | (0.01) | 0.38 | (0.02) | -0.07 | (0.01) | **0.46** | (0.02) | -0.98 | (0.01) | -0.16 | (0.00) | 0.44 | (0.00) | 1.36 | (0.01) |
| | Thailand | 0.73 | (0.02) | 0.72 | (0.03) | 0.74 | (0.02) | -0.02 | (0.03) | -0.13 | (0.02) | 0.52 | (0.00) | 0.97 | (0.01) | 1.56 | (0.01) |
| | Tunisia | 1.02 | (0.02) | 1.03 | (0.03) | 1.01 | (0.02) | 0.02 | (0.03) | -0.10 | (0.02) | 0.92 | (0.01) | 1.36 | (0.00) | 1.88 | (0.01) |
| | Uruguay | 0.09 | (0.02) | -0.02 | (0.02) | 0.19 | (0.02) | **-0.21** | (0.03) | -1.08 | (0.02) | -0.15 | (0.01) | 0.36 | (0.01) | 1.22 | (0.01) |

Note: Values that are statistically significant are indicated in bold (see Annex A3).
1. Results based on students' self-reports.
StatLink 📈 http://dx.doi.org/10.1787/142102278412

Pour consulter la version française intégrale de ce tableau, suivre ce lien :
StatLink 📈 http://dx.doi.org/10.1787/152630454851

[Part 2/2]

**Table 3.9** Index of enjoyment of science and performance on the science scale, by quarters of the index[1]

Tableau 3.9 Indice du plaisir apporté par les sciences et scores sur l'échelle de culture scientifique, par quartile de l'indice

| | Performance on the science scale, by quarters of this index | | | | | | | Change in the science score per unit of this index | | Increased likelihood of students in the bottom quarter of this index scoring in the bottom quarter of the science performance distribution | | Explained variance in student performance (r-squared x 100) | |
| | Bottom quarter | | Second quarter | | Third quarter | | Top quarter | | | | | | | |
| | Mean score | S.E. | Mean score | S.E. | Mean score | S.E. | Mean score | S.E | Effect | S.E. | Ratio | S.E. | Percentage | S.E. |
|---|---|---|---|---|---|---|---|---|---|---|---|---|---|---|
| **Australia** | **474** | (2.4) | 507 | (2.49) | 545 | (2.82) | **583** | (3.4) | **41.8** | (1.07) | **2.2** | (0.09) | 18.7 | (0.90) |
| Austria | **478** | (4.5) | 499 | (4.02) | 522 | (4.50) | **546** | (6.0) | **25.0** | (1.90) | **1.8** | (0.12) | 8.0 | (1.25) |
| Belgium | **472** | (4.1) | 497 | (3.75) | 528 | (3.44) | **546** | (4.0) | **31.2** | (2.16) | **1.8** | (0.13) | 9.3 | (1.28) |
| Canada | **493** | (2.9) | 523 | (2.67) | 548 | (2.49) | **581** | (3.3) | **32.6** | (1.04) | **2.0** | (0.07) | 13.0 | (0.79) |
| Czech Republic | **487** | (4.9) | 505 | (4.72) | 522 | (3.95) | **537** | (4.9) | **21.7** | (2.21) | **1.5** | (0.09) | 3.8 | (0.80) |
| Denmark | **464** | (3.9) | 479 | (4.57) | 503 | (4.03) | **539** | (4.9) | **31.3** | (1.63) | **1.6** | (0.10) | 10.8 | (1.08) |
| Finland | **524** | (3.1) | 559 | (3.07) | 575 | (3.60) | **596** | (3.1) | **32.1** | (1.57) | **2.1** | (0.11) | 11.2 | (1.07) |
| France | **459** | (4.2) | 481 | (4.06) | 505 | (4.24) | **541** | (4.2) | **33.2** | (1.81) | **1.7** | (0.12) | 10.5 | (1.09) |
| Germany | **476** | (5.2) | 506 | (4.36) | 530 | (4.05) | **559** | (4.5) | **30.8** | (1.78) | **1.9** | (0.13) | 11.4 | (1.14) |
| Greece | **446** | (4.5) | 462 | (3.63) | 484 | (3.54) | **503** | (4.3) | **22.3** | (1.49) | **1.5** | (0.10) | 6.2 | (0.83) |
| Hungary | **474** | (3.6) | 501 | (3.84) | 510 | (3.65) | **531** | (4.4) | **24.3** | (2.04) | **1.8** | (0.12) | 6.3 | (1.01) |
| Iceland | **434** | (2.8) | 475 | (3.71) | 510 | (3.38) | **549** | (3.3) | **39.8** | (1.37) | **2.6** | (0.18) | 22.0 | (1.38) |
| Ireland | **461** | (4.4) | 495 | (3.54) | 525 | (4.30) | **557** | (3.6) | **36.8** | (1.43) | **2.2** | (0.16) | 16.2 | (1.12) |
| Italy | **449** | (2.6) | 469 | (2.72) | 486 | (2.91) | **499** | (3.3) | **24.4** | (1.72) | **1.5** | (0.08) | 4.8 | (0.67) |
| Japan | **487** | (4.7) | 520 | (3.50) | 545 | (4.08) | **574** | (3.6) | **33.4** | (1.71) | **2.0** | (0.12) | 12.2 | (1.11) |
| Korea | **482** | (4.6) | 498 | (3.74) | 535 | (3.54) | **574** | (4.5) | **36.7** | (1.94) | **1.9** | (0.12) | 16.7 | (1.50) |
| Luxembourg | **452** | (2.6) | 477 | (3.25) | 494 | (2.73) | **523** | (3.3) | **24.9** | (1.35) | **1.7** | (0.11) | 8.2 | (0.87) |
| Mexico | **407** | (3.7) | 410 | (3.40) | 407 | (2.83) | **416** | (4.2) | **4.7** | (2.05) | **1.0** | (0.07) | 0.2 | (0.16) |
| Netherlands | **496** | (3.8) | 506 | (3.56) | 535 | (3.93) | **564** | (4.2) | **29.6** | (1.75) | **1.5** | (0.12) | 8.3 | (0.98) |
| New Zealand | **483** | (2.9) | 510 | (4.21) | 551 | (3.64) | **583** | (4.1) | **40.3** | (1.44) | **1.9** | (0.12) | 13.8 | (1.03) |
| Norway | **440** | (3.6) | 475 | (3.09) | 509 | (3.63) | **532** | (3.8) | **34.5** | (1.26) | **2.2** | (0.13) | 15.7 | (0.98) |
| Poland | **489** | (3.5) | 483 | (3.91) | 497 | (3.46) | **523** | (3.4) | **14.9** | (1.51) | **1.0** | (0.08) | 2.4 | (0.48) |
| Portugal | **444** | (3.9) | 467 | (3.87) | 479 | (4.50) | **508** | (3.7) | **31.0** | (2.09) | **1.7** | (0.12) | 7.6 | (1.04) |
| Slovak Republic | **469** | (4.0) | 481 | (4.65) | 496 | (4.53) | **508** | (4.6) | **18.2** | (2.74) | **1.4** | (0.10) | 2.7 | (0.76) |
| Spain | **451** | (2.7) | 473 | (2.99) | 501 | (3.25) | **530** | (3.3) | **32.4** | (1.24) | **1.8** | (0.09) | 11.9 | (0.85) |
| Sweden | **461** | (3.7) | 493 | (3.18) | 517 | (3.81) | **546** | (3.6) | **32.6** | (1.64) | **2.1** | (0.16) | 13.2 | (1.23) |
| Switzerland | **470** | (3.1) | 499 | (3.50) | 520 | (3.64) | **558** | (4.5) | **34.7** | (1.42) | **1.8** | (0.09) | 12.7 | (0.99) |
| Turkey | **398** | (3.1) | 416 | (4.25) | 426 | (5.25) | **455** | (6.2) | **22.3** | (2.09) | **1.4** | (0.14) | 6.9 | (1.05) |
| United Kingdom | **470** | (3.6) | 497 | (3.10) | 528 | (3.21) | **567** | (3.4) | **42.9** | (1.73) | **1.8** | (0.10) | 13.5 | (1.02) |
| United States | **452** | (2.9) | 480 | (4.35) | 501 | (5.65) | **526** | (7.6) | **30.1** | (2.47) | **1.5** | (0.13) | 8.2 | (1.42) |
| **OECD total** | **467** | (1.2) | 487 | (1.38) | 499 | (1.56) | **513** | (2.1) | **19.8** | (0.74) | **1.3** | (0.03) | 3.7 | (0.28) |
| **OECD average** | **465** | (0.7) | 488 | (0.68) | 511 | (0.70) | **539** | (0.8) | **29.7** | (0.32) | **1.8** | (0.02) | 10.2 | (0.19) |
| Argentina | 389 | (7.3) | 408 | (6.55) | 391 | (6.84) | 384 | (6.6) | -1.4 | (2.87) | 1.0 | (0.11) | 0.0 | (0.10) |
| Azerbaijan | 382 | (3.5) | 385 | (4.04) | 381 | (3.02) | 383 | (3.2) | 0.9 | (1.49) | 1.1 | (0.09) | 0.0 | (0.07) |
| Brazil | 391 | (3.6) | 397 | (4.26) | 383 | (3.74) | 392 | (3.9) | 0.5 | (1.86) | 0.9 | (0.06) | 0.0 | (0.03) |
| Bulgaria | **420** | (6.0) | 444 | (6.35) | 436 | (7.29) | 445 | (7.8) | **12.1** | (2.89) | 1.3 | (0.10) | 0.9 | (0.42) |
| Chile | **422** | (4.5) | 431 | (4.71) | 441 | (4.90) | 459 | (6.9) | **16.2** | (2.05) | 1.2 | (0.09) | 2.7 | (0.65) |
| Colombia | 396 | (4.4) | 391 | (4.48) | 383 | (4.54) | 384 | (5.6) | -5.9 | (2.70) | 0.9 | (0.08) | 0.3 | (0.28) |
| Croatia | **476** | (3.0) | 489 | (2.99) | 499 | (3.42) | 509 | (3.8) | **13.8** | (1.72) | 1.4 | (0.09) | 2.1 | (0.52) |
| Estonia | **509** | (3.5) | 527 | (3.53) | 538 | (3.47) | 553 | (4.1) | **20.2** | (1.85) | 1.5 | (0.10) | 4.3 | (0.80) |
| Hong Kong-China | **496** | (3.3) | 537 | (3.58) | 553 | (3.56) | 584 | (3.3) | **36.0** | (1.45) | 2.2 | (0.15) | 12.4 | (0.86) |
| Indonesia | 393 | (8.1) | 388 | (5.91) | 393 | (5.79) | 401 | (5.0) | 5.1 | (3.55) | 1.0 | (0.09) | 0.3 | (0.37) |
| Israel | **417** | (4.7) | 457 | (4.38) | 473 | (4.57) | 484 | (6.2) | **22.1** | (1.92) | 1.7 | (0.13) | 5.8 | (1.02) |
| Jordan | **403** | (3.6) | 416 | (3.36) | 426 | (3.94) | 445 | (4.5) | **18.8** | (2.07) | 1.4 | (0.10) | 3.3 | (0.70) |
| Kyrgyzstan | **347** | (4.9) | 325 | (3.24) | 314 | (3.56) | 307 | (4.1) | -18.8 | (2.66) | 0.7 | (0.07) | 2.9 | (0.77) |
| Latvia | **482** | (4.2) | 482 | (3.85) | 494 | (3.59) | 501 | (4.2) | **12.1** | (2.66) | 1.1 | (0.08) | 1.0 | (0.43) |
| Liechtenstein | **490** | (10.8) | 496 | (10.23) | 541 | (9.58) | 566 | (9.4) | **29.0** | (4.87) | 1.7 | (0.42) | 11.0 | (3.33) |
| Lithuania | **467** | (3.6) | 483 | (3.52) | 489 | (4.11) | 514 | (4.0) | **21.8** | (1.77) | 1.4 | (0.09) | 3.9 | (0.60) |
| Macao-China | **483** | (2.4) | 507 | (2.81) | 514 | (3.16) | 540 | (2.6) | **26.0** | (1.58) | 1.8 | (0.12) | 7.5 | (0.89) |
| Montenegro | **420** | (3.1) | 416 | (3.06) | 407 | (2.78) | 407 | (3.3) | -4.4 | (1.79) | 0.7 | (0.07) | 0.3 | (0.22) |
| Qatar | **331** | (1.9) | 351 | (2.31) | 360 | (2.08) | 364 | (2.2) | **12.5** | (0.84) | 1.4 | (0.08) | 2.7 | (0.35) |
| Romania | 407 | (4.5) | 427 | (5.76) | 416 | (5.00) | 426 | (5.5) | 8.3 | (2.43) | 1.1 | (0.09) | 0.7 | (0.38) |
| Russian Federation | **470** | (5.0) | 477 | (4.18) | 482 | (3.93) | 488 | (6.0) | **10.9** | (2.31) | 1.2 | (0.08) | 0.9 | (0.39) |
| Serbia | **446** | (3.6) | 441 | (3.41) | 432 | (3.82) | 426 | (4.7) | -8.8 | (1.83) | 0.8 | (0.06) | 0.9 | (0.35) |
| Slovenia | **504** | (2.7) | 512 | (3.58) | 522 | (3.68) | 538 | (4.0) | **15.0** | (1.86) | 1.3 | (0.08) | 2.2 | (0.56) |
| Chinese Taipei | **498** | (3.7) | 525 | (4.50) | 538 | (4.42) | 570 | (4.0) | **28.9** | (1.53) | 1.8 | (0.10) | 8.0 | (0.77) |
| Thailand | **406** | (2.6) | 407 | (2.80) | 426 | (3.57) | 444 | (3.7) | **23.6** | (2.00) | 1.3 | (0.08) | 4.2 | (0.68) |
| Tunisia | **372** | (3.0) | 376 | (4.32) | 385 | (4.33) | 410 | (4.7) | **14.7** | (1.83) | 1.2 | (0.08) | 2.1 | (0.49) |
| Uruguay | 424 | (4.0) | 429 | (3.99) | 432 | (4.06) | 431 | (4.7) | 3.4 | (2.08) | 1.0 | (0.08) | 0.1 | (0.15) |

Note: Values that are statistically significant are indicated in bold (see Annex A3).
1. Results based on students' self-reports.
StatLink http://dx.doi.org/10.1787/142102278412

Pour consulter la version française intégrale de ce tableau, suivre ce lien :
StatLink http://dx.doi.org/10.1787/152630454851

[Part 1/2]

**Table 3.10** Index of instrumental motivation to learn science and performance on the science scale, by quarters of the index[1]

Tableau 3.10 Indice de motivation instrumentale pour l'apprentissage des sciences et scores sur l'échelle de culture scientifique, par quartile de l'indice

| | Index of instrumental motivation to learn science | | | | | | | | | | | | | | | |
|---|---|---|---|---|---|---|---|---|---|---|---|---|---|---|---|---|
| | All students | | Males | | Females | | Gender difference (M - F) | | Bottom quarter | | Second quarter | | Third quarter | | Top quarter | |
| | Mean index | S.E. | Mean index | S.E. | Mean index | S.E. | Dif. | S.E. | Mean index | S.E. | Mean index | S.E. | Mean index | S.E. | Mean index | S.E. |
| **OECD** | | | | | | | | | | | | | | | | |
| Australia | 0.11 | (0.02) | 0.11 | (0.02) | 0.10 | (0.02) | 0.02 | (0.02) | -1.22 | (0.01) | -0.29 | (0.00) | 0.39 | (0.00) | 1.54 | (0.01) |
| Austria | -0.40 | (0.03) | -0.29 | (0.03) | -0.51 | (0.04) | **0.22** | (0.04) | -1.71 | (0.01) | -0.78 | (0.01) | -0.15 | (0.01) | 1.05 | (0.02) |
| Belgium | -0.22 | (0.02) | -0.18 | (0.02) | -0.26 | (0.02) | **0.08** | (0.03) | -1.40 | (0.01) | -0.56 | (0.00) | 0.09 | (0.01) | 1.01 | (0.01) |
| Canada | 0.32 | (0.02) | 0.28 | (0.02) | 0.36 | (0.02) | **-0.08** | (0.03) | -1.01 | (0.01) | -0.02 | (0.01) | 0.62 | (0.01) | 1.70 | (0.01) |
| Czech Republic | -0.24 | (0.02) | -0.30 | (0.02) | -0.15 | (0.03) | **-0.15** | (0.04) | -1.26 | (0.02) | -0.51 | (0.00) | 0.01 | (0.01) | 0.82 | (0.02) |
| Denmark | 0.04 | (0.01) | 0.00 | (0.02) | 0.08 | (0.02) | **-0.08** | (0.03) | -1.12 | (0.01) | -0.34 | (0.01) | 0.27 | (0.00) | 1.34 | (0.01) |
| Finland | -0.22 | (0.02) | -0.28 | (0.02) | -0.15 | (0.02) | **-0.13** | (0.03) | -1.26 | (0.02) | -0.53 | (0.01) | 0.00 | (0.01) | 0.92 | (0.02) |
| France | -0.07 | (0.02) | -0.02 | (0.04) | -0.12 | (0.02) | 0.10 | (0.04) | -1.40 | (0.02) | -0.44 | (0.00) | 0.23 | (0.01) | 1.31 | (0.01) |
| Germany | -0.07 | (0.02) | 0.01 | (0.03) | -0.16 | (0.02) | **0.17** | (0.03) | -1.34 | (0.01) | -0.47 | (0.01) | 0.20 | (0.01) | 1.33 | (0.01) |
| Greece | 0.08 | (0.02) | 0.21 | (0.03) | -0.04 | (0.02) | **0.25** | (0.04) | -1.12 | (0.02) | -0.25 | (0.01) | 0.40 | (0.01) | 1.29 | (0.01) |
| Hungary | -0.07 | (0.02) | -0.06 | (0.02) | -0.09 | (0.03) | 0.03 | (0.03) | -1.11 | (0.01) | -0.39 | (0.00) | 0.19 | (0.01) | 1.01 | (0.02) |
| Iceland | 0.09 | (0.02) | 0.13 | (0.02) | 0.04 | (0.03) | **0.09** | (0.03) | -1.32 | (0.02) | -0.32 | (0.01) | 0.41 | (0.01) | 1.58 | (0.01) |
| Ireland | 0.15 | (0.02) | 0.04 | (0.03) | 0.27 | (0.03) | **-0.23** | (0.04) | -1.18 | (0.02) | -0.22 | (0.01) | 0.46 | (0.01) | 1.55 | (0.01) |
| Italy | 0.12 | (0.01) | 0.19 | (0.01) | 0.04 | (0.02) | **0.15** | (0.02) | -0.93 | (0.01) | -0.18 | (0.00) | 0.37 | (0.00) | 1.21 | (0.01) |
| Japan | -0.43 | (0.03) | -0.33 | (0.03) | -0.54 | (0.03) | **0.21** | (0.04) | -1.74 | (0.01) | -0.78 | (0.00) | -0.17 | (0.01) | 0.96 | (0.02) |
| Korea | -0.26 | (0.02) | -0.18 | (0.03) | -0.34 | (0.03) | **0.15** | (0.03) | -1.40 | (0.02) | -0.58 | (0.01) | 0.03 | (0.01) | 0.92 | (0.03) |
| Luxembourg | -0.15 | (0.02) | -0.18 | (0.02) | -0.11 | (0.02) | **-0.08** | (0.03) | -1.49 | (0.01) | -0.54 | (0.01) | 0.13 | (0.01) | 1.31 | (0.01) |
| Mexico | 0.54 | (0.01) | 0.52 | (0.02) | 0.55 | (0.02) | -0.03 | (0.02) | -0.46 | (0.01) | 0.32 | (0.00) | 0.76 | (0.00) | 1.53 | (0.01) |
| Netherlands | -0.22 | (0.02) | -0.22 | (0.03) | -0.23 | (0.02) | 0.00 | (0.03) | -1.45 | (0.02) | -0.56 | (0.01) | 0.07 | (0.01) | 1.05 | (0.02) |
| New Zealand | 0.17 | (0.02) | 0.15 | (0.02) | 0.20 | (0.02) | -0.04 | (0.04) | -1.07 | (0.02) | -0.21 | (0.01) | 0.44 | (0.01) | 1.54 | (0.01) |
| Norway | -0.16 | (0.02) | -0.15 | (0.02) | -0.17 | (0.02) | 0.02 | (0.02) | -1.32 | (0.02) | -0.49 | (0.01) | 0.14 | (0.01) | 1.04 | (0.02) |
| Poland | 0.16 | (0.02) | 0.11 | (0.02) | 0.21 | (0.02) | **-0.10** | (0.03) | -0.90 | (0.02) | -0.12 | (0.01) | 0.37 | (0.00) | 1.28 | (0.02) |
| Portugal | 0.47 | (0.02) | 0.37 | (0.02) | 0.56 | (0.03) | **-0.19** | (0.03) | -0.77 | (0.03) | 0.26 | (0.01) | 0.68 | (0.01) | 1.71 | (0.01) |
| Slovak Republic | -0.19 | (0.02) | -0.19 | (0.03) | -0.18 | (0.03) | -0.01 | (0.04) | -1.22 | (0.02) | -0.49 | (0.00) | 0.08 | (0.01) | 0.88 | (0.02) |
| Spain | 0.06 | (0.02) | 0.10 | (0.02) | 0.01 | (0.02) | **0.09** | (0.03) | -1.25 | (0.01) | -0.31 | (0.01) | 0.37 | (0.01) | 1.43 | (0.01) |
| Sweden | -0.05 | (0.02) | -0.04 | (0.02) | -0.07 | (0.02) | 0.02 | (0.03) | -1.26 | (0.02) | -0.40 | (0.01) | 0.23 | (0.01) | 1.21 | (0.02) |
| Switzerland | -0.25 | (0.02) | -0.20 | (0.02) | -0.31 | (0.02) | **0.11** | (0.03) | -1.43 | (0.01) | -0.61 | (0.00) | -0.01 | (0.01) | 1.05 | (0.02) |
| Turkey | 0.34 | (0.02) | 0.30 | (0.03) | 0.38 | (0.03) | **-0.08** | (0.03) | -0.93 | (0.02) | 0.12 | (0.01) | 0.61 | (0.01) | 1.54 | (0.01) |
| United Kingdom | 0.17 | (0.01) | 0.23 | (0.02) | 0.11 | (0.02) | **0.12** | (0.03) | -0.98 | (0.02) | -0.19 | (0.01) | 0.39 | (0.00) | 1.46 | (0.01) |
| United States | 0.29 | (0.02) | 0.28 | (0.02) | 0.29 | (0.02) | -0.01 | (0.03) | -0.86 | (0.02) | 0.02 | (0.01) | 0.48 | (0.01) | 1.51 | (0.01) |
| **OECD total** | 0.11 | (0.01) | 0.13 | (0.01) | 0.09 | (0.01) | **0.04** | (0.01) | -1.14 | (0.01) | -0.23 | (0.00) | 0.41 | (0.00) | 1.40 | (0.00) |
| **OECD average** | 0.00 | (0.00) | 0.01 | (0.00) | -0.01 | (0.00) | **0.02** | (0.01) | -1.20 | (0.00) | -0.33 | (0.00) | 0.27 | (0.00) | 1.27 | (0.00) |
| **Partners** | | | | | | | | | | | | | | | | |
| Argentina | 0.44 | (0.02) | 0.43 | (0.03) | 0.44 | (0.02) | -0.01 | (0.03) | -0.68 | (0.02) | 0.21 | (0.01) | 0.68 | (0.01) | 1.54 | (0.01) |
| Azerbaijan | 0.55 | (0.02) | 0.53 | (0.03) | 0.57 | (0.03) | -0.04 | (0.03) | -0.58 | (0.01) | 0.29 | (0.01) | 0.89 | (0.01) | 1.60 | (0.01) |
| Brazil | 0.48 | (0.01) | 0.44 | (0.02) | 0.52 | (0.02) | **-0.08** | (0.03) | -0.55 | (0.02) | 0.25 | (0.01) | 0.69 | (0.01) | 1.54 | (0.01) |
| Bulgaria | 0.36 | (0.02) | 0.31 | (0.02) | 0.41 | (0.02) | **-0.10** | (0.02) | -0.68 | (0.02) | 0.17 | (0.01) | 0.52 | (0.01) | 1.42 | (0.01) |
| Chile | 0.52 | (0.03) | 0.48 | (0.03) | 0.56 | (0.04) | **-0.07** | (0.03) | -0.77 | (0.02) | 0.21 | (0.01) | 0.91 | (0.01) | 1.73 | (0.01) |
| Colombia | 0.65 | (0.02) | 0.62 | (0.03) | 0.67 | (0.02) | -0.05 | (0.03) | -0.41 | (0.02) | 0.35 | (0.01) | 0.97 | (0.01) | 1.68 | (0.01) |
| Croatia | 0.05 | (0.03) | 0.02 | (0.03) | 0.07 | (0.03) | -0.05 | (0.04) | -1.15 | (0.02) | -0.23 | (0.00) | 0.35 | (0.00) | 1.21 | (0.01) |
| Estonia | 0.06 | (0.01) | 0.06 | (0.02) | 0.05 | (0.02) | 0.01 | (0.02) | -0.87 | (0.02) | -0.24 | (0.00) | 0.24 | (0.00) | 1.09 | (0.01) |
| Hong Kong-China | 0.16 | (0.02) | 0.28 | (0.02) | 0.05 | (0.02) | **0.23** | (0.03) | -1.03 | (0.02) | -0.06 | (0.01) | 0.38 | (0.01) | 1.36 | (0.01) |
| Indonesia | 0.76 | (0.02) | 0.72 | (0.03) | 0.80 | (0.02) | -0.08 | (0.03) | -0.04 | (0.02) | 0.44 | (0.00) | 0.98 | (0.01) | 1.67 | (0.01) |
| Israel | -0.37 | (0.03) | -0.30 | (0.04) | -0.44 | (0.04) | **0.14** | (0.04) | -1.70 | (0.01) | -0.78 | (0.01) | -0.13 | (0.01) | 1.15 | (0.02) |
| Jordan | 0.80 | (0.02) | 0.73 | (0.02) | 0.88 | (0.02) | **-0.15** | (0.02) | -0.20 | (0.02) | 0.60 | (0.01) | 1.11 | (0.00) | 1.70 | (0.01) |
| Kyrgyzstan | 0.84 | (0.02) | 0.78 | (0.02) | 0.90 | (0.02) | **-0.12** | (0.02) | -0.15 | (0.01) | 0.62 | (0.01) | 1.17 | (0.01) | 1.73 | (0.01) |
| Latvia | 0.01 | (0.02) | 0.01 | (0.02) | 0.00 | (0.02) | 0.01 | (0.03) | -0.86 | (0.01) | -0.28 | (0.01) | 0.22 | (0.01) | 0.96 | (0.02) |
| Liechtenstein | -0.32 | (0.05) | -0.14 | (0.08) | -0.48 | (0.07) | **0.34** | (0.11) | -1.55 | (0.04) | -0.68 | (0.02) | -0.08 | (0.03) | 1.05 | (0.06) |
| Lithuania | 0.37 | (0.01) | 0.40 | (0.02) | 0.34 | (0.02) | 0.07 | (0.03) | -0.64 | (0.01) | 0.10 | (0.01) | 0.55 | (0.01) | 1.47 | (0.01) |
| Macao-China | 0.39 | (0.02) | 0.43 | (0.02) | 0.34 | (0.02) | **0.09** | (0.03) | -0.61 | (0.02) | 0.24 | (0.01) | 0.46 | (0.01) | 1.46 | (0.02) |
| Montenegro | 0.45 | (0.02) | 0.42 | (0.02) | 0.47 | (0.02) | -0.05 | (0.03) | -0.80 | (0.02) | 0.22 | (0.01) | 0.75 | (0.01) | 1.62 | (0.01) |
| Qatar | 0.52 | (0.01) | 0.53 | (0.02) | 0.51 | (0.01) | 0.02 | (0.02) | -0.76 | (0.02) | 0.26 | (0.00) | 0.90 | (0.01) | 1.70 | (0.01) |
| Romania | 0.40 | (0.02) | 0.37 | (0.03) | 0.43 | (0.02) | -0.06 | (0.03) | -0.61 | (0.02) | 0.23 | (0.01) | 0.60 | (0.01) | 1.38 | (0.01) |
| Russian Federation | 0.21 | (0.02) | 0.28 | (0.02) | 0.15 | (0.02) | **0.13** | (0.02) | -0.78 | (0.01) | -0.06 | (0.01) | 0.43 | (0.00) | 1.27 | (0.01) |
| Serbia | 0.11 | (0.02) | 0.13 | (0.03) | 0.09 | (0.03) | 0.03 | (0.03) | -1.08 | (0.02) | -0.19 | (0.01) | 0.42 | (0.01) | 1.29 | (0.01) |
| Slovenia | 0.06 | (0.01) | 0.06 | (0.02) | 0.06 | (0.02) | 0.00 | (0.03) | -1.05 | (0.01) | -0.21 | (0.01) | 0.34 | (0.00) | 1.17 | (0.02) |
| Chinese Taipei | 0.27 | (0.01) | 0.44 | (0.02) | 0.09 | (0.02) | **0.35** | (0.02) | -0.80 | (0.01) | 0.07 | (0.01) | 0.41 | (0.00) | 1.40 | (0.01) |
| Thailand | 0.72 | (0.01) | 0.63 | (0.02) | 0.78 | (0.01) | **-0.14** | (0.02) | 0.03 | (0.01) | 0.37 | (0.00) | 0.88 | (0.00) | 1.58 | (0.01) |
| Tunisia | 0.84 | (0.02) | 0.78 | (0.03) | 0.89 | (0.02) | **-0.10** | (0.03) | -0.28 | (0.02) | 0.66 | (0.01) | 1.20 | (0.01) | 1.76 | (0.01) |
| Uruguay | 0.19 | (0.02) | 0.14 | (0.03) | 0.24 | (0.02) | **-0.10** | (0.04) | -1.01 | (0.02) | -0.12 | (0.01) | 0.45 | (0.01) | 1.44 | (0.01) |

Note: Values that are statistically significant are indicated in bold (see Annex A3).
1. Results based on students' self-reports.
*StatLink* http://dx.doi.org/10.1787/142102278412

Pour consulter la version française intégrale de ce tableau, suivre ce lien :
*StatLink* http://dx.doi.org/10.1787/152630454851

[Part 2/2]

**Table 3.10** Index of instrumental motivation to learn science and performance on the science scale, by quarters of the index[1]

Tableau 3.10 Indice de motivation instrumentale pour l'apprentissage des sciences et scores sur l'échelle de culture scientifique, par quartile de l'indice

| | Performance on the science scale, by quarters of this index | | | | | | | Change in the science score per unit of this index | | Increased likelihood of students in the bottom quarter of this index scoring in the bottom quarter of the science performance distribution | | Explained variance in student performance (r-squared x 100) | |
| | Bottom quarter | | Second quarter | | Third quarter | | Top quarter | | | | | | | |
| | Mean score | S.E. | Mean score | S.E. | Mean score | S.E. | Mean score | S.E | Effect | S.E. | Ratio | S.E. | Percentage | S.E. |
|---|---|---|---|---|---|---|---|---|---|---|---|---|---|---|
| **OECD** | | | | | | | | | | | | | | |
| Australia | **494** | (3.0) | 528 | (3.2) | 536 | (3.1) | **581** | (2.7) | **29.5** | (0.94) | **1.8** | (0.08) | 9.9 | (0.57) |
| Austria | **503** | (4.2) | 521 | (4.1) | 518 | (6.0) | 520 | (7.3) | 5.6 | (2.68) | 1.2 | (0.09) | 0.4 | (0.39) |
| Belgium | **502** | (4.2) | 527 | (3.1) | 530 | (3.7) | **540** | (4.6) | **17.0** | (1.97) | **1.4** | (0.09) | 2.9 | (0.63) |
| Canada | **514** | (2.9) | 528 | (3.1) | 540 | (3.1) | **578** | (2.4) | **22.8** | (1.06) | **1.5** | (0.07) | 6.4 | (0.55) |
| Czech Republic | **511** | (4.8) | 521 | (4.6) | 518 | (4.9) | 526 | (4.9) | 6.4 | (2.36) | 1.1 | (0.10) | 0.3 | (0.24) |
| Denmark | **482** | (4.1) | 495 | (3.8) | 493 | (4.6) | 528 | (3.7) | **17.6** | (1.82) | **1.3** | (0.10) | 3.5 | (0.69) |
| Finland | **530** | (2.8) | 555 | (3.2) | 573 | (3.3) | **599** | (3.4) | **30.5** | (1.54) | **1.8** | (0.13) | 10.2 | (1.02) |
| France | **470** | (3.7) | 491 | (3.8) | 499 | (4.7) | **541** | (4.8) | **25.5** | (1.83) | **1.4** | (0.10) | 7.4 | (1.02) |
| Germany | **510** | (4.2) | 522 | (4.1) | 520 | (5.2) | 542 | (5.4) | **12.2** | (1.50) | 1.1 | (0.07) | 1.7 | (0.42) |
| Greece | **472** | (4.0) | 464 | (4.6) | 472 | (4.3) | 490 | (4.0) | 9.9 | (1.68) | 0.9 | (0.07) | 1.1 | (0.37) |
| Hungary | 510 | (3.8) | 506 | (4.0) | 495 | (3.6) | 510 | (4.7) | 1.9 | (2.61) | **0.8** | (0.08) | 0.0 | (0.10) |
| Iceland | **456** | (3.8) | 483 | (3.5) | 500 | (3.5) | **540** | (3.5) | **28.1** | (1.56) | **1.8** | (0.10) | 10.7 | (1.10) |
| Ireland | **480** | (3.7) | 511 | (4.2) | 522 | (4.4) | **550** | (4.3) | **24.8** | (1.48) | **1.8** | (0.11) | 7.9 | (0.92) |
| Italy | **461** | (2.6) | 471 | (2.8) | 476 | (2.8) | 489 | (3.6) | **14.2** | (1.73) | 1.1 | (0.06) | 1.6 | (0.40) |
| Japan | **498** | (4.0) | 519 | (3.8) | 544 | (4.2) | 570 | (4.2) | **27.5** | (1.62) | **1.7** | (0.11) | 8.6 | (0.96) |
| Korea | **499** | (4.7) | 515 | (3.5) | 524 | (3.8) | 551 | (5.9) | **23.3** | (2.73) | **1.5** | (0.10) | 6.0 | (1.38) |
| Luxembourg | **481** | (2.7) | 491 | (3.5) | 481 | (3.6) | 502 | (3.1) | 7.6 | (1.37) | 1.1 | (0.07) | 0.7 | (0.26) |
| Mexico | 416 | (3.2) | 412 | (2.9) | 406 | (3.2) | 415 | (3.9) | -1.1 | (1.44) | 0.9 | (0.06) | 0.0 | (0.04) |
| Netherlands | **521** | (3.8) | 521 | (3.5) | 522 | (5.0) | 556 | (5.8) | **14.0** | (1.59) | 1.1 | (0.07) | 2.2 | (0.52) |
| New Zealand | **504** | (3.3) | 528 | (3.5) | 535 | (4.4) | **584** | (3.6) | **29.2** | (1.53) | **1.5** | (0.09) | 7.7 | (0.83) |
| Norway | **462** | (3.4) | 490 | (3.9) | 497 | (3.2) | 516 | (3.3) | **22.2** | (1.52) | **1.5** | (0.09) | 5.2 | (0.70) |
| Poland | 504 | (3.5) | 497 | (3.8) | 487 | (3.2) | 506 | (3.3) | 2.8 | (1.39) | **0.8** | (0.06) | 0.1 | (0.07) |
| Portugal | **437** | (4.0) | 459 | (4.2) | 468 | (4.9) | 524 | (3.7) | **32.9** | (1.65) | **1.6** | (0.13) | 11.8 | (1.14) |
| Slovak Republic | 484 | (4.5) | 493 | (3.4) | 491 | (3.9) | 495 | (5.1) | 5.0 | (2.45) | 1.1 | (0.10) | 0.2 | (0.22) |
| Spain | **471** | (2.6) | 479 | (3.4) | 488 | (3.6) | 523 | (3.5) | **19.6** | (1.12) | **1.3** | (0.08) | 5.2 | (0.60) |
| Sweden | **479** | (3.2) | 499 | (3.2) | 509 | (3.3) | 542 | (3.8) | **25.9** | (1.59) | **1.6** | (0.11) | 7.7 | (0.95) |
| Switzerland | **493** | (4.2) | 517 | (3.8) | 517 | (3.7) | 541 | (5.6) | **19.6** | (1.76) | **1.4** | (0.08) | 3.7 | (0.68) |
| Turkey | **413** | (3.6) | 417 | (4.5) | 422 | (4.7) | 453 | (6.0) | 15.6 | (1.92) | 1.1 | (0.08) | 3.4 | (0.73) |
| United Kingdom | **491** | (3.7) | 512 | (3.5) | 510 | (3.1) | 556 | (3.3) | **26.1** | (1.50) | **1.4** | (0.09) | 5.5 | (0.65) |
| United States | **482** | (4.3) | 479 | (6.3) | 480 | (5.0) | 520 | (5.3) | 18.1 | (2.01) | 1.0 | (0.09) | 2.5 | (0.58) |
| **OECD total** | **489** | (1.2) | 491 | (1.7) | 482 | (1.6) | **510** | (2.0) | 9.3 | (0.70) | **0.9** | (0.03) | 0.8 | (0.12) |
| **OECD average** | **484** | (0.7) | 498 | (0.7) | 502 | (0.7) | **530** | (0.8) | **17.8** | (0.33) | **1.3** | (0.02) | 4.5 | (0.13) |
| **Partners** | | | | | | | | | | | | | | |
| Argentina | **413** | (6.5) | 399 | (6.4) | 397 | (6.7) | 396 | (8.2) | -5.6 | (2.87) | **0.8** | (0.07) | 0.3 | (0.26) |
| Azerbaijan | 388 | (3.9) | 383 | (3.6) | 383 | (3.6) | 384 | (3.6) | -1.7 | (1.76) | 1.0 | (0.08) | 0.1 | (0.15) |
| Brazil | **407** | (4.5) | 394 | (3.6) | 385 | (4.5) | 392 | (3.8) | -5.5 | (1.93) | **0.8** | (0.07) | 0.3 | (0.18) |
| Bulgaria | **456** | (6.1) | 435 | (6.7) | 432 | (7.3) | 436 | (7.2) | -6.5 | (2.76) | **0.7** | (0.07) | 0.3 | (0.22) |
| Chile | **445** | (4.6) | 430 | (4.4) | 432 | (5.4) | 460 | (6.0) | 4.7 | (2.06) | **0.8** | (0.08) | 0.3 | (0.23) |
| Colombia | **405** | (4.8) | 393 | (3.5) | 384 | (5.7) | 384 | (5.1) | -9.6 | (2.90) | **0.7** | (0.10) | 0.9 | (0.49) |
| Croatia | **494** | (3.2) | 506 | (3.6) | 502 | (3.6) | 497 | (4.1) | 2.4 | (1.87) | 1.1 | (0.08) | 0.1 | (0.11) |
| Estonia | 534 | (3.4) | 531 | (3.5) | 529 | (3.8) | 534 | (4.0) | 2.6 | (2.13) | 0.9 | (0.08) | 0.1 | (0.11) |
| Hong Kong-China | **537** | (4.5) | 553 | (4.4) | 544 | (3.9) | **589** | (3.7) | **19.1** | (1.81) | **1.3** | (0.15) | 4.0 | (0.77) |
| Indonesia | 398 | (9.2) | 396 | (8.7) | 386 | (4.1) | 400 | (4.1) | 0.1 | (4.80) | 0.9 | (0.08) | 0.0 | (0.15) |
| Israel | **496** | (5.0) | 475 | (5.0) | 446 | (4.6) | **432** | (5.4) | **-22.4** | (2.08) | **0.6** | (0.06) | 5.0 | (0.88) |
| Jordan | 398 | (3.7) | 419 | (3.7) | 428 | (3.7) | 452 | (4.1) | **25.6** | (1.99) | **1.7** | (0.10) | 4.8 | (0.72) |
| Kyrgyzstan | **351** | (4.7) | 326 | (3.7) | 314 | (3.8) | 323 | (3.5) | **-18.3** | (2.40) | **0.8** | (0.08) | 2.8 | (0.70) |
| Latvia | 491 | (3.8) | 493 | (3.2) | 490 | (4.8) | 487 | (4.8) | -1.2 | (2.22) | 0.9 | (0.08) | 0.0 | (0.06) |
| Liechtenstein | **509** | (10.3) | 527 | (10.8) | 511 | (14.6) | 543 | (10.8) | 13.6 | (4.90) | 1.1 | (0.28) | 2.0 | (1.40) |
| Lithuania | **490** | (4.0) | 481 | (4.3) | 483 | (4.2) | 502 | (3.9) | 6.5 | (1.95) | 0.9 | (0.07) | 0.4 | (0.21) |
| Macao-China | **494** | (3.0) | 500 | (4.1) | 507 | (3.6) | 533 | (3.5) | **19.7** | (2.21) | **1.3** | (0.11) | 3.7 | (0.83) |
| Montenegro | **428** | (2.5) | 417 | (2.7) | 409 | (3.1) | 405 | (2.8) | -9.4 | (1.34) | **0.7** | (0.07) | 1.3 | (0.36) |
| Qatar | **338** | (2.1) | 345 | (2.3) | 354 | (1.9) | 373 | (2.5) | **13.8** | (1.23) | **1.4** | (0.08) | 2.5 | (0.44) |
| Romania | 419 | (6.4) | 415 | (4.2) | 418 | (4.6) | 425 | (5.8) | 4.1 | (2.53) | 1.1 | (0.12) | 0.2 | (0.20) |
| Russian Federation | **499** | (4.5) | 480 | (4.1) | 472 | (3.9) | 471 | (5.3) | **-11.1** | (2.09) | **0.6** | (0.06) | 1.0 | (0.38) |
| Serbia | **447** | (3.4) | 442 | (3.5) | 428 | (3.9) | 428 | (4.7) | -7.7 | (1.82) | **0.7** | (0.07) | 0.7 | (0.34) |
| Slovenia | **518** | (3.2) | 520 | (3.0) | 520 | (4.1) | 538 | (3.8) | **10.2** | (2.03) | 1.1 | (0.08) | 0.9 | (0.34) |
| Chinese Taipei | **523** | (3.9) | 525 | (4.2) | 522 | (4.9) | 560 | (3.8) | **17.4** | (1.40) | 1.1 | (0.07) | 2.5 | (0.40) |
| Thailand | **410** | (3.6) | 411 | (2.4) | 413 | (3.1) | 449 | (3.3) | **23.3** | (2.06) | **1.2** | (0.10) | 3.7 | (0.67) |
| Tunisia | **367** | (3.5) | 379 | (3.9) | 389 | (3.9) | 420 | (4.4) | 20.8 | (1.82) | **1.4** | (0.13) | 4.3 | (0.64) |
| Uruguay | 442 | (3.8) | 435 | (3.8) | 422 | (4.0) | 435 | (4.4) | -2.8 | (1.64) | **0.7** | (0.07) | 0.1 | (0.09) |

Note: Values that are statistically significant are indicated in bold (see Annex A3).
1. Results based on students' self-reports.
StatLink ᴍᴤ http://dx.doi.org/10.1787/142102278412

Pour consulter la version française intégrale de ce tableau, suivre ce lien :
StatLink ᴍᴤ http://dx.doi.org/10.1787/152630454851

[Part 1/2]

**Table 3.11 Index of future-oriented motivation to learn science and performance on the science scale, by quarters of the index[1]**

Tableau 3.11 Indice de motivation prospective pour l'apprentissage des sciences et scores sur l'échelle de culture scientifique, par quartile de l'indice

| | | All students | | Males | | Females | | Gender difference (M - F) | | Bottom quarter | | Second quarter | | Third quarter | | Top quarter | |
|---|---|---|---|---|---|---|---|---|---|---|---|---|---|---|---|---|---|
| | | Mean index | S.E. | Mean index | S.E. | Mean index | S.E. | Dif. | S.E. | Mean index | S.E. | Mean index | S.E. | Mean index | S.E. | Mean index | S.E. |
| OECD | Australia | -0.07 | (0.01) | -0.03 | (0.02) | -0.12 | (0.02) | **0.09** | (0.02) | -1.39 | (0.00) | -0.40 | (0.01) | 0.24 | (0.01) | 1.26 | (0.01) |
| | Austria | -0.33 | (0.02) | -0.29 | (0.03) | -0.37 | (0.03) | **0.08** | (0.03) | -1.42 | (0.00) | -0.86 | (0.01) | -0.07 | (0.01) | 1.03 | (0.02) |
| | Belgium | -0.03 | (0.02) | 0.05 | (0.03) | -0.12 | (0.02) | **0.18** | (0.03) | -1.32 | (0.00) | -0.29 | (0.01) | 0.22 | (0.01) | 1.27 | (0.01) |
| | Canada | 0.20 | (0.01) | 0.22 | (0.02) | 0.19 | (0.02) | 0.03 | (0.02) | -1.22 | (0.01) | -0.14 | (0.00) | 0.58 | (0.01) | 1.59 | (0.01) |
| | Czech Republic | -0.12 | (0.02) | -0.21 | (0.02) | 0.00 | (0.03) | **-0.21** | (0.04) | -1.32 | (0.01) | -0.20 | (0.01) | 0.06 | (0.01) | 1.00 | (0.02) |
| | Denmark | -0.17 | (0.02) | -0.21 | (0.03) | -0.14 | (0.02) | **-0.08** | (0.03) | -1.42 | (0.00) | -0.49 | (0.01) | 0.05 | (0.00) | 1.16 | (0.02) |
| | Finland | -0.17 | (0.02) | -0.22 | (0.02) | -0.12 | (0.02) | **-0.11** | (0.03) | -1.33 | (0.00) | -0.32 | (0.01) | 0.04 | (0.01) | 0.93 | (0.01) |
| | France | -0.03 | (0.02) | 0.06 | (0.03) | -0.12 | (0.02) | **0.18** | (0.03) | -1.35 | (0.00) | -0.42 | (0.01) | 0.28 | (0.01) | 1.36 | (0.02) |
| | Germany | -0.15 | (0.02) | -0.05 | (0.03) | -0.26 | (0.02) | **0.21** | (0.03) | -1.39 | (0.00) | -0.60 | (0.01) | 0.14 | (0.01) | 1.25 | (0.02) |
| | Greece | 0.15 | (0.02) | 0.33 | (0.03) | -0.02 | (0.02) | **0.35** | (0.04) | -1.22 | (0.01) | -0.09 | (0.00) | 0.43 | (0.01) | 1.48 | (0.01) |
| | Hungary | 0.07 | (0.02) | 0.07 | (0.03) | 0.08 | (0.03) | -0.02 | (0.03) | -1.07 | (0.01) | -0.10 | (0.00) | 0.25 | (0.01) | 1.22 | (0.02) |
| | Iceland | -0.02 | (0.02) | 0.13 | (0.02) | -0.17 | (0.03) | **0.30** | (0.03) | -1.36 | (0.00) | -0.31 | (0.01) | 0.28 | (0.01) | 1.30 | (0.02) |
| | Ireland | -0.05 | (0.02) | -0.10 | (0.02) | 0.00 | (0.03) | **-0.09** | (0.03) | -1.36 | (0.00) | -0.34 | (0.01) | 0.27 | (0.01) | 1.25 | (0.02) |
| | Italy | 0.20 | (0.02) | 0.30 | (0.02) | 0.10 | (0.02) | **0.20** | (0.02) | -0.99 | (0.01) | -0.06 | (0.00) | 0.48 | (0.00) | 1.36 | (0.01) |
| | Japan | -0.24 | (0.02) | -0.02 | (0.02) | -0.46 | (0.03) | **0.44** | (0.03) | -1.42 | (0.00) | -0.64 | (0.01) | 0.02 | (0.01) | 1.08 | (0.02) |
| | Korea | -0.25 | (0.02) | -0.11 | (0.03) | -0.39 | (0.03) | **0.28** | (0.03) | -1.42 | (0.00) | -0.57 | (0.01) | -0.01 | (0.00) | 0.99 | (0.03) |
| | Luxembourg | -0.05 | (0.02) | -0.04 | (0.02) | -0.06 | (0.02) | 0.02 | (0.03) | -1.39 | (0.00) | -0.43 | (0.01) | 0.26 | (0.01) | 1.38 | (0.01) |
| | Mexico | 0.60 | (0.02) | 0.65 | (0.02) | 0.55 | (0.02) | **0.10** | (0.02) | -0.43 | (0.01) | 0.35 | (0.00) | 0.91 | (0.00) | 1.57 | (0.01) |
| | Netherlands | -0.24 | (0.02) | -0.11 | (0.02) | -0.37 | (0.02) | **0.26** | (0.03) | -1.42 | (0.00) | -0.50 | (0.01) | 0.01 | (0.00) | 0.96 | (0.02) |
| | New Zealand | 0.00 | (0.02) | 0.03 | (0.02) | -0.02 | (0.03) | 0.05 | (0.03) | -1.32 | (0.01) | -0.25 | (0.01) | 0.30 | (0.01) | 1.27 | (0.02) |
| | Norway | -0.22 | (0.02) | -0.15 | (0.03) | -0.30 | (0.02) | **0.16** | (0.04) | -1.42 | (0.00) | -0.61 | (0.01) | 0.04 | (0.01) | 1.10 | (0.02) |
| | Poland | 0.16 | (0.01) | 0.09 | (0.02) | 0.22 | (0.02) | **-0.13** | (0.03) | -1.03 | (0.01) | -0.05 | (0.00) | 0.40 | (0.01) | 1.31 | (0.01) |
| | Portugal | 0.27 | (0.02) | 0.29 | (0.02) | 0.25 | (0.02) | 0.04 | (0.03) | -1.02 | (0.01) | -0.03 | (0.00) | 0.60 | (0.01) | 1.51 | (0.02) |
| | Slovak Republic | 0.08 | (0.02) | 0.03 | (0.02) | 0.14 | (0.03) | **-0.11** | (0.04) | -1.04 | (0.02) | -0.05 | (0.00) | 0.17 | (0.01) | 1.25 | (0.02) |
| | Spain | 0.08 | (0.02) | 0.13 | (0.02) | 0.02 | (0.02) | **0.12** | (0.03) | -1.30 | (0.01) | -0.25 | (0.01) | 0.38 | (0.01) | 1.47 | (0.01) |
| | Sweden | -0.21 | (0.02) | -0.18 | (0.02) | -0.25 | (0.02) | **0.07** | (0.03) | -1.42 | (0.00) | -0.57 | (0.01) | 0.06 | (0.01) | 1.09 | (0.02) |
| | Switzerland | -0.22 | (0.02) | -0.17 | (0.02) | -0.27 | (0.02) | **0.10** | (0.03) | -1.37 | (0.00) | -0.68 | (0.01) | 0.06 | (0.00) | 1.11 | (0.02) |
| | Turkey | 0.65 | (0.03) | 0.70 | (0.03) | 0.59 | (0.03) | **0.11** | (0.03) | -0.70 | (0.02) | 0.35 | (0.01) | 1.05 | (0.01) | 1.91 | (0.01) |
| | United Kingdom | -0.12 | (0.02) | -0.03 | (0.02) | -0.20 | (0.02) | **0.18** | (0.03) | -1.37 | (0.00) | -0.41 | (0.01) | 0.15 | (0.00) | 1.17 | (0.01) |
| | United States | 0.20 | (0.01) | 0.27 | (0.02) | 0.13 | (0.02) | **0.13** | (0.03) | -1.10 | (0.01) | -0.05 | (0.00) | 0.53 | (0.01) | 1.43 | (0.01) |
| | **OECD total** | 0.11 | (0.01) | 0.18 | (0.01) | 0.03 | (0.01) | **0.15** | (0.01) | -1.24 | (0.00) | -0.16 | (0.00) | 0.41 | (0.00) | 1.40 | (0.01) |
| | **OECD average** | 0.00 | (0.00) | 0.05 | (0.00) | -0.05 | (0.00) | **0.10** | (0.01) | -1.24 | (0.00) | -0.30 | (0.00) | 0.27 | (0.00) | 1.27 | (0.00) |
| Partners | Argentina | 0.31 | (0.03) | 0.32 | (0.04) | 0.31 | (0.03) | 0.00 | (0.04) | -1.03 | (0.02) | 0.05 | (0.01) | 0.70 | (0.01) | 1.53 | (0.02) |
| | Azerbaijan | 0.68 | (0.02) | 0.69 | (0.03) | 0.68 | (0.03) | 0.01 | (0.03) | -0.51 | (0.02) | 0.40 | (0.01) | 1.07 | (0.00) | 1.78 | (0.01) |
| | Brazil | 0.46 | (0.02) | 0.48 | (0.03) | 0.44 | (0.02) | 0.05 | (0.02) | -0.67 | (0.02) | 0.13 | (0.01) | 0.78 | (0.01) | 1.59 | (0.01) |
| | Bulgaria | 0.38 | (0.03) | 0.33 | (0.03) | 0.43 | (0.03) | **-0.11** | (0.03) | -0.77 | (0.02) | 0.07 | (0.01) | 0.73 | (0.01) | 1.49 | (0.01) |
| | Chile | 0.24 | (0.02) | 0.24 | (0.02) | 0.24 | (0.03) | 0.00 | (0.03) | -1.06 | (0.01) | -0.03 | (0.00) | 0.55 | (0.01) | 1.51 | (0.01) |
| | Colombia | 0.74 | (0.02) | 0.75 | (0.04) | 0.73 | (0.03) | 0.01 | (0.05) | -0.38 | (0.02) | 0.43 | (0.01) | 1.03 | (0.01) | 1.87 | (0.01) |
| | Croatia | 0.22 | (0.02) | 0.20 | (0.02) | 0.23 | (0.02) | -0.03 | (0.02) | -0.85 | (0.01) | -0.05 | (0.00) | 0.45 | (0.01) | 1.32 | (0.01) |
| | Estonia | -0.09 | (0.02) | -0.12 | (0.02) | -0.06 | (0.02) | -0.06 | (0.03) | -1.19 | (0.01) | -0.32 | (0.01) | 0.15 | (0.01) | 1.00 | (0.02) |
| | Hong Kong-China | 0.29 | (0.01) | 0.46 | (0.02) | 0.12 | (0.02) | **0.34** | (0.03) | -0.82 | (0.02) | -0.05 | (0.00) | 0.58 | (0.01) | 1.44 | (0.01) |
| | Indonesia | 0.81 | (0.03) | 0.77 | (0.04) | 0.85 | (0.02) | -0.08 | (0.04) | -0.06 | (0.02) | 0.64 | (0.01) | 1.03 | (0.00) | 1.62 | (0.01) |
| | Israel | 0.31 | (0.02) | 0.39 | (0.02) | 0.22 | (0.03) | **0.17** | (0.04) | -1.26 | (0.01) | -0.02 | (0.00) | 0.78 | (0.01) | 1.72 | (0.01) |
| | Jordan | 1.07 | (0.02) | 1.14 | (0.02) | 1.00 | (0.03) | **0.14** | (0.03) | -0.01 | (0.02) | 0.89 | (0.01) | 1.36 | (0.01) | 2.04 | (0.01) |
| | Kyrgyzstan | 1.03 | (0.02) | 1.01 | (0.02) | 1.04 | (0.02) | -0.03 | (0.02) | 0.01 | (0.02) | 0.89 | (0.00) | 1.30 | (0.01) | 1.92 | (0.01) |
| | Latvia | -0.09 | (0.02) | -0.09 | (0.02) | -0.09 | (0.02) | 0.00 | (0.03) | -1.17 | (0.01) | -0.18 | (0.01) | 0.07 | (0.01) | 0.92 | (0.01) |
| | Liechtenstein | -0.30 | (0.05) | -0.21 | (0.07) | -0.37 | (0.06) | 0.16 | (0.10) | -1.36 | (0.02) | -0.76 | (0.02) | -0.05 | (0.02) | 1.00 | (0.06) |
| | Lithuania | 0.12 | (0.02) | 0.09 | (0.02) | 0.16 | (0.02) | **-0.08** | (0.03) | -0.89 | (0.02) | -0.05 | (0.00) | 0.26 | (0.01) | 1.18 | (0.01) |
| | Macao-China | 0.17 | (0.01) | 0.27 | (0.02) | 0.06 | (0.01) | **0.20** | (0.02) | -0.80 | (0.01) | -0.05 | (0.00) | 0.33 | (0.01) | 1.19 | (0.01) |
| | Montenegro | 0.32 | (0.02) | 0.32 | (0.02) | 0.33 | (0.02) | -0.02 | (0.03) | -0.98 | (0.02) | 0.00 | (0.00) | 0.71 | (0.01) | 1.57 | (0.01) |
| | Qatar | 0.60 | (0.01) | 0.78 | (0.02) | 0.43 | (0.02) | **0.35** | (0.03) | -0.87 | (0.01) | 0.35 | (0.01) | 1.03 | (0.00) | 1.89 | (0.01) |
| | Romania | 0.55 | (0.02) | 0.55 | (0.02) | 0.54 | (0.02) | 0.02 | (0.03) | -0.49 | (0.02) | 0.27 | (0.01) | 0.87 | (0.01) | 1.54 | (0.02) |
| | Russian Federation | 0.33 | (0.02) | 0.37 | (0.02) | 0.29 | (0.02) | **0.08** | (0.02) | -0.58 | (0.02) | 0.04 | (0.00) | 0.57 | (0.01) | 1.28 | (0.01) |
| | Serbia | 0.28 | (0.02) | 0.34 | (0.02) | 0.22 | (0.03) | **0.11** | (0.03) | -0.93 | (0.02) | 0.02 | (0.00) | 0.57 | (0.01) | 1.47 | (0.01) |
| | Slovenia | 0.01 | (0.02) | -0.01 | (0.02) | 0.02 | (0.02) | -0.03 | (0.03) | -1.20 | (0.01) | -0.24 | (0.01) | 0.24 | (0.01) | 1.24 | (0.02) |
| | Chinese Taipei | 0.14 | (0.01) | 0.39 | (0.02) | -0.14 | (0.01) | **0.53** | (0.02) | -1.04 | (0.01) | -0.05 | (0.00) | 0.33 | (0.01) | 1.31 | (0.01) |
| | Thailand | 0.86 | (0.02) | 0.84 | (0.02) | 0.87 | (0.02) | -0.03 | (0.02) | -0.07 | (0.01) | 0.75 | (0.01) | 1.08 | (0.00) | 1.66 | (0.01) |
| | Tunisia | 1.07 | (0.02) | 1.10 | (0.02) | 1.04 | (0.02) | **0.06** | (0.03) | -0.04 | (0.02) | 0.89 | (0.01) | 1.39 | (0.00) | 2.04 | (0.01) |
| | Uruguay | 0.14 | (0.02) | 0.08 | (0.03) | 0.20 | (0.03) | **-0.12** | (0.04) | -1.25 | (0.01) | -0.14 | (0.01) | 0.45 | (0.01) | 1.52 | (0.02) |

Note: Values that are statistically significant are indicated in bold (see Annex A3).
1. Results based on students' self-reports.
StatLink ⌦ http://dx.doi.org/10.1787/142102278412

Pour consulter la version française intégrale de ce tableau, suivre ce lien :
StatLink ⌦ http://dx.doi.org/10.1787/152630454851

[Part 2/2]

**Table 3.11** Index of future-oriented motivation to learn science and performance on the science scale, by quarters of the index[1]

Tableau 3.11 Indice de motivation prospective pour l'apprentissage des sciences et scores sur l'échelle de culture scientifique, par quartile de l'indice

| | | Performance on the science scale, by quarters of this index | | | | | | | Change in the science score per unit of this index | | Increased likelihood of students in the bottom quarter of this index scoring in the bottom quarter of the science performance distribution | | Explained variance in student performance (r-squared x 100) | |
| | | Bottom quarter | | Second quarter | | Third quarter | | Top quarter | | | | | | | |
| | | Mean score | S.E. | Mean score | S.E. | Mean score | S.E. | Mean score | S.E | Effect | S.E. | Ratio | S.E. | Percentage | S.E. |
|---|---|---|---|---|---|---|---|---|---|---|---|---|---|---|---|
| OECD | Australia | **490** | (2.5) | 520 | (2.6) | 528 | (2.8) | **574** | (3.3) | **30.2** | (1.04) | **1.8** | (0.08) | 9.7 | (0.62) |
| | Austria | **490** | (3.7) | 508 | (4.4) | 511 | (4.5) | **540** | (6.6) | **19.1** | (2.46) | **1.4** | (0.11) | 3.7 | (1.02) |
| | Belgium | **489** | (3.2) | 505 | (3.1) | 514 | (3.1) | **556** | (3.7) | **25.1** | (1.55) | **1.5** | (0.07) | 6.6 | (0.79) |
| | Canada | **508** | (2.8) | 518 | (2.4) | 547 | (2.7) | **573** | (3.2) | **25.0** | (1.09) | **1.6** | (0.07) | 8.2 | (0.70) |
| | Czech Republic | **510** | (4.4) | 516 | (4.4) | 512 | (4.6) | **536** | (6.2) | **10.0** | (2.25) | 1.1 | (0.09) | 0.9 | (0.39) |
| | Denmark | **481** | (3.5) | 491 | (4.3) | 487 | (4.0) | **531** | (4.6) | **20.3** | (1.50) | **1.2** | (0.08) | 4.9 | (0.74) |
| | Finland | **531** | (2.8) | 556 | (3.4) | 562 | (3.1) | **606** | (2.9) | **32.4** | (1.45) | **1.8** | (0.11) | 10.6 | (0.96) |
| | France | **469** | (3.6) | 486 | (3.6) | 492 | (4.5) | **547** | (5.1) | **27.2** | (1.83) | **1.5** | (0.10) | 8.1 | (1.10) |
| | Germany | **499** | (5.4) | 520 | (4.0) | 522 | (4.3) | **553** | (5.2) | **20.3** | (1.33) | **1.5** | (0.11) | 4.7 | (0.63) |
| | Greece | **469** | (3.7) | 465 | (3.8) | 469 | (4.6) | **496** | (4.6) | **10.4** | (1.61) | 1.0 | (0.07) | 1.4 | (0.44) |
| | Hungary | **504** | (3.8) | 497 | (3.8) | 500 | (4.2) | **518** | (5.7) | **9.0** | (2.75) | 0.9 | (0.09) | 0.8 | (0.51) |
| | Iceland | **452** | (3.1) | 485 | (3.1) | 496 | (3.6) | **536** | (4.2) | **30.9** | (1.80) | **1.9** | (0.12) | 10.6 | (1.18) |
| | Ireland | **474** | (3.8) | 500 | (4.2) | 512 | (4.0) | **554** | (4.5) | **28.6** | (1.58) | **1.8** | (0.10) | 9.3 | (1.04) |
| | Italy | **469** | (2.5) | 465 | (2.3) | 480 | (3.0) | **493** | (3.5) | **12.4** | (1.58) | 1.0 | (0.05) | 1.4 | (0.36) |
| | Japan | **500** | (4.5) | 523 | (3.9) | 532 | (4.1) | **573** | (4.3) | **28.6** | (1.58) | **1.6** | (0.10) | 8.1 | (0.99) |
| | Korea | **501** | (3.8) | 520 | (3.5) | 507 | (4.4) | **562** | (5.9) | **23.2** | (2.63) | **1.3** | (0.08) | 5.8 | (1.40) |
| | Luxembourg | **472** | (2.7) | 484 | (2.6) | 487 | (2.6) | **507** | (3.2) | **13.3** | (1.45) | **1.2** | (0.08) | 2.2 | (0.48) |
| | Mexico | **422** | (2.9) | 416 | (2.7) | 409 | (3.7) | **396** | (4.7) | **-11.0** | (2.32) | **0.7** | (0.07) | 1.2 | (0.49) |
| | Netherlands | **507** | (3.4) | 526 | (4.0) | 520 | (3.6) | **567** | (5.8) | **23.8** | (2.16) | **1.4** | (0.08) | 5.6 | (1.08) |
| | New Zealand | **501** | (3.1) | 518 | (4.7) | 534 | (4.1) | **577** | (4.7) | **29.5** | (1.61) | **1.4** | (0.09) | 7.6 | (0.89) |
| | Norway | **461** | (3.5) | 494 | (3.4) | 498 | (3.5) | **512** | (3.9) | **18.2** | (1.50) | **1.5** | (0.09) | 3.7 | (0.60) |
| | Poland | 503 | (3.4) | 489 | (2.9) | 493 | (3.3) | 508 | (3.6) | **3.7** | (1.43) | **0.8** | (0.06) | 0.1 | (0.11) |
| | Portugal | **455** | (4.0) | 447 | (4.0) | 482 | (3.8) | **516** | (3.8) | **25.9** | (1.51) | **1.3** | (0.08) | 8.3 | (0.93) |
| | Slovak Republic | **494** | (3.5) | 483 | (4.1) | 477 | (4.5) | **507** | (4.4) | **5.3** | (2.17) | **0.8** | (0.06) | 0.3 | (0.21) |
| | Spain | **468** | (2.6) | 475 | (3.2) | 487 | (3.7) | **528** | (3.2) | **22.7** | (1.18) | **1.4** | (0.08) | 7.1 | (0.75) |
| | Sweden | **472** | (3.1) | 507 | (3.0) | 497 | (4.1) | **545** | (4.0) | **25.5** | (1.48) | **1.7** | (0.11) | 7.0 | (0.85) |
| | Switzerland | **486** | (3.6) | 510 | (3.1) | 510 | (3.3) | **542** | (5.4) | **22.5** | (2.05) | **1.4** | (0.07) | 4.9 | (0.92) |
| | Turkey | **417** | (3.5) | 418 | (3.6) | 414 | (4.4) | **452** | (6.9) | **11.3** | (2.09) | 1.0 | (0.09) | 2.0 | (0.65) |
| | United Kingdom | **485** | (3.3) | 510 | (3.4) | 507 | (3.1) | **564** | (4.0) | **29.2** | (1.63) | **1.5** | (0.09) | 7.3 | (0.86) |
| | United States | **478** | (4.0) | 472 | (3.8) | 496 | (5.0) | **514** | (7.3) | **17.9** | (2.09) | 1.1 | (0.08) | 2.7 | (0.65) |
| | **OECD total** | **487** | (1.2) | 488 | (1.1) | 492 | (1.5) | **504** | (2.3) | **8.3** | (0.74) | **0.9** | (0.02) | 0.7 | (0.12) |
| | **OECD average** | **482** | (0.6) | 494 | (0.7) | 499 | (0.7) | **533** | (0.9) | **19.7** | (0.33) | **1.3** | (0.02) | 5.2 | (0.15) |
| Partners | Argentina | **407** | (6.0) | 398 | (6.3) | 394 | (8.1) | **391** | (8.2) | **-4.8** | (2.56) | **0.8** | (0.09) | 0.2 | (0.26) |
| | Azerbaijan | **391** | (3.8) | 384 | (3.7) | 382 | (3.8) | **379** | (3.5) | **-5.1** | (1.39) | **0.8** | (0.09) | 0.7 | (0.36) |
| | Brazil | **406** | (3.6) | 394 | (4.4) | 389 | (3.9) | **382** | (3.7) | **-8.6** | (1.75) | **0.7** | (0.06) | 0.8 | (0.31) |
| | Bulgaria | **454** | (5.8) | 445 | (5.8) | 433 | (8.0) | **420** | (8.6) | **-11.1** | (3.13) | **0.6** | (0.06) | 0.9 | (0.51) |
| | Chile | **433** | (4.7) | 425 | (4.0) | 441 | (4.9) | **458** | (6.8) | **10.4** | (1.98) | 1.0 | (0.08) | 1.2 | (0.46) |
| | Colombia | **401** | (4.0) | 393 | (4.2) | 385 | (4.9) | **378** | (5.5) | **-10.1** | (2.40) | **0.7** | (0.10) | 1.2 | (0.51) |
| | Croatia | **492** | (3.2) | 488 | (3.0) | 490 | (3.2) | **506** | (4.1) | **6.7** | (1.63) | 1.0 | (0.07) | 0.5 | (0.23) |
| | Estonia | **524** | (3.2) | 533 | (3.1) | 531 | (3.6) | **540** | (4.4) | **7.1** | (1.88) | 1.1 | (0.10) | 0.5 | (0.28) |
| | Hong Kong-China | **524** | (3.4) | 526 | (3.1) | 547 | (3.4) | **572** | (4.1) | **23.6** | (1.56) | **1.3** | (0.08) | 5.5 | (0.72) |
| | Indonesia | **409** | (9.6) | 391 | (6.2) | 387 | (4.9) | **389** | (5.2) | **-11.5** | (5.55) | **0.6** | (0.07) | 1.2 | (1.13) |
| | Israel | **438** | (5.0) | 463 | (4.3) | 463 | (5.5) | **479** | (5.6) | **13.7** | (2.00) | **1.2** | (0.11) | 2.0 | (0.58) |
| | Jordan | **411** | (3.6) | 413 | (3.4) | 420 | (4.3) | **451** | (4.4) | **16.4** | (2.13) | 1.1 | (0.07) | 2.3 | (0.55) |
| | Kyrgyzstan | **367** | (4.6) | 324 | (3.9) | 309 | (3.4) | **306** | (3.4) | **-30.8** | (2.33) | **0.5** | (0.05) | 8.2 | (1.12) |
| | Latvia | 490 | (4.1) | 486 | (3.4) | 488 | (4.8) | 497 | (5.3) | **4.8** | (2.75) | 0.9 | (0.09) | 0.2 | (0.25) |
| | Liechtenstein | **502** | (9.4) | 523 | (11.3) | 515 | (9.8) | **549** | (12.7) | **17.9** | (5.83) | **1.3** | (0.29) | 3.0 | (1.93) |
| | Lithuania | **486** | (3.5) | 484 | (3.9) | 481 | (4.9) | **503** | (4.7) | **8.1** | (2.07) | 1.0 | (0.07) | 0.6 | (0.28) |
| | Macao-China | **507** | (2.4) | 508 | (2.5) | 509 | (2.6) | **521** | (3.0) | **8.7** | (1.84) | 1.0 | (0.08) | 0.8 | (0.33) |
| | Montenegro | **427** | (2.5) | 420 | (2.5) | 405 | (2.8) | **399** | (3.0) | **-11.1** | (1.38) | **0.6** | (0.06) | 2.0 | (0.47) |
| | Qatar | **347** | (2.2) | 352 | (2.2) | 347 | (1.9) | **362** | (2.6) | **5.4** | (1.00) | 1.0 | (0.06) | 0.5 | (0.17) |
| | Romania | **428** | (4.9) | 423 | (4.5) | 415 | (6.6) | **411** | (5.5) | **-6.7** | (2.12) | **0.7** | (0.09) | 0.3 | (0.30) |
| | Russian Federation | **493** | (4.3) | 485 | (4.1) | 473 | (4.1) | **468** | (6.1) | **-11.7** | (2.27) | **0.7** | (0.07) | 1.0 | (0.38) |
| | Serbia | **442** | (3.2) | 438 | (3.6) | 437 | (3.6) | **430** | (5.1) | **-4.3** | (1.81) | **0.8** | (0.06) | 0.2 | (0.20) |
| | Slovenia | **503** | (3.3) | 512 | (3.7) | 518 | (3.5) | **553** | (3.2) | **21.3** | (1.87) | **1.3** | (0.10) | 4.3 | (0.75) |
| | Chinese Taipei | **521** | (3.9) | 515 | (4.3) | 534 | (4.7) | **561** | (4.8) | **19.6** | (1.68) | **1.2** | (0.06) | 3.6 | (0.62) |
| | Thailand | **426** | (3.4) | 417 | (2.8) | 410 | (3.2) | **432** | (3.8) | **0.6** | (2.41) | **0.8** | (0.07) | 0.0 | (0.05) |
| | Tunisia | **378** | (2.6) | 376 | (4.7) | 386 | (3.9) | **409** | (4.6) | **12.2** | (1.96) | 1.0 | (0.07) | 1.5 | (0.44) |
| | Uruguay | **437** | (3.7) | 430 | (3.5) | 432 | (3.9) | **433** | (5.2) | **0.0** | (1.88) | **0.9** | (0.06) | 0.0 | (0.04) |

Note: Values that are statistically significant are indicated in bold (see Annex A3).
1. Results based on students' self-reports.
StatLink ⬛⬛ http://dx.doi.org/10.1787/142102278412

Pour consulter la version française intégrale de ce tableau, suivre ce lien :
StatLink ⬛⬛ http://dx.doi.org/10.1787/152630454851

[Part 1/1]

**Table 3.12  Percentage of students expecting a science-related career[1] at age 30 and performance on the science scale, by gender[2]**

Tableau 3.12  Pourcentage d'élèves envisageant d'exercer une profession à caractère scientifique à l'âge de 30 ans et scores sur l'échelle de culture scientifique, selon le sexe

| | | All students | | | | | | Males | | | | | | Females | | | | | |
|---|---|---|---|---|---|---|---|---|---|---|---|---|---|---|---|---|---|---|---|
| | | Students expecting a science career | | | | Students not expecting a science career | | Students expecting a science career | | | | Students not expecting a science career | | Students expecting a science career | | | | Students not expecting a science career | |
| | | % | S.E. | Mean score | S.E. | Mean score | S.E. | % | S.E. | Mean score | S.E. | Mean score | S.E. | % | S.E. | Mean score | S.E. | Mean score | S.E. |
| OECD | Australia | 27.8 | (0.6) | 570 | (2.8) | 512 | (2.2) | 27.0 | (0.7) | 581 | (4.1) | 509 | (3.0) | 28.7 | (0.8) | 559 | (3.2) | 515 | (2.8) |
| | Austria | 20.0 | (1.1) | 542 | (5.7) | 504 | (3.7) | 17.8 | (1.6) | 561 | (5.7) | 505 | (4.3) | 22.3 | (1.2) | 527 | (8.0) | 502 | (4.5) |
| | Belgium | 27.0 | (0.7) | 555 | (3.0) | 496 | (2.7) | 25.7 | (1.0) | 570 | (3.7) | 493 | (3.6) | 28.4 | (0.9) | 541 | (3.8) | 499 | (3.4) |
| | Canada | 37.1 | (0.7) | 561 | (2.1) | 521 | (2.3) | 32.7 | (0.8) | 578 | (3.0) | 520 | (2.7) | 41.4 | (0.9) | 548 | (2.3) | 523 | (2.7) |
| | Czech Republic | 17.4 | (0.8) | 570 | (4.3) | 502 | (3.5) | 17.0 | (1.1) | 576 | (4.6) | 504 | (4.1) | 18.0 | (1.3) | 563 | (6.5) | 499 | (5.1) |
| | Denmark | 21.8 | (0.7) | 530 | (3.8) | 487 | (3.0) | 18.9 | (0.9) | 545 | (5.0) | 491 | (3.9) | 24.8 | (0.9) | 518 | (4.9) | 483 | (3.7) |
| | Finland | 18.1 | (0.6) | 595 | (3.6) | 557 | (2.2) | 15.1 | (0.7) | 610 | (5.8) | 553 | (2.7) | 21.1 | (1.0) | 583 | (4.0) | 560 | (2.6) |
| | France | 28.3 | (0.9) | 529 | (4.8) | 486 | (3.3) | 26.6 | (1.3) | 547 | (6.4) | 482 | (4.3) | 29.9 | (1.0) | 514 | (5.3) | 489 | (3.5) |
| | Germany | 18.4 | (0.6) | 564 | (3.7) | 509 | (3.9) | 18.0 | (0.9) | 577 | (4.9) | 511 | (5.0) | 18.8 | (0.8) | 552 | (5.4) | 507 | (3.8) |
| | Greece | 25.1 | (0.7) | 515 | (3.2) | 461 | (3.4) | 23.7 | (1.1) | 522 | (4.5) | 453 | (4.5) | 26.4 | (1.0) | 508 | (4.7) | 469 | (3.5) |
| | Hungary | 16.8 | (1.0) | 557 | (4.7) | 494 | (2.7) | 17.3 | (1.2) | 569 | (5.8) | 495 | (3.2) | 16.2 | (1.1) | 541 | (6.3) | 493 | (3.7) |
| | Iceland | 32.3 | (0.8) | 525 | (2.6) | 478 | (2.0) | 27.4 | (1.1) | 534 | (3.9) | 476 | (3.1) | 37.1 | (1.1) | 518 | (3.6) | 481 | (2.5) |
| | Ireland | 29.3 | (0.8) | 546 | (3.6) | 495 | (3.3) | 28.3 | (1.2) | 553 | (4.9) | 492 | (4.3) | 30.2 | (0.9) | 538 | (4.4) | 497 | (3.5) |
| | Italy | 31.6 | (0.9) | 505 | (3.0) | 463 | (2.1) | 32.3 | (1.1) | 513 | (3.9) | 462 | (3.0) | 31.0 | (1.0) | 498 | (3.9) | 464 | (2.6) |
| | Japan | 7.8 | (0.9) | 567 | (12.4) | 529 | (3.3) | 4.3 | (0.5) | 605 | (7.6) | 531 | (5.0) | 11.5 | (1.6) | 552 | (14.7) | 527 | (4.7) |
| | Korea | 18.5 | (0.6) | 550 | (4.3) | 516 | (3.5) | 20.4 | (0.8) | 552 | (5.6) | 514 | (5.0) | 16.6 | (0.9) | 548 | (6.0) | 518 | (3.8) |
| | Luxembourg | 24.2 | (0.7) | 518 | (2.8) | 477 | (1.2) | 23.4 | (0.8) | 528 | (3.8) | 481 | (2.1) | 24.9 | (1.0) | 509 | (3.7) | 473 | (2.1) |
| | Mexico | 34.5 | (0.9) | 432 | (2.8) | 399 | (2.9) | 35.6 | (1.3) | 438 | (3.4) | 401 | (3.5) | 33.6 | (1.0) | 427 | (3.5) | 398 | (2.6) |
| | Netherlands | 22.9 | (0.7) | 555 | (3.8) | 517 | (3.0) | 15.9 | (0.8) | 579 | (5.0) | 520 | (3.5) | 30.0 | (1.1) | 542 | (4.5) | 514 | (3.6) |
| | New Zealand | 24.2 | (0.7) | 575 | (3.3) | 519 | (2.8) | 20.5 | (1.0) | 584 | (5.1) | 518 | (4.1) | 27.6 | (1.0) | 570 | (4.5) | 519 | (3.9) |
| | Norway | 25.0 | (0.6) | 522 | (3.5) | 480 | (2.8) | 20.8 | (0.9) | 538 | (4.5) | 476 | (3.6) | 29.3 | (1.0) | 510 | (4.4) | 483 | (3.1) |
| | Poland | 31.3 | (0.7) | 530 | (2.7) | 484 | (2.6) | 33.9 | (1.1) | 529 | (3.8) | 485 | (3.0) | 28.7 | (1.0) | 531 | (3.3) | 482 | (2.8) |
| | Portugal | 38.8 | (0.9) | 508 | (2.4) | 453 | (3.6) | 35.4 | (1.4) | 519 | (3.9) | 455 | (4.2) | 42.1 | (1.0) | 500 | (2.6) | 452 | (3.9) |
| | Slovak Republic | 19.7 | (1.1) | 535 | (4.0) | 478 | (2.7) | 21.7 | (1.2) | 542 | (5.3) | 478 | (4.0) | 17.5 | (1.3) | 526 | (5.1) | 478 | (3.4) |
| | Spain | 27.7 | (0.8) | 532 | (2.6) | 473 | (2.5) | 25.2 | (1.0) | 544 | (2.9) | 474 | (2.9) | 30.3 | (0.9) | 521 | (3.1) | 471 | (2.9) |
| | Sweden | 22.4 | (0.7) | 530 | (3.7) | 497 | (2.5) | 20.3 | (1.0) | 547 | (5.1) | 495 | (2.9) | 24.6 | (1.0) | 515 | (4.7) | 500 | (3.2) |
| | Switzerland | 21.9 | (0.4) | 543 | (4.0) | 503 | (3.2) | 20.7 | (0.6) | 557 | (4.5) | 504 | (3.3) | 23.2 | (0.8) | 531 | (4.9) | 502 | (3.6) |
| | Turkey | 24.1 | (1.3) | 474 | (7.0) | 409 | (2.7) | 23.1 | (1.5) | 472 | (8.5) | 404 | (3.3) | 25.3 | (1.3) | 476 | (7.1) | 415 | (3.4) |
| | United Kingdom | 24.6 | (0.7) | 556 | (3.3) | 503 | (2.5) | 22.5 | (0.9) | 578 | (4.2) | 506 | (3.3) | 26.6 | (0.8) | 537 | (4.8) | 501 | (3.1) |
| | United States | 38.1 | (0.8) | 511 | (4.5) | 477 | (4.4) | 32.0 | (1.2) | 533 | (5.3) | 471 | (5.2) | 44.4 | (1.1) | 496 | (4.5) | 484 | (4.5) |
| | **OECD total** | 28.2 | (0.3) | 516 | (1.7) | 483 | (1.1) | 25.7 | (0.4) | 529 | (2.0) | 482 | (1.4) | 30.8 | (0.4) | 505 | (1.9) | 484 | (1.2) |
| | **OECD average** | 25.2 | (0.1) | 537 | (0.8) | 489 | (0.5) | 23.5 | (0.2) | 549 | (0.9) | 489 | (0.7) | 27.0 | (0.2) | 527 | (1.0) | 490 | (0.6) |
| Partners | Argentina | 30.7 | (1.2) | 428 | (5.2) | 382 | (6.0) | 27.6 | (1.4) | 428 | (6.3) | 375 | (6.3) | 33.5 | (1.5) | 428 | (6.9) | 389 | (6.7) |
| | Azerbaijan | 18.3 | (0.9) | 400 | (3.5) | 380 | (2.9) | 15.0 | (1.2) | 400 | (5.1) | 377 | (3.2) | 21.7 | (1.2) | 400 | (3.6) | 384 | (2.9) |
| | Brazil | 35.8 | (0.9) | 409 | (3.6) | 383 | (2.8) | 28.6 | (1.1) | 428 | (3.2) | 385 | (3.2) | 41.9 | (1.1) | 399 | (3.6) | 380 | (3.3) |
| | Bulgaria | 24.0 | (0.6) | 450 | (7.7) | 432 | (5.9) | 22.8 | (0.9) | 444 | (8.5) | 424 | (6.5) | 25.3 | (0.9) | 456 | (8.8) | 441 | (6.7) |
| | Chile | 40.3 | (1.2) | 468 | (4.6) | 420 | (4.5) | 39.8 | (1.4) | 482 | (5.7) | 427 | (5.1) | 40.9 | (1.8) | 451 | (5.7) | 411 | (5.1) |
| | Colombia | 47.8 | (0.9) | 402 | (3.3) | 377 | (3.8) | 46.1 | (1.2) | 418 | (4.3) | 374 | (4.4) | 49.3 | (1.1) | 390 | (3.9) | 379 | (5.1) |
| | Croatia | 17.1 | (1.4) | 531 | (4.2) | 486 | (2.5) | 17.4 | (1.7) | 538 | (4.8) | 483 | (3.4) | 16.8 | (1.3) | 524 | (5.8) | 489 | (3.1) |
| | Estonia | 21.1 | (0.7) | 561 | (3.3) | 524 | (2.6) | 19.3 | (0.9) | 570 | (4.5) | 520 | (3.1) | 22.9 | (1.0) | 553 | (4.6) | 528 | (3.2) |
| | Hong Kong-China | 20.8 | (0.7) | 586 | (3.6) | 531 | (2.6) | 21.4 | (0.9) | 596 | (4.4) | 532 | (3.7) | 20.2 | (1.0) | 575 | (5.3) | 530 | (3.4) |
| | Indonesia | 24.0 | (2.0) | 413 | (11.6) | 388 | (3.9) | 23.0 | (3.2) | 427 | (18.0) | 391 | (5.2) | 25.1 | (1.5) | 400 | (5.5) | 384 | (3.6) |
| | Israel | 23.0 | (1.0) | 496 | (4.6) | 446 | (4.0) | 17.7 | (1.3) | 511 | (7.8) | 450 | (5.7) | 28.3 | (1.3) | 486 | (5.1) | 441 | (4.6) |
| | Jordan | 39.2 | (1.1) | 460 | (3.5) | 399 | (2.6) | 37.5 | (1.7) | 454 | (5.4) | 382 | (4.2) | 40.8 | (1.2) | 464 | (3.7) | 417 | (3.2) |
| | Kyrgyzstan | 21.3 | (0.8) | 336 | (3.7) | 323 | (3.0) | 13.7 | (0.8) | 361 | (6.3) | 319 | (3.4) | 27.7 | (1.0) | 326 | (3.8) | 327 | (3.3) |
| | Latvia | 19.1 | (0.6) | 523 | (4.1) | 482 | (2.9) | 19.5 | (0.9) | 529 | (5.5) | 476 | (3.3) | 18.9 | (0.9) | 518 | (5.1) | 488 | (3.3) |
| | Liechtenstein | 19.8 | (2.0) | 546 | (13.3) | 516 | (5.0) | 21.3 | (2.9) | 549 | (17.7) | 507 | (8.7) | 18.5 | (2.8) | 543 | (18.9) | 524 | (7.3) |
| | Lithuania | 21.2 | (0.7) | 525 | (3.3) | 479 | (2.8) | 21.2 | (1.0) | 526 | (4.0) | 473 | (3.3) | 21.2 | (0.9) | 523 | (4.4) | 485 | (3.1) |
| | Macao-China | 17.7 | (0.5) | 544 | (2.6) | 504 | (1.1) | 18.1 | (1.0) | 553 | (3.9) | 504 | (1.9) | 17.3 | (0.8) | 534 | (3.6) | 504 | (1.8) |
| | Montenegro | 16.2 | (0.6) | 434 | (3.5) | 408 | (1.2) | 14.4 | (0.9) | 436 | (5.3) | 408 | (1.9) | 18.1 | (0.8) | 433 | (4.5) | 409 | (1.9) |
| | Qatar | m | m | m | m | m | m | m | m | m | m | m | m | m | m | m | m | m | m |
| | Romania | 21.8 | (1.3) | 457 | (5.5) | 408 | (4.6) | 21.3 | (1.5) | 474 | (5.8) | 402 | (4.3) | 22.3 | (1.4) | 441 | (6.2) | 413 | (5.5) |
| | Russian Federation | 20.9 | (0.8) | 502 | (4.2) | 474 | (3.7) | 21.2 | (1.2) | 520 | (4.6) | 471 | (4.1) | 20.5 | (0.8) | 485 | (5.4) | 476 | (3.9) |
| | Serbia | 22.8 | (1.7) | 470 | (4.0) | 426 | (3.0) | 22.7 | (1.3) | 469 | (5.0) | 423 | (3.2) | 22.8 | (2.5) | 470 | (5.2) | 430 | (3.9) |
| | Slovenia | 31.4 | (0.7) | 547 | (2.6) | 507 | (1.4) | 32.2 | (0.9) | 548 | (3.5) | 500 | (2.4) | 30.6 | (1.1) | 547 | (3.6) | 513 | (2.5) |
| | Chinese Taipei | 23.1 | (1.1) | 561 | (6.0) | 524 | (3.7) | 28.1 | (0.8) | 569 | (4.9) | 524 | (4.5) | 17.6 | (2.0) | 548 | (13.0) | 525 | (4.6) |
| | Thailand | 25.5 | (0.9) | 467 | (3.3) | 405 | (2.0) | 16.9 | (1.0) | 485 | (5.4) | 396 | (3.4) | 31.9 | (1.2) | 460 | (3.4) | 413 | (2.3) |
| | Tunisia | 34.8 | (1.0) | 426 | (4.9) | 366 | (2.3) | 33.4 | (1.2) | 427 | (4.7) | 364 | (2.9) | 36.2 | (1.3) | 426 | (6.0) | 368 | (2.7) |
| | Uruguay | 32.5 | (1.1) | 456 | (4.2) | 419 | (2.9) | 28.7 | (1.4) | 465 | (7.2) | 416 | (4.2) | 36.0 | (1.3) | 449 | (4.3) | 422 | (3.2) |

Note: Values that are statistically significant are indicated in bold (see Annex A3).
1. See Annex A10 for the list of PISA science-related careers.
2. Results based on students' self-reports.
StatLink ᔕᕯ http://dx.doi.org/10.1787/142102278412

Pour consulter la version française intégrale de ce tableau, suivre ce lien :
StatLink ᔕᕯ http://dx.doi.org/10.1787/152630454851

[Part 1/1]

**Table 3.13** **Percentage of students having at least one parent in a science-related career[1] and performance on the science scale, by gender[2]**

Tableau 3.13  Pourcentage d'élèves dont au moins un parent exerce une profession à caractère scientifique et scores sur l'échelle de culture scientifique, selon le sexe

| | All students | | | | | | Males | | | | | | Females | | | | | |
|---|---|---|---|---|---|---|---|---|---|---|---|---|---|---|---|---|---|---|
| | Students with at least one parent in a science-related career | | | | Students without a parent in a science-related career | | Students with at least one parent in a science-related career | | | | Students without a parent in a science-related career | | Students with at least one parent in a science-related career | | | | Students without a parent in a science-related career | |
| | % | S.E. | Mean score | S.E. | Mean score | S.E. | % | S.E. | Mean score | S.E. | Mean score | S.E. | % | S.E. | Mean score | S.E. | Mean score | S.E. |
| Australia | 22.8 | (0.5) | **555** | (3.0) | **521** | (2.2) | 22.6 | (0.7) | **554** | (4.6) | **523** | (3.0) | 23.1 | (0.8) | **557** | (4.1) | **520** | (2.5) |
| Austria | 16.8 | (0.6) | **548** | (4.0) | **504** | (4.3) | 15.9 | (0.8) | **549** | (4.8) | **509** | (4.5) | 17.7 | (0.9) | **548** | (5.1) | **498** | (5.7) |
| Belgium | 19.5 | (0.5) | **555** | (3.2) | **502** | (2.6) | 20.0 | (0.8) | **554** | (4.9) | **503** | (3.2) | 19.0 | (0.9) | **555** | (3.9) | **501** | (3.4) |
| Canada | 23.6 | (0.5) | **561** | (2.8) | **529** | (2.0) | 24.5 | (0.8) | **565** | (3.2) | **531** | (2.6) | 22.7 | (0.6) | **558** | (3.8) | **527** | (2.1) |
| Czech Republic | 17.6 | (0.6) | **553** | (5.5) | **506** | (3.3) | 17.8 | (0.8) | **545** | (7.1) | **510** | (4.2) | 17.3 | (0.9) | **563** | (7.0) | **501** | (4.7) |
| Denmark | 20.5 | (0.9) | **533** | (4.0) | **489** | (3.0) | 20.7 | (1.1) | **532** | (5.7) | **496** | (3.5) | 20.2 | (1.0) | **533** | (4.1) | **483** | (3.4) |
| Finland | 25.4 | (0.7) | **586** | (2.8) | **557** | (2.2) | 25.1 | (0.8) | **583** | (4.1) | **556** | (2.8) | 25.6 | (1.0) | **589** | (3.4) | **558** | (2.6) |
| France | 18.9 | (0.9) | **550** | (4.3) | **487** | (3.3) | 19.4 | (1.2) | **552** | (6.0) | **488** | (4.3) | 18.4 | (1.0) | **548** | (5.0) | **485** | (3.5) |
| Germany | 20.0 | (0.8) | **568** | (3.6) | **509** | (3.5) | 20.5 | (1.1) | **568** | (4.9) | **514** | (4.4) | 19.6 | (1.0) | **567** | (4.2) | **504** | (3.7) |
| Greece | 12.1 | (0.7) | **519** | (3.9) | **469** | (3.1) | 11.6 | (0.7) | **515** | (6.0) | **464** | (4.3) | 12.7 | (0.9) | **522** | (5.2) | **473** | (3.4) |
| Hungary | 15.9 | (0.7) | **539** | (4.6) | **498** | (2.5) | 15.6 | (0.8) | **547** | (5.5) | **501** | (3.2) | 16.2 | (1.0) | **531** | (6.6) | **495** | (3.5) |
| Iceland | 24.7 | (0.8) | **520** | (3.8) | **484** | (1.8) | 25.7 | (1.1) | **521** | (5.0) | **480** | (2.6) | 23.6 | (1.0) | **519** | (4.9) | **488** | (2.6) |
| Ireland | 17.3 | (0.8) | **542** | (4.6) | **504** | (3.0) | 17.9 | (1.0) | **538** | (6.7) | **505** | (4.1) | 16.7 | (1.1) | **546** | (5.4) | **504** | (3.2) |
| Italy | 14.0 | (0.4) | **511** | (3.2) | **470** | (2.0) | 14.8 | (0.6) | **512** | (4.5) | **472** | (2.9) | 13.2 | (0.5) | **511** | (4.5) | **469** | (2.5) |
| Japan | 8.5 | (0.4) | **540** | (7.1) | **534** | (3.3) | 8.2 | (0.6) | **547** | (8.3) | **538** | (4.7) | 8.7 | (0.7) | **533** | (9.6) | **531** | (5.2) |
| Korea | 10.9 | (0.6) | **535** | (6.8) | **521** | (3.2) | 10.5 | (0.9) | **535** | (9.6) | **520** | (4.6) | 11.2 | (0.8) | **535** | (7.0) | **522** | (3.9) |
| Luxembourg | 15.1 | (0.5) | **538** | (3.3) | **478** | (1.1) | 15.7 | (0.7) | **541** | (4.8) | **483** | (1.9) | 14.5 | (0.7) | **535** | (4.6) | **474** | (1.9) |
| Mexico | 9.2 | (0.5) | **458** | (4.5) | **406** | (2.5) | 9.1 | (0.5) | **461** | (5.4) | **410** | (3.0) | 9.3 | (0.8) | **455** | (5.3) | **403** | (2.5) |
| Netherlands | 28.1 | (0.8) | **557** | (2.8) | **515** | (3.4) | 27.2 | (1.1) | **561** | (4.0) | **519** | (3.6) | 29.0 | (1.0) | **553** | (3.6) | **511** | (3.8) |
| New Zealand | 21.3 | (0.7) | **570** | (4.2) | **525** | (2.8) | 21.6 | (0.9) | **563** | (6.4) | **525** | (4.0) | 21.1 | (1.1) | **577** | (5.3) | **524** | (3.6) |
| Norway | 34.4 | (0.9) | **506** | (3.1) | **482** | (3.0) | 34.3 | (1.2) | **508** | (3.9) | **481** | (4.0) | 34.4 | (1.3) | **504** | (4.1) | **483** | (3.2) |
| Poland | 18.8 | (0.7) | **527** | (3.7) | **492** | (2.5) | 19.0 | (0.9) | **526** | (4.5) | **494** | (2.9) | 18.7 | (0.9) | **528** | (5.3) | **489** | (2.7) |
| Portugal | 9.7 | (0.6) | **534** | (5.0) | **469** | (3.0) | 10.7 | (0.9) | **535** | (7.4) | **471** | (3.6) | 8.9 | (0.6) | **533** | (5.7) | **466** | (3.2) |
| Slovak Republic | 15.4 | (0.6) | **532** | (4.1) | **481** | (2.5) | 16.7 | (1.0) | **540** | (5.4) | **483** | (3.8) | 14.1 | (0.8) | **522** | (5.8) | **480** | (3.1) |
| Spain | 11.8 | (0.6) | **533** | (4.0) | **483** | (2.5) | 11.5 | (0.5) | **539** | (5.5) | **485** | (3.0) | 12.0 | (0.8) | **528** | (4.5) | **482** | (2.6) |
| Sweden | 24.1 | (0.7) | **533** | (4.4) | **497** | (2.3) | 25.5 | (0.9) | **531** | (5.0) | **498** | (2.7) | 22.7 | (1.0) | **535** | (5.4) | **495** | (3.0) |
| Switzerland | 25.5 | (0.7) | **546** | (3.7) | **500** | (3.1) | 25.0 | (0.9) | **548** | (4.3) | **504** | (3.3) | 26.0 | (0.9) | **545** | (4.2) | **496** | (3.7) |
| Turkey | 4.8 | (0.5) | **495** | (12.4) | **421** | (3.4) | 4.6 | (0.5) | **501** | (14.6) | **415** | (4.1) | 5.0 | (0.6) | **488** | (13.3) | **428** | (3.8) |
| United Kingdom | 19.9 | (0.5) | **555** | (3.4) | **509** | (2.4) | 19.6 | (0.7) | **563** | (4.8) | **515** | (3.0) | 20.1 | (0.7) | **548** | (4.6) | **504** | (2.9) |
| United States | 22.1 | (0.8) | **527** | (5.0) | **484** | (4.0) | 22.3 | (1.3) | **527** | (6.8) | **485** | (5.0) | 22.0 | (1.0) | **527** | (5.5) | **482** | (3.8) |
| **OECD total** | 17.0 | (0.2) | **535** | (1.8) | **487** | (1.1) | 17.1 | (0.4) | **536** | (2.5) | **487** | (1.4) | 16.9 | (0.3) | **533** | (2.2) | **483** | (1.2) |
| **OECD average** | 18.3 | (0.1) | **538** | (0.9) | **494** | (0.5) | 18.5 | (0.2) | **539** | (1.1) | **496** | (0.6) | 18.1 | (0.2) | **536** | (1.0) | **493** | (0.6) |
| Argentina | 11.9 | (1.2) | **433** | (12.1) | **389** | (5.9) | 11.5 | (1.3) | **429** | (15.1) | **383** | (6.3) | 12.3 | (1.4) | **437** | (11.5) | **395** | (6.7) |
| Azerbaijan | 16.0 | (0.7) | **400** | (3.5) | **380** | (2.8) | 15.0 | (0.9) | **396** | (4.7) | **377** | (3.2) | 17.2 | (0.8) | **404** | (3.7) | **383** | (2.8) |
| Brazil | 7.8 | (0.4) | **442** | (6.5) | **388** | (2.7) | 8.4 | (0.6) | **448** | (9.4) | **393** | (3.0) | 7.3 | (0.5) | **436** | (7.1) | **383** | (2.9) |
| Bulgaria | 18.5 | (1.0) | **490** | (8.3) | **427** | (5.5) | 17.1 | (1.2) | **483** | (9.6) | **421** | (6.2) | 19.9 | (1.2) | **496** | (9.0) | **433** | (6.4) |
| Chile | 8.5 | (0.6) | **506** | (5.9) | **432** | (4.2) | 8.6 | (0.8) | **513** | (9.6) | **443** | (5.2) | 8.4 | (0.9) | **497** | (9.7) | **420** | (4.1) |
| Colombia | 8.6 | (0.5) | **418** | (8.7) | **386** | (3.6) | 7.8 | (1.0) | **420** | (15.4) | **391** | (4.3) | 9.2 | (1.0) | **417** | (8.4) | **381** | (4.2) |
| Croatia | 17.9 | (0.6) | **525** | (3.4) | **487** | (2.5) | 16.7 | (0.8) | **524** | (4.9) | **487** | (3.3) | 19.0 | (0.7) | **527** | (4.3) | **488** | (3.2) |
| Estonia | 12.8 | (0.6) | **552** | (4.1) | **529** | (2.5) | 13.2 | (1.0) | **550** | (5.9) | **528** | (3.1) | 12.5 | (0.6) | **553** | (4.4) | **531** | (3.0) |
| Hong Kong-China | 5.8 | (0.4) | **573** | (7.0) | **542** | (2.4) | 5.0 | (0.6) | **584** | (9.3) | **546** | (3.3) | 6.5 | (0.6) | **566** | (9.5) | **538** | (3.3) |
| Indonesia | 1.8 | (0.2) | c | c | **394** | (5.9) | 1.9 | (0.4) | c | c | **399** | (8.5) | 1.8 | (0.3) | c | c | **387** | (3.8) |
| Israel | 17.4 | (0.7) | **505** | (5.7) | **452** | (3.7) | 18.0 | (1.0) | **517** | (7.2) | **456** | (5.5) | 16.8 | (0.9) | **492** | (7.3) | **449** | (4.4) |
| Jordan | 11.7 | (0.7) | **466** | (5.8) | **420** | (2.6) | 12.6 | (1.1) | **457** | (8.8) | **406** | (4.0) | 10.8 | (0.9) | **475** | (6.0) | **432** | (3.2) |
| Kyrgyzstan | 15.5 | (0.7) | **344** | (4.7) | **320** | (2.9) | 15.3 | (0.9) | **349** | (6.4) | **317** | (3.4) | 15.7 | (0.9) | **340** | (5.0) | **323** | (3.1) |
| Latvia | 14.3 | (0.6) | **514** | (5.1) | **488** | (3.0) | 14.0 | (0.7) | **513** | (5.9) | **484** | (3.4) | 14.7 | (0.7) | **516** | (7.2) | **491** | (3.1) |
| Liechtenstein | 25.1 | (2.3) | **558** | (8.5) | **511** | (5.3) | 26.7 | (3.7) | **548** | (12.7) | **504** | (9.2) | 23.6 | (2.6) | **568** | (11.8) | **516** | (7.8) |
| Lithuania | 13.4 | (0.6) | **525** | (4.9) | **484** | (2.7) | 12.8 | (0.8) | **523** | (7.0) | **480** | (2.9) | 14.0 | (0.9) | **527** | (5.5) | **489** | (3.2) |
| Macao-China | 3.6 | (0.3) | **523** | (7.8) | **511** | (1.1) | 3.6 | (0.5) | **514** | (12.3) | **514** | (1.9) | 3.6 | (0.4) | **532** | (8.3) | **508** | (1.7) |
| Montenegro | 14.4 | (0.6) | **437** | (3.5) | **410** | (1.2) | 14.9 | (0.9) | **432** | (4.9) | **410** | (2.0) | 13.8 | (0.9) | **443** | (5.3) | **410** | (1.9) |
| Qatar | m | m | m | m | m | m | m | m | m | m | m | m | m | m | m | m | m | m |
| Romania | 7.8 | (0.9) | **476** | (8.8) | **414** | (4.1) | 8.8 | (0.9) | **476** | (10.5) | **412** | (4.1) | 6.8 | (1.1) | **476** | (10.3) | **416** | (4.7) |
| Russian Federation | 15.6 | (0.5) | **505** | (5.3) | **476** | (3.6) | 15.8 | (0.7) | **503** | (6.7) | **479** | (4.0) | 15.5 | (0.9) | **506** | (5.2) | **473** | (3.9) |
| Serbia | 20.2 | (0.8) | **470** | (3.5) | **428** | (3.2) | 19.2 | (0.9) | **471** | (4.8) | **425** | (3.5) | 21.2 | (1.2) | **469** | (4.3) | **431** | (4.1) |
| Slovenia | 24.4 | (0.5) | **555** | (3.2) | **509** | (1.4) | 22.6 | (0.9) | **549** | (5.6) | **507** | (2.2) | 26.2 | (0.9) | **560** | (4.2) | **511** | (2.4) |
| Chinese Taipei | 10.9 | (0.4) | **556** | (5.0) | **534** | (3.5) | 10.9 | (0.5) | **559** | (5.7) | **538** | (4.3) | 10.9 | (0.5) | **553** | (7.3) | **529** | (5.0) |
| Thailand | 3.0 | (0.3) | **495** | (9.9) | **421** | (2.0) | 2.7 | (0.5) | c | c | **413** | (3.3) | 3.3 | (0.4) | **500** | (8.8) | **427** | (2.3) |
| Tunisia | 9.9 | (0.7) | **428** | (8.7) | **382** | (2.4) | 9.5 | (0.9) | **415** | (10.3) | **382** | (2.8) | 10.3 | (1.2) | **439** | (10.6) | **382** | (2.8) |
| Uruguay | 13.3 | (0.6) | **473** | (5.2) | **423** | (3.0) | 13.6 | (0.9) | **474** | (6.2) | **422** | (4.4) | 13.0 | (0.8) | **472** | (5.5) | **424** | (3.1) |

Note: Values that are statistically significant are indicated in bold (see Annex A3).
1. See Annex A10 for the list of PISA science-related careers.
2. Results based on students' self-reports.
StatLink ⧉ http://dx.doi.org/10.1787/142102278412

Pour consulter la version française intégrale de ce tableau, suivre ce lien :
StatLink ⧉ http://dx.doi.org/10.1787/152630454851

[Part 1/1]

**Table 3.14** — Percentage of students expecting a science-related career[1] at age 30 with or without at least one parent in a science-related career and performance on the science scale[2]

Tableau 3.14 — Pourcentage d'élèves envisageant d'exercer une profession à caractère scientifique à l'âge de 30 ans, ayant ou non au moins un parent qui exerce une profession scientifique, et scores sur l'échelle de culture scientifique

| | Students expecting a science career with at least one parent in a science-related career | | | | Students expecting a science career without a parent in a science-related career | | | | Students not expecting a science career with at least one parent in a science-related career | | | | Students not expecting a science career without a parent in a science-related career | | | |
|---|---|---|---|---|---|---|---|---|---|---|---|---|---|---|---|---|
| | % | S.E. | Mean score | S.E. | % | S.E. | Mean score | S.E. | % | S.E. | Mean score | S.E. | % | S.E. | Mean score | S.E. |
| **OECD** | | | | | | | | | | | | | | | | |
| Australia | 8.0 | (0.27) | 586 | (3.91) | 20.0 | (0.49) | 564 | (3.00) | 14.9 | (0.41) | 539 | (3.25) | 57.2 | (0.69) | 507 | (2.17) |
| Austria | 4.9 | (0.43) | 558 | (7.58) | 15.1 | (0.90) | 537 | (6.66) | 11.9 | (0.48) | 544 | (4.39) | 68.1 | (1.12) | 497 | (4.05) |
| Belgium | 7.5 | (0.37) | 583 | (4.53) | 19.7 | (0.63) | 545 | (3.27) | 12.1 | (0.42) | 538 | (3.61) | 60.7 | (0.74) | 490 | (2.80) |
| Canada | 10.4 | (0.34) | 582 | (4.03) | 27.0 | (0.55) | 554 | (2.16) | 13.2 | (0.44) | 546 | (3.34) | 49.4 | (0.65) | 516 | (2.36) |
| Czech Republic | 4.6 | (0.35) | 587 | (5.51) | 13.1 | (0.72) | 565 | (4.99) | 13.1 | (0.55) | 541 | (6.72) | 69.3 | (0.92) | 496 | (3.21) |
| Denmark | 6.5 | (0.43) | 556 | (5.09) | 15.8 | (0.60) | 521 | (4.11) | 14.0 | (0.69) | 522 | (4.62) | 63.7 | (0.91) | 482 | (3.13) |
| Finland | 6.1 | (0.36) | 606 | (5.20) | 12.1 | (0.53) | 589 | (4.57) | 19.2 | (0.62) | 580 | (3.26) | 62.6 | (0.79) | 551 | (2.26) |
| France | 7.2 | (0.48) | 574 | (5.28) | 21.2 | (0.73) | 517 | (4.95) | 11.8 | (0.62) | 535 | (5.19) | 59.8 | (1.06) | 478 | (3.41) |
| Germany | 5.7 | (0.36) | 594 | (5.52) | 13.1 | (0.51) | 553 | (4.60) | 14.4 | (0.65) | 560 | (4.13) | 66.8 | (0.91) | 502 | (3.55) |
| Greece | 5.0 | (0.41) | 537 | (5.07) | 20.2 | (0.60) | 509 | (3.64) | 7.2 | (0.43) | 507 | (5.91) | 67.6 | (0.93) | 457 | (3.29) |
| Hungary | 4.6 | (0.41) | 579 | (7.01) | 12.3 | (0.76) | 548 | (4.55) | 11.4 | (0.56) | 523 | (4.72) | 71.8 | (1.04) | 490 | (2.63) |
| Iceland | 10.3 | (0.51) | 540 | (5.16) | 22.1 | (0.63) | 519 | (3.55) | 14.3 | (0.58) | 508 | (4.55) | 53.3 | (0.92) | 472 | (1.92) |
| Ireland | 6.7 | (0.50) | 565 | (6.95) | 22.8 | (0.73) | 541 | (3.63) | 10.6 | (0.52) | 528 | (5.38) | 59.9 | (1.01) | 491 | (3.27) |
| Italy | 6.3 | (0.32) | 525 | (4.27) | 25.4 | (0.83) | 501 | (3.19) | 7.7 | (0.28) | 501 | (3.82) | 60.6 | (0.92) | 458 | (2.16) |
| Japan | 1.8 | (0.34) | c | c | 6.4 | (0.70) | 570 | (11.55) | 6.7 | (0.31) | 535 | (6.16) | 85.1 | (1.01) | 532 | (3.29) |
| Korea | 2.5 | (0.23) | c | c | 16.0 | (0.59) | 548 | (4.41) | 8.4 | (0.51) | 526 | (7.72) | 73.1 | (0.82) | 515 | (3.33) |
| Luxembourg | 4.8 | (0.31) | 559 | (5.01) | 19.6 | (0.63) | 508 | (3.29) | 10.3 | (0.38) | 529 | (4.25) | 65.3 | (0.70) | 470 | (1.26) |
| Mexico | 4.4 | (0.31) | 467 | (5.38) | 30.4 | (0.79) | 427 | (2.69) | 4.8 | (0.33) | 450 | (5.60) | 60.3 | (0.93) | 397 | (2.68) |
| Netherlands | 7.7 | (0.40) | 575 | (4.81) | 15.3 | (0.59) | 547 | (5.11) | 20.4 | (0.72) | 550 | (3.23) | 56.7 | (0.77) | 508 | (3.46) |
| New Zealand | 7.0 | (0.42) | 601 | (6.50) | 17.4 | (0.59) | 567 | (3.48) | 14.3 | (0.54) | 555 | (5.13) | 61.2 | (0.80) | 513 | (2.98) |
| Norway | 10.0 | (0.45) | 533 | (4.39) | 15.3 | (0.53) | 516 | (4.29) | 24.6 | (0.80) | 497 | (3.49) | 50.2 | (0.84) | 475 | (3.08) |
| Poland | 7.4 | (0.41) | 551 | (4.38) | 24.0 | (0.62) | 524 | (3.00) | 11.4 | (0.53) | 512 | (4.60) | 57.2 | (0.85) | 478 | (2.75) |
| Portugal | 5.1 | (0.37) | 548 | (6.05) | 33.9 | (0.80) | 502 | (2.51) | 4.7 | (0.41) | 519 | (6.97) | 56.4 | (0.94) | 449 | (3.47) |
| Slovak Republic | 4.5 | (0.38) | 564 | (5.33) | 15.3 | (0.90) | 527 | (4.20) | 11.0 | (0.52) | 519 | (5.10) | 69.1 | (1.23) | 472 | (2.63) |
| Spain | 5.0 | (0.43) | 554 | (4.91) | 22.8 | (0.63) | 527 | (2.59) | 6.8 | (0.38) | 518 | (4.90) | 65.4 | (0.93) | 469 | (2.49) |
| Sweden | 6.7 | (0.42) | 556 | (6.16) | 15.7 | (0.59) | 520 | (3.81) | 17.4 | (0.61) | 524 | (4.74) | 60.2 | (0.80) | 491 | (2.46) |
| Switzerland | 7.6 | (0.39) | 571 | (5.37) | 14.4 | (0.34) | 529 | (4.18) | 18.0 | (0.53) | 536 | (3.71) | 60.1 | (0.67) | 494 | (3.17) |
| Turkey | 2.3 | (0.37) | c | c | 21.9 | (1.04) | 468 | (6.52) | 2.5 | (0.32) | c | c | 73.3 | (1.37) | 408 | (2.48) |
| United Kingdom | 6.7 | (0.42) | 582 | (5.17) | 18.2 | (0.65) | 549 | (4.39) | 13.1 | (0.37) | 543 | (3.97) | 61.9 | (0.71) | 499 | (2.50) |
| United States | 10.3 | (0.58) | 547 | (5.80) | 28.8 | (0.75) | 502 | (4.22) | 11.9 | (0.56) | 511 | (5.77) | 49.1 | (0.77) | 474 | (4.37) |
| **OECD total** | 6.6 | (0.17) | 553 | (2.37) | 22.0 | (0.27) | 506 | (1.66) | 10.4 | (0.15) | 523 | (2.08) | 61.0 | (0.28) | 478 | (1.07) |
| **OECD average** | 6.3 | (0.07) | 561 | (1.25) | 19.2 | (0.12) | 530 | (0.83) | 12.1 | (0.09) | 525 | (0.99) | 62.5 | (0.17) | 484 | (0.54) |
| **Partners** | | | | | | | | | | | | | | | | |
| Argentina | 4.9 | (0.70) | 460 | (8.84) | 26.5 | (1.12) | 422 | (5.27) | 7.1 | (0.75) | 419 | (15.18) | 61.5 | (1.43) | 381 | (5.90) |
| Azerbaijan | 4.5 | (0.35) | 417 | (4.86) | 14.1 | (0.81) | 394 | (3.75) | 12.0 | (0.66) | 395 | (4.01) | 69.5 | (0.89) | 378 | (2.94) |
| Brazil | 3.6 | (0.25) | 452 | (7.90) | 32.4 | (0.90) | 405 | (3.70) | 4.3 | (0.32) | 434 | (8.04) | 59.6 | (0.91) | 380 | (2.68) |
| Bulgaria | 4.8 | (0.38) | 495 | (13.91) | 19.4 | (0.60) | 441 | (6.93) | 13.7 | (0.77) | 489 | (7.56) | 62.1 | (1.06) | 424 | (5.48) |
| Chile | 5.0 | (0.41) | 512 | (6.87) | 35.4 | (1.15) | 462 | (4.54) | 3.6 | (0.35) | 496 | (9.43) | 56.0 | (1.27) | 416 | (4.20) |
| Colombia | 3.8 | (0.38) | 433 | (7.99) | 44.1 | (0.87) | 400 | (3.45) | 4.8 | (0.65) | 407 | (11.01) | 47.3 | (0.94) | 374 | (4.00) |
| Croatia | 4.3 | (0.37) | 547 | (5.45) | 13.0 | (1.10) | 526 | (4.46) | 13.6 | (0.48) | 519 | (3.67) | 69.1 | (1.34) | 480 | (2.53) |
| Estonia | 3.4 | (0.28) | 586 | (5.90) | 17.6 | (0.65) | 557 | (3.80) | 9.4 | (0.52) | 540 | (4.51) | 69.5 | (0.74) | 522 | (2.63) |
| Hong Kong-China | 1.8 | (0.23) | c | c | 19.4 | (0.68) | 585 | (3.65) | 4.0 | (0.31) | 560 | (7.52) | 74.9 | (0.82) | 531 | (2.52) |
| Indonesia | 0.6 | (0.13) | c | c | 23.4 | (2.04) | 413 | (12.08) | 1.2 | (0.19) | c | c | 74.8 | (2.03) | 388 | (4.01) |
| Israel | m | m | m | m | m | m | m | m | m | m | m | m | m | m | m | m |
| Jordan | 6.4 | (0.44) | 484 | (6.71) | 33.3 | (0.89) | 455 | (3.28) | 5.3 | (0.47) | 444 | (6.78) | 55.0 | (1.10) | 399 | (2.41) |
| Kyrgyzstan | 4.1 | (0.37) | 358 | (8.50) | 17.7 | (0.71) | 331 | (4.07) | 11.7 | (0.56) | 343 | (5.40) | 66.6 | (0.86) | 321 | (2.94) |
| Latvia | 3.8 | (0.28) | 540 | (7.58) | 15.6 | (0.54) | 521 | (4.48) | 10.5 | (0.49) | 505 | (6.13) | 70.1 | (0.74) | 480 | (2.74) |
| Liechtenstein | 8.1 | (1.49) | 583 | (17.87) | 11.3 | (1.71) | 525 | (17.31) | 17.0 | (2.03) | 546 | (11.41) | 63.7 | (2.19) | 508 | (6.09) |
| Lithuania | 4.6 | (0.32) | 550 | (6.37) | 16.8 | (0.57) | 520 | (3.58) | 8.8 | (0.52) | 512 | (6.40) | 69.8 | (0.75) | 476 | (2.70) |
| Macao-China | 0.9 | (0.13) | c | c | 16.9 | (0.50) | 544 | (2.82) | 2.7 | (0.30) | c | c | 79.5 | (0.57) | 504 | (1.17) |
| Montenegro | 2.6 | (0.26) | c | c | 13.9 | (0.57) | 432 | (3.69) | 11.7 | (0.53) | 434 | (3.91) | 71.8 | (0.73) | 406 | (1.39) |
| Qatar | m | m | m | m | m | m | m | m | m | m | m | m | m | m | m | m |
| Romania | 3.3 | (0.67) | 502 | (8.53) | 18.7 | (1.02) | 449 | (4.88) | 4.5 | (0.50) | 458 | (10.51) | 73.5 | (1.57) | 405 | (4.71) |
| Russian Federation | 4.1 | (0.35) | 515 | (8.02) | 16.8 | (0.65) | 499 | (4.54) | 11.5 | (0.44) | 501 | (5.66) | 67.5 | (0.81) | 470 | (3.66) |
| Serbia | 5.8 | (0.58) | 488 | (5.26) | 17.2 | (1.28) | 464 | (4.83) | 14.4 | (0.65) | 463 | (3.94) | 62.6 | (1.64) | 419 | (3.10) |
| Slovenia | 9.2 | (0.48) | 577 | (5.78) | 22.4 | (0.60) | 536 | (2.72) | 15.3 | (0.60) | 541 | (4.34) | 53.1 | (0.78) | 498 | (1.70) |
| Chinese Taipei | 3.3 | (0.25) | 573 | (9.24) | 20.2 | (1.01) | 562 | (6.01) | 7.7 | (0.28) | 549 | (5.09) | 68.9 | (1.06) | 526 | (3.76) |
| Thailand | 1.7 | (0.25) | c | c | 24.7 | (0.59) | 464 | (2.93) | 1.4 | (0.22) | c | c | 72.3 | (0.74) | 407 | (1.98) |
| Tunisia | 5.3 | (0.59) | 468 | (9.24) | 29.8 | (0.74) | 419 | (4.25) | 4.6 | (0.43) | 389 | (10.16) | 60.4 | (1.16) | 366 | (2.06) |
| Uruguay | 6.6 | (0.50) | 482 | (6.88) | 26.3 | (0.93) | 450 | (4.59) | 6.8 | (0.48) | 468 | (5.35) | 60.3 | (1.23) | 415 | (3.07) |

1. See Annex A10 for the list of PISA science-related careers.
2. Results based on students' self-reports.
*StatLink* http://dx.doi.org/10.1787/142102278412

Pour consulter la version française intégrale de ce tableau, suivre ce lien :
*StatLink* http://dx.doi.org/10.1787/152630454851

[Part 1/2]

**Table 3.15** Index of students' science-related activities and performance on the science scale, by quarters of the index[1]

Tableau 3.15 Indice de participation à des activités scientifiques et scores sur l'échelle de culture scientifique, par quartile de l'indice

| | Index of students' science-related activities | | | | | | | | | | | | | | | |
| --- | --- | --- | --- | --- | --- | --- | --- | --- | --- | --- | --- | --- | --- | --- | --- | --- |
| | All students | | Males | | Females | | Gender difference (M - F) | | Bottom quarter | | Second quarter | | Third quarter | | Top quarter | |
| | Mean index | S.E. | Mean index | S.E. | Mean index | S.E. | Dif. | S.E. | Mean index | S.E. | Mean index | S.E. | Mean index | S.E. | Mean index | S.E. |
| **OECD** | | | | | | | | | | | | | | | | |
| Australia | -0.29 | (0.01) | -0.20 | (0.02) | -0.39 | (0.02) | **0.19** | (0.03) | -1.59 | (0.01) | -0.61 | (0.00) | 0.09 | (0.01) | 0.95 | (0.01) |
| Austria | 0.01 | (0.02) | 0.05 | (0.02) | -0.02 | (0.03) | 0.07 | (0.03) | -1.29 | (0.01) | -0.21 | (0.01) | 0.41 | (0.01) | 1.15 | (0.01) |
| Belgium | 0.01 | (0.01) | 0.07 | (0.02) | -0.05 | (0.02) | **0.12** | (0.03) | -1.30 | (0.01) | -0.21 | (0.01) | 0.41 | (0.00) | 1.14 | (0.01) |
| Canada | -0.15 | (0.01) | -0.05 | (0.02) | -0.25 | (0.02) | **0.19** | (0.03) | -1.47 | (0.01) | -0.50 | (0.01) | 0.28 | (0.00) | 1.08 | (0.01) |
| Czech Republic | 0.05 | (0.02) | -0.02 | (0.02) | 0.14 | (0.02) | **-0.16** | (0.03) | -1.09 | (0.02) | -0.15 | (0.01) | 0.36 | (0.01) | 1.10 | (0.01) |
| Denmark | -0.15 | (0.02) | -0.11 | (0.03) | -0.19 | (0.02) | **0.08** | (0.03) | -1.41 | (0.01) | -0.50 | (0.01) | 0.23 | (0.01) | 1.07 | (0.01) |
| Finland | -0.16 | (0.01) | -0.18 | (0.02) | -0.15 | (0.02) | -0.03 | (0.03) | -1.23 | (0.01) | -0.46 | (0.01) | 0.13 | (0.01) | 0.91 | (0.01) |
| France | -0.01 | (0.02) | 0.07 | (0.03) | -0.08 | (0.02) | **0.15** | (0.03) | -1.28 | (0.01) | -0.24 | (0.01) | 0.38 | (0.01) | 1.12 | (0.01) |
| Germany | 0.11 | (0.02) | 0.16 | (0.02) | 0.06 | (0.02) | **0.09** | (0.03) | -1.16 | (0.02) | -0.10 | (0.01) | 0.50 | (0.01) | 1.21 | (0.01) |
| Greece | 0.28 | (0.02) | 0.35 | (0.03) | 0.20 | (0.03) | **0.16** | (0.04) | -1.15 | (0.01) | -0.01 | (0.01) | 0.74 | (0.01) | 1.53 | (0.02) |
| Hungary | 0.32 | (0.02) | 0.33 | (0.02) | 0.31 | (0.02) | 0.02 | (0.02) | -0.83 | (0.02) | 0.08 | (0.01) | 0.69 | (0.01) | 1.36 | (0.01) |
| Iceland | -0.21 | (0.02) | 0.06 | (0.02) | -0.49 | (0.02) | **0.55** | (0.03) | -1.63 | (0.01) | -0.57 | (0.01) | 0.23 | (0.01) | 1.12 | (0.01) |
| Ireland | -0.43 | (0.02) | -0.34 | (0.03) | -0.52 | (0.03) | **0.17** | (0.04) | -1.69 | (0.00) | -0.86 | (0.01) | -0.09 | (0.01) | 0.91 | (0.01) |
| Italy | 0.26 | (0.01) | 0.35 | (0.02) | 0.17 | (0.02) | **0.18** | (0.03) | -0.93 | (0.01) | 0.04 | (0.00) | 0.64 | (0.00) | 1.30 | (0.01) |
| Japan | -0.62 | (0.02) | -0.45 | (0.02) | -0.80 | (0.02) | **0.35** | (0.03) | -1.69 | (0.00) | -1.09 | (0.01) | -0.37 | (0.01) | 0.66 | (0.01) |
| Korea | -0.19 | (0.02) | -0.04 | (0.03) | -0.33 | (0.03) | **0.29** | (0.04) | -1.50 | (0.01) | -0.51 | (0.01) | 0.23 | (0.01) | 1.04 | (0.01) |
| Luxembourg | 0.10 | (0.01) | 0.16 | (0.02) | 0.05 | (0.02) | **0.11** | (0.03) | -1.24 | (0.01) | -0.12 | (0.01) | 0.53 | (0.01) | 1.25 | (0.01) |
| Mexico | 0.73 | (0.02) | 0.77 | (0.02) | 0.70 | (0.02) | **0.07** | (0.02) | -0.41 | (0.01) | 0.56 | (0.00) | 1.06 | (0.00) | 1.72 | (0.02) |
| Netherlands | -0.26 | (0.02) | -0.09 | (0.02) | -0.44 | (0.03) | **0.35** | (0.03) | -1.59 | (0.01) | -0.61 | (0.01) | 0.11 | (0.01) | 1.03 | (0.02) |
| New Zealand | -0.26 | (0.02) | -0.19 | (0.02) | -0.33 | (0.02) | **0.14** | (0.03) | -1.54 | (0.01) | -0.57 | (0.01) | 0.12 | (0.01) | 0.95 | (0.01) |
| Norway | -0.11 | (0.02) | 0.05 | (0.02) | -0.27 | (0.02) | **0.32** | (0.03) | -1.44 | (0.01) | -0.46 | (0.01) | 0.30 | (0.01) | 1.17 | (0.01) |
| Poland | 0.64 | (0.01) | 0.62 | (0.02) | 0.67 | (0.02) | **-0.05** | (0.02) | -0.41 | (0.02) | 0.47 | (0.01) | 0.96 | (0.01) | 1.55 | (0.01) |
| Portugal | 0.45 | (0.02) | 0.48 | (0.02) | 0.42 | (0.02) | **0.06** | (0.03) | -0.78 | (0.02) | 0.29 | (0.01) | 0.84 | (0.00) | 1.46 | (0.01) |
| Slovak Republic | 0.23 | (0.02) | 0.26 | (0.03) | 0.20 | (0.02) | **0.06** | (0.03) | -0.81 | (0.02) | 0.00 | (0.01) | 0.53 | (0.00) | 1.20 | (0.01) |
| Spain | -0.15 | (0.02) | -0.07 | (0.02) | -0.22 | (0.02) | **0.14** | (0.02) | -1.48 | (0.01) | -0.45 | (0.01) | 0.27 | (0.00) | 1.08 | (0.01) |
| Sweden | -0.41 | (0.02) | -0.31 | (0.04) | -0.52 | (0.03) | **0.21** | (0.04) | -1.68 | (0.00) | -0.70 | (0.01) | -0.09 | (0.01) | 0.83 | (0.01) |
| Switzerland | 0.03 | (0.02) | 0.09 | (0.02) | -0.04 | (0.02) | **0.13** | (0.02) | -1.26 | (0.01) | -0.18 | (0.00) | 0.39 | (0.01) | 1.16 | (0.01) |
| Turkey | 0.57 | (0.02) | 0.63 | (0.03) | 0.49 | (0.03) | **0.14** | (0.03) | -0.66 | (0.03) | 0.39 | (0.01) | 0.93 | (0.00) | 1.62 | (0.01) |
| United Kingdom | -0.35 | (0.02) | -0.25 | (0.03) | -0.45 | (0.03) | **0.20** | (0.03) | -1.66 | (0.00) | -0.67 | (0.01) | 0.02 | (0.01) | 0.90 | (0.01) |
| United States | -0.09 | (0.02) | 0.04 | (0.02) | -0.21 | (0.02) | **0.25** | (0.03) | -1.42 | (0.01) | -0.40 | (0.01) | 0.33 | (0.01) | 1.13 | (0.01) |
| **OECD total** | 0.02 | (0.01) | 0.11 | (0.01) | -0.07 | (0.01) | **0.18** | (0.01) | -1.36 | (0.00) | -0.27 | (0.00) | 0.44 | (0.00) | 1.26 | (0.00) |
| **OECD average** | 0.00 | (0.00) | 0.07 | (0.00) | -0.08 | (0.00) | **0.15** | (0.01) | -1.25 | (0.00) | -0.28 | (0.00) | 0.37 | (0.00) | 1.16 | (0.00) |
| **Partners** | | | | | | | | | | | | | | | | |
| Argentina | 0.43 | (0.03) | 0.47 | (0.03) | 0.40 | (0.03) | **0.07** | (0.03) | -0.85 | (0.02) | 0.18 | (0.01) | 0.81 | (0.01) | 1.60 | (0.02) |
| Azerbaijan | 1.22 | (0.02) | 1.29 | (0.02) | 1.15 | (0.02) | **0.15** | (0.02) | 0.23 | (0.02) | 1.04 | (0.00) | 1.47 | (0.00) | 2.14 | (0.02) |
| Brazil | 0.53 | (0.02) | 0.56 | (0.02) | 0.51 | (0.02) | 0.05 | (0.03) | -0.80 | (0.02) | 0.29 | (0.01) | 0.94 | (0.01) | 1.69 | (0.01) |
| Bulgaria | 0.78 | (0.02) | 0.79 | (0.03) | 0.76 | (0.02) | 0.02 | (0.03) | -0.30 | (0.02) | 0.63 | (0.01) | 1.06 | (0.00) | 1.71 | (0.01) |
| Chile | 0.49 | (0.02) | 0.54 | (0.02) | 0.43 | (0.03) | **0.11** | (0.03) | -0.78 | (0.02) | 0.26 | (0.01) | 0.87 | (0.01) | 1.60 | (0.02) |
| Colombia | 1.00 | (0.02) | 1.02 | (0.02) | 0.98 | (0.03) | 0.04 | (0.03) | -0.04 | (0.01) | 0.84 | (0.01) | 1.30 | (0.01) | 1.89 | (0.01) |
| Croatia | 0.36 | (0.01) | 0.36 | (0.02) | 0.36 | (0.02) | 0.00 | (0.03) | -0.78 | (0.02) | 0.18 | (0.01) | 0.71 | (0.00) | 1.33 | (0.01) |
| Estonia | 0.40 | (0.01) | 0.37 | (0.02) | 0.43 | (0.02) | **-0.06** | (0.03) | -0.69 | (0.01) | 0.23 | (0.00) | 0.74 | (0.00) | 1.30 | (0.01) |
| Hong Kong-China | 0.26 | (0.02) | 0.39 | (0.02) | 0.13 | (0.02) | **0.26** | (0.03) | -1.12 | (0.01) | 0.07 | (0.01) | 0.72 | (0.00) | 1.36 | (0.01) |
| Indonesia | 0.57 | (0.02) | 0.57 | (0.02) | 0.57 | (0.02) | -0.01 | (0.02) | -0.30 | (0.03) | 0.38 | (0.01) | 0.80 | (0.00) | 1.39 | (0.01) |
| Israel | 0.12 | (0.02) | 0.18 | (0.04) | 0.07 | (0.03) | **0.10** | (0.05) | -1.47 | (0.01) | -0.31 | (0.01) | 0.64 | (0.01) | 1.64 | (0.02) |
| Jordan | 0.97 | (0.02) | 1.04 | (0.03) | 0.90 | (0.03) | **0.14** | (0.04) | -0.24 | (0.02) | 0.84 | (0.00) | 1.34 | (0.00) | 1.94 | (0.01) |
| Kyrgyzstan | 1.33 | (0.02) | 1.34 | (0.02) | 1.33 | (0.02) | 0.01 | (0.02) | 0.39 | (0.01) | 1.18 | (0.00) | 1.59 | (0.00) | 2.17 | (0.01) |
| Latvia | 0.25 | (0.02) | 0.24 | (0.03) | 0.25 | (0.02) | -0.01 | (0.03) | -0.81 | (0.02) | 0.03 | (0.00) | 0.59 | (0.01) | 1.18 | (0.02) |
| Liechtenstein | -0.12 | (0.05) | -0.01 | (0.09) | -0.21 | (0.06) | 0.20 | (0.11) | -1.40 | (0.04) | -0.34 | (0.02) | 0.24 | (0.02) | 1.04 | (0.05) |
| Lithuania | 0.26 | (0.02) | 0.22 | (0.02) | 0.30 | (0.02) | **-0.08** | (0.03) | -0.81 | (0.01) | 0.00 | (0.01) | 0.60 | (0.01) | 1.24 | (0.01) |
| Macao-China | 0.27 | (0.01) | 0.38 | (0.02) | 0.16 | (0.02) | **0.23** | (0.03) | -0.87 | (0.02) | 0.03 | (0.01) | 0.63 | (0.01) | 1.29 | (0.01) |
| Montenegro | 0.75 | (0.01) | 0.76 | (0.02) | 0.74 | (0.02) | 0.01 | (0.03) | -0.38 | (0.02) | 0.60 | (0.01) | 1.07 | (0.00) | 1.71 | (0.01) |
| Qatar | 0.64 | (0.01) | 0.81 | (0.02) | 0.47 | (0.02) | **0.35** | (0.03) | -0.87 | (0.02) | 0.41 | (0.01) | 1.09 | (0.00) | 1.92 | (0.02) |
| Romania | 0.64 | (0.02) | 0.66 | (0.02) | 0.62 | (0.02) | 0.05 | (0.03) | -0.38 | (0.02) | 0.48 | (0.00) | 0.92 | (0.01) | 1.53 | (0.02) |
| Russian Federation | 0.56 | (0.03) | 0.57 | (0.02) | 0.55 | (0.03) | 0.02 | (0.03) | -0.48 | (0.02) | 0.38 | (0.01) | 0.85 | (0.01) | 1.49 | (0.03) |
| Serbia | 0.54 | (0.02) | 0.56 | (0.02) | 0.52 | (0.03) | 0.04 | (0.02) | -0.55 | (0.01) | 0.34 | (0.01) | 0.86 | (0.01) | 1.51 | (0.02) |
| Slovenia | 0.43 | (0.01) | 0.45 | (0.02) | 0.42 | (0.02) | 0.04 | (0.03) | -0.82 | (0.02) | 0.27 | (0.01) | 0.84 | (0.00) | 1.44 | (0.01) |
| Chinese Taipei | 0.40 | (0.01) | 0.51 | (0.02) | 0.27 | (0.02) | **0.24** | (0.02) | -0.87 | (0.01) | 0.29 | (0.00) | 0.81 | (0.01) | 1.36 | (0.01) |
| Thailand | 1.10 | (0.01) | 1.07 | (0.02) | 1.13 | (0.01) | **-0.06** | (0.02) | 0.35 | (0.01) | 0.98 | (0.00) | 1.29 | (0.00) | 1.79 | (0.01) |
| Tunisia | 1.11 | (0.01) | 1.15 | (0.02) | 1.08 | (0.01) | **0.07** | (0.02) | 0.16 | (0.02) | 1.02 | (0.00) | 1.40 | (0.00) | 1.87 | (0.01) |
| Uruguay | 0.15 | (0.02) | 0.18 | (0.02) | 0.12 | (0.02) | 0.05 | (0.03) | -1.11 | (0.02) | -0.12 | (0.01) | 0.51 | (0.01) | 1.32 | (0.01) |

Note: Values that are statistically significant are indicated in bold (see Annex A3).
1. Results based on students' self-reports.
StatLink ⌨⬛ http://dx.doi.org/10.1787/142102278412

Pour consulter la version française intégrale de ce tableau, suivre ce lien :
StatLink ⌨⬛ http://dx.doi.org/10.1787/152630454851

[Part 2/2]

**Table 3.15**  Index of students' science-related activities and performance on the science scale, by quarters of the index[1]

Tableau 3.15  Indice de participation à des activités scientifiques et scores sur l'échelle de culture scientifique, par quartile de l'indice

| | | Performance on the science scale, by quarters of this index | | | | | | | Change in the science score per unit of this index | | Increased likelihood of students in the bottom quarter of this index scoring in the bottom quarter of the science performance distribution | | Explained variance in student performance (r-squared x 100) | |
| | | Bottom quarter | | Second quarter | | Third quarter | | Top quarter | | | | | | | |
| | | Mean score | S.E. | Mean score | S.E. | Mean score | S.E. | Mean score | S.E | Effect | S.E. | Ratio | S.E. | Percentage | S.E. |
|---|---|---|---|---|---|---|---|---|---|---|---|---|---|---|---|
| OECD | Australia | **489** | (2.4) | 518 | (2.8) | 539 | (3.2) | **564** | (3.3) | **28.6** | (1.25) | **1.7** | (0.07) | 7.8 | (0.65) |
| | Austria | **479** | (4.4) | 513 | (4.0) | 524 | (5.2) | **529** | (5.9) | **20.3** | (2.38) | **1.7** | (0.14) | 3.9 | (0.95) |
| | Belgium | **477** | (3.4) | 509 | (3.1) | 527 | (3.1) | **531** | (4.4) | **22.1** | (1.82) | **1.7** | (0.09) | 4.5 | (0.74) |
| | Canada | **506** | (2.8) | 529 | (2.7) | 549 | (2.6) | **561** | (3.2) | **21.1** | (1.33) | **1.7** | (0.10) | 5.1 | (0.63) |
| | Czech Republic | **491** | (4.9) | 514 | (4.2) | 524 | (4.3) | **521** | (5.7) | **11.6** | (2.76) | **1.4** | (0.09) | 1.0 | (0.52) |
| | Denmark | **461** | (4.1) | 486 | (3.7) | 511 | (3.8) | **527** | (4.6) | **25.8** | (1.72) | **1.8** | (0.12) | 7.3 | (0.92) |
| | Finland | **532** | (3.1) | 560 | (3.1) | 574 | (3.4) | **588** | (3.0) | **25.5** | (1.73) | **1.8** | (0.10) | 6.4 | (0.86) |
| | France | **458** | (4.1) | 492 | (3.8) | 512 | (3.8) | **523** | (5.3) | **25.8** | (2.23) | **1.8** | (0.10) | 5.8 | (0.96) |
| | Germany | **482** | (4.9) | 516 | (4.4) | 532 | (3.5) | **540** | (5.1) | **23.0** | (1.92) | **1.7** | (0.11) | 4.7 | (0.74) |
| | Greece | **450** | (3.8) | 475 | (3.7) | 484 | (4.3) | **487** | (5.0) | **12.7** | (1.65) | **1.5** | (0.10) | 2.2 | (0.57) |
| | Hungary | **482** | (3.7) | 502 | (3.6) | 517 | (3.6) | **517** | (4.5) | **15.9** | (2.16) | **1.4** | (0.11) | 2.5 | (0.66) |
| | Iceland | **448** | (3.4) | 480 | (3.2) | 509 | (2.9) | **531** | (3.9) | **29.2** | (1.65) | **2.0** | (0.12) | 10.2 | (1.04) |
| | Ireland | **472** | (3.7) | 503 | (4.3) | 523 | (4.1) | **540** | (4.4) | **24.8** | (1.57) | **1.8** | (0.14) | 7.0 | (0.88) |
| | Italy | **454** | (2.5) | 474 | (2.5) | 489 | (2.9) | **485** | (3.1) | **14.5** | (1.47) | **1.4** | (0.07) | 1.9 | (0.37) |
| | Japan | **500** | (4.9) | 521 | (4.0) | 547 | (3.7) | **559** | (3.8) | **22.8** | (1.78) | **1.7** | (0.10) | 4.7 | (0.68) |
| | Korea | **489** | (4.2) | 514 | (3.5) | 537 | (3.7) | **550** | (6.2) | **24.5** | (2.22) | **1.8** | (0.10) | 7.2 | (1.23) |
| | Luxembourg | **455** | (2.3) | 487 | (2.5) | 503 | (2.8) | **502** | (3.5) | **17.5** | (1.68) | **1.6** | (0.08) | 3.1 | (0.60) |
| | Mexico | **411** | (3.1) | 415 | (2.8) | 418 | (3.6) | **396** | (4.7) | **-6.1** | (2.16) | **0.8** | (0.06) | 0.4 | (0.31) |
| | Netherlands | **498** | (3.6) | 522 | (4.0) | 543 | (3.6) | **539** | (5.0) | **15.1** | (2.16) | **1.5** | (0.11) | 2.6 | (0.73) |
| | New Zealand | **499** | (3.5) | 521 | (3.7) | 542 | (3.9) | **564** | (4.7) | **25.0** | (2.00) | **1.4** | (0.11) | 5.1 | (0.85) |
| | Norway | **453** | (3.3) | 483 | (3.3) | 506 | (3.7) | **513** | (3.9) | **22.0** | (1.64) | **1.7** | (0.10) | 5.7 | (0.82) |
| | Poland | **490** | (3.4) | 494 | (3.9) | 501 | (3.6) | **506** | (3.6) | **7.3** | (1.79) | **1.1** | (0.07) | 0.4 | (0.20) |
| | Portugal | **450** | (3.8) | 475 | (3.6) | 488 | (4.4) | **484** | (4.3) | **15.9** | (1.88) | **1.5** | (0.10) | 2.6 | (0.65) |
| | Slovak Republic | **473** | (5.5) | 489 | (3.4) | 495 | (4.2) | **498** | (5.0) | **11.7** | (4.28) | **1.3** | (0.13) | 1.0 | (0.73) |
| | Spain | **462** | (2.6) | 486 | (3.3) | 500 | (3.3) | **509** | (3.8) | **17.9** | (1.37) | **1.6** | (0.10) | 3.9 | (0.58) |
| | Sweden | **469** | (3.3) | 498 | (2.9) | 514 | (3.6) | **537** | (3.8) | **25.1** | (1.79) | **1.8** | (0.11) | 6.5 | (0.90) |
| | Switzerland | **480** | (3.2) | 513 | (3.3) | 525 | (3.7) | **529** | (5.2) | **19.4** | (1.95) | **1.6** | (0.07) | 3.4 | (0.68) |
| | Turkey | **397** | (3.4) | 424 | (3.8) | 431 | (4.6) | **445** | (6.4) | **19.5** | (2.32) | **1.5** | (0.11) | 4.7 | (0.95) |
| | United Kingdom | **474** | (3.5) | 512 | (3.4) | 528 | (4.0) | **548** | (4.2) | **27.7** | (1.95) | **1.8** | (0.08) | 6.4 | (0.89) |
| | United States | **465** | (3.9) | 489 | (4.1) | 502 | (5.6) | **503** | (7.6) | **14.3** | (2.22) | **1.3** | (0.10) | 1.8 | (0.59) |
| | **OECD total** | **478** | (1.4) | 496 | (1.5) | 502 | (1.6) | **489** | (1.8) | **4.4** | (0.69) | **1.1** | (0.03) | 0.2 | (0.06) |
| | **OECD average** | **472** | (0.7) | 497 | (0.6) | 513 | (0.7) | **521** | (0.9) | **19.4** | (0.37) | **1.6** | (0.02) | 4.3 | (0.14) |
| Partners | Argentina | **399** | (8.4) | 403 | (6.1) | 401 | (5.9) | **371** | (7.1) | **-10.6** | (2.85) | 0.9 | (0.11) | 1.1 | (0.58) |
| | Azerbaijan | 384 | (3.7) | 385 | (3.3) | 384 | (3.3) | 380 | (3.5) | -1.6 | (1.77) | 1.0 | (0.09) | 0.1 | (0.12) |
| | Brazil | **396** | (3.7) | 397 | (3.6) | 395 | (4.1) | **375** | (4.0) | **-8.0** | (1.46) | **0.8** | (0.06) | 0.8 | (0.28) |
| | Bulgaria | 426 | (5.2) | 442 | (6.6) | 446 | (7.8) | 434 | (8.2) | 3.8 | (3.02) | 1.0 | (0.08) | 0.1 | (0.16) |
| | Chile | **422** | (3.7) | 439 | (5.3) | 452 | (4.9) | **440** | (6.6) | **7.3** | (2.06) | **1.3** | (0.09) | 0.6 | (0.32) |
| | Colombia | 395 | (4.4) | 392 | (3.9) | 388 | (5.1) | 378 | (4.9) | -10.7 | (2.67) | 0.8 | (0.07) | 1.0 | (0.46) |
| | Croatia | **473** | (2.9) | 494 | (3.8) | 500 | (3.4) | **506** | (3.6) | **14.6** | (1.41) | **1.4** | (0.09) | 2.1 | (0.41) |
| | Estonia | 523 | (3.7) | 534 | (3.1) | 538 | (3.8) | 531 | (4.3) | 5.0 | (2.13) | 1.1 | (0.09) | 0.2 | (0.20) |
| | Hong Kong-China | **509** | (3.7) | 541 | (3.4) | 548 | (3.8) | **571** | (4.1) | **23.3** | (1.54) | **1.8** | (0.12) | 6.3 | (0.80) |
| | Indonesia | 387 | (7.1) | 397 | (6.6) | 399 | (6.5) | 390 | (5.1) | 3.1 | (2.96) | 1.1 | (0.08) | 0.1 | (0.18) |
| | Israel | **439** | (6.1) | 471 | (4.0) | 477 | (4.3) | **444** | (7.1) | 1.3 | (2.44) | **1.3** | (0.12) | 0.0 | (0.09) |
| | Jordan | **428** | (3.8) | 427 | (3.4) | 423 | (4.2) | **415** | (4.7) | **-5.4** | (2.07) | 0.9 | (0.08) | 0.3 | (0.23) |
| | Kyrgyzstan | **358** | (5.3) | 332 | (3.3) | 313 | (3.1) | **291** | (3.9) | **-34.3** | (2.91) | **0.5** | (0.06) | 9.0 | (1.39) |
| | Latvia | 483 | (4.2) | 492 | (3.2) | 496 | (3.9) | 489 | (4.0) | 4.2 | (2.10) | 1.1 | (0.09) | 0.2 | (0.20) |
| | Liechtenstein | 506 | (9.6) | 519 | (13.0) | 534 | (10.4) | 530 | (10.5) | 10.6 | (5.59) | 1.1 | (0.27) | 1.1 | (1.08) |
| | Lithuania | 481 | (4.2) | 488 | (3.7) | 495 | (3.9) | 488 | (4.1) | 2.2 | (2.22) | 1.1 | (0.08) | 0.0 | (0.08) |
| | Macao-China | **491** | (2.4) | 511 | (2.6) | 518 | (2.6) | **524** | (2.8) | **15.0** | (1.40) | **1.4** | (0.10) | 2.8 | (0.53) |
| | Montenegro | **411** | (2.8) | 422 | (2.9) | 414 | (3.3) | **401** | (2.5) | **-4.1** | (1.72) | 0.9 | (0.09) | 0.2 | (0.17) |
| | Qatar | **345** | (2.0) | 368 | (2.6) | 361 | (2.3) | **332** | (2.0) | **-2.2** | (0.89) | 1.1 | (0.06) | 0.1 | (0.07) |
| | Romania | **404** | (4.6) | 425 | (4.8) | 429 | (4.9) | **416** | (5.8) | **7.7** | (2.46) | 1.3 | (0.17) | 0.6 | (0.34) |
| | Russian Federation | 473 | (4.4) | 481 | (3.4) | 488 | (4.1) | 476 | (7.6) | 2.5 | (3.32) | 1.1 | (0.09) | 0.1 | (0.16) |
| | Serbia | 431 | (3.7) | 439 | (3.4) | 439 | (3.8) | 435 | (4.8) | 1.9 | (2.11) | 1.0 | (0.07) | 0.0 | (0.08) |
| | Slovenia | **495** | (2.8) | 518 | (3.0) | 530 | (3.1) | **534** | (3.8) | **16.7** | (1.92) | **1.4** | (0.09) | 2.4 | (0.53) |
| | Chinese Taipei | **506** | (4.0) | 536 | (4.1) | 535 | (4.0) | **554** | (4.3) | **18.0** | (1.47) | **1.6** | (0.07) | 3.0 | (0.49) |
| | Thailand | **403** | (2.7) | 414 | (2.8) | 430 | (2.7) | **438** | (3.3) | **21.8** | (1.93) | **1.4** | (0.08) | 2.8 | (0.51) |
| | Tunisia | **393** | (3.3) | 395 | (4.3) | 385 | (3.9) | **371** | (4.2) | **-8.7** | (2.05) | **0.7** | (0.07) | 0.6 | (0.26) |
| | Uruguay | 426 | (4.0) | 434 | (3.5) | 433 | (4.9) | 423 | (4.1) | -2.6 | (1.96) | 1.0 | (0.09) | 0.1 | (0.11) |

Note: Values that are statistically significant are indicated in bold (see Annex A3).
1. Results based on students' self-reports.
*StatLink* ⫘ http://dx.doi.org/10.1787/142102278412

Pour consulter la version française intégrale de ce tableau, suivre ce lien :
*StatLink* ⫘ http://dx.doi.org/10.1787/152630454851

[Part 1/2]

**Table 3.16** Index of students' awareness of environmental issues and performance on the science scale, by quarters of the index[1]

Tableau 3.16 Indice de sensibilisation aux problèmes environnementaux et scores sur l'échelle de culture scientifique, par quartile de l'indice

| | Index of students' awareness of environmental issues | | | | | | | | | | | | | | | |
| | All students | | Males | | Females | | Gender difference (M - F) | | Bottom quarter | | Second quarter | | Third quarter | | Top quarter | |
| | Mean index | S.E. | Mean index | S.E. | Mean index | S.E. | Dif. | S.E. | Mean index | S.E. | Mean index | S.E. | Mean index | S.E. | Mean index | S.E. |
| **OECD** | | | | | | | | | | | | | | | | |
| Australia | 0.10 | (0.02) | 0.19 | (0.02) | 0.01 | (0.02) | **0.18** | (0.03) | -1.10 | (0.01) | -0.19 | (0.00) | 0.37 | (0.00) | 1.33 | (0.02) |
| Austria | 0.23 | (0.02) | 0.32 | (0.03) | 0.14 | (0.03) | **0.18** | (0.04) | -0.99 | (0.02) | -0.05 | (0.01) | 0.52 | (0.01) | 1.46 | (0.02) |
| Belgium | -0.16 | (0.02) | -0.06 | (0.02) | -0.27 | (0.02) | **0.21** | (0.03) | -1.37 | (0.02) | -0.42 | (0.01) | 0.14 | (0.00) | 1.00 | (0.02) |
| Canada | 0.27 | (0.01) | 0.36 | (0.02) | 0.18 | (0.02) | **0.18** | (0.02) | -0.93 | (0.01) | -0.05 | (0.00) | 0.52 | (0.00) | 1.55 | (0.02) |
| Czech Republic | 0.07 | (0.02) | 0.14 | (0.02) | -0.02 | (0.03) | **0.16** | (0.03) | -0.94 | (0.02) | -0.18 | (0.00) | 0.30 | (0.00) | 1.08 | (0.02) |
| Denmark | -0.21 | (0.02) | -0.06 | (0.03) | -0.35 | (0.03) | **0.29** | (0.03) | -1.39 | (0.02) | -0.51 | (0.01) | 0.08 | (0.00) | 1.00 | (0.02) |
| Finland | -0.02 | (0.02) | 0.08 | (0.02) | -0.12 | (0.02) | **0.20** | (0.03) | -1.06 | (0.01) | -0.26 | (0.01) | 0.21 | (0.01) | 1.04 | (0.02) |
| France | -0.16 | (0.02) | -0.02 | (0.03) | -0.30 | (0.02) | **0.28** | (0.03) | -1.38 | (0.02) | -0.44 | (0.01) | 0.12 | (0.01) | 1.04 | (0.02) |
| Germany | 0.15 | (0.02) | 0.31 | (0.04) | -0.01 | (0.03) | **0.32** | (0.04) | -1.19 | (0.03) | -0.12 | (0.01) | 0.47 | (0.01) | 1.44 | (0.02) |
| Greece | 0.09 | (0.02) | 0.13 | (0.03) | 0.05 | (0.03) | **0.08** | (0.04) | -1.07 | (0.02) | -0.21 | (0.00) | 0.35 | (0.00) | 1.28 | (0.01) |
| Hungary | 0.10 | (0.01) | 0.13 | (0.02) | 0.08 | (0.02) | 0.05 | (0.03) | -0.91 | (0.02) | -0.18 | (0.00) | 0.33 | (0.00) | 1.16 | (0.02) |
| Iceland | -0.39 | (0.02) | -0.18 | (0.02) | -0.61 | (0.02) | **0.43** | (0.03) | -1.77 | (0.02) | -0.73 | (0.01) | -0.08 | (0.01) | 1.01 | (0.03) |
| Ireland | 0.38 | (0.02) | 0.44 | (0.04) | 0.32 | (0.03) | **0.12** | (0.04) | -0.83 | (0.02) | 0.08 | (0.01) | 0.66 | (0.01) | 1.59 | (0.02) |
| Italy | 0.18 | (0.02) | 0.25 | (0.02) | 0.12 | (0.02) | **0.12** | (0.03) | -0.96 | (0.01) | -0.08 | (0.00) | 0.44 | (0.00) | 1.34 | (0.01) |
| Japan | -0.13 | (0.02) | -0.07 | (0.03) | -0.19 | (0.02) | **0.13** | (0.03) | -1.10 | (0.02) | -0.37 | (0.00) | 0.08 | (0.00) | 0.86 | (0.02) |
| Korea | -0.22 | (0.02) | -0.19 | (0.03) | -0.26 | (0.03) | 0.08 | (0.04) | -1.20 | (0.02) | -0.50 | (0.01) | 0.00 | (0.01) | 0.80 | (0.02) |
| Luxembourg | -0.26 | (0.02) | -0.08 | (0.02) | -0.44 | (0.02) | **0.36** | (0.02) | -1.69 | (0.02) | -0.60 | (0.01) | 0.12 | (0.01) | 1.14 | (0.02) |
| Mexico | -0.45 | (0.02) | -0.44 | (0.02) | -0.47 | (0.02) | 0.03 | (0.02) | -1.60 | (0.01) | -0.74 | (0.01) | -0.16 | (0.00) | 0.70 | (0.01) |
| Netherlands | -0.08 | (0.02) | 0.02 | (0.02) | -0.17 | (0.02) | **0.19** | (0.02) | -1.12 | (0.02) | -0.30 | (0.01) | 0.16 | (0.01) | 0.95 | (0.02) |
| New Zealand | -0.12 | (0.02) | -0.02 | (0.02) | -0.21 | (0.02) | **0.19** | (0.03) | -1.30 | (0.02) | -0.41 | (0.01) | 0.15 | (0.01) | 1.08 | (0.02) |
| Norway | 0.06 | (0.02) | 0.19 | (0.03) | -0.07 | (0.02) | **0.26** | (0.03) | -1.18 | (0.02) | -0.20 | (0.01) | 0.35 | (0.00) | 1.29 | (0.02) |
| Poland | 0.37 | (0.02) | 0.38 | (0.03) | 0.37 | (0.02) | 0.01 | (0.03) | -0.81 | (0.02) | 0.06 | (0.01) | 0.59 | (0.01) | 1.66 | (0.02) |
| Portugal | 0.12 | (0.02) | 0.18 | (0.03) | 0.05 | (0.03) | **0.13** | (0.03) | -1.02 | (0.02) | -0.17 | (0.01) | 0.38 | (0.00) | 1.27 | (0.02) |
| Slovak Republic | 0.15 | (0.02) | 0.21 | (0.03) | 0.09 | (0.03) | **0.12** | (0.04) | -0.98 | (0.02) | -0.16 | (0.01) | 0.38 | (0.00) | 1.37 | (0.02) |
| Spain | 0.06 | (0.02) | 0.13 | (0.02) | -0.01 | (0.02) | **0.15** | (0.02) | -1.09 | (0.01) | -0.24 | (0.00) | 0.30 | (0.00) | 1.27 | (0.02) |
| Sweden | -0.24 | (0.02) | -0.08 | (0.02) | -0.41 | (0.03) | **0.33** | (0.03) | -1.62 | (0.02) | -0.60 | (0.01) | 0.09 | (0.01) | 1.17 | (0.02) |
| Switzerland | -0.22 | (0.02) | -0.04 | (0.02) | -0.41 | (0.03) | **0.37** | (0.03) | -1.54 | (0.02) | -0.50 | (0.01) | 0.13 | (0.01) | 1.04 | (0.01) |
| Turkey | 0.07 | (0.03) | -0.01 | (0.04) | 0.17 | (0.03) | **-0.17** | (0.04) | -1.19 | (0.02) | -0.23 | (0.01) | 0.37 | (0.00) | 1.34 | (0.02) |
| United Kingdom | 0.25 | (0.01) | 0.40 | (0.02) | 0.11 | (0.02) | **0.29** | (0.03) | -1.00 | (0.02) | -0.06 | (0.01) | 0.51 | (0.01) | 1.54 | (0.02) |
| United States | 0.01 | (0.03) | 0.11 | (0.03) | -0.10 | (0.03) | **0.21** | (0.03) | -1.28 | (0.02) | -0.32 | (0.01) | 0.29 | (0.01) | 1.34 | (0.02) |
| **OECD total** | -0.01 | (0.01) | 0.07 | (0.01) | -0.09 | (0.01) | **0.16** | (0.01) | -1.23 | (0.01) | -0.31 | (0.01) | 0.26 | (0.00) | 1.24 | (0.01) |
| **OECD average** | 0.00 | (0.00) | 0.09 | (0.00) | -0.09 | (0.00) | **0.18** | (0.01) | -1.19 | (0.00) | -0.29 | (0.00) | 0.27 | (0.00) | 1.21 | (0.00) |
| **Partners** | | | | | | | | | | | | | | | | |
| Argentina | -0.63 | (0.04) | -0.62 | (0.04) | -0.63 | (0.04) | 0.01 | (0.04) | -1.85 | (0.02) | -0.93 | (0.01) | -0.32 | (0.01) | 0.59 | (0.02) |
| Azerbaijan | -0.56 | (0.03) | -0.56 | (0.03) | -0.55 | (0.03) | -0.01 | (0.04) | -1.94 | (0.02) | -0.89 | (0.01) | -0.24 | (0.01) | 0.86 | (0.02) |
| Brazil | -0.26 | (0.02) | -0.24 | (0.03) | -0.28 | (0.03) | 0.03 | (0.03) | -1.45 | (0.02) | -0.62 | (0.01) | -0.01 | (0.01) | 1.04 | (0.02) |
| Bulgaria | -0.10 | (0.03) | -0.19 | (0.04) | -0.02 | (0.03) | **-0.17** | (0.04) | -1.35 | (0.03) | -0.32 | (0.01) | 0.22 | (0.01) | 1.03 | (0.02) |
| Chile | -0.27 | (0.03) | -0.19 | (0.03) | -0.36 | (0.03) | **0.17** | (0.03) | -1.39 | (0.02) | -0.59 | (0.01) | -0.03 | (0.01) | 0.93 | (0.02) |
| Colombia | -0.43 | (0.03) | -0.44 | (0.04) | -0.43 | (0.04) | -0.01 | (0.04) | -1.62 | (0.02) | -0.74 | (0.01) | -0.12 | (0.01) | 0.76 | (0.02) |
| Croatia | 0.32 | (0.02) | 0.32 | (0.03) | 0.33 | (0.02) | 0.00 | (0.03) | -0.78 | (0.02) | 0.05 | (0.00) | 0.54 | (0.01) | 1.49 | (0.02) |
| Estonia | 0.24 | (0.02) | 0.24 | (0.02) | 0.24 | (0.02) | 0.00 | (0.03) | -0.85 | (0.02) | -0.06 | (0.01) | 0.45 | (0.01) | 1.42 | (0.02) |
| Hong Kong-China | 0.34 | (0.02) | 0.38 | (0.02) | 0.31 | (0.02) | **0.07** | (0.03) | -0.62 | (0.02) | 0.11 | (0.01) | 0.56 | (0.01) | 1.31 | (0.01) |
| Indonesia | -1.09 | (0.02) | -1.12 | (0.03) | -1.04 | (0.02) | **-0.08** | (0.03) | -2.03 | (0.02) | -1.32 | (0.00) | -0.85 | (0.00) | -0.14 | (0.02) |
| Israel | -0.66 | (0.03) | -0.57 | (0.04) | -0.74 | (0.04) | **0.17** | (0.06) | -2.19 | (0.02) | -0.97 | (0.01) | -0.31 | (0.01) | 0.84 | (0.03) |
| Jordan | -0.04 | (0.02) | -0.25 | (0.03) | 0.17 | (0.03) | **-0.41** | (0.04) | -1.36 | (0.02) | -0.32 | (0.01) | 0.28 | (0.01) | 1.25 | (0.02) |
| Kyrgyzstan | -0.45 | (0.02) | -0.57 | (0.03) | -0.35 | (0.03) | **-0.22** | (0.04) | -1.79 | (0.02) | -0.74 | (0.01) | -0.12 | (0.01) | 0.84 | (0.02) |
| Latvia | -0.02 | (0.02) | 0.01 | (0.03) | -0.04 | (0.03) | 0.04 | (0.03) | -1.04 | (0.02) | -0.25 | (0.01) | 0.23 | (0.01) | 0.99 | (0.01) |
| Liechtenstein | 0.01 | (0.05) | 0.16 | (0.07) | -0.12 | (0.07) | **0.27** | (0.10) | -1.17 | (0.07) | -0.19 | (0.01) | 0.33 | (0.02) | 1.07 | (0.05) |
| Lithuania | -0.02 | (0.02) | 0.00 | (0.03) | -0.05 | (0.03) | 0.06 | (0.03) | -1.18 | (0.02) | -0.31 | (0.01) | 0.27 | (0.01) | 1.13 | (0.02) |
| Macao-China | 0.06 | (0.01) | 0.08 | (0.02) | 0.03 | (0.02) | 0.05 | (0.03) | -0.95 | (0.02) | -0.17 | (0.00) | 0.29 | (0.01) | 1.05 | (0.02) |
| Montenegro | 0.03 | (0.02) | -0.02 | (0.02) | 0.09 | (0.02) | **-0.12** | (0.03) | -1.25 | (0.03) | -0.27 | (0.01) | 0.33 | (0.01) | 1.32 | (0.02) |
| Qatar | -0.72 | (0.02) | -0.68 | (0.02) | -0.76 | (0.02) | **0.08** | (0.03) | -2.26 | (0.02) | -1.05 | (0.00) | -0.38 | (0.01) | 0.81 | (0.02) |
| Romania | -0.37 | (0.03) | -0.40 | (0.04) | -0.34 | (0.03) | -0.06 | (0.04) | -1.55 | (0.02) | -0.64 | (0.01) | -0.08 | (0.01) | 0.81 | (0.02) |
| Russian Federation | 0.18 | (0.03) | 0.18 | (0.03) | 0.18 | (0.03) | 0.00 | (0.03) | -0.99 | (0.02) | -0.09 | (0.01) | 0.42 | (0.01) | 1.38 | (0.02) |
| Serbia | 0.02 | (0.02) | -0.03 | (0.03) | 0.06 | (0.02) | **-0.09** | (0.03) | -1.15 | (0.02) | -0.27 | (0.01) | 0.28 | (0.01) | 1.20 | (0.02) |
| Slovenia | 0.30 | (0.01) | 0.33 | (0.03) | 0.27 | (0.02) | 0.06 | (0.04) | -0.80 | (0.02) | 0.07 | (0.00) | 0.52 | (0.01) | 1.40 | (0.02) |
| Chinese Taipei | 0.46 | (0.02) | 0.51 | (0.02) | 0.40 | (0.02) | **0.11** | (0.03) | -0.55 | (0.02) | 0.22 | (0.00) | 0.61 | (0.00) | 1.54 | (0.02) |
| Thailand | -0.20 | (0.02) | -0.31 | (0.03) | -0.11 | (0.02) | **-0.21** | (0.03) | -1.30 | (0.02) | -0.44 | (0.01) | 0.11 | (0.01) | 0.85 | (0.01) |
| Tunisia | -0.73 | (0.02) | -0.68 | (0.03) | -0.78 | (0.03) | **0.10** | (0.03) | -1.85 | (0.02) | -1.01 | (0.01) | -0.47 | (0.01) | 0.41 | (0.02) |
| Uruguay | -0.34 | (0.02) | -0.32 | (0.03) | -0.35 | (0.02) | 0.03 | (0.03) | -1.46 | (0.02) | -0.64 | (0.01) | -0.08 | (0.01) | 0.83 | (0.02) |

Note: Values that are statistically significant are indicated in bold (see Annex A3).
1. Results based on students' self-reports.
StatLink 🔗 http://dx.doi.org/10.1787/142102278412

Pour consulter la version française intégrale de ce tableau, suivre ce lien :
StatLink 🔗 http://dx.doi.org/10.1787/152630454851

[Part 2/2]

**Table 3.16  Index of students' awareness of environmental issues and performance on the science scale, by quarters of the index[1]**

Tableau 3.16  Indice de sensibilisation aux problèmes environnementaux et scores sur l'échelle de culture scientifique, par quartile de l'indice

| | Performance on the science scale, by quarters of this index | | | | | | | | Change in the science score per unit of this index | | Increased likelihood of students in the bottom quarter of this index scoring in the bottom quarter of the science performance distribution | | Explained variance in student performance (r-squared x 100) | |
| | Bottom quarter | | Second quarter | | Third quarter | | Top quarter | | | | | | | |
| | Mean score | S.E. | Mean score | S.E. | Mean score | S.E. | Mean score | S.E | Effect | S.E. | Ratio | S.E. | Percentage | S.E. |
|---|---|---|---|---|---|---|---|---|---|---|---|---|---|---|
| Australia | **459** | (2.2) | 522 | (2.5) | 545 | (2.5) | 585 | (3.3) | **46.4** | (1.12) | **3.0** | (0.12) | 21.4 | (1.02) |
| Austria | **440** | (5.2) | 503 | (4.2) | 539 | (3.8) | 568 | (4.2) | **49.8** | (1.92) | **3.4** | (0.23) | 25.9 | (1.49) |
| Belgium | **437** | (3.7) | 507 | (2.6) | 544 | (2.7) | 574 | (2.8) | **52.7** | (1.74) | **3.9** | (0.21) | 27.4 | (1.45) |
| Canada | **481** | (2.7) | 530 | (2.5) | 555 | (3.0) | 580 | (2.7) | **36.2** | (1.15) | **2.7** | (0.14) | 15.4 | (0.95) |
| Czech Republic | **464** | (4.5) | 513 | (4.5) | 537 | (3.7) | 560 | (4.4) | **44.2** | (2.22) | **2.5** | (0.14) | 15.5 | (1.04) |
| Denmark | **431** | (3.7) | 482 | (3.6) | 515 | (3.5) | 558 | (3.7) | **46.7** | (1.91) | **3.1** | (0.20) | 23.8 | (1.59) |
| Finland | **510** | (2.8) | 558 | (2.5) | 580 | (2.8) | 607 | (3.4) | **42.6** | (1.51) | **2.8** | (0.14) | 18.4 | (1.14) |
| France | **419** | (4.2) | 490 | (3.5) | 524 | (3.9) | 556 | (4.0) | **50.1** | (1.95) | **3.5** | (0.24) | 24.1 | (1.43) |
| Germany | **451** | (4.9) | 516 | (3.5) | 547 | (4.0) | 577 | (3.7) | **43.9** | (1.26) | **3.4** | (0.19) | 23.9 | (1.22) |
| Greece | **425** | (4.4) | 464 | (3.7) | 487 | (3.4) | 521 | (3.6) | **37.5** | (1.86) | **2.4** | (0.14) | 15.2 | (1.25) |
| Hungary | **460** | (3.4) | 497 | (4.1) | 515 | (3.6) | 546 | (3.8) | **38.5** | (1.87) | **2.2** | (0.16) | 13.8 | (1.22) |
| Iceland | **427** | (3.3) | 475 | (2.9) | 516 | (3.1) | 551 | (3.2) | **41.3** | (1.54) | **2.9** | (0.21) | 23.8 | (1.64) |
| Ireland | **450** | (3.6) | 504 | (3.8) | 530 | (3.4) | 555 | (3.6) | **41.4** | (1.52) | **2.7** | (0.16) | 18.1 | (1.16) |
| Italy | **416** | (2.5) | 468 | (2.6) | 498 | (2.5) | 522 | (3.1) | **43.9** | (1.42) | **2.8** | (0.16) | 18.6 | (1.10) |
| Japan | **460** | (4.5) | 524 | (4.1) | 562 | (4.1) | 582 | (3.4) | **56.0** | (2.07) | **3.3** | (0.22) | 21.2 | (1.47) |
| Korea | **466** | (4.9) | 509 | (2.7) | 542 | (3.3) | 572 | (4.8) | **47.2** | (2.20) | **2.7** | (0.15) | 19.0 | (1.30) |
| Luxembourg | **418** | (2.5) | 472 | (2.3) | 514 | (2.9) | 544 | (2.9) | **40.7** | (1.29) | **3.1** | (0.18) | 23.8 | (1.29) |
| Mexico | **377** | (2.8) | 401 | (2.9) | 419 | (3.1) | 444 | (4.0) | **27.3** | (1.53) | **1.8** | (0.11) | 10.1 | (1.04) |
| Netherlands | **458** | (4.6) | 523 | (3.8) | 554 | (3.5) | 585 | (3.7) | **57.4** | (1.90) | **3.7** | (0.27) | 27.6 | (1.60) |
| New Zealand | **454** | (3.9) | 523 | (3.9) | 555 | (3.6) | 598 | (3.3) | **54.5** | (1.66) | **3.3** | (0.21) | 25.0 | (1.37) |
| Norway | **431** | (3.4) | 484 | (3.0) | 508 | (3.1) | 537 | (3.7) | **37.8** | (1.75) | **2.7** | (0.15) | 16.9 | (1.35) |
| Poland | **442** | (3.1) | 484 | (2.8) | 513 | (3.4) | 555 | (2.9) | **41.6** | (1.49) | **2.6** | (0.16) | 21.3 | (1.20) |
| Portugal | **410** | (3.7) | 469 | (3.6) | 494 | (3.4) | 526 | (3.1) | **46.3** | (1.85) | **3.4** | (0.22) | 23.2 | (1.41) |
| Slovak Republic | **435** | (3.5) | 476 | (3.4) | 513 | (3.6) | 536 | (3.4) | **40.4** | (1.76) | **2.5** | (0.15) | 17.2 | (1.28) |
| Spain | **427** | (3.0) | 483 | (3.0) | 508 | (3.0) | 539 | (2.9) | **43.5** | (1.82) | **3.1** | (0.21) | 21.4 | (1.50) |
| Sweden | **446** | (3.1) | 490 | (2.6) | 523 | (3.4) | 561 | (3.6) | **38.1** | (1.37) | **2.6** | (0.16) | 21.6 | (1.29) |
| Switzerland | **436** | (3.1) | 499 | (2.7) | 541 | (3.2) | 572 | (3.7) | **49.6** | (1.38) | **3.5** | (0.17) | 27.5 | (1.23) |
| Turkey | **378** | (3.6) | 412 | (3.4) | 439 | (4.3) | 468 | (6.7) | **32.9** | (2.96) | **2.3** | (0.18) | 16.6 | (2.19) |
| United Kingdom | **441** | (3.2) | 501 | (3.2) | 539 | (3.0) | 583 | (3.1) | **50.4** | (1.41) | **3.1** | (0.16) | 23.4 | (1.13) |
| United States | **422** | (4.1) | 481 | (4.4) | 512 | (4.5) | 545 | (4.5) | **40.8** | (1.63) | **2.7** | (0.17) | 17.5 | (1.07) |
| **OECD total** | **425** | (1.4) | 483 | (1.2) | 514 | (1.4) | 546 | (1.4) | **43.8** | (0.59) | **2.7** | (0.05) | 18.4 | (0.39) |
| **OECD average** | **439** | (0.7) | 492 | (0.6) | 522 | (0.6) | 554 | (0.7) | **44.0** | (0.32) | **2.9** | (0.03) | 20.6 | (0.24) |
| Argentina | **341** | (6.0) | 384 | (6.4) | 414 | (5.5) | 438 | (6.7) | **38.8** | (2.66) | **2.2** | (0.18) | 14.8 | (1.75) |
| Azerbaijan | **367** | (3.0) | 379 | (3.4) | 389 | (3.4) | 398 | (3.9) | **10.4** | (1.18) | **1.6** | (0.14) | 4.4 | (1.01) |
| Brazil | **336** | (2.6) | 373 | (3.0) | 410 | (3.4) | 445 | (4.6) | **40.4** | (2.01) | **2.5** | (0.17) | 20.9 | (1.41) |
| Bulgaria | **370** | (4.6) | 428 | (5.9) | 465 | (6.7) | 487 | (7.8) | **44.5** | (2.60) | **2.7** | (0.22) | 17.6 | (1.74) |
| Chile | **382** | (3.8) | 426 | (4.3) | 454 | (4.8) | 492 | (5.2) | **43.5** | (1.88) | **2.6** | (0.18) | 19.9 | (1.35) |
| Colombia | **348** | (4.8) | 384 | (4.8) | 400 | (5.1) | 422 | (4.2) | **30.1** | (2.10) | **2.1** | (0.16) | 11.7 | (1.77) |
| Croatia | **434** | (3.0) | 484 | (2.8) | 513 | (3.2) | 544 | (3.4) | **45.7** | (1.66) | **3.0** | (0.17) | 24.1 | (1.41) |
| Estonia | **481** | (3.0) | 522 | (3.5) | 548 | (3.2) | 576 | (3.4) | **38.6** | (1.79) | **2.7** | (0.16) | 18.3 | (1.49) |
| Hong Kong-China | **483** | (3.8) | 539 | (3.4) | 557 | (3.2) | 591 | (3.0) | **52.0** | (1.82) | **3.0** | (0.20) | 20.7 | (1.31) |
| Indonesia | **372** | (6.3) | 382 | (4.6) | 398 | (6.3) | 421 | (6.7) | **26.0** | (2.36) | **1.6** | (0.10) | 8.2 | (1.35) |
| Israel | **415** | (4.7) | 448 | (4.8) | 477 | (5.2) | 500 | (4.8) | **25.2** | (1.66) | **1.8** | (0.14) | 7.9 | (0.94) |
| Jordan | **372** | (2.8) | 412 | (3.1) | 439 | (3.8) | 471 | (4.3) | **35.8** | (1.68) | **2.5** | (0.14) | 18.3 | (1.32) |
| Kyrgyzstan | **303** | (3.7) | 318 | (3.5) | 334 | (3.5) | 344 | (4.1) | **15.8** | (1.47) | **1.5** | (0.08) | 4.1 | (0.68) |
| Latvia | **443** | (3.9) | 477 | (3.6) | 506 | (3.4) | 534 | (4.1) | **43.1** | (1.96) | **2.4** | (0.15) | 17.9 | (1.57) |
| Liechtenstein | **467** | (9.8) | 511 | (11.4) | 543 | (11.6) | 567 | (9.6) | **39.8** | (5.12) | **2.5** | (0.48) | 14.5 | (3.49) |
| Lithuania | **431** | (3.3) | 477 | (3.5) | 506 | (3.3) | 540 | (3.6) | **43.5** | (1.69) | **2.8** | (0.16) | 20.5 | (1.27) |
| Macao-China | **465** | (2.9) | 506 | (2.8) | 526 | (2.4) | 547 | (2.3) | **38.1** | (1.40) | **2.5** | (0.15) | 16.4 | (1.17) |
| Montenegro | **366** | (2.3) | 399 | (2.9) | 430 | (2.4) | 458 | (2.9) | **33.4** | (1.45) | **2.6** | (0.16) | 19.3 | (1.30) |
| Qatar | **320** | (1.8) | 344 | (2.0) | 356 | (1.9) | 387 | (2.5) | **19.4** | (0.92) | **1.6** | (0.08) | 8.3 | (0.69) |
| Romania | **374** | (4.5) | 410 | (4.4) | 431 | (5.1) | 460 | (5.6) | **34.5** | (1.99) | **2.3** | (0.23) | 17.0 | (1.57) |
| Russian Federation | **430** | (4.2) | 469 | (3.6) | 495 | (3.8) | 525 | (4.1) | **37.8** | (1.77) | **2.5** | (0.20) | 16.1 | (1.31) |
| Serbia | **384** | (3.8) | 428 | (3.8) | 453 | (3.7) | 481 | (3.5) | **38.1** | (1.79) | **2.6** | (0.17) | 18.8 | (1.40) |
| Slovenia | **458** | (2.9) | 515 | (2.7) | 539 | (3.4) | 572 | (3.4) | **46.5** | (1.59) | **2.8** | (0.13) | 18.7 | (1.20) |
| Chinese Taipei | **465** | (4.3) | 531 | (3.6) | 554 | (3.6) | 580 | (3.1) | **48.4** | (2.14) | **3.3** | (0.18) | 19.6 | (1.20) |
| Thailand | **383** | (3.1) | 414 | (3.2) | 435 | (3.1) | 452 | (3.0) | **30.7** | (1.51) | **2.1** | (0.14) | 12.1 | (1.05) |
| Tunisia | **357** | (2.6) | 380 | (3.2) | 391 | (3.8) | 416 | (5.5) | **23.9** | (2.54) | **1.7** | (0.11) | 7.3 | (1.32) |
| Uruguay | **385** | (3.4) | 422 | (3.5) | 445 | (3.7) | 469 | (5.6) | **35.3** | (1.99) | **2.2** | (0.12) | 12.4 | (1.28) |

Note: Values that are statistically significant are indicated in bold (see Annex A3).
1. Results based on students' self-reports.
StatLink ᔦᔦ http://dx.doi.org/10.1787/142102278412

Pour consulter la version française intégrale de ce tableau, suivre ce lien :
StatLink ᔦᔦ http://dx.doi.org/10.1787/152630454851

[Part 1/2]

**Table 3.17  Index of students' level of concern for environmental issues and performance on the science scale, by quarters of the index[1]**

Tableau 3.17  Indice d'inquiétude suscitée par les problèmes environnementaux et scores sur l'échelle de culture scientifique, par quartile de l'indice

| | | Index of students' level of concern for environmental issues | | | | | | | | | | | | | | | |
|---|---|---|---|---|---|---|---|---|---|---|---|---|---|---|---|---|---|
| | | All students | | Males | | Females | | Gender difference (M - F) | | Bottom quarter | | Second quarter | | Third quarter | | Top quarter | |
| | | Mean index | S.E. | Mean index | S.E. | Mean index | S.E. | Dif. | S.E. | Mean index | S.E. | Mean index | S.E. | Mean index | S.E. | Mean index | S.E. |
| OECD | Australia | -0.19 | (0.01) | -0.29 | (0.01) | -0.07 | (0.01) | **-0.22** | (0.02) | -1.31 | (0.02) | -0.48 | (0.00) | 0.01 | (0.00) | 1.03 | (0.01) |
| | Austria | -0.03 | (0.02) | -0.16 | (0.02) | 0.10 | (0.02) | **-0.26** | (0.03) | -1.13 | (0.02) | -0.42 | (0.01) | 0.18 | (0.01) | 1.25 | (0.01) |
| | Belgium | -0.09 | (0.02) | -0.15 | (0.02) | -0.01 | (0.02) | **-0.14** | (0.03) | -1.14 | (0.03) | -0.44 | (0.00) | 0.08 | (0.00) | 1.15 | (0.01) |
| | Canada | -0.10 | (0.01) | -0.21 | (0.02) | 0.01 | (0.02) | **-0.22** | (0.02) | -1.29 | (0.02) | -0.45 | (0.00) | 0.13 | (0.00) | 1.20 | (0.01) |
| | Czech Republic | 0.02 | (0.02) | -0.05 | (0.02) | 0.12 | (0.02) | **-0.17** | (0.03) | -1.03 | (0.02) | -0.40 | (0.01) | 0.21 | (0.01) | 1.31 | (0.01) |
| | Denmark | -0.35 | (0.02) | -0.44 | (0.02) | -0.27 | (0.02) | **-0.17** | (0.03) | -1.46 | (0.02) | -0.66 | (0.00) | -0.16 | (0.00) | 0.87 | (0.02) |
| | Finland | -0.52 | (0.01) | -0.65 | (0.02) | -0.38 | (0.02) | **-0.27** | (0.03) | -1.46 | (0.01) | -0.81 | (0.00) | -0.38 | (0.01) | 0.58 | (0.02) |
| | France | 0.04 | (0.02) | -0.01 | (0.02) | 0.09 | (0.02) | **-0.10** | (0.03) | -1.05 | (0.02) | -0.31 | (0.01) | 0.24 | (0.01) | 1.27 | (0.01) |
| | Germany | 0.08 | (0.02) | -0.04 | (0.02) | 0.20 | (0.02) | **-0.24** | (0.03) | -1.05 | (0.02) | -0.28 | (0.00) | 0.30 | (0.01) | 1.35 | (0.00) |
| | Greece | 0.14 | (0.02) | 0.05 | (0.02) | 0.23 | (0.02) | **-0.18** | (0.03) | -0.91 | (0.02) | -0.20 | (0.01) | 0.35 | (0.01) | 1.32 | (0.01) |
| | Hungary | 0.26 | (0.02) | 0.17 | (0.02) | 0.34 | (0.02) | **-0.17** | (0.03) | -0.75 | (0.02) | -0.06 | (0.01) | 0.44 | (0.01) | 1.39 | (0.00) |
| | Iceland | -0.42 | (0.02) | -0.47 | (0.02) | -0.36 | (0.02) | **-0.11** | (0.03) | -1.62 | (0.01) | -0.88 | (0.01) | -0.24 | (0.01) | 1.08 | (0.01) |
| | Ireland | -0.26 | (0.02) | -0.37 | (0.03) | -0.16 | (0.02) | **-0.20** | (0.03) | -1.50 | (0.02) | -0.59 | (0.00) | -0.04 | (0.01) | 1.08 | (0.01) |
| | Italy | 0.14 | (0.01) | 0.06 | (0.02) | 0.22 | (0.01) | **-0.16** | (0.02) | -0.96 | (0.01) | -0.26 | (0.01) | 0.40 | (0.01) | 1.39 | (0.00) |
| | Japan | 0.01 | (0.01) | -0.07 | (0.02) | 0.09 | (0.02) | **-0.16** | (0.03) | -1.07 | (0.02) | -0.35 | (0.00) | 0.20 | (0.01) | 1.28 | (0.01) |
| | Korea | 0.07 | (0.01) | 0.08 | (0.02) | 0.07 | (0.02) | 0.01 | (0.02) | -0.81 | (0.02) | -0.25 | (0.00) | 0.16 | (0.01) | 1.19 | (0.01) |
| | Luxembourg | -0.02 | (0.02) | -0.12 | (0.02) | 0.09 | (0.02) | **-0.21** | (0.03) | -1.32 | (0.02) | -0.40 | (0.01) | 0.28 | (0.01) | 1.38 | (0.00) |
| | Mexico | 0.57 | (0.02) | 0.47 | (0.02) | 0.66 | (0.02) | **-0.19** | (0.03) | -0.59 | (0.02) | 0.29 | (0.00) | 1.20 | (0.01) | 1.39 | (0.00) |
| | Netherlands | -0.01 | (0.02) | -0.10 | (0.02) | 0.08 | (0.02) | **-0.19** | (0.03) | -1.11 | (0.01) | -0.40 | (0.00) | 0.18 | (0.00) | 1.28 | (0.01) |
| | New Zealand | -0.31 | (0.01) | -0.42 | (0.02) | -0.22 | (0.02) | **-0.19** | (0.03) | -1.47 | (0.02) | -0.62 | (0.00) | -0.10 | (0.01) | 0.94 | (0.01) |
| | Norway | -0.40 | (0.02) | -0.54 | (0.03) | -0.25 | (0.02) | **-0.30** | (0.03) | -1.72 | (0.03) | -0.75 | (0.00) | -0.15 | (0.01) | 1.03 | (0.01) |
| | Poland | 0.01 | (0.02) | -0.13 | (0.02) | 0.16 | (0.02) | **-0.29** | (0.02) | -1.15 | (0.02) | -0.33 | (0.01) | 0.25 | (0.01) | 1.29 | (0.01) |
| | Portugal | 0.60 | (0.01) | 0.53 | (0.02) | 0.66 | (0.02) | **-0.13** | (0.02) | -0.56 | (0.02) | 0.32 | (0.00) | 1.24 | (0.01) | 1.40 | (0.00) |
| | Slovak Republic | 0.18 | (0.02) | 0.13 | (0.02) | 0.23 | (0.02) | **-0.10** | (0.03) | -0.91 | (0.02) | -0.19 | (0.01) | 0.41 | (0.01) | 1.39 | (0.01) |
| | Spain | 0.58 | (0.01) | 0.47 | (0.01) | 0.70 | (0.01) | **-0.23** | (0.02) | -0.57 | (0.01) | 0.29 | (0.01) | 1.22 | (0.01) | 1.40 | (0.01) |
| | Sweden | -0.43 | (0.02) | -0.57 | (0.02) | -0.27 | (0.02) | **-0.30** | (0.03) | -1.63 | (0.02) | -0.78 | (0.00) | -0.25 | (0.01) | 0.96 | (0.02) |
| | Switzerland | -0.12 | (0.01) | -0.21 | (0.02) | -0.04 | (0.02) | **-0.17** | (0.02) | -1.20 | (0.01) | -0.47 | (0.00) | 0.05 | (0.00) | 1.13 | (0.01) |
| | Turkey | 0.88 | (0.02) | 0.76 | (0.03) | 1.03 | (0.02) | **-0.27** | (0.02) | -0.45 | (0.04) | 1.19 | (0.01) | 1.39 | (0.00) | 1.40 | (0.00) |
| | United Kingdom | -0.30 | (0.01) | -0.35 | (0.02) | -0.25 | (0.02) | **-0.10** | (0.02) | -1.48 | (0.02) | -0.60 | (0.01) | -0.09 | (0.01) | 0.97 | (0.01) |
| | United States | -0.08 | (0.02) | -0.21 | (0.03) | 0.06 | (0.02) | **-0.27** | (0.04) | -1.40 | (0.03) | -0.44 | (0.01) | 0.21 | (0.01) | 1.30 | (0.01) |
| | **OECD total** | **0.08** | **(0.01)** | **-0.02** | **(0.01)** | **0.18** | **(0.01)** | **-0.20** | **(0.01)** | **-1.16** | **(0.01)** | **-0.29** | **(0.00)** | **0.39** | **(0.00)** | **1.39** | **(0.00)** |
| | **OECD average** | **0.00** | **(0.00)** | **-0.10** | **(0.00)** | **0.10** | **(0.00)** | **-0.19** | **(0.01)** | **-1.14** | **(0.00)** | **-0.32** | **(0.00)** | **0.26** | **(0.00)** | **1.20** | **(0.00)** |
| Partners | Argentina | 0.42 | (0.02) | 0.33 | (0.03) | 0.51 | (0.02) | **-0.18** | (0.03) | -0.78 | (0.02) | 0.08 | (0.01) | 1.00 | (0.01) | 1.39 | (0.00) |
| | Azerbaijan | 0.29 | (0.03) | 0.21 | (0.03) | 0.36 | (0.03) | **-0.15** | (0.03) | -1.03 | (0.02) | -0.11 | (0.01) | 0.89 | (0.02) | 1.39 | (0.00) |
| | Brazil | 0.52 | (0.02) | 0.38 | (0.02) | 0.64 | (0.02) | **-0.26** | (0.03) | -0.75 | (0.02) | 0.22 | (0.01) | 1.21 | (0.01) | 1.39 | (0.00) |
| | Bulgaria | 0.37 | (0.02) | 0.24 | (0.03) | 0.50 | (0.03) | **-0.27** | (0.04) | -0.87 | (0.02) | 0.01 | (0.00) | 0.94 | (0.01) | 1.39 | (0.00) |
| | Chile | 0.52 | (0.01) | 0.45 | (0.02) | 0.60 | (0.02) | **-0.15** | (0.03) | -0.54 | (0.01) | 0.19 | (0.01) | 1.03 | (0.01) | 1.39 | (0.00) |
| | Colombia | 0.71 | (0.03) | 0.60 | (0.04) | 0.80 | (0.03) | **-0.20** | (0.04) | -0.57 | (0.03) | 0.62 | (0.02) | 1.39 | (0.00) | 1.40 | (0.00) |
| | Croatia | 0.44 | (0.02) | 0.35 | (0.02) | 0.53 | (0.02) | **-0.19** | (0.02) | -0.72 | (0.02) | 0.07 | (0.01) | 1.01 | (0.01) | 1.39 | (0.00) |
| | Estonia | -0.04 | (0.01) | -0.10 | (0.02) | 0.03 | (0.02) | **-0.12** | (0.03) | -1.01 | (0.01) | -0.35 | (0.00) | 0.11 | (0.01) | 1.10 | (0.01) |
| | Hong Kong-China | -0.02 | (0.02) | -0.04 | (0.02) | 0.00 | (0.02) | -0.04 | (0.03) | -1.16 | (0.02) | -0.43 | (0.01) | 0.21 | (0.01) | 1.30 | (0.01) |
| | Indonesia | 0.38 | (0.02) | 0.24 | (0.03) | 0.52 | (0.02) | **-0.28** | (0.03) | -0.94 | (0.02) | 0.04 | (0.01) | 1.02 | (0.01) | 1.39 | (0.00) |
| | Israel | -0.26 | (0.02) | -0.32 | (0.03) | -0.20 | (0.03) | **-0.11** | (0.04) | -1.43 | (0.04) | -0.48 | (0.01) | -0.02 | (0.01) | 0.90 | (0.02) |
| | Jordan | -0.01 | (0.02) | -0.09 | (0.02) | 0.08 | (0.02) | **-0.18** | (0.02) | -1.10 | (0.02) | -0.38 | (0.01) | 0.20 | (0.01) | 1.27 | (0.01) |
| | Kyrgyzstan | 0.01 | (0.02) | -0.13 | (0.03) | 0.12 | (0.03) | **-0.26** | (0.04) | -1.50 | (0.03) | -0.36 | (0.01) | 0.49 | (0.01) | 1.39 | (0.01) |
| | Latvia | -0.06 | (0.01) | -0.16 | (0.02) | 0.03 | (0.02) | **-0.19** | (0.03) | -1.07 | (0.01) | -0.40 | (0.01) | 0.11 | (0.01) | 1.11 | (0.01) |
| | Liechtenstein | -0.13 | (0.06) | -0.15 | (0.09) | -0.12 | (0.07) | -0.03 | (0.12) | -1.32 | (0.08) | -0.51 | (0.02) | 0.08 | (0.02) | 1.21 | (0.04) |
| | Lithuania | 0.06 | (0.01) | 0.00 | (0.02) | 0.13 | (0.02) | **-0.13** | (0.03) | -0.94 | (0.02) | -0.27 | (0.01) | 0.22 | (0.01) | 1.23 | (0.01) |
| | Macao-China | 0.11 | (0.02) | 0.01 | (0.02) | 0.22 | (0.02) | **-0.20** | (0.03) | -1.19 | (0.02) | -0.25 | (0.01) | 0.50 | (0.01) | 1.39 | (0.00) |
| | Montenegro | 0.22 | (0.02) | 0.17 | (0.02) | 0.28 | (0.02) | **-0.12** | (0.03) | -1.00 | (0.02) | -0.14 | (0.01) | 0.64 | (0.02) | 1.39 | (0.00) |
| | Qatar | -0.23 | (0.01) | -0.28 | (0.02) | -0.18 | (0.02) | **-0.10** | (0.03) | -1.54 | (0.02) | -0.60 | (0.01) | 0.00 | (0.01) | 1.23 | (0.01) |
| | Romania | -0.16 | (0.02) | -0.24 | (0.03) | -0.08 | (0.03) | **-0.16** | (0.05) | -1.31 | (0.03) | -0.47 | (0.01) | 0.04 | (0.01) | 1.11 | (0.01) |
| | Russian Federation | 0.17 | (0.02) | 0.09 | (0.03) | 0.25 | (0.03) | **-0.16** | (0.03) | -0.88 | (0.02) | -0.15 | (0.00) | 0.34 | (0.00) | 1.37 | (0.00) |
| | Serbia | 0.25 | (0.02) | 0.20 | (0.02) | 0.31 | (0.02) | **-0.11** | (0.03) | -0.94 | (0.02) | -0.09 | (0.00) | 0.66 | (0.01) | 1.39 | (0.01) |
| | Slovenia | 0.11 | (0.01) | 0.05 | (0.02) | 0.17 | (0.02) | **-0.13** | (0.03) | -1.01 | (0.02) | -0.23 | (0.01) | 0.36 | (0.01) | 1.33 | (0.01) |
| | Chinese Taipei | 0.52 | (0.02) | 0.45 | (0.02) | 0.59 | (0.02) | **-0.14** | (0.02) | -1.01 | (0.03) | 0.30 | (0.01) | 1.39 | (0.00) | 1.40 | (0.00) |
| | Thailand | 0.29 | (0.02) | 0.09 | (0.03) | 0.43 | (0.02) | **-0.34** | (0.03) | -0.99 | (0.03) | -0.06 | (0.01) | 0.81 | (0.01) | 1.39 | (0.00) |
| | Tunisia | -0.16 | (0.02) | -0.19 | (0.02) | -0.14 | (0.02) | -0.05 | (0.03) | -1.14 | (0.02) | -0.47 | (0.01) | 0.00 | (0.01) | 0.96 | (0.02) |
| | Uruguay | 0.15 | (0.02) | 0.10 | (0.02) | 0.19 | (0.02) | **-0.09** | (0.03) | -0.87 | (0.02) | -0.14 | (0.00) | 0.37 | (0.01) | 1.24 | (0.01) |

Note: Values that are statistically significant are indicated in bold (see Annex A3).
1. Results based on students' self-reports.
StatLink ⌨ http://dx.doi.org/10.1787/142102278412

Pour consulter la version française intégrale de ce tableau, suivre ce lien :
StatLink ⌨ http://dx.doi.org/10.1787/152630454851

[Part 2/2]

**Table 3.17  Index of students' level of concern for environmental issues and performance on the science scale, by quarters of the index[1]**

Tableau 3.17  Indice d'inquiétude suscitée par les problèmes environnementaux et scores sur l'échelle de culture scientifique, par quartile de l'indice

| | | Performance on the science scale, by quarters of this index | | | | | | | Change in the science score per unit of this index | | Increased likelihood of students in the bottom quarter of this index scoring in the bottom quarter of the science performance distribution | | Explained variance in student performance (r-squared x 100) | |
| | | Bottom quarter | | Second quarter | | Third quarter | | Top quarter | | | | | | | |
| | | Mean score | S.E. | Mean score | S.E. | Mean score | S.E. | Mean score | S.E | Effect | S.E. | Ratio | S.E. | Percentage | S.E. |
|---|---|---|---|---|---|---|---|---|---|---|---|---|---|---|---|
| *OECD* | Australia | **509** | (3.4) | 537 | (2.7) | 541 | (2.7) | **526** | (2.4) | **8.4** | (1.11) | **1.5** | (0.06) | 0.7 | (0.19) |
| | Austria | 504 | (5.5) | 519 | (5.8) | 519 | (4.5) | 510 | (4.2) | 3.7 | (1.89) | **1.3** | (0.08) | 0.1 | (0.12) |
| | Belgium | 503 | (4.7) | 528 | (3.2) | 522 | (2.6) | 510 | (2.7) | **6.0** | (2.42) | **1.4** | (0.09) | 0.3 | (0.26) |
| | Canada | 527 | (3.1) | 541 | (2.4) | 545 | (2.7) | 533 | (2.7) | **4.6** | (1.21) | **1.3** | (0.06) | 0.3 | (0.13) |
| | Czech Republic | **526** | (5.8) | 529 | (5.1) | 512 | (3.9) | **508** | (4.0) | **-7.0** | (2.31) | 1.0 | (0.08) | 0.4 | (0.29) |
| | Denmark | 490 | (4.5) | 500 | (4.1) | 502 | (4.7) | 496 | (4.2) | 3.2 | (2.01) | **1.2** | (0.08) | 0.1 | (0.14) |
| | Finland | 562 | (3.5) | 565 | (3.4) | 572 | (2.8) | 555 | (3.3) | -1.6 | (1.81) | 1.0 | (0.07) | 0.0 | (0.06) |
| | France | 461 | (5.2) | 507 | (4.4) | 512 | (3.8) | 513 | (3.8) | **23.3** | (1.91) | **2.1** | (0.12) | 4.6 | (0.73) |
| | Germany | **501** | (5.4) | 535 | (4.0) | 530 | (4.5) | 526 | (4.8) | **11.2** | (1.84) | **1.5** | (0.08) | 1.2 | (0.39) |
| | Greece | **440** | (4.8) | 483 | (3.8) | 488 | (3.6) | **486** | (3.9) | **20.1** | (1.92) | **2.0** | (0.11) | 3.6 | (0.70) |
| | Hungary | 500 | (4.4) | 513 | (3.7) | 507 | (3.5) | 498 | (3.5) | 0.9 | (2.26) | **1.3** | (0.11) | 0.0 | (0.05) |
| | Iceland | **503** | (3.5) | 507 | (3.1) | 491 | (3.9) | 471 | (3.7) | **-9.9** | (1.72) | 0.8 | (0.08) | 1.2 | (0.40) |
| | Ireland | 508 | (4.1) | 511 | (4.6) | 512 | (4.0) | 510 | (3.9) | **3.3** | (1.40) | 1.1 | (0.07) | 0.1 | (0.11) |
| | Italy | **465** | (2.8) | 481 | (2.7) | 482 | (2.7) | 477 | (2.8) | **5.1** | (1.41) | **1.4** | (0.08) | 0.2 | (0.14) |
| | Japan | **510** | (4.7) | 536 | (4.4) | 548 | (3.8) | **533** | (4.3) | **9.6** | (1.74) | **1.5** | (0.07) | 0.9 | (0.32) |
| | Korea | 516 | (4.6) | 532 | (3.9) | 529 | (4.1) | 512 | (3.9) | -0.6 | (2.12) | **1.2** | (0.06) | 0.0 | (0.04) |
| | Luxembourg | **477** | (3.3) | 489 | (3.3) | 496 | (3.0) | **489** | (2.8) | **7.7** | (1.47) | **1.3** | (0.09) | 0.7 | (0.28) |
| | Mexico | 376 | (4.5) | 425 | (2.8) | 421 | (3.3) | 420 | (2.8) | **21.1** | (1.96) | **2.3** | (0.13) | 5.0 | (0.98) |
| | Netherlands | 524 | (4.6) | 543 | (4.1) | 531 | (4.4) | 521 | (3.9) | -0.8 | (1.82) | **1.3** | (0.09) | 0.0 | (0.05) |
| | New Zealand | 525 | (4.3) | 542 | (4.1) | 541 | (3.6) | 521 | (3.6) | 0.7 | (1.71) | **1.2** | (0.07) | 0.0 | (0.03) |
| | Norway | 485 | (3.8) | 503 | (3.7) | 496 | (3.9) | 478 | (3.8) | 1.2 | (1.62) | **1.2** | (0.08) | 0.0 | (0.07) |
| | Poland | 478 | (3.3) | 503 | (3.0) | 508 | (3.4) | 503 | (2.9) | **10.6** | (2.04) | **1.6** | (0.08) | 1.3 | (0.31) |
| | Portugal | 466 | (5.5) | 489 | (3.4) | 472 | (3.8) | 472 | (4.1) | 2.9 | (1.88) | **1.4** | (0.10) | 0.1 | (0.11) |
| | Slovak Republic | 494 | (4.7) | 491 | (3.7) | 490 | (3.6) | 485 | (3.7) | -2.9 | (2.16) | 1.1 | (0.08) | 0.1 | (0.12) |
| | Spain | **480** | (3.3) | 498 | (3.2) | 491 | (3.5) | **488** | (3.3) | **5.1** | (1.47) | **1.3** | (0.07) | 0.2 | (0.13) |
| | Sweden | 496 | (4.4) | 510 | (4.2) | 519 | (2.9) | 496 | (3.6) | 2.4 | (1.50) | **1.3** | (0.11) | 0.1 | (0.10) |
| | Switzerland | **494** | (4.9) | 522 | (4.4) | 519 | (3.4) | 514 | (3.1) | **11.4** | (1.76) | **1.4** | (0.07) | 1.1 | (0.36) |
| | Turkey | **403** | (5.2) | 430 | (5.2) | 433 | (4.7) | **431** | (4.8) | **19.1** | (2.35) | **1.8** | (0.16) | 4.1 | (0.95) |
| | United Kingdom | **499** | (3.8) | 514 | (3.5) | 531 | (2.9) | **523** | (3.6) | **11.7** | (1.38) | **1.4** | (0.06) | 1.3 | (0.29) |
| | United States | **469** | (6.3) | 500 | (5.4) | 505 | (4.4) | 487 | (4.0) | **8.9** | (1.37) | **1.6** | (0.10) | 0.9 | (0.26) |
| | **OECD total** | **481** | (2.1) | **508** | (1.7) | **501** | (1.2) | **479** | (1.3) | **1.2** | (0.76) | **1.4** | (0.03) | 0.0 | (0.02) |
| | **OECD average** | **490** | (0.8) | **509** | (0.7) | **509** | (0.7) | **500** | (0.7) | **6.0** | (0.33) | **1.4** | (0.02) | 1.0 | (0.07) |
| *Partners* | Argentina | **360** | (8.0) | 399 | (7.1) | 411 | (5.2) | **407** | (5.7) | **23.2** | (2.88) | **2.1** | (0.13) | 4.5 | (1.14) |
| | Azerbaijan | **368** | (3.3) | 385 | (3.3) | 389 | (3.5) | 392 | (3.5) | **8.4** | (1.04) | **1.6** | (0.11) | 2.3 | (0.58) |
| | Brazil | **349** | (3.5) | 398 | (4.2) | 408 | (3.8) | **410** | (3.5) | **24.2** | (1.81) | **2.3** | (0.14) | 6.4 | (0.79) |
| | Bulgaria | **414** | (7.5) | 453 | (6.9) | 447 | (6.3) | **435** | (6.0) | **10.1** | (2.36) | **1.7** | (0.14) | 0.8 | (0.39) |
| | Chile | **420** | (5.4) | 441 | (5.0) | 447 | (5.5) | **448** | (5.0) | **15.1** | (1.83) | **1.6** | (0.10) | 1.8 | (0.43) |
| | Colombia | 361 | (5.2) | 401 | (4.0) | 397 | (4.2) | 395 | (5.4) | **18.4** | (2.23) | **1.9** | (0.15) | 3.8 | (0.98) |
| | Croatia | 495 | (3.6) | 502 | (3.5) | 490 | (3.9) | 487 | (3.7) | -2.0 | (1.84) | **1.2** | (0.08) | 0.0 | (0.08) |
| | Estonia | 532 | (4.1) | 539 | (3.8) | 527 | (2.9) | 530 | (3.5) | -0.2 | (2.05) | 1.1 | (0.08) | 0.0 | (0.04) |
| | Hong Kong-China | **548** | (3.9) | 553 | (3.4) | 541 | (3.9) | **528** | (3.6) | **-7.3** | (1.75) | 0.9 | (0.06) | 0.6 | (0.28) |
| | Indonesia | 360 | (5.6) | 405 | (9.3) | 405 | (5.0) | 405 | (4.2) | **15.5** | (1.67) | **2.3** | (0.15) | 5.0 | (1.32) |
| | Israel | **423** | (5.1) | 467 | (4.8) | 477 | (4.3) | 473 | (4.7) | **18.0** | (2.20) | **1.8** | (0.10) | 2.7 | (0.65) |
| | Jordan | **389** | (3.7) | 425 | (3.9) | 442 | (3.7) | 437 | (3.4) | **19.8** | (1.59) | **2.0** | (0.12) | 4.4 | (0.68) |
| | Kyrgyzstan | **301** | (3.5) | 329 | (4.6) | 334 | (3.8) | **337** | (3.3) | **11.9** | (1.17) | **1.7** | (0.12) | 2.9 | (0.64) |
| | Latvia | 491 | (5.2) | 492 | (3.5) | 492 | (3.0) | 484 | (3.8) | -2.0 | (1.85) | 1.1 | (0.07) | 0.0 | (0.07) |
| | Liechtenstein | 513 | (9.4) | 530 | (11.1) | 536 | (9.4) | 515 | (8.8) | 1.6 | (4.01) | **1.2** | (0.28) | 0.0 | (0.22) |
| | Lithuania | **489** | (4.7) | 499 | (4.2) | 492 | (3.9) | 474 | (3.0) | **-4.4** | (2.14) | 1.1 | (0.08) | 0.2 | (0.17) |
| | Macao-China | **493** | (2.8) | 514 | (2.6) | 520 | (2.6) | **518** | (2.9) | **8.4** | (1.33) | **1.6** | (0.11) | 1.2 | (0.39) |
| | Montenegro | 399 | (2.5) | 419 | (2.3) | 425 | (3.9) | **411** | (3.4) | **5.9** | (1.27) | **1.5** | (0.09) | 0.5 | (0.23) |
| | Qatar | **336** | (2.4) | 354 | (2.1) | 369 | (2.1) | **349** | (2.4) | **4.8** | (1.14) | **1.5** | (0.10) | 0.4 | (0.20) |
| | Romania | 396 | (4.6) | 423 | (5.7) | 433 | (4.4) | **423** | (4.8) | **11.4** | (1.82) | **1.7** | (0.10) | 1.8 | (0.63) |
| | Russian Federation | **460** | (5.9) | 487 | (4.0) | 494 | (3.9) | **478** | (4.2) | **9.0** | (2.62) | **1.5** | (0.13) | 0.8 | (0.44) |
| | Serbia | 428 | (4.1) | 442 | (4.0) | 441 | (3.8) | 435 | (3.8) | 2.8 | (1.50) | **1.3** | (0.08) | 0.1 | (0.11) |
| | Slovenia | 509 | (3.5) | 536 | (3.4) | 524 | (3.2) | 515 | (3.1) | 2.4 | (1.72) | **1.4** | (0.09) | 0.1 | (0.08) |
| | Chinese Taipei | **490** | (5.2) | 554 | (3.2) | 544 | (4.3) | **543** | (4.4) | **18.3** | (1.27) | **2.4** | (0.12) | 4.7 | (0.60) |
| | Thailand | **380** | (2.9) | 432 | (3.2) | 438 | (3.2) | **435** | (3.2) | **20.5** | (1.30) | **2.5** | (0.15) | 6.9 | (0.78) |
| | Tunisia | **360** | (4.0) | 387 | (4.1) | 401 | (3.9) | **398** | (3.1) | **16.0** | (1.54) | **1.8** | (0.10) | 2.7 | (0.53) |
| | Uruguay | 431 | (4.2) | 434 | (3.6) | 433 | (3.9) | 423 | (3.9) | -1.8 | (1.98) | 1.1 | (0.07) | 0.0 | (0.06) |

Note: Values that are statistically significant are indicated in bold (see Annex A3).
1. Results based on students' self-reports.
*StatLink* ⧉ http://dx.doi.org/10.1787/142102278412

Pour consulter la version française intégrale de ce tableau, suivre ce lien :
*StatLink* ⧉ http://dx.doi.org/10.1787/152630454851

[Part 1/2]

**Table 3.18** Index of students' optimism regarding environmental issues and performance on the science scale, by quarters of the index[1]

Tableau 3.18 Indice d'optimisme à l'égard des problèmes environnementaux et scores sur l'échelle de culture scientifique, par quartile de l'indice

| | Index of students' optimism regarding environmental issues | | | | | | | | | | | | | | | | |
| | All students | | Males | | Females | | Gender difference (M - F) | | Bottom quarter | | Second quarter | | Third quarter | | Top quarter | |
| | Mean index | S.E. | Mean index | S.E. | Mean index | S.E. | Dif. | S.E. | Mean index | S.E. | Mean index | S.E. | Mean index | S.E. | Mean index | S.E. |
|---|---|---|---|---|---|---|---|---|---|---|---|---|---|---|---|---|
| **OECD** | | | | | | | | | | | | | | | | |
| Australia | -0.13 | (0.01) | -0.03 | (0.02) | -0.24 | (0.02) | **0.21** | (0.02) | -1.43 | (0.01) | -0.42 | (0.00) | 0.20 | (0.00) | 1.13 | (0.01) |
| Austria | -0.21 | (0.02) | -0.12 | (0.02) | -0.31 | (0.02) | **0.20** | (0.02) | -1.29 | (0.01) | -0.40 | (0.01) | 0.08 | (0.00) | 0.76 | (0.01) |
| Belgium | -0.17 | (0.01) | -0.11 | (0.02) | -0.23 | (0.02) | **0.12** | (0.02) | -1.41 | (0.01) | -0.40 | (0.01) | 0.15 | (0.00) | 0.98 | (0.02) |
| Canada | -0.22 | (0.01) | -0.07 | (0.01) | -0.37 | (0.02) | **0.30** | (0.02) | -1.54 | (0.00) | -0.49 | (0.00) | 0.15 | (0.00) | 1.02 | (0.01) |
| Czech Republic | 0.06 | (0.02) | 0.14 | (0.02) | -0.04 | (0.02) | **0.18** | (0.03) | -1.14 | (0.02) | -0.15 | (0.00) | 0.36 | (0.01) | 1.17 | (0.02) |
| Denmark | 0.07 | (0.02) | 0.16 | (0.02) | -0.01 | (0.02) | **0.17** | (0.03) | -1.01 | (0.02) | -0.11 | (0.01) | 0.36 | (0.00) | 1.06 | (0.02) |
| Finland | 0.00 | (0.01) | 0.10 | (0.02) | -0.10 | (0.02) | **0.20** | (0.02) | -1.13 | (0.01) | -0.15 | (0.00) | 0.30 | (0.00) | 0.98 | (0.02) |
| France | -0.11 | (0.02) | -0.09 | (0.02) | -0.13 | (0.02) | 0.03 | (0.03) | -1.30 | (0.01) | -0.36 | (0.01) | 0.18 | (0.00) | 1.04 | (0.02) |
| Germany | -0.10 | (0.01) | -0.01 | (0.02) | -0.20 | (0.02) | **0.19** | (0.03) | -1.25 | (0.01) | -0.28 | (0.01) | 0.19 | (0.00) | 0.92 | (0.02) |
| Greece | 0.06 | (0.02) | 0.20 | (0.02) | -0.08 | (0.02) | **0.29** | (0.02) | -1.25 | (0.02) | -0.19 | (0.00) | 0.40 | (0.01) | 1.28 | (0.02) |
| Hungary | -0.05 | (0.02) | -0.02 | (0.02) | -0.09 | (0.02) | **0.07** | (0.03) | -1.30 | (0.01) | -0.24 | (0.01) | 0.25 | (0.00) | 1.09 | (0.02) |
| Iceland | 0.03 | (0.01) | 0.09 | (0.02) | -0.02 | (0.02) | **0.12** | (0.03) | -1.17 | (0.01) | -0.15 | (0.00) | 0.35 | (0.00) | 1.10 | (0.02) |
| Ireland | 0.12 | (0.02) | 0.24 | (0.02) | 0.01 | (0.02) | **0.23** | (0.03) | -1.10 | (0.01) | -0.10 | (0.01) | 0.43 | (0.01) | 1.26 | (0.02) |
| Italy | 0.03 | (0.01) | 0.11 | (0.02) | -0.04 | (0.02) | **0.15** | (0.02) | -1.15 | (0.01) | -0.17 | (0.01) | 0.33 | (0.00) | 1.14 | (0.01) |
| Japan | 0.10 | (0.02) | 0.16 | (0.03) | 0.04 | (0.02) | **0.12** | (0.03) | -1.30 | (0.01) | -0.09 | (0.01) | 0.48 | (0.00) | 1.32 | (0.02) |
| Korea | 0.37 | (0.02) | 0.42 | (0.03) | 0.31 | (0.02) | **0.11** | (0.03) | -1.08 | (0.01) | 0.11 | (0.01) | 0.68 | (0.00) | 1.76 | (0.02) |
| Luxembourg | -0.18 | (0.01) | -0.09 | (0.02) | -0.26 | (0.02) | **0.17** | (0.02) | -1.43 | (0.01) | -0.41 | (0.01) | 0.13 | (0.00) | 0.99 | (0.02) |
| Mexico | -0.14 | (0.02) | -0.14 | (0.03) | -0.14 | (0.03) | 0.00 | (0.03) | -1.55 | (0.00) | -0.52 | (0.00) | 0.14 | (0.01) | 1.35 | (0.02) |
| Netherlands | 0.09 | (0.02) | 0.16 | (0.02) | 0.02 | (0.02) | **0.15** | (0.04) | -1.15 | (0.02) | -0.12 | (0.01) | 0.42 | (0.00) | 1.22 | (0.02) |
| New Zealand | -0.22 | (0.02) | -0.14 | (0.02) | -0.30 | (0.02) | **0.15** | (0.03) | -1.53 | (0.01) | -0.49 | (0.01) | 0.13 | (0.00) | 1.01 | (0.02) |
| Norway | 0.42 | (0.02) | 0.54 | (0.02) | 0.30 | (0.02) | **0.24** | (0.03) | -0.80 | (0.02) | 0.19 | (0.01) | 0.67 | (0.00) | 1.64 | (0.02) |
| Poland | 0.19 | (0.02) | 0.26 | (0.02) | 0.12 | (0.02) | **0.15** | (0.03) | -1.10 | (0.02) | -0.06 | (0.00) | 0.50 | (0.00) | 1.42 | (0.02) |
| Portugal | -0.20 | (0.02) | -0.09 | (0.03) | -0.30 | (0.03) | **0.21** | (0.03) | -1.59 | (0.00) | -0.57 | (0.00) | 0.04 | (0.01) | 1.32 | (0.02) |
| Slovak Republic | -0.08 | (0.02) | -0.02 | (0.02) | -0.15 | (0.02) | **0.12** | (0.03) | -1.34 | (0.01) | -0.33 | (0.01) | 0.24 | (0.00) | 1.10 | (0.02) |
| Spain | 0.17 | (0.01) | 0.24 | (0.02) | 0.10 | (0.02) | **0.14** | (0.03) | -1.12 | (0.01) | -0.07 | (0.00) | 0.50 | (0.00) | 1.38 | (0.01) |
| Sweden | 0.19 | (0.02) | 0.29 | (0.02) | 0.10 | (0.02) | **0.19** | (0.03) | -1.06 | (0.01) | -0.01 | (0.01) | 0.51 | (0.00) | 1.33 | (0.02) |
| Switzerland | -0.10 | (0.01) | -0.02 | (0.01) | -0.18 | (0.01) | **0.16** | (0.02) | -1.26 | (0.01) | -0.29 | (0.01) | 0.18 | (0.00) | 0.98 | (0.01) |
| Turkey | -0.08 | (0.03) | 0.04 | (0.03) | -0.22 | (0.04) | **0.25** | (0.05) | -1.61 | (0.00) | -0.61 | (0.00) | 0.31 | (0.01) | 1.60 | (0.03) |
| United Kingdom | -0.07 | (0.01) | 0.05 | (0.02) | -0.19 | (0.02) | **0.24** | (0.02) | -1.45 | (0.01) | -0.36 | (0.01) | 0.27 | (0.01) | 1.25 | (0.02) |
| United States | 0.14 | (0.03) | 0.32 | (0.03) | -0.04 | (0.03) | **0.36** | (0.03) | -1.33 | (0.01) | -0.11 | (0.00) | 0.49 | (0.01) | 1.50 | (0.02) |
| **OECD total** | 0.03 | (0.01) | 0.14 | (0.01) | -0.07 | (0.01) | **0.20** | (0.01) | -1.34 | (0.00) | -0.24 | (0.00) | 0.38 | (0.00) | 1.34 | (0.01) |
| **OECD average** | 0.00 | (0.00) | 0.09 | (0.00) | -0.09 | (0.00) | **0.17** | (0.01) | -1.27 | (0.00) | -0.25 | (0.00) | 0.31 | (0.00) | 1.20 | (0.00) |
| **Partners** | | | | | | | | | | | | | | | | |
| Argentina | 0.15 | (0.03) | 0.12 | (0.03) | 0.19 | (0.04) | -0.07 | (0.04) | -1.34 | (0.01) | -0.15 | (0.01) | 0.55 | (0.01) | 1.57 | (0.02) |
| Azerbaijan | 0.63 | (0.04) | 0.54 | (0.04) | 0.72 | (0.04) | **-0.18** | (0.04) | -1.01 | (0.03) | 0.33 | (0.01) | 1.01 | (0.01) | 2.19 | (0.02) |
| Brazil | 0.01 | (0.02) | 0.01 | (0.02) | 0.01 | (0.02) | 0.00 | (0.03) | -1.60 | (0.00) | -0.43 | (0.01) | 0.41 | (0.01) | 1.66 | (0.02) |
| Bulgaria | 0.68 | (0.03) | 0.82 | (0.03) | 0.54 | (0.03) | **0.28** | (0.04) | -0.89 | (0.02) | 0.39 | (0.01) | 1.02 | (0.01) | 2.22 | (0.01) |
| Chile | 0.29 | (0.03) | 0.31 | (0.03) | 0.27 | (0.03) | 0.04 | (0.04) | -1.08 | (0.01) | 0.03 | (0.01) | 0.64 | (0.01) | 1.58 | (0.02) |
| Colombia | 0.30 | (0.06) | 0.35 | (0.04) | 0.26 | (0.08) | 0.09 | (0.06) | -1.29 | (0.02) | -0.10 | (0.01) | 0.68 | (0.01) | 1.91 | (0.02) |
| Croatia | -0.29 | (0.02) | -0.20 | (0.02) | -0.38 | (0.03) | **0.18** | (0.03) | -1.61 | (0.00) | -0.62 | (0.01) | 0.00 | (0.01) | 1.06 | (0.02) |
| Estonia | 0.02 | (0.02) | 0.09 | (0.02) | -0.06 | (0.02) | **0.15** | (0.03) | -1.18 | (0.01) | -0.20 | (0.01) | 0.29 | (0.01) | 1.18 | (0.02) |
| Hong Kong-China | 0.33 | (0.02) | 0.36 | (0.02) | 0.30 | (0.02) | 0.05 | (0.03) | -0.94 | (0.02) | 0.09 | (0.01) | 0.65 | (0.00) | 1.52 | (0.02) |
| Indonesia | 0.16 | (0.02) | 0.18 | (0.03) | 0.13 | (0.02) | 0.05 | (0.03) | -1.26 | (0.01) | -0.09 | (0.01) | 0.50 | (0.00) | 1.49 | (0.02) |
| Israel | 0.48 | (0.02) | 0.55 | (0.03) | 0.42 | (0.03) | **0.13** | (0.05) | -0.98 | (0.02) | 0.22 | (0.01) | 0.82 | (0.01) | 1.86 | (0.02) |
| Jordan | 0.24 | (0.03) | 0.32 | (0.04) | 0.17 | (0.04) | **0.15** | (0.05) | -1.39 | (0.01) | -0.13 | (0.01) | 0.66 | (0.01) | 1.82 | (0.02) |
| Kyrgyzstan | 0.72 | (0.03) | 0.65 | (0.03) | 0.79 | (0.03) | **-0.15** | (0.04) | -0.83 | (0.02) | 0.50 | (0.01) | 1.10 | (0.01) | 2.12 | (0.02) |
| Latvia | 0.16 | (0.02) | 0.22 | (0.03) | 0.10 | (0.02) | **0.11** | (0.03) | -0.86 | (0.02) | -0.07 | (0.01) | 0.40 | (0.00) | 1.18 | (0.02) |
| Liechtenstein | -0.26 | (0.05) | -0.24 | (0.09) | -0.28 | (0.07) | 0.05 | (0.12) | -1.50 | (0.03) | -0.48 | (0.02) | 0.07 | (0.02) | 0.89 | (0.06) |
| Lithuania | 0.18 | (0.02) | 0.21 | (0.03) | 0.15 | (0.02) | 0.06 | (0.03) | -1.07 | (0.02) | -0.08 | (0.01) | 0.47 | (0.01) | 1.42 | (0.02) |
| Macao-China | 0.36 | (0.02) | 0.46 | (0.03) | 0.25 | (0.02) | **0.21** | (0.04) | -0.99 | (0.02) | 0.06 | (0.01) | 0.66 | (0.01) | 1.70 | (0.02) |
| Montenegro | 0.60 | (0.02) | 0.64 | (0.03) | 0.56 | (0.03) | **0.08** | (0.04) | -0.79 | (0.02) | 0.31 | (0.01) | 0.88 | (0.01) | 1.99 | (0.02) |
| Qatar | 0.73 | (0.02) | 0.75 | (0.02) | 0.72 | (0.02) | 0.03 | (0.03) | -0.78 | (0.02) | 0.46 | (0.01) | 1.01 | (0.01) | 2.24 | (0.02) |
| Romania | 0.51 | (0.02) | 0.58 | (0.03) | 0.45 | (0.02) | **0.13** | (0.03) | -0.76 | (0.02) | 0.23 | (0.01) | 0.78 | (0.01) | 1.80 | (0.04) |
| Russian Federation | 0.57 | (0.01) | 0.60 | (0.02) | 0.55 | (0.02) | **0.06** | (0.03) | -0.56 | (0.02) | 0.29 | (0.00) | 0.80 | (0.01) | 1.76 | (0.02) |
| Serbia | 0.28 | (0.02) | 0.37 | (0.03) | 0.19 | (0.03) | **0.19** | (0.04) | -1.19 | (0.01) | -0.05 | (0.01) | 0.61 | (0.01) | 1.75 | (0.02) |
| Slovenia | -0.12 | (0.02) | 0.00 | (0.02) | -0.24 | (0.02) | **0.24** | (0.03) | -1.34 | (0.01) | -0.37 | (0.01) | 0.19 | (0.01) | 1.04 | (0.02) |
| Chinese Taipei | 0.03 | (0.02) | 0.06 | (0.02) | -0.01 | (0.03) | 0.07 | (0.04) | -1.44 | (0.01) | -0.32 | (0.01) | 0.40 | (0.01) | 1.48 | (0.02) |
| Thailand | 0.58 | (0.02) | 0.61 | (0.03) | 0.56 | (0.03) | 0.05 | (0.03) | -1.02 | (0.02) | 0.26 | (0.01) | 0.94 | (0.01) | 2.12 | (0.02) |
| Tunisia | 0.30 | (0.03) | 0.29 | (0.03) | 0.31 | (0.03) | -0.02 | (0.04) | -1.13 | (0.02) | 0.11 | (0.01) | 0.72 | (0.01) | 1.49 | (0.02) |
| Uruguay | -0.03 | (0.02) | -0.04 | (0.03) | -0.01 | (0.03) | -0.03 | (0.05) | -1.49 | (0.01) | -0.40 | (0.01) | 0.34 | (0.01) | 1.44 | (0.02) |

Note: Values that are statistically significant are indicated in bold (see Annex A3).
1. Results based on students' self-reports.
StatLink ▄▆▊▎ http://dx.doi.org/10.1787/142102278412

Pour consulter la version française intégrale de ce tableau, suivre ce lien :
StatLink ▄▆▊▎ http://dx.doi.org/10.1787/152630454851

[Part 2/2]

**Table 3.18** **Index of students' optimism regarding environmental issues and performance on the science scale, by quarters of the index[1]**

Tableau 3.18 Indice d'optimisme à l'égard des problèmes environnementaux et scores sur l'échelle de culture scientifique, par quartile de l'indice

| | | Performance on the science scale, by quarters of this index | | | | | | | Change in the science score per unit of this index | | Increased likelihood of students in the bottom quarter of this index scoring in the bottom quarter of the science performance distribution | | Explained variance in student performance (r-squared x 100) | |
| | | Bottom quarter | | Second quarter | | Third quarter | | Top quarter | | | | | | | |
| | | Mean score | S.E. | Mean score | S.E. | Mean score | S.E. | Mean score | S.E | Effect | S.E. | Ratio | S.E. | Percentage | S.E. |
|---|---|---|---|---|---|---|---|---|---|---|---|---|---|---|---|
| *OECD* | Australia | **536** | (2.7) | 537 | (2.8) | 535 | (2.7) | **505** | (3.6) | **-12.2** | (1.11) | 0.8 | (0.04) | 1.6 | (0.29) |
| | Austria | **525** | (4.6) | 525 | (4.6) | 511 | (4.7) | **488** | (6.8) | **-19.5** | (2.61) | 0.8 | (0.06) | 2.7 | (0.68) |
| | Belgium | **532** | (2.4) | 534 | (2.9) | 521 | (2.8) | **476** | (4.4) | **-22.6** | (1.80) | 0.6 | (0.04) | 4.9 | (0.72) |
| | Canada | **540** | (2.6) | 545 | (2.7) | 542 | (2.3) | **520** | (2.6) | **-8.6** | (1.02) | 0.9 | (0.05) | 0.9 | (0.21) |
| | Czech Republic | **531** | (3.9) | 527 | (4.1) | 524 | (4.3) | **495** | (6.2) | **-15.1** | (2.1) | 0.7 | (0.05) | 2.1 | (0.60) |
| | Denmark | **506** | (4.0) | 502 | (3.9) | 498 | (4.3) | **483** | (4.8) | **-9.7** | (2.34) | 0.8 | (0.06) | 0.8 | (0.38) |
| | Finland | **579** | (3.0) | 574 | (2.9) | 563 | (3.9) | **539** | (3.3) | **-17.4** | (1.49) | 0.7 | (0.05) | 3.0 | (0.51) |
| | France | **532** | (4.2) | 523 | (3.7) | 495 | (4.5) | **441** | (4.9) | **-35.6** | (2.06) | 0.5 | (0.05) | 11.0 | (1.11) |
| | Germany | **524** | (4.8) | 533 | (4.0) | 528 | (5.2) | **506** | (5.5) | **-8.5** | (1.99) | 0.9 | (0.07) | 0.6 | (0.27) |
| | Greece | **501** | (3.4) | 498 | (3.7) | 473 | (4.1) | **424** | (4.2) | **-28.3** | (1.48) | 0.5 | (0.05) | 9.5 | (0.90) |
| | Hungary | **523** | (3.4) | 519 | (3.2) | 505 | (4.0) | **471** | (3.8) | **-21.3** | (1.67) | 0.6 | (0.06) | 5.2 | (0.81) |
| | Iceland | **509** | (3.0) | 504 | (3.4) | 492 | (3.1) | **465** | (3.6) | **-19.5** | (1.70) | 0.7 | (0.06) | 3.4 | (0.58) |
| | Ireland | **527** | (3.8) | 517 | (3.8) | 510 | (4.3) | **486** | (4.5) | **-17.3** | (1.55) | 0.7 | (0.05) | 3.1 | (0.52) |
| | Italy | **509** | (2.5) | 498 | (2.6) | 473 | (2.6) | **425** | (2.8) | **-32.9** | (1.38) | 0.4 | (0.03) | 10.0 | (0.75) |
| | Japan | **532** | (4.5) | 539 | (4.0) | 533 | (4.3) | **522** | (4.3) | **-4.6** | (1.50) | 1.0 | (0.07) | 0.2 | (0.15) |
| | Korea | **523** | (3.3) | 530 | (4.2) | 531 | (4.3) | **505** | (5.1) | **-6.6** | (1.50) | 0.9 | (0.07) | 0.7 | (0.30) |
| | Luxembourg | **505** | (2.4) | 506 | (2.5) | 488 | (2.8) | **451** | (2.8) | **-21.9** | (1.29) | 0.7 | (0.05) | 4.7 | (0.56) |
| | Mexico | **439** | (3.0) | 430 | (2.5) | 409 | (3.5) | **363** | (3.7) | **-25.1** | (1.49) | 0.5 | (0.05) | 12.2 | (1.24) |
| | Netherlands | **533** | (3.5) | 534 | (3.6) | 536 | (4.4) | **515** | (5.6) | **-8.1** | (2.08) | 0.8 | (0.07) | 0.7 | (0.34) |
| | New Zealand | **550** | (3.4) | 551 | (3.7) | 533 | (3.5) | **495** | (4.4) | **-22.9** | (1.39) | 0.7 | (0.05) | 4.6 | (0.57) |
| | Norway | **496** | (3.4) | 508 | (3.0) | 486 | (4.2) | **472** | (3.8) | **-10.4** | (1.55) | 0.8 | (0.06) | 1.2 | (0.36) |
| | Poland | **512** | (3.1) | 513 | (3.0) | 496 | (3.4) | **472** | (3.6) | **-15.6** | (1.25) | 0.6 | (0.05) | 3.1 | (0.49) |
| | Portugal | **502** | (3.0) | 491 | (3.5) | 480 | (4.2) | **426** | (4.6) | **-24.8** | (1.40) | 0.5 | (0.04) | 10.3 | (1.06) |
| | Slovak Republic | **505** | (3.9) | 504 | (3.4) | 495 | (4.0) | **456** | (4.2) | **-19.4** | (1.82) | 0.6 | (0.07) | 4.1 | (0.79) |
| | Spain | **505** | (3.4) | 505 | (3.1) | 492 | (3.1) | **455** | (3.2) | **-20.3** | (1.21) | 0.6 | (0.05) | 5.0 | (0.59) |
| | Sweden | **514** | (3.3) | 513 | (3.4) | 506 | (4.1) | **489** | (3.8) | **-11.5** | (1.44) | 0.8 | (0.06) | 1.5 | (0.35) |
| | Switzerland | **528** | (3.5) | 523 | (3.2) | 515 | (3.8) | **482** | (4.9) | **-19.7** | (1.76) | 0.7 | (0.04) | 3.1 | (0.53) |
| | Turkey | **450** | (5.3) | 447 | (5.1) | 416 | (4.6) | **383** | (2.9) | **-21.2** | (1.68) | 0.5 | (0.05) | 10.5 | (1.15) |
| | United Kingdom | **530** | (3.4) | 530 | (3.4) | 525 | (3.6) | **482** | (4.2) | **-17.7** | (1.43) | 0.7 | (0.06) | 3.1 | (0.49) |
| | United States | **508** | (4.1) | 509 | (4.2) | 487 | (5.6) | **456** | (6.9) | **-19.4** | (2.23) | 0.6 | (0.05) | 4.2 | (0.90) |
| | **OECD total** | **505** | (1.5) | 507 | (1.3) | 498 | (1.4) | **460** | (2.3) | **-16.5** | (0.89) | 0.7 | (0.02) | 2.8 | (0.30) |
| | **OECD average** | **517** | (0.7) | 516 | (0.6) | 503 | (0.7) | **472** | (0.8) | **-17.9** | (0.31) | 0.7 | (0.01) | 4.3 | (0.12) |
| *Partners* | Argentina | **431** | (5.3) | 424 | (5.3) | 385 | (7.9) | **338** | (6.2) | **-31.4** | (1.90) | 0.4 | (0.05) | 12.8 | (1.34) |
| | Azerbaijan | 385 | (3.4) | 387 | (3.7) | 382 | (3.4) | 379 | (3.3) | -1.7 | (0.85) | 1.0 | (0.08) | 0.1 | (0.14) |
| | Brazil | **429** | (3.7) | 415 | (3.6) | 381 | (3.6) | **340** | (2.9) | **-26.8** | (1.03) | 0.4 | (0.04) | 14.3 | (0.99) |
| | Bulgaria | **475** | (6.2) | 452 | (7.9) | 418 | (6.5) | **407** | (5.6) | **-20.3** | (2.01) | 0.4 | (0.06) | 5.5 | (0.95) |
| | Chile | **480** | (4.7) | 456 | (4.5) | 428 | (4.4) | **390** | (4.2) | **-32.7** | (1.16) | 0.3 | (0.03) | 14.1 | (0.88) |
| | Colombia | **428** | (4.4) | 408 | (4.3) | 375 | (4.4) | **344** | (4.8) | **-25.5** | (1.86) | 0.3 | (0.05) | 13.9 | (1.61) |
| | Croatia | **512** | (3.1) | 509 | (2.9) | 502 | (3.2) | **451** | (3.6) | **-23.6** | (1.30) | 0.6 | (0.05) | 8.3 | (0.91) |
| | Estonia | **558** | (3.3) | 546 | (3.1) | 531 | (3.1) | **491** | (4.0) | **-25.6** | (1.65) | 0.5 | (0.05) | 8.2 | (0.98) |
| | Hong Kong-China | **548** | (4.3) | 556 | (3.5) | 541 | (3.5) | **526** | (3.7) | **-9.6** | (1.72) | 0.9 | (0.07) | 1.1 | (0.38) |
| | Indonesia | **417** | (6.1) | 399 | (6.1) | 384 | (7.2) | **374** | (5.0) | **-14.9** | (1.45) | 0.5 | (0.04) | 5.3 | (0.78) |
| | Israel | **496** | (4.3) | 487 | (4.5) | 436 | (5.4) | **423** | (4.9) | **-23.8** | (1.19) | 0.5 | (0.05) | 5.9 | (0.87) |
| | Jordan | **464** | (3.6) | 445 | (4.1) | 406 | (3.5) | **377** | (3.1) | **-27.1** | (1.19) | 0.4 | (0.04) | 14.4 | (1.07) |
| | Kyrgyzstan | 328 | (4.8) | 325 | (3.7) | 326 | (3.7) | 321 | (3.4) | -1.0 | (1.54) | 1.0 | (0.09) | 0.0 | (0.07) |
| | Latvia | **504** | (3.2) | 504 | (4.0) | 490 | (4.1) | **461** | (5.0) | **-19.2** | (2.05) | 0.7 | (0.06) | 3.6 | (0.74) |
| | Liechtenstein | **527** | (10.3) | 542 | (10.2) | 528 | (10.6) | **492** | (11.1) | **-11.5** | (5.12) | 0.9 | (0.26) | 1.3 | (1.10) |
| | Lithuania | **501** | (3.5) | 498 | (3.4) | 489 | (4.4) | **465** | (4.1) | **-14.0** | (1.37) | 0.7 | (0.06) | 2.4 | (0.49) |
| | Macao-China | **520** | (2.7) | 521 | (2.6) | 515 | (2.6) | **488** | (2.5) | **-11.4** | (1.42) | 0.8 | (0.06) | 2.5 | (0.61) |
| | Montenegro | **447** | (2.8) | 429 | (2.6) | 402 | (2.6) | **373** | (2.1) | **-24.5** | (1.17) | 0.4 | (0.04) | 11.6 | (1.05) |
| | Qatar | **381** | (2.6) | 359 | (2.3) | 340 | (2.3) | **328** | (1.9) | **-15.9** | (1.16) | 0.6 | (0.06) | 5.1 | (0.70) |
| | Romania | **446** | (4.7) | 434 | (4.9) | 402 | (5.2) | **392** | (4.9) | **-19.7** | (1.45) | 0.5 | (0.05) | 6.3 | (0.84) |
| | Russian Federation | **489** | (4.0) | 495 | (4.5) | 471 | (4.5) | **463** | (4.3) | **-9.8** | (1.48) | 0.8 | (0.06) | 1.1 | (0.32) |
| | Serbia | **468** | (3.3) | 460 | (3.7) | 425 | (3.8) | **391** | (3.7) | **-25.5** | (1.38) | 0.4 | (0.05) | 12.0 | (1.16) |
| | Slovenia | **523** | (2.9) | 530 | (3.0) | 526 | (3.8) | **505** | (4.0) | **-7.9** | (1.90) | 0.9 | (0.07) | 0.6 | (0.30) |
| | Chinese Taipei | **528** | (4.2) | 549 | (3.4) | 543 | (4.2) | **511** | (5.0) | **-8.8** | (1.29) | 1.0 | (0.06) | 1.2 | (0.34) |
| | Thailand | **460** | (3.2) | 433 | (2.7) | 402 | (3.4) | **391** | (2.9) | **-21.9** | (1.22) | 0.4 | (0.05) | 12.0 | (1.14) |
| | Tunisia | **435** | (4.5) | 405 | (4.6) | 357 | (3.3) | **349** | (2.8) | **-32.5** | (1.75) | 0.3 | (0.04) | 17.0 | (1.30) |
| | Uruguay | **464** | (3.0) | 447 | (3.9) | 428 | (4.3) | **382** | (4.0) | **-27.7** | (1.42) | 0.4 | (0.05) | 11.4 | (1.13) |

Note: Values that are statistically significant are indicated in bold (see Annex A3).
1. Results based on students' self-reports.
*StatLink* ᴬᴵᴸᴾ http://dx.doi.org/10.1787/142102278412

Pour consulter la version française intégrale de ce tableau, suivre ce lien :
*StatLink* ᴬᴵᴸᴾ http://dx.doi.org/10.1787/152630454851

[Part 1/2]

**Table 3.19** Index of students' responsibility for sustainable development and performance on the science scale, by quarters of the index[1]

Tableau 3.19 Indice de responsabilisation à l'égard du développement durable et scores sur l'échelle de culture scientifique, par quartile de l'indice

| | Index of students' responsibility for sustainable development | | | | | | | | | | | | | | | |
| | All students | | Males | | Females | | Gender difference (M - F) | | Bottom quarter | | Second quarter | | Third quarter | | Top quarter | |
| | Mean index | S.E. | Mean index | S.E. | Mean index | S.E. | Dif. | S.E. | Mean index | S.E. | Mean index | S.E. | Mean index | S.E. | Mean index | S.E. |
|---|---|---|---|---|---|---|---|---|---|---|---|---|---|---|---|---|
| **OECD** | | | | | | | | | | | | | | | | |
| Australia | -0.25 | (0.01) | -0.34 | (0.02) | -0.16 | (0.01) | **-0.18** | (0.02) | -1.24 | (0.01) | -0.57 | (0.00) | -0.12 | (0.00) | 0.93 | (0.01) |
| Austria | 0.01 | (0.02) | -0.07 | (0.03) | 0.09 | (0.03) | **-0.16** | (0.04) | -1.24 | (0.01) | -0.34 | (0.01) | 0.33 | (0.01) | 1.28 | (0.02) |
| Belgium | 0.01 | (0.02) | -0.03 | (0.03) | 0.06 | (0.02) | **-0.09** | (0.03) | -1.07 | (0.02) | -0.36 | (0.00) | 0.23 | (0.00) | 1.25 | (0.01) |
| Canada | 0.02 | (0.02) | -0.10 | (0.02) | 0.13 | (0.02) | **-0.23** | (0.02) | -1.13 | (0.01) | -0.42 | (0.00) | 0.20 | (0.01) | 1.43 | (0.02) |
| Czech Republic | -0.29 | (0.02) | -0.28 | (0.02) | -0.30 | (0.02) | 0.03 | (0.03) | -1.21 | (0.02) | -0.61 | (0.01) | -0.14 | (0.01) | 0.81 | (0.03) |
| Denmark | -0.25 | (0.01) | -0.37 | (0.02) | -0.13 | (0.02) | **-0.24** | (0.03) | -1.25 | (0.01) | -0.58 | (0.00) | -0.11 | (0.01) | 0.94 | (0.02) |
| Finland | -0.10 | (0.02) | -0.36 | (0.02) | 0.15 | (0.03) | **-0.51** | (0.03) | -1.26 | (0.02) | -0.51 | (0.00) | 0.09 | (0.01) | 1.27 | (0.02) |
| France | 0.28 | (0.02) | 0.27 | (0.02) | 0.28 | (0.03) | -0.01 | (0.03) | -0.88 | (0.02) | -0.11 | (0.01) | 0.53 | (0.01) | 1.57 | (0.02) |
| Germany | -0.10 | (0.02) | -0.13 | (0.03) | -0.07 | (0.03) | **-0.06** | (0.03) | -1.34 | (0.03) | -0.42 | (0.01) | 0.18 | (0.00) | 1.17 | (0.02) |
| Greece | 0.17 | (0.02) | 0.12 | (0.03) | 0.21 | (0.02) | **-0.09** | (0.04) | -0.92 | (0.01) | -0.18 | (0.01) | 0.40 | (0.01) | 1.37 | (0.02) |
| Hungary | 0.22 | (0.02) | 0.20 | (0.02) | 0.24 | (0.02) | -0.04 | (0.03) | -0.87 | (0.01) | -0.14 | (0.01) | 0.44 | (0.01) | 1.45 | (0.02) |
| Iceland | -0.28 | (0.02) | -0.41 | (0.03) | -0.14 | (0.02) | **-0.27** | (0.03) | -1.44 | (0.02) | -0.64 | (0.01) | -0.08 | (0.01) | 1.05 | (0.02) |
| Ireland | -0.01 | (0.02) | -0.10 | (0.02) | 0.08 | (0.02) | **-0.18** | (0.02) | -1.08 | (0.02) | -0.37 | (0.01) | 0.23 | (0.01) | 1.19 | (0.01) |
| Italy | 0.08 | (0.01) | 0.04 | (0.02) | 0.13 | (0.02) | **-0.10** | (0.02) | -0.88 | (0.01) | -0.24 | (0.01) | 0.28 | (0.00) | 1.19 | (0.01) |
| Japan | 0.04 | (0.02) | -0.01 | (0.02) | 0.09 | (0.02) | **-0.09** | (0.03) | -1.10 | (0.02) | -0.34 | (0.00) | 0.26 | (0.01) | 1.33 | (0.02) |
| Korea | 0.43 | (0.02) | 0.38 | (0.02) | 0.47 | (0.02) | **-0.09** | (0.03) | -0.64 | (0.01) | 0.02 | (0.01) | 0.62 | (0.01) | 1.70 | (0.02) |
| Luxembourg | 0.08 | (0.02) | 0.03 | (0.02) | 0.12 | (0.02) | **-0.09** | (0.03) | -1.26 | (0.02) | -0.28 | (0.01) | 0.37 | (0.01) | 1.47 | (0.02) |
| Mexico | 0.39 | (0.01) | 0.37 | (0.02) | 0.41 | (0.02) | -0.03 | (0.03) | -0.72 | (0.02) | 0.08 | (0.01) | 0.62 | (0.00) | 1.59 | (0.01) |
| Netherlands | -0.48 | (0.01) | -0.48 | (0.02) | -0.47 | (0.02) | 0.00 | (0.02) | -1.37 | (0.01) | -0.79 | (0.01) | -0.35 | (0.01) | 0.61 | (0.02) |
| New Zealand | -0.34 | (0.01) | -0.44 | (0.02) | -0.26 | (0.02) | **-0.17** | (0.03) | -1.30 | (0.02) | -0.66 | (0.00) | -0.21 | (0.01) | 0.79 | (0.02) |
| Norway | -0.27 | (0.02) | -0.41 | (0.03) | -0.13 | (0.02) | **-0.28** | (0.03) | -1.49 | (0.03) | -0.61 | (0.01) | -0.08 | (0.01) | 1.09 | (0.02) |
| Poland | 0.17 | (0.01) | 0.12 | (0.02) | 0.21 | (0.02) | **-0.09** | (0.03) | -0.88 | (0.01) | -0.27 | (0.00) | 0.36 | (0.01) | 1.46 | (0.02) |
| Portugal | 0.52 | (0.01) | 0.50 | (0.02) | 0.55 | (0.02) | **-0.06** | (0.02) | -0.54 | (0.02) | 0.12 | (0.01) | 0.74 | (0.01) | 1.78 | (0.01) |
| Slovak Republic | -0.25 | (0.02) | -0.17 | (0.02) | -0.33 | (0.02) | 0.16 | (0.03) | -1.17 | (0.01) | -0.56 | (0.00) | -0.09 | (0.01) | 0.83 | (0.02) |
| Spain | 0.31 | (0.01) | 0.30 | (0.02) | 0.33 | (0.02) | -0.03 | (0.03) | -0.75 | (0.01) | -0.06 | (0.00) | 0.52 | (0.00) | 1.54 | (0.01) |
| Sweden | -0.33 | (0.02) | -0.46 | (0.03) | -0.19 | (0.02) | **-0.27** | (0.03) | -1.50 | (0.02) | -0.65 | (0.01) | -0.15 | (0.01) | 0.97 | (0.02) |
| Switzerland | 0.04 | (0.02) | -0.01 | (0.02) | 0.11 | (0.02) | **-0.12** | (0.03) | -1.19 | (0.01) | -0.32 | (0.01) | 0.33 | (0.00) | 1.36 | (0.01) |
| Turkey | 0.73 | (0.03) | 0.66 | (0.04) | 0.81 | (0.04) | **-0.15** | (0.03) | -0.66 | (0.07) | 0.32 | (0.01) | 1.06 | (0.01) | 2.20 | (0.01) |
| United Kingdom | -0.27 | (0.01) | -0.31 | (0.02) | -0.23 | (0.02) | **-0.08** | (0.03) | -1.29 | (0.01) | -0.63 | (0.01) | -0.15 | (0.01) | 1.00 | (0.01) |
| United States | -0.33 | (0.02) | -0.39 | (0.02) | -0.27 | (0.02) | **-0.12** | (0.03) | -1.34 | (0.02) | -0.65 | (0.01) | -0.22 | (0.01) | 0.90 | (0.02) |
| **OECD total** | 0.00 | (0.01) | -0.04 | (0.01) | 0.05 | (0.01) | **-0.09** | (0.01) | -1.15 | (0.01) | -0.40 | (0.00) | 0.22 | (0.00) | 1.34 | (0.01) |
| **OECD average** | 0.00 | (0.00) | -0.06 | (0.00) | 0.06 | (0.00) | **-0.12** | (0.01) | -1.10 | (0.00) | -0.36 | (0.00) | 0.20 | (0.00) | 1.25 | (0.00) |
| **Partners** | | | | | | | | | | | | | | | | |
| Argentina | 0.04 | (0.02) | 0.08 | (0.03) | 0.00 | (0.02) | **0.08** | (0.03) | -1.01 | (0.02) | -0.30 | (0.00) | 0.26 | (0.01) | 1.20 | (0.02) |
| Azerbaijan | 0.02 | (0.02) | 0.02 | (0.03) | 0.02 | (0.03) | 0.00 | (0.03) | -1.06 | (0.02) | -0.34 | (0.01) | 0.19 | (0.01) | 1.30 | (0.02) |
| Brazil | 0.06 | (0.01) | 0.06 | (0.02) | 0.05 | (0.02) | 0.01 | (0.03) | -0.90 | (0.01) | -0.31 | (0.01) | 0.23 | (0.01) | 1.22 | (0.02) |
| Bulgaria | 0.04 | (0.02) | 0.01 | (0.02) | 0.06 | (0.02) | -0.05 | (0.03) | -0.96 | (0.02) | -0.32 | (0.00) | 0.19 | (0.01) | 1.24 | (0.02) |
| Chile | 0.37 | (0.02) | 0.43 | (0.02) | 0.30 | (0.03) | **0.12** | (0.04) | -0.73 | (0.02) | 0.04 | (0.01) | 0.60 | (0.01) | 1.57 | (0.02) |
| Colombia | 0.19 | (0.02) | 0.25 | (0.03) | 0.14 | (0.02) | **0.11** | (0.04) | -0.82 | (0.01) | -0.13 | (0.01) | 0.39 | (0.01) | 1.34 | (0.02) |
| Croatia | 0.00 | (0.01) | 0.02 | (0.02) | -0.02 | (0.02) | 0.04 | (0.02) | -0.92 | (0.01) | -0.31 | (0.00) | 0.19 | (0.00) | 1.04 | (0.01) |
| Estonia | -0.17 | (0.02) | -0.21 | (0.02) | -0.13 | (0.03) | **-0.08** | (0.03) | -1.19 | (0.01) | -0.50 | (0.01) | 0.04 | (0.01) | 0.98 | (0.01) |
| Hong Kong-China | 0.29 | (0.02) | 0.30 | (0.02) | 0.28 | (0.02) | 0.02 | (0.03) | -0.66 | (0.01) | -0.10 | (0.01) | 0.47 | (0.01) | 1.46 | (0.02) |
| Indonesia | -0.02 | (0.02) | 0.02 | (0.03) | -0.06 | (0.02) | **0.08** | (0.03) | -0.89 | (0.02) | -0.30 | (0.01) | 0.17 | (0.00) | 0.96 | (0.02) |
| Israel | m | m | m | m | m | m | m | m | m | m | m | m | m | m | m | m |
| Jordan | 0.25 | (0.02) | 0.16 | (0.03) | 0.34 | (0.03) | **-0.19** | (0.04) | -0.94 | (0.02) | -0.06 | (0.01) | 0.51 | (0.00) | 1.49 | (0.02) |
| Kyrgyzstan | 0.02 | (0.02) | -0.01 | (0.02) | 0.05 | (0.02) | **-0.06** | (0.02) | -1.02 | (0.01) | -0.33 | (0.00) | 0.22 | (0.01) | 1.23 | (0.02) |
| Latvia | -0.38 | (0.02) | -0.38 | (0.02) | -0.39 | (0.02) | 0.01 | (0.02) | -1.22 | (0.01) | -0.66 | (0.01) | -0.24 | (0.01) | 0.58 | (0.02) |
| Liechtenstein | 0.05 | (0.06) | 0.02 | (0.11) | 0.08 | (0.06) | -0.06 | (0.12) | -1.20 | (0.07) | -0.32 | (0.02) | 0.31 | (0.02) | 1.42 | (0.06) |
| Lithuania | -0.04 | (0.02) | -0.05 | (0.02) | -0.02 | (0.02) | -0.03 | (0.02) | -1.01 | (0.01) | -0.39 | (0.01) | 0.15 | (0.01) | 1.10 | (0.02) |
| Macao-China | 0.36 | (0.01) | 0.33 | (0.02) | 0.39 | (0.02) | **-0.06** | (0.03) | -0.62 | (0.01) | 0.02 | (0.01) | 0.55 | (0.01) | 1.49 | (0.01) |
| Montenegro | 0.27 | (0.01) | 0.27 | (0.02) | 0.27 | (0.02) | 0.00 | (0.03) | -0.84 | (0.02) | -0.10 | (0.01) | 0.48 | (0.01) | 1.55 | (0.02) |
| Qatar | 0.21 | (0.01) | 0.13 | (0.02) | 0.28 | (0.02) | **-0.16** | (0.03) | -1.18 | (0.02) | -0.21 | (0.01) | 0.50 | (0.01) | 1.72 | (0.01) |
| Romania | -0.11 | (0.02) | -0.08 | (0.02) | -0.13 | (0.02) | **0.05** | (0.03) | -1.10 | (0.02) | -0.45 | (0.01) | 0.07 | (0.01) | 1.05 | (0.03) |
| Russian Federation | 0.00 | (0.01) | 0.02 | (0.02) | -0.01 | (0.01) | 0.03 | (0.02) | -0.94 | (0.01) | -0.35 | (0.00) | 0.18 | (0.01) | 1.10 | (0.02) |
| Serbia | 0.15 | (0.02) | 0.21 | (0.03) | 0.10 | (0.02) | **0.11** | (0.03) | -0.90 | (0.02) | -0.24 | (0.01) | 0.34 | (0.01) | 1.42 | (0.02) |
| Slovenia | 0.17 | (0.02) | 0.11 | (0.02) | 0.23 | (0.02) | **-0.12** | (0.03) | -0.94 | (0.02) | -0.20 | (0.01) | 0.39 | (0.01) | 1.44 | (0.02) |
| Chinese Taipei | 0.76 | (0.01) | 0.72 | (0.02) | 0.81 | (0.02) | **-0.08** | (0.03) | -0.43 | (0.01) | 0.40 | (0.00) | 1.04 | (0.01) | 2.06 | (0.01) |
| Thailand | 0.30 | (0.01) | 0.19 | (0.02) | 0.38 | (0.02) | **-0.19** | (0.03) | -0.67 | (0.01) | -0.09 | (0.01) | 0.52 | (0.00) | 1.43 | (0.02) |
| Tunisia | 0.19 | (0.02) | 0.16 | (0.03) | 0.22 | (0.02) | -0.06 | (0.04) | -0.96 | (0.02) | -0.12 | (0.01) | 0.45 | (0.01) | 1.39 | (0.02) |
| Uruguay | 0.04 | (0.02) | 0.05 | (0.03) | 0.04 | (0.02) | 0.02 | (0.03) | -0.96 | (0.02) | -0.31 | (0.00) | 0.24 | (0.01) | 1.21 | (0.02) |

Note: Values that are statistically significant are indicated in bold (see Annex A3).
1. Results based on students' self-reports.
*StatLink* http://dx.doi.org/10.1787/142102278412

Pour consulter la version française intégrale de ce tableau, suivre ce lien :
*StatLink* http://dx.doi.org/10.1787/152630454851

[Part 2/2]

**Table 3.19** Index of students' responsibility for sustainable development and performance on the science scale, by quarters of the index[1]

Tableau 3.19 Indice de responsabilisation à l'égard du développement durable et scores sur l'échelle de culture scientifique, par quartile de l'indice

| | | Performance on the science scale, by quarters of this index | | | | | | | Change in the science score per unit of this index | | Increased likelihood of students in the bottom quarter of this index scoring in the bottom quarter of the science performance distribution | | Explained variance in student performance (r-squared x 100) | |
| | | Bottom quarter | | Second quarter | | Third quarter | | Top quarter | | | | | | | |
| | | Mean score | S.E. | Mean score | S.E. | Mean score | S.E. | Mean score | S.E | Effect | S.E. | Ratio | S.E. | Percentage | S.E. |
|---|---|---|---|---|---|---|---|---|---|---|---|---|---|---|---|
| *OECD* | Australia | 495 | (2.8) | 511 | (2.6) | 538 | (2.8) | 570 | (2.6) | 31.7 | (1.16) | 1.8 | (0.06) | 8.2 | (0.56) |
| | Austria | 474 | (4.7) | 503 | (5.1) | 528 | (4.8) | 545 | (4.1) | 26.6 | (1.77) | 1.9 | (0.11) | 7.6 | (0.83) |
| | Belgium | 488 | (3.7) | 508 | (3.5) | 525 | (3.2) | 542 | (2.9) | 22.4 | (1.84) | 1.6 | (0.08) | 4.7 | (0.78) |
| | Canada | 509 | (2.4) | 519 | (2.9) | 549 | (2.9) | 570 | (2.7) | 23.8 | (1.07) | 1.6 | (0.07) | 6.9 | (0.62) |
| | Czech Republic | 487 | (4.7) | 511 | (4.6) | 528 | (4.4) | 548 | (4.4) | 25.3 | (2.25) | 1.7 | (0.14) | 4.9 | (0.84) |
| | Denmark | 462 | (4.4) | 484 | (3.8) | 509 | (3.9) | 535 | (3.3) | 29.8 | (2.02) | 1.8 | (0.11) | 8.5 | (0.98) |
| | Finland | 528 | (3.0) | 552 | (2.9) | 575 | (2.3) | 599 | (2.7) | 25.6 | (1.22) | 2.0 | (0.10) | 9.3 | (0.87) |
| | France | 452 | (5.3) | 488 | (4.0) | 514 | (4.1) | 538 | (3.7) | 33.4 | (1.63) | 2.2 | (0.16) | 11.1 | (1.05) |
| | Germany | 489 | (5.6) | 518 | (3.6) | 534 | (4.6) | 552 | (4.8) | 23.3 | (2.24) | 1.7 | (0.10) | 6.0 | (1.09) |
| | Greece | 426 | (3.9) | 467 | (3.9) | 495 | (4.1) | 510 | (3.7) | 33.4 | (1.85) | 2.5 | (0.16) | 11.5 | (1.18) |
| | Hungary | 473 | (3.8) | 497 | (4.0) | 519 | (3.7) | 529 | (3.6) | 22.5 | (1.97) | 1.8 | (0.12) | 5.8 | (0.99) |
| | Iceland | 447 | (3.7) | 483 | (3.6) | 509 | (3.7) | 532 | (3.7) | 30.3 | (1.97) | 2.1 | (0.15) | 10.4 | (1.26) |
| | Ireland | 467 | (4.2) | 500 | (4.2) | 525 | (3.9) | 547 | (3.8) | 32.5 | (1.62) | 2.1 | (0.12) | 10.1 | (0.95) |
| | Italy | 447 | (2.8) | 466 | (2.5) | 488 | (2.5) | 504 | (2.8) | 25.4 | (1.44) | 1.7 | (0.08) | 5.1 | (0.58) |
| | Japan | 496 | (4.6) | 521 | (4.0) | 552 | (3.5) | 558 | (4.6) | 24.1 | (1.82) | 1.8 | (0.09) | 5.8 | (0.87) |
| | Korea | 487 | (4.6) | 531 | (3.6) | 535 | (4.1) | 536 | (4.3) | 17.9 | (2.03) | 1.9 | (0.10) | 3.4 | (0.71) |
| | Luxembourg | 455 | (2.5) | 479 | (3.1) | 499 | (3.2) | 517 | (2.9) | 21.5 | (1.25) | 1.6 | (0.08) | 6.1 | (0.69) |
| | Mexico | 373 | (3.5) | 407 | (3.3) | 424 | (3.2) | 438 | (3.2) | 26.8 | (1.44) | 2.2 | (0.12) | 9.5 | (0.95) |
| | Netherlands | 505 | (4.5) | 525 | (4.6) | 537 | (4.0) | 552 | (4.4) | 20.6 | (1.73) | 1.5 | (0.10) | 3.3 | (0.56) |
| | New Zealand | 503 | (3.9) | 518 | (4.2) | 536 | (4.0) | 573 | (4.2) | 31.0 | (1.79) | 1.5 | (0.09) | 6.4 | (0.74) |
| | Norway | 450 | (3.5) | 481 | (3.8) | 504 | (3.7) | 529 | (3.4) | 27.5 | (1.52) | 2.0 | (0.13) | 10.0 | (1.22) |
| | Poland | 459 | (3.6) | 487 | (3.2) | 514 | (3.2) | 533 | (3.0) | 27.9 | (1.41) | 2.0 | (0.10) | 8.9 | (0.84) |
| | Portugal | 433 | (4.1) | 475 | (3.4) | 494 | (3.8) | 497 | (3.6) | 23.9 | (1.61) | 2.3 | (0.15) | 6.2 | (0.78) |
| | Slovak Republic | 456 | (3.8) | 483 | (3.9) | 497 | (3.8) | 525 | (4.0) | 29.8 | (2.41) | 1.8 | (0.10) | 6.8 | (0.94) |
| | Spain | 454 | (4.0) | 487 | (2.9) | 503 | (3.1) | 515 | (3.1) | 23.2 | (1.41) | 2.0 | (0.10) | 5.7 | (0.68) |
| | Sweden | 472 | (2.9) | 495 | (4.5) | 514 | (3.5) | 541 | (3.7) | 26.6 | (1.44) | 1.8 | (0.11) | 8.4 | (0.87) |
| | Switzerland | 473 | (3.6) | 500 | (3.6) | 525 | (3.8) | 551 | (3.7) | 29.0 | (1.37) | 1.8 | (0.09) | 9.0 | (0.72) |
| | Turkey | 390 | (3.9) | 427 | (4.4) | 440 | (5.1) | 441 | (5.1) | 17.1 | (1.66) | 2.1 | (0.14) | 5.5 | (0.94) |
| | United Kingdom | 472 | (3.9) | 499 | (3.2) | 525 | (3.2) | 570 | (3.3) | 38.7 | (1.49) | 2.0 | (0.13) | 11.6 | (0.92) |
| | United States | 461 | (4.5) | 479 | (5.4) | 490 | (4.9) | 531 | (5.3) | 28.1 | (1.97) | 1.6 | (0.10) | 6.2 | (0.78) |
| | **OECD total** | 467 | (1.8) | 483 | (1.6) | 504 | (1.5) | 515 | (1.3) | 18.0 | (0.69) | 1.5 | (0.04) | 3.1 | (0.22) |
| | **OECD average** | 466 | (0.7) | 493 | (0.7) | 514 | (0.7) | 534 | (0.7) | 26.7 | (0.31) | 1.9 | (0.02) | 7.4 | (0.16) |
| *Partners* | Argentina | 362 | (6.1) | 393 | (6.1) | 408 | (7.7) | 419 | (6.6) | 22.4 | (2.55) | 1.7 | (0.14) | 4.2 | (0.94) |
| | Azerbaijan | 370 | (3.2) | 384 | (3.2) | 389 | (3.2) | 392 | (3.8) | 8.6 | (1.25) | 1.5 | (0.12) | 2.2 | (0.59) |
| | Brazil | 361 | (3.5) | 391 | (3.4) | 398 | (3.8) | 416 | (3.7) | 22.8 | (1.80) | 1.8 | (0.09) | 4.8 | (0.74) |
| | Bulgaria | 413 | (6.4) | 431 | (6.6) | 455 | (6.7) | 452 | (6.7) | 14.2 | (2.66) | 1.4 | (0.11) | 1.5 | (0.54) |
| | Chile | 402 | (4.6) | 434 | (4.7) | 453 | (5.1) | 466 | (5.6) | 25.6 | (2.05) | 1.9 | (0.14) | 6.6 | (0.92) |
| | Colombia | 358 | (4.8) | 387 | (4.6) | 400 | (4.9) | 409 | (3.9) | 21.6 | (2.33) | 1.7 | (0.16) | 5.0 | (0.92) |
| | Croatia | 470 | (3.4) | 487 | (2.9) | 508 | (3.2) | 510 | (3.1) | 19.6 | (1.64) | 1.5 | (0.09) | 3.4 | (0.53) |
| | Estonia | 501 | (3.3) | 524 | (2.8) | 542 | (3.6) | 559 | (3.5) | 24.9 | (1.54) | 1.8 | (0.15) | 6.9 | (0.83) |
| | Hong Kong-China | 503 | (4.0) | 540 | (3.8) | 562 | (4.5) | 565 | (3.9) | 25.8 | (2.18) | 2.0 | (0.13) | 5.9 | (0.97) |
| | Indonesia | 361 | (3.1) | 391 | (5.8) | 408 | (7.3) | 415 | (7.0) | 25.3 | (2.58) | 2.0 | (0.15) | 7.4 | (1.10) |
| | Israel | m | m | m | m | m | m | m | m | m | m | m | m | m | m |
| | Jordan | 380 | (4.1) | 424 | (3.5) | 442 | (3.6) | 445 | (3.7) | 24.7 | (1.73) | 2.3 | (0.13) | 7.3 | (0.91) |
| | Kyrgyzstan | 310 | (4.2) | 326 | (3.5) | 335 | (3.8) | 331 | (4.2) | 8.9 | (2.14) | 1.5 | (0.10) | 1.0 | (0.47) |
| | Latvia | 476 | (3.9) | 480 | (4.0) | 491 | (4.4) | 513 | (4.8) | 16.4 | (2.68) | 1.3 | (0.13) | 2.1 | (0.63) |
| | Liechtenstein | 484 | (11.3) | 512 | (12.2) | 544 | (12.0) | 549 | (8.6) | 25.3 | (4.30) | 1.8 | (0.34) | 7.6 | (2.52) |
| | Lithuania | 466 | (4.4) | 479 | (3.7) | 501 | (4.1) | 508 | (3.2) | 19.3 | (1.85) | 1.5 | (0.10) | 3.4 | (0.60) |
| | Macao-China | 487 | (3.0) | 510 | (2.7) | 522 | (2.5) | 526 | (2.6) | 15.6 | (1.66) | 1.7 | (0.11) | 2.8 | (0.60) |
| | Montenegro | 394 | (2.9) | 415 | (2.4) | 422 | (2.7) | 422 | (3.0) | 8.3 | (1.62) | 1.5 | (0.10) | 1.0 | (0.40) |
| | Qatar | 324 | (2.3) | 357 | (2.5) | 368 | (1.9) | 358 | (2.1) | 10.0 | (0.95) | 1.8 | (0.10) | 2.0 | (0.37) |
| | Romania | 380 | (4.7) | 409 | (4.4) | 437 | (5.4) | 450 | (5.2) | 27.8 | (2.20) | 2.1 | (0.18) | 9.3 | (1.17) |
| | Russian Federation | 466 | (5.3) | 471 | (5.0) | 485 | (3.8) | 496 | (4.2) | 13.8 | (2.02) | 1.4 | (0.10) | 1.6 | (0.45) |
| | Serbia | 424 | (4.2) | 431 | (3.5) | 446 | (3.6) | 444 | (4.1) | 7.2 | (1.69) | 1.3 | (0.10) | 0.7 | (0.30) |
| | Slovenia | 492 | (3.4) | 509 | (3.7) | 537 | (3.6) | 547 | (3.3) | 21.8 | (1.64) | 1.6 | (0.10) | 4.7 | (0.73) |
| | Chinese Taipei | 495 | (5.3) | 543 | (4.3) | 552 | (3.7) | 540 | (3.4) | 16.4 | (1.61) | 2.0 | (0.10) | 2.9 | (0.56) |
| | Thailand | 386 | (2.7) | 412 | (2.9) | 437 | (3.3) | 451 | (3.2) | 28.7 | (1.70) | 2.0 | (0.18) | 9.9 | (0.95) |
| | Tunisia | 349 | (3.5) | 386 | (4.2) | 401 | (4.4) | 410 | (3.3) | 24.5 | (1.45) | 2.2 | (0.18) | 8.0 | (0.92) |
| | Uruguay | 406 | (3.9) | 424 | (4.2) | 441 | (3.7) | 455 | (3.8) | 19.3 | (2.02) | 1.5 | (0.10) | 3.4 | (0.67) |

Note: Values that are statistically significant are indicated in bold (see Annex A3).
1. Results based on students' self-reports.
*StatLink* ᴍᵍ￫ http://dx.doi.org/10.1787/142102278412

Pour consulter la version française intégrale de ce tableau, suivre ce lien :
*StatLink* ᴍᵍ￫ http://dx.doi.org/10.1787/152630454851

[Part 1/2]

**Table 3.20** Proportion of between-school variance for science attitudinal indices[1]

Tableau 3.20 Part de variance inter-établissements des indices d'attitude en sciences

| | | General value of science | | Personal value of science | | Self-efficacy in science | | Self-concept in science | | General interest of science | | Enjoyment of science | | Instrumental motivation to learn science | |
|---|---|---|---|---|---|---|---|---|---|---|---|---|---|---|---|
| | | Propor-tion | S.E. | Propor-tion | S.E. | Propor-tion | S.E. | Propor-tion | S.E. | Propor-tion | S.E. | Propor-tion | S.E. | Propor-tion | S.E. |
| OECD | Australia | 0.04 | (0.004) | 0.04 | (0.005) | 0.08 | (0.008) | 0.04 | (0.005) | 0.04 | (0.004) | 0.06 | (0.007) | 0.04 | (0.004) |
| | Austria | 0.08 | (0.015) | 0.05 | (0.009) | 0.13 | (0.012) | 0.08 | (0.014) | 0.06 | (0.009) | 0.15 | (0.016) | 0.14 | (0.018) |
| | Belgium | 0.04 | (0.007) | 0.04 | (0.005) | 0.10 | (0.010) | 0.07 | (0.008) | 0.13 | (0.016) | 0.10 | (0.011) | 0.06 | (0.006) |
| | Canada | 0.05 | (0.003) | 0.05 | (0.003) | 0.06 | (0.003) | 0.06 | (0.005) | 0.03 | (0.004) | 0.05 | (0.004) | 0.07 | (0.005) |
| | Czech Republic | 0.03 | (0.007) | 0.05 | (0.008) | 0.06 | (0.007) | 0.03 | (0.005) | 0.05 | (0.008) | 0.05 | (0.006) | 0.06 | (0.006) |
| | Denmark | 0.02 | (0.006) | 0.02 | (0.012) | 0.06 | (0.011) | 0.05 | (0.010) | 0.06 | (0.013) | 0.05 | (0.009) | 0.02 | (0.013) |
| | Finland | 0.02 | (0.006) | 0.01 | (0.006) | 0.03 | (0.006) | 0.01 | (0.006) | 0.03 | (0.008) | 0.02 | (0.006) | 0.02 | (0.006) |
| | France | 0.06 | (0.009) | 0.06 | (0.011) | 0.07 | (0.010) | 0.03 | (0.009) | 0.08 | (0.009) | 0.08 | (0.011) | 0.07 | (0.010) |
| | Germany | 0.05 | (0.007) | 0.03 | (0.011) | 0.10 | (0.011) | 0.03 | (0.009) | 0.05 | (0.009) | 0.08 | (0.011) | 0.05 | (0.010) |
| | Greece | 0.03 | (0.006) | 0.03 | (0.007) | 0.05 | (0.006) | 0.03 | (0.009) | 0.05 | (0.010) | 0.05 | (0.008) | 0.02 | (0.009) |
| | Hungary | 0.04 | (0.008) | 0.04 | (0.008) | 0.05 | (0.007) | 0.05 | (0.009) | 0.04 | (0.010) | 0.07 | (0.009) | 0.07 | (0.009) |
| | Iceland | 0.04 | (0.022) | 0.05 | (0.029) | 0.02 | (0.021) | 0.05 | (0.026) | 0.06 | (0.035) | 0.06 | (0.031) | 0.04 | (0.028) |
| | Ireland | 0.03 | (0.006) | 0.04 | (0.008) | 0.06 | (0.010) | 0.04 | (0.010) | 0.04 | (0.009) | 0.05 | (0.009) | 0.05 | (0.009) |
| | Italy | 0.05 | (0.004) | 0.05 | (0.003) | 0.05 | (0.005) | 0.06 | (0.003) | 0.06 | (0.004) | 0.06 | (0.004) | 0.08 | (0.004) |
| | Japan | 0.06 | (0.008) | 0.03 | (0.005) | 0.05 | (0.008) | 0.05 | (0.008) | 0.06 | (0.007) | 0.07 | (0.009) | 0.11 | (0.011) |
| | Korea | 0.04 | (0.009) | 0.04 | (0.013) | 0.06 | (0.010) | 0.06 | (0.012) | 0.06 | (0.010) | 0.07 | (0.016) | 0.05 | (0.020) |
| | Luxembourg | 0.03 | (0.009) | 0.01 | (0.006) | 0.06 | (0.008) | 0.02 | (0.009) | 0.03 | (0.008) | 0.04 | (0.009) | 0.01 | (0.007) |
| | Mexico | 0.05 | (0.002) | 0.02 | (0.002) | 0.04 | (0.003) | 0.02 | (0.002) | 0.04 | (0.003) | 0.04 | (0.002) | 0.03 | (0.003) |
| | Netherlands | 0.05 | (0.005) | 0.02 | (0.005) | 0.07 | (0.008) | 0.04 | (0.007) | 0.06 | (0.008) | 0.07 | (0.008) | 0.03 | (0.007) |
| | New Zealand | 0.05 | (0.007) | 0.04 | (0.008) | 0.04 | (0.008) | 0.02 | (0.009) | 0.05 | (0.009) | 0.05 | (0.007) | 0.04 | (0.009) |
| | Norway | 0.04 | (0.014) | 0.03 | (0.012) | 0.03 | (0.012) | 0.03 | (0.009) | 0.04 | (0.014) | 0.03 | (0.011) | 0.02 | (0.010) |
| | Poland | 0.02 | (0.005) | 0.02 | (0.005) | 0.03 | (0.006) | 0.02 | (0.004) | 0.02 | (0.004) | 0.03 | (0.006) | 0.02 | (0.004) |
| | Portugal | 0.02 | (0.006) | 0.02 | (0.005) | 0.03 | (0.005) | 0.02 | (0.006) | 0.02 | (0.006) | 0.02 | (0.003) | 0.06 | (0.007) |
| | Slovak Republic | 0.05 | (0.011) | 0.05 | (0.010) | 0.06 | (0.012) | 0.04 | (0.008) | 0.07 | (0.018) | 0.04 | (0.009) | 0.10 | (0.015) |
| | Spain | 0.03 | (0.002) | 0.03 | (0.002) | 0.06 | (0.003) | 0.03 | (0.003) | 0.03 | (0.003) | 0.04 | (0.003) | 0.04 | (0.004) |
| | Sweden | 0.05 | (0.011) | 0.04 | (0.011) | 0.05 | (0.011) | 0.02 | (0.009) | 0.05 | (0.010) | 0.05 | (0.010) | 0.04 | (0.011) |
| | Switzerland | 0.05 | (0.008) | 0.05 | (0.008) | 0.08 | (0.008) | 0.05 | (0.008) | 0.06 | (0.006) | 0.09 | (0.008) | 0.05 | (0.010) |
| | Turkey | 0.10 | (0.011) | 0.07 | (0.011) | 0.10 | (0.016) | 0.06 | (0.008) | 0.05 | (0.007) | 0.06 | (0.008) | 0.05 | (0.007) |
| | United Kingdom | 0.03 | (0.003) | 0.03 | (0.003) | 0.05 | (0.003) | 0.03 | (0.003) | 0.04 | (0.004) | 0.04 | (0.003) | 0.03 | (0.003) |
| | United States | 0.04 | (0.007) | 0.02 | (0.007) | 0.04 | (0.008) | 0.03 | (0.006) | 0.03 | (0.007) | 0.03 | (0.006) | 0.01 | (0.005) |
| | **OECD average** | 0.04 | (0.002) | 0.04 | (0.002) | 0.06 | (0.002) | 0.04 | (0.002) | 0.05 | (0.002) | 0.06 | (0.002) | 0.05 | (0.002) |
| Partners | Argentina | 0.04 | (0.009) | 0.05 | (0.010) | 0.05 | (0.010) | 0.05 | (0.012) | 0.10 | (0.025) | 0.08 | (0.012) | 0.05 | (0.011) |
| | Azerbaijan | 0.08 | (0.014) | 0.06 | (0.016) | 0.13 | (0.028) | 0.09 | (0.011) | 0.06 | (0.009) | 0.07 | (0.009) | 0.06 | (0.009) |
| | Brazil | 0.05 | (0.005) | 0.06 | (0.006) | 0.08 | (0.006) | 0.04 | (0.004) | 0.06 | (0.005) | 0.05 | (0.004) | 0.05 | (0.004) |
| | Bulgaria | 0.06 | (0.015) | 0.03 | (0.010) | 0.15 | (0.043) | 0.05 | (0.014) | 0.05 | (0.019) | 0.05 | (0.011) | 0.03 | (0.008) |
| | Chile | 0.04 | (0.009) | 0.03 | (0.008) | 0.08 | (0.009) | 0.03 | (0.008) | 0.03 | (0.006) | 0.05 | (0.008) | 0.05 | (0.008) |
| | Colombia | 0.02 | (0.008) | 0.03 | (0.007) | 0.04 | (0.007) | 0.03 | (0.005) | 0.06 | (0.009) | 0.04 | (0.007) | 0.04 | (0.007) |
| | Croatia | 0.02 | (0.007) | 0.02 | (0.006) | 0.06 | (0.005) | 0.03 | (0.007) | 0.03 | (0.006) | 0.04 | (0.005) | 0.08 | (0.010) |
| | Estonia | 0.04 | (0.005) | 0.03 | (0.006) | 0.03 | (0.006) | 0.02 | (0.005) | 0.02 | (0.004) | 0.04 | (0.006) | 0.02 | (0.006) |
| | Hong Kong-China | 0.02 | (0.007) | 0.01 | (0.007) | 0.04 | (0.007) | 0.02 | (0.008) | 0.03 | (0.006) | 0.02 | (0.005) | 0.01 | (0.011) |
| | Indonesia | 0.04 | (0.004) | 0.03 | (0.004) | 0.05 | (0.005) | 0.08 | (0.006) | 0.04 | (0.004) | 0.04 | (0.004) | 0.05 | (0.004) |
| | Israel | 0.10 | (0.013) | 0.12 | (0.015) | 0.07 | (0.012) | 0.11 | (0.013) | 0.23 | (0.022) | 0.15 | (0.015) | 0.09 | (0.020) |
| | Jordan | 0.05 | (0.007) | 0.02 | (0.004) | 0.04 | (0.005) | 0.03 | (0.004) | 0.03 | (0.005) | 0.03 | (0.006) | 0.03 | (0.004) |
| | Kyrgyzstan | 0.04 | (0.006) | 0.05 | (0.006) | 0.07 | (0.010) | 0.07 | (0.007) | 0.06 | (0.006) | 0.09 | (0.006) | 0.07 | (0.005) |
| | Latvia | 0.02 | (0.006) | 0.03 | (0.005) | 0.03 | (0.005) | 0.02 | (0.005) | 0.02 | (0.004) | 0.03 | (0.007) | 0.03 | (0.005) |
| | Liechtenstein | 0.06 | (0.050) | 0.02 | (0.026) | 0.07 | (0.042) | 0.00 | (0.012) | 0.10 | (0.042) | 0.11 | (0.039) | 0.04 | (0.036) |
| | Lithuania | 0.03 | (0.006) | 0.03 | (0.007) | 0.04 | (0.006) | 0.02 | (0.006) | 0.02 | (0.004) | 0.03 | (0.007) | 0.02 | (0.007) |
| | Macao-China | 0.02 | (0.006) | 0.01 | (0.003) | 0.03 | (0.008) | 0.03 | (0.009) | 0.02 | (0.005) | 0.01 | (0.004) | 0.03 | (0.008) |
| | Montenegro | 0.02 | (0.006) | 0.04 | (0.009) | 0.06 | (0.013) | 0.03 | (0.007) | 0.05 | (0.010) | 0.06 | (0.009) | 0.08 | (0.026) |
| | Qatar | 0.06 | (0.021) | 0.04 | (0.015) | 0.07 | (0.019) | 0.04 | (0.014) | 0.06 | (0.021) | 0.06 | (0.013) | 0.04 | (0.012) |
| | Romania | 0.06 | (0.010) | 0.01 | (0.007) | 0.07 | (0.016) | 0.03 | (0.009) | 0.04 | (0.009) | 0.02 | (0.006) | 0.03 | (0.006) |
| | Russian Federation | 0.02 | (0.005) | 0.05 | (0.006) | 0.07 | (0.008) | 0.04 | (0.005) | 0.05 | (0.007) | 0.05 | (0.006) | 0.04 | (0.005) |
| | Serbia | 0.02 | (0.008) | 0.05 | (0.006) | 0.06 | (0.009) | 0.04 | (0.007) | 0.05 | (0.014) | 0.06 | (0.007) | 0.06 | (0.007) |
| | Slovenia | 0.07 | (0.022) | 0.06 | (0.026) | 0.10 | (0.024) | 0.04 | (0.018) | 0.05 | (0.022) | 0.06 | (0.022) | 0.07 | (0.021) |
| | Chinese Taipei | 0.04 | (0.005) | 0.02 | (0.003) | 0.07 | (0.007) | 0.04 | (0.005) | 0.05 | (0.006) | 0.04 | (0.005) | 0.02 | (0.003) |
| | Thailand | 0.05 | (0.008) | 0.03 | (0.004) | 0.03 | (0.005) | 0.04 | (0.010) | 0.04 | (0.006) | 0.02 | (0.004) | 0.02 | (0.003) |
| | Tunisia | 0.05 | (0.007) | 0.03 | (0.006) | 0.03 | (0.006) | 0.02 | (0.006) | 0.03 | (0.006) | 0.02 | (0.006) | 0.03 | (0.006) |
| | Uruguay | 0.02 | (0.016) | 0.06 | (0.010) | 0.05 | (0.013) | 0.03 | (0.012) | 0.05 | (0.014) | 0.05 | (0.012) | 0.04 | (0.016) |

1. Results based on students' self-reports.
StatLink ⌨️ http://dx.doi.org/10.1787/142102278412

Pour consulter la version française intégrale de ce tableau, suivre ce lien :
StatLink ⌨️ http://dx.doi.org/10.1787/152630454851

[Part 2/2]
**Table 3.20** **Proportion of between-school variance for science attitudinal indices[1]**

Tableau 3.20   Part de variance inter-établissements des indices d'attitude en sciences

| | | Proportion of between-school variance for: | | | | | | | | | | |
|---|---|---|---|---|---|---|---|---|---|---|---|---|
| | | Future-oriented motivation to learn science | | Science-related activities | | Awareness of environmental issues | | Level of concern for environmental issues | | Optimism regarding environmental issues | | Responsibility for sustainable development | |
| | | Proportion | S.E. | Proportion | S.E. | Proportion | S.E. | Proportion | S.E. | Proportion | S.E. | Proportion | S.E. |
| **OECD** | Australia | 0.03 | (0.004) | 0.04 | (0.005) | 0.10 | (0.008) | 0.02 | (0.004) | 0.02 | (0.004) | 0.03 | (0.003) |
| | Austria | 0.09 | (0.009) | 0.07 | (0.009) | 0.15 | (0.018) | 0.02 | (0.009) | 0.03 | (0.006) | 0.08 | (0.010) |
| | Belgium | 0.06 | (0.006) | 0.04 | (0.005) | 0.14 | (0.012) | 0.03 | (0.008) | 0.03 | (0.007) | 0.08 | (0.010) |
| | Canada | 0.06 | (0.004) | 0.05 | (0.003) | 0.07 | (0.004) | 0.04 | (0.005) | 0.03 | (0.003) | 0.11 | (0.005) |
| | Czech Republic | 0.05 | (0.006) | 0.04 | (0.005) | 0.05 | (0.005) | 0.04 | (0.007) | 0.03 | (0.006) | 0.03 | (0.005) |
| | Denmark | 0.03 | (0.011) | 0.04 | (0.008) | 0.06 | (0.010) | 0.02 | (0.010) | 0.02 | (0.006) | 0.02 | (0.009) |
| | Finland | 0.01 | (0.006) | 0.01 | (0.006) | 0.03 | (0.005) | 0.01 | (0.006) | 0.01 | (0.005) | 0.02 | (0.008) |
| | France | 0.07 | (0.010) | 0.06 | (0.009) | 0.15 | (0.013) | 0.03 | (0.007) | 0.06 | (0.008) | 0.07 | (0.009) |
| | Germany | 0.04 | (0.009) | 0.04 | (0.007) | 0.11 | (0.012) | 0.02 | (0.008) | 0.02 | (0.010) | 0.05 | (0.006) |
| | Greece | 0.03 | (0.009) | 0.05 | (0.011) | 0.08 | (0.013) | 0.03 | (0.006) | 0.09 | (0.015) | 0.06 | (0.010) |
| | Hungary | 0.09 | (0.010) | 0.05 | (0.010) | 0.07 | (0.008) | 0.02 | (0.010) | 0.06 | (0.015) | 0.04 | (0.010) |
| | Iceland | 0.03 | (0.022) | 0.03 | (0.023) | 0.04 | (0.025) | 0.03 | (0.023) | 0.01 | (0.012) | 0.04 | (0.023) |
| | Ireland | 0.03 | (0.009) | 0.04 | (0.008) | 0.07 | (0.010) | 0.01 | (0.013) | 0.01 | (0.010) | 0.04 | (0.006) |
| | Italy | 0.09 | (0.005) | 0.05 | (0.003) | 0.13 | (0.009) | 0.03 | (0.002) | 0.07 | (0.006) | 0.04 | (0.004) |
| | Japan | 0.09 | (0.009) | 0.03 | (0.005) | 0.09 | (0.009) | 0.01 | (0.006) | 0.01 | (0.008) | 0.05 | (0.007) |
| | Korea | 0.05 | (0.024) | 0.06 | (0.016) | 0.07 | (0.008) | 0.01 | (0.005) | 0.02 | (0.010) | 0.03 | (0.006) |
| | Luxembourg | 0.02 | (0.007) | 0.02 | (0.006) | 0.14 | (0.012) | 0.01 | (0.006) | 0.02 | (0.005) | 0.03 | (0.008) |
| | Mexico | 0.05 | (0.003) | 0.05 | (0.002) | 0.08 | (0.006) | 0.05 | (0.003) | 0.11 | (0.005) | 0.06 | (0.003) |
| | Netherlands | 0.05 | (0.006) | 0.05 | (0.008) | 0.11 | (0.010) | 0.02 | (0.007) | 0.02 | (0.007) | 0.02 | (0.005) |
| | New Zealand | 0.03 | (0.007) | 0.03 | (0.007) | 0.06 | (0.009) | 0.01 | (0.010) | 0.02 | (0.008) | 0.03 | (0.005) |
| | Norway | 0.03 | (0.009) | 0.03 | (0.014) | 0.03 | (0.011) | 0.02 | (0.015) | 0.02 | (0.011) | 0.05 | (0.014) |
| | Poland | 0.02 | (0.005) | 0.01 | (0.004) | 0.04 | (0.007) | 0.01 | (0.008) | 0.01 | (0.007) | 0.02 | (0.005) |
| | Portugal | 0.04 | (0.005) | 0.02 | (0.006) | 0.07 | (0.008) | 0.01 | (0.007) | 0.07 | (0.011) | 0.02 | (0.007) |
| | Slovak Republic | 0.07 | (0.013) | 0.05 | (0.008) | 0.07 | (0.009) | 0.02 | (0.006) | 0.04 | (0.007) | 0.03 | (0.010) |
| | Spain | 0.04 | (0.004) | 0.04 | (0.003) | 0.07 | (0.003) | 0.02 | (0.002) | 0.03 | (0.003) | 0.03 | (0.002) |
| | Sweden | 0.03 | (0.009) | 0.04 | (0.007) | 0.07 | (0.010) | 0.01 | (0.012) | 0.01 | (0.009) | 0.03 | (0.011) |
| | Switzerland | 0.07 | (0.009) | 0.05 | (0.005) | 0.12 | (0.009) | 0.03 | (0.005) | 0.03 | (0.004) | 0.08 | (0.006) |
| | Turkey | 0.06 | (0.008) | 0.05 | (0.010) | 0.15 | (0.015) | 0.08 | (0.019) | 0.12 | (0.015) | 0.10 | (0.019) |
| | United Kingdom | 0.03 | (0.003) | 0.05 | (0.004) | 0.05 | (0.003) | 0.02 | (0.004) | 0.02 | (0.004) | 0.03 | (0.003) |
| | United States | 0.01 | (0.007) | 0.03 | (0.005) | 0.07 | (0.009) | 0.02 | (0.008) | 0.04 | (0.010) | 0.02 | (0.005) |
| | **OECD average** | 0.05 | (0.002) | 0.04 | (0.002) | 0.08 | (0.002) | 0.02 | (0.002) | 0.04 | (0.002) | 0.04 | (0.002) |
| **Partners** | Argentina | 0.06 | (0.012) | 0.10 | (0.020) | 0.12 | (0.014) | 0.06 | (0.010) | 0.14 | (0.019) | 0.04 | (0.007) |
| | Azerbaijan | 0.09 | (0.009) | 0.05 | (0.008) | 0.09 | (0.016) | 0.08 | (0.011) | 0.06 | (0.010) | 0.04 | (0.009) |
| | Brazil | 0.06 | (0.005) | 0.06 | (0.005) | 0.17 | (0.011) | 0.04 | (0.006) | 0.13 | (0.010) | 0.04 | (0.004) |
| | Bulgaria | 0.08 | (0.011) | 0.04 | (0.010) | 0.19 | (0.032) | 0.06 | (0.016) | 0.15 | (0.029) | 0.02 | (0.011) |
| | Chile | 0.04 | (0.008) | 0.03 | (0.007) | 0.13 | (0.022) | 0.02 | (0.008) | 0.10 | (0.013) | 0.04 | (0.008) |
| | Colombia | 0.06 | (0.011) | 0.03 | (0.006) | 0.13 | (0.020) | 0.04 | (0.005) | 0.16 | (0.022) | 0.03 | (0.006) |
| | Croatia | 0.03 | (0.005) | 0.02 | (0.005) | 0.08 | (0.008) | 0.01 | (0.007) | 0.07 | (0.016) | 0.01 | (0.006) |
| | Estonia | 0.05 | (0.005) | 0.02 | (0.005) | 0.04 | (0.005) | 0.02 | (0.006) | 0.14 | (0.011) | 0.02 | (0.006) |
| | Hong Kong-China | 0.01 | (0.008) | 0.03 | (0.008) | 0.06 | (0.008) | 0.01 | (0.008) | 0.02 | (0.008) | 0.02 | (0.004) |
| | Indonesia | 0.05 | (0.003) | 0.06 | (0.007) | 0.07 | (0.005) | 0.09 | (0.007) | 0.06 | (0.008) | 0.05 | (0.005) |
| | Israel | 0.12 | (0.016) | 0.32 | (0.022) | 0.09 | (0.012) | 0.03 | (0.011) | 0.05 | (0.011) | m | m |
| | Jordan | 0.02 | (0.004) | 0.05 | (0.006) | 0.08 | (0.008) | 0.03 | (0.005) | 0.08 | (0.012) | 0.04 | (0.009) |
| | Kyrgyzstan | 0.10 | (0.006) | 0.12 | (0.006) | 0.07 | (0.007) | 0.05 | (0.009) | 0.05 | (0.022) | 0.04 | (0.009) |
| | Latvia | 0.04 | (0.005) | 0.07 | (0.008) | 0.05 | (0.007) | 0.02 | (0.004) | 0.03 | (0.005) | 0.01 | (0.004) |
| | Liechtenstein | 0.03 | (0.019) | 0.08 | (0.042) | 0.08 | (0.040) | 0.02 | (0.050) | 0.04 | (0.050) | 0.05 | (0.039) |
| | Lithuania | 0.02 | (0.006) | 0.02 | (0.006) | 0.06 | (0.012) | 0.01 | (0.008) | 0.03 | (0.011) | 0.03 | (0.006) |
| | Macao-China | 0.01 | (0.004) | 0.03 | (0.006) | 0.09 | (0.013) | 0.03 | (0.007) | 0.03 | (0.011) | 0.01 | (0.005) |
| | Montenegro | 0.09 | (0.016) | 0.03 | (0.009) | 0.09 | (0.011) | 0.01 | (0.005) | 0.05 | (0.017) | 0.01 | (0.007) |
| | Qatar | 0.08 | (0.018) | 0.07 | (0.017) | 0.18 | (0.024) | 0.03 | (0.014) | 0.08 | (0.021) | 0.06 | (0.016) |
| | Romania | 0.02 | (0.006) | 0.02 | (0.005) | 0.11 | (0.013) | 0.03 | (0.008) | 0.05 | (0.006) | 0.04 | (0.007) |
| | Russian Federation | 0.06 | (0.007) | 0.08 | (0.008) | 0.12 | (0.012) | 0.04 | (0.010) | 0.02 | (0.006) | 0.02 | (0.005) |
| | Serbia | 0.06 | (0.007) | 0.03 | (0.005) | 0.09 | (0.012) | 0.01 | (0.009) | 0.11 | (0.016) | 0.02 | (0.009) |
| | Slovenia | 0.10 | (0.019) | 0.07 | (0.020) | 0.11 | (0.018) | 0.04 | (0.020) | 0.05 | (0.025) | 0.05 | (0.023) |
| | Chinese Taipei | 0.04 | (0.005) | 0.03 | (0.004) | 0.08 | (0.007) | 0.03 | (0.005) | 0.04 | (0.008) | 0.02 | (0.004) |
| | Thailand | 0.03 | (0.004) | 0.03 | (0.003) | 0.07 | (0.009) | 0.05 | (0.011) | 0.10 | (0.013) | 0.03 | (0.005) |
| | Tunisia | 0.02 | (0.005) | 0.02 | (0.004) | 0.07 | (0.012) | 0.02 | (0.005) | 0.16 | (0.014) | 0.05 | (0.007) |
| | Uruguay | 0.05 | (0.017) | 0.06 | (0.013) | 0.07 | (0.008) | 0.03 | (0.010) | 0.09 | (0.013) | 0.04 | (0.011) |

1. Results based on students' self-reports.
*StatLink* http://dx.doi.org/10.1787/142102278412

Pour consulter la version française intégrale de ce tableau, suivre ce lien :
*StatLink* http://dx.doi.org/10.1787/152630454851

89

[Part 1/2]

**Table 3.21  Effect sizes for gender differences (females minus males) in science performance scales and attitudinal indices[1]**

Tableau 3.21  Différences entre les sexes (filles moins garçons) en termes d'ampleur de l'effet sur les échelles de culture scientifique et indices d'attitude en sciences

Effect sizes in favour of females:
- from 0.2 to 0.5
- from 0.5 to 0.8
- Equal or greater than 0.8

Effect sizes in favour of males:
- from -0.2 to -0.5
- from -0.5 to -0.8
- Equal or less than -0.8

| | Combined science scale | | Identifying scientific issues | | Explaining phenomena scientifically | | Using scientific evidence | | General value of science | | Personal value of science | | Self-efficacy in science | | Self-concept in science | |
|---|---|---|---|---|---|---|---|---|---|---|---|---|---|---|---|---|
| | Effect size | S.E. | Effect size | S.E. | Effect size | S.E. | Effect size | S.E. | Effect size | S.E. | Effect size | S.E. | Effect size | S.E. | Effect size | S.E. |
| **OECD** | | | | | | | | | | | | | | | | |
| Australia | 0.00 | (0.03) | 0.21 | (0.09) | -0.13 | (0.06) | 0.03 | (0.03) | -0.13 | (0.06) | -0.12 | (0.05) | -0.09 | (0.04) | -0.22 | (0.09) |
| Austria | -0.08 | (0.05) | 0.24 | (0.09) | -0.19 | (0.08) | -0.08 | (0.05) | -0.02 | (0.03) | -0.19 | (0.09) | -0.17 | (0.07) | -0.22 | (0.09) |
| Belgium | -0.01 | (0.03) | 0.14 | (0.07) | -0.16 | (0.07) | 0.08 | (0.05) | -0.11 | (0.05) | -0.15 | (0.07) | -0.16 | (0.07) | -0.27 | (0.11) |
| Canada | -0.04 | (0.03) | 0.14 | (0.06) | -0.17 | (0.07) | 0.01 | (0.02) | -0.16 | (0.07) | -0.14 | (0.06) | -0.07 | (0.03) | -0.27 | (0.10) |
| Czech Republic | -0.05 | (0.05) | 0.20 | (0.09) | -0.21 | (0.09) | -0.01 | (0.05) | -0.07 | (0.04) | -0.13 | (0.06) | 0.15 | (0.06) | -0.13 | (0.06) |
| Denmark | -0.10 | (0.05) | 0.12 | (0.05) | -0.22 | (0.09) | -0.02 | (0.03) | -0.24 | (0.09) | -0.13 | (0.06) | -0.01 | (0.03) | -0.43 | (0.17) |
| Finland | 0.04 | (0.03) | 0.31 | (0.13) | -0.11 | (0.05) | 0.07 | (0.04) | -0.11 | (0.05) | -0.06 | (0.04) | 0.10 | (0.05) | -0.24 | (0.10) |
| France | -0.03 | (0.03) | 0.15 | (0.07) | -0.15 | (0.07) | 0.03 | (0.04) | -0.28 | (0.12) | -0.09 | (0.05) | -0.16 | (0.07) | -0.41 | (0.16) |
| Germany | -0.07 | (0.04) | 0.16 | (0.07) | -0.20 | (0.08) | -0.03 | (0.03) | -0.14 | (0.07) | -0.23 | (0.10) | -0.19 | (0.08) | -0.38 | (0.15) |
| Greece | 0.12 | (0.06) | 0.35 | (0.14) | -0.03 | (0.04) | 0.19 | (0.08) | -0.16 | (0.07) | -0.07 | (0.04) | -0.15 | (0.06) | -0.36 | (0.14) |
| Hungary | -0.07 | (0.05) | 0.16 | (0.07) | -0.24 | (0.10) | 0.01 | (0.04) | -0.13 | (0.06) | -0.14 | (0.06) | 0.03 | (0.03) | -0.30 | (0.12) |
| Iceland | 0.06 | (0.04) | 0.29 | (0.12) | -0.07 | (0.04) | 0.07 | (0.04) | -0.30 | (0.12) | -0.14 | (0.06) | -0.22 | (0.08) | -0.40 | (0.14) |
| Ireland | 0.00 | (0.04) | 0.17 | (0.08) | -0.09 | (0.05) | 0.07 | (0.04) | -0.14 | (0.06) | -0.09 | (0.04) | 0.07 | (0.04) | -0.07 | (0.04) |
| Italy | -0.03 | (0.03) | 0.17 | (0.07) | -0.15 | (0.07) | 0.02 | (0.03) | -0.14 | (0.06) | -0.17 | (0.08) | -0.16 | (0.07) | -0.29 | (0.12) |
| Japan | -0.03 | (0.06) | 0.17 | (0.09) | -0.17 | (0.08) | 0.02 | (0.06) | -0.09 | (0.04) | -0.28 | (0.12) | -0.32 | (0.13) | -0.49 | (0.21) |
| Korea | 0.02 | (0.05) | 0.24 | (0.11) | -0.12 | (0.07) | 0.07 | (0.06) | -0.04 | (0.04) | -0.09 | (0.04) | -0.21 | (0.09) | -0.30 | (0.12) |
| Luxembourg | -0.10 | (0.04) | 0.12 | (0.05) | -0.26 | (0.10) | -0.03 | (0.03) | -0.16 | (0.07) | -0.12 | (0.05) | -0.07 | (0.03) | -0.18 | (0.07) |
| Mexico | -0.08 | (0.04) | 0.08 | (0.03) | -0.21 | (0.09) | -0.03 | (0.03) | 0.06 | (0.03) | -0.05 | (0.03) | 0.00 | (0.02) | -0.03 | (0.02) |
| Netherlands | -0.08 | (0.04) | 0.12 | (0.05) | -0.20 | (0.08) | -0.02 | (0.03) | -0.12 | (0.05) | -0.27 | (0.11) | -0.32 | (0.13) | -0.44 | (0.17) |
| New Zealand | 0.03 | (0.04) | 0.21 | (0.09) | -0.10 | (0.05) | 0.08 | (0.05) | -0.13 | (0.06) | -0.11 | (0.05) | -0.05 | (0.03) | -0.24 | (0.09) |
| Norway | 0.05 | (0.03) | 0.25 | (0.10) | -0.06 | (0.04) | 0.06 | (0.03) | -0.17 | (0.08) | -0.15 | (0.07) | -0.15 | (0.07) | -0.45 | (0.17) |
| Poland | -0.04 | (0.03) | 0.16 | (0.07) | -0.18 | (0.07) | 0.04 | (0.03) | 0.05 | (0.03) | 0.01 | (0.03) | 0.15 | (0.07) | -0.11 | (0.05) |
| Portugal | -0.06 | (0.04) | 0.14 | (0.06) | -0.18 | (0.07) | -0.02 | (0.03) | -0.04 | (0.03) | -0.12 | (0.04) | -0.02 | (0.02) | -0.12 | (0.06) |
| Slovak Republic | -0.07 | (0.05) | 0.21 | (0.09) | -0.23 | (0.10) | 0.00 | (0.04) | -0.12 | (0.05) | -0.15 | (0.07) | -0.06 | (0.04) | -0.17 | (0.08) |
| Spain | -0.05 | (0.03) | 0.16 | (0.07) | -0.18 | (0.07) | 0.01 | (0.02) | -0.07 | (0.03) | -0.15 | (0.06) | -0.09 | (0.04) | -0.24 | (0.09) |
| Sweden | -0.01 | (0.03) | 0.17 | (0.07) | -0.12 | (0.05) | 0.05 | (0.03) | -0.21 | (0.09) | -0.11 | (0.05) | -0.05 | (0.03) | -0.31 | (0.12) |
| Switzerland | -0.06 | (0.03) | 0.11 | (0.05) | -0.18 | (0.07) | -0.02 | (0.02) | -0.17 | (0.07) | -0.16 | (0.07) | -0.16 | (0.06) | -0.35 | (0.14) |
| Turkey | 0.14 | (0.07) | 0.38 | (0.15) | -0.01 | (0.04) | 0.17 | (0.08) | 0.10 | (0.05) | 0.18 | (0.07) | 0.08 | (0.04) | -0.07 | (0.04) |
| United Kingdom | -0.09 | (0.05) | 0.07 | (0.03) | -0.20 | (0.08) | -0.05 | (0.04) | -0.26 | (0.10) | -0.27 | (0.11) | -0.18 | (0.07) | -0.40 | (0.15) |
| United States | -0.01 | (0.03) | 0.16 | (0.06) | -0.12 | (0.05) | 0.04 | (0.03) | -0.17 | (0.06) | -0.13 | (0.06) | -0.09 | (0.04) | -0.30 | (0.11) |
| **OECD average** | **-0.02** | (0.01) | **0.19** | (0.02) | **-0.15** | (0.01) | **0.03** | (0.01) | **-0.12** | (0.01) | **-0.13** | (0.01) | **-0.09** | (0.01) | **-0.27** | (0.02) |
| **Partners** | | | | | | | | | | | | | | | | |
| Argentina | 0.13 | (0.07) | 0.27 | (0.11) | 0.00 | (0.05) | 0.19 | (0.08) | 0.03 | (0.03) | -0.09 | (0.05) | -0.01 | (0.03) | -0.10 | (0.05) |
| Azerbaijan | 0.14 | (0.06) | 0.12 | (0.05) | 0.15 | (0.06) | 0.07 | (0.04) | -0.06 | (0.04) | 0.09 | (0.04) | 0.16 | (0.07) | 0.01 | (0.03) |
| Brazil | -0.10 | (0.04) | 0.08 | (0.04) | -0.21 | (0.08) | -0.06 | (0.03) | 0.08 | (0.04) | -0.08 | (0.04) | 0.10 | (0.04) | -0.14 | (0.06) |
| Bulgaria | 0.16 | (0.08) | 0.31 | (0.13) | 0.05 | (0.05) | 0.21 | (0.09) | 0.11 | (0.05) | 0.12 | (0.06) | 0.13 | (0.06) | -0.11 | (0.05) |
| Chile | -0.24 | (0.10) | -0.03 | (0.04) | -0.37 | (0.15) | -0.16 | (0.08) | -0.03 | (0.03) | -0.19 | (0.08) | -0.06 | (0.04) | -0.22 | (0.09) |
| Colombia | -0.11 | (0.06) | 0.03 | (0.04) | -0.20 | (0.09) | -0.05 | (0.05) | 0.00 | (0.04) | -0.05 | (0.04) | 0.12 | (0.06) | -0.05 | (0.03) |
| Croatia | 0.03 | (0.04) | 0.32 | (0.13) | -0.13 | (0.06) | 0.06 | (0.04) | 0.05 | (0.03) | -0.08 | (0.04) | -0.03 | (0.03) | -0.12 | (0.06) |
| Estonia | 0.04 | (0.03) | 0.32 | (0.13) | -0.07 | (0.04) | 0.05 | (0.04) | 0.03 | (0.03) | -0.08 | (0.04) | 0.06 | (0.04) | -0.15 | (0.07) |
| Hong Kong-China | -0.07 | (0.05) | 0.15 | (0.07) | -0.22 | (0.10) | -0.02 | (0.05) | -0.18 | (0.07) | -0.10 | (0.05) | -0.18 | (0.08) | -0.47 | (0.19) |
| Indonesia | -0.17 | (0.10) | -0.11 | (0.08) | -0.24 | (0.11) | -0.06 | (0.07) | 0.01 | (0.03) | 0.04 | (0.03) | 0.01 | (0.04) | -0.09 | (0.05) |
| Israel | -0.03 | (0.05) | 0.11 | (0.06) | -0.14 | (0.08) | 0.06 | (0.05) | -0.14 | (0.06) | -0.04 | (0.04) | -0.12 | (0.06) | -0.14 | (0.06) |
| Jordan | 0.32 | (0.14) | 0.36 | (0.15) | 0.21 | (0.10) | 0.39 | (0.17) | 0.19 | (0.08) | 0.20 | (0.09) | 0.07 | (0.04) | -0.06 | (0.04) |
| Kyrgyzstan | 0.07 | (0.04) | 0.21 | (0.09) | -0.02 | (0.03) | 0.14 | (0.06) | 0.02 | (0.03) | 0.17 | (0.08) | 0.14 | (0.06) | -0.07 | (0.04) |
| Latvia | 0.08 | (0.04) | 0.38 | (0.15) | -0.11 | (0.05) | 0.14 | (0.06) | 0.08 | (0.04) | -0.03 | (0.03) | 0.05 | (0.04) | -0.23 | (0.08) |
| Liechtenstein | 0.12 | (0.10) | 0.29 | (0.14) | -0.06 | (0.10) | 0.18 | (0.11) | -0.29 | (0.16) | -0.16 | (0.12) | -0.24 | (0.14) | -0.37 | (0.17) |
| Lithuania | 0.10 | (0.05) | 0.31 | (0.12) | -0.09 | (0.04) | 0.17 | (0.07) | 0.04 | (0.03) | 0.13 | (0.06) | 0.19 | (0.08) | -0.24 | (0.10) |
| Macao-China | -0.05 | (0.04) | 0.19 | (0.08) | -0.17 | (0.07) | 0.00 | (0.03) | -0.14 | (0.06) | 0.09 | (0.04) | -0.10 | (0.05) | -0.51 | (0.21) |
| Montenegro | 0.02 | (0.03) | 0.20 | (0.08) | -0.11 | (0.05) | 0.09 | (0.04) | 0.07 | (0.04) | -0.04 | (0.03) | 0.02 | (0.03) | -0.04 | (0.03) |
| Qatar | 0.39 | (0.15) | 0.48 | (0.19) | 0.33 | (0.13) | 0.34 | (0.14) | -0.15 | (0.06) | 0.11 | (0.05) | -0.03 | (0.02) | -0.14 | (0.05) |
| Romania | 0.03 | (0.03) | 0.22 | (0.09) | -0.12 | (0.06) | 0.09 | (0.05) | -0.01 | (0.03) | 0.00 | (0.03) | 0.02 | (0.04) | -0.08 | (0.05) |
| Russian Federation | -0.03 | (0.03) | 0.22 | (0.09) | -0.21 | (0.09) | 0.05 | (0.03) | 0.06 | (0.04) | -0.10 | (0.05) | 0.03 | (0.02) | -0.09 | (0.04) |
| Serbia | 0.06 | (0.04) | 0.26 | (0.11) | -0.06 | (0.04) | 0.11 | (0.06) | 0.06 | (0.04) | -0.11 | (0.05) | -0.04 | (0.04) | -0.08 | (0.04) |
| Slovenia | 0.08 | (0.04) | 0.31 | (0.12) | -0.10 | (0.05) | 0.12 | (0.05) | -0.10 | (0.05) | -0.02 | (0.03) | 0.04 | (0.03) | -0.25 | (0.10) |
| Chinese Taipei | -0.08 | (0.06) | 0.06 | (0.06) | -0.19 | (0.09) | 0.00 | (0.05) | -0.04 | (0.03) | -0.16 | (0.06) | -0.32 | (0.12) | -0.53 | (0.21) |
| Thailand | 0.22 | (0.10) | 0.40 | (0.17) | 0.04 | (0.04) | 0.27 | (0.12) | 0.15 | (0.07) | 0.22 | (0.09) | 0.13 | (0.06) | -0.09 | (0.04) |
| Tunisia | 0.06 | (0.04) | 0.23 | (0.09) | -0.06 | (0.04) | 0.11 | (0.05) | -0.07 | (0.04) | 0.09 | (0.05) | 0.07 | (0.04) | -0.16 | (0.06) |
| Uruguay | 0.03 | (0.04) | 0.23 | (0.09) | -0.11 | (0.05) | 0.07 | (0.04) | 0.04 | (0.03) | 0.03 | (0.03) | 0.16 | (0.06) | 0.03 | (0.03) |

Note: Values that are statistically significant are indicated in bold (see Annex A3).
1. Results based on students' self-reports.
StatLink http://dx.doi.org/10.1787/142102278412

Pour consulter la version française intégrale de ce tableau, suivre ce lien :
StatLink http://dx.doi.org/10.1787/152630454851

[Part 2/2]

**Table 3.21 Effect sizes for gender differences (females minus males) in science performance scales and attitudinal indices[1]**

**Tableau 3.21 Différences entre les sexes (filles moins garçons) en termes d'ampleur de l'effet sur les échelles de culture scientifique et indices d'attitude en sciences**

Effect sizes in favour of females:
- from 0.2 to 0.5
- from 0.5 to 0.8
- Equal or greater than 0.8

Effect sizes in favour of males:
- from -0.2 to -0.5
- from -0.5 to -0.8
- Equal or less than -0.8

| | | General interest in science | | Enjoyment of science | | Instrumental motivation to learn science | | Future-oriented motivation to learn science | | Science-related activities | | Awareness of environmental issues | | Level of concern for environmental issues | | Optimism regarding environmental issues | | Responsibility for sustainable development | |
|---|---|---|---|---|---|---|---|---|---|---|---|---|---|---|---|---|---|---|---|
| | | Effect size | S.E. | Effect size | S.E. | Effect size | S.E. | Effect size | S.E. | Effect size | S.E. | Effect size | S.E. | Effect size | S.E. | Effect size | S.E. | Effect size | S.E. |
| OECD | Australia | 0.02 | (0.02) | **-0.09** | (0.04) | -0.01 | (0.02) | **-0.09** | (0.04) | **-0.19** | (0.08) | **-0.18** | (0.08) | **0.22** | (0.09) | **-0.21** | (0.08) | **0.20** | (0.08) |
| | Austria | -0.06 | (0.03) | -0.04 | (0.03) | **-0.21** | (0.08) | -0.08 | (0.04) | -0.07 | (0.04) | **-0.18** | (0.08) | **0.28** | (0.11) | **-0.25** | (0.10) | **0.16** | (0.07) |
| | Belgium | 0.06 | (0.04) | **-0.08** | (0.04) | **-0.08** | (0.04) | **-0.18** | (0.07) | **-0.13** | (0.05) | **-0.22** | (0.09) | **0.15** | (0.06) | **-0.13** | (0.05) | **0.09** | (0.05) |
| | Canada | 0.02 | (0.02) | **-0.08** | (0.04) | **0.08** | (0.04) | -0.03 | (0.02) | **-0.20** | (0.08) | **-0.18** | (0.07) | **0.22** | (0.08) | **-0.31** | (0.12) | **0.23** | (0.09) |
| | Czech Republic | 0.03 | (0.03) | **0.24** | (0.10) | **0.18** | (0.07) | **0.24** | (0.10) | **0.18** | (0.08) | **-0.19** | (0.08) | **0.19** | (0.08) | **-0.20** | (0.08) | -0.03 | (0.03) |
| | Denmark | -0.01 | (0.03) | -0.01 | (0.03) | **0.08** | (0.03) | **0.08** | (0.03) | -0.08 | (0.04) | **-0.31** | (0.13) | **0.18** | (0.07) | **-0.20** | (0.09) | **0.27** | (0.11) |
| | Finland | -0.01 | (0.03) | **0.21** | (0.09) | **0.15** | (0.06) | **0.12** | (0.05) | 0.04 | (0.03) | **-0.23** | (0.10) | **0.33** | (0.13) | **-0.24** | (0.10) | **0.52** | (0.19) |
| | France | -0.05 | (0.03) | **-0.16** | (0.07) | **-0.10** | (0.05) | **-0.17** | (0.07) | **-0.16** | (0.07) | **-0.29** | (0.12) | **0.11** | (0.04) | -0.04 | (0.03) | 0.01 | (0.02) |
| | Germany | **-0.08** | (0.04) | **-0.14** | (0.06) | **-0.16** | (0.07) | **-0.21** | (0.09) | **-0.10** | (0.05) | **-0.30** | (0.13) | **0.26** | (0.11) | **-0.22** | (0.09) | 0.06 | (0.03) |
| | Greece | 0.01 | (0.03) | **-0.19** | (0.08) | **-0.26** | (0.10) | **-0.35** | (0.13) | **-0.15** | (0.07) | -0.08 | (0.05) | **0.21** | (0.09) | **-0.29** | (0.11) | 0.10 | (0.05) |
| | Hungary | -0.02 | (0.03) | **0.12** | (0.05) | -0.03 | (0.03) | 0.02 | (0.03) | -0.02 | (0.03) | -0.06 | (0.04) | **0.21** | (0.09) | **-0.08** | (0.04) | 0.05 | (0.03) |
| | Iceland | **-0.10** | (0.05) | **-0.17** | (0.07) | **-0.08** | (0.04) | **-0.30** | (0.11) | **-0.54** | (0.20) | **-0.39** | (0.16) | **0.11** | (0.05) | **-0.13** | (0.06) | **0.27** | (0.10) |
| | Ireland | **0.08** | (0.04) | 0.06 | (0.04) | **0.22** | (0.09) | **0.09** | (0.04) | **-0.17** | (0.07) | **-0.12** | (0.06) | **0.20** | (0.07) | **-0.25** | (0.09) | **0.19** | (0.08) |
| | Italy | 0.00 | (0.02) | **-0.09** | (0.04) | **-0.18** | (0.07) | **-0.22** | (0.08) | **-0.20** | (0.09) | **-0.13** | (0.06) | **0.18** | (0.07) | **-0.17** | (0.07) | **0.11** | (0.05) |
| | Japan | **-0.18** | (0.08) | **-0.49** | (0.19) | **-0.20** | (0.07) | **-0.46** | (0.18) | **-0.37** | (0.15) | **-0.15** | (0.07) | **0.17** | (0.07) | **-0.12** | (0.05) | **0.10** | (0.04) |
| | Korea | -0.06 | (0.04) | **-0.26** | (0.11) | **-0.16** | (0.07) | **-0.30** | (0.12) | **-0.30** | (0.12) | -0.09 | (0.05) | -0.01 | (0.02) | **-0.10** | (0.05) | **0.10** | (0.05) |
| | Luxembourg | 0.03 | (0.03) | 0.05 | (0.03) | 0.07 | (0.04) | -0.02 | (0.02) | **-0.11** | (0.05) | **-0.32** | (0.13) | **0.20** | (0.08) | **-0.18** | (0.08) | **0.08** | (0.04) |
| | Mexico | 0.05 | (0.03) | 0.04 | (0.03) | 0.04 | (0.03) | **-0.12** | (0.05) | **-0.09** | (0.04) | -0.03 | (0.03) | **0.23** | (0.09) | 0.00 | (0.02) | 0.04 | (0.03) |
| | Netherlands | -0.04 | (0.03) | **-0.29** | (0.12) | 0.00 | (0.03) | **-0.29** | (0.12) | **-0.36** | (0.14) | **-0.22** | (0.09) | **0.20** | (0.08) | **-0.16** | (0.07) | 0.00 | (0.02) |
| | New Zealand | 0.06 | (0.04) | **-0.10** | (0.05) | 0.04 | (0.03) | -0.05 | (0.03) | **-0.15** | (0.06) | **-0.19** | (0.08) | **0.20** | (0.08) | **-0.15** | (0.07) | **0.20** | (0.08) |
| | Norway | **-0.09** | (0.04) | **-0.22** | (0.09) | -0.02 | (0.03) | **-0.16** | (0.07) | **-0.32** | (0.12) | **-0.26** | (0.11) | **0.27** | (0.12) | **-0.25** | (0.11) | **0.27** | (0.11) |
| | Poland | 0.04 | (0.03) | **0.13** | (0.05) | **0.11** | (0.05) | **0.15** | (0.06) | 0.06 | (0.04) | -0.01 | (0.02) | **0.30** | (0.12) | **-0.14** | (0.06) | 0.10 | (0.05) |
| | Portugal | 0.01 | (0.02) | 0.04 | (0.03) | **0.20** | (0.08) | -0.04 | (0.03) | **-0.07** | (0.03) | **-0.14** | (0.06) | **0.16** | (0.07) | **-0.18** | (0.08) | 0.06 | (0.03) |
| | Slovak Republic | -0.05 | (0.04) | -0.03 | (0.03) | 0.01 | (0.04) | **0.13** | (0.06) | **-0.08** | (0.04) | **-0.12** | (0.06) | **0.11** | (0.05) | **-0.13** | (0.06) | **-0.20** | (0.09) |
| | Spain | 0.04 | (0.03) | 0.03 | (0.03) | **-0.09** | (0.04) | **-0.11** | (0.04) | **-0.15** | (0.06) | **-0.15** | (0.06) | **0.27** | (0.11) | **-0.14** | (0.06) | 0.03 | (0.03) |
| | Sweden | 0.03 | (0.03) | -0.01 | (0.04) | -0.02 | (0.03) | **-0.07** | (0.03) | **-0.23** | (0.09) | **-0.30** | (0.12) | **0.29** | (0.12) | **-0.20** | (0.08) | **0.27** | (0.11) |
| | Switzerland | -0.04 | (0.02) | **-0.07** | (0.03) | **-0.11** | (0.05) | **-0.11** | (0.05) | **-0.14** | (0.06) | **-0.35** | (0.14) | **0.19** | (0.08) | **-0.19** | (0.08) | **0.12** | (0.06) |
| | Turkey | 0.02 | (0.03) | 0.03 | (0.03) | **0.08** | (0.04) | **-0.11** | (0.05) | **-0.16** | (0.07) | **0.17** | (0.08) | **0.32** | (0.15) | **-0.20** | (0.08) | **0.14** | (0.06) |
| | United Kingdom | **-0.14** | (0.06) | **-0.24** | (0.10) | **-0.13** | (0.05) | **-0.18** | (0.07) | **-0.20** | (0.08) | **-0.28** | (0.12) | **0.10** | (0.04) | **-0.23** | (0.09) | **0.08** | (0.04) |
| | United States | -0.04 | (0.02) | **-0.18** | (0.07) | 0.01 | (0.03) | **-0.14** | (0.05) | **-0.25** | (0.09) | **-0.20** | (0.08) | **0.25** | (0.10) | **-0.33** | (0.13) | **0.13** | (0.06) |
| | **OECD average** | **-0.02** | (0.01) | **-0.07** | (0.01) | **-0.02** | (0.01) | **-0.10** | (0.01) | **-0.16** | (0.02) | **-0.18** | (0.02) | **0.20** | (0.02) | **-0.18** | (0.01) | **0.12** | (0.01) |
| Partners | Argentina | **0.16** | (0.07) | **0.18** | (0.08) | 0.01 | (0.03) | 0.00 | (0.03) | -0.08 | (0.04) | -0.01 | (0.03) | **0.20** | (0.09) | 0.06 | (0.03) | -0.09 | (0.05) |
| | Azerbaijan | 0.06 | (0.03) | **0.13** | (0.06) | 0.05 | (0.04) | -0.01 | (0.03) | **-0.19** | (0.07) | 0.01 | (0.03) | **0.15** | (0.06) | **0.15** | (0.06) | 0.00 | (0.03) |
| | Brazil | **0.13** | (0.06) | **0.14** | (0.06) | 0.09 | (0.05) | **-0.05** | (0.03) | -0.05 | (0.03) | -0.03 | (0.03) | **0.28** | (0.12) | 0.00 | (0.02) | -0.02 | (0.02) |
| | Bulgaria | **0.14** | (0.06) | **0.17** | (0.08) | **0.12** | (0.05) | **0.12** | (0.05) | -0.03 | (0.03) | **0.17** | (0.08) | **0.28** | (0.12) | **-0.23** | (0.09) | 0.06 | (0.04) |
| | Chile | **0.11** | (0.05) | -0.01 | (0.03) | 0.08 | (0.04) | 0.00 | (0.03) | **-0.11** | (0.05) | **-0.19** | (0.08) | **0.19** | (0.08) | -0.04 | (0.03) | **-0.13** | (0.06) |
| | Colombia | 0.07 | (0.04) | 0.05 | (0.03) | 0.07 | (0.04) | -0.01 | (0.04) | -0.06 | (0.04) | 0.01 | (0.04) | **0.22** | (0.09) | -0.07 | (0.05) | **-0.12** | (0.06) |
| | Croatia | **0.12** | (0.06) | **0.11** | (0.05) | 0.05 | (0.04) | 0.03 | (0.03) | 0.00 | (0.02) | 0.00 | (0.03) | **0.21** | (0.09) | **-0.18** | (0.07) | -0.05 | (0.03) |
| | Estonia | 0.00 | (0.02) | **0.15** | (0.06) | -0.01 | (0.03) | 0.07 | (0.04) | 0.08 | (0.04) | 0.00 | (0.02) | **0.15** | (0.07) | **-0.16** | (0.07) | **0.09** | (0.04) |
| | Hong Kong-China | **-0.28** | (0.11) | **-0.37** | (0.14) | **-0.25** | (0.10) | **-0.38** | (0.15) | **-0.27** | (0.10) | -0.09 | (0.05) | 0.04 | (0.03) | -0.05 | (0.03) | -0.02 | (0.03) |
| | Indonesia | 0.02 | (0.02) | 0.05 | (0.04) | **0.12** | (0.06) | 0.12 | (0.07) | 0.01 | (0.03) | **0.10** | (0.05) | **0.28** | (0.11) | -0.05 | (0.03) | -0.10 | (0.05) |
| | Israel | -0.06 | (0.04) | -0.02 | (0.04) | **-0.13** | (0.06) | **-0.15** | (0.06) | -0.09 | (0.05) | **-0.14** | (0.07) | **0.11** | (0.06) | **-0.12** | (0.06) | m | m |
| | Jordan | 0.07 | (0.04) | -0.06 | (0.04) | **0.20** | (0.08) | **-0.18** | (0.07) | **-0.15** | (0.07) | **0.40** | (0.17) | **0.19** | (0.08) | **-0.12** | (0.06) | **0.19** | (0.09) |
| | Kyrgyzstan | 0.05 | (0.03) | **0.18** | (0.08) | **0.16** | (0.07) | 0.04 | (0.03) | -0.02 | (0.02) | **0.21** | (0.09) | **0.22** | (0.09) | **0.13** | (0.05) | 0.06 | (0.04) |
| | Latvia | -0.04 | (0.04) | **0.13** | (0.06) | -0.01 | (0.03) | 0.00 | (0.03) | 0.01 | (0.03) | -0.05 | (0.04) | **0.22** | (0.10) | **-0.14** | (0.06) | -0.02 | (0.02) |
| | Liechtenstein | 0.05 | (0.07) | -0.06 | (0.10) | **-0.34** | (0.16) | -0.17 | (0.11) | -0.21 | (0.13) | -0.30 | (0.15) | 0.03 | (0.10) | -0.05 | (0.10) | 0.06 | (0.09) |
| | Lithuania | 0.07 | (0.04) | **0.21** | (0.09) | **-0.08** | (0.04) | **0.10** | (0.05) | **0.10** | (0.05) | -0.06 | (0.04) | **0.15** | (0.07) | -0.06 | (0.03) | 0.04 | (0.03) |
| | Macao-China | **-0.25** | (0.11) | **-0.26** | (0.10) | **-0.11** | (0.05) | **-0.26** | (0.10) | **-0.26** | (0.11) | -0.06 | (0.04) | **0.20** | (0.08) | **-0.20** | (0.08) | 0.07 | (0.04) |
| | Montenegro | **0.15** | (0.07) | **0.11** | (0.05) | 0.05 | (0.03) | 0.02 | (0.03) | -0.02 | (0.03) | **0.11** | (0.05) | **0.12** | (0.05) | -0.07 | (0.04) | 0.00 | (0.03) |
| | Qatar | **-0.14** | (0.06) | **-0.18** | (0.07) | -0.02 | (0.02) | **-0.33** | (0.11) | **-0.31** | (0.12) | -0.06 | (0.03) | **0.09** | (0.04) | -0.02 | (0.02) | **0.13** | (0.06) |
| | Romania | 0.06 | (0.03) | 0.06 | (0.04) | 0.07 | (0.04) | -0.02 | (0.03) | -0.06 | (0.04) | 0.06 | (0.04) | **0.17** | (0.08) | **-0.13** | (0.06) | -0.06 | (0.03) |
| | Russian Federation | **0.14** | (0.06) | **0.09** | (0.05) | **-0.16** | (0.06) | **-0.10** | (0.05) | -0.02 | (0.03) | 0.00 | (0.02) | **0.18** | (0.07) | -0.06 | (0.03) | -0.04 | (0.03) |
| | Serbia | **0.14** | (0.06) | -0.03 | (0.03) | -0.04 | (0.03) | **-0.12** | (0.05) | -0.05 | (0.03) | **0.09** | (0.05) | **0.12** | (0.05) | **-0.16** | (0.07) | **-0.11** | (0.05) |
| | Slovenia | **-0.14** | (0.06) | 0.06 | (0.04) | 0.00 | (0.03) | 0.03 | (0.03) | -0.04 | (0.03) | -0.06 | (0.04) | **0.14** | (0.06) | **-0.26** | (0.11) | **0.13** | (0.06) |
| | Chinese Taipei | **-0.29** | (0.11) | **-0.51** | (0.20) | **-0.41** | (0.16) | **-0.61** | (0.24) | **-0.27** | (0.10) | **-0.13** | (0.06) | **0.12** | (0.05) | -0.06 | (0.03) | **0.09** | (0.04) |
| | Thailand | **0.25** | (0.10) | 0.03 | (0.03) | **0.23** | (0.09) | 0.05 | (0.03) | 0.10 | (0.05) | **0.23** | (0.10) | **0.34** | (0.14) | -0.04 | (0.03) | **0.23** | (0.09) |
| | Tunisia | 0.07 | (0.04) | -0.03 | (0.03) | **0.13** | (0.06) | -0.07 | (0.04) | **-0.10** | (0.04) | **-0.11** | (0.05) | 0.05 | (0.04) | 0.02 | (0.03) | 0.06 | (0.04) |
| | Uruguay | 0.05 | (0.03) | **0.23** | (0.09) | **0.10** | (0.05) | **0.12** | (0.05) | -0.06 | (0.03) | -0.03 | (0.03) | **0.11** | (0.05) | 0.02 | (0.03) | -0.02 | (0.03) |

Note: Values that are statistically significant are indicated in bold (see Annex A3).
1. Results based on students' self-reports.
StatLink http://dx.doi.org/10.1787/142102278412

Pour consulter la version française intégrale de ce tableau, suivre ce lien :
StatLink http://dx.doi.org/10.1787/152630454851

[Part 1/2]

**Table 3.22** Effect sizes for the difference between the top and bottom quarters of the PISA index of economic, social and cultural status (ESCS) for science attitudinal indices[1]

Tableau 3.22 Différences entre les quartiles supérieur et inférieur de l'indice PISA de statut économique, social et culturel (SESC) en termes d'ampleur de l'effet dans les indices d'attitude en sciences

Effect sizes in favour of students from more advantaged background:
- from 0.2 to 0.5
- from 0.5 to 0.8
- Equal or greater than 0.8

Effect sizes in favour of students from less advantaged background:
- from -0.2 to -0.5
- from -0.5 to -0.8
- Equal or less than -0.8

| | General value of science | | Personal value of science | | Self-efficacy in science | | Self-concept in science | | General interest in science | | Enjoyment of science | | Instrumental motivation to learn science | |
|---|---|---|---|---|---|---|---|---|---|---|---|---|---|---|
| | Effect size | S.E. | Effect size | S.E. | Effect size | S.E. | Effect size | S.E. | Effect size | S.E. | Effect size | S.E. | Effect size | S.E. |
| **OECD** | | | | | | | | | | | | | | |
| Australia | 0.60 | (0.22) | 0.49 | (0.19) | 0.72 | (0.27) | 0.51 | (0.19) | 0.40 | (0.13) | 0.51 | (0.19) | 0.40 | (0.15) |
| Austria | 0.44 | (0.17) | 0.25 | (0.11) | 0.76 | (0.28) | 0.37 | (0.14) | 0.39 | (0.14) | 0.41 | (0.17) | 0.03 | (0.05) |
| Belgium | 0.41 | (0.15) | 0.44 | (0.16) | 0.60 | (0.21) | 0.34 | (0.12) | 0.51 | (0.16) | 0.47 | (0.17) | 0.28 | (0.10) |
| Canada | 0.44 | (0.16) | 0.46 | (0.18) | 0.63 | (0.22) | 0.46 | (0.17) | 0.35 | (0.12) | 0.43 | (0.16) | 0.40 | (0.16) |
| Czech Republic | 0.23 | (0.09) | 0.05 | (0.04) | 0.50 | (0.20) | 0.18 | (0.08) | 0.20 | (0.08) | 0.14 | (0.06) | 0.09 | (0.05) |
| Denmark | 0.45 | (0.18) | 0.45 | (0.19) | 0.75 | (0.28) | 0.47 | (0.18) | 0.48 | (0.16) | 0.53 | (0.20) | 0.28 | (0.12) |
| Finland | 0.54 | (0.21) | 0.51 | (0.19) | 0.63 | (0.23) | 0.53 | (0.20) | 0.45 | (0.16) | 0.41 | (0.15) | 0.50 | (0.19) |
| France | 0.46 | (0.17) | 0.49 | (0.18) | 0.77 | (0.26) | 0.43 | (0.16) | 0.52 | (0.16) | 0.50 | (0.19) | 0.46 | (0.18) |
| Germany | 0.48 | (0.17) | 0.36 | (0.14) | 0.70 | (0.24) | 0.33 | (0.13) | 0.31 | (0.11) | 0.51 | (0.20) | 0.17 | (0.08) |
| Greece | 0.40 | (0.15) | 0.48 | (0.19) | 0.61 | (0.24) | 0.49 | (0.19) | 0.50 | (0.18) | 0.47 | (0.18) | 0.25 | (0.11) |
| Hungary | 0.46 | (0.17) | 0.16 | (0.07) | 0.63 | (0.23) | 0.22 | (0.10) | 0.26 | (0.09) | 0.29 | (0.11) | 0.04 | (0.05) |
| Iceland | 0.49 | (0.19) | 0.51 | (0.19) | 0.66 | (0.24) | 0.71 | (0.26) | 0.45 | (0.16) | 0.55 | (0.20) | 0.52 | (0.20) |
| Ireland | 0.61 | (0.22) | 0.65 | (0.23) | 0.75 | (0.27) | 0.56 | (0.20) | 0.57 | (0.18) | 0.53 | (0.19) | 0.46 | (0.15) |
| Italy | 0.45 | (0.17) | 0.29 | (0.11) | 0.49 | (0.18) | 0.24 | (0.10) | 0.31 | (0.11) | 0.29 | (0.11) | 0.32 | (0.13) |
| Japan | 0.36 | (0.14) | 0.33 | (0.13) | 0.44 | (0.15) | 0.21 | (0.09) | 0.37 | (0.13) | 0.31 | (0.12) | 0.40 | (0.16) |
| Korea | 0.28 | (0.11) | 0.39 | (0.15) | 0.60 | (0.22) | 0.49 | (0.20) | 0.46 | (0.16) | 0.44 | (0.18) | 0.24 | (0.11) |
| Luxembourg | 0.52 | (0.19) | 0.34 | (0.13) | 0.71 | (0.25) | 0.41 | (0.16) | 0.44 | (0.14) | 0.47 | (0.18) | 0.19 | (0.08) |
| Mexico | 0.39 | (0.15) | 0.02 | (0.03) | 0.53 | (0.19) | 0.21 | (0.09) | -0.10 | (0.05) | -0.24 | (0.10) | -0.16 | (0.07) |
| Netherlands | 0.51 | (0.20) | 0.37 | (0.15) | 0.54 | (0.19) | 0.38 | (0.15) | 0.38 | (0.13) | 0.47 | (0.19) | 0.15 | (0.07) |
| New Zealand | 0.59 | (0.23) | 0.49 | (0.19) | 0.75 | (0.27) | 0.49 | (0.18) | 0.32 | (0.11) | 0.49 | (0.18) | 0.43 | (0.16) |
| Norway | 0.45 | (0.17) | 0.39 | (0.14) | 0.59 | (0.20) | 0.45 | (0.17) | 0.40 | (0.13) | 0.41 | (0.16) | 0.31 | (0.12) |
| Poland | 0.38 | (0.15) | 0.06 | (0.04) | 0.68 | (0.26) | 0.31 | (0.13) | 0.21 | (0.09) | 0.17 | (0.08) | 0.01 | (0.03) |
| Portugal | 0.50 | (0.18) | 0.39 | (0.15) | 0.66 | (0.23) | 0.41 | (0.15) | 0.34 | (0.11) | 0.26 | (0.10) | 0.63 | (0.24) |
| Slovak Republic | 0.36 | (0.15) | -0.03 | (0.05) | 0.54 | (0.21) | 0.25 | (0.11) | 0.35 | (0.12) | 0.12 | (0.06) | 0.04 | (0.04) |
| Spain | 0.40 | (0.15) | 0.47 | (0.18) | 0.61 | (0.22) | 0.54 | (0.20) | 0.41 | (0.14) | 0.45 | (0.18) | 0.46 | (0.18) |
| Sweden | 0.55 | (0.21) | 0.59 | (0.22) | 0.62 | (0.23) | 0.55 | (0.21) | 0.40 | (0.15) | 0.46 | (0.18) | 0.44 | (0.16) |
| Switzerland | 0.40 | (0.14) | 0.36 | (0.13) | 0.74 | (0.27) | 0.42 | (0.16) | 0.50 | (0.16) | 0.49 | (0.18) | 0.31 | (0.11) |
| Turkey | 0.37 | (0.14) | 0.32 | (0.14) | 0.55 | (0.20) | 0.14 | (0.07) | 0.24 | (0.10) | 0.23 | (0.10) | 0.09 | (0.05) |
| United Kingdom | 0.53 | (0.20) | 0.46 | (0.18) | 0.76 | (0.29) | 0.40 | (0.17) | 0.36 | (0.12) | 0.46 | (0.18) | 0.31 | (0.13) |
| United States | 0.60 | (0.22) | 0.47 | (0.18) | 0.67 | (0.24) | 0.48 | (0.17) | 0.18 | (0.07) | 0.41 | (0.15) | 0.31 | (0.13) |
| **OECD average** | 0.46 | (0.03) | 0.37 | (0.03) | 0.64 | (0.04) | 0.40 | (0.03) | 0.37 | (0.02) | 0.38 | (0.03) | 0.28 | (0.02) |
| **Partners** | | | | | | | | | | | | | | |
| Argentina | 0.24 | (0.10) | -0.16 | (0.07) | 0.50 | (0.19) | 0.11 | (0.07) | -0.10 | (0.07) | -0.13 | (0.07) | -0.15 | (0.07) |
| Azerbaijan | 0.27 | (0.10) | 0.03 | (0.05) | 0.50 | (0.17) | 0.10 | (0.07) | 0.26 | (0.10) | -0.06 | (0.05) | -0.03 | (0.05) |
| Brazil | 0.28 | (0.11) | -0.09 | (0.05) | 0.67 | (0.24) | 0.07 | (0.04) | -0.04 | (0.05) | -0.13 | (0.06) | -0.15 | (0.07) |
| Bulgaria | 0.27 | (0.11) | 0.01 | (0.04) | 0.64 | (0.20) | 0.16 | (0.08) | 0.20 | (0.08) | 0.08 | (0.05) | -0.11 | (0.06) |
| Chile | 0.38 | (0.14) | 0.18 | (0.08) | 0.74 | (0.27) | 0.36 | (0.13) | 0.00 | (0.04) | 0.24 | (0.10) | 0.16 | (0.08) |
| Colombia | 0.25 | (0.09) | -0.11 | (0.07) | 0.57 | (0.22) | 0.19 | (0.09) | -0.25 | (0.11) | -0.16 | (0.08) | -0.16 | (0.09) |
| Croatia | 0.29 | (0.11) | 0.05 | (0.04) | 0.61 | (0.24) | 0.17 | (0.10) | 0.18 | (0.07) | 0.06 | (0.04) | -0.03 | (0.04) |
| Estonia | 0.48 | (0.18) | 0.35 | (0.14) | 0.54 | (0.21) | 0.43 | (0.16) | 0.41 | (0.14) | 0.27 | (0.11) | 0.14 | (0.06) |
| Hong Kong-China | 0.28 | (0.11) | 0.26 | (0.10) | 0.56 | (0.21) | 0.22 | (0.09) | 0.31 | (0.11) | 0.32 | (0.13) | 0.04 | (0.05) |
| Indonesia | 0.29 | (0.12) | 0.08 | (0.05) | 0.58 | (0.20) | -0.09 | (0.06) | 0.26 | (0.09) | 0.05 | (0.05) | 0.13 | (0.08) |
| Israel | 0.35 | (0.13) | 0.21 | (0.09) | 0.35 | (0.14) | 0.23 | (0.09) | 0.07 | (0.05) | 0.03 | (0.05) | -0.09 | (0.06) |
| Jordan | 0.49 | (0.17) | 0.33 | (0.13) | 0.46 | (0.17) | 0.39 | (0.15) | 0.28 | (0.10) | 0.16 | (0.08) | 0.30 | (0.11) |
| Kyrgyzstan | 0.17 | (0.07) | -0.14 | (0.06) | 0.30 | (0.12) | -0.21 | (0.09) | -0.06 | (0.04) | -0.30 | (0.13) | -0.33 | (0.14) |
| Latvia | 0.41 | (0.16) | 0.21 | (0.11) | 0.46 | (0.19) | 0.17 | (0.09) | 0.20 | (0.10) | 0.06 | (0.06) | 0.03 | (0.05) |
| Liechtenstein | 0.53 | (0.25) | 0.35 | (0.19) | 0.69 | (0.28) | 0.42 | (0.23) | 0.45 | (0.19) | 0.78 | (0.33) | 0.16 | (0.13) |
| Lithuania | 0.38 | (0.15) | 0.20 | (0.09) | 0.60 | (0.22) | 0.37 | (0.15) | 0.29 | (0.12) | 0.21 | (0.09) | 0.06 | (0.04) |
| Macao-China | 0.22 | (0.09) | 0.27 | (0.12) | 0.50 | (0.19) | 0.23 | (0.10) | 0.15 | (0.07) | 0.13 | (0.06) | 0.06 | (0.06) |
| Montenegro | 0.23 | (0.09) | -0.05 | (0.04) | 0.70 | (0.25) | 0.18 | (0.07) | 0.16 | (0.06) | -0.15 | (0.07) | -0.16 | (0.07) |
| Qatar | m | m | m | m | m | m | m | m | m | m | m | m | m | m |
| Romania | 0.43 | (0.16) | 0.18 | (0.08) | 0.56 | (0.20) | 0.19 | (0.09) | 0.27 | (0.10) | 0.05 | (0.04) | -0.05 | (0.05) |
| Russian Federation | 0.30 | (0.12) | -0.01 | (0.04) | 0.47 | (0.17) | 0.25 | (0.11) | -0.01 | (0.05) | 0.04 | (0.04) | -0.13 | (0.07) |
| Serbia | 0.15 | (0.06) | -0.12 | (0.06) | 0.55 | (0.21) | 0.08 | (0.05) | 0.07 | (0.04) | -0.27 | (0.11) | -0.11 | (0.06) |
| Slovenia | 0.35 | (0.14) | 0.17 | (0.08) | 0.70 | (0.27) | 0.11 | (0.06) | 0.24 | (0.10) | 0.11 | (0.06) | 0.16 | (0.07) |
| Chinese Taipei | 0.43 | (0.16) | 0.35 | (0.13) | 0.65 | (0.23) | 0.35 | (0.14) | 0.41 | (0.14) | 0.40 | (0.15) | 0.29 | (0.12) |
| Thailand | 0.29 | (0.11) | 0.23 | (0.09) | 0.36 | (0.14) | 0.02 | (0.04) | 0.09 | (0.06) | 0.10 | (0.05) | 0.15 | (0.07) |
| Tunisia | 0.32 | (0.12) | 0.25 | (0.10) | 0.41 | (0.17) | 0.18 | (0.08) | 0.13 | (0.07) | -0.06 | (0.05) | 0.13 | (0.07) |
| Uruguay | 0.16 | (0.07) | -0.13 | (0.07) | 0.48 | (0.16) | 0.20 | (0.08) | -0.06 | (0.05) | -0.05 | (0.05) | 0.04 | (0.04) |

Note: Values that are statistically significant are indicated in bold (see Annex A3).
1. Results based on students' self-reports.
*StatLink* http://dx.doi.org/10.1787/142102278412

Pour consulter la version française intégrale de ce tableau, suivre ce lien :
*StatLink* http://dx.doi.org/10.1787/152630454851

[Part 2/2]

**Table 3.22** Effect sizes for the difference between the top and bottom quarters of the PISA index of economic, social and cultural status (ESCS) for science attitudinal indices[1]

*Tableau 3.22* Différences entre les quartiles supérieur et inférieur de l'indice PISA de statut économique, social et culturel (SESC) en termes d'ampleur de l'effet dans les indices d'attitude en sciences

Effect sizes in favour of students from more advantaged background:
- from 0.2 to 0.5
- from 0.5 to 0.8
- Equal or greater than 0.8

Effect sizes in favour of students from less advantaged background:
- from -0.2 to -0.5
- from -0.5 to -0.8
- Equal or less than -0.8

| | Future-oriented motivation to learn science | | Science-related activities | | Awareness of environmental issues | | Level of concern for environmental issues | | Optimism regarding environmental issues | | Responsibility for sustainable development | |
|---|---|---|---|---|---|---|---|---|---|---|---|---|
| | Effect size | S.E. | Effect size | S.E. | Effect size | S.E. | Effect size | S.E. | Effect size | S.E. | Effect size | S.E. |
| **OECD** | | | | | | | | | | | | |
| Australia | 0.33 | (0.13) | 0.45 | (0.17) | 0.68 | (0.24) | 0.12 | (0.04) | -0.07 | (0.03) | 0.43 | (0.17) |
| Austria | 0.29 | (0.13) | 0.32 | (0.13) | 0.69 | (0.25) | 0.05 | (0.04) | -0.25 | (0.09) | 0.33 | (0.13) |
| Belgium | 0.38 | (0.15) | 0.40 | (0.14) | 0.83 | (0.27) | 0.03 | (0.03) | -0.28 | (0.10) | 0.37 | (0.14) |
| Canada | 0.40 | (0.16) | 0.37 | (0.14) | 0.60 | (0.22) | 0.05 | (0.03) | -0.08 | (0.04) | 0.29 | (0.11) |
| Czech Republic | 0.11 | (0.05) | 0.13 | (0.06) | 0.49 | (0.19) | -0.20 | (0.08) | -0.11 | (0.06) | 0.18 | (0.08) |
| Denmark | 0.32 | (0.14) | 0.46 | (0.17) | 0.68 | (0.24) | 0.04 | (0.05) | -0.10 | (0.05) | 0.40 | (0.16) |
| Finland | 0.47 | (0.18) | 0.37 | (0.14) | 0.52 | (0.20) | 0.02 | (0.04) | -0.14 | (0.06) | 0.36 | (0.14) |
| France | 0.43 | (0.18) | 0.55 | (0.19) | 0.91 | (0.29) | 0.33 | (0.12) | -0.52 | (0.18) | 0.53 | (0.20) |
| Germany | 0.38 | (0.16) | 0.53 | (0.18) | 0.74 | (0.25) | 0.08 | (0.05) | -0.10 | (0.06) | 0.28 | (0.11) |
| Greece | 0.35 | (0.14) | 0.44 | (0.16) | 0.62 | (0.24) | 0.20 | (0.08) | -0.38 | (0.14) | 0.50 | (0.19) |
| Hungary | 0.14 | (0.07) | 0.29 | (0.10) | 0.63 | (0.22) | -0.02 | (0.04) | -0.31 | (0.11) | 0.30 | (0.12) |
| Iceland | 0.48 | (0.19) | 0.44 | (0.17) | 0.63 | (0.24) | -0.15 | (0.06) | -0.15 | (0.06) | 0.30 | (0.13) |
| Ireland | 0.44 | (0.17) | 0.49 | (0.18) | 0.63 | (0.22) | 0.00 | (0.04) | -0.15 | (0.08) | 0.48 | (0.17) |
| Italy | 0.29 | (0.12) | 0.37 | (0.14) | 0.57 | (0.20) | 0.07 | (0.03) | -0.29 | (0.11) | 0.29 | (0.11) |
| Japan | 0.35 | (0.14) | 0.32 | (0.13) | 0.52 | (0.20) | 0.08 | (0.04) | 0.03 | (0.04) | 0.28 | (0.10) |
| Korea | 0.21 | (0.10) | 0.52 | (0.20) | 0.61 | (0.23) | 0.06 | (0.04) | -0.02 | (0.04) | 0.21 | (0.09) |
| Luxembourg | 0.25 | (0.10) | 0.46 | (0.16) | 0.88 | (0.29) | 0.11 | (0.05) | -0.37 | (0.14) | 0.41 | (0.16) |
| Mexico | -0.39 | (0.16) | -0.01 | (0.04) | 0.54 | (0.19) | 0.17 | (0.07) | -0.36 | (0.13) | 0.40 | (0.16) |
| Netherlands | 0.33 | (0.14) | 0.43 | (0.16) | 0.78 | (0.28) | -0.01 | (0.04) | -0.12 | (0.05) | 0.38 | (0.14) |
| New Zealand | 0.36 | (0.15) | 0.45 | (0.17) | 0.75 | (0.27) | 0.00 | (0.04) | -0.19 | (0.07) | 0.40 | (0.15) |
| Norway | 0.24 | (0.09) | 0.38 | (0.13) | 0.51 | (0.19) | 0.03 | (0.03) | -0.05 | (0.04) | 0.38 | (0.14) |
| Poland | 0.03 | (0.04) | 0.23 | (0.09) | 0.54 | (0.21) | 0.06 | (0.04) | -0.10 | (0.05) | 0.19 | (0.08) |
| Portugal | 0.42 | (0.18) | 0.31 | (0.11) | 0.86 | (0.30) | -0.10 | (0.05) | -0.35 | (0.12) | 0.27 | (0.10) |
| Slovak Republic | -0.05 | (0.04) | 0.10 | (0.06) | 0.59 | (0.23) | -0.04 | (0.04) | -0.20 | (0.08) | 0.28 | (0.12) |
| Spain | 0.47 | (0.19) | 0.40 | (0.15) | 0.71 | (0.26) | -0.03 | (0.04) | -0.16 | (0.06) | 0.22 | (0.08) |
| Sweden | 0.48 | (0.19) | 0.50 | (0.20) | 0.65 | (0.24) | 0.04 | (0.05) | -0.14 | (0.06) | 0.41 | (0.15) |
| Switzerland | 0.41 | (0.17) | 0.38 | (0.13) | 0.74 | (0.23) | 0.07 | (0.03) | -0.21 | (0.08) | 0.50 | (0.19) |
| Turkey | 0.02 | (0.05) | 0.37 | (0.15) | 0.57 | (0.21) | 0.17 | (0.07) | -0.40 | (0.15) | 0.19 | (0.09) |
| United Kingdom | 0.30 | (0.12) | 0.50 | (0.18) | 0.75 | (0.27) | 0.09 | (0.04) | -0.18 | (0.07) | 0.51 | (0.20) |
| United States | 0.26 | (0.10) | 0.24 | (0.08) | 0.73 | (0.26) | 0.16 | (0.06) | -0.23 | (0.10) | 0.45 | (0.18) |
| **OECD average** | 0.28 | (0.03) | 0.37 | (0.03) | 0.66 | (0.04) | 0.05 | (0.01) | -0.20 | (0.02) | 0.35 | (0.03) |
| **Partners** | | | | | | | | | | | | |
| Argentina | -0.15 | (0.07) | -0.10 | (0.06) | 0.79 | (0.29) | 0.14 | (0.07) | -0.43 | (0.15) | 0.45 | (0.19) |
| Azerbaijan | -0.23 | (0.10) | 0.18 | (0.07) | 0.35 | (0.13) | 0.06 | (0.05) | -0.10 | (0.06) | 0.14 | (0.07) |
| Brazil | -0.14 | (0.07) | 0.05 | (0.04) | 0.75 | (0.30) | 0.12 | (0.06) | -0.34 | (0.12) | 0.23 | (0.09) |
| Bulgaria | -0.24 | (0.10) | 0.33 | (0.12) | 0.72 | (0.23) | 0.06 | (0.05) | -0.26 | (0.11) | 0.19 | (0.08) |
| Chile | 0.21 | (0.09) | 0.15 | (0.06) | 0.88 | (0.33) | 0.09 | (0.04) | -0.44 | (0.16) | 0.40 | (0.15) |
| Colombia | -0.31 | (0.14) | 0.10 | (0.05) | 0.64 | (0.21) | -0.02 | (0.05) | -0.45 | (0.16) | 0.25 | (0.10) |
| Croatia | 0.06 | (0.04) | 0.23 | (0.09) | 0.61 | (0.23) | -0.10 | (0.05) | -0.26 | (0.09) | 0.12 | (0.05) |
| Estonia | 0.17 | (0.08) | 0.18 | (0.07) | 0.43 | (0.16) | -0.10 | (0.05) | -0.11 | (0.06) | 0.26 | (0.11) |
| Hong Kong-China | 0.09 | (0.05) | 0.49 | (0.18) | 0.53 | (0.20) | -0.02 | (0.04) | 0.01 | (0.03) | 0.32 | (0.12) |
| Indonesia | 0.10 | (0.07) | 0.66 | (0.22) | 0.59 | (0.23) | 0.18 | (0.07) | -0.05 | (0.04) | 0.32 | (0.12) |
| Israel | 0.08 | (0.05) | -0.09 | (0.06) | 0.40 | (0.14) | 0.17 | (0.07) | -0.35 | (0.13) | m | m |
| Jordan | 0.26 | (0.11) | 0.15 | (0.07) | 0.46 | (0.17) | 0.11 | (0.05) | -0.34 | (0.13) | 0.29 | (0.11) |
| Kyrgyzstan | -0.49 | (0.21) | -0.23 | (0.10) | 0.24 | (0.10) | 0.09 | (0.05) | 0.03 | (0.05) | -0.06 | (0.06) |
| Latvia | 0.05 | (0.06) | 0.19 | (0.10) | 0.54 | (0.23) | -0.05 | (0.04) | -0.13 | (0.06) | 0.22 | (0.11) |
| Liechtenstein | 0.45 | (0.22) | 0.34 | (0.20) | 0.44 | (0.20) | -0.12 | (0.12) | -0.02 | (0.13) | 0.44 | (0.23) |
| Lithuania | 0.10 | (0.06) | 0.14 | (0.07) | 0.64 | (0.24) | -0.12 | (0.06) | -0.09 | (0.05) | 0.18 | (0.08) |
| Macao-China | 0.02 | (0.04) | 0.46 | (0.18) | 0.47 | (0.18) | -0.02 | (0.04) | 0.02 | (0.04) | 0.08 | (0.05) |
| Montenegro | -0.25 | (0.11) | 0.21 | (0.09) | 0.59 | (0.23) | 0.03 | (0.04) | -0.24 | (0.10) | 0.06 | (0.04) |
| Qatar | m | m | m | m | m | m | m | m | m | m | m | m |
| Romania | -0.10 | (0.05) | 0.39 | (0.14) | 0.54 | (0.21) | -0.10 | (0.06) | -0.19 | (0.08) | 0.52 | (0.20) |
| Russian Federation | -0.29 | (0.12) | 0.06 | (0.07) | 0.55 | (0.21) | 0.04 | (0.04) | -0.07 | (0.05) | 0.22 | (0.09) |
| Serbia | -0.16 | (0.07) | 0.16 | (0.06) | 0.55 | (0.21) | -0.06 | (0.04) | -0.34 | (0.12) | 0.06 | (0.04) |
| Slovenia | 0.25 | (0.11) | 0.24 | (0.10) | 0.62 | (0.24) | -0.12 | (0.05) | -0.04 | (0.04) | 0.24 | (0.10) |
| Chinese Taipei | 0.32 | (0.13) | 0.52 | (0.18) | 0.64 | (0.24) | 0.29 | (0.10) | -0.17 | (0.06) | 0.26 | (0.10) |
| Thailand | -0.01 | (0.04) | 0.39 | (0.15) | 0.45 | (0.17) | 0.15 | (0.06) | -0.33 | (0.13) | 0.35 | (0.13) |
| Tunisia | 0.12 | (0.06) | 0.11 | (0.06) | 0.43 | (0.17) | 0.00 | (0.03) | -0.47 | (0.19) | 0.19 | (0.08) |
| Uruguay | -0.03 | (0.05) | -0.06 | (0.05) | 0.64 | (0.23) | -0.13 | (0.06) | -0.21 | (0.08) | 0.25 | (0.10) |

Note: Values that are statistically significant are indicated in bold (see Annex A3).
1. Results based on students' self-reports.
*StatLink* ☞ http://dx.doi.org/10.1787/142102278412

Pour consulter la version française intégrale de ce tableau, suivre ce lien :
*StatLink* ☞ http://dx.doi.org/10.1787/152630454851

[Part 1/2]

**Table 3.23** Effect sizes for the difference between students with an immigrant background and native students for science attitudinal indices[1]

Tableau 3.23  Différences en termes d'ampleur de l'effet dans les indices d'attitude en sciences entre les élèves allochtones et autochtones

Effect sizes in favour of native students:
  from -0.2 to -0.5
  from -0.5 to -0.8
  Equal or less than -0.8

Effect sizes in favour of students with an immigrant background:
  from 0.2 to 0.5
  from 0.5 to 0.8
  Equal or greater than 0.8

| | Percentage of students with an immigrant background | Awareness of environmental issues | | Optimism regarding environmental issues | | Level of concern for environmental issues | | Responsibility for sustainable development | | General value of science | | Personal value of science | |
|---|---|---|---|---|---|---|---|---|---|---|---|---|---|
| | | Effect size | S.E. | Effect size | S.E. | Effect size | S.E. | Effect size | S.E. | Effect size | S.E. | Effect size | S.E. |
| **Australia** | 21.9 | **0.13** | (0.06) | **0.14** | (0.05) | -0.02 | (0.02) | **0.08** | (0.04) | **0.23** | (0.09) | **0.22** | (0.09) |
| Austria | 13.2 | **-0.40** | (0.16) | **0.29** | (0.11) | -0.10 | (0.06) | **-0.16** | (0.06) | 0.03 | (0.04) | **0.16** | (0.06) |
| Belgium | 13.3 | **-0.43** | (0.17) | **0.25** | (0.10) | 0.01 | (0.04) | 0.04 | (0.04) | 0.07 | (0.04) | **0.15** | (0.07) |
| Canada | 21.1 | 0.06 | (0.04) | **0.11** | (0.05) | -0.05 | (0.03) | -0.02 | (0.03) | **0.25** | (0.10) | **0.25** | (0.10) |
| Czech Republic | 1.9 | c | c | c | c | c | c | c | c | c | c | c | c |
| Denmark | 7.6 | **-0.17** | (0.09) | **0.34** | (0.14) | -0.09 | (0.06) | -0.17 | (0.09) | **0.14** | (0.07) | **0.29** | (0.12) |
| Finland | 1.5 | c | c | c | c | c | c | c | c | c | c | c | c |
| France | 13.0 | **-0.19** | (0.09) | **0.32** | (0.13) | **-0.18** | (0.08) | **-0.13** | (0.06) | **0.15** | (0.07) | **0.16** | (0.07) |
| Germany | 14.2 | **-0.53** | (0.21) | **0.19** | (0.09) | -0.07 | (0.07) | **-0.20** | (0.09) | **-0.17** | (0.07) | **-0.15** | (0.06) |
| Greece | 7.6 | **-0.25** | (0.12) | **0.24** | (0.12) | -0.01 | (0.05) | **-0.29** | (0.11) | 0.01 | (0.04) | -0.00 | (0.05) |
| Hungary | 1.7 | c | c | c | c | c | c | c | c | c | c | c | c |
| Iceland | 1.8 | c | c | c | c | c | c | c | c | c | c | c | c |
| Ireland | 5.6 | -0.08 | (0.07) | 0.16 | (0.08) | 0.03 | (0.06) | 0.05 | (0.06) | **0.13** | (0.07) | **0.23** | (0.09) |
| Italy | 3.8 | **-0.47** | (0.20) | **0.34** | (0.14) | **-0.26** | (0.11) | **-0.36** | (0.14) | -0.13 | (0.07) | -0.06 | (0.06) |
| Japan | 0.4 | c | c | c | c | c | c | c | c | c | c | c | c |
| Korea | 0.0 | c | c | c | c | c | c | c | c | c | c | c | c |
| Luxembourg | 36.1 | **-0.34** | (0.14) | **0.24** | (0.10) | **-0.12** | (0.06) | -0.03 | (0.03) | **-0.19** | (0.07) | -0.00 | (0.03) |
| Mexico | 2.4 | c | c | c | c | c | c | c | c | c | c | c | c |
| Netherlands | 11.3 | **-0.31** | (0.14) | 0.09 | (0.07) | -0.06 | (0.05) | -0.06 | (0.05) | 0.02 | (0.04) | **0.17** | (0.07) |
| New Zealand | 21.3 | **0.11** | (0.05) | **0.20** | (0.08) | 0.08 | (0.05) | **0.22** | (0.08) | **0.34** | (0.13) | **0.34** | (0.13) |
| Norway | 6.1 | -0.08 | (0.06) | 0.15 | (0.08) | -0.07 | (0.07) | -0.13 | (0.07) | 0.05 | (0.05) | 0.14 | (0.08) |
| Poland | 0.2 | c | c | c | c | c | c | c | c | c | c | c | c |
| Portugal | 5.9 | **-0.29** | (0.12) | **0.23** | (0.10) | **-0.20** | (0.09) | **-0.17** | (0.07) | **-0.14** | (0.06) | -0.12 | (0.07) |
| Slovak Republic | 0.5 | c | c | c | c | c | c | c | c | c | c | c | c |
| Spain | 6.9 | **-0.24** | (0.12) | **0.18** | (0.07) | **-0.22** | (0.09) | **-0.18** | (0.09) | -0.01 | (0.05) | **0.19** | (0.08) |
| Sweden | 10.8 | **-0.16** | (0.07) | **0.20** | (0.08) | 0.07 | (0.05) | -0.06 | (0.04) | **0.15** | (0.07) | **0.26** | (0.11) |
| Switzerland | 22.4 | **-0.37** | (0.16) | **0.30** | (0.12) | **-0.13** | (0.07) | **-0.21** | (0.08) | 0.04 | (0.03) | 0.03 | (0.03) |
| Turkey | 1.5 | c | c | c | c | c | c | c | c | c | c | c | c |
| United Kingdom | 8.6 | **0.12** | (0.06) | 0.10 | (0.06) | 0.06 | (0.05) | **0.13** | (0.06) | **0.29** | (0.12) | **0.36** | (0.14) |
| United States | 15.2 | **-0.23** | (0.10) | 0.10 | (0.05) | 0.06 | (0.04) | **0.10** | (0.04) | 0.03 | (0.04) | 0.01 | (0.04) |
| **OECD average** | 9.3 | **-0.21** | (0.03) | **0.21** | (0.02) | **-0.06** | (0.01) | **-0.08** | (0.02) | **0.07** | (0.02) | **0.13** | (0.02) |
| Argentina | 2.7 | c | c | c | c | c | c | c | c | c | c | c | c |
| Azerbaijan | 2.4 | c | c | c | c | c | c | c | c | c | c | c | c |
| Brazil | 2.4 | c | c | c | c | c | c | c | c | c | c | c | c |
| Bulgaria | 0.2 | c | c | c | c | c | c | c | c | c | c | c | c |
| Chile | 0.6 | c | c | c | c | c | c | c | c | c | c | c | c |
| Colombia | 0.4 | c | c | c | c | c | c | c | c | c | c | c | c |
| Croatia | 12.0 | **-0.15** | (0.07) | 0.18 | (0.08) | 0.04 | (0.03) | -0.03 | (0.03) | 0.05 | (0.04) | 0.04 | (0.04) |
| Estonia | 11.6 | -0.05 | (0.05) | **0.52** | (0.21) | **-0.15** | (0.07) | 0.05 | (0.05) | **-0.25** | (0.10) | -0.03 | (0.04) |
| Hong Kong-China | 43.8 | 0.01 | (0.03) | 0.03 | (0.04) | -0.01 | (0.03) | -0.04 | (0.03) | **0.08** | (0.04) | **0.09** | (0.04) |
| Indonesia | 0.2 | c | c | c | c | c | c | c | c | c | c | c | c |
| Israel | 23.0 | -0.03 | (0.04) | 0.05 | (0.04) | -0.08 | (0.05) | m | m | -0.05 | (0.04) | -0.07 | (0.04) |
| Jordan | 16.8 | 0.08 | (0.05) | **-0.14** | (0.06) | **0.09** | (0.04) | 0.01 | (0.04) | 0.07 | (0.04) | -0.05 | (0.04) |
| Kyrgyzstan | 2.6 | c | c | c | c | c | c | c | c | c | c | c | c |
| Latvia | 7.1 | 0.02 | (0.05) | **0.23** | (0.11) | **-0.24** | (0.11) | 0.04 | (0.06) | 0.05 | (0.05) | **0.26** | (0.12) |
| Liechtenstein | 36.8 | -0.16 | (0.12) | **0.33** | (0.15) | -0.00 | (0.09) | -0.06 | (0.09) | 0.06 | (0.10) | **0.32** | (0.15) |
| Lithuania | 2.1 | c | c | c | c | c | c | c | c | c | c | c | c |
| Macao-China | 73.6 | 0.02 | (0.03) | -0.05 | (0.03) | 0.07 | (0.04) | -0.01 | (0.03) | 0.08 | (0.04) | -0.00 | (0.03) |
| Montenegro | 7.2 | **0.32** | (0.14) | **-0.29** | (0.12) | 0.01 | (0.05) | -0.11 | (0.07) | 0.02 | (0.06) | -0.03 | (0.06) |
| Qatar | 40.5 | **0.28** | (0.10) | **-0.30** | (0.11) | **0.15** | (0.05) | **0.21** | (0.07) | **0.36** | (0.12) | **0.26** | (0.09) |
| Romania | 0.1 | c | c | c | c | c | c | c | c | c | c | c | c |
| Russian Federation | 8.7 | -0.06 | (0.05) | -0.07 | (0.05) | 0.01 | (0.05) | -0.07 | (0.05) | -0.03 | (0.04) | -0.04 | (0.04) |
| Serbia | 9.0 | -0.05 | (0.04) | -0.08 | (0.06) | -0.09 | (0.06) | -0.08 | (0.05) | -0.03 | (0.05) | **-0.18** | (0.07) |
| Slovenia | 10.3 | **-0.38** | (0.15) | 0.05 | (0.04) | -0.10 | (0.05) | **-0.19** | (0.08) | **-0.22** | (0.09) | **-0.21** | (0.09) |
| Chinese Taipei | 0.6 | c | c | c | c | c | c | c | c | c | c | c | c |
| Thailand | 0.3 | c | c | c | c | c | c | c | c | c | c | c | c |
| Tunisia | 0.8 | c | c | c | c | c | c | c | c | c | c | c | c |
| Uruguay | 0.4 | c | c | c | c | c | c | c | c | c | c | c | c |

*OECD* (row group label for Australia–OECD average)
*Partners* (row group label for Argentina–Uruguay)

Note: Values that are statistically significant are indicated in bold (see Annex A3).
1. Results based on students' self-reports.
*StatLink* http://dx.doi.org/10.1787/142102278412

Pour consulter la version française intégrale de ce tableau, suivre ce lien :
*StatLink* http://dx.doi.org/10.1787/152630454851

[Part 2/2]

**Table 3.23** **Effect sizes for the difference between students with an immigrant background and native students for science attitudinal indices[1]**

Tableau 3.23 Différences en termes d'ampleur de l'effet dans les indices d'attitude en sciences entre les élèves allochtones et autochtones

Effect sizes in favour of native students:
from -0.2 to -0.5
from -0.5 to -0.8
Equal or less than -0.8

Effect sizes in favour of students with an immigrant background:
from 0.2 to 0.5
from 0.5 to 0.8
Equal or greater than 0.8

| | General interest in science | | Enjoyment of science | | Instrumental motivation to learn science | | Future-oriented motivation to learn science | | Science-related activities | | Self-concept in science | | Self-efficacy in science | |
|---|---|---|---|---|---|---|---|---|---|---|---|---|---|---|
| | Effect size | S.E. | Effect size | S.E. | Effect size | S.E. | Effect size | S.E. | Effect size | S.E. | Effect size | S.E. | Effect size | S.E. |
| **OECD** | | | | | | | | | | | | | | |
| Australia | **0.27** | (0.10) | **0.28** | (0.11) | **0.25** | (0.10) | **0.27** | (0.11) | **0.29** | (0.11) | **0.13** | (0.05) | **0.17** | (0.07) |
| Austria | 0.07 | (0.06) | **0.10** | (0.05) | **0.24** | (0.11) | **0.18** | (0.07) | **0.15** | (0.07) | **-0.18** | (0.09) | 0.06 | (0.05) |
| Belgium | 0.05 | (0.04) | **0.18** | (0.08) | **0.31** | (0.13) | **0.14** | (0.06) | **0.16** | (0.07) | -0.06 | (0.04) | **0.24** | (0.10) |
| Canada | **0.23** | (0.08) | **0.24** | (0.09) | **0.21** | (0.08) | **0.26** | (0.10) | **0.28** | (0.11) | 0.06 | (0.04) | 0.01 | (0.02) |
| Czech Republic | c | c | c | c | c | c | c | c | c | c | c | c | c | c |
| Denmark | **0.25** | (0.11) | **0.23** | (0.09) | 0.09 | (0.07) | **0.31** | (0.13) | **0.17** | (0.08) | -0.07 | (0.06) | 0.13 | (0.07) |
| Finland | c | c | c | c | c | c | c | c | c | c | c | c | c | c |
| France | 0.09 | (0.06) | **0.22** | (0.09) | **0.15** | (0.07) | **0.19** | (0.08) | **0.22** | (0.09) | -0.05 | (0.05) | 0.08 | (0.05) |
| Germany | -0.08 | (0.04) | **-0.14** | (0.06) | **-0.11** | (0.05) | -0.02 | (0.04) | -0.04 | (0.04) | **-0.31** | (0.11) | **-0.14** | (0.06) |
| Greece | 0.04 | (0.05) | 0.09 | (0.06) | 0.05 | (0.06) | -0.04 | (0.04) | 0.05 | (0.05) | -0.07 | (0.06) | -0.09 | (0.06) |
| Hungary | c | c | c | c | c | c | c | c | c | c | c | c | c | c |
| Iceland | c | c | c | c | c | c | c | c | c | c | c | c | c | c |
| Ireland | **0.20** | (0.09) | **0.26** | (0.11) | **0.26** | (0.11) | **0.29** | (0.13) | **0.34** | (0.14) | 0.11 | (0.07) | **0.24** | (0.11) |
| Italy | -0.04 | (0.05) | 0.02 | (0.05) | 0.03 | (0.05) | 0.07 | (0.06) | 0.09 | (0.06) | **-0.30** | (0.12) | **-0.20** | (0.09) |
| Japan | c | c | c | c | c | c | c | c | c | c | c | c | c | c |
| Korea | c | c | c | c | c | c | c | c | c | c | c | c | c | c |
| Luxembourg | -0.08 | (0.04) | -0.03 | (0.03) | **0.08** | (0.04) | 0.02 | (0.02) | -0.06 | (0.03) | **-0.14** | (0.06) | **-0.16** | (0.06) |
| Mexico | c | c | c | c | c | c | c | c | c | c | c | c | c | c |
| Netherlands | 0.13 | (0.07) | **0.28** | (0.11) | -0.10 | (0.06) | **0.15** | (0.07) | **0.24** | (0.10) | 0.01 | (0.04) | 0.06 | (0.06) |
| New Zealand | **0.37** | (0.13) | **0.39** | (0.14) | **0.39** | (0.15) | **0.39** | (0.15) | **0.41** | (0.15) | **0.11** | (0.05) | **0.28** | (0.10) |
| Norway | 0.17 | (0.09) | **0.19** | (0.09) | **0.28** | (0.13) | **0.35** | (0.15) | **0.28** | (0.13) | -0.00 | (0.05) | 0.12 | (0.08) |
| Poland | c | c | c | c | c | c | c | c | c | c | c | c | c | c |
| Portugal | -0.01 | (0.06) | -0.02 | (0.05) | -0.14 | (0.08) | -0.15 | (0.08) | 0.06 | (0.06) | **-0.28** | (0.11) | -0.00 | (0.08) |
| Slovak Republic | c | c | c | c | c | c | c | c | c | c | c | c | c | c |
| Spain | **0.23** | (0.09) | **0.27** | (0.10) | **0.27** | (0.11) | **0.23** | (0.09) | **0.41** | (0.16) | -0.09 | (0.05) | 0.09 | (0.05) |
| Sweden | **0.28** | (0.10) | **0.29** | (0.11) | **0.29** | (0.12) | **0.32** | (0.13) | **0.32** | (0.12) | 0.05 | (0.04) | 0.08 | (0.04) |
| Switzerland | 0.03 | (0.02) | -0.03 | (0.03) | -0.00 | (0.03) | **0.10** | (0.04) | **0.09** | (0.04) | -0.10 | (0.05) | **-0.12** | (0.05) |
| Turkey | c | c | c | c | c | c | c | c | c | c | c | c | c | c |
| United Kingdom | **0.29** | (0.12) | **0.33** | (0.14) | **0.27** | (0.11) | **0.31** | (0.13) | **0.55** | (0.21) | **0.16** | (0.07) | **0.28** | (0.12) |
| United States | **0.16** | (0.06) | **0.11** | (0.05) | **0.12** | (0.05) | **0.13** | (0.06) | **0.26** | (0.12) | **-0.26** | (0.10) | **-0.14** | (0.06) |
| **OECD average** | **0.13** | (0.02) | **0.16** | (0.02) | **0.15** | (0.02) | **0.18** | (0.02) | **0.21** | (0.02) | **-0.06** | (0.02) | **0.05** | (0.02) |
| **Partners** | | | | | | | | | | | | | | |
| Argentina | c | c | c | c | c | c | c | c | c | c | c | c | c | c |
| Azerbaijan | c | c | c | c | c | c | c | c | c | c | c | c | c | c |
| Brazil | c | c | c | c | c | c | c | c | c | c | c | c | c | c |
| Bulgaria | c | c | c | c | c | c | c | c | c | c | c | c | c | c |
| Chile | c | c | c | c | c | c | c | c | c | c | c | c | c | c |
| Colombia | c | c | c | c | c | c | c | c | c | c | c | c | c | c |
| Croatia | -0.06 | (0.05) | 0.02 | (0.04) | 0.03 | (0.04) | -0.03 | (0.03) | -0.02 | (0.04) | **-0.13** | (0.06) | 0.01 | (0.04) |
| Estonia | **0.15** | (0.07) | 0.01 | (0.04) | **0.17** | (0.08) | **0.39** | (0.14) | **0.12** | (0.06) | 0.02 | (0.04) | 0.07 | (0.04) |
| Hong Kong-China | 0.05 | (0.04) | 0.05 | (0.03) | **0.14** | (0.06) | **0.08** | (0.04) | -0.02 | (0.04) | -0.06 | (0.04) | **0.10** | (0.05) |
| Indonesia | c | c | c | c | c | c | c | c | c | c | c | c | c | c |
| Israel | 0.01 | (0.03) | -0.00 | (0.03) | -0.06 | (0.04) | 0.02 | (0.03) | -0.08 | (0.04) | -0.06 | (0.04) | **-0.13** | (0.05) |
| Jordan | -0.00 | (0.04) | -0.05 | (0.04) | 0.03 | (0.04) | -0.04 | (0.04) | **-0.12** | (0.06) | -0.02 | (0.04) | -0.00 | (0.04) |
| Kyrgyzstan | c | c | c | c | c | c | c | c | c | c | c | c | c | c |
| Latvia | **0.19** | (0.10) | 0.17 | (0.10) | **0.23** | (0.11) | **0.29** | (0.12) | **0.32** | (0.13) | **0.21** | (0.10) | 0.13 | (0.08) |
| Liechtenstein | 0.24 | (0.13) | 0.16 | (0.12) | **0.23** | (0.13) | 0.27 | (0.14) | **0.34** | (0.15) | 0.03 | (0.10) | 0.19 | (0.12) |
| Lithuania | c | c | c | c | c | c | c | c | c | c | c | c | c | c |
| Macao-China | **0.11** | (0.05) | **0.11** | (0.04) | **0.13** | (0.06) | -0.03 | (0.03) | -0.05 | (0.04) | 0.02 | (0.03) | 0.07 | (0.05) |
| Montenegro | -0.04 | (0.06) | -0.01 | (0.05) | -0.00 | (0.05) | -0.05 | (0.06) | -0.02 | (0.05) | **0.24** | (0.11) | 0.06 | (0.06) |
| Qatar | **0.25** | (0.08) | **0.35** | (0.13) | **0.28** | (0.10) | **0.26** | (0.10) | **0.07** | (0.03) | **0.18** | (0.07) | **0.19** | (0.07) |
| Romania | c | c | c | c | c | c | c | c | c | c | c | c | c | c |
| Russian Federation | 0.02 | (0.04) | -0.01 | (0.04) | -0.01 | (0.03) | -0.06 | (0.04) | 0.04 | (0.04) | -0.07 | (0.05) | -0.07 | (0.05) |
| Serbia | **-0.19** | (0.08) | **-0.17** | (0.08) | **-0.19** | (0.08) | **-0.17** | (0.07) | **-0.19** | (0.07) | **-0.12** | (0.06) | **-0.13** | (0.06) |
| Slovenia | -0.06 | (0.04) | **-0.13** | (0.06) | -0.11 | (0.06) | **-0.14** | (0.07) | **-0.24** | (0.10) | **-0.20** | (0.08) | -0.02 | (0.04) |
| Chinese Taipei | c | c | c | c | c | c | c | c | c | c | c | c | c | c |
| Thailand | c | c | c | c | c | c | c | c | c | c | c | c | c | c |
| Tunisia | c | c | c | c | c | c | c | c | c | c | c | c | c | c |
| Uruguay | c | c | c | c | c | c | c | c | c | c | c | c | c | c |

Note: Values that are statistically significant are indicated in bold (see Annex A3).
1. Results based on students' self-reports.

StatLink http://dx.doi.org/10.1787/142102278412

Pour consulter la version française intégrale de ce tableau, suivre ce lien :
StatLink http://dx.doi.org/10.1787/152630454851

[Part 1/2]

**Table 4.1a** Between-school and within-school variance in student performance on the science scale in PISA 2006

Tableau 4.1a Variance inter- et intra-établissements des scores sur l'échelle de culture scientifique du cycle PISA 2006

| | | Variance expressed as a percentage of the average variance in student performance (SP) across OECD countries[1] | | | Variance explained by the PISA index of economic, social and cultural status of students | |
| | Total variance in SP[2] | Total variance in SP expressed as a percentage of the average variance in student performance across OECD countries[3] | Total variance in SP between schools[4] | Total variance in SP within schools | Between-school variance explained | Within-school variance explained |
|---|---|---|---|---|---|---|
| **OECD** | | | | | | |
| Australia | 9 926 | 110.6 | 19.8 | 91.1 | 7.8 | 4.3 |
| Austria | 9 551 | 106.5 | 60.7 | 50.7 | 7.9 | 0.6 |
| Belgium | 9 791 | 109.1 | 57.0 | 53.0 | 11.7 | 2.0 |
| Canada | 8 743 | 97.5 | 17.9 | 79.3 | 4.3 | 3.2 |
| Czech Republic | 9 687 | 108.0 | 62.4 | 55.9 | 12.7 | 1.7 |
| Denmark | 8 580 | 95.6 | 14.8 | 82.0 | 6.0 | 8.1 |
| Finland | 7 301 | 81.4 | 4.7 | 76.7 | 1.2 | 5.5 |
| France | w | w | w | w | w | w |
| Germany | 9 908 | 110.4 | 66.2 | 50.8 | 11.6 | 1.4 |
| Greece | 8 420 | 93.9 | 48.5 | 55.1 | 11.3 | 1.7 |
| Hungary | 7 720 | 86.1 | 60.5 | 38.5 | 9.4 | 0.2 |
| Iceland | 9 263 | 103.2 | 9.3 | 95.4 | 0.1 | 6.4 |
| Ireland | 8 871 | 98.9 | 16.9 | 82.6 | 7.4 | 4.9 |
| Italy | 9 045 | 100.8 | 52.6 | 51.8 | 4.8 | 0.4 |
| Japan | 9 812 | 109.4 | 53.0 | 59.4 | 2.9 | 0.1 |
| Korea | 8 093 | 90.2 | 31.8 | 59.3 | 3.8 | 0.4 |
| Luxembourg | 9 356 | 104.3 | 30.5 | 72.7 | 12.4 | 6.0 |
| Mexico | 6 490 | 72.3 | 25.5 | 38.2 | 4.2 | 0.3 |
| Netherlands | 9 081 | 101.2 | 59.6 | 40.0 | 6.8 | 0.7 |
| New Zealand | 11 230 | 125.2 | 20.0 | 106.0 | 10.6 | 10.1 |
| Norway | 8 894 | 99.1 | 9.9 | 88.8 | 2.8 | 5.2 |
| Poland | 8 047 | 89.7 | 12.2 | 78.9 | 5.5 | 8.6 |
| Portugal | 7 824 | 87.2 | 27.8 | 58.5 | 8.8 | 3.6 |
| Slovak Republic | 8 648 | 96.4 | 40.9 | 55.6 | 11.7 | 2.6 |
| Spain | 8 150 | 90.8 | 12.7 | 74.2 | 5.0 | 5.3 |
| Sweden | 8 635 | 96.3 | 11.5 | 85.8 | 4.4 | 6.2 |
| Switzerland | 9 830 | 109.6 | 37.5 | 66.7 | 8.0 | 4.8 |
| Turkey | 6 928 | 77.2 | 40.8 | 35.8 | 5.9 | 0.7 |
| United Kingdom | 11 156 | 124.4 | 23.5 | 97.8 | 8.6 | 6.1 |
| United States | 11 186 | 124.7 | 29.1 | 94.0 | 12.7 | 7.7 |
| **OECD average** | **8 971** | **100.0** | **33.0** | **68.1** | **7.2** | **3.8** |
| **Partners** | | | | | | |
| Argentina | 10 197 | 113.7 | 53.2 | 58.4 | 12.2 | 1.6 |
| Azerbaijan | 3 106 | 34.6 | 17.9 | 18.1 | 1.4 | 0.4 |
| Brazil | 7 970 | 88.8 | 41.4 | 46.6 | 8.2 | 0.6 |
| Bulgaria | 11 352 | 126.5 | 69.6 | 59.4 | 16.4 | 1.0 |
| Chile | 8 446 | 94.1 | 53.0 | 52.2 | 14.2 | 0.8 |
| Colombia | 7 200 | 80.3 | 25.2 | 57.0 | 7.5 | 1.3 |
| Croatia | 7 356 | 82.0 | 33.8 | 50.0 | 6.0 | 1.3 |
| Estonia | 6 986 | 77.9 | 16.0 | 61.5 | 3.8 | 2.9 |
| Hong Kong-China | 8 381 | 93.4 | 34.1 | 58.3 | 3.6 | 0.6 |
| Indonesia | 4 909 | 54.7 | 19.4 | 25.4 | 0.7 | 0.0 |
| Israel | 12 299 | 137.1 | 44.4 | 96.1 | 9.9 | 4.1 |
| Jordan | 7 989 | 89.1 | 19.7 | 67.5 | 5.1 | 3.3 |
| Kyrgyzstan | 6 991 | 77.9 | 30.7 | 48.3 | 3.0 | 0.2 |
| Latvia | 7 056 | 78.7 | 14.5 | 64.2 | 4.3 | 3.1 |
| Liechtenstein | 9 330 | 104.0 | c | c | c | c |
| Lithuania | 8 082 | 90.1 | 25.5 | 65.4 | 9.0 | 3.8 |
| Macao-China | 6 095 | 67.9 | 19.2 | 55.0 | 1.0 | 0.3 |
| Montenegro | 6 390 | 71.2 | 20.2 | 50.8 | 3.5 | 0.8 |
| Qatar | 7 012 | 78.2 | 47.3 | 41.9 | c | c |
| Romania | 6 585 | 73.4 | 35.5 | 37.7 | 6.8 | 1.0 |
| Russian Federation | 8 023 | 89.4 | 24.1 | 66.9 | 4.6 | 2.2 |
| Serbia | 7 224 | 80.5 | 34.3 | 48.7 | 6.6 | 1.0 |
| Slovenia | 9 628 | 107.3 | 64.8 | 42.8 | 6.2 | 0.3 |
| Chinese Taipei | 8 889 | 99.1 | 45.8 | 51.7 | 6.0 | 1.0 |
| Thailand | 5 958 | 66.4 | 25.6 | 43.6 | 7.7 | 0.4 |
| Tunisia | 6 768 | 75.4 | 32.3 | 43.9 | 3.0 | 0.2 |
| Uruguay | 8 887 | 99.1 | 39.6 | 57.7 | 11.8 | 1.9 |

1. The variance components were estimated for all students in participating countries with data on socio-economic background and study programmes.
2. The total variance in student performance is calculated from the square of the standard deviation for the students used in the analysis. The statistical variance in student performance and not the standard deviation is used for this comparison to allow for the decomposition.
3. The sum of the between- and within-school variance components, as an estimate from a sample, does not necessarily add up to the total.
4. In some countries, sub-units within schools were sampled instead of schools and this may affect the estimation of the between-school variance components (see Annex A2).
5. This index is often referred to as the intra-class correlation (rho).
**StatLink** http://dx.doi.org/10.1787/142104560611

Pour consulter la version française intégrale de ce tableau, suivre ce lien :
**StatLink** http://dx.doi.org/10.1787/152684743050

[Part 2/2]

**Table 4.1a** Between-school and within-school variance in student performance on the science scale in PISA 2006

*Tableau 4.1a* Variance inter- et intra-établissements des scores sur l'échelle de culture scientifique du cycle PISA 2006

| | Variance expressed as a percentage of the average variance in student performance (SP) across OECD countries[1] | | | | | | Total variance between schools expressed as a percentage of the total variance within the country[5] |
| | Variance explained by the PISA index of economic, social and cultural status of students and schools | | Variance explained by students' study programmes | | Variance explained by students' study programmes and the PISA index of economic, social and cultural status of students and schools | | |
| | Between-school variance explained | Within-school variance explained | Between-school variance explained | Within-school variance explained | Between-school variance explained | Within-school variance explained | |
|---|---|---|---|---|---|---|---|
| **OECD** | | | | | | | |
| Australia | 12.5 | 4.4 | 1.9 | 3.9 | 13.0 | 7.9 | 17.9 |
| Austria | 40.1 | 0.6 | 45.2 | 0.3 | 49.5 | 0.8 | 57.0 |
| Belgium | 40.7 | 2.0 | 45.4 | 12.7 | 50.6 | 13.3 | 52.3 |
| Canada | 7.1 | 3.2 | 2.0 | 3.2 | 7.2 | 5.9 | 18.4 |
| Czech Republic | 43.5 | 1.8 | 50.2 | 0.4 | 52.2 | 2.0 | 57.8 |
| Denmark | 8.2 | 8.3 | 1.6 | 0.1 | 8.6 | 8.4 | 15.4 |
| Finland | 1.3 | 5.5 | 0.0 | 0.0 | 1.3 | 5.5 | 5.8 |
| France | w | w | w | w | w | w | w |
| Germany | 49.4 | 1.4 | 56.0 | 2.0 | 58.1 | 3.3 | 59.9 |
| Greece | 29.1 | 1.8 | 37.3 | 0.0 | 41.7 | 1.7 | 51.7 |
| Hungary | 47.5 | 0.2 | 46.2 | 0.0 | 51.6 | 0.3 | 70.4 |
| Iceland | 0.2 | 6.3 | 1.8 | 0.3 | 2.0 | 6.6 | 9.0 |
| Ireland | 11.4 | 5.0 | 1.1 | 3.6 | 11.4 | 8.3 | 17.0 |
| Italy | 27.6 | 0.5 | 26.4 | 0.1 | 31.9 | 0.5 | 52.1 |
| Japan | 29.0 | 0.1 | 9.7 | 0.0 | 30.2 | 0.1 | 48.5 |
| Korea | 16.9 | 0.4 | 15.2 | 0.4 | 20.9 | 0.8 | 35.3 |
| Luxembourg | 27.3 | 6.0 | 26.4 | 22.0 | 28.1 | 23.9 | 29.2 |
| Mexico | 13.3 | 0.4 | 9.1 | 0.0 | 16.8 | 0.4 | 35.3 |
| Netherlands | 41.1 | 0.8 | 55.7 | 8.8 | 56.3 | 9.1 | 58.9 |
| New Zealand | 14.9 | 10.2 | 0.2 | 1.9 | 14.9 | 11.7 | 15.9 |
| Norway | 3.7 | 5.2 | 0.8 | 0.1 | 4.0 | 5.2 | 9.9 |
| Poland | 5.8 | 8.7 | 1.0 | 0.5 | 6.0 | 8.9 | 13.6 |
| Portugal | 14.7 | 3.6 | 20.7 | 11.9 | 23.6 | 13.6 | 31.9 |
| Slovak Republic | 23.3 | 2.5 | 23.2 | 1.3 | 29.4 | 3.6 | 42.4 |
| Spain | 6.2 | 5.4 | 0.0 | 0.1 | 6.2 | 5.5 | 13.9 |
| Sweden | 6.1 | 6.1 | 4.2 | 0.0 | 6.7 | 5.9 | 12.0 |
| Switzerland | 17.0 | 4.8 | 5.9 | 1.0 | 18.0 | 5.6 | 34.2 |
| Turkey | 24.3 | 0.7 | 23.9 | 0.2 | 29.6 | 0.9 | 52.8 |
| United Kingdom | 14.8 | 6.4 | 0.6 | 1.2 | 14.9 | 7.4 | 18.9 |
| United States | 18.9 | 7.7 | 5.8 | 4.3 | 20.8 | 10.7 | 23.3 |
| **OECD average** | **20.5** | **3.8** | **17.8** | **2.8** | **24.3** | **6.1** | |
| **Partners** | | | | | | | |
| Argentina | 31.4 | 1.6 | 26.2 | 5.2 | 40.4 | 6.6 | 46.8 |
| Azerbaijan | 2.5 | 0.4 | 0.8 | 0.2 | 3.1 | 0.5 | 51.8 |
| Brazil | 24.1 | 0.7 | 14.5 | 3.8 | 28.7 | 4.5 | 46.6 |
| Bulgaria | 47.5 | 0.9 | 23.6 | 0.2 | 48.2 | 1.2 | 55.0 |
| Chile | 38.8 | 0.7 | 14.6 | 0.7 | 42.6 | 1.5 | 56.3 |
| Colombia | 14.1 | 1.4 | 6.5 | 6.6 | 15.0 | 7.3 | 31.3 |
| Croatia | 20.4 | 1.3 | 25.7 | 8.2 | 26.4 | 8.5 | 41.3 |
| Estonia | 6.5 | 2.9 | 0.1 | 0.5 | 6.4 | 3.3 | 20.5 |
| Hong Kong-China | 13.6 | 0.6 | 8.3 | 4.9 | 16.4 | 5.0 | 36.5 |
| Indonesia | 8.0 | 0.0 | 4.7 | 0.0 | 9.0 | 0.0 | 35.5 |
| Israel | 20.0 | 4.1 | 5.4 | 0.8 | 21.7 | 4.8 | 32.4 |
| Jordan | 7.8 | 3.3 | 0.0 | 0.0 | 7.8 | 3.3 | 22.1 |
| Kyrgyzstan | 17.4 | 0.2 | 0.0 | 1.0 | 17.0 | 1.1 | 39.4 |
| Latvia | 6.7 | 3.1 | 0.6 | 1.6 | 6.8 | 4.5 | 18.4 |
| Liechtenstein | c | c | c | c | c | c | c |
| Lithuania | 15.0 | 3.9 | 12.2 | 0.5 | 17.5 | 4.3 | 28.3 |
| Macao-China | 2.2 | 0.3 | 7.7 | 8.5 | 7.8 | 8.7 | 28.3 |
| Montenegro | 12.0 | 0.9 | 15.4 | 5.0 | 16.4 | 5.2 | 28.3 |
| Qatar | c | c | 17.6 | 0.6 | c | c | 60.5 |
| Romania | 19.8 | 1.0 | 19.5 | 0.0 | 25.2 | 1.0 | 48.3 |
| Russian Federation | 8.2 | 2.2 | 5.0 | 4.1 | 9.4 | 5.5 | 27.0 |
| Serbia | 22.9 | 1.0 | 22.2 | 3.2 | 25.5 | 3.7 | 42.6 |
| Slovenia | 46.2 | 0.3 | 52.0 | 0.1 | 54.3 | 0.4 | 60.4 |
| Chinese Taipei | 26.4 | 1.0 | 23.2 | 1.3 | 30.7 | 2.2 | 46.2 |
| Thailand | 18.0 | 0.6 | 7.4 | 1.3 | 19.4 | 1.9 | 38.5 |
| Tunisia | 12.6 | 0.2 | 25.0 | 2.1 | 26.5 | 2.2 | 42.8 |
| Uruguay | 23.9 | 2.0 | 26.3 | 2.6 | 32.8 | 4.2 | 39.9 |

1. The variance components were estimated for all students in participating countries with data on socio-economic background and study programmes.
2. The total variance in student performance is calculated from the square of the standard deviation for the students used in the analysis. The statistical variance in student performance and not the standard deviation is used for this comparison to allow for the decomposition.
3. The sum of the between- and within-school variance components, as an estimate from a sample, does not necessarily add up to the total.
4. In some countries, sub-units within schools were sampled instead of schools and this may affect the estimation of the between-school variance components (see Annex A2).
5. This index is often referred to as the intra-class correlation (rho).
*StatLink* ᘍ᠍᠍ http://dx.doi.org/10.1787/142104560611

Pour consulter la version française intégrale de ce tableau, suivre ce lien :
*StatLink* ᘍ᠍᠍ http://dx.doi.org/10.1787/152684743050

[Part 1/1]

**Table 4.1b** Between-school and within-school variance in student performance on the science scale in PISA 2003

Tableau 4.1b  Variance inter- et intra-établissements des scores sur l'échelle de culture scientifique du cycle PISA 2003

| | Total variance in SP[2] | Variance expressed as a percentage of the average variance in student performance (SP) across OECD countries[1] | | | | | | | | | | | Total variance between schools expressed as a percentage of the total variance within the country[5] |
|---|---|---|---|---|---|---|---|---|---|---|---|---|---|
| | | Total variance in SP expressed as a percentage of the average variance in student performance across OECD countries[3] | Total variance in SP between schools[4] | Total variance in SP within schools | Variance explained by the PISA index of economic, social and cultural status of students | | Variance explained by the PISA index of economic, social and cultural status of students and schools | | Variance explained by students' study programmes | | Variance explained by students' study programmes and the PISA index of economic, social and cultural status of students and schools | | |
| | | | | | Between-school variance explained | Within-school variance explained | Between-school variance explained | Within-school variance explained | Between-school variance explained | Within-school variance explained | Between-school variance explained | Within-school variance explained | |
| **OECD** | | | | | | | | | | | | | |
| Australia | 10 283 | 103.4 | 20.5 | 82.4 | 9.2 | 4.9 | 14.6 | 5.0 | 1.3 | 2.4 | 15.5 | 7.1 | 19.9 |
| Austria | 9 146 | 91.9 | 51.6 | 44.8 | 8.2 | 0.7 | 35.8 | 0.5 | 41.0 | 0.0 | 44.4 | 0.8 | 56.1 |
| Belgium | 10 308 | 103.6 | 43.6 | 61.2 | 15.5 | 4.1 | 34.2 | 4.2 | 31.6 | 11.8 | 36.7 | 13.3 | 42.1 |
| Canada | 9 845 | 99.0 | 15.3 | 82.3 | 5.0 | 5.6 | 7.0 | 5.6 | 3.0 | 5.2 | 7.3 | 9.9 | 15.5 |
| Czech Republic | 9 746 | 98.0 | 39.9 | 62.5 | 11.9 | 2.2 | 29.7 | 2.3 | 17.3 | 0.0 | 33.0 | 2.2 | 40.8 |
| Denmark | 10 263 | 103.2 | 12.8 | 91.3 | 7.4 | 9.9 | 8.8 | 9.9 | 1.2 | 0.2 | 9.0 | 10.1 | 12.4 |
| Finland | 8 209 | 82.5 | 3.5 | 79.0 | 0.7 | 7.5 | 0.7 | 7.5 | 0.0 | 0.0 | 0.7 | 7.5 | 4.3 |
| France | w | w | w | w | w | w | w | w | w | w | w | w | w |
| Germany | 11 004 | 110.6 | 56.3 | 55.3 | 17.5 | 3.6 | 44.7 | 3.7 | 1.8 | 0.1 | 44.7 | 3.8 | 50.9 |
| Greece | 10 069 | 101.2 | 27.2 | 75.3 | 8.5 | 2.1 | 19.0 | 2.1 | 20.0 | 0.1 | 23.7 | 2.2 | 26.9 |
| Hungary | 8 795 | 88.4 | 36.4 | 52.8 | 8.5 | 0.5 | 31.0 | 0.5 | 26.6 | 0.0 | 32.2 | 0.6 | 41.2 |
| Iceland | 9 077 | 91.2 | 3.6 | 87.6 | 0.8 | 5.2 | 0.8 | 5.3 | 0.0 | 0.0 | 0.8 | 5.3 | 3.9 |
| Ireland | 8 592 | 86.4 | 13.4 | 73.8 | 8.5 | 7.2 | 11.4 | 7.4 | 1.5 | 4.0 | 11.5 | 10.8 | 15.5 |
| Italy | 11 611 | 116.7 | 57.1 | 61.8 | 7.7 | 0.8 | 33.5 | 0.9 | 22.6 | 0.0 | 36.0 | 0.9 | 48.9 |
| Japan | 11 892 | 119.5 | 55.4 | 65.0 | 4.4 | 0.2 | 36.4 | 0.2 | 4.4 | 0.0 | 37.1 | 0.2 | 46.3 |
| Korea | 10 089 | 101.4 | 38.9 | 63.2 | 5.8 | 0.7 | 23.1 | 0.7 | 20.3 | 0.6 | 27.2 | 1.2 | 38.3 |
| Luxembourg | 10 538 | 105.9 | 30.5 | 75.5 | 10.5 | 4.0 | 27.5 | 4.0 | 9.0 | 7.4 | 27.2 | 10.0 | 28.8 |
| Mexico | 7 524 | 75.6 | 19.5 | 48.9 | 4.5 | 0.6 | 11.6 | 0.8 | 7.0 | 0.0 | 13.9 | 0.8 | 25.7 |
| Netherlands | 9 366 | 94.1 | 52.5 | 43.6 | 8.2 | 1.1 | 40.3 | 1.1 | 48.7 | 3.6 | 50.0 | 4.6 | 55.8 |
| New Zealand | 10 658 | 107.1 | 18.8 | 89.1 | 9.4 | 8.6 | 14.3 | 8.7 | 0.6 | 2.9 | 14.3 | 11.1 | 17.6 |
| Norway | 10 717 | 107.7 | 8.2 | 99.5 | 3.0 | 10.9 | 3.3 | 10.9 | 0.1 | 0.1 | 3.3 | 10.9 | 7.6 |
| Poland | 10 472 | 105.3 | 14.9 | 90.9 | 8.9 | 9.8 | 10.5 | 10.0 | 1.0 | 0.1 | 10.7 | 10.0 | 14.1 |
| Portugal | 8 687 | 87.3 | 27.3 | 61.6 | 8.1 | 3.9 | 14.9 | 3.9 | 23.4 | 7.6 | 25.2 | 9.9 | 31.2 |
| Slovak Republic | 9 496 | 95.5 | 34.8 | 60.4 | 11.4 | 2.8 | 27.3 | 2.8 | 22.9 | 0.1 | 28.7 | 3.0 | 36.4 |
| Spain | 9 982 | 100.3 | 16.7 | 80.7 | 6.3 | 4.9 | 8.9 | 4.9 | 0.0 | 1.1 | 7.4 | 5.5 | 16.6 |
| Sweden | 11 291 | 113.5 | 10.0 | 103.8 | 4.5 | 11.7 | 5.3 | 11.7 | 1.3 | 0.6 | 6.2 | 12.1 | 8.9 |
| Switzerland | 11 439 | 115.0 | 33.1 | 77.1 | 10.8 | 7.2 | 19.4 | 7.3 | 5.5 | 0.9 | 19.7 | 8.0 | 28.7 |
| Turkey | 9 174 | 92.2 | 47.5 | 42.4 | 7.8 | 0.6 | 33.6 | 0.6 | 9.0 | 0.1 | 34.1 | 0.6 | 51.6 |
| United Kingdom | m | m | m | m | m | m | m | m | m | m | m | m | m |
| United States | 10 271 | 103.2 | 22.8 | 80.3 | 11.1 | 7.2 | 16.1 | 7.4 | 2.0 | 1.7 | 16.2 | 8.5 | 22.1 |
| **OECD average** | **9 948** | **100.0** | **29.0** | **71.1** | **8.0** | **4.6** | **20.1** | **4.6** | **11.5** | **1.8** | **22.0** | **6.1** | |
| **Partners** | | | | | | | | | | | | | |
| Brazil | 9 702 | 97.5 | 32.4 | 60.5 | 4.2 | 0.0 | 19.1 | 0.1 | 12.6 | 2.3 | 24.6 | 2.4 | 33.3 |
| Hong Kong-China | 8 764 | 88.1 | 39.1 | 47.0 | 2.5 | 0.2 | 16.1 | 0.2 | 12.0 | 2.9 | 21.5 | 3.0 | 44.4 |
| Indonesia | 4 633 | 46.6 | 16.1 | 27.5 | 1.3 | 0.1 | 7.4 | 0.1 | 3.8 | 0.0 | 7.9 | 0.1 | 34.6 |
| Latvia | 8 554 | 86.0 | 17.5 | 69.7 | 4.6 | 4.0 | 7.3 | 4.0 | 0.5 | 0.9 | 7.3 | 4.7 | 20.3 |
| Liechtenstein | 10 694 | 107.5 | c | c | c | c | c | c | c | c | c | c | c |
| Macao-China | 7 724 | 77.6 | 13.6 | 67.0 | 0.6 | 0.1 | 2.6 | 0.1 | 4.7 | 5.1 | 6.2 | 5.1 | 17.6 |
| Russian Federation | 9 945 | 100.0 | 20.9 | 78.9 | 5.3 | 2.9 | 10.0 | 2.8 | 3.6 | 2.1 | 10.6 | 4.4 | 20.9 |
| Thailand | 6 622 | 66.6 | 22.0 | 46.6 | 6.3 | 0.6 | 13.7 | 0.7 | 4.7 | 1.2 | 14.9 | 1.9 | 33.0 |
| Tunisia | 7 622 | 76.6 | 25.7 | 50.9 | 2.4 | 0.1 | 12.0 | 0.1 | 20.3 | 1.4 | 21.1 | 1.6 | 33.5 |
| Uruguay | 11 872 | 119.3 | 41.0 | 83.9 | 12.6 | 1.7 | 28.5 | 2.0 | 29.9 | 1.6 | 36.0 | 3.6 | 34.3 |

1. The variance components were estimated for all students in participating countries with data on socio-economic background and study programmes. Students in special education programmes were excluded from these analyses.
2. The total variance in student performance is calculated from the square of the standard deviation for the students used in the analysis. The statistical variance in student performance and not the standard deviation is used for this comparison to allow for the decomposition.
3. The sum of the between- and within-school variance components, as an estimate from a sample, does not necessarily add up to the total.
4. In some countries, sub-units within schools were sampled instead of schools and this may affect the estimation of the between-school variance components (see Annex A2).
5. This index is often referred to as the intra-class correlation (rho).
StatLink ▄▆▊ http://dx.doi.org/10.1787/142104560611

Pour consulter la version française intégrale de ce tableau, suivre ce lien :
StatLink ▄▆▊ http://dx.doi.org/10.1787/152684743050

[Part 1/1]

**Table 4.1c** **Between-school and within-school variance in student performance on the science scale in PISA 2000**

Tableau 4.1c  Variance inter- et intra-établissements des scores sur l'échelle de culture scientifique du cycle PISA 2000

| | Total variance in SP[2] | Variance expressed as a percentage of the average variance in student performance (SP) across OECD countries[1] | | | | | | | |
|---|---|---|---|---|---|---|---|---|---|
| | | Total variance in SP expressed as a percentage of the average variance in student performance across OECD countries[3] | Total variance in SP between schools[4] | Total variance in SP within schools | Variance explained by the PISA index of economic, social and cultural status of students | | Variance explained by the PISA index of economic, social and cultural status of students and schools | | Total variance between schools expressed as a percentage of the total variance within the country[5] |
| | | | | | Between-school variance explained | Within-school variance explained | Between-school variance explained | Within-school variance explained | |
| **OECD** Australia | 8 866 | 101.1 | 17.0 | 83.7 | 8.7 | 5.3 | 11.5 | 5.8 | 16.8 |
| Austria | 8 548 | 97.5 | 56.4 | 49.1 | 8.6 | 0.4 | 36.9 | 0.5 | 57.8 |
| Belgium | 10 897 | 124.3 | 65.0 | 64.2 | 15.3 | 2.7 | 43.5 | 2.8 | 52.3 |
| Canada | 7 830 | 89.3 | 14.4 | 73.9 | 4.3 | 5.2 | 5.6 | 5.4 | 16.1 |
| Czech Republic | 7 968 | 90.9 | 32.8 | 59.2 | 11.4 | 3.1 | 22.7 | 3.2 | 36.0 |
| Denmark | 10 391 | 118.5 | 17.2 | 102.1 | 7.8 | 12.3 | 10.1 | 12.5 | 14.5 |
| Finland | 7 351 | 83.9 | 4.1 | 79.7 | 0.7 | 5.2 | 0.7 | 5.2 | 4.9 |
| France | w | w | w | w | w | w | w | w | w |
| Germany | 9 791 | 111.7 | 54.2 | 59.4 | 16.3 | 2.9 | 43.9 | 3.1 | 48.5 |
| Greece | 9 382 | 107.0 | 43.1 | 64.7 | 6.4 | 0.8 | 21.3 | 0.8 | 40.3 |
| Hungary | 9 871 | 112.6 | 52.5 | 58.1 | 11.2 | 0.3 | 43.4 | 0.4 | 46.6 |
| Iceland | 7 660 | 87.4 | 6.3 | 81.2 | 1.5 | 3.1 | 1.7 | 3.1 | 7.2 |
| Ireland | 8 365 | 95.4 | 13.6 | 82.3 | 6.8 | 5.6 | 10.0 | 5.9 | 14.3 |
| Italy | 9 569 | 109.2 | 48.6 | 64.9 | 5.9 | 0.5 | 23.2 | 0.5 | 44.5 |
| Japan | m | m | m | m | m | m | m | m | m |
| Korea | 6 508 | 74.2 | 29.4 | 45.9 | 2.9 | 0.1 | 15.7 | 0.1 | 39.6 |
| Luxembourg | m | m | m | m | m | m | m | m | m |
| Mexico | 5 947 | 67.8 | 27.5 | 39.9 | 6.4 | 0.1 | 18.4 | 0.2 | 40.5 |
| Netherlands | m | m | m | m | m | m | m | m | m |
| New Zealand | 9 868 | 112.6 | 19.2 | 93.2 | 9.8 | 8.1 | 13.9 | 8.4 | 17.1 |
| Norway | 8 969 | 102.3 | 9.1 | 93.3 | 3.1 | 10.4 | 3.3 | 10.4 | 8.9 |
| Poland | 9 059 | 103.3 | 50.7 | 51.7 | 4.6 | 0.0 | 31.1 | 0.1 | 49.1 |
| Portugal | 7 837 | 89.4 | 27.2 | 60.6 | 8.6 | 2.8 | 17.4 | 2.8 | 30.4 |
| Spain | 9 042 | 103.1 | 17.5 | 86.2 | 9.9 | 5.8 | 11.8 | 6.0 | 17.0 |
| Sweden | 8 650 | 98.7 | 7.7 | 91.1 | 3.4 | 5.9 | 4.5 | 5.9 | 7.8 |
| Switzerland | 10 018 | 114.3 | 45.8 | 64.2 | 13.2 | 6.2 | 25.2 | 6.1 | 40.1 |
| United Kingdom | m | m | m | m | m | m | m | m | m |
| United States | 9 226 | 105.3 | 34.5 | 72.2 | 15.9 | 5.4 | 27.2 | 5.7 | 32.8 |
| **OECD average** | **8 766** | **100.0** | **30.2** | **70.5** | **7.9** | **4.0** | **19.3** | **4.1** | |
| **Partners** Argentina | 11 458 | 130.7 | 57.1 | 74.7 | 11.4 | 0.2 | 37.0 | 0.5 | 43.7 |
| Brazil | 8 153 | 93.0 | 27.8 | 66.7 | 10.5 | 0.6 | 17.3 | 1.7 | 29.9 |
| Bulgaria | 8 859 | 101.1 | 42.5 | 63.7 | 14.4 | 1.0 | 34.6 | 1.3 | 42.1 |
| Chile | 8 869 | 101.2 | 41.2 | 64.6 | 14.1 | 1.0 | 28.4 | 1.1 | 40.7 |
| Hong Kong-China | 7 135 | 81.4 | 35.9 | 44.8 | 4.2 | 0.6 | 16.2 | 0.7 | 44.1 |
| Indonesia | 5 520 | 63.0 | 19.4 | 39.2 | 1.1 | 0.0 | 6.7 | 0.1 | 30.8 |
| Israel | 14 913 | 170.1 | 58.2 | 109.1 | 16.2 | 3.6 | 34.9 | 4.1 | 34.2 |
| Latvia | 9 461 | 107.9 | 31.7 | 76.5 | 6.6 | 1.6 | 17.3 | 1.7 | 29.4 |
| Liechtenstein | 8 806 | 100.5 | c | c | c | c | c | c | c |
| Romania | 8 879 | 101.3 | 36.4 | 66.8 | 0.9 | 0.0 | 15.3 | 0.0 | 35.9 |
| Russian Federation | 9 782 | 111.6 | 34.4 | 76.6 | 5.3 | 1.6 | 13.1 | 1.5 | 30.8 |
| Thailand | 5 870 | 67.0 | 20.2 | 47.4 | 3.0 | 0.0 | 9.9 | 0.1 | 30.2 |

1. The variance components were estimated for all students in participating countries with data on socio-economic background and study programmes. Students in special education programmes were excluded from these analyses.
2. The total variance in student performance is calculated from the square of the standard deviation for the students used in the analysis. The statistical variance in student performance and not the standard deviation is used for this comparison to allow for the decomposition.
3. The sum of the between- and within-school variance components, as an estimate from a sample, does not necessarily add up to the total.
4. In some countries, sub-units within schools were sampled instead of schools and this may affect the estimation of the between-school variance components (see Annex A2).
5. This index is often referred to as the intra-class correlation (rho).
*StatLink* ᘖᔢ http://dx.doi.org/10.1787/142104560611

Pour consulter la version française intégrale de ce tableau, suivre ce lien :
*StatLink* ᘖᔢ http://dx.doi.org/10.1787/152684743050

[Part 1/2]

### Table 4.1d   Between-school and within-school variance in student performance on the reading scale in PISA 2006

Variance inter- et intra-établissements des scores sur l'échelle de compréhension de l'écrit du cycle PISA 2006

| | Total variance in SP[2] | Variance expressed as a percentage of the average variance in student performance (SP) across OECD countries[1] | | | | |
| | | Total variance in SP expressed as a percentage of the average variance in student performance across OECD countries[3] | Total variance in SP between schools[4] | Total variance in SP within schools | Variance explained by the PISA index of economic, social and cultural status of students | |
| | | | | | Between-school variance explained | Within-school variance explained |
|---|---|---|---|---|---|---|
| **OECD** | | | | | | |
| Australia | 8 687 | 89.4 | 18.8 | 71.9 | 7.0 | 3.5 |
| Austria | 11 667 | 120.1 | 70.3 | 54.8 | 5.3 | 0.2 |
| Belgium | 11 853 | 122.0 | 66.9 | 57.2 | 9.9 | 1.3 |
| Canada | 9 142 | 94.1 | 21.6 | 72.6 | 4.8 | 3.5 |
| Czech Republic | 12 332 | 127.0 | 75.0 | 59.1 | 9.4 | 0.7 |
| Denmark | 7 844 | 80.8 | 15.8 | 67.0 | 4.8 | 4.6 |
| Finland | 6 575 | 67.7 | 6.5 | 61.3 | 1.5 | 3.7 |
| France | w | w | w | w | w | w |
| Germany | 12 245 | 126.1 | 100.5 | 48.0 | 8.5 | 0.6 |
| Greece | 10 449 | 107.6 | 56.2 | 59.5 | 7.1 | 0.5 |
| Hungary | 8 846 | 91.1 | 74.0 | 34.6 | 3.5 | 0.0 |
| Iceland | 9 143 | 94.1 | 11.6 | 85.0 | 0.9 | 3.8 |
| Ireland | 8 426 | 86.7 | 20.1 | 67.3 | 6.5 | 3.7 |
| Italy | 11 683 | 120.3 | 63.5 | 58.7 | 2.1 | 0.0 |
| Japan | 10 132 | 104.3 | 54.0 | 55.0 | 2.4 | 0.1 |
| Korea | 7 790 | 80.2 | 33.0 | 48.7 | 2.1 | 0.1 |
| Luxembourg | 10 015 | 103.1 | 28.9 | 71.8 | 11.2 | 5.6 |
| Mexico | 9 147 | 94.2 | 33.9 | 48.8 | 3.9 | 0.2 |
| Netherlands | 9 248 | 95.2 | 57.3 | 35.0 | 4.1 | 0.3 |
| New Zealand | 10 749 | 110.7 | 20.3 | 91.7 | 8.0 | 8.8 |
| Norway | 10 687 | 110.0 | 13.4 | 96.5 | 3.1 | 5.3 |
| Poland | 9 985 | 102.8 | 16.2 | 87.9 | 6.5 | 8.2 |
| Portugal | 9 731 | 100.2 | 35.4 | 64.1 | 11.0 | 4.2 |
| Slovak Republic | 11 009 | 113.3 | 57.0 | 58.3 | 9.2 | 1.3 |
| Spain | 7 827 | 80.6 | 13.0 | 63.7 | 3.7 | 3.0 |
| Sweden | 9 362 | 96.4 | 17.0 | 81.0 | 4.6 | 4.2 |
| Switzerland | 8 776 | 90.3 | 31.7 | 53.9 | 6.0 | 2.8 |
| Turkey | 8 559 | 88.1 | 41.8 | 44.5 | 4.7 | 0.4 |
| United Kingdom | 10 071 | 103.7 | 21.9 | 78.5 | 6.4 | 3.8 |
| United States | m | m | m | m | m | m |
| **OECD average** | **9 714** | **100.0** | **38.4** | **63.4** | **5.6** | **2.6** |
| **Partners** | | | | | | |
| Argentina | 15 354 | 158.1 | 71.0 | 84.9 | 10.3 | 0.8 |
| Azerbaijan | 4 943 | 50.9 | 24.3 | 29.1 | 2.3 | 0.2 |
| Brazil | 10 486 | 107.9 | 47.0 | 55.3 | 6.5 | 0.2 |
| Bulgaria | 13 721 | 141.3 | 81.4 | 64.2 | 15.1 | 0.7 |
| Chile | 10 678 | 109.9 | 62.1 | 63.2 | 12.2 | 0.4 |
| Colombia | 11 631 | 119.7 | 35.8 | 83.0 | 9.3 | 1.8 |
| Croatia | 7 887 | 81.2 | 39.1 | 43.7 | 4.1 | 0.5 |
| Estonia | 7 142 | 73.5 | 22.7 | 50.1 | 3.2 | 1.6 |
| Hong Kong-China | 6 677 | 68.7 | 26.8 | 41.5 | 2.2 | 0.3 |
| Indonesia | 5 596 | 57.6 | 25.0 | 24.5 | 0.5 | 0.0 |
| Israel | 14 072 | 144.9 | 58.5 | 91.9 | 8.3 | 3.0 |
| Jordan | 8 720 | 89.8 | 26.5 | 61.0 | 5.3 | 3.4 |
| Kyrgyzstan | 10 395 | 107.0 | 44.5 | 63.5 | 5.6 | 0.8 |
| Latvia | 8 171 | 84.1 | 22.3 | 62.7 | 4.5 | 2.2 |
| Liechtenstein | 8 740 | 90.0 | c | c | c | c |
| Lithuania | 9 087 | 93.5 | 27.3 | 67.5 | 8.8 | 3.5 |
| Macao-China | 5 843 | 60.2 | 17.4 | 48.0 | 0.7 | 0.3 |
| Montenegro | 8 052 | 82.9 | 27.9 | 57.9 | 3.1 | 0.4 |
| Qatar | 11 731 | 120.8 | 71.9 | 61.7 | c | c |
| Romania | 8 423 | 86.7 | 47.9 | 41.6 | 2.5 | 0.0 |
| Russian Federation | 8 692 | 89.5 | 32.1 | 60.7 | 5.2 | 1.6 |
| Serbia | 8 405 | 86.5 | 40.5 | 48.8 | 7.2 | 1.0 |
| Slovenia | 7 735 | 79.6 | 68.4 | 25.5 | 3.4 | 0.1 |
| Chinese Taipei | 7 076 | 72.8 | 32.7 | 38.7 | 4.9 | 1.0 |
| Thailand | 6 701 | 69.0 | 29.6 | 41.1 | 5.5 | 0.2 |
| Tunisia | 9 448 | 97.3 | 47.7 | 53.4 | 2.1 | 0.0 |
| Uruguay | 14 703 | 151.4 | 62.4 | 87.8 | 12.4 | 1.2 |

1. The variance components were estimated for all students in participating countries with data on socio-economic background and study programmes.
2. The total variance in student performance is calculated from the square of the standard deviation for the students used in the analysis. The statistical variance in student performance and not the standard deviation is used for this comparison to allow for the decomposition.
3. The sum of the between- and within-school variance components, as an estimate from a sample, does not necessarily add up to the total.
4. In some countries, sub-units within schools were sampled instead of schools and this may affect the estimation of the between-school variance components (see Annex A2).
5. This index is often referred to as the intra-class correlation (rho).
StatLink ⟐ http://dx.doi.org/10.1787/142104560611

Pour consulter la version française intégrale de ce tableau, suivre ce lien :
StatLink ⟐ http://dx.doi.org/10.1787/152684743050

[Part 2/2]

## Table 4.1d  Between-school and within-school variance in student performance on the reading scale in PISA 2006

Variance inter- et intra-établissements des scores sur l'échelle de compréhension de l'écrit du cycle PISA 2006

| | Variance expressed as a percentage of the average variance in student performance (SP) across OECD countries[1] | | | | | | Total variance between schools expressed as a percentage of the total variance within the country[5] |
|---|---|---|---|---|---|---|---|
| | Variance explained by the PISA index of economic, social and cultural status of students and schools | | Variance explained by students' study programmes | | Variance explained by students' study programmes and the PISA index of economic, social and cultural status of students and schools | | |
| | Between-school variance explained | Within-school variance explained | Between-school variance explained | Within-school variance explained | Between-school variance explained | Within-school variance explained | |
| Australia | 11.8 | 3.5 | 1.2 | 3.7 | 11.9 | 6.8 | 21.1 |
| Austria | 41.7 | 0.2 | 54.1 | 1.2 | 56.2 | 1.3 | 58.5 |
| Belgium | 43.3 | 1.3 | 53.5 | 13.0 | 58.0 | 13.2 | 54.8 |
| Canada | 8.1 | 3.5 | 2.0 | 3.7 | 8.0 | 6.7 | 23.0 |
| Czech Republic | 47.3 | 0.9 | 59.8 | 0.3 | 61.2 | 1.0 | 59.1 |
| Denmark | 7.5 | 4.7 | 3.1 | 0.1 | 8.9 | 4.9 | 19.5 |
| Finland | 2.0 | 3.7 | 0.0 | 0.0 | 2.0 | 3.7 | 9.7 |
| France | w | w | w | w | w | w | w |
| Germany | 63.9 | 0.5 | 86.2 | 1.7 | 88.7 | 2.1 | 79.7 |
| Greece | 29.4 | 0.5 | 39.9 | 0.0 | 44.5 | 0.5 | 52.3 |
| Hungary | 53.6 | 0.0 | 53.7 | 0.0 | 60.1 | 0.0 | 81.2 |
| Iceland | 0.9 | 3.8 | 2.0 | 0.3 | 2.7 | 4.0 | 12.3 |
| Ireland | 11.5 | 3.7 | 0.8 | 3.5 | 11.4 | 7.0 | 23.2 |
| Italy | 32.0 | 0.1 | 35.0 | 0.1 | 38.7 | 0.1 | 52.8 |
| Japan | 30.1 | 0.1 | 10.4 | 0.0 | 30.9 | 0.1 | 51.8 |
| Korea | 14.6 | 0.1 | 13.1 | 0.5 | 18.2 | 0.6 | 41.1 |
| Luxembourg | 24.0 | 5.6 | 27.2 | 25.9 | 27.7 | 27.3 | 28.1 |
| Mexico | 15.9 | 0.2 | 12.3 | 0.0 | 21.1 | 0.3 | 36.0 |
| Netherlands | 34.8 | 0.3 | 50.8 | 7.8 | 51.1 | 7.9 | 60.2 |
| New Zealand | 10.9 | 8.8 | 0.0 | 2.2 | 10.7 | 10.5 | 18.4 |
| Norway | 4.1 | 5.3 | 0.8 | 0.0 | 4.4 | 5.2 | 12.9 |
| Poland | 7.4 | 8.3 | 1.2 | 0.6 | 7.6 | 8.5 | 15.8 |
| Portugal | 19.1 | 4.2 | 24.1 | 13.3 | 28.9 | 15.2 | 35.4 |
| Slovak Republic | 24.3 | 1.3 | 31.9 | 3.0 | 35.6 | 4.1 | 50.3 |
| Spain | 5.2 | 3.0 | 0.0 | 0.0 | 5.2 | 3.1 | 16.1 |
| Sweden | 7.9 | 4.0 | 4.4 | 0.0 | 5.6 | 6.6 | 17.7 |
| Switzerland | 15.2 | 2.7 | 4.3 | 0.6 | 15.7 | 3.2 | 35.1 |
| Turkey | 22.8 | 0.4 | 22.4 | 0.0 | 27.1 | 0.5 | 47.5 |
| United Kingdom | 12.3 | 4.0 | 0.8 | 1.7 | 12.4 | 5.6 | 21.2 |
| United States | m | m | m | m | m | m | m |
| **OECD average** | **21.5** | **2.7** | **21.2** | **3.0** | **26.9** | **5.4** | |
| Argentina | 35.0 | 0.8 | 32.7 | 6.1 | 47.9 | 6.8 | 44.9 |
| Azerbaijan | 8.6 | 0.2 | 0.5 | 0.4 | 8.8 | 0.6 | 47.8 |
| Brazil | 23.6 | 0.3 | 17.1 | 5.0 | 29.9 | 5.3 | 43.5 |
| Bulgaria | 52.8 | 0.6 | 27.1 | 0.6 | 53.6 | 1.1 | 57.7 |
| Chile | 40.8 | 0.4 | 18.4 | 0.8 | 47.0 | 1.2 | 56.5 |
| Colombia | 16.8 | 1.9 | 9.4 | 11.4 | 18.2 | 12.2 | 29.9 |
| Croatia | 21.9 | 0.5 | 28.0 | 8.3 | 29.1 | 8.3 | 48.1 |
| Estonia | 7.2 | 1.6 | 0.0 | 0.9 | 6.9 | 2.4 | 30.8 |
| Hong Kong-China | 9.6 | 0.3 | 6.2 | 3.0 | 11.9 | 3.1 | 38.9 |
| Indonesia | 10.1 | 0.0 | 6.5 | 0.0 | 11.8 | 0.0 | 43.3 |
| Israel | 18.7 | 3.0 | 8.3 | 0.5 | 24.2 | 3.4 | 40.4 |
| Jordan | 8.2 | 3.4 | 0.0 | 0.0 | 8.2 | 3.4 | 29.5 |
| Kyrgyzstan | 20.6 | 0.9 | 0.0 | 1.5 | 20.1 | 2.2 | 41.6 |
| Latvia | 8.9 | 2.1 | 2.6 | 2.0 | 11.6 | 4.0 | 26.6 |
| Liechtenstein | c | c | c | c | c | c | c |
| Lithuania | 15.3 | 3.5 | 11.4 | 0.5 | 17.1 | 4.0 | 29.2 |
| Macao-China | 1.1 | 0.3 | 5.2 | 6.6 | 5.2 | 6.8 | 29.0 |
| Montenegro | 17.0 | 0.4 | 21.2 | 6.5 | 22.3 | 6.5 | 33.6 |
| Qatar | c | c | 26.6 | 0.7 | c | c | 59.5 |
| Romania | 23.5 | 0.1 | 26.8 | 0.0 | 32.7 | 0.1 | 55.2 |
| Russian Federation | 12.2 | 1.6 | 5.5 | 4.5 | 12.8 | 5.4 | 35.9 |
| Serbia | 26.7 | 1.0 | 26.2 | 4.8 | 30.1 | 5.3 | 46.6 |
| Slovenia | 39.7 | 0.0 | 54.0 | 0.0 | 54.7 | 0.1 | 85.9 |
| Chinese Taipei | 18.9 | 1.0 | 15.3 | 0.5 | 21.8 | 1.5 | 44.9 |
| Thailand | 18.0 | 0.3 | 8.9 | 1.9 | 20.4 | 2.2 | 42.9 |
| Tunisia | 16.3 | 0.0 | 32.0 | 3.0 | 34.2 | 3.0 | 49.0 |
| Uruguay | 31.4 | 1.3 | 35.2 | 4.1 | 44.1 | 5.0 | 41.2 |

1. The variance components were estimated for all students in participating countries with data on socio-economic background and study programmes.
2. The total variance in student performance is calculated from the square of the standard deviation for the students used in the analysis. The statistical variance in student performance and not the standard deviation is used for this comparison to allow for the decomposition.
3. The sum of the between- and within-school variance components, as an estimate from a sample, does not necessarily add up to the total.
4. In some countries, sub-units within schools were sampled instead of schools and this may affect the estimation of the between-school variance components (see Annex A2).
5. This index is often referred to as the intra-class correlation (rho).
StatLink ⏍ http://dx.doi.org/10.1787/142104560611

Pour consulter la version française intégrale de ce tableau, suivre ce lien :
StatLink ⏍ http://dx.doi.org/10.1787/152684743050

[Part 1/1]

### Table 4.1e  Between-school and within-school variance in student performance on the reading scale in PISA 2003

Variance inter- et intra-établissements des scores sur l'échelle de compréhension de l'écrit du cycle PISA 2003

| | Total variance in SP[2] | Total variance in SP expressed as a percentage of the average variance in student performance across OECD countries[3] | Total variance in SP between schools[4] | Total variance in SP within schools | Variance explained by the PISA index of economic, social and cultural status of students | | Variance explained by the PISA index of economic, social and cultural status of students and schools | | Variance explained by students' study programmes | | Variance explained by students' study programmes and the PISA index of economic, social and cultural status of students and schools | | Total variance between schools expressed as a percentage of the total variance within the country[5] |
|---|---|---|---|---|---|---|---|---|---|---|---|---|---|
| | | | | | Between-school variance explained | Within-school variance explained | Between-school variance explained | Within-school variance explained | Between-school variance explained | Within-school variance explained | Between-school variance explained | Within-school variance explained | |
| **OECD** | | | | | | | | | | | | | |
| Australia | 9 345 | 103.8 | 21.7 | 80.9 | 8.9 | 4.3 | 15.1 | 4.4 | 1.4 | 2.2 | 16.1 | 6.3 | 20.9 |
| Austria | 9 894 | 109.9 | 65.3 | 51.2 | 12.5 | 1.4 | 47.2 | 1.2 | 53.7 | 0.0 | 57.9 | 1.5 | 59.4 |
| Belgium | 10 249 | 113.9 | 52.6 | 63.0 | 15.3 | 3.3 | 39.2 | 3.3 | 35.1 | 11.6 | 42.7 | 12.6 | 46.2 |
| Canada | 7 771 | 86.3 | 13.7 | 72.0 | 4.0 | 4.2 | 5.7 | 4.2 | 2.8 | 4.3 | 6.3 | 7.8 | 15.8 |
| Czech Republic | 7 913 | 87.9 | 38.0 | 53.7 | 9.5 | 1.4 | 27.9 | 1.5 | 18.3 | 0.0 | 31.8 | 1.5 | 43.2 |
| Denmark | 7 729 | 85.9 | 15.7 | 72.2 | 7.5 | 7.3 | 9.8 | 7.4 | 2.5 | 0.1 | 10.6 | 7.5 | 18.3 |
| Finland | 6 521 | 72.5 | 2.8 | 69.7 | 0.6 | 6.3 | 0.6 | 6.3 | 0.0 | 0.0 | 0.6 | 6.3 | 3.9 |
| France | w | w | w | w | w | w | w | w | w | w | w | w | w |
| Germany | 10 218 | 113.5 | 59.6 | 54.9 | 14.4 | 2.1 | 46.1 | 2.1 | 1.0 | 0.1 | 46.2 | 2.2 | 52.5 |
| Greece | 10 842 | 120.5 | 44.1 | 82.7 | 7.8 | 0.9 | 28.1 | 0.8 | 32.7 | 0.0 | 37.4 | 0.7 | 36.6 |
| Hungary | 8 008 | 89.0 | 42.8 | 47.1 | 6.7 | 0.2 | 35.7 | 0.2 | 33.2 | 0.0 | 37.9 | 0.3 | 48.1 |
| Iceland | 9 545 | 106.0 | 4.1 | 102.0 | 0.8 | 3.3 | 0.8 | 3.3 | 0.0 | 0.0 | 0.8 | 3.3 | 3.8 |
| Ireland | 7 375 | 81.9 | 17.8 | 65.3 | 8.3 | 5.3 | 13.1 | 5.4 | 2.2 | 4.7 | 13.7 | 9.7 | 21.7 |
| Italy | 10 097 | 112.2 | 55.4 | 58.1 | 6.8 | 0.6 | 32.8 | 0.6 | 24.4 | 0.0 | 34.5 | 0.7 | 49.4 |
| Japan | 10 907 | 121.2 | 54.3 | 68.3 | 5.4 | 0.3 | 35.6 | 0.4 | 3.4 | 0.0 | 36.5 | 0.4 | 44.8 |
| Korea | 6 768 | 75.2 | 27.6 | 48.9 | 4.6 | 0.6 | 16.7 | 0.6 | 14.4 | 0.3 | 19.6 | 0.9 | 36.7 |
| Luxembourg | 9 816 | 109.1 | 29.5 | 79.2 | 10.6 | 4.5 | 25.2 | 4.5 | 7.9 | 8.3 | 24.6 | 11.3 | 27.1 |
| Mexico | 9 041 | 100.4 | 31.4 | 55.1 | 4.7 | 0.4 | 18.5 | 0.5 | 12.6 | 0.0 | 23.0 | 0.5 | 31.2 |
| Netherlands | 6 647 | 73.9 | 40.4 | 35.0 | 5.4 | 0.6 | 30.1 | 0.6 | 36.1 | 2.1 | 37.3 | 2.7 | 54.8 |
| New Zealand | 10 744 | 119.4 | 20.4 | 100.0 | 10.0 | 10.0 | 14.7 | 10.0 | 0.8 | 3.7 | 14.7 | 13.1 | 17.1 |
| Norway | 10 376 | 115.3 | 8.9 | 106.5 | 2.9 | 10.6 | 3.2 | 10.6 | 0.1 | 0.1 | 3.2 | 10.6 | 7.7 |
| Poland | 9 185 | 102.0 | 14.9 | 87.4 | 7.9 | 8.3 | 9.7 | 8.4 | 0.8 | 0.1 | 9.9 | 8.4 | 14.6 |
| Portugal | 8 551 | 95.0 | 36.7 | 60.9 | 7.8 | 2.3 | 19.9 | 2.3 | 31.0 | 8.6 | 33.9 | 9.7 | 38.6 |
| Slovak Republic | 8 362 | 92.9 | 37.1 | 55.6 | 11.1 | 2.5 | 28.7 | 2.5 | 25.7 | 0.3 | 31.0 | 2.8 | 39.9 |
| Spain | 9 071 | 100.8 | 18.9 | 78.7 | 5.9 | 3.6 | 9.2 | 3.7 | 0.0 | 1.5 | 6.6 | 4.7 | 18.8 |
| Sweden | 8 985 | 99.8 | 9.0 | 91.2 | 4.1 | 10.3 | 4.8 | 10.3 | 1.7 | 0.5 | 6.0 | 10.6 | 9.0 |
| Switzerland | 8 893 | 98.8 | 28.6 | 67.1 | 9.0 | 5.5 | 16.9 | 5.5 | 4.7 | 0.6 | 17.2 | 6.0 | 28.9 |
| Turkey | 9 023 | 100.3 | 52.9 | 47.4 | 7.5 | 0.5 | 37.1 | 0.4 | 12.0 | 0.1 | 38.7 | 0.5 | 52.8 |
| United Kingdom | m | m | m | m | m | m | m | m | m | m | m | m | m |
| United States | 10 139 | 112.7 | 27.4 | 85.9 | 12.4 | 7.2 | 18.9 | 7.4 | 3.4 | 3.3 | 19.4 | 9.9 | 24.3 |
| **OECD average** | **9 001** | **100.0** | **31.1** | **69.3** | **7.6** | **3.8** | **21.1** | **3.9** | **12.9** | **1.9** | **23.5** | **5.4** | |
| **Partners** | | | | | | | | | | | | | |
| Brazil | 12 395 | 137.7 | 38.4 | 95.1 | 4.7 | 0.0 | 21.6 | 0.1 | 18.9 | 4.6 | 30.4 | 4.7 | 27.9 |
| Hong Kong-China | 7 016 | 77.9 | 32.2 | 44.1 | 1.3 | 0.1 | 12.8 | 0.1 | 10.4 | 2.0 | 17.8 | 2.0 | 41.3 |
| Indonesia | 5 822 | 64.7 | 22.1 | 38.9 | 1.1 | 0.0 | 10.0 | 0.1 | 6.0 | 0.0 | 11.2 | 0.1 | 34.1 |
| Latvia | 8 116 | 90.2 | 17.9 | 73.4 | 3.9 | 3.5 | 6.0 | 3.5 | 0.5 | 1.0 | 6.0 | 4.3 | 19.9 |
| Liechtenstein | 8 019 | 89.1 | c | c | c | c | c | c | c | c | c | c | c |
| Macao-China | 4 484 | 49.8 | 12.3 | 40.7 | 0.4 | 0.0 | 1.9 | 0.0 | 3.9 | 3.5 | 5.1 | 3.5 | 24.6 |
| Russian Federation | 8 690 | 96.6 | 22.6 | 73.9 | 6.3 | 3.3 | 12.2 | 3.2 | 4.3 | 2.9 | 12.9 | 5.5 | 23.5 |
| Thailand | 6 103 | 67.8 | 23.4 | 46.6 | 4.1 | 0.1 | 13.4 | 0.2 | 5.0 | 1.4 | 14.8 | 1.6 | 34.5 |
| Tunisia | 9 134 | 101.5 | 33.8 | 67.4 | 3.6 | 0.2 | 16.0 | 0.2 | 26.8 | 1.7 | 27.9 | 2.0 | 33.3 |
| Uruguay | 14 744 | 163.8 | 61.7 | 111.7 | 17.0 | 2.0 | 43.3 | 2.2 | 45.8 | 3.3 | 54.7 | 5.5 | 37.7 |

1. The variance components were estimated for all students in participating countries with data on socio-economic background and study programmes. Students in special education programmes were excluded from these analyses.
2. The total variance in student performance is calculated from the square of the standard deviation for the students used in the analysis. The statistical variance in student performance and not the standard deviation is used for this comparison to allow for the decomposition.
3. The sum of the between- and within-school variance components, as an estimate from a sample, does not necessarily add up to the total.
4. In some countries, sub-units within schools were sampled instead of schools and this may affect the estimation of the between-school variance components (see Annex A2).
5. This index is often referred to as the intra-class correlation (rho).
StatLink ⟐ http://dx.doi.org/10.1787/142104560611

Pour consulter la version française intégrale de ce tableau, suivre ce lien :
StatLink ⟐ http://dx.doi.org/10.1787/152684743050

[Part 1/1]

**Table 4.1f  Between-school and within-school variance in student performance on the reading scale in PISA 2000**

Variance inter- et intra-établissements des scores sur l'échelle de compréhension de l'écrit du cycle PISA 2000

| | Total variance in SP[2] | Variance expressed as a percentage of the average variance in student performance (SP) across OECD countries[1] | | | | | | | Total variance between schools expressed as a percentage of the total variance within the country[5] |
|---|---|---|---|---|---|---|---|---|---|
| | | Total variance in SP expressed as a percentage of the average variance in student performance across OECD countries[3] | Total variance in SP between schools[4] | Total variance in SP within schools | Variance explained by the PISA index of economic, social and cultural status of students | | Variance explained by the PISA index of economic, social and cultural status of students and schools | | |
| | | | | | Between-school variance explained | Within-school variance explained | Between-school variance explained | Within-school variance explained | |
| **OECD** | | | | | | | | | |
| Australia | 10 313 | 116.2 | 20.6 | 94.9 | 11.6 | 8.0 | 14.9 | 8.3 | 17.8 |
| Austria | 8 954 | 100.9 | 63.5 | 49.2 | 8.8 | 0.6 | 43.2 | 0.6 | 62.9 |
| Belgium | 10 485 | 118.1 | 69.5 | 53.9 | 11.7 | 1.7 | 44.2 | 1.7 | 58.8 |
| Canada | 8 875 | 100.0 | 17.6 | 83.1 | 6.3 | 6.1 | 8.9 | 6.3 | 17.6 |
| Czech Republic | 7 393 | 83.3 | 36.2 | 48.0 | 9.9 | 2.6 | 24.8 | 2.7 | 43.5 |
| Denmark | 9 258 | 104.3 | 17.3 | 89.2 | 7.7 | 10.1 | 9.7 | 10.1 | 16.6 |
| Finland | 7 484 | 84.3 | 5.3 | 79.1 | 1.0 | 5.9 | 1.0 | 5.9 | 6.3 |
| France | w | w | w | w | w | w | w | w | w |
| Germany | 10 062 | 113.3 | 61.7 | 53.9 | 14.3 | 2.2 | 49.5 | 2.2 | 54.5 |
| Greece | 9 405 | 105.9 | 56.7 | 55.1 | 7.1 | 1.0 | 27.1 | 1.0 | 53.5 |
| Hungary | 7 892 | 88.9 | 51.8 | 36.2 | 5.4 | 0.1 | 41.9 | 0.1 | 58.2 |
| Iceland | 8 347 | 94.0 | 7.4 | 86.7 | 1.8 | 4.7 | 2.0 | 4.6 | 7.9 |
| Ireland | 8 682 | 97.8 | 17.1 | 81.6 | 6.9 | 5.1 | 11.2 | 5.2 | 17.5 |
| Italy | 8 298 | 93.5 | 54.9 | 44.8 | 2.9 | 0.1 | 29.1 | 0.1 | 58.7 |
| Japan | m | m | m | m | m | m | m | m | m |
| Korea | 4 836 | 54.5 | 20.8 | 34.6 | 2.3 | 0.3 | 10.4 | 0.2 | 38.1 |
| Luxembourg | m | m | m | m | m | m | m | m | m |
| Mexico | 7 399 | 83.3 | 44.5 | 39.3 | 6.3 | 0.2 | 29.1 | 0.2 | 53.4 |
| Netherlands | m | m | m | m | m | m | m | m | m |
| New Zealand | 11 359 | 128.0 | 20.7 | 106.9 | 9.8 | 8.9 | 14.4 | 9.1 | 16.2 |
| Norway | 10 552 | 118.9 | 12.1 | 107.3 | 4.0 | 11.0 | 4.6 | 11.0 | 10.2 |
| Poland | 9 475 | 106.7 | 67.3 | 40.7 | 2.6 | 0.0 | 38.0 | 0.0 | 63.1 |
| Portugal | 9 362 | 105.5 | 38.5 | 66.0 | 11.3 | 3.7 | 25.1 | 3.7 | 36.5 |
| Spain | 7 111 | 80.1 | 16.1 | 64.2 | 7.8 | 4.2 | 10.5 | 4.3 | 20.1 |
| Sweden | 8 404 | 94.7 | 8.5 | 86.5 | 4.4 | 6.8 | 5.8 | 6.8 | 9.0 |
| Switzerland | 10 374 | 116.9 | 49.3 | 65.2 | 12.4 | 5.4 | 27.4 | 5.3 | 42.2 |
| United Kingdom | m | m | m | m | m | m | m | m | m |
| United States | 9 865 | 111.1 | 31.2 | 83.1 | 15.4 | 6.5 | 24.9 | 6.7 | 28.1 |
| **OECD average** | **8 878** | **100.0** | **34.3** | **67.4** | **7.5** | **4.1** | **21.6** | **4.2** | |
| **Partners** | | | | | | | | | |
| Argentina | 11 421 | 129.4 | 67.9 | 61.3 | 10.9 | 0.6 | 43.9 | 0.6 | 52.4 |
| Brazil | 7 369 | 83.0 | 37.8 | 48.8 | 7.9 | 0.4 | 23.3 | 0.6 | 45.5 |
| Bulgaria | 10 161 | 115.1 | 69.8 | 53.6 | 14.2 | 1.3 | 53.8 | 1.4 | 60.6 |
| Chile | 8 043 | 91.1 | 56.2 | 44.6 | 11.5 | 0.9 | 34.7 | 0.9 | 61.6 |
| Hong Kong-China | 6 937 | 78.1 | 36.7 | 40.8 | 2.5 | 0.2 | 15.6 | 0.2 | 47.0 |
| Indonesia | 5 162 | 58.1 | 22.9 | 30.0 | 1.7 | 0.2 | 8.9 | 0.2 | 39.3 |
| Israel | 11 333 | 128.4 | 59.1 | 68.5 | 14.3 | 2.6 | 36.1 | 2.7 | 46.0 |
| Latvia | 10 345 | 116.5 | 37.2 | 80.8 | 6.8 | 2.1 | 20.3 | 2.2 | 31.9 |
| Liechtenstein | 9 152 | 103.1 | c | c | c | c | c | c | c |
| Romania | 10 301 | 116.7 | 57.6 | 62.2 | 1.6 | 0.0 | 26.6 | 0.0 | 49.3 |
| Russian Federation | 8 418 | 94.8 | 34.3 | 60.2 | 5.4 | 1.7 | 16.2 | 1.6 | 36.2 |
| Thailand | 5 847 | 65.9 | 20.7 | 46.3 | 3.1 | 0.2 | 8.6 | 0.3 | 31.4 |

1. The variance components were estimated for all students in participating countries with data on socio-economic background and study programmes. Students in special education programmes were excluded from these analyses.
2. The total variance in student performance is calculated from the square of the standard deviation for the students used in the analysis. The statistical variance in student performance and not the standard deviation is used for this comparison to allow for the decomposition.
3. The sum of the between- and within-school variance components, as an estimate from a sample, does not necessarily add up to the total.
4. In some countries, sub-units within schools were sampled instead of schools and this may affect the estimation of the between-school variance components (see Annex A2).
5. This index is often referred to as the intra-class correlation (rho).
*StatLink* ᠁᠍ http://dx.doi.org/10.1787/142104560611

Pour consulter la version française intégrale de ce tableau, suivre ce lien :
*StatLink* ᠁᠍ http://dx.doi.org/10.1787/152684743050

[Part 1/2]

### Table 4.1g Between-school and within-school variance in student performance on the mathematics scale in PISA 2006

Variance inter- et intra-établissements des scores sur l'échelle de culture mathématique du cycle PISA 2006

| | Total variance in SP[2] | Variance expressed as a percentage of the average variance in student performance (SP) across OECD countries[1] | | | | |
| | | Total variance in SP expressed as a percentage of the average variance in student performance across OECD countries[3] | Total variance in SP between schools[4] | Total variance in SP within schools | Variance explained by the PISA index of economic, social and cultural status of students | |
| | | | | | Between-school variance explained | Within-school variance explained |
|---|---|---|---|---|---|---|
| **OECD** | | | | | | |
| Australia | 7 658 | 92.1 | 19.7 | 72.4 | 6.7 | 3.3 |
| Austria | 9 619 | 115.7 | 69.5 | 54.5 | 7.7 | 0.5 |
| Belgium | 11 090 | 133.4 | 69.4 | 62.4 | 12.8 | 2.1 |
| Canada | 7 268 | 87.4 | 18.2 | 69.9 | 3.9 | 3.1 |
| Czech Republic | 10 604 | 127.5 | 77.1 | 64.2 | 15.2 | 1.9 |
| Denmark | 7 111 | 85.5 | 14.9 | 72.8 | 5.4 | 6.7 |
| Finland | 6 499 | 78.2 | 5.8 | 72.4 | 1.4 | 6.4 |
| France | w | w | w | w | w | w |
| Germany | 9 665 | 116.2 | 74.0 | 47.9 | 11.6 | 1.3 |
| Greece | 8 476 | 101.9 | 46.5 | 65.2 | 13.2 | 2.8 |
| Hungary | 8 229 | 99.0 | 74.0 | 39.7 | 12.6 | 0.6 |
| Iceland | 7 715 | 92.8 | 8.5 | 85.3 | 0.6 | 6.7 |
| Ireland | 6 687 | 80.4 | 15.5 | 65.4 | 6.3 | 4.3 |
| Italy | 9 067 | 109.0 | 59.1 | 54.0 | 4.1 | 0.3 |
| Japan | 8 086 | 97.2 | 52.8 | 46.4 | 3.8 | 0.3 |
| Korea | 8 561 | 102.9 | 41.9 | 61.9 | 6.0 | 0.8 |
| Luxembourg | 8 692 | 104.5 | 33.2 | 70.6 | 10.2 | 3.3 |
| Mexico | 7 266 | 87.4 | 31.0 | 42.2 | 3.8 | 0.2 |
| Netherlands | 7 790 | 93.7 | 58.5 | 33.9 | 5.6 | 0.5 |
| New Zealand | 8 468 | 101.8 | 15.7 | 86.8 | 7.9 | 7.2 |
| Norway | 8 260 | 99.3 | 10.7 | 88.6 | 3.1 | 5.0 |
| Poland | 7 471 | 89.8 | 13.3 | 78.1 | 5.9 | 8.5 |
| Portugal | 8 209 | 98.7 | 33.1 | 65.6 | 10.2 | 4.0 |
| Slovak Republic | 8 921 | 107.3 | 54.5 | 57.3 | 13.0 | 2.4 |
| Spain | 7 868 | 94.6 | 14.8 | 77.0 | 5.5 | 4.9 |
| Sweden | 7 906 | 95.1 | 14.1 | 82.4 | 4.8 | 6.6 |
| Switzerland | 9 463 | 113.8 | 39.4 | 70.0 | 7.2 | 3.7 |
| Turkey | 8 693 | 104.5 | 54.7 | 47.9 | 7.8 | 0.9 |
| United Kingdom | 7 779 | 93.6 | 20.1 | 69.7 | 6.5 | 4.0 |
| United States | 8 028 | 97.1 | 26.4 | 68.6 | 10.3 | 5.5 |
| **OECD average** | **8 316** | **100.0** | **36.8** | **64.6** | **7.3** | **3.4** |
| **Partners** | | | | | | |
| Argentina | 10 199 | 122.6 | 60.9 | 59.2 | 11.9 | 1.2 |
| Azerbaijan | 2 308 | 27.8 | 19.9 | 15.0 | 0.1 | 0.1 |
| Brazil | 8 462 | 101.8 | 52.2 | 46.6 | 8.9 | 0.6 |
| Bulgaria | 10 179 | 122.4 | 62.9 | 60.0 | 16.0 | 1.2 |
| Chile | 7 707 | 92.7 | 58.2 | 46.4 | 14.8 | 0.9 |
| Colombia | 7 759 | 93.3 | 35.8 | 61.0 | 9.7 | 1.3 |
| Croatia | 6 954 | 83.6 | 32.7 | 52.4 | 5.5 | 1.1 |
| Estonia | 6 467 | 77.8 | 19.2 | 57.8 | 4.9 | 3.4 |
| Hong Kong-China | 8 694 | 104.6 | 41.1 | 62.6 | 3.5 | 0.4 |
| Indonesia | 6 403 | 77.0 | 33.0 | 33.3 | 0.9 | 0.0 |
| Israel | 11 447 | 137.7 | 56.9 | 83.6 | 10.6 | 3.5 |
| Jordan | 6 891 | 82.9 | 19.6 | 60.5 | 5.6 | 3.3 |
| Kyrgyzstan | 7 489 | 90.1 | 37.9 | 51.5 | 5.2 | 0.6 |
| Latvia | 6 823 | 82.1 | 18.4 | 63.9 | 5.2 | 3.8 |
| Liechtenstein | 8 610 | 103.5 | c | c | c | c |
| Lithuania | 8 042 | 96.7 | 32.0 | 67.2 | 11.6 | 4.5 |
| Macao-China | 7 107 | 85.5 | 20.7 | 70.6 | 1.0 | 0.2 |
| Montenegro | 7 216 | 86.8 | 20.9 | 62.6 | 3.6 | 1.2 |
| Qatar | 8 343 | 100.3 | 60.5 | 53.5 | c | c |
| Romania | 7 036 | 84.6 | 43.4 | 40.7 | 7.7 | 1.1 |
| Russian Federation | 8 015 | 96.4 | 27.9 | 71.0 | 4.7 | 3.2 |
| Serbia | 8 378 | 100.7 | 44.5 | 61.3 | 7.8 | 0.9 |
| Slovenia | 7 945 | 95.5 | 55.5 | 36.9 | 5.1 | 0.3 |
| Chinese Taipei | 10 584 | 127.3 | 60.1 | 62.4 | 7.3 | 1.1 |
| Thailand | 6 642 | 79.9 | 29.8 | 52.0 | 7.6 | 0.4 |
| Tunisia | 8 455 | 101.7 | 48.1 | 53.0 | 8.1 | 1.0 |
| Uruguay | 9 859 | 118.6 | 47.5 | 69.2 | 14.8 | 2.5 |

1. The variance components were estimated for all students in participating countries with data on socio-economic background and study programmes.
2. The total variance in student performance is calculated from the square of the standard deviation for the students used in the analysis. The statistical variance in student performance and not the standard deviation is used for this comparison to allow for the decomposition.
3. The sum of the between- and within-school variance components, as an estimate from a sample, does not necessarily add up to the total.
4. In some countries, sub-units within schools were sampled instead of schools and this may affect the estimation of the between-school variance components (see Annex A2).
5. This index is often referred to as the intra-class correlation (rho).
*StatLink* http://dx.doi.org/10.1787/142104560611

Pour consulter la version française intégrale de ce tableau, suivre ce lien :
*StatLink* http://dx.doi.org/10.1787/152684743050

[Part 2/2]

**Table 4.1g** Between-school and within-school variance in student performance on the mathematics scale in PISA 2006

Variance inter- et intra-établissements des scores sur l'échelle de culture mathématique du cycle PISA 2006

| | Variance expressed as a percentage of the average variance in student performance (SP) across OECD countries[1] | | | | | | Total variance between schools expressed as a percentage of the total variance within the country[5] |
|---|---|---|---|---|---|---|---|
| | Variance explained by the PISA index of economic, social and cultural status of students and schools | | Variance explained by students' study programmes | | Variance explained by students' study programmes and the PISA index of economic, social and cultural status of students and schools | | |
| | Between-school variance explained | Within-school variance explained | Between-school variance explained | Within-school variance explained | Between-school variance explained | Within-school variance explained | |
| Australia | 11.7 | 3.4 | 1.7 | 3.7 | 12.4 | 6.6 | 21.4 |
| Austria | 40.7 | 0.5 | 53.5 | 0.7 | 56.0 | 1.1 | 60.1 |
| Belgium | 45.7 | 2.1 | 55.5 | 15.0 | 60.3 | 15.5 | 52.0 |
| Canada | 6.2 | 3.2 | 0.7 | 3.7 | 5.2 | 6.4 | 20.8 |
| Czech Republic | 54.6 | 2.1 | 61.1 | 0.3 | 64.5 | 2.2 | 60.4 |
| Denmark | 7.4 | 6.8 | 2.7 | 0.1 | 8.5 | 7.0 | 17.4 |
| Finland | 1.5 | 6.4 | 0.0 | 0.0 | 1.5 | 6.4 | 7.4 |
| France | w | w | w | w | w | w | w |
| Germany | 54.2 | 1.3 | 61.0 | 1.9 | 63.6 | 3.0 | 63.7 |
| Greece | 27.6 | 2.8 | 33.8 | 0.0 | 38.4 | 2.8 | 45.6 |
| Hungary | 53.1 | 0.5 | 52.7 | 0.0 | 58.8 | 0.6 | 74.8 |
| Iceland | 0.6 | 6.7 | 1.3 | 0.2 | 1.8 | 6.9 | 9.1 |
| Ireland | 9.9 | 4.4 | 0.9 | 3.6 | 9.7 | 7.6 | 19.2 |
| Italy | 27.0 | 0.3 | 24.9 | 0.0 | 31.6 | 0.4 | 54.2 |
| Japan | 28.7 | 0.3 | 8.8 | 0.0 | 29.6 | 0.3 | 54.3 |
| Korea | 24.0 | 0.8 | 19.5 | 0.5 | 28.8 | 1.3 | 40.7 |
| Luxembourg | 29.8 | 3.3 | 28.1 | 21.2 | 30.8 | 21.7 | 31.8 |
| Mexico | 15.0 | 0.3 | 11.5 | 0.0 | 19.7 | 0.3 | 35.5 |
| Netherlands | 37.6 | 0.5 | 53.0 | 9.3 | 53.3 | 9.5 | 62.5 |
| New Zealand | 11.2 | 7.3 | 0.1 | 1.6 | 11.1 | 8.5 | 15.4 |
| Norway | 4.3 | 4.9 | 0.9 | 0.1 | 4.7 | 4.9 | 10.8 |
| Poland | 6.4 | 8.7 | 1.3 | 0.6 | 6.6 | 8.9 | 14.9 |
| Portugal | 17.1 | 4.0 | 24.0 | 13.1 | 27.5 | 15.0 | 33.5 |
| Slovak Republic | 29.6 | 2.3 | 27.2 | 1.5 | 34.9 | 3.6 | 50.8 |
| Spain | 7.2 | 4.9 | 0.0 | 0.1 | 7.3 | 5.0 | 15.6 |
| Sweden | 6.9 | 6.5 | 5.1 | 0.0 | 8.8 | 5.6 | 14.8 |
| Switzerland | 16.9 | 3.7 | 5.5 | 1.1 | 17.7 | 4.7 | 34.6 |
| Turkey | 31.9 | 0.9 | 30.3 | 0.2 | 39.7 | 1.1 | 52.3 |
| United Kingdom | 12.4 | 4.3 | 0.7 | 0.8 | 12.4 | 5.0 | 21.5 |
| United States | 16.4 | 5.6 | 5.1 | 4.2 | 18.1 | 8.6 | 27.3 |
| **OECD average** | **21.9** | **3.4** | **19.7** | **2.9** | **26.3** | **5.9** | |
| Argentina | 35.7 | 1.2 | 28.1 | 4.1 | 44.8 | 5.2 | 49.6 |
| Azerbaijan | 0.2 | 0.1 | 0.6 | 0.2 | 0.7 | 0.2 | 71.7 |
| Brazil | 29.7 | 0.6 | 15.1 | 3.5 | 34.1 | 4.1 | 51.3 |
| Bulgaria | 41.0 | 1.1 | 18.9 | 0.7 | 39.9 | 1.7 | 51.3 |
| Chile | 40.3 | 0.9 | 17.8 | 1.5 | 45.2 | 2.3 | 62.8 |
| Colombia | 21.6 | 1.4 | 9.1 | 8.8 | 22.5 | 9.3 | 38.3 |
| Croatia | 19.8 | 1.1 | 23.3 | 7.9 | 24.2 | 8.1 | 39.1 |
| Estonia | 8.8 | 3.4 | 0.2 | 0.7 | 8.8 | 4.0 | 24.6 |
| Hong Kong-China | 17.8 | 0.4 | 10.4 | 6.4 | 21.2 | 6.5 | 39.3 |
| Indonesia | 12.2 | 0.0 | 6.7 | 0.0 | 13.6 | 0.0 | 42.9 |
| Israel | 25.5 | 3.5 | 7.4 | 1.1 | 28.4 | 4.4 | 41.3 |
| Jordan | 9.0 | 3.3 | 0.0 | 0.0 | 9.0 | 3.3 | 23.6 |
| Kyrgyzstan | 21.5 | 0.7 | 0.0 | 1.3 | 20.7 | 1.8 | 42.1 |
| Latvia | 8.2 | 3.8 | 0.8 | 1.6 | 8.7 | 5.2 | 22.4 |
| Liechtenstein | c | c | c | c | c | c | c |
| Lithuania | 20.3 | 4.5 | 14.8 | 0.5 | 22.8 | 5.0 | 33.1 |
| Macao-China | 3.0 | 0.1 | 9.3 | 10.2 | 9.7 | 10.2 | 24.3 |
| Montenegro | 11.6 | 1.2 | 11.5 | 5.3 | 13.5 | 5.7 | 24.1 |
| Qatar | 22.0 | 0.0 | c | c | 29.8 | 1.3 | 60.3 |
| Romania | 23.7 | 1.1 | 21.2 | 0.0 | 28.9 | 1.1 | 51.3 |
| Russian Federation | 7.1 | 3.1 | 5.9 | 6.7 | 8.8 | 8.7 | 29.0 |
| Serbia | 30.7 | 0.9 | 27.8 | 4.9 | 32.9 | 5.2 | 44.2 |
| Slovenia | 37.4 | 0.2 | 42.6 | 0.0 | 44.8 | 0.3 | 58.1 |
| Chinese Taipei | 35.5 | 1.1 | 29.9 | 0.9 | 41.7 | 2.0 | 47.2 |
| Thailand | 19.0 | 0.6 | 6.0 | 1.1 | 19.7 | 1.7 | 37.4 |
| Tunisia | 24.4 | 1.0 | 33.1 | 2.1 | 39.2 | 3.1 | 47.3 |
| Uruguay | 29.2 | 2.6 | 29.1 | 3.7 | 38.7 | 5.9 | 40.1 |

*(OECD countries listed above OECD average; Partners listed below)*

1. The variance components were estimated for all students in participating countries with data on socio-economic background and study programmes.
2. The total variance in student performance is calculated from the square of the standard deviation for the students used in the analysis. The statistical variance in student performance and not the standard deviation is used for this comparison to allow for the decomposition.
3. The sum of the between- and within-school variance components, as an estimate from a sample, does not necessarily add up to the total.
4. In some countries, sub-units within schools were sampled instead of schools and this may affect the estimation of the between-school variance components (see Annex A2).
5. This index is often referred to as the intra-class correlation (rho).

*StatLink* http://dx.doi.org/10.1787/142104560611

Pour consulter la version française intégrale de ce tableau, suivre ce lien :
*StatLink* http://dx.doi.org/10.1787/152684743050

[Part 1/1]
**Table 4.1h   Between-school and within-school variance in student performance on the mathematics scale in PISA 2003**

Variance inter- et intra-établissements des scores sur l'échelle de culture mathématique du cycle PISA 2003

| | | Variance expressed as a percentage of the average variance in student performance (SP) across OECD countries[1] | | | | | | | | | | | |
| | Total variance in SP[2] | Total variance in SP expressed as a percentage of the average variance in student performance across OECD countries[3] | Total variance in SP between schools[4] | Total variance in SP within schools | Variance explained by the PISA index of economic, social and cultural status of students | | Variance explained by the PISA index of economic, social and cultural status of students and schools | | Variance explained by students' study programmes | | Variance explained by students' study programmes and the PISA index of economic, social and cultural status of students and schools | | Total variance between schools expressed as a percentage of the total variance within the country[5] |
| | | | | | Between-school variance explained | Within-school variance explained | Between-school variance explained | Within-school variance explained | Between-school variance explained | Within-school variance explained | Between-school variance explained | Within-school variance explained | |
|---|---|---|---|---|---|---|---|---|---|---|---|---|---|
| **OECD** | | | | | | | | | | | | | |
| Australia | 9 036 | 105.1 | 22.0 | 82.3 | 9.0 | 4.2 | 15.3 | 4.3 | 1.8 | 2.8 | 16.6 | 6.8 | 21.0 |
| Austria | 8 455 | 98.4 | 55.4 | 49.5 | 7.6 | 0.6 | 35.1 | 0.5 | 41.4 | 0.1 | 44.9 | 0.8 | 56.4 |
| Belgium | 10 463 | 121.7 | 56.9 | 66.7 | 17.7 | 4.4 | 41.9 | 4.4 | 38.3 | 15.0 | 44.6 | 16.2 | 46.7 |
| Canada | 7 626 | 88.7 | 15.1 | 72.6 | 4.7 | 4.2 | 7.1 | 4.3 | 2.6 | 5.0 | 7.0 | 8.5 | 17.1 |
| Czech Republic | 8 581 | 99.8 | 50.5 | 55.2 | 13.8 | 2.5 | 36.9 | 2.6 | 18.4 | 0.0 | 40.0 | 2.6 | 50.5 |
| Denmark | 8 289 | 96.4 | 13.0 | 84.1 | 7.7 | 9.7 | 9.3 | 9.8 | 1.2 | 0.1 | 9.4 | 9.9 | 13.5 |
| Finland | 6 974 | 81.1 | 3.9 | 77.2 | 0.9 | 7.9 | 0.9 | 7.9 | 0.0 | 0.0 | 0.9 | 7.9 | 4.8 |
| France | w | w | w | w | w | w | w | w | w | w | w | w | w |
| Germany | 9 306 | 108.3 | 56.4 | 52.6 | 14.1 | 2.2 | 43.8 | 2.2 | 1.1 | 0.1 | 43.9 | 2.3 | 52.1 |
| Greece | 8 751 | 101.8 | 38.8 | 68.0 | 10.3 | 2.5 | 25.2 | 2.3 | 28.3 | 0.0 | 32.9 | 2.3 | 38.1 |
| Hungary | 8 200 | 95.4 | 49.0 | 47.3 | 11.7 | 1.0 | 41.6 | 1.0 | 34.3 | 0.1 | 42.7 | 1.0 | 51.4 |
| Iceland | 8 123 | 94.5 | 3.6 | 90.9 | 1.3 | 4.7 | 1.3 | 4.7 | 0.0 | 0.0 | 1.3 | 4.7 | 3.8 |
| Ireland | 7 213 | 83.9 | 13.4 | 71.2 | 7.8 | 6.0 | 11.0 | 6.1 | 1.3 | 4.3 | 11.0 | 9.9 | 16.0 |
| Italy | 9 153 | 106.5 | 56.8 | 52.0 | 6.6 | 0.7 | 30.5 | 0.7 | 17.5 | 0.0 | 31.7 | 0.7 | 53.3 |
| Japan | 9 994 | 116.3 | 62.1 | 55.0 | 3.3 | 0.1 | 42.0 | 0.1 | 5.2 | 0.0 | 42.8 | 0.1 | 53.4 |
| Korea | 8 531 | 99.3 | 42.0 | 58.1 | 7.7 | 1.1 | 27.8 | 1.1 | 21.5 | 0.6 | 31.2 | 1.6 | 42.3 |
| Luxembourg | 8 432 | 98.1 | 31.1 | 67.6 | 9.2 | 3.0 | 27.8 | 2.9 | 9.3 | 8.1 | 27.6 | 9.9 | 31.7 |
| Mexico | 7 295 | 84.9 | 29.0 | 44.8 | 4.2 | 0.3 | 16.5 | 0.4 | 11.1 | 0.0 | 20.7 | 0.5 | 34.2 |
| Netherlands | 7 897 | 91.9 | 54.5 | 39.5 | 8.7 | 1.3 | 40.8 | 1.3 | 49.2 | 3.2 | 50.7 | 4.4 | 59.3 |
| New Zealand | 9 457 | 110.0 | 20.1 | 90.9 | 9.8 | 8.7 | 15.2 | 8.8 | 0.8 | 3.1 | 15.2 | 11.4 | 18.2 |
| Norway | 8 432 | 98.1 | 6.5 | 91.6 | 2.7 | 11.1 | 2.9 | 11.2 | 0.2 | 0.1 | 2.9 | 11.2 | 6.6 |
| Poland | 8 138 | 94.7 | 12.0 | 83.1 | 7.1 | 8.9 | 8.2 | 9.0 | 0.8 | 0.1 | 8.3 | 9.0 | 12.7 |
| Portugal | 7 647 | 89.0 | 30.3 | 60.0 | 9.5 | 4.8 | 17.2 | 4.8 | 26.5 | 8.6 | 28.6 | 11.6 | 34.1 |
| Slovak Republic | 8 478 | 98.6 | 41.5 | 58.0 | 12.9 | 3.1 | 32.3 | 3.1 | 25.9 | 0.2 | 33.7 | 3.3 | 42.1 |
| Spain | 7 803 | 90.8 | 17.2 | 70.1 | 6.4 | 4.1 | 9.8 | 4.2 | 0.0 | 1.8 | 7.2 | 5.4 | 19.0 |
| Sweden | 8 880 | 103.3 | 10.9 | 92.7 | 4.7 | 11.2 | 5.8 | 11.2 | 1.4 | 0.5 | 6.9 | 11.4 | 10.5 |
| Switzerland | 9 541 | 111.0 | 36.4 | 70.2 | 9.4 | 5.1 | 19.3 | 5.1 | 6.0 | 1.0 | 19.9 | 5.9 | 32.8 |
| Turkey | 10 952 | 127.4 | 68.6 | 56.5 | 10.0 | 0.7 | 48.9 | 0.6 | 13.5 | 0.2 | 49.9 | 0.7 | 53.9 |
| United Kingdom | m | m | m | m | m | m | m | m | m | m | m | m | m |
| United States | 9 016 | 104.9 | 27.1 | 78.3 | 12.1 | 7.0 | 18.7 | 7.2 | 3.2 | 2.8 | 19.2 | 9.2 | 25.8 |
| **OECD average** | **8 595** | **100.0** | **33.0** | **67.4** | **8.3** | **4.3** | **22.6** | **4.3** | **12.9** | **2.1** | **24.7** | **6.0** | |
| **Partners** | | | | | | | | | | | | | |
| Brazil | 10 000 | 116.3 | 49.2 | 59.8 | 6.3 | 0.2 | 28.6 | 0.3 | 18.7 | 3.6 | 36.8 | 3.9 | 42.3 |
| Hong Kong-China | 9 946 | 115.7 | 52.8 | 60.4 | 2.6 | 0.1 | 22.7 | 0.2 | 15.3 | 4.6 | 29.2 | 4.6 | 45.6 |
| Indonesia | 6 480 | 75.4 | 31.6 | 39.5 | 0.7 | 0.0 | 13.1 | 0.0 | 7.2 | 0.0 | 14.4 | 0.0 | 41.9 |
| Latvia | 7 749 | 90.2 | 20.6 | 71.0 | 5.3 | 4.6 | 8.4 | 4.6 | 0.6 | 1.4 | 8.3 | 5.7 | 22.8 |
| Liechtenstein | 9 816 | 114.2 | c | c | c | c | c | c | c | c | c | c | c |
| Macao-China | 7 566 | 88.0 | 16.9 | 74.5 | 1.4 | 0.2 | 4.5 | 0.2 | 6.1 | 7.4 | 9.0 | 7.5 | 19.2 |
| Russian Federation | 8 501 | 98.9 | 29.7 | 69.1 | 5.6 | 2.7 | 11.9 | 2.6 | 4.5 | 2.9 | 12.6 | 4.9 | 30.1 |
| Thailand | 6 723 | 78.2 | 30.3 | 51.0 | 5.9 | 0.4 | 16.4 | 0.5 | 4.8 | 1.6 | 17.0 | 2.0 | 38.8 |
| Tunisia | 6 707 | 78.0 | 32.8 | 44.9 | 5.3 | 0.6 | 18.1 | 0.7 | 25.2 | 1.8 | 27.6 | 2.4 | 42.1 |
| Uruguay | 9 915 | 115.4 | 53.5 | 68.6 | 13.0 | 1.4 | 38.2 | 1.5 | 37.6 | 2.7 | 47.4 | 4.1 | 46.4 |

1. The variance components were estimated for all students in participating countries with data on socio-economic background and study programmes. Students in special education programmes were excluded from these analyses.
2. The total variance in student performance is calculated from the square of the standard deviation for the students used in the analysis. The statistical variance in student performance and not the standard deviation is used for this comparison to allow for the decomposition.
3. The sum of the between- and within-school variance components, as an estimate from a sample, does not necessarily add up to the total.
4. In some countries, sub-units within schools were sampled instead of schools and this may affect the estimation of the between-school variance components (see Annex A2).
5. This index is often referred to as the intra-class correlation (rho).
*StatLink* ᵃᵍᵏ http://dx.doi.org/10.1787/142104560611

Pour consulter la version française intégrale de ce tableau, suivre ce lien :
*StatLink* ᵃᵍᵏ http://dx.doi.org/10.1787/152684743050

[Part 1/1]

**Table 4.1i   Between-school and within-school variance in student performance on the mathematics scale in PISA 2000**

Variance inter- et intra-établissements des scores sur l'échelle de culture mathématique du cycle PISA 2000

| | | Variance expressed as a percentage of the average variance in student performance (SP) across OECD countries[1] | | | | | | | |
|---|---|---|---|---|---|---|---|---|---|
| | Total variance in SP[2] | Total variance in SP expressed as a percentage of the average variance in student performance across OECD countries[3] | Total variance in SP between schools[4] | Total variance in SP within schools | Variance explained by the PISA index of economic, social and cultural status of students | | Variance explained by the PISA index of economic, social and cultural status of students and schools | | Total variance between schools expressed as a percentage of the total variance within the country[5] |
| | | | | | Between-school variance explained | Within-school variance explained | Between-school variance explained | Within-school variance explained | |
| **OECD** | | | | | | | | | |
| Australia | 8 066 | 95.5 | 16.3 | 78.5 | 9.9 | 5.9 | 12.1 | 6.5 | 17.0 |
| Austria | 8 648 | 102.4 | 57.5 | 53.9 | 9.5 | 0.6 | 36.1 | 0.6 | 56.1 |
| Belgium | 10 315 | 122.1 | 64.5 | 61.4 | 14.0 | 2.0 | 43.1 | 2.1 | 52.8 |
| Canada | 7 104 | 84.1 | 14.8 | 68.8 | 3.8 | 4.6 | 5.2 | 4.8 | 17.6 |
| Czech Republic | 8 544 | 101.2 | 40.9 | 61.1 | 12.2 | 3.5 | 28.4 | 3.6 | 40.4 |
| Denmark | 7 195 | 85.2 | 12.7 | 73.2 | 6.0 | 6.7 | 7.2 | 6.9 | 14.9 |
| Finland | 6 316 | 74.8 | 3.4 | 71.5 | 0.2 | 6.1 | 0.3 | 6.1 | 4.5 |
| France | w | w | w | w | w | w | w | w | w |
| Germany | 9 654 | 114.3 | 59.5 | 56.2 | 15.0 | 2.2 | 44.8 | 2.4 | 52.0 |
| Greece | 11 736 | 139.0 | 65.8 | 77.2 | 11.9 | 2.3 | 33.5 | 2.3 | 47.3 |
| Hungary | 9 193 | 108.9 | 54.0 | 54.7 | 13.9 | 0.8 | 45.4 | 0.9 | 49.6 |
| Iceland | 6 979 | 82.6 | 4.4 | 78.4 | 1.0 | 4.5 | 1.0 | 4.5 | 5.4 |
| Ireland | 6 916 | 81.9 | 9.3 | 72.7 | 5.3 | 5.8 | 7.5 | 6.1 | 11.4 |
| Italy | 8 079 | 95.7 | 41.7 | 57.7 | 3.9 | 0.2 | 19.7 | 0.2 | 43.6 |
| Japan | m | m | m | m | m | m | m | m | m |
| Korea | 7 108 | 84.2 | 34.1 | 50.7 | 4.7 | 0.4 | 20.8 | 0.4 | 40.5 |
| Luxembourg | m | m | m | m | m | m | m | m | m |
| Mexico | 6 897 | 81.7 | 41.3 | 41.8 | 7.5 | 0.2 | 26.6 | 0.1 | 50.5 |
| Netherlands | m | m | m | m | m | m | m | m | m |
| New Zealand | 9 432 | 111.7 | 20.0 | 91.8 | 9.8 | 8.0 | 14.0 | 8.2 | 17.9 |
| Norway | 8 359 | 99.0 | 8.7 | 90.3 | 1.7 | 8.8 | 1.8 | 8.8 | 8.8 |
| Poland | 9 949 | 117.8 | 63.2 | 53.3 | 6.9 | 0.4 | 35.9 | 0.4 | 53.7 |
| Portugal | 8 263 | 97.8 | 29.0 | 67.7 | 10.4 | 3.8 | 19.3 | 3.9 | 29.6 |
| Spain | 8 139 | 96.4 | 16.8 | 78.8 | 8.1 | 5.4 | 10.3 | 5.5 | 17.4 |
| Sweden | 8 638 | 102.3 | 7.7 | 94.7 | 4.8 | 7.7 | 5.5 | 7.7 | 7.6 |
| Switzerland | 9 886 | 117.1 | 46.0 | 69.8 | 11.0 | 3.4 | 25.3 | 3.1 | 39.3 |
| United Kingdom | m | m | m | m | m | m | m | m | m |
| United States | 8 825 | 104.5 | 33.0 | 73.2 | 16.9 | 7.7 | 26.7 | 7.9 | 31.6 |
| **OECD average** | **8 445** | **100.0** | **32.4** | **68.6** | **8.2** | **3.9** | **20.5** | **4.0** | |
| **Partners** | | | | | | | | | |
| Argentina | 14 513 | 163.0 | 72.5 | 88.9 | 18.3 | 1.0 | 49.0 | 1.3 | 44.5 |
| Brazil | 9 496 | 112.4 | 42.1 | 73.0 | 16.6 | 1.0 | 28.9 | 2.3 | 37.4 |
| Bulgaria | 11 616 | 130.5 | 64.3 | 71.1 | 18.5 | 2.0 | 50.3 | 2.3 | 49.3 |
| Chile | 8 735 | 98.1 | 47.3 | 56.9 | 13.6 | 0.7 | 32.3 | 0.7 | 48.2 |
| Hong Kong-China | 8 642 | 102.3 | 46.0 | 56.1 | 2.5 | 0.2 | 18.6 | 0.2 | 45.0 |
| Indonesia | 7 095 | 84.0 | 26.3 | 51.7 | 1.6 | 0.1 | 8.7 | 0.2 | 31.3 |
| Israel | 16 845 | 189.2 | 65.6 | 117.2 | 21.3 | 4.6 | 42.3 | 5.6 | 34.7 |
| Latvia | 10 614 | 125.7 | 33.8 | 92.4 | 5.3 | 1.4 | 17.2 | 1.5 | 26.9 |
| Liechtenstein | 9 080 | 107.5 | c | c | c | c | c | c | c |
| Romania | 13 323 | 149.6 | 60.5 | 91.3 | 4.4 | 1.0 | 25.4 | 0.1 | 40.4 |
| Russian Federation | 10 772 | 127.6 | 45.5 | 81.9 | 5.4 | 2.1 | 12.8 | 2.0 | 35.6 |
| Thailand | 6 799 | 80.5 | 27.4 | 54.9 | 5.2 | 0.5 | 11.1 | 0.6 | 34.0 |

1. The variance components were estimated for all students in participating countries with data on socio-economic background and study programmes. Students in special education programmes were excluded from these analyses.
2. The total variance in student performance is calculated from the square of the standard deviation for the students used in the analysis. The statistical variance in student performance and not the standard deviation is used for this comparison to allow for the decomposition.
3. The sum of the between- and within-school variance components, as an estimate from a sample, does not necessarily add up to the total.
4. In some countries, sub-units within schools were sampled instead of schools and this may affect the estimation of the between-school variance components (see Annex A2).
5. This index is often referred to as the intra-class correlation (rho).
StatLink http://dx.doi.org/10.1787/142104560611

Pour consulter la version française intégrale de ce tableau, suivre ce lien :
StatLink http://dx.doi.org/10.1787/152684743050

[Part 1/3]

**Table 4.2a Distribution of student performance on the science scale, by immigrant status**

Tableau 4.2a Répartition des scores sur l'échelle de culture scientifique selon l'ascendance autochtone ou allochtone

| | | Native students | | | | | | | | | | | | |
|---|---|---|---|---|---|---|---|---|---|---|---|---|---|---|
| | | | | Percentiles of the science performance distribution | | | | | | | | | | |
| | | Mean score | | 5th | | 10th | | 25th | | 75th | | 90th | | 95th | |
| | | Mean | S.E. | Score | S.E. | Score | S.E. | Score | S.E. | Score | S.E. | Score | S.E. | Score | S.E. |
| OECD | Australia | 529 | (2.0) | 364 | (3.8) | 400 | (3.5) | 463 | (2.6) | 598 | (2.1) | 653 | (2.4) | 684 | (3.5) |
| | Austria | 523 | (3.5) | 368 | (5.3) | 400 | (4.6) | 460 | (5.0) | 589 | (4.1) | 638 | (3.8) | 667 | (3.8) |
| | Belgium | 523 | (2.4) | 357 | (6.6) | 394 | (4.7) | 460 | (3.5) | 593 | (2.2) | 639 | (2.0) | 664 | (2.8) |
| | Canada | 541 | (1.8) | 385 | (4.3) | 421 | (3.3) | 480 | (2.2) | 605 | (2.0) | 655 | (2.6) | 684 | (2.7) |
| | Czech Republic | 515 | (3.5) | 354 | (5.9) | 388 | (4.8) | 445 | (4.5) | 584 | (3.9) | 642 | (4.4) | 673 | (4.8) |
| | Denmark | 503 | (2.9) | 356 | (5.9) | 385 | (4.2) | 441 | (3.3) | 566 | (3.3) | 619 | (4.4) | 649 | (4.4) |
| | Finland | 566 | (2.0) | 425 | (4.4) | 457 | (2.8) | 509 | (2.6) | 623 | (2.4) | 674 | (2.8) | 700 | (2.9) |
| | France | 505 | (3.5) | 337 | (6.9) | 374 | (5.5) | 436 | (5.7) | 576 | (3.6) | 628 | (3.7) | 657 | (3.5) |
| | Germany | 532 | (3.2) | 373 | (6.2) | 408 | (5.1) | 468 | (4.8) | 599 | (3.5) | 650 | (3.2) | 678 | (3.2) |
| | Greece | 478 | (3.2) | 323 | (7.7) | 360 | (5.2) | 418 | (4.2) | 540 | (3.2) | 591 | (3.7) | 621 | (3.7) |
| | Hungary | 505 | (2.7) | 360 | (4.1) | 389 | (4.3) | 443 | (3.6) | 566 | (3.4) | 618 | (3.2) | 647 | (4.3) |
| | Iceland | 494 | (1.7) | 336 | (4.0) | 371 | (2.9) | 429 | (2.5) | 562 | (2.3) | 616 | (3.0) | 645 | (3.7) |
| | Ireland | 510 | (3.0) | 356 | (4.5) | 390 | (4.2) | 447 | (4.0) | 576 | (3.3) | 630 | (3.6) | 660 | (5.1) |
| | Italy | 479 | (2.0) | 325 | (3.3) | 357 | (2.9) | 414 | (2.7) | 545 | (2.5) | 600 | (2.7) | 632 | (2.8) |
| | Japan | 532 | (3.4) | 357 | (6.1) | 397 | (6.3) | 466 | (5.1) | 603 | (3.1) | 655 | (3.0) | 685 | (3.6) |
| | Korea | 523 | (3.3) | 371 | (7.8) | 405 | (5.8) | 464 | (4.0) | 587 | (3.8) | 635 | (4.7) | 663 | (6.0) |
| | Luxembourg | 511 | (1.6) | 364 | (5.2) | 399 | (4.3) | 454 | (2.4) | 572 | (2.6) | 620 | (3.4) | 650 | (4.4) |
| | Mexico | 415 | (2.6) | 290 | (3.6) | 315 | (3.7) | 361 | (2.9) | 468 | (2.9) | 519 | (3.2) | 547 | (3.8) |
| | Netherlands | 534 | (2.3) | 376 | (5.0) | 408 | (4.0) | 469 | (4.1) | 602 | (2.4) | 651 | (3.1) | 679 | (3.7) |
| | New Zealand | 536 | (2.6) | 361 | (6.9) | 401 | (4.5) | 465 | (3.9) | 610 | (2.9) | 667 | (3.5) | 700 | (4.8) |
| | Norway | 493 | (2.5) | 343 | (5.9) | 377 | (3.9) | 429 | (3.0) | 557 | (2.6) | 613 | (3.5) | 643 | (3.7) |
| | Poland | 499 | (2.3) | 354 | (3.9) | 383 | (3.0) | 436 | (2.8) | 563 | (3.2) | 616 | (3.4) | 645 | (3.3) |
| | Portugal | 479 | (2.9) | 336 | (5.5) | 364 | (4.5) | 417 | (3.9) | 541 | (2.8) | 590 | (2.8) | 618 | (3.8) |
| | Slovak Republic | 490 | (2.6) | 336 | (5.5) | 369 | (3.7) | 427 | (3.3) | 555 | (4.1) | 610 | (4.1) | 639 | (3.7) |
| | Spain | 494 | (2.4) | 348 | (3.6) | 378 | (3.9) | 433 | (3.1) | 556 | (3.0) | 606 | (2.8) | 635 | (3.0) |
| | Sweden | 512 | (2.3) | 361 | (4.4) | 395 | (3.3) | 450 | (3.1) | 575 | (2.9) | 626 | (2.9) | 657 | (3.7) |
| | Switzerland | 531 | (2.9) | 379 | (5.0) | 413 | (3.5) | 470 | (3.4) | 595 | (3.2) | 644 | (4.4) | 672 | (4.5) |
| | Turkey | 425 | (3.8) | 301 | (3.0) | 326 | (3.1) | 367 | (2.6) | 476 | (5.8) | 540 | (9.6) | 575 | (9.7) |
| | United Kingdom | 519 | (2.0) | 344 | (4.1) | 382 | (3.3) | 446 | (3.0) | 594 | (2.7) | 655 | (3.1) | 688 | (3.8) |
| | United States | 499 | (4.3) | 328 | (6.5) | 361 | (6.7) | 423 | (5.5) | 576 | (4.4) | 635 | (3.8) | 667 | (4.5) |
| | **OECD total** | **497** | **(1.2)** | **330** | **(2.0)** | **362** | **(1.9)** | **423** | **(1.5)** | **571** | **(1.3)** | **629** | **(1.3)** | **662** | **(1.6)** |
| | **OECD average** | **506** | **(0.5)** | **352** | **(1.0)** | **386** | **(0.8)** | **443** | **(0.7)** | **572** | **(0.6)** | **624** | **(0.7)** | **654** | **(0.8)** |
| Partners | Argentina | 393 | (6.2) | 219 | (10.8) | 261 | (9.2) | 326 | (7.2) | 463 | (6.6) | 521 | (6.4) | 557 | (6.6) |
| | Azerbaijan | 384 | (2.8) | 301 | (3.0) | 317 | (2.7) | 345 | (2.8) | 416 | (3.7) | 458 | (6.6) | 487 | (7.5) |
| | Brazil | 393 | (6.4) | 256 | (4.3) | 283 | (3.3) | 330 | (2.6) | 450 | (4.5) | 512 | (6.0) | 550 | (5.2) |
| | Bulgaria | 436 | (6.1) | 268 | (7.7) | 302 | (7.0) | 359 | (6.5) | 511 | (7.7) | 578 | (8.0) | 613 | (8.3) |
| | Chile | 440 | (4.4) | 296 | (4.7) | 325 | (4.5) | 375 | (4.1) | 502 | (6.0) | 562 | (6.6) | 597 | (6.1) |
| | Colombia | 391 | (3.3) | 252 | (5.7) | 283 | (4.9) | 335 | (4.8) | 447 | (4.4) | 497 | (4.5) | 529 | (4.3) |
| | Croatia | 497 | (2.6) | 355 | (5.2) | 386 | (4.7) | 437 | (3.4) | 556 | (2.9) | 608 | (3.4) | 637 | (4.1) |
| | Estonia | 537 | (2.6) | 398 | (3.8) | 429 | (4.2) | 482 | (3.0) | 593 | (3.5) | 643 | (3.5) | 670 | (3.6) |
| | Hong Kong-China | 547 | (3.0) | 384 | (5.2) | 423 | (5.8) | 489 | (4.2) | 611 | (3.5) | 658 | (4.7) | 685 | (4.2) |
| | Indonesia | 395 | (5.7) | 288 | (4.3) | 309 | (3.6) | 346 | (4.2) | 439 | (7.9) | 489 | (11.4) | 518 | (11.6) |
| | Israel | 462 | (3.6) | 284 | (5.6) | 320 | (5.4) | 383 | (4.7) | 541 | (4.6) | 605 | (4.3) | 640 | (6.6) |
| | Jordan | 422 | (2.9) | 280 | (5.1) | 312 | (4.0) | 362 | (3.1) | 482 | (3.8) | 535 | (4.6) | 567 | (5.7) |
| | Kyrgyzstan | 324 | (2.8) | 196 | (4.0) | 224 | (3.3) | 270 | (3.2) | 372 | (3.3) | 427 | (4.5) | 466 | (6.5) |
| | Latvia | 492 | (3.0) | 352 | (5.2) | 383 | (4.5) | 436 | (3.8) | 549 | (3.5) | 598 | (3.6) | 628 | (3.0) |
| | Liechtenstein | 540 | (5.8) | 407 | (20.1) | 437 | (16.8) | 480 | (11.6) | 596 | (9.4) | 642 | (10.1) | 679 | (21.6) |
| | Lithuania | 489 | (2.9) | 342 | (3.7) | 372 | (3.3) | 427 | (3.5) | 552 | (3.7) | 605 | (4.4) | 633 | (5.5) |
| | Macao-China | 504 | (2.2) | 370 | (6.4) | 398 | (5.8) | 448 | (3.4) | 561 | (3.6) | 609 | (3.9) | 636 | (6.9) |
| | Montenegro | 411 | (1.2) | 286 | (2.8) | 312 | (2.2) | 355 | (2.3) | 464 | (2.1) | 516 | (3.1) | 548 | (3.9) |
| | Qatar | 330 | (1.1) | 223 | (2.9) | 245 | (1.8) | 283 | (1.9) | 371 | (2.0) | 421 | (2.8) | 454 | (3.3) |
| | Romania | 418 | (4.2) | 291 | (4.5) | 314 | (5.0) | 361 | (5.2) | 473 | (5.7) | 526 | (5.5) | 556 | (8.1) |
| | Russian Federation | 481 | (3.8) | 336 | (6.0) | 367 | (5.6) | 420 | (4.7) | 542 | (4.4) | 598 | (3.9) | 629 | (4.6) |
| | Serbia | 436 | (3.1) | 297 | (5.2) | 326 | (4.1) | 376 | (3.9) | 495 | (3.9) | 546 | (3.8) | 577 | (3.9) |
| | Slovenia | 525 | (1.2) | 366 | (3.3) | 399 | (3.1) | 458 | (2.9) | 595 | (1.9) | 653 | (2.9) | 683 | (3.9) |
| | Chinese Taipei | 535 | (3.5) | 372 | (4.7) | 405 | (4.6) | 470 | (5.3) | 603 | (3.3) | 651 | (2.6) | 677 | (3.5) |
| | Thailand | 422 | (2.1) | 303 | (4.3) | 328 | (3.2) | 370 | (2.6) | 472 | (3.3) | 525 | (4.0) | 554 | (4.8) |
| | Tunisia | 387 | (2.9) | 257 | (3.8) | 284 | (3.3) | 331 | (2.8) | 441 | (4.2) | 496 | (6.0) | 528 | (6.9) |
| | Uruguay | 430 | (2.7) | 276 | (7.1) | 309 | (5.2) | 366 | (3.9) | 495 | (3.2) | 551 | (3.7) | 585 | (4.4) |

StatLink ⟓⟔ http://dx.doi.org/10.1787/142104560611

Pour consulter la version française intégrale de ce tableau, suivre ce lien :
StatLink ⟓⟔ http://dx.doi.org/10.1787/152684743050

[Part 2/3]
**Table 4.2a**  **Distribution of student performance on the science scale, by immigrant status**

Tableau 4.2a  Répartition des scores sur l'échelle de culture scientifique selon l'ascendance autochtone ou allochtone

| | | | Second-generation students | | | | | | | | | | |
|---|---|---|---|---|---|---|---|---|---|---|---|---|---|
| | | | | | Percentiles of the science performance distribution | | | | | | | | |
| | Mean score | | 5th | | 10th | | 25th | | 75th | | 90th | | 95th | |
| | Mean | S.E. | Score | S.E. | Score | S.E. | Score | S.E. | Score | S.E. | Score | S.E. | Score | S.E. |
| Australia | 528 | (5.7) | 361 | (6.6) | 396 | (7.1) | 461 | (6.1) | 598 | (7.4) | 656 | (8.9) | 688 | (9.3) |
| Austria | 431 | (13.4) | 285 | (15.7) | 312 | (11.5) | 352 | (13.1) | 496 | (16.5) | 572 | (20.5) | 616 | (22.2) |
| Belgium | 443 | (7.3) | 292 | (14.7) | 327 | (11.6) | 376 | (8.7) | 507 | (9.7) | 563 | (8.9) | 599 | (10.7) |
| Canada | 528 | (4.8) | 366 | (8.4) | 401 | (8.5) | 461 | (7.7) | 598 | (5.8) | 645 | (6.7) | 671 | (7.9) |
| Czech Republic | c | c | c | c | c | c | c | c | c | c | c | c | c | c |
| Denmark | 418 | (11.0) | 277 | (23.0) | 308 | (14.3) | 351 | (14.0) | 483 | (16.2) | 532 | (15.3) | 568 | (18.1) |
| Finland | c | c | c | c | c | c | c | c | c | c | c | c | c | c |
| France | 456 | (10.4) | 294 | (11.9) | 321 | (14.1) | 381 | (12.9) | 534 | (12.1) | 593 | (14.1) | 624 | (16.9) |
| Germany | 439 | (8.7) | 276 | (15.6) | 308 | (15.0) | 368 | (12.6) | 508 | (9.1) | 569 | (11.0) | 603 | (18.8) |
| Greece | c | c | c | c | c | c | c | c | c | c | c | c | c | c |
| Hungary | c | c | c | c | c | c | c | c | c | c | c | c | c | c |
| Iceland | c | c | c | c | c | c | c | c | c | c | c | c | c | c |
| Ireland | c | c | c | c | c | c | c | c | c | c | c | c | c | c |
| Italy | c | c | c | c | c | c | c | c | c | c | c | c | c | c |
| Japan | c | c | c | c | c | c | c | c | c | c | c | c | c | c |
| Korea | c | c | c | c | c | c | c | c | c | c | c | c | c | c |
| Luxembourg | 445 | (3.0) | 303 | (6.8) | 332 | (6.3) | 382 | (4.2) | 507 | (4.6) | 569 | (6.3) | 604 | (8.1) |
| Mexico | c | c | c | c | c | c | c | c | c | c | c | c | c | c |
| Netherlands | 455 | (11.2) | 315 | (13.0) | 341 | (15.7) | 389 | (15.9) | 517 | (14.0) | 583 | (16.1) | 612 | (14.1) |
| New Zealand | 508 | (8.0) | 319 | (14.4) | 368 | (17.3) | 424 | (10.3) | 597 | (10.3) | 651 | (10.7) | 685 | (11.6) |
| Norway | c | c | c | c | c | c | c | c | c | c | c | c | c | c |
| Poland | c | c | c | c | c | c | c | c | c | c | c | c | c | c |
| Portugal | c | c | c | c | c | c | c | c | c | c | c | c | c | c |
| Slovak Republic | c | c | c | c | c | c | c | c | c | c | c | c | c | c |
| Spain | c | c | c | c | c | c | c | c | c | c | c | c | c | c |
| Sweden | 464 | (6.0) | 321 | (15.1) | 349 | (9.3) | 400 | (9.8) | 529 | (7.9) | 578 | (11.0) | 614 | (18.4) |
| Switzerland | 462 | (4.8) | 305 | (7.8) | 338 | (6.9) | 391 | (6.3) | 530 | (6.1) | 590 | (6.7) | 624 | (7.8) |
| Turkey | c | c | c | c | c | c | c | c | c | c | c | c | c | c |
| United Kingdom | 493 | (8.9) | 332 | (20.3) | 367 | (15.8) | 421 | (12.9) | 564 | (11.8) | 627 | (17.4) | 668 | (22.5) |
| United States | 456 | (6.7) | 306 | (12.6) | 332 | (9.8) | 382 | (9.6) | 524 | (10.5) | 589 | (9.6) | 627 | (14.4) |
| **OECD total** | **463** | **(3.5)** | **303** | **(8.8)** | **333** | **(5.7)** | **388** | **(5.0)** | **534** | **(3.6)** | **598** | **(5.1)** | **639** | **(6.3)** |
| **OECD average** | **466** | **(2.2)** | **311** | **(3.8)** | **342** | **(3.3)** | **395** | **(2.9)** | **535** | **(2.9)** | **594** | **(3.3)** | **629** | **(4.1)** |
| Argentina | c | c | c | c | c | c | c | c | c | c | c | c | c | c |
| Azerbaijan | c | c | c | c | c | c | c | c | c | c | c | c | c | c |
| Brazil | c | c | c | c | c | c | c | c | c | c | c | c | c | c |
| Bulgaria | c | c | c | c | c | c | c | c | c | c | c | c | c | c |
| Chile | c | c | c | c | c | c | c | c | c | c | c | c | c | c |
| Colombia | c | c | c | c | c | c | c | c | c | c | c | c | c | c |
| Croatia | 481 | (6.3) | 360 | (7.5) | 380 | (8.9) | 423 | (9.1) | 536 | (9.7) | 583 | (9.2) | 610 | (14.3) |
| Estonia | 505 | (4.6) | 378 | (11.2) | 406 | (8.5) | 447 | (6.1) | 558 | (8.3) | 615 | (9.8) | 651 | (10.8) |
| Hong Kong-China | 551 | (3.6) | 395 | (7.3) | 432 | (7.8) | 491 | (6.2) | 615 | (4.4) | 660 | (6.6) | 686 | (6.4) |
| Indonesia | c | c | c | c | c | c | c | c | c | c | c | c | c | c |
| Israel | 445 | (6.6) | 268 | (16.7) | 309 | (11.5) | 370 | (10.1) | 518 | (11.8) | 588 | (10.8) | 620 | (11.5) |
| Jordan | 445 | (5.4) | 308 | (7.3) | 336 | (9.4) | 387 | (7.4) | 505 | (9.3) | 555 | (7.2) | 584 | (9.5) |
| Kyrgyzstan | c | c | c | c | c | c | c | c | c | c | c | c | c | c |
| Latvia | 489 | (6.1) | 357 | (11.8) | 383 | (8.3) | 427 | (6.7) | 547 | (9.5) | 602 | (11.3) | 632 | (13.4) |
| Liechtenstein | 510 | (13.7) | 358 | (22.9) | 382 | (29.8) | 433 | (24.1) | 595 | (33.2) | 658 | (15.8) | 669 | (17.6) |
| Lithuania | c | c | c | c | c | c | c | c | c | c | c | c | c | c |
| Macao-China | 519 | (1.4) | 390 | (5.4) | 420 | (3.5) | 469 | (3.0) | 572 | (2.4) | 613 | (2.4) | 637 | (3.3) |
| Montenegro | c | c | c | c | c | c | c | c | c | c | c | c | c | c |
| Qatar | 366 | (2.3) | 251 | (6.0) | 274 | (4.5) | 311 | (3.0) | 414 | (3.0) | 469 | (5.9) | 502 | (7.9) |
| Romania | a | a | a | a | a | a | a | a | a | a | a | a | a | a |
| Russian Federation | 468 | (6.7) | 312 | (17.7) | 355 | (15.2) | 409 | (9.9) | 527 | (10.2) | 582 | (13.6) | 617 | (21.7) |
| Serbia | 444 | (6.1) | 324 | (20.7) | 344 | (13.9) | 388 | (9.1) | 500 | (11.4) | 551 | (13.5) | 576 | (19.9) |
| Slovenia | 468 | (5.5) | 328 | (8.0) | 356 | (10.8) | 402 | (8.5) | 531 | (9.9) | 591 | (15.4) | 620 | (11.0) |
| Chinese Taipei | c | c | c | c | c | c | c | c | c | c | c | c | c | c |
| Thailand | c | c | c | c | c | c | c | c | c | c | c | c | c | c |
| Tunisia | c | c | c | c | c | c | c | c | c | c | c | c | c | c |
| Uruguay | c | c | c | c | c | c | c | c | c | c | c | c | c | c |

*StatLink* http://dx.doi.org/10.1787/142104560611

Pour consulter la version française intégrale de ce tableau, suivre ce lien :
*StatLink* http://dx.doi.org/10.1787/152684743050

[Part 3/3]

**Table 4.2a**   **Distribution of student performance on the science scale, by immigrant status**

Tableau 4.2a   Répartition des scores sur l'échelle de culture scientifique selon l'ascendance autochtone ou allochtone

|  |  | First-generation students | | | | | | | | | | | | |
|---|---|---|---|---|---|---|---|---|---|---|---|---|---|---|
|  |  |  |  | Percentiles of the science performance distribution | | | | | | | | | | |
|  |  | Mean score | | 5th | | 10th | | 25th | | 75th | | 90th | | 95th | |
|  |  | Mean | S.E. | Score | S.E. | Score | S.E. | Score | S.E. | Score | S.E. | Score | S.E. | Score | S.E. |
| OECD | Australia | 527 | (5.7) | 343 | (10.7) | 383 | (9.4) | 448 | (7.2) | 606 | (7.9) | 664 | (9.5) | 696 | (10.1) |
|  | Austria | 435 | (10.9) | 265 | (25.1) | 299 | (19.4) | 359 | (16.5) | 510 | (10.7) | 577 | (11.0) | 604 | (9.4) |
|  | Belgium | 430 | (8.3) | 273 | (14.9) | 304 | (12.1) | 360 | (11.0) | 500 | (9.2) | 558 | (14.6) | 597 | (15.3) |
|  | Canada | 519 | (5.2) | 342 | (13.8) | 381 | (11.2) | 444 | (8.6) | 592 | (7.1) | 648 | (7.1) | 678 | (8.7) |
|  | Czech Republic | c | c | c | c | c | c | c | c | c | c | c | c | c | c |
|  | Denmark | 414 | (8.0) | 272 | (25.5) | 299 | (18.3) | 352 | (11.5) | 477 | (12.6) | 534 | (20.7) | 581 | (31.5) |
|  | Finland | c | c | c | c | c | c | c | c | c | c | c | c | c | c |
|  | France | 438 | (10.1) | 250 | (33.2) | 301 | (21.8) | 367 | (19.5) | 510 | (15.1) | 587 | (17.8) | 617 | (25.0) |
|  | Germany | 455 | (8.8) | 292 | (15.9) | 320 | (16.3) | 378 | (13.6) | 531 | (12.6) | 590 | (14.2) | 622 | (14.9) |
|  | Greece | 428 | (10.3) | 276 | (28.7) | 312 | (14.7) | 364 | (12.9) | 490 | (15.4) | 550 | (14.3) | 579 | (17.1) |
|  | Hungary | c | c | c | c | c | c | c | c | c | c | c | c | c | c |
|  | Iceland | c | c | c | c | c | c | c | c | c | c | c | c | c | c |
|  | Ireland | 500 | (14.6) | 303 | (27.8) | 333 | (24.4) | 418 | (19.1) | 585 | (15.8) | 654 | (16.0) | 693 | (20.1) |
|  | Italy | 418 | (8.2) | 255 | (37.0) | 300 | (17.6) | 353 | (7.8) | 489 | (9.8) | 544 | (8.5) | 576 | (13.2) |
|  | Japan | c | c | c | c | c | c | c | c | c | c | c | c | c | c |
|  | Korea | a | a | a | a | a | a | a | a | a | a | a | a | a | a |
|  | Luxembourg | 445 | (3.7) | 283 | (7.9) | 310 | (6.1) | 367 | (6.5) | 521 | (7.8) | 587 | (7.2) | 627 | (9.7) |
|  | Mexico | c | c | c | c | c | c | c | c | c | c | c | c | c | c |
|  | Netherlands | 467 | (10.2) | 318 | (15.2) | 335 | (14.0) | 393 | (15.7) | 532 | (12.5) | 602 | (17.0) | 642 | (28.1) |
|  | New Zealand | 526 | (6.6) | 315 | (12.0) | 364 | (14.9) | 439 | (9.5) | 619 | (7.6) | 680 | (7.2) | 708 | (7.1) |
|  | Norway | 433 | (11.2) | 267 | (19.0) | 303 | (15.4) | 363 | (13.7) | 501 | (17.3) | 582 | (25.1) | 631 | (39.7) |
|  | Poland | c | c | c | c | c | c | c | c | c | c | c | c | c | c |
|  | Portugal | 412 | (11.1) | 265 | (33.2) | 304 | (18.2) | 356 | (15.0) | 465 | (18.5) | 535 | (19.7) | 558 | (16.5) |
|  | Slovak Republic | c | c | c | c | c | c | c | c | c | c | c | c | c | c |
|  | Spain | 428 | (7.2) | 268 | (19.5) | 303 | (14.5) | 359 | (9.4) | 496 | (9.3) | 564 | (13.0) | 596 | (11.7) |
|  | Sweden | 434 | (8.1) | 287 | (18.2) | 312 | (15.7) | 365 | (11.1) | 497 | (13.1) | 567 | (18.2) | 617 | (34.9) |
|  | Switzerland | 436 | (6.9) | 272 | (10.0) | 302 | (10.2) | 357 | (8.1) | 509 | (11.4) | 589 | (11.8) | 630 | (10.1) |
|  | Turkey | c | c | c | c | c | c | c | c | c | c | c | c | c | c |
|  | United Kingdom | 479 | (14.7) | 264 | (40.8) | 316 | (33.1) | 389 | (25.1) | 570 | (17.7) | 638 | (14.7) | 673 | (20.3) |
|  | United States | 442 | (7.9) | 283 | (10.7) | 308 | (9.5) | 365 | (10.6) | 513 | (12.8) | 570 | (16.3) | 608 | (14.4) |
|  | **OECD total** | **448** | **(3.0)** | **275** | **(6.6)** | **305** | **(4.8)** | **366** | **(4.9)** | **526** | **(5.9)** | **594** | **(4.5)** | **634** | **(6.7)** |
|  | **OECD average** | **453** | **(2.1)** | **284** | **(5.2)** | **319** | **(3.8)** | **379** | **(3.0)** | **526** | **(2.8)** | **591** | **(3.4)** | **627** | **(4.5)** |
| Partners | Argentina | c | c | c | c | c | c | c | c | c | c | c | c | c | c |
|  | Azerbaijan | c | c | c | c | c | c | c | c | c | c | c | c | c | c |
|  | Brazil | c | c | c | c | c | c | c | c | c | c | c | c | c | c |
|  | Bulgaria | c | c | c | c | c | c | c | c | c | c | c | c | c | c |
|  | Chile | c | c | c | c | c | c | c | c | c | c | c | c | c | c |
|  | Colombia | c | c | c | c | c | c | c | c | c | c | c | c | c | c |
|  | Croatia | 475 | (5.6) | 359 | (10.9) | 380 | (5.4) | 418 | (5.3) | 530 | (10.7) | 580 | (9.2) | 607 | (12.5) |
|  | Estonia | c | c | c | c | c | c | c | c | c | c | c | c | c | c |
|  | Hong Kong-China | 521 | (4.9) | 363 | (10.4) | 395 | (10.3) | 457 | (6.6) | 590 | (5.5) | 638 | (7.2) | 666 | (6.7) |
|  | Indonesia | c | c | c | c | c | c | c | c | c | c | c | c | c | c |
|  | Israel | 468 | (7.8) | 286 | (16.9) | 323 | (12.3) | 385 | (9.1) | 553 | (13.2) | 617 | (9.3) | 654 | (10.8) |
|  | Jordan | 451 | (4.7) | 324 | (13.9) | 352 | (9.3) | 403 | (6.6) | 502 | (7.6) | 545 | (8.8) | 573 | (11.7) |
|  | Kyrgyzstan | c | c | c | c | c | c | c | c | c | c | c | c | c | c |
|  | Latvia | c | c | c | c | c | c | c | c | c | c | c | c | c | c |
|  | Liechtenstein | 483 | (11.1) | 326 | (27.3) | 349 | (18.1) | 399 | (19.5) | 558 | (25.5) | 641 | (31.0) | 684 | (30.1) |
|  | Lithuania | c | c | c | c | c | c | c | c | c | c | c | c | c | c |
|  | Macao-China | 500 | (3.5) | 374 | (10.1) | 402 | (6.8) | 445 | (5.8) | 553 | (5.0) | 603 | (7.4) | 630 | (11.2) |
|  | Montenegro | 436 | (6.6) | 301 | (17.8) | 331 | (12.4) | 373 | (10.8) | 497 | (11.0) | 549 | (14.0) | 573 | (16.4) |
|  | Qatar | 414 | (3.1) | 268 | (7.0) | 295 | (4.9) | 342 | (4.3) | 478 | (6.6) | 555 | (5.2) | 596 | (7.7) |
|  | Romania | c | c | c | c | c | c | c | c | c | c | c | c | c | c |
|  | Russian Federation | 467 | (7.8) | 322 | (13.9) | 352 | (11.3) | 403 | (13.7) | 533 | (9.6) | 580 | (11.2) | 614 | (16.5) |
|  | Serbia | 444 | (6.4) | 328 | (16.0) | 350 | (11.6) | 393 | (8.9) | 495 | (11.1) | 536 | (10.2) | 564 | (16.0) |
|  | Slovenia | c | c | c | c | c | c | c | c | c | c | c | c | c | c |
|  | Chinese Taipei | c | c | c | c | c | c | c | c | c | c | c | c | c | c |
|  | Thailand | c | c | c | c | c | c | c | c | c | c | c | c | c | c |
|  | Tunisia | c | c | c | c | c | c | c | c | c | c | c | c | c | c |
|  | Uruguay | c | c | c | c | c | c | c | c | c | c | c | c | c | c |

*StatLink* ᵃₛᶫ http://dx.doi.org/10.1787/142104560611

Pour consulter la version française intégrale de ce tableau, suivre ce lien :
*StatLink* ᵃₛᶫ http://dx.doi.org/10.1787/152684743050

[Part 1/3]

**Table 4.2b** Percentage of students at each proficiency level on the science scale, by immigrant status

Tableau 4.2b Pourcentage d'élèves à chaque niveau de compétence sur l'échelle de culture scientifique selon l'ascendance autochtone ou allochtone

| | Native students - Proficiency levels | | | | | | | | | | | | | |
|---|---|---|---|---|---|---|---|---|---|---|---|---|---|---|
| | Below Level 1 (below 334.94 score points) | | Level 1 (from 334.94 to 409.54 score points) | | Level 2 (from 409.54 to 484.14 score points) | | Level 3 (from 484.14 to 558.73 score points) | | Level 4 (from 558.73 to 633.33 score points) | | Level 5 (from 633.33 to 707.93 score points) | | Level 6 (above 707.93 score points) | |
| | % | S.E. | % | S.E. | % | S.E. | % | S.E. | % | S.E. | % | S.E. | % | S.E. |
| Australia | 2.6 | (0.3) | 9.1 | (0.5) | 20.2 | (0.6) | 28.3 | (0.6) | 25.1 | (0.6) | 11.8 | (0.5) | 2.7 | (0.3) |
| Austria | 2.0 | (0.4) | 9.8 | (0.9) | 21.2 | (1.1) | 30.0 | (1.1) | 25.8 | (1.2) | 9.8 | (0.8) | 1.3 | (0.2) |
| Belgium | 3.0 | (0.5) | 9.8 | (0.6) | 19.7 | (0.8) | 28.9 | (0.8) | 27.2 | (0.9) | 10.3 | (0.5) | 1.1 | (0.2) |
| Canada | 1.6 | (0.2) | 6.5 | (0.4) | 18.3 | (0.7) | 29.5 | (0.8) | 28.7 | (0.8) | 12.8 | (0.6) | 2.6 | (0.3) |
| Czech Republic | 3.0 | (0.6) | 11.7 | (0.8) | 23.4 | (1.2) | 28.0 | (1.1) | 22.0 | (0.9) | 9.9 | (0.9) | 1.9 | (0.3) |
| Denmark | 3.0 | (0.6) | 12.6 | (0.7) | 26.0 | (1.1) | 30.4 | (1.1) | 20.8 | (1.0) | 6.5 | (0.7) | 0.7 | (0.2) |
| Finland | 0.4 | (0.1) | 3.1 | (0.4) | 13.1 | (0.6) | 29.4 | (1.1) | 32.7 | (0.9) | 17.3 | (0.7) | 4.0 | (0.4) |
| France | 4.8 | (0.6) | 13.1 | (1.0) | 22.3 | (1.1) | 28.4 | (1.1) | 22.5 | (1.1) | 8.0 | (0.6) | 0.9 | (0.2) |
| Germany | 1.9 | (0.4) | 8.4 | (0.9) | 20.0 | (1.2) | 29.4 | (1.2) | 26.5 | (0.9) | 11.7 | (0.7) | 2.2 | (0.3) |
| Greece | 6.3 | (0.8) | 16.0 | (0.9) | 28.8 | (1.2) | 30.5 | (0.9) | 14.9 | (0.9) | 3.3 | (0.3) | 0.3 | (0.1) |
| Hungary | 2.5 | (0.3) | 12.3 | (0.9) | 25.9 | (1.1) | 31.2 | (1.1) | 21.1 | (0.9) | 6.3 | (0.6) | 0.6 | (0.2) |
| Iceland | 4.8 | (0.5) | 14.2 | (0.8) | 26.0 | (0.7) | 28.9 | (0.9) | 19.5 | (0.8) | 5.8 | (0.5) | 0.8 | (0.2) |
| Ireland | 3.0 | (0.4) | 11.5 | (0.8) | 24.1 | (0.9) | 30.2 | (1.0) | 21.8 | (0.9) | 8.4 | (0.6) | 1.1 | (0.2) |
| Italy | 6.3 | (0.4) | 17.4 | (0.6) | 27.8 | (0.8) | 28.0 | (0.6) | 15.7 | (0.6) | 4.4 | (0.3) | 0.4 | (0.1) |
| Japan | 3.1 | (0.4) | 8.8 | (0.7) | 18.5 | (0.9) | 27.5 | (0.9) | 27.0 | (1.1) | 12.4 | (0.6) | 2.6 | (0.3) |
| Korea | 2.3 | (0.5) | 8.5 | (0.8) | 21.1 | (1.0) | 32.0 | (1.2) | 25.7 | (0.9) | 9.3 | (0.8) | 1.1 | (0.3) |
| Luxembourg | 2.4 | (0.3) | 9.7 | (0.7) | 23.8 | (0.8) | 33.9 | (1.3) | 22.6 | (1.0) | 6.9 | (0.5) | 0.6 | (0.2) |
| Mexico | 15.6 | (1.1) | 32.8 | (0.9) | 32.2 | (0.9) | 15.7 | (0.7) | 3.4 | (0.4) | 0.3 | (0.1) | 0.0 | a |
| Netherlands | 1.3 | (0.2) | 8.9 | (0.7) | 19.6 | (0.9) | 27.7 | (0.9) | 28.0 | (1.0) | 12.6 | (0.9) | 1.8 | (0.3) |
| New Zealand | 2.9 | (0.4) | 8.6 | (0.5) | 19.1 | (0.9) | 27.0 | (1.0) | 24.6 | (0.8) | 13.7 | (0.8) | 4.1 | (0.5) |
| Norway | 4.2 | (0.6) | 14.1 | (0.9) | 27.6 | (0.9) | 29.5 | (1.0) | 18.1 | (0.7) | 5.7 | (0.4) | 0.6 | (0.1) |
| Poland | 3.0 | (0.4) | 13.4 | (0.6) | 27.4 | (1.0) | 29.7 | (1.0) | 19.6 | (0.8) | 6.2 | (0.4) | 0.7 | (0.1) |
| Portugal | 4.8 | (0.7) | 17.5 | (1.0) | 29.2 | (1.0) | 29.9 | (1.2) | 15.3 | (0.9) | 3.2 | (0.4) | 0.1 | (0.1) |
| Slovak Republic | 4.9 | (0.6) | 14.8 | (0.9) | 28.0 | (1.0) | 28.3 | (1.0) | 18.1 | (1.0) | 5.3 | (0.5) | 0.6 | (0.1) |
| Spain | 3.6 | (0.4) | 14.0 | (0.7) | 27.1 | (0.9) | 31.3 | (0.7) | 18.7 | (0.7) | 4.8 | (0.4) | 0.4 | (0.1) |
| Sweden | 2.4 | (0.4) | 10.7 | (0.6) | 24.6 | (0.9) | 30.9 | (1.0) | 22.8 | (1.0) | 7.3 | (0.5) | 1.2 | (0.2) |
| Switzerland | 1.7 | (0.3) | 7.7 | (0.5) | 20.2 | (0.9) | 30.7 | (1.0) | 27.2 | (1.1) | 10.7 | (0.9) | 1.7 | (0.3) |
| Turkey | 12.5 | (0.8) | 33.4 | (1.3) | 31.6 | (1.4) | 15.3 | (1.1) | 6.3 | (1.2) | 0.9 | (0.3) | 0.0 | a |
| United Kingdom | 4.1 | (0.4) | 11.2 | (0.6) | 21.3 | (0.8) | 26.4 | (0.7) | 22.6 | (0.6) | 11.4 | (0.6) | 3.0 | (0.3) |
| United States | 5.8 | (0.9) | 15.2 | (1.0) | 23.8 | (1.1) | 24.7 | (0.9) | 20.2 | (1.0) | 8.5 | (0.7) | 1.7 | (0.3) |
| **OECD total** | **5.7** | **(0.3)** | **15.4** | **(0.3)** | **24.1** | **(0.4)** | **25.8** | **(0.3)** | **19.7** | **(0.3)** | **7.8** | **(0.2)** | **1.4** | **(0.1)** |
| **OECD average** | **4.0** | **(0.1)** | **12.8** | **(0.1)** | **23.7** | **(0.2)** | **28.4** | **(0.2)** | **21.5** | **(0.2)** | **8.2** | **(0.1)** | **1.4** | **(0.0)** |
| Argentina | 27.7 | (2.4) | 27.8 | (1.4) | 25.8 | (1.3) | 14.0 | (1.3) | 4.2 | (0.7) | 0.5 | (0.1) | 0.0 | a |
| Azerbaijan | 18.6 | (1.5) | 52.9 | (1.6) | 23.2 | (1.4) | 5.0 | (0.9) | 0.4 | (0.2) | 0.0 | a | a | a |
| Brazil | 26.7 | (1.0) | 33.1 | (1.0) | 24.4 | (0.9) | 11.7 | (0.9) | 3.5 | (0.4) | 0.5 | (0.2) | 0.0 | (0.0) |
| Bulgaria | 17.7 | (1.7) | 24.2 | (1.3) | 25.2 | (1.2) | 19.3 | (1.2) | 10.5 | (1.1) | 2.6 | (0.5) | 0.5 | (0.2) |
| Chile | 12.5 | (1.1) | 26.5 | (1.6) | 30.1 | (1.2) | 20.3 | (1.5) | 8.6 | (1.0) | 1.8 | (0.3) | 0.1 | (0.1) |
| Colombia | 24.9 | (1.7) | 34.2 | (1.5) | 27.9 | (1.5) | 10.9 | (1.1) | 2.0 | (0.4) | 0.2 | (0.1) | 0.0 | a |
| Croatia | 3.0 | (0.4) | 13.0 | (0.7) | 28.4 | (1.0) | 31.7 | (1.1) | 18.4 | (0.9) | 4.9 | (0.5) | 0.6 | (0.1) |
| Estonia | 0.9 | (0.2) | 5.7 | (0.6) | 19.3 | (0.9) | 34.2 | (1.1) | 27.7 | (1.1) | 10.8 | (0.8) | 1.5 | (0.3) |
| Hong Kong-China | 1.7 | (0.3) | 6.4 | (0.7) | 15.5 | (1.1) | 28.9 | (1.1) | 30.5 | (1.4) | 14.9 | (1.1) | 2.2 | (0.4) |
| Indonesia | 19.5 | (1.7) | 41.6 | (2.2) | 27.9 | (1.4) | 9.6 | (2.0) | 1.4 | (0.5) | 0.0 | a | a | a |
| Israel | 12.7 | (1.2) | 20.4 | (1.0) | 24.3 | (1.2) | 22.3 | (1.2) | 14.6 | (0.9) | 4.8 | (0.6) | 0.9 | (0.2) |
| Jordan | 15.7 | (0.9) | 29.2 | (1.0) | 30.8 | (1.1) | 18.2 | (0.9) | 5.4 | (0.7) | 0.6 | (0.2) | 0.0 | a |
| Kyrgyzstan | 57.4 | (1.5) | 29.0 | (1.1) | 10.1 | (0.8) | 2.9 | (0.4) | 0.7 | (0.2) | 0.0 | a | a | a |
| Latvia | 3.2 | (0.5) | 13.2 | (1.0) | 28.7 | (1.2) | 33.7 | (1.0) | 17.0 | (1.0) | 3.9 | (0.4) | 0.3 | (0.1) |
| Liechtenstein | 0.7 | (0.6) | 5.2 | (2.3) | 19.8 | (4.4) | 31.2 | (4.0) | 30.6 | (3.3) | 9.7 | (2.3) | 2.8 | (1.2) |
| Lithuania | 3.9 | (0.4) | 15.7 | (0.8) | 27.4 | (0.9) | 30.2 | (0.9) | 17.7 | (0.9) | 4.6 | (0.6) | 0.4 | (0.2) |
| Macao-China | 1.6 | (0.5) | 11.2 | (1.1) | 28.1 | (2.1) | 33.1 | (1.6) | 20.7 | (1.5) | 5.0 | (0.7) | 0.3 | (0.2) |
| Montenegro | 17.1 | (0.8) | 33.3 | (1.3) | 31.3 | (1.0) | 14.6 | (0.7) | 3.5 | (0.4) | 0.3 | (0.1) | 0.0 | a |
| Qatar | 55.9 | (0.9) | 31.5 | (1.0) | 10.0 | (0.7) | 2.3 | (0.3) | 0.2 | (0.1) | 0.0 | a | a | a |
| Romania | 15.9 | (1.5) | 30.9 | (1.5) | 31.9 | (1.6) | 16.6 | (1.2) | 4.2 | (0.6) | 0.5 | (0.1) | 0.0 | a |
| Russian Federation | 4.8 | (0.7) | 16.6 | (1.2) | 30.2 | (1.0) | 28.7 | (1.3) | 15.3 | (1.1) | 3.8 | (0.5) | 0.5 | (0.1) |
| Serbia | 12.0 | (0.9) | 26.5 | (1.2) | 32.0 | (1.3) | 22.0 | (1.3) | 6.7 | (0.6) | 0.8 | (0.2) | 0.0 | a |
| Slovenia | 2.4 | (0.4) | 9.7 | (0.7) | 22.2 | (0.8) | 27.9 | (1.2) | 23.7 | (1.2) | 11.7 | (0.6) | 2.4 | (0.3) |
| Chinese Taipei | 1.6 | (0.3) | 9.3 | (0.8) | 18.4 | (0.9) | 27.5 | (0.8) | 28.3 | (1.0) | 13.2 | (0.8) | 1.7 | (0.2) |
| Thailand | 11.9 | (0.8) | 33.5 | (1.0) | 33.6 | (0.9) | 16.6 | (0.8) | 4.1 | (0.4) | 0.4 | (0.1) | 0.0 | a |
| Tunisia | 26.8 | (1.1) | 35.3 | (0.9) | 25.4 | (1.0) | 10.5 | (1.0) | 2.0 | (0.5) | 0.1 | (0.1) | 0.0 | a |
| Uruguay | 15.9 | (1.2) | 25.1 | (1.2) | 30.1 | (1.6) | 20.2 | (1.2) | 7.1 | (0.6) | 1.3 | (0.2) | 0.1 | (0.1) |

*StatLink* http://dx.doi.org/10.1787/142104560611

Pour consulter la version française intégrale de ce tableau, suivre ce lien :
*StatLink* http://dx.doi.org/10.1787/152684743050

[Part 2/3]

**Table 4.2b** **Percentage of students at each proficiency level on the science scale, by immigrant status**

Tableau 4.2b  Pourcentage d'élèves à chaque niveau de compétence sur l'échelle de culture scientifique selon l'ascendance autochtone ou allochtone

| | Second-generation students - Proficiency levels | | | | | | | | | | | | | |
|---|---|---|---|---|---|---|---|---|---|---|---|---|---|---|
| | Below Level 1 (below 334.94 score points) | | Level 1 (from 334.94 to 409.54 score points) | | Level 2 (from 409.54 to 484.14 score points) | | Level 3 (from 484.14 to 558.73 score points) | | Level 4 (from 558.73 to 633.33 score points) | | Level 5 (from 633.33 to 707.93 score points) | | Level 6 (above 707.93 score points) | |
| | % | S.E. | % | S.E. | % | S.E. | % | S.E. | % | S.E. | % | S.E. | % | S.E. |
| **OECD** | | | | | | | | | | | | | | |
| Australia | 2.6 | (0.6) | 10.2 | (1.2) | 20.2 | (1.5) | 28.0 | (1.4) | 24.0 | (1.3) | 12.0 | (1.5) | 3.1 | (0.8) |
| Austria | 18.5 | (4.4) | 26.8 | (6.0) | 26.5 | (4.6) | 16.0 | (3.7) | 8.4 | (2.2) | 3.6 | (1.6) | 0.3 | c |
| Belgium | 12.2 | (3.0) | 25.4 | (4.2) | 29.5 | (2.7) | 22.2 | (2.8) | 8.6 | (1.7) | 2.2 | (0.8) | 0.0 | c |
| Canada | 2.0 | (0.6) | 9.5 | (1.3) | 20.6 | (1.9) | 26.9 | (1.7) | 28.2 | (2.2) | 11.1 | (1.6) | 1.6 | (0.5) |
| Czech Republic | c | c | c | c | c | c | c | c | c | c | c | c | c | c |
| Denmark | 19.4 | (4.7) | 28.4 | (4.6) | 26.8 | (4.7) | 18.9 | (4.0) | 5.5 | (2.3) | 0.5 | c | 0.4 | c |
| Finland | c | c | c | c | c | c | c | c | c | c | c | c | c | c |
| France | 12.7 | (2.9) | 22.4 | (2.7) | 25.6 | (2.8) | 22.1 | (2.9) | 13.3 | (2.6) | 3.5 | (1.7) | 0.5 | (0.3) |
| Germany | 14.3 | (2.9) | 25.8 | (3.1) | 26.6 | (2.7) | 21.3 | (2.9) | 9.2 | (1.8) | 2.5 | (1.2) | 0.2 | c |
| Greece | c | c | c | c | c | c | c | c | c | c | c | c | c | c |
| Hungary | c | c | c | c | c | c | c | c | c | c | c | c | c | c |
| Iceland | c | c | c | c | c | c | c | c | c | c | c | c | c | c |
| Ireland | c | c | c | c | c | c | c | c | c | c | c | c | c | c |
| Italy | c | c | c | c | c | c | c | c | c | c | c | c | c | c |
| Japan | c | c | c | c | c | c | c | c | c | c | c | c | c | c |
| Korea | c | c | c | c | c | c | c | c | c | c | c | c | c | c |
| Luxembourg | 10.6 | (1.4) | 26.8 | (2.1) | 29.6 | (1.9) | 21.1 | (1.5) | 9.7 | (1.4) | 2.0 | (0.8) | 0.2 | (0.2) |
| Mexico | c | c | c | c | c | c | c | c | c | c | c | c | c | c |
| Netherlands | 8.6 | (3.3) | 24.2 | (5.3) | 31.1 | (4.1) | 22.2 | (3.9) | 10.7 | (2.3) | 2.9 | (1.4) | 0.3 | c |
| New Zealand | 6.7 | (1.7) | 14.1 | (2.5) | 23.3 | (3.3) | 18.9 | (2.9) | 22.6 | (3.0) | 12.5 | (2.2) | 1.9 | (1.0) |
| Norway | c | c | c | c | c | c | c | c | c | c | c | c | c | c |
| Poland | c | c | c | c | c | c | c | c | c | c | c | c | c | c |
| Portugal | c | c | c | c | c | c | c | c | c | c | c | c | c | c |
| Slovak Republic | c | c | c | c | c | c | c | c | c | c | c | c | c | c |
| Spain | c | c | c | c | c | c | c | c | c | c | c | c | c | c |
| Sweden | 7.0 | (1.9) | 21.5 | (3.1) | 30.3 | (3.6) | 26.9 | (3.8) | 11.0 | (2.1) | 3.0 | (1.5) | 0.3 | c |
| Switzerland | 9.3 | (1.2) | 22.0 | (1.6) | 28.5 | (1.8) | 23.8 | (1.8) | 12.5 | (1.6) | 3.3 | (0.8) | 0.5 | (0.3) |
| Turkey | c | c | c | c | c | c | c | c | c | c | c | c | c | c |
| United Kingdom | 4.6 | (1.5) | 15.9 | (3.8) | 27.4 | (3.7) | 25.5 | (3.6) | 17.7 | (2.9) | 6.3 | (1.8) | 2.5 | (1.2) |
| United States | 10.5 | (2.2) | 24.6 | (2.8) | 27.8 | (2.5) | 21.6 | (2.4) | 10.8 | (1.7) | 4.2 | (1.1) | 0.5 | (0.4) |
| **OECD total** | **10.3** | **(1.2)** | **22.4** | **(1.5)** | **26.5** | **(1.4)** | **22.3** | **(1.3)** | **12.9** | **(0.9)** | **4.8** | **(0.6)** | **0.7** | **(0.2)** |
| **OECD average** | **9.9** | **(0.7)** | **21.3** | **(0.9)** | **26.7** | **(0.8)** | **22.5** | **(0.8)** | **13.7** | **(0.6)** | **5.0** | **(0.4)** | **0.9** | **(0.2)** |
| **Partners** | | | | | | | | | | | | | | |
| Argentina | c | c | c | c | c | c | c | c | c | c | c | c | c | c |
| Azerbaijan | c | c | c | c | c | c | c | c | c | c | c | c | c | c |
| Brazil | c | c | c | c | c | c | c | c | c | c | c | c | c | c |
| Bulgaria | c | c | c | c | c | c | c | c | c | c | c | c | c | c |
| Chile | c | c | c | c | c | c | c | c | c | c | c | c | c | c |
| Colombia | c | c | c | c | c | c | c | c | c | c | c | c | c | c |
| Croatia | 2.2 | (1.3) | 17.1 | (3.4) | 33.3 | (3.5) | 30.4 | (3.9) | 14.5 | (2.6) | 2.5 | (1.4) | 0.1 | c |
| Estonia | 1.3 | (0.7) | 9.7 | (1.8) | 30.9 | (2.7) | 33.6 | (2.2) | 17.5 | (2.2) | 6.4 | (1.2) | 0.7 | (0.5) |
| Hong Kong-China | 1.1 | (0.5) | 5.7 | (0.9) | 15.9 | (1.8) | 28.4 | (1.6) | 31.4 | (1.7) | 14.9 | (1.4) | 2.6 | (0.7) |
| Indonesia | c | c | c | c | c | c | c | c | c | c | c | c | c | c |
| Israel | 15.8 | (2.3) | 22.0 | (2.8) | 25.7 | (2.9) | 20.2 | (2.1) | 12.5 | (1.8) | 3.3 | (1.0) | 0.4 | (0.4) |
| Jordan | 9.6 | (1.5) | 24.1 | (2.5) | 33.2 | (3.4) | 24.1 | (2.5) | 8.0 | (1.9) | 0.9 | (0.5) | 0.0 | c |
| Kyrgyzstan | c | c | c | c | c | c | c | c | c | c | c | c | c | c |
| Latvia | 2.3 | (0.9) | 15.7 | (2.6) | 31.6 | (4.1) | 29.7 | (2.5) | 16.0 | (2.9) | 4.6 | (1.8) | 0.2 | c |
| Liechtenstein | 2.2 | | 14.9 | (7.4) | 25.7 | (7.2) | 23.8 | (7.9) | 17.5 | (5.7) | 15.0 | (5.4) | 0.9 | c |
| Lithuania | c | c | c | c | c | c | c | c | c | c | c | c | c | c |
| Macao-China | 0.9 | (0.3) | 6.9 | (0.6) | 23.5 | (1.0) | 37.7 | (1.4) | 25.5 | (1.0) | 5.4 | (0.5) | 0.2 | (0.1) |
| Montenegro | c | c | c | c | c | c | c | c | c | c | c | c | c | c |
| Qatar | 36.9 | (1.4) | 36.0 | (1.6) | 19.4 | (1.4) | 6.5 | (0.9) | 1.1 | (0.4) | 0.1 | 0 | c | 0 |
| Romania | a | a | a | a | a | a | a | a | a | a | a | a | a | a |
| Russian Federation | 7.4 | (2.1) | 17.8 | (3.6) | 31.3 | (4.1) | 27.7 | (4.8) | 13.2 | (3.4) | 2.4 | (1.6) | 0.2 | c |
| Serbia | 7.4 | (3.1) | 28.1 | (5.0) | 33.5 | (5.0) | 22.6 | (4.3) | 7.5 | (2.5) | 0.9 | 0 | c | 0 |
| Slovenia | 6.2 | (1.4) | 21.5 | (2.8) | 30.2 | (2.7) | 25.6 | (2.4) | 13.3 | (2.2) | 2.9 | (1.1) | 0.3 | (0.4) |
| Chinese Taipei | c | c | c | c | c | c | c | c | c | c | c | c | c | c |
| Thailand | c | c | c | c | c | c | c | c | c | c | c | c | c | c |
| Tunisia | c | c | c | c | c | c | c | c | c | c | c | c | c | c |
| Uruguay | c | c | c | c | c | c | c | c | c | c | c | c | c | c |

*StatLink* http://dx.doi.org/10.1787/142104560611

Pour consulter la version française intégrale de ce tableau, suivre ce lien :
*StatLink* http://dx.doi.org/10.1787/152684743050

[Part 3/3]

**Table 4.2b** **Percentage of students at each proficiency level on the science scale, by immigrant status**

Tableau 4.2b  Pourcentage d'élèves à chaque niveau de compétence sur l'échelle de culture scientifique selon l'ascendance autochtone ou allochtone

| | First-generation students - Proficiency levels | | | | | | | | | | | | |
|---|---|---|---|---|---|---|---|---|---|---|---|---|---|
| | Below Level 1 (below 334.94 score points) | | Level 1 (from 334.94 to 409.54 score points) | | Level 2 (from 409.54 to 484.14 score points) | | Level 3 (from 484.14 to 558.73 score points) | | Level 4 (from 558.73 to 633.33 score points) | | Level 5 (from 633.33 to 707.93 score points) | | Level 6 (above 707.93 score points) | |
| | % | S.E. | % | S.E. | % | S.E. | % | S.E. | % | S.E. | % | S.E. | % | S.E. |
| **OECD** | | | | | | | | | | | | | | |
| Australia | 4.1 | (0.8) | 11.6 | (1.4) | 18.9 | (2.0) | 24.5 | (1.8) | 23.6 | (1.9) | 13.2 | (1.8) | 4.0 | (1.0) |
| Austria | 18.5 | (4.8) | 23.9 | (2.9) | 23.9 | (3.3) | 19.7 | (2.9) | 11.7 | (2.0) | 2.0 | (0.8) | 0.2 | (0.2) |
| Belgium | 17.4 | (3.5) | 26.1 | (3.0) | 25.8 | (3.3) | 20.8 | (3.0) | 8.0 | (2.0) | 1.9 | (0.7) | 0.0 | c |
| Canada | 4.2 | (1.1) | 11.6 | (1.8) | 20.2 | (1.9) | 26.6 | (2.2) | 23.9 | (2.1) | 10.9 | (1.8) | 2.6 | (0.9) |
| Czech Republic | c | c | c | c | c | c | c | c | c | c | c | c | c | c |
| Denmark | 18.5 | (4.1) | 33.0 | (4.9) | 26.2 | (4.7) | 15.0 | (3.4) | 5.1 | (1.9) | 1.6 | (1.4) | 0.6 | c |
| Finland | c | c | c | c | c | c | c | c | c | c | c | c | c | c |
| France | 17.9 | (3.8) | 20.0 | (3.9) | 28.9 | (4.4) | 18.9 | (4.3) | 10.9 | (3.3) | 3.2 | (2.1) | 0.2 | c |
| Germany | 13.1 | (2.9) | 21.4 | (3.2) | 26.0 | (3.7) | 22.2 | (3.4) | 13.9 | (2.9) | 2.9 | (1.3) | 0.5 | (0.6) |
| Greece | 15.5 | (3.3) | 26.1 | (4.2) | 31.3 | (4.1) | 19.4 | (4.6) | 6.2 | (2.5) | 1.4 | (1.0) | 0.0 | c |
| Hungary | c | c | c | c | c | c | c | c | c | c | c | c | c | c |
| Iceland | c | c | c | c | c | c | c | c | c | c | c | c | c | c |
| Ireland | 10.3 | (4.0) | 12.6 | (3.0) | 20.3 | (3.9) | 23.1 | (3.5) | 19.8 | (3.8) | 11.1 | (3.0) | 2.9 | (2.2) |
| Italy | 18.8 | (3.3) | 29.1 | (3.7) | 24.4 | (3.6) | 20.6 | (3.4) | 6.0 | (1.6) | 0.9 | (0.5) | 0.1 | c |
| Japan | c | c | c | c | c | c | c | c | c | c | c | c | c | c |
| Korea | a | a | a | a | a | a | a | a | a | a | a | a | a | a |
| Luxembourg | 15.7 | (1.5) | 23.7 | (2.3) | 26.0 | (2.5) | 18.7 | (1.8) | 11.5 | (1.5) | 3.7 | (0.8) | 0.7 | (0.4) |
| Mexico | c | c | c | c | c | c | c | c | c | c | c | c | c | c |
| Netherlands | 10.0 | (3.8) | 20.2 | (4.3) | 28.1 | (5.0) | 23.5 | (4.1) | 12.8 | (3.5) | 4.6 | (1.9) | 0.8 | (0.7) |
| New Zealand | 7.1 | (1.5) | 10.7 | (1.7) | 19.6 | (1.8) | 19.5 | (1.9) | 22.4 | (2.1) | 15.6 | (1.6) | 5.0 | (0.9) |
| Norway | 17.1 | (3.8) | 28.5 | (4.5) | 24.7 | (4.0) | 16.5 | (3.9) | 8.2 | (3.2) | 4.9 | (2.3) | a | a |
| Poland | c | c | c | c | c | c | c | c | c | c | c | c | c | c |
| Portugal | 17.4 | (4.7) | 36.5 | (5.0) | 25.0 | (3.9) | 16.2 | (3.9) | 3.5 | (2.0) | 1.5 | (1.3) | a | a |
| Slovak Republic | c | c | c | c | c | c | c | c | c | c | c | c | c | c |
| Spain | 17.3 | (2.5) | 24.9 | (3.0) | 28.8 | (2.8) | 18.2 | (2.4) | 9.1 | (2.1) | 1.6 | (1.0) | 0.0 | c |
| Sweden | 14.4 | (3.4) | 29.0 | (4.9) | 27.7 | (4.4) | 17.0 | (3.3) | 8.0 | (2.8) | 3.6 | (1.7) | 0.3 | c |
| Switzerland | 17.7 | (2.4) | 25.8 | (1.9) | 25.2 | (2.1) | 16.4 | (1.8) | 10.4 | (1.6) | 4.1 | (1.1) | 0.4 | (0.5) |
| Turkey | c | c | c | c | c | c | c | c | c | c | c | c | c | c |
| United Kingdom | 12.2 | (4.5) | 17.2 | (4.3) | 21.5 | (3.2) | 21.3 | (3.6) | 16.8 | (2.9) | 9.2 | (2.6) | 1.8 | (1.5) |
| United States | 16.5 | (3.0) | 22.2 | (3.1) | 26.8 | (3.4) | 22.3 | (3.0) | 8.9 | (2.2) | 2.0 | (1.0) | 1.3 | (1.0) |
| **OECD total** | **16.7** | **(1.3)** | **21.1** | **(1.3)** | **24.5** | **(1.4)** | **21.0** | **(1.4)** | **11.7** | **(1.0)** | **3.9** | **(0.4)** | **1.2** | **(0.4)** |
| **OECD average** | **14.2** | **(0.7)** | **22.7** | **(0.8)** | **25.0** | **(0.8)** | **20.0** | **(0.7)** | **12.0** | **(0.6)** | **5.0** | **(0.4)** | **1.2** | **(0.3)** |
| **Partners** | | | | | | | | | | | | | | |
| Argentina | c | c | c | c | c | c | c | c | c | c | c | c | c | c |
| Azerbaijan | c | c | c | c | c | c | c | c | c | c | c | c | c | c |
| Brazil | c | c | c | c | c | c | c | c | c | c | c | c | c | c |
| Bulgaria | c | c | c | c | c | c | c | c | c | c | c | c | c | c |
| Chile | c | c | c | c | c | c | c | c | c | c | c | c | c | c |
| Colombia | c | c | c | c | c | c | c | c | c | c | c | c | c | c |
| Croatia | 1.9 | (0.7) | 19.1 | (2.3) | 35.9 | (3.2) | 27.5 | (3.6) | 13.2 | (2.7) | 2.2 | (1.0) | 0.2 | c |
| Estonia | c | c | c | c | c | c | c | c | c | c | c | c | c | c |
| Hong Kong-China | 2.3 | (1.0) | 10.0 | (1.5) | 22.2 | (1.8) | 29.1 | (2.1) | 25.5 | (2.4) | 10.0 | (1.4) | 1.0 | (0.4) |
| Indonesia | c | c | c | c | c | c | c | c | c | c | c | c | c | c |
| Israel | 12.6 | (2.4) | 19.3 | (3.0) | 24.9 | (2.5) | 19.7 | (2.2) | 16.0 | (2.0) | 6.2 | (1.4) | 1.3 | (0.8) |
| Jordan | 6.3 | (1.6) | 22.0 | (2.9) | 38.5 | (3.0) | 26.4 | (2.7) | 6.6 | (1.6) | 0.3 | c | 0.0 | c |
| Kyrgyzstan | c | c | c | c | c | c | c | c | c | c | c | c | c | c |
| Latvia | c | c | c | c | c | c | c | c | c | c | c | c | c | c |
| Liechtenstein | 7.0 | (3.2) | 21.7 | (5.5) | 22.5 | (4.9) | 23.4 | (5.7) | 15.4 | (5.0) | 8.6 | (3.4) | 1.5 | (1.5) |
| Lithuania | c | c | c | c | c | c | c | c | c | c | c | c | c | c |
| Macao-China | 1.8 | (0.8) | 10.4 | (1.4) | 30.3 | (2.9) | 34.9 | (3.3) | 18.0 | (2.3) | 4.4 | (1.1) | 0.3 | (0.2) |
| Montenegro | 11.2 | (2.7) | 28.0 | (4.2) | 30.8 | (4.3) | 22.1 | (3.3) | 7.8 | (2.7) | 0.1 | c | 0.0 | c |
| Qatar | 22.4 | (1.6) | 30.6 | (1.8) | 23.5 | (1.8) | 14.0 | (1.4) | 7.6 | (0.8) | 1.7 | (0.5) | 0.1 | (0.1) |
| Romania | c | c | c | c | c | c | c | c | c | c | c | c | c | c |
| Russian Federation | 6.8 | (2.1) | 19.6 | (3.3) | 31.1 | (3.3) | 27.1 | (4.1) | 13.2 | (3.1) | 1.9 | (1.8) | 0.3 | c |
| Serbia | 6.3 | (2.5) | 25.3 | (4.1) | 39.0 | (3.1) | 24.0 | (4.0) | 4.9 | (1.9) | 0.5 | (0.5) | 0.0 | c |
| Slovenia | c | c | c | c | c | c | c | c | c | c | c | c | c | c |
| Chinese Taipei | c | c | c | c | c | c | c | c | c | c | c | c | c | c |
| Thailand | c | c | c | c | c | c | c | c | c | c | c | c | c | c |
| Tunisia | c | c | c | c | c | c | c | c | c | c | c | c | c | c |
| Uruguay | c | c | c | c | c | c | c | c | c | c | c | c | c | c |

*StatLink* ᵇ http://dx.doi.org/10.1787/142104560611

Pour consulter la version française intégrale de ce tableau, suivre ce lien :
*StatLink* ᵇ http://dx.doi.org/10.1787/152684743050

[Part 1/2]

**Table 4.2c** **Percentage of students, performance on the science scale and difference in the PISA index of economic, social and cultural status (ESCS), by students' immigrant background[1]**

Tableau 4.2c  Pourcentage d'élèves, score sur l'échelle de culture scientifique et variation de l'indice de statut économique, social et culturel (SESC), selon l'ascendance autochtone ou allochtone

| | | Native students (born in the country of assessment with at least one of their parents born in the same country) | | | | Second-generation students (born in the country of assessment but whose parents were born in another country) | | | | First-generation students (born in another country and whose parents were born in another country) | | | | Increased likelihood of first-generation students scoring in the bottom quarter of the science performance distribution | |
| | | | | Performance on the science scale | | | | Performance on the science scale | | | | Performance on the science scale | | | |
| | | % of students | S.E. | Mean score | S.E. | % of students | S.E. | Mean score | S.E. | % of students | S.E. | Mean score | S.E. | Ratio | S.E. |
|---|---|---|---|---|---|---|---|---|---|---|---|---|---|---|---|
| OECD | Australia | 78.1 | (1.2) | 529 | (2.0) | 12.8 | (0.7) | 528 | (5.7) | 9.0 | (0.6) | 527 | (5.7) | 1.1 | (0.1) |
| | Austria | 86.8 | (1.2) | 523 | (3.5) | 5.3 | (0.7) | 431 | (13.4) | 7.9 | (0.7) | 435 | (10.9) | 2.4 | (0.2) |
| | Belgium | 86.7 | (1.0) | 523 | (2.4) | 7.0 | (0.7) | 443 | (7.3) | 6.3 | (0.7) | 430 | (8.3) | 2.4 | (0.2) |
| | Canada | 78.9 | (1.2) | 541 | (1.8) | 11.2 | (0.7) | 528 | (4.8) | 9.9 | (0.7) | 519 | (5.2) | 1.4 | (0.1) |
| | Czech Republic | 98.1 | (0.2) | 515 | (3.5) | 0.7 | (0.1) | c | c | 1.2 | (0.2) | c | c | c | c |
| | Denmark | 92.4 | (0.8) | 503 | (2.9) | 4.2 | (0.6) | 418 | (11.0) | 3.4 | (0.4) | 414 | (8.0) | 2.5 | (0.2) |
| | Finland | 98.5 | (0.3) | 566 | (2.0) | 0.2 | c | c | c | 1.3 | (0.3) | c | c | c | c |
| | France | 87.0 | (1.0) | 505 | (3.5) | 9.6 | (0.9) | 456 | (10.4) | 3.4 | (0.3) | 438 | (10.1) | 1.8 | (0.2) |
| | Germany | 85.8 | (1.0) | 532 | (3.2) | 7.7 | (0.7) | 439 | (8.7) | 6.6 | (0.5) | 455 | (8.8) | 2.1 | (0.2) |
| | Greece | 92.4 | (0.7) | 478 | (3.2) | 1.2 | (0.2) | c | c | 6.4 | (0.7) | 428 | (10.3) | 1.9 | (0.2) |
| | Hungary | 98.3 | (0.3) | 505 | (2.7) | 0.4 | c | c | c | 1.3 | (0.2) | c | c | c | c |
| | Iceland | 98.2 | (0.2) | 494 | (1.7) | 0.4 | c | c | c | 1.4 | (0.2) | c | c | c | c |
| | Ireland | 94.4 | (0.5) | 510 | (3.0) | 1.1 | (0.1) | c | c | 4.5 | (0.5) | 500 | (14.6) | 1.3 | (0.2) |
| | Italy | 96.2 | (0.3) | 479 | (2.4) | 0.7 | (0.1) | c | c | 3.1 | (0.3) | 418 | (8.2) | 2.0 | (0.2) |
| | Japan | 99.6 | (0.1) | 532 | (3.4) | 0.1 | c | c | c | 0.3 | c | c | c | c | c |
| | Korea | 100.0 | (0.0) | 523 | (3.3) | 0.0 | c | c | c | a | a | a | a | a | a |
| | Luxembourg | 63.9 | (0.6) | 511 | (1.6) | 19.5 | (0.5) | 445 | (3.0) | 16.6 | (0.5) | 445 | (3.7) | 2.1 | (0.1) |
| | Mexico | 97.6 | (0.3) | 415 | (2.6) | 0.6 | (0.1) | c | c | 1.9 | (0.3) | c | c | c | c |
| | Netherlands | 88.7 | (1.1) | 534 | (2.3) | 7.8 | (0.8) | 455 | (11.2) | 3.5 | (0.4) | 467 | (10.2) | 2.0 | (0.2) |
| | New Zealand | 78.7 | (1.0) | 536 | (2.6) | 6.9 | (0.6) | 508 | (8.0) | 14.3 | (0.7) | 526 | (6.6) | 1.3 | (0.1) |
| | Norway | 93.9 | (0.7) | 493 | (2.5) | 3.0 | (0.5) | c | c | 3.1 | (0.3) | 433 | (11.2) | 2.1 | (0.2) |
| | Poland | 99.8 | (0.1) | 499 | (2.3) | 0.1 | c | c | c | 0.1 | c | c | c | c | c |
| | Portugal | 94.1 | (0.8) | 479 | (2.9) | 2.4 | (0.4) | c | c | 3.5 | (0.6) | 412 | (11.1) | 2.3 | (0.2) |
| | Slovak Republic | 99.5 | (0.1) | 490 | (2.6) | 0.3 | c | c | c | 0.1 | c | c | c | c | c |
| | Spain | 93.1 | (0.7) | 494 | (2.4) | 0.8 | (0.1) | c | c | 6.1 | (0.7) | 428 | (7.2) | 2.1 | (0.2) |
| | Sweden | 89.2 | (0.9) | 512 | (2.3) | 6.2 | (0.6) | 464 | (6.0) | 4.7 | (0.6) | 434 | (8.1) | 2.4 | (0.2) |
| | Switzerland | 77.6 | (0.7) | 531 | (2.9) | 11.8 | (0.5) | 462 | (4.8) | 10.6 | (0.4) | 436 | (6.9) | 2.7 | (0.1) |
| | Turkey | 98.5 | (0.4) | 425 | (3.8) | 0.8 | (0.3) | c | c | 0.6 | c | c | c | c | c |
| | United Kingdom | 91.4 | (0.9) | 519 | (2.0) | 5.0 | (0.6) | 493 | (8.9) | 3.7 | (0.5) | 479 | (14.7) | 1.6 | (0.2) |
| | United States | 84.8 | (1.2) | 499 | (4.3) | 9.4 | (0.9) | 456 | (6.7) | 5.8 | (0.5) | 442 | (7.9) | 1.7 | (0.2) |
| | **OECD total** | 90.9 | (0.4) | 497 | (1.2) | 5.1 | (0.3) | 463 | (3.5) | 3.9 | (0.1) | 448 | (3.0) | 1.7 | (0.1) |
| | **OECD average** | 90.7 | (0.1) | 506 | (0.5) | 4.6 | (0.1) | 466 | (2.2) | 4.8 | (0.1) | 453 | (2.1) | 2.0 | (0.0) |
| Partners | Argentina | 97.3 | (0.3) | 393 | (6.2) | 1.6 | (0.2) | c | c | 1.1 | (0.2) | c | c | c | c |
| | Azerbaijan | 97.6 | (0.5) | 384 | (2.8) | 1.4 | (0.4) | c | c | 1.1 | (0.1) | c | c | c | c |
| | Brazil | 97.6 | (0.2) | 393 | (2.8) | 2.2 | (0.2) | c | c | 0.2 | c | c | c | c | c |
| | Bulgaria | 99.8 | (0.1) | 436 | (6.1) | 0.1 | c | c | c | 0.1 | c | c | c | c | c |
| | Chile | 99.4 | (0.1) | 440 | (4.4) | 0.2 | c | c | c | 0.4 | c | c | c | c | c |
| | Colombia | 99.6 | (0.1) | 391 | (3.3) | 0.2 | c | c | c | 0.1 | c | c | c | c | c |
| | Croatia | 88.0 | (0.7) | 497 | (2.6) | 4.8 | (0.4) | 481 | (6.3) | 7.2 | (0.6) | 475 | (5.6) | 1.4 | (0.1) |
| | Estonia | 88.4 | (0.6) | 537 | (2.6) | 10.5 | (0.6) | 505 | (4.6) | 1.1 | (0.2) | c | c | c | c |
| | Hong Kong-China | 56.2 | (1.4) | 547 | (3.0) | 24.6 | (0.8) | 551 | (3.6) | 19.2 | (1.1) | 521 | (4.9) | 1.5 | (0.1) |
| | Indonesia | 99.8 | (0.1) | 395 | (5.7) | 0.0 | c | c | c | 0.1 | c | c | c | c | c |
| | Israel | 77.0 | (1.2) | 462 | (3.6) | 11.5 | (0.6) | 445 | (6.6) | 11.5 | (1.1) | 468 | (7.8) | 0.9 | (0.1) |
| | Jordan | 83.2 | (0.9) | 422 | (2.9) | 10.4 | (0.7) | 445 | (5.4) | 6.4 | (0.4) | 451 | (4.7) | 0.5 | (0.1) |
| | Kyrgyzstan | 97.4 | (0.4) | 324 | (2.8) | 1.7 | (0.3) | c | c | 0.9 | (0.2) | c | c | c | c |
| | Latvia | 92.9 | (0.6) | 492 | (3.0) | 6.6 | (0.6) | 489 | (6.1) | 0.5 | c | c | c | c | c |
| | Liechtenstein | 63.2 | (2.7) | 540 | (5.8) | 13.1 | (1.8) | 510 | (13.7) | 23.6 | (2.4) | 483 | (11.1) | 2.3 | (0.5) |
| | Lithuania | 97.9 | (0.4) | 489 | (2.9) | 1.7 | (0.3) | c | c | 0.4 | c | c | c | c | c |
| | Macao-China | 26.4 | (0.6) | 504 | (2.2) | 57.8 | (0.7) | 519 | (1.4) | 15.8 | (0.5) | 500 | (3.5) | 1.3 | (0.1) |
| | Montenegro | 92.8 | (0.5) | 411 | (1.2) | 1.8 | (0.2) | c | c | 5.4 | (0.4) | 436 | (6.6) | 0.7 | (0.1) |
| | Qatar | 59.5 | (0.5) | 330 | (1.1) | 22.0 | (0.6) | 366 | (2.3) | 18.5 | (0.5) | 414 | (3.1) | 0.4 | (0.1) |
| | Romania | 99.9 | (0.0) | 418 | (4.2) | a | a | a | a | 0.1 | c | c | c | c | c |
| | Russian Federation | 91.3 | (0.5) | 481 | (3.8) | 4.0 | (0.3) | 468 | (6.7) | 4.8 | (0.5) | 467 | (7.8) | 1.2 | (0.2) |
| | Serbia | 91.0 | (0.5) | 436 | (3.1) | 3.2 | (0.3) | 444 | (6.1) | 5.9 | (0.4) | 444 | (6.4) | 0.8 | (0.1) |
| | Slovenia | 89.7 | (0.5) | 525 | (1.2) | 8.5 | (0.4) | 468 | (5.5) | 1.8 | (0.2) | c | c | c | c |
| | Chinese Taipei | 99.4 | (0.1) | 535 | (3.5) | 0.4 | (0.1) | c | c | 0.2 | c | c | c | c | c |
| | Thailand | 99.7 | (0.1) | 422 | (2.1) | 0.3 | c | c | c | 0.0 | c | c | c | c | c |
| | Tunisia | 99.2 | (0.1) | 387 | (2.9) | 0.5 | c | c | c | 0.3 | c | c | c | c | c |
| | Uruguay | 99.6 | (0.1) | 430 | (2.7) | 0.1 | c | c | c | 0.3 | c | c | c | c | c |

Note: Values that are statistically significant are indicated in bold (see Annex A3).
1. Results based on students' self-reports.
*StatLink* http://dx.doi.org/10.1787/142104560611

Pour consulter la version française intégrale de ce tableau, suivre ce lien :
*StatLink* http://dx.doi.org/10.1787/152684743050

[Part 2/2]

**Table 4.2c** Percentage of students, performance on the science scale and difference in the PISA index of economic, social and cultural status (ESCS), by students' immigrant background[1]

Tableau 4.2c Pourcentage d'élèves, score sur l'échelle de culture scientifique et variation de l'indice de statut économique, social et culturel (SESC), selon l'ascendance autochtone ou allochtone

| | Difference in science performance between second-generation and native students | | Difference in science performance between first-generation and native students | | Difference in science performance between first- and second-generation students | | Difference in science performance between students with an immigrant background (first- and second-generation) and native students | | | | | | Difference in the ESCS between students with an immigrant background (first- and second-generation) and native students | |
| | | | | | | | PISA 2006 | | PISA 2003 | | PISA 2000 | | | |
| | Dif. | S.E. | Dif. | S.E. | Dif. | S.E. | Dif. | S.E. | Dif. | S.E. | Dif. | S.E. | Dif. | S.E. |
|---|---|---|---|---|---|---|---|---|---|---|---|---|---|---|
| Australia | -2 | (5.4) | -3 | (5.6) | -1 | (4.5) | -2 | (5.0) | -12 | (4.2) | -13 | (7.7) | -0.02 | (0.04) |
| Austria | -92 | (13.7) | -89 | (11.1) | 4 | (10.3) | -90 | (11.1) | -76 | (5.8) | -98 | (9.2) | -0.60 | (0.09) |
| Belgium | -80 | (7.3) | -93 | (8.5) | -13 | (8.7) | -86 | (6.5) | -98 | (6.9) | -105 | (8.6) | -0.63 | (0.06) |
| Canada | -12 | (4.9) | -22 | (5.3) | -9 | (4.6) | c | c | -18 | (4.6) | -22 | (3.3) | -0.06 | (0.04) |
| Czech Republic | c | c | c | c | c | c | -60 | (13.5) | c | c | c | c | c | c |
| Denmark | -85 | (10.8) | -89 | (7.9) | -3 | (11.4) | -87 | (7.7) | -73 | (9.6) | -82 | (10.6) | -0.90 | (0.07) |
| Finland | c | c | c | c | c | c | c | c | c | c | c | c | c | c |
| France | -48 | (10.9) | -67 | (10.7) | -19 | (13.0) | -53 | (9.2) | -64 | (8.8) | -66 | (8.0) | -0.58 | (0.07) |
| Germany | -93 | (7.9) | -77 | (8.5) | 16 | (9.7) | -85 | (6.7) | -99 | (7.5) | -93 | (7.1) | -0.73 | (0.05) |
| Greece | c | c | -49 | (10.4) | c | c | -44 | (9.6) | -45 | (7.2) | -66 | (17.4) | -0.48 | (0.06) |
| Hungary | c | c | c | c | c | c | c | c | c | c | c | c | c | c |
| Iceland | c | c | c | c | c | c | c | c | c | c | c | c | c | c |
| Ireland | c | c | -10 | (14.0) | c | c | -11 | (11.7) | -6 | (10.6) | c | c | 0.11 | (0.08) |
| Italy | c | c | -61 | (8.3) | c | c | -58 | (7.8) | c | c | c | c | -0.45 | (0.05) |
| Japan | c | c | c | c | c | c | c | c | c | c | c | c | c | c |
| Korea | c | c | a | a | a | a | c | c | c | c | m | m | c | c |
| Luxembourg | -66 | (3.8) | -67 | (4.3) | -1 | (4.6) | -67 | (3.3) | -48 | (3.2) | m | m | -0.92 | (0.03) |
| Mexico | c | c | c | c | c | c | c | c | c | c | -61 | (9.2) | c | c |
| Netherlands | -79 | (11.5) | -68 | (9.9) | 11 | (11.4) | -75 | (9.7) | -75 | (8.9) | m | m | -0.81 | (0.07) |
| New Zealand | -28 | (8.1) | -10 | (6.8) | 18 | (8.7) | -16 | (6.0) | -26 | (6.2) | -27 | (6.9) | 0.02 | (0.04) |
| Norway | c | c | -60 | (11.1) | c | c | -59 | (8.5) | -80 | (8.6) | -65 | (8.3) | -0.55 | (0.05) |
| Poland | c | c | c | c | c | c | c | c | c | c | c | c | c | c |
| Portugal | c | c | -67 | (11.3) | c | c | -55 | (10.8) | -44 | (18.7) | -31 | (11.0) | 0.05 | (0.14) |
| Slovak Republic | c | c | c | c | c | c | c | c | c | c | a | a | c | c |
| Spain | c | c | -66 | (6.9) | c | c | -60 | (6.9) | -54 | (10.5) | c | c | -0.29 | (0.08) |
| Sweden | -48 | (5.5) | -78 | (7.7) | -31 | (8.6) | -61 | (5.1) | -79 | (9.3) | -58 | (6.6) | -0.39 | (0.06) |
| Switzerland | -69 | (4.4) | -95 | (6.1) | -26 | (6.4) | -81 | (4.2) | -88 | (5.2) | -85 | (5.9) | -0.51 | (0.03) |
| Turkey | c | c | c | c | c | c | c | c | c | c | a | a | c | c |
| United Kingdom | -26 | (8.8) | -41 | (14.4) | -14 | (15.2) | -33 | (9.0) | m | m | m | m | -0.22 | (0.07) |
| United States | -43 | (6.9) | -57 | (8.0) | -14 | (7.4) | -48 | (6.4) | -34 | (7.2) | -39 | (15.3) | -0.63 | (0.08) |
| **OECD total** | **-34** | **(3.6)** | **-48** | **(3.2)** | **-15** | **(3.8)** | | | | | | | **-0.27** | **(0.04)** |
| **OECD average** | **-55** | **(2.2)** | **-58** | **(2.1)** | **-6** | **(2.5)** | **-57** | **(1.9)** | **-57** | **(2.0)** | **-61** | **(2.5)** | **-0.43** | **(0.02)** |
| Argentina | c | c | c | c | c | c | c | c | a | a | c | c | c | c |
| Azerbaijan | c | c | c | c | c | c | c | c | a | a | a | a | c | c |
| Brazil | c | c | c | c | c | c | c | c | c | c | c | c | c | c |
| Bulgaria | c | c | c | c | c | c | c | c | c | c | c | c | c | c |
| Chile | c | c | c | c | c | c | c | c | c | c | c | c | c | c |
| Colombia | c | c | c | c | c | c | c | c | c | c | c | c | c | c |
| Croatia | -16 | (6.4) | -22 | (5.7) | -6 | (8.3) | -19 | (4.4) | a | a | a | a | -0.36 | (0.04) |
| Estonia | -32 | (4.8) | c | c | c | c | -33 | (4.9) | a | a | a | a | -0.06 | (0.05) |
| Hong Kong-China | 4 | (4.1) | -26 | (5.6) | -30 | (5.2) | -9 | (4.1) | -10 | (3.5) | -7 | (4.6) | -0.63 | (0.04) |
| Indonesia | c | c | c | c | c | c | c | c | c | c | c | c | c | c |
| Israel | -17 | (5.7) | 6 | (7.6) | 23 | (8.4) | -6 | (5.4) | a | a | 5 | (11.0) | -0.25 | (0.04) |
| Jordan | 24 | (5.3) | 29 | (5.3) | 5 | (5.7) | 26 | (4.5) | a | a | a | a | 0.35 | (0.06) |
| Kyrgyzstan | c | c | c | c | c | c | c | c | a | a | a | a | c | c |
| Latvia | -3 | (6.2) | c | c | c | c | -3 | (6.2) | 1 | (7.2) | -16 | (8.8) | 0.10 | (0.06) |
| Liechtenstein | -30 | (16.5) | -57 | (13.3) | -27 | (18.2) | -47 | (11.7) | -54 | (19.1) | -75 | (18.9) | -0.27 | (0.10) |
| Lithuania | c | c | c | c | c | c | c | c | a | a | a | a | c | c |
| Macao-China | 15 | (2.6) | -4 | (4.2) | -19 | (3.9) | 11 | (2.6) | -1 | (8.2) | a | a | -0.44 | (0.02) |
| Montenegro | c | c | 24 | (6.8) | c | c | 17 | (5.9) | a | a | a | a | 0.18 | (0.06) |
| Qatar | 36 | (2.6) | 84 | (3.6) | 48 | (3.8) | 58 | (2.4) | a | a | a | a | -0.05 | (0.02) |
| Romania | a | a | c | c | a | a | c | c | c | c | c | c | c | c |
| Russian Federation | -13 | (7.1) | -14 | (8.0) | -1 | (9.4) | -14 | (6.0) | -22 | (4.6) | 1 | (10.0) | -0.05 | (0.06) |
| Serbia | 8 | (6.2) | 9 | (6.3) | 0 | (8.7) | 9 | (4.7) | a | a | a | a | -0.06 | (0.05) |
| Slovenia | -57 | (5.9) | c | c | c | c | -56 | (5.5) | a | a | a | a | -0.61 | (0.04) |
| Chinese Taipei | c | c | c | c | c | c | c | c | a | a | a | a | c | c |
| Thailand | c | c | c | c | c | c | c | c | c | c | c | c | c | c |
| Tunisia | c | c | c | c | c | c | c | c | c | c | -19 | (33.5) | c | c |
| Uruguay | c | c | c | c | c | c | c | c | a | a | a | a | c | c |

Note: Values that are statistically significant are indicated in bold (see Annex A3).
1. Results based on students' self-reports.
*StatLink* ⌖ http://dx.doi.org/10.1787/142104560611

Pour consulter la version française intégrale de ce tableau, suivre ce lien :
*StatLink* ⌖ http://dx.doi.org/10.1787/152684743050

[Part 1/1]

**Table 4.2d   Differences in student performance in reading, by immigrant status**

Tableau 4.2d   Variation de la performance des élèves en compréhension de l'écrit selon l'ascendance autochtone ou allochtone

| | | Performance on the reading scale | | | | | | Difference in reading performance | | | | | |
|---|---|---|---|---|---|---|---|---|---|---|---|---|---|
| | | Native students | | Second-generation students | | First-generation students | | Second-generation students minus native students | | First-generation students minus native students | | First-generation students minus second-generation students | |
| | | Mean score | S.E. | Mean score | S.E. | Mean score | S.E. | Difference | S.E. | Difference | S.E. | Difference | S.E. |
| OECD | Australia | 514 | (1.9) | 521 | (4.9) | 514 | (5.3) | 7 | (4.6) | 1 | (5.2) | -7 | (4.1) |
| | Austria | 499 | (3.4) | 420 | (18.8) | 451 | (12.6) | **-79** | (18.8) | **-48** | (12.6) | **31** | (14.9) |
| | Belgium | 515 | (2.9) | 434 | (9.1) | 413 | (8.2) | **-81** | (8.8) | **-101** | (8.1) | -21 | (11.8) |
| | Canada | 532 | (2.2) | 532 | (4.7) | 512 | (5.5) | 0 | (4.5) | **-19** | (5.2) | **-20** | (4.9) |
| | Czech Republic | 486 | (4.1) | c | c | c | c | c | c | c | c | c | c |
| | Denmark | 500 | (2.9) | 436 | (11.3) | 422 | (8.6) | **-64** | (10.8) | **-79** | (8.2) | -14 | (11.8) |
| | Finland | 549 | (2.1) | c | c | c | c | c | c | c | c | c | c |
| | France | 495 | (4.4) | 459 | (8.7) | 449 | (12.6) | **-36** | (9.8) | **-45** | (13.2) | -9 | (14.8) |
| | Germany | 510 | (3.8) | 427 | (10.8) | 440 | (11.3) | **-83** | (10.1) | **-70** | (10.3) | 12 | (13.7) |
| | Greece | 464 | (4.1) | c | c | 427 | (9.9) | c | c | **-37** | (10.4) | c | c |
| | Hungary | 483 | (3.3) | c | c | c | c | c | c | c | c | c | c |
| | Iceland | 489 | (2.0) | c | c | c | c | c | c | c | c | c | c |
| | Ireland | 520 | (3.4) | c | c | 506 | (15.5) | c | c | -14 | (15.3) | c | c |
| | Italy | 473 | (2.4) | c | c | 404 | (9.4) | c | c | **-69** | (9.2) | c | c |
| | Japan | 498 | (3.6) | c | c | c | c | c | c | c | c | c | c |
| | Korea | 557 | (3.8) | c | c | a | a | c | c | a | a | a | a |
| | Luxembourg | 504 | (1.7) | 443 | (3.3) | 435 | (3.9) | **-61** | (3.9) | **-69** | (4.4) | -7 | (4.9) |
| | Mexico | 417 | (3.0) | c | c | c | c | c | c | c | c | c | c |
| | Netherlands | 515 | (2.7) | 454 | (11.3) | 449 | (11.1) | **-61** | (11.8) | **-65** | (10.5) | -5 | (13.7) |
| | New Zealand | 526 | (3.0) | 519 | (8.2) | 507 | (6.3) | -7 | (8.3) | **-19** | (6.3) | -13 | (8.5) |
| | Norway | 491 | (2.8) | c | c | 427 | (12.2) | c | c | **-63** | (12.3) | c | c |
| | Poland | 509 | (2.8) | c | c | c | c | c | c | c | c | c | c |
| | Portugal | 477 | (3.5) | c | c | 408 | (13.6) | c | c | **-69** | (14.2) | c | c |
| | Slovak Republic | 468 | (3.0) | c | c | c | c | c | c | c | c | c | c |
| | Spain | 465 | (2.2) | c | c | 410 | (7.1) | c | c | **-55** | (7.0) | c | c |
| | Sweden | 514 | (3.6) | 486 | (6.5) | 446 | (8.7) | **-29** | (6.2) | **-68** | (8.6) | **-40** | (10.0) |
| | Switzerland | 515 | (2.8) | 467 | (4.6) | 430 | (6.6) | **-48** | (4.1) | **-85** | (5.6) | **-37** | (6.3) |
| | Turkey | 448 | (4.2) | c | c | c | c | c | c | c | c | c | c |
| | United Kingdom | 499 | (1.9) | 492 | (10.3) | 455 | (14.2) | -7 | (10.2) | **-44** | (13.9) | **-37** | (13.4) |
| | United States | m | m | m | m | m | m | m | m | m | m | m | m |
| | **OECD total** | **488** | **(1.0)** | **467** | **(3.7)** | **443** | **(3.5)** | **-22** | **(3.8)** | **-46** | **(3.3)** | **-24** | **(4.1)** |
| | **OECD average** | **498** | **(0.6)** | **457** | **(3.2)** | **448** | **(2.3)** | **-42** | **(2.6)** | **-54** | **(2.3)** | **-13** | **(3.0)** |
| Partners | Argentina | 377 | (7.3) | c | c | c | c | c | c | c | c | c | c |
| | Azerbaijan | 355 | (3.2) | c | c | c | c | c | c | c | c | c | c |
| | Brazil | 396 | (3.8) | c | c | c | c | c | c | c | c | c | c |
| | Bulgaria | 405 | (6.8) | c | c | c | c | c | c | c | c | c | c |
| | Chile | 444 | (5.1) | c | c | c | c | c | c | c | c | c | c |
| | Colombia | 388 | (5.0) | c | c | c | c | c | c | c | c | c | c |
| | Croatia | 481 | (2.9) | 464 | (5.9) | 464 | (5.1) | **-16** | (6.1) | **-16** | (5.5) | 0 | (7.8) |
| | Estonia | 508 | (2.8) | 463 | (5.7) | c | c | **-45** | (5.5) | **-87** | (14.9) | **-42** | (13.7) |
| | Hong Kong-China | 539 | (2.8) | 547 | (3.2) | 516 | (4.5) | 8 | (3.7) | **-23** | (4.9) | **-31** | (4.9) |
| | Indonesia | 394 | (5.9) | c | c | c | c | c | c | c | c | c | c |
| | Israel | 447 | (4.4) | 439 | (8.3) | 447 | (8.6) | -7 | (7.2) | 1 | (8.5) | 8 | (10.1) |
| | Jordan | 400 | (3.2) | 425 | (6.3) | 435 | (6.1) | **25** | (6.2) | **35** | (6.2) | 9 | (7.4) |
| | Kyrgyzstan | 287 | (3.3) | c | c | c | c | c | c | c | c | c | c |
| | Latvia | 483 | (3.8) | 464 | (6.9) | c | c | **-19** | (7.0) | c | c | c | c |
| | Liechtenstein | 530 | (5.7) | 508 | (12.4) | 463 | (10.8) | -21 | (14.7) | **-67** | (13.1) | **-46** | (18.0) |
| | Lithuania | 472 | (3.1) | c | c | c | c | c | c | c | c | c | c |
| | Macao-China | 484 | (2.4) | 498 | (1.6) | 492 | (3.2) | **14** | (3.1) | **8** | (3.9) | -6 | (3.7) |
| | Montenegro | 392 | (1.3) | c | c | 413 | (7.0) | c | c | **21** | (7.1) | c | c |
| | Qatar | 291 | (1.5) | 330 | (3.1) | 391 | (3.4) | **38** | (3.4) | **99** | (3.9) | **61** | (4.7) |
| | Romania | 396 | (4.7) | a | a | c | c | a | a | c | c | a | a |
| | Russian Federation | 441 | (4.5) | 432 | (7.3) | 438 | (8.0) | -10 | (7.7) | -4 | (8.3) | 6 | (9.6) |
| | Serbia | 401 | (3.4) | 412 | (8.1) | 413 | (8.0) | 11 | (8.1) | 12 | (7.7) | 1 | (9.8) |
| | Slovenia | 499 | (1.1) | 467 | (4.5) | c | c | **-31** | (4.8) | c | c | c | c |
| | Chinese Taipei | 498 | (3.2) | c | c | c | c | c | c | c | c | c | c |
| | Thailand | 418 | (2.6) | c | c | c | c | c | c | c | c | c | c |
| | Tunisia | 382 | (4.0) | c | c | c | c | c | c | c | c | c | c |
| | Uruguay | 416 | (3.5) | c | c | c | c | c | c | c | c | c | c |

Note: Values that are statistically significant are indicated in bold (see Annex A3).
*StatLink* ᴍᴤ᷁ http://dx.doi.org/10.1787/142104560611

Pour consulter la version française intégrale de ce tableau, suivre ce lien :
*StatLink* ᴍᴤ᷁ http://dx.doi.org/10.1787/152684743050

[Part 1/1]

**Table 4.2e** Differences in student performance in mathematics, by immigrant status

Tableau 4.2e Variation de la performance des élèves en mathématiques selon l'ascendance autochtone ou allochtone

| | Performance on the mathematics scale | | | | | | Difference in mathematics performance | | | | | |
| | Native students | | Second-generation students | | First-generation students | | Second-generation students minus native students | | First-generation students minus native students | | First-generation students minus second-generation students | |
| | Mean score | S.E. | Mean score | S.E. | Mean score | S.E. | Difference | S.E. | Difference | S.E. | Difference | S.E. |
|---|---|---|---|---|---|---|---|---|---|---|---|---|
| **OECD** | | | | | | | | | | | | |
| Australia | 519 | (1.9) | 531 | (5.5) | 530 | (5.6) | 12 | (5.1) | 11 | (5.3) | -1 | (4.0) |
| Austria | 515 | (3.6) | 435 | (13.6) | 450 | (8.7) | -81 | (13.8) | -65 | (9.0) | 16 | (11.4) |
| Belgium | 535 | (2.7) | 451 | (10.0) | 423 | (8.3) | -84 | (9.4) | -112 | (8.5) | -29 | (11.2) |
| Canada | 531 | (1.8) | 524 | (4.4) | 524 | (5.4) | -8 | (4.5) | -7 | (5.5) | 0 | (5.0) |
| Czech Republic | 512 | (3.6) | c | c | c | c | c | c | c | c | c | c |
| Denmark | 519 | (2.5) | 456 | (8.8) | 439 | (7.6) | -63 | (8.4) | -80 | (7.6) | -17 | (10.5) |
| Finland | 550 | (2.2) | c | c | c | c | c | c | c | c | c | c |
| France | 504 | (3.3) | 458 | (9.8) | 442 | (12.2) | -47 | (10.3) | -62 | (12.4) | -15 | (13.8) |
| Germany | 519 | (3.4) | 441 | (8.4) | 454 | (7.9) | -78 | (7.7) | -65 | (7.5) | 13 | (9.0) |
| Greece | 463 | (3.0) | c | c | 418 | (8.1) | c | c | -45 | (8.5) | c | c |
| Hungary | 492 | (2.9) | c | c | c | c | c | c | c | c | c | c |
| Iceland | 509 | (1.8) | c | c | c | c | c | c | c | c | c | c |
| Ireland | 504 | (2.7) | c | c | 485 | (12.0) | c | c | -19 | (11.8) | c | c |
| Italy | 465 | (2.2) | c | c | 421 | (7.5) | c | c | -44 | (7.6) | c | c |
| Japan | 523 | (3.3) | c | c | c | c | c | c | c | c | c | c |
| Korea | 549 | (3.7) | c | c | a | a | c | c | a | a | a | a |
| Luxembourg | 509 | (1.5) | 464 | (2.7) | 454 | (3.8) | -46 | (3.4) | -55 | (4.2) | -10 | (4.5) |
| Mexico | 411 | (2.7) | c | c | c | c | c | c | c | c | c | c |
| Netherlands | 539 | (2.3) | 472 | (9.8) | 481 | (8.6) | -66 | (10.0) | -58 | (8.3) | 9 | (9.7) |
| New Zealand | 524 | (2.5) | 511 | (6.9) | 530 | (5.3) | -13 | (6.9) | 6 | (5.7) | 19 | (7.8) |
| Norway | 495 | (2.4) | c | c | 437 | (9.9) | c | c | -58 | (9.8) | c | c |
| Poland | 497 | (2.4) | c | c | c | c | c | c | c | c | c | c |
| Portugal | 470 | (2.9) | c | c | 411 | (11.0) | c | c | -59 | (11.4) | c | c |
| Slovak Republic | 493 | (2.8) | c | c | c | c | c | c | c | c | c | c |
| Spain | 485 | (2.2) | c | c | 426 | (6.9) | c | c | -59 | (6.8) | c | c |
| Sweden | 510 | (2.4) | 467 | (7.1) | 446 | (7.2) | -42 | (6.7) | -64 | (7.2) | -21 | (8.0) |
| Switzerland | 547 | (2.9) | 485 | (4.8) | 459 | (6.5) | -62 | (4.2) | -88 | (5.8) | -26 | (6.0) |
| Turkey | 425 | (4.9) | c | c | c | c | c | c | c | c | c | c |
| United Kingdom | 499 | (2.0) | 474 | (7.9) | 474 | (10.9) | -25 | (7.7) | -25 | (10.7) | 0 | (11.5) |
| United States | 481 | (4.1) | 458 | (5.8) | 444 | (7.4) | -23 | (6.0) | -37 | (7.2) | -14 | (5.9) |
| **OECD total** | 489 | (1.1) | 464 | (3.1) | 451 | (3.0) | -25 | (3.3) | -38 | (3.0) | -13 | (3.2) |
| **OECD average** | 503 | (0.5) | 473 | (2.1) | 457 | (1.9) | -45 | (2.1) | -49 | (1.9) | -5 | (2.4) |
| **Partners** | | | | | | | | | | | | |
| Argentina | 383 | (6.3) | c | c | c | c | c | c | c | c | c | c |
| Azerbaijan | 477 | (2.3) | c | c | c | c | c | c | c | c | c | c |
| Brazil | 372 | (3.0) | c | c | c | c | c | c | c | c | c | c |
| Bulgaria | 415 | (6.1) | c | c | c | c | c | c | c | c | c | c |
| Chile | 412 | (4.6) | c | c | c | c | c | c | c | c | c | c |
| Colombia | 373 | (3.7) | c | c | c | c | c | c | c | c | c | c |
| Croatia | 470 | (2.5) | 464 | (6.3) | 451 | (4.9) | -6 | (6.2) | -19 | (5.1) | -13 | (8.2) |
| Estonia | 519 | (2.7) | 496 | (5.2) | c | c | -23 | (4.9) | c | c | c | c |
| Hong Kong-China | 554 | (3.1) | 555 | (3.9) | 521 | (4.8) | 1 | (4.2) | -32 | (5.4) | -34 | (5.2) |
| Indonesia | 393 | (5.6) | c | c | c | c | c | c | c | c | c | c |
| Israel | 448 | (4.2) | 438 | (7.5) | 457 | (7.5) | -10 | (6.4) | 9 | (7.4) | 19 | (8.7) |
| Jordan | 383 | (3.3) | 407 | (5.7) | 413 | (5.3) | 24 | (5.5) | 30 | (5.6) | 6 | (6.5) |
| Kyrgyzstan | 312 | (3.2) | c | c | c | c | c | c | c | c | c | c |
| Latvia | 488 | (3.1) | 489 | (5.6) | c | c | 1 | (5.8) | c | c | c | c |
| Liechtenstein | 541 | (6.1) | 516 | (13.2) | 489 | (10.9) | -25 | (16.5) | -52 | (12.7) | -27 | (17.7) |
| Lithuania | 488 | (3.0) | c | c | c | c | c | c | c | c | c | c |
| Macao-China | 519 | (2.5) | 531 | (1.7) | 520 | (3.4) | 12 | (2.9) | 1 | (4.4) | -11 | (3.9) |
| Montenegro | 400 | (1.4) | c | c | 420 | (7.3) | c | c | 20 | (7.4) | c | c |
| Qatar | 299 | (1.4) | 336 | (2.7) | 380 | (2.9) | 37 | (2.9) | 81 | (3.4) | 44 | (4.2) |
| Romania | 415 | (4.2) | a | a | c | c | a | a | c | c | a | a |
| Russian Federation | 478 | (4.1) | 447 | (7.2) | 464 | (7.9) | -31 | (8.6) | -14 | (8.1) | 17 | (9.4) |
| Serbia | 435 | (3.5) | 457 | (7.6) | 447 | (7.2) | 22 | (7.3) | 11 | (6.9) | -11 | (8.8) |
| Slovenia | 509 | (1.1) | 474 | (5.3) | c | c | -36 | (5.6) | c | c | c | c |
| Chinese Taipei | 552 | (3.9) | c | c | c | c | c | c | c | c | c | c |
| Thailand | 419 | (2.3) | c | c | c | c | c | c | c | c | c | c |
| Tunisia | 367 | (4.0) | c | c | c | c | c | c | c | c | c | c |
| Uruguay | 429 | (2.7) | c | c | c | c | c | c | c | c | c | c |

Note: Values that are statistically significant are indicated in bold (see Annex A3).
StatLink ᗅᗰᔆ http://dx.doi.org/10.1787/142104560611

Pour consulter la version française intégrale de ce tableau, suivre ce lien :
StatLink ᗅᗰᔆ http://dx.doi.org/10.1787/152684743050

[Part 1/2]

**Table 4.3a** **Percentage of students and performance on the science scale, by language spoken at home[1]**

Tableau 4.3a Pourcentage d'élèves et score sur l'échelle de culture scientifique selon la langue parlée en famille

| | | Language spoken at home most of the time is DIFFERENT from the language of assessment, from other official languages or from other national dialects | | | | Language spoken at home most of the time is the SAME as the language of assessment, other official languages or another national dialects | | | |
|---|---|---|---|---|---|---|---|---|---|
| | | Percentage of students | S.E. | Performance on the science scale | | Percentage of students | S.E. | Performance on the science scale | |
| | | | | Mean score | S.E. | | | Mean score | S.E. |
| OECD | Australia | 8.0 | (0.7) | 511 | (7.6) | 92.0 | (0.7) | 530 | (2.0) |
| | Austria | 10.0 | (1.1) | 429 | (13.4) | 90.0 | (1.1) | 523 | (3.4) |
| | Belgium | 5.7 | (0.5) | 425 | (8.0) | 94.3 | (0.5) | 522 | (2.2) |
| | Canada | 10.6 | (0.7) | 517 | (5.4) | 89.4 | (0.7) | 540 | (1.8) |
| | Czech Republic | 0.8 | (0.2) | c | c | 99.2 | (0.2) | 515 | (3.5) |
| | Denmark | 4.5 | (0.5) | 415 | (8.7) | 95.5 | (0.5) | 502 | (3.0) |
| | Finland | 1.3 | (0.2) | c | c | 98.7 | (0.2) | 565 | (2.0) |
| | France | 5.4 | (0.5) | 457 | (9.0) | 94.6 | (0.5) | 500 | (3.4) |
| | Germany | 9.0 | (0.7) | 441 | (8.7) | 91.0 | (0.7) | 532 | (3.2) |
| | Greece | 3.9 | (0.5) | 398 | (11.1) | 96.1 | (0.5) | 477 | (3.1) |
| | Hungary | 0.8 | (0.2) | c | c | 99.2 | (0.2) | 505 | (2.7) |
| | Iceland | 2.2 | (0.3) | c | c | 97.8 | (0.3) | 494 | (1.7) |
| | Ireland | 2.0 | (0.3) | c | c | 98.0 | (0.3) | 511 | (3.1) |
| | Italy | 2.9 | (0.3) | c | c | 97.1 | (0.3) | 485 | (2.0) |
| | Japan | 0.3 | c | c | c | 99.7 | (0.1) | 534 | (3.3) |
| | Korea | 0.1 | c | c | c | 99.9 | (0.0) | 523 | (3.4) |
| | Luxembourg | 23.7 | (0.6) | 430 | (3.0) | 76.3 | (0.6) | 514 | (1.4) |
| | Mexico | 0.2 | (0.1) | c | c | 99.8 | (0.1) | 410 | (2.7) |
| | Netherlands | 5.9 | (0.7) | 449 | (11.0) | 94.1 | (0.7) | 531 | (2.2) |
| | New Zealand | 8.7 | (0.6) | 498 | (8.2) | 91.3 | (0.6) | 538 | (2.4) |
| | Norway | 4.7 | (0.5) | 442 | (10.3) | 95.3 | (0.5) | 492 | (2.5) |
| | Poland | 0.4 | c | c | c | 99.6 | (0.2) | 498 | (2.3) |
| | Portugal | 2.3 | (0.4) | c | c | 97.7 | (0.4) | 477 | (2.9) |
| | Slovak Republic | 0.4 | c | c | c | 99.6 | (0.1) | 489 | (2.6) |
| | Spain | 2.6 | (0.3) | c | c | 97.4 | (0.3) | 491 | (2.5) |
| | Sweden | 7.8 | (0.7) | 444 | (5.9) | 92.2 | (0.7) | 511 | (2.2) |
| | Switzerland | 12.9 | (0.6) | 438 | (5.4) | 87.1 | (0.6) | 528 | (2.9) |
| | Turkey | 2.4 | (0.4) | c | c | 97.6 | (0.4) | 425 | (3.9) |
| | United Kingdom | 3.8 | (0.6) | 464 | (14.8) | 96.2 | (0.6) | 519 | (2.0) |
| | United States | 10.7 | (1.0) | 434 | (6.4) | 89.3 | (1.0) | 498 | (4.3) |
| | **OECD total** | **5.5** | **(0.3)** | **444** | **(3.5)** | **94.5** | **(0.3)** | **496** | **(1.2)** |
| | **OECD average** | **5.1** | **(0.1)** | **448** | **(3.0)** | **94.9** | **(0.1)** | **506** | **(0.5)** |
| Partners | Argentina | 0.5 | c | c | c | 99.5 | (0.2) | 392 | (6.1) |
| | Azerbaijan | 2.2 | (0.7) | c | c | 97.8 | (0.7) | 383 | (2.8) |
| | Brazil | 0.3 | (0.1) | c | c | 99.7 | (0.1) | 390 | (2.8) |
| | Bulgaria | 4.7 | (0.9) | 346 | (9.1) | 95.3 | (0.9) | 440 | (5.8) |
| | Chile | 0.2 | c | c | c | 99.8 | (0.1) | 438 | (4.5) |
| | Colombia | 0.5 | c | c | c | 99.5 | (0.2) | 388 | (3.4) |
| | Croatia | 0.4 | c | c | c | 99.6 | (0.1) | 494 | (2.4) |
| | Estonia | 0.5 | c | c | c | 99.5 | (0.1) | 533 | (2.5) |
| | Hong Kong-China | 2.7 | (0.7) | c | c | 97.3 | (0.7) | 546 | (2.4) |
| | Indonesia | 1.5 | (0.3) | c | c | 98.5 | (0.3) | 394 | (5.6) |
| | Israel | 11.4 | (1.1) | 457 | (7.9) | 88.6 | (1.1) | 460 | (3.7) |
| | Jordan | 2.9 | (0.3) | c | c | 97.1 | (0.3) | 425 | (2.7) |
| | Kyrgyzstan | 1.2 | (0.3) | c | c | 98.8 | (0.3) | 323 | (2.9) |
| | Latvia | 0.5 | c | c | c | 99.5 | (0.1) | 491 | (2.9) |
| | Liechtenstein | 12.2 | (1.6) | 434 | (17.4) | 87.8 | (1.6) | 536 | (4.7) |
| | Lithuania | 0.1 | c | c | c | 99.9 | (0.0) | 489 | (2.8) |
| | Macao-China | 3.9 | (0.3) | 480 | (8.9) | 96.1 | (0.3) | 513 | (1.1) |
| | Montenegro | 2.4 | (0.2) | 403 | (8.2) | 97.6 | (0.2) | 413 | (1.3) |
| | Qatar | 4.1 | (0.2) | 398 | (6.6) | 95.9 | (0.2) | 350 | (1.0) |
| | Romania | 0.6 | c | c | c | 99.4 | (0.2) | 419 | (4.2) |
| | Russian Federation | 9.5 | (2.0) | 427 | (6.8) | 90.5 | (2.0) | 485 | (3.4) |
| | Serbia | 0.5 | c | c | c | 99.5 | (0.1) | 436 | (3.0) |
| | Slovenia | 5.6 | (0.4) | 450 | (6.7) | 94.4 | (0.4) | 525 | (1.1) |
| | Chinese Taipei | 0.6 | (0.1) | c | c | 99.4 | (0.1) | 536 | (3.4) |
| | Thailand | 1.6 | (0.2) | c | c | 98.4 | (0.2) | 422 | (2.1) |
| | Tunisia | 4.7 | (0.5) | 390 | (8.7) | 95.3 | (0.5) | 385 | (2.8) |
| | Uruguay | 1.4 | (0.3) | c | c | 98.6 | (0.3) | 430 | (2.7) |

Note: Values that are statistically significant are indicated in bold (see Annex A3).
1. Results based on students' self-reports.
*StatLink* http://dx.doi.org/10.1787/142104560611

Pour consulter la version française intégrale de ce tableau, suivre ce lien :
*StatLink* http://dx.doi.org/10.1787/152684743050

[Part 2/2]

**Table 4.3a** **Percentage of students and performance on the science scale, by language spoken at home[1]**

Tableau 4.3a Pourcentage d'élèves et score sur l'échelle de culture scientifique selon la langue parlée en famille

| | Difference in science performance between students who do not speak the language of assessment at home and students who speak the language of assessment at home | | | | | | Increased likelihood of students who do not speak the language of assessment at home scoring in the bottom quarter of the science performance distribution | | Effect size (language spoken at home is different from the language of assessment minus the same language) | |
| | PISA 2006 | | PISA 2003 | | PISA 2000 | | | | | |
| | Difference | S.E. | Difference | S.E. | Difference | S.E. | Ratio | S.E. | Effect size | S.E. |
|---|---|---|---|---|---|---|---|---|---|---|
| Australia | -19 | (7.0) | -24 | (6.0) | -38 | (9.1) | 1.4 | (0.10) | -0.19 | (0.09) |
| Austria | -94 | (13.6) | -74 | (7.5) | -95 | (10.5) | 2.8 | (0.30) | -0.98 | (0.41) |
| Belgium | -97 | (7.7) | -95 | (9.3) | -126 | (9.5) | 2.6 | (0.19) | -1.00 | (0.39) |
| Canada | -23 | (5.1) | -35 | (5.0) | -36 | (4.4) | 1.4 | (0.10) | -0.24 | (0.10) |
| Czech Republic | c | c | c | c | c | c | c | c | c | c |
| Denmark | -87 | (8.2) | -36 | (13.9) | -83 | (11.3) | 2.5 | (0.23) | -0.96 | (0.36) |
| Finland | c | c | c | c | -67 | (18.6) | c | c | c | c |
| France | -43 | (9.3) | -78 | (11.8) | -75 | (10.2) | 1.7 | (0.21) | -0.42 | (0.18) |
| Germany | -90 | (7.9) | -108 | (7.0) | -113 | (11.3) | 2.5 | (0.19) | -0.95 | (0.37) |
| Greece | -79 | (10.6) | -57 | (10.4) | c | c | 2.3 | (0.24) | -0.86 | (0.35) |
| Hungary | c | c | -40 | (22.8) | m | m | c | c | c | c |
| Iceland | c | c | c | c | c | c | c | c | c | c |
| Ireland | c | c | c | c | c | c | c | c | c | c |
| Italy | c | c | -65 | (19.4) | 18 | (27.0) | c | c | c | c |
| Japan | c | c | c | c | c | c | c | c | c | c |
| Korea | c | c | c | c | m | m | c | c | c | c |
| Luxembourg | -84 | (3.5) | -53 | (3.7) | m | m | 3.3 | (0.21) | -0.95 | (0.36) |
| Mexico | c | c | -67 | (25.2) | c | c | c | c | c | c |
| Netherlands | -82 | (10.5) | -84 | (9.9) | m | m | 2.4 | (0.26) | -0.86 | (0.34) |
| New Zealand | -40 | (7.8) | -45 | (7.1) | -66 | (9.8) | 1.8 | (0.15) | -0.35 | (0.16) |
| Norway | -50 | (9.3) | -75 | (10.2) | -57 | (9.7) | 1.9 | (0.18) | -0.50 | (0.22) |
| Poland | c | c | c | c | c | c | c | c | c | c |
| Portugal | c | c | c | c | c | c | c | c | c | c |
| Slovak Republic | c | c | -157 | (41.1) | a | a | c | c | c | c |
| Spain | c | c | -16 | (19.9) | -51 | (23.3) | c | c | c | c |
| Sweden | -67 | (5.6) | -79 | (10.6) | -69 | (9.4) | 2.2 | (0.16) | -0.72 | (0.27) |
| Switzerland | -90 | (4.4) | -91 | (6.9) | -90 | (6.2) | 2.8 | (0.13) | -0.94 | (0.38) |
| Turkey | c | c | c | c | a | a | c | c | c | c |
| United Kingdom | -54 | (14.4) | m | m | m | m | 1.8 | (0.24) | -0.49 | (0.22) |
| United States | -64 | (6.8) | -52 | (6.9) | -68 | (13.7) | 2.0 | (0.17) | -0.64 | (0.22) |
| **OECD total** | **-52** | (3.7) | **-55** | (4.0) | **-63** | (8.9) | **1.8** | (0.08) | **-0.51** | (0.19) |
| **OECD average** | **-59** | (2.6) | **-63** | (3.9) | **-57** | (4.2) | **2.0** | (0.07) | **-0.60** | (0.06) |
| Argentina | c | c | a | a | c | c | c | c | c | c |
| Azerbaijan | c | c | a | a | a | a | c | c | c | c |
| Brazil | c | c | c | c | c | c | c | c | c | c |
| Bulgaria | -94 | (9.2) | a | a | -97 | (16.9) | 2.5 | (0.26) | -1.00 | (0.31) |
| Chile | c | c | a | a | c | c | c | c | c | c |
| Colombia | c | c | a | a | a | a | c | c | c | c |
| Croatia | c | c | a | a | a | a | c | c | c | c |
| Estonia | c | c | a | a | a | a | c | c | c | c |
| Hong Kong-China | c | c | -60 | (8.4) | -61 | (8.9) | c | c | c | c |
| Indonesia | c | c | -9 | (12.4) | -16 | (13.5) | c | c | c | c |
| Israel | 4 | (7.8) | a | a | a | a | 1.1 | (0.13) | -0.03 | (0.06) |
| Jordan | c | c | a | a | a | a | c | c | c | c |
| Kyrgyzstan | c | c | a | a | a | a | c | c | c | c |
| Latvia | c | c | -4 | (23.6) | -162 | (71.8) | c | c | c | c |
| Liechtenstein | -102 | (18.3) | -52 | (14.2) | -55 | (20.1) | 3.2 | (0.59) | -1.09 | (0.47) |
| Lithuania | c | c | a | a | a | a | c | c | c | c |
| Macao-China | -33 | (9.1) | -55 | (14.9) | a | a | 1.6 | (0.23) | -0.41 | (0.18) |
| Montenegro | c | c | a | a | a | a | c | c | c | c |
| Qatar | 48 | (6.8) | a | a | a | a | 0.8 | (0.12) | 0.47 | (0.23) |
| Romania | c | c | a | a | c | c | c | c | c | c |
| Russian Federation | -58 | (7.1) | -60 | (10.3) | -26 | (11.0) | 1.9 | (0.20) | -0.68 | (0.24) |
| Serbia | c | c | a | a | a | a | c | c | c | c |
| Slovenia | -75 | (6.8) | a | a | a | a | 2.3 | (0.18) | -0.81 | (0.28) |
| Chinese Taipei | c | c | a | a | a | a | c | c | c | c |
| Thailand | c | c | -36 | (14.5) | -50 | (23.2) | c | c | c | c |
| Tunisia | 5 | (7.7) | 13 | (26.4) | a | a | 1.0 | (0.16) | 0.05 | (0.08) |
| Uruguay | c | c | c | c | a | a | c | c | c | c |

Note: Values that are statistically significant are indicated in bold (see Annex A3).
1. Results based on students' self-reports.
*StatLink* ᵃᵖ http://dx.doi.org/10.1787/142104560611

Pour consulter la version française intégrale de ce tableau, suivre ce lien :
*StatLink* ᵃᵖ http://dx.doi.org/10.1787/152684743050

[Part 1/1]

**Table 4.3b** Performance of students on the reading and mathematics scales, by language spoken at home[1]

Tableau 4.3b Scores des élèves sur les échelles de compréhension de l'écrit et de culture mathématique selon la langue parlée en famille

| | | Language spoken at home most of the time is DIFFERENT from the language of assessment, from other official languages or from other national dialects | | | | Language spoken at home most of the time is THE SAME as the language of assessment, other official languages or another national dialect | | | | Difference of performance between students with an immigrant background who speak a language at home that is different from the language of instruction and native students | | | |
|---|---|---|---|---|---|---|---|---|---|---|---|---|---|
| | | Reading | | Mathematics | | Reading | | Mathematics | | Reading | | Mathematics | |
| | | Mean score | S.E. | Mean score | S.E. | Mean score | S.E. | Mean score | S.E. | Dif. | S.E. | Dif. | S.E. |
| OECD | Australia | 495 | (7.1) | 523 | (7.7) | 516 | (1.8) | 521 | (2.0) | -10 | (6.8) | 11 | (7.3) |
| | Austria | 436 | (17.7) | 442 | (12.8) | 500 | (3.4) | 515 | (3.5) | **-63** | (16.9) | **-74** | (12.4) |
| | Belgium | 491 | (7.5) | 515 | (6.7) | 512 | (2.7) | 530 | (2.6) | **-114** | (9.2) | **-103** | (10.2) |
| | Canada | 504 | (4.6) | 522 | (4.3) | 534 | (2.2) | 531 | (1.8) | **-21** | (5.4) | -4 | (5.4) |
| | Czech Republic | c | c | c | c | 487 | (4.0) | 513 | (3.6) | c | c | c | c |
| | Denmark | 422 | (9.0) | 440 | (7.0) | 501 | (3.0) | 519 | (2.6) | **-84** | (8.5) | **-85** | (7.4) |
| | Finland | c | c | c | c | 548 | (2.1) | 550 | (2.2) | c | c | c | c |
| | France | 444 | (9.2) | 441 | (10.1) | 493 | (4.2) | 502 | (3.2) | **-41** | (10.9) | **-61** | (11.6) |
| | Germany | 423 | (9.7) | 438 | (8.4) | 511 | (3.8) | 519 | (3.3) | **-93** | (8.9) | **-85** | (7.2) |
| | Greece | 392 | (13.2) | 408 | (9.7) | 463 | (4.0) | 462 | (2.9) | **-57** | (11.2) | **-63** | (8.7) |
| | Hungary | c | c | c | c | 484 | (3.3) | 492 | (2.9) | c | c | c | c |
| | Iceland | c | c | c | c | 489 | (1.9) | 508 | (1.8) | c | c | c | c |
| | Ireland | c | c | c | c | 521 | (3.3) | 504 | (2.7) | c | c | c | c |
| | Italy | c | c | c | c | 484 | (2.4) | 473 | (2.4) | c | c | c | c |
| | Japan | c | c | c | c | 500 | (3.6) | 526 | (3.3) | c | c | c | c |
| | Korea | c | c | c | c | 557 | (3.8) | 548 | (3.8) | a | a | a | a |
| | Luxembourg | 485 | (1.6) | 494 | (1.3) | 511 | (4.9) | 525 | (4.7) | **-79** | (3.7) | **-63** | (3.4) |
| | Mexico | c | c | c | c | 414 | (2.7) | 408 | (2.8) | c | c | c | c |
| | Netherlands | 438 | (12.3) | 472 | (10.3) | 512 | (2.4) | 536 | (2.2) | **-76** | (12.9) | **-67** | (11.0) |
| | New Zealand | 485 | (7.8) | 522 | (6.7) | 529 | (2.7) | 526 | (2.3) | **-41** | (8.4) | -2 | (7.7) |
| | Norway | 429 | (9.4) | 448 | (7.5) | 491 | (2.8) | 495 | (2.4) | **-57** | (11.0) | **-53** | (9.7) |
| | Poland | c | c | c | c | 508 | (2.7) | 496 | (2.4) | c | c | c | c |
| | Portugal | 416 | (17.3) | 445 | (15.3) | 475 | (3.6) | 468 | (3.0) | c | c | c | c |
| | Slovak Republic | c | c | c | c | 475 | (3.4) | 501 | (3.2) | c | c | c | c |
| | Spain | c | c | c | c | 464 | (2.4) | 483 | (2.5) | c | c | c | c |
| | Sweden | c | c | c | c | 515 | (3.3) | 509 | (2.2) | **-52** | (7.0) | **-54** | (6.9) |
| | Switzerland | 442 | (5.3) | 473 | (5.5) | 515 | (2.8) | 546 | (2.9) | **-81** | (4.1) | **-84** | (4.4) |
| | Turkey | c | c | c | c | 448 | (4.3) | 425 | (5.0) | c | c | c | c |
| | United Kingdom | 450 | (12.8) | 458 | (9.8) | 499 | (2.0) | 499 | (2.0) | **-43** | (15.5) | **-34** | (11.1) |
| | United States | m | m | 440 | (5.9) | m | m | 480 | (4.2) | m | m | **-38** | (6.5) |
| | **OECD total** | 439 | (4.3) | 447 | (2.3) | 489 | (1.0) | 488 | (1.2) | **-42** | (3.8) | **-38** | (3.5) |
| | **OECD average** | 450 | (2.7) | 467 | (2.2) | 498 | (0.6) | 504 | (0.5) | **-61** | (2.6) | **-54** | (2.1) |
| Partners | Argentina | c | c | c | c | 376 | (7.2) | 382 | (6.3) | c | c | c | c |
| | Azerbaijan | c | c | c | c | 351 | (3.1) | 475 | (2.3) | c | c | c | c |
| | Brazil | c | c | c | c | 393 | (3.8) | 370 | (3.0) | c | c | c | c |
| | Bulgaria | 319 | (10.7) | 343 | (8.9) | 414 | (6.4) | 423 | (5.9) | c | c | c | c |
| | Chile | c | c | c | c | 443 | (5.2) | 411 | (4.7) | a | a | a | a |
| | Colombia | c | c | c | c | 385 | (5.1) | 370 | (3.8) | a | a | a | a |
| | Croatia | c | c | c | c | 478 | (2.9) | 468 | (2.4) | c | c | c | c |
| | Estonia | c | c | c | c | 503 | (3.0) | 516 | (2.8) | c | c | c | c |
| | Hong Kong-China | c | c | c | c | 539 | (2.4) | 552 | (2.7) | **-19** | (8.6) | **-42** | (10.3) |
| | Indonesia | c | c | c | c | 409 | (10.3) | 402 | (11.7) | c | c | c | c |
| | Israel | 428 | (7.9) | 445 | (7.6) | 449 | (4.5) | 449 | (4.1) | -3 | (8.8) | 10 | (7.2) |
| | Jordan | c | c | c | c | 404 | (3.0) | 387 | (3.1) | c | c | c | c |
| | Kyrgyzstan | c | c | c | c | 281 | (3.4) | 307 | (3.3) | c | c | c | c |
| | Latvia | c | c | c | c | 481 | (3.8) | 489 | (3.1) | c | c | c | c |
| | Liechtenstein | 420 | (17.6) | 448 | (18.7) | 524 | (4.5) | 537 | (4.5) | **-112** | (19.7) | **-93** | (20.3) |
| | Lithuania | c | c | c | c | 472 | (3.0) | 488 | (3.0) | c | c | c | c |
| | Macao-China | 493 | (1.1) | 526 | (1.3) | 523 | (12.6) | 531 | (16.4) | **12** | (3.0) | **9** | (2.9) |
| | Montenegro | c | c | c | c | 404 | (2.1) | 411 | (2.1) | c | c | c | c |
| | Qatar | 300 | (2.4) | 344 | (2.1) | 321 | (1.6) | 311 | (1.5) | **56** | (5.5) | **82** | (4.6) |
| | Romania | c | c | c | c | 397 | (4.7) | 415 | (4.3) | c | c | c | c |
| | Russian Federation | 377 | (8.0) | 444 | (9.4) | 447 | (3.9) | 479 | (3.7) | c | c | c | c |
| | Serbia | c | c | c | c | 401 | (3.4) | 436 | (3.5) | c | c | c | c |
| | Slovenia | 454 | (5.6) | 459 | (6.2) | 498 | (1.0) | 509 | (1.1) | **-45** | (5.6) | **-52** | (6.6) |
| | Chinese Taipei | c | c | c | c | 510 | (3.0) | 565 | (3.7) | c | c | c | c |
| | Thailand | c | c | c | c | 430 | (3.7) | 431 | (3.7) | c | c | c | c |
| | Tunisia | 399 | (9.8) | 385 | (10.2) | 380 | (3.9) | 365 | (3.7) | c | c | c | c |
| | Uruguay | c | c | c | c | 416 | (3.5) | 430 | (2.6) | c | c | c | c |

Note: Values that are statistically significant are indicated in bold (see Annex A3).
1. Results based on students' self-reports.
*StatLink* http://dx.doi.org/10.1787/142104560611

Pour consulter la version française intégrale de ce tableau, suivre ce lien :
*StatLink* http://dx.doi.org/10.1787/152684743050

[Part 1/1]

**Table 4.3c** Differences in science performance between students with an immigrant background (first- and second-generation) and native students associated with students' immigrant background and home language[1]

Tableau 4.3c Variation de la performance des élèves en sciences selon l'ascendance autochtone ou allochtone (1ère et 2e générations) et la langue parlée en famille

| | Difference in science performance | | | | | | | |
|---|---|---|---|---|---|---|---|---|
| | WITHOUT ACCOUNTING for the economic, social and cultural status of students | | | | WITH ACCOUNTING for the economic, social and cultural status of students | | | |
| | Students with an immigrant background minus native students | | Students with an immigrant background who speak a language at home that is different from the language of instruction minus native students | | Students with an immigrant background minus native students | | Students with an immigrant background who speak a language at home that is different from the language of instruction minus native students | |
| | Difference | S.E. | Difference | S.E. | Difference | S.E. | Difference | S.E. |
| **OECD** | | | | | | | | |
| Australia | -2.0 | (5.0) | -15.2 | (7.4) | -0.4 | (4.4) | 3.0 | (3.9) |
| Austria | -90.1 | (11.1) | -96.4 | (13.2) | -60.9 | (8.4) | -36.8 | (9.4) |
| Belgium | -86.4 | (6.5) | -102.4 | (7.9) | -57.2 | (5.4) | -51.8 | (6.0) |
| Canada | -16.9 | (4.5) | -20.7 | (5.8) | -12.8 | (4.1) | -10.1 | (4.9) |
| Czech Republic | c | c | c | c | c | c | c | c |
| Denmark | -86.9 | (7.7) | -95.7 | (8.8) | -48.9 | (7.6) | -33.3 | (9.3) |
| Finland | c | c | c | c | c | c | c | c |
| France | -53.1 | (9.2) | -58.8 | (10.9) | -18.1 | (7.6) | -18.2 | (8.4) |
| Germany | -85.4 | (6.7) | -96.9 | (8.0) | -45.8 | (6.5) | -24.3 | (8.3) |
| Greece | -44.3 | (9.6) | -78.9 | (11.0) | -25.1 | (8.6) | -10.4 | (11.5) |
| Hungary | c | c | c | c | c | c | c | c |
| Iceland | c | c | c | c | c | c | c | c |
| Ireland | -10.5 | (11.7) | c | c | -12.8 | (10.3) | c | c |
| Italy | -58.4 | (7.8) | c | c | -46.9 | (8.1) | c | c |
| Japan | c | c | c | c | c | c | c | c |
| Korea | c | c | c | c | c | c | c | c |
| Luxembourg | -66.5 | (3.3) | -82.3 | (3.6) | -31.7 | (3.9) | 0.0 | (5.4) |
| Mexico | c | c | c | c | c | c | c | c |
| Netherlands | -75.5 | (9.7) | -85.6 | (11.6) | -41.0 | (7.9) | -36.9 | (9.4) |
| New Zealand | -15.9 | (6.0) | -38.6 | (8.7) | -16.7 | (4.5) | -7.4 | (4.7) |
| Norway | -58.6 | (8.5) | -59.8 | (10.9) | -35.3 | (9.0) | -24.0 | (11.8) |
| Poland | c | c | c | c | c | c | c | c |
| Portugal | -54.9 | (10.8) | c | c | -56.5 | (8.3) | c | c |
| Slovak Republic | c | c | c | c | c | c | c | c |
| Spain | -59.7 | (6.9) | c | c | -48.2 | (6.1) | c | c |
| Sweden | -60.8 | (5.1) | -67.6 | (6.1) | -43.4 | (4.5) | -32.0 | (7.6) |
| Switzerland | -81.4 | (4.2) | -95.5 | (4.4) | -56.3 | (4.1) | -37.2 | (5.5) |
| Turkey | c | c | c | c | c | c | c | c |
| United Kingdom | -32.5 | (9.0) | -49.1 | (14.3) | -14.2 | (6.0) | -8.3 | (6.7) |
| United States | -48.3 | (6.4) | -62.2 | (6.9) | -16.8 | (6.1) | -9.5 | (7.0) |
| **OECD total** | **-40.1** | (2.9) | **-51.7** | (3.7) | **-24.5** | (2.6) | **-16.4** | (2.9) |
| **OECD average** | **-54.4** | (1.8) | **-69.1** | (2.3) | **-34.4** | (1.5) | **-21.1** | (2.0) |
| **Partners** | | | | | | | | |
| Argentina | c | c | c | c | c | c | c | c |
| Azerbaijan | c | c | c | c | c | c | c | c |
| Brazil | c | c | c | c | c | c | c | c |
| Bulgaria | c | c | c | c | c | c | c | c |
| Chile | c | c | a | a | c | c | a | a |
| Colombia | c | c | a | a | c | c | a | a |
| Croatia | -19.4 | (4.4) | c | c | -7.1 | (4.4) | c | c |
| Estonia | -32.8 | (4.9) | c | c | -30.2 | (4.8) | c | c |
| Hong Kong-China | -9.1 | (4.1) | -38.7 | (11.2) | 8.4 | (3.8) | c | c |
| Indonesia | c | c | c | c | c | c | c | c |
| Israel | -5.7 | (5.4) | 3.6 | (7.6) | 9.0 | (4.9) | 1.4 | (5.4) |
| Jordan | 25.8 | (4.5) | c | c | 15.1 | (4.1) | c | c |
| Kyrgyzstan | c | c | c | c | c | c | c | c |
| Latvia | -3.3 | (6.2) | c | c | -6.0 | (5.8) | c | c |
| Liechtenstein | -47.2 | (11.7) | -107.3 | (20.1) | -34.0 | (10.9) | -23.8 | (12.3) |
| Lithuania | c | c | c | c | c | c | c | c |
| Macao-China | 11.0 | (2.6) | 10.1 | (2.6) | 17.3 | (2.7) | 34.7 | (14.5) |
| Montenegro | 16.7 | (5.9) | c | c | 16.0 | (5.8) | c | c |
| Qatar | 58.0 | (2.4) | 62.5 | (4.4) | 58.9 | (2.4) | 58.2 | (2.7) |
| Romania | c | c | c | c | c | c | c | c |
| Russian Federation | -13.6 | (6.0) | c | c | -11.7 | (5.5) | -1.1 | (5.1) |
| Serbia | 8.6 | (4.7) | c | c | 10.8 | (4.0) | c | c |
| Slovenia | -56.0 | (5.5) | -78.5 | (7.1) | -29.0 | (5.5) | -10.4 | (7.7) |
| Chinese Taipei | c | c | c | c | c | c | c | c |
| Thailand | c | c | c | c | c | c | c | c |
| Tunisia | c | c | c | c | c | c | c | c |
| Uruguay | c | c | c | c | c | c | c | c |

Note: Values that are statistically significant are indicated in bold (see Annex A3).
1. Results based on students' self-reports.
*StatLink* http://dx.doi.org/10.1787/142104560611

Pour consulter la version française intégrale de ce tableau, suivre ce lien :
*StatLink* http://dx.doi.org/10.1787/152684743050

[Part 1/1]

**Table 4.3d** **Characteristics of schools attended by native students and students with an immigrant background (scores standardised within each country)**

Tableau 4.3d Caractéristiques des établissements fréquentés par des élèves autochtones et allochtones (scores normalisés pour chaque pays)

| | Positive value indicates more favourable characteristics | | | | | | | | Negative value indicates more favourable characteristics | | | | | | | |
|---|---|---|---|---|---|---|---|---|---|---|---|---|---|---|---|---|
| | PISA index of economic, social and cultural status | | | | Quality of educational resources | | | | Student/teacher ratio | | | | Teacher shortage | | | |
| | Native students | | Students with an immigrant background | | Native students | | Students with an immigrant background | | Native students | | Students with an immigrant background | | Native students | | Students with an immigrant background | |
| | Mean index | S.E. | Mean index | S.E. | Mean index | S.E. | Mean index | S.E. | Mean index | S.E. | Mean index | S.E. | Mean index | S.E. | Mean index | S.E. |
| **OECD** Australia | 0.01 | (0.02) | -0.02 | (0.05) | -0.02 | (0.05) | 0.08 | (0.08) | -0.05 | (0.05) | 0.18 | (0.15) | 0.02 | (0.05) | -0.08 | (0.08) |
| Austria | 0.09 | (0.03) | -0.63 | (0.10) | 0.02 | (0.08) | -0.11 | (0.15) | 0.03 | (0.06) | -0.17 | (0.07) | -0.02 | (0.08) | 0.10 | (0.13) |
| Belgium | 0.09 | (0.02) | -0.60 | (0.07) | 0.00 | (0.06) | 0.03 | (0.14) | 0.04 | (0.04) | -0.27 | (0.10) | -0.06 | (0.06) | 0.41 | (0.09) |
| Canada | 0.02 | (0.02) | -0.06 | (0.05) | -0.01 | (0.05) | 0.04 | (0.11) | 0.00 | (0.04) | 0.00 | (0.09) | 0.04 | (0.05) | -0.13 | (0.08) |
| Czech Republic | 0.01 | (0.03) | c | c | 0.00 | (0.08) | c | c | 0.00 | (0.07) | c | c | -0.01 | (0.07) | c | c |
| Denmark | 0.07 | (0.03) | -0.93 | (0.07) | 0.02 | (0.07) | -0.23 | (0.13) | 0.00 | (0.07) | -0.02 | (0.11) | 0.01 | (0.08) | -0.07 | (0.14) |
| Finland | 0.01 | (0.02) | c | c | 0.00 | (0.08) | c | c | 0.00 | (0.07) | c | c | 0.00 | (0.08) | c | c |
| France | 0.09 | (0.03) | -0.59 | (0.09) | w | w | w | w | w | w | w | w | w | w | w | w |
| Germany | 0.11 | (0.03) | -0.67 | (0.05) | 0.02 | (0.07) | -0.11 | (0.11) | 0.01 | (0.06) | -0.08 | (0.10) | -0.07 | (0.06) | 0.41 | (0.08) |
| Greece | 0.04 | (0.04) | -0.46 | (0.06) | 0.02 | (0.09) | -0.27 | (0.09) | 0.00 | (0.07) | -0.02 | (0.11) | 0.00 | (0.08) | -0.02 | (0.13) |
| Hungary | 0.00 | (0.03) | c | c | 0.00 | (0.07) | c | c | 0.00 | (0.07) | c | c | 0.00 | (0.07) | c | c |
| Iceland | 0.01 | (0.01) | c | c | 0.00 | (0.01) | c | c | 0.00 | (0.01) | c | c | 0.00 | (0.01) | c | c |
| Ireland | -0.01 | (0.03) | 0.12 | (0.10) | -0.01 | (0.08) | 0.11 | (0.11) | 0.00 | (0.06) | -0.07 | (0.12) | 0.00 | (0.08) | 0.03 | (0.10) |
| Italy | 0.02 | (0.02) | -0.44 | (0.05) | 0.00 | (0.05) | 0.04 | (0.07) | 0.01 | (0.04) | -0.19 | (0.08) | 0.00 | (0.07) | 0.00 | (0.09) |
| Japan | 0.00 | (0.02) | c | c | 0.00 | (0.07) | c | c | 0.00 | (0.07) | c | c | 0.00 | (0.07) | c | c |
| Korea | 0.00 | (0.03) | c | c | 0.00 | (0.08) | c | c | 0.00 | (0.06) | c | c | 0.00 | (0.08) | c | c |
| Luxembourg | 0.30 | (0.01) | -0.53 | (0.02) | -0.04 | (0.01) | 0.07 | (0.02) | 0.01 | (0.01) | -0.01 | (0.02) | 0.03 | (0.01) | -0.04 | (0.02) |
| Mexico | 0.01 | (0.03) | c | c | 0.01 | (0.05) | c | c | 0.00 | (0.06) | c | c | -0.01 | (0.05) | c | c |
| Netherlands | 0.10 | (0.02) | -0.81 | (0.08) | 0.02 | (0.07) | -0.18 | (0.09) | 0.03 | (0.08) | -0.25 | (0.13) | -0.01 | (0.07) | 0.09 | (0.10) |
| New Zealand | -0.01 | (0.02) | 0.02 | (0.05) | -0.03 | (0.07) | 0.12 | (0.07) | -0.06 | (0.07) | 0.22 | (0.09) | 0.04 | (0.06) | -0.14 | (0.06) |
| Norway | 0.04 | (0.02) | -0.69 | (0.08) | -0.02 | (0.08) | 0.24 | (0.15) | -0.01 | (0.07) | 0.14 | (0.09) | 0.01 | (0.08) | -0.12 | (0.13) |
| Poland | 0.00 | (0.02) | c | c | 0.00 | (0.07) | c | c | 0.00 | (0.06) | c | c | 0.00 | (0.08) | c | c |
| Portugal | 0.00 | (0.03) | 0.04 | (0.11) | 0.02 | (0.08) | -0.25 | (0.14) | 0.01 | (0.07) | -0.18 | (0.17) | 0.00 | (0.08) | -0.07 | (0.14) |
| Slovak Republic | 0.00 | (0.03) | c | c | 0.00 | (0.06) | c | c | 0.00 | (0.08) | c | c | 0.00 | (0.06) | c | c |
| Spain | 0.02 | (0.03) | -0.25 | (0.08) | 0.00 | (0.05) | -0.04 | (0.11) | 0.03 | (0.04) | -0.41 | (0.06) | 0.01 | (0.04) | -0.16 | (0.08) |
| Sweden | 0.05 | (0.02) | -0.44 | (0.08) | -0.02 | (0.08) | 0.15 | (0.13) | 0.04 | (0.08) | -0.34 | (0.13) | 0.00 | (0.07) | 0.00 | (0.14) |
| Switzerland | 0.13 | (0.02) | -0.45 | (0.04) | 0.01 | (0.07) | -0.02 | (0.06) | 0.04 | (0.06) | -0.13 | (0.06) | -0.02 | (0.06) | 0.08 | (0.06) |
| Turkey | -0.01 | (0.04) | c | c | 0.00 | (0.09) | c | c | 0.00 | (0.08) | c | c | 0.00 | (0.08) | c | c |
| United Kingdom | 0.02 | (0.02) | -0.25 | (0.09) | -0.01 | (0.07) | 0.15 | (0.18) | 0.04 | (0.05) | -0.41 | (0.12) | 0.01 | (0.06) | -0.07 | (0.14) |
| United States | 0.11 | (0.04) | -0.59 | (0.09) | -0.01 | (0.09) | 0.04 | (0.13) | -0.07 | (0.09) | 0.42 | (0.14) | 0.00 | (0.09) | 0.00 | (0.13) |
| **OECD total** | **0.02** | (0.01) | **-0.24** | (0.04) | **-0.02** | (0.03) | **0.16** | (0.07) | **-0.01** | (0.02) | **0.06** | (0.05) | **-0.01** | (0.03) | **0.08** | (0.06) |
| **OECD average** | **0.04** | (0.00) | **-0.41** | (0.02) | **0.00** | (0.01) | **-0.01** | (0.03) | **0.00** | (0.01) | **-0.08** | (0.02) | **0.00** | (0.01) | **0.01** | (0.02) |
| **Partners** Argentina | 0.01 | (0.06) | c | c | 0.00 | (0.06) | c | c | 0.00 | (0.10) | c | c | 0.00 | (0.08) | c | c |
| Azerbaijan | -0.01 | (0.03) | c | c | 0.00 | (0.07) | c | c | 0.00 | (0.08) | c | c | 0.01 | (0.08) | c | c |
| Brazil | 0.01 | (0.03) | c | c | 0.00 | (0.04) | c | c | 0.00 | (0.06) | c | c | 0.00 | (0.05) | c | c |
| Bulgaria | 0.00 | (0.05) | c | c | 0.00 | (0.08) | c | c | 0.00 | (0.10) | c | c | 0.00 | (0.08) | c | c |
| Chile | 0.00 | (0.05) | c | c | 0.00 | (0.09) | c | c | 0.00 | (0.10) | c | c | 0.00 | (0.09) | c | c |
| Colombia | 0.00 | (0.04) | c | c | 0.00 | (0.07) | c | c | 0.00 | (0.12) | c | c | 0.00 | (0.10) | c | c |
| Croatia | 0.05 | (0.02) | -0.36 | (0.04) | 0.01 | (0.07) | -0.09 | (0.11) | 0.00 | (0.07) | 0.00 | (0.09) | 0.00 | (0.07) | 0.03 | (0.08) |
| Estonia | 0.01 | (0.02) | -0.07 | (0.06) | -0.01 | (0.07) | 0.04 | (0.17) | 0.00 | (0.04) | -0.01 | (0.13) | 0.05 | (0.06) | -0.40 | (0.13) |
| Hong Kong-China | 0.30 | (0.04) | -0.38 | (0.03) | 0.01 | (0.09) | -0.02 | (0.08) | 0.00 | (0.07) | -0.01 | (0.07) | -0.03 | (0.09) | 0.03 | (0.10) |
| Indonesia | 0.00 | (0.05) | c | c | 0.00 | (0.07) | c | c | 0.00 | (0.07) | c | c | 0.00 | (0.06) | c | c |
| Israel | 0.07 | (0.03) | -0.22 | (0.05) | -0.03 | (0.08) | 0.10 | (0.11) | 0.04 | (0.07) | -0.14 | (0.09) | 0.04 | (0.10) | -0.12 | (0.11) |
| Jordan | -0.05 | (0.03) | 0.26 | (0.05) | -0.05 | (0.08) | 0.23 | (0.09) | -0.07 | (0.05) | 0.35 | (0.11) | 0.03 | (0.08) | -0.16 | (0.09) |
| Kyrgyzstan | -0.01 | (0.03) | c | c | 0.00 | (0.06) | c | c | -0.01 | (0.07) | c | c | 0.00 | (0.08) | c | c |
| Latvia | -0.01 | (0.03) | 0.10 | (0.06) | -0.03 | (0.07) | 0.44 | (0.11) | -0.01 | (0.09) | 0.13 | (0.06) | 0.00 | (0.08) | 0.03 | (0.11) |
| Liechtenstein | c | c | c | c | c | c | c | c | c | c | c | c | c | c | c | c |
| Lithuania | 0.00 | (0.03) | c | c | 0.01 | (0.07) | c | c | 0.01 | (0.07) | c | c | 0.01 | (0.08) | c | c |
| Macao-China | 0.38 | (0.03) | -0.13 | (0.02) | -0.10 | (0.02) | 0.04 | (0.01) | -0.01 | (0.02) | 0.00 | (0.01) | 0.06 | (0.02) | -0.02 | (0.01) |
| Montenegro | -0.01 | (0.02) | 0.18 | (0.07) | 0.00 | (0.00) | -0.03 | (0.05) | -0.01 | (0.00) | 0.09 | (0.04) | -0.01 | (0.01) | 0.14 | (0.07) |
| Qatar | 0.02 | (0.02) | -0.03 | (0.02) | -0.04 | (0.01) | 0.06 | (0.02) | -0.09 | (0.02) | 0.13 | (0.03) | 0.04 | (0.01) | -0.06 | (0.01) |
| Romania | 0.00 | (0.04) | c | c | 0.00 | (0.08) | c | c | 0.00 | (0.07) | c | c | 0.00 | (0.09) | c | c |
| Russian Federation | 0.01 | (0.04) | -0.05 | (0.07) | -0.01 | (0.05) | 0.08 | (0.08) | 0.00 | (0.06) | 0.02 | (0.08) | 0.00 | (0.07) | -0.02 | (0.06) |
| Serbia | 0.01 | (0.03) | -0.06 | (0.06) | 0.00 | (0.07) | -0.01 | (0.10) | -0.02 | (0.09) | 0.21 | (0.09) | 0.01 | (0.07) | -0.09 | (0.09) |
| Slovenia | 0.07 | (0.01) | -0.63 | (0.04) | 0.01 | (0.01) | -0.13 | (0.03) | 0.00 | (0.01) | 0.02 | (0.04) | -0.01 | (0.01) | 0.07 | (0.05) |
| Chinese Taipei | 0.00 | (0.03) | c | c | 0.00 | (0.08) | c | c | 0.00 | (0.07) | c | c | 0.00 | (0.08) | c | c |
| Thailand | 0.00 | (0.03) | c | c | 0.00 | (0.06) | c | c | 0.00 | (0.08) | c | c | 0.00 | (0.07) | c | c |
| Tunisia | 0.00 | (0.05) | c | c | 0.00 | (0.07) | c | c | 0.00 | (0.07) | c | c | 0.00 | (0.08) | c | c |
| Uruguay | 0.00 | (0.03) | c | c | 0.00 | (0.05) | c | c | 0.00 | (0.05) | c | c | 0.00 | (0.05) | c | c |

StatLink http://dx.doi.org/10.1787/142104560611

Pour consulter la version française intégrale de ce tableau, suivre ce lien :
StatLink http://dx.doi.org/10.1787/152684743050

[Part 1/2]

## Table 4.4a  Relationship between student performance in science and the PISA index of economic, social and cultural status (ESCS)

Tableau 4.4a  Relation entre la performance des élèves en sciences et l'indice PISA de statut économique, social et culturel (SESC)

| | Unadjusted mean score | | Mean score if the mean ESCS would be equal in all OECD countries | | Strength of the relationship between student performance and the ESCS | | Slope of the socio-economic gradient[1] | | Length of the projection of the gradient line | | | | | |
| | | | | | | | | | 5th percentile of the ESCS | | 95th percentile of the ESCS | | Difference between 95th and 5th percentile of the ESCS | |
| | Mean score | S.E. | Mean score | S.E. | Percentage of explained variance in student performance | S.E. | Score point difference associated with one unit on the ESCS | S.E. | Index | S.E. | Index | S.E. | Dif. | S.E. |
|---|---|---|---|---|---|---|---|---|---|---|---|---|---|---|
| **OECD** | | | | | | | | | | | | | | |
| Australia | **527** | (2.3) | **519** | (1.7) | **11.3** | (0.78) | **43** | (1.5) | -1.08 | (0.02) | 1.39 | (0.03) | 2.47 | (0.03) |
| Austria | **511** | (3.9) | 502 | (3.7) | 15.4 | (2.02) | 46 | (3.1) | -1.04 | (0.07) | 1.63 | (0.05) | 2.67 | (0.09) |
| Belgium | **510** | (2.5) | 503 | (2.2) | **19.4** | (1.29) | 48 | (1.9) | -1.29 | (0.04) | 1.58 | (0.02) | 2.87 | (0.05) |
| Canada | **534** | (2.0) | **524** | (1.8) | 8.2 | (0.68) | 33 | (1.4) | -0.99 | (0.02) | 1.60 | (0.02) | 2.59 | (0.03) |
| Czech Republic | **513** | (3.5) | **512** | (3.2) | 15.6 | (1.35) | 51 | (2.6) | -1.14 | (0.02) | 1.30 | (0.02) | 2.44 | (0.03) |
| Denmark | 496 | (3.1) | 485 | (2.5) | 14.1 | (1.43) | 39 | (2.0) | -1.14 | (0.04) | 1.72 | (0.03) | 2.86 | (0.04) |
| Finland | **563** | (2.0) | **556** | (1.8) | 8.3 | (0.87) | 31 | (1.6) | -1.04 | (0.03) | 1.48 | (0.02) | 2.52 | (0.03) |
| France | 495 | (3.4) | 502 | (2.7) | **21.2** | (1.77) | 54 | (2.5) | -1.50 | (0.06) | 1.30 | (0.03) | 2.81 | (0.07) |
| Germany | **516** | (3.8) | 505 | (3.1) | **19.0** | (1.45) | 46 | (2.1) | -1.16 | (0.05) | 1.82 | (0.04) | 2.99 | (0.06) |
| Greece | 473 | (3.2) | **479** | (2.6) | 15.0 | (1.72) | 37 | (2.2) | -1.72 | (0.04) | 1.45 | (0.06) | 3.18 | (0.05) |
| Hungary | 504 | (2.7) | **508** | (2.2) | **21.4** | (1.58) | 44 | (1.8) | -1.53 | (0.03) | 1.50 | (0.03) | 3.02 | (0.05) |
| Iceland | 491 | (1.6) | **470** | (2.1) | 6.7 | (0.80) | 29 | (1.8) | -0.67 | (0.04) | 2.11 | (0.02) | 2.79 | (0.04) |
| Ireland | **508** | (3.2) | **510** | (2.5) | 12.7 | (1.37) | 39 | (2.2) | -1.38 | (0.04) | 1.43 | (0.04) | 2.81 | (0.05) |
| Italy | 475 | (2.0) | **478** | (1.9) | 10.0 | (0.94) | 31 | (1.6) | -1.59 | (0.03) | 1.67 | (0.04) | 3.25 | (0.05) |
| Japan | **531** | (3.4) | **533** | (3.1) | 7.4 | (0.95) | 39 | (2.7) | -1.08 | (0.02) | 1.13 | (0.01) | 2.22 | (0.02) |
| Korea | **522** | (3.4) | **522** | (3.0) | 8.1 | (1.49) | 32 | (3.1) | -1.32 | (0.05) | 1.30 | (0.04) | 2.62 | (0.07) |
| Luxembourg | **486** | (1.1) | **483** | (1.1) | **21.7** | (1.12) | 41 | (1.2) | -1.96 | (0.02) | 1.72 | (0.02) | 3.68 | (0.03) |
| Mexico | 410 | (2.7) | **435** | (2.4) | 16.8 | (1.72) | 25 | (1.3) | -2.95 | (0.06) | 1.21 | (0.06) | 4.16 | (0.08) |
| Netherlands | **525** | (2.7) | **515** | (2.4) | 16.7 | (1.65) | 44 | (2.2) | -1.23 | (0.06) | 1.60 | (0.03) | 2.83 | (0.06) |
| New Zealand | 530 | (2.7) | **528** | (2.3) | **16.4** | (1.11) | 52 | (1.8) | -1.27 | (0.04) | 1.40 | (0.04) | 2.67 | (0.05) |
| Norway | 487 | (3.1) | 474 | (2.8) | 8.3 | (1.10) | 36 | (2.5) | -0.73 | (0.03) | 1.62 | (0.03) | 2.35 | (0.04) |
| Poland | 498 | (2.3) | 510 | (2.1) | 14.5 | (1.13) | 39 | (1.8) | -1.56 | (0.03) | 1.31 | (0.07) | 2.87 | (0.07) |
| Portugal | **474** | (3.0) | **492** | (2.3) | 16.6 | (1.50) | 28 | (1.4) | -2.46 | (0.03) | 1.70 | (0.03) | 4.16 | (0.04) |
| Slovak Republic | **488** | (2.6) | **495** | (2.2) | **19.2** | (1.96) | 45 | (2.6) | -1.40 | (0.07) | 1.48 | (0.02) | 2.88 | (0.07) |
| Spain | **488** | (2.6) | 499 | (1.9) | 13.9 | (1.21) | 31 | (1.3) | -1.93 | (0.05) | 1.56 | (0.01) | 3.48 | (0.05) |
| Sweden | 503 | (2.4) | 496 | (2.2) | **10.6** | (0.97) | 38 | (2.1) | -1.04 | (0.03) | 1.47 | (0.04) | 2.50 | (0.03) |
| Switzerland | **512** | (3.2) | **508** | (2.6) | 15.7 | (1.20) | 44 | (1.8) | -1.37 | (0.03) | 1.54 | (0.03) | 2.91 | (0.04) |
| Turkey | 424 | (3.8) | **463** | (6.4) | 16.5 | (2.96) | 31 | (3.2) | -2.85 | (0.04) | 0.77 | (0.08) | 3.62 | (0.08) |
| United Kingdom | **515** | (2.3) | **508** | (1.9) | 13.9 | (1.12) | 48 | (1.9) | -1.12 | (0.03) | 1.50 | (0.01) | 2.62 | (0.03) |
| United States | **489** | (4.2) | **483** | (3.0) | 17.9 | (1.63) | 49 | (2.5) | -1.39 | (0.06) | 1.59 | (0.04) | 2.98 | (0.07) |
| **OECD total** | 491 | (1.2) | 496 | (0.9) | **20.2** | (0.57) | 45 | (0.6) | -2.00 | (0.03) | 1.47 | (0.01) | 3.47 | (0.03) |
| **OECD average** | 500 | (0.5) | 500 | (0.5) | 14.4 | (0.26) | 40 | (0.4) | -1.43 | (0.01) | 1.50 | (0.01) | 2.93 | (0.01) |
| **Partners** | | | | | | | | | | | | | | |
| Argentina | **391** | (6.1) | **416** | (4.7) | **19.5** | (2.33) | 38 | (2.4) | -2.54 | (0.06) | 1.27 | (0.07) | 3.81 | (0.08) |
| Azerbaijan | **382** | (2.8) | **388** | (2.7) | **4.7** | (1.71) | 11 | (2.0) | -2.06 | (0.04) | 1.31 | (0.04) | 3.37 | (0.05) |
| Brazil | **390** | (2.8) | **424** | (3.6) | 17.1 | (1.92) | 30 | (1.9) | -3.04 | (0.02) | 0.89 | (0.04) | 3.93 | (0.05) |
| Bulgaria | 434 | (6.1) | 446 | (4.4) | 24.1 | (2.76) | 52 | (3.6) | -1.77 | (0.09) | 1.44 | (0.06) | 3.20 | (0.11) |
| Chile | **438** | (4.3) | **465** | (3.3) | **23.3** | (1.92) | 38 | (1.8) | -2.55 | (0.08) | 1.30 | (0.07) | 3.85 | (0.10) |
| Colombia | 388 | (3.4) | 411 | (3.0) | 11.4 | (1.57) | 23 | (1.6) | -2.95 | (0.07) | 1.06 | (0.08) | 4.01 | (0.10) |
| Croatia | **493** | (2.4) | 497 | (2.3) | 12.3 | (1.21) | 34 | (1.9) | -1.46 | (0.04) | 1.46 | (0.04) | 2.92 | (0.05) |
| Estonia | 531 | (2.5) | 527 | (2.4) | 9.3 | (1.12) | 31 | (2.0) | -1.11 | (0.03) | 1.44 | (0.02) | 2.56 | (0.03) |
| Hong Kong-China | **542** | (2.5) | **560** | (2.9) | **6.9** | (1.26) | 26 | (2.3) | -2.17 | (0.04) | 0.98 | (0.08) | 3.14 | (0.09) |
| Indonesia | 393 | (5.7) | **425** | (7.5) | 10.2 | (2.31) | 21 | (2.6) | -3.11 | (0.04) | 0.35 | (0.07) | 3.46 | (0.08) |
| Israel | **454** | (3.7) | **448** | (3.5) | **10.9** | (1.10) | 43 | (2.7) | -1.29 | (0.04) | 1.50 | (0.06) | 2.79 | (0.07) |
| Jordan | 422 | (2.8) | 438 | (2.8) | 11.2 | (1.35) | 27 | (1.8) | -2.57 | (0.09) | 1.03 | (0.05) | 3.59 | (0.09) |
| Kyrgyzstan | 322 | (2.9) | 340 | (2.8) | 8.2 | (1.42) | 27 | (2.6) | -2.02 | (0.02) | 0.83 | (0.04) | 2.85 | (0.04) |
| Latvia | 490 | (3.0) | 491 | (2.6) | 9.7 | (1.41) | 29 | (2.3) | -1.40 | (0.03) | 1.42 | (0.04) | 2.82 | (0.05) |
| Liechtenstein | **522** | (4.1) | **513** | (4.3) | 20.4 | (4.42) | 49 | (5.5) | -1.34 | (0.08) | 1.70 | (0.11) | 3.04 | (0.12) |
| Lithuania | 488 | (2.8) | 487 | (2.3) | 15.2 | (1.33) | 38 | (2.0) | -1.37 | (0.02) | 1.49 | (0.03) | 2.86 | (0.04) |
| Macao-China | **511** | (1.1) | **523** | (1.8) | **2.2** | (0.49) | 13 | (1.5) | -2.28 | (0.02) | 0.55 | (0.03) | 2.83 | (0.03) |
| Montenegro | 412 | (1.1) | 412 | (1.1) | 7.5 | (0.90) | 24 | (1.4) | -1.44 | (0.03) | 1.42 | (0.02) | 2.87 | (0.03) |
| Qatar | m | m | m | m | m | m | m | m | m | m | m | m | m | m |
| Romania | 418 | (4.2) | 431 | (3.9) | 16.6 | (3.15) | 35 | (3.4) | -1.89 | (0.06) | 1.27 | (0.06) | 3.16 | (0.09) |
| Russian Federation | 479 | (3.7) | **483** | (3.2) | 8.1 | (1.23) | 32 | (2.6) | -1.31 | (0.03) | 1.18 | (0.01) | 2.48 | (0.03) |
| Serbia | 436 | (3.0) | 440 | (2.5) | 13.2 | (1.27) | 33 | (1.8) | -1.56 | (0.03) | 1.52 | (0.04) | 3.08 | (0.05) |
| Slovenia | **519** | (1.1) | **513** | (1.2) | 16.7 | (1.11) | 46 | (1.6) | -1.25 | (0.04) | 1.57 | (0.02) | 2.82 | (0.04) |
| Chinese Taipei | **532** | (3.6) | **546** | (2.8) | 12.5 | (1.19) | 42 | (2.1) | -1.60 | (0.04) | 1.04 | (0.03) | 2.63 | (0.05) |
| Thailand | **421** | (2.1) | **461** | (3.3) | 15.9 | (2.00) | 28 | (1.6) | -2.84 | (0.04) | 0.77 | (0.07) | 3.62 | (0.07) |
| Tunisia | 386 | (3.0) | 408 | (4.4) | 9.5 | (2.11) | 19 | (2.2) | -3.26 | (0.03) | 1.08 | (0.08) | 4.34 | (0.08) |
| Uruguay | **428** | (2.7) | **446** | (2.5) | 18.3 | (1.23) | 34 | (1.4) | -2.47 | (0.04) | 1.43 | (0.04) | 3.90 | (0.05) |

Note: Values that are statistically significant are indicated in bold (see Annex A3).
1. Single-level bivariate regression of science performance on the ESCS, the slope is the regression coefficient for the ESCS.
2. Student-level regression of science performance on the ESCS and the squared term of the ESCS, the index of curvelinearity is the regression coefficient for the squared term.
StatLink  http://dx.doi.org/10.1787/142104560611

Pour consulter la version française intégrale de ce tableau, suivre ce lien :
StatLink http://dx.doi.org/10.1787/152684743050

[Part 2/2]

**Table 4.4a** Relationship between student performance in science and the PISA index of economic, social and cultural status (ESCS)

Tableau 4.4a  Relation entre la performance des élèves en sciences et l'indice PISA de statut économique, social et culturel (SESC)

| | | ESCS mean | | Variability in the ESCS | | Index of curvilinearity[2] | | Index of skewness in the distribution of the ESCS | | Percentage of students that fall within the lowest 15 per cent of the international distribution on the ESCS | |
| --- | --- | --- | --- | --- | --- | --- | --- | --- | --- | --- | --- |
| | | Mean index | S.E. | Standard deviation | S.E. | Score point difference associated with one unit on the ESCS squared | S.E. | Index | S.E. | Approximated by the percentage of students with a value on the PISA index of economic, social and cultural status smaller than -1 | S.E. |
| OECD | Australia | 0.21 | (0.01) | 0.78 | (0.01) | -1.23 | (1.38) | -0.22 | (0.03) | 6.1 | (0.3) |
| | Austria | 0.20 | (0.02) | 0.83 | (0.02) | **-7.84** | (1.73) | 0.09 | (0.08) | 6.0 | (0.7) |
| | Belgium | 0.17 | (0.02) | 0.91 | (0.01) | **-2.01** | (0.97) | -0.26 | (0.04) | 8.6 | (0.5) |
| | Canada | 0.37 | (0.02) | 0.81 | (0.01) | **-2.57** | (1.14) | -0.29 | (0.03) | 4.7 | (0.3) |
| | Czech Republic | 0.03 | (0.02) | 0.76 | (0.01) | -3.37 | (1.96) | 0.03 | (0.06) | 7.8 | (0.5) |
| | Denmark | 0.31 | (0.03) | 0.89 | (0.01) | -1.00 | (1.27) | -0.16 | (0.05) | 6.5 | (0.5) |
| | Finland | 0.26 | (0.02) | 0.79 | (0.01) | 1.89 | (1.56) | -0.17 | (0.04) | 5.6 | (0.4) |
| | France | -0.09 | (0.03) | 0.86 | (0.02) | 1.14 | (1.88) | -0.19 | (0.04) | 14.1 | (0.8) |
| | Germany | 0.29 | (0.03) | 0.93 | (0.01) | **-3.60** | (1.17) | -0.09 | (0.05) | 6.8 | (0.6) |
| | Greece | -0.15 | (0.03) | 0.97 | (0.02) | **-4.04** | (1.39) | 0.04 | (0.03) | 20.2 | (1.1) |
| | Hungary | -0.09 | (0.03) | 0.92 | (0.02) | **-3.28** | (1.25) | 0.12 | (0.04) | 15.4 | (1.0) |
| | Iceland | 0.77 | (0.01) | 0.87 | (0.01) | -2.61 | (1.69) | -0.24 | (0.04) | 2.4 | (0.3) |
| | Ireland | -0.02 | (0.03) | 0.86 | (0.01) | -1.05 | (1.34) | 0.02 | (0.04) | 12.0 | (0.7) |
| | Italy | -0.07 | (0.02) | 0.98 | (0.01) | **-4.57** | (0.94) | 0.21 | (0.02) | 18.7 | (0.6) |
| | Japan | -0.01 | (0.02) | 0.70 | (0.01) | **-11.25** | (2.49) | 0.06 | (0.03) | 6.9 | (0.5) |
| | Korea | -0.01 | (0.02) | 0.81 | (0.01) | 2.51 | (1.77) | -0.14 | (0.04) | 10.7 | (0.6) |
| | Luxembourg | 0.09 | (0.01) | 1.10 | (0.01) | -1.71 | (0.93) | -0.36 | (0.03) | 17.6 | (0.5) |
| | Mexico | -0.99 | (0.04) | 1.31 | (0.02) | **1.61** | (0.62) | 0.20 | (0.04) | 52.5 | (1.4) |
| | Netherlands | 0.25 | (0.03) | 0.89 | (0.02) | 2.11 | (1.65) | -0.12 | (0.04) | 7.5 | (0.7) |
| | New Zealand | 0.10 | (0.02) | 0.83 | (0.01) | 2.68 | (1.61) | -0.28 | (0.08) | 9.0 | (0.4) |
| | Norway | 0.42 | (0.02) | 0.76 | (0.01) | **-4.10** | (1.65) | -0.32 | (0.05) | 2.3 | (0.3) |
| | Poland | -0.30 | (0.02) | 0.87 | (0.01) | 0.60 | (1.09) | -0.25 | (0.04) | 20.8 | (0.9) |
| | Portugal | -0.62 | (0.04) | 1.28 | (0.02) | 0.80 | (0.78) | 0.42 | (0.03) | 43.5 | (1.5) |
| | Slovak Republic | -0.15 | (0.02) | 0.91 | (0.02) | -3.39 | (2.75) | 0.20 | (0.12) | 13.5 | (0.9) |
| | Spain | -0.31 | (0.03) | 1.07 | (0.01) | **-2.44** | (0.99) | 0.23 | (0.03) | 29.1 | (1.0) |
| | Sweden | 0.24 | (0.02) | 0.79 | (0.01) | -1.49 | (1.84) | -0.33 | (0.09) | 5.6 | (0.4) |
| | Switzerland | 0.09 | (0.02) | 0.89 | (0.01) | **-2.30** | (1.24) | -0.04 | (0.03) | 11.7 | (0.5) |
| | Turkey | -1.28 | (0.04) | 1.10 | (0.03) | **5.72** | (1.39) | 0.15 | (0.05) | 62.7 | (1.6) |
| | United Kingdom | 0.19 | (0.01) | 0.81 | (0.01) | -0.33 | (1.62) | -0.13 | (0.05) | 6.6 | (0.5) |
| | United States | 0.14 | (0.04) | 0.91 | (0.02) | **3.30** | (1.38) | -0.21 | (0.04) | 11.0 | (0.9) |
| | **OECD total** | -0.10 | (0.01) | 1.04 | (0.01) | **-0.86** | (0.40) | -0.10 | (0.02) | 17.9 | (0.3) |
| | **OECD average** | 0.00 | (0.00) | 0.91 | (0.00) | **-1.39** | (0.28) | -0.07 | (0.01) | 14.9 | (0.1) |
| Partners | Argentina | -0.64 | (0.07) | 1.16 | (0.02) | 3.11 | (1.65) | -0.06 | (0.06) | 37.9 | (2.2) |
| | Azerbaijan | -0.45 | (0.03) | 1.06 | (0.02) | **3.86** | (1.16) | 0.13 | (0.05) | 33.7 | (1.2) |
| | Brazil | -1.12 | (0.03) | 1.25 | (0.01) | **6.10** | (1.33) | 0.05 | (0.03) | 52.9 | (1.1) |
| | Bulgaria | -0.21 | (0.05) | 1.01 | (0.02) | -1.55 | (1.99) | -0.05 | (0.08) | 21.1 | (1.4) |
| | Chile | -0.70 | (0.06) | 1.18 | (0.03) | **4.30** | (1.12) | 0.15 | (0.05) | 42.3 | (2.2) |
| | Colombia | -1.00 | (0.05) | 1.23 | (0.03) | **4.03** | (1.12) | 0.04 | (0.05) | 49.9 | (2.0) |
| | Croatia | -0.11 | (0.02) | 0.87 | (0.01) | 0.01 | (1.16) | 0.23 | (0.03) | 13.5 | (0.6) |
| | Estonia | 0.14 | (0.02) | 0.81 | (0.01) | 5.04 | (2.20) | 0.02 | (0.04) | 7.3 | (0.7) |
| | Hong Kong-China | -0.67 | (0.03) | 0.93 | (0.02) | -1.24 | (1.50) | 0.18 | (0.03) | 37.6 | (1.2) |
| | Indonesia | -1.52 | (0.05) | 1.08 | (0.02) | **4.01** | (1.25) | 0.29 | (0.07) | 68.6 | (2.1) |
| | Israel | 0.22 | (0.02) | 0.86 | (0.01) | **5.25** | (1.84) | -0.60 | (0.05) | 8.3 | (0.6) |
| | Jordan | -0.57 | (0.03) | 1.11 | (0.02) | **2.93** | (0.95) | -0.46 | (0.05) | 34.0 | (1.2) |
| | Kyrgyzstan | -0.66 | (0.02) | 0.88 | (0.01) | **4.65** | (1.54) | 0.00 | (0.05) | 35.0 | (1.1) |
| | Latvia | -0.02 | (0.02) | 0.90 | (0.01) | -1.99 | (1.84) | 0.03 | (0.04) | 14.7 | (0.8) |
| | Liechtenstein | 0.19 | (0.05) | 0.89 | (0.03) | **-9.11** | (4.43) | -0.09 | (0.12) | 9.2 | (1.3) |
| | Lithuania | 0.04 | (0.03) | 0.92 | (0.01) | -2.32 | (1.72) | 0.04 | (0.03) | 14.6 | (0.6) |
| | Macao-China | -0.91 | (0.01) | 0.87 | (0.01) | **-2.81** | (1.10) | 0.23 | (0.03) | 48.6 | (0.8) |
| | Montenegro | -0.02 | (0.01) | 0.90 | (0.01) | 0.30 | (1.36) | -0.82 | (0.02) | 14.4 | (0.5) |
| | Qatar | m | m | m | m | m | m | m | m | m | m |
| | Romania | -0.37 | (0.04) | 0.95 | (0.03) | 1.05 | (1.69) | 0.08 | (0.05) | 24.1 | (1.3) |
| | Russian Federation | -0.10 | (0.03) | 0.79 | (0.01) | 0.28 | (2.32) | 0.20 | (0.04) | 12.6 | (0.9) |
| | Serbia | -0.14 | (0.03) | 0.94 | (0.01) | -1.21 | (1.61) | -0.03 | (0.06) | 16.9 | (0.9) |
| | Slovenia | 0.13 | (0.01) | 0.87 | (0.01) | -1.09 | (1.71) | 0.09 | (0.03) | 8.7 | (0.4) |
| | Chinese Taipei | -0.31 | (0.02) | 0.80 | (0.01) | 1.38 | (1.32) | 0.41 | (0.04) | 20.3 | (1.1) |
| | Thailand | -1.43 | (0.03) | 1.11 | (0.02) | **4.96** | (1.15) | 0.01 | (0.03) | 69.4 | (1.1) |
| | Tunisia | -1.20 | (0.07) | 1.36 | (0.03) | **4.59** | (0.96) | 0.68 | (0.04) | 56.9 | (2.3) |
| | Uruguay | -0.51 | (0.03) | 1.19 | (0.01) | **3.70** | (0.98) | -0.05 | (0.04) | 34.7 | (1.1) |

Note: Values that are statistically significant are indicated in bold (see Annex A3).
1. Single-level bivariate regression of science performance on the ESCS, the slope is the regression coefficient for the ESCS.
2. Student-level regression of science performance on the ESCS and the squared term of the ESCS, the index of curvilinearity is the regression coefficient for the squared term.
*StatLink* ⟳ http://dx.doi.org/10.1787/142104560611

Pour consulter la version française intégrale de ce tableau, suivre ce lien :
*StatLink* ⟳ http://dx.doi.org/10.1787/152684743050

[Part 1/2]

**Table 4.4b** **Decomposition of the gradient of the PISA index of economic, social and cultural status (ESCS) into between-school and within-school components[1]**

*Tableau 4.4b* Décomposition du gradient de l'indice PISA de statut économique, social et culturel (SESC) en composantes inter- et intra-établissements

| | Overall effect of ESCS[2] | | Within-school effects of ESCS[3] | | | | Student variability in the distribution of ESCS | | | | | |
|---|---|---|---|---|---|---|---|---|---|---|---|---|
| | Score point difference associated with one unit on the ESCS | S.E. | Student-level score point difference associated with one unit of the student-level ESCS | S.E. | Explained within-school variance | S.E. | 25th percentile of the student distribution of ESCS | S.E. | 75th percentile of the student distribution of ESCS | S.E. | Interquartile range of the distribution of the student-level ESCS | S.E. |
| **OECD** | | | | | | | | | | | | |
| Australia | 43 | (1.5) | 29 | (1.4) | 4.9 | (0.5) | -0.33 | (0.02) | 0.79 | (0.02) | 1.12 | (0.02) |
| Austria | 46 | (3.1) | 10 | (1.7) | 1.1 | (0.4) | -0.37 | (0.03) | 0.73 | (0.03) | 1.09 | (0.03) |
| Belgium | 48 | (1.9) | 17 | (1.2) | 3.9 | (0.5) | -0.45 | (0.02) | 0.86 | (0.02) | 1.31 | (0.02) |
| Canada | 33 | (1.4) | 23 | (1.5) | 4.1 | (0.5) | -0.17 | (0.01) | 0.96 | (0.02) | 1.13 | (0.01) |
| Czech Republic | 51 | (2.6) | 19 | (1.6) | 3.2 | (0.5) | -0.52 | (0.03) | 0.55 | (0.03) | 1.06 | (0.03) |
| Denmark | 39 | (2.0) | 32 | (1.9) | 10.1 | (1.0) | -0.31 | (0.02) | 0.96 | (0.04) | 1.28 | (0.03) |
| Finland | 31 | (1.6) | 30 | (1.6) | 7.2 | (0.8) | -0.30 | (0.02) | 0.83 | (0.03) | 1.13 | (0.02) |
| France | w | w | w | w | w | w | w | w | w | w | w | w |
| Germany | 46 | (2.1) | 14 | (1.5) | 2.8 | (0.6) | -0.33 | (0.04) | 0.93 | (0.04) | 1.26 | (0.03) |
| Greece | 37 | (2.2) | 16 | (1.5) | 3.2 | (0.6) | -0.86 | (0.03) | 0.59 | (0.05) | 1.45 | (0.04) |
| Hungary | 44 | (1.8) | 7 | (1.3) | 0.6 | (0.3) | -0.72 | (0.03) | 0.57 | (0.05) | 1.29 | (0.05) |
| Iceland | 29 | (1.8) | 29 | (1.9) | 6.7 | (0.8) | 0.17 | (0.02) | 1.43 | (0.01) | 1.26 | (0.02) |
| Ireland | 39 | (2.2) | 28 | (2.0) | 6.1 | (0.8) | -0.61 | (0.03) | 0.59 | (0.05) | 1.20 | (0.03) |
| Italy | 31 | (1.6) | 7 | (1.0) | 0.9 | (0.2) | -0.79 | (0.02) | 0.56 | (0.02) | 1.35 | (0.02) |
| Japan | 39 | (2.7) | 5 | (2.2) | 0.2 | (0.2) | -0.54 | (0.03) | 0.51 | (0.02) | 1.05 | (0.04) |
| Korea | 32 | (3.1) | 9 | (1.9) | 0.7 | (0.3) | -0.56 | (0.03) | 0.59 | (0.04) | 1.14 | (0.04) |
| Luxembourg | 41 | (1.2) | 24 | (1.4) | 8.2 | (0.9) | -0.58 | (0.02) | 0.88 | (0.02) | 1.46 | (0.03) |
| Mexico | 25 | (1.3) | 6 | (0.8) | 1.0 | (0.2) | -2.04 | (0.05) | 0.03 | (0.07) | 2.07 | (0.06) |
| Netherlands | 44 | (2.2) | 11 | (1.3) | 1.9 | (0.5) | -0.35 | (0.03) | 0.93 | (0.04) | 1.28 | (0.03) |
| New Zealand | 52 | (1.8) | 41 | (1.9) | 9.7 | (0.9) | -0.45 | (0.02) | 0.70 | (0.03) | 1.15 | (0.02) |
| Norway | 36 | (2.5) | 31 | (2.0) | 5.8 | (0.8) | -0.10 | (0.02) | 0.95 | (0.02) | 1.05 | (0.04) |
| Poland | 39 | (1.8) | 35 | (1.6) | 11.1 | (0.9) | -0.89 | (0.02) | 0.17 | (0.03) | 1.06 | (0.04) |
| Portugal | 28 | (1.4) | 17 | (1.2) | 6.1 | (0.9) | -1.65 | (0.04) | 0.24 | (0.06) | 1.89 | (0.05) |
| Slovak Republic | 45 | (2.6) | 21 | (1.9) | 4.6 | (0.9) | -0.75 | (0.01) | 0.43 | (0.05) | 1.18 | (0.04) |
| Spain | 31 | (1.3) | 24 | (1.3) | 7.2 | (0.8) | -1.13 | (0.03) | 0.45 | (0.05) | 1.58 | (0.04) |
| Sweden | 38 | (2.1) | 32 | (2.9) | 7.1 | (1.3) | -0.29 | (0.02) | 0.82 | (0.03) | 1.11 | (0.03) |
| Switzerland | 44 | (1.8) | 26 | (1.5) | 7.2 | (0.7) | -0.51 | (0.02) | 0.69 | (0.02) | 1.20 | (0.02) |
| Turkey | 31 | (3.2) | 9 | (1.2) | 1.9 | (0.5) | -2.11 | (0.03) | -0.55 | (0.07) | 1.56 | (0.06) |
| United Kingdom | 48 | (1.9) | 32 | (2.0) | 6.6 | (0.7) | -0.36 | (0.02) | 0.76 | (0.02) | 1.12 | (0.02) |
| United States | 49 | (2.5) | 34 | (1.9) | 8.2 | (0.8) | -0.49 | (0.04) | 0.80 | (0.04) | 1.30 | (0.03) |
| **OECD total** | 45 | (0.6) | 20 | (0.5) | 17.0 | (0.9) | -0.73 | (0.01) | 0.65 | (0.02) | 1.38 | (0.01) |
| **OECD average** | 40 | (0.4) | 21 | (0.3) | 4.9 | (0.1) | -0.63 | (0.01) | 0.64 | (0.01) | 1.28 | (0.01) |
| **Partners** | | | | | | | | | | | | |
| Argentina | 38 | (2.4) | 13 | (1.7) | 2.8 | (0.7) | -1.49 | (0.08) | 0.23 | (0.09) | 1.72 | (0.06) |
| Azerbaijan | 11 | (2.0) | 7 | (0.9) | 2.1 | (0.5) | -1.23 | (0.04) | 0.39 | (0.06) | 1.62 | (0.05) |
| Brazil | 30 | (1.9) | 8 | (1.2) | 1.4 | (0.5) | -2.13 | (0.03) | -0.11 | (0.04) | 2.02 | (0.03) |
| Bulgaria | 52 | (3.6) | 13 | (1.7) | 1.6 | (0.5) | -0.92 | (0.06) | 0.55 | (0.08) | 1.47 | (0.07) |
| Chile | 38 | (1.8) | 11 | (1.4) | 1.4 | (0.4) | -1.57 | (0.07) | 0.14 | (0.09) | 1.71 | (0.07) |
| Colombia | 23 | (1.6) | 11 | (1.8) | 2.4 | (0.8) | -1.95 | (0.07) | -0.11 | (0.07) | 1.83 | (0.07) |
| Croatia | 34 | (1.9) | 14 | (1.4) | 2.7 | (0.5) | -0.70 | (0.02) | 0.46 | (0.03) | 1.16 | (0.03) |
| Estonia | 31 | (2.0) | 22 | (1.8) | 4.7 | (0.8) | -0.49 | (0.03) | 0.79 | (0.03) | 1.28 | (0.03) |
| Hong Kong-China | 26 | (2.3) | 9 | (1.7) | 1.0 | (0.4) | -1.33 | (0.02) | -0.06 | (0.04) | 1.27 | (0.03) |
| Indonesia | 21 | (2.6) | 1 | (1.1) | 0.1 | (0.1) | -2.37 | (0.05) | -0.72 | (0.09) | 1.64 | (0.07) |
| Israel | 43 | (2.7) | 26 | (2.3) | 4.3 | (0.8) | -0.30 | (0.03) | 0.80 | (0.03) | 1.11 | (0.02) |
| Jordan | 27 | (1.8) | 18 | (1.3) | 4.9 | (0.7) | -1.30 | (0.03) | 0.30 | (0.04) | 1.61 | (0.04) |
| Kyrgyzstan | 27 | (2.6) | 6 | (1.4) | 0.4 | (0.2) | -1.26 | (0.03) | -0.07 | (0.05) | 1.19 | (0.04) |
| Latvia | 29 | (2.3) | 21 | (2.1) | 4.8 | (0.9) | -0.74 | (0.01) | 0.70 | (0.04) | 1.43 | (0.04) |
| Liechtenstein | 49 | (5.5) | c | c | c | c | -0.36 | (0.06) | 0.82 | (0.08) | 1.18 | (0.08) |
| Lithuania | 38 | (2.0) | 24 | (1.5) | 5.9 | (0.8) | -0.71 | (0.03) | 0.79 | (0.04) | 1.49 | (0.03) |
| Macao-China | 13 | (1.5) | 7 | (1.6) | 0.5 | (0.2) | -1.52 | (0.03) | -0.33 | (0.02) | 1.19 | (0.02) |
| Montenegro | 24 | (1.4) | 11 | (1.5) | 1.7 | (0.5) | -0.66 | (0.02) | 0.65 | (0.02) | 1.31 | (0.02) |
| Qatar | m | m | m | m | m | m | m | m | m | m | m | m |
| Romania | 35 | (3.4) | 12 | (2.8) | 2.7 | (1.2) | -0.97 | (0.04) | 0.25 | (0.05) | 1.22 | (0.05) |
| Russian Federation | 32 | (2.6) | 20 | (1.8) | 3.2 | (0.6) | -0.71 | (0.02) | 0.53 | (0.05) | 1.24 | (0.03) |
| Serbia | 33 | (1.8) | 12 | (1.2) | 2.1 | (0.4) | -0.80 | (0.03) | 0.50 | (0.04) | 1.30 | (0.04) |
| Slovenia | 46 | (1.6) | 7 | (1.4) | 0.7 | (0.3) | -0.51 | (0.02) | 0.80 | (0.03) | 1.31 | (0.03) |
| Chinese Taipei | 42 | (2.1) | 14 | (1.6) | 1.9 | (0.5) | -0.87 | (0.03) | 0.22 | (0.02) | 1.09 | (0.02) |
| Thailand | 28 | (1.6) | 8 | (1.3) | 1.5 | (0.4) | -2.28 | (0.02) | -0.73 | (0.08) | 1.56 | (0.08) |
| Tunisia | 19 | (2.2) | 4 | (1.1) | 0.4 | (0.3) | -2.28 | (0.06) | -0.20 | (0.12) | 2.08 | (0.09) |
| Uruguay | 34 | (1.4) | 14 | (1.4) | 3.4 | (0.6) | -1.40 | (0.04) | 0.35 | (0.04) | 1.76 | (0.04) |

1. In some countries, sub-units within schools were sampled instead of schools as administrative units and this may affect the estimation of school-level effects.
2. Single-level bivariate regression of science performance on the ESCS, the slope is the regression coefficient for the ESCS.
3. Two-level regression of science performance on student ESCS and school mean ESCS: within-school slope for ESCS and explained variance at the student level by the model.
4. Two-level regression of science performance on student ESCS and school mean ESCS: between-school slope for ESCS and explained variance at the school level by the model.
5. Distribution of the school mean ESCS, percentiles calculated at student-level.
6. The index of inclusion is derived from the intra-class correlation for ESCS as 1-rho.
*StatLink* http://dx.doi.org/10.1787/142104560611

Pour consulter la version française intégrale de ce tableau, suivre ce lien :
*StatLink* http://dx.doi.org/10.1787/152684743050

[Part 2/2]

**Table 4.4b** Decomposition of the gradient of the PISA index of economic, social and cultural status (ESCS) into between-school and within-school components[1]

Tableau 4.4b Décomposition du gradient de l'indice PISA de statut économique, social et culturel (SESC) en composantes inter- et intra-établissements

| | | Between-school effects of ESCS[4] | | | School variability in the distribution of ESCS[5] | | | | | | | Index of inclusion[6] | |
|---|---|---|---|---|---|---|---|---|---|---|---|---|---|
| | | School-level score point difference associated with one unit on the school mean ESCS | S.E. | Explained between-school variance | S.E. | 25th percentile of the school mean distribution of ESCS | S.E. | 75th percentile of the school mean distribution of ESCS | S.E. | Interquartile range of the distribution of school mean distribution of ESCS | S.E. | Proportion of ESCS variance within schools | S.E. |
| OECD | Australia | 56 | (2.2) | 63.2 | (2.1) | -0.09 | (0.02) | 0.49 | (0.01) | 0.57 | (0.02) | 0.77 | (0.01) |
| | Austria | 110 | (2.7) | 66.2 | (1.6) | -0.11 | (0.03) | 0.52 | (0.03) | 0.64 | (0.04) | 0.71 | (0.01) |
| | Belgium | 102 | (1.5) | 71.4 | (1.1) | -0.17 | (0.03) | 0.55 | (0.04) | 0.73 | (0.04) | 0.73 | (0.01) |
| | Canada | 44 | (2.3) | 39.4 | (1.7) | 0.08 | (0.02) | 0.60 | (0.03) | 0.52 | (0.03) | 0.81 | (0.01) |
| | Czech Republic | 120 | (2.6) | 69.8 | (1.3) | -0.22 | (0.03) | 0.20 | (0.04) | 0.42 | (0.04) | 0.73 | (0.02) |
| | Denmark | 41 | (4.3) | 55.3 | (5.9) | 0.06 | (0.03) | 0.50 | (0.05) | 0.44 | (0.05) | 0.87 | (0.02) |
| | Finland | 10 | (3.7) | 27.2 | (9.9) | 0.07 | (0.03) | 0.44 | (0.02) | 0.36 | (0.03) | 0.91 | (0.01) |
| | France | w | w | w | w | w | w | w | w | w | w | w | w |
| | Germany | 114 | (2.2) | 74.6 | (1.7) | -0.11 | (0.04) | 0.64 | (0.04) | 0.75 | (0.05) | 0.75 | (0.01) |
| | Greece | 66 | (1.9) | 59.9 | (2.2) | -0.52 | (0.05) | 0.17 | (0.04) | 0.69 | (0.06) | 0.66 | (0.02) |
| | Hungary | 85 | (2.6) | 78.5 | (1.7) | -0.46 | (0.08) | 0.35 | (0.09) | 0.81 | (0.11) | 0.54 | (0.02) |
| | Iceland | -5 | (7.0) | 2.6 | (5.4) | 0.51 | (0.00) | 1.05 | (0.00) | 0.54 | (0.00) | 0.85 | (0.03) |
| | Ireland | 48 | (3.1) | 67.4 | (3.9) | -0.25 | (0.03) | 0.21 | (0.04) | 0.46 | (0.05) | 0.79 | (0.02) |
| | Italy | 87 | (1.3) | 52.4 | (1.0) | -0.45 | (0.02) | 0.28 | (0.03) | 0.73 | (0.04) | 0.76 | (0.01) |
| | Japan | 133 | (3.1) | 54.8 | (1.1) | -0.30 | (0.03) | 0.22 | (0.03) | 0.52 | (0.04) | 0.76 | (0.01) |
| | Korea | 80 | (2.4) | 53.0 | (2.3) | -0.32 | (0.04) | 0.27 | (0.04) | 0.58 | (0.05) | 0.74 | (0.01) |
| | Luxembourg | 69 | (2.3) | 89.6 | (1.6) | -0.29 | (0.00) | 0.56 | (0.00) | 0.85 | (0.00) | 0.77 | (0.01) |
| | Mexico | 37 | (0.9) | 52.0 | (1.0) | -1.69 | (0.10) | -0.43 | (0.07) | 1.25 | (0.11) | 0.60 | (0.01) |
| | Netherlands | 123 | (1.9) | 68.9 | (1.3) | -0.04 | (0.02) | 0.59 | (0.03) | 0.63 | (0.04) | 0.78 | (0.01) |
| | New Zealand | 55 | (3.7) | 74.4 | (5.3) | -0.16 | (0.02) | 0.37 | (0.02) | 0.54 | (0.03) | 0.82 | (0.01) |
| | Norway | 29 | (5.8) | 37.6 | (7.0) | 0.24 | (0.03) | 0.57 | (0.04) | 0.33 | (0.04) | 0.88 | (0.02) |
| | Poland | 21 | (3.4) | 48.0 | (5.7) | -0.62 | (0.04) | -0.03 | (0.05) | 0.59 | (0.07) | 0.76 | (0.02) |
| | Portugal | 32 | (1.9) | 52.8 | (2.7) | -1.18 | (0.10) | -0.15 | (0.11) | 1.03 | (0.14) | 0.69 | (0.01) |
| | Slovak Republic | 56 | (3.9) | 57.1 | (4.4) | -0.47 | (0.05) | 0.12 | (0.08) | 0.59 | (0.09) | 0.63 | (0.02) |
| | Spain | 21 | (1.5) | 49.2 | (1.9) | -0.71 | (0.05) | 0.03 | (0.06) | 0.73 | (0.07) | 0.76 | (0.01) |
| | Sweden | 34 | (7.6) | 52.6 | (8.5) | -0.01 | (0.01) | 0.44 | (0.03) | 0.44 | (0.03) | 0.87 | (0.01) |
| | Switzerland | 70 | (2.1) | 45.2 | (1.9) | -0.21 | (0.03) | 0.37 | (0.03) | 0.58 | (0.04) | 0.82 | (0.01) |
| | Turkey | 65 | (1.6) | 59.7 | (1.5) | -1.69 | (0.05) | -0.91 | (0.07) | 0.78 | (0.08) | 0.69 | (0.01) |
| | United Kingdom | 71 | (2.6) | 62.7 | (3.7) | -0.09 | (0.04) | 0.45 | (0.01) | 0.54 | (0.04) | 0.83 | (0.01) |
| | United States | 51 | (2.6) | 65.0 | (2.2) | -0.19 | (0.08) | 0.43 | (0.05) | 0.63 | (0.08) | 0.74 | (0.01) |
| | **OECD total** | 55 | (1.2) | 65.8 | (0.9) | -0.43 | (0.02) | 0.36 | (0.02) | 0.79 | (0.03) | | |
| | **OECD average** | 64 | (0.6) | 57.2 | (0.7) | -0.33 | (0.01) | 0.30 | (0.01) | 0.63 | (0.01) | 0.76 | (0.00) |
| Partners | Argentina | 57 | (2.3) | 59.0 | (2.6) | -1.23 | (0.12) | -0.04 | (0.13) | 1.19 | (0.15) | 0.61 | (0.02) |
| | Azerbaijan | 15 | (1.2) | 13.9 | (1.1) | -0.89 | (0.04) | -0.02 | (0.09) | 0.86 | (0.10) | 0.63 | (0.01) |
| | Brazil | 48 | (1.5) | 58.3 | (1.7) | -1.67 | (0.03) | -0.68 | (0.12) | 0.98 | (0.12) | 0.61 | (0.01) |
| | Bulgaria | 68 | (3.6) | 68.3 | (3.1) | -0.65 | (0.06) | 0.23 | (0.11) | 0.88 | (0.12) | 0.49 | (0.02) |
| | Chile | 54 | (1.8) | 73.3 | (2.5) | -1.31 | (0.04) | -0.12 | (0.09) | 1.18 | (0.08) | 0.47 | (0.01) |
| | Colombia | 31 | (2.2) | 55.9 | (2.5) | -1.49 | (0.06) | -0.59 | (0.04) | 0.90 | (0.07) | 0.60 | (0.02) |
| | Croatia | 83 | (2.1) | 60.3 | (1.8) | -0.43 | (0.04) | 0.13 | (0.03) | 0.56 | (0.04) | 0.78 | (0.01) |
| | Estonia | 42 | (3.0) | 40.4 | (3.3) | -0.11 | (0.04) | 0.38 | (0.04) | 0.49 | (0.05) | 0.81 | (0.01) |
| | Hong Kong-China | 64 | (2.3) | 39.8 | (2.3) | -1.02 | (0.05) | -0.43 | (0.08) | 0.60 | (0.09) | 0.76 | (0.01) |
| | Indonesia | 42 | (1.3) | 41.1 | (1.4) | -2.02 | (0.05) | -1.12 | (0.16) | 0.89 | (0.16) | 0.67 | (0.01) |
| | Israel | 69 | (3.3) | 45.2 | (2.8) | -0.12 | (0.03) | 0.54 | (0.04) | 0.65 | (0.05) | 0.76 | (0.01) |
| | Jordan | 28 | (1.8) | 39.5 | (3.9) | -0.93 | (0.05) | -0.33 | (0.08) | 0.60 | (0.09) | 0.75 | (0.01) |
| | Kyrgyzstan | 75 | (2.3) | 56.7 | (2.2) | -0.99 | (0.02) | -0.40 | (0.06) | 0.59 | (0.07) | 0.74 | (0.01) |
| | Latvia | 35 | (3.5) | 46.1 | (4.8) | -0.34 | (0.02) | 0.24 | (0.06) | 0.58 | (0.06) | 0.80 | (0.01) |
| | Liechtenstein | c | c | c | c | c | c | c | c | c | c | c | c |
| | Lithuania | 47 | (2.3) | 58.7 | (2.5) | -0.32 | (0.04) | 0.33 | (0.03) | 0.65 | (0.05) | 0.73 | (0.02) |
| | Macao-China | 15 | (5.6) | 11.3 | (3.7) | -1.20 | (0.00) | -0.73 | (0.11) | 0.48 | (0.11) | 0.67 | (0.03) |
| | Montenegro | 65 | (4.6) | 59.7 | (5.0) | -0.38 | (0.00) | 0.23 | (0.00) | 0.60 | (0.00) | 0.80 | (0.03) |
| | Qatar | m | m | m | m | m | m | m | m | m | m | m | m |
| | Romania | 60 | (3.2) | 55.7 | (2.2) | -0.70 | (0.06) | -0.10 | (0.05) | 0.60 | (0.08) | 0.66 | (0.01) |
| | Russian Federation | 39 | (3.8) | 34.1 | (4.8) | -0.36 | (0.05) | 0.14 | (0.05) | 0.50 | (0.06) | 0.76 | (0.02) |
| | Serbia | 75 | (1.8) | 66.6 | (2.1) | -0.51 | (0.03) | 0.17 | (0.07) | 0.68 | (0.07) | 0.74 | (0.02) |
| | Slovenia | 121 | (2.6) | 71.3 | (1.3) | -0.20 | (0.01) | 0.51 | (0.01) | 0.71 | (0.01) | 0.74 | (0.02) |
| | Chinese Taipei | 107 | (1.9) | 57.7 | (1.2) | -0.61 | (0.03) | -0.02 | (0.03) | 0.60 | (0.04) | 0.77 | (0.01) |
| | Thailand | 42 | (1.5) | 70.4 | (2.8) | -2.00 | (0.03) | -1.04 | (0.08) | 0.96 | (0.08) | 0.50 | (0.01) |
| | Tunisia | 36 | (1.3) | 39.1 | (2.4) | -1.89 | (0.09) | -0.67 | (0.07) | 1.22 | (0.09) | 0.64 | (0.01) |
| | Uruguay | 45 | (1.8) | 60.4 | (1.7) | -1.06 | (0.08) | -0.07 | (0.06) | 0.99 | (0.09) | 0.62 | (0.01) |

1. In some countries, sub-units within schools were sampled instead of schools as administrative units and this may affect the estimation of school-level effects.
2. Single-level bivariate regression of science performance on the ESCS, the slope is the regression coefficient for the ESCS.
3. Two-level regression of science performance on student ESCS and school mean ESCS: within-school slope for ESCS and explained variance at the student level by the model.
4. Two-level regression of science performance on student ESCS and school mean ESCS: between-school slope for ESCS and explained variance at the school level by the model.
5. Distribution of the school mean ESCS, percentiles calculated at student-level.
6. The index of inclusion is derived from the intra-class correlation for ESCS as 1-rho.
*StatLink* http://dx.doi.org/10.1787/142104560611

Pour consulter la version française intégrale de ce tableau, suivre ce lien :
*StatLink* http://dx.doi.org/10.1787/152684743050

[Part 1/2]

**Table 4.4c** Relationship between student performance in science and the PISA index of economic, social and cultural status (ESCS) for PISA 2000, PISA 2003 and PISA 2006

**Tableau 4.4c** Relation entre la performance des élèves en sciences et l'indice PISA de statut économique, social et culturel (SESC) pour les cycles PISA 2000, PISA 2003 et PISA 2006

| | Slope of ESCS for science,[1] PISA 2006 | | Strength of the relationship between science in PISA 2006 and the ESCS | | Slope of ESCS for science,[1] PISA 2003 | | Strength of the relationship between science in PISA 2003 and the ESCS | | Slope of ESCS for science,[1] PISA 2000 | | Strength of the relationship between science in PISA 2000 and the ESCS | |
|---|---|---|---|---|---|---|---|---|---|---|---|---|
| | Score point difference associated with one unit on the ESCS | S.E. | Percentage of explained variance in student performance | S.E. | Score point difference associated with one unit on the ESCS | S.E. | Percentage of explained variance in student performance | S.E. | Score point difference associated with one unit on the ESCS | S.E. | Percentage of explained variance in student performance | S.E. |
| **Australia** | **43** | (1.5) | **11.3** | (0.78) | 47 | (2.1) | 14.6 | (1.15) | 42 | (2.6) | 14.3 | (1.75) |
| Austria | **46** | (3.1) | 15.4 | (2.02) | 49 | (2.2) | 18.7 | (1.48) | 42 | (2.7) | 15.3 | (1.70) |
| Belgium | **48** | (1.9) | **19.4** | (1.29) | **55** | (1.8) | **24.5** | (1.32) | 53 | (2.7) | **20.0** | (1.51) |
| Canada | 33 | (1.4) | **8.2** | (0.68) | 40 | (1.6) | **11.4** | (0.82) | 33 | (1.5) | **10.6** | (0.88) |
| Czech Republic | 51 | (2.6) | 15.6 | (1.35) | 50 | (2.2) | 16.4 | (1.38) | 56 | (2.7) | 20.9 | (1.83) |
| Denmark | 39 | (2.0) | 14.1 | (1.43) | 47 | (2.3) | 16.3 | (1.40) | 46 | (2.6) | 16.6 | (1.80) |
| **Finland** | **31** | (1.6) | **8.3** | (0.87) | 34 | (1.7) | **9.9** | (0.97) | 26 | (2.3) | **7.3** | (1.24) |
| France | 54 | (2.5) | 21.2 | (1.77) | 54 | (2.8) | 20.9 | (1.97) | 47 | (2.5) | 18.5 | (1.90) |
| Germany | **46** | (2.1) | **19.0** | (1.45) | 54 | (1.7) | 25.9 | (1.51) | 54 | (2.6) | 23.4 | (2.19) |
| Greece | 37 | (2.2) | 15.0 | (1.72) | 36 | (2.0) | 13.0 | (1.48) | 30 | (2.8) | 10.5 | (1.93) |
| **Hungary** | **44** | (1.8) | **21.4** | (1.58) | 51 | (2.4) | 21.4 | (1.75) | 60 | (3.6) | 23.3 | (2.44) |
| Iceland | 29 | (1.8) | **6.7** | (0.80) | 31 | (2.1) | **6.8** | (0.95) | 22 | (2.4) | 5.7 | (1.19) |
| Ireland | 39 | (2.2) | 12.7 | (1.37) | 44 | (2.1) | 17.8 | (1.62) | 34 | (2.3) | 12.8 | (1.62) |
| Italy | **31** | (1.6) | **10.0** | (0.94) | 40 | (2.2) | 14.1 | (1.32) | 30 | (2.4) | **9.3** | (1.34) |
| Japan | 39 | (2.7) | **7.4** | (0.95) | 48 | (4.5) | **10.6** | (1.67) | m | m | m | m |
| Korea | 32 | (3.1) | **8.1** | (1.49) | 39 | (3.3) | **10.9** | (1.75) | 27 | (2.8) | **8.4** | (1.70) |
| **Luxembourg** | **41** | (1.2) | **21.7** | (1.12) | 40 | (1.6) | 17.7 | (1.27) | m | m | m | m |
| Mexico | **25** | (1.3) | 16.8 | (1.72) | 28 | (1.9) | 15.1 | (1.82) | 26 | (2.2) | 16.2 | (2.67) |
| Netherlands | 44 | (2.2) | 16.7 | (1.65) | 47 | (2.4) | 17.3 | (1.62) | m | m | m | m |
| New Zealand | 52 | (1.8) | 16.4 | (1.11) | 46 | (1.7) | 16.8 | (1.13) | 44 | (2.5) | 16.2 | (1.60) |
| Norway | 36 | (2.5) | **8.3** | (1.10) | 47 | (2.3) | **12.9** | (1.21) | 38 | (2.2) | 13.1 | (1.44) |
| Poland | 39 | (1.8) | 14.5 | (1.13) | 52 | (2.1) | 17.5 | (1.29) | 42 | (3.5) | 14.1 | (2.11) |
| **Portugal** | **28** | (1.4) | 16.6 | (1.50) | **29** | (1.6) | 15.1 | (1.55) | 33 | (2.2) | 15.6 | (2.23) |
| Slovak Republic | 45 | (2.6) | 19.2 | (1.96) | **58** | (3.6) | 21.8 | (2.29) | a | a | a | a |
| **Spain** | **31** | (1.3) | 13.9 | (1.21) | 36 | (2.0) | **13.3** | (1.38) | 35 | (2.1) | 15.3 | (1.71) |
| Sweden | 38 | (2.1) | **10.6** | (0.97) | 46 | (2.4) | 14.2 | (1.36) | 33 | (2.3) | **9.3** | (1.20) |
| Switzerland | 44 | (1.8) | 15.7 | (1.20) | **56** | (2.5) | **19.4** | (1.54) | 52 | (2.3) | 23.0 | (1.92) |
| Turkey | 31 | (3.2) | 16.5 | (2.96) | 41 | (4.4) | 22.2 | (3.76) | a | a | a | a |
| United Kingdom | **48** | (1.9) | 13.9 | (1.12) | m | m | m | m | m | m | m | m |
| United States | **49** | (2.5) | 17.9 | (1.63) | 48 | (1.7) | 18.5 | (1.33) | 46 | (3.6) | 21.2 | (2.93) |
| **OECD average** | 40 | (0.4) | 14.4 | (0.26) | 45 | (0.5) | 16.4 | (0.30) | 40 | (0.5) | 15.1 | (0.38) |
| Argentina | 38 | (2.4) | **19.5** | (2.33) | a | a | a | a | a | a | a | a |
| Azerbaijan | 11 | (2.0) | **4.7** | (1.71) | a | a | a | a | a | a | a | a |
| Brazil | 30 | (1.9) | 17.1 | (1.92) | 30 | (2.6) | 11.6 | (1.84) | 28 | (2.9) | 12.2 | (2.29) |
| Bulgaria | 52 | (3.6) | 24.1 | (2.76) | a | a | a | a | a | a | a | a |
| Chile | 38 | (1.8) | 23.3 | (1.92) | a | a | a | a | a | a | a | a |
| Colombia | 23 | (1.6) | 11.4 | (1.57) | a | a | a | a | a | a | a | a |
| Croatia | 34 | (1.9) | 12.3 | (1.21) | a | a | a | a | a | a | a | a |
| Estonia | 31 | (2.0) | **9.3** | (1.12) | a | a | a | a | a | a | a | a |
| Hong Kong-China | 26 | (2.3) | **6.9** | (1.26) | 30 | (2.5) | **6.7** | (1.20) | 32 | (3.0) | 9.4 | (1.93) |
| Indonesia | 21 | (2.6) | 10.2 | (2.31) | 19 | (2.2) | **8.0** | (1.62) | 18 | (3.5) | 5.6 | (1.97) |
| Israel | 43 | (2.7) | **10.9** | (1.10) | a | a | a | a | a | a | a | a |
| Jordan | 27 | (1.8) | 11.2 | (1.35) | a | a | a | a | a | a | a | a |
| Kyrgyzstan | 27 | (2.6) | 8.2 | (1.42) | a | a | a | a | a | a | a | a |
| Latvia | 29 | (2.3) | **9.7** | (1.41) | 38 | (3.0) | **9.5** | (1.53) | 36 | (4.7) | 8.9 | (2.17) |
| Liechtenstein | 49 | (5.5) | 20.4 | (4.42) | **61** | (6.7) | 23.0 | (4.47) | 43 | (7.6) | 19.2 | (6.74) |
| Lithuania | 38 | (2.0) | 15.2 | (1.33) | a | a | a | a | a | a | a | a |
| Macao-China | 13 | (1.5) | 2.2 | (0.49) | 10 | (3.1) | **0.9** | (0.59) | a | a | a | a |
| Montenegro | 24 | (1.4) | 7.5 | (0.90) | a | a | a | a | a | a | a | a |
| Qatar | m | m | m | m | m | m | m | m | m | m | m | m |
| Romania | 35 | (3.4) | 16.6 | (3.15) | a | a | a | a | a | a | a | a |
| Russian Federation | 32 | (2.6) | **8.1** | (1.23) | 40 | (2.3) | **9.0** | (1.01) | 38 | (3.3) | 8.0 | (1.29) |
| Serbia | 33 | (1.8) | 13.2 | (1.27) | a | a | a | a | a | a | a | a |
| Slovenia | 46 | (1.6) | 16.7 | (1.11) | a | a | a | a | a | a | a | a |
| Chinese Taipei | 42 | (2.1) | 12.5 | (1.19) | a | a | a | a | a | a | a | a |
| Thailand | 28 | (1.6) | 15.9 | (2.00) | 28 | (2.2) | 12.8 | (1.85) | 22 | (2.7) | 7.0 | (1.70) |
| Tunisia | 19 | (2.2) | 9.5 | (2.11) | 19 | (2.5) | 7.2 | (1.83) | a | a | a | a |
| Uruguay | 34 | (1.4) | 18.3 | (1.23) | 37 | (2.3) | 12.7 | (1.47) | a | a | a | a |

Note: Values that are statistically significant are indicated in bold (see Annex A3). Differences are later cycle minus the earlier cycle.
1. Single-level bivariate regression of science performance on the ESCS, the slope is the regression coefficient for the ESCS.
*StatLink*  http://dx.doi.org/10.1787/142104560611

Pour consulter la version française intégrale de ce tableau, suivre ce lien :
*StatLink* http://dx.doi.org/10.1787/152684743050

[Part 2/2]

**Table 4.4c** Relationship between student performance in science and the PISA index of economic, social and cultural status (ESCS) for PISA 2000, PISA 2003 and PISA 2006

Tableau 4.4c Relation entre la performance des élèves en sciences et l'indice PISA de statut économique, social et culturel (SESC) pour les cycles PISA 2000, PISA 2003 et PISA 2006

| | Difference in ESCS slope between 2006 and 2000 | | Difference in ESCS slope between 2006 and 2003 | | Difference in ESCS slope between 2003 and 2000 | | Difference in ESCS percent explained between 2006 and 2000 | | Difference in ESCS percent explained between 2006 and 2003 | | Difference in ESCS percent explained between 2003 and 2000 | |
|---|---|---|---|---|---|---|---|---|---|---|---|---|
| | Dif. | S.E. | Dif. | S.E. | Dif. | S.E. | Dif. | S.E. | Dif. | S.E. | Dif. | S.E. |
| **Australia** | 1.5 | (3.1) | -3.7 | (2.6) | 5.2 | (3.4) | -3.0 | (1.9) | **-3.3** | (1.4) | 0.2 | (2.1) |
| Austria | 4.3 | (4.1) | -2.5 | (3.8) | **6.8** | (3.5) | 0.1 | (2.6) | -3.2 | (2.5) | 3.3 | (2.3) |
| Belgium | -5.7 | (3.3) | **-7.3** | (2.6) | 1.5 | (3.2) | -0.6 | (2.0) | **-5.1** | (1.8) | **4.5** | (2.0) |
| Canada | 0.3 | (2.1) | **-7.2** | (2.1) | **7.5** | (2.2) | **-2.4** | (1.1) | **-3.1** | (1.1) | 0.7 | (1.2) |
| Czech Republic | -4.9 | (3.7) | 0.6 | (3.4) | -5.5 | (3.5) | **-5.3** | (2.3) | -0.9 | (1.9) | **-4.4** | (2.3) |
| Denmark | **-6.7** | (3.3) | **-8.5** | (3.1) | 1.8 | (3.5) | -2.4 | (2.3) | -2.1 | (2.0) | -0.3 | (2.3) |
| Finland | 5.4 | (2.8) | -3.2 | (2.3) | **8.6** | (2.8) | 0.9 | (1.5) | -1.6 | (1.3) | 2.6 | (1.6) |
| France | 6.4 | (3.5) | -0.2 | (3.8) | 6.5 | (3.8) | 2.7 | (2.6) | 0.2 | (2.6) | 2.4 | (2.7) |
| Germany | **-7.6** | (3.3) | **-7.5** | (2.7) | -0.1 | (3.1) | -4.5 | (2.6) | **-6.9** | (2.1) | 2.5 | (2.7) |
| Greece | 7.0 | (3.6) | 0.6 | (3.0) | 6.4 | (3.4) | 4.5 | (2.6) | 2.0 | (2.3) | 2.5 | (2.4) |
| Hungary | **-16.0** | (4.0) | **-6.6** | (3.0) | **-9.4** | (4.3) | -1.9 | (2.9) | 0.1 | (2.4) | -2.0 | (3.0) |
| Iceland | **6.5** | (3.0) | -2.1 | (2.8) | **8.6** | (3.2) | 1.0 | (1.4) | -0.1 | (1.2) | 1.1 | (1.5) |
| Ireland | 4.7 | (3.2) | -4.9 | (3.1) | **9.5** | (3.1) | -0.2 | (2.1) | **-5.1** | (2.1) | **4.9** | (2.3) |
| Italy | 0.6 | (2.9) | **-8.7** | (2.7) | **9.3** | (3.3) | 0.7 | (1.6) | **-4.1** | (1.6) | **4.8** | (1.9) |
| Japan | m | m | -9.6 | (5.2) | m | m | m | m | -3.2 | (1.9) | m | m |
| Korea | 4.3 | (4.2) | -7.4 | (4.6) | **11.7** | (4.3) | -0.3 | (2.3) | -2.8 | (2.3) | 2.5 | (2.4) |
| Luxembourg | m | m | 1.4 | (2.0) | m | (1.6) | m | m | **4.0** | (1.7) | m | m |
| Mexico | -1.3 | (2.6) | -2.8 | (2.3) | 1.5 | (2.9) | 0.5 | (3.2) | 1.7 | (2.5) | -1.2 | (3.2) |
| Netherlands | m | m | -3.3 | (3.3) | m | (2.4) | m | m | -0.5 | (2.3) | m | m |
| New Zealand | **7.9** | (3.0) | **5.6** | (2.4) | 2.3 | (3.0) | 0.2 | (1.9) | -0.4 | (1.6) | 0.6 | (2.0) |
| Norway | -2.3 | (3.3) | **-11.6** | (3.4) | **9.3** | (3.2) | **-4.9** | (1.8) | **-4.6** | (1.6) | -0.2 | (1.9) |
| Poland | -2.7 | (3.9) | **-12.6** | (2.7) | **9.9** | (4.1) | 0.4 | (2.4) | -3.0 | (1.7) | 3.4 | (2.5) |
| Portugal | -4.3 | (2.6) | -0.3 | (2.1) | -4.0 | (2.7) | 1.0 | (2.7) | 1.5 | (2.2) | -0.5 | (2.7) |
| Slovak Republic | a | a | **-12.7** | (4.4) | a | a | a | a | -2.6 | (3.0) | a | a |
| Spain | -3.4 | (2.5) | **-4.7** | (2.4) | 1.4 | (2.9) | -1.4 | (2.1) | 0.6 | (1.8) | -2.0 | (2.2) |
| Sweden | 5.0 | (3.1) | **-7.4** | (3.1) | **12.5** | (3.3) | 1.2 | (1.5) | **-3.6** | (1.7) | **4.8** | (1.8) |
| Switzerland | **-7.4** | (3.0) | **-11.7** | (3.1) | 4.3 | (3.4) | **-7.3** | (2.3) | -3.7 | (1.9) | **-3.6** | (2.5) |
| Turkey | a | a | -10.3 | (5.5) | a | a | a | a | -5.7 | (4.8) | a | a |
| United Kingdom | m | m | m | m | m | m | m | m | m | m | m | m |
| United States | 2.9 | (4.4) | 1.4 | (3.0) | 1.4 | (3.9) | -3.3 | (3.3) | -0.6 | (2.1) | -2.7 | (3.2) |
| **OECD average** | -0.2 | (0.7) | **-5.1** | (0.6) | **4.5** | (0.7) | **-1.0** | (0.5) | **-1.9** | (0.4) | **1.0** | (0.5) |
| Argentina | a | a | a | a | a | a | a | a | a | a | a | a |
| Azerbaijan | a | a | a | a | a | a | a | a | a | a | a | a |
| Brazil | 1.4 | (3.5) | -0.5 | (3.2) | 2.0 | (3.9) | **4.9** | (3.0) | **5.5** | (2.7) | -0.6 | (2.9) |
| Bulgaria | a | a | a | a | a | a | a | a | a | a | a | a |
| Chile | a | a | a | a | a | a | a | a | a | a | a | a |
| Colombia | a | a | a | a | a | a | a | a | a | a | a | a |
| Croatia | a | a | a | a | a | a | a | a | a | a | a | a |
| Estonia | a | a | a | a | a | a | a | a | a | a | a | a |
| Hong Kong-China | -6.0 | (3.8) | -4.0 | (3.4) | -2.0 | (3.9) | -2.5 | (2.3) | 0.2 | (1.7) | -2.6 | (2.3) |
| Indonesia | 2.5 | (4.4) | 1.5 | (3.4) | 0.9 | (4.1) | 4.7 | (3.0) | 2.3 | (2.8) | 2.4 | (2.5) |
| Israel | a | a | a | a | a | a | a | a | a | a | a | a |
| Jordan | a | a | a | a | a | a | a | a | a | a | a | a |
| Kyrgyzstan | a | a | a | a | a | a | a | a | a | a | a | a |
| Latvia | -6.9 | (5.2) | **-8.9** | (3.8) | 2.0 | (5.6) | 0.9 | (2.6) | 0.3 | (2.1) | 0.6 | (2.7) |
| Liechtenstein | 5.4 | (9.4) | -11.8 | (8.7) | 17.2 | (10.2) | 1.3 | (8.1) | -2.6 | (6.3) | 3.9 | (8.1) |
| Lithuania | a | a | a | a | a | a | a | a | a | a | a | a |
| Macao-China | a | a | 3.4 | (3.5) | a | a | a | a | 1.3 | (0.8) | a | a |
| Montenegro | a | a | a | a | a | a | a | a | a | a | a | a |
| Qatar | m | m | m | m | m | m | m | m | m | m | m | m |
| Romania | a | a | a | a | a | a | a | a | a | a | a | a |
| Russian Federation | -5.7 | (4.2) | **-7.8** | (3.5) | 2.2 | (4.0) | 0.1 | (1.8) | -0.9 | (1.6) | 1.0 | (1.6) |
| Serbia | a | a | a | a | a | a | a | a | a | a | a | a |
| Slovenia | a | a | a | a | a | a | a | a | a | a | a | a |
| Chinese Taipei | a | a | a | a | a | a | a | a | a | a | a | a |
| Thailand | 6.0 | (3.2) | -0.6 | (2.8) | 6.6 | (3.5) | **8.9** | (2.6) | 3.1 | (2.7) | **5.8** | (2.5) |
| Tunisia | a | a | -0.4 | (3.3) | a | a | a | a | 2.3 | (2.8) | a | a |
| Uruguay | a | a | -2.9 | (2.7) | a | a | a | a | **5.5** | (1.9) | a | a |

Note: Values that are statistically significant are indicated in bold (see Annex A3). Differences are later cycle minus the earlier cycle.
1. Single-level bivariate regression of science performance on the ESCS, the slope is the regression coefficient for the ESCS.
StatLink ᴿᴱᴮ http://dx.doi.org/10.1787/142104560611

Pour consulter la version française intégrale de ce tableau, suivre ce lien :
StatLink ᴿᴱᴮ http://dx.doi.org/10.1787/152684743050

[Part 1/2]

**Table 4.4d** Relationship between student performance in mathematics and the PISA index of economic, social and cultural status (ESCS) for PISA 2000, PISA 2003 and PISA 2006

Tableau 4.4d Relation entre la performance des élèves en mathématiques et l'indice PISA de statut économique, social et culturel (SESC) pour les cycles PISA 2000, PISA 2003 et PISA 2006

| | Slope of ESCS for mathematics,[1] PISA 2006 | | Strength of the relationship between mathematics in PISA 2006 and the ESCS | | Slope of ESCS for mathematics,[1] PISA 2003 | | Strength of the relationship between mathematics in PISA 2003 and the ESCS | | Slope of ESCS for mathematics,[1] PISA 2000 | | Strength of the relationship between mathematics in PISA 2000 and the ESCS | |
| | Score point difference associated with one unit on the ESCS | S.E. | Percentage of explained variance in student performance | S.E. | Score point difference associated with one unit on the ESCS | S.E. | Percentage of explained variance in student performance | S.E. | Score point difference associated with one unit on the ESCS | S.E. | Percentage of explained variance in student performance | S.E. |
|---|---|---|---|---|---|---|---|---|---|---|---|---|
| **OECD** | | | | | | | | | | | | |
| Australia | 38 | (1.4) | **11.5** | (0.79) | 42 | (2.2) | **13.7** | (1.19) | 44 | (2.6) | 17.1 | (1.82) |
| Austria | 43 | (3.3) | 13.6 | (2.04) | 43 | (2.3) | 16.0 | (1.57) | 41 | (2.8) | 14.7 | (1.89) |
| Belgium | **49** | (2.3) | **17.9** | (1.17) | **55** | (1.7) | **24.1** | (1.32) | **49** | (2.7) | **19.3** | (1.76) |
| Canada | 30 | (1.3) | 7.9 | (0.70) | 34 | (1.4) | 10.5 | (0.82) | 30 | (1.2) | 9.8 | (0.72) |
| Czech Republic | **54** | (2.7) | 16.1 | (1.43) | **51** | (2.1) | 19.5 | (1.44) | **59** | (2.8) | **21.3** | (1.88) |
| Denmark | 34 | (1.9) | 13.0 | (1.37) | 44 | (2.0) | 17.6 | (1.41) | 36 | (2.3) | 14.4 | (1.84) |
| Finland | **32** | (1.5) | **10.0** | (0.96) | **33** | (1.6) | **10.8** | (1.05) | **26** | (1.7) | **8.7** | (1.08) |
| France | 51 | (2.5) | 21.3 | (1.88) | 43 | (2.2) | 19.6 | (1.78) | 38 | (2.4) | 15.5 | (1.90) |
| Germany | **47** | (2.4) | **19.5** | (1.59) | **47** | (1.7) | **22.8** | (1.47) | **54** | (2.8) | **22.8** | (2.38) |
| Greece | 37 | (2.4) | 15.5 | (1.81) | 37 | (2.2) | 15.9 | (1.91) | 37 | (3.4) | 13.3 | (2.28) |
| Hungary | **48** | (2.0) | **23.4** | (1.64) | **55** | (2.3) | **27.0** | (1.81) | **60** | (3.1) | **26.2** | (2.38) |
| Iceland | 28 | (1.7) | 8.0 | (0.92) | 28 | (1.7) | 6.5 | (0.83) | 24 | (2.6) | 6.7 | (1.42) |
| Ireland | 35 | (2.0) | 13.6 | (1.46) | 39 | (2.0) | 16.2 | (1.55) | 32 | (1.8) | 13.4 | (1.39) |
| Italy | 29 | (1.5) | 8.8 | (0.83) | 34 | (2.0) | **13.6** | (1.34) | 25 | (2.2) | **7.3** | (1.30) |
| Japan | 40 | (2.5) | **9.4** | (0.99) | 46 | (4.1) | **11.6** | (1.69) | m | m | m | m |
| Korea | 38 | (3.7) | 11.0 | (1.79) | 41 | (3.1) | 14.2 | (1.95) | 32 | (2.4) | **11.0** | (1.55) |
| Luxembourg | 36 | (1.0) | 17.8 | (0.90) | 35 | (1.2) | 17.1 | (1.01) | m | m | m | m |
| Mexico | 26 | (1.5) | 15.9 | (1.59) | 29 | (1.9) | 17.1 | (2.06) | 30 | (2.2) | 17.8 | (2.59) |
| Netherlands | 39 | (2.3) | 15.5 | (1.68) | 45 | (2.4) | 18.6 | (1.71) | m | m | m | m |
| New Zealand | **43** | (1.6) | 14.8 | (1.01) | 44 | (1.6) | 16.8 | (1.20) | 42 | (2.6) | 16.1 | (1.79) |
| Norway | 35 | (2.4) | 8.3 | (1.14) | 44 | (1.7) | **14.1** | (1.09) | 34 | (2.7) | **10.6** | (1.58) |
| Poland | 38 | (1.6) | 14.6 | (1.12) | 45 | (1.8) | 16.7 | (1.21) | 44 | (3.6) | 14.0 | (2.12) |
| Portugal | **29** | (1.5) | 16.6 | (1.59) | **29** | (1.2) | 17.5 | (1.50) | **34** | (2.1) | 16.6 | (2.15) |
| Slovak Republic | 46 | (3.2) | 19.4 | (2.30) | 53 | (2.6) | 22.3 | (1.85) | a | a | a | a |
| Spain | 30 | (1.3) | 12.9 | (1.16) | 33 | (1.7) | **14.0** | (1.33) | 33 | (2.0) | 14.6 | (1.76) |
| Sweden | 38 | (1.9) | **11.6** | (0.99) | 42 | (2.1) | 15.3 | (1.32) | 38 | (2.2) | **12.1** | (1.39) |
| Switzerland | 40 | (1.8) | 13.4 | (1.06) | **47** | (2.1) | 16.8 | (1.27) | **44** | (2.3) | 17.1 | (1.76) |
| Turkey | 35 | (3.9) | 16.8 | (2.99) | 45 | (4.8) | 22.3 | (3.70) | a | a | a | a |
| United Kingdom | 41 | (1.7) | 14.1 | (1.19) | m | m | m | m | m | m | m | m |
| United States | 42 | (2.4) | 18.2 | (1.59) | 45 | (1.6) | 19.0 | (1.20) | 50 | (2.8) | 23.8 | (2.61) |
| **OECD average** | 38 | (0.4) | 14.4 | (0.27) | 42 | (0.4) | 16.8 | (0.30) | 39 | (0.5) | 15.2 | (0.38) |
| **Partners** | | | | | | | | | | | | |
| Argentina | 38 | (2.9) | **19.3** | (2.39) | a | a | a | a | a | a | a | a |
| Azerbaijan | **3** | (1.5) | **0.3** | (0.41) | a | a | a | a | a | a | a | a |
| Brazil | 32 | (2.4) | 18.6 | (2.20) | 35 | (3.1) | 15.3 | (2.39) | 35 | (3.0) | 16.7 | (2.81) |
| Bulgaria | 47 | (3.7) | 22.8 | (2.82) | a | a | a | a | a | a | a | a |
| Chile | 38 | (1.9) | 25.4 | (2.16) | a | a | a | a | a | a | a | a |
| Colombia | 26 | (2.2) | 13.5 | (1.99) | a | a | a | a | a | a | a | a |
| Croatia | 32 | (1.8) | **11.2** | (1.13) | a | a | a | a | a | a | a | a |
| Estonia | 34 | (2.2) | 12.0 | (1.40) | a | a | a | a | a | a | a | a |
| Hong Kong-China | 26 | (2.5) | 6.8 | (1.28) | 31 | (2.9) | 6.5 | (1.27) | 27 | (3.3) | 5.7 | (1.50) |
| Indonesia | 24 | (2.9) | 10.1 | (2.23) | 21 | (2.6) | **7.0** | (1.61) | 20 | (4.0) | 5.5 | (1.95) |
| Israel | 43 | (2.7) | **11.9** | (1.14) | a | a | a | a | a | a | a | a |
| Jordan | 27 | (1.9) | 12.9 | (1.61) | a | a | a | a | a | a | a | a |
| Kyrgyzstan | 33 | (2.6) | **11.1** | (1.62) | a | a | a | a | a | a | a | a |
| Latvia | 31 | (2.4) | 11.6 | (1.64) | 38 | (2.3) | 10.5 | (1.28) | 31 | (3.8) | 5.6 | (1.28) |
| Liechtenstein | 44 | (5.9) | 17.8 | (4.73) | 55 | (5.9) | 20.6 | (3.71) | 33 | (8.6) | 10.4 | (4.67) |
| Lithuania | 41 | (1.9) | 17.3 | (1.41) | a | a | a | a | a | a | a | a |
| Macao-China | 14 | (1.6) | 2.2 | (0.49) | 14 | (3.3) | 1.9 | (0.89) | a | a | a | a |
| Montenegro | 27 | (1.8) | 8.4 | (1.10) | a | a | a | a | a | a | a | a |
| Qatar | m | m | m | m | m | m | m | m | m | m | m | m |
| Romania | 37 | (3.6) | 17.4 | (3.12) | a | a | a | a | a | a | a | a |
| Russian Federation | 33 | (2.8) | 8.4 | (1.40) | 39 | (2.3) | 10.0 | (1.08) | 38 | (4.0) | 7.2 | (1.47) |
| Serbia | 35 | (2.1) | 12.6 | (1.30) | a | a | a | a | a | a | a | a |
| Slovenia | 42 | (1.8) | 17.0 | (1.44) | a | a | a | a | a | a | a | a |
| Chinese Taipei | 46 | (2.7) | 12.9 | (1.34) | a | a | a | a | a | a | a | a |
| Thailand | 28 | (1.8) | 14.6 | (1.85) | 27 | (2.6) | **11.4** | (1.94) | 26 | (3.0) | 8.6 | (1.86) |
| Tunisia | 27 | (2.4) | 15.8 | (2.70) | 24 | (2.4) | 13.0 | (2.43) | a | a | a | a |
| Uruguay | 36 | (1.6) | **18.8** | (1.55) | 38 | (2.1) | 15.9 | (1.64) | a | a | a | a |

Note: Values that are statistically significant are indicated in bold (see Annex A3). Differences are later cycle minus the earlier cycle.
1. Single-level bivariate regression of mathematics performance on the ESCS, the slope is the regression coefficient for the ESCS.
StatLink  http://dx.doi.org/10.1787/142104560611

Pour consulter la version française intégrale de ce tableau, suivre ce lien :
StatLink  http://dx.doi.org/10.1787/152684743050

[Part 2/2]

**Table 4.4d** Relationship between student performance in mathematics and the PISA index of economic, social and cultural status (ESCS) for PISA 2000, PISA 2003 and PISA 2006

*Tableau 4.4d* Relation entre la performance des élèves en mathématiques et l'indice PISA de statut économique, social et culturel (SESC) pour les cycles PISA 2000, PISA 2003 et PISA 2006

| | Difference in ESCS slope between PISA 2006 and PISA 2000 | | Difference in ESCS slope between PISA 2006 and PISA 2003 | | Difference in ESCS slope between PISA 2003 and PISA 2000 | | Difference in ESCS percent explained between PISA 2006 and PISA 2000 | | Difference in ESCS percent explained between PISA 2006 and PISA 2003 | | Difference in ESCS percent explained between PISA 2003 and PISA 2000 | |
|---|---|---|---|---|---|---|---|---|---|---|---|---|
| | Dif. | S.E. | Dif. | S.E. | Dif. | S.E. | Dif. | S.E. | Dif. | S.E. | Dif. | S.E. |
| **OECD** | | | | | | | | | | | | |
| Australia | -5.6 | (3.0) | -4.3 | (2.6) | -1.3 | (3.4) | **-5.6** | (2.0) | -2.1 | (1.4) | -3.5 | (2.2) |
| Austria | 2.9 | (4.4) | 0.2 | (4.0) | 2.8 | (3.6) | -1.1 | (2.8) | -2.4 | (2.6) | 1.3 | (2.5) |
| Belgium | -0.5 | (3.5) | **-6.4** | (2.9) | 5.9 | (3.2) | -1.4 | (2.1) | **-6.2** | (1.8) | **4.8** | (2.2) |
| Canada | -0.5 | (1.8) | **-4.6** | (2.0) | **4.1** | (1.9) | -2.0 | (1.0) | **-2.6** | (1.1) | 0.7 | (1.1) |
| Czech Republic | -4.7 | (3.9) | 2.8 | (3.5) | **-7.5** | (3.5) | **-5.2** | (2.4) | -3.3 | (2.0) | -1.8 | (2.4) |
| Denmark | -1.7 | (2.9) | **-10.3** | (2.7) | **8.6** | (3.0) | -1.4 | (2.3) | **-4.6** | (2.0) | 3.2 | (2.3) |
| Finland | **6.4** | (2.2) | -0.9 | (2.2) | **7.3** | (2.3) | 1.3 | (1.4) | -0.8 | (1.4) | 2.1 | (1.5) |
| France | **12.9** | (3.5) | **7.6** | (3.3) | 5.3 | (3.3) | **5.8** | (2.7) | 1.7 | (2.6) | 4.1 | (2.6) |
| Germany | **-7.2** | (3.7) | 0.0 | (2.9) | **-7.2** | (3.3) | -3.2 | (2.9) | -3.3 | (2.2) | 0.1 | (2.8) |
| Greece | -0.1 | (4.2) | 0.3 | (3.3) | -0.4 | (4.1) | 2.2 | (2.9) | -0.4 | (2.6) | 2.6 | (3.0) |
| Hungary | **-12.2** | (3.7) | **-7.3** | (3.1) | -5.0 | (3.8) | -2.8 | (2.9) | -3.6 | (2.4) | 0.8 | (3.0) |
| Iceland | 4.9 | (3.2) | 0.3 | (2.5) | 4.6 | (3.2) | 1.4 | (1.7) | 1.6 | (1.2) | -0.2 | (1.6) |
| Ireland | 2.7 | (2.7) | -3.4 | (2.8) | **6.1** | (2.7) | 0.2 | (2.0) | -2.6 | (2.1) | 2.8 | (2.1) |
| Italy | 4.0 | (2.7) | **-5.7** | (2.5) | **9.7** | (3.0) | 1.4 | (1.5) | **-4.8** | (1.6) | **6.3** | (1.9) |
| Japan | m | m | -6.7 | (4.8) | m | m | m | m | -2.2 | (2.0) | m | m |
| Korea | 5.4 | (4.3) | -3.2 | (4.8) | **8.6** | (3.9) | 0.0 | (2.4) | -3.2 | (2.6) | 3.2 | (2.5) |
| Luxembourg | m | m | 0.9 | (1.6) | m | m | m | m | 0.7 | (1.4) | m | m |
| Mexico | -4.5 | (2.6) | -3.4 | (2.4) | -1.0 | (2.9) | -1.9 | (3.0) | -1.2 | (2.6) | -0.7 | (3.3) |
| Netherlands | m | m | -5.8 | (3.3) | m | m | m | m | -3.1 | (2.4) | m | m |
| New Zealand | 0.5 | (3.0) | -0.9 | (2.3) | 1.4 | (3.0) | -1.4 | (2.1) | -2.0 | (1.6) | 0.7 | (2.2) |
| Norway | 1.0 | (3.7) | **-9.4** | (3.0) | **10.4** | (3.2) | -2.2 | (1.9) | **-5.8** | (1.6) | 3.5 | (1.9) |
| Poland | -6.3 | (3.9) | **-6.7** | (2.4) | 0.4 | (4.0) | 0.5 | (2.4) | -2.1 | (1.6) | 2.6 | (2.4) |
| Portugal | -5.1 | (2.6) | 0.1 | (2.0) | **-5.2** | (2.4) | 0.0 | (2.7) | -0.9 | (2.2) | 0.9 | (2.6) |
| Slovak Republic | a | a | -7.4 | (4.1) | a | a | a | a | -2.9 | (3.0) | a | a |
| Spain | -2.8 | (2.4) | -3.1 | (2.1) | 0.2 | (2.6) | -1.7 | (2.1) | -1.1 | (1.8) | -0.6 | (2.2) |
| Sweden | 0.6 | (2.9) | -3.8 | (2.8) | 4.4 | (3.0) | -0.5 | (1.7) | **-3.7** | (1.7) | 3.2 | (1.9) |
| Switzerland | -3.5 | (2.9) | **-7.4** | (2.8) | 4.0 | (3.2) | -3.7 | (2.1) | **-3.4** | (1.7) | -0.3 | (2.2) |
| Turkey | a | a | -10.2 | (6.2) | a | a | a | a | -5.5 | (4.8) | a | a |
| United Kingdom | m | m | m | m | m | m | m | m | m | m | m | m |
| United States | **-7.8** | (3.7) | -3.2 | (2.9) | -4.5 | (3.2) | -5.5 | (3.1) | -0.8 | (2.0) | -4.7 | (2.9) |
| **OECD average** | **-0.9** | **(0.7)** | **-3.5** | **(0.6)** | **2.1** | **(0.7)** | **-1.1** | **(0.5)** | **-2.4** | **(0.4)** | **1.3** | **(0.5)** |
| **Partners** | | | | | | | | | | | | |
| Argentina | a | a | a | a | a | a | a | a | a | a | a | a |
| Azerbaijan | a | a | a | a | a | a | a | a | a | a | a | a |
| Brazil | -3.1 | (3.8) | -3.3 | (4.0) | 0.2 | (4.3) | 1.9 | (3.6) | 3.3 | (3.2) | -1.4 | (3.7) |
| Bulgaria | a | a | a | a | a | a | a | a | a | a | a | a |
| Chile | a | a | a | a | a | a | a | a | a | a | a | a |
| Colombia | a | a | a | a | a | a | a | a | a | a | a | a |
| Croatia | a | a | a | a | a | a | a | a | a | a | a | a |
| Estonia | a | a | a | a | a | a | a | a | a | a | a | a |
| Hong Kong-China | -0.5 | (4.2) | -5.1 | (3.9) | 4.5 | (4.4) | 1.1 | (2.0) | 0.3 | (1.8) | 0.8 | (2.0) |
| Indonesia | 3.2 | (4.9) | 2.4 | (3.9) | 0.8 | (4.8) | 4.6 | (3.0) | 3.2 | (2.7) | 1.5 | (2.5) |
| Israel | a | a | a | a | a | a | a | a | a | a | a | a |
| Jordan | a | a | a | a | a | a | a | a | a | a | a | a |
| Kyrgyzstan | a | a | a | a | a | a | a | a | a | a | a | a |
| Latvia | 0.4 | (4.5) | **-6.8** | (3.3) | 7.2 | (4.4) | **5.9** | (2.1) | 1.1 | (2.1) | **4.8** | (1.8) |
| Liechtenstein | 10.8 | (10.4) | -11.3 | (8.3) | **22.1** | (10.4) | 7.3 | (6.6) | -2.9 | (6.0) | 10.2 | (6.0) |
| Lithuania | a | a | a | a | a | a | a | a | a | a | a | a |
| Macao-China | a | a | 0.3 | (3.6) | a | a | a | a | 0.3 | (1.0) | a | a |
| Montenegro | a | a | a | a | a | a | a | a | a | a | a | a |
| Qatar | m | m | m | m | m | m | m | m | m | m | m | m |
| Romania | a | a | a | a | a | a | a | a | a | a | a | a |
| Russian Federation | -5.1 | (4.8) | -6.2 | (3.6) | 1.1 | (4.6) | 1.1 | (2.0) | -1.6 | (1.8) | 2.8 | (1.8) |
| Serbia | a | a | a | a | a | a | a | a | a | a | a | a |
| Slovenia | a | a | a | a | a | a | a | a | a | a | a | a |
| Chinese Taipei | a | a | a | a | a | a | a | a | a | a | a | a |
| Thailand | 2.1 | (3.5) | 1.1 | (3.1) | 1.0 | (3.9) | **6.0** | (2.6) | 3.2 | (2.7) | 2.8 | (2.7) |
| Tunisia | a | a | 2.9 | (3.4) | a | a | a | a | 2.8 | (3.6) | a | a |
| Uruguay | a | a | -1.3 | (2.6) | a | a | a | a | 2.9 | (2.3) | a | a |

Note: Values that are statistically significant are indicated in bold (see Annex A3). Differences are later cycle minus the earlier cycle.
1. Single-level bivariate regression of mathematics performance on the ESCS, the slope is the regression coefficient for the ESCS.
StatLink ⟶ http://dx.doi.org/10.1787/142104560611

Pour consulter la version française intégrale de ce tableau, suivre ce lien :
StatLink ⟶ http://dx.doi.org/10.1787/152684743050

I. DATA/*DONNÉES*

[Part 1/2]

**Table 4.4e** **Relationship between student performance in reading and the PISA index of economic, social and cultural status (ESCS) for PISA 2000, PISA 2003 and PISA 2006**

Tableau 4.4e Relation entre la performance des élèves en compréhension de l'écrit et l'indice PISA de statut économique, social et culturel (SESC) pour les cycles PISA 2000, PISA 2003 et PISA 2006

| | Slope of ESCS for reading,[1] PISA 2006 | | Strength of the relationship between reading in PISA 2006 and the ESCS | | Slope of ESCS for reading,[1] PISA 2003 | | Strength of the relationship between reading in PISA 2003 and the ESCS | | Slope of ESCS for reading,[1] PISA 2000 | | Strength of the relationship between reading in PISA 2000 and the ESCS | |
|---|---|---|---|---|---|---|---|---|---|---|---|---|
| | Score point difference associated with one unit on the ESCS | S.E. | Percentage of explained variance in student performance | S.E. | Score point difference associated with one unit on the ESCS | S.E. | Percentage of explained variance in student performance | S.E. | Score point difference associated with one unit on the ESCS | S.E. | Percentage of explained variance in student performance | S.E. |
| **OECD** | | | | | | | | | | | | |
| Australia | 41 | (1.4) | 11.8 | (0.77) | 44 | (1.9) | 14.2 | (1.08) | 50 | (2.4) | 17.4 | (1.65) |
| Austria | 46 | (3.7) | 12.9 | (2.01) | 54 | (2.3) | 21.3 | (1.61) | 44 | (2.3) | 16.6 | (1.36) |
| Belgium | 48 | (2.2) | 16.0 | (1.18) | 54 | (2.0) | 22.8 | (1.37) | 50 | (2.1) | 18.9 | (1.32) |
| Canada | 36 | (1.6) | 9.5 | (0.77) | 34 | (1.3) | 9.9 | (0.75) | 37 | (1.2) | 12.2 | (0.63) |
| Czech Republic | 51 | (3.4) | 12.5 | (1.37) | 44 | (2.2) | 15.5 | (1.45) | 60 | (2.5) | 22.9 | (1.82) |
| Denmark | 32 | (2.1) | 10.7 | (1.27) | 41 | (1.9) | 16.3 | (1.27) | 43 | (2.0) | 16.1 | (1.44) |
| Finland | 29 | (1.7) | 7.7 | (0.92) | 30 | (1.6) | 9.6 | (0.97) | 28 | (2.0) | 8.6 | (0.98) |
| France | 48 | (2.8) | 16.4 | (1.70) | 45 | (2.7) | 19.5 | (1.95) | 43 | (2.1) | 19.0 | (1.67) |
| Germany | 47 | (2.6) | 15.9 | (1.46) | 48 | (1.7) | 22.5 | (1.35) | 59 | (2.8) | 23.6 | (2.48) |
| Greece | 34 | (2.9) | 10.7 | (1.64) | 34 | (2.1) | 10.9 | (1.43) | 32 | (2.7) | 12.2 | (1.91) |
| Hungary | 45 | (2.5) | 19.4 | (1.71) | 48 | (2.3) | 21.7 | (1.83) | 57 | (2.8) | 25.4 | (2.18) |
| Iceland | 24 | (1.9) | 4.9 | (0.73) | 24 | (2.2) | 4.0 | (0.75) | 27 | (1.6) | 7.4 | (0.86) |
| Ireland | 38 | (2.3) | 12.3 | (1.36) | 39 | (2.1) | 16.5 | (1.69) | 34 | (1.8) | 12.3 | (1.25) |
| Italy | 30 | (1.8) | 7.5 | (0.82) | 37 | (2.0) | 14.1 | (1.27) | 30 | (2.0) | 10.4 | (1.17) |
| Japan | 39 | (3.0) | 7.3 | (1.00) | 47 | (3.8) | 10.8 | (1.50) | m | m | m | m |
| Korea | 28 | (3.2) | 6.6 | (1.34) | 32 | (2.8) | 10.9 | (1.69) | 24 | (2.3) | 8.6 | (1.56) |
| Luxembourg | 41 | (1.2) | 20.6 | (1.07) | 38 | (1.4) | 17.4 | (1.12) | m | m | m | m |
| Mexico | 28 | (1.8) | 14.5 | (1.68) | 32 | (2.3) | 16.9 | (2.29) | 33 | (2.0) | 19.8 | (2.44) |
| Netherlands | 40 | (2.5) | 13.7 | (1.58) | 37 | (2.2) | 15.5 | (1.62) | m | m | m | m |
| New Zealand | 49 | (2.2) | 14.9 | (1.23) | 46 | (1.8) | 16.7 | (1.20) | 46 | (2.3) | 15.2 | (1.43) |
| Norway | 38 | (2.7) | 7.8 | (1.01) | 44 | (2.1) | 11.7 | (1.14) | 41 | (2.0) | 12.6 | (1.22) |
| Poland | 42 | (1.9) | 13.3 | (1.09) | 46 | (2.3) | 15.8 | (1.30) | 44 | (3.4) | 14.3 | (1.90) |
| Portugal | 33 | (1.8) | 17.9 | (1.63) | 26 | (1.8) | 12.8 | (1.60) | 38 | (2.1) | 18.0 | (2.06) |
| Slovak Republic | 45 | (3.4) | 14.9 | (2.05) | 51 | (2.5) | 20.9 | (1.89) | a | a | a | a |
| Spain | 27 | (1.5) | 10.5 | (1.20) | 32 | (2.1) | 11.4 | (1.33) | 32 | (1.5) | 15.8 | (1.47) |
| Sweden | 36 | (2.5) | 8.5 | (1.07) | 41 | (2.1) | 14.2 | (1.26) | 37 | (1.6) | 11.7 | (1.01) |
| Switzerland | 39 | (1.6) | 14.0 | (1.04) | 47 | (2.2) | 17.9 | (1.51) | 51 | (2.1) | 21.4 | (1.63) |
| Turkey | 31 | (2.9) | 13.1 | (2.37) | 39 | (4.1) | 20.3 | (3.55) | a | a | a | a |
| United Kingdom | 43 | (1.9) | 12.2 | (1.07) | m | m | m | m | m | m | m | m |
| United States | m | m | m | m | 47 | (1.7) | 18.0 | (1.24) | 47 | (2.8) | 19.3 | (2.05) |
| **OECD average** | 38 | (0.4) | 12.3 | (0.26) | 41 | (0.4) | 15.5 | (0.29) | 41 | (0.5) | 15.8 | (0.33) |
| **Partners** | | | | | | | | | | | | |
| Argentina | 39 | (2.9) | 13.5 | (2.11) | a | a | a | a | a | a | a | a |
| Azerbaijan | 18 | (2.7) | 7.2 | (1.99) | a | a | a | a | a | a | a | a |
| Brazil | 30 | (2.7) | 13.7 | (1.84) | 29 | (2.6) | 8.6 | (1.52) | 28 | (1.9) | 13.9 | (1.85) |
| Bulgaria | 55 | (4.2) | 22.7 | (2.88) | a | a | a | a | a | a | a | a |
| Chile | 38 | (2.4) | 18.6 | (2.06) | a | a | a | a | a | a | a | a |
| Colombia | 28 | (2.3) | 10.3 | (1.70) | a | a | a | a | a | a | a | a |
| Croatia | 32 | (2.0) | 10.2 | (1.13) | a | a | a | a | a | a | a | a |
| Estonia | 29 | (2.5) | 7.7 | (1.21) | a | a | a | a | a | a | a | a |
| Hong Kong-China | 22 | (2.4) | 6.3 | (1.34) | 24 | (2.5) | 5.3 | (1.13) | 28 | (2.8) | 7.8 | (1.64) |
| Indonesia | 23 | (2.6) | 10.8 | (2.22) | 20 | (2.2) | 6.8 | (1.39) | 23 | (2.9) | 9.1 | (2.04) |
| Israel | 40 | (3.3) | 8.2 | (1.16) | a | a | a | a | a | a | a | a |
| Jordan | 28 | (2.2) | 11.3 | (1.68) | a | a | a | a | a | a | a | a |
| Kyrgyzstan | 36 | (3.0) | 9.8 | (1.45) | a | a | a | a | a | a | a | a |
| Latvia | 31 | (2.5) | 9.4 | (1.43) | 33 | (3.1) | 7.7 | (1.49) | 38 | (3.6) | 9.0 | (1.57) |
| Liechtenstein | 45 | (4.8) | 18.1 | (4.02) | 47 | (5.9) | 18.6 | (4.47) | 43 | (5.6) | 17.1 | (4.53) |
| Lithuania | 39 | (2.2) | 14.0 | (1.46) | a | a | a | a | a | a | a | a |
| Macao-China | 12 | (1.8) | 1.8 | (0.54) | 8 | (2.5) | 0.9 | (0.62) | a | a | a | a |
| Montenegro | 24 | (1.7) | 6.0 | (0.85) | a | a | a | a | a | a | a | a |
| Qatar | m | m | m | m | m | m | m | m | m | m | m | m |
| Romania | 32 | (3.6) | 11.0 | (2.42) | a | a | a | a | a | a | a | a |
| Russian Federation | 34 | (3.0) | 8.3 | (1.37) | 41 | (2.1) | 10.9 | (1.03) | 40 | (2.9) | 10.2 | (1.45) |
| Serbia | 36 | (2.1) | 14.0 | (1.36) | a | a | a | a | a | a | a | a |
| Slovenia | 39 | (1.7) | 15.1 | (1.32) | a | a | a | a | a | a | a | a |
| Chinese Taipei | 38 | (2.0) | 13.0 | (1.21) | a | a | a | a | a | a | a | a |
| Thailand | 28 | (1.8) | 14.7 | (2.00) | 24 | (2.2) | 9.9 | (1.71) | 22 | (2.7) | 7.3 | (1.71) |
| Tunisia | 21 | (2.4) | 8.5 | (2.04) | 21 | (2.5) | 7.6 | (1.77) | a | a | a | a |
| Uruguay | 38 | (2.2) | 13.5 | (1.39) | 41 | (2.3) | 12.8 | (1.39) | a | a | a | a |

Note: Values that are statistically significant are indicated in bold (see Annex A3). Differences are later cycle minus the earlier cycle.
1. Single-level bivariate regression of reading performance on the ESCS, the slope is the regression coefficient for the ESCS.
*StatLink*  http://dx.doi.org/10.1787/142104560611

Pour consulter la version française intégrale de ce tableau, suivre ce lien :
*StatLink* http://dx.doi.org/10.1787/152684743050

131

[Part 2/2]

**Table 4.4e** Relationship between student performance in reading and the PISA index of economic, social and cultural status (ESCS) for PISA 2000, PISA 2003 and PISA 2006

**Tableau 4.4e** Relation entre la performance des élèves en compréhension de l'écrit et l'indice PISA de statut économique, social et culturel (SESC) pour les cycles PISA 2000, PISA 2003 et PISA 2006

| | Difference in ESCS slope between PISA 2006 and PISA 2000 | | Difference in ESCS slope between PISA 2006 and PISA 2003 | | Difference in ESCS slope between PISA 2003 and PISA 2000 | | Difference in ESCS percent explained between PISA 2006 and PISA 2000 | | Difference in ESCS percent explained between PISA 2006 and PISA 2003 | | Difference in ESCS percent explained between PISA 2003 and PISA 2000 | |
|---|---|---|---|---|---|---|---|---|---|---|---|---|
| | Dif. | S.E. | Dif. | S.E. | Dif. | S.E. | Dif. | S.E. | Dif. | S.E. | Dif. | S.E. |
| **OECD** | | | | | | | | | | | | |
| Australia | **-9.0** | (2.8) | -2.9 | (2.4) | -6.1 | (3.1) | **-5.7** | (1.8) | -2.4 | (1.3) | -3.2 | (2.0) |
| Austria | 2.2 | (4.3) | -7.4 | (4.4) | **9.6** | (3.2) | -3.7 | (2.4) | **-8.4** | (2.6) | **4.6** | (2.1) |
| Belgium | -1.9 | (3.0) | **-5.9** | (3.0) | 4.0 | (2.9) | -2.9 | (1.8) | **-6.9** | (1.8) | **3.9** | (1.9) |
| Canada | -0.9 | (2.0) | 3.0 | (2.1) | **-3.8** | (1.8) | -2.7 | (1.0) | -0.4 | (1.1) | **-2.3** | (1.0) |
| Czech Republic | **-8.5** | (4.3) | 7.4 | (4.1) | **-15.9** | (3.3) | **-10.4** | (2.3) | -3.0 | (2.0) | **-7.4** | (2.3) |
| Denmark | **-10.3** | (2.9) | **-8.8** | (2.8) | -1.5 | (2.8) | **-5.4** | (1.9) | **-5.6** | (1.8) | 0.2 | (1.9) |
| Finland | 0.1 | (2.6) | -1.5 | (2.3) | 1.7 | (2.5) | -0.9 | (1.3) | -1.8 | (1.3) | 1.0 | (1.4) |
| France | 5.4 | (3.5) | 2.9 | (3.9) | 2.6 | (3.4) | -2.6 | (2.4) | -3.1 | (2.6) | 0.6 | (2.6) |
| Germany | **-11.6** | (3.8) | -1.2 | (3.1) | **-10.4** | (3.3) | **-7.7** | (2.9) | **-6.6** | (2.0) | -1.1 | (2.8) |
| Greece | 2.4 | (4.0) | 0.3 | (3.5) | 2.1 | (3.4) | -1.5 | (2.5) | -0.2 | (2.2) | -1.3 | (2.4) |
| Hungary | **-12.0** | (3.8) | -3.5 | (3.4) | **-8.6** | (3.6) | **-6.0** | (2.8) | -2.3 | (2.5) | -3.7 | (2.8) |
| Iceland | -2.2 | (2.5) | 0.3 | (2.9) | -2.5 | (2.7) | **-2.4** | (1.1) | 0.9 | (1.0) | **-3.4** | (1.1) |
| Ireland | 3.4 | (3.0) | -1.7 | (3.1) | 5.1 | (2.8) | 0.0 | (1.9) | -4.2 | (2.2) | **4.2** | (2.1) |
| Italy | 0.2 | (2.7) | **-6.7** | (2.6) | **6.8** | (2.8) | **-3.0** | (1.4) | **-6.6** | (1.5) | **3.6** | (1.7) |
| Japan | m | m | -7.5 | (4.8) | m | m | m | m | -3.4 | (1.8) | m | m |
| Korea | 4.0 | (4.0) | -4.1 | (4.2) | **8.1** | (3.6) | -2.0 | (2.1) | **-4.3** | (2.2) | 2.4 | (2.3) |
| Luxembourg | m | m | 3.4 | (1.9) | m | m | m | m | **3.2** | (1.5) | m | m |
| Mexico | -5.0 | (2.6) | -4.7 | (2.9) | -0.3 | (3.0) | -5.2 | (3.0) | -2.4 | (2.8) | -2.9 | (3.3) |
| Netherlands | m | m | 2.4 | (3.3) | m | m | m | m | -1.8 | (2.3) | m | m |
| New Zealand | 3.0 | (3.2) | 2.1 | (2.8) | 0.9 | (2.9) | -0.2 | (1.9) | -1.7 | (1.7) | 1.5 | (1.9) |
| Norway | -3.1 | (3.4) | -6.4 | (3.4) | 3.3 | (2.9) | **-4.8** | (1.6) | **-3.9** | (1.5) | -0.9 | (1.7) |
| Poland | -1.6 | (3.9) | -4.4 | (3.0) | 2.8 | (4.1) | -1.1 | (2.2) | -2.6 | (1.7) | 1.5 | (2.3) |
| Portugal | -5.3 | (2.8) | 6.5 | (2.5) | **-11.8** | (2.7) | -0.1 | (2.6) | **5.1** | (2.3) | **-5.2** | (2.6) |
| Slovak Republic | a | a | -6.5 | (4.2) | a | a | a | a | **-6.1** | (2.8) | a | a |
| Spain | **-4.8** | (2.1) | **-5.1** | (2.6) | 0.3 | (2.5) | **-5.3** | (1.9) | -0.9 | (1.8) | **-4.4** | (2.0) |
| Sweden | -0.9 | (3.0) | -5.1 | (3.3) | 4.3 | (2.7) | **-3.2** | (1.5) | **-5.7** | (1.7) | 2.5 | (1.6) |
| Switzerland | **-11.0** | (2.6) | **-7.7** | (2.7) | -3.3 | (3.0) | **-7.3** | (1.9) | **-3.9** | (1.8) | -3.5 | (2.2) |
| Turkey | a | a | -8.5 | (5.0) | a | a | a | a | -7.2 | (4.3) | a | a |
| United Kingdom | m | m | m | m | m | m | m | m | m | m | m | m |
| United States | m | m | m | m | -0.2 | (3.3) | m | m | m | m | -1.4 | (2.4) |
| **OECD average** | **-2.9** | (0.7) | **-2.5** | (0.6) | -0.5 | (0.6) | **-3.7** | (0.4) | **-3.1** | (0.4) | -0.6 | (0.4) |
| **Partners** | | | | | | | | | | | | |
| Argentina | a | a | a | a | a | a | a | a | a | a | a | a |
| Azerbaijan | a | a | a | a | a | a | a | a | a | a | a | a |
| Brazil | 1.8 | (3.3) | 1.1 | (3.7) | 0.8 | (3.2) | -0.2 | (2.6) | **5.1** | (2.4) | **-5.3** | (2.4) |
| Bulgaria | a | a | a | a | a | a | a | a | a | a | a | a |
| Chile | a | a | a | a | a | a | a | a | a | a | a | a |
| Colombia | a | a | a | a | a | a | a | a | a | a | a | a |
| Croatia | a | a | a | a | a | a | a | a | a | a | a | a |
| Estonia | a | a | a | a | a | a | a | a | a | a | a | a |
| Hong Kong-China | -6.0 | (3.7) | -1.5 | (3.4) | -4.5 | (3.8) | -1.5 | (2.1) | 1.0 | (1.8) | -2.5 | (2.0) |
| Indonesia | 0.0 | (3.9) | 2.8 | (3.4) | -2.8 | (3.6) | 1.6 | (3.0) | 3.9 | (2.6) | -2.3 | (2.5) |
| Israel | a | a | a | a | a | a | a | a | a | a | a | a |
| Jordan | a | a | a | a | a | a | a | a | a | a | a | a |
| Kyrgyzstan | a | a | a | a | a | a | a | a | a | a | a | a |
| Latvia | -7.6 | (4.4) | -2.6 | (4.0) | -5.0 | (4.7) | 0.5 | (2.1) | 1.8 | (2.1) | -1.3 | (2.2) |
| Liechtenstein | 1.3 | (7.4) | -2.6 | (7.6) | 3.9 | (8.1) | 1.0 | (6.1) | -0.5 | (6.0) | 1.4 | (6.4) |
| Lithuania | a | a | a | a | a | a | a | a | a | a | a | a |
| Macao-China | a | a | 4.3 | (3.1) | a | a | a | a | 0.9 | (0.8) | a | a |
| Montenegro | a | a | a | a | a | a | a | a | a | a | a | a |
| Qatar | m | m | m | m | m | m | m | m | m | m | m | m |
| Romania | a | a | a | a | a | a | a | a | a | a | a | a |
| Russian Federation | -5.9 | (4.2) | **-7.3** | (3.7) | 1.4 | (3.6) | -1.9 | (2.0) | -2.6 | (1.7) | 0.7 | (1.8) |
| Serbia | a | a | a | a | a | a | a | a | a | a | a | a |
| Slovenia | a | a | a | a | a | a | a | a | a | a | a | a |
| Chinese Taipei | a | a | a | a | a | a | a | a | a | a | a | a |
| Thailand | 6.3 | (3.2) | 4.3 | (2.9) | 2.0 | (3.5) | **7.4** | (2.6) | 4.8 | (2.6) | 2.6 | (2.4) |
| Tunisia | a | a | -0.6 | (3.5) | a | a | a | a | 0.9 | (2.7) | a | a |
| Uruguay | a | a | -3.6 | (3.2) | a | a | a | a | 0.7 | (2.0) | a | a |

Note: Values that are statistically significant are indicated in bold (see Annex A3). Differences are later cycle minus the earlier cycle.
1. Single-level bivariate regression of reading performance on the ESCS, the slope is the regression coefficient for the ESCS.
StatLink ᴴᴵᴸ http://dx.doi.org/10.1787/142104560611

Pour consulter la version française intégrale de ce tableau, suivre ce lien :
StatLink ᴴᴵᴸ http://dx.doi.org/10.1787/152684743050

[Part 1/1]

**Table 4.5    Relationship between science motivational indices and the PISA index of economic, social and cultural status (ESCS)**

Tableau 4.5    Relation entre les indices de motivation et l'indice PISA de statut économique, social et culturel (SESC)

| | Percentage of variance for the following indices explained by ESCS | | | | | | | | | |
|---|---|---|---|---|---|---|---|---|---|---|
| | Interest in learning science topics | | General interest in science | | Enjoyment of science | | Instrumental motivation to learn science | | Future-oriented motivation to learn science | |
| | Percentage | S.E. | Percentage | S.E. | Percentage | S.E. | Percentage | S.E. | Percentage | S.E. |
| **OECD** | | | | | | | | | | |
| Australia | 0.4 | (0.15) | 2.4 | (0.35) | 3.4 | (0.41) | 2.1 | (0.34) | 1.4 | (0.25) |
| Austria | 0.0 | (0.04) | 1.9 | (0.49) | 2.2 | (0.54) | 0.0 | (0.03) | 1.0 | (0.35) |
| Belgium | 0.0 | (0.05) | 3.8 | (0.66) | 3.0 | (0.57) | 1.1 | (0.32) | 2.0 | (0.44) |
| Canada | 0.2 | (0.09) | 1.7 | (0.29) | 2.5 | (0.34) | 2.1 | (0.38) | 2.2 | (0.36) |
| Czech Republic | 0.0 | (0.09) | 0.7 | (0.34) | 0.4 | (0.19) | 0.1 | (0.09) | 0.2 | (0.14) |
| Denmark | 1.5 | (0.48) | 2.9 | (0.58) | 3.6 | (0.61) | 1.0 | (0.29) | 1.5 | (0.45) |
| Finland | 1.5 | (0.45) | 2.7 | (0.54) | 2.2 | (0.49) | 3.2 | (0.55) | 3.1 | (0.58) |
| France | 0.4 | (0.24) | 3.6 | (0.60) | 3.3 | (0.68) | 2.8 | (0.61) | 2.5 | (0.54) |
| Germany | 0.4 | (0.21) | 1.8 | (0.52) | 4.0 | (0.57) | 0.6 | (0.27) | 2.2 | (0.49) |
| Greece | 0.1 | (0.13) | 3.6 | (0.63) | 3.4 | (0.55) | 0.9 | (0.33) | 1.8 | (0.39) |
| Hungary | 0.1 | (0.15) | 1.1 | (0.40) | 1.3 | (0.47) | 0.0 | (0.06) | 0.4 | (0.32) |
| Iceland | 1.4 | (0.41) | 3.1 | (0.58) | 4.5 | (0.70) | 3.7 | (0.67) | 3.3 | (0.58) |
| Ireland | 1.5 | (0.47) | 4.9 | (0.60) | 4.5 | (0.59) | 3.3 | (0.55) | 3.0 | (0.54) |
| Italy | 0.0 | (0.06) | 1.6 | (0.31) | 1.4 | (0.29) | 1.7 | (0.37) | 1.3 | (0.26) |
| Japan | 0.8 | (0.25) | 2.2 | (0.45) | 1.5 | (0.39) | 2.5 | (0.45) | 1.9 | (0.44) |
| Korea | 2.6 | (0.77) | 3.5 | (0.70) | 3.2 | (0.79) | 1.1 | (0.50) | 1.0 | (0.49) |
| Luxembourg | 0.3 | (0.17) | 2.5 | (0.48) | 2.5 | (0.42) | 0.4 | (0.18) | 0.6 | (0.22) |
| Mexico | 1.5 | (0.44) | 0.2 | (0.15) | 0.8 | (0.31) | 0.3 | (0.14) | 2.2 | (0.49) |
| Netherlands | 0.1 | (0.21) | 2.1 | (0.60) | 2.4 | (0.50) | 0.5 | (0.23) | 1.5 | (0.47) |
| New Zealand | 0.3 | (0.23) | 1.7 | (0.51) | 3.8 | (0.59) | 2.4 | (0.53) | 1.9 | (0.43) |
| Norway | 1.0 | (0.50) | 3.0 | (0.59) | 2.8 | (0.53) | 1.8 | (0.47) | 1.0 | (0.29) |
| Poland | 0.4 | (0.20) | 0.9 | (0.28) | 0.7 | (0.27) | 0.0 | (0.03) | 0.0 | (0.05) |
| Portugal | 1.4 | (0.57) | 1.1 | (0.37) | 0.9 | (0.38) | 5.0 | (0.83) | 2.0 | (0.52) |
| Slovak Republic | 0.0 | (0.05) | 2.5 | (0.78) | 0.4 | (0.29) | 0.0 | (0.08) | 0.0 | (0.05) |
| Spain | 0.0 | (0.04) | 2.3 | (0.39) | 3.0 | (0.55) | 3.1 | (0.47) | 2.9 | (0.49) |
| Sweden | 1.5 | (0.47) | 2.8 | (0.70) | 3.1 | (0.73) | 2.6 | (0.63) | 3.1 | (0.54) |
| Switzerland | 0.5 | (0.20) | 3.2 | (0.44) | 3.2 | (0.40) | 1.4 | (0.27) | 2.3 | (0.34) |
| Turkey | 0.8 | (0.38) | 0.9 | (0.35) | 0.7 | (0.37) | 0.1 | (0.12) | 0.0 | (0.06) |
| United Kingdom | 0.7 | (0.26) | 1.8 | (0.39) | 2.9 | (0.52) | 1.5 | (0.34) | 1.2 | (0.32) |
| United States | 0.5 | (0.31) | 0.5 | (0.24) | 2.3 | (0.49) | 1.2 | (0.34) | 0.8 | (0.29) |
| **OECD total** | 2.2 | (0.24) | 0.0 | (0.02) | 0.1 | (0.03) | 0.1 | (0.03) | 0.0 | (0.03) |
| **OECD average** | 0.7 | (0.06) | 2.2 | (0.09) | 2.5 | (0.09) | 1.6 | (0.07) | 1.6 | (0.07) |
| **Partners** | | | | | | | | | | |
| Argentina | 3.7 | (1.03) | 0.2 | (0.20) | 0.4 | (0.29) | 0.4 | (0.27) | 0.3 | (0.21) |
| Azerbaijan | 1.3 | (0.51) | 1.0 | (0.41) | 0.1 | (0.14) | 0.1 | (0.16) | 0.8 | (0.35) |
| Brazil | 1.7 | (0.61) | 0.0 | (0.06) | 0.2 | (0.17) | 0.3 | (0.17) | 0.4 | (0.18) |
| Bulgaria | 0.0 | (0.12) | 1.1 | (0.45) | 0.3 | (0.25) | 0.1 | (0.11) | 0.5 | (0.35) |
| Chile | 4.3 | (0.87) | 0.0 | (0.03) | 0.7 | (0.28) | 0.4 | (0.29) | 0.6 | (0.30) |
| Colombia | 0.4 | (0.27) | 1.0 | (0.39) | 0.3 | (0.27) | 0.5 | (0.44) | 1.6 | (0.62) |
| Croatia | 0.9 | (0.31) | 0.4 | (0.19) | 0.0 | (0.07) | 0.0 | (0.06) | 0.0 | (0.06) |
| Estonia | 0.1 | (0.14) | 2.1 | (0.53) | 1.0 | (0.34) | 0.2 | (0.14) | 0.4 | (0.23) |
| Hong Kong-China | 0.7 | (0.29) | 1.4 | (0.45) | 1.5 | (0.43) | 0.0 | (0.06) | 0.1 | (0.11) |
| Indonesia | 0.7 | (0.29) | 1.0 | (0.36) | 0.1 | (0.14) | 0.3 | (0.34) | 0.2 | (0.25) |
| Israel | 1.5 | (0.50) | 0.0 | (0.05) | 0.0 | (0.05) | 0.0 | (0.05) | 0.0 | (0.05) |
| Jordan | 0.0 | (0.04) | 1.3 | (0.40) | 0.5 | (0.32) | 1.2 | (0.31) | 1.2 | (0.38) |
| Kyrgyzstan | 0.0 | (0.08) | 0.0 | (0.08) | 1.2 | (0.43) | 1.6 | (0.57) | 3.2 | (0.70) |
| Latvia | 0.0 | (0.11) | 0.6 | (0.36) | 0.1 | (0.14) | 0.0 | (0.05) | 0.1 | (0.09) |
| Liechtenstein | 1.1 | (1.05) | 2.9 | (1.51) | 7.1 | (2.57) | 0.8 | (0.84) | 3.1 | (1.81) |
| Lithuania | 0.3 | (0.20) | 1.3 | (0.39) | 0.5 | (0.19) | 0.0 | (0.04) | 0.1 | (0.09) |
| Macao-China | 1.0 | (0.34) | 0.4 | (0.22) | 0.5 | (0.23) | 0.1 | (0.14) | 0.0 | (0.06) |
| Montenegro | 0.0 | (0.04) | 0.4 | (0.22) | 0.5 | (0.24) | 0.4 | (0.21) | 1.1 | (0.40) |
| Qatar | m | m | m | m | m | m | m | m | m | m |
| Romania | 0.3 | (0.33) | 1.2 | (0.43) | 0.2 | (0.17) | 0.0 | (0.04) | 0.1 | (0.11) |
| Russian Federation | 0.2 | (0.18) | 0.0 | (0.05) | 0.0 | (0.06) | 0.2 | (0.19) | 1.1 | (0.39) |
| Serbia | 0.9 | (0.35) | 0.0 | (0.05) | 1.1 | (0.36) | 0.1 | (0.15) | 0.5 | (0.25) |
| Slovenia | 0.0 | (0.04) | 0.9 | (0.26) | 0.2 | (0.11) | 0.2 | (0.13) | 0.8 | (0.30) |
| Chinese Taipei | 1.7 | (0.38) | 2.6 | (0.38) | 2.4 | (0.41) | 1.3 | (0.28) | 1.7 | (0.34) |
| Thailand | 0.1 | (0.16) | 0.1 | (0.15) | 0.3 | (0.19) | 0.4 | (0.23) | 0.0 | (0.04) |
| Tunisia | 0.2 | (0.18) | 0.4 | (0.25) | 0.0 | (0.09) | 0.3 | (0.24) | 0.2 | (0.18) |
| Uruguay | 2.5 | (0.68) | 0.1 | (0.16) | 0.0 | (0.08) | 0.0 | (0.06) | 0.0 | (0.05) |

StatLink ⏱ http://dx.doi.org/10.1787/142104560611

Pour consulter la version française intégrale de ce tableau, suivre ce lien :
StatLink ⏱ http://dx.doi.org/10.1787/152684743050

[Part 1/1]

**Table 4.6** Relationship between student perceptions of science and the PISA index of economic, social and cultural status (ESCS)

Tableau 4.6   Relation entre les indices d'attitude à l'égard des sciences et l'indice PISA de statut économique, social et culturel (SESC)

| | Percentage of variance for the following indices explained by ESCS | | | | | | | | | |
|---|---|---|---|---|---|---|---|---|---|---|
| | Support for scientific enquiry | | General value of science | | Personal value of science | | Self-efficacy in science | | Self-concept in science | |
| | Percentage | S.E. | Percentage | S.E. | Percentage | S.E. | Percentage | S.E. | Percentage | S.E. |
| Australia | 3.7 | (0.43) | 4.5 | (0.43) | 3.1 | (0.36) | 7.4 | (0.53) | 3.7 | (0.41) |
| Austria | 2.1 | (0.49) | 2.8 | (0.54) | 0.7 | (0.26) | 7.6 | (0.79) | 1.7 | (0.43) |
| Belgium | 2.6 | (0.51) | 2.2 | (0.43) | 2.6 | (0.49) | 4.9 | (0.59) | 1.9 | (0.42) |
| Canada | 1.9 | (0.32) | 2.7 | (0.38) | 2.9 | (0.37) | 5.8 | (0.57) | 3.1 | (0.47) |
| Czech Republic | 0.6 | (0.33) | 1.1 | (0.33) | 0.1 | (0.09) | 3.8 | (0.60) | 0.5 | (0.23) |
| Denmark | 5.4 | (0.89) | 3.2 | (0.59) | 2.9 | (0.54) | 8.0 | (0.97) | 3.1 | (0.60) |
| Finland | 2.5 | (0.57) | 3.9 | (0.57) | 3.5 | (0.57) | 5.3 | (0.80) | 3.7 | (0.67) |
| France | 2.9 | (0.64) | 3.4 | (0.63) | 3.2 | (0.66) | 7.6 | (0.85) | 2.6 | (0.59) |
| Germany | 3.0 | (0.56) | 3.7 | (0.54) | 2.2 | (0.50) | 8.2 | (0.91) | 1.9 | (0.43) |
| Greece | 3.8 | (0.74) | 2.3 | (0.45) | 3.3 | (0.55) | 5.6 | (0.79) | 3.3 | (0.58) |
| Hungary | 1.5 | (0.52) | 3.0 | (0.67) | 0.4 | (0.26) | 5.6 | (0.70) | 0.7 | (0.40) |
| Iceland | 2.5 | (0.56) | 3.6 | (0.62) | 4.0 | (0.66) | 6.6 | (0.86) | 7.6 | (0.94) |
| Ireland | 4.7 | (0.80) | 5.6 | (0.74) | 6.2 | (0.73) | 8.1 | (0.89) | 4.6 | (0.70) |
| Italy | 2.5 | (0.42) | 3.0 | (0.35) | 1.3 | (0.27) | 3.8 | (0.49) | 1.0 | (0.22) |
| Japan | 1.7 | (0.44) | 2.2 | (0.45) | 2.0 | (0.36) | 3.1 | (0.52) | 0.7 | (0.23) |
| Korea | 3.6 | (0.86) | 1.6 | (0.47) | 2.8 | (0.89) | 5.5 | (0.99) | 3.9 | (0.77) |
| Luxembourg | 3.3 | (0.54) | 3.4 | (0.55) | 1.5 | (0.38) | 6.9 | (0.64) | 2.3 | (0.43) |
| Mexico | 1.6 | (0.36) | 2.1 | (0.60) | 0.0 | (0.04) | 3.8 | (0.61) | 0.7 | (0.23) |
| Netherlands | 2.9 | (0.72) | 3.4 | (0.54) | 1.7 | (0.40) | 4.3 | (0.57) | 2.0 | (0.54) |
| New Zealand | 4.9 | (0.76) | 4.7 | (0.65) | 3.3 | (0.63) | 7.5 | (0.70) | 3.3 | (0.58) |
| Norway | 4.1 | (1.00) | 4.1 | (0.71) | 2.9 | (0.55) | 5.9 | (0.86) | 3.5 | (0.67) |
| Poland | 1.9 | (0.48) | 2.4 | (0.44) | 0.1 | (0.07) | 7.8 | (0.75) | 1.7 | (0.39) |
| Portugal | 2.7 | (0.65) | 3.1 | (0.56) | 1.8 | (0.38) | 5.9 | (0.84) | 2.3 | (0.59) |
| Slovak Republic | 3.0 | (0.77) | 2.2 | (0.57) | 0.0 | (0.06) | 4.4 | (0.79) | 1.1 | (0.37) |
| Spain | 1.5 | (0.41) | 2.3 | (0.39) | 3.2 | (0.49) | 5.5 | (0.70) | 4.0 | (0.58) |
| Sweden | 4.7 | (0.82) | 4.6 | (0.64) | 4.7 | (0.71) | 6.6 | (1.06) | 4.6 | (0.71) |
| Switzerland | 2.1 | (0.44) | 2.3 | (0.34) | 1.8 | (0.31) | 7.1 | (0.54) | 2.7 | (0.42) |
| Turkey | 2.0 | (0.75) | 2.0 | (0.58) | 1.4 | (0.59) | 4.6 | (0.99) | 0.3 | (0.25) |
| United Kingdom | 3.1 | (0.57) | 4.0 | (0.45) | 2.9 | (0.40) | 8.1 | (0.68) | 2.3 | (0.40) |
| United States | 3.2 | (0.66) | 4.8 | (0.64) | 3.1 | (0.52) | 6.7 | (0.93) | 3.1 | (0.73) |
| **OECD total** | 0.3 | (0.06) | 1.0 | (0.11) | 0.3 | (0.06) | 4.6 | (0.26) | 0.6 | (0.11) |
| **OECD average** | 2.9 | (0.11) | 3.1 | (0.10) | 2.3 | (0.09) | 6.1 | (0.14) | 2.6 | (0.10) |
| Argentina | 0.7 | (0.48) | 0.7 | (0.42) | 0.3 | (0.21) | 3.7 | (0.83) | 0.1 | (0.17) |
| Azerbaijan | 0.1 | (0.14) | 1.3 | (0.39) | 0.0 | (0.04) | 3.9 | (0.85) | 0.1 | (0.15) |
| Brazil | 1.4 | (0.43) | 1.4 | (0.36) | 0.0 | (0.07) | 6.4 | (0.83) | 0.2 | (0.13) |
| Bulgaria | 3.1 | (0.90) | 1.3 | (0.48) | 0.1 | (0.08) | 6.5 | (1.11) | 0.6 | (0.36) |
| Chile | 1.9 | (0.53) | 2.2 | (0.40) | 0.6 | (0.25) | 7.5 | (0.95) | 1.9 | (0.40) |
| Colombia | 1.9 | (0.57) | 1.0 | (0.37) | 0.3 | (0.23) | 4.9 | (0.78) | 0.6 | (0.48) |
| Croatia | 0.7 | (0.27) | 1.3 | (0.32) | 0.1 | (0.07) | 5.1 | (0.62) | 0.5 | (0.21) |
| Estonia | 1.7 | (0.46) | 3.5 | (0.63) | 1.7 | (0.36) | 4.3 | (0.63) | 2.8 | (0.49) |
| Hong Kong-China | 0.8 | (0.45) | 1.2 | (0.42) | 1.0 | (0.29) | 5.0 | (0.75) | 0.9 | (0.35) |
| Indonesia | 2.5 | (0.57) | 1.1 | (0.37) | 0.1 | (0.14) | 4.8 | (0.84) | 0.1 | (0.17) |
| Israel | 0.3 | (0.24) | 1.3 | (0.44) | 0.3 | (0.20) | 1.8 | (0.52) | 0.6 | (0.29) |
| Jordan | 2.1 | (0.66) | 3.6 | (0.63) | 1.7 | (0.47) | 3.0 | (0.69) | 2.3 | (0.57) |
| Kyrgyzstan | 0.3 | (0.24) | 0.6 | (0.26) | 0.2 | (0.15) | 1.3 | (0.38) | 0.7 | (0.30) |
| Latvia | 1.4 | (0.52) | 2.0 | (0.50) | 0.6 | (0.34) | 3.4 | (0.65) | 0.5 | (0.29) |
| Liechtenstein | 3.7 | (2.46) | 4.3 | (1.84) | 1.5 | (1.42) | 6.4 | (2.38) | 3.4 | (1.96) |
| Lithuania | 2.2 | (0.59) | 1.9 | (0.42) | 0.6 | (0.25) | 5.6 | (0.79) | 1.6 | (0.47) |
| Macao-China | 1.2 | (0.46) | 0.6 | (0.24) | 1.1 | (0.37) | 4.2 | (0.73) | 0.7 | (0.35) |
| Montenegro | 0.5 | (0.22) | 0.6 | (0.25) | 0.1 | (0.09) | 6.7 | (0.75) | 0.3 | (0.19) |
| Qatar | m | m | m | m | m | m | m | m | m | m |
| Romania | 3.5 | (1.09) | 3.1 | (0.83) | 0.8 | (0.30) | 4.8 | (0.95) | 0.7 | (0.27) |
| Russian Federation | 1.8 | (0.57) | 1.3 | (0.40) | 0.0 | (0.04) | 3.2 | (0.66) | 0.8 | (0.41) |
| Serbia | 0.9 | (0.33) | 0.3 | (0.15) | 0.2 | (0.15) | 4.1 | (0.60) | 0.1 | (0.13) |
| Slovenia | 1.5 | (0.49) | 1.8 | (0.43) | 0.4 | (0.19) | 6.3 | (0.79) | 0.2 | (0.14) |
| Chinese Taipei | 2.7 | (0.40) | 2.4 | (0.43) | 1.8 | (0.37) | 6.5 | (0.58) | 2.0 | (0.39) |
| Thailand | 3.1 | (0.71) | 1.4 | (0.40) | 0.9 | (0.33) | 2.0 | (0.43) | 0.0 | (0.04) |
| Tunisia | 1.2 | (0.50) | 1.4 | (0.47) | 1.1 | (0.51) | 2.9 | (0.65) | 0.6 | (0.30) |
| Uruguay | 0.9 | (0.32) | 0.5 | (0.22) | 0.3 | (0.24) | 3.5 | (0.74) | 0.7 | (0.29) |

*StatLink* ᵐˢᵖ http://dx.doi.org/10.1787/142104560611

Pour consulter la version française intégrale de ce tableau, suivre ce lien :
*StatLink* ᵐˢᵖ http://dx.doi.org/10.1787/152684743050

[Part 1/2]

**Table 4.7a Percentage of students and performance on the science, reading and mathematics scales, by level of education of parents[1]**

Tableau 4.7a  Pourcentage d'élèves et scores sur les échelles de culture scientifique, de compréhension de l'écrit et de culture mathématique, selon le niveau de formation des parents

| | Parents with completed lower secondary education or below (ISCED Levels 0, 1 or 2) | | | | | | | | Parents with completed tertiary education (ISCED Levels 5 or 6) | | | | | | | |
| | | | Performance | | | | | | | | Performance | | | | | |
| | | | Science | | Reading | | Mathematics | | | | Science | | Reading | | Mathematics | |
| | % of students | S.E. | Mean score | S.E. | Mean score | S.E. | Mean score | S.E. | % of students | S.E. | Mean score | S.E. | Mean score | S.E. | Mean score | S.E. |
|---|---|---|---|---|---|---|---|---|---|---|---|---|---|---|---|---|
| Australia | 10.9 | (0.4) | 486 | (3.3) | 477 | (3.1) | 487 | (3.0) | 54.0 | (0.7) | 548 | (2.5) | 532 | (2.3) | 539 | (2.7) |
| Austria | 4.5 | (0.6) | 414 | (15.0) | 417 | (20.0) | 426 | (14.7) | 50.9 | (1.1) | 522 | (3.8) | 500 | (4.0) | 514 | (3.7) |
| Belgium | 7.1 | (0.5) | 437 | (7.6) | 425 | (9.4) | 444 | (11.8) | 57.7 | (0.9) | 536 | (2.4) | 525 | (3.0) | 546 | (2.6) |
| Canada | 3.5 | (0.3) | 476 | (6.7) | 466 | (7.7) | 485 | (5.9) | 69.4 | (0.6) | 547 | (2.0) | 540 | (2.4) | 537 | (2.0) |
| Czech Republic | 2.1 | (0.3) | c | c | c | c | c | c | 33.1 | (0.9) | 533 | (4.8) | 499 | (5.5) | 533 | (5.0) |
| Denmark | 6.9 | (0.5) | 427 | (5.8) | 435 | (6.4) | 456 | (5.2) | 63.3 | (1.1) | 513 | (3.5) | 509 | (3.5) | 527 | (3.0) |
| Finland | 6.4 | (0.4) | 532 | (5.7) | 518 | (5.1) | 517 | (6.0) | 76.6 | (0.8) | 572 | (2.2) | 556 | (2.3) | 556 | (2.3) |
| France | 15.8 | (0.8) | 446 | (5.7) | 445 | (6.4) | 448 | (5.0) | 39.1 | (1.2) | 529 | (4.5) | 517 | (4.8) | 526 | (4.3) |
| Germany | 15.1 | (0.9) | 449 | (6.8) | 420 | (7.4) | 446 | (6.9) | 45.8 | (1.1) | 543 | (3.6) | 521 | (4.2) | 531 | (3.8) |
| Greece | 17.8 | (1.0) | 418 | (4.8) | 409 | (6.6) | 404 | (5.0) | 44.3 | (1.3) | 498 | (3.7) | 480 | (4.3) | 485 | (3.7) |
| Hungary | 6.6 | (0.6) | 426 | (4.6) | 406 | (8.5) | 407 | (5.5) | 34.7 | (1.2) | 543 | (3.6) | 520 | (3.8) | 533 | (4.2) |
| Iceland | 11.4 | (0.6) | 450 | (5.3) | 449 | (5.3) | 469 | (5.0) | 50.2 | (0.8) | 511 | (2.3) | 505 | (2.8) | 526 | (2.4) |
| Ireland | 11.4 | (0.6) | 467 | (5.9) | 478 | (6.7) | 463 | (5.1) | 46.0 | (1.2) | 533 | (3.5) | 541 | (3.6) | 523 | (3.1) |
| Italy | 28.2 | (0.7) | 443 | (3.0) | 437 | (3.8) | 433 | (2.7) | 26.1 | (0.7) | 491 | (3.2) | 482 | (3.7) | 477 | (3.4) |
| Japan | 2.5 | (0.3) | c | c | c | c | c | c | 60.7 | (1.1) | 554 | (3.3) | 521 | (3.6) | 545 | (3.1) |
| Korea | 8.6 | (0.5) | 486 | (7.1) | 529 | (7.5) | 507 | (7.3) | 42.8 | (1.3) | 541 | (4.8) | 573 | (4.4) | 570 | (5.8) |
| Luxembourg | 21.1 | (0.5) | 431 | (3.0) | 426 | (3.3) | 449 | (2.7) | 44.5 | (0.6) | 518 | (2.3) | 510 | (2.3) | 516 | (2.1) |
| Mexico | 53.4 | (1.2) | 388 | (2.9) | 386 | (3.7) | 383 | (3.3) | 35.6 | (1.0) | 437 | (3.8) | 441 | (4.0) | 434 | (3.7) |
| Netherlands | 11.3 | (0.7) | 476 | (6.4) | 460 | (6.9) | 490 | (6.0) | 53.3 | (1.0) | 546 | (2.9) | 524 | (3.2) | 549 | (2.7) |
| New Zealand | 8.6 | (0.4) | 475 | (5.5) | 472 | (5.9) | 480 | (5.2) | 53.2 | (1.0) | 557 | (3.1) | 545 | (3.4) | 544 | (2.9) |
| Norway | 2.6 | (0.3) | c | c | c | c | c | c | 67.6 | (0.9) | 501 | (2.9) | 498 | (3.0) | 502 | (2.5) |
| Poland | 4.6 | (0.4) | 432 | (4.9) | 440 | (6.8) | 434 | (5.3) | 18.6 | (0.8) | 553 | (3.9) | 561 | (4.5) | 545 | (3.7) |
| Portugal | 53.9 | (1.4) | 454 | (3.3) | 450 | (4.2) | 446 | (3.5) | 22.5 | (1.1) | 513 | (4.1) | 515 | (4.5) | 504 | (4.4) |
| Slovak Republic | 3.1 | (0.6) | 376 | (17.9) | 348 | (26.0) | 356 | (24.3) | 28.8 | (0.9) | 529 | (4.2) | 506 | (4.4) | 532 | (4.6) |
| Spain | 36.3 | (1.1) | 461 | (2.9) | 438 | (2.9) | 456 | (2.6) | 34.8 | (1.1) | 518 | (3.0) | 483 | (3.0) | 506 | (3.2) |
| Sweden | 7.6 | (0.5) | 456 | (4.9) | 463 | (5.9) | 462 | (5.4) | 69.4 | (0.8) | 515 | (2.4) | 519 | (3.4) | 514 | (2.5) |
| Switzerland | 19.0 | (0.7) | 458 | (3.5) | 453 | (3.5) | 481 | (3.6) | 50.2 | (0.9) | 534 | (3.7) | 520 | (3.7) | 549 | (3.6) |
| Turkey | 58.4 | (1.5) | 404 | (2.4) | 429 | (3.7) | 401 | (2.7) | 15.9 | (1.2) | 477 | (10.6) | 494 | (9.6) | 485 | (13.2) |
| United Kingdom | 5.3 | (0.3) | 450 | (5.9) | 444 | (5.9) | 450 | (4.8) | 51.4 | (0.8) | 537 | (2.9) | 516 | (2.8) | 512 | (2.6) |
| United States | 6.9 | (0.7) | 414 | (6.0) | m | m | 412 | (5.1) | 58.1 | (1.4) | 511 | (4.9) | m | m | 494 | (4.7) |
| **OECD total** | 16.7 | (0.3) | 420 | (1.4) | 421 | (1.8) | 417 | (1.6) | 46.8 | (0.5) | 521 | (1.7) | 513 | (1.1) | 511 | (1.6) |
| **OECD average** | 15.0 | (0.1) | 446 | (1.3) | 443 | (1.7) | 448 | (1.4) | 46.6 | (0.2) | 525 | (0.7) | 516 | (0.7) | 522 | (0.8) |
| Argentina | 34.2 | (1.8) | 353 | (6.0) | 338 | (7.2) | 344 | (6.0) | 45.5 | (1.8) | 422 | (5.8) | 402 | (7.4) | 408 | (6.4) |
| Azerbaijan | 2.8 | (0.3) | c | c | c | c | c | c | 60.1 | (1.3) | 388 | (3.0) | 362 | (3.3) | 476 | (2.4) |
| Brazil | 47.4 | (1.0) | 365 | (2.8) | 367 | (4.1) | 342 | (3.3) | 35.9 | (1.0) | 416 | (4.4) | 417 | (4.9) | 397 | (4.9) |
| Bulgaria | 7.1 | (0.8) | 340 | (11.2) | 295 | (15.1) | 328 | (12.9) | 36.0 | (1.8) | 477 | (8.1) | 446 | (8.5) | 453 | (8.1) |
| Chile | 28.4 | (1.9) | 391 | (3.8) | 397 | (4.9) | 363 | (4.2) | 31.0 | (1.7) | 485 | (4.6) | 490 | (6.3) | 456 | (4.7) |
| Colombia | 42.3 | (1.9) | 368 | (4.1) | 361 | (6.4) | 346 | (5.1) | 42.7 | (1.4) | 410 | (4.1) | 411 | (5.6) | 394 | (4.2) |
| Croatia | 5.9 | (0.4) | 443 | (5.2) | 426 | (5.4) | 415 | (5.4) | 43.9 | (0.8) | 504 | (2.8) | 485 | (3.1) | 476 | (2.6) |
| Estonia | 1.8 | (0.3) | c | c | c | c | c | c | 50.9 | (1.0) | 543 | (3.0) | 510 | (3.1) | 527 | (3.0) |
| Hong Kong-China | 44.1 | (1.3) | 523 | (3.0) | 521 | (3.2) | 529 | (3.2) | 13.6 | (1.0) | 575 | (6.8) | 561 | (6.3) | 580 | (7.3) |
| Indonesia | 53.7 | (2.2) | 378 | (4.2) | 377 | (4.6) | 375 | (4.2) | 17.8 | (1.3) | 416 | (7.0) | 414 | (7.7) | 416 | (8.1) |
| Israel | 6.4 | (0.5) | 393 | (7.6) | 387 | (8.2) | 378 | (7.7) | 68.2 | (1.0) | 474 | (4.1) | 457 | (5.0) | 462 | (4.5) |
| Jordan | 23.3 | (1.1) | 387 | (3.4) | 364 | (4.2) | 348 | (3.9) | 48.4 | (1.3) | 447 | (3.7) | 425 | (4.4) | 409 | (4.0) |
| Kyrgyzstan | 1.8 | (0.2) | c | c | c | c | c | c | 77.5 | (1.0) | 328 | (2.9) | 294 | (3.5) | 318 | (3.6) |
| Latvia | 2.3 | (0.3) | c | c | c | c | c | c | 50.8 | (1.0) | 503 | (3.6) | 493 | (4.2) | 502 | (3.5) |
| Liechtenstein | 20.0 | (1.9) | 466 | (12.1) | 464 | (11.9) | 479 | (13.2) | 51.2 | (2.7) | 550 | (6.2) | 536 | (5.8) | 548 | (6.2) |
| Lithuania | 0.5 | (0.1) | c | c | c | c | c | c | 57.6 | (1.2) | 507 | (3.4) | 489 | (3.7) | 508 | (3.6) |
| Macao-China | 56.8 | (0.9) | 504 | (1.5) | 487 | (1.5) | 518 | (1.9) | 9.9 | (0.5) | 516 | (4.5) | 499 | (4.7) | 525 | (4.5) |
| Montenegro | 3.9 | (0.3) | 361 | (5.6) | 339 | (6.4) | 350 | (6.4) | 61.2 | (0.8) | 421 | (1.5) | 402 | (1.8) | 410 | (1.8) |
| Qatar | 15.1 | (0.4) | 331 | (2.1) | 288 | (2.8) | 291 | (2.4) | 60.9 | (0.5) | 361 | (1.2) | 327 | (1.7) | 334 | (1.5) |
| Romania | 6.9 | (0.9) | 357 | (7.3) | 339 | (11.0) | 357 | (9.9) | 48.7 | (1.5) | 429 | (5.6) | 402 | (6.1) | 425 | (5.5) |
| Russian Federation | 1.0 | (0.2) | c | c | c | c | c | c | 42.5 | (1.3) | 498 | (4.2) | 457 | (5.0) | 493 | (4.6) |
| Serbia | 6.2 | (0.4) | 378 | (6.5) | 335 | (7.5) | 370 | (6.8) | 49.9 | (0.9) | 447 | (3.2) | 413 | (3.5) | 446 | (3.7) |
| Slovenia | 6.7 | (0.5) | 448 | (7.0) | 437 | (7.4) | 441 | (6.7) | 36.1 | (0.7) | 559 | (2.4) | 528 | (2.0) | 542 | (2.3) |
| Chinese Taipei | 20.6 | (1.0) | 491 | (4.8) | 459 | (4.6) | 504 | (6.2) | 16.1 | (0.7) | 589 | (3.9) | 544 | (3.8) | 605 | (4.6) |
| Thailand | 64.2 | (1.1) | 405 | (2.0) | 402 | (2.6) | 400 | (2.2) | 12.8 | (0.9) | 482 | (5.7) | 475 | (5.9) | 477 | (5.3) |
| Tunisia | 45.0 | (1.8) | 369 | (2.5) | 365 | (3.3) | 342 | (3.1) | 24.7 | (1.6) | 408 | (6.8) | 401 | (8.1) | 403 | (7.9) |
| Uruguay | 34.4 | (1.0) | 392 | (3.3) | 373 | (5.0) | 385 | (3.2) | 54.3 | (1.0) | 452 | (2.9) | 438 | (4.0) | 451 | (2.9) |

Note: Values that are statistically significant are indicated in bold (see Annex A3).
1. Results based on students' self-reports.
StatLink ⟲ http://dx.doi.org/10.1787/142104560611

Pour consulter la version française intégrale de ce tableau, suivre ce lien :
StatLink ⟲ http://dx.doi.org/10.1787/152684743050

[Part 2/2]

**Table 4.7a**   **Percentage of students and performance on the science, reading and mathematics scales, by level of education of parents[1]**

*Tableau 4.7a*   *Pourcentage d'élèves et scores sur les échelles de culture scientifique, de compréhension de l'écrit et de culture mathématique, selon le niveau de formation des parents*

| | | Increased likelihood of students, whose parents have completed lower secondary education or below, scoring in the bottom quarter of the science performance distribution | | Difference in science performance between students whose parents have completed tertiary education minus students whose parents have completed lower secondary education or below | | | | | |
| | | | | PISA 2006 | | PISA 2003 | | PISA 2000 | |
| | | Ratio | S.E. | Dif. | S.E. | Dif. | S.E. | Dif. | S.E. |
|---|---|---|---|---|---|---|---|---|---|
| OECD | Australia | 1.7 | (0.08) | 62 | (3.5) | 53 | (4.6) | 64 | (6.4) |
| | Austria | 2.8 | (0.30) | 108 | (14.8) | 85 | (8.8) | 70 | (7.5) |
| | Belgium | 2.4 | (0.16) | 98 | (7.5) | 95 | (6.1) | 80 | (6.3) |
| | Canada | 2.1 | (0.14) | 71 | (6.4) | 64 | (4.7) | 62 | (3.5) |
| | Czech Republic | c | c | c | c | c | c | c | c |
| | Denmark | 2.3 | (0.18) | 86 | (6.6) | 78 | (6.7) | 104 | (7.7) |
| | Finland | 1.6 | (0.16) | 39 | (5.9) | 39 | (5.2) | 43 | (6.0) |
| | France | 2.1 | (0.17) | 84 | (6.8) | 81 | (7.8) | 70 | (7.0) |
| | Germany | 2.7 | (0.16) | 94 | (6.0) | 124 | (6.5) | 117 | (9.9) |
| | Greece | 2.3 | (0.16) | 80 | (5.5) | 62 | (6.3) | 53 | (6.8) |
| | Hungary | 2.7 | (0.19) | 118 | (5.3) | 123 | (7.9) | 146 | (9.7) |
| | Iceland | 1.9 | (0.16) | 62 | (5.9) | 44 | (4.9) | 40 | (5.8) |
| | Ireland | 1.8 | (0.12) | 66 | (5.9) | 66 | (5.9) | 47 | (5.9) |
| | Italy | 1.8 | (0.09) | 49 | (4.0) | 62 | (5.5) | 56 | (7.7) |
| | Japan | c | c | c | c | 65 | (15.2) | m | m |
| | Korea | 1.7 | (0.14) | 55 | (8.1) | 62 | (6.5) | 45 | (6.0) |
| | Luxembourg | 2.6 | (0.15) | 86 | (3.7) | 76 | (4.5) | 67 | (6.6) |
| | Mexico | 2.0 | (0.15) | 49 | (4.2) | 47 | (5.0) | 60 | (7.5) |
| | Netherlands | 1.9 | (0.15) | 70 | (6.4) | 58 | (7.1) | 59 | (7.2) |
| | New Zealand | 1.9 | (0.15) | 82 | (5.6) | 83 | (6.1) | 73 | (8.2) |
| | Norway | c | c | c | c | 65 | (9.5) | 56 | (8.5) |
| | Poland | 2.4 | (0.16) | 121 | (6.2) | c | c | 109 | (15.5) |
| | Portugal | 2.0 | (0.16) | 59 | (4.5) | 44 | (5.0) | 47 | (7.4) |
| | Slovak Republic | 2.9 | (0.39) | 152 | (18.9) | 175 | (26.0) | a | a |
| | Spain | 1.8 | (0.12) | 56 | (3.6) | 57 | (4.6) | 64 | (5.6) |
| | Sweden | 1.9 | (0.16) | 59 | (5.2) | 68 | (6.3) | 43 | (6.5) |
| | Switzerland | 2.2 | (0.11) | 76 | (3.8) | 85 | (5.2) | 82 | (6.5) |
| | Turkey | 1.7 | (0.18) | 74 | (10.8) | 89 | (13.1) | a | a |
| | United Kingdom | 2.1 | (0.17) | 87 | (6.2) | 84 | (7.7) | 74 | (7.8) |
| | United States | 2.2 | (0.19) | 97 | (7.1) | 84 | (7.8) | 99 | (11.2) |
| | **OECD total** | 1.7 | (0.05) | 100 | (2.1) | 99 | (2.1) | 88 | (2.9) |
| | **OECD average** | 2.1 | (0.03) | 79 | (1.4) | 76 | (1.6) | 70 | (1.5) |
| Partners | Argentina | 2.0 | (0.19) | 69 | (6.0) | a | a | 69 | (9.1) |
| | Azerbaijan | c | c | c | c | a | a | a | a |
| | Brazil | 1.8 | (0.12) | 51 | (5.0) | 33 | (5.5) | 60 | (7.6) |
| | Bulgaria | 2.7 | (0.29) | 137 | (13.2) | a | a | 117 | (20.4) |
| | Chile | 2.2 | (0.21) | 93 | (5.3) | a | a | 81 | (6.3) |
| | Colombia | 1.6 | (0.16) | 42 | (4.7) | a | a | a | a |
| | Croatia | 2.1 | (0.15) | 61 | (5.3) | a | a | a | a |
| | Estonia | c | c | c | c | a | a | a | a |
| | Hong Kong-China | 1.8 | (0.13) | 52 | (6.6) | 38 | (6.8) | 54 | (7.7) |
| | Indonesia | 1.6 | (0.17) | 38 | (7.1) | 26 | (6.1) | 37 | (9.3) |
| | Israel | 1.9 | (0.18) | 81 | (7.6) | a | a | 101 | (14.8) |
| | Jordan | 1.7 | (0.12) | 60 | (4.5) | a | a | a | a |
| | Kyrgyzstan | c | c | c | c | a | a | a | a |
| | Latvia | c | c | c | c | c | c | 89 | (13.2) |
| | Liechtenstein | 2.3 | (0.54) | 84 | (15.2) | 81 | (13.4) | 56 | (17.9) |
| | Lithuania | c | c | c | c | a | a | a | a |
| | Macao-China | 1.3 | (0.08) | 12 | (4.8) | 23 | (10.5) | a | a |
| | Montenegro | 2.0 | (0.20) | 60 | (5.9) | a | a | a | a |
| | Qatar | 1.1 | (0.08) | 31 | (2.5) | a | a | a | a |
| | Romania | 2.4 | (0.36) | 72 | (10.1) | a | a | 45 | (9.0) |
| | Russian Federation | c | c | c | c | c | c | 70 | (9.8) |
| | Serbia | 2.1 | (0.17) | 69 | (6.7) | a | a | a | a |
| | Slovenia | 2.2 | (0.20) | 111 | (7.4) | a | a | a | a |
| | Chinese Taipei | 1.9 | (0.12) | 98 | (5.7) | a | a | a | a |
| | Thailand | 1.7 | (0.17) | 77 | (6.2) | 71 | (6.4) | 64 | (6.9) |
| | Tunisia | 1.4 | (0.11) | 39 | (7.4) | 38 | (8.4) | a | a |
| | Uruguay | 2.1 | (0.15) | 60 | (3.4) | 56 | (4.5) | a | a |

Note: Values that are statistically significant are indicated in bold (see Annex A3).
1. Results based on students' self-reports.
*StatLink* http://dx.doi.org/10.1787/142104560611

Pour consulter la version française intégrale de ce tableau, suivre ce lien :
*StatLink* http://dx.doi.org/10.1787/152684743050

[Part 1/4]

**Table 4.7b** **Percentage of students and performance on the science, reading and mathematics scales, by level of mothers' education[1]**

Tableau 4.7b Pourcentage d'élèves et scores sur les échelles de culture scientifique, de compréhension de l'écrit et de culture mathématique, selon le niveau de formation de la mère

| | | | Mothers without completed primary education (ISCED Level 0) | | | | | | | | Mothers with completed primary or lower secondary education (ISCED Levels 1 or 2) | | | | | | | | |
|---|---|---|---|---|---|---|---|---|---|---|---|---|---|---|---|---|---|---|
| | | | | | Performance | | | | | | | | | Performance | | | | |
| | | | | | Science | | Reading | | Mathematics | | | | | Science | | Reading | | Mathematics |
| | | % of students | S.E. | Mean score | S.E. | Mean score | S.E. | Mean score | S.E. | % of students | S.E. | Mean score | S.E. | Mean score | S.E. | Mean score | S.E. |
| **OECD** | Australia | 1.7 | (0.1) | c | c | c | c | c | c | 20.2 | (0.5) | 507 | (2.6) | 498 | (2.6) | 504 | (2.4) |
| | Austria | 1.8 | (0.3) | c | c | c | c | c | c | 9.3 | (0.7) | 458 | (10.6) | 445 | (12.3) | 458 | (10.0) |
| | Belgium | 3.5 | (0.3) | 409 | (8.9) | 392 | (11.3) | 418 | (10.9) | 10.1 | (0.4) | 482 | (5.9) | 476 | (6.6) | 490 | (7.2) |
| | Canada | 1.1 | (0.1) | c | c | c | c | c | c | 6.1 | (0.3) | 497 | (4.0) | 490 | (4.9) | 498 | (3.9) |
| | Czech Republic | 0.7 | (0.2) | c | c | c | c | c | c | 4.4 | (0.4) | 451 | (9.4) | 429 | (15.2) | 426 | (8.4) |
| | Denmark | 2.0 | (0.3) | c | c | c | c | c | c | 11.3 | (0.7) | 457 | (4.7) | 463 | (5.0) | 483 | (4.1) |
| | Finland | 1.2 | (0.2) | c | c | c | c | c | c | 11.1 | (0.6) | 542 | (3.9) | 525 | (3.8) | 526 | (4.2) |
| | France | 4.4 | (0.4) | 426 | (8.4) | 434 | (8.2) | 430 | (8.2) | 20.6 | (0.8) | 466 | (4.5) | 461 | (5.4) | 468 | (4.4) |
| | Germany | 4.3 | (0.5) | 418 | (10.2) | 393 | (11.4) | 420 | (10.4) | 17.2 | (0.8) | 473 | (6.7) | 444 | (7.7) | 463 | (6.5) |
| | Greece | 0.8 | (0.2) | c | c | c | c | c | c | 28.1 | (1.2) | 436 | (4.3) | 423 | (5.3) | 423 | (4.0) |
| | Hungary | 0.8 | (0.2) | c | c | c | c | c | c | 14.4 | (0.9) | 444 | (4.4) | 427 | (6.2) | 430 | (5.1) |
| | Iceland | 3.8 | (0.3) | 438 | (7.6) | 446 | (7.7) | 450 | (7.7) | 25.0 | (0.7) | 469 | (3.2) | 467 | (3.1) | 484 | (3.3) |
| | Ireland | 0.9 | (0.2) | c | c | c | c | c | c | 19.7 | (0.8) | 479 | (4.6) | 493 | (5.0) | 472 | (4.0) |
| | Italy | 1.4 | (0.1) | c | c | c | c | c | c | 38.5 | (0.9) | 454 | (2.4) | 447 | (2.9) | 442 | (2.4) |
| | Japan | 0.0 | c | c | c | c | c | c | c | 4.4 | (0.3) | 474 | (7.1) | 446 | (8.5) | 471 | (6.4) |
| | Korea | 1.5 | (0.2) | c | c | c | c | c | c | 14.9 | (0.7) | 497 | (5.7) | 536 | (6.3) | 518 | (5.9) |
| | Luxembourg | 14.4 | (0.5) | 430 | (4.1) | 428 | (4.0) | 448 | (4.1) | 18.8 | (0.6) | 465 | (3.4) | 458 | (3.6) | 476 | (3.1) |
| | Mexico | 18.7 | (1.0) | 371 | (3.5) | 367 | (4.9) | 365 | (4.2) | 47.1 | (0.9) | 404 | (2.4) | 405 | (2.9) | 399 | (2.8) |
| | Netherlands | 3.2 | (0.3) | 450 | (10.1) | 436 | (10.9) | 462 | (9.4) | 17.9 | (0.8) | 504 | (4.8) | 487 | (5.4) | 515 | (5.2) |
| | New Zealand | 3.9 | (0.3) | 485 | (8.3) | 470 | (8.3) | 481 | (7.9) | 13.0 | (0.6) | 503 | (5.1) | 501 | (5.6) | 504 | (4.2) |
| | Norway | 1.1 | (0.2) | c | c | c | c | c | c | 5.2 | (0.5) | 451 | (8.2) | 457 | (9.4) | 450 | (7.9) |
| | Poland | 0.2 | (0.1) | c | c | c | c | c | c | 8.7 | (0.6) | 446 | (4.5) | 455 | (5.4) | 445 | (4.4) |
| | Portugal | 29.6 | (1.2) | 442 | (3.8) | 435 | (4.5) | 434 | (4.1) | 33.3 | (1.0) | 473 | (3.5) | 473 | (4.3) | 464 | (3.5) |
| | Slovak Republic | 0.6 | (0.2) | c | c | c | c | c | c | 5.2 | (0.7) | 396 | (12.4) | 374 | (17.5) | 387 | (17.0) |
| | Spain | 8.2 | (0.5) | 436 | (5.0) | 417 | (4.9) | 433 | (5.3) | 41.6 | (1.0) | 478 | (2.1) | 453 | (2.1) | 470 | (1.8) |
| | Sweden | 1.9 | (0.2) | c | c | c | c | c | c | 11.0 | (0.5) | 473 | (4.4) | 476 | (6.0) | 471 | (4.9) |
| | Switzerland | 3.9 | (0.2) | 445 | (6.6) | 445 | (6.9) | 467 | (7.4) | 26.3 | (0.6) | 476 | (3.5) | 470 | (3.5) | 499 | (3.8) |
| | Turkey | 16.5 | (1.0) | 394 | (3.9) | 418 | (6.0) | 388 | (5.8) | 62.0 | (1.3) | 417 | (2.9) | 442 | (3.8) | 417 | (3.6) |
| | United Kingdom | 2.1 | (0.2) | c | c | c | c | c | c | 6.5 | (0.3) | 482 | (6.4) | 470 | (5.6) | 478 | (5.0) |
| | United States | 2.1 | (0.3) | c | c | m | m | c | c | 8.8 | (0.6) | 428 | (5.8) | m | m | 421 | (4.9) |
| | **OECD total** | 4.7 | (0.2) | 400 | (2.3) | 399 | (3.2) | 399 | (2.8) | 19.2 | (0.3) | 441 | (1.3) | 443 | (1.4) | 438 | (1.4) |
| | **OECD average** | 4.5 | (0.1) | 429 | (2.1) | 423 | (2.3) | 433 | (2.2) | 18.7 | (0.1) | 466 | (1.0) | 462 | (1.3) | 465 | (1.1) |
| **Partners** | Argentina | 11.8 | (0.9) | 332 | (6.9) | 327 | (8.7) | 323 | (7.6) | 32.6 | (1.3) | 371 | (6.6) | 352 | (7.9) | 361 | (6.6) |
| | Azerbaijan | 2.3 | (0.3) | c | c | c | c | c | c | 4.3 | (0.5) | 371 | (4.2) | 358 | (8.3) | 475 | (6.7) |
| | Brazil | 15.5 | (0.6) | 349 | (3.8) | 355 | (3.9) | 321 | (3.7) | 43.7 | (0.8) | 377 | (3.0) | 379 | (5.3) | 357 | (3.8) |
| | Bulgaria | 1.3 | (0.3) | c | c | c | c | c | c | 11.8 | (1.1) | 355 | (8.1) | 319 | (11.4) | 345 | (10.0) |
| | Chile | 10.6 | (0.8) | 396 | (4.9) | 401 | (6.0) | 370 | (5.2) | 29.4 | (1.4) | 402 | (4.0) | 408 | (5.3) | 373 | (4.4) |
| | Colombia | 16.7 | (0.9) | 366 | (4.8) | 362 | (8.1) | 345 | (6.9) | 37.8 | (1.6) | 376 | (4.2) | 373 | (6.5) | 353 | (4.7) |
| | Croatia | 0.3 | (0.1) | c | c | c | c | c | c | 15.0 | (0.6) | 463 | (4.3) | 448 | (5.1) | 437 | (4.3) |
| | Estonia | 0.2 | (0.1) | c | c | c | c | c | c | 4.2 | (0.4) | 494 | (8.5) | 458 | (9.8) | 471 | (9.8) |
| | Hong Kong-China | 9.8 | (0.5) | 515 | (6.6) | 517 | (6.0) | 523 | (6.1) | 47.2 | (1.2) | 533 | (2.9) | 528 | (3.0) | 537 | (3.1) |
| | Indonesia | 14.2 | (1.0) | 375 | (5.9) | 373 | (6.1) | 369 | (6.0) | 53.5 | (1.9) | 384 | (4.6) | 384 | (4.9) | 381 | (4.6) |
| | Israel | 3.6 | (0.3) | 386 | (8.7) | 362 | (10.6) | 369 | (9.1) | 7.6 | (0.6) | 408 | (6.5) | 411 | (7.7) | 391 | (8.2) |
| | Jordan | 12.2 | (0.9) | 381 | (4.3) | 352 | (5.5) | 338 | (4.7) | 26.5 | (0.9) | 403 | (2.9) | 387 | (3.2) | 367 | (3.5) |
| | Kyrgyzstan | 1.9 | (0.2) | c | c | c | c | c | c | 3.1 | (0.3) | 292 | (8.1) | 243 | (16.5) | 280 | (8.9) |
| | Latvia | 0.7 | (0.2) | c | c | c | c | c | c | 3.1 | (0.3) | 439 | (10.7) | 434 | (15.5) | 430 | (13.5) |
| | Liechtenstein | 1.2 | (0.7) | c | c | c | c | c | c | 32.7 | (2.3) | 485 | (9.0) | 479 | (8.5) | 497 | (9.9) |
| | Lithuania | 0.3 | (0.1) | c | c | c | c | c | c | 1.7 | (0.2) | c | c | c | c | c | c |
| | Macao-China | 14.6 | (0.6) | 502 | (3.1) | 486 | (3.1) | 513 | (3.5) | 58.2 | (0.7) | 510 | (1.5) | 491 | (1.6) | 525 | (1.8) |
| | Montenegro | 0.7 | (0.1) | c | c | c | c | c | c | 9.6 | (0.4) | 377 | (3.8) | 358 | (3.9) | 360 | (3.9) |
| | Qatar | 13.6 | (0.4) | 333 | (2.7) | 292 | (3.9) | 294 | (3.3) | 13.0 | (0.4) | 337 | (2.6) | 301 | (3.9) | 299 | (3.2) |
| | Romania | 1.2 | (0.4) | c | c | c | c | c | c | 12.4 | (1.2) | 377 | (6.2) | 355 | (7.5) | 376 | (7.8) |
| | Russian Federation | 0.1 | (0.1) | c | c | c | c | c | c | 2.3 | (0.2) | c | c | c | c | c | c |
| | Serbia | 0.7 | (0.1) | c | c | c | c | c | c | 14.8 | (0.7) | 391 | (4.2) | 349 | (5.0) | 386 | (5.1) |
| | Slovenia | 0.6 | (0.1) | c | c | c | c | c | c | 14.8 | (0.5) | 471 | (3.7) | 457 | (3.9) | 463 | (3.4) |
| | Chinese Taipei | 1.1 | (0.2) | c | c | c | c | c | c | 31.7 | (1.1) | 502 | (4.5) | 470 | (4.1) | 518 | (5.4) |
| | Thailand | 10.2 | (0.8) | 402 | (5.7) | 401 | (8.2) | 395 | (5.2) | 64.8 | (1.0) | 411 | (2.0) | 407 | (2.5) | 407 | (2.4) |
| | Tunisia | 22.6 | (1.5) | 371 | (3.3) | 358 | (4.7) | 343 | (3.7) | 43.3 | (1.3) | 377 | (3.3) | 377 | (4.6) | 355 | (4.0) |
| | Uruguay | 6.6 | (0.4) | 374 | (5.4) | 355 | (7.4) | 358 | (6.3) | 38.9 | (1.1) | 404 | (3.3) | 385 | (4.7) | 400 | (3.0) |

Note: Values that are statistically significant are indicated in bold (see Annex A3).
1. Results based on students' self-reports.
*StatLink* http://dx.doi.org/10.1787/142104560611

Pour consulter la version française intégrale de ce tableau, suivre ce lien :
*StatLink* http://dx.doi.org/10.1787/152684743050

[Part 2/4]

**Table 4.7b** Percentage of students and performance on the science, reading and mathematics scales, by level of mothers' education[1]

Tableau 4.7b Pourcentage d'élèves et scores sur les échelles de culture scientifique, de compréhension de l'écrit et de culture mathématique, selon le niveau de formation de la mère

| | | Mothers with completed upper secondary education (ISCED Level 3) | | | | | | | Mothers with completed tertiary education (ISCED Levels 5 or 6) | | | | | | | |
| | | | | Performance | | | | | | | | Performance | | | | | |
| | | | | Science | | Reading | | Mathematics | | | | Science | | Reading | | Mathematics | |
| | | % of students | S.E. | Mean score | S.E. | Mean score | S.E. | Mean score | S.E. | % of students | S.E. | Mean score | S.E. | Mean score | S.E. | Mean score | S.E. |
|---|---|---|---|---|---|---|---|---|---|---|---|---|---|---|---|---|---|
| OECD | Australia | 36.8 | (0.6) | 521 | (2.2) | 507 | (2.0) | 515 | (2.1) | 41.2 | (0.7) | 551 | (2.7) | 534 | (2.4) | 539 | (2.8) |
| | Austria | 61.7 | (1.0) | 515 | (3.6) | 493 | (3.6) | 510 | (3.8) | 27.3 | (1.0) | 530 | (4.6) | 510 | (4.9) | 521 | (4.2) |
| | Belgium | 39.4 | (0.7) | 505 | (2.9) | 501 | (3.5) | 518 | (3.3) | 46.9 | (0.9) | 541 | (2.6) | 529 | (3.1) | 551 | (2.7) |
| | Canada | 34.8 | (0.6) | 527 | (2.4) | 519 | (2.6) | 520 | (2.3) | 58.0 | (0.7) | 549 | (2.2) | 542 | (2.6) | 539 | (2.1) |
| | Czech Republic | 71.1 | (0.9) | 513 | (3.3) | 485 | (3.7) | 510 | (3.3) | 23.8 | (0.8) | 535 | (5.5) | 500 | (6.1) | 539 | (5.7) |
| | Denmark | 31.4 | (0.8) | 488 | (3.1) | 489 | (2.9) | 507 | (2.8) | 55.2 | (1.1) | 516 | (3.6) | 511 | (3.7) | 529 | (3.1) |
| | Finland | 19.3 | (0.6) | 547 | (3.2) | 527 | (3.3) | 535 | (3.2) | 68.4 | (0.8) | 574 | (2.3) | 558 | (2.3) | 558 | (2.4) |
| | France | 46.1 | (0.9) | 504 | (3.7) | 497 | (4.6) | 505 | (3.5) | 28.9 | (1.0) | 534 | (4.7) | 520 | (5.0) | 529 | (4.7) |
| | Germany | 51.2 | (0.9) | 533 | (2.7) | 520 | (3.0) | 518 | (2.8) | 27.3 | (0.9) | 545 | (4.7) | 522 | (5.5) | 536 | (5.2) |
| | Greece | 40.2 | (0.8) | 482 | (3.4) | 468 | (4.3) | 465 | (3.2) | 31.0 | (1.2) | 500 | (3.4) | 485 | (4.9) | 487 | (4.4) |
| | Hungary | 56.9 | (1.1) | 501 | (2.5) | 479 | (3.1) | 487 | (2.4) | 27.9 | (1.2) | 547 | (3.9) | 525 | (4.1) | 537 | (4.6) |
| | Iceland | 36.5 | (0.8) | 490 | (2.5) | 480 | (2.8) | 505 | (2.6) | 34.7 | (0.8) | 521 | (2.8) | 514 | (3.3) | 534 | (3.1) |
| | Ireland | 45.8 | (1.0) | 508 | (3.1) | 519 | (3.4) | 503 | (2.8) | 33.6 | (1.0) | 535 | (3.9) | 542 | (4.0) | 525 | (3.6) |
| | Italy | 41.3 | (0.8) | 493 | (2.3) | 487 | (2.9) | 477 | (2.7) | 18.7 | (0.5) | 492 | (3.6) | 483 | (4.2) | 478 | (3.7) |
| | Japan | 48.2 | (0.9) | 517 | (3.9) | 486 | (4.0) | 508 | (3.9) | 47.4 | (1.0) | 557 | (3.5) | 521 | (3.9) | 548 | (3.5) |
| | Korea | 58.9 | (1.1) | 520 | (3.0) | 552 | (3.7) | 544 | (3.2) | 24.7 | (1.2) | 549 | (6.2) | 581 | (5.4) | 579 | (7.5) |
| | Luxembourg | 33.2 | (0.7) | 498 | (2.4) | 491 | (2.4) | 499 | (2.3) | 33.5 | (0.7) | 519 | (2.7) | 511 | (2.8) | 516 | (2.6) |
| | Mexico | 9.7 | (0.4) | 443 | (4.2) | 445 | (5.1) | 443 | (4.1) | 24.4 | (0.8) | 439 | (4.0) | 444 | (4.3) | 436 | (3.9) |
| | Netherlands | 43.7 | (0.9) | 525 | (3.2) | 511 | (3.4) | 529 | (3.0) | 35.2 | (1.1) | 549 | (3.5) | 526 | (3.7) | 554 | (3.0) |
| | New Zealand | 39.8 | (0.9) | 534 | (3.1) | 526 | (3.2) | 523 | (2.9) | 43.3 | (1.0) | 559 | (3.3) | 546 | (3.5) | 545 | (3.2) |
| | Norway | 39.2 | (1.0) | 481 | (3.0) | 484 | (3.4) | 484 | (3.2) | 54.5 | (1.0) | 504 | (3.3) | 499 | (3.6) | 505 | (2.9) |
| | Poland | 76.6 | (0.7) | 495 | (2.1) | 505 | (2.7) | 492 | (2.3) | 14.5 | (0.6) | 555 | (4.0) | 565 | (4.8) | 548 | (3.9) |
| | Portugal | 19.3 | (0.8) | 495 | (3.5) | 496 | (4.4) | 487 | (3.5) | 17.7 | (1.0) | 518 | (4.4) | 520 | (4.8) | 509 | (4.7) |
| | Slovak Republic | 74.5 | (1.0) | 485 | (2.8) | 463 | (3.4) | 490 | (2.8) | 19.8 | (0.7) | 531 | (4.8) | 509 | (5.0) | 532 | (5.5) |
| | Spain | 26.3 | (0.6) | 500 | (3.4) | 472 | (3.1) | 491 | (3.1) | 24.0 | (1.0) | 521 | (3.8) | 487 | (3.9) | 509 | (4.1) |
| | Sweden | 26.0 | (0.8) | 506 | (3.4) | 513 | (4.0) | 501 | (3.6) | 61.1 | (0.9) | 516 | (2.5) | 519 | (3.5) | 515 | (2.5) |
| | Switzerland | 40.2 | (0.6) | 529 | (3.2) | 514 | (2.9) | 546 | (3.2) | 29.6 | (0.8) | 536 | (4.1) | 522 | (4.1) | 550 | (3.8) |
| | Turkey | 15.1 | (0.9) | 461 | (7.3) | 484 | (7.3) | 464 | (9.0) | 6.4 | (0.8) | 492 | (15.3) | 500 | (14.6) | 507 | (17.1) |
| | United Kingdom | 50.9 | (0.8) | 521 | (2.5) | 501 | (2.5) | 499 | (2.4) | 40.5 | (0.7) | 538 | (2.9) | 517 | (2.8) | 512 | (2.7) |
| | United States | 41.5 | (1.1) | 480 | (4.1) | m | m | 466 | (3.8) | 47.7 | (1.5) | 514 | (5.1) | m | m | 496 | (4.7) |
| | **OECD total** | 40.9 | (0.4) | 501 | (1.4) | 502 | (1.0) | 494 | (1.3) | 35.3 | (0.5) | 524 | (1.9) | 516 | (1.2) | 513 | (1.8) |
| | **OECD average** | 41.9 | (0.2) | 504 | (0.6) | 497 | (0.7) | 501 | (0.6) | 34.9 | (0.2) | 529 | (0.9) | 519 | (0.9) | 525 | (0.9) |
| Partners | Argentina | 17.6 | (0.9) | 411 | (7.6) | 394 | (9.3) | 406 | (7.3) | 38.0 | (1.5) | 423 | (6.0) | 402 | (7.8) | 409 | (6.6) |
| | Azerbaijan | 50.7 | (1.4) | 379 | (3.6) | 343 | (3.7) | 476 | (3.0) | 42.6 | (1.3) | 390 | (3.2) | 366 | (3.9) | 476 | (2.4) |
| | Brazil | 14.5 | (0.7) | 425 | (5.2) | 432 | (6.4) | 407 | (4.9) | 26.3 | (0.9) | 420 | (4.9) | 420 | (5.8) | 401 | (5.5) |
| | Bulgaria | 56.5 | (1.6) | 429 | (4.8) | 399 | (5.7) | 408 | (4.7) | 30.4 | (1.7) | 483 | (8.7) | 450 | (8.9) | 457 | (8.7) |
| | Chile | 38.9 | (1.3) | 450 | (4.8) | 452 | (4.8) | 425 | (4.6) | 21.2 | (1.3) | 493 | (5.0) | 500 | (7.1) | 464 | (5.2) |
| | Colombia | 13.8 | (1.0) | 394 | (5.8) | 386 | (6.9) | 386 | (5.2) | 31.7 | (1.5) | 413 | (4.6) | 415 | (6.2) | 397 | (4.6) |
| | Croatia | 52.9 | (0.7) | 494 | (2.7) | 481 | (3.1) | 470 | (2.7) | 31.7 | (0.7) | 508 | (2.9) | 489 | (3.3) | 478 | (2.7) |
| | Estonia | 54.3 | (0.9) | 522 | (2.8) | 494 | (3.5) | 505 | (3.0) | 41.3 | (0.9) | 548 | (3.1) | 515 | (3.3) | 532 | (3.2) |
| | Hong Kong-China | 35.3 | (1.0) | 557 | (3.3) | 549 | (3.3) | 563 | (3.7) | 7.7 | (0.7) | 573 | (8.8) | 555 | (7.8) | 574 | (9.4) |
| | Indonesia | 21.7 | (1.9) | 419 | (8.6) | 421 | (8.6) | 417 | (8.5) | 10.6 | (1.1) | 417 | (8.9) | 411 | (9.5) | 417 | (10.2) |
| | Israel | 35.3 | (0.9) | 443 | (4.1) | 430 | (5.0) | 430 | (5.1) | 53.5 | (1.2) | 482 | (4.4) | 464 | (5.3) | 471 | (4.7) |
| | Jordan | 29.4 | (0.8) | 429 | (2.8) | 410 | (3.3) | 392 | (3.0) | 31.9 | (1.2) | 451 | (4.6) | 427 | (5.6) | 412 | (4.8) |
| | Kyrgyzstan | 31.8 | (0.9) | 311 | (3.9) | 265 | (3.8) | 297 | (3.6) | 63.2 | (1.0) | 332 | (3.0) | 300 | (3.8) | 322 | (3.8) |
| | Latvia | 53.4 | (1.0) | 482 | (2.8) | 472 | (3.5) | 476 | (2.8) | 42.8 | (1.0) | 507 | (3.7) | 496 | (4.5) | 505 | (3.7) |
| | Liechtenstein | 39.5 | (2.6) | 544 | (7.4) | 531 | (7.5) | 543 | (8.0) | 26.6 | (2.3) | 548 | (11.0) | 533 | (10.0) | 543 | (10.2) |
| | Lithuania | 47.0 | (1.3) | 470 | (2.8) | 454 | (3.1) | 465 | (2.9) | 51.0 | (1.2) | 508 | (3.6) | 491 | (3.8) | 510 | (3.8) |
| | Macao-China | 20.6 | (0.5) | 519 | (3.0) | 500 | (2.9) | 535 | (3.2) | 6.6 | (0.4) | 519 | (5.5) | 501 | (6.3) | 522 | (6.0) |
| | Montenegro | 40.4 | (0.7) | 410 | (2.1) | 390 | (2.3) | 397 | (2.5) | 49.3 | (0.7) | 423 | (1.8) | 403 | (2.0) | 412 | (2.1) |
| | Qatar | 30.3 | (0.6) | 350 | (1.6) | 315 | (2.3) | 315 | (1.9) | 43.2 | (0.5) | 361 | (1.4) | 326 | (2.1) | 336 | (1.8) |
| | Romania | 46.9 | (1.2) | 421 | (3.8) | 403 | (4.7) | 417 | (4.3) | 39.6 | (1.4) | 432 | (6.6) | 403 | (6.9) | 428 | (6.3) |
| | Russian Federation | 65.1 | (1.1) | 472 | (3.6) | 433 | (4.3) | 468 | (3.8) | 32.5 | (1.2) | 499 | (4.6) | 460 | (5.3) | 495 | (5.0) |
| | Serbia | 47.8 | (0.8) | 441 | (3.3) | 409 | (3.8) | 443 | (3.7) | 36.7 | (0.9) | 450 | (3.3) | 416 | (3.6) | 448 | (3.9) |
| | Slovenia | 56.5 | (0.8) | 512 | (2.0) | 488 | (1.7) | 497 | (1.7) | 28.2 | (0.7) | 564 | (2.9) | 530 | (2.4) | 547 | (2.9) |
| | Chinese Taipei | 58.2 | (1.0) | 541 | (3.1) | 505 | (3.0) | 560 | (3.4) | 9.0 | (0.5) | 597 | (4.2) | 549 | (4.2) | 610 | (4.9) |
| | Thailand | 15.9 | (0.6) | 436 | (3.8) | 431 | (4.0) | 435 | (4.1) | 9.0 | (0.7) | 490 | (6.2) | 483 | (5.8) | 487 | (5.8) |
| | Tunisia | 21.1 | (1.1) | 405 | (5.1) | 403 | (5.8) | 387 | (6.5) | 13.1 | (1.3) | 413 | (9.2) | 400 | (11.3) | 406 | (10.6) |
| | Uruguay | 12.9 | (0.6) | 449 | (5.3) | 437 | (7.5) | 452 | (7.4) | 41.7 | (1.0) | 457 | (3.1) | 445 | (4.4) | 458 | (3.1) |

Note: Values that are statistically significant are indicated in bold (see Annex A3).
1. Results based on students' self-reports.
StatLink ᴗᴗ http://dx.doi.org/10.1787/142104560611

Pour consulter la version française intégrale de ce tableau, suivre ce lien :
StatLink ᴗᴗ http://dx.doi.org/10.1787/152684743050

[Part 3/4]

**Table 4.7b** **Percentage of students and performance on the science, reading and mathematics scales, by level of mothers' education[1]**

Tableau 4.7b Pourcentage d'élèves et scores sur les échelles de culture scientifique, de compréhension de l'écrit et de culture mathématique, selon le niveau de formation de la mère

| | Increased likelihood of students whose mothers have not completed upper secondary education scoring in the bottom quarter of the science performance distribution | | Difference in performance between students whose mother completed primary or lower secondary education and students whose mother did not complete primary education | | | | | |
| | | | Science | | Reading | | Mathematics | |
| | Ratio | S.E. | Dif. | S.E. | Dif. | S.E. | Dif. | S.E. |
|---|---|---|---|---|---|---|---|---|
| Australia | 1.5 | (0.06) | c | c | c | c | c | c |
| Austria | 2.3 | (0.22) | c | c | c | c | c | c |
| Belgium | 2.1 | (0.14) | **73** | (7.9) | **84** | (9.8) | **72** | (8.6) |
| Canada | 1.8 | (0.11) | c | c | c | c | c | c |
| Czech Republic | 2.2 | (0.22) | c | c | c | c | c | c |
| Denmark | 2.0 | (0.16) | c | c | c | c | c | c |
| Finland | 1.5 | (0.12) | c | c | c | c | c | c |
| France | 2.0 | (0.16) | **40** | (7.7) | **28** | (8.1) | **38** | (8.3) |
| Germany | 2.6 | (0.17) | **55** | (9.2) | **51** | (11.6) | **44** | (9.0) |
| Greece | 2.1 | (0.15) | c | c | c | c | c | c |
| Hungary | 2.6 | (0.16) | c | c | c | c | c | c |
| Iceland | 1.7 | (0.09) | **31** | (8.8) | **21** | (8.9) | **33** | (9.4) |
| Ireland | 1.7 | (0.12) | c | c | c | c | c | c |
| Italy | 1.6 | (0.09) | c | c | c | c | c | c |
| Japan | 1.9 | (0.16) | c | c | c | c | c | c |
| Korea | 1.6 | (0.11) | c | c | c | c | c | c |
| Luxembourg | 2.4 | (0.14) | **35** | (5.8) | **30** | (5.5) | **28** | (5.9) |
| Mexico | 2.0 | (0.16) | **32** | (3.3) | **38** | (4.8) | **34** | (4.0) |
| Netherlands | 1.6 | (0.12) | **54** | (8.9) | **51** | (10.1) | **52** | (8.3) |
| New Zealand | 1.6 | (0.11) | 18 | (9.8) | **32** | (9.5) | 23 | (9.0) |
| Norway | 1.7 | (0.16) | c | c | c | c | c | c |
| Poland | 2.1 | (0.12) | c | c | c | c | c | c |
| Portugal | 2.1 | (0.20) | **31** | (3.7) | **37** | (4.3) | **30** | (3.9) |
| Slovak Republic | 2.7 | (0.30) | c | c | c | c | c | c |
| Spain | 1.6 | (0.11) | **41** | (4.8) | **35** | (4.7) | **37** | (5.3) |
| Sweden | 1.7 | (0.11) | c | c | c | c | c | c |
| Switzerland | 2.1 | (0.11) | **31** | (7.6) | **25** | (7.8) | **32** | (8.5) |
| Turkey | 2.0 | (0.25) | **22** | (4.2) | **24** | (5.8) | **29** | (6.1) |
| United Kingdom | 1.9 | (0.14) | c | c | c | c | c | c |
| United States | 2.1 | (0.18) | c | c | m | m | c | c |
| **OECD total** | **2.5** | (0.08) | **41** | (2.4) | **44** | (3.0) | **39** | (2.8) |
| **OECD average** | **2.0** | (0.03) | **39** | (2.1) | **38** | (2.3) | **38** | (2.1) |
| Argentina | 2.1 | (0.21) | **40** | (8.1) | 25 | (10.5) | **38** | (8.0) |
| Azerbaijan | 1.4 | (0.14) | c | c | c | c | c | c |
| Brazil | 1.8 | (0.12) | **27** | (4.2) | **24** | (6.3) | **36** | (4.7) |
| Bulgaria | 2.7 | (0.28) | c | c | c | c | c | c |
| Chile | 2.4 | (0.23) | 6 | (5.4) | 7 | (6.5) | 3 | (5.1) |
| Colombia | 1.5 | (0.16) | 10 | (4.8) | 11 | (8.3) | 8 | (6.2) |
| Croatia | 1.7 | (0.13) | c | c | c | c | c | c |
| Estonia | 1.7 | (0.23) | c | c | c | c | c | c |
| Hong Kong-China | 1.7 | (0.13) | 18 | (7.1) | 11 | (6.3) | 13 | (6.6) |
| Indonesia | 1.6 | (0.18) | 9 | (3.6) | 11 | (4.2) | 12 | (4.7) |
| Israel | 1.9 | (0.16) | 22 | (9.3) | **49** | (12.0) | 22 | (10.0) |
| Jordan | 1.8 | (0.13) | **22** | (5.0) | **35** | (5.8) | **29** | (5.1) |
| Kyrgyzstan | 1.6 | (0.18) | c | c | c | c | c | c |
| Latvia | 1.9 | (0.22) | c | c | c | c | c | c |
| Liechtenstein | 2.2 | (0.57) | c | c | c | c | c | c |
| Lithuania | 2.2 | (0.28) | c | c | c | c | c | c |
| Macao-China | 1.1 | (0.09) | 8 | (3.6) | 5 | (3.7) | **12** | (4.0) |
| Montenegro | 1.8 | (0.13) | c | c | c | c | c | c |
| Qatar | 1.1 | (0.06) | 5 | (3.7) | 9 | (5.4) | 5 | (5.1) |
| Romania | 2.2 | (0.31) | c | c | c | c | c | c |
| Russian Federation | 1.7 | (0.27) | c | c | c | c | c | c |
| Serbia | 2.1 | (0.16) | c | c | c | c | c | c |
| Slovenia | 2.0 | (0.10) | c | c | c | c | c | c |
| Chinese Taipei | 1.9 | (0.12) | c | c | c | c | c | c |
| Thailand | 1.8 | (0.20) | 8 | (6.0) | 6 | (8.4) | **12** | (5.5) |
| Tunisia | 1.4 | (0.15) | 6 | (4.0) | **19** | (5.5) | **11** | (4.2) |
| Uruguay | 2.1 | (0.17) | **31** | (5.7) | **31** | (7.4) | **42** | (6.8) |

Note: Values that are statistically significant are indicated in bold (see Annex A3).
1. Results based on students' self-reports.
*StatLink* http://dx.doi.org/10.1787/142104560611

Pour consulter la version française intégrale de ce tableau, suivre ce lien :
*StatLink* http://dx.doi.org/10.1787/152684743050

[Part 4/4]

**Table 4.7b** **Percentage of students and performance on the science, reading and mathematics scales, by level of mothers' education[1]**

Tableau 4.7b   Pourcentage d'élèves et scores sur les échelles de culture scientifique, de compréhension de l'écrit et de culture mathématique, selon le niveau de formation de la mère

| | | Difference in performance between students whose mother completed upper secondary education and students whose mother completed primary or lower secondary education | | | | | | Difference in performance between students whose mother completed tertiary education and students whose mother completed upper secondary education | | | | | |
|---|---|---|---|---|---|---|---|---|---|---|---|---|---|
| | | Science | | Reading | | Mathematics | | Science | | Reading | | Mathematics | |
| | | Dif. | S.E. | Dif. | S.E. | Dif. | S.E. | Dif. | S.E. | Dif. | S.E. | Dif. | S.E. |
| OECD | Australia | 14 | (2.5) | 10 | (2.5) | 11 | (2.3) | 30 | (2.5) | 27 | (2.3) | 24 | (2.2) |
| | Austria | 57 | (9.9) | 48 | (11.5) | 52 | (9.6) | 15 | (4.1) | 18 | (4.6) | 11 | (4.0) |
| | Belgium | 24 | (6.0) | 25 | (6.9) | 28 | (7.8) | 36 | (3.3) | 29 | (3.8) | 33 | (3.4) |
| | Canada | 30 | (4.2) | 29 | (4.7) | 22 | (4.0) | 22 | (2.5) | 23 | (2.6) | 18 | (2.2) |
| | Czech Republic | 62 | (9.6) | 55 | (14.8) | 84 | (8.4) | 22 | (4.7) | 16 | (4.8) | 29 | (5.0) |
| | Denmark | 31 | (5.0) | 26 | (4.7) | 24 | (4.6) | 28 | (3.7) | 22 | (3.5) | 22 | (3.3) |
| | Finland | 5 | (5.0) | 2 | (4.8) | 9 | (4.7) | 27 | (3.4) | 31 | (3.4) | 24 | (2.9) |
| | France | 39 | (5.2) | 36 | (5.5) | 37 | (5.1) | 29 | (4.8) | 22 | (4.9) | 24 | (4.9) |
| | Germany | 60 | (6.2) | 76 | (6.9) | 55 | (6.2) | 12 | (4.3) | 2 | (4.8) | 17 | (4.4) |
| | Greece | 45 | (4.0) | 46 | (5.2) | 42 | (4.1) | 18 | (4.1) | 17 | (4.6) | 22 | (4.3) |
| | Hungary | 57 | (4.3) | 52 | (6.1) | 57 | (5.3) | 46 | (4.0) | 46 | (4.0) | 50 | (4.3) |
| | Iceland | 22 | (4.3) | 13 | (4.0) | 21 | (4.0) | 30 | (3.5) | 34 | (3.7) | 29 | (3.5) |
| | Ireland | 29 | (4.4) | 26 | (4.3) | 31 | (3.8) | 27 | (3.7) | 23 | (3.6) | 22 | (3.5) |
| | Italy | 39 | (2.8) | 40 | (3.1) | 34 | (2.9) | -1 | (3.2) | -4 | (4.1) | 1 | (3.3) |
| | Japan | 42 | (6.6) | 41 | (7.6) | 37 | (5.8) | 40 | (3.6) | 35 | (3.9) | 40 | (3.6) |
| | Korea | 23 | (5.2) | 16 | (4.7) | 25 | (5.2) | 29 | (5.9) | 29 | (5.2) | 36 | (7.0) |
| | Luxembourg | 33 | (4.7) | 34 | (4.6) | 23 | (4.1) | 21 | (4.2) | 20 | (3.8) | 17 | (4.0) |
| | Mexico | 40 | (4.6) | 40 | (5.7) | 44 | (4.3) | -4 | (3.9) | -1 | (4.9) | -7 | (3.9) |
| | Netherlands | 21 | (4.6) | 24 | (4.9) | 14 | (5.0) | 24 | (4.4) | 15 | (4.5) | 24 | (3.7) |
| | New Zealand | 31 | (5.1) | 24 | (4.9) | 19 | (4.7) | 25 | (3.7) | 21 | (3.6) | 22 | (3.3) |
| | Norway | 30 | (7.6) | 28 | (9.0) | 34 | (7.3) | 23 | (3.4) | 15 | (4.0) | 22 | (3.5) |
| | Poland | 48 | (4.3) | 49 | (5.4) | 47 | (4.1) | 61 | (3.7) | 60 | (4.2) | 56 | (3.3) |
| | Portugal | 22 | (4.0) | 23 | (5.0) | 23 | (3.9) | 24 | (4.3) | 24 | (4.6) | 22 | (4.6) |
| | Slovak Republic | 89 | (13.6) | 90 | (18.3) | 103 | (18.0) | 46 | (4.7) | 45 | (4.9) | 42 | (5.3) |
| | Spain | 22 | (3.2) | 20 | (3.2) | 21 | (3.1) | 21 | (4.1) | 15 | (4.5) | 18 | (4.3) |
| | Sweden | 33 | (5.2) | 36 | (5.8) | 29 | (6.2) | 11 | (3.4) | 7 | (3.5) | 14 | (3.3) |
| | Switzerland | 53 | (3.0) | 44 | (3.0) | 47 | (3.0) | 6 | (3.4) | 8 | (3.4) | 4 | (3.2) |
| | Turkey | 44 | (6.4) | 43 | (6.8) | 47 | (7.5) | 31 | (11.5) | 15 | (11.4) | 43 | (11.4) |
| | United Kingdom | 40 | (6.9) | 31 | (5.7) | 21 | (5.3) | 17 | (3.3) | 15 | (3.3) | 13 | (2.9) |
| | United States | 52 | (5.9) | m | m | 46 | (4.6) | 34 | (4.5) | m | m | 30 | (3.5) |
| | **OECD total** | 60 | (1.8) | 58 | (1.4) | 56 | (1.8) | 23 | (1.7) | 14 | (1.3) | 19 | (1.5) |
| | **OECD average** | 38 | (1.1) | 35 | (1.3) | 36 | (1.1) | 25 | (0.8) | 22 | (0.8) | 24 | (0.8) |
| Partners | Argentina | 39 | (8.3) | 42 | (9.8) | 45 | (7.0) | 12 | (6.7) | 8 | (8.9) | 3 | (6.4) |
| | Azerbaijan | 7 | (5.0) | -15 | (7.4) | 1 | (6.9) | 12 | (3.7) | 23 | (4.3) | 0 | (3.0) |
| | Brazil | 48 | (5.0) | 53 | (5.7) | 51 | (5.2) | -5 | (5.9) | -13 | (7.5) | -7 | (6.1) |
| | Bulgaria | 75 | (8.2) | 80 | (10.8) | 63 | (9.8) | 53 | (7.4) | 50 | (7.8) | 50 | (7.0) |
| | Chile | 48 | (4.6) | 44 | (5.5) | 53 | (4.4) | 43 | (5.4) | 48 | (6.2) | 39 | (5.2) |
| | Colombia | 18 | (6.2) | 13 | (6.0) | 33 | (5.6) | 19 | (6.8) | 29 | (8.9) | 11 | (6.7) |
| | Croatia | 31 | (4.0) | 33 | (4.6) | 34 | (4.1) | 14 | (3.0) | 7 | (3.3) | 8 | (2.9) |
| | Estonia | 28 | (8.9) | 35 | (9.8) | 34 | (9.8) | 26 | (3.0) | 22 | (3.4) | 27 | (3.0) |
| | Hong Kong-China | 24 | (3.8) | 21 | (3.7) | 26 | (4.2) | 16 | (8.8) | 6 | (7.9) | 11 | (9.2) |
| | Indonesia | 36 | (5.8) | 38 | (5.9) | 36 | (6.4) | -2 | (9.2) | -10 | (9.7) | -1 | (10.1) |
| | Israel | 35 | (6.7) | 19 | (7.1) | 40 | (8.2) | 39 | (4.4) | 34 | (5.2) | 40 | (4.6) |
| | Jordan | 26 | (3.1) | 23 | (3.6) | 25 | (3.3) | 22 | (4.5) | 17 | (5.1) | 19 | (4.0) |
| | Kyrgyzstan | 19 | (7.9) | 22 | (15.2) | 17 | (9.5) | 21 | (4.2) | 35 | (4.5) | 25 | (3.8) |
| | Latvia | 42 | (10.2) | 38 | (15.4) | 46 | (13.4) | 25 | (3.3) | 24 | (4.5) | 29 | (3.0) |
| | Liechtenstein | 59 | (13.8) | 53 | (12.8) | 46 | (14.2) | 4 | (14.1) | 2 | (13.3) | -1 | (14.1) |
| | Lithuania | c | c | c | c | c | c | 38 | (4.1) | 37 | (4.2) | 44 | (4.1) |
| | Macao-China | 8 | (3.6) | 9 | (3.5) | 9 | (3.9) | 0 | (6.1) | 1 | (7.0) | -13 | (6.6) |
| | Montenegro | 33 | (4.4) | 32 | (4.6) | 38 | (4.6) | 12 | (3.0) | 12 | (3.3) | 15 | (3.5) |
| | Qatar | 12 | (3.1) | 15 | (4.8) | 16 | (3.7) | 12 | (2.3) | 11 | (3.3) | 22 | (2.7) |
| | Romania | 44 | (6.5) | 48 | (7.2) | 42 | (8.1) | 12 | (5.1) | 0 | (6.2) | 10 | (5.1) |
| | Russian Federation | c | c | c | c | c | c | 27 | (3.6) | 27 | (4.0) | 27 | (3.9) |
| | Serbia | 51 | (4.2) | 60 | (4.9) | 56 | (4.9) | 8 | (3.3) | 7 | (3.6) | 6 | (3.5) |
| | Slovenia | 41 | (4.6) | 31 | (4.5) | 34 | (4.2) | 52 | (4.1) | 42 | (3.4) | 49 | (3.6) |
| | Chinese Taipei | 39 | (3.5) | 35 | (3.0) | 41 | (4.2) | 56 | (4.2) | 44 | (4.2) | 50 | (4.9) |
| | Thailand | 26 | (3.7) | 24 | (3.6) | 28 | (4.1) | 54 | (5.2) | 52 | (4.8) | 52 | (5.2) |
| | Tunisia | 28 | (5.8) | 26 | (6.5) | 32 | (6.7) | 8 | (6.8) | -3 | (9.0) | 20 | (8.2) |
| | Uruguay | 44 | (5.9) | 52 | (8.8) | 53 | (7.6) | 8 | (4.5) | 8 | (6.4) | 6 | (6.9) |

Note: Values that are statistically significant are indicated in bold (see Annex A3).
1. Results based on students' self-reports.
*StatLink* http://dx.doi.org/10.1787/142104560611

Pour consulter la version française intégrale de ce tableau, suivre ce lien :
*StatLink* http://dx.doi.org/10.1787/152684743050

[Part 1/4]

**Table 4.7c** **Percentage of students and performance on the science, reading and mathematics scales, by level of fathers' education[1]**

Tableau 4.7c — Pourcentage d'élèves et scores sur les échelles de culture scientifique, de compréhension de l'écrit et de culture mathématique, selon le niveau de formation du père

| | Fathers without completed primary education (ISCED Level 0) | | | | | | | | Fathers with completed primary or lower secondary education (ISCED Levels 1 or 2) | | | | | | | |
| | | | Science | | Reading | | Mathematics | | | | Science | | Reading | | Mathematics | |
| | % of students | S.E. | Mean score | S.E. | Mean score | S.E. | Mean score | S.E. | % of students | S.E. | Mean score | S.E. | Mean score | S.E. | Mean score | S.E. |
|---|---|---|---|---|---|---|---|---|---|---|---|---|---|---|---|---|
| **OECD** | | | | | | | | | | | | | | | | |
| Australia | 2.3 | (0.2) | c | c | c | c | c | c | 20.1 | (0.6) | 505 | (2.7) | 493 | (2.4) | 500 | (2.5) |
| Austria | 1.5 | (0.2) | c | c | c | c | c | c | 6.7 | (0.6) | 457 | (13.7) | 456 | (17.3) | 469 | (12.9) |
| Belgium | 3.5 | (0.3) | 426 | (7.5) | 406 | (9.5) | 437 | (7.3) | 10.5 | (0.4) | 491 | (4.2) | 487 | (4.8) | 505 | (4.2) |
| Canada | 1.1 | (0.1) | c | c | c | c | c | c | 9.0 | (0.4) | 506 | (3.9) | 497 | (4.2) | 505 | (3.3) |
| Czech Republic | 1.0 | (0.2) | c | c | c | c | c | c | 2.6 | (0.3) | c | c | c | c | c | c |
| Denmark | 1.6 | (0.2) | c | c | c | c | c | c | 13.3 | (0.7) | 461 | (4.9) | 463 | (4.9) | 484 | (4.3) |
| Finland | 2.2 | (0.2) | c | c | c | c | c | c | 15.9 | (0.7) | 557 | (3.8) | 537 | (3.4) | 540 | (3.6) |
| France | 4.9 | (0.4) | 428 | (9.8) | 434 | (10.3) | 428 | (9.3) | 21.6 | (0.9) | 476 | (4.5) | 473 | (5.4) | 479 | (4.1) |
| Germany | 3.6 | (0.4) | 421 | (8.2) | 398 | (10.0) | 429 | (10.3) | 17.0 | (0.6) | 473 | (5.4) | 449 | (6.0) | 468 | (4.7) |
| Greece | 1.4 | (0.2) | c | c | c | c | c | c | 29.1 | (1.1) | 437 | (4.2) | 431 | (5.6) | 420 | (4.0) |
| Hungary | 1.1 | (0.2) | c | c | c | c | c | c | 9.9 | (0.7) | 450 | (4.6) | 430 | (7.0) | 432 | (4.9) |
| Iceland | 3.1 | (0.3) | 441 | (8.1) | 444 | (9.2) | 451 | (7.1) | 14.5 | (0.6) | 464 | (4.4) | 459 | (4.5) | 488 | (4.5) |
| Ireland | 1.5 | (0.2) | c | c | c | c | c | c | 24.3 | (0.9) | 484 | (4.7) | 492 | (5.0) | 479 | (3.9) |
| Italy | 1.3 | (0.1) | c | c | c | c | c | c | 39.8 | (0.6) | 456 | (2.5) | 451 | (3.3) | 445 | (2.2) |
| Japan | 0.0 | c | c | c | c | c | c | c | 7.0 | (0.5) | 479 | (6.6) | 446 | (7.6) | 482 | (6.3) |
| Korea | 1.5 | (0.2) | c | c | c | c | c | c | 11.5 | (0.7) | 497 | (5.6) | 531 | (6.4) | 516 | (6.1) |
| Luxembourg | 11.0 | (0.4) | 420 | (4.1) | 419 | (5.0) | 441 | (3.9) | 15.1 | (0.5) | 463 | (3.9) | 452 | (4.1) | 472 | (3.2) |
| Mexico | 16.0 | (0.9) | 372 | (3.8) | 363 | (5.9) | 367 | (5.7) | 45.0 | (1.0) | 398 | (2.9) | 400 | (3.3) | 394 | (3.1) |
| Netherlands | 2.7 | (0.4) | c | c | c | c | c | c | 16.3 | (0.6) | 502 | (4.6) | 488 | (5.3) | 512 | (4.2) |
| New Zealand | 4.1 | (0.3) | 468 | (8.5) | 460 | (8.8) | 469 | (8.1) | 12.2 | (0.6) | 505 | (4.8) | 504 | (4.8) | 502 | (4.3) |
| Norway | 1.3 | (0.2) | c | c | c | c | c | c | 7.1 | (0.4) | 474 | (5.5) | 479 | (5.7) | 478 | (5.6) |
| Poland | 0.4 | (0.1) | c | c | c | c | c | c | 8.2 | (0.5) | 457 | (4.0) | 462 | (4.8) | 454 | (4.2) |
| Portugal | 31.0 | (1.1) | 450 | (3.6) | 444 | (4.7) | 441 | (3.8) | 31.5 | (0.9) | 472 | (3.3) | 473 | (3.8) | 465 | (3.5) |
| Slovak Republic | 1.0 | (0.2) | c | c | c | c | c | c | 3.4 | (0.6) | 395 | (15.3) | 369 | (22.9) | 374 | (20.8) |
| Spain | 9.5 | (0.6) | 449 | (5.0) | 425 | (4.9) | 440 | (4.5) | 37.8 | (1.0) | 476 | (2.5) | 452 | (2.5) | 470 | (2.3) |
| Sweden | 2.5 | (0.3) | c | c | c | c | c | c | 18.4 | (0.7) | 489 | (3.5) | 494 | (3.9) | 486 | (3.3) |
| Switzerland | 3.7 | (0.3) | 441 | (6.0) | 436 | (6.1) | 466 | (6.6) | 22.3 | (0.6) | 474 | (3.7) | 467 | (3.6) | 496 | (3.8) |
| Turkey | 5.5 | (0.5) | 390 | (5.3) | 410 | (8.5) | 387 | (7.6) | 56.9 | (1.5) | 406 | (2.4) | 432 | (3.6) | 403 | (2.6) |
| United Kingdom | 2.4 | (0.2) | c | c | c | c | c | c | 11.7 | (0.5) | 494 | (4.4) | 478 | (4.3) | 483 | (4.0) |
| United States | 2.6 | (0.4) | c | c | m | m | m | m | 9.6 | (0.6) | 433 | (4.7) | m | m | 426 | (4.6) |
| **OECD total** | **4.1** | **(0.1)** | **408** | **(2.6)** | **399** | **(3.6)** | **405** | **(3.4)** | **19.5** | **(0.3)** | **442** | **(1.3)** | **443** | **(1.4)** | **438** | **(1.4)** |
| **OECD average** | **4.2** | **(0.1)** | **428** | **(2.0)** | **422** | **(2.4)** | **432** | **(2.1)** | **18.3** | **(0.1)** | **470** | **(1.0)** | **466** | **(1.3)** | **470** | **(1.1)** |
| **Partners** | | | | | | | | | | | | | | | | |
| Argentina | 13.4 | (0.9) | 336 | (6.3) | 327 | (8.7) | 321 | (7.7) | 33.6 | (1.5) | 382 | (5.7) | 366 | (7.1) | 375 | (5.5) |
| Azerbaijan | 2.6 | (0.3) | c | c | c | c | c | c | 4.5 | (0.5) | 366 | (5.2) | 358 | (7.1) | 471 | (4.3) |
| Brazil | 18.2 | (0.6) | 349 | (3.2) | 347 | (5.6) | 320 | (3.8) | 41.4 | (0.9) | 381 | (3.0) | 384 | (4.3) | 360 | (3.3) |
| Bulgaria | 1.1 | (0.2) | c | c | c | c | c | c | 9.6 | (0.8) | 360 | (9.0) | 320 | (11.7) | 348 | (9.4) |
| Chile | 9.6 | (0.8) | 394 | (5.3) | 396 | (6.3) | 369 | (6.4) | 28.4 | (1.4) | 405 | (3.6) | 408 | (4.7) | 377 | (3.9) |
| Colombia | 18.0 | (1.3) | 367 | (4.6) | 354 | (8.0) | 343 | (7.7) | 34.8 | (1.3) | 372 | (4.2) | 370 | (6.4) | 354 | (4.4) |
| Croatia | 0.6 | (0.1) | c | c | c | c | c | c | 10.0 | (0.5) | 454 | (4.9) | 435 | (5.4) | 428 | (5.3) |
| Estonia | 0.6 | (0.1) | c | c | c | c | c | c | 6.7 | (0.5) | 516 | (5.1) | 486 | (6.6) | 490 | (6.6) |
| Hong Kong-China | 8.6 | (0.4) | 523 | (5.2) | 518 | (4.9) | 528 | (5.6) | 47.0 | (1.3) | 529 | (3.1) | 527 | (3.1) | 534 | (3.2) |
| Indonesia | 10.6 | (0.8) | 369 | (6.0) | 369 | (6.3) | 364 | (6.6) | 48.1 | (2.0) | 381 | (3.9) | 378 | (4.3) | 377 | (3.9) |
| Israel | 3.5 | (0.4) | 405 | (11.2) | 384 | (12.5) | 390 | (10.3) | 8.5 | (0.5) | 414 | (7.3) | 407 | (7.5) | 402 | (8.4) |
| Jordan | 7.8 | (0.7) | 376 | (5.5) | 348 | (7.8) | 335 | (5.4) | 25.1 | (0.8) | 400 | (2.8) | 380 | (3.2) | 362 | (3.5) |
| Kyrgyzstan | 1.7 | (0.2) | c | c | c | c | c | c | 3.1 | (0.4) | 301 | (8.8) | 258 | (8.7) | 279 | (8.7) |
| Latvia | 0.8 | (0.1) | c | c | c | c | c | c | 5.2 | (0.5) | 469 | (8.0) | 453 | (8.7) | 468 | (11.0) |
| Liechtenstein | 2.1 | (0.8) | c | c | c | c | c | c | 24.1 | (2.5) | 483 | (10.7) | 479 | (10.5) | 490 | (11.6) |
| Lithuania | 0.9 | (0.1) | c | c | c | c | c | c | 1.9 | (0.2) | c | c | c | c | c | c |
| Macao-China | 12.1 | (0.6) | 494 | (3.7) | 482 | (4.3) | 507 | (4.3) | 55.0 | (0.9) | 510 | (1.6) | 492 | (1.5) | 524 | (1.8) |
| Montenegro | 1.0 | (0.2) | c | c | c | c | c | c | 5.5 | (0.4) | 372 | (4.8) | 350 | (5.6) | 361 | (5.4) |
| Qatar | 7.9 | (0.3) | 324 | (3.1) | 283 | (4.1) | 280 | (3.9) | 13.1 | (0.4) | 332 | (2.4) | 288 | (3.1) | 298 | (2.7) |
| Romania | 1.4 | (0.3) | c | c | c | c | c | c | 10.1 | (0.8) | 374 | (7.5) | 354 | (10.2) | 373 | (9.5) |
| Russian Federation | 0.2 | (0.1) | c | c | c | c | c | c | 3.5 | (0.3) | 439 | (9.0) | 404 | (11.5) | 447 | (10.6) |
| Serbia | 0.5 | (0.1) | c | c | c | c | c | c | 10.9 | (0.7) | 394 | (4.9) | 351 | (5.7) | 384 | (5.2) |
| Slovenia | 0.8 | (0.2) | c | c | c | c | c | c | 11.5 | (0.5) | 472 | (5.1) | 452 | (6.1) | 463 | (4.8) |
| Chinese Taipei | 1.1 | (0.2) | c | c | c | c | c | c | 29.6 | (1.1) | 501 | (4.6) | 469 | (4.1) | 515 | (5.6) |
| Thailand | 8.5 | (0.7) | 406 | (6.5) | 399 | (9.1) | 399 | (6.0) | 60.9 | (1.1) | 407 | (1.9) | 404 | (2.3) | 402 | (2.2) |
| Tunisia | 10.1 | (0.8) | 363 | (4.3) | 353 | (5.3) | 331 | (4.7) | 41.2 | (1.4) | 373 | (2.5) | 370 | (3.3) | 347 | (3.2) |
| Uruguay | 8.9 | (0.5) | 381 | (5.0) | 355 | (7.1) | 376 | (5.3) | 40.3 | (0.9) | 410 | (3.4) | 396 | (4.6) | 410 | (3.5) |

Note: Values that are statistically significant are indicated in bold (see Annex A3).
1. Results based on students' self-reports.
StatLink ⌦ http://dx.doi.org/10.1787/142104560611

Pour consulter la version française intégrale de ce tableau, suivre ce lien :
StatLink ⌦ http://dx.doi.org/10.1787/152684743050

[Part 2/4]

**Table 4.7c** Percentage of students and performance on the science, reading and mathematics scales, by level of fathers' education[1]

Tableau 4.7c Pourcentage d'élèves et scores sur les échelles de culture scientifique, de compréhension de l'écrit et de culture mathématique, selon le niveau de formation du père

| | Fathers with completed upper secondary education (ISCED Level 3) | | | | | | | | Fathers with completed tertiary education (ISCED Levels 5 or 6) | | | | | | | |
| | | | Performance | | | | | | | | Performance | | | | | |
| | | | Science | | Reading | | Mathematics | | | | Science | | Reading | | Mathematics | |
| | % of students | S.E. | Mean score | S.E. | Mean score | S.E. | Mean score | S.E. | % of students | S.E. | Mean score | S.E. | Mean score | S.E. | Mean score | S.E. |
|---|---|---|---|---|---|---|---|---|---|---|---|---|---|---|---|---|
| **OECD** | | | | | | | | | | | | | | | | |
| Australia | 37.3 | (0.6) | 522 | (2.3) | 508 | (2.2) | 514 | (2.2) | 40.4 | (0.8) | 556 | (2.8) | 541 | (2.5) | 548 | (3.0) |
| Austria | 47.3 | (1.0) | 514 | (3.9) | 492 | (4.0) | 509 | (3.9) | 44.6 | (1.0) | 521 | (3.9) | 499 | (4.1) | 513 | (3.9) |
| Belgium | 40.4 | (0.7) | 510 | (2.9) | 505 | (3.3) | 523 | (3.2) | 45.7 | (0.9) | 537 | (2.7) | 527 | (3.3) | 548 | (3.0) |
| Canada | 37.5 | (0.7) | 532 | (2.3) | 523 | (2.7) | 523 | (2.3) | 52.4 | (0.7) | 550 | (2.2) | 544 | (2.6) | 541 | (2.2) |
| Czech Republic | 72.4 | (0.8) | 512 | (3.4) | 483 | (3.7) | 511 | (3.4) | 24.0 | (0.8) | 537 | (5.1) | 504 | (5.8) | 535 | (5.4) |
| Denmark | 42.3 | (1.0) | 491 | (3.4) | 492 | (3.4) | 510 | (2.8) | 42.9 | (1.3) | 523 | (4.0) | 517 | (4.0) | 535 | (3.6) |
| Finland | 23.0 | (0.6) | 555 | (2.9) | 537 | (3.1) | 542 | (3.0) | 58.9 | (0.9) | 573 | (2.5) | 558 | (2.6) | 558 | (2.6) |
| France | 42.6 | (1.1) | 503 | (3.7) | 495 | (4.9) | 505 | (3.5) | 30.9 | (1.3) | 536 | (5.0) | 522 | (5.0) | 533 | (4.9) |
| Germany | 40.5 | (0.8) | 528 | (3.0) | 518 | (3.6) | 515 | (3.2) | 38.8 | (1.0) | 548 | (3.6) | 525 | (4.2) | 534 | (4.0) |
| Greece | 34.3 | (0.9) | 479 | (3.4) | 468 | (4.3) | 464 | (3.1) | 35.2 | (1.3) | 502 | (3.7) | 480 | (4.7) | 490 | (3.7) |
| Hungary | 65.2 | (1.1) | 499 | (2.7) | 478 | (3.3) | 485 | (2.6) | 23.9 | (1.1) | 550 | (4.4) | 526 | (4.7) | 541 | (5.0) |
| Iceland | 44.9 | (0.9) | 492 | (2.4) | 487 | (2.7) | 503 | (2.5) | 37.5 | (0.7) | 512 | (2.6) | 503 | (2.7) | 526 | (2.6) |
| Ireland | 41.7 | (0.9) | 509 | (3.0) | 520 | (3.4) | 503 | (2.8) | 32.4 | (1.2) | 537 | (4.1) | 545 | (4.1) | 526 | (3.5) |
| Italy | 39.9 | (0.6) | 492 | (2.4) | 484 | (2.8) | 474 | (2.9) | 19.0 | (0.6) | 495 | (3.6) | 487 | (4.1) | 482 | (3.8) |
| Japan | 42.3 | (1.1) | 515 | (4.5) | 483 | (4.6) | 506 | (4.4) | 50.7 | (1.2) | 561 | (3.1) | 528 | (3.6) | 551 | (3.2) |
| Korea | 46.8 | (1.2) | 514 | (3.3) | 549 | (4.2) | 538 | (3.4) | 40.2 | (1.3) | 544 | (4.9) | 574 | (4.5) | 573 | (6.0) |
| Luxembourg | 37.6 | (0.7) | 492 | (2.3) | 485 | (2.4) | 493 | (2.3) | 36.2 | (0.7) | 523 | (2.7) | 516 | (2.6) | 521 | (2.5) |
| Mexico | 9.7 | (0.5) | 435 | (2.6) | 439 | (3.6) | 434 | (2.8) | 29.3 | (0.9) | 441 | (4.0) | 444 | (4.3) | 437 | (3.9) |
| Netherlands | 37.8 | (1.0) | 520 | (3.1) | 505 | (3.3) | 528 | (3.0) | 43.3 | (1.2) | 551 | (3.0) | 530 | (3.5) | 552 | (2.9) |
| New Zealand | 47.8 | (1.0) | 536 | (3.0) | 526 | (3.3) | 524 | (2.6) | 35.9 | (1.0) | 565 | (3.6) | 555 | (3.8) | 556 | (3.4) |
| Norway | 40.5 | (1.0) | 481 | (3.5) | 482 | (4.0) | 485 | (3.5) | 51.1 | (1.1) | 506 | (3.0) | 503 | (3.0) | 507 | (2.6) |
| Poland | 79.9 | (0.8) | 496 | (2.3) | 507 | (2.8) | 495 | (2.4) | 11.5 | (0.7) | 559 | (5.3) | 566 | (5.4) | 548 | (4.7) |
| Portugal | 21.2 | (0.7) | 497 | (4.1) | 496 | (4.8) | 489 | (3.9) | 16.3 | (1.0) | 512 | (4.8) | 514 | (5.2) | 503 | (4.9) |
| Slovak Republic | 75.2 | (1.0) | 483 | (2.7) | 462 | (3.3) | 488 | (2.7) | 20.4 | (0.9) | 535 | (4.7) | 512 | (5.0) | 540 | (5.0) |
| Spain | 25.9 | (0.6) | 496 | (2.9) | 471 | (3.0) | 487 | (2.7) | 26.8 | (0.9) | 522 | (3.4) | 486 | (3.7) | 510 | (3.6) |
| Sweden | 28.2 | (0.8) | 513 | (3.8) | 514 | (4.7) | 509 | (3.6) | 50.9 | (0.9) | 515 | (2.9) | 520 | (3.7) | 514 | (2.9) |
| Switzerland | 29.5 | (0.7) | 519 | (3.0) | 506 | (2.9) | 537 | (3.3) | 44.4 | (0.9) | 537 | (3.8) | 523 | (3.7) | 553 | (3.6) |
| Turkey | 23.0 | (1.0) | 441 | (5.1) | 462 | (5.4) | 445 | (6.3) | 14.6 | (1.2) | 480 | (10.9) | 499 | (9.7) | 487 | (13.6) |
| United Kingdom | 47.7 | (0.9) | 523 | (2.6) | 502 | (2.4) | 500 | (2.4) | 38.2 | (0.9) | 546 | (3.6) | 525 | (3.5) | 521 | (3.3) |
| United States | 43.2 | (1.2) | 481 | (3.8) | m | m | 467 | (3.6) | 44.6 | (1.5) | 520 | (5.3) | m | m | 502 | (4.9) |
| **OECD total** | 39.6 | (0.4) | 498 | (1.4) | 498 | (1.0) | 490 | (1.3) | 36.8 | (0.5) | 527 | (1.7) | 518 | (1.2) | 517 | (1.6) |
| **OECD average** | 41.5 | (0.2) | 503 | (0.6) | 496 | (0.7) | 500 | (0.6) | 36.0 | (0.2) | 530 | (0.8) | 520 | (0.8) | 526 | (0.8) |
| **Partners** | | | | | | | | | | | | | | | | |
| Argentina | 19.9 | (0.9) | 404 | (8.2) | 382 | (10.5) | 398 | (8.4) | 33.1 | (1.7) | 424 | (6.7) | 408 | (8.2) | 410 | (7.5) |
| Azerbaijan | 40.6 | (1.4) | 376 | (3.7) | 341 | (4.2) | 476 | (2.9) | 52.3 | (1.3) | 391 | (3.1) | 365 | (3.4) | 477 | (2.5) |
| Brazil | 13.8 | (0.6) | 424 | (4.5) | 430 | (6.0) | 406 | (4.4) | 26.5 | (0.8) | 422 | (5.4) | 423 | (6.0) | 403 | (6.0) |
| Bulgaria | 64.9 | (1.3) | 431 | (5.1) | 399 | (5.8) | 409 | (4.9) | 24.4 | (1.5) | 483 | (9.1) | 455 | (9.6) | 459 | (9.5) |
| Chile | 38.0 | (1.2) | 447 | (4.4) | 453 | (5.1) | 422 | (4.5) | 24.0 | (1.6) | 489 | (5.2) | 492 | (6.7) | 459 | (5.3) |
| Colombia | 13.0 | (0.8) | 393 | (6.1) | 399 | (8.0) | 378 | (5.9) | 34.1 | (1.2) | 415 | (4.6) | 414 | (6.5) | 399 | (4.9) |
| Croatia | 56.6 | (0.8) | 496 | (2.8) | 481 | (3.2) | 470 | (2.7) | 32.8 | (0.8) | 505 | (3.4) | 487 | (3.5) | 479 | (3.2) |
| Estonia | 57.8 | (0.9) | 529 | (2.9) | 502 | (3.6) | 513 | (2.9) | 34.9 | (0.9) | 543 | (3.4) | 505 | (3.5) | 528 | (3.3) |
| Hong Kong-China | 33.5 | (0.9) | 556 | (3.2) | 546 | (3.2) | 559 | (3.4) | 10.8 | (0.9) | 576 | (7.3) | 565 | (6.8) | 585 | (8.0) |
| Indonesia | 26.8 | (1.9) | 411 | (9.0) | 414 | (8.2) | 410 | (8.8) | 14.4 | (1.1) | 421 | (7.7) | 419 | (8.5) | 421 | (8.8) |
| Israel | 30.8 | (0.7) | 444 | (4.2) | 435 | (5.2) | 433 | (5.1) | 57.2 | (0.9) | 479 | (4.3) | 460 | (5.2) | 466 | (4.7) |
| Jordan | 27.0 | (0.8) | 417 | (3.3) | 399 | (3.5) | 380 | (3.1) | 40.1 | (1.2) | 452 | (3.9) | 430 | (4.5) | 414 | (4.3) |
| Kyrgyzstan | 30.2 | (1.0) | 311 | (3.8) | 264 | (4.8) | 295 | (3.7) | 65.0 | (1.1) | 329 | (2.9) | 295 | (3.6) | 320 | (3.6) |
| Latvia | 61.2 | (1.1) | 488 | (2.9) | 480 | (3.4) | 483 | (3.1) | 32.7 | (1.0) | 502 | (4.7) | 496 | (5.7) | 504 | (4.7) |
| Liechtenstein | 28.5 | (2.3) | 526 | (7.4) | 510 | (8.2) | 528 | (7.6) | 45.3 | (2.6) | 552 | (6.4) | 539 | (6.1) | 552 | (6.2) |
| Lithuania | 59.7 | (1.2) | 477 | (2.7) | 460 | (3.1) | 475 | (3.1) | 37.5 | (1.2) | 513 | (4.1) | 495 | (4.2) | 514 | (4.0) |
| Macao-China | 25.7 | (0.8) | 522 | (2.5) | 499 | (3.2) | 539 | (3.2) | 7.2 | (0.4) | 514 | (5.6) | 497 | (5.8) | 522 | (5.7) |
| Montenegro | 42.3 | (0.8) | 407 | (2.0) | 387 | (2.3) | 394 | (2.4) | 51.1 | (0.8) | 422 | (1.7) | 403 | (1.9) | 410 | (2.0) |
| Qatar | 26.7 | (0.5) | 337 | (2.1) | 303 | (2.7) | 299 | (2.4) | 52.3 | (0.6) | 367 | (1.4) | 333 | (1.8) | 340 | (1.7) |
| Romania | 51.0 | (1.3) | 421 | (4.7) | 400 | (4.7) | 415 | (4.5) | 37.5 | (1.6) | 431 | (5.8) | 405 | (6.3) | 429 | (5.9) |
| Russian Federation | 68.9 | (1.0) | 471 | (3.8) | 433 | (4.3) | 469 | (4.1) | 27.4 | (1.1) | 506 | (4.9) | 463 | (5.8) | 499 | (5.1) |
| Serbia | 49.8 | (0.7) | 438 | (3.2) | 403 | (3.9) | 440 | (3.6) | 38.8 | (0.9) | 448 | (3.4) | 415 | (3.9) | 447 | (4.0) |
| Slovenia | 63.9 | (0.7) | 514 | (1.7) | 490 | (1.4) | 500 | (1.6) | 23.8 | (0.7) | 564 | (3.2) | 536 | (2.6) | 546 | (3.2) |
| Chinese Taipei | 54.8 | (0.9) | 537 | (3.4) | 500 | (3.3) | 556 | (3.8) | 14.5 | (0.6) | 590 | (4.2) | 546 | (4.0) | 606 | (4.9) |
| Thailand | 20.4 | (0.7) | 438 | (3.5) | 434 | (4.1) | 440 | (4.2) | 10.2 | (0.7) | 486 | (6.0) | 477 | (6.7) | 479 | (5.9) |
| Tunisia | 27.2 | (1.0) | 394 | (4.1) | 387 | (4.5) | 374 | (5.2) | 21.5 | (1.6) | 412 | (6.5) | 408 | (8.0) | 409 | (7.8) |
| Uruguay | 10.8 | (0.6) | 448 | (5.1) | 436 | (7.1) | 450 | (7.1) | 40.0 | (1.0) | 457 | (3.4) | 443 | (4.3) | 455 | (3.4) |

Note: Values that are statistically significant are indicated in bold (see Annex A3).
1. Results based on students' self-reports.
StatLink http://dx.doi.org/10.1787/142104560611

Pour consulter la version française intégrale de ce tableau, suivre ce lien :
StatLink http://dx.doi.org/10.1787/152684743050

[Part 3/4]

**Table 4.7c** Percentage of students and performance on the science, reading and mathematics scales, by level of fathers' education[1]

Tableau 4.7c Pourcentage d'élèves et scores sur les échelles de culture scientifique, de compréhension de l'écrit et de culture mathématique, selon le niveau de formation du père

| | Increased likelihood of students whose fathers have not completed upper secondary education scoring in the bottom quarter of the science performance distribution | | Difference in performance between students whose father completed primary or lower secondary education and students whose father did not complete primary education | | | | | |
| | | | Science | | Reading | | Mathematics | |
| | Ratio | S.E. | Dif. | S.E. | Dif. | S.E. | Dif. | S.E. |
|---|---|---|---|---|---|---|---|---|
| **OECD** | | | | | | | | |
| Australia | 1.6 | (0.06) | c | c | c | c | c | c |
| Austria | 2.2 | (0.25) | c | c | c | c | c | c |
| Belgium | 1.8 | (0.10) | **66** | (8.0) | **82** | (10.0) | **68** | (7.8) |
| Canada | 1.7 | (0.08) | c | c | c | c | c | c |
| Czech Republic | 2.1 | (0.23) | c | c | c | c | c | c |
| Denmark | 1.8 | (0.13) | c | c | c | c | c | c |
| Finland | 1.3 | (0.08) | c | c | c | c | c | c |
| France | 1.8 | (0.15) | **49** | (9.5) | **39** | (10.4) | **51** | (9.6) |
| Germany | 2.5 | (0.16) | **51** | (7.6) | **51** | (9.7) | **40** | (9.3) |
| Greece | 2.1 | (0.17) | c | c | c | c | c | c |
| Hungary | 2.3 | (0.16) | c | c | c | c | c | c |
| Iceland | 1.7 | (0.12) | **23** | (8.5) | 15 | (9.0) | **37** | (9.0) |
| Ireland | 1.6 | (0.11) | c | c | c | c | c | c |
| Italy | 1.7 | (0.08) | c | c | c | c | c | c |
| Japan | 2.0 | (0.15) | c | c | c | c | c | c |
| Korea | 1.6 | (0.13) | c | c | c | c | c | c |
| Luxembourg | 2.4 | (0.14) | **43** | (5.8) | **33** | (6.7) | **32** | (5.3) |
| Mexico | 2.1 | (0.18) | **25** | (3.6) | **37** | (5.5) | **26** | (5.3) |
| Netherlands | 1.7 | (0.14) | c | c | c | c | c | c |
| New Zealand | 1.7 | (0.11) | **37** | (10.8) | **44** | (10.3) | **33** | (9.8) |
| Norway | 1.4 | (0.16) | c | c | c | c | c | c |
| Poland | 1.8 | (0.11) | c | c | c | c | c | c |
| Portugal | 1.8 | (0.17) | **22** | (3.4) | **29** | (4.0) | **24** | (3.7) |
| Slovak Republic | 2.8 | (0.33) | c | c | c | c | c | c |
| Spain | 1.6 | (0.12) | **27** | (4.6) | **27** | (4.8) | **30** | (4.5) |
| Sweden | 1.4 | (0.12) | c | c | c | c | c | c |
| Switzerland | 2.0 | (0.11) | **33** | (6.6) | **31** | (6.4) | **30** | (6.8) |
| Turkey | 1.8 | (0.19) | **16** | (5.2) | **21** | (8.2) | **16** | (7.4) |
| United Kingdom | 1.6 | (0.10) | c | c | c | c | c | c |
| United States | 2.0 | (0.14) | c | c | m | m | c | c |
| **OECD total** | **2.4** | **(0.07)** | **34** | **(2.6)** | **44** | **(3.3)** | **33** | **(3.3)** |
| **OECD average** | **1.9** | **(0.03)** | **36** | **(2.1)** | **37** | **(2.4)** | **35** | **(2.2)** |
| **Partners** | | | | | | | | |
| Argentina | 1.8 | (0.17) | **46** | (6.6) | **39** | (9.1) | **54** | (7.0) |
| Azerbaijan | 1.5 | (0.18) | c | c | c | c | c | c |
| Brazil | 1.8 | (0.12) | **32** | (3.8) | **37** | (5.4) | **40** | (4.1) |
| Bulgaria | 2.4 | (0.23) | c | c | c | c | c | c |
| Chile | 2.2 | (0.19) | **11** | (5.2) | **13** | (5.8) | 9 | (5.1) |
| Colombia | 1.7 | (0.18) | 5 | (4.2) | **16** | (7.8) | 12 | (5.8) |
| Croatia | 1.8 | (0.13) | c | c | c | c | c | c |
| Estonia | 1.1 | (0.14) | c | c | c | c | c | c |
| Hong Kong-China | 1.7 | (0.14) | 7 | (5.9) | 9 | (5.1) | 6 | (6.2) |
| Indonesia | 1.7 | (0.19) | **12** | (3.9) | **10** | (4.3) | **14** | (5.0) |
| Israel | 1.7 | (0.16) | 9 | (12.2) | **23** | (14.0) | 12 | (12.1) |
| Jordan | 1.7 | (0.11) | **24** | (5.6) | **32** | (8.0) | **27** | (5.2) |
| Kyrgyzstan | 1.6 | (0.16) | c | c | c | c | c | c |
| Latvia | 1.6 | (0.19) | c | c | c | c | c | c |
| Liechtenstein | 2.3 | (0.51) | c | c | c | c | c | c |
| Lithuania | 1.4 | (0.19) | c | c | c | c | c | c |
| Macao-China | 1.2 | (0.08) | **16** | (4.3) | **10** | (4.3) | **17** | (4.8) |
| Montenegro | 1.8 | (0.18) | c | c | c | c | c | c |
| Qatar | 1.2 | (0.08) | **8** | (4.2) | 5 | (5.5) | **18** | (5.4) |
| Romania | 2.0 | (0.26) | c | c | c | c | c | c |
| Russian Federation | 1.7 | (0.20) | c | c | c | c | c | c |
| Serbia | 1.9 | (0.13) | c | c | c | c | c | c |
| Slovenia | 1.9 | (0.16) | c | c | c | c | c | c |
| Chinese Taipei | 1.9 | (0.13) | c | c | c | c | c | c |
| Thailand | 1.8 | (0.20) | 1 | (6.6) | 4 | (9.0) | 3 | (6.5) |
| Tunisia | 1.4 | (0.11) | **10** | (4.5) | **17** | (5.1) | **16** | (5.1) |
| Uruguay | 2.1 | (0.16) | **29** | (5.5) | **41** | (7.5) | **34** | (6.2) |

Note: Values that are statistically significant are indicated in bold (see Annex A3).
1. Results based on students' self-reports.
*StatLink* http://dx.doi.org/10.1787/142104560611

Pour consulter la version française intégrale de ce tableau, suivre ce lien :
*StatLink* http://dx.doi.org/10.1787/152684743050

[Part 4/4]

**Table 4.7c** Percentage of students and performance on the science, reading and mathematics scales, by level of fathers' education[1]

Tableau 4.7c Pourcentage d'élèves et scores sur les échelles de culture scientifique, de compréhension de l'écrit et de culture mathématique, selon le niveau de formation du père

| | Difference in performance between students whose father completed upper secondary education and students whose father completed primary or lower secondary education | | | | | | Difference in performance between students whose father completed tertiary education and students whose father completed upper secondary education | | | | | |
| | Science | | Reading | | Mathematics | | Science | | Reading | | Mathematics | |
| | Dif. | S.E. | Dif. | S.E. | Dif. | S.E. | Dif. | S.E. | Dif. | S.E. | Dif. | S.E. |
|---|---|---|---|---|---|---|---|---|---|---|---|---|
| **OECD** | | | | | | | | | | | | |
| Australia | 17 | (2.9) | 15 | (2.7) | 14 | (2.7) | 34 | (2.9) | 33 | (2.8) | 34 | (2.9) |
| Austria | 57 | (12.8) | 37 | (16.1) | 40 | (12.4) | 7 | (3.1) | 6 | (3.9) | 4 | (3.7) |
| Belgium | 19 | (4.7) | 17 | (4.9) | 18 | (4.4) | 27 | (2.9) | 22 | (3.2) | 26 | (2.9) |
| Canada | 26 | (4.0) | 26 | (4.2) | 18 | (3.4) | 18 | (2.5) | 21 | (2.7) | 18 | (2.4) |
| Czech Republic | c | c | c | c | c | c | 25 | (4.4) | 21 | (4.5) | 24 | (4.6) |
| Denmark | 31 | (5.4) | 29 | (5.1) | 26 | (4.9) | 31 | (4.5) | 25 | (4.6) | 25 | (3.9) |
| Finland | -2 | (4.5) | 0 | (3.9) | 3 | (4.0) | 18 | (3.5) | 21 | (3.6) | 16 | (3.1) |
| France | 27 | (4.9) | 22 | (5.2) | 26 | (4.7) | 33 | (5.5) | 27 | (5.4) | 28 | (5.3) |
| Germany | 55 | (4.9) | 69 | (5.4) | 47 | (4.4) | 20 | (3.3) | 7 | (3.8) | 19 | (3.3) |
| Greece | 42 | (3.9) | 37 | (5.3) | 44 | (4.1) | 23 | (3.8) | 12 | (5.1) | 26 | (3.9) |
| Hungary | 49 | (4.9) | 48 | (7.3) | 53 | (5.1) | 51 | (4.6) | 48 | (4.7) | 56 | (4.8) |
| Iceland | 28 | (5.1) | 28 | (5.0) | 15 | (5.1) | 20 | (3.3) | 17 | (3.4) | 23 | (3.0) |
| Ireland | 25 | (4.1) | 28 | (4.5) | 25 | (3.4) | 28 | (4.1) | 25 | (3.6) | 22 | (3.8) |
| Italy | 36 | (2.8) | 32 | (3.0) | 29 | (2.5) | 3 | (3.5) | 3 | (4.3) | 7 | (3.7) |
| Japan | 36 | (5.9) | 37 | (6.6) | 24 | (5.4) | 46 | (4.2) | 45 | (4.7) | 45 | (4.4) |
| Korea | 17 | (5.4) | 18 | (5.1) | 22 | (5.4) | 30 | (5.2) | 25 | (4.9) | 35 | (6.2) |
| Luxembourg | 29 | (4.6) | 33 | (4.8) | 21 | (3.9) | 31 | (3.9) | 30 | (3.6) | 28 | (3.6) |
| Mexico | 37 | (3.7) | 39 | (5.0) | 40 | (3.8) | 6 | (3.8) | 5 | (4.3) | 3 | (3.5) |
| Netherlands | 18 | (5.2) | 17 | (5.6) | 16 | (4.5) | 31 | (3.5) | 25 | (4.2) | 24 | (3.4) |
| New Zealand | 31 | (5.2) | 22 | (4.7) | 22 | (4.6) | 29 | (3.5) | 29 | (3.4) | 32 | (3.3) |
| Norway | 8 | (5.8) | 3 | (6.6) | 7 | (5.6) | 25 | (3.7) | 21 | (3.9) | 22 | (3.6) |
| Poland | 39 | (3.8) | 44 | (4.7) | 40 | (3.8) | 63 | (5.2) | 60 | (4.9) | 53 | (4.4) |
| Portugal | 25 | (4.3) | 23 | (4.8) | 25 | (4.0) | 16 | (4.6) | 18 | (5.0) | 14 | (4.7) |
| Slovak Republic | 88 | (15.9) | 92 | (23.4) | 114 | (21.4) | 52 | (4.6) | 50 | (5.2) | 52 | (4.7) |
| Spain | 19 | (3.1) | 19 | (3.3) | 17 | (3.1) | 26 | (3.2) | 15 | (4.1) | 23 | (3.1) |
| Sweden | 24 | (5.5) | 20 | (5.1) | 23 | (4.8) | 2 | (3.6) | 7 | (3.9) | 5 | (3.5) |
| Switzerland | 45 | (3.4) | 39 | (3.4) | 41 | (3.8) | 18 | (3.5) | 17 | (3.0) | 16 | (3.5) |
| Turkey | 35 | (4.8) | 30 | (4.9) | 42 | (5.3) | 39 | (8.7) | 37 | (7.9) | 42 | (10.6) |
| United Kingdom | 29 | (4.2) | 23 | (4.0) | 17 | (3.5) | 24 | (4.4) | 23 | (3.9) | 21 | (3.9) |
| United States | c | c | m | m | c | c | 38 | (4.6) | m | m | 35 | (3.8) |
| **OECD total** | **56** | (1.9) | **55** | (1.6) | **52** | (1.8) | **29** | (1.6) | **20** | (1.4) | **27** | (1.4) |
| **OECD average** | **32** | (1.1) | **30** | (1.4) | **30** | (1.2) | **27** | (0.8) | **24** | (0.8) | **26** | (0.8) |
| **Partners** | | | | | | | | | | | | |
| Argentina | 22 | (6.9) | 16 | (10.1) | 23 | (6.6) | 20 | (7.5) | 27 | (9.4) | 12 | (7.7) |
| Azerbaijan | 10 | (5.7) | -17 | (6.3) | 5 | (4.5) | 14 | (3.7) | 25 | (4.2) | 1 | (2.7) |
| Brazil | 43 | (4.6) | 46 | (4.9) | 46 | (4.6) | -2 | (5.6) | -7 | (6.8) | -3 | (6.3) |
| Bulgaria | 71 | (8.4) | 79 | (10.5) | 61 | (8.9) | 52 | (7.5) | 56 | (8.6) | 49 | (7.6) |
| Chile | 42 | (4.3) | 44 | (5.4) | 44 | (4.2) | 42 | (5.3) | 40 | (6.4) | 38 | (5.4) |
| Colombia | 21 | (5.8) | 29 | (9.1) | 23 | (6.3) | 22 | (5.3) | 15 | (7.5) | 21 | (6.3) |
| Croatia | 42 | (4.4) | 46 | (4.6) | 42 | (4.9) | 9 | (3.6) | 5 | (3.7) | 9 | (3.5) |
| Estonia | 13 | (4.4) | 16 | (5.7) | 23 | (5.8) | 14 | (3.9) | 3 | (4.1) | 15 | (3.4) |
| Hong Kong-China | 26 | (4.1) | 19 | (3.9) | 25 | (4.2) | 21 | (7.4) | 19 | (7.0) | 26 | (7.8) |
| Indonesia | 31 | (6.9) | 36 | (5.9) | 33 | (7.2) | 10 | (8.4) | 5 | (7.8) | 11 | (8.7) |
| Israel | 30 | (7.3) | 29 | (7.3) | 32 | (7.7) | 35 | (4.3) | 24 | (4.7) | 32 | (4.0) |
| Jordan | 17 | (3.7) | 18 | (3.9) | 17 | (3.5) | 35 | (4.3) | 31 | (4.6) | 34 | (3.9) |
| Kyrgyzstan | 10 | (8.3) | 6 | (8.2) | 15 | (8.9) | 18 | (3.9) | 31 | (5.0) | 26 | (3.7) |
| Latvia | 19 | (8.1) | 27 | (9.4) | 15 | (11.5) | 14 | (4.6) | 16 | (5.3) | 21 | (4.6) |
| Liechtenstein | 43 | (13.5) | 31 | (14.6) | 38 | (14.0) | 26 | (9.6) | 28 | (9.7) | 24 | (9.2) |
| Lithuania | c | c | c | c | c | c | 36 | (4.0) | 35 | (4.1) | 39 | (3.7) |
| Macao-China | 13 | (3.1) | 7 | (3.7) | 15 | (3.5) | -9 | (6.1) | -2 | (6.8) | -17 | (6.9) |
| Montenegro | 35 | (5.1) | 37 | (6.1) | 33 | (5.7) | 14 | (2.9) | 16 | (3.2) | 16 | (3.2) |
| Qatar | 5 | (3.1) | 15 | (4.1) | 1 | (3.8) | 29 | (2.7) | 30 | (3.4) | 41 | (3.0) |
| Romania | 47 | (7.0) | 46 | (9.1) | 42 | (8.9) | 10 | (5.4) | 5 | (5.4) | 13 | (5.5) |
| Russian Federation | 32 | (8.5) | 29 | (10.6) | 22 | (10.6) | 35 | (4.8) | 30 | (4.9) | 30 | (5.0) |
| Serbia | 44 | (4.8) | 52 | (5.8) | 56 | (4.9) | 10 | (3.0) | 12 | (3.5) | 7 | (3.3) |
| Slovenia | 42 | (5.9) | 38 | (6.6) | 38 | (5.5) | 50 | (3.8) | 47 | (3.3) | 46 | (3.7) |
| Chinese Taipei | 35 | (4.3) | 32 | (3.5) | 42 | (5.4) | 54 | (4.2) | 46 | (3.7) | 50 | (4.8) |
| Thailand | 31 | (3.4) | 30 | (3.7) | 38 | (4.1) | 48 | (5.3) | 43 | (5.9) | 38 | (5.4) |
| Tunisia | 21 | (4.5) | 17 | (5.3) | 27 | (5.4) | 18 | (5.1) | 21 | (6.3) | 35 | (6.1) |
| Uruguay | 38 | (5.1) | 39 | (7.7) | 40 | (7.5) | 9 | (5.3) | 7 | (6.8) | 5 | (6.8) |

Note: Values that are statistically significant are indicated in bold (see Annex A3).
1. Results based on students' self-reports.
*StatLink* http://dx.doi.org/10.1787/142104560611

Pour consulter la version française intégrale de ce tableau, suivre ce lien :
*StatLink* http://dx.doi.org/10.1787/152684743050

[Part 1/2]

**Table 4.8a** **Percentage of students and performance on the science, reading and mathematics scales, by occupational status of parents[1]**

Tableau 4.8a Pourcentage d'élèves et scores sur les échelles de culture scientifique, de compréhension de l'écrit et de culture mathématique, selon le type de profession exercée par les parents

| | Blue-collar low-skill parents | | | | | | | | White-collar high-skill parents | | | | | | | |
| | | | Performance | | | | | | | | Performance | | | | | |
| | | | Science | | Reading | | Mathematics | | | | Science | | Reading | | Mathematics | |
| | % of students | S.E. | Mean score | S.E. | Mean score | S.E. | Mean score | S.E. | % of students | S.E. | Mean score | S.E. | Mean score | S.E. | Mean score | S.E. |
|---|---|---|---|---|---|---|---|---|---|---|---|---|---|---|---|---|
| Australia | 6.2 | (0.3) | 473 | (3.8) | 464 | (3.6) | 472 | (3.5) | 66.3 | (0.7) | 547 | (2.2) | 532 | (2.0) | 537 | (2.2) |
| Austria | 7.3 | (0.5) | 444 | (7.8) | 423 | (8.9) | 440 | (8.0) | 51.0 | (1.1) | 541 | (3.5) | 523 | (3.8) | 534 | (3.7) |
| Belgium | 9.0 | (0.4) | 453 | (4.6) | 441 | (5.9) | 461 | (4.9) | 55.2 | (1.0) | 545 | (2.4) | 536 | (2.7) | 556 | (2.8) |
| Canada | 5.6 | (0.3) | 492 | (4.3) | 488 | (5.2) | 493 | (4.6) | 66.6 | (0.7) | 552 | (2.0) | 545 | (2.3) | 542 | (2.1) |
| Czech Republic | 6.9 | (0.5) | 460 | (6.2) | 431 | (7.5) | 450 | (6.7) | 57.9 | (1.1) | 544 | (4.1) | 516 | (4.2) | 542 | (4.1) |
| Denmark | 6.6 | (0.5) | 448 | (5.6) | 453 | (5.5) | 471 | (5.9) | 59.4 | (1.4) | 520 | (3.3) | 515 | (3.5) | 533 | (2.9) |
| Finland | 5.2 | (0.4) | 526 | (6.0) | 510 | (5.6) | 511 | (5.7) | 56.5 | (1.0) | 579 | (2.4) | 562 | (2.5) | 564 | (2.7) |
| France | 6.9 | (0.5) | 433 | (6.7) | 430 | (6.7) | 439 | (6.1) | 51.8 | (1.5) | 538 | (3.3) | 528 | (3.8) | 534 | (3.5) |
| Germany | 8.1 | (0.5) | 454 | (6.2) | 430 | (7.7) | 443 | (6.0) | 51.9 | (1.2) | 553 | (3.0) | 534 | (3.6) | 542 | (3.3) |
| Greece | 10.6 | (0.6) | 434 | (5.3) | 418 | (7.3) | 419 | (4.9) | 54.0 | (1.3) | 499 | (3.2) | 487 | (3.7) | 485 | (3.3) |
| Hungary | 7.0 | (0.5) | 458 | (6.0) | 436 | (6.9) | 445 | (5.8) | 44.5 | (1.2) | 536 | (3.5) | 517 | (3.8) | 526 | (3.8) |
| Iceland | 2.8 | (0.2) | c | c | c | c | c | c | 69.9 | (0.7) | 505 | (2.0) | 497 | (2.3) | 519 | (2.0) |
| Ireland | 6.4 | (0.4) | 470 | (8.2) | 482 | (7.9) | 467 | (6.8) | 56.1 | (1.3) | 531 | (3.1) | 540 | (3.3) | 522 | (2.9) |
| Italy | 13.1 | (0.5) | 446 | (3.4) | 439 | (3.6) | 434 | (3.7) | 48.0 | (0.7) | 497 | (2.7) | 490 | (2.9) | 482 | (2.9) |
| Japan | 3.4 | (0.3) | 496 | (8.2) | 462 | (8.8) | 489 | (7.6) | 41.4 | (0.9) | 553 | (3.7) | 522 | (3.9) | 545 | (3.8) |
| Korea | 5.0 | (0.3) | 508 | (7.5) | 544 | (7.1) | 530 | (8.0) | 67.7 | (1.0) | 530 | (3.7) | 563 | (4.0) | 556 | (4.2) |
| Luxembourg | 10.4 | (0.4) | 428 | (3.7) | 423 | (4.4) | 437 | (3.8) | 46.9 | (0.7) | 527 | (1.8) | 523 | (2.0) | 528 | (1.9) |
| Mexico | 21.0 | (0.7) | 393 | (2.8) | 394 | (2.9) | 389 | (3.5) | 32.9 | (1.1) | 445 | (3.4) | 449 | (3.6) | 441 | (3.5) |
| Netherlands | 6.4 | (0.4) | 456 | (7.5) | 443 | (9.0) | 472 | (8.0) | 66.6 | (1.1) | 549 | (2.2) | 530 | (2.4) | 552 | (2.3) |
| New Zealand | 5.4 | (0.5) | 462 | (7.0) | 454 | (8.4) | 468 | (6.1) | 64.6 | (0.9) | 558 | (2.8) | 547 | (2.9) | 544 | (2.6) |
| Norway | 3.1 | (0.3) | 439 | (9.8) | 427 | (11.3) | 441 | (9.3) | 73.8 | (1.0) | 503 | (2.6) | 502 | (2.7) | 504 | (2.5) |
| Poland | 5.3 | (0.3) | 468 | (6.3) | 478 | (6.6) | 466 | (6.0) | 44.3 | (1.1) | 528 | (2.7) | 540 | (3.4) | 524 | (2.8) |
| Portugal | 12.6 | (0.6) | 438 | (5.3) | 428 | (7.2) | 429 | (5.8) | 26.9 | (1.2) | 526 | (3.3) | 529 | (3.9) | 519 | (3.4) |
| Slovak Republic | 9.6 | (0.6) | 439 | (5.9) | 421 | (8.2) | 441 | (7.6) | 47.3 | (1.2) | 526 | (3.3) | 504 | (3.9) | 528 | (3.4) |
| Spain | 10.4 | (0.5) | 463 | (3.3) | 440 | (4.0) | 454 | (3.6) | 40.0 | (1.2) | 522 | (2.8) | 490 | (2.5) | 511 | (2.8) |
| Sweden | 5.1 | (0.4) | 461 | (6.7) | 461 | (8.5) | 464 | (7.8) | 65.7 | (0.8) | 524 | (2.5) | 528 | (3.5) | 522 | (2.4) |
| Switzerland | 5.7 | (0.3) | 453 | (6.5) | 452 | (5.8) | 477 | (6.5) | 58.2 | (1.0) | 540 | (3.2) | 526 | (3.0) | 555 | (3.2) |
| Turkey | 12.8 | (0.6) | 402 | (4.1) | 428 | (4.9) | 399 | (4.1) | 36.1 | (1.4) | 449 | (6.8) | 474 | (6.2) | 454 | (8.6) |
| United Kingdom | 5.3 | (0.4) | 450 | (5.1) | 442 | (5.3) | 440 | (4.2) | 62.0 | (0.8) | 542 | (2.6) | 521 | (2.5) | 518 | (2.5) |
| United States | 6.5 | (0.5) | 429 | (6.9) | m | m | 427 | (6.7) | 64.8 | (1.4) | 516 | (4.0) | m | m | 497 | (3.8) |
| **OECD total** | 8.3 | (0.2) | 433 | (2.0) | 431 | (1.5) | 430 | (2.1) | 53.6 | (0.4) | 523 | (1.3) | 518 | (0.9) | 513 | (1.2) |
| **OECD average** | 7.7 | (0.1) | 454 | (1.1) | 448 | (1.3) | 454 | (1.1) | 54.3 | (0.2) | 527 | (0.6) | 520 | (0.6) | 524 | (0.6) |
| Argentina | 11.7 | (0.9) | 361 | (8.8) | 345 | (10.2) | 355 | (9.1) | 41.6 | (2.2) | 431 | (7.1) | 418 | (8.8) | 420 | (6.8) |
| Azerbaijan | 14.1 | (1.1) | 375 | (4.6) | 339 | (4.1) | 475 | (3.6) | 56.9 | (1.4) | 392 | (2.8) | 368 | (3.7) | 478 | (2.3) |
| Brazil | 32.7 | (1.1) | 362 | (3.4) | 362 | (6.3) | 339 | (4.4) | 43.1 | (1.1) | 425 | (4.0) | 428 | (4.7) | 404 | (4.4) |
| Bulgaria | 12.6 | (0.8) | 385 | (6.9) | 348 | (9.5) | 368 | (6.6) | 47.8 | (1.9) | 482 | (6.5) | 454 | (6.6) | 457 | (6.9) |
| Chile | 24.6 | (1.3) | 402 | (4.5) | 405 | (5.9) | 375 | (5.5) | 30.2 | (1.7) | 493 | (4.5) | 499 | (6.2) | 466 | (4.7) |
| Colombia | 20.1 | (1.2) | 369 | (4.9) | 365 | (7.0) | 350 | (4.2) | 39.7 | (1.6) | 411 | (3.8) | 412 | (5.0) | 395 | (4.7) |
| Croatia | 6.8 | (0.4) | 453 | (6.3) | 442 | (6.5) | 428 | (6.6) | 41.7 | (0.9) | 525 | (2.9) | 508 | (2.9) | 497 | (3.0) |
| Estonia | 8.7 | (0.6) | 494 | (5.9) | 456 | (6.1) | 476 | (6.0) | 55.5 | (1.1) | 554 | (2.8) | 523 | (2.8) | 538 | (2.8) |
| Hong Kong-China | 15.7 | (0.7) | 518 | (4.5) | 516 | (4.3) | 524 | (4.9) | 35.3 | (1.4) | 563 | (3.9) | 554 | (3.5) | 569 | (4.3) |
| Indonesia | 25.6 | (1.6) | 385 | (4.5) | 383 | (4.6) | 381 | (4.7) | 26.2 | (1.4) | 415 | (8.6) | 418 | (8.3) | 418 | (8.5) |
| Israel | 6.5 | (0.5) | 409 | (7.7) | 394 | (8.2) | 396 | (9.0) | 72.7 | (1.0) | 481 | (3.8) | 468 | (4.5) | 470 | (3.9) |
| Jordan | 14.4 | (0.6) | 398 | (4.4) | 380 | (4.8) | 363 | (4.4) | 65.4 | (1.2) | 449 | (3.5) | 429 | (4.0) | 411 | (3.9) |
| Kyrgyzstan | 10.9 | (0.6) | 295 | (5.3) | 255 | (5.3) | 287 | (4.8) | 45.6 | (1.1) | 343 | (3.6) | 313 | (4.4) | 335 | (4.3) |
| Latvia | 7.1 | (0.6) | 464 | (8.1) | 450 | (7.7) | 460 | (6.1) | 52.8 | (1.3) | 513 | (3.2) | 504 | (3.8) | 509 | (3.4) |
| Liechtenstein | 8.1 | (1.3) | 436 | (20.1) | 429 | (19.2) | 450 | (19.3) | 65.0 | (2.5) | 543 | (5.6) | 529 | (5.1) | 543 | (6.0) |
| Lithuania | 11.2 | (0.5) | 449 | (5.7) | 429 | (5.5) | 446 | (6.1) | 51.5 | (1.3) | 516 | (3.5) | 499 | (3.8) | 517 | (3.5) |
| Macao-China | 18.9 | (0.6) | 503 | (2.5) | 486 | (2.9) | 518 | (2.7) | 33.3 | (0.8) | 519 | (2.0) | 499 | (2.2) | 535 | (2.2) |
| Montenegro | 11.6 | (0.5) | 386 | (3.5) | 366 | (4.0) | 372 | (3.8) | 49.2 | (0.8) | 436 | (1.9) | 419 | (2.1) | 425 | (2.3) |
| Qatar | m | m | m | m | m | m | m | m | m | m | m | m | m | m | m | m |
| Romania | 24.6 | (0.9) | 388 | (6.1) | 365 | (6.5) | 384 | (5.7) | 29.7 | (1.6) | 461 | (6.2) | 438 | (6.2) | 460 | (6.3) |
| Russian Federation | 9.9 | (0.7) | 447 | (6.0) | 405 | (6.9) | 444 | (6.5) | 54.6 | (1.4) | 498 | (3.9) | 458 | (4.8) | 494 | (4.2) |
| Serbia | 8.7 | (0.6) | 394 | (5.2) | 353 | (5.7) | 391 | (5.1) | 48.0 | (1.3) | 465 | (2.8) | 433 | (3.1) | 466 | (3.3) |
| Slovenia | 7.6 | (0.4) | 478 | (4.6) | 460 | (4.7) | 469 | (5.0) | 50.3 | (0.6) | 552 | (1.9) | 523 | (1.7) | 535 | (1.9) |
| Chinese Taipei | 10.2 | (0.5) | 506 | (5.4) | 471 | (4.8) | 522 | (5.9) | 55.1 | (1.0) | 554 | (3.1) | 517 | (2.9) | 572 | (3.5) |
| Thailand | 15.7 | (0.9) | 403 | (3.5) | 401 | (3.4) | 399 | (4.3) | 29.2 | (1.0) | 460 | (3.9) | 456 | (3.9) | 456 | (4.2) |
| Tunisia | 37.3 | (1.9) | 363 | (2.5) | 356 | (3.5) | 334 | (3.2) | 33.6 | (2.3) | 419 | (5.7) | 419 | (6.6) | 414 | (6.5) |
| Uruguay | 17.0 | (0.7) | 390 | (4.1) | 369 | (7.3) | 389 | (4.8) | 38.6 | (1.1) | 466 | (3.1) | 455 | (4.6) | 466 | (3.4) |

Note: Values that are statistically significant are indicated in bold (see Annex A3).
1. Results based on students' self-reports.
StatLink ⌐⌐⌐ http://dx.doi.org/10.1787/142104560611

Pour consulter la version française intégrale de ce tableau, suivre ce lien :
StatLink ⌐⌐⌐ http://dx.doi.org/10.1787/152684743050

[Part 2/2]

**Table 4.8a** Percentage of students and performance on the science, reading and mathematics scales, by occupational status of parents[1]

Tableau 4.8a Pourcentage d'élèves et scores sur les échelles de culture scientifique, de compréhension de l'écrit et de culture mathématique, selon le type de profession exercée par les parents

| | Increased likelihood of students, with blue-collar low-skill parents, scoring in the bottom quarter of the science performance distribution | | Difference in science performance between students with white-collar high-skill parents and students with blue-collar low-skill parents | | | | | |
| | | | PISA 2006 | | PISA 2003 | | PISA 2000 | |
| | Ratio | S.E. | Dif. | S.E. | Dif. | S.E. | Dif. | S.E. |
|---|---|---|---|---|---|---|---|---|
| Australia | 2.0 | (0.10) | 74 | (4.0) | 74 | (6.0) | 68 | (10.7) |
| Austria | 2.3 | (0.16) | 97 | (8.0) | 82 | (5.9) | 79 | (9.6) |
| Belgium | 2.3 | (0.12) | 92 | (4.9) | 98 | (6.4) | 104 | (11.2) |
| Canada | 1.8 | (0.13) | 60 | (4.5) | 65 | (5.1) | 72 | (5.1) |
| Czech Republic | 1.9 | (0.20) | 83 | (7.0) | 70 | (8.1) | 79 | (7.5) |
| Denmark | 1.9 | (0.16) | 72 | (6.3) | 65 | (9.7) | 85 | (9.0) |
| Finland | 1.7 | (0.16) | 53 | (6.4) | 43 | (7.5) | 50 | (11.1) |
| France | 2.2 | (0.19) | 105 | (8.1) | 96 | (9.4) | 95 | (7.6) |
| Germany | 2.2 | (0.17) | 99 | (6.3) | 112 | (7.9) | 114 | (11.2) |
| Greece | 1.9 | (0.14) | 65 | (5.9) | 56 | (8.0) | 59 | (8.4) |
| Hungary | 1.9 | (0.19) | 78 | (6.7) | 70 | (8.9) | 105 | (10.2) |
| Iceland | c | c | c | c | c | c | 22 | (10.1) |
| Ireland | 1.7 | (0.16) | 60 | (7.9) | 75 | (8.0) | 72 | (7.5) |
| Italy | 1.5 | (0.08) | 51 | (3.9) | 63 | (5.6) | 41 | (6.8) |
| Japan | 1.6 | (0.19) | 57 | (8.7) | 64 | (11.2) | 16 | (8.6) |
| Korea | 1.3 | (0.16) | 22 | (6.9) | 37 | (6.6) | 35 | (6.7) |
| Luxembourg | 2.1 | (0.14) | 100 | (4.2) | 96 | (5.9) | m | m |
| Mexico | 1.3 | (0.08) | 52 | (3.8) | 34 | (3.8) | 45 | (6.8) |
| Netherlands | 2.4 | (0.20) | 93 | (7.8) | 87 | (8.9) | m | m |
| New Zealand | 2.2 | (0.17) | 96 | (7.1) | 72 | (7.8) | 97 | (11.6) |
| Norway | 1.9 | (0.18) | 64 | (9.6) | c | c | 73 | (10.1) |
| Poland | 1.5 | (0.16) | 60 | (6.7) | 67 | (6.7) | 66 | (11.2) |
| Portugal | 1.7 | (0.14) | 87 | (6.3) | 78 | (6.9) | 54 | (7.0) |
| Slovak Republic | 2.0 | (0.18) | 87 | (7.1) | 83 | (7.8) | a | a |
| Spain | 1.5 | (0.10) | 59 | (4.2) | 57 | (5.8) | 57 | (7.4) |
| Sweden | 1.8 | (0.19) | 63 | (7.0) | 74 | (10.7) | 51 | (8.9) |
| Switzerland | 2.0 | (0.13) | 88 | (6.7) | 95 | (8.6) | 113 | (9.8) |
| Turkey | 1.3 | (0.11) | 48 | (7.7) | 56 | (10.1) | a | a |
| United Kingdom | 2.1 | (0.14) | 92 | (5.2) | m | m | m | m |
| United States | 2.1 | (0.14) | 88 | (6.5) | 72 | (7.6) | 81 | (9.1) |
| **OECD total** | **2.1** | **(0.05)** | **89** | **(2.1)** | **88** | **(2.4)** | **72** | **(3.4)** |
| **OECD average** | **1.9** | **(0.03)** | **74** | **(1.2)** | **72** | **(1.5)** | **69** | **(1.8)** |
| Argentina | 1.6 | (0.16) | 70 | (9.0) | a | a | 86 | (11.6) |
| Azerbaijan | 1.3 | (0.18) | 16 | (4.0) | a | a | a | a |
| Brazil | 1.7 | (0.11) | 64 | (4.7) | 76 | (7.6) | 51 | (8.3) |
| Bulgaria | 2.0 | (0.18) | 98 | (8.5) | a | a | 64 | (11.2) |
| Chile | 1.8 | (0.11) | 91 | (5.2) | a | a | 80 | (5.3) |
| Colombia | 1.4 | (0.14) | 42 | (4.9) | a | a | a | a |
| Croatia | 1.8 | (0.15) | 72 | (6.3) | a | a | a | a |
| Estonia | 1.7 | (0.13) | 59 | (5.6) | a | a | a | a |
| Hong Kong-China | 1.5 | (0.11) | 44 | (5.9) | 36 | (5.0) | 45 | (7.3) |
| Indonesia | 1.1 | (0.11) | 30 | (7.3) | 42 | (4.8) | 39 | (7.4) |
| Israel | 1.8 | (0.18) | 73 | (8.2) | a | a | 62 | (17.6) |
| Jordan | 1.7 | (0.19) | 51 | (5.6) | a | a | a | a |
| Kyrgyzstan | 1.6 | (0.15) | 47 | (5.9) | a | a | a | a |
| Latvia | 1.5 | (0.18) | 48 | (8.1) | 53 | (7.5) | 63 | (9.4) |
| Liechtenstein | 2.6 | (0.61) | 106 | (21.4) | 113 | (18.1) | 87 | (27.9) |
| Lithuania | 1.8 | (0.13) | 68 | (6.1) | a | a | a | a |
| Macao-China | 1.2 | (0.07) | 16 | (3.2) | -5 | (9.9) | a | a |
| Montenegro | 1.6 | (0.12) | 50 | (4.3) | a | a | a | a |
| Qatar | m | m | m | m | a | a | a | a |
| Romania | 2.0 | (0.22) | 73 | (9.2) | a | a | 42 | (9.1) |
| Russian Federation | 1.6 | (0.12) | 51 | (5.6) | 46 | (7.8) | 51 | (8.6) |
| Serbia | 1.9 | (0.17) | 70 | (5.4) | a | a | a | a |
| Slovenia | 1.7 | (0.15) | 75 | (5.1) | a | a | a | a |
| Chinese Taipei | 1.5 | (0.12) | 48 | (4.9) | a | a | a | a |
| Thailand | 1.4 | (0.11) | 57 | (5.1) | 57 | (6.4) | 49 | (7.2) |
| Tunisia | 1.6 | (0.12) | 56 | (6.7) | 51 | (7.1) | a | a |
| Uruguay | 1.9 | (0.18) | 76 | (4.2) | 75 | (7.4) | a | a |

Note: Values that are statistically significant are indicated in bold (see Annex A3).
1. Results based on students' self-reports.
*StatLink* ▨▱ http://dx.doi.org/10.1787/142104560611

Pour consulter la version française intégrale de ce tableau, suivre ce lien :
*StatLink* ▨▱ http://dx.doi.org/10.1787/152684743050

[Part 1/3]

**Table 4.8b** **International socio-economic index of occupational status (HISEI) and performance on the science scale, by quarters of the index[1]**

Tableau 4.8b Indice socioéconomique international de statut professionnel (ISEI+) et score des élèves sur l'échelle de culture scientifique, par quartile de l'indice

| | | All students | | International socio-economic index of occupational status (HISEI) | | | | | | | |
| | | | | Bottom quarter | | Second quarter | | Third quarter | | Top quarter | |
| | | Mean index | S.E. | Mean index | S.E. | Mean index | S.E. | Mean index | S.E. | Mean index | S.E. |
|---|---|---|---|---|---|---|---|---|---|---|---|
| OECD | Australia | 53.0 | (0.28) | 31.2 | (0.14) | 47.8 | (0.06) | 59.9 | (0.09) | 73.2 | (0.13) |
| | Austria | 48.3 | (0.42) | 28.1 | (0.20) | 41.3 | (0.11) | 52.9 | (0.07) | 70.9 | (0.28) |
| | Belgium | 49.8 | (0.35) | 28.7 | (0.14) | 43.8 | (0.14) | 54.7 | (0.09) | 72.2 | (0.21) |
| | Canada | 53.5 | (0.28) | 32.7 | (0.16) | 49.0 | (0.09) | 59.3 | (0.12) | 73.2 | (0.15) |
| | Czech Republic | 48.2 | (0.33) | 31.2 | (0.15) | 43.4 | (0.12) | 51.9 | (0.04) | 66.5 | (0.28) |
| | Denmark | 49.4 | (0.47) | 28.1 | (0.16) | 41.3 | (0.14) | 56.3 | (0.15) | 72.0 | (0.23) |
| | Finland | 48.8 | (0.38) | 27.5 | (0.10) | 41.4 | (0.15) | 54.8 | (0.10) | 71.6 | (0.25) |
| | France | 48.6 | (0.54) | 27.9 | (0.16) | 42.5 | (0.13) | 53.2 | (0.05) | 71.0 | (0.23) |
| | Germany | 49.0 | (0.45) | 29.0 | (0.17) | 42.1 | (0.13) | 53.7 | (0.07) | 71.4 | (0.23) |
| | Greece | 48.3 | (0.51) | 27.7 | (0.17) | 41.9 | (0.15) | 52.6 | (0.07) | 70.9 | (0.27) |
| | Hungary | 47.8 | (0.43) | 29.5 | (0.17) | 41.9 | (0.08) | 51.3 | (0.09) | 68.5 | (0.30) |
| | Iceland | 53.9 | (0.26) | 31.7 | (0.18) | 47.5 | (0.13) | 61.9 | (0.19) | 74.6 | (0.22) |
| | Ireland | 49.0 | (0.51) | 28.3 | (0.16) | 42.7 | (0.10) | 53.5 | (0.09) | 71.4 | (0.26) |
| | Italy | 46.4 | (0.30) | 27.2 | (0.11) | 39.8 | (0.10) | 50.2 | (0.04) | 68.4 | (0.25) |
| | Japan | 50.3 | (0.24) | 34.2 | (0.16) | 43.5 | (0.05) | 50.8 | (0.09) | 72.6 | (0.18) |
| | Korea | 50.0 | (0.31) | 32.7 | (0.22) | 47.2 | (0.10) | 53.3 | (0.07) | 66.9 | (0.37) |
| | Luxembourg | 47.7 | (0.21) | 26.8 | (0.18) | 41.4 | (0.14) | 52.5 | (0.04) | 70.0 | (0.25) |
| | Mexico | 41.9 | (0.48) | 21.9 | (0.07) | 31.1 | (0.12) | 45.9 | (0.17) | 68.8 | (0.24) |
| | Netherlands | 51.5 | (0.38) | 31.3 | (0.19) | 46.1 | (0.15) | 56.7 | (0.19) | 71.8 | (0.18) |
| | New Zealand | 51.6 | (0.33) | 30.9 | (0.17) | 46.5 | (0.11) | 56.6 | (0.15) | 72.3 | (0.21) |
| | Norway | 53.1 | (0.40) | 34.3 | (0.21) | 46.5 | (0.11) | 58.5 | (0.19) | 73.2 | (0.21) |
| | Poland | 44.4 | (0.33) | 26.8 | (0.19) | 38.2 | (0.12) | 48.7 | (0.11) | 63.8 | (0.29) |
| | Portugal | 41.7 | (0.48) | 25.3 | (0.17) | 32.6 | (0.05) | 44.6 | (0.16) | 64.3 | (0.46) |
| | Slovak Republic | 47.2 | (0.39) | 28.5 | (0.26) | 40.5 | (0.12) | 50.6 | (0.11) | 69.4 | (0.20) |
| | Spain | 44.8 | (0.45) | 26.7 | (0.12) | 34.8 | (0.08) | 49.4 | (0.10) | 68.3 | (0.32) |
| | Sweden | 50.7 | (0.31) | 30.5 | (0.16) | 44.8 | (0.15) | 55.8 | (0.17) | 71.6 | (0.21) |
| | Switzerland | 49.2 | (0.34) | 29.1 | (0.12) | 43.0 | (0.11) | 54.3 | (0.03) | 70.6 | (0.29) |
| | Turkey | 39.6 | (0.55) | 22.3 | (0.14) | 30.7 | (0.07) | 45.3 | (0.13) | 60.1 | (0.55) |
| | United Kingdom | 50.7 | (0.30) | 30.0 | (0.12) | 45.5 | (0.13) | 55.3 | (0.09) | 71.8 | (0.17) |
| | United States | 52.5 | (0.56) | 29.9 | (0.13) | 47.6 | (0.13) | 59.5 | (0.15) | 73.1 | (0.28) |
| | **OECD total** | **48.8** | **(0.17)** | **27.8** | **(0.05)** | **42.2** | **(0.04)** | **53.8** | **(0.03)** | **71.6** | **(0.09)** |
| | **OECD average** | **48.7** | **(0.07)** | **29.0** | **(0.03)** | **42.2** | **(0.02)** | **53.5** | **(0.02)** | **70.2** | **(0.05)** |
| Partners | Argentina | 45.7 | (0.88) | 26.2 | (0.21) | 37.1 | (0.22) | 49.7 | (0.14) | 69.7 | (0.39) |
| | Azerbaijan | 49.4 | (0.57) | 27.2 | (0.22) | 39.9 | (0.27) | 56.5 | (0.31) | 74.0 | (0.25) |
| | Brazil | 41.1 | (0.46) | 19.2 | (0.16) | 30.6 | (0.11) | 49.7 | (0.12) | 64.8 | (0.37) |
| | Bulgaria | 47.4 | (0.64) | 29.1 | (0.16) | 38.9 | (0.14) | 50.8 | (0.11) | 71.0 | (0.25) |
| | Chile | 40.6 | (0.71) | 21.9 | (0.21) | 32.0 | (0.07) | 44.4 | (0.13) | 64.1 | (0.53) |
| | Colombia | 42.3 | (0.54) | 22.3 | (0.22) | 33.1 | (0.14) | 47.9 | (0.14) | 65.9 | (0.45) |
| | Croatia | 46.6 | (0.28) | 29.8 | (0.18) | 39.6 | (0.09) | 49.4 | (0.10) | 67.6 | (0.25) |
| | Estonia | 50.3 | (0.38) | 29.9 | (0.14) | 41.7 | (0.13) | 57.8 | (0.16) | 71.8 | (0.18) |
| | Hong Kong-China | 42.8 | (0.38) | 26.9 | (0.18) | 36.7 | (0.11) | 47.5 | (0.12) | 60.1 | (0.32) |
| | Indonesia | 37.6 | (0.56) | 20.5 | (0.24) | 28.8 | (0.06) | 42.1 | (0.17) | 58.9 | (0.49) |
| | Israel | 53.4 | (0.37) | 31.7 | (0.26) | 50.0 | (0.09) | 58.9 | (0.20) | 72.9 | (0.23) |
| | Jordan | 51.0 | (0.49) | 28.3 | (0.17) | 44.9 | (0.22) | 58.5 | (0.23) | 72.4 | (0.25) |
| | Kyrgyzstan | 45.7 | (0.44) | 27.1 | (0.18) | 37.8 | (0.13) | 45.0 | (0.12) | 72.8 | (0.27) |
| | Latvia | 48.5 | (0.46) | 28.1 | (0.17) | 40.7 | (0.16) | 52.7 | (0.13) | 72.4 | (0.24) |
| | Liechtenstein | 51.1 | (0.83) | 30.6 | (0.64) | 48.4 | (0.51) | 55.0 | (0.03) | 70.8 | (0.97) |
| | Lithuania | 49.7 | (0.47) | 27.8 | (0.12) | 41.1 | (0.14) | 56.7 | (0.24) | 73.3 | (0.24) |
| | Macao-China | 41.8 | (0.22) | 26.0 | (0.15) | 34.9 | (0.10) | 46.9 | (0.11) | 59.4 | (0.29) |
| | Montenegro | 49.2 | (0.26) | 29.9 | (0.14) | 42.7 | (0.10) | 52.5 | (0.09) | 71.9 | (0.25) |
| | Qatar | m | m | m | m | m | m | m | m | m | m |
| | Romania | 43.2 | (0.59) | 25.2 | (0.39) | 35.7 | (0.14) | 45.8 | (0.16) | 66.1 | (0.59) |
| | Russian Federation | 50.7 | (0.48) | 29.5 | (0.15) | 42.1 | (0.09) | 58.5 | (0.22) | 72.7 | (0.17) |
| | Serbia | 48.4 | (0.42) | 29.1 | (0.20) | 42.5 | (0.06) | 51.0 | (0.08) | 71.1 | (0.29) |
| | Slovenia | 49.9 | (0.22) | 30.3 | (0.13) | 43.1 | (0.07) | 54.2 | (0.15) | 71.9 | (0.21) |
| | Chinese Taipei | 48.5 | (0.37) | 28.0 | (0.10) | 42.6 | (0.15) | 53.3 | (0.06) | 70.1 | (0.16) |
| | Thailand | 36.6 | (0.39) | 21.9 | (0.11) | 26.3 | (0.12) | 38.7 | (0.19) | 59.4 | (0.39) |
| | Tunisia | 38.4 | (1.00) | 19.4 | (0.11) | 26.1 | (0.17) | 42.3 | (0.25) | 65.6 | (0.48) |
| | Uruguay | 44.1 | (0.41) | 23.8 | (0.20) | 34.7 | (0.15) | 48.9 | (0.15) | 69.1 | (0.34) |

Note: Values that are statistically significant are indicated in bold (see Annex A3).
1. Results based on students' self-reports.
StatLink ⟨⟩ http://dx.doi.org/10.1787/142104560611

Pour consulter la version française intégrale de ce tableau, suivre ce lien :
StatLink ⟨⟩ http://dx.doi.org/10.1787/152684743050

147

[Part 2/3]

**Table 4.8b** International socio-economic index of occupational status (HISEI) and performance on the science scale, by quarters of the index[1]

Tableau 4.8b  Indice socioéconomique international de statut professionnel (ISEI+) et score des élèves sur l'échelle de culture scientifique, par quartile de l'indice

| | Performance on the science scale, by quarters of this index | | | | | | | |
|---|---|---|---|---|---|---|---|---|
| | Bottom quarter | | Second quarter | | Third quarter | | Top quarter | |
| | Mean score | S.E. | Mean score | S.E. | Mean score | S.E. | Mean score | S.E. |
| Australia | 490 | (2.4) | 522 | (2.5) | 538 | (2.5) | 569 | (3.0) |
| Austria | 466 | (6.7) | 496 | (4.2) | 532 | (4.3) | 554 | (3.8) |
| Belgium | 464 | (3.5) | 501 | (3.1) | 532 | (2.8) | 564 | (3.0) |
| Canada | 502 | (2.8) | 533 | (2.6) | 545 | (2.4) | 569 | (2.7) |
| Czech Republic | 469 | (4.6) | 501 | (4.5) | 530 | (4.0) | 564 | (4.5) |
| Denmark | 463 | (3.5) | 487 | (4.1) | 509 | (3.5) | 537 | (4.5) |
| Finland | 545 | (3.0) | 548 | (2.7) | 569 | (3.4) | 596 | (3.1) |
| France | 448 | (4.8) | 482 | (4.5) | 515 | (3.8) | 559 | (4.1) |
| Germany | 474 | (4.7) | 502 | (4.2) | 542 | (3.7) | 569 | (3.5) |
| Greece | 436 | (4.7) | 461 | (4.2) | 486 | (3.5) | 518 | (3.6) |
| Hungary | 469 | (3.7) | 490 | (3.4) | 517 | (3.7) | 552 | (4.1) |
| Iceland | 468 | (3.5) | 481 | (2.9) | 499 | (3.6) | 525 | (3.9) |
| Ireland | 476 | (4.5) | 505 | (3.6) | 519 | (3.5) | 548 | (3.5) |
| Italy | 442 | (3.1) | 468 | (2.8) | 486 | (2.6) | 512 | (3.2) |
| Japan | 506 | (4.7) | 532 | (4.3) | 543 | (4.1) | 559 | (4.2) |
| Korea | 506 | (3.8) | 514 | (4.0) | 527 | (4.2) | 545 | (5.4) |
| Luxembourg | 429 | (2.6) | 471 | (3.0) | 512 | (2.6) | 540 | (2.7) |
| Mexico | 377 | (3.8) | 398 | (2.7) | 425 | (2.8) | 448 | (4.1) |
| Netherlands | 478 | (3.9) | 523 | (3.4) | 540 | (3.5) | 573 | (2.8) |
| New Zealand | 487 | (4.1) | 526 | (3.8) | 552 | (3.2) | 578 | (3.8) |
| Norway | 457 | (4.8) | 480 | (3.7) | 499 | (3.2) | 529 | (4.1) |
| Poland | 469 | (3.1) | 485 | (3.1) | 504 | (2.8) | 539 | (3.8) |
| Portugal | 440 | (4.0) | 454 | (3.6) | 487 | (3.3) | 521 | (3.5) |
| Slovak Republic | 446 | (3.9) | 482 | (3.3) | 503 | (3.9) | 538 | (4.1) |
| Spain | 455 | (2.9) | 475 | (2.8) | 502 | (2.7) | 530 | (3.5) |
| Sweden | 467 | (3.3) | 497 | (3.5) | 515 | (3.6) | 547 | (3.6) |
| Switzerland | 463 | (3.5) | 504 | (3.1) | 525 | (4.1) | 559 | (3.9) |
| Turkey | 404 | (3.4) | 409 | (4.0) | 428 | (4.3) | 461 | (8.2) |
| United Kingdom | 472 | (2.8) | 508 | (3.1) | 531 | (3.5) | 568 | (3.4) |
| United States | 445 | (5.6) | 485 | (4.4) | 508 | (4.0) | 541 | (4.7) |
| **OECD total** | **443** | (1.5) | **486** | (1.5) | **509** | (1.3) | **541** | (1.5) |
| **OECD average** | **464** | (0.7) | **491** | (0.6) | **514** | (0.6) | **544** | (0.7) |
| Argentina | 355 | (5.3) | 381 | (6.7) | 410 | (7.0) | 442 | (8.3) |
| Azerbaijan | 377 | (4.6) | 378 | (2.9) | 385 | (3.2) | 403 | (3.5) |
| Brazil | 358 | (3.9) | 371 | (3.0) | 409 | (3.2) | 433 | (5.3) |
| Bulgaria | 381 | (5.8) | 425 | (5.5) | 456 | (5.6) | 500 | (7.7) |
| Chile | 398 | (4.5) | 418 | (4.6) | 444 | (4.3) | 496 | (4.9) |
| Colombia | 366 | (4.0) | 376 | (4.8) | 398 | (3.8) | 420 | (4.6) |
| Croatia | 459 | (3.5) | 484 | (3.3) | 504 | (3.3) | 535 | (3.3) |
| Estonia | 499 | (4.1) | 518 | (2.9) | 546 | (3.0) | 568 | (4.0) |
| Hong Kong-China | 526 | (3.8) | 537 | (4.0) | 554 | (3.5) | 564 | (4.2) |
| Indonesia | 381 | (3.6) | 368 | (3.9) | 417 | (9.5) | 416 | (8.4) |
| Israel | 422 | (5.1) | 457 | (5.2) | 482 | (5.0) | 503 | (5.5) |
| Jordan | 400 | (3.5) | 432 | (3.3) | 437 | (4.4) | 466 | (5.0) |
| Kyrgyzstan | 299 | (4.8) | 318 | (3.7) | 329 | (3.0) | 357 | (4.5) |
| Latvia | 464 | (4.0) | 475 | (4.5) | 503 | (3.3) | 527 | (4.1) |
| Liechtenstein | 472 | (10.0) | 525 | (9.1) | 542 | (9.4) | 554 | (12.0) |
| Lithuania | 454 | (3.3) | 475 | (3.5) | 510 | (3.5) | 525 | (4.2) |
| Macao-China | 503 | (2.5) | 510 | (3.1) | 517 | (2.5) | 518 | (2.7) |
| Montenegro | 387 | (2.5) | 407 | (2.5) | 425 | (2.8) | 447 | (2.7) |
| Qatar | m | m | m | m | m | m | m | m |
| Romania | 388 | (6.1) | 406 | (5.2) | 425 | (6.0) | 469 | (6.6) |
| Russian Federation | 451 | (4.2) | 469 | (4.3) | 497 | (4.3) | 507 | (3.8) |
| Serbia | 401 | (4.3) | 422 | (3.4) | 451 | (3.3) | 476 | (3.3) |
| Slovenia | 476 | (2.6) | 499 | (2.9) | 535 | (2.8) | 572 | (3.1) |
| Chinese Taipei | 505 | (5.0) | 528 | (3.6) | 549 | (3.6) | 567 | (3.6) |
| Thailand | 401 | (3.3) | 405 | (3.4) | 428 | (3.7) | 462 | (4.0) |
| Tunisia | 361 | (3.1) | 371 | (3.2) | 388 | (4.2) | 427 | (6.3) |
| Uruguay | 392 | (4.0) | 411 | (3.8) | 440 | (3.9) | 478 | (4.0) |

Note: Values that are statistically significant are indicated in bold (see Annex A3).
1. Results based on students' self-reports.
*StatLink* http://dx.doi.org/10.1787/142104560611

Pour consulter la version française intégrale de ce tableau, suivre ce lien :
*StatLink* http://dx.doi.org/10.1787/152684743050

[Part 3/3]

**Table 4.8b** International socio-economic index of occupational status (HISEI) and performance on the science scale, by quarters of the index[1]

Tableau 4.8b  Indice socioéconomique international de statut professionnel (ISEI+) et score des élèves sur l'échelle de culture scientifique, par quartile de l'indice

| | | Change in the science score per 17.1 units of this index[2] | | Increased likelihood of students in the bottom quarter of this index scoring in the bottom quarter of the science performance distribution | | Explained variance in student performance (r-squared x 100) | |
|---|---|---|---|---|---|---|---|
| | | Effect | S.E. | Ratio | S.E. | Percentage | S.E. |
| *OECD* | Australia | 30.6 | (1.15) | 1.9 | (0.08) | 8.9 | (0.63) |
| | Austria | 34.3 | (2.50) | 2.3 | (0.16) | 11.7 | (1.42) |
| | Belgium | 38.3 | (1.66) | 2.4 | (0.12) | 14.8 | (1.24) |
| | Canada | 26.8 | (1.26) | 1.8 | (0.08) | 7.1 | (0.63) |
| | Czech Republic | 45.2 | (2.28) | 2.1 | (0.13) | 14.3 | (1.13) |
| | Denmark | 27.8 | (1.91) | 1.9 | (0.14) | 9.3 | (1.22) |
| | Finland | 20.3 | (1.38) | 1.5 | (0.09) | 5.7 | (0.78) |
| | France | 42.3 | (2.32) | 2.3 | (0.17) | 17.1 | (1.63) |
| | Germany | 37.6 | (1.91) | 2.2 | (0.13) | 13.6 | (1.17) |
| | Greece | 32.5 | (2.18) | 2.0 | (0.13) | 12.2 | (1.41) |
| | Hungary | 36.1 | (2.11) | 2.0 | (0.16) | 13.4 | (1.41) |
| | Iceland | 22.6 | (1.55) | 1.5 | (0.10) | 5.5 | (0.73) |
| | Ireland | 27.8 | (1.81) | 1.8 | (0.11) | 8.3 | (1.02) |
| | Italy | 28.0 | (1.58) | 1.8 | (0.09) | 8.0 | (0.84) |
| | Japan | 18.9 | (2.09) | 1.7 | (0.11) | 2.7 | (0.58) |
| | Korea | 19.1 | (2.66) | 1.3 | (0.08) | 2.8 | (0.74) |
| | Luxembourg | 42.4 | (1.47) | 2.8 | (0.17) | 18.3 | (1.14) |
| | Mexico | 25.7 | (1.64) | 1.9 | (0.14) | 12.2 | (1.40) |
| | Netherlands | 38.4 | (1.93) | 2.4 | (0.16) | 14.2 | (1.28) |
| | New Zealand | 37.8 | (1.78) | 2.1 | (0.13) | 11.4 | (1.01) |
| | Norway | 29.2 | (1.94) | 1.8 | (0.15) | 8.0 | (1.01) |
| | Poland | 33.8 | (1.73) | 1.7 | (0.09) | 10.7 | (0.96) |
| | Portugal | 35.6 | (1.91) | 2.0 | (0.13) | 14.5 | (1.43) |
| | Slovak Republic | 37.1 | (2.30) | 2.3 | (0.15) | 14.2 | (1.50) |
| | Spain | 28.7 | (1.52) | 1.9 | (0.15) | 10.1 | (1.07) |
| | Sweden | 31.3 | (1.57) | 1.9 | (0.12) | 10.0 | (0.90) |
| | Switzerland | 36.3 | (1.69) | 2.3 | (0.10) | 12.1 | (1.03) |
| | Turkey | 29.0 | (3.67) | 1.4 | (0.10) | 9.9 | (2.21) |
| | United Kingdom | 38.8 | (1.67) | 2.1 | (0.11) | 11.9 | (1.09) |
| | United States | 36.1 | (2.20) | 2.2 | (0.15) | 11.5 | (1.26) |
| | **OECD total** | **36.9** | **(0.75)** | **2.3** | **(0.05)** | **12.4** | **(0.48)** |
| | **OECD average** | **32.3** | **(0.36)** | **2.0** | **(0.02)** | **10.8** | **(0.22)** |
| *Partners* | Argentina | 33.4 | (3.45) | 1.9 | (0.19) | 11.4 | (2.46) |
| | Azerbaijan | 9.9 | (1.60) | 1.4 | (0.12) | 3.7 | (1.26) |
| | Brazil | 30.4 | (2.11) | 1.7 | (0.12) | 13.3 | (1.63) |
| | Bulgaria | 45.8 | (3.59) | 2.5 | (0.23) | 17.4 | (2.23) |
| | Chile | 39.4 | (2.05) | 2.0 | (0.19) | 17.8 | (1.80) |
| | Colombia | 22.7 | (1.97) | 1.5 | (0.13) | 7.3 | (1.29) |
| | Croatia | 32.4 | (1.96) | 2.1 | (0.15) | 11.3 | (1.19) |
| | Estonia | 26.9 | (1.59) | 1.9 | (0.12) | 9.9 | (1.04) |
| | Hong Kong-China | 21.7 | (2.56) | 1.4 | (0.10) | 3.7 | (0.86) |
| | Indonesia | 19.4 | (3.14) | 1.2 | (0.12) | 6.4 | (1.63) |
| | Israel | 33.1 | (2.32) | 1.8 | (0.14) | 8.1 | (1.02) |
| | Jordan | 25.3 | (1.92) | 1.9 | (0.17) | 8.7 | (1.19) |
| | Kyrgyzstan | 19.7 | (2.16) | 1.6 | (0.14) | 6.0 | (1.16) |
| | Latvia | 24.1 | (2.24) | 1.8 | (0.12) | 8.2 | (1.33) |
| | Liechtenstein | 37.4 | (6.30) | 2.3 | (0.40) | 12.3 | (3.98) |
| | Lithuania | 27.3 | (1.90) | 2.0 | (0.12) | 10.3 | (1.25) |
| | Macao-China | 8.7 | (1.59) | 1.2 | (0.09) | 0.8 | (0.29) |
| | Montenegro | 24.1 | (1.44) | 1.8 | (0.13) | 8.3 | (0.98) |
| | Qatar | m | m | m | m | m | m |
| | Romania | 34.1 | (3.38) | 2.0 | (0.22) | 15.9 | (3.03) |
| | Russian Federation | 22.2 | (1.70) | 1.7 | (0.12) | 6.3 | (0.93) |
| | Serbia | 30.2 | (1.71) | 2.0 | (0.15) | 11.6 | (1.11) |
| | Slovenia | 39.4 | (1.55) | 2.1 | (0.11) | 14.1 | (1.11) |
| | Chinese Taipei | 25.3 | (1.75) | 1.8 | (0.11) | 6.6 | (0.83) |
| | Thailand | 28.5 | (1.98) | 1.5 | (0.17) | 11.9 | (1.58) |
| | Tunisia | 23.8 | (2.59) | 1.5 | (0.13) | 10.1 | (2.12) |
| | Uruguay | 32.8 | (1.39) | 1.9 | (0.16) | 13.5 | (1.06) |

Note: Values that are statistically significant are indicated in bold (see Annex A3).
1. Results based on students' self-reports.
2. 17.1 refers to one standard deviaiton on the index.
StatLink ⫘⫙ http://dx.doi.org/10.1787/142104560611

Pour consulter la version française intégrale de ce tableau, suivre ce lien :
StatLink ⫘⫙ http://dx.doi.org/10.1787/152684743050

149

[Part 1/2]

**Table 4.9a   Percentage of students and performance on the science, reading and mathematics scales, by level of cultural possessions at home[1]**

Tableau 4.9a   Pourcentage d'élèves et scores sur les échelles de culture scientifique, de compréhension de l'écrit et de culture mathématique, selon le patrimoine culturel familial

| | | Students with a low level of cultural possessions at home (bottom quarter of the index of cultural possessions at home) | | | | | | Students with a high level of cultural possessions at home (top quarter of the index of cultural possessions at home) | | | | | |
| | | Performance | | | | | | Performance | | | | | |
| | | Science | | Reading | | Mathematics | | Science | | Reading | | Mathematics | |
| | | Mean score | S.E. | Mean score | S.E. | Mean score | S.E. | Mean score | S.E. | Mean score | S.E. | Mean score | S.E. |
|---|---|---|---|---|---|---|---|---|---|---|---|---|---|
| OECD | Australia | 504 | (2.7) | 490 | (2.9) | 504 | (2.5) | 564 | (2.8) | 547 | (2.5) | 548 | (2.9) |
| | Austria | 486 | (4.7) | 458 | (4.8) | 484 | (4.8) | 552 | (4.0) | 537 | (4.7) | 544 | (4.2) |
| | Belgium | 474 | (3.3) | 461 | (4.5) | 487 | (3.7) | 555 | (2.6) | 549 | (2.7) | 563 | (2.8) |
| | Canada | 515 | (2.7) | 500 | (3.1) | 512 | (2.6) | 561 | (2.6) | 558 | (3.0) | 549 | (2.4) |
| | Czech Republic | 480 | (5.3) | 446 | (5.9) | 480 | (5.3) | 550 | (4.2) | 523 | (4.5) | 545 | (4.7) |
| | Denmark | 462 | (4.1) | 460 | (4.3) | 484 | (3.6) | 538 | (4.0) | 533 | (3.9) | 548 | (3.6) |
| | Finland | 535 | (2.9) | 514 | (3.1) | 523 | (3.0) | 586 | (3.1) | 570 | (3.0) | 569 | (3.3) |
| | France | 444 | (4.1) | 433 | (5.1) | 451 | (3.8) | 546 | (4.3) | 537 | (4.3) | 541 | (4.5) |
| | Germany | 493 | (4.2) | 466 | (5.2) | 481 | (3.9) | 563 | (3.4) | 547 | (3.7) | 551 | (3.8) |
| | Greece | 448 | (4.8) | 432 | (5.5) | 439 | (4.3) | 498 | (4.4) | 484 | (5.3) | 481 | (4.6) |
| | Hungary | 455 | (3.5) | 426 | (4.5) | 446 | (3.9) | 534 | (3.2) | 515 | (3.5) | 520 | (4.1) |
| | Iceland | 462 | (2.9) | 453 | (3.1) | 479 | (2.6) | 509 | (3.0) | 502 | (3.4) | 521 | (3.1) |
| | Ireland | 483 | (4.4) | 493 | (4.6) | 484 | (3.8) | 552 | (3.8) | 557 | (3.8) | 534 | (3.5) |
| | Italy | 443 | (2.7) | 431 | (3.9) | 434 | (2.6) | 497 | (2.6) | 492 | (3.0) | 481 | (2.9) |
| | Japan | 505 | (4.4) | 468 | (5.1) | 502 | (4.1) | 561 | (3.8) | 529 | (4.4) | 548 | (3.9) |
| | Korea | 482 | (4.8) | 515 | (6.1) | 506 | (4.8) | 550 | (4.4) | 584 | (4.1) | 579 | (5.5) |
| | Luxembourg | 450 | (2.6) | 439 | (3.0) | 458 | (2.6) | 533 | (2.9) | 529 | (2.9) | 532 | (2.8) |
| | Mexico | 394 | (2.5) | 392 | (3.6) | 389 | (3.4) | 437 | (3.9) | 438 | (4.2) | 433 | (3.9) |
| | Netherlands | 496 | (4.9) | 478 | (5.1) | 504 | (4.7) | 561 | (3.4) | 540 | (3.7) | 563 | (3.0) |
| | New Zealand | 508 | (3.3) | 498 | (3.4) | 506 | (3.0) | 579 | (3.3) | 567 | (3.5) | 561 | (3.0) |
| | Norway | 454 | (3.1) | 443 | (3.6) | 460 | (3.1) | 518 | (3.5) | 520 | (3.8) | 519 | (3.3) |
| | Poland | 467 | (3.2) | 465 | (3.5) | 468 | (3.1) | 522 | (3.1) | 542 | (3.6) | 518 | (3.2) |
| | Portugal | 440 | (4.1) | 428 | (5.2) | 432 | (4.5) | 511 | (3.5) | 516 | (4.0) | 503 | (3.6) |
| | Slovak Republic | 459 | (4.3) | 426 | (5.0) | 463 | (5.1) | 506 | (3.4) | 487 | (4.0) | 507 | (3.6) |
| | Spain | 453 | (2.5) | 430 | (2.5) | 451 | (2.6) | 520 | (2.9) | 489 | (3.1) | 506 | (2.9) |
| | Sweden | 475 | (3.5) | 475 | (4.3) | 476 | (3.5) | 530 | (5.0) | 536 | (6.1) | 526 | (4.5) |
| | Switzerland | 489 | (3.3) | 476 | (3.2) | 513 | (3.4) | 546 | (4.1) | 531 | (4.1) | 558 | (4.3) |
| | Turkey | 396 | (3.6) | 411 | (5.0) | 400 | (4.0) | 453 | (6.2) | 478 | (5.7) | 449 | (8.0) |
| | United Kingdom | 484 | (3.2) | 465 | (3.0) | 473 | (3.0) | 559 | (3.6) | 538 | (3.6) | 530 | (3.1) |
| | United States | 452 | (4.0) | m | m | 447 | (3.9) | 524 | (5.1) | m | m | 502 | (4.7) |
| | **OECD total** | 457 | (1.2) | 449 | (1.5) | 456 | (1.3) | 530 | (1.5) | 528 | (1.1) | 518 | (1.3) |
| | **OECD average** | 470 | (0.7) | 458 | (0.8) | 471 | (0.7) | 534 | (0.7) | 527 | (0.7) | 528 | (0.7) |
| Partners | Argentina | 367 | (6.4) | 349 | (7.5) | 364 | (6.0) | 426 | (5.9) | 410 | (7.4) | 410 | (7.0) |
| | Azerbaijan | 379 | (4.4) | 343 | (4.8) | 475 | (3.6) | 390 | (3.3) | 362 | (4.2) | 481 | (2.8) |
| | Brazil | 382 | (3.7) | 376 | (6.3) | 363 | (4.3) | 406 | (4.4) | 413 | (4.8) | 386 | (4.8) |
| | Bulgaria | 379 | (5.5) | 337 | (6.9) | 364 | (6.3) | 473 | (6.3) | 449 | (6.4) | 447 | (6.4) |
| | Chile | 413 | (4.2) | 419 | (5.2) | 389 | (4.8) | 477 | (5.3) | 481 | (6.7) | 446 | (5.1) |
| | Colombia | 375 | (4.6) | 365 | (6.9) | 355 | (5.4) | 410 | (4.4) | 411 | (5.9) | 396 | (4.9) |
| | Croatia | 465 | (3.5) | 443 | (4.3) | 444 | (3.3) | 532 | (3.5) | 519 | (3.4) | 498 | (3.5) |
| | Estonia | 506 | (3.4) | 474 | (4.5) | 491 | (3.6) | 547 | (3.5) | 517 | (3.4) | 529 | (3.6) |
| | Hong Kong-China | 518 | (3.7) | 512 | (3.9) | 528 | (4.5) | 565 | (4.7) | 559 | (3.8) | 568 | (4.6) |
| | Indonesia | 390 | (6.4) | 390 | (6.2) | 387 | (6.4) | 394 | (5.4) | 395 | (6.6) | 391 | (5.5) |
| | Israel | 414 | (5.0) | 401 | (6.3) | 412 | (6.1) | 487 | (5.1) | 470 | (5.9) | 470 | (5.2) |
| | Jordan | 415 | (3.4) | 389 | (3.8) | 380 | (3.7) | 438 | (4.4) | 421 | (4.6) | 398 | (4.8) |
| | Kyrgyzstan | 304 | (3.9) | 264 | (4.3) | 295 | (4.0) | 349 | (3.4) | 315 | (4.2) | 337 | (4.1) |
| | Latvia | 460 | (3.9) | 441 | (4.4) | 462 | (4.1) | 507 | (3.8) | 502 | (4.3) | 502 | (4.1) |
| | Liechtenstein | 492 | (8.6) | 480 | (8.6) | 500 | (9.1) | 576 | (9.4) | 560 | (9.3) | 573 | (9.3) |
| | Lithuania | 450 | (3.5) | 422 | (3.8) | 452 | (3.6) | 520 | (3.9) | 509 | (4.5) | 517 | (3.9) |
| | Macao-China | 496 | (2.8) | 476 | (2.7) | 509 | (3.0) | 527 | (2.3) | 510 | (2.6) | 543 | (2.6) |
| | Montenegro | 380 | (2.2) | 354 | (2.5) | 367 | (2.6) | 437 | (2.7) | 424 | (2.7) | 426 | (2.9) |
| | Qatar | 344 | (1.9) | 308 | (2.4) | 312 | (2.3) | 365 | (2.5) | 331 | (2.8) | 339 | (2.9) |
| | Romania | 382 | (7.0) | 356 | (7.1) | 377 | (6.3) | 442 | (5.5) | 421 | (6.5) | 441 | (5.3) |
| | Russian Federation | 461 | (4.6) | 416 | (5.4) | 456 | (4.8) | 489 | (3.6) | 454 | (4.2) | 489 | (4.2) |
| | Serbia | 399 | (3.9) | 354 | (3.9) | 399 | (4.0) | 464 | (3.0) | 435 | (3.7) | 464 | (3.8) |
| | Slovenia | 474 | (3.6) | 452 | (3.0) | 467 | (3.1) | 553 | (2.8) | 528 | (2.4) | 535 | (2.7) |
| | Chinese Taipei | 490 | (4.3) | 456 | (3.9) | 507 | (5.2) | 565 | (3.4) | 528 | (3.2) | 583 | (3.6) |
| | Thailand | 413 | (3.0) | 406 | (3.7) | 411 | (3.4) | 428 | (2.9) | 427 | (3.5) | 422 | (3.1) |
| | Tunisia | 367 | (3.1) | 357 | (3.9) | 344 | (3.6) | 408 | (5.3) | 407 | (6.0) | 391 | (6.5) |
| | Uruguay | 398 | (3.5) | 379 | (4.6) | 401 | (3.3) | 468 | (4.0) | 457 | (4.6) | 466 | (4.0) |

Note: Values that are statistically significant are indicated in bold (see Annex A3).
1. Results based on students' self-reports.
*StatLink* http://dx.doi.org/10.1787/142104560611

Pour consulter la version française intégrale de ce tableau, suivre ce lien :
*StatLink* http://dx.doi.org/10.1787/152684743050

[Part 2/2]

**Table 4.9a** **Percentage of students and performance on the science, reading and mathematics scales, by level of cultural possessions at home[1]**

Tableau 4.9a  Pourcentage d'élèves et scores sur les échelles de culture scientifique, de compréhension de l'écrit et de culture mathématique, selon le patrimoine culturel familial

| | Increased likelihood of students, who are in the bottom quarter of the index of cultural possessions at home, scoring in the bottom quarter of the science performance distribution | | Difference in science performance between students with a high level of cultural possessions at home and students with a low level of cultural possessions at home | | | | | |
| | | | PISA 2006 | | PISA 2003 | | PISA 2000 | |
| | Ratio | S.E. | Dif. | S.E. | Dif. | S.E. | Dif. | S.E. |
|---|---|---|---|---|---|---|---|---|
| **OECD** | | | | | | | | |
| Australia | 1.5 | (0.05) | 60 | (3.2) | 66 | (4.0) | 73 | (5.9) |
| Austria | 1.5 | (0.10) | 66 | (4.6) | 80 | (5.0) | 48 | (6.8) |
| Belgium | 1.9 | (0.09) | 80 | (3.8) | 83 | (5.1) | 84 | (6.2) |
| Canada | 1.4 | (0.08) | 46 | (3.2) | 56 | (3.5) | 45 | (3.0) |
| Czech Republic | 1.7 | (0.12) | 70 | (5.6) | 61 | (5.8) | 61 | (6.3) |
| Denmark | 1.8 | (0.12) | 76 | (4.5) | 93 | (4.5) | 70 | (5.6) |
| Finland | 1.8 | (0.10) | 51 | (4.0) | 63 | (3.7) | 41 | (5.0) |
| France | 2.3 | (0.14) | 102 | (5.9) | 110 | (6.9) | 76 | (6.3) |
| Germany | 1.5 | (0.09) | 69 | (4.7) | 81 | (4.7) | 79 | (7.1) |
| Greece | 1.7 | (0.13) | 50 | (5.9) | 69 | (6.4) | 57 | (7.4) |
| Hungary | 2.5 | (0.17) | 80 | (4.7) | 87 | (5.6) | 82 | (7.3) |
| Iceland | 1.7 | (0.10) | 47 | (4.1) | 40 | (5.6) | 31 | (7.3) |
| Ireland | 1.6 | (0.12) | 69 | (4.8) | 65 | (4.2) | 49 | (7.3) |
| Italy | 1.8 | (0.09) | 54 | (3.7) | 69 | (5.5) | 39 | (6.3) |
| Japan | 1.6 | (0.12) | 55 | (4.9) | 64 | (6.8) | 52 | (6.4) |
| Korea | 2.1 | (0.12) | 68 | (6.1) | 70 | (6.9) | 41 | (5.0) |
| Luxembourg | 1.9 | (0.12) | 82 | (4.0) | 78 | (4.7) | m | m |
| Mexico | 1.4 | (0.08) | 43 | (4.1) | 60 | (5.9) | 55 | (6.4) |
| Netherlands | 1.7 | (0.11) | 65 | (6.0) | 60 | (5.7) | m | m |
| New Zealand | 1.5 | (0.10) | 71 | (4.1) | 67 | (4.7) | 58 | (7.2) |
| Norway | 1.9 | (0.11) | 64 | (3.9) | 73 | (5.6) | 65 | (6.4) |
| Poland | 1.8 | (0.11) | 55 | (3.6) | 69 | (5.5) | 56 | (8.5) |
| Portugal | 2.0 | (0.13) | 71 | (5.0) | 75 | (5.6) | 66 | (5.9) |
| Slovak Republic | 1.8 | (0.14) | 47 | (5.4) | 58 | (7.6) | a | a |
| Spain | 1.9 | (0.11) | 66 | (3.3) | 68 | (5.0) | 66 | (5.5) |
| Sweden | 1.7 | (0.13) | 55 | (6.9) | 84 | (7.0) | 57 | (6.1) |
| Switzerland | 1.4 | (0.09) | 57 | (4.2) | 59 | (4.9) | 67 | (6.8) |
| Turkey | 1.6 | (0.11) | 57 | (6.2) | 66 | (10.5) | a | a |
| United Kingdom | 1.6 | (0.08) | 75 | (4.4) | m | m | m | m |
| United States | 1.7 | (0.12) | 72 | (5.5) | 84 | (4.9) | 80 | (9.3) |
| **OECD total** | **1.7** | **(0.04)** | **72** | **(1.6)** | **83** | **(2.1)** | **70** | **(2.9)** |
| **OECD average** | **1.7** | **(0.02)** | **64** | **(0.9)** | **71** | **(1.1)** | **60** | **(1.3)** |
| **Partners** | | | | | | | | |
| Argentina | 1.5 | (0.13) | 59 | (7.6) | a | a | 60 | (13.7) |
| Azerbaijan | 1.3 | (0.10) | 12 | (4.3) | a | a | a | a |
| Brazil | 1.1 | (0.07) | 24 | (5.6) | 31 | (5.7) | 34 | (6.9) |
| Bulgaria | 2.4 | (0.19) | 94 | (6.8) | a | a | 59 | (8.2) |
| Chile | 1.5 | (0.12) | 64 | (6.1) | a | a | 67 | (6.0) |
| Colombia | 1.3 | (0.10) | 36 | (5.3) | a | a | a | a |
| Croatia | 1.7 | (0.09) | 66 | (4.3) | a | a | a | a |
| Estonia | 1.6 | (0.10) | 41 | (4.2) | a | a | a | a |
| Hong Kong-China | 1.6 | (0.10) | 47 | (6.0) | 50 | (6.0) | 39 | (6.9) |
| Indonesia | 1.1 | (0.08) | 4 | (4.5) | 17 | (3.4) | 5 | (4.7) |
| Israel | 1.8 | (0.14) | 73 | (6.1) | a | a | 82 | (13.8) |
| Jordan | 1.2 | (0.08) | 23 | (4.5) | a | a | a | a |
| Kyrgyzstan | 1.4 | (0.08) | 45 | (5.0) | a | a | a | a |
| Latvia | 1.8 | (0.14) | 47 | (5.0) | 59 | (5.2) | 53 | (9.1) |
| Liechtenstein | 1.6 | (0.31) | 84 | (12.8) | 85 | (16.1) | 66 | (21.5) |
| Lithuania | 2.1 | (0.15) | 70 | (4.8) | a | a | a | a |
| Macao-China | 1.4 | (0.09) | 31 | (3.5) | 23 | (7.4) | a | a |
| Montenegro | 2.0 | (0.11) | 57 | (3.7) | a | a | a | a |
| Qatar | 1.1 | (0.07) | 21 | (3.4) | a | a | a | a |
| Romania | 2.2 | (0.19) | 60 | (9.0) | a | a | 48 | (10.0) |
| Russian Federation | 1.5 | (0.08) | 29 | (4.4) | 47 | (4.7) | 30 | (5.6) |
| Serbia | 2.2 | (0.12) | 65 | (4.0) | a | a | a | a |
| Slovenia | 2.2 | (0.14) | 79 | (4.6) | a | a | a | a |
| Chinese Taipei | 2.1 | (0.13) | 75 | (4.2) | a | a | a | a |
| Thailand | 1.1 | (0.08) | 15 | (3.6) | 30 | (4.9) | 1 | (4.8) |
| Tunisia | 1.4 | (0.10) | 41 | (5.5) | 48 | (6.9) | a | a |
| Uruguay | 1.8 | (0.12) | 70 | (4.4) | 77 | (6.4) | a | a |

Note: Values that are statistically significant are indicated in bold (see Annex A3).
1. Results based on students' self-reports.
*StatLink* ⌐⌐⌐ http://dx.doi.org/10.1787/142104560611

Pour consulter la version française intégrale de ce tableau, suivre ce lien :
*StatLink* ⌐⌐⌐ http://dx.doi.org/10.1787/152684743050

[Part 1/3]

**Table 4.9b** Index of cultural possessions in the home and performance on the science scale, by quarters of the index[1]

Tableau 4.9b  Indice de patrimoine culturel familial et score sur l'échelle de culture scientifique, par quartile de l'indice

| | | | Index of cultural possessions in the home | | | | | | | |
| | All students | | Bottom quarter | | Second quarter | | Third quarter | | Top quarter | |
| | Mean index | S.E. | Mean index | S.E. | Mean index | S.E. | Mean index | S.E. | Mean index | S.E. |
|---|---|---|---|---|---|---|---|---|---|---|
| **OECD** | | | | | | | | | | |
| Australia | -0.11 | (0.02) | -1.44 | (0.01) | -0.57 | (0.00) | 0.32 | (0.01) | 1.25 | (0.00) |
| Austria | 0.07 | (0.02) | -1.16 | (0.01) | -0.27 | (0.01) | 0.50 | (0.02) | 1.21 | (0.00) |
| Belgium | -0.27 | (0.02) | -1.52 | (0.00) | -0.62 | (0.01) | 0.02 | (0.01) | 1.02 | (0.01) |
| Canada | -0.10 | (0.02) | -1.49 | (0.01) | -0.58 | (0.00) | 0.38 | (0.01) | 1.28 | (0.00) |
| Czech Republic | -0.01 | (0.02) | -1.23 | (0.01) | -0.29 | (0.01) | 0.38 | (0.01) | 1.12 | (0.00) |
| Denmark | -0.10 | (0.03) | -1.48 | (0.01) | -0.59 | (0.00) | 0.38 | (0.01) | 1.32 | (0.00) |
| Finland | 0.15 | (0.02) | -1.18 | (0.02) | -0.17 | (0.01) | 0.79 | (0.01) | 1.18 | (0.00) |
| France | -0.17 | (0.03) | -1.52 | (0.00) | -0.50 | (0.00) | 0.20 | (0.00) | 1.13 | (0.00) |
| Germany | 0.08 | (0.02) | -1.13 | (0.01) | -0.21 | (0.01) | 0.52 | (0.02) | 1.14 | (0.00) |
| Greece | 0.03 | (0.02) | -1.20 | (0.02) | -0.24 | (0.01) | 0.33 | (0.01) | 1.22 | (0.00) |
| Hungary | 0.33 | (0.02) | -1.10 | (0.02) | 0.19 | (0.00) | 0.91 | (0.02) | 1.33 | (0.00) |
| Iceland | 0.73 | (0.01) | -0.42 | (0.02) | 0.89 | (0.01) | 1.21 | (0.00) | 1.22 | (0.00) |
| Ireland | -0.19 | (0.03) | -1.44 | (0.01) | -0.54 | (0.00) | 0.12 | (0.01) | 1.13 | (0.00) |
| Italy | 0.26 | (0.01) | -0.86 | (0.01) | 0.05 | (0.00) | 0.83 | (0.01) | 1.02 | (0.00) |
| Japan | -0.48 | (0.02) | -1.45 | (0.00) | -0.97 | (0.01) | -0.22 | (0.01) | 0.71 | (0.01) |
| Korea | 0.11 | (0.02) | -1.17 | (0.01) | -0.15 | (0.01) | 0.57 | (0.02) | 1.20 | (0.00) |
| Luxembourg | 0.02 | (0.01) | -1.31 | (0.01) | -0.35 | (0.01) | 0.51 | (0.01) | 1.23 | (0.00) |
| Mexico | -0.32 | (0.02) | -1.44 | (0.00) | -0.69 | (0.01) | -0.01 | (0.01) | 0.83 | (0.01) |
| Netherlands | -0.32 | (0.03) | -1.65 | (0.01) | -0.59 | (0.00) | -0.05 | (0.01) | 1.02 | (0.01) |
| New Zealand | -0.11 | (0.02) | -1.48 | (0.01) | -0.61 | (0.00) | 0.30 | (0.00) | 1.34 | (0.00) |
| Norway | 0.29 | (0.03) | -1.15 | (0.02) | -0.09 | (0.02) | 1.08 | (0.01) | 1.35 | (0.00) |
| Poland | 0.11 | (0.02) | -1.20 | (0.02) | -0.18 | (0.01) | 0.56 | (0.01) | 1.27 | (0.00) |
| Portugal | -0.11 | (0.03) | -1.43 | (0.00) | -0.42 | (0.01) | 0.32 | (0.01) | 1.08 | (0.00) |
| Slovak Republic | 0.31 | (0.02) | -0.89 | (0.01) | 0.13 | (0.00) | 0.98 | (0.01) | 1.02 | (0.00) |
| Spain | 0.10 | (0.02) | -1.07 | (0.01) | -0.13 | (0.01) | 0.51 | (0.01) | 1.08 | (0.00) |
| Sweden | 0.11 | (0.02) | -1.32 | (0.02) | -0.35 | (0.01) | 0.67 | (0.02) | 1.42 | (0.00) |
| Switzerland | -0.17 | (0.02) | -1.42 | (0.01) | -0.57 | (0.00) | 0.18 | (0.00) | 1.13 | (0.01) |
| Turkey | -0.04 | (0.02) | -1.27 | (0.01) | -0.31 | (0.01) | 0.19 | (0.00) | 1.24 | (0.01) |
| United Kingdom | -0.13 | (0.02) | -1.42 | (0.00) | -0.51 | (0.00) | 0.33 | (0.01) | 1.11 | (0.00) |
| United States | -0.09 | (0.03) | -1.43 | (0.01) | -0.51 | (0.00) | 0.41 | (0.01) | 1.17 | (0.00) |
| **OECD total** | -0.09 | (0.01) | -1.40 | (0.00) | -0.46 | (0.00) | 0.31 | (0.00) | 1.17 | (0.00) |
| **OECD average** | 0.00 | (0.00) | -1.28 | (0.00) | -0.33 | (0.00) | 0.44 | (0.00) | 1.16 | (0.00) |
| **Partners** | | | | | | | | | | |
| Argentina | -0.21 | (0.03) | -1.37 | (0.01) | -0.53 | (0.00) | 0.14 | (0.00) | 0.93 | (0.01) |
| Azerbaijan | 0.52 | (0.02) | -0.56 | (0.02) | 0.39 | (0.01) | 1.12 | (0.00) | 1.13 | (0.00) |
| Brazil | -0.15 | (0.02) | -1.24 | (0.01) | -0.41 | (0.00) | 0.14 | (0.00) | 0.90 | (0.01) |
| Bulgaria | 0.24 | (0.03) | -1.00 | (0.02) | 0.05 | (0.01) | 0.82 | (0.01) | 1.07 | (0.00) |
| Chile | -0.08 | (0.02) | -1.18 | (0.01) | -0.37 | (0.01) | 0.17 | (0.01) | 1.05 | (0.00) |
| Colombia | 0.01 | (0.03) | -1.14 | (0.02) | -0.22 | (0.01) | 0.34 | (0.01) | 1.08 | (0.00) |
| Croatia | -0.21 | (0.02) | -1.44 | (0.00) | -0.59 | (0.01) | 0.09 | (0.01) | 1.08 | (0.00) |
| Estonia | 0.34 | (0.01) | -0.83 | (0.02) | 0.14 | (0.00) | 0.96 | (0.01) | 1.08 | (0.00) |
| Hong Kong-China | -0.31 | (0.02) | -1.47 | (0.00) | -0.62 | (0.01) | 0.03 | (0.01) | 0.83 | (0.01) |
| Indonesia | -0.61 | (0.02) | -1.55 | (0.00) | -0.99 | (0.02) | -0.43 | (0.01) | 0.55 | (0.02) |
| Israel | 0.10 | (0.02) | -1.13 | (0.01) | -0.18 | (0.01) | 0.68 | (0.01) | 1.03 | (0.00) |
| Jordan | -0.34 | (0.02) | -1.40 | (0.00) | -0.63 | (0.01) | -0.08 | (0.01) | 0.73 | (0.01) |
| Kyrgyzstan | 0.12 | (0.02) | -0.93 | (0.02) | -0.07 | (0.01) | 0.43 | (0.01) | 1.07 | (0.00) |
| Latvia | 0.37 | (0.02) | -0.81 | (0.02) | 0.16 | (0.00) | 1.00 | (0.01) | 1.13 | (0.00) |
| Liechtenstein | 0.05 | (0.04) | -1.24 | (0.05) | -0.29 | (0.04) | 0.54 | (0.05) | 1.21 | (0.00) |
| Lithuania | 0.16 | (0.02) | -1.10 | (0.01) | -0.12 | (0.01) | 0.80 | (0.01) | 1.03 | (0.00) |
| Macao-China | -0.45 | (0.01) | -1.41 | (0.00) | -0.86 | (0.01) | -0.17 | (0.01) | 0.66 | (0.01) |
| Montenegro | 0.38 | (0.01) | -0.74 | (0.02) | 0.18 | (0.01) | 1.03 | (0.00) | 1.04 | (0.00) |
| Qatar | -0.12 | (0.01) | -1.31 | (0.01) | -0.50 | (0.01) | 0.18 | (0.00) | 1.15 | (0.01) |
| Romania | 0.54 | (0.03) | -0.76 | (0.03) | 0.29 | (0.00) | 1.16 | (0.02) | 1.47 | (0.00) |
| Russian Federation | 0.57 | (0.02) | -0.51 | (0.02) | 0.20 | (0.00) | 1.22 | (0.01) | 1.37 | (0.00) |
| Serbia | 0.20 | (0.02) | -1.01 | (0.01) | -0.03 | (0.01) | 0.79 | (0.01) | 1.03 | (0.00) |
| Slovenia | 0.19 | (0.01) | -1.04 | (0.02) | -0.10 | (0.01) | 0.80 | (0.01) | 1.09 | (0.00) |
| Chinese Taipei | 0.08 | (0.02) | -1.16 | (0.01) | -0.17 | (0.01) | 0.64 | (0.01) | 1.01 | (0.00) |
| Thailand | -0.13 | (0.02) | -1.24 | (0.01) | -0.51 | (0.00) | 0.16 | (0.00) | 1.07 | (0.00) |
| Tunisia | -0.42 | (0.03) | -1.40 | (0.00) | -0.83 | (0.01) | -0.13 | (0.01) | 0.66 | (0.01) |
| Uruguay | -0.05 | (0.02) | -1.24 | (0.01) | -0.29 | (0.01) | 0.26 | (0.01) | 1.06 | (0.00) |

Note: Values that are statistically significant are indicated in bold (see Annex A3).
1. Results based on students' self-reports.
StatLink ⟲ http://dx.doi.org/10.1787/142104560611

Pour consulter la version française intégrale de ce tableau, suivre ce lien :
StatLink ⟲ http://dx.doi.org/10.1787/152684743050

[Part 2/3]

**Table 4.9b** **Index of cultural possessions in the home and performance on the science scale, by quarters of the index[1]**

Tableau 4.9b   Indice de patrimoine culturel familial et score sur l'échelle de culture scientifique, par quartile de l'indice

| | | Performance on the science scale, by quarters of the index | | | | | | |
|---|---|---|---|---|---|---|---|---|
| | | Bottom quarter | | Second quarter | | Third quarter | | Top quarter | |
| | | Mean score | S.E. | Mean score | S.E. | Mean score | S.E. | Mean score | S.E. |
| OECD | Australia | **503** | (3.0) | 515 | (2.4) | 534 | (2.9) | **564** | (2.8) |
| | Austria | **485** | (5.2) | 495 | (5.4) | 514 | (5.2) | **553** | (4.2) |
| | Belgium | **475** | (3.4) | 505 | (3.9) | 517 | (3.4) | **554** | (2.7) |
| | Canada | **515** | (2.6) | 528 | (2.5) | 541 | (2.9) | **561** | (2.6) |
| | Czech Republic | **481** | (5.3) | 502 | (4.4) | 521 | (4.9) | **550** | (4.2) |
| | Denmark | **462** | (4.0) | 482 | (3.7) | 504 | (3.5) | **539** | (4.1) |
| | Finland | **536** | (3.2) | 555 | (4.0) | 579 | (3.3) | **585** | (3.1) |
| | France | **443** | (4.1) | 480 | (4.1) | 518 | (4.3) | **545** | (4.3) |
| | Germany | **492** | (4.6) | 502 | (5.0) | 523 | (5.2) | **561** | (4.0) |
| | Greece | **447** | (5.2) | 471 | (4.0) | 483 | (4.4) | **497** | (4.5) |
| | Hungary | **455** | (3.5) | 507 | (3.5) | 521 | (3.4) | **536** | (3.4) |
| | Iceland | **461** | (3.5) | 497 | (4.8) | 505 | (3.8) | **503** | (3.4) |
| | Ireland | **483** | (4.2) | 498 | (3.8) | 506 | (3.6) | **552** | (3.8) |
| | Italy | **443** | (2.9) | 473 | (2.5) | 491 | (3.5) | **497** | (3.2) |
| | Japan | **503** | (5.0) | 520 | (4.4) | 546 | (3.8) | **560** | (3.8) |
| | Korea | **486** | (5.1) | 517 | (4.4) | 538 | (4.7) | **549** | (4.9) |
| | Luxembourg | **452** | (2.9) | 471 | (3.1) | 494 | (2.8) | **532** | (3.1) |
| | Mexico | **394** | (2.6) | 404 | (3.1) | 419 | (3.1) | **437** | (3.8) |
| | Netherlands | **495** | (5.0) | 517 | (4.4) | 529 | (3.8) | **561** | (3.9) |
| | New Zealand | **508** | (3.7) | 522 | (3.4) | 524 | (3.8) | **579** | (3.3) |
| | Norway | **455** | (4.1) | 477 | (4.5) | 509 | (3.4) | **518** | (4.1) |
| | Poland | **466** | (3.3) | 495 | (4.0) | 510 | (3.5) | **523** | (3.4) |
| | Portugal | **439** | (4.0) | 460 | (4.4) | 489 | (4.0) | **511** | (3.8) |
| | Slovak Republic | **459** | (4.3) | 486 | (3.5) | 504 | (3.9) | **506** | (4.1) |
| | Spain | **454** | (3.0) | 480 | (3.0) | 503 | (3.2) | **520** | (3.2) |
| | Sweden | **474** | (3.9) | 495 | (3.4) | 521 | (4.7) | **530** | (4.9) |
| | Switzerland | **490** | (3.4) | 504 | (3.2) | 509 | (4.0) | **547** | (4.2) |
| | Turkey | **396** | (3.6) | 417 | (3.9) | 431 | (4.5) | **453** | (6.3) |
| | United Kingdom | **484** | (3.2) | 498 | (3.4) | 525 | (3.6) | **559** | (3.6) |
| | United States | **451** | (4.3) | 484 | (4.8) | 500 | (5.6) | **526** | (5.2) |
| | **OECD total** | **457** | (1.2) | **482** | (1.6) | **501** | (1.6) | **530** | (1.5) |
| | **OECD average** | **470** | (0.7) | **492** | (0.7) | **510** | (0.7) | **534** | (0.7) |
| Partners | Argentina | **369** | (6.2) | 381 | (6.6) | 404 | (7.1) | **428** | (7.1) |
| | Azerbaijan | **379** | (4.4) | 378 | (3.0) | 390 | (3.6) | **390** | (3.3) |
| | Brazil | **381** | (4.7) | 386 | (3.9) | 395 | (3.7) | **406** | (4.4) |
| | Bulgaria | **379** | (6.0) | 429 | (6.6) | 463 | (7.2) | **473** | (6.8) |
| | Chile | **411** | (4.4) | 424 | (4.8) | 440 | (5.8) | **478** | (5.3) |
| | Colombia | **375** | (4.5) | 386 | (4.7) | 390 | (4.8) | **409** | (4.9) |
| | Croatia | **464** | (3.5) | 483 | (3.6) | 504 | (3.0) | **532** | (3.5) |
| | Estonia | **506** | (3.4) | 531 | (3.4) | 543 | (4.6) | **547** | (4.4) |
| | Hong Kong-China | **518** | (3.8) | 532 | (4.2) | 555 | (4.3) | **564** | (5.2) |
| | Indonesia | 389 | (5.1) | 394 | (6.9) | 397 | (7.8) | 396 | (6.1) |
| | Israel | **416** | (5.0) | 448 | (5.8) | 474 | (4.7) | **492** | (4.8) |
| | Jordan | **414** | (3.5) | 419 | (4.6) | 429 | (4.5) | **438** | (4.6) |
| | Kyrgyzstan | **304** | (3.7) | 319 | (5.0) | 331 | (4.6) | **349** | (3.5) |
| | Latvia | **460** | (4.0) | 489 | (3.5) | 505 | (5.4) | **507** | (4.4) |
| | Liechtenstein | **492** | (9.6) | 496 | (14.1) | 536 | (11.2) | **572** | (9.3) |
| | Lithuania | **451** | (3.5) | 479 | (3.6) | 508 | (3.8) | **521** | (3.8) |
| | Macao-China | **496** | (3.4) | 501 | (3.0) | 520 | (2.9) | **529** | (2.4) |
| | Montenegro | **379** | (2.2) | 403 | (2.4) | 435 | (3.1) | **436** | (3.5) |
| | Qatar | **346** | (2.5) | 347 | (3.0) | 353 | (2.1) | **366** | (2.5) |
| | Romania | **382** | (5.5) | 421 | (5.5) | 435 | (4.6) | **440** | (5.2) |
| | Russian Federation | **458** | (5.1) | 484 | (4.8) | 487 | (4.6) | **491** | (4.3) |
| | Serbia | **399** | (3.9) | 431 | (3.8) | 454 | (3.5) | **462** | (3.3) |
| | Slovenia | **475** | (3.4) | 511 | (3.2) | 540 | (3.7) | **551** | (3.5) |
| | Chinese Taipei | **488** | (4.8) | 523 | (4.6) | 553 | (3.7) | **567** | (3.4) |
| | Thailand | **412** | (2.8) | 417 | (3.0) | 426 | (2.9) | **428** | (3.0) |
| | Tunisia | **368** | (3.3) | 376 | (3.8) | 395 | (4.2) | **408** | (5.5) |
| | Uruguay | **397** | (3.9) | 420 | (4.3) | 435 | (3.8) | **469** | (4.0) |

Note: Values that are statistically significant are indicated in bold (see Annex A3).
1. Results based on students' self-reports.
StatLink ⬛🖳 http://dx.doi.org/10.1787/142104560611

Pour consulter la version française intégrale de ce tableau, suivre ce lien :
StatLink ⬛🖳 http://dx.doi.org/10.1787/152684743050

153

[Part 3/3]

**Table 4.9b** Index of cultural possessions in the home and performance on the science scale, by quarters of the index[1]

Tableau 4.9b Indice de patrimoine culturel familial et score sur l'échelle de culture scientifique, par quartile de l'indice

| | | Change in the science score per unit of this index | | Increased likelihood of students in the bottom quarter of this index scoring in the bottom quarter of the science performance distribution | | Explained variance in student performance (r-squared x 100) | |
|---|---|---|---|---|---|---|---|
| | | Effect | S.E. | Ratio | S.E. | Percentage | S.E. |
| OECD | Australia | 21.8 | (1.10) | 1.5 | (0.08) | 5.3 | (0.50) |
| | Austria | 27.7 | (1.68) | 1.5 | (0.11) | 7.5 | (0.79) |
| | Belgium | 31.9 | (1.54) | 1.9 | (0.09) | 9.6 | (0.79) |
| | Canada | 16.5 | (1.05) | 1.4 | (0.07) | 3.7 | (0.45) |
| | Czech Republic | 29.1 | (1.93) | 1.7 | (0.14) | 7.5 | (0.93) |
| | Denmark | 26.2 | (1.40) | 1.8 | (0.12) | 9.4 | (0.92) |
| | Finland | 21.3 | (1.31) | 1.7 | (0.12) | 6.2 | (0.72) |
| | France | 39.4 | (2.23) | 2.3 | (0.14) | 14.6 | (1.41) |
| | Germany | 28.6 | (1.82) | 1.6 | (0.09) | 7.1 | (0.77) |
| | Greece | 21.1 | (2.27) | 1.7 | (0.14) | 4.8 | (0.95) |
| | Hungary | 30.7 | (1.70) | 2.5 | (0.17) | 12.1 | (1.24) |
| | Iceland | 27.8 | (1.86) | 1.7 | (0.11) | 5.0 | (0.65) |
| | Ireland | 26.4 | (1.81) | 1.6 | (0.13) | 7.2 | (0.90) |
| | Italy | 28.2 | (1.88) | 1.8 | (0.09) | 5.6 | (0.71) |
| | Japan | 25.9 | (2.04) | 1.7 | (0.12) | 5.4 | (0.78) |
| | Korea | 27.4 | (2.34) | 2.0 | (0.11) | 8.6 | (1.22) |
| | Luxembourg | 30.9 | (1.53) | 1.9 | (0.14) | 10.7 | (1.03) |
| | Mexico | 20.1 | (1.82) | 1.4 | (0.08) | 5.1 | (0.85) |
| | Netherlands | 24.6 | (2.06) | 1.7 | (0.11) | 6.9 | (1.07) |
| | New Zealand | 22.9 | (1.35) | 1.4 | (0.09) | 5.5 | (0.65) |
| | Norway | 25.0 | (1.44) | 1.8 | (0.11) | 8.4 | (0.90) |
| | Poland | 23.1 | (1.34) | 1.8 | (0.11) | 6.7 | (0.73) |
| | Portugal | 29.0 | (1.92) | 2.0 | (0.13) | 9.8 | (1.09) |
| | Slovak Republic | 24.6 | (2.29) | 1.8 | (0.14) | 4.6 | (0.81) |
| | Spain | 30.0 | (1.42) | 1.9 | (0.11) | 8.4 | (0.75) |
| | Sweden | 20.3 | (1.81) | 1.7 | (0.13) | 6.1 | (1.07) |
| | Switzerland | 22.4 | (1.56) | 1.4 | (0.07) | 4.8 | (0.66) |
| | Turkey | 23.0 | (2.38) | 1.6 | (0.10) | 6.9 | (1.08) |
| | United Kingdom | 29.3 | (1.65) | 1.6 | (0.08) | 7.1 | (0.76) |
| | United States | 27.5 | (1.91) | 1.7 | (0.11) | 7.0 | (0.90) |
| | **OECD total** | **26.0** | (0.55) | **1.7** | (0.04) | **6.1** | (0.25) |
| | **OECD average** | **26.1** | (0.33) | **1.7** | (0.02) | **7.3** | (0.16) |
| Partners | Argentina | 26.2 | (3.18) | 1.4 | (0.12) | 5.4 | (1.25) |
| | Azerbaijan | 5.9 | (2.37) | 1.2 | (0.10) | 0.7 | (0.55) |
| | Brazil | 11.8 | (2.39) | 1.1 | (0.09) | 1.2 | (0.47) |
| | Bulgaria | 44.3 | (3.23) | 2.4 | (0.20) | 13.3 | (1.42) |
| | Chile | 29.2 | (2.56) | 1.5 | (0.14) | 7.2 | (1.16) |
| | Colombia | 14.4 | (2.04) | 1.3 | (0.12) | 2.3 | (0.59) |
| | Croatia | 27.0 | (1.57) | 1.8 | (0.10) | 8.8 | (0.93) |
| | Estonia | 19.7 | (1.78) | 1.6 | (0.10) | 3.7 | (0.63) |
| | Hong Kong-China | 20.9 | (2.57) | 1.6 | (0.12) | 4.2 | (0.94) |
| | Indonesia | 3.4 | (1.81) | 1.0 | (0.07) | 0.2 | (0.19) |
| | Israel | 34.2 | (2.31) | 1.7 | (0.12) | 7.7 | (0.96) |
| | Jordan | 13.4 | (1.97) | 1.2 | (0.08) | 1.6 | (0.45) |
| | Kyrgyzstan | 20.3 | (2.18) | 1.4 | (0.10) | 3.8 | (0.72) |
| | Latvia | 22.5 | (1.93) | 1.8 | (0.14) | 5.2 | (0.84) |
| | Liechtenstein | 30.5 | (4.78) | 1.5 | (0.37) | 10.0 | (2.99) |
| | Lithuania | 31.8 | (1.99) | 2.1 | (0.13) | 10.3 | (1.10) |
| | Macao-China | 16.2 | (1.46) | 1.4 | (0.11) | 3.1 | (0.55) |
| | Montenegro | 30.6 | (1.45) | 2.0 | (0.14) | 8.9 | (0.82) |
| | Qatar | 8.7 | (1.27) | 1.1 | (0.07) | 1.0 | (0.28) |
| | Romania | 24.7 | (2.42) | 2.2 | (0.20) | 8.8 | (1.52) |
| | Russian Federation | 15.7 | (2.29) | 1.5 | (0.09) | 2.3 | (0.62) |
| | Serbia | 30.6 | (1.67) | 2.2 | (0.13) | 9.7 | (0.92) |
| | Slovenia | 35.5 | (1.91) | 2.1 | (0.13) | 10.6 | (1.09) |
| | Chinese Taipei | 36.2 | (1.86) | 2.2 | (0.15) | 11.7 | (0.99) |
| | Thailand | 7.0 | (1.43) | 1.2 | (0.07) | 0.6 | (0.25) |
| | Tunisia | 21.1 | (2.73) | 1.4 | (0.11) | 4.6 | (1.06) |
| | Uruguay | 29.7 | (1.69) | 1.8 | (0.16) | 7.7 | (0.85) |

Note: Values that are statistically significant are indicated in bold (see Annex A3).
1. Results based on students' self-reports.
StatLink ⟨⟩ http://dx.doi.org/10.1787/142104560611

Pour consulter la version française intégrale de ce tableau, suivre ce lien :
StatLink ⟨⟩ http://dx.doi.org/10.1787/152684743050

[Part 1/2]

**Table 4.10** **Student performance on the science, reading and mathematics scales, by level of home educational resources[1]**

Tableau 4.10 Score sur les échelles de culture scientifique, de compréhension de l'écrit et de culture mathématique, selon les ressources éducatives à la maison

| | Students with a low level of home educational resources (bottom quarter of the index of home educational resources) | | | | | | Students with a high level of home educational resources (top quarter of the index of home educational resources) | | | | | |
|---|---|---|---|---|---|---|---|---|---|---|---|---|
| | Performance | | | | | | Performance | | | | | |
| | Science | | Reading | | Mathematics | | Science | | Reading | | Mathematics | |
| | Mean score | S.E. | Mean score | S.E. | Mean score | S.E. | Mean score | S.E. | Mean score | S.E. | Mean score | S.E. |
| **OECD** | | | | | | | | | | | | |
| Australia | 502 | (3.0) | 487 | (2.9) | 497 | (2.7) | 541 | (2.8) | 528 | (2.6) | 533 | (2.7) |
| Austria | 487 | (5.6) | 461 | (5.9) | 481 | (5.4) | 521 | (4.4) | 503 | (4.6) | 516 | (4.4) |
| Belgium | 474 | (4.6) | 459 | (6.0) | 482 | (5.2) | 518 | (3.4) | 511 | (3.7) | 527 | (3.4) |
| Canada | 515 | (2.7) | 500 | (3.2) | 508 | (2.7) | 545 | (2.7) | 543 | (2.8) | 538 | (2.5) |
| Czech Republic | 466 | (5.1) | 433 | (7.2) | 461 | (5.2) | 532 | (3.4) | 502 | (4.0) | 526 | (3.8) |
| Denmark | 478 | (3.9) | 477 | (3.9) | 493 | (3.5) | 503 | (3.9) | 502 | (4.2) | 523 | (3.4) |
| Finland | 545 | (3.1) | 531 | (3.2) | 526 | (3.5) | 562 | (3.2) | 547 | (3.3) | 553 | (3.1) |
| France | 445 | (4.9) | 436 | (5.8) | 448 | (4.7) | 516 | (4.1) | 511 | (4.4) | 515 | (3.8) |
| Germany | 485 | (5.4) | 455 | (6.6) | 472 | (5.5) | 536 | (4.5) | 520 | (5.0) | 527 | (4.4) |
| Greece | 428 | (4.9) | 414 | (6.3) | 416 | (4.9) | 506 | (3.7) | 493 | (4.6) | 493 | (4.0) |
| Hungary | 456 | (3.8) | 432 | (5.5) | 442 | (4.2) | 533 | (3.4) | 512 | (3.9) | 519 | (3.8) |
| Iceland | 473 | (3.4) | 473 | (3.3) | 487 | (3.1) | 502 | (3.3) | 494 | (3.5) | 515 | (3.1) |
| Ireland | 480 | (4.3) | 488 | (4.8) | 478 | (3.4) | 529 | (3.2) | 542 | (3.3) | 519 | (2.9) |
| Italy | 440 | (3.0) | 433 | (3.8) | 428 | (2.8) | 497 | (2.8) | 488 | (2.6) | 483 | (2.9) |
| Japan | 503 | (4.7) | 469 | (5.1) | 498 | (4.3) | 545 | (4.0) | 513 | (4.2) | 534 | (3.9) |
| Korea | 495 | (4.7) | 529 | (5.7) | 515 | (4.8) | 543 | (4.2) | 577 | (4.1) | 572 | (5.0) |
| Luxembourg | 463 | (2.5) | 453 | (2.7) | 465 | (2.4) | 495 | (2.8) | 488 | (3.4) | 501 | (2.7) |
| Mexico | 379 | (3.4) | 375 | (3.8) | 374 | (3.9) | 450 | (3.6) | 455 | (3.9) | 447 | (3.5) |
| Netherlands | 487 | (4.6) | 469 | (5.1) | 493 | (4.8) | 547 | (3.7) | 528 | (3.8) | 551 | (3.5) |
| New Zealand | 493 | (4.4) | 482 | (5.0) | 490 | (3.5) | 556 | (3.5) | 548 | (3.9) | 544 | (3.3) |
| Norway | 466 | (4.3) | 458 | (4.7) | 467 | (4.0) | 498 | (3.5) | 498 | (3.6) | 501 | (3.3) |
| Poland | 461 | (3.2) | 464 | (3.8) | 457 | (2.8) | 514 | (3.2) | 528 | (3.9) | 512 | (3.4) |
| Portugal | 432 | (4.6) | 421 | (5.6) | 422 | (4.8) | 487 | (3.7) | 490 | (3.9) | 481 | (3.5) |
| Slovak Republic | 435 | (4.5) | 409 | (6.2) | 436 | (5.9) | 521 | (3.3) | 501 | (4.0) | 528 | (3.9) |
| Spain | 454 | (3.7) | 426 | (3.1) | 445 | (2.9) | 502 | (2.6) | 476 | (2.4) | 494 | (2.5) |
| Sweden | 480 | (3.8) | 480 | (5.1) | 476 | (3.5) | 513 | (3.3) | 520 | (3.6) | 514 | (3.0) |
| Switzerland | 491 | (4.2) | 478 | (3.9) | 510 | (4.2) | 521 | (4.0) | 509 | (3.4) | 539 | (3.9) |
| Turkey | 384 | (3.4) | 406 | (4.9) | 381 | (4.2) | 457 | (6.9) | 479 | (6.2) | 464 | (9.1) |
| United Kingdom | 482 | (3.9) | 462 | (3.9) | 466 | (3.7) | 532 | (2.9) | 514 | (2.8) | 512 | (2.6) |
| United States | 455 | (6.6) | m | m | 445 | (5.9) | 513 | (4.8) | m | m | 495 | (4.2) |
| **OECD total** | 450 | (2.1) | 436 | (1.7) | 443 | (2.0) | 517 | (0.9) | 513 | (1.0) | 514 | (1.0) |
| **OECD average** | 468 | (0.8) | 457 | (0.9) | 465 | (0.8) | 518 | (0.7) | 511 | (0.7) | 516 | (0.7) |
| **Partners** | | | | | | | | | | | | |
| Argentina | 344 | (7.0) | 320 | (8.6) | 338 | (7.2) | 442 | (6.5) | 430 | (7.8) | 433 | (6.1) |
| Azerbaijan | 366 | (4.2) | 332 | (5.0) | 472 | (3.6) | 397 | (3.7) | 375 | (4.9) | 480 | (2.5) |
| Brazil | 356 | (2.8) | 360 | (5.4) | 334 | (3.4) | 444 | (4.6) | 446 | (5.5) | 425 | (5.1) |
| Bulgaria | 372 | (6.2) | 332 | (8.9) | 357 | (6.8) | 482 | (6.8) | 458 | (6.5) | 459 | (7.0) |
| Chile | 402 | (3.7) | 407 | (5.0) | 376 | (4.8) | 478 | (5.1) | 483 | (5.9) | 451 | (4.8) |
| Colombia | 358 | (4.6) | 344 | (7.0) | 337 | (5.7) | 430 | (4.4) | 438 | (5.5) | 418 | (4.3) |
| Croatia | 452 | (3.4) | 433 | (4.3) | 428 | (3.6) | 512 | (3.2) | 499 | (3.1) | 486 | (3.2) |
| Estonia | 512 | (3.6) | 482 | (4.7) | 491 | (3.6) | 539 | (3.2) | 510 | (3.5) | 526 | (3.4) |
| Hong Kong-China | 516 | (4.2) | 507 | (4.1) | 523 | (4.5) | 556 | (3.2) | 554 | (2.7) | 561 | (3.6) |
| Indonesia | 373 | (4.1) | 371 | (4.4) | 368 | (4.6) | 417 | (8.2) | 417 | (8.2) | 418 | (8.0) |
| Israel | 420 | (5.6) | 402 | (6.9) | 412 | (6.8) | 474 | (4.6) | 458 | (5.7) | 460 | (5.1) |
| Jordan | 383 | (3.3) | 357 | (4.2) | 347 | (3.8) | 454 | (4.3) | 435 | (4.8) | 414 | (4.7) |
| Kyrgyzstan | 297 | (4.5) | 253 | (5.2) | 285 | (4.1) | 345 | (3.9) | 314 | (5.1) | 337 | (5.0) |
| Latvia | 462 | (4.3) | 450 | (5.6) | 453 | (4.4) | 507 | (4.0) | 498 | (4.5) | 507 | (3.9) |
| Liechtenstein | 502 | (7.8) | 491 | (8.2) | 507 | (8.8) | 527 | (10.6) | 514 | (9.9) | 531 | (9.9) |
| Lithuania | 444 | (3.5) | 426 | (4.1) | 441 | (3.6) | 520 | (3.6) | 502 | (4.0) | 520 | (3.7) |
| Macao-China | 486 | (2.6) | 468 | (2.3) | 500 | (2.6) | 531 | (3.1) | 511 | (2.5) | 546 | (3.6) |
| Montenegro | 378 | (2.3) | 356 | (2.6) | 365 | (2.6) | 436 | (2.8) | 415 | (3.3) | 424 | (2.9) |
| Qatar | 321 | (1.7) | 278 | (2.4) | 283 | (1.9) | 375 | (2.6) | 344 | (3.1) | 350 | (2.7) |
| Romania | 385 | (5.2) | 366 | (7.0) | 378 | (6.3) | 456 | (5.9) | 430 | (6.5) | 458 | (6.2) |
| Russian Federation | 446 | (4.9) | 407 | (5.5) | 442 | (4.6) | 505 | (4.0) | 468 | (4.7) | 503 | (4.2) |
| Serbia | 402 | (4.3) | 362 | (4.7) | 397 | (4.8) | 461 | (3.3) | 431 | (3.8) | 463 | (3.7) |
| Slovenia | 495 | (3.9) | 471 | (3.0) | 483 | (3.1) | 535 | (2.7) | 509 | (2.4) | 520 | (2.5) |
| Chinese Taipei | 502 | (4.5) | 466 | (4.3) | 511 | (5.7) | 556 | (3.3) | 520 | (3.3) | 577 | (3.7) |
| Thailand | 389 | (2.8) | 378 | (3.7) | 388 | (4.1) | 467 | (3.9) | 466 | (3.8) | 461 | (3.9) |
| Tunisia | 352 | (2.9) | 338 | (4.4) | 325 | (3.4) | 429 | (6.1) | 430 | (7.0) | 424 | (6.8) |
| Uruguay | 382 | (3.7) | 358 | (5.1) | 379 | (3.4) | 471 | (3.4) | 458 | (4.8) | 470 | (3.9) |

Note: Values that are statistically significant are indicated in bold (see Annex A3).
1. Results based on students' self-reports.
*StatLink* ▨▧ http://dx.doi.org/10.1787/142104560611

Pour consulter la version française intégrale de ce tableau, suivre ce lien :
*StatLink* ▨▧ http://dx.doi.org/10.1787/152684743050

[Part 2/2]

**Table 4.10** Student performance on the science, reading and mathematics scales, by level of home educational resources[1]

Tableau 4.10 Score sur les échelles de culture scientifique, de compréhension de l'écrit et de culture mathématique, selon les ressources éducatives à la maison

| | | Increased likelihood of students, who are in the bottom quarter of the index of home educational resources, scoring in the bottom quarter of the science performance distribution | | Difference in science performance between students with a high level of home educational resources and students with a low level of home educational resources | | | | | |
| | | | | PISA 2006 | | PISA 2003 | | PISA 2000 | |
| | | Ratio | S.E. | Dif. | S.E. | Dif. | S.E. | Dif. | S.E. |
|---|---|---|---|---|---|---|---|---|---|
| OECD | Australia | 1.6 | (0.07) | 39 | (3.0) | 42 | (4.0) | 45 | (6.8) |
| | Austria | 1.6 | (0.12) | 34 | (4.3) | 35 | (4.3) | 40 | (5.7) |
| | Belgium | 2.0 | (0.10) | 44 | (5.3) | 74 | (4.9) | 74 | (10.1) |
| | Canada | 1.5 | (0.06) | 30 | (3.0) | 36 | (3.3) | 28 | (3.6) |
| | Czech Republic | 2.4 | (0.20) | 66 | (4.9) | 64 | (5.0) | 54 | (4.9) |
| | Denmark | 1.3 | (0.08) | 25 | (4.2) | 65 | (5.3) | 59 | (7.1) |
| | Finland | 1.4 | (0.07) | 17 | (3.6) | 31 | (4.0) | 26 | (6.1) |
| | France | 2.4 | (0.14) | 71 | (5.6) | 48 | (5.7) | 49 | (6.9) |
| | Germany | 1.8 | (0.09) | 50 | (4.8) | 50 | (5.5) | 47 | (8.6) |
| | Greece | 2.3 | (0.15) | 78 | (5.3) | 69 | (6.3) | 40 | (8.5) |
| | Hungary | 2.6 | (0.19) | 77 | (4.8) | 52 | (5.6) | 63 | (7.5) |
| | Iceland | 1.5 | (0.08) | 29 | (5.0) | 21 | (5.0) | 18 | (6.6) |
| | Ireland | 1.8 | (0.09) | 49 | (4.1) | 53 | (5.3) | 46 | (6.3) |
| | Italy | 1.9 | (0.10) | 56 | (3.7) | 46 | (4.9) | 35 | (6.4) |
| | Japan | 1.6 | (0.10) | 42 | (4.7) | 53 | (6.7) | 30 | (6.5) |
| | Korea | 1.6 | (0.10) | 48 | (5.7) | 57 | (6.2) | 29 | (5.5) |
| | Luxembourg | 1.6 | (0.09) | 32 | (3.8) | 36 | (4.6) | m | m |
| | Mexico | 1.8 | (0.11) | 72 | (5.0) | 73 | (6.2) | 69 | (7.0) |
| | Netherlands | 2.1 | (0.13) | 60 | (4.4) | 74 | (6.1) | m | m |
| | New Zealand | 1.9 | (0.11) | 63 | (4.9) | 55 | (5.0) | 60 | (6.5) |
| | Norway | 1.6 | (0.08) | 32 | (4.5) | 45 | (4.9) | 65 | (6.2) |
| | Poland | 2.0 | (0.11) | 54 | (4.3) | 46 | (4.6) | 63 | (9.2) |
| | Portugal | 2.3 | (0.16) | 56 | (4.9) | 58 | (5.6) | 50 | (6.3) |
| | Slovak Republic | 2.6 | (0.22) | 86 | (5.6) | 66 | (7.5) | a | a |
| | Spain | 1.9 | (0.09) | 48 | (3.5) | 39 | (5.2) | 36 | (5.8) |
| | Sweden | 1.5 | (0.09) | 34 | (4.9) | 57 | (5.6) | 27 | (6.0) |
| | Switzerland | 1.4 | (0.07) | 30 | (3.8) | 60 | (6.3) | 38 | (5.7) |
| | Turkey | 2.0 | (0.15) | 73 | (7.9) | 85 | (9.3) | a | a |
| | United Kingdom | 1.8 | (0.07) | 51 | (4.5) | m | m | m | m |
| | United States | 1.7 | (0.16) | 58 | (7.4) | 51 | (4.6) | 80 | (13.4) |
| | **OECD total** | **2.0** | **(0.06)** | **67** | **(2.2)** | **64** | **(1.9)** | **61** | **(3.7)** |
| | **OECD average** | **1.8** | **(0.02)** | **50** | **(0.9)** | **53** | **(1.0)** | **47** | **(1.4)** |
| Partners | Argentina | 2.0 | (0.19) | 98 | (7.7) | a | a | 100 | (9.8) |
| | Azerbaijan | 1.7 | (0.16) | 30 | (5.1) | a | a | a | a |
| | Brazil | 1.7 | (0.12) | 88 | (5.2) | 74 | (8.1) | 62 | (8.1) |
| | Bulgaria | 2.7 | (0.24) | 110 | (9.0) | a | a | 70 | (7.2) |
| | Chile | 1.9 | (0.13) | 76 | (5.4) | a | a | 68 | (6.8) |
| | Colombia | 1.8 | (0.17) | 72 | (5.9) | a | a | a | a |
| | Croatia | 2.2 | (0.12) | 60 | (3.9) | a | a | a | a |
| | Estonia | 1.5 | (0.09) | 27 | (3.9) | a | a | a | a |
| | Hong Kong-China | 1.7 | (0.12) | 41 | (5.2) | 50 | (5.5) | 51 | (6.4) |
| | Indonesia | 1.5 | (0.13) | 43 | (7.3) | 38 | (4.7) | 34 | (7.8) |
| | Israel | 1.6 | (0.10) | 54 | (6.0) | a | a | 62 | (14.1) |
| | Jordan | 2.1 | (0.13) | 71 | (5.3) | a | a | a | a |
| | Kyrgyzstan | 1.6 | (0.12) | 49 | (5.3) | a | a | a | a |
| | Latvia | 1.7 | (0.14) | 45 | (4.7) | 40 | (5.0) | 31 | (8.3) |
| | Liechtenstein | 1.5 | (0.28) | 26 | (14.7) | 77 | (15.3) | 52 | (19.2) |
| | Lithuania | 2.3 | (0.13) | 76 | (4.2) | a | a | a | a |
| | Macao-China | 1.7 | (0.10) | 44 | (3.9) | 26 | (9.4) | a | a |
| | Montenegro | 1.9 | (0.10) | 57 | (3.5) | a | a | a | a |
| | Qatar | 1.6 | (0.08) | 54 | (3.2) | a | a | a | a |
| | Romania | 2.0 | (0.18) | 71 | (7.9) | a | a | 56 | (11.3) |
| | Russian Federation | 1.8 | (0.12) | 59 | (5.7) | 41 | (4.5) | 47 | (5.2) |
| | Serbia | 1.9 | (0.13) | 59 | (4.5) | a | a | a | a |
| | Slovenia | 1.6 | (0.11) | 40 | (5.0) | a | a | a | a |
| | Chinese Taipei | 1.8 | (0.10) | 55 | (3.6) | a | a | a | a |
| | Thailand | 1.8 | (0.15) | 79 | (4.6) | 55 | (5.1) | 55 | (7.0) |
| | Tunisia | 1.8 | (0.13) | 77 | (6.9) | 60 | (7.2) | a | a |
| | Uruguay | 2.3 | (0.16) | 88 | (4.5) | 47 | (6.4) | a | a |

Note: Values that are statistically significant are indicated in bold (see Annex A3).
1. Results based on students' self-reports.
*StatLink* ⟐⟐ http://dx.doi.org/10.1787/142104560611

Pour consulter la version française intégrale de ce tableau, suivre ce lien :
*StatLink* ⟐⟐ http://dx.doi.org/10.1787/152684743050

[Part 1/2]
**Table 4.11** Student performance on the science, reading and mathematics scales, by economic, social and cultural status[1]

Tableau 4.11  Score sur les échelles de culture scientifique, de compréhension de l'écrit et de culture mathématique, selon le statut économique, social et culturel

| | Students with a less advantaged economic, social and cultural status (bottom quarter of the PISA index of economic, social and cultural status) | | | | | | Students with a more advantaged economic, social and cultural status (top quarter of the PISA index of economic, social and cultural status) | | | | | |
|---|---|---|---|---|---|---|---|---|---|---|---|---|
| | Performance | | | | | | Performance | | | | | |
| | Science | | Reading | | Mathematics | | Science | | Reading | | Mathematics | |
| | Mean score | S.E. | Mean score | S.E. | Mean score | S.E. | Mean score | S.E. | Mean score | S.E. | Mean score | S.E. |
| **OECD** | | | | | | | | | | | | |
| Australia | 484 | (2.2) | 472 | (2.3) | 482 | (2.1) | 572 | (2.8) | 555 | (2.4) | 561 | (2.8) |
| Austria | 462 | (6.7) | 441 | (7.6) | 459 | (6.8) | 559 | (3.6) | 539 | (4.3) | 553 | (4.1) |
| Belgium | 456 | (4.2) | 446 | (5.2) | 463 | (5.7) | 566 | (2.9) | 555 | (3.1) | 576 | (3.0) |
| Canada | 501 | (2.8) | 490 | (3.4) | 498 | (2.6) | 569 | (2.5) | 566 | (2.7) | 561 | (2.4) |
| Czech Republic | 465 | (4.3) | 436 | (6.3) | 457 | (4.4) | 564 | (4.6) | 535 | (4.8) | 564 | (4.8) |
| Denmark | 453 | (3.7) | 459 | (4.1) | 475 | (3.3) | 543 | (4.1) | 534 | (4.1) | 553 | (3.8) |
| Finland | 535 | (3.0) | 519 | (3.0) | 519 | (3.1) | 598 | (2.8) | 578 | (3.2) | 585 | (2.8) |
| France | 437 | (4.8) | 432 | (5.3) | 441 | (4.3) | 559 | (4.3) | 544 | (4.6) | 556 | (4.7) |
| Germany | 460 | (5.2) | 438 | (6.3) | 450 | (5.4) | 572 | (3.3) | 550 | (4.1) | 561 | (3.7) |
| Greece | 427 | (4.8) | 416 | (6.2) | 412 | (4.7) | 520 | (4.0) | 504 | (5.0) | 507 | (4.3) |
| Hungary | 450 | (3.6) | 426 | (5.2) | 435 | (3.8) | 559 | (3.7) | 536 | (4.1) | 552 | (4.3) |
| Iceland | 458 | (3.2) | 457 | (3.2) | 473 | (3.6) | 522 | (3.1) | 512 | (3.4) | 536 | (3.0) |
| Ireland | 467 | (4.7) | 478 | (4.9) | 465 | (4.0) | 555 | (3.3) | 562 | (3.4) | 545 | (3.3) |
| Italy | 435 | (3.0) | 428 | (4.2) | 424 | (2.7) | 511 | (3.3) | 502 | (3.4) | 496 | (3.6) |
| Japan | 493 | (5.3) | 460 | (5.6) | 485 | (5.0) | 562 | (4.2) | 530 | (4.5) | 556 | (4.0) |
| Korea | 494 | (4.7) | 532 | (5.7) | 513 | (5.0) | 558 | (5.4) | 588 | (4.9) | 590 | (6.6) |
| Luxembourg | 424 | (2.5) | 416 | (3.0) | 437 | (2.4) | 543 | (2.7) | 535 | (3.0) | 543 | (2.4) |
| Mexico | 370 | (3.4) | 365 | (5.1) | 364 | (4.6) | 457 | (3.6) | 461 | (3.8) | 453 | (3.4) |
| Netherlands | 478 | (4.8) | 465 | (5.2) | 490 | (4.8) | 578 | (2.9) | 555 | (3.1) | 579 | (3.3) |
| New Zealand | 480 | (4.4) | 473 | (4.8) | 482 | (3.5) | 589 | (3.3) | 577 | (3.5) | 571 | (3.3) |
| Norway | 453 | (3.8) | 447 | (4.3) | 458 | (3.9) | 523 | (3.6) | 521 | (3.9) | 525 | (3.2) |
| Poland | 460 | (3.1) | 465 | (3.6) | 456 | (3.1) | 546 | (3.4) | 557 | (4.0) | 540 | (3.2) |
| Portugal | 433 | (4.2) | 421 | (5.5) | 424 | (4.3) | 526 | (3.2) | 529 | (3.9) | 519 | (3.4) |
| Slovak Republic | 437 | (4.0) | 414 | (5.4) | 439 | (5.2) | 540 | (4.0) | 517 | (4.7) | 543 | (4.4) |
| Spain | 446 | (3.0) | 423 | (3.1) | 440 | (2.7) | 533 | (3.5) | 498 | (3.7) | 522 | (3.7) |
| Sweden | 466 | (3.6) | 470 | (4.7) | 464 | (3.4) | 543 | (4.2) | 542 | (5.8) | 542 | (3.6) |
| Switzerland | 458 | (3.1) | 452 | (3.4) | 481 | (3.4) | 563 | (3.7) | 546 | (3.4) | 576 | (3.7) |
| Turkey | 390 | (3.3) | 409 | (5.3) | 387 | (3.9) | 474 | (8.5) | 494 | (7.7) | 480 | (10.6) |
| United Kingdom | 467 | (3.3) | 452 | (3.2) | 456 | (2.9) | 570 | (3.3) | 546 | (3.4) | 543 | (3.8) |
| United States | 435 | (5.4) | m | m | 428 | (5.0) | 552 | (4.3) | m | m | 529 | (4.2) |
| **OECD total** | 428 | (1.4) | 427 | (1.6) | 425 | (1.5) | 548 | (1.4) | 537 | (1.1) | 537 | (1.3) |
| **OECD average** | 456 | (0.7) | 448 | (0.9) | 455 | (0.8) | 547 | (0.7) | 537 | (0.8) | 544 | (0.8) |
| **Partners** | | | | | | | | | | | | |
| Argentina | 338 | (5.1) | 323 | (6.3) | 328 | (5.9) | 455 | (6.1) | 441 | (8.4) | 445 | (7.5) |
| Azerbaijan | 373 | (4.6) | 336 | (5.9) | 476 | (3.6) | 404 | (3.6) | 384 | (4.5) | 484 | (3.0) |
| Brazil | 352 | (3.6) | 351 | (6.2) | 327 | (4.7) | 443 | (5.2) | 444 | (6.2) | 424 | (6.1) |
| Bulgaria | 367 | (6.3) | 334 | (9.0) | 354 | (6.5) | 506 | (7.8) | 478 | (7.6) | 480 | (8.3) |
| Chile | 387 | (3.8) | 391 | (4.8) | 358 | (4.9) | 503 | (5.1) | 508 | (6.9) | 475 | (5.1) |
| Colombia | 358 | (3.9) | 345 | (6.3) | 334 | (4.9) | 431 | (3.7) | 434 | (5.2) | 417 | (4.3) |
| Croatia | 454 | (3.7) | 439 | (4.2) | 431 | (3.5) | 532 | (3.3) | 513 | (3.4) | 503 | (3.2) |
| Estonia | 504 | (3.7) | 475 | (5.1) | 483 | (4.1) | 570 | (3.6) | 535 | (3.8) | 555 | (3.6) |
| Hong Kong-China | 511 | (3.9) | 509 | (4.3) | 517 | (4.2) | 573 | (4.6) | 561 | (4.3) | 579 | (4.8) |
| Indonesia | 373 | (5.1) | 369 | (5.1) | 366 | (4.9) | 429 | (7.9) | 432 | (7.5) | 431 | (8.0) |
| Israel | 406 | (4.8) | 392 | (6.2) | 394 | (6.2) | 505 | (5.1) | 483 | (6.6) | 492 | (4.8) |
| Jordan | 387 | (3.2) | 363 | (3.5) | 349 | (3.5) | 465 | (4.7) | 443 | (5.8) | 426 | (5.2) |
| Kyrgyzstan | 299 | (4.5) | 251 | (5.6) | 282 | (4.4) | 357 | (4.4) | 332 | (5.5) | 355 | (4.9) |
| Latvia | 457 | (4.7) | 447 | (5.5) | 450 | (5.0) | 525 | (4.3) | 517 | (5.0) | 523 | (4.6) |
| Liechtenstein | 461 | (8.2) | 452 | (8.1) | 473 | (10.3) | 578 | (10.2) | 561 | (8.7) | 576 | (9.8) |
| Lithuania | 445 | (3.2) | 426 | (3.9) | 440 | (3.5) | 537 | (4.5) | 519 | (5.0) | 538 | (4.4) |
| Macao-China | 493 | (2.6) | 477 | (2.3) | 506 | (2.7) | 518 | (2.7) | 499 | (2.9) | 535 | (3.0) |
| Montenegro | 386 | (2.3) | 364 | (2.9) | 369 | (3.0) | 444 | (2.8) | 423 | (3.0) | 435 | (3.1) |
| Qatar | m | m | m | m | m | m | m | m | m | m | m | m |
| Romania | 377 | (4.8) | 358 | (6.9) | 373 | (6.0) | 463 | (6.9) | 438 | (6.6) | 463 | (6.7) |
| Russian Federation | 446 | (4.2) | 406 | (4.9) | 441 | (4.3) | 515 | (4.3) | 477 | (5.0) | 512 | (4.8) |
| Serbia | 399 | (4.3) | 359 | (4.8) | 396 | (5.0) | 478 | (3.1) | 447 | (3.3) | 479 | (3.6) |
| Slovenia | 467 | (2.9) | 452 | (3.1) | 458 | (2.7) | 573 | (2.9) | 541 | (2.5) | 555 | (2.9) |
| Chinese Taipei | 492 | (4.9) | 459 | (4.7) | 503 | (5.8) | 577 | (3.3) | 536 | (3.3) | 596 | (3.7) |
| Thailand | 395 | (2.9) | 388 | (4.2) | 391 | (3.6) | 468 | (4.2) | 463 | (4.5) | 466 | (4.3) |
| Tunisia | 363 | (3.2) | 354 | (3.5) | 334 | (3.6) | 427 | (6.5) | 424 | (7.4) | 424 | (7.3) |
| Uruguay | 381 | (3.6) | 358 | (6.0) | 373 | (4.4) | 484 | (3.6) | 472 | (5.2) | 484 | (3.7) |

Note: Values that are statistically significant are indicated in bold (see Annex A3).
1. Results based on students' self-reports.

StatLink ⌨ http://dx.doi.org/10.1787/142104560611

Pour consulter la version française intégrale de ce tableau, suivre ce lien :
StatLink ⌨ http://dx.doi.org/10.1787/152684743050

[Part 2/2]

**Table 4.11** Student performance on the science, reading and mathematics scales, by economic, social and cultural status[1]

Tableau 4.11 Score sur les échelles de culture scientifique, de compréhension de l'écrit et de culture mathématique, selon le statut économique, social et culturel

| | Increased likelihood of students with a less advantaged PISA index of economic, social and cultural status scoring in the bottom quarter of the science performance distribution | | Difference in science performance between students with a more advantaged PISA index of economic, social and cultural status and students with a less advantaged PISA index of economic, social and cultural status | | | | | |
| | | | PISA 2006 | | PISA 2003 | | PISA 2000 | |
| | Ratio | S.E. | Dif. | S.E. | Dif. | S.E. | Dif. | S.E. |
|---|---|---|---|---|---|---|---|---|
| Australia | 2.0 | (0.08) | 88 | (3.3) | 102 | (4.4) | 95 | (5.8) |
| Austria | 2.3 | (0.17) | 97 | (7.1) | 107 | (5.5) | 93 | (7.2) |
| Belgium | 2.6 | (0.13) | 110 | (5.2) | 133 | (5.2) | 123 | (7.1) |
| Canada | 1.8 | (0.08) | 68 | (3.4) | 88 | (3.8) | 72 | (3.9) |
| Czech Republic | 2.1 | (0.13) | 99 | (5.6) | 104 | (5.4) | 109 | (5.8) |
| Denmark | 2.2 | (0.13) | 90 | (5.0) | 108 | (5.9) | 108 | (6.9) |
| Finland | 1.7 | (0.11) | 63 | (3.5) | 74 | (3.9) | 61 | (5.5) |
| France | 2.6 | (0.20) | 122 | (6.4) | 133 | (7.4) | 113 | (6.6) |
| Germany | 2.6 | (0.14) | 111 | (5.5) | 139 | (5.4) | 126 | (7.0) |
| Greece | 2.3 | (0.16) | 93 | (6.4) | 95 | (5.5) | 83 | (8.4) |
| Hungary | 2.7 | (0.24) | 108 | (5.0) | 118 | (6.4) | 128 | (8.7) |
| Iceland | 1.8 | (0.10) | 64 | (4.1) | 66 | (5.2) | 52 | (6.5) |
| Ireland | 2.0 | (0.13) | 88 | (5.4) | 98 | (6.0) | 82 | (6.6) |
| Italy | 2.0 | (0.09) | 76 | (4.4) | 104 | (6.2) | 78 | (7.0) |
| Japan | 2.0 | (0.15) | 69 | (5.7) | 91 | (8.9) | m | m |
| Korea | 1.7 | (0.11) | 64 | (7.0) | 85 | (7.9) | 59 | (6.4) |
| Luxembourg | 3.0 | (0.17) | 119 | (3.7) | 116 | (4.4) | m | m |
| Mexico | 2.1 | (0.13) | 87 | (4.8) | 86 | (6.2) | 79 | (7.0) |
| Netherlands | 2.2 | (0.16) | 100 | (5.7) | 105 | (6.9) | m | m |
| New Zealand | 2.2 | (0.14) | 109 | (4.8) | 112 | (4.3) | 108 | (6.3) |
| Norway | 1.8 | (0.11) | 69 | (4.8) | 95 | (6.0) | 81 | (5.9) |
| Poland | 2.0 | (0.10) | 86 | (4.4) | 110 | (5.3) | 93 | (9.5) |
| Portugal | 2.2 | (0.13) | 93 | (5.3) | 94 | (5.9) | 84 | (7.5) |
| Slovak Republic | 2.5 | (0.22) | 103 | (6.1) | 122 | (8.2) | a | a |
| Spain | 2.1 | (0.12) | 87 | (4.3) | 93 | (5.6) | 96 | (6.7) |
| Sweden | 1.9 | (0.12) | 77 | (4.6) | 99 | (6.1) | 75 | (5.4) |
| Switzerland | 2.4 | (0.13) | 105 | (4.0) | 122 | (6.3) | 128 | (6.7) |
| Turkey | 1.8 | (0.17) | 84 | (9.3) | 108 | (12.0) | a | a |
| United Kingdom | 2.2 | (0.13) | 103 | (4.9) | m | m | m | m |
| United States | 2.2 | (0.15) | 117 | (7.0) | 115 | (4.6) | 113 | (9.8) |
| **OECD total** | **2.7** | **(0.07)** | **120** | **(2.1)** | **124** | **(2.2)** | **116** | **(3.2)** |
| **OECD average** | **2.2** | **(0.03)** | **92** | **(1.0)** | **104** | **(1.2)** | **93** | **(1.4)** |
| Argentina | 2.2 | (0.22) | 117 | (7.8) | a | a | a | a |
| Azerbaijan | 1.4 | (0.11) | 31 | (5.2) | a | a | a | a |
| Brazil | 1.8 | (0.13) | 91 | (6.4) | 84 | (7.8) | 80 | (10.0) |
| Bulgaria | 2.7 | (0.29) | 138 | (10.4) | a | a | a | a |
| Chile | 2.4 | (0.19) | 116 | (5.9) | a | a | a | a |
| Colombia | 1.6 | (0.18) | 73 | (5.4) | a | a | a | a |
| Croatia | 2.1 | (0.13) | 78 | (4.9) | a | a | a | a |
| Estonia | 1.7 | (0.11) | 66 | (4.5) | a | a | a | a |
| Hong Kong-China | 1.8 | (0.14) | 62 | (6.4) | 60 | (6.0) | 68 | (7.3) |
| Indonesia | 1.5 | (0.13) | 56 | (7.3) | 48 | (5.7) | 45 | (9.0) |
| Israel | 2.0 | (0.13) | 99 | (6.2) | a | a | a | a |
| Jordan | 1.8 | (0.11) | 79 | (5.6) | a | a | a | a |
| Kyrgyzstan | 1.4 | (0.10) | 58 | (6.3) | a | a | a | a |
| Latvia | 1.9 | (0.18) | 68 | (6.4) | 71 | (6.1) | 74 | (10.2) |
| Liechtenstein | 2.6 | (0.50) | 117 | (13.5) | 134 | (14.2) | 109 | (20.8) |
| Lithuania | 2.2 | (0.13) | 92 | (5.3) | a | a | a | a |
| Macao-China | 1.4 | (0.10) | 25 | (3.8) | 28 | (7.2) | a | a |
| Montenegro | 1.7 | (0.11) | 58 | (3.7) | a | a | a | a |
| Qatar | m | m | m | m | a | a | a | a |
| Romania | 2.3 | (0.26) | 85 | (9.7) | a | a | a | a |
| Russian Federation | 1.8 | (0.12) | 69 | (5.5) | 77 | (4.8) | 71 | (7.1) |
| Serbia | 2.0 | (0.14) | 79 | (4.6) | a | a | a | a |
| Slovenia | 2.3 | (0.12) | 106 | (4.2) | a | a | a | a |
| Chinese Taipei | 2.0 | (0.13) | 84 | (5.1) | a | a | a | a |
| Thailand | 1.5 | (0.14) | 73 | (5.2) | 70 | (6.1) | 44 | (7.3) |
| Tunisia | 1.4 | (0.12) | 64 | (7.4) | 57 | (8.4) | a | a |
| Uruguay | 2.3 | (0.16) | 103 | (4.6) | 101 | (6.8) | a | a |

Note: Values that are statistically significant are indicated in bold (see Annex A3).
1. Results based on students' self-reports.
StatLink ᔡᔟ http://dx.doi.org/10.1787/142104560611

Pour consulter la version française intégrale de ce tableau, suivre ce lien :
StatLink ᔡᔟ http://dx.doi.org/10.1787/152684743050

【Part 1/1】

**Table 4.12** Parents' perceptions of school and student performance in science[1]

Tableau 4.12 Point de vue des parents sur la performance en sciences de leur enfant et sur l'établissement qu'il fréquente

| | | Score point difference between parents answering "strongly agree or agree" versus "disagree or strongly disagree" to the following statements: | | | | | | | | | | |
| | | Standards of achievement are high in my child's school | | | | I am satisfied with the disciplinary atmosphere in my child's school | | | | My child's school does a good job in educating students | | | |
| | | Before accounting for ESCS[2] | | After accounting for ESCS | | Before accounting for ESCS | | After accounting for ESCS | | Before accounting for ESCS | | After accounting for ESCS | |
| | | Dif. | S.E. | Dif. | S.E. | Dif. | S.E. | Dif. | S.E. | Dif. | S.E. | Dif. | S.E. |
|---|---|---|---|---|---|---|---|---|---|---|---|---|---|
| *OECD* | Denmark | **18.0** | (4.80) | **18.6** | (4.54) | **15.4** | (5.12) | **12.2** | (4.75) | **29.7** | (5.01) | **25.0** | (4.75) |
| | Germany | **30.5** | (3.94) | **30.3** | (3.64) | **20.8** | (4.07) | **19.4** | (3.63) | **14.9** | (3.90) | **18.1** | (3.74) |
| | Iceland | **9.0** | (4.23) | **10.3** | (3.90) | **12.5** | (4.85) | 7.9 | (4.71) | **24.1** | (5.46) | **21.7** | (5.13) |
| | Italy | **24.0** | (3.68) | **22.6** | (3.50) | **8.2** | (3.74) | **8.5** | (3.47) | 7.3 | (4.03) | **11.6** | (3.84) |
| | Korea | **30.2** | (5.14) | **26.0** | (4.34) | **11.5** | (4.11) | **10.7** | (3.55) | **10.4** | (4.33) | **9.8** | (3.79) |
| | Luxembourg | **26.0** | (3.65) | **23.6** | (3.65) | **11.1** | (4.20) | **14.8** | (4.09) | **9.7** | (3.97) | **16.7** | (3.63) |
| | New Zealand | **13.9** | (5.52) | **13.1** | (5.12) | **24.7** | (4.33) | **19.3** | (3.97) | **32.3** | (6.79) | **27.1** | (6.44) |
| | Poland | 4.9 | (4.02) | 5.9 | (3.79) | 2.2 | (3.34) | 3.5 | (2.93) | -6.2 | (4.41) | 2.4 | (4.29) |
| | Portugal | **16.9** | (4.00) | **10.6** | (3.64) | 5.6 | (4.20) | **9.7** | (3.83) | -5.0 | (5.54) | 5.5 | (5.14) |
| | Turkey | **24.4** | (4.31) | **24.3** | (3.74) | 6.2 | (4.32) | 5.1 | (3.76) | 6.7 | (4.48) | **11.2** | (4.17) |
| *Partners* | Bulgaria | **14.9** | (7.30) | 10.6 | (5.85) | -6.9 | (4.94) | -2.2 | (4.26) | -3.4 | (8.99) | 3.1 | (7.82) |
| | Colombia | **15.0** | (5.79) | 10.2 | (5.29) | 0.8 | (4.57) | 0.8 | (4.06) | -6.8 | (6.52) | -6.1 | (6.03) |
| | Croatia | **43.3** | (3.26) | **33.9** | (2.87) | **10.9** | (3.66) | **10.9** | (3.46) | 7.8 | (4.40) | **10.0** | (4.18) |
| | Hong Kong-China | **48.0** | (4.04) | **41.0** | (3.52) | **48.8** | (5.60) | **46.6** | (5.42) | **26.3** | (3.68) | **25.1** | (3.37) |
| | Macao-China | **17.5** | (2.64) | **15.4** | (2.72) | **14.0** | (3.62) | **13.0** | (3.59) | **12.3** | (3.85) | **11.0** | (3.80) |
| | Qatar | 5.7 | (3.14) | 5.7 | (3.24) | 1.1 | (3.62) | 0.7 | (3.70) | **11.1** | (4.20) | **10.1** | (4.17) |

Note: Values that are statistically signifcant are indicated in bold (see Annex A3).
1. Results based on reports from parents.
2. ESCS: PISA index of economic, social and cultural status.
*StatLink* ﹃᧒ http://dx.doi.org/10.1787/142104560611

Pour consulter la version française intégrale de ce tableau, suivre ce lien :
*StatLink* ﹃᧒ http://dx.doi.org/10.1787/152684743050

【Part 1/1】

**Table 4.13** Parents' perceptions of school[1]

Tableau 4.13 Point de vue des parents sur l'établissement que leur enfant fréquente

| | | Percentage of parents strongly agreeing or agreeing with the following statements: | | | | | | |
| | | Most of my child's school teachers seem competent and dedicated | Standards of achievement are high in my child's school | I am happy with the content taught and the instructional methods used in my child's school | I am satisfied with the disciplinary atmosphere in my child's school | My child's progress is carefully monitored by the school | My child's school provides regular and useful information on my child's progress | My child's school does a good job in educating students |
|---|---|---|---|---|---|---|---|---|
| *OECD* | Denmark | 87.8 | 77.3 | 77.3 | 74.3 | 71.6 | 68.4 | 78.0 |
| | Germany | 79.7 | 71.4 | 71.2 | 73.8 | 61.4 | 46.2 | 76.2 |
| | Iceland | 85.9 | 72.4 | 78.3 | 76.2 | 81.6 | 81.2 | 82.6 |
| | Italy | 91.2 | 80.1 | 85.8 | 80.9 | 84.6 | 83.2 | 92.1 |
| | Korea | 83.3 | 71.5 | 76.8 | 78.4 | 66.1 | 62.7 | 79.4 |
| | Luxembourg | 84.5 | 76.6 | 75.4 | 82.9 | 71.7 | 58.1 | 83.5 |
| | New Zealand | 93.4 | 87.1 | 86.5 | 82.7 | 85.3 | 82.3 | 91.2 |
| | Poland | 90.1 | 88.4 | 83.8 | 79.9 | 82.4 | 92.7 | 90.0 |
| | Portugal | 93.8 | 76.1 | 86.6 | 80.4 | 83.6 | 83.4 | 89.1 |
| | Turkey | 86.7 | 72.9 | 73.4 | 81.9 | 63.8 | 66.9 | 85.0 |
| *Partners* | Bulgaria | 95.4 | 87.2 | 90.6 | 80.3 | 83.5 | 84.8 | 94.3 |
| | Colombia | 94.4 | 86.2 | 92.6 | 82.7 | 93.4 | 92.5 | 95.8 |
| | Croatia | 92.2 | 65.8 | 85.0 | 82.2 | 78.0 | 83.8 | 91.7 |
| | Hong Kong-China | 89.7 | 53.8 | 82.1 | 88.5 | 75.3 | 57.1 | 78.8 |
| | Macao-China | 89.0 | 73.9 | 84.2 | 83.7 | 83.1 | 75.0 | 82.0 |
| | Qatar | 86.7 | 80.2 | 78.4 | 79.4 | 75.7 | 64.7 | 84.7 |

1. Results based on reports from parents.
*StatLink* ﹃᧒ http://dx.doi.org/10.1787/142104560611

Pour consulter la version française intégrale de ce tableau, suivre ce lien :
*StatLink* ﹃᧒ http://dx.doi.org/10.1787/152684743050

[Part 1/1]
**Table 4.14** Parents' reports of child's past science activities and student performance in science[1]

*Tableau 4.14* Performance des élèves en sciences selon le compte-rendu des parents sur les activités scientifiques antérieures de leur enfant

| | | Scores associated with parents answering "very often or regularly" versus "never or only sometimes" to the question: "Thinking back to when your child was about 10 years old, how often would your child have read books on scientific discoveries?" | | | | | | | | Difference in score before accounting for ESCS[2] | | Difference in score after accounting for ESCS[2] | |
| | | Very often or regularly | | | | Never or only sometimes | | | | | | | |
| | | Mean score | S.E. | % of students | S.E. | Mean score | S.E. | % of students | S.E. | Dif. | S.E. | Dif. | S.E. |
|---|---|---|---|---|---|---|---|---|---|---|---|---|---|
| OECD | Denmark | 557 | (6.10) | 9.8 | (0.62) | 508 | (3.00) | 90.2 | (0.62) | **49.2** | (6.51) | **43.9** | (6.11) |
| | Germany | 567 | (6.04) | 12.7 | (0.63) | 522 | (3.50) | 87.3 | (0.63) | **44.7** | (5.27) | **33.2** | (5.55) |
| | Iceland | 556 | (7.25) | 10.7 | (0.63) | 502 | (1.84) | 89.3 | (0.63) | **53.7** | (7.51) | **46.8** | (7.40) |
| | Italy | 517 | (4.25) | 12.5 | (0.44) | 477 | (1.97) | 87.5 | (0.44) | **39.6** | (3.67) | **31.5** | (3.10) |
| | Korea | 558 | (5.50) | 17.8 | (0.77) | 516 | (3.13) | 82.2 | (0.77) | **42.0** | (4.69) | **31.6** | (3.64) |
| | Luxembourg | 545 | (3.86) | 16.7 | (0.57) | 485 | (1.44) | 83.3 | (0.57) | **60.0** | (4.12) | **43.7** | (4.06) |
| | New Zealand | 601 | (5.73) | 12.5 | (0.52) | 544 | (2.76) | 87.5 | (0.52) | **57.4** | (6.31) | **47.2** | (5.90) |
| | Poland | m | m | m | m | m | m | m | m | m | m | m | m |
| | Portugal | 510 | (6.07) | 10.8 | (0.52) | 474 | (3.01) | 89.2 | (0.52) | **36.4** | (6.19) | **24.3** | (5.64) |
| | Turkey | 440 | (6.61) | 16.0 | (0.63) | 421 | (3.66) | 84.0 | (0.63) | **18.6** | (5.26) | **11.5** | (4.31) |
| Partners | Bulgaria | 478 | (9.22) | 11.3 | (0.68) | 429 | (5.96) | 88.7 | (0.68) | **49.7** | (7.10) | **33.3** | (5.21) |
| | Colombia | 392 | (4.30) | 24.9 | (0.99) | 388 | (3.45) | 75.1 | (0.99) | 3.9 | (3.79) | 1.6 | (4.11) |
| | Croatia | 540 | (4.55) | 11.3 | (0.49) | 490 | (2.51) | 88.7 | (0.49) | **50.4** | (4.30) | **38.3** | (4.10) |
| | Hong Kong-China | 581 | (5.45) | 9.2 | (0.50) | 541 | (2.49) | 90.8 | (0.50) | **40.0** | (5.52) | **30.8** | (5.38) |
| | Macao-China | 533 | (5.56) | 7.4 | (0.41) | 509 | (1.15) | 92.6 | (0.41) | **23.8** | (5.82) | **20.3** | (5.81) |
| | Qatar | 374 | (3.87) | 15.4 | (0.57) | 360 | (1.37) | 84.6 | (0.57) | **13.5** | (4.12) | **11.7** | (4.32) |

Note: Values that are statistically signifcant are indicated in bold (see Annex A3).
1. Results based on reports from parents.
2. ESCS: PISA index of economic, social and cultural status.
*StatLink* 🔗 http://dx.doi.org/10.1787/142104560611

Pour consulter la version française intégrale de ce tableau, suivre ce lien :
*StatLink* 🔗 http://dx.doi.org/10.1787/152684743050

[Part 1/1]
**Table 5.1** **School admittance policies[1]**

Tableau 5.1  Politiques d'admission des établissements

| | | Percentage of students in schools where the principal reported the following statements as a "prerequisite" or a "high priority" for admittance at their school | | | | | | | | | | | |
|---|---|---|---|---|---|---|---|---|---|---|---|---|---|
| | | Residence in a particular area | | Students' academic records | | Recommendations of feeder schools | | Parents' endorsement of the instructional or religious philosophy of the school | | Students' needs or desires for a special programme | | Attendance of other family members at the school | |
| | | % | S.E. | % | S.E. | % | S.E. | % | S.E. | % | S.E. | % | S.E. |
| *OECD* | Australia | 41.5 | (2.5) | 9.3 | (1.8) | 18.2 | (2.3) | 27.5 | (1.6) | 24.6 | (2.6) | 41.9 | (2.4) |
| | Austria | 25.0 | (2.9) | 65.2 | (2.1) | 5.2 | (1.6) | 10.5 | (2.3) | 43.9 | (3.8) | 12.5 | (2.6) |
| | Belgium | 2.4 | (1.1) | 25.6 | (2.5) | 7.4 | (1.9) | 40.3 | (3.3) | 13.2 | (2.5) | 9.9 | (1.8) |
| | Canada | 77.6 | (1.7) | 10.4 | (1.2) | 22.2 | (2.1) | 15.2 | (2.0) | 36.9 | (2.4) | 26.4 | (2.3) |
| | Czech Republic | 21.0 | (2.5) | 42.2 | (3.2) | 3.1 | (1.3) | 10.8 | (2.1) | 10.3 | (3.1) | 4.3 | (1.5) |
| | Denmark | 55.5 | (4.0) | 3.9 | (1.5) | 8.7 | (1.7) | 19.5 | (3.4) | 16.6 | (3.2) | 24.2 | (3.6) |
| | Finland | 75.2 | (3.7) | 4.2 | (1.9) | 2.1 | (1.2) | 9.9 | (2.7) | 16.6 | (3.5) | 12.8 | (3.0) |
| | France | w | w | w | w | w | w | w | w | w | w | w | w |
| | Germany | 64.8 | (3.3) | 38.8 | (3.7) | 37.8 | (3.4) | 10.6 | (2.2) | 21.5 | (3.0) | 17.4 | (2.6) |
| | Greece | 71.3 | (3.3) | 4.5 | (1.7) | 1.3 | (0.8) | 4.0 | (1.4) | 13.6 | (2.5) | 24.3 | (3.4) |
| | Hungary | 3.9 | (1.3) | 64.4 | (3.8) | 1.2 | (0.8) | 22.9 | (3.8) | 30.4 | (3.5) | 3.9 | (1.7) |
| | Iceland | 93.7 | (0.1) | 1.1 | (0.0) | 6.5 | (0.2) | 9.7 | (0.1) | 18.5 | (0.2) | 9.9 | (0.1) |
| | Ireland | 42.0 | (4.1) | 2.5 | (1.2) | 11.8 | (2.6) | 27.3 | (3.2) | 13.7 | (2.9) | 37.5 | (3.6) |
| | Italy | 11.3 | (2.2) | 7.1 | (1.7) | 6.6 | (1.5) | 10.2 | (1.5) | 33.2 | (2.6) | 11.3 | (1.8) |
| | Japan | 20.1 | (3.1) | 86.3 | (2.5) | 26.1 | (3.4) | 8.7 | (2.3) | 28.9 | (3.7) | 5.8 | (1.9) |
| | Korea | 22.6 | (3.5) | 59.1 | (4.0) | 11.4 | (2.8) | 3.6 | (1.5) | 15.3 | (3.3) | 0.7 | (0.7) |
| | Luxembourg | 42.3 | (0.1) | 41.6 | (0.1) | 7.8 | (0.0) | 7.3 | (0.0) | 11.2 | (0.0) | 40.8 | (0.1) |
| | Mexico | 9.9 | (1.8) | 38.1 | (2.8) | 8.7 | (1.7) | 5.9 | (1.1) | 12.2 | (1.3) | 10.5 | (2.6) |
| | Netherlands | 10.3 | (2.2) | 65.3 | (3.9) | 90.3 | (2.3) | 19.5 | (3.3) | 19.6 | (3.1) | 4.5 | (1.4) |
| | New Zealand | 49.3 | (2.7) | 9.3 | (2.1) | 15.8 | (2.5) | 19.2 | (2.3) | 19.0 | (2.6) | 30.7 | (3.0) |
| | Norway | 78.7 | (2.8) | a | a | 0.8 | (0.6) | 2.2 | (1.0) | 3.1 | (1.3) | 4.9 | (1.7) |
| | Poland | 81.8 | (3.1) | 13.5 | (2.5) | 6.1 | (1.7) | 5.7 | (1.7) | 4.7 | (1.7) | 5.0 | (1.7) |
| | Portugal | 56.8 | (3.6) | 6.7 | (2.1) | 1.2 | (0.9) | 10.2 | (2.0) | 41.4 | (4.0) | 31.5 | (4.0) |
| | Slovak Republic | 19.3 | (3.0) | 46.5 | (2.6) | 3.2 | (1.4) | 7.4 | (1.8) | 18.4 | (3.4) | 2.6 | (1.2) |
| | Spain | 67.9 | (3.1) | 3.0 | (0.9) | 2.4 | (0.8) | 13.8 | (1.9) | 13.0 | (1.9) | 47.6 | (2.9) |
| | Sweden | 57.3 | (3.5) | 1.9 | (0.7) | 0.5 | (0.5) | 3.2 | (1.3) | 10.2 | (2.2) | 12.0 | (2.2) |
| | Switzerland | 80.1 | (2.0) | 51.1 | (2.5) | 40.0 | (2.7) | 1.6 | (0.5) | 21.2 | (2.7) | 1.7 | (0.8) |
| | Turkey | 35.3 | (3.7) | 29.0 | (3.5) | 1.4 | (0.9) | 1.3 | (0.9) | 5.4 | (1.9) | 2.6 | (1.4) |
| | United Kingdom | 60.6 | (3.2) | 9.8 | (1.3) | 7.0 | (1.6) | 12.4 | (1.9) | 9.6 | (1.9) | 32.6 | (2.9) |
| | United States | 81.1 | (3.2) | 7.9 | (1.9) | 9.3 | (2.1) | 5.0 | (1.5) | 22.4 | (3.7) | 9.7 | (2.2) |
| | **OECD total** | 51.6 | (1.1) | 27.0 | (0.9) | 13.5 | (0.7) | 8.3 | (0.5) | 19.5 | (1.3) | 12.9 | (0.8) |
| | **OECD average** | 46.9 | (0.5) | 26.7 | (0.5) | 12.6 | (0.3) | 11.9 | (0.4) | 18.9 | (0.5) | 16.5 | (0.4) |
| *Partners* | Argentina | 9.9 | (2.2) | 7.1 | (2.0) | 9.7 | (3.5) | 16.3 | (3.2) | 20.4 | (4.1) | 27.0 | (3.8) |
| | Azerbaijan | 47.3 | (4.1) | 17.3 | (3.1) | 6.8 | (2.1) | 17.4 | (3.2) | 5.3 | (1.8) | 6.3 | (2.1) |
| | Brazil | 20.2 | (2.4) | 8.1 | (1.6) | 4.7 | (1.2) | 10.6 | (1.9) | 5.7 | (1.3) | 6.1 | (1.3) |
| | Bulgaria | 28.6 | (3.6) | 83.9 | (2.7) | 9.5 | (2.9) | 47.7 | (4.2) | 75.1 | (3.7) | 51.4 | (4.5) |
| | Chile | 6.8 | (2.1) | 33.0 | (3.7) | 7.5 | (2.5) | 12.5 | (2.9) | 12.3 | (2.7) | 16.2 | (3.6) |
| | Colombia | 15.4 | (3.4) | 19.8 | (3.3) | 11.3 | (2.8) | 19.0 | (3.5) | 20.3 | (4.2) | 5.3 | (1.6) |
| | Croatia | 1.6 | (1.0) | 90.6 | (1.9) | 2.6 | (0.1) | 0.7 | (0.5) | 7.7 | (2.0) | 1.3 | (0.7) |
| | Estonia | 41.6 | (3.0) | 44.3 | (3.4) | 9.4 | (2.1) | 9.2 | (2.1) | 9.2 | (2.3) | 9.9 | (2.2) |
| | Hong Kong-China | 5.1 | (1.8) | 82.7 | (3.2) | 20.5 | (3.8) | 13.2 | (2.9) | 7.0 | (2.2) | 16.9 | (3.3) |
| | Indonesia | 20.4 | (3.4) | 62.9 | (4.4) | 18.5 | (3.2) | 34.5 | (3.6) | 24.6 | (2.8) | 7.9 | (1.8) |
| | Israel | 38.9 | (4.4) | 35.5 | (4.5) | 19.2 | (3.7) | 32.8 | (3.6) | 26.2 | (4.0) | 12.2 | (3.1) |
| | Jordan | 64.8 | (3.8) | 26.9 | (3.4) | 13.9 | (2.6) | 12.2 | (2.6) | 16.0 | (3.0) | 13.4 | (2.5) |
| | Kyrgyzstan | 49.7 | (3.7) | 22.8 | (3.2) | 12.6 | (2.7) | 7.5 | (1.9) | 15.3 | (2.5) | 10.6 | (2.5) |
| | Latvia | 20.4 | (2.9) | 17.6 | (2.4) | 1.8 | (1.1) | 10.1 | (2.4) | 46.4 | (4.2) | 10.7 | (2.1) |
| | Liechtenstein | c | c | c | c | c | c | c | c | c | c | c | c |
| | Lithuania | 52.9 | (3.7) | 11.0 | (2.3) | 1.6 | (0.8) | 4.3 | (1.9) | 7.7 | (2.0) | 15.4 | (2.5) |
| | Macao-China | 1.8 | (0.0) | 66.4 | (0.1) | 58.9 | (0.1) | 11.6 | (0.1) | 10.9 | (0.0) | 25.0 | (0.1) |
| | Montenegro | 10.0 | (0.2) | 66.8 | (0.2) | a | a | 3.6 | (0.0) | 9.2 | (0.0) | 1.7 | (0.0) |
| | Qatar | 74.4 | (0.1) | 53.4 | (0.1) | 21.8 | (0.1) | 35.2 | (0.1) | 16.9 | (0.1) | 34.1 | (0.1) |
| | Romania | 12.3 | (2.7) | 61.6 | (4.2) | 9.3 | (2.7) | 12.0 | (2.8) | 47.6 | (5.7) | 6.9 | (1.9) |
| | Russian Federation | 41.2 | (3.7) | 10.9 | (2.1) | 8.0 | (2.5) | 17.0 | (2.8) | 18.8 | (3.2) | 12.8 | (3.0) |
| | Serbia | 8.5 | (2.4) | 91.3 | (2.2) | 7.0 | (1.9) | 7.7 | (2.3) | 70.7 | (3.8) | 10.4 | (2.6) |
| | Slovenia | 5.8 | (0.5) | 38.2 | (0.2) | 1.3 | (0.0) | 4.9 | (0.1) | 63.9 | (0.3) | 5.8 | (0.2) |
| | Chinese Taipei | 32.8 | (3.1) | 52.7 | (3.1) | 15.7 | (2.8) | 16.2 | (2.3) | 22.5 | (3.0) | 8.8 | (1.8) |
| | Thailand | 70.7 | (3.2) | 43.6 | (4.0) | 32.9 | (3.5) | 47.6 | (4.0) | 44.1 | (3.5) | 19.2 | (2.8) |
| | Tunisia | 83.4 | (3.2) | 23.7 | (3.6) | 14.5 | (3.1) | 3.3 | (1.4) | 26.6 | (4.1) | 12.3 | (3.0) |
| | Uruguay | 22.0 | (2.3) | 9.0 | (1.7) | 1.2 | (0.6) | 6.1 | (1.2) | 10.6 | (2.3) | 6.7 | (1.2) |

1. Results based on reports from school principals and reported proportionate to the number of 15-year-olds enrolled in the school.
*StatLink* http://dx.doi.org/10.1787/142127877152

Pour consulter la version française intégrale de ce tableau, suivre ce lien :
*StatLink* http://dx.doi.org/10.1787/152751048643

[Part 1/2]

**Table 5.2  Structural features of school systems**

Tableau 5.2  Caractéristiques structurelles des systèmes d'éducation

| | | Number of school types or distinct educational programmes available to 15-year-olds | Proportion of 15-year-olds enrolled in programmes that give access to vocational studies at the next programme level or direct access to the labour market[1] | First age of selection in the education system | Proportion of repeaters in participating schools | |
|---|---|---|---|---|---|---|
| | | | | | Lower secondary education | Upper secondary education |
| OECD | Australia | 1 | 1.2 | 16.0 | 0.2 | 0.5 |
| | Austria | 4 | 41.5 | 10.0 | 2.8 | 5.0 |
| | Belgium | 4 | 22.4 | 12.0 | 5.7 | 9.3 |
| | Canada | 1 | 0.0 | 16.0 | 4.1 | 4.1 |
| | Czech Republic | 5 | 15.6 | 11.0 | 0.6 | 2.1 |
| | Denmark | 1 | 0.0 | 16.0 | 0.1 | 0.1 |
| | Finland | 1 | 0.0 | 16.0 | 0.3 | 0.0 |
| | France | w | w | w | w | w |
| | Germany | 4 | a | 10.0 | 3.9 | 3.8 |
| | Greece | 2 | 13.7 | 15.0 | 2.4 | 2.9 |
| | Hungary | 3 | 17.8 | 11.0 | 1.2 | 3.5 |
| | Iceland | 1 | 0.1 | 16.0 | 0.4 | 0.0 |
| | Ireland | 4 | 22.5 | 15.0 | 0.2 | 2.1 |
| | Italy | 3 | 2.2 | 14.0 | 1.9 | 8.1 |
| | Japan | 2 | 26.1 | 15.0 | 0.0 | 0.0 |
| | Korea | 3 | 23.2 | 14.0 | 0.0 | 0.0 |
| | Luxembourg | 4 | 5.5 | 13.0 | 7.6 | 9.8 |
| | Mexico | 3 | 5.1 | 12.0 | 2.2 | 3.0 |
| | Netherlands | 4 | 54.7 | 12.0 | 3.2 | 7.2 |
| | New Zealand | 1 | 0.0 | 16.0 | 0.1 | 1.4 |
| | Norway | 1 | 0.0 | 16.0 | 0.0 | 0.0 |
| | Poland | 1 | m | 16.0 | 2.2 | 2.8 |
| | Portugal | 3 | 14.0 | 15.0 | 12.8 | 16.9 |
| | Slovak Republic | 5 | 10.8 | 11.0 | 0.9 | 1.2 |
| | Spain | 1 | 0.0 | 16.0 | 16.0 | 15.8 |
| | Sweden | 1 | 0.0 | 16.0 | 0.3 | 1.1 |
| | Switzerland | 4 | 6.2 | 12.0 | 2.3 | 4.4 |
| | Turkey | 3 | m | 11.0 | 1.5 | 2.5 |
| | United Kingdom | 1 | m | 16.0 | 0.0 | 0.0 |
| | United States | 1 | 0.0 | 16.0 | 6.3 | 4.3 |
| | **OECD average** | 2.5 | 11.3 | 14.0 | 2.7 | 3.9 |
| Partners | Argentina | 3 | 1.0 | 12.0 | 15.0 | 12.9 |
| | Azerbaijan | 2 | 0.5 | 15.0 | 0.9 | 0.7 |
| | Brazil | 1 | 0.0 | 17.0 | 10.6 | 10.5 |
| | Bulgaria | 2 | 0.0 | 11.0 | 1.8 | 0.4 |
| | Chile | 2 | 0.0 | 13.0 | 4.7 | 7.5 |
| | Colombia | 2 | 0.0 | 15.0 | 4.1 | 2.2 |
| | Croatia | 3 | 26.2 | 14.0 | 0.0 | 2.2 |
| | Estonia | 1 | 1.8 | 15.0 | 3.9 | 1.1 |
| | Hong Kong-China | 3 | 0.0 | 15.0 | 2.9 | 3.1 |
| | Indonesia | 1 | 17.4 | 15.0 | 0.6 | 1.0 |
| | Israel | 2 | 18.3 | 15.0 | 0.0 | 0.0 |
| | Jordan | 1 | 0.0 | 16.0 | 4.1 | 0.9 |
| | Kyrgyzstan | 1 | 0.0 | 15.0 | 0.4 | 0.5 |
| | Latvia | 3 | 3.4 | 16.0 | 3.3 | 0.5 |
| | Liechtenstein | 3 | 0.0 | 11.0 | c | c |
| | Lithuania | 3 | 0.2 | 15.0 | 0.9 | 0.3 |
| | Macao-China | 2 | 1.3 | 12.0 | 11.1 | 5.9 |
| | Montenegro | 4 | 68.0 | 14.0 | 5.0 | 2.3 |
| | Qatar | 4 | 0.0 | 15.0 | 4.9 | 7.2 |
| | Romania | 3 | 23.4 | 14.0 | 1.9 | 0.5 |
| | Russian Federation | 3 | 4.9 | 14.5 | 0.8 | 0.3 |
| | Serbia | 1 | 75.7 | 14.0 | 2.4 | 3.1 |
| | Slovenia | 3 | 52.1 | 14.0 | 1.1 | 3.7 |
| | Chinese Taipei | 3 | 0.0 | 15.0 | 0.0 | 0.7 |
| | Thailand | 2 | 14.8 | 16.0 | 0.7 | 0.6 |
| | Tunisia | 1 | 0.0 | 16.0 | 19.8 | 18.2 |
| | Uruguay | 1 | 6.7 | 12.0 | 17.1 | 16.4 |

1. Based on the designation of the study programme (ISCED categories B and C).
*StatLink* http://dx.doi.org/10.1787/142127877152

Pour consulter la version française intégrale de ce tableau, suivre ce lien :
*StatLink* http://dx.doi.org/10.1787/152751048643

[Part 2/2]

**Table 5.2** **Structural features of school systems**

Tableau 5.2  Caractéristiques structurelles des systèmes d'éducation

| | | Performance on the science scale | | | Variance expressed as a percentage of the average variance in student performance across OECD countries | | Existence of standards-based external examinations[2] |
|---|---|---|---|---|---|---|---|
| | Mean score | S.E. | Standard deviation | S.E. | Total variance in student performance | Total variance in student performance between schools | |
| **OECD** | | | | | | | |
| Australia | 527 | (2.3) | 100 | (1.0) | 110 | 20 | 0.81 |
| Austria | 511 | (3.9) | 98 | (2.4) | 106 | 60 | 0.00 |
| Belgium | 510 | (2.5) | 100 | (2.0) | 109 | 57 | 0.00 |
| Canada | 534 | (2.0) | 94 | (1.1) | 97 | 18 | 0.51 |
| Czech Republic | 513 | (3.5) | 98 | (2.0) | 108 | 62 | 1.00 |
| Denmark | 496 | (3.1) | 93 | (1.4) | 95 | 15 | 1.00 |
| Finland | 563 | (2.0) | 86 | (1.0) | 81 | 5 | 1.00 |
| France | 495 | (3.4) | 102 | (2.1) | 112 | w | w |
| Germany | 516 | (3.8) | 100 | (2.0) | 110 | 66 | 0.35 |
| Greece | 473 | (3.2) | 92 | (2.0) | 93 | 48 | 0.00 |
| Hungary | 504 | (2.7) | 88 | (1.6) | 86 | 60 | 1.00 |
| Iceland | 491 | (1.6) | 97 | (1.2) | 103 | 9 | 0.00 |
| Ireland | 508 | (3.2) | 94 | (1.5) | 98 | 17 | 1.00 |
| Italy | 475 | (2.0) | 96 | (1.3) | 100 | 52 | 1.00 |
| Japan | 531 | (3.4) | 100 | (2.0) | 109 | 53 | 1.00 |
| Korea | 522 | (3.4) | 90 | (2.4) | 90 | 32 | 1.00 |
| Luxembourg | 486 | (1.1) | 97 | (0.9) | 104 | 30 | 1.00 |
| Mexico | 410 | (2.7) | 81 | (1.5) | 72 | 25 | 0.00 |
| Netherlands | 525 | (2.7) | 96 | (1.6) | 101 | 59 | 0.00 |
| New Zealand | 530 | (2.7) | 107 | (1.4) | 125 | 20 | 1.00 |
| Norway | 487 | (3.1) | 96 | (2.0) | 99 | 10 | 0.30 |
| Poland | 498 | (2.3) | 90 | (1.1) | 89 | 12 | 1.00 |
| Portugal | 474 | (3.0) | 89 | (1.7) | 87 | 28 | 0.00 |
| Slovak Republic | 488 | (2.6) | 93 | (1.8) | 96 | 41 | 1.00 |
| Spain | 488 | (2.6) | 91 | (1.0) | 90 | 13 | 0.00 |
| Sweden | 503 | (2.4) | 94 | (1.4) | 96 | 11 | 0.00 |
| Switzerland | 512 | (3.2) | 99 | (1.7) | 109 | 37 | 0.00 |
| Turkey | 424 | (3.8) | 83 | (3.2) | 77 | 41 | 1.00 |
| United Kingdom | 515 | (2.3) | 107 | (1.5) | 124 | 23 | 1.00 |
| United States | 489 | (4.2) | 106 | (1.7) | 124 | 29 | 0.07 |
| **OECD average** | 500 | (0.5) | 95 | (0.3) | 100 | 33 | 0.59 |
| **Partners** | | | | | | | |
| Argentina | 391 | (6.1) | 101 | (2.6) | 113 | 53 | 0.00 |
| Azerbaijan | 382 | (2.8) | 56 | (1.9) | 34 | 18 | 1.00 |
| Brazil | 390 | (2.8) | 89 | (1.9) | 88 | 41 | 0.00 |
| Bulgaria | 434 | (6.1) | 107 | (3.2) | 126 | 69 | 0.47 |
| Chile | 438 | (4.3) | 92 | (1.8) | 94 | 53 | 0.00 |
| Colombia | 388 | (3.4) | 85 | (1.8) | 80 | 25 | 0.00 |
| Croatia | 493 | (2.4) | 86 | (1.4) | 82 | 34 | 0.00 |
| Estonia | 531 | (2.5) | 84 | (1.1) | 78 | 16 | 1.00 |
| Hong Kong-China | 542 | (2.5) | 92 | (1.9) | 93 | 34 | 1.00 |
| Indonesia | 393 | (5.7) | 70 | (3.3) | 54 | 19 | 0.00 |
| Israel | 454 | (3.7) | 111 | (2.0) | 137 | 44 | 1.00 |
| Jordan | 422 | (2.8) | 90 | (1.9) | 89 | 20 | 1.00 |
| Kyrgyzstan | 322 | (2.9) | 84 | (2.0) | 78 | 31 | 1.00 |
| Latvia | 490 | (3.0) | 84 | (1.3) | 78 | 14 | 1.00 |
| Liechtenstein | 522 | (4.1) | 97 | (3.1) | c | c | 1.00 |
| Lithuania | 488 | (2.8) | 90 | (1.6) | 90 | 25 | 1.00 |
| Macao-China | 511 | (1.1) | 78 | (0.8) | 68 | 19 | 0.00 |
| Montenegro | 412 | (1.1) | 80 | (0.9) | 71 | 20 | 0.00 |
| Qatar | 349 | (0.9) | 84 | (0.8) | 78 | 47 | 1.00 |
| Romania | 418 | (4.2) | 81 | (2.4) | 73 | 35 | 0.00 |
| Russian Federation | 479 | (3.7) | 90 | (1.4) | 89 | 24 | 1.00 |
| Serbia | 436 | (3.0) | 85 | (1.6) | 80 | 34 | 0.26 |
| Slovenia | 519 | (1.1) | 98 | (1.0) | 107 | 65 | 1.00 |
| Chinese Taipei | 532 | (3.6) | 94 | (1.6) | 99 | 46 | 1.00 |
| Thailand | 421 | (2.1) | 77 | (1.5) | 66 | 25 | 1.00 |
| Tunisia | 386 | (3.0) | 82 | (2.0) | 75 | 32 | 0.00 |
| Uruguay | 428 | (2.7) | 94 | (1.8) | 99 | 39 | 0.00 |

2. This column indicates the extent to which standards-based external examinations exist in the system. Where there is a value between 0 and 1, standards-based external examinations exist in some parts of the system concerned, but not throughout the system (*e.g.* regional variation or variation between different types of education programmes).
StatLink ᵃᵍᵉ http://dx.doi.org/10.1787/142127877152

Pour consulter la version française intégrale de ce tableau, suivre ce lien :
StatLink ᵃᵍᵉ http://dx.doi.org/10.1787/152751048643

[Part 1/1]

**Table 5.3** Ability grouping and performance in science[1]

Tableau 5.3 Regroupement des élèves par aptitude et performances en sciences

| | Percentage of students in schools where the principal reported that within the school (between and/or within classes) there was | | | | | | Performance on the science scale | | | | | | | |
| | No ability grouping | | Ability grouping for *some* subjects | | Ability grouping for *all* subjects | | *No* ability grouping or ability grouping for *some* subjects | | Ability grouping for *all* subjects | | Observed difference (Ability grouping for *all* subjects – *No* ability grouping or ability grouping for *some* subjects) | | After accounting for the PISA index of economic, social and cultural status | |
| | % of students | S.E. | % of students | S.E. | % of students | S.E. | Mean | S.E. | Mean | S.E. | Score dif. | S.E. | Score dif. | S.E. |
|---|---|---|---|---|---|---|---|---|---|---|---|---|---|---|
| **OECD** | | | | | | | | | | | | | | |
| Australia | 5.5 | (1.1) | 89.6 | (1.7) | 4.9 | (1.3) | 528 | (2.3) | 508 | (12.9) | -19.9 | (13.1) | -14.0 | (11.8) |
| Austria | 56.0 | (2.7) | 39.9 | (2.7) | 4.1 | (1.4) | 512 | (3.7) | 491 | (38.2) | -21.4 | (37.8) | -15.9 | (27.9) |
| Belgium | 56.3 | (3.1) | 21.6 | (2.6) | 22.2 | (2.7) | 513 | (3.1) | 502 | (12.2) | -11.3 | (13.9) | -6.8 | (10.9) |
| Canada | 8.7 | (1.2) | 76.5 | (2.0) | 14.8 | (1.7) | 536 | (2.2) | 532 | (5.9) | -3.9 | (6.4) | 1.1 | (5.0) |
| Czech Republic | 34.5 | (3.4) | 53.7 | (4.2) | 11.8 | (3.1) | 514 | (4.5) | 494 | (10.4) | -19.8 | (12.5) | **-21.0** | (9.6) |
| Denmark | 17.9 | (3.3) | 74.9 | (3.3) | 7.2 | (2.0) | 497 | (3.1) | 492 | (11.3) | -4.8 | (11.1) | -5.0 | (9.1) |
| Finland | 49.8 | (3.9) | 48.1 | (3.8) | 2.1 | (1.1) | 563 | (2.1) | c | c | c | c | c | c |
| France | w | w | w | w | w | w | w | w | w | w | w | w | w | w |
| Germany | 58.0 | (2.6) | 31.4 | (2.4) | 10.5 | (2.2) | 519 | (4.1) | 490 | (13.9) | **-29.1** | (14.8) | **-23.7** | (11.0) |
| Greece | 85.0 | (2.9) | 14.4 | (2.8) | 0.6 | (0.6) | 476 | (3.9) | c | c | c | c | c | c |
| Hungary | 30.6 | (3.6) | 67.2 | (3.4) | 2.2 | (1.2) | 505 | (3.2) | c | c | c | c | c | c |
| Iceland | 19.8 | (0.2) | 74.0 | (0.2) | 6.2 | (0.1) | 490 | (1.7) | 479 | (6.6) | -11.5 | (6.9) | -8.1 | (6.6) |
| Ireland | 2.0 | (1.1) | 90.6 | (2.3) | 7.4 | (2.0) | 508 | (3.5) | 508 | (12.8) | 0.4 | (13.5) | 1.8 | (9.2) |
| Italy | 53.1 | (2.5) | 25.1 | (2.3) | 21.8 | (2.3) | 479 | (3.0) | 465 | (5.5) | **-14.2** | (7.0) | -10.4 | (5.5) |
| Japan | 44.3 | (3.5) | 45.9 | (3.7) | 9.8 | (2.5) | 529 | (3.6) | 551 | (10.3) | 21.9 | (11.2) | 12.8 | (9.4) |
| Korea | 11.5 | (2.9) | 81.6 | (3.7) | 6.8 | (2.5) | 521 | (3.7) | 532 | (15.8) | 10.2 | (17.0) | 15.2 | (12.8) |
| Luxembourg | 26.8 | (0.1) | 27.0 | (0.0) | 46.1 | (0.1) | 493 | (1.5) | 478 | (1.5) | **-15.3** | (2.2) | **-6.6** | (2.1) |
| Mexico | 28.1 | (2.8) | 42.7 | (3.0) | 29.3 | (2.9) | 414 | (3.5) | 404 | (5.5) | -9.4 | (6.8) | -4.6 | (5.6) |
| Netherlands | 18.8 | (2.8) | 32.9 | (3.7) | 48.3 | (4.0) | 525 | (7.2) | 523 | (5.9) | -1.4 | (11.8) | -1.6 | (8.8) |
| New Zealand | 3.2 | (1.4) | 91.0 | (2.0) | 5.8 | (1.7) | 531 | (3.0) | 541 | (15.6) | 9.9 | (16.0) | 3.8 | (11.1) |
| Norway | 58.0 | (4.2) | 39.1 | (4.0) | 2.9 | (1.2) | 486 | (3.3) | c | c | c | c | c | c |
| Poland | 52.5 | (3.6) | 44.2 | (3.7) | 3.3 | (1.4) | 497 | (2.5) | 514 | (11.3) | 16.9 | (11.8) | 11.5 | (8.3) |
| Portugal | 47.4 | (4.3) | 38.9 | (4.0) | 13.7 | (2.8) | 479 | (3.4) | 447 | (12.9) | **-31.3** | (14.2) | **-28.8** | (11.2) |
| Slovak Republic | 27.3 | (3.4) | 57.2 | (4.1) | 15.5 | (3.0) | 488 | (3.3) | 491 | (12.4) | 3.2 | (14.1) | 1.7 | (9.9) |
| Spain | 28.6 | (3.2) | 56.2 | (3.3) | 15.2 | (2.5) | 487 | (2.9) | 497 | (5.9) | 10.8 | (6.9) | 7.2 | (4.9) |
| Sweden | 24.5 | (3.1) | 70.0 | (3.5) | 5.5 | (1.6) | 504 | (2.2) | 484 | (14.4) | -20.8 | (14.2) | **-21.0** | (9.0) |
| Switzerland | 23.6 | (2.5) | 36.2 | (3.2) | 40.1 | (2.7) | 526 | (4.4) | 489 | (3.7) | **-36.9** | (5.9) | **-30.4** | (4.8) |
| Turkey | 59.4 | (4.4) | 22.0 | (3.6) | 18.6 | (3.2) | 425 | (5.0) | 413 | (9.7) | -11.7 | (11.9) | -6.3 | (9.4) |
| United Kingdom | 0.3 | (0.1) | 91.7 | (1.9) | 8.1 | (1.9) | 521 | (2.3) | 469 | (18.2) | **-52.4** | (18.8) | **-37.6** | (15.4) |
| United States | 12.7 | (2.8) | 79.9 | (3.4) | 7.4 | (2.2) | 490 | (3.4) | 513 | (14.8) | 22.8 | (15.3) | 15.5 | (9.3) |
| **OECD average** | 32.6 | (0.5) | 53.9 | (0.6) | 13.5 | (0.4) | 502 | (0.6) | 492 | (2.7) | **-8.8** | (2.8) | **-6.9** | (2.1) |
| **Partners** | | | | | | | | | | | | | | |
| Argentina | 37.5 | (4.1) | 40.1 | (4.8) | 22.4 | (3.3) | 402 | (7.4) | 365 | (9.0) | **-36.6** | (11.2) | **-19.8** | (9.5) |
| Azerbaijan | 5.8 | (1.9) | 77.7 | (3.9) | 16.5 | (3.6) | 382 | (3.1) | 382 | (7.0) | -0.2 | (7.8) | -1.0 | (7.4) |
| Brazil | 45.2 | (2.7) | 11.4 | (2.1) | 43.4 | (2.6) | 398 | (3.7) | 380 | (5.2) | **-17.7** | (6.9) | **-11.8** | (5.1) |
| Bulgaria | 47.5 | (4.3) | 40.4 | (4.3) | 12.1 | (2.7) | 441 | (7.3) | 425 | (17.4) | -16.3 | (20.1) | -10.2 | (13.0) |
| Chile | 36.0 | (4.3) | 44.7 | (4.4) | 19.3 | (3.2) | 445 | (5.0) | 430 | (8.5) | -15.1 | (10.1) | 3.9 | (7.6) |
| Colombia | 40.6 | (5.3) | 17.0 | (3.4) | 42.4 | (5.4) | 389 | (4.9) | 387 | (6.3) | -1.7 | (8.9) | -4.7 | (7.3) |
| Croatia | 53.6 | (3.7) | 19.7 | (3.1) | 26.7 | (3.3) | 498 | (3.3) | 481 | (7.2) | -17.0 | (9.0) | -12.3 | (7.4) |
| Estonia | 43.1 | (3.6) | 42.1 | (3.6) | 14.8 | (2.5) | 531 | (2.9) | 535 | (6.4) | 4.5 | (7.3) | -0.6 | (6.4) |
| Hong Kong-China | 31.8 | (3.6) | 50.8 | (3.8) | 17.3 | (3.0) | 542 | (3.2) | 542 | (11.8) | -0.5 | (13.6) | 1.8 | (11.8) |
| Indonesia | 25.1 | (2.8) | 10.6 | (2.4) | 64.3 | (3.4) | 396 | (7.3) | 393 | (8.8) | -3.0 | (11.9) | -5.3 | (10.2) |
| Israel | 2.7 | (1.4) | 77.9 | (3.6) | 19.5 | (3.7) | 459 | (5.1) | 440 | (9.9) | -18.8 | (12.3) | -13.4 | (10.0) |
| Jordan | 10.3 | (2.4) | 58.8 | (3.7) | 31.0 | (3.1) | 423 | (3.6) | 418 | (5.7) | -4.6 | (7.5) | -2.8 | (6.3) |
| Kyrgyzstan | 33.0 | (3.6) | 52.0 | (3.8) | 15.0 | (2.7) | 320 | (3.3) | 333 | (12.1) | 13.0 | (13.2) | 10.5 | (11.2) |
| Latvia | 49.9 | (3.6) | 33.0 | (3.8) | 17.1 | (3.1) | 490 | (2.9) | 489 | (10.4) | -0.9 | (11.0) | -4.9 | (8.3) |
| Liechtenstein | c | c | c | c | c | c | c | c | c | c | c | c | c | c |
| Lithuania | 34.2 | (3.8) | 57.2 | (3.9) | 8.6 | (2.2) | 488 | (2.9) | 490 | (13.2) | 2.3 | (13.8) | -5.2 | (11.6) |
| Macao-China | 59.1 | (0.1) | 27.6 | (0.1) | 13.4 | (0.1) | 511 | (0.9) | 511 | (5.3) | 0.1 | (5.5) | 0.2 | (5.3) |
| Montenegro | 31.3 | (0.2) | 7.2 | (0.0) | 61.5 | (0.2) | 430 | (1.8) | 400 | (1.4) | **-29.4** | (2.3) | **-24.3** | (2.3) |
| Qatar | 24.8 | (0.1) | 24.7 | (0.1) | 50.5 | (0.1) | 347 | (1.3) | 354 | (1.4) | **6.4** | (1.9) | **5.1** | (2.0) |
| Romania | 19.5 | (3.8) | 51.9 | (5.1) | 28.6 | (4.0) | 423 | (5.8) | 407 | (10.3) | -15.3 | (13.6) | -8.6 | (10.4) |
| Russian Federation | 20.0 | (3.5) | 39.6 | (4.0) | 40.4 | (3.7) | 477 | (4.4) | 484 | (5.8) | 7.5 | (6.7) | 3.0 | (5.9) |
| Serbia | 53.5 | (3.9) | 11.8 | (2.6) | 34.7 | (3.7) | 437 | (4.8) | 435 | (5.7) | -2.6 | (8.6) | -1.8 | (7.4) |
| Slovenia | 57.0 | (0.2) | 39.5 | (0.3) | 3.5 | (0.3) | 522 | (1.2) | 437 | (13.4) | **-85.3** | (13.6) | **-60.8** | (19.4) |
| Chinese Taipei | 55.1 | (3.1) | 36.7 | (3.0) | 8.2 | (1.6) | 531 | (3.8) | 553 | (14.0) | 21.8 | (14.5) | 11.3 | (12.2) |
| Thailand | 7.5 | (2.3) | 42.4 | (3.6) | 50.2 | (4.1) | 426 | (3.8) | 416 | (4.7) | -10.1 | (7.2) | -4.9 | (5.5) |
| Tunisia | 19.1 | (3.2) | 3.4 | (1.6) | 77.5 | (3.4) | 387 | (8.8) | 386 | (4.0) | -1.0 | (11.0) | 0.3 | (9.4) |
| Uruguay | 67.2 | (2.8) | 15.6 | (2.4) | 17.2 | (2.2) | 428 | (3.7) | 428 | (9.2) | 0.3 | (11.3) | 1.4 | (7.6) |

Note: Values that are statistically significant are indicated in bold (see Annex A3).
1. Results based on reports from school principals and reported proportionate to the number of 15-year-olds enrolled in school.
*StatLink* http://dx.doi.org/10.1787/142127877152

Pour consulter la version française intégrale de ce tableau, suivre ce lien :
*StatLink* http://dx.doi.org/10.1787/152751048643

[Part 1/3]

**Table 5.4** Percentage of students and student performance on the science, reading and mathematics scales, by type of school[1]

Tableau 5.4 Pourcentage d'élèves et scores des élèves sur les échelles de culture scientifique, de compréhension de l'écrit et de culture mathématique, selon le type d'établissement

| | Government or public schools[2] | | | | | | | | Government-dependent private schools[3] | | | | | | | |
| | % of students | S.E. | Performance on the science scale | | Performance on the reading scale | | Performance on the mathematics scale | | % of students | S.E. | Performance on the science scale | | Performance on the reading scale | | Performance on the mathematics scale | |
| | | | Mean score | S.E. | Mean score | S.E. | Mean score | S.E. | | | Mean score | S.E. | Mean score | S.E. | Mean score | S.E. |
|---|---|---|---|---|---|---|---|---|---|---|---|---|---|---|---|---|
| **OECD** | | | | | | | | | | | | | | | | |
| Australia | w | w | w | w | w | w | w | w | w | w | w | w | w | w | w | w |
| Austria | 90.7 | (2.2) | 511 | (3.9) | 491 | (3.7) | 506 | (3.8) | 8.4 | (2.2) | 503 | (19.8) | 479 | (24.3) | 488 | (17.3) |
| Belgium | w | w | w | w | w | w | w | w | w | w | w | w | w | w | w | w |
| Canada | 93.0 | (0.7) | 532 | (2.1) | 524 | (2.6) | 524 | (2.0) | 4.3 | (0.3) | 578 | (5.9) | 578 | (7.5) | 582 | (8.0) |
| Czech Republic | 96.2 | (1.8) | 514 | (3.7) | 482 | (4.7) | 510 | (3.9) | 3.5 | (1.8) | 492 | (29.3) | 481 | (43.6) | 487 | (24.2) |
| Denmark | 76.1 | (3.1) | 492 | (3.1) | 493 | (3.1) | 511 | (2.8) | 22.8 | (3.0) | 507 | (8.3) | 499 | (8.2) | 521 | (7.5) |
| Finland | 97.6 | (1.1) | 564 | (2.0) | 547 | (2.2) | 549 | (2.3) | 2.4 | (1.1) | c | c | c | c | c | c |
| France | w | w | w | w | w | w | w | w | w | w | w | w | w | w | w | w |
| Germany | 94.3 | (1.8) | 514 | (3.8) | 494 | (4.4) | 502 | (3.9) | 5.5 | (1.8) | 555 | (21.6) | 535 | (19.2) | 544 | (25.7) |
| Greece | 94.9 | (1.2) | 469 | (3.2) | 455 | (4.1) | 455 | (2.9) | 0.0 | (0.0) | a | a | a | a | a | a |
| Hungary | 84.2 | (3.4) | 500 | (4.0) | 478 | (4.5) | 485 | (4.3) | 13.1 | (3.1) | 533 | (17.5) | 516 | (16.7) | 529 | (17.9) |
| Iceland | 98.9 | (0.1) | 490 | (1.6) | 484 | (1.9) | 505 | (1.7) | 1.0 | (0.1) | c | c | c | c | c | c |
| Ireland | 41.8 | (1.4) | 488 | (5.3) | 494 | (5.2) | 483 | (4.9) | 54.8 | (2.0) | 519 | (3.9) | 530 | (4.5) | 511 | (3.2) |
| Italy | 96.4 | (0.7) | 476 | (2.0) | 469 | (2.5) | 462 | (2.3) | 1.2 | (0.4) | c | c | c | c | c | c |
| Japan | 70.1 | (1.4) | 537 | (3.6) | 501 | (4.2) | 528 | (3.2) | 1.0 | (1.0) | c | c | c | c | c | c |
| Korea | 53.7 | (3.9) | 524 | (5.4) | 554 | (5.5) | 549 | (6.3) | 31.5 | (3.7) | 505 | (7.1) | 543 | (8.4) | 527 | (7.2) |
| Luxembourg | 85.6 | (0.0) | 490 | (1.0) | 481 | (1.3) | 495 | (1.0) | 14.4 | (0.0) | 465 | (3.5) | 470 | (3.6) | 460 | (3.0) |
| Mexico | 89.7 | (1.5) | 402 | (2.7) | 402 | (3.2) | 398 | (2.9) | 0.0 | (0.0) | c | c | c | c | c | c |
| Netherlands | 33.0 | (4.3) | 524 | (10.1) | 505 | (9.6) | 526 | (9.2) | 67.0 | (4.3) | 527 | (4.1) | 509 | (4.4) | 534 | (3.7) |
| New Zealand | 95.5 | (0.6) | 527 | (2.8) | 518 | (3.1) | 519 | (2.5) | 0.0 | (0.0) | a | a | a | a | a | a |
| Norway | 98.1 | (0.9) | 484 | (3.2) | 482 | (3.3) | 488 | (2.7) | 1.9 | (0.9) | c | c | c | c | c | c |
| Poland | 98.4 | (0.1) | 497 | (2.4) | 507 | (2.8) | 495 | (2.5) | 1.0 | (0.2) | c | c | c | c | c | c |
| Portugal | 91.1 | (1.3) | 471 | (3.2) | 469 | (3.8) | 463 | (3.3) | 6.9 | (1.3) | 484 | (8.8) | 470 | (13.1) | 479 | (8.1) |
| Slovak Republic | 92.3 | (1.9) | 487 | (2.9) | 465 | (3.5) | 491 | (3.1) | 7.2 | (1.8) | 506 | (12.9) | 484 | (18.9) | 507 | (12.2) |
| Spain | 65.3 | (1.0) | 475 | (3.0) | 446 | (2.5) | 466 | (2.6) | 24.6 | (1.4) | 503 | (4.1) | 482 | (4.1) | 495 | (3.5) |
| Sweden | 91.7 | (0.8) | 501 | (2.4) | 504 | (3.5) | 501 | (2.4) | 8.3 | (0.8) | 531 | (7.1) | 539 | (7.5) | 522 | (9.6) |
| Switzerland | 95.5 | (0.6) | 511 | (3.1) | 499 | (3.1) | 530 | (3.2) | 0.9 | (0.4) | c | c | c | c | c | c |
| Turkey | 99.5 | (0.5) | 424 | (3.9) | 447 | (4.3) | 423 | (5.0) | 0.0 | (0.0) | a | a | a | a | a | a |
| United Kingdom | 93.8 | (1.0) | 510 | (2.4) | 492 | (2.5) | 492 | (2.2) | 0.2 | (0.1) | c | c | c | c | c | c |
| United States | 92.6 | (1.2) | 485 | (4.2) | m | m | 470 | (4.0) | 0.8 | (0.8) | c | c | m | m | m | m |
| **OECD total** | 86.6 | (0.5) | 485 | (1.3) | 477 | (1.1) | 476 | (1.3) | 5.8 | (0.4) | 516 | (3.2) | 517 | (3.6) | 521 | (3.4) |
| **OECD average** | 85.6 | (0.3) | 496 | (0.7) | 488 | (0.8) | 494 | (0.7) | 10.5 | (0.3) | 515 | (3.6) | 508 | (4.5) | 513 | (3.5) |
| **Partners** | | | | | | | | | | | | | | | | |
| Argentina | 67.5 | (3.7) | 364 | (5.4) | 342 | (6.9) | 354 | (5.9) | 24.8 | (3.1) | 441 | (10.3) | 430 | (12.0) | 430 | (9.2) |
| Azerbaijan | 99.1 | (0.4) | 382 | (2.7) | 351 | (3.0) | 475 | (2.3) | 0.0 | (0.0) | a | a | a | a | a | a |
| Brazil | 92.4 | (1.4) | 375 | (2.7) | 378 | (3.8) | 353 | (2.8) | 0.0 | (0.0) | a | a | a | a | a | a |
| Bulgaria | m | m | m | m | m | m | m | m | m | m | m | m | m | m | m | m |
| Chile | 46.9 | (2.9) | 409 | (6.3) | 412 | (6.8) | 385 | (7.2) | 44.9 | (3.3) | 447 | (5.6) | 453 | (7.2) | 418 | (5.7) |
| Colombia | 82.7 | (2.8) | 379 | (4.0) | 378 | (5.9) | 361 | (4.6) | 5.1 | (2.5) | 431 | (16.4) | 440 | (22.2) | 415 | (16.2) |
| Croatia | 98.6 | (1.0) | 494 | (2.5) | 478 | (2.9) | 467 | (2.4) | 0.6 | (0.4) | c | c | c | c | c | c |
| Estonia | 98.1 | (0.9) | 531 | (2.4) | 500 | (2.8) | 514 | (1.4) | 1.4 | (0.8) | c | c | c | c | c | c |
| Hong Kong-China | 7.5 | (0.2) | 570 | (9.6) | 562 | (10.3) | 575 | (15.9) | 90.7 | (1.4) | 541 | (2.9) | 535 | (2.7) | 546 | (2.9) |
| Indonesia | 60.7 | (3.6) | 403 | (7.2) | 403 | (6.8) | 404 | (7.6) | 13.5 | (3.0) | 352 | (6.1) | 344 | (5.1) | 341 | (6.5) |
| Israel | 73.4 | (4.0) | 449 | (4.9) | 435 | (5.7) | 438 | (5.5) | 20.3 | (3.6) | 471 | (11.6) | 457 | (13.1) | 461 | (10.1) |
| Jordan | 80.6 | (1.7) | 410 | (2.8) | 390 | (3.3) | 373 | (3.4) | 1.3 | (0.9) | c | c | c | c | c | c |
| Kyrgyzstan | 99.4 | (0.4) | 320 | (3.1) | 283 | (3.7) | 308 | (3.6) | 0.0 | (0.0) | a | a | a | a | a | a |
| Latvia | 100.0 | (0.0) | 490 | (3.0) | 479 | (3.7) | 486 | (3.0) | 0.0 | (0.0) | a | a | a | a | a | a |
| Liechtenstein | c | c | c | c | c | c | c | c | c | c | c | c | c | c | c | c |
| Lithuania | 99.3 | (0.7) | 487 | (2.6) | 469 | (2.9) | 485 | (2.8) | 0.7 | (0.7) | c | c | c | c | c | c |
| Macao-China | 3.8 | (0.0) | 463 | (4.6) | 453 | (4.5) | 473 | (5.2) | 68.5 | (0.1) | 504 | (1.4) | 487 | (1.4) | 517 | (1.7) |
| Montenegro | 99.8 | (0.0) | 412 | (1.1) | 393 | (1.2) | 400 | (1.3) | 0.0 | (0.0) | a | a | a | a | a | a |
| Qatar | 91.1 | (0.1) | 338 | (0.9) | 301 | (1.2) | 304 | (1.0) | 0.1 | (0.0) | c | c | c | c | c | c |
| Romania | 100.0 | (0.0) | 418 | (4.2) | 396 | (4.7) | 415 | (4.2) | 0.0 | (0.0) | a | a | a | a | a | a |
| Russian Federation | 100.0 | (0.0) | 479 | (3.7) | 440 | (4.3) | 476 | (3.9) | 0.0 | (0.0) | a | a | a | a | a | a |
| Serbia | 99.4 | (0.7) | 436 | (3.1) | 401 | (3.5) | 436 | (3.6) | 0.6 | (0.7) | c | c | c | c | c | c |
| Slovenia | 97.7 | (0.0) | 517 | (1.1) | 493 | (1.0) | 503 | (1.0) | 2.3 | (0.0) | c | c | c | c | c | c |
| Chinese Taipei | 65.0 | (2.4) | 549 | (3.5) | 509 | (3.5) | 567 | (4.3) | 0.0 | (0.0) | a | a | a | a | a | a |
| Thailand | 83.5 | (0.7) | 422 | (2.2) | 417 | (2.8) | 418 | (2.4) | 6.1 | (1.7) | 389 | (10.3) | 385 | (11.8) | 379 | (9.6) |
| Tunisia | 98.2 | (1.0) | 388 | (3.0) | 384 | (4.1) | 368 | (4.0) | 1.8 | (1.0) | c | c | c | c | c | c |
| Uruguay | 84.9 | (0.8) | 416 | (3.0) | 397 | (3.8) | 414 | (2.8) | 0.0 | (0.0) | a | a | a | a | a | a |

Note: Values that are statistically significant are indicated in bold (see Annex A3).
1. Results based on reports from school principals and reported proportionate to the number of 15-year-olds enrolled in the school.
2. Schools which are directly controlled or managed by: i) a public education authority or agency, or ii) a government agency directly or a governing body, most of whose members are either appointed by a public authority or elected by public franchise.
3. Schools which receive 50% or more of their core funding - funding that supports the basic educational services of the institution - from government agencies.
StatLink ᐊᔑᔈ http://dx.doi.org/10.1787/142127877152

Pour consulter la version française intégrale de ce tableau, suivre ce lien :
StatLink ᐊᔑᔈ http://dx.doi.org/10.1787/152751048643

[Part 2/3]
**Table 5.4** **Percentage of students and student performance on the science, reading and mathematics scales, by type of school[1]**

Tableau 5.4 Pourcentage d'élèves et scores des élèves sur les échelles de culture scientifique, de compréhension de l'écrit et de culture mathématique, selon le type d'établissement

| | | | Government-independent private schools[4] | | | | | | Difference in performance on the science scale between public and private schools (government-dependent and government-independent schools combined) | |
| | % of students | S.E. | Performance on the science scale | | Performance on the reading scale | | Performance on the mathematics scale | | Dif. (Pub. - Priv.) | S.E. |
| | | | Mean score | S.E. | Mean score | S.E. | Mean score | S.E. | | |
|---|---|---|---|---|---|---|---|---|---|---|
| **OECD** | | | | | | | | | | |
| Australia | w | w | w | w | w | w | w | w | w | w |
| Austria | 0.9 | (0.6) | c | c | c | c | c | c | 1 | (19.5) |
| Belgium | w | w | w | w | w | w | w | w | w | w |
| Canada | 2.7 | (0.7) | c | c | c | c | c | c | **-44** | (5.2) |
| Czech Republic | 0.2 | (0.2) | c | c | c | c | c | c | 23 | (27.7) |
| Denmark | 1.1 | (0.8) | c | c | c | c | c | c | **-17** | (8.1) |
| Finland | 0.0 | (0.0) | a | a | a | a | a | a | c | c |
| France | w | w | w | w | w | w | w | w | w | w |
| Germany | 0.2 | (0.2) | c | c | c | c | c | c | **-40** | (21.7) |
| Greece | 5.1 | (1.2) | 545 | (6.0) | 543 | (7.9) | 527 | (9.0) | **-76** | (7.1) |
| Hungary | 2.7 | (1.6) | c | c | c | c | c | c | **-34** | (16.8) |
| Iceland | 0.1 | (0.1) | c | c | c | c | c | c | c | c |
| Ireland | 3.4 | (1.5) | 558 | (10.9) | 544 | (12.6) | 556 | (11.2) | **-34** | (6.5) |
| Italy | 2.4 | (0.6) | c | c | c | c | c | c | 18 | (18.3) |
| Japan | 28.9 | (1.6) | 526 | (7.1) | 498 | (6.6) | 518 | (8.1) | 13 | (8.1) |
| Korea | 14.8 | (2.5) | 552 | (8.7) | 591 | (9.3) | 584 | (10.4) | 4 | (8.8) |
| Luxembourg | 0.0 | (0.0) | a | a | a | a | a | a | 25 | (3.6) |
| Mexico | 10.3 | (1.5) | 455 | (9.6) | 455 | (9.1) | 454 | (9.6) | **-53** | (9.9) |
| Netherlands | 0.0 | (0.0) | a | a | a | a | a | a | -3 | (12.9) |
| New Zealand | 4.5 | (0.6) | 603 | (6.4) | 573 | (9.6) | 578 | (9.4) | **-77** | (6.9) |
| Norway | 0.0 | (0.0) | a | a | a | a | a | a | c | c |
| Poland | 0.6 | (0.2) | c | c | c | c | c | c | c | c |
| Portugal | 2.1 | (0.3) | c | c | c | c | c | c | **-24** | (9.8) |
| Slovak Republic | 0.5 | (0.5) | c | c | c | c | c | c | -15 | (13.4) |
| Spain | 10.1 | (1.5) | 537 | (9.5) | 505 | (9.1) | 527 | (10.1) | **-38** | (4.2) |
| Sweden | 0.0 | (0.0) | a | a | a | a | a | a | **-30** | (7.4) |
| Switzerland | 3.6 | (0.4) | 513 | (13.4) | 500 | (10.2) | 518 | (9.0) | 2 | (16.3) |
| Turkey | 0.5 | (0.5) | c | c | c | c | c | c | c | c |
| United Kingdom | 6.0 | (1.0) | 597 | (8.7) | 577 | (9.3) | 571 | (7.5) | **-86** | (8.8) |
| United States | 6.6 | (0.9) | 554 | (13.6) | m | m | 534 | (10.5) | **-63** | (13.9) |
| **OECD total** | 7.6 | (0.4) | 531 | (5.3) | 510 | (4.6) | 523 | (4.8) | **-39** | (3.6) |
| **OECD average** | 4.1 | (0.2) | 544 | (3.1) | 532 | (3.1) | 537 | (3.0) | **-25** | (2.8) |
| **Partners** | | | | | | | | | | |
| Argentina | 7.7 | (2.6) | 447 | (18.1) | 435 | (22.4) | 437 | (23.9) | **-78** | (9.4) |
| Azerbaijan | 0.9 | (0.4) | c | c | c | c | c | c | c | c |
| Brazil | 7.6 | (1.4) | 482 | (11.5) | 482 | (11.4) | 462 | (13.3) | **-107** | (11.9) |
| Bulgaria | m | m | m | m | m | m | m | m | m | m |
| Chile | 8.2 | (2.0) | 514 | (15.8) | 513 | (16.1) | 483 | (14.5) | **-48** | (8.1) |
| Colombia | 12.3 | (2.2) | 412 | (9.2) | 405 | (10.1) | 397 | (11.1) | **-38** | (9.2) |
| Croatia | 0.7 | (0.5) | c | c | c | c | c | c | c | c |
| Estonia | 0.6 | (0.4) | c | c | c | c | c | c | c | c |
| Hong Kong-China | 1.9 | (1.4) | c | c | c | c | c | c | 30 | (10.0) |
| Indonesia | 25.8 | (2.9) | 389 | (6.0) | 390 | (6.3) | 382 | (5.6) | 26 | (8.3) |
| Israel | 6.3 | (1.9) | 475 | (17.9) | 454 | (24.8) | 463 | (19.3) | -22 | (11.6) |
| Jordan | 18.1 | (1.5) | 468 | (5.4) | 443 | (8.7) | 427 | (6.7) | **-61** | (6.5) |
| Kyrgyzstan | 0.6 | (0.4) | c | c | c | c | c | c | c | c |
| Latvia | 0.0 | (0.0) | a | a | a | a | a | a | a | a |
| Liechtenstein | c | c | c | c | c | c | c | c | c | c |
| Lithuania | 0.0 | (0.0) | a | a | a | a | a | a | c | c |
| Macao-China | 27.6 | (0.1) | 535 | (1.8) | 511 | (2.0) | 553 | (2.1) | **-49** | (4.5) |
| Montenegro | 0.2 | c | c | c | c | c | c | c | c | c |
| Qatar | 8.8 | (0.1) | 434 | (4.1) | 412 | (5.4) | 420 | (3.9) | **-96** | (4.2) |
| Romania | 0.0 | a | a | a | a | a | a | a | a | a |
| Russian Federation | 0.0 | a | a | a | a | a | a | a | a | a |
| Serbia | 0.0 | a | a | a | a | a | a | a | c | c |
| Slovenia | 0.1 | c | c | c | c | c | c | c | c | c |
| Chinese Taipei | 35.0 | (2.4) | 501 | (7.2) | 472 | (6.6) | 516 | (8.3) | 48 | (8.7) |
| Thailand | 10.5 | (1.7) | 433 | (8.4) | 432 | (9.2) | 429 | (10.9) | 5 | (6.8) |
| Tunisia | 0.0 | a | a | a | a | a | a | a | c | c |
| Uruguay | 15.1 | (0.8) | 496 | (5.6) | 495 | (7.1) | 495 | (5.9) | **-80** | (6.4) |

Note: Values that are statistically significant are indicated in bold (see Annex A3).
1. Results based on reports from school principals and reported proportionate to the number of 15-year-olds enrolled in the school.
4. Schools which receive less than 50% of their core funding – funding that supports the basic educational services of the institution – from government agencies.
StatLink ⟪⟫ http://dx.doi.org/10.1787/142127877152

Pour consulter la version française intégrale de ce tableau, suivre ce lien :
StatLink ⟪⟫ http://dx.doi.org/10.1787/152751048643

[Part 3/3]

**Table 5.4** **Percentage of students and student performance on the science, reading and mathematics scales, by type of school[1]**

Tableau 5.4 Pourcentage d'élèves et scores des élèves sur les échelles de culture scientifique, de compréhension de l'écrit et de culture mathématique, selon le type d'établissement

| | PISA index of economic, social and cultural status | | | | | | Difference in performance on the science scales between public and private schools after accounting for the PISA index of economic, social and cultural status of: | | | |
| | Public schools | | Private schools (government-dependent and government-independent) | | Difference | | Students | | Students and schools | |
| | Mean index | S.E | Mean index | S.E. | Dif. (Pub. - Priv.) | S.E | Dif. (Pub. - Priv.) | S.E | Dif. (Pub. - Priv.) | S.E |
|---|---|---|---|---|---|---|---|---|---|---|
| **OECD** | | | | | | | | | | |
| Australia | w | w | w | w | w | w | w | w | w | w |
| Austria | 0.18 | (0.02) | 0.32 | (0.16) | -0.14 | (0.16) | 8 | (13.9) | 19 | (10.2) |
| Belgium | w | w | w | w | w | w | w | w | w | w |
| Canada | 0.34 | (0.02) | 0.86 | (0.06) | **-0.52** | (0.06) | **-26** | (4.2) | **-10** | (4.3) |
| Czech Republic | 0.02 | (0.02) | 0.14 | (0.19) | -0.13 | (0.18) | 30 | (18.9) | 41 | (7.7) |
| Denmark | 0.23 | (0.03) | 0.48 | (0.06) | **-0.25** | (0.07) | -8 | (6.5) | -1 | (6.7) |
| Finland | 0.25 | (0.02) | c | c | c | c | c | c | c | c |
| France | w | w | w | w | w | w | w | w | w | w |
| Germany | 0.26 | (0.03) | 0.64 | (0.09) | **-0.38** | (0.10) | -20 | (19.6) | 12 | (18.3) |
| Greece | -0.22 | (0.03) | 1.11 | (0.11) | **-1.33** | (0.12) | **-30** | (6.7) | 39 | (12.1) |
| Hungary | -0.16 | (0.04) | 0.35 | (0.13) | **-0.51** | (0.15) | -12 | (12.7) | 15 | (10.0) |
| Iceland | 0.77 | (0.01) | c | c | c | c | c | c | c | c |
| Ireland | -0.24 | (0.04) | 0.13 | (0.04) | **-0.37** | (0.06) | **-20** | (5.2) | -7 | (4.8) |
| Italy | -0.08 | (0.02) | 0.14 | (0.17) | -0.22 | (0.17) | 24 | (15.1) | 38 | (14.1) |
| Japan | -0.09 | (0.02) | 0.18 | (0.04) | **-0.27** | (0.04) | **26** | (7.2) | **58** | (6.9) |
| Korea | 0.02 | (0.04) | -0.04 | (0.04) | 0.06 | (0.07) | 2 | (7.3) | -1 | (6.2) |
| Luxembourg | 0.11 | (0.01) | -0.03 | (0.04) | **0.13** | (0.04) | **20** | (3.5) | **13** | (3.4) |
| Mexico | -1.20 | (0.04) | 0.31 | (0.14) | **-1.52** | (0.16) | **-17** | (6.9) | **21** | (6.3) |
| Netherlands | 0.28 | (0.08) | 0.24 | (0.03) | 0.04 | (0.09) | -4 | (9.2) | -7 | (5.7) |
| New Zealand | 0.07 | (0.02) | 0.76 | (0.10) | **-0.70** | (0.10) | **-39** | (4.7) | -10 | (6.9) |
| Norway | 0.41 | (0.02) | c | c | c | c | c | c | c | c |
| Poland | -0.32 | (0.02) | c | c | c | c | c | c | c | c |
| Portugal | -0.67 | (0.05) | -0.38 | (0.09) | **-0.29** | (0.10) | -16 | (8.7) | -9 | (8.7) |
| Slovak Republic | -0.18 | (0.03) | 0.19 | (0.10) | **-0.36** | (0.10) | 2 | (10.8) | 18 | (9.6) |
| Spain | -0.57 | (0.04) | 0.15 | (0.06) | **-0.72** | (0.06) | **-16** | (3.5) | -5 | (4.3) |
| Sweden | 0.21 | (0.02) | 0.51 | (0.06) | **-0.30** | (0.06) | -17 | (6.9) | -9 | (7.0) |
| Switzerland | 0.06 | (0.02) | 0.60 | (0.11) | **-0.54** | (0.11) | 26 | (16.3) | **63** | (19.2) |
| Turkey | -1.30 | (0.04) | c | c | c | c | c | c | c | c |
| United Kingdom | 0.15 | (0.02) | 0.85 | (0.10) | **-0.70** | (0.10) | **-51** | (7.4) | **-16** | (10.0) |
| United States | 0.08 | (0.04) | 0.80 | (0.12) | **-0.72** | (0.12) | **-28** | (9.7) | 0 | (8.8) |
| **OECD total** | **-0.18** | **(0.01)** | **0.31** | **(0.03)** | **-0.49** | **(0.03)** | **-17** | **(2.9)** | **-3** | **(2.7)** |
| **OECD average** | **-0.06** | **(0.01)** | **0.38** | **(0.02)** | **-0.44** | **(0.02)** | **-8** | **(2.2)** | **12** | **(2.0)** |
| **Partners** | | | | | | | | | | |
| Argentina | -0.98 | (0.05) | 0.01 | (0.10) | **-0.99** | (0.11) | **-48** | (9.1) | -11 | (11.1) |
| Azerbaijan | -0.46 | (0.03) | c | c | c | c | c | c | c | c |
| Brazil | -1.35 | (0.03) | 0.28 | (0.09) | **-1.63** | (0.09) | **-77** | (11.4) | **-35** | (12.6) |
| Bulgaria | m | m | m | m | m | m | m | m | m | m |
| Chile | -1.17 | (0.08) | -0.40 | (0.08) | **-0.77** | (0.11) | **-21** | (6.7) | -2 | (6.8) |
| Colombia | -1.21 | (0.07) | -0.20 | (0.14) | **-1.00** | (0.16) | **-19** | (9.5) | 1 | (12.0) |
| Croatia | -0.12 | (0.01) | c | c | c | c | c | c | c | c |
| Estonia | 0.13 | (0.02) | c | c | c | c | c | c | c | c |
| Hong Kong-China | -0.46 | (0.17) | -0.69 | (0.03) | 0.23 | (0.18) | **23** | (6.3) | 12 | (6.4) |
| Indonesia | -1.41 | (0.06) | -1.71 | (0.07) | **0.30** | (0.09) | **21** | (7.3) | 12 | (6.3) |
| Israel | 0.19 | (0.03) | 0.31 | (0.06) | -0.12 | (0.08) | -19 | (9.9) | -14 | (9.5) |
| Jordan | -0.71 | (0.04) | -0.02 | (0.07) | **-0.69** | (0.08) | **-45** | (5.3) | **-34** | (5.7) |
| Kyrgyzstan | -0.68 | (0.02) | c | c | c | c | c | c | c | c |
| Latvia | -0.02 | (0.02) | a | a | a | a | a | a | a | a |
| Liechtenstein | c | c | c | c | c | c | c | c | c | c |
| Lithuania | 0.03 | (0.02) | c | c | c | c | c | c | c | c |
| Macao-China | -1.50 | (0.05) | -0.90 | (0.01) | **-0.61** | (0.04) | **-42** | (4.6) | **-28** | (4.5) |
| Montenegro | 0.00 | (0.01) | c | c | c | c | c | c | c | c |
| Qatar | 0.11 | (0.01) | 0.75 | (0.03) | **-0.64** | (0.03) | **-90** | (4.4) | **-74** | (4.4) |
| Romania | -0.37 | (0.04) | a | a | a | a | a | a | a | a |
| Russian Federation | -0.10 | (0.03) | a | a | a | a | a | a | a | a |
| Serbia | -0.13 | (0.03) | c | c | c | c | c | c | c | c |
| Slovenia | 0.12 | (0.01) | c | c | c | c | c | c | c | c |
| Chinese Taipei | -0.31 | (0.03) | -0.32 | (0.06) | 0.02 | (0.07) | **47** | (6.2) | **46** | (4.3) |
| Thailand | -1.49 | (0.03) | -1.15 | (0.11) | **-0.33** | (0.12) | **14** | (5.8) | **21** | (6.6) |
| Tunisia | -1.20 | (0.07) | c | c | c | c | c | c | c | c |
| Uruguay | -0.74 | (0.03) | 0.77 | (0.05) | **-1.50** | (0.06) | **-36** | (6.6) | **27** | (8.3) |

Note: Values that are statistically significant are indicated in bold (see Annex A3).
1. Results based on reports from school principals and reported proportionate to the number of 15-year-olds enrolled in the school.
*StatLink* http://dx.doi.org/10.1787/142127877152

Pour consulter la version française intégrale de ce tableau, suivre ce lien :
*StatLink* http://dx.doi.org/10.1787/152751048643

[Part 1/1]

**Table 5.5   School choice[1]**

Tableau 5.5   Choix de l'établissement

| | | Number of schools competing for students in the same area | | | | | |
|---|---|---|---|---|---|---|---|
| | | Two or more other schools | | One other school | | No other schools | |
| | | % | S.E. | % | S.E. | % | S.E. |
| OECD | Australia | 88.4 | (1.5) | 5.2 | (1.1) | 6.4 | (1.1) |
| | Austria | 45.2 | (3.7) | 19.2 | (3.1) | 35.6 | (3.4) |
| | Belgium | 71.9 | (2.9) | 18.6 | (2.8) | 9.4 | (2.0) |
| | Canada | 58.8 | (2.5) | 18.5 | (2.4) | 22.7 | (2.2) |
| | Czech Republic | 73.9 | (3.2) | 12.1 | (2.1) | 14.1 | (2.5) |
| | Denmark | 59.2 | (3.9) | 18.2 | (3.1) | 22.6 | (3.3) |
| | Finland | 40.5 | (4.2) | 15.5 | (2.9) | 44.0 | (3.7) |
| | France | w | w | w | w | w | w |
| | Germany | 68.8 | (3.3) | 14.2 | (2.2) | 17.0 | (2.6) |
| | Greece | 44.8 | (3.9) | 14.9 | (3.1) | 40.3 | (3.4) |
| | Hungary | 59.7 | (3.9) | 15.9 | (3.1) | 24.4 | (3.6) |
| | Iceland | 22.8 | (0.2) | 5.0 | (0.1) | 72.2 | (0.2) |
| | Ireland | 73.8 | (3.5) | 9.8 | (2.4) | 16.4 | (2.7) |
| | Italy | 68.8 | (2.6) | 12.0 | (1.7) | 19.2 | (2.5) |
| | Japan | 82.0 | (2.8) | 7.6 | (1.8) | 10.4 | (2.2) |
| | Korea | 75.7 | (3.6) | 8.7 | (2.2) | 15.6 | (3.0) |
| | Luxembourg | 51.0 | (0.1) | 15.7 | (0.0) | 33.3 | (0.1) |
| | Mexico | 67.6 | (2.7) | 16.7 | (2.8) | 15.7 | (2.0) |
| | Netherlands | 74.2 | (3.0) | 15.3 | (2.5) | 10.5 | (2.2) |
| | New Zealand | 82.1 | (2.7) | 7.1 | (2.0) | 10.8 | (2.0) |
| | Norway | 21.8 | (3.3) | 12.4 | (2.6) | 65.9 | (3.6) |
| | Poland | 44.4 | (3.1) | 20.5 | (3.3) | 35.1 | (3.5) |
| | Portugal | 48.2 | (4.3) | 24.7 | (3.7) | 27.1 | (3.9) |
| | Slovak Republic | 85.0 | (2.7) | 6.4 | (1.9) | 8.6 | (2.1) |
| | Spain | 62.1 | (2.6) | 17.7 | (2.2) | 20.2 | (2.2) |
| | Sweden | 49.6 | (3.6) | 13.5 | (2.5) | 36.8 | (3.7) |
| | Switzerland | 27.5 | (2.8) | 14.1 | (2.0) | 58.4 | (2.7) |
| | Turkey | 52.7 | (4.5) | 15.6 | (3.5) | 31.7 | (3.9) |
| | United Kingdom | 83.7 | (2.3) | 8.7 | (1.9) | 7.6 | (1.5) |
| | United States | 63.6 | (3.7) | 10.5 | (2.6) | 25.9 | (3.1) |
| | **OECD total** | 66.3 | (1.2) | 12.6 | (0.9) | 21.1 | (1.0) |
| | **OECD average** | 60.3 | (0.6) | 13.6 | (0.5) | 26.1 | (0.5) |
| Partners | Argentina | 71.3 | (4.0) | 9.4 | (2.4) | 19.3 | (3.5) |
| | Azerbaijan | 48.0 | (3.7) | 26.6 | (3.5) | 25.4 | (3.3) |
| | Brazil | 28.4 | (2.3) | 38.8 | (2.6) | 32.8 | (2.4) |
| | Bulgaria | 67.4 | (3.9) | 17.4 | (2.7) | 15.2 | (3.2) |
| | Chile | 63.9 | (3.6) | 17.3 | (3.4) | 18.8 | (3.3) |
| | Colombia | 57.6 | (5.9) | 18.2 | (3.9) | 24.2 | (5.0) |
| | Croatia | 65.4 | (4.1) | 11.6 | (2.2) | 23.0 | (3.5) |
| | Estonia | 56.4 | (2.8) | 22.2 | (2.6) | 21.4 | (2.6) |
| | Hong Kong-China | 89.6 | (2.5) | 9.2 | (2.4) | 1.2 | (0.9) |
| | Indonesia | 90.0 | (2.6) | 4.8 | (2.1) | 5.2 | (1.4) |
| | Israel | 69.1 | (3.8) | 13.6 | (3.4) | 17.4 | (3.2) |
| | Jordan | 36.4 | (3.9) | 19.4 | (3.0) | 44.1 | (3.9) |
| | Kyrgyzstan | 47.6 | (3.2) | 17.3 | (3.0) | 35.1 | (2.9) |
| | Latvia | 80.7 | (3.1) | 15.2 | (2.9) | 4.1 | (1.6) |
| | Liechtenstein | c | c | c | c | c | c |
| | Lithuania | 42.1 | (3.6) | 30.4 | (3.2) | 27.5 | (2.9) |
| | Macao-China | 80.8 | (0.1) | 8.6 | (0.1) | 10.6 | (0.1) |
| | Montenegro | 73.6 | (0.2) | 24.9 | (0.1) | 1.5 | (0.1) |
| | Qatar | 27.7 | (0.1) | 15.7 | (0.1) | 56.6 | (0.1) |
| | Romania | 31.1 | (4.5) | 23.7 | (4.0) | 45.2 | (5.4) |
| | Russian Federation | 51.1 | (4.8) | 16.9 | (2.6) | 32.0 | (4.3) |
| | Serbia | 49.6 | (4.4) | 23.4 | (3.8) | 27.1 | (3.6) |
| | Slovenia | 40.2 | (0.5) | 12.2 | (0.3) | 47.6 | (0.5) |
| | Chinese Taipei | 80.9 | (3.4) | 12.7 | (2.8) | 6.4 | (2.1) |
| | Thailand | 65.8 | (4.4) | 22.5 | (3.9) | 11.7 | (2.9) |
| | Tunisia | 29.3 | (4.5) | 21.8 | (3.7) | 48.9 | (5.1) |
| | Uruguay | 34.5 | (2.4) | 13.5 | (2.0) | 52.0 | (2.9) |

1. Results based on reports from school principals and reported proportionate to the number of 15-year-olds enrolled in the school.
**StatLink** 🔍🖉 http://dx.doi.org/10.1787/142127877152

Pour consulter la version française intégrale de ce tableau, suivre ce lien :
**StatLink** 🔍🖉 http://dx.doi.org/10.1787/152751048643

[Part 1/1]
**Table 5.6   Parental expectations for high academic standards[1]**

Tableau 5.6   Pressions parentales en faveur de performances scolaires élevées

| | | Parental expectations are characterised by pressure on the school to achieve high academic standards among students from | | | | | |
|---|---|---|---|---|---|---|---|
| | | Many parents | | A minority of parents | | Very few parents | |
| | | % | S.E. | % | S.E. | % | S.E. |
| *OECD* | Australia | 37.0 | (2.8) | 52.8 | (2.8) | 10.2 | (1.8) |
| | Austria | 4.0 | (1.5) | 30.2 | (3.3) | 65.8 | (3.4) |
| | Belgium | 8.4 | (1.8) | 33.1 | (2.8) | 58.5 | (2.9) |
| | Canada | 31.9 | (2.4) | 50.2 | (2.6) | 17.9 | (2.0) |
| | Czech Republic | 28.0 | (3.4) | 60.3 | (3.7) | 11.7 | (2.4) |
| | Denmark | 25.7 | (3.1) | 40.8 | (3.6) | 33.4 | (3.8) |
| | Finland | 1.4 | (1.0) | 19.7 | (3.4) | 78.9 | (3.4) |
| | France | w | w | w | w | w | w |
| | Germany | 5.0 | (1.6) | 52.4 | (3.5) | 42.6 | (3.3) |
| | Greece | 15.2 | (2.8) | 20.7 | (3.2) | 64.1 | (4.0) |
| | Hungary | 29.1 | (3.0) | 49.0 | (4.1) | 21.9 | (3.4) |
| | Iceland | 13.4 | (0.2) | 37.8 | (0.2) | 48.8 | (0.3) |
| | Ireland | 42.5 | (3.9) | 47.1 | (4.0) | 10.4 | (2.4) |
| | Italy | 21.7 | (2.1) | 56.0 | (3.0) | 22.3 | (2.4) |
| | Japan | 39.2 | (2.8) | 49.3 | (3.2) | 11.5 | (2.6) |
| | Korea | 17.2 | (3.0) | 65.2 | (3.8) | 17.6 | (2.9) |
| | Luxembourg | 1.8 | (0.0) | 43.6 | (0.1) | 54.6 | (0.1) |
| | Mexico | 23.3 | (2.0) | 40.7 | (2.5) | 36.0 | (3.0) |
| | Netherlands | 8.7 | (2.5) | 45.8 | (4.4) | 45.5 | (3.9) |
| | New Zealand | 43.5 | (3.4) | 49.4 | (3.3) | 7.1 | (1.7) |
| | Norway | 8.8 | (2.0) | 52.1 | (3.5) | 39.1 | (3.4) |
| | Poland | 23.5 | (3.0) | 50.2 | (4.0) | 26.3 | (3.8) |
| | Portugal | 7.1 | (2.0) | 68.8 | (3.7) | 24.1 | (3.4) |
| | Slovak Republic | 14.4 | (3.2) | 63.0 | (3.9) | 22.6 | (2.9) |
| | Spain | 8.9 | (1.7) | 31.0 | (2.5) | 60.1 | (3.0) |
| | Sweden | 43.4 | (3.8) | 56.6 | (3.8) | 0.0 | (0.0) |
| | Switzerland | 10.2 | (1.5) | 53.1 | (3.0) | 36.7 | (2.9) |
| | Turkey | 14.2 | (2.9) | 46.8 | (4.0) | 39.0 | (3.9) |
| | United Kingdom | 37.8 | (2.8) | 50.6 | (2.9) | 11.7 | (1.7) |
| | United States | 35.5 | (4.3) | 48.5 | (4.6) | 16.0 | (3.4) |
| | **OECD total** | 26.5 | (1.5) | 48.7 | (1.5) | 24.8 | (1.1) |
| | **OECD average** | 20.7 | (0.5) | 47.1 | (0.6) | 32.2 | (0.5) |
| *Partners* | Argentina | 11.1 | (2.6) | 33.8 | (4.4) | 55.2 | (4.4) |
| | Azerbaijan | 17.6 | (3.2) | 49.3 | (4.7) | 33.1 | (4.1) |
| | Brazil | 21.1 | (2.1) | 49.2 | (2.8) | 29.7 | (2.6) |
| | Bulgaria | 22.8 | (3.6) | 55.5 | (4.5) | 21.7 | (3.7) |
| | Chile | 19.0 | (2.9) | 52.2 | (4.5) | 28.8 | (4.0) |
| | Colombia | 11.8 | (5.0) | 38.4 | (4.9) | 49.8 | (4.5) |
| | Croatia | 5.8 | (1.6) | 39.6 | (3.7) | 54.6 | (3.7) |
| | Estonia | 24.2 | (2.8) | 52.3 | (3.5) | 23.5 | (2.9) |
| | Hong Kong-China | 3.2 | (1.4) | 73.4 | (3.5) | 23.4 | (3.4) |
| | Indonesia | 23.4 | (3.8) | 60.4 | (4.9) | 16.2 | (2.7) |
| | Israel | 33.3 | (4.5) | 38.2 | (4.5) | 28.5 | (3.8) |
| | Jordan | 23.1 | (2.9) | 52.2 | (4.1) | 24.7 | (3.3) |
| | Kyrgyzstan | 36.9 | (3.6) | 52.8 | (4.0) | 10.3 | (2.4) |
| | Latvia | 14.4 | (2.8) | 31.4 | (3.7) | 54.2 | (3.8) |
| | Liechtenstein | c | c | c | c | c | c |
| | Lithuania | 7.6 | (2.2) | 54.6 | (4.0) | 37.9 | (3.7) |
| | Macao-China | 1.6 | (0.0) | 54.4 | (0.1) | 44.0 | (0.1) |
| | Montenegro | 8.6 | (0.1) | 63.2 | (0.1) | 28.2 | (0.1) |
| | Qatar | 26.6 | (0.1) | 38.2 | (0.1) | 35.2 | (0.1) |
| | Romania | 11.6 | (2.9) | 27.4 | (4.0) | 61.1 | (4.9) |
| | Russian Federation | 14.4 | (3.0) | 61.6 | (4.6) | 24.1 | (4.1) |
| | Serbia | 2.0 | (1.0) | 53.1 | (3.9) | 45.0 | (4.0) |
| | Slovenia | 21.2 | (0.4) | 43.4 | (0.6) | 35.4 | (0.5) |
| | Chinese Taipei | 27.7 | (3.1) | 66.4 | (3.2) | 5.9 | (1.5) |
| | Thailand | 28.3 | (2.8) | 40.9 | (3.9) | 30.8 | (3.5) |
| | Tunisia | 5.8 | (2.0) | 37.1 | (4.4) | 57.1 | (4.6) |
| | Uruguay | 6.8 | (1.2) | 36.6 | (3.1) | 56.6 | (3.0) |

1. Results based on reports from school principals and reported proportionate to the number of 15-year-olds enrolled in the school.
*StatLink* http://dx.doi.org/10.1787/142127877152

Pour consulter la version française intégrale de ce tableau, suivre ce lien :
*StatLink* http://dx.doi.org/10.1787/152751048643

[Part 1/3]

**Table 5.7** Parents' perceptions of school quality[1]

Tableau 5.7 Qualité des établissements selon l'avis des parents

| | Percentage of students whose parents agree or strongly agree with the following statements regarding the school their children attend: | | | | | | | | | | | | | |
|---|---|---|---|---|---|---|---|---|---|---|---|---|---|---|
| | Most of the teachers in the school seem competent and dedicated | | Standards of achievement are high in the school | | I am happy with the content taught and the instructional methods used in the school | | I am satisfied with the disciplinary atmosphere in the school | | My child's progress is carefully monitored by the school | | The school provides regular and useful information on my child's progress | | The school does a good job in educating students | |
| | % | S.E. | % | S.E. | % | S.E. | % | S.E. | % | S.E. | % | S.E. | % | S.E. |
| **OECD** Denmark | 87.8 | (0.7) | 77.3 | (1.3) | 77.3 | (1.0) | 74.3 | (1.3) | 71.6 | (1.1) | 68.4 | (1.1) | 78.0 | (1.2) |
| Germany | 79.7 | (0.7) | 71.4 | (1.1) | 71.2 | (0.9) | 73.8 | (1.1) | 61.4 | (1.1) | 46.2 | (1.1) | 76.2 | (0.9) |
| Iceland | 85.9 | (0.6) | 72.4 | (0.9) | 78.3 | (0.8) | 76.2 | (0.7) | 81.6 | (0.7) | 81.2 | (0.7) | 82.6 | (0.7) |
| Italy | 91.2 | (0.3) | 80.1 | (0.5) | 85.8 | (0.5) | 80.9 | (0.6) | 84.6 | (0.5) | 83.2 | (0.6) | 92.1 | (0.4) |
| Korea | 83.3 | (0.7) | 71.5 | (1.1) | 76.8 | (0.8) | 78.4 | (0.8) | 66.1 | (1.0) | 62.7 | (0.9) | 79.4 | (0.8) |
| Luxembourg | 84.5 | (0.7) | 76.6 | (0.7) | 75.4 | (0.8) | 82.9 | (0.7) | 71.7 | (0.7) | 58.1 | (0.9) | 83.5 | (0.6) |
| New Zealand | 93.4 | (0.4) | 87.1 | (0.7) | 86.5 | (0.6) | 82.7 | (0.8) | 85.3 | (0.7) | 82.3 | (0.8) | 91.2 | (0.6) |
| Poland | 90.1 | (0.5) | 88.4 | (0.7) | 83.8 | (0.7) | 79.9 | (0.9) | 82.4 | (0.8) | 92.7 | (0.4) | 90.0 | (0.5) |
| Portugal | 93.8 | (0.4) | 76.1 | (0.9) | 86.6 | (0.7) | 80.4 | (1.0) | 83.6 | (0.7) | 83.4 | (0.8) | 89.1 | (0.7) |
| Turkey | 86.7 | (0.6) | 72.9 | (0.9) | 73.4 | (0.9) | 81.9 | (0.7) | 63.8 | (1.2) | 66.9 | (1.1) | 85.0 | (0.7) |
| **Partners** Bulgaria | 95.4 | (0.4) | 87.2 | (0.8) | 90.6 | (0.6) | 80.3 | (0.9) | 83.5 | (0.8) | 84.8 | (0.8) | 94.3 | (0.4) |
| Colombia | 94.4 | (0.6) | 86.2 | (1.3) | 92.6 | (0.5) | 82.7 | (1.1) | 93.4 | (0.5) | 92.5 | (0.7) | 95.8 | (0.5) |
| Croatia | 92.2 | (0.4) | 65.8 | (1.0) | 85.0 | (0.6) | 82.2 | (0.7) | 78.0 | (0.8) | 83.8 | (0.6) | 91.7 | (0.5) |
| Hong Kong-China | 89.7 | (0.6) | 53.8 | (1.3) | 82.1 | (0.7) | 88.5 | (0.7) | 75.3 | (0.9) | 57.1 | (1.0) | 78.8 | (0.8) |
| Macao-China | 89.0 | (0.5) | 73.9 | (0.7) | 84.2 | (0.6) | 83.7 | (0.6) | 83.1 | (0.6) | 75.0 | (0.7) | 82.0 | (0.6) |
| Qatar | 86.7 | (0.5) | 80.2 | (0.6) | 78.4 | (0.7) | 79.4 | (0.7) | 75.7 | (0.6) | 64.7 | (0.7) | 84.7 | (0.7) |
| **Country average** | 89.0 | (0.1) | 76.3 | (0.2) | 81.8 | (0.2) | 80.5 | (0.2) | 77.6 | (0.2) | 73.9 | (0.2) | 85.9 | (0.2) |

| | Performance on the science scale by parents' agreement with "most of the teachers in the school seem competent and dedicated" | | | | | | Performance on the science scale by parents' agreement with "standards of achievement are high in the school" | | | | | |
|---|---|---|---|---|---|---|---|---|---|---|---|---|
| | Strongly agree or agree | | Disagree or strongly disagree | | Difference in science performance between "strongly agree or agree" and "disagree or strongly disagree" | | Strongly agree or agree | | Disagree or strongly disagree | | Difference in science performance between "strongly agree or agree" and "disagree or strongly disagree" | |
| | Mean score | S.E. | Mean score | S.E. | Dif. (agree - disagree) | S.E. | Mean score | S.E. | Mean score | S.E. | Dif. (agree - disagree) | S.E. |
| **OECD** Denmark | 516 | (2.9) | 486 | (5.3) | **30.3** | (5.6) | 517 | (2.9) | 499 | (4.6) | **18.0** | (4.8) |
| Germany | 530 | (3.7) | 524 | (4.6) | 5.7 | (4.2) | 537 | (3.5) | 507 | (4.6) | **30.5** | (3.9) |
| Iceland | 512 | (1.8) | 485 | (5.1) | **26.6** | (5.1) | 510 | (2.2) | 501 | (3.5) | **9.0** | (4.2) |
| Italy | 481 | (2.1) | 483 | (4.4) | -1.7 | (4.1) | 486 | (2.2) | 462 | (3.5) | **24.0** | (3.7) |
| Korea | 523 | (3.6) | 523 | (3.9) | -0.3 | (4.3) | 532 | (3.7) | 502 | (4.4) | **30.2** | (5.1) |
| Luxembourg | 496 | (1.6) | 493 | (4.3) | 2.5 | (4.8) | 501 | (1.7) | 475 | (3.1) | **26.0** | (3.6) |
| New Zealand | 553 | (2.6) | 530 | (7.0) | **22.7** | (7.3) | 553 | (2.8) | 539 | (4.9) | **13.9** | (5.5) |
| Poland | 500 | (2.4) | 507 | (4.2) | -6.5 | (4.0) | 502 | (2.4) | 498 | (4.2) | 4.9 | (4.0) |
| Portugal | 477 | (2.9) | 479 | (6.8) | -1.2 | (6.7) | 482 | (3.1) | 465 | (3.8) | **16.9** | (4.0) |
| Turkey | 424 | (3.6) | 427 | (7.2) | -3.3 | (5.5) | 431 | (4.6) | 407 | (3.3) | **24.4** | (4.3) |
| **Partners** Bulgaria | 433 | (6.2) | 436 | (10.0) | -2.6 | (9.2) | 435 | (6.5) | 420 | (7.3) | **14.9** | (7.3) |
| Colombia | 388 | (3.4) | 396 | (6.8) | -8.2 | (6.8) | 391 | (3.4) | 376 | (5.8) | **15.0** | (5.8) |
| Croatia | 495 | (2.5) | 502 | (5.3) | -7.2 | (5.3) | 510 | (2.6) | 467 | (3.1) | **43.3** | (3.3) |
| Hong Kong-China | 547 | (2.5) | 519 | (4.8) | **28.1** | (4.8) | 567 | (3.4) | 519 | (2.7) | **48.0** | (4.0) |
| Macao-China | 513 | (1.3) | 496 | (3.5) | **16.7** | (3.9) | 515 | (1.3) | 498 | (2.2) | **17.5** | (2.6) |
| Qatar | 362 | (1.3) | 360 | (3.8) | 1.8 | (4.1) | 363 | (1.5) | 357 | (2.7) | 5.7 | (3.1) |
| **Country average** | 484 | (0.8) | 478 | (1.4) | **6.4** | (1.4) | 490 | (0.8) | 468 | (1.0) | **21.4** | (1.1) |

Note: Values that are statistically significant are indicated in bold (see Annex A3).
1. Results based on reports from parents of the students who were assessed and reported proportionate to the number of 15-year-olds enrolled in the school.
StatLink 🔗 http://dx.doi.org/10.1787/142127877152

Pour consulter la version française intégrale de ce tableau, suivre ce lien :
StatLink 🔗 http://dx.doi.org/10.1787/152751048643

[Part 2/3]

**Table 5.7** Parents' perceptions of school quality[1]

Tableau 5.7 Qualité des établissements selon l'avis des parents

| | | Performance on the science scale by parents' agreement with "I am happy with the content taught and the instructional methods used in the school" | | | | | | Performance on the science scale by parents' agreement with "I am satisfied with the disciplinary atmosphere in the school" | | | | | |
|---|---|---|---|---|---|---|---|---|---|---|---|---|---|
| | | Strongly agree or agree | | Disagree or strongly disagree | | Difference in science performance between "strongly agree or agree" and "disagree or strongly disagree" | | Strongly agree or agree | | Disagree or strongly disagree | | Difference in science performance between "strongly agree or agree" and "disagree or strongly disagree" | |
| | | Mean score | S.E. | Mean score | S.E. | Dif. (agree - disagree) | S.E. | Mean score | S.E. | Mean score | S.E. | Dif. (agree - disagree) | S.E. |
| OECD | Denmark | 518 | (3.0) | 496 | (4.3) | **21.8** | (4.6) | 516 | (3.2) | 501 | (4.3) | **15.4** | (5.1) |
| | Germany | 529 | (4.0) | 525 | (3.7) | 4.0 | (3.7) | 534 | (3.9) | 513 | (3.9) | **20.8** | (4.1) |
| | Iceland | 510 | (2.0) | 498 | (4.1) | **12.0** | (4.6) | 510 | (2.2) | 498 | (4.0) | **12.5** | (4.8) |
| | Italy | 481 | (2.1) | 482 | (4.2) | -0.8 | (4.0) | 483 | (2.4) | 475 | (3.3) | **8.2** | (3.7) |
| | Korea | 523 | (3.6) | 522 | (3.7) | 1.0 | (3.5) | 526 | (3.6) | 514 | (3.9) | **11.5** | (4.1) |
| | Luxembourg | 491 | (1.7) | 505 | (2.8) | **-13.9** | (3.5) | 497 | (1.5) | 486 | (3.9) | **11.1** | (4.2) |
| | New Zealand | 553 | (2.7) | 539 | (5.1) | **14.0** | (5.6) | 555 | (2.7) | 531 | (4.2) | **24.7** | (4.3) |
| | Poland | 500 | (2.5) | 509 | (4.0) | **-9.2** | (4.1) | 502 | (2.4) | 500 | (3.5) | 2.2 | (3.3) |
| | Portugal | 477 | (3.1) | 479 | (4.5) | -1.3 | (4.9) | 479 | (3.2) | 473 | (3.8) | 5.6 | (4.2) |
| | Turkey | 421 | (4.0) | 434 | (5.1) | **-12.6** | (4.4) | 426 | (4.0) | 420 | (5.0) | 6.2 | (4.3) |
| Partners | Bulgaria | 431 | (6.3) | 456 | (7.9) | **-25.3** | (7.3) | 432 | (6.6) | 439 | (5.9) | -6.9 | (4.9) |
| | Colombia | 387 | (3.4) | 404 | (6.6) | **-16.2** | (6.9) | 389 | (3.6) | 388 | (4.2) | 0.8 | (4.6) |
| | Croatia | 492 | (2.7) | 513 | (3.7) | **-21.2** | (4.0) | 497 | (2.7) | 486 | (3.6) | **10.9** | (3.7) |
| | Hong Kong-China | 548 | (2.5) | 527 | (3.7) | **21.1** | (3.5) | 550 | (2.4) | 501 | (5.4) | **48.8** | (5.6) |
| | Macao-China | 512 | (1.3) | 505 | (2.8) | 6.3 | (3.3) | 513 | (1.3) | 499 | (3.2) | **14.0** | (3.6) |
| | Qatar | 363 | (1.6) | 358 | (3.1) | 4.6 | (3.8) | 362 | (1.4) | 361 | (3.2) | 1.1 | (3.6) |
| | **Country average** | 484 | (0.8) | 485 | (1.1) | -1.0 | (1.2) | 486 | (0.8) | 474 | (1.0) | **11.7** | (1.1) |

| | | Performance on the science scale by parents' agreement with "my child's progress is carefully monitored by the school" | | | | | | Performance on the science scale by parents' agreement with "the school provides regular and useful information on my child's progress" | | | | | |
|---|---|---|---|---|---|---|---|---|---|---|---|---|---|
| | | Strongly agree or agree | | Disagree or strongly disagree | | Difference in science performance between "strongly agree or agree" and "disagree or strongly disagree" | | Strongly agree or agree | | Disagree or strongly disagree | | Difference in science performance between "strongly agree or agree" and "disagree or strongly disagree" | |
| | | Mean score | S.E. | Mean score | S.E. | Dif. (agree - disagree) | S.E. | Mean score | S.E. | Mean score | S.E. | Dif. (agree - disagree) | S.E. |
| OECD | Denmark | 517 | (2.9) | 501 | (4.1) | **15.4** | (3.8) | 518 | (3.0) | 500 | (3.8) | **17.5** | (3.9) |
| | Germany | 525 | (4.2) | 534 | (4.0) | **-9.8** | (4.1) | 515 | (4.7) | 541 | (3.3) | **-26.1** | (4.1) |
| | Iceland | 512 | (1.9) | 487 | (4.7) | **25.7** | (5.1) | 512 | (2.1) | 489 | (4.3) | **23.3** | (4.9) |
| | Italy | 481 | (2.1) | 481 | (3.6) | 0.6 | (3.2) | 479 | (2.1) | 492 | (3.2) | **-13.5** | (2.7) |
| | Korea | 525 | (3.8) | 520 | (3.4) | 4.2 | (3.5) | 521 | (4.0) | 526 | (3.3) | -4.8 | (3.5) |
| | Luxembourg | 491 | (1.9) | 505 | (2.6) | **-14.4** | (3.6) | 483 | (2.1) | 512 | (2.1) | **-28.4** | (3.2) |
| | New Zealand | 554 | (2.7) | 532 | (5.4) | **22.7** | (5.6) | 554 | (2.7) | 537 | (5.1) | **17.4** | (5.3) |
| | Poland | 501 | (2.3) | 505 | (4.0) | -3.4 | (3.7) | 501 | (2.3) | 508 | (5.2) | -7.4 | (4.8) |
| | Portugal | 476 | (3.0) | 485 | (4.0) | **-9.3** | (3.6) | 473 | (3.0) | 500 | (4.1) | **-27.1** | (4.1) |
| | Turkey | 421 | (4.0) | 431 | (4.6) | **-9.6** | (3.3) | 419 | (4.2) | 436 | (4.3) | **-16.6** | (3.6) |
| Partners | Bulgaria | 427 | (6.2) | 465 | (7.2) | **-37.8** | (5.7) | 427 | (6.1) | 472 | (9.1) | **-45.1** | (7.6) |
| | Colombia | 390 | (3.3) | 382 | (6.9) | 7.7 | (6.2) | 388 | (3.3) | 400 | (6.2) | -11.3 | (6.0) |
| | Croatia | 492 | (2.7) | 507 | (3.4) | **-15.0** | (3.4) | 493 | (2.7) | 508 | (3.9) | **-14.7** | (3.9) |
| | Hong Kong-China | 546 | (2.6) | 539 | (3.8) | 7.7 | (3.8) | 545 | (3.1) | 544 | (2.6) | 1.0 | (3.1) |
| | Macao-China | 511 | (1.2) | 508 | (3.2) | 3.4 | (3.6) | 510 | (1.4) | 513 | (2.3) | -3.2 | (2.9) |
| | Qatar | 362 | (1.5) | 363 | (3.1) | -0.8 | (3.8) | 359 | (1.6) | 368 | (2.7) | **-8.6** | (3.4) |
| | **Country average** | 483 | (0.8) | 484 | (1.1) | -0.8 | (1.1) | 481 | (0.8) | 490 | (1.1) | **-9.2** | (1.1) |

Note: Values that are statistically significant are indicated in bold (see Annex A3).
1. Results based on reports from parents of the students who were assessed and reported proportionate to the number of 15-year-olds enrolled in the school.
*StatLink* http://dx.doi.org/10.1787/142127877152

Pour consulter la version française intégrale de ce tableau, suivre ce lien :
*StatLink* http://dx.doi.org/10.1787/152751048643

[Part 3/3]
**Table 5.7** **Parents' perceptions of school quality[1]**

Tableau 5.7 Qualité des établissements selon l'avis des parents

| | | Performance on the science scale by parents' agreement with "the school does a good job in educating students" | | | | | |
| | | Strongly agree or agree | | Disagree or strongly disagree | | Difference in science performance between "strongly agree or agree" and "disagree or strongly disagree" | |
| | | Mean score | S.E. | Mean score | S.E. | Dif. (agree – disagree) | S.E. |
|---|---|---|---|---|---|---|---|
| OECD | Denmark | 519 | (3.1) | 489 | (4.5) | 29.7 | (5.0) |
| | Germany | 532 | (3.7) | 517 | (4.4) | 14.9 | (3.9) |
| | Iceland | 512 | (2.0) | 488 | (5.0) | 24.1 | (5.5) |
| | Italy | 482 | (2.1) | 474 | (4.3) | 7.3 | (4.0) |
| | Korea | 525 | (3.6) | 515 | (4.2) | 10.4 | (4.3) |
| | Luxembourg | 497 | (1.5) | 487 | (3.7) | 9.7 | (4.0) |
| | New Zealand | 554 | (2.7) | 522 | (6.3) | 32.3 | (6.8) |
| | Poland | 501 | (2.3) | 508 | (4.9) | -6.2 | (4.4) |
| | Portugal | 477 | (3.1) | 482 | (5.3) | -5.0 | (5.5) |
| | Turkey | 426 | (4.0) | 419 | (5.0) | 6.7 | (4.5) |
| Partners | Bulgaria | 433 | (6.4) | 437 | (8.6) | -3.4 | (9.0) |
| | Colombia | 388 | (3.4) | 395 | (6.4) | -6.8 | (6.5) |
| | Croatia | 496 | (2.6) | 488 | (4.7) | 7.8 | (4.4) |
| | Hong Kong-China | 550 | (2.6) | 524 | (3.5) | 26.3 | (3.7) |
| | Macao-China | 513 | (1.3) | 501 | (3.3) | 12.3 | (3.9) |
| | Qatar | 364 | (1.5) | 353 | (3.7) | 11.1 | (4.2) |
| | **Country average** | 486 | (0.8) | 475 | (1.3) | 10.7 | (1.3) |

Note: Values that are statistically significant are indicated in bold (see Annex A3).
1. Results based on reports from parents of the students who were assessed and reported proportionate to the number of 15-year-olds enrolled in the school.
*StatLink* http://dx.doi.org/10.1787/142127877152

Pour consulter la version française intégrale de ce tableau, suivre ce lien :
*StatLink* http://dx.doi.org/10.1787/152751048643

[Part 1/1]

**Table 5.8   Use of achievement data for accountability purposes[1]**

Tableau 5.8   Usage des résultats scolaires aux fins de responsabilisation

| | Percentage of students in schools where the principal reported that achievement data are | | | | | | | | | |
|---|---|---|---|---|---|---|---|---|---|---|
| | Posted publicly | | Used in evaluation of the principal's performance | | Used in evaluation of teachers' performance | | Used in decisions about instructional resource allocation to the school | | Tracked over time by an administrative authority | |
| | % | S.E. | % | S.E. | % | S.E. | % | S.E. | % | S.E. |
| **OECD** | | | | | | | | | | |
| Australia | 60.3 | (2.6) | 47.6 | (3.1) | 43.0 | (3.0) | 57.6 | (3.0) | 87.9 | (2.1) |
| Austria | 7.9 | (2.2) | 22.0 | (3.7) | 26.3 | (3.7) | 19.5 | (3.0) | 60.4 | (3.7) |
| Belgium | 5.0 | (1.4) | 6.7 | (1.8) | 14.5 | (2.3) | 23.4 | (2.5) | 56.3 | (3.2) |
| Canada | 64.2 | (2.7) | 22.0 | (2.3) | 19.0 | (2.0) | 56.6 | (2.5) | 90.8 | (1.1) |
| Czech Republic | 46.7 | (4.2) | 62.4 | (4.2) | 90.7 | (2.0) | 8.9 | (2.8) | 56.0 | (4.1) |
| Denmark | 43.7 | (3.6) | 15.0 | (2.8) | 21.6 | (3.2) | 31.4 | (3.8) | 33.8 | (3.4) |
| Finland | 4.5 | (1.4) | 3.0 | (1.3) | 13.8 | (2.9) | 7.3 | (2.1) | 54.2 | (4.1) |
| France | w | w | w | w | w | w | w | w | w | w |
| Germany | 14.2 | (2.0) | 19.5 | (2.7) | 28.5 | (2.7) | 26.0 | (2.9) | 55.2 | (2.8) |
| Greece | 31.9 | (3.9) | 6.0 | (2.0) | 9.2 | (2.5) | 1.5 | (0.9) | 48.8 | (4.1) |
| Hungary | 27.8 | (3.4) | 69.2 | (3.9) | 91.8 | (2.5) | 8.8 | (2.5) | 40.4 | (3.8) |
| Iceland | 26.1 | (0.2) | 9.8 | (0.2) | 24.9 | (0.2) | 3.3 | (0.1) | 82.0 | (0.2) |
| Ireland | 18.1 | (2.9) | 5.8 | (1.9) | 29.5 | (3.9) | 46.9 | (4.2) | 47.8 | (4.3) |
| Italy | 33.2 | (2.9) | 20.6 | (2.2) | 24.6 | (2.0) | 53.5 | (2.6) | 21.7 | (2.4) |
| Japan | 10.8 | (2.7) | 10.0 | (2.3) | 25.7 | (3.7) | 6.1 | (1.9) | 15.7 | (2.5) |
| Korea | 16.5 | (3.3) | 23.1 | (3.2) | 34.4 | (3.7) | 30.1 | (4.1) | 51.8 | (4.1) |
| Luxembourg | 51.8 | (0.1) | a | a | 4.8 | (0.0) | 7.1 | (0.0) | 80.1 | (0.0) |
| Mexico | 37.8 | (2.8) | 36.8 | (2.9) | 82.7 | (2.3) | 18.2 | (2.3) | 91.4 | (1.1) |
| Netherlands | 82.9 | (3.0) | 30.7 | (3.6) | 72.8 | (3.5) | 14.2 | (2.7) | 86.2 | (2.6) |
| New Zealand | 66.9 | (3.1) | 38.3 | (3.1) | 46.7 | (3.2) | 69.3 | (2.8) | 91.8 | (1.8) |
| Norway | 47.1 | (3.4) | 34.9 | (3.6) | 39.7 | (3.7) | 11.4 | (2.4) | 52.9 | (4.1) |
| Poland | 42.6 | (3.9) | 78.3 | (3.0) | 88.6 | (2.1) | 12.2 | (2.3) | 77.9 | (3.2) |
| Portugal | 33.1 | (4.1) | 14.0 | (2.8) | 39.5 | (4.3) | 57.2 | (3.9) | 69.4 | (4.2) |
| Slovak Republic | 28.3 | (3.2) | 51.3 | (3.6) | 75.3 | (3.4) | 15.3 | (2.9) | 76.1 | (3.8) |
| Spain | 11.4 | (2.3) | 13.7 | (2.2) | 41.8 | (3.1) | 43.1 | (3.5) | 64.4 | (2.6) |
| Sweden | 66.6 | (3.3) | 39.7 | (4.2) | 48.7 | (4.0) | 45.9 | (4.1) | 83.4 | (3.0) |
| Switzerland | 6.6 | (1.3) | 5.5 | (1.4) | 8.3 | (1.3) | 24.7 | (2.8) | 35.9 | (2.3) |
| Turkey | 35.3 | (4.0) | 51.3 | (4.1) | 75.4 | (3.5) | 32.8 | (3.6) | 80.6 | (3.3) |
| United Kingdom | 92.7 | (1.6) | 91.1 | (1.5) | 93.7 | (1.3) | 63.5 | (3.8) | 92.4 | (1.5) |
| United States | 90.6 | (1.9) | 56.8 | (3.6) | 41.6 | (3.6) | 79.4 | (3.2) | 96.6 | (1.1) |
| **OECD total** | 51.6 | (1.0) | 41.4 | (1.2) | 49.0 | (1.2) | 44.2 | (1.2) | 73.1 | (0.7) |
| **OECD average** | 38.1 | (0.5) | 31.6 | (0.6) | 43.3 | (0.5) | 30.2 | (0.5) | 64.9 | (0.6) |
| **Partners** | | | | | | | | | | |
| Argentina | 5.9 | (1.7) | 19.2 | (3.5) | 53.8 | (4.3) | 31.0 | (4.2) | 50.1 | (4.5) |
| Azerbaijan | 81.2 | (3.3) | 87.1 | (2.9) | 98.2 | (1.2) | 69.0 | (4.3) | 68.8 | (4.4) |
| Brazil | 25.9 | (2.8) | 53.8 | (2.7) | 78.1 | (2.3) | 70.7 | (2.6) | 87.9 | (1.5) |
| Bulgaria | 19.5 | (3.3) | 31.4 | (4.0) | 58.9 | (4.2) | 15.0 | (3.2) | 71.4 | (3.8) |
| Chile | 37.8 | (4.5) | 39.4 | (4.4) | 56.2 | (4.5) | 86.5 | (2.8) | 78.9 | (3.9) |
| Colombia | 34.8 | (5.4) | 41.4 | (5.1) | 72.8 | (4.2) | 66.0 | (4.7) | 80.0 | (3.9) |
| Croatia | 32.5 | (3.4) | 24.4 | (3.7) | 39.1 | (4.0) | 11.0 | (2.5) | 83.0 | (3.2) |
| Estonia | 50.7 | (3.5) | 57.1 | (3.4) | 86.0 | (2.4) | 18.7 | (2.4) | 88.4 | (2.4) |
| Hong Kong-China | 56.3 | (4.6) | 28.2 | (3.5) | 63.4 | (3.9) | 51.2 | (3.9) | 61.7 | (4.1) |
| Indonesia | 13.7 | (2.6) | 88.4 | (2.3) | 96.9 | (1.6) | 85.5 | (2.6) | 63.0 | (3.3) |
| Israel | 36.1 | (3.6) | 73.6 | (4.2) | 93.6 | (2.1) | 72.5 | (3.6) | 70.9 | (3.8) |
| Jordan | 28.6 | (3.6) | 47.6 | (3.7) | 82.5 | (2.9) | 52.5 | (3.7) | 80.5 | (3.4) |
| Kyrgyzstan | 61.2 | (3.6) | 84.6 | (2.9) | 99.5 | (0.4) | 74.2 | (3.0) | 97.6 | (1.0) |
| Latvia | 32.0 | (3.8) | 36.5 | (4.3) | 90.6 | (2.1) | 32.7 | (3.8) | 51.6 | (4.0) |
| Liechtenstein | c | c | c | c | c | c | c | c | c | c |
| Lithuania | 26.9 | (3.1) | 46.8 | (4.1) | 84.3 | (2.8) | 26.7 | (3.2) | 73.6 | (3.0) |
| Macao-China | 10.3 | (0.0) | 4.3 | (0.0) | 41.1 | (0.1) | 30.8 | (0.1) | 50.2 | (0.1) |
| Montenegro | 82.5 | (0.1) | 37.8 | (0.2) | 71.3 | (0.2) | 20.9 | (0.1) | 89.6 | (0.1) |
| Qatar | 56.6 | (0.1) | 66.7 | (0.1) | 93.3 | (0.1) | 42.4 | (0.2) | 83.6 | (0.1) |
| Romania | 68.6 | (5.2) | 89.1 | (2.4) | 97.1 | (1.0) | 77.5 | (3.4) | 70.3 | (4.1) |
| Russian Federation | 75.3 | (3.6) | 88.8 | (2.2) | 100.0 | (0.0) | 66.2 | (4.8) | 100.0 | (0.0) |
| Serbia | 52.9 | (4.0) | 38.4 | (4.3) | 66.1 | (4.2) | 14.0 | (2.9) | 65.7 | (4.0) |
| Slovenia | 35.8 | (0.3) | 24.3 | (0.3) | 27.4 | (0.3) | a | a | 69.6 | (0.4) |
| Chinese Taipei | 31.8 | (3.5) | 13.8 | (2.3) | 30.2 | (2.5) | 19.3 | (2.8) | 31.9 | (3.1) |
| Thailand | 72.2 | (3.7) | 75.0 | (3.6) | 86.4 | (3.0) | 76.0 | (3.2) | 81.7 | (2.9) |
| Tunisia | 18.4 | (3.4) | 68.7 | (4.4) | 82.4 | (2.8) | 63.9 | (5.0) | 81.6 | (4.0) |
| Uruguay | 13.2 | (2.2) | 14.8 | (2.2) | 46.1 | (3.3) | 13.9 | (2.0) | 66.0 | (2.6) |

1. Results based on reports from school principals and reported proportionate to the number of 15-year-olds enrolled in the school.
*StatLink* ⟦⟧ http://dx.doi.org/10.1787/142127877152

Pour consulter la version française intégrale de ce tableau, suivre ce lien :
*StatLink* ⟦⟧ http://dx.doi.org/10.1787/152751048643

[Part 1/1]

**Table 5.9** School accountability to parents[1]

Tableau 5.9 Responsabilité des établissements à l'égard des parents

| | Percentage of students in schools where the principal reported that the school provided information to parents on student performance relative to | | | | | |
|---|---|---|---|---|---|---|
| | Other students in the same school | | Other students in other schools | | National or regional benchmarks | |
| | % | S.E. | % | S.E. | % | S.E. |
| Australia | 59.4 | (2.5) | 19.7 | (2.2) | 50.2 | (2.6) |
| Austria | 28.5 | (3.1) | 10.3 | (2.0) | 8.8 | (2.1) |
| Belgium | 35.1 | (2.6) | 0.8 | (0.6) | 14.1 | (2.1) |
| Canada | 79.3 | (1.5) | 33.9 | (2.6) | 61.2 | (2.4) |
| Czech Republic | 65.7 | (3.6) | 34.8 | (3.1) | 57.1 | (3.1) |
| Denmark | 31.4 | (3.9) | 42.7 | (4.1) | 49.5 | (3.8) |
| Finland | 15.4 | (3.0) | 16.2 | (3.0) | 47.1 | (4.2) |
| France | w | w | w | w | w | w |
| Germany | 67.8 | (3.2) | 27.4 | (2.9) | 31.4 | (2.8) |
| Greece | 70.5 | (3.6) | 5.9 | (1.9) | 16.5 | (2.8) |
| Hungary | 70.8 | (3.9) | 20.6 | (3.4) | 32.9 | (3.9) |
| Iceland | 41.4 | (0.2) | 32.3 | (0.2) | 49.1 | (0.2) |
| Ireland | 38.9 | (3.7) | 7.4 | (2.1) | 26.3 | (3.8) |
| Italy | 18.8 | (2.2) | 8.2 | (1.4) | 19.7 | (2.3) |
| Japan | 40.2 | (3.4) | a | a | 80.0 | (3.3) |
| Korea | 84.1 | (3.1) | 42.0 | (4.1) | 78.0 | (3.3) |
| Luxembourg | 78.3 | (0.1) | 13.2 | (0.0) | 13.2 | (0.0) |
| Mexico | 87.7 | (1.9) | 38.7 | (2.4) | 36.2 | (2.5) |
| Netherlands | 35.4 | (3.8) | 11.5 | (2.6) | 18.7 | (3.3) |
| New Zealand | 49.9 | (3.4) | 36.8 | (3.3) | 74.2 | (2.9) |
| Norway | 39.2 | (3.5) | 30.5 | (3.5) | 65.3 | (3.9) |
| Poland | 78.7 | (3.0) | 45.6 | (3.7) | 78.6 | (3.2) |
| Portugal | 47.3 | (4.5) | 3.5 | (1.4) | 31.8 | (3.6) |
| Slovak Republic | 94.3 | (1.7) | 56.4 | (3.9) | 61.2 | (3.5) |
| Spain | 50.0 | (3.2) | 9.7 | (1.8) | 10.7 | (2.0) |
| Sweden | 12.0 | (2.5) | 23.3 | (3.5) | 94.4 | (1.7) |
| Switzerland | 49.1 | (3.1) | 17.1 | (2.1) | 23.2 | (1.9) |
| Turkey | 88.1 | (3.2) | 74.1 | (3.7) | 71.7 | (3.7) |
| United Kingdom | 54.7 | (3.2) | 36.2 | (3.1) | 80.2 | (2.6) |
| United States | 65.9 | (4.2) | 64.1 | (4.5) | 85.9 | (3.1) |
| **OECD total** | 63.1 | (1.4) | 43.0 | (1.7) | 62.9 | (1.1) |
| **OECD average** | 54.4 | (0.6) | 27.2 | (0.5) | 47.1 | (0.5) |
| Argentina | 65.0 | (4.6) | 21.6 | (3.6) | 66.5 | (3.7) |
| Azerbaijan | 97.7 | (1.5) | 71.5 | (3.5) | 87.1 | (2.8) |
| Brazil | 84.9 | (2.0) | 59.9 | (2.8) | 59.7 | (2.9) |
| Bulgaria | 81.2 | (3.2) | 34.4 | (4.1) | 46.0 | (4.9) |
| Chile | 73.0 | (4.4) | 47.9 | (4.8) | 89.2 | (3.1) |
| Colombia | 87.9 | (2.7) | 24.9 | (3.9) | 91.8 | (2.5) |
| Croatia | 60.0 | (3.7) | 22.7 | (3.4) | a | a |
| Estonia | 40.6 | (3.4) | 21.1 | (3.0) | 62.9 | (3.6) |
| Hong Kong-China | 85.6 | (2.7) | 5.8 | (1.9) | 14.7 | (3.6) |
| Indonesia | 97.8 | (1.5) | 74.4 | (3.3) | 88.7 | (2.4) |
| Israel | 55.1 | (3.9) | 23.7 | (3.7) | 31.7 | (3.6) |
| Jordan | 91.0 | (2.2) | 38.2 | (4.0) | 40.8 | (4.1) |
| Kyrgyzstan | 90.7 | (2.2) | 64.7 | (3.4) | 80.5 | (3.0) |
| Latvia | 31.9 | (3.3) | 25.0 | (3.6) | 30.8 | (4.1) |
| Liechtenstein | c | c | c | c | c | c |
| Lithuania | 56.7 | (3.9) | 24.5 | (3.5) | a | a |
| Macao-China | 38.9 | (0.1) | 4.0 | (0.0) | 1.5 | (0.0) |
| Montenegro | 82.6 | (0.1) | 17.6 | (0.2) | 20.8 | (0.2) |
| Qatar | 89.0 | (0.1) | 50.8 | (0.1) | 58.2 | (0.1) |
| Romania | 94.8 | (1.7) | 67.3 | (4.2) | 74.1 | (4.0) |
| Russian Federation | 90.6 | (2.1) | 61.0 | (3.9) | 74.4 | (3.8) |
| Serbia | 92.1 | (2.3) | 28.1 | (3.3) | 28.1 | (3.2) |
| Slovenia | 27.5 | (0.3) | 2.3 | (0.2) | 36.8 | (0.4) |
| Chinese Taipei | 66.4 | (3.9) | 20.1 | (2.5) | 21.1 | (3.1) |
| Thailand | 83.3 | (3.0) | 42.6 | (3.9) | 52.1 | (4.0) |
| Tunisia | 73.7 | (3.9) | 27.3 | (3.9) | 30.0 | (3.9) |
| Uruguay | 47.9 | (3.1) | 4.2 | (1.1) | 14.7 | (2.1) |

1. Results based on reports from school principals and reported proportionate to the number of 15-year-olds enrolled in the school.
*StatLink* http://dx.doi.org/10.1787/142127877152

Pour consulter la version française intégrale de ce tableau, suivre ce lien :
*StatLink* http://dx.doi.org/10.1787/152751048643

[Part 1/4]

**Table 5.10 Involvement of schools in decision making[1]**

Tableau 5.10 Participation des établissements à la prise de décisions

Percentage of students in schools where the principal reported that only the school, only the government, or both the school and the government have considerable responsibility for the following aspects of school policy and management

| Cross-country correlation between the percentage of schools having considerable responsibility ("school only" and "school and government") and performance in science[2] | Selecting teachers for hire: Correlation coefficient | Selecting teachers for hire: P-value | Dismissing teachers: Correlation coefficient | Dismissing teachers: P-value | Establishing teachers' starting salaries: Correlation coefficient | Establishing teachers' starting salaries: P-value |
|---|---|---|---|---|---|---|
| | **0.43** | (0.00) | **0.32** | (0.02) | 0.20 | (0.14) |

**Selecting teachers for hire**

| | | School only | | School and government | | Government only | |
|---|---|---|---|---|---|---|---|
| | | % | S.E. | % | S.E. | % | S.E. |
| OECD | Australia | 58.1 | (1.5) | 15.7 | (2.0) | 26.2 | (2.1) |
| | Austria | 7.5 | (2.5) | 25.7 | (3.9) | 66.8 | (4.3) |
| | Belgium | 72.2 | (2.5) | 15.7 | (2.7) | 12.1 | (1.5) |
| | Canada | 49.4 | (2.5) | 34.2 | (2.8) | 16.4 | (1.8) |
| | Czech Republic | 98.8 | (0.5) | 1.2 | (0.5) | 0.0 | (0.0) |
| | Denmark | 94.9 | (1.7) | 2.7 | (1.3) | 2.3 | (1.2) |
| | Finland | 27.5 | (3.0) | 35.9 | (4.2) | 36.6 | (4.0) |
| | France | w | w | w | w | w | w |
| | Germany | 15.0 | (2.5) | 29.8 | (2.8) | 55.2 | (3.3) |
| | Greece | 4.8 | (1.5) | 0.3 | (0.3) | 94.8 | (1.2) |
| | Hungary | 97.0 | (1.4) | 2.9 | (1.4) | 0.1 | (0.1) |
| | Iceland | 98.3 | (0.1) | 1.5 | (0.1) | 0.2 | (0.1) |
| | Ireland | 76.2 | (1.8) | 6.6 | (2.0) | 17.2 | (1.9) |
| | Italy | 5.2 | (0.8) | 17.5 | (2.3) | 77.3 | (2.3) |
| | Japan | 32.3 | (1.2) | 1.2 | (0.8) | 66.5 | (1.5) |
| | Korea | 37.0 | (3.9) | 7.1 | (2.0) | 55.9 | (4.1) |
| | Luxembourg | 15.7 | (0.0) | 44.8 | (0.1) | 39.5 | (0.1) |
| | Mexico | 49.6 | (2.2) | 3.1 | (0.7) | 47.3 | (2.3) |
| | Netherlands | 100.0 | (0.0) | 0.0 | (0.0) | 0.0 | (0.0) |
| | New Zealand | 100.0 | (0.0) | 0.0 | (0.0) | 0.0 | (0.0) |
| | Norway | 58.9 | (3.8) | 15.1 | (2.6) | 25.9 | (3.2) |
| | Poland | 90.1 | (2.4) | 9.8 | (2.4) | 0.1 | (0.1) |
| | Portugal | 13.7 | (2.0) | 8.4 | (2.3) | 78.0 | (2.9) |
| | Slovak Republic | 100.0 | (0.0) | 0.0 | (0.0) | 0.0 | (0.0) |
| | Spain | 34.0 | (1.1) | 0.7 | (0.5) | 65.2 | (1.0) |
| | Sweden | 97.8 | (1.1) | 2.2 | (1.1) | 0.0 | (0.0) |
| | Switzerland | 86.1 | (1.5) | 9.9 | (1.4) | 4.0 | (0.3) |
| | Turkey | 3.0 | (1.6) | 3.1 | (1.4) | 93.9 | (2.1) |
| | United Kingdom | 94.3 | (0.9) | 5.6 | (0.9) | 0.1 | (0.1) |
| | United States | 97.7 | (1.7) | 2.3 | (1.7) | 0.0 | (0.0) |
| | **OECD average** | 59.1 | (0.4) | 10.5 | (0.4) | 30.4 | (0.4) |
| Partners | Argentina | 49.2 | (3.7) | 6.1 | (2.0) | 44.7 | (3.5) |
| | Azerbaijan | 79.7 | (3.1) | 9.2 | (2.3) | 11.2 | (2.3) |
| | Brazil | 28.6 | (2.3) | 13.8 | (2.1) | 57.6 | (2.5) |
| | Bulgaria | 92.9 | (2.3) | 7.0 | (2.3) | 0.2 | (0.1) |
| | Chile | 59.2 | (2.8) | 2.7 | (1.5) | 38.1 | (2.8) |
| | Colombia | 19.2 | (2.4) | 1.6 | (0.9) | 79.1 | (2.6) |
| | Croatia | 94.5 | (1.4) | 5.5 | (1.4) | 0.0 | (0.0) |
| | Estonia | 95.3 | (1.4) | 3.0 | (1.4) | 1.7 | (1.0) |
| | Hong Kong-China | 89.7 | (1.6) | 7.6 | (1.6) | 2.7 | (0.1) |
| | Indonesia | 32.8 | (3.6) | 18.6 | (3.3) | 48.6 | (4.2) |
| | Israel | 52.2 | (4.2) | 42.3 | (4.4) | 5.5 | (1.6) |
| | Jordan | 9.1 | (1.4) | 0.3 | (0.3) | 90.6 | (1.3) |
| | Kyrgyzstan | 56.2 | (3.4) | 18.2 | (3.1) | 25.6 | (3.2) |
| | Latvia | 93.7 | (1.8) | 6.3 | (1.8) | 0.0 | (0.0) |
| | Liechtenstein | c | c | c | c | c | c |
| | Lithuania | 97.2 | (1.1) | 2.2 | (1.0) | 0.6 | (0.4) |
| | Macao-China | 96.2 | (0.0) | 2.2 | (0.0) | 1.6 | (0.0) |
| | Montenegro | 96.8 | (0.1) | 3.2 | (0.1) | 0.0 | (0.0) |
| | Qatar | 31.1 | (0.1) | 0.3 | (0.0) | 68.6 | (0.1) |
| | Romania | 2.6 | (1.2) | 6.3 | (1.9) | 91.1 | (2.3) |
| | Russian Federation | 92.9 | (2.0) | 6.9 | (2.1) | 0.1 | (0.1) |
| | Serbia | 89.9 | (2.3) | 10.1 | (2.3) | 0.0 | (0.0) |
| | Slovenia | 86.8 | (0.2) | 13.2 | (0.2) | 0.0 | (0.0) |
| | Chinese Taipei | 81.4 | (2.8) | 16.8 | (2.9) | 1.8 | (1.0) |
| | Thailand | 30.4 | (2.6) | 14.9 | (3.1) | 54.7 | (3.7) |
| | Tunisia | 3.7 | (1.4) | 0.6 | (0.6) | 95.7 | (1.5) |
| | Uruguay | 16.7 | (0.9) | 2.8 | (0.7) | 80.6 | (1.1) |

**Dismissing teachers**

| | | School only | | School and government | | Government only | |
|---|---|---|---|---|---|---|---|
| | | % | S.E. | % | S.E. | % | S.E. |
| OECD | Australia | 37.3 | (1.9) | 8.1 | (1.7) | 54.5 | (2.3) |
| | Austria | 4.5 | (2.1) | 18.5 | (3.1) | 77.1 | (3.4) |
| | Belgium | 61.7 | (2.1) | 20.1 | (2.7) | 18.2 | (2.3) |
| | Canada | 22.1 | (1.8) | 24.8 | (2.5) | 53.1 | (2.6) |
| | Czech Republic | 98.8 | (0.5) | 1.2 | (0.5) | 0.0 | (0.0) |
| | Denmark | 49.6 | (3.4) | 18.2 | (2.7) | 32.2 | (3.5) |
| | Finland | 13.6 | (2.4) | 18.0 | (3.2) | 68.4 | (3.4) |
| | France | w | w | w | w | w | w |
| | Germany | 7.4 | (1.9) | 10.0 | (1.9) | 82.6 | (2.6) |
| | Greece | 4.6 | (1.5) | 0.8 | (0.5) | 94.6 | (1.2) |
| | Hungary | 94.5 | (1.8) | 4.7 | (1.6) | 0.8 | (0.7) |
| | Iceland | 90.6 | (0.1) | 4.1 | (0.1) | 5.2 | (0.1) |
| | Ireland | 62.2 | (2.4) | 11.4 | (2.0) | 26.4 | (2.0) |
| | Italy | 4.8 | (0.8) | 9.2 | (1.4) | 86.0 | (1.6) |
| | Japan | 32.3 | (1.2) | 1.2 | (0.8) | 66.5 | (1.5) |
| | Korea | 33.8 | (3.7) | 5.7 | (1.7) | 60.4 | (4.0) |
| | Luxembourg | 20.1 | (0.0) | 27.2 | (0.1) | 52.7 | (0.1) |
| | Mexico | 36.1 | (2.3) | 2.7 | (0.7) | 61.2 | (2.4) |
| | Netherlands | 99.5 | (0.5) | 0.0 | (0.0) | 0.5 | (0.5) |
| | New Zealand | 96.9 | (1.4) | 2.4 | (1.2) | 0.7 | (0.7) |
| | Norway | 35.5 | (3.7) | 16.1 | (2.6) | 48.4 | (3.6) |
| | Poland | 88.8 | (2.5) | 9.7 | (2.4) | 1.4 | (0.9) |
| | Portugal | 10.6 | (1.4) | 0.5 | (0.6) | 88.9 | (1.5) |
| | Slovak Republic | 99.0 | (0.6) | 1.0 | (0.6) | 0.0 | (0.0) |
| | Spain | 34.8 | (1.0) | 0.1 | (0.1) | 65.0 | (1.0) |
| | Sweden | 57.7 | (3.7) | 22.4 | (3.8) | 19.9 | (3.0) |
| | Switzerland | 73.8 | (2.1) | 13.4 | (1.7) | 12.8 | (1.6) |
| | Turkey | 2.3 | (1.4) | 1.5 | (1.1) | 96.2 | (1.8) |
| | United Kingdom | 71.6 | (2.7) | 22.1 | (2.8) | 6.3 | (0.4) |
| | United States | 99.8 | (0.2) | 0.2 | (0.2) | 0.0 | (0.0) |
| | **OECD average** | 49.8 | (0.4) | 9.5 | (0.3) | 40.7 | (0.4) |
| Partners | Argentina | 35.9 | (4.3) | 7.5 | (2.9) | 56.6 | (3.8) |
| | Azerbaijan | 91.8 | (2.1) | 2.9 | (1.1) | 5.3 | (1.7) |
| | Brazil | 22.2 | (2.0) | 7.6 | (1.4) | 70.2 | (2.4) |
| | Bulgaria | 92.5 | (2.4) | 7.5 | (2.4) | 0.0 | (0.0) |
| | Chile | 57.6 | (2.7) | 2.6 | (1.5) | 39.7 | (2.8) |
| | Colombia | 20.0 | (2.5) | 3.4 | (2.1) | 76.6 | (3.1) |
| | Croatia | 86.7 | (2.4) | 11.9 | (2.3) | 1.3 | (1.0) |
| | Estonia | 96.9 | (1.1) | 1.9 | (1.1) | 1.1 | (0.8) |
| | Hong Kong-China | 82.4 | (2.4) | 12.2 | (2.7) | 5.4 | (1.1) |
| | Indonesia | 36.0 | (3.9) | 15.7 | (3.4) | 48.3 | (4.2) |
| | Israel | 41.7 | (4.4) | 41.2 | (4.4) | 17.1 | (2.8) |
| | Jordan | 9.3 | (1.2) | 0.0 | (0.0) | 90.7 | (1.2) |
| | Kyrgyzstan | 52.1 | (3.3) | 14.9 | (2.8) | 33.0 | (3.0) |
| | Latvia | 96.5 | (1.4) | 3.5 | (1.4) | 0.0 | (0.0) |
| | Liechtenstein | c | c | c | c | c | c |
| | Lithuania | 97.3 | (1.2) | 2.5 | (1.2) | 0.2 | (0.2) |
| | Macao-China | 96.2 | (0.0) | 0.0 | (0.0) | 3.8 | (0.0) |
| | Montenegro | 88.2 | (0.1) | 11.8 | (0.1) | 0.0 | (0.0) |
| | Qatar | 31.2 | (0.1) | 0.8 | (0.0) | 68.0 | (0.1) |
| | Romania | 9.1 | (2.7) | 13.1 | (2.7) | 77.9 | (3.6) |
| | Russian Federation | 94.1 | (1.9) | 5.4 | (1.9) | 0.5 | (0.4) |
| | Serbia | 82.8 | (3.3) | 15.2 | (3.1) | 2.0 | (1.0) |
| | Slovenia | 79.3 | (0.3) | 18.8 | (0.3) | 1.9 | (0.0) |
| | Chinese Taipei | 79.9 | (3.0) | 19.5 | (3.1) | 0.6 | (0.4) |
| | Thailand | 58.0 | (4.2) | 14.8 | (2.9) | 27.2 | (3.9) |
| | Tunisia | 2.4 | (1.0) | 1.0 | (1.0) | 96.7 | (1.4) |
| | Uruguay | 15.7 | (0.9) | 0.6 | (0.1) | 83.7 | (0.9) |

**Establishing teachers' starting salaries**

| | | School only | | School and government | | Government only | |
|---|---|---|---|---|---|---|---|
| | | % | S.E. | % | S.E. | % | S.E. |
| OECD | Australia | 13.1 | (1.1) | 4.7 | (1.4) | 82.1 | (1.6) |
| | Austria | 0.9 | (0.7) | 0.0 | (0.0) | 99.1 | (0.7) |
| | Belgium | 0.4 | (0.4) | 0.7 | (0.5) | 98.8 | (0.7) |
| | Canada | 11.4 | (1.3) | 9.1 | (1.5) | 79.5 | (1.9) |
| | Czech Republic | 72.7 | (3.6) | 18.1 | (3.1) | 9.2 | (2.0) |
| | Denmark | 16.4 | (2.9) | 20.6 | (3.2) | 63.0 | (3.7) |
| | Finland | 5.1 | (1.7) | 5.8 | (2.0) | 89.1 | (2.3) |
| | France | w | w | w | w | w | w |
| | Germany | 3.7 | (1.1) | 1.5 | (1.0) | 94.8 | (1.8) |
| | Greece | 0.7 | (0.6) | 0.4 | (0.4) | 98.9 | (0.7) |
| | Hungary | 48.7 | (4.0) | 13.5 | (2.5) | 37.8 | (3.9) |
| | Iceland | 11.5 | (0.2) | 0.8 | (0.1) | 87.6 | (0.2) |
| | Ireland | 3.8 | (1.5) | 2.5 | (1.3) | 93.7 | (1.8) |
| | Italy | 2.7 | (1.1) | 0.2 | (0.2) | 97.1 | (1.1) |
| | Japan | 32.3 | (1.2) | 0.0 | (0.0) | 67.7 | (1.2) |
| | Korea | 13.3 | (2.7) | 3.1 | (1.4) | 83.6 | (3.0) |
| | Luxembourg | 12.8 | (0.0) | 0.0 | (0.0) | 87.2 | (0.0) |
| | Mexico | 22.2 | (2.3) | 0.6 | (0.4) | 77.1 | (2.4) |
| | Netherlands | 74.6 | (3.0) | 6.6 | (1.7) | 18.8 | (2.8) |
| | New Zealand | 12.8 | (2.1) | 2.5 | (0.8) | 84.7 | (2.2) |
| | Norway | 11.1 | (2.3) | 4.5 | (1.6) | 84.4 | (2.6) |
| | Poland | 14.0 | (2.9) | 12.9 | (2.8) | 73.1 | (3.8) |
| | Portugal | 4.6 | (1.1) | 0.0 | (0.0) | 95.4 | (1.1) |
| | Slovak Republic | 40.6 | (3.9) | 19.8 | (2.8) | 39.6 | (3.9) |
| | Spain | 6.2 | (1.4) | 2.8 | (1.0) | 91.0 | (1.7) |
| | Sweden | 57.5 | (3.5) | 21.3 | (3.3) | 21.2 | (3.1) |
| | Switzerland | 6.9 | (1.1) | 6.9 | (1.4) | 86.2 | (1.8) |
| | Turkey | 3.8 | (1.4) | 0.0 | (0.0) | 96.2 | (1.4) |
| | United Kingdom | 54.9 | (3.0) | 26.9 | (3.1) | 18.2 | (1.9) |
| | United States | 79.5 | (3.3) | 11.2 | (2.2) | 9.3 | (2.8) |
| | **OECD average** | 22.0 | (0.4) | 6.8 | (0.3) | 71.2 | (0.4) |
| Partners | Argentina | 4.0 | (2.2) | 2.1 | (1.2) | 94.0 | (2.5) |
| | Azerbaijan | 31.8 | (3.8) | 2.1 | (1.2) | 66.1 | (3.9) |
| | Brazil | 15.4 | (1.5) | 0.8 | (0.5) | 83.9 | (1.5) |
| | Bulgaria | 8.5 | (2.3) | 6.1 | (2.0) | 85.4 | (3.0) |
| | Chile | 47.6 | (3.0) | 6.0 | (2.0) | 46.4 | (2.9) |
| | Colombia | 12.9 | (1.9) | 2.2 | (0.6) | 84.9 | (2.0) |
| | Croatia | 1.4 | (0.8) | 1.3 | (0.9) | 97.3 | (1.2) |
| | Estonia | 11.1 | (2.0) | 23.2 | (3.0) | 65.7 | (3.3) |
| | Hong Kong-China | 18.0 | (2.6) | 25.0 | (3.7) | 57.0 | (4.2) |
| | Indonesia | 37.4 | (3.6) | 13.2 | (2.6) | 49.4 | (4.1) |
| | Israel | 16.7 | (3.3) | 3.6 | (1.9) | 79.7 | (3.8) |
| | Jordan | 8.5 | (0.9) | 0.0 | (0.0) | 91.5 | (0.9) |
| | Kyrgyzstan | 21.5 | (3.1) | 3.1 | (1.2) | 75.5 | (3.2) |
| | Latvia | 15.5 | (2.9) | 24.0 | (3.6) | 60.5 | (4.2) |
| | Liechtenstein | c | c | c | c | c | c |
| | Lithuania | 11.4 | (2.3) | 8.0 | (2.1) | 80.6 | (2.6) |
| | Macao-China | 96.2 | (0.0) | 0.0 | (0.0) | 3.8 | (0.0) |
| | Montenegro | 0.3 | (0.0) | 3.9 | (0.0) | 95.8 | (0.0) |
| | Qatar | 25.5 | (0.1) | 4.0 | (0.1) | 70.5 | (0.1) |
| | Romania | 5.3 | (2.1) | 2.8 | (1.4) | 91.9 | (2.7) |
| | Russian Federation | 19.6 | (2.8) | 17.5 | (3.2) | 62.9 | (4.0) |
| | Serbia | 6.6 | (2.0) | 8.6 | (2.1) | 84.8 | (2.6) |
| | Slovenia | 2.9 | (0.1) | 9.7 | (0.2) | 87.4 | (0.2) |
| | Chinese Taipei | 22.6 | (2.9) | 9.3 | (2.5) | 68.1 | (2.5) |
| | Thailand | 27.2 | (2.9) | 7.9 | (2.1) | 64.9 | (3.2) |
| | Tunisia | 2.3 | (1.0) | 0.0 | (0.0) | 97.7 | (1.0) |
| | Uruguay | 13.3 | (0.8) | 0.6 | (0.1) | 86.2 | (0.8) |

Note: Values that are statistically significant at the 5% level ($p<0.05$) are indicated in bold.
1. Results based on reports from school principals and reported proportionate to the number of 15-year-olds enrolled in the school.
2. The cross-country correlation is based on all participating countries where the data are available.

StatLink http://dx.doi.org/10.1787/142127877152

Pour consulter la version française intégrale de ce tableau, suivre ce lien :
StatLink http://dx.doi.org/10.1787/152751048643

[Part 2/4]

**Table 5.10**   Involvement of schools in decision making[1]

Tableau 5.10   Participation des établissements à la prise de décisions

Percentage of students in schools where the principal reported that only the school, only the government, or both the school and the government have considerable responsibility for the following aspects of school policy and management

| Cross-country correlation between the percentage of schools having considerable responsibility ("school only" and "school and government") and performance in science[2] | Determining teachers' salary increases | | | | | | Formulating the school budget | | | | | | Deciding on budget allocations within the school | | | | | |
|---|---|---|---|---|---|---|---|---|---|---|---|---|---|---|---|---|---|---|
| | Correlation coefficient | | | P-value | | | Correlation coefficient | | | P-value | | | Correlation coefficient | | | P-value | | |
| | 0.22 | | | (0.11) | | | **0.47** | | | (0.00) | | | **0.54** | | | (0.00) | | |
| | School only | | School and government | | Government only | | School only | | School and government | | Government only | | School only | | School and government | | Government only | |
| | % | S.E. | % | S.E. | % | S.E. | % | S.E. | % | S.E. | % | S.E. | % | S.E. | % | S.E. | % | S.E. |
| **OECD** | | | | | | | | | | | | | | | | | | |
| Australia | 16.1 | (1.6) | 7.2 | (1.5) | 76.7 | (1.6) | 71.0 | (2.6) | 17.8 | (2.2) | 11.2 | (1.7) | 93.3 | (1.5) | 5.7 | (1.4) | 1.0 | (0.6) |
| Austria | 0.0 | (0.0) | 0.0 | (0.0) | 100.0 | (0.0) | 15.7 | (2.3) | 6.8 | (2.0) | 77.5 | (2.9) | 92.1 | (2.2) | 6.3 | (2.1) | 1.6 | (0.8) |
| Belgium | 0.4 | (0.4) | 0.7 | (0.5) | 98.8 | (0.7) | 55.8 | (2.2) | 22.4 | (2.4) | 21.8 | (2.0) | 67.6 | (2.4) | 21.9 | (2.5) | 10.5 | (1.8) |
| Canada | 11.7 | (1.5) | 10.8 | (1.6) | 77.4 | (2.0) | 29.1 | (1.8) | 37.4 | (2.7) | 33.5 | (2.6) | 78.7 | (2.1) | 14.9 | (1.5) | 6.5 | (1.3) |
| Czech Republic | 64.6 | (3.8) | 23.9 | (3.6) | 11.5 | (2.2) | 54.7 | (4.4) | 35.0 | (4.2) | 10.3 | (2.1) | 76.0 | (3.8) | 23.0 | (3.7) | 1.0 | (0.7) |
| Denmark | 16.2 | (3.0) | 23.2 | (3.2) | 60.6 | (3.6) | 81.5 | (3.0) | 14.0 | (2.8) | 4.5 | (1.6) | 97.2 | (1.2) | 2.8 | (1.2) | 0.0 | (0.0) |
| Finland | 5.3 | (1.9) | 4.0 | (1.6) | 90.7 | (2.5) | 30.0 | (4.0) | 37.7 | (3.9) | 32.3 | (4.1) | 86.8 | (3.0) | 11.8 | (2.8) | 1.4 | (1.2) |
| France | w | w | w | w | w | w | w | w | w | w | w | w | w | w | w | w | w | w |
| Germany | 3.8 | (1.1) | 5.6 | (1.8) | 90.6 | (2.3) | 79.0 | (2.8) | 12.6 | (2.1) | 8.4 | (2.0) | 96.3 | (1.3) | 3.1 | (1.1) | 0.6 | (0.6) |
| Greece | 1.9 | (1.3) | 0.9 | (0.6) | 97.3 | (1.5) | 60.8 | (3.9) | 8.8 | (2.2) | 30.4 | (3.7) | 55.8 | (4.2) | 4.7 | (1.6) | 39.4 | (4.2) |
| Hungary | 51.2 | (4.1) | 19.7 | (3.2) | 29.2 | (3.6) | 73.7 | (3.7) | 15.7 | (2.8) | 10.6 | (2.5) | 92.4 | (2.0) | 5.0 | (1.9) | 2.6 | (1.3) |
| Iceland | 5.1 | (0.1) | 11.3 | (0.1) | 83.6 | (0.2) | 45.0 | (0.2) | 26.3 | (0.2) | 28.6 | (0.2) | 75.5 | (0.3) | 14.9 | (0.2) | 9.5 | (0.2) |
| Ireland | 2.9 | (1.3) | 1.9 | (1.1) | 95.2 | (1.7) | 66.0 | (2.7) | 10.9 | (2.3) | 23.2 | (2.3) | 95.0 | (1.3) | 3.2 | (1.4) | 1.8 | (0.7) |
| Italy | 2.7 | (1.1) | 0.2 | (0.0) | 97.0 | (1.1) | 17.9 | (2.6) | 14.3 | (2.3) | 67.7 | (3.1) | 87.9 | (1.5) | 8.6 | (1.4) | 3.5 | (1.0) |
| Japan | 32.3 | (1.2) | 1.1 | (0.8) | 66.6 | (1.5) | 38.7 | (2.1) | 6.2 | (1.8) | 55.1 | (2.6) | 88.1 | (2.2) | 4.9 | (1.7) | 7.0 | (1.8) |
| Korea | 6.1 | (1.9) | 1.2 | (0.9) | 92.7 | (2.1) | 68.8 | (3.8) | 11.0 | (2.5) | 20.2 | (3.5) | 91.1 | (1.9) | 2.5 | (1.3) | 6.4 | (1.9) |
| Luxembourg | 12.8 | (0.0) | 0.0 | (0.0) | 87.2 | (0.0) | 38.7 | (0.0) | 46.1 | (0.0) | 15.2 | (0.0) | 83.6 | (0.0) | 16.4 | (0.0) | 0.0 | (0.0) |
| Mexico | 21.8 | (2.4) | 0.2 | (0.1) | 78.0 | (2.4) | 58.4 | (2.7) | 2.7 | (0.6) | 38.9 | (2.7) | 85.9 | (1.4) | 1.8 | (0.5) | 12.3 | (1.4) |
| Netherlands | 61.1 | (3.8) | 8.6 | (2.2) | 30.3 | (3.8) | 98.5 | (0.9) | 0.0 | (0.0) | 1.5 | (0.9) | 99.1 | (0.7) | 0.5 | (0.5) | 0.5 | (0.5) |
| New Zealand | 22.7 | (2.6) | 12.6 | (1.9) | 64.7 | (3.0) | 92.1 | (1.6) | 4.8 | (0.8) | 3.2 | (1.4) | 99.4 | (0.6) | 0.6 | (0.6) | 0.0 | (0.0) |
| Norway | 7.7 | (2.0) | 16.7 | (3.0) | 75.6 | (3.4) | 55.7 | (3.4) | 17.9 | (2.9) | 26.4 | (3.5) | 93.6 | (1.8) | 4.8 | (1.6) | 1.6 | (0.9) |
| Poland | 6.0 | (1.6) | 16.6 | (2.9) | 77.3 | (3.3) | 6.0 | (1.7) | 36.0 | (3.8) | 57.9 | (3.8) | 27.6 | (3.2) | 36.6 | (3.8) | 35.8 | (3.7) |
| Portugal | 4.0 | (1.0) | 0.8 | (0.6) | 95.2 | (1.2) | 69.8 | (3.9) | 13.7 | (2.8) | 16.5 | (3.1) | 56.5 | (3.9) | 24.0 | (3.4) | 19.5 | (3.0) |
| Slovak Republic | 32.9 | (4.0) | 19.0 | (2.5) | 48.1 | (3.9) | 52.1 | (3.9) | 32.3 | (3.5) | 15.6 | (3.4) | 79.3 | (2.7) | 18.6 | (2.7) | 2.2 | (1.0) |
| Spain | 6.7 | (1.4) | 2.3 | (0.7) | 91.1 | (1.6) | 77.0 | (2.8) | 10.1 | (2.3) | 12.9 | (2.2) | 95.8 | (1.2) | 2.9 | (1.0) | 1.2 | (0.6) |
| Sweden | 61.4 | (3.6) | 32.0 | (3.5) | 6.6 | (2.0) | 56.9 | (3.8) | 32.0 | (4.2) | 11.0 | (2.4) | 96.4 | (1.3) | 2.2 | (1.0) | 1.3 | (0.8) |
| Switzerland | 10.1 | (1.5) | 11.2 | (1.7) | 78.7 | (2.1) | 52.0 | (2.8) | 24.5 | (2.4) | 23.5 | (2.2) | 82.4 | (1.6) | 12.7 | (1.6) | 4.8 | (1.1) |
| Turkey | 2.3 | (1.4) | 0.0 | (0.0) | 97.7 | (1.4) | 62.4 | (3.9) | 9.9 | (2.5) | 27.7 | (3.7) | 69.5 | (4.4) | 4.7 | (1.8) | 25.8 | (4.1) |
| United Kingdom | 69.1 | (3.0) | 21.0 | (3.0) | 10.0 | (0.9) | 62.5 | (3.2) | 25.0 | (2.6) | 12.5 | (1.9) | 97.3 | (0.9) | 2.6 | (0.9) | 0.1 | (0.1) |
| United States | 78.3 | (3.1) | 15.7 | (3.1) | 5.9 | (1.4) | 85.7 | (3.0) | 12.4 | (3.0) | 1.9 | (1.0) | 95.3 | (1.7) | 3.9 | (1.6) | 0.8 | (0.6) |
| **OECD average** | 21.3 | (0.4) | 9.3 | (0.4) | 69.5 | (0.4) | 57.1 | (0.6) | 18.8 | (0.5) | 24.1 | (0.5) | 84.0 | (0.4) | 9.2 | (0.3) | 6.8 | (0.3) |
| **Partners** | | | | | | | | | | | | | | | | | | |
| Argentina | 2.5 | (1.7) | 0.9 | (0.8) | 96.6 | (1.9) | 30.2 | (4.2) | 11.6 | (3.4) | 58.2 | (4.3) | 62.6 | (4.3) | 9.7 | (3.1) | 27.6 | (3.7) |
| Azerbaijan | 4.9 | (1.6) | 1.4 | (1.0) | 93.7 | (1.9) | 9.0 | (2.4) | 2.0 | (1.2) | 88.9 | (2.7) | 39.5 | (4.5) | 0.5 | (0.5) | 60.1 | (4.5) |
| Brazil | 14.8 | (1.3) | 1.8 | (1.0) | 83.4 | (1.5) | 25.4 | (2.2) | 13.2 | (2.0) | 61.4 | (2.6) | 48.8 | (2.6) | 14.4 | (2.0) | 36.8 | (2.8) |
| Bulgaria | 8.7 | (2.1) | 11.5 | (2.5) | 79.8 | (3.3) | 28.8 | (3.8) | 27.9 | (3.9) | 43.3 | (4.1) | 57.1 | (3.6) | 27.7 | (3.3) | 15.1 | (2.8) |
| Chile | 43.2 | (3.3) | 7.6 | (2.3) | 49.1 | (3.4) | 62.1 | (2.9) | 8.1 | (2.0) | 29.8 | (3.0) | 78.6 | (2.6) | 10.5 | (2.7) | 10.9 | (2.1) |
| Colombia | 13.2 | (1.9) | 2.5 | (0.7) | 84.3 | (1.9) | 87.8 | (2.8) | 2.2 | (1.0) | 10.0 | (2.6) | 95.9 | (1.5) | 2.4 | (1.2) | 1.7 | (1.0) |
| Croatia | 1.3 | (0.8) | 0.6 | (0.6) | 98.1 | (1.0) | 36.4 | (3.8) | 39.5 | (3.9) | 24.1 | (3.1) | 66.7 | (3.5) | 24.2 | (3.1) | 9.1 | (2.4) |
| Estonia | 14.8 | (2.6) | 48.9 | (3.4) | 36.3 | (3.4) | 37.2 | (3.5) | 56.4 | (3.8) | 6.4 | (1.8) | 85.1 | (2.5) | 12.5 | (2.4) | 2.4 | (0.8) |
| Hong Kong-China | 19.0 | (2.9) | 13.8 | (2.8) | 67.2 | (3.6) | 92.0 | (1.9) | 6.7 | (1.7) | 1.3 | (1.0) | 94.1 | (2.0) | 5.9 | (2.0) | 0.0 | (0.0) |
| Indonesia | 39.7 | (3.7) | 10.7 | (2.1) | 49.6 | (4.0) | 92.6 | (2.1) | 5.2 | (1.6) | 2.2 | (1.3) | 84.5 | (2.6) | 7.0 | (2.0) | 8.4 | (1.8) |
| Israel | 15.0 | (3.3) | 6.7 | (2.2) | 78.3 | (4.1) | 47.5 | (3.9) | 41.3 | (4.1) | 11.2 | (2.6) | 73.1 | (3.4) | 22.9 | (3.4) | 3.9 | (1.3) |
| Jordan | 8.8 | (2.0) | 0.0 | (0.0) | 91.2 | (2.0) | 94.5 | (2.0) | 0.2 | (0.0) | 5.3 | (2.0) | 86.2 | (2.8) | 1.3 | (0.9) | 12.5 | (2.7) |
| Kyrgyzstan | 7.7 | (2.1) | 3.1 | (1.2) | 89.2 | (2.5) | 35.4 | (3.6) | 6.2 | (1.9) | 58.4 | (4.2) | 52.3 | (4.0) | 9.6 | (2.3) | 38.1 | (3.9) |
| Latvia | 17.2 | (3.3) | 25.0 | (3.8) | 57.8 | (3.9) | 68.8 | (3.1) | 24.9 | (3.2) | 6.3 | (1.7) | 26.2 | (3.4) | 10.9 | (3.0) | 62.9 | (3.6) |
| Liechtenstein | c | c | c | c | c | c | c | c | c | c | c | c | c | c | c | c | c | c |
| Lithuania | 6.0 | (1.9) | 11.2 | (2.3) | 82.8 | (2.9) | 32.5 | (3.2) | 36.9 | (3.7) | 30.5 | (3.3) | 58.1 | (3.6) | 21.4 | (3.1) | 20.5 | (2.7) |
| Macao-China | 96.2 | (0.0) | 0.0 | (0.0) | 3.8 | (0.0) | 94.4 | (0.0) | 4.0 | (0.0) | 1.6 | (0.0) | 94.4 | (0.0) | 4.0 | (0.0) | 1.6 | (0.0) |
| Montenegro | 6.8 | (0.1) | 10.7 | (0.1) | 82.5 | (0.2) | 14.7 | (0.2) | 15.6 | (0.1) | 69.8 | (0.1) | 72.2 | (0.2) | 12.5 | (0.1) | 15.3 | (0.1) |
| Qatar | 31.9 | (0.1) | 0.0 | (0.0) | 68.1 | (0.1) | 30.9 | (0.1) | 4.3 | (0.1) | 64.8 | (0.1) | 58.0 | (0.1) | 2.0 | (0.0) | 40.0 | (0.1) |
| Romania | 5.1 | (2.1) | 5.3 | (1.9) | 89.6 | (2.9) | 53.4 | (6.1) | 12.4 | (2.8) | 34.2 | (6.7) | 42.4 | (5.5) | 5.4 | (1.8) | 52.2 | (5.8) |
| Russian Federation | 8.1 | (1.7) | 21.1 | (3.3) | 70.8 | (4.0) | 10.1 | (1.8) | 32.2 | (3.9) | 57.8 | (3.6) | 43.3 | (3.4) | 32.8 | (4.0) | 23.8 | (3.2) |
| Serbia | 30.0 | (3.7) | 17.8 | (2.9) | 52.2 | (4.0) | 11.4 | (2.5) | 25.3 | (3.3) | 63.3 | (3.5) | 72.7 | (3.6) | 14.8 | (2.8) | 12.5 | (2.7) |
| Slovenia | 4.4 | (0.0) | 27.1 | (0.5) | 68.4 | (0.5) | 23.1 | (0.5) | 52.7 | (0.5) | 24.1 | (0.4) | 72.6 | (0.2) | 25.2 | (0.2) | 2.3 | (0.1) |
| Chinese Taipei | 29.5 | (3.0) | 7.4 | (1.9) | 63.1 | (3.0) | 52.4 | (3.4) | 19.8 | (3.1) | 27.6 | (3.0) | 87.4 | (2.6) | 9.7 | (2.4) | 2.9 | (1.2) |
| Thailand | 72.9 | (3.3) | 19.5 | (3.1) | 7.6 | (1.9) | 68.4 | (4.1) | 12.5 | (2.8) | 19.0 | (3.4) | 92.0 | (2.1) | 4.2 | (1.5) | 3.8 | (1.5) |
| Tunisia | 2.3 | (1.0) | 0.6 | (0.6) | 97.1 | (1.2) | 20.5 | (3.1) | 12.4 | (3.1) | 67.1 | (4.3) | 88.5 | (2.6) | 7.7 | (2.2) | 3.8 | (1.7) |
| Uruguay | 12.3 | (1.0) | 0.9 | (0.3) | 86.9 | (1.0) | 19.8 | (1.3) | 6.5 | (1.9) | 73.7 | (1.9) | 53.1 | (2.9) | 12.1 | (2.3) | 34.8 | (2.7) |

Note: Values that are statistically significant at the 5% level (p<0.05) are indicated in bold.
1. Results based on reports from school principals and reported proportionate to the number of 15-year-olds enrolled in the school.
2. The cross-country correlation is based on all participating countries where the data are available.
StatLink ⟐ http://dx.doi.org/10.1787/142127877152

Pour consulter la version française intégrale de ce tableau, suivre ce lien :
StatLink ⟐ http://dx.doi.org/10.1787/152751048643

[Part 3/4]

**Table 5.10  Involvement of schools in decision making[1]**

Tableau 5.10  Participation des établissements à la prise de décisions

**Percentage of students in schools where the principal reported that only the school, only the government, or both the school and the government have considerable responsibility for the following aspects of school policy and management**

| Cross-country correlation between the percentage of schools having considerable responsibility ("school only" and "school and government") and performance in science[2] | Establishing student disciplinary policies | | | | Establishing student assessment policies | | | | Approving students for admission to the school | | | |
|---|---|---|---|---|---|---|---|---|---|---|---|---|
| | Correlation coefficient | | P-value | | Correlation coefficient | | P-value | | Correlation coefficient | | P-value | |
| | **0.41** | | (0.00) | | **0.43** | | (0.00) | | **0.27** | | (0.04) | |
| | School only | | School and government | Government only | School only | | School and government | Government only | School only | | School and government | Government only |
| | % | S.E. | % | S.E. | % | S.E. | % | S.E. | % | S.E. | % | S.E. | % | S.E. | % | S.E. | % | S.E. |


| Country | Disc. School only % | S.E. | Disc. School and gov % | S.E. | Disc. Gov only % | S.E. | Assess. School only % | S.E. | Assess. School and gov % | S.E. | Assess. Gov only % | S.E. | Admiss. School only % | S.E. | Admiss. School and gov % | S.E. | Admiss. Gov only % | S.E. |
|---|---|---|---|---|---|---|---|---|---|---|---|---|---|---|---|---|---|---|
| **OECD** | | | | | | | | | | | | | | | | | | |
| Australia | 67.8 | (2.6) | 30.8 | (2.6) | 1.4 | (0.5) | 50.1 | (2.7) | 46.4 | (2.6) | 3.5 | (0.9) | 72.9 | (2.5) | 22.9 | (2.4) | 4.2 | (1.2) |
| Austria | 83.0 | (3.1) | 16.3 | (3.1) | 0.7 | (0.6) | 50.2 | (4.1) | 23.9 | (3.3) | 25.9 | (3.4) | 72.5 | (4.3) | 19.7 | (3.8) | 7.8 | (2.1) |
| Belgium | 81.4 | (2.7) | 15.5 | (2.4) | 3.1 | (1.3) | 78.2 | (2.7) | 17.6 | (2.6) | 4.2 | (1.3) | 71.6 | (2.6) | 19.6 | (2.3) | 8.8 | (1.8) |
| Canada | 45.0 | (2.2) | 46.6 | (2.5) | 8.4 | (1.7) | 24.7 | (1.8) | 56.2 | (2.5) | 19.1 | (2.0) | 51.8 | (2.5) | 40.5 | (2.5) | 7.7 | (1.4) |
| Czech Republic | 95.7 | (1.9) | 4.3 | (1.9) | 0.0 | (0.0) | 94.5 | (1.9) | 5.0 | (1.8) | 0.5 | (0.5) | 86.3 | (2.9) | 13.7 | (2.9) | 0.0 | (0.0) |
| Denmark | 100.0 | (0.0) | 0.0 | (0.0) | 0.0 | (0.0) | 71.6 | (3.3) | 19.0 | (3.1) | 9.4 | (2.1) | 76.0 | (3.2) | 18.7 | (3.1) | 5.2 | (1.8) |
| Finland | 78.5 | (3.6) | 20.0 | (3.6) | 1.5 | (1.2) | 79.3 | (3.6) | 19.8 | (3.6) | 0.9 | (0.7) | 48.7 | (4.8) | 30.3 | (4.2) | 21.1 | (3.3) |
| France | w | w | w | w | w | w | w | w | w | w | w | w | w | w | w | w | w | w |
| Germany | 82.1 | (2.5) | 17.4 | (2.5) | 0.5 | (0.5) | 55.2 | (3.6) | 34.5 | (3.7) | 10.3 | (2.5) | 76.8 | (2.8) | 20.9 | (3.0) | 2.3 | (1.0) |
| Greece | 78.6 | (3.3) | 11.5 | (2.6) | 9.9 | (2.4) | 17.3 | (3.1) | 6.4 | (2.0) | 76.3 | (3.5) | 69.6 | (3.4) | 4.9 | (1.6) | 25.5 | (3.5) |
| Hungary | 94.8 | (2.0) | 4.4 | (1.8) | 0.8 | (0.8) | 93.5 | (2.3) | 5.7 | (2.1) | 0.8 | (0.8) | 94.1 | (1.8) | 4.3 | (1.6) | 1.6 | (1.1) |
| Iceland | 93.5 | (0.1) | 6.5 | (0.1) | 0.0 | (0.0) | 86.7 | (0.1) | 11.7 | (0.1) | 1.7 | (0.0) | 69.9 | (0.3) | 16.3 | (0.2) | 13.8 | (0.2) |
| Ireland | 90.8 | (2.4) | 9.2 | (2.4) | 0.0 | (0.0) | 86.4 | (2.7) | 13.1 | (2.8) | 0.5 | (0.6) | 94.2 | (1.9) | 5.8 | (1.9) | a | a |
| Italy | 97.4 | (1.1) | 2.3 | (1.1) | 0.3 | (0.2) | 92.3 | (1.8) | 5.4 | (1.3) | 2.3 | (1.2) | 93.1 | (1.4) | 4.1 | (1.1) | 2.8 | (1.0) |
| Japan | 98.4 | (0.9) | 1.6 | (0.9) | 0.0 | (0.0) | 98.1 | (1.0) | 1.7 | (1.0) | 0.2 | (0.2) | 99.0 | (0.7) | 1.0 | (0.7) | 0.0 | (0.0) |
| Korea | 85.1 | (2.7) | 9.8 | (2.4) | 5.0 | (1.9) | 65.6 | (3.8) | 19.5 | (3.3) | 14.9 | (3.0) | 82.5 | (3.5) | 8.8 | (2.4) | 8.7 | (2.7) |
| Luxembourg | 53.3 | (0.0) | 38.4 | (0.0) | 8.3 | (0.0) | 4.6 | (0.0) | 20.8 | (0.1) | 74.6 | (0.1) | 62.5 | (0.1) | 33.6 | (0.1) | 3.9 | (0.0) |
| Mexico | 89.0 | (1.4) | 6.8 | (1.1) | 4.1 | (0.9) | 58.4 | (2.4) | 12.9 | (1.8) | 28.6 | (2.8) | 67.0 | (2.5) | 9.0 | (1.7) | 24.0 | (2.5) |
| Netherlands | 99.5 | (0.5) | 0.0 | (0.0) | 0.5 | (0.5) | 98.7 | (0.7) | 0.6 | (0.5) | 0.7 | (0.6) | 96.7 | (1.3) | 2.1 | (1.1) | 1.2 | (0.8) |
| New Zealand | 95.6 | (1.4) | 4.4 | (1.4) | 0.0 | (0.0) | 82.0 | (2.6) | 17.3 | (2.6) | 0.7 | (0.7) | 87.1 | (2.1) | 9.4 | (1.9) | 3.4 | (1.1) |
| Norway | 78.0 | (2.9) | 16.5 | (2.6) | 5.5 | (1.7) | 37.2 | (3.9) | 23.3 | (2.9) | 39.4 | (3.9) | 48.4 | (3.8) | 13.6 | (2.7) | 38.0 | (3.6) |
| Poland | 95.5 | (1.7) | 4.5 | (1.7) | 0.0 | (0.0) | 90.2 | (2.3) | 9.8 | (2.3) | a | a | 85.9 | (2.6) | 13.3 | (2.8) | 0.8 | (0.7) |
| Portugal | 45.9 | (4.2) | 29.5 | (4.1) | 24.6 | (3.5) | 32.7 | (4.1) | 38.2 | (4.1) | 29.1 | (3.7) | 61.8 | (4.2) | 29.8 | (4.2) | 8.5 | (2.2) |
| Slovak Republic | 94.1 | (1.9) | 4.7 | (1.7) | 1.2 | (0.8) | 62.3 | (3.9) | 25.0 | (3.4) | 12.7 | (2.8) | 92.2 | (1.9) | 7.8 | (1.9) | 0.0 | (0.0) |
| Spain | 70.8 | (2.7) | 26.8 | (2.7) | 2.4 | (1.0) | 47.1 | (3.2) | 34.7 | (3.0) | 18.2 | (2.6) | 39.0 | (2.9) | 23.2 | (2.4) | 37.8 | (2.5) |
| Sweden | 97.0 | (1.4) | 2.9 | (1.4) | 0.1 | (0.1) | 63.3 | (3.2) | 32.8 | (3.1) | 3.9 | (1.5) | 66.9 | (3.9) | 22.2 | (3.4) | 10.9 | (2.5) |
| Switzerland | 79.4 | (2.4) | 18.1 | (2.3) | 2.6 | (1.0) | 37.5 | (2.9) | 38.7 | (3.3) | 23.8 | (2.4) | 66.1 | (2.4) | 21.8 | (2.8) | 12.2 | (2.0) |
| Turkey | 34.8 | (4.1) | 7.1 | (1.8) | 58.1 | (4.4) | 44.3 | (4.3) | 6.4 | (1.9) | 49.3 | (4.1) | 77.4 | (3.5) | 6.4 | (1.8) | 16.2 | (3.1) |
| United Kingdom | 90.2 | (1.7) | 9.8 | (1.7) | 0.0 | (0.0) | 86.2 | (1.9) | 13.5 | (1.9) | 0.3 | (0.2) | 54.9 | (3.4) | 23.5 | (2.7) | 21.6 | (2.5) |
| United States | 91.7 | (1.6) | 7.9 | (1.7) | 0.4 | (0.4) | 51.6 | (3.7) | 42.4 | (3.8) | 6.0 | (1.9) | 88.2 | (2.7) | 7.3 | (2.4) | 4.4 | (1.7) |
| **OECD average** | 82.3 | (0.4) | 12.9 | (0.4) | 4.8 | (0.3) | 63.4 | (0.5) | 20.8 | (0.5) | 16.4 | (0.4) | 74.2 | (0.5) | 15.7 | (0.5) | 10.4 | (0.4) |
| **Partners** | | | | | | | | | | | | | | | | | | |
| Argentina | 64.9 | (4.2) | 30.3 | (3.8) | 4.7 | (1.6) | 42.3 | (4.8) | 36.6 | (4.5) | 21.1 | (3.8) | 79.3 | (3.2) | 8.9 | (2.1) | 11.8 | (2.5) |
| Azerbaijan | 99.4 | (0.6) | 0.0 | (0.0) | 0.6 | (0.6) | 76.6 | (3.5) | 3.7 | (1.5) | 19.7 | (3.3) | 97.9 | (1.2) | 1.5 | (1.0) | 0.6 | (0.6) |
| Brazil | 77.0 | (2.3) | 16.6 | (2.3) | 6.4 | (1.3) | 56.5 | (2.5) | 29.1 | (2.6) | 14.4 | (1.8) | 76.1 | (2.6) | 15.7 | (2.4) | 8.2 | (1.4) |
| Bulgaria | 44.3 | (4.2) | 52.9 | (4.3) | 2.8 | (1.3) | 8.6 | (2.6) | 33.0 | (3.8) | 58.4 | (3.8) | 44.9 | (4.0) | 34.1 | (4.0) | 21.0 | (3.4) |
| Chile | 85.0 | (2.8) | 14.1 | (2.8) | 0.8 | (0.7) | 66.9 | (3.7) | 25.5 | (3.7) | 7.6 | (2.1) | 91.4 | (1.9) | 6.9 | (1.7) | 1.7 | (0.9) |
| Colombia | 96.1 | (1.4) | 3.9 | (1.4) | 0.0 | (0.0) | 61.0 | (5.5) | 21.8 | (5.5) | 17.3 | (4.5) | 79.8 | (5.1) | 11.7 | (4.9) | 8.5 | (2.3) |
| Croatia | 56.7 | (3.2) | 40.0 | (3.4) | 3.2 | (1.4) | 14.1 | (2.8) | 21.4 | (3.2) | 64.5 | (3.8) | 30.8 | (3.5) | 37.7 | (3.8) | 31.5 | (3.8) |
| Estonia | 95.0 | (1.3) | 5.0 | (1.3) | 0.0 | (0.0) | 50.6 | (3.6) | 46.9 | (3.6) | 2.5 | (1.3) | 69.5 | (3.6) | 30.0 | (3.6) | 0.5 | (0.5) |
| Hong Kong-China | 100.0 | (0.0) | 0.0 | (0.0) | 0.0 | (0.0) | 93.5 | (1.8) | 6.5 | (1.8) | 0.0 | (0.0) | 91.2 | (2.2) | 8.8 | (2.2) | 0.0 | (0.0) |
| Indonesia | 89.9 | (4.1) | 5.4 | (1.3) | 4.7 | (3.9) | 72.0 | (4.5) | 16.7 | (2.5) | 11.3 | (4.2) | 72.2 | (4.5) | 17.2 | (2.8) | 10.6 | (4.2) |
| Israel | 80.1 | (3.5) | 18.3 | (3.4) | 1.6 | (1.2) | 82.3 | (3.2) | 16.1 | (3.4) | 1.6 | (1.2) | 56.3 | (4.3) | 32.4 | (4.1) | 11.3 | (2.8) |
| Jordan | 40.1 | (4.0) | 2.1 | (1.1) | 57.8 | (4.0) | 43.5 | (4.0) | 1.3 | (0.9) | 55.2 | (4.0) | 73.8 | (3.5) | 1.8 | (1.0) | 24.4 | (3.4) |
| Kyrgyzstan | 79.9 | (3.0) | 11.2 | (2.5) | 8.9 | (2.1) | 60.7 | (3.7) | 12.0 | (2.2) | 27.3 | (3.5) | 95.7 | (1.5) | 2.6 | (1.1) | 1.7 | (0.9) |
| Latvia | 92.3 | (1.4) | 7.7 | (1.4) | 0.0 | (0.0) | 46.1 | (4.1) | 44.6 | (3.6) | 9.3 | (2.3) | 82.0 | (2.8) | 16.6 | (2.7) | 1.4 | (0.8) |
| Liechtenstein | c | c | c | c | c | c | c | c | c | c | c | c | c | c | c | c | c | c |
| Lithuania | 95.7 | (1.5) | 3.8 | (1.4) | 0.5 | (0.5) | 63.4 | (3.7) | 32.8 | (3.7) | 3.8 | (1.5) | 84.0 | (3.0) | 14.1 | (2.7) | 1.9 | (1.3) |
| Macao-China | 100.0 | (0.0) | 0.0 | (0.0) | 0.0 | (0.0) | 99.3 | (0.0) | 0.0 | (0.0) | 0.7 | (0.0) | 97.4 | (0.0) | 2.6 | (0.0) | 0.0 | (0.0) |
| Montenegro | 40.1 | (0.2) | 22.2 | (0.1) | 37.6 | (0.2) | 46.7 | (0.2) | 25.9 | (0.1) | 27.4 | (0.2) | 24.3 | (0.2) | 27.4 | (0.1) | 48.4 | (0.1) |
| Qatar | 52.4 | (0.1) | 10.3 | (0.1) | 37.3 | (0.1) | 56.2 | (0.1) | 5.2 | (0.1) | 38.6 | (0.1) | 70.6 | (0.1) | 5.9 | (0.0) | 23.6 | (0.1) |
| Romania | 100.0 | (0.0) | 0.0 | (0.0) | 0.0 | (0.0) | 35.6 | (5.6) | 23.6 | (3.8) | 40.7 | (4.4) | 17.7 | (3.1) | 9.8 | (2.4) | 72.5 | (3.7) |
| Russian Federation | 93.7 | (1.9) | 5.8 | (1.7) | 0.5 | (0.8) | 41.8 | (3.6) | 33.9 | (4.8) | 24.4 | (2.8) | 88.2 | (2.4) | 11.1 | (2.3) | 0.6 | (0.6) |
| Serbia | 88.1 | (2.5) | 11.9 | (2.5) | 0.0 | (0.0) | 39.4 | (3.7) | 46.7 | (4.3) | 14.0 | (2.8) | 11.2 | (2.4) | 51.2 | (3.8) | 37.6 | (3.8) |
| Slovenia | 80.2 | (0.5) | 19.4 | (0.4) | 0.4 | (0.2) | 19.6 | (0.4) | 58.2 | (0.4) | 22.2 | (0.4) | 34.6 | (0.5) | 43.4 | (0.4) | 22.0 | (0.5) |
| Chinese Taipei | 64.0 | (4.1) | 26.7 | (3.3) | 9.3 | (2.6) | 64.4 | (3.7) | 26.7 | (3.2) | 8.9 | (2.2) | 32.7 | (3.4) | 25.6 | (3.2) | 41.7 | (3.7) |
| Thailand | 88.1 | (2.5) | 10.6 | (2.3) | 1.2 | (0.9) | 83.0 | (3.1) | 12.2 | (2.6) | 4.7 | (1.7) | 65.5 | (3.5) | 25.7 | (3.5) | 8.7 | (2.0) |
| Tunisia | 74.6 | (3.7) | 7.3 | (2.3) | 18.1 | (3.3) | 25.2 | (3.4) | 4.4 | (1.5) | 70.5 | (3.4) | 45.2 | (4.5) | 16.7 | (3.4) | 38.1 | (4.5) |
| Uruguay | 45.2 | (2.9) | 32.7 | (2.8) | 22.2 | (2.4) | 19.7 | (2.1) | 29.1 | (3.2) | 51.2 | (3.2) | 41.1 | (2.7) | 16.8 | (2.7) | 42.0 | (2.9) |

Note: Values that are statistically significant at the 5% level (p<0.05) are indicated in bold.
1. Results based on reports from school principals and reported proportionate to the number of 15-year-olds enrolled in the school.
2. The cross-country correlation is based on all participating countries where the data are available.
*StatLink* ☜ http://dx.doi.org/10.1787/142127877152

Pour consulter la version française intégrale de ce tableau, suivre ce lien :
*StatLink* ☜ http://dx.doi.org/10.1787/152751048643

[Part 4/4]

**Table 5.10** Involvement of schools in decision making[1]

Tableau 5.10 Participation des établissements à la prise de décisions

| | Percentage of students in schools where the principal reported that only the school, only the government, or both the school and the government have considerable responsibility for the following aspects of school policy and management | | | | | | | | |
|---|---|---|---|---|---|---|---|---|---|
| | **Choosing which textbooks are used** | | | **Determining course content** | | | **Deciding which courses are offered** | | |
| Cross-country correlation between the percentage of schools having considerable responsibility ("school only" and "school and government") and performance in science[2] | Correlation coefficient | | P-value | Correlation coefficient | | P-value | Correlation coefficient | | P-value |
| | **0.51** | | (0.00) | **0.52** | | (0.00) | **0.58** | | (0.00) |
| | School only | School and government | Government only | School only | School and government | Government only | School only | School and government | Government only |
| | % S.E. | % S.E. | % S.E. | % S.E. | % S.E. | % S.E. | % S.E. | % S.E. | % S.E. |
| **OECD** | | | | | | | | | |
| Australia | 90.8 (1.6) | 8.5 (1.6) | 0.6 (0.4) | 30.6 (2.6) | 51.2 (2.9) | 18.2 (2.2) | 72.3 (2.6) | 26.0 (2.5) | 1.7 (0.8) |
| Austria | 94.8 (1.9) | 5.2 (1.9) | 0.0 (0.0) | 44.0 (4.0) | 34.8 (3.8) | 21.2 (3.4) | 39.3 (3.6) | 41.6 (3.8) | 19.1 (2.5) |
| Belgium | 96.9 (1.0) | 2.8 (0.9) | 0.3 (0.3) | 30.7 (2.8) | 33.7 (2.8) | 35.6 (3.1) | 36.6 (3.2) | 47.1 (3.3) | 16.3 (2.6) |
| Canada | 39.3 (2.4) | 42.2 (2.7) | 18.5 (2.0) | 12.2 (1.3) | 41.3 (2.5) | 46.5 (2.4) | 43.8 (2.5) | 51.3 (2.5) | 4.9 (1.0) |
| Czech Republic | 62.6 (4.3) | 28.3 (3.5) | 9.1 (2.6) | 72.2 (4.3) | 24.2 (3.6) | 3.6 (2.1) | 87.0 (2.7) | 12.4 (2.6) | 0.5 (0.5) |
| Denmark | 100.0 (0.0) | 0.0 (0.0) | 0.0 (0.0) | 57.2 (3.6) | 33.3 (3.4) | 9.5 (2.4) | 53.7 (4.0) | 40.6 (3.8) | 5.7 (1.6) |
| Finland | 98.3 (1.0) | 1.7 (1.0) | 0.0 (0.0) | 38.0 (4.1) | 33.0 (4.0) | 28.9 (3.6) | 64.1 (4.2) | 29.1 (4.2) | 6.8 (2.0) |
| France | w w | w w | w w | w w | w w | w w | w w | w w | w w |
| Germany | 79.4 (3.1) | 19.4 (3.2) | 1.3 (1.0) | 23.3 (2.4) | 40.7 (3.4) | 36.0 (3.0) | 79.0 (3.0) | 18.0 (2.7) | 2.9 (1.4) |
| Greece | 0.7 (0.6) | 4.7 (1.7) | 94.6 (1.8) | 0.0 (0.0) | 1.5 (0.8) | 98.5 (0.8) | 4.4 (1.6) | 5.0 (1.6) | 90.7 (2.0) |
| Hungary | 95.3 (1.8) | 2.8 (1.4) | 1.8 (1.1) | 50.5 (3.9) | 37.5 (3.8) | 12.0 (2.6) | 52.5 (4.5) | 39.3 (4.1) | 8.1 (2.4) |
| Iceland | 84.8 (0.2) | 7.4 (0.1) | 7.7 (0.1) | 39.0 (0.2) | 27.6 (0.2) | 33.5 (0.2) | 31.4 (0.3) | 34.9 (0.2) | 33.7 (0.3) |
| Ireland | 100.0 (0.0) | 0.0 (0.0) | 0.0 (0.0) | 35.1 (3.8) | 25.0 (3.5) | 40.0 (3.9) | 82.4 (3.1) | 16.4 (3.1) | 1.2 (0.9) |
| Italy | 98.7 (0.8) | 0.4 (0.2) | 0.9 (0.8) | 53.3 (2.9) | 29.3 (2.5) | 17.5 (2.2) | 54.9 (3.0) | 25.9 (2.4) | 19.2 (2.3) |
| Japan | 89.1 (2.3) | 6.1 (1.8) | 4.8 (1.4) | 93.0 (1.8) | 4.8 (1.4) | 2.2 (1.1) | 92.9 (1.8) | 3.9 (1.4) | 3.2 (1.3) |
| Korea | 95.4 (1.5) | 4.6 (1.5) | 0.0 (0.0) | 92.6 (2.1) | 5.6 (1.9) | 1.8 (0.9) | 81.9 (3.2) | 14.8 (2.9) | 3.3 (1.5) |
| Luxembourg | 10.1 (0.0) | 33.1 (0.1) | 56.8 (0.1) | 0.0 (0.0) | 40.3 (0.0) | 59.7 (0.0) | 0.0 (0.0) | 42.1 (0.1) | 57.9 (0.1) |
| Mexico | 59.6 (2.6) | 7.9 (1.2) | 32.5 (2.6) | 21.0 (2.2) | 4.4 (0.6) | 74.6 (2.3) | 15.7 (2.2) | 4.2 (0.7) | 80.2 (2.3) |
| Netherlands | 99.5 (0.5) | 0.0 (0.0) | 0.5 (0.5) | 78.8 (3.0) | 14.0 (2.6) | 7.1 (2.2) | 76.9 (3.6) | 18.0 (3.1) | 5.1 (2.0) |
| New Zealand | 100.0 (0.0) | 0.0 (0.0) | 0.0 (0.0) | 68.8 (2.7) | 26.9 (2.5) | 4.2 (1.6) | 90.2 (2.2) | 9.8 (2.2) | 0.0 (0.0) |
| Norway | 96.7 (1.2) | 3.3 (1.2) | 0.0 (0.0) | 30.9 (3.6) | 30.9 (3.4) | 38.2 (3.9) | 23.2 (3.3) | 24.8 (3.4) | 52.0 (4.1) |
| Poland | 92.5 (2.1) | 7.5 (2.1) | 0.0 (0.0) | 93.0 (2.1) | 7.0 (2.1) | 0.0 (0.0) | 44.1 (3.5) | 26.7 (3.4) | 29.2 (3.6) |
| Portugal | 99.1 (0.7) | 0.9 (0.7) | 0.0 (0.0) | 24.5 (3.4) | 22.8 (3.5) | 52.7 (3.4) | 44.1 (4.0) | 32.7 (4.0) | 23.2 (3.5) |
| Slovak Republic | 55.5 (3.6) | 33.3 (3.7) | 11.2 (2.2) | 25.6 (3.5) | 37.7 (4.1) | 36.7 (3.9) | 38.1 (4.0) | 39.7 (4.3) | 22.2 (3.1) |
| Spain | 93.6 (1.7) | 5.7 (1.6) | 0.8 (0.5) | 25.8 (2.8) | 32.3 (3.3) | 41.9 (3.5) | 33.1 (3.1) | 25.0 (3.1) | 41.9 (2.9) |
| Sweden | 100.0 (0.0) | 0.0 (0.0) | 0.0 (0.0) | 57.5 (4.0) | 35.4 (3.9) | 7.1 (1.8) | 48.7 (4.0) | 29.3 (3.4) | 22.0 (3.2) |
| Switzerland | 37.2 (2.4) | 39.9 (2.7) | 22.9 (1.9) | 15.5 (1.8) | 44.2 (3.1) | 40.4 (3.0) | 13.7 (1.9) | 53.5 (3.1) | 32.7 (2.7) |
| Turkey | 57.3 (4.3) | 15.5 (2.9) | 27.2 (4.0) | 8.4 (2.3) | 2.2 (1.3) | 89.4 (2.6) | 26.8 (3.9) | 15.7 (2.9) | 57.5 (4.1) |
| United Kingdom | 99.1 (0.4) | 0.8 (0.4) | 0.1 (0.0) | 74.2 (2.8) | 19.7 (2.5) | 6.1 (1.6) | 86.5 (2.2) | 13.4 (2.2) | 0.1 (0.0) |
| United States | 82.4 (2.9) | 17.1 (2.8) | 0.5 (0.5) | 50.1 (4.3) | 39.9 (4.3) | 10.0 (2.4) | 69.1 (3.8) | 29.1 (4.0) | 1.8 (1.0) |
| **OECD average** | 79.6 (0.4) | 10.3 (0.3) | 10.1 (0.2) | 43.0 (0.5) | 26.9 (0.5) | 30.1 (0.5) | 51.3 (0.6) | 26.6 (0.6) | 22.2 (0.4) |
| **Partners** | | | | | | | | | |
| Argentina | 86.4 (2.8) | 7.6 (2.0) | 6.0 (2.0) | 42.0 (4.1) | 42.1 (4.2) | 15.9 (3.1) | 52.1 (4.1) | 23.2 (3.8) | 24.6 (3.9) |
| Azerbaijan | 43.2 (4.4) | 4.3 (1.7) | 52.4 (4.5) | 42.1 (4.2) | 0.7 (0.7) | 57.2 (4.2) | 31.9 (4.1) | 9.5 (2.7) | 58.6 (4.2) |
| Brazil | 84.5 (1.6) | 13.8 (1.5) | 1.7 (0.6) | 51.5 (2.9) | 27.5 (2.6) | 21.0 (2.5) | 28.9 (2.2) | 26.4 (2.3) | 44.7 (2.9) |
| Bulgaria | 74.0 (3.8) | 23.6 (3.7) | 2.3 (1.4) | 8.5 (2.2) | 20.4 (3.3) | 71.1 (3.8) | 10.2 (2.2) | 43.8 (3.8) | 46.0 (4.0) |
| Chile | 79.4 (3.4) | 17.5 (3.2) | 3.1 (1.4) | 42.0 (3.8) | 26.1 (3.7) | 31.8 (4.4) | 73.6 (3.5) | 19.4 (3.1) | 7.0 (1.9) |
| Colombia | 96.7 (1.3) | 1.4 (0.7) | 1.9 (1.2) | 71.9 (5.2) | 15.3 (3.0) | 12.8 (5.0) | 76.8 (5.2) | 17.2 (5.1) | 6.0 (2.0) |
| Croatia | 38.2 (4.0) | 46.3 (4.0) | 15.6 (2.5) | 4.9 (1.6) | 36.6 (3.3) | 58.5 (3.3) | 2.5 (1.1) | 16.9 (2.8) | 80.6 (3.0) |
| Estonia | 72.2 (3.0) | 25.9 (3.0) | 1.9 (0.8) | 65.3 (3.0) | 31.7 (3.0) | 3.1 (1.1) | 84.5 (2.7) | 13.1 (2.5) | 2.3 (1.0) |
| Hong Kong-China | 97.4 (1.3) | 2.6 (1.3) | 0.0 (0.0) | 86.5 (2.6) | 12.9 (2.6) | 0.6 (0.6) | 93.2 (1.8) | 6.8 (1.8) | 0.0 (0.0) |
| Indonesia | 75.8 (3.1) | 16.4 (2.1) | 7.7 (2.3) | 59.0 (4.4) | 20.0 (3.1) | 21.0 (4.2) | 58.5 (3.8) | 19.4 (2.8) | 22.1 (3.1) |
| Israel | 57.8 (4.8) | 36.4 (4.5) | 5.8 (2.0) | 37.9 (4.4) | 43.4 (4.4) | 18.7 (3.3) | 66.6 (4.6) | 31.1 (4.7) | 2.3 (1.4) |
| Jordan | 6.0 (1.8) | 0.3 (0.3) | 93.7 (1.9) | 6.0 (2.1) | 0.0 (0.0) | 94.0 (2.1) | 12.0 (2.5) | 1.0 (0.8) | 86.9 (2.6) |
| Kyrgyzstan | 49.4 (3.7) | 13.2 (2.5) | 37.4 (3.4) | 36.5 (3.6) | 9.7 (1.8) | 53.8 (3.9) | 34.8 (4.0) | 10.6 (2.2) | 54.6 (4.1) |
| Latvia | 56.9 (4.1) | 41.6 (4.0) | 1.5 (1.0) | 12.0 (2.7) | 40.7 (3.5) | 47.3 (3.4) | 47.6 (4.1) | 42.1 (4.4) | 10.3 (2.5) |
| Liechtenstein | c c | c c | c c | c c | c c | c c | c c | c c | c c |
| Lithuania | 77.5 (3.4) | 21.4 (3.4) | 1.1 (0.7) | 45.7 (4.2) | 37.0 (4.0) | 17.3 (2.7) | 76.2 (3.4) | 19.2 (3.2) | 4.6 (1.6) |
| Macao-China | 100.0 (0.0) | 0.0 (0.0) | 0.0 (0.0) | 96.8 (0.0) | 2.4 (0.0) | 0.7 (0.0) | 89.6 (0.0) | 10.4 (0.0) | 0.0 (0.0) |
| Montenegro | 6.5 (0.2) | 10.9 (0.1) | 82.6 (0.2) | 3.6 (0.0) | 17.6 (0.1) | 78.8 (0.1) | 13.1 (0.2) | 13.8 (0.2) | 73.1 (0.2) |
| Qatar | 27.1 (0.1) | 0.3 (0.0) | 72.6 (0.1) | 21.8 (0.1) | 2.6 (0.1) | 75.6 (0.1) | 21.2 (0.1) | 2.7 (0.1) | 76.1 (0.1) |
| Romania | 81.0 (5.5) | 10.7 (2.7) | 8.3 (6.2) | 20.2 (3.9) | 24.3 (3.6) | 55.4 (5.3) | 65.1 (6.3) | 13.4 (2.8) | 21.5 (6.7) |
| Russian Federation | 51.2 (4.9) | 36.8 (4.1) | 12.0 (3.0) | 20.9 (3.8) | 46.1 (3.9) | 33.1 (4.0) | 63.5 (3.5) | 30.3 (3.4) | 6.1 (1.5) |
| Serbia | 17.3 (3.2) | 49.0 (3.4) | 33.6 (3.8) | 2.8 (1.2) | 27.7 (3.4) | 69.5 (3.2) | 2.4 (0.8) | 7.7 (2.1) | 89.9 (2.0) |
| Slovenia | 47.2 (0.5) | 47.7 (0.5) | 5.2 (0.1) | 13.6 (0.3) | 50.2 (0.5) | 36.2 (0.3) | 22.0 (0.5) | 51.5 (0.6) | 26.5 (0.3) |
| Chinese Taipei | 92.5 (1.9) | 7.5 (1.9) | 0.0 (0.0) | 76.1 (3.3) | 18.1 (2.5) | 5.8 (2.3) | 81.0 (2.9) | 16.6 (2.8) | 2.3 (1.2) |
| Thailand | 93.0 (1.5) | 3.8 (1.3) | 3.2 (1.2) | 94.8 (1.9) | 4.5 (1.8) | 0.7 (0.7) | 93.4 (1.8) | 6.0 (1.7) | 0.5 (0.5) |
| Tunisia | 0.0 (0.0) | 0.0 (0.0) | 100.0 (0.0) | 1.6 (0.9) | 1.1 (0.8) | 97.3 (1.2) | 0.6 (0.6) | 0.0 (0.0) | 99.4 (0.6) |
| Uruguay | 17.1 (2.0) | 28.4 (2.8) | 54.5 (2.8) | 4.3 (1.0) | 9.0 (1.4) | 86.7 (1.5) | 17.7 (2.0) | 13.2 (2.5) | 69.1 (2.6) |

Note: Values that are statistically significant at the 5% level (p< 0.05) are indicated in bold.
1. Results based on reports from school principals and reported proportionate to the number of 15-year-olds enrolled in the school.
2. The cross-country correlation is based on all participating countries where the data are available.
StatLink http://dx.doi.org/10.1787/142127877152

Pour consulter la version française intégrale de ce tableau, suivre ce lien :
StatLink http://dx.doi.org/10.1787/152751048643

[Part 1/1]

**Table 5.11　Influence of business and industry on the school curriculum[1]**

Tableau 5.11　Influence du monde de l'entreprise et de l'industrie sur les programmes de cours

| | Percentage of students in schools where the principal reported that business and industry have | | | | | |
| | No influence on the curriculum | | A minor or indirect influence on the curriculum | | A considerable influence on the curriculum | |
| | % | S.E. | % | S.E. | % | S.E. |
|---|---|---|---|---|---|---|
| Australia | 16.5 | (2.2) | 74.6 | (2.5) | 8.9 | (1.7) |
| Austria | 5.3 | (1.7) | 42.0 | (3.4) | 52.7 | (3.2) |
| Belgium | 33.4 | (2.9) | 56.1 | (3.0) | 10.5 | (2.2) |
| Canada | 17.1 | (1.9) | 72.7 | (2.0) | 10.2 | (1.1) |
| Czech Republic | 46.1 | (3.0) | 42.5 | (4.1) | 11.4 | (3.2) |
| Denmark | 63.6 | (4.1) | 34.9 | (4.2) | 1.5 | (0.9) |
| Finland | 22.5 | (3.5) | 73.4 | (3.8) | 4.1 | (1.7) |
| France | w | w | w | w | w | w |
| Germany | 12.5 | (2.3) | 62.1 | (3.4) | 25.4 | (3.1) |
| Greece | 76.6 | (3.3) | 19.1 | (3.2) | 4.3 | (1.5) |
| Hungary | 27.7 | (3.7) | 63.4 | (4.3) | 9.0 | (2.3) |
| Iceland | 29.3 | (0.2) | 66.0 | (0.2) | 4.7 | (0.1) |
| Ireland | 25.2 | (3.3) | 60.9 | (3.8) | 13.9 | (2.8) |
| Italy | 36.2 | (2.4) | 52.2 | (2.3) | 11.6 | (1.6) |
| Japan | 62.8 | (3.5) | 36.2 | (3.5) | 1.0 | (0.6) |
| Korea | 44.9 | (3.9) | 47.5 | (4.1) | 7.5 | (2.3) |
| Luxembourg | 36.5 | (0.1) | 59.7 | (0.1) | 3.8 | (0.0) |
| Mexico | 56.4 | (3.0) | 21.8 | (2.4) | 21.8 | (2.3) |
| Netherlands | 54.0 | (3.5) | 41.1 | (3.6) | 5.0 | (1.5) |
| New Zealand | 18.4 | (2.3) | 77.1 | (2.7) | 4.5 | (1.5) |
| Norway | 37.8 | (3.6) | 58.9 | (3.4) | 3.2 | (1.4) |
| Poland | m | m | m | m | m | m |
| Portugal | 55.0 | (4.2) | 40.3 | (4.2) | 4.6 | (1.2) |
| Slovak Republic | 35.0 | (3.8) | 48.2 | (4.0) | 16.8 | (2.9) |
| Spain | 64.9 | (3.1) | 31.8 | (3.0) | 3.3 | (1.2) |
| Sweden | 43.1 | (3.9) | 51.8 | (4.1) | 5.1 | (1.6) |
| Switzerland | 17.4 | (1.9) | 66.9 | (2.6) | 15.8 | (2.4) |
| Turkey | 48.6 | (4.2) | 44.2 | (4.5) | 7.2 | (2.1) |
| United Kingdom | 10.5 | (1.9) | 74.3 | (3.0) | 15.2 | (2.6) |
| United States | 18.1 | (3.3) | 67.2 | (3.5) | 14.7 | (2.9) |
| **OECD total** | 33.5 | (1.2) | 53.7 | (1.4) | 12.8 | (1.0) |
| **OECD average** | 36.3 | (0.6) | 53.1 | (0.6) | 10.6 | (0.4) |
| Argentina | 56.8 | (4.5) | 29.6 | (4.3) | 13.5 | (3.4) |
| Azerbaijan | 30.6 | (4.2) | 40.1 | (4.2) | 29.4 | (3.9) |
| Brazil | 60.5 | (2.8) | 27.8 | (2.9) | 11.7 | (2.0) |
| Bulgaria | 46.5 | (4.5) | 39.1 | (4.4) | 14.4 | (3.0) |
| Chile | 53.4 | (4.6) | 33.4 | (4.9) | 13.2 | (3.9) |
| Colombia | 29.8 | (4.1) | 42.8 | (5.9) | 27.4 | (4.9) |
| Croatia | 28.3 | (3.1) | 57.5 | (3.6) | 14.2 | (2.2) |
| Estonia | 31.5 | (3.1) | 59.2 | (3.4) | 9.3 | (2.1) |
| Hong Kong-China | 20.0 | (3.2) | 68.4 | (3.6) | 11.6 | (2.8) |
| Indonesia | 9.1 | (1.9) | 40.0 | (3.2) | 50.9 | (3.3) |
| Israel | 52.1 | (3.7) | 42.1 | (4.0) | 5.8 | (2.0) |
| Jordan | 13.0 | (2.6) | 61.0 | (4.4) | 26.0 | (4.0) |
| Kyrgyzstan | 27.2 | (3.0) | 51.1 | (4.0) | 21.8 | (3.1) |
| Latvia | 30.3 | (4.1) | 53.4 | (4.2) | 16.3 | (3.1) |
| Liechtenstein | c | c | c | c | c | c |
| Lithuania | 18.4 | (2.9) | 65.1 | (3.3) | 16.5 | (3.0) |
| Macao-China | 57.6 | (0.1) | 40.9 | (0.1) | 1.5 | (0.0) |
| Montenegro | 23.6 | (0.1) | 44.9 | (0.2) | 31.5 | (0.2) |
| Qatar | 38.6 | (0.2) | 46.1 | (0.1) | 15.3 | (0.1) |
| Romania | 28.1 | (3.9) | 47.2 | (4.8) | 24.7 | (3.9) |
| Russian Federation | 16.0 | (3.4) | 51.6 | (4.2) | 32.5 | (3.5) |
| Serbia | 42.6 | (3.8) | 47.6 | (4.0) | 9.8 | (2.3) |
| Slovenia | 61.1 | (0.4) | 33.7 | (0.4) | 5.2 | (0.1) |
| Chinese Taipei | 32.9 | (3.3) | 55.3 | (3.4) | 11.7 | (2.5) |
| Thailand | 10.0 | (2.4) | 41.7 | (4.2) | 48.3 | (3.8) |
| Tunisia | 23.4 | (3.8) | 43.7 | (4.1) | 32.9 | (4.2) |
| Uruguay | 83.9 | (1.5) | 13.5 | (1.4) | 2.6 | (0.8) |

1. Results based on reports from school principals and reported proportionate to the number of 15-year-olds enrolled in the school.
StatLink ⌨️ http://dx.doi.org/10.1787/142127877152

Pour consulter la version française intégrale de ce tableau, suivre ce lien :
StatLink ⌨️ http://dx.doi.org/10.1787/152751048643

[Part 1/1]
**Table 5.12a  Direct influence of stakeholders on decision making at school: staffing[1]**

Tableau 5.12a  Influence directe des acteurs intervenant dans les décisions relatives au recrutement du personnel de l'établissement

| | | Percentage of students in schools where the principal reported that the following stakeholders exert a direct influence on decision making about staffing | | | | | | | | | | |
|---|---|---|---|---|---|---|---|---|---|---|---|---|
| | | Regional or national education authorities (e.g. inspectorates) | | The school's governing board | | Parent groups | | Teacher groups | | Student groups | | External examination board | |
| | | % | S.E. | % | S.E. | % | S.E. | % | S.E. | % | S.E. | % | S.E. |
| OECD | Australia | 63.3 | (2.5) | 22.4 | (2.4) | 5.6 | (1.5) | 43.1 | (2.7) | 1.2 | (0.6) | 1.8 | (0.8) |
| | Austria | 95.0 | (2.1) | 4.0 | (1.6) | 0.5 | (0.5) | 34.3 | (3.7) | 1.5 | (0.9) | a | a |
| | Belgium | 62.9 | (3.0) | 82.7 | (2.5) | 6.8 | (1.4) | 44.5 | (2.5) | 3.0 | (1.0) | 1.5 | (0.7) |
| | Canada | 47.3 | (2.7) | 44.8 | (2.6) | 4.5 | (0.9) | 37.1 | (2.5) | 1.6 | (0.5) | 2.5 | (0.8) |
| | Czech Republic | 26.1 | (3.4) | 16.0 | (3.4) | 4.2 | (1.6) | 28.0 | (4.0) | 3.7 | (1.5) | 2.4 | (1.4) |
| | Denmark | 42.2 | (3.4) | 3.7 | (1.7) | 2.1 | (1.2) | 63.7 | (4.1) | 42.4 | (4.2) | 8.4 | (2.4) |
| | Finland | 42.9 | (4.0) | 22.7 | (3.5) | 1.3 | (1.1) | 37.0 | (4.0) | 2.8 | (1.6) | 0.7 | (0.7) |
| | France | w | w | w | w | w | w | w | w | w | w | w | w |
| | Germany | 93.6 | (1.9) | 9.4 | (1.8) | 1.3 | (0.7) | 17.8 | (2.4) | 1.0 | (0.7) | 2.0 | (0.8) |
| | Greece | 90.7 | (2.4) | 2.2 | (0.7) | 2.1 | (1.3) | 10.7 | (2.4) | 3.0 | (1.5) | a | a |
| | Hungary | 20.0 | (3.3) | 90.6 | (2.3) | 5.9 | (1.9) | 44.4 | (4.2) | 2.7 | (1.4) | 40.3 | (4.3) |
| | Iceland | 11.3 | (0.2) | 25.3 | (0.2) | 0.6 | (0.1) | 10.0 | (0.2) | a | a | a | a |
| | Ireland | 90.7 | (2.4) | 59.4 | (3.4) | 1.9 | (1.1) | 22.5 | (3.3) | 0.6 | (0.6) | 4.5 | (1.7) |
| | Italy | 90.2 | (1.6) | 2.9 | (1.1) | 0.9 | (0.8) | 2.3 | (0.8) | 0.8 | (0.8) | 1.3 | (0.6) |
| | Japan | 66.7 | (1.4) | 27.2 | (1.9) | a | a | 4.0 | (1.0) | a | a | a | a |
| | Korea | 80.2 | (3.0) | 7.8 | (2.2) | 2.5 | (1.2) | 25.1 | (3.7) | 2.4 | (1.2) | 6.2 | (1.9) |
| | Luxembourg | 87.5 | (0.0) | 17.7 | (0.1) | a | a | 8.8 | (0.0) | a | a | 24.3 | (0.1) |
| | Mexico | 50.1 | (2.7) | 44.5 | (2.5) | 17.7 | (2.2) | 37.4 | (2.5) | 24.2 | (2.7) | 13.5 | (1.8) |
| | Netherlands | 36.9 | (4.2) | 66.4 | (3.9) | 4.3 | (1.3) | 65.1 | (3.5) | 4.7 | (1.5) | 1.5 | (0.9) |
| | New Zealand | 73.3 | (3.1) | 74.6 | (3.0) | 0.9 | (0.6) | 46.2 | (3.3) | 2.5 | (1.2) | 3.1 | (1.2) |
| | Norway | 17.3 | (2.9) | 6.2 | (1.7) | a | a | 34.9 | (3.5) | a | a | a | a |
| | Poland | 37.4 | (3.6) | 0.6 | (0.6) | 0.1 | (0.1) | 20.0 | (2.8) | a | a | 0.6 | (0.6) |
| | Portugal | 86.8 | (1.7) | 38.4 | (4.0) | a | a | 2.6 | (1.2) | a | a | a | a |
| | Slovak Republic | 17.4 | (3.1) | 17.6 | (3.1) | 1.8 | (0.9) | 49.1 | (3.9) | a | a | 0.6 | (0.6) |
| | Spain | 71.0 | (2.1) | 20.8 | (2.0) | 1.7 | (0.8) | 13.1 | (2.1) | 0.1 | (0.0) | a | a |
| | Sweden | 7.4 | (2.0) | 10.0 | (2.2) | 3.9 | (1.5) | 76.7 | (3.0) | 20.2 | (3.5) | a | a |
| | Switzerland | 54.9 | (2.9) | 83.8 | (1.8) | a | a | 7.7 | (1.7) | 0.6 | (0.6) | 2.3 | (1.0) |
| | Turkey | 26.9 | (4.1) | 3.5 | (1.7) | 1.9 | (1.3) | 1.8 | (1.1) | 3.0 | (1.5) | 1.0 | (0.8) |
| | United Kingdom | 29.1 | (2.9) | 88.4 | (1.9) | 0.8 | (0.5) | 20.1 | (2.6) | 13.9 | (2.5) | 4.3 | (1.4) |
| | United States | 58.1 | (3.7) | 86.5 | (2.9) | 11.5 | (2.4) | 36.9 | (4.3) | 12.1 | (2.8) | 13.7 | (2.9) |
| | **OECD total** | 58.0 | (1.3) | 45.9 | (1.0) | 6.2 | (0.8) | 26.5 | (1.3) | 7.8 | (0.9) | 7.1 | (0.9) |
| | **OECD average** | 54.4 | (0.5) | 33.8 | (0.4) | 3.5 | (0.3) | 29.1 | (0.5) | 6.7 | (0.4) | 6.5 | (0.4) |
| Partners | Argentina | 65.3 | (3.9) | 39.5 | (4.2) | 2.9 | (1.4) | 15.7 | (3.0) | 6.4 | (1.9) | 5.1 | (1.5) |
| | Azerbaijan | 37.5 | (4.2) | 13.6 | (2.5) | 5.3 | (1.6) | 10.8 | (2.5) | 2.0 | (1.1) | 0.8 | (0.4) |
| | Brazil | 74.8 | (2.1) | 37.4 | (2.4) | 13.6 | (1.7) | 5.9 | (1.4) | 1.2 | (0.6) | 2.7 | (1.1) |
| | Bulgaria | 12.5 | (2.4) | 9.0 | (2.2) | 6.1 | (2.1) | 28.0 | (3.7) | 1.4 | (1.0) | 2.8 | (0.9) |
| | Chile | 43.1 | (3.9) | 74.5 | (3.3) | 5.8 | (2.6) | 10.5 | (2.7) | 6.7 | (2.7) | 8.7 | (2.9) |
| | Colombia | 61.5 | (4.1) | 5.7 | (1.8) | 2.2 | (1.4) | 2.7 | (1.6) | 0.7 | (0.5) | 7.6 | (2.3) |
| | Croatia | 26.0 | (3.3) | 30.9 | (3.6) | a | a | 7.0 | (2.0) | a | a | 1.2 | (0.7) |
| | Estonia | 9.2 | (2.2) | 37.2 | (3.2) | 3.2 | (1.1) | 15.9 | (2.8) | 3.9 | (1.4) | 3.1 | (1.5) |
| | Hong Kong-China | 45.0 | (4.3) | 85.5 | (2.6) | 1.8 | (1.0) | 9.8 | (3.2) | a | a | 1.4 | (1.0) |
| | Indonesia | 66.3 | (3.6) | 33.3 | (3.7) | a | a | 6.0 | (2.8) | 1.0 | (0.7) | 8.1 | (2.6) |
| | Israel | 66.9 | (4.1) | 15.2 | (2.8) | 6.6 | (2.2) | 62.9 | (3.9) | 2.1 | (1.2) | a | a |
| | Jordan | 83.7 | (2.5) | 9.0 | (1.7) | 0.3 | (0.0) | 9.9 | (2.4) | 2.3 | (1.1) | 3.6 | (1.5) |
| | Kyrgyzstan | 65.7 | (3.6) | 32.4 | (3.3) | 2.1 | (1.1) | 21.2 | (2.9) | 6.4 | (2.0) | 9.4 | (2.4) |
| | Latvia | 62.1 | (4.2) | 35.4 | (3.9) | 33.0 | (3.8) | 51.6 | (4.5) | 20.6 | (3.5) | 1.5 | (0.9) |
| | Liechtenstein | c | c | c | c | c | c | c | c | c | c | c | c |
| | Lithuania | 23.4 | (3.0) | 34.0 | (3.4) | 18.6 | (2.8) | 42.3 | (3.6) | 9.0 | (2.1) | 1.1 | (0.6) |
| | Macao-China | 42.8 | (0.1) | 69.2 | (0.1) | 1.9 | (0.0) | 1.9 | (0.0) | a | a | 2.0 | (0.0) |
| | Montenegro | 13.2 | (0.1) | 41.4 | (0.2) | 19.5 | (0.1) | 7.4 | (0.1) | 13.2 | (0.1) | a | a |
| | Qatar | 63.9 | (0.1) | 29.5 | (0.1) | 1.2 | (0.1) | 8.3 | (0.1) | 2.3 | (0.1) | 4.1 | (0.1) |
| | Romania | 95.7 | (1.6) | 37.6 | (4.1) | 1.4 | (1.0) | 12.1 | (2.7) | 0.6 | (0.6) | 9.0 | (2.0) |
| | Russian Federation | 17.9 | (2.9) | 26.6 | (2.7) | 8.4 | (1.9) | 33.3 | (4.5) | 5.4 | (1.5) | 11.6 | (2.2) |
| | Serbia | 40.4 | (3.4) | 89.7 | (2.3) | 12.6 | (2.6) | 22.1 | (3.2) | 6.9 | (2.3) | 8.0 | (2.1) |
| | Slovenia | 68.3 | (0.4) | 14.0 | (0.1) | 0.7 | (0.0) | 22.4 | (0.2) | a | a | 1.7 | (0.0) |
| | Chinese Taipei | 53.1 | (4.3) | 90.3 | (1.9) | 5.8 | (1.5) | 16.3 | (2.4) | 1.1 | (0.6) | 12.3 | (2.4) |
| | Thailand | 79.6 | (2.9) | 48.8 | (4.0) | 17.8 | (3.0) | 43.2 | (3.8) | 14.5 | (2.9) | 40.6 | (3.6) |
| | Tunisia | 86.1 | (2.9) | 2.1 | (1.0) | a | a | 1.7 | (0.9) | a | a | 5.6 | (2.0) |
| | Uruguay | 80.2 | (1.7) | 21.8 | (1.5) | 0.8 | (0.5) | 3.8 | (1.1) | 0.4 | (0.3) | 2.7 | (0.6) |

1. Results based on reports from school principals and reported proportionate to the number of 15-year-olds enrolled in the school.
StatLink 🛢 http://dx.doi.org/10.1787/142127877152

Pour consulter la version française intégrale de ce tableau, suivre ce lien :
StatLink 🛢 http://dx.doi.org/10.1787/152751048643

[Part 1/1]

**Table 5.12b  Direct influence of stakeholders on decision making at school: budgeting[1]**

Tableau 5.12b  Influence directe des acteurs intervenant dans les décisions relatives au budget de l'établissement

| | Percentage of students in schools where the principal reported that the following stakeholders exert a direct influence on decision making about budgeting | | | | | | | | | | | |
|---|---|---|---|---|---|---|---|---|---|---|---|---|
| | Regional or national education authorities (e.g. inspectorates) | | The school's governing board | | Parent groups | | Teacher groups | | Student groups | | External examination board | |
| | % | S.E. | % | S.E. | % | S.E. | % | S.E. | % | S.E. | % | S.E. |
| **OECD** | | | | | | | | | | | | |
| Australia | 59.4 | (2.6) | 65.9 | (2.4) | 25.0 | (2.4) | 38.8 | (2.6) | 6.8 | (1.5) | 1.6 | (0.8) |
| Austria | 65.6 | (3.3) | 21.0 | (3.3) | 7.8 | (2.2) | 28.8 | (3.5) | 0.9 | (0.6) | a | a |
| Belgium | 55.1 | (3.0) | 86.2 | (2.2) | 10.8 | (2.0) | 29.2 | (2.8) | 3.9 | (1.2) | 0.4 | (0.4) |
| Canada | 66.6 | (2.4) | 68.7 | (2.4) | 23.0 | (1.9) | 25.8 | (2.4) | 7.3 | (1.5) | 2.9 | (0.8) |
| Czech Republic | 59.8 | (4.6) | 77.3 | (3.5) | 8.4 | (2.0) | 16.3 | (2.9) | 1.9 | (1.1) | 0.4 | (0.3) |
| Denmark | 77.2 | (3.4) | 3.1 | (1.4) | 52.1 | (3.5) | 38.6 | (3.7) | 16.8 | (3.0) | 80.6 | (3.5) |
| Finland | 53.8 | (3.9) | 31.7 | (3.8) | 2.2 | (1.4) | 31.9 | (3.7) | 5.5 | (1.7) | 1.5 | (0.9) |
| France | w | w | w | w | w | w | w | w | w | w | w | w |
| Germany | 23.9 | (2.9) | 60.1 | (3.0) | 11.1 | (2.3) | 46.1 | (3.5) | 10.9 | (2.2) | 1.8 | (0.9) |
| Greece | 20.2 | (3.1) | 85.5 | (2.9) | 7.4 | (2.1) | 1.9 | (0.9) | 6.4 | (1.7) | a | a |
| Hungary | 31.9 | (3.3) | 77.6 | (3.5) | 11.6 | (2.4) | 28.2 | (3.6) | 10.9 | (2.3) | 64.4 | (4.1) |
| Iceland | 4.7 | (0.1) | 78.3 | (0.2) | 4.3 | (0.1) | 3.0 | (0.1) | 2.5 | (0.0) | 4.9 | (0.1) |
| Ireland | 73.2 | (3.4) | 70.5 | (3.0) | 5.1 | (1.8) | 7.2 | (2.1) | 4.6 | (1.7) | 4.5 | (1.7) |
| Italy | 24.0 | (2.4) | 88.3 | (1.8) | 12.4 | (1.7) | 12.0 | (1.7) | 11.1 | (1.5) | 2.4 | (1.1) |
| Japan | 60.7 | (2.4) | 32.1 | (1.8) | 10.8 | (2.3) | 21.9 | (2.9) | 5.4 | (1.8) | 4.3 | (2.1) |
| Korea | 64.0 | (3.8) | 82.4 | (3.5) | 8.0 | (2.2) | 46.0 | (4.1) | 6.1 | (1.7) | 5.7 | (1.6) |
| Luxembourg | 55.6 | (0.0) | 84.2 | (0.0) | 12.5 | (0.0) | 16.2 | (0.1) | 12.0 | (0.1) | a | a |
| Mexico | 48.9 | (2.8) | 25.7 | (2.6) | 31.8 | (2.7) | 6.9 | (1.2) | 4.7 | (1.0) | 2.6 | (0.6) |
| Netherlands | 58.3 | (4.1) | 77.6 | (3.6) | 11.4 | (2.5) | 62.8 | (3.7) | 2.1 | (1.1) | a | a |
| New Zealand | 58.9 | (3.2) | 94.5 | (1.6) | 2.5 | (1.2) | 24.4 | (2.8) | 4.1 | (1.3) | 4.5 | (1.4) |
| Norway | 28.7 | (3.5) | 55.5 | (3.9) | 11.5 | (2.4) | 47.0 | (4.0) | 11.1 | (2.2) | 2.1 | (0.8) |
| Poland | 30.8 | (3.2) | 4.8 | (1.6) | 9.6 | (2.2) | 24.3 | (3.3) | 1.2 | (0.9) | 1.2 | (0.9) |
| Portugal | 81.0 | (3.1) | 76.8 | (3.7) | 4.2 | (1.5) | 1.1 | (0.8) | 0.8 | (0.7) | a | a |
| Slovak Republic | 52.9 | (4.1) | 41.2 | (4.3) | 14.3 | (3.5) | 15.0 | (3.0) | 0.5 | (0.5) | a | a |
| Spain | 56.5 | (2.9) | 81.7 | (2.2) | 11.6 | (2.0) | 6.7 | (1.4) | 4.8 | (1.3) | a | a |
| Sweden | 8.0 | (2.0) | 31.2 | (3.2) | 3.9 | (1.4) | 66.2 | (3.6) | 10.4 | (2.9) | a | a |
| Switzerland | 71.8 | (1.8) | 74.2 | (2.4) | 1.1 | (0.5) | 10.3 | (1.6) | 0.5 | (0.0) | 3.8 | (1.1) |
| Turkey | 11.1 | (2.7) | 38.1 | (3.7) | 49.5 | (4.5) | 5.5 | (1.9) | 4.7 | (1.8) | 1.3 | (0.8) |
| United Kingdom | 59.1 | (3.4) | 90.8 | (1.8) | 2.5 | (1.0) | 7.7 | (1.7) | 2.2 | (0.9) | 3.5 | (1.0) |
| United States | 76.6 | (2.9) | 93.5 | (1.7) | 24.9 | (3.4) | 35.7 | (3.9) | 16.2 | (2.9) | 10.5 | (2.7) |
| **OECD total** | 54.9 | (1.1) | 65.8 | (0.8) | 19.1 | (1.1) | 26.3 | (1.3) | 8.8 | (0.9) | 6.0 | (0.9) |
| **OECD average** | 49.6 | (0.6) | 62.0 | (0.5) | 13.5 | (0.4) | 24.3 | (0.5) | 6.1 | (0.3) | 9.8 | (0.4) |
| **Partners** | | | | | | | | | | | | |
| Argentina | 66.4 | (4.3) | 38.1 | (4.4) | 11.7 | (2.7) | 10.8 | (2.6) | 3.9 | (1.6) | 1.8 | (0.8) |
| Azerbaijan | 58.1 | (3.4) | 2.9 | (1.3) | 4.1 | (1.5) | 1.7 | (1.1) | 2.3 | (1.3) | 0.7 | (0.7) |
| Brazil | 66.8 | (2.2) | 54.2 | (2.5) | 43.7 | (2.4) | 28.5 | (2.5) | 18.7 | (2.4) | 3.2 | (0.7) |
| Bulgaria | 61.2 | (3.8) | 6.4 | (1.8) | 10.4 | (2.3) | 12.2 | (2.6) | 3.2 | (1.4) | 11.5 | (2.8) |
| Chile | 43.3 | (3.6) | 71.1 | (3.0) | 35.1 | (3.9) | 11.3 | (2.8) | 8.2 | (1.9) | 8.0 | (3.0) |
| Colombia | 8.3 | (2.3) | 77.7 | (3.8) | 21.2 | (3.7) | 12.4 | (3.2) | 15.5 | (3.7) | 5.1 | (1.9) |
| Croatia | 65.1 | (3.8) | 80.1 | (3.1) | 2.2 | (1.3) | 3.2 | (1.4) | 0.6 | (0.8) | a | a |
| Estonia | 51.2 | (3.4) | 78.1 | (3.0) | 6.7 | (1.9) | 29.1 | (3.1) | 13.4 | (2.5) | a | a |
| Hong Kong-China | 65.1 | (4.0) | 91.8 | (2.4) | 15.6 | (2.9) | 28.9 | (3.6) | 5.0 | (1.5) | 1.4 | (1.0) |
| Indonesia | 27.4 | (3.0) | 79.6 | (3.2) | 57.4 | (3.3) | 14.1 | (2.2) | 18.8 | (2.7) | 2.8 | (1.1) |
| Israel | 80.5 | (3.6) | 16.3 | (3.2) | 39.1 | (4.3) | 34.6 | (4.1) | 7.5 | (2.7) | a | a |
| Jordan | 19.8 | (3.2) | 65.9 | (4.0) | 5.8 | (1.6) | 19.2 | (2.6) | 9.6 | (2.3) | 2.7 | (1.2) |
| Kyrgyzstan | 44.1 | (3.3) | 13.1 | (2.6) | 64.2 | (3.6) | 8.8 | (1.8) | 5.4 | (1.6) | 13.0 | (2.0) |
| Latvia | 31.2 | (3.3) | 69.4 | (3.6) | 44.1 | (3.7) | 42.9 | (4.5) | 26.1 | (3.7) | 0.2 | (0.2) |
| Liechtenstein | c | c | c | c | c | c | c | c | c | c | c | c |
| Lithuania | 74.7 | (2.8) | 74.0 | (2.9) | 33.1 | (3.4) | 37.1 | (3.7) | 9.7 | (2.0) | 0.9 | (0.6) |
| Macao-China | 59.1 | (0.1) | 77.6 | (0.1) | a | a | 1.3 | (0.0) | a | a | 4.6 | (0.0) |
| Montenegro | 44.4 | (0.1) | 72.1 | (0.2) | 0.9 | (0.1) | 3.4 | (0.0) | a | a | a | a |
| Qatar | 61.1 | (0.1) | 27.2 | (0.1) | 0.5 | (0.0) | 3.6 | (0.1) | 1.7 | (0.0) | 1.9 | (0.0) |
| Romania | 37.8 | (5.7) | 77.3 | (5.9) | 26.9 | (5.4) | 12.9 | (3.0) | 3.0 | (1.8) | 7.0 | (1.6) |
| Russian Federation | 91.2 | (2.0) | 39.3 | (3.4) | 29.1 | (3.2) | 7.8 | (1.9) | 2.1 | (1.0) | 2.0 | (1.1) |
| Serbia | 86.7 | (2.4) | 68.3 | (4.5) | 25.3 | (3.9) | 9.3 | (2.3) | 0.6 | (0.6) | 1.8 | (1.1) |
| Slovenia | 91.2 | (0.4) | 69.4 | (0.4) | 21.7 | (0.2) | 9.7 | (0.1) | 4.2 | (0.1) | 0.6 | (0.0) |
| Chinese Taipei | 74.6 | (2.9) | 3.7 | (1.3) | 8.1 | (2.3) | 6.6 | (1.5) | 1.3 | (0.7) | 20.9 | (3.2) |
| Thailand | 77.6 | (3.2) | 75.3 | (3.3) | 40.7 | (4.2) | 40.2 | (3.9) | 22.3 | (3.1) | 29.1 | (2.9) |
| Tunisia | 43.0 | (4.3) | 60.5 | (4.5) | 0.6 | (0.7) | 1.5 | (1.1) | 1.0 | (0.6) | a | a |
| Uruguay | 69.5 | (1.8) | 17.7 | (1.4) | 6.5 | (2.0) | 5.8 | (1.3) | 1.3 | (0.7) | 5.4 | (1.0) |

1. Results based on reports from school principals and reported proportionate to the number of 15-year-olds enrolled in the school.
*StatLink* http://dx.doi.org/10.1787/142127877152

Pour consulter la version française intégrale de ce tableau, suivre ce lien :
*StatLink* http://dx.doi.org/10.1787/152751048643

[Part 1/1]

**Table 5.12c** Direct influence of stakeholders on decision making at school: instructional content[1]

**Tableau 5.12c** Influence directe des acteurs intervenant dans les décisions relatives aux contenus d'enseignement de l'établissement

| | | Percentage of students in schools where the principal reported that the following stakeholders exert a direct influence on decision making about instructional content | | | | | | | | | | |
|---|---|---|---|---|---|---|---|---|---|---|---|---|
| | | Regional or national education authorities (e.g. inspectorates) | | The school's governing board | | Parent groups | | Teacher groups | | Student groups | | External examination board | |
| | | % | S.E. | % | S.E. | % | S.E. | % | S.E. | % | S.E. | % | S.E. |
| OECD | Australia | 81.9 | (2.1) | 7.3 | (1.4) | 11.1 | (1.7) | 66.0 | (2.6) | 13.4 | (2.2) | 71.3 | (2.3) |
| | Austria | 65.3 | (3.4) | 43.5 | (3.8) | 10.2 | (2.2) | 69.1 | (3.6) | 16.5 | (3.0) | a | a |
| | Belgium | 80.5 | (2.4) | 27.2 | (2.4) | 8.0 | (1.6) | 37.1 | (3.4) | 9.1 | (2.0) | 6.9 | (1.1) |
| | Canada | 88.7 | (1.5) | 23.4 | (1.8) | 9.9 | (1.4) | 61.5 | (2.4) | 7.6 | (1.1) | 19.4 | (2.1) |
| | Czech Republic | 45.5 | (4.0) | 32.9 | (3.7) | 21.5 | (3.8) | 84.7 | (2.5) | 29.6 | (4.3) | 47.5 | (4.0) |
| | Denmark | 11.6 | (2.6) | 45.6 | (4.1) | 14.2 | (2.6) | 11.9 | (2.4) | 58.6 | (3.8) | 20.4 | (3.2) |
| | Finland | 86.8 | (3.1) | 28.2 | (3.9) | 40.2 | (4.1) | 86.3 | (2.9) | 37.9 | (3.8) | 11.1 | (2.4) |
| | France | w | w | w | w | w | w | w | w | w | w | w | w |
| | Germany | 76.1 | (2.7) | 33.0 | (3.1) | 1.9 | (0.9) | 72.3 | (2.7) | 23.6 | (2.8) | 6.0 | (1.6) |
| | Greece | 88.8 | (2.6) | 1.1 | (0.8) | 0.7 | (0.7) | 14.3 | (2.5) | 3.3 | (1.5) | a | a |
| | Hungary | 58.8 | (4.3) | 80.9 | (3.5) | 30.1 | (3.9) | 95.2 | (1.7) | 36.2 | (4.0) | 41.2 | (4.2) |
| | Iceland | 65.8 | (0.2) | 0.5 | (0.0) | 1.7 | (0.1) | 9.6 | (0.2) | 2.7 | (0.1) | 2.0 | (0.1) |
| | Ireland | 72.2 | (3.4) | 16.9 | (2.5) | 14.1 | (2.9) | 34.0 | (3.7) | 9.5 | (2.2) | 47.1 | (3.9) |
| | Italy | 44.1 | (2.7) | 9.8 | (1.8) | 13.5 | (1.6) | 76.2 | (2.0) | 19.8 | (1.9) | 5.5 | (1.2) |
| | Japan | 36.5 | (3.8) | 14.7 | (2.7) | 15.3 | (3.1) | 90.2 | (2.2) | 8.5 | (2.6) | 6.0 | (1.9) |
| | Korea | 30.7 | (3.8) | 20.4 | (3.0) | 23.8 | (3.4) | 69.2 | (3.8) | 34.4 | (3.6) | 28.3 | (3.5) |
| | Luxembourg | 96.1 | (0.0) | 3.8 | (0.0) | 1.9 | (0.0) | 39.3 | (0.1) | 1.9 | (0.0) | 0.3 | (0.0) |
| | Mexico | 64.9 | (2.6) | 27.4 | (2.5) | 4.5 | (0.9) | 47.1 | (2.9) | 17.5 | (2.4) | 23.3 | (2.4) |
| | Netherlands | 56.5 | (4.2) | 14.8 | (3.0) | 23.6 | (3.3) | 77.6 | (3.7) | 23.9 | (3.4) | 8.5 | (2.2) |
| | New Zealand | 77.2 | (2.9) | 11.3 | (2.3) | 12.4 | (1.9) | 58.5 | (3.3) | 12.2 | (2.2) | 44.7 | (3.0) |
| | Norway | 82.8 | (3.0) | 3.8 | (1.5) | 6.2 | (1.7) | 61.9 | (3.5) | 18.5 | (2.7) | 4.0 | (1.3) |
| | Poland | 28.5 | (3.7) | 13.3 | (2.7) | 38.0 | (3.6) | 90.2 | (2.2) | 15.5 | (3.0) | 12.3 | (2.4) |
| | Portugal | 86.5 | (2.6) | 9.2 | (1.8) | 1.0 | (0.6) | 33.5 | (3.3) | 1.5 | (0.9) | 14.1 | (2.6) |
| | Slovak Republic | 60.9 | (3.7) | 27.6 | (3.3) | 26.5 | (3.5) | 15.8 | (2.5) | 13.9 | (2.9) | 5.2 | (1.8) |
| | Spain | 85.2 | (2.3) | 19.7 | (2.6) | 5.9 | (1.6) | 30.4 | (2.8) | 5.6 | (1.5) | a | a |
| | Sweden | 45.0 | (4.0) | 7.0 | (1.8) | 17.4 | (2.9) | 80.9 | (2.8) | 71.5 | (3.3) | 1.0 | (1.0) |
| | Switzerland | 87.5 | (1.9) | 17.8 | (2.1) | 2.0 | (0.8) | 60.0 | (2.9) | 6.6 | (1.3) | 12.1 | (2.1) |
| | Turkey | 56.9 | (4.1) | 17.3 | (2.9) | 14.3 | (2.9) | 48.0 | (3.9) | 27.1 | (3.9) | 16.3 | (3.1) |
| | United Kingdom | 62.1 | (3.1) | 18.9 | (2.9) | 4.6 | (1.4) | 21.2 | (2.7) | 14.7 | (2.5) | 72.4 | (2.8) |
| | United States | 83.4 | (3.1) | 67.6 | (3.8) | 25.0 | (3.8) | 81.7 | (3.2) | 17.3 | (3.1) | 33.6 | (3.8) |
| | **OECD total** | 65.7 | (1.0) | 34.6 | (1.2) | 16.2 | (1.2) | 67.4 | (1.3) | 18.2 | (1.1) | 25.3 | (1.3) |
| | **OECD average** | 65.8 | (0.6) | 22.2 | (0.5) | 13.8 | (0.5) | 56.0 | (0.5) | 19.3 | (0.5) | 21.6 | (0.5) |
| Partners | Argentina | 80.8 | (3.4) | 31.2 | (3.4) | 10.1 | (1.7) | 54.1 | (3.9) | 16.3 | (2.7) | 11.6 | (2.6) |
| | Azerbaijan | 32.9 | (3.4) | 38.2 | (4.0) | 34.9 | (3.6) | 50.6 | (4.1) | 35.1 | (3.7) | 9.5 | (2.4) |
| | Brazil | 44.9 | (2.8) | 69.1 | (2.4) | 24.5 | (2.6) | 66.8 | (2.4) | 28.6 | (2.5) | 13.6 | (1.9) |
| | Bulgaria | 94.8 | (1.7) | 24.9 | (3.9) | 4.6 | (1.8) | 27.8 | (3.8) | 6.6 | (2.0) | 19.5 | (3.0) |
| | Chile | 80.0 | (2.9) | 52.2 | (4.9) | 11.0 | (2.7) | 52.4 | (4.7) | 23.2 | (3.2) | 31.0 | (3.9) |
| | Colombia | 54.6 | (5.3) | 59.6 | (5.2) | 23.0 | (4.0) | 90.3 | (2.8) | 42.6 | (5.6) | 33.6 | (4.5) |
| | Croatia | 84.4 | (2.5) | 7.8 | (2.0) | 12.1 | (2.8) | 73.3 | (3.4) | 20.8 | (3.4) | 13.1 | (2.7) |
| | Estonia | 66.7 | (3.0) | 44.8 | (3.7) | 23.1 | (2.8) | 95.1 | (1.6) | 55.7 | (3.4) | 60.5 | (3.5) |
| | Hong Kong-China | 71.7 | (3.7) | 18.5 | (3.1) | 24.7 | (4.1) | 77.7 | (3.3) | 25.4 | (4.2) | 81.1 | (3.3) |
| | Indonesia | 42.2 | (4.4) | 3.8 | (1.3) | 2.5 | (1.2) | 83.7 | (2.9) | 18.0 | (2.8) | 11.5 | (2.4) |
| | Israel | 72.9 | (3.5) | 53.1 | (4.2) | 7.3 | (2.3) | 7.3 | (2.3) | 15.2 | (3.2) | a | a |
| | Jordan | 65.2 | (3.6) | 8.1 | (2.3) | 6.4 | (1.8) | 39.4 | (3.9) | 12.8 | (2.5) | 18.2 | (2.8) |
| | Kyrgyzstan | 52.3 | (4.3) | 48.8 | (4.0) | 17.8 | (3.0) | 52.0 | (3.9) | 31.9 | (3.6) | 29.9 | (3.7) |
| | Latvia | 68.9 | (3.9) | 22.6 | (3.3) | 17.7 | (2.9) | 78.9 | (3.0) | 19.8 | (3.1) | 56.3 | (4.1) |
| | Liechtenstein | c | c | c | c | c | c | c | c | c | c | c | c |
| | Lithuania | 82.1 | (3.1) | 72.9 | (3.4) | 58.3 | (3.7) | 78.6 | (2.9) | 73.3 | (3.4) | 54.6 | (3.6) |
| | Macao-China | 45.5 | (0.1) | 50.1 | (0.1) | 26.4 | (0.1) | 58.4 | (0.1) | 32.3 | (0.1) | 31.6 | (0.1) |
| | Montenegro | 80.5 | (0.1) | 3.5 | (0.1) | 19.7 | (0.1) | 38.4 | (0.2) | 17.0 | (0.1) | 20.0 | (0.2) |
| | Qatar | 71.8 | (0.1) | 19.0 | (0.1) | 11.0 | (0.1) | 41.0 | (0.1) | 7.1 | (0.1) | 14.8 | (0.1) |
| | Romania | 84.5 | (2.8) | 28.5 | (3.4) | 27.1 | (3.8) | 65.2 | (5.7) | 48.5 | (4.7) | 19.2 | (3.4) |
| | Russian Federation | 86.1 | (3.9) | 64.7 | (3.4) | 47.1 | (3.9) | 75.3 | (3.6) | 44.1 | (3.4) | 45.9 | (3.7) |
| | Serbia | 92.0 | (2.6) | 3.4 | (1.4) | 16.1 | (2.9) | 64.0 | (4.1) | 26.5 | (3.4) | 34.6 | (3.3) |
| | Slovenia | 86.4 | (0.3) | 7.1 | (0.3) | 17.5 | (0.4) | 82.0 | (0.3) | 21.3 | (0.3) | 63.6 | (0.5) |
| | Chinese Taipei | 59.5 | (3.9) | 27.0 | (2.7) | 51.1 | (3.5) | 56.4 | (3.3) | 44.3 | (3.3) | 25.2 | (2.8) |
| | Thailand | 32.3 | (3.9) | 61.4 | (3.6) | 60.0 | (3.9) | 83.6 | (2.6) | 72.2 | (3.5) | 69.0 | (3.7) |
| | Tunisia | 84.6 | (3.2) | 0.6 | (0.6) | 0.6 | (0.6) | 3.5 | (1.4) | a | a | 7.0 | (1.8) |
| | Uruguay | 92.7 | (1.2) | 17.2 | (2.3) | 1.9 | (0.7) | 25.4 | (2.6) | 4.0 | (0.9) | 6.7 | (1.4) |

1. Results based on reports from school principals and reported proportionate to the number of 15-year-olds enrolled in the school.
StatLink ᗧᔆᗰ http://dx.doi.org/10.1787/142127877152

Pour consulter la version française intégrale de ce tableau, suivre ce lien :
StatLink ᗧᔆᗰ http://dx.doi.org/10.1787/152751048643

[Part 1/1]

**Table 5.12d** **Direct influence of stakeholders on decision making at school: assessment practices[1]**

Tableau 5.12d  Influence directe des acteurs intervenant dans les décisions relatives aux pratiques d'évaluation de l'établissement

| | Percentage of students in schools where the principal reported that the following stakeholders exert a direct influence on decision making about assessment practices | | | | | | | | | | | |
|---|---|---|---|---|---|---|---|---|---|---|---|---|
| | Regional or national education authorities (*e.g.* inspectorates) | | The school's governing board | | Parent groups | | Teacher groups | | Student groups | | External examination board | |
| | % | S.E. | % | S.E. | % | S.E. | % | S.E. | % | S.E. | % | S.E. |
| Australia | 84.3 | (2.3) | 7.0 | (1.4) | 10.0 | (1.6) | 69.6 | (2.8) | 13.2 | (2.2) | 82.0 | (1.7) |
| Austria | 47.5 | (4.0) | 14.1 | (2.9) | 4.7 | (1.6) | 61.0 | (4.1) | 9.0 | (2.4) | a | a |
| Belgium | 58.1 | (3.2) | 49.9 | (3.0) | 23.3 | (3.3) | 56.1 | (3.3) | 23.8 | (2.3) | 18.0 | (2.5) |
| Canada | 79.9 | (1.9) | 28.6 | (2.0) | 10.5 | (1.8) | 66.6 | (2.4) | 7.0 | (1.1) | 36.7 | (2.7) |
| Czech Republic | 60.4 | (4.1) | 72.1 | (3.5) | 35.2 | (3.6) | 74.5 | (3.4) | 37.6 | (4.0) | 48.0 | (4.3) |
| Denmark | 45.7 | (4.1) | 93.1 | (2.1) | a | a | 80.2 | (2.9) | 47.6 | (3.7) | 24.7 | (3.6) |
| Finland | 83.5 | (3.1) | 22.2 | (3.4) | 25.6 | (3.9) | 73.8 | (3.7) | 14.0 | (3.2) | 22.6 | (3.7) |
| France | w | w | w | w | w | w | w | w | w | w | w | w |
| Germany | 53.6 | (3.5) | 39.7 | (3.3) | 2.4 | (1.0) | 76.2 | (2.6) | 6.9 | (1.8) | 12.7 | (2.0) |
| Greece | 73.5 | (3.6) | 1.1 | (0.8) | 0.8 | (0.8) | 40.6 | (4.2) | 2.9 | (1.5) | a | a |
| Hungary | 51.4 | (4.3) | 86.8 | (2.6) | 45.5 | (3.9) | 96.1 | (1.6) | 87.6 | (3.0) | 36.0 | (4.3) |
| Iceland | 49.0 | (0.2) | 12.0 | (0.2) | 18.9 | (0.2) | 7.4 | (0.1) | 7.3 | (0.2) | 36.8 | (0.2) |
| Ireland | 57.9 | (3.6) | 24.9 | (3.0) | 14.9 | (2.7) | 46.2 | (4.3) | 13.4 | (2.5) | 84.3 | (2.9) |
| Italy | 16.6 | (2.2) | 12.3 | (1.8) | 8.7 | (1.7) | 78.4 | (2.2) | 9.8 | (1.3) | 24.3 | (2.5) |
| Japan | 23.3 | (2.9) | 17.4 | (3.0) | 8.4 | (1.9) | 84.8 | (3.0) | 6.3 | (2.0) | 6.6 | (1.9) |
| Korea | 42.2 | (3.8) | 20.3 | (3.3) | 21.3 | (3.1) | 66.3 | (4.3) | 18.2 | (3.2) | 32.6 | (3.6) |
| Luxembourg | 98.1 | (0.0) | 16.7 | (0.1) | a | a | 29.9 | (0.1) | a | a | 24.2 | (0.1) |
| Mexico | 43.7 | (2.7) | 39.6 | (2.5) | 6.2 | (1.2) | 46.0 | (2.7) | 24.7 | (2.3) | 51.0 | (2.1) |
| Netherlands | 53.6 | (3.7) | 6.8 | (2.0) | 9.4 | (2.2) | 63.4 | (4.2) | 17.9 | (3.1) | 78.7 | (3.1) |
| New Zealand | 79.3 | (2.8) | 10.6 | (2.0) | 5.2 | (1.5) | 58.9 | (3.2) | 5.3 | (1.6) | 95.7 | (1.4) |
| Norway | 62.0 | (3.0) | 3.3 | (1.3) | 10.4 | (2.2) | 80.2 | (3.2) | 25.3 | (3.2) | 20.7 | (3.3) |
| Poland | 30.9 | (3.8) | 18.1 | (2.8) | 62.2 | (3.4) | 90.6 | (2.4) | 74.5 | (3.4) | 30.3 | (3.6) |
| Portugal | 72.3 | (3.7) | 43.9 | (4.1) | 24.4 | (3.2) | 40.1 | (3.3) | 16.3 | (2.7) | 67.4 | (3.9) |
| Slovak Republic | 62.4 | (4.0) | 18.3 | (3.1) | 26.5 | (3.6) | 15.9 | (3.1) | 19.8 | (3.1) | 18.6 | (3.1) |
| Spain | 64.4 | (2.8) | 25.4 | (2.9) | 6.3 | (1.5) | 34.9 | (2.8) | 8.6 | (1.5) | a | a |
| Sweden | 49.6 | (3.9) | 1.7 | (0.9) | 3.7 | (1.5) | 77.0 | (2.8) | 15.5 | (3.3) | 2.8 | (1.4) |
| Switzerland | 69.7 | (2.5) | 32.4 | (2.7) | 2.0 | (0.8) | 45.3 | (2.9) | 3.4 | (1.0) | 22.5 | (2.7) |
| Turkey | 46.5 | (4.6) | 48.2 | (4.0) | 28.4 | (3.8) | 59.5 | (4.0) | 42.6 | (4.2) | 29.1 | (4.1) |
| United Kingdom | 60.9 | (3.0) | 21.2 | (3.0) | 8.1 | (1.8) | 30.0 | (2.9) | 17.6 | (2.6) | 84.9 | (2.5) |
| United States | 79.7 | (3.4) | 58.9 | (4.3) | 10.7 | (2.7) | 66.5 | (3.6) | 9.7 | (2.9) | 41.9 | (3.9) |
| **OECD total** | 56.9 | (1.2) | 37.2 | (1.4) | 13.4 | (0.9) | 64.4 | (1.2) | 17.6 | (1.1) | 37.8 | (1.3) |
| **OECD average** | 58.6 | (0.6) | 29.2 | (0.5) | 16.1 | (0.5) | 59.2 | (0.6) | 20.9 | (0.5) | 39.7 | (0.6) |
| Argentina | 63.1 | (4.1) | 31.1 | (3.8) | 6.5 | (1.7) | 47.5 | (4.3) | 9.2 | (2.2) | 22.4 | (2.9) |
| Azerbaijan | 20.5 | (2.8) | 35.6 | (4.0) | 24.7 | (3.6) | 32.0 | (3.5) | 21.8 | (3.4) | 46.5 | (4.3) |
| Brazil | 37.6 | (2.7) | 71.7 | (2.4) | 24.3 | (2.6) | 69.7 | (2.2) | 29.7 | (2.6) | 31.2 | (2.6) |
| Bulgaria | 87.1 | (2.9) | 50.5 | (4.2) | 11.0 | (2.4) | 32.0 | (4.1) | 12.4 | (2.6) | 43.0 | (3.8) |
| Chile | 55.5 | (3.8) | 56.7 | (4.9) | 11.1 | (2.1) | 55.5 | (4.7) | 25.7 | (3.9) | 30.4 | (3.6) |
| Colombia | 45.9 | (5.6) | 55.8 | (5.6) | 32.9 | (5.4) | 81.2 | (3.7) | 60.7 | (5.1) | 64.3 | (4.7) |
| Croatia | 83.9 | (2.4) | 11.4 | (2.5) | 42.3 | (3.8) | 75.0 | (3.5) | 45.7 | (3.9) | 34.0 | (3.6) |
| Estonia | 62.2 | (3.3) | 43.6 | (3.7) | 19.2 | (2.8) | 95.2 | (1.2) | 50.7 | (3.5) | 66.7 | (3.3) |
| Hong Kong-China | 67.8 | (3.9) | 20.3 | (3.2) | 22.4 | (3.7) | 69.4 | (3.9) | 17.1 | (3.4) | 92.8 | (2.5) |
| Indonesia | 30.0 | (3.3) | 4.4 | (1.3) | 10.3 | (2.1) | 66.3 | (4.9) | 9.2 | (1.8) | 49.8 | (4.8) |
| Israel | 33.5 | (4.0) | 69.3 | (3.7) | 11.5 | (2.7) | 9.6 | (2.6) | 34.8 | (3.8) | a | a |
| Jordan | 43.9 | (3.6) | 42.2 | (3.7) | 51.4 | (3.9) | 41.4 | (3.7) | 36.8 | (3.9) | 47.6 | (3.8) |
| Kyrgyzstan | 33.7 | (4.1) | 30.2 | (3.9) | 6.1 | (2.2) | 48.1 | (3.5) | 20.1 | (3.4) | 38.3 | (3.9) |
| Latvia | 66.0 | (3.8) | 27.2 | (3.7) | 25.4 | (3.7) | 87.6 | (2.4) | 42.0 | (4.0) | 65.7 | (3.5) |
| Liechtenstein | c | c | c | c | c | c | c | c | c | c | c | c |
| Lithuania | 49.2 | (4.0) | 66.8 | (3.7) | 48.0 | (3.3) | 76.6 | (3.2) | 66.7 | (3.2) | 65.1 | (3.5) |
| Macao-China | 45.3 | (0.1) | 47.0 | (0.1) | 30.1 | (0.1) | 50.9 | (0.1) | 23.5 | (0.1) | 36.7 | (0.1) |
| Montenegro | 58.2 | (0.2) | 12.3 | (0.1) | 32.6 | (0.1) | 45.0 | (0.1) | 41.0 | (0.2) | 58.7 | (0.2) |
| Qatar | 59.3 | (0.1) | 38.4 | (0.1) | 19.2 | (0.1) | 36.7 | (0.1) | 12.0 | (0.1) | 26.8 | (0.1) |
| Romania | 69.4 | (5.8) | 43.7 | (6.0) | 12.3 | (2.6) | 77.2 | (4.0) | 23.6 | (4.2) | 71.2 | (4.2) |
| Russian Federation | 60.0 | (3.4) | 47.0 | (3.3) | 15.4 | (3.0) | 63.4 | (3.3) | 30.7 | (3.7) | 66.5 | (3.5) |
| Serbia | 75.4 | (3.7) | 5.4 | (1.9) | 43.4 | (4.1) | 57.0 | (4.2) | 51.4 | (4.1) | 44.2 | (4.2) |
| Slovenia | 80.6 | (0.3) | 12.8 | (0.1) | 31.6 | (0.3) | 91.5 | (0.2) | 52.8 | (0.6) | 67.8 | (0.6) |
| Chinese Taipei | 48.1 | (3.4) | 26.1 | (3.0) | 41.3 | (3.0) | 47.3 | (3.4) | 31.7 | (3.2) | 26.6 | (3.0) |
| Thailand | 36.6 | (3.6) | 51.6 | (3.7) | 58.0 | (3.7) | 67.6 | (3.6) | 60.0 | (3.8) | 89.3 | (2.6) |
| Tunisia | 64.9 | (4.2) | 18.8 | (3.4) | 9.0 | (2.5) | 8.0 | (2.1) | 4.6 | (1.7) | 29.1 | (4.0) |
| Uruguay | 90.4 | (1.5) | 26.3 | (2.8) | 0.9 | (0.5) | 30.1 | (2.7) | 2.7 | (0.9) | 19.1 | (2.4) |

1. Results based on reports from school principals and reported proportionate to the number of 15-year-olds enrolled in the school.
*StatLink* ᴍᔕᔭ http://dx.doi.org/10.1787/142127877152

Pour consulter la version française intégrale de ce tableau, suivre ce lien :
*StatLink* ᴍᔕᔭ http://dx.doi.org/10.1787/152751048643

183

[Part 1/1]

**Table 5.13** School principals' perceptions of vacant science teaching positions and lack of qualified science teachers[1]

Tableau 5.13 Postes vacants d'enseignants et offre correspondante d'enseignants qualifiés dans les matières scientifiques

| | Percentage of student in schools where the principal reported | | | | | | | | | |
|---|---|---|---|---|---|---|---|---|---|---|
| | No vacant science teaching positions to be filled | | All vacant science teaching positions filled | | One or more vacant science teaching positions not filled | | No vacant science teaching positions to be filled or all vacant science teaching positions filled — of which a lack of qualified science teachers hinders instruction to some extent or a lot | | One or more vacant science teaching positions not filled — of which a lack of qualified science teachers hinders instruction to some extent or a lot | |
| | % | S.E. | % | S.E. | % | S.E. | % | S.E. | % | S.E. |
| **OECD** | | | | | | | | | | |
| Australia | 21.7 | (2.3) | 74.6 | (2.6) | 3.7 | (1.1) | 29.3 | (2.5) | 65.8 | (16.2) |
| Austria | 55.6 | (3.7) | 41.2 | (3.9) | 3.2 | (1.0) | 6.7 | (1.8) | 73.8 | (19.9) |
| Belgium | 25.1 | (2.5) | 73.8 | (2.6) | 1.2 | (0.7) | 27.0 | (3.1) | c | c |
| Canada | 18.0 | (1.7) | 80.3 | (1.8) | 1.7 | (0.5) | 20.2 | (2.0) | c | c |
| Czech Republic | 53.8 | (3.4) | 44.1 | (3.3) | 2.1 | (1.1) | 15.4 | (2.7) | c | c |
| Denmark | 37.0 | (3.7) | 61.2 | (3.7) | 1.8 | (1.0) | 24.0 | (3.5) | c | c |
| Finland | 59.5 | (3.8) | 37.0 | (3.9) | 3.5 | (1.3) | 2.0 | (1.1) | 7.6 | (7.9) |
| France | w | w | w | w | w | w | w | w | w | w |
| Germany | 40.2 | (2.9) | 48.0 | (3.0) | 11.8 | (2.3) | 30.5 | (3.1) | 85.6 | (6.3) |
| Greece | 30.9 | (4.4) | 69.1 | (4.4) | 0.0 | (0.0) | 10.1 | (2.2) | c | c |
| Hungary | 57.4 | (4.4) | 39.6 | (4.3) | 3.0 | (1.4) | 3.9 | (1.7) | 43.2 | (24.4) |
| Iceland | 31.2 | (0.2) | 67.2 | (0.2) | 1.6 | (0.1) | 24.3 | (0.2) | c | c |
| Ireland | 55.5 | (3.9) | 44.0 | (3.9) | 0.5 | (0.5) | 8.1 | (2.1) | c | c |
| Italy | 33.4 | (2.6) | 66.5 | (2.6) | 0.2 | (0.1) | 12.6 | (2.0) | c | c |
| Japan | 11.1 | (2.5) | 86.0 | (2.7) | 3.0 | (1.2) | 2.9 | (1.2) | c | c |
| Korea | 80.0 | (3.2) | 18.8 | (3.2) | 1.3 | (0.9) | 3.6 | (1.5) | c | c |
| Luxembourg | 38.4 | (0.0) | 42.6 | (0.0) | 19.0 | (0.0) | 25.2 | (0.0) | 71.4 | (0.1) |
| Mexico | 48.9 | (2.9) | 48.7 | (3.0) | 2.4 | (0.6) | 32.6 | (2.8) | c | c |
| Netherlands | 34.1 | (3.6) | 63.0 | (3.7) | 2.9 | (1.1) | 7.3 | (2.1) | c | c |
| New Zealand | 19.2 | (2.7) | 79.3 | (2.8) | 1.5 | (0.5) | 15.1 | (2.6) | c | c |
| Norway | m | m | m | m | m | m | m | m | m | m |
| Poland | 73.1 | (3.6) | 26.8 | (3.6) | 0.1 | (0.1) | 1.9 | (1.1) | c | c |
| Portugal | 25.1 | (3.2) | 74.9 | (3.2) | 0.0 | (0.0) | 0.0 | (0.0) | c | c |
| Slovak Republic | 2.6 | (1.3) | 96.6 | (1.4) | 0.8 | (0.4) | 7.0 | (1.9) | c | c |
| Spain | 36.0 | (2.4) | 63.6 | (2.4) | 0.4 | (0.3) | 4.0 | (1.4) | c | c |
| Sweden | 27.4 | (3.3) | 71.7 | (3.5) | 0.9 | (0.6) | 7.2 | (2.2) | c | c |
| Switzerland | 42.1 | (3.0) | 56.9 | (3.0) | 1.0 | (0.2) | 15.6 | (1.7) | c | c |
| Turkey | 62.9 | (4.2) | 29.6 | (3.9) | 7.5 | (2.7) | 62.2 | (4.1) | 100.0 | (0.0) |
| United Kingdom | 18.6 | (2.5) | 72.6 | (3.0) | 8.8 | (1.8) | 11.1 | (2.3) | 72.0 | (11.3) |
| United States | 26.5 | (3.6) | 70.7 | (3.6) | 2.8 | (0.8) | 19.7 | (3.4) | c | c |
| **OECD total** | 35.8 | (1.2) | 60.7 | (1.3) | 3.5 | (0.4) | 18.4 | (1.1) | 73.6 | (4.9) |
| **OECD average** | 38.0 | (0.6) | 58.9 | (0.6) | 3.3 | (0.2) | 15.9 | (0.4) | 64.9 | (4.8) |
| **Partners** | | | | | | | | | | |
| Argentina | 37.2 | (4.7) | 61.1 | (4.7) | 1.7 | (0.5) | 11.8 | (3.0) | c | c |
| Azerbaijan | 54.7 | (3.9) | 32.3 | (3.7) | 13.0 | (3.4) | 59.0 | (4.0) | 58.4 | (16.4) |
| Brazil | 9.2 | (1.5) | 80.9 | (1.9) | 9.9 | (1.7) | 23.3 | (2.4) | 51.2 | (10.4) |
| Bulgaria | 69.4 | (4.0) | 30.6 | (4.0) | 0.0 | (0.0) | 1.3 | (0.8) | c | c |
| Chile | 35.4 | (4.4) | 62.1 | (4.5) | 2.5 | (1.3) | 33.7 | (5.0) | c | c |
| Colombia | 56.0 | (5.0) | 38.7 | (4.7) | 5.3 | (2.0) | 19.8 | (5.8) | 74.3 | (16.1) |
| Croatia | 27.4 | (3.2) | 70.9 | (3.2) | 1.8 | (1.2) | 14.8 | (2.7) | c | c |
| Estonia | 55.2 | (3.7) | 43.0 | (3.6) | 1.9 | (1.3) | 22.0 | (3.0) | c | c |
| Hong Kong-China | 49.7 | (4.6) | 50.3 | (4.6) | 0.0 | (0.0) | 8.7 | (2.3) | c | c |
| Indonesia | 6.4 | (1.2) | 59.8 | (3.3) | 33.8 | (3.2) | 23.1 | (3.3) | 63.4 | (5.5) |
| Israel | 23.4 | (3.9) | 69.2 | (4.3) | 7.4 | (2.4) | 10.3 | (3.1) | 38.7 | (17.5) |
| Jordan | 8.6 | (2.5) | 85.0 | (2.7) | 6.4 | (1.9) | 58.4 | (4.0) | 92.5 | (11.1) |
| Kyrgyzstan | 2.7 | (1.1) | 72.2 | (3.2) | 25.1 | (3.1) | 60.5 | (4.3) | 74.9 | (6.2) |
| Latvia | 34.1 | (3.8) | 64.7 | (3.8) | 1.2 | (0.8) | 15.5 | (2.9) | c | c |
| Liechtenstein | c | c | c | c | c | c | c | c | c | c |
| Lithuania | 54.2 | (4.1) | 45.2 | (4.1) | 0.6 | (0.6) | 15.1 | (2.6) | c | c |
| Macao-China | 13.8 | (0.0) | 84.5 | (0.0) | 1.7 | (0.0) | 15.9 | (0.1) | c | c |
| Montenegro | 48.5 | (0.2) | 49.7 | (0.2) | 1.8 | (0.0) | 7.2 | (0.1) | c | c |
| Qatar | 19.6 | (0.1) | 77.9 | (0.1) | 2.5 | (0.1) | 25.2 | (0.1) | c | c |
| Romania | 40.7 | (5.0) | 58.4 | (5.0) | 0.9 | (0.7) | 2.0 | (1.1) | c | c |
| Russian Federation | 6.8 | (2.0) | 90.2 | (2.2) | 3.0 | (1.1) | 32.4 | (3.5) | 100.0 | (0.0) |
| Serbia | 40.9 | (4.0) | 55.8 | (4.1) | 3.3 | (1.4) | 1.6 | (1.0) | 0.0 | (0.0) |
| Slovenia | 22.6 | (0.3) | 70.5 | (0.3) | 7.0 | (0.1) | 0.3 | (0.2) | 0.0 | (0.0) |
| Chinese Taipei | 19.2 | (2.8) | 71.1 | (3.6) | 9.8 | (2.4) | 12.3 | (3.1) | 29.9 | (12.3) |
| Thailand | 41.3 | (4.2) | 56.7 | (4.1) | 2.1 | (0.8) | 18.2 | (3.2) | c | c |
| Tunisia | 68.9 | (4.0) | 31.1 | (4.0) | 0.0 | (0.0) | 1.4 | (1.0) | c | c |
| Uruguay | 44.9 | (2.7) | 52.4 | (2.7) | 2.7 | (0.7) | 20.5 | (2.1) | c | c |

1. Results based on reports from school principals and reported proportionate to the number of 15-year-olds enrolled in the school.
StatLink http://dx.doi.org/10.1787/142127877152

Pour consulter la version française intégrale de ce tableau, suivre ce lien :
StatLink http://dx.doi.org/10.1787/152751048643

[Part 1/2]

**Table 5.14   Index of teacher shortage and student performance on the science scale, by quarters of the index[1] and student/teacher ratio**

Tableau 5.14   Indice de pénurie d'enseignants et performance des élèves sur l'échelle de culture scientifique, par quartile de l'indice, et nombre d'élèves par enseignant

| | Index of teacher shortage | | | | | | | | | | Performance on the science scale by quarters of the index of teacher shortage | | | | | | | |
|---|---|---|---|---|---|---|---|---|---|---|---|---|---|---|---|---|---|---|
| | All students | | Bottom quarter | | Second quarter | | Third quarter | | Top quarter | | Bottom quarter | | Second quarter | | Third quarter | | Top quarter | |
| | Mean index | S.E. | Mean index | S.E. | Mean index | S.E. | Mean index | S.E. | Mean index | S.E. | Mean score | S.E. | Mean score | S.E. | Mean score | S.E. | Mean score | S.E. |
| **OECD** | | | | | | | | | | | | | | | | | | |
| Australia | 0.33 | (0.05) | -1.06 | (0.00) | 0.00 | (0.03) | 0.79 | (0.02) | 1.59 | (0.03) | **550** | (5.4) | 528 | (4.3) | 520 | (4.8) | **509** | (5.5) |
| Austria | -0.36 | (0.06) | -1.06 | (0.00) | -1.03 | (0.01) | -0.05 | (0.03) | 0.69 | (0.07) | 516 | (7.7) | 512 | (6.8) | 523 | (9.2) | 494 | (11.2) |
| Belgium | 0.49 | (0.06) | -0.92 | (0.03) | 0.18 | (0.03) | 0.87 | (0.02) | 1.82 | (0.06) | **546** | (6.1) | 508 | (10.4) | 512 | (8.0) | **482** | (8.5) |
| Canada | 0.17 | (0.05) | -1.06 | (0.00) | -0.37 | (0.03) | 0.54 | (0.02) | 1.56 | (0.07) | 539 | (4.3) | 541 | (4.9) | 532 | (4.1) | 529 | (3.7) |
| Czech Republic | 0.15 | (0.05) | -0.65 | (0.05) | -0.08 | (0.02) | 0.30 | (0.02) | 1.05 | (0.07) | **553** | (8.9) | 515 | (7.0) | 509 | (8.7) | 479 | (9.1) |
| Denmark | 0.10 | (0.06) | -0.90 | (0.03) | -0.09 | (0.03) | 0.41 | (0.02) | 0.97 | (0.04) | 501 | (5.1) | 496 | (5.2) | 496 | (5.5) | 493 | (7.3) |
| Finland | -0.28 | (0.05) | -1.06 | (0.00) | -0.44 | (0.03) | -0.12 | (0.02) | 0.49 | (0.05) | 572 | (3.7) | 561 | (4.1) | 559 | (3.7) | 561 | (4.3) |
| France | w | w | w | w | w | w | w | w | w | w | w | w | w | w | w | w | w | w |
| Germany | 0.36 | (0.05) | -0.99 | (0.02) | 0.20 | (0.04) | 0.83 | (0.03) | 1.42 | (0.03) | **538** | (7.4) | 531 | (8.0) | 522 | (7.0) | 474 | (11.6) |
| Greece | -0.34 | (0.08) | c | c | c | c | c | c | c | c | c | c | c | c | c | c | c | c |
| Hungary | -0.56 | (0.05) | c | c | c | c | c | c | c | c | c | c | c | c | c | c | c | c |
| Iceland | 0.04 | (0.01) | -1.06 | (0.00) | -0.38 | (0.01) | 0.36 | (0.00) | 1.22 | (0.01) | **494** | (3.8) | 496 | (3.5) | 487 | (3.3) | 484 | (3.6) |
| Ireland | -0.21 | (0.07) | -1.06 | (0.00) | -0.83 | (0.04) | 0.10 | (0.02) | 0.93 | (0.09) | 510 | (5.6) | 508 | (6.1) | 502 | (6.8) | 513 | (6.4) |
| Italy | 0.06 | (0.07) | -1.06 | (0.00) | -0.52 | (0.03) | 0.52 | (0.02) | 1.30 | (0.07) | 464 | (7.2) | 467 | (5.4) | 489 | (5.3) | 484 | (5.8) |
| Japan | -0.51 | (0.05) | c | c | c | c | c | c | c | c | c | c | c | c | c | c | c | c |
| Korea | -0.51 | (0.07) | c | c | c | c | c | c | c | c | c | c | c | c | c | c | c | c |
| Luxembourg | 1.06 | (0.00) | -0.08 | (0.01) | 0.86 | (0.00) | 1.35 | (0.01) | 2.11 | (0.00) | 483 | (2.6) | 502 | (2.4) | 479 | (2.4) | 482 | (2.2) |
| Mexico | 0.66 | (0.05) | -0.70 | (0.03) | 0.52 | (0.02) | 1.02 | (0.02) | 1.81 | (0.05) | **427** | (4.1) | 414 | (5.4) | 404 | (6.0) | **392** | (7.2) |
| Netherlands | 0.13 | (0.06) | -1.06 | (0.00) | -0.21 | (0.04) | 0.53 | (0.03) | 1.26 | (0.07) | **538** | (8.6) | 530 | (7.7) | 521 | (12.0) | **510** | (9.7) |
| New Zealand | 0.37 | (0.04) | -0.73 | (0.05) | 0.19 | (0.02) | 0.71 | (0.02) | 1.33 | (0.04) | **551** | (6.9) | 532 | (5.7) | 520 | (6.2) | **523** | (4.9) |
| Norway | 0.35 | (0.05) | -0.78 | (0.05) | 0.23 | (0.02) | 0.78 | (0.01) | 1.15 | (0.02) | 479 | (9.2) | 492 | (4.4) | 487 | (4.2) | 485 | (4.0) |
| Poland | -0.84 | (0.04) | c | c | c | c | c | c | c | c | c | c | c | c | c | c | c | c |
| Portugal | -0.84 | (0.03) | c | c | c | c | c | c | c | c | c | c | c | c | c | c | c | c |
| Slovak Republic | -0.05 | (0.05) | -1.06 | (0.00) | -0.36 | (0.03) | 0.21 | (0.01) | 1.01 | (0.08) | **509** | (7.6) | 492 | (8.3) | 487 | (8.4) | **466** | (6.7) |
| Spain | -0.64 | (0.04) | c | c | c | c | c | c | c | c | c | c | c | c | c | c | c | c |
| Sweden | -0.36 | (0.06) | -1.06 | (0.00) | -0.97 | (0.02) | -0.13 | (0.02) | 0.71 | (0.06) | 506 | (4.4) | 508 | (4.4) | 504 | (4.0) | 496 | (6.0) |
| Switzerland | -0.06 | (0.04) | -1.06 | (0.00) | -0.44 | (0.03) | 0.28 | (0.02) | 0.97 | (0.03) | 525 | (7.0) | 512 | (4.6) | 510 | (7.9) | 501 | (7.6) |
| Turkey | 1.41 | (0.10) | -0.09 | (0.13) | 1.21 | (0.03) | 1.71 | (0.02) | 2.81 | (0.10) | 417 | (10.7) | 432 | (11.4) | 432 | (10.0) | 420 | (5.4) |
| United Kingdom | 0.08 | (0.06) | -1.06 | (0.00) | -0.40 | (0.04) | 0.43 | (0.04) | 1.34 | (0.07) | **527** | (7.6) | 527 | (5.9) | 512 | (6.4) | **501** | (6.1) |
| United States | -0.02 | (0.08) | -1.06 | (0.00) | -0.63 | (0.05) | 0.41 | (0.04) | 1.21 | (0.07) | 492 | (7.5) | 497 | (6.1) | 487 | (8.0) | 483 | (12.1) |
| **OECD total** | 0.04 | (0.03) | -1.06 | (0.00) | -0.65 | (0.02) | 0.44 | (0.02) | 1.43 | (0.03) | **505** | (2.3) | 506 | (2.3) | 490 | (3.4) | **462** | (4.2) |
| **OECD average** | 0.01 | (0.01) | -0.89 | (0.01) | -0.15 | (0.01) | 0.54 | (0.00) | 1.31 | (0.01) | **511** | (1.4) | 505 | (1.4) | 500 | (1.5) | **489** | (1.5) |
| **Partners** | | | | | | | | | | | | | | | | | | |
| Argentina | -0.26 | (0.07) | -1.06 | (0.00) | -1.02 | (0.01) | 0.04 | (0.05) | 1.02 | (0.05) | **416** | (9.2) | 410 | (9.6) | 376 | (9.3) | **366** | (12.8) |
| Azerbaijan | 0.63 | (0.09) | -0.90 | (0.04) | 0.54 | (0.04) | 1.13 | (0.02) | 1.75 | (0.08) | 375 | (5.3) | 397 | (6.2) | 389 | (6.0) | 372 | (3.7) |
| Brazil | 0.14 | (0.06) | -1.06 | (0.00) | -0.62 | (0.04) | 0.60 | (0.02) | 1.64 | (0.08) | **417** | (6.6) | 403 | (5.0) | 382 | (4.8) | **361** | (5.6) |
| Bulgaria | -0.41 | (0.05) | -1.06 | (0.00) | -0.82 | (0.03) | -0.18 | (0.02) | 0.44 | (0.05) | 424 | (10.2) | 429 | (9.3) | 437 | (9.4) | 450 | (15.3) |
| Chile | 0.50 | (0.09) | -0.90 | (0.04) | 0.16 | (0.04) | 1.01 | (0.03) | 1.71 | (0.06) | 450 | (10.8) | 437 | (8.9) | 436 | (9.3) | 435 | (8.8) |
| Colombia | 0.23 | (0.12) | -1.06 | (0.00) | -0.39 | (0.06) | 0.67 | (0.03) | 1.69 | (0.15) | **401** | (7.5) | 394 | (5.9) | 378 | (7.7) | **381** | (6.0) |
| Croatia | -0.26 | (0.05) | -1.06 | (0.00) | -0.82 | (0.05) | 0.09 | (0.02) | 0.76 | (0.05) | **509** | (5.1) | 501 | (5.3) | 480 | (7.2) | **480** | (6.5) |
| Estonia | 0.37 | (0.05) | -0.81 | (0.05) | 0.12 | (0.02) | 0.68 | (0.02) | 1.51 | (0.05) | 522 | (6.1) | 537 | (5.4) | 534 | (5.1) | 535 | (4.4) |
| Hong Kong-China | -0.20 | (0.09) | -1.06 | (0.00) | -0.92 | (0.03) | 0.08 | (0.04) | 1.11 | (0.11) | 549 | (6.5) | 547 | (6.0) | 537 | (9.9) | 532 | (8.9) |
| Indonesia | 0.71 | (0.06) | -0.60 | (0.07) | 0.47 | (0.04) | 1.01 | (0.02) | 1.94 | (0.08) | **413** | (8.6) | 395 | (12.6) | 385 | (9.9) | **376** | (6.3) |
| Israel | -0.25 | (0.09) | -1.06 | (0.00) | -0.98 | (0.02) | -0.03 | (0.04) | 1.05 | (0.14) | 469 | (7.8) | 467 | (7.4) | 439 | (8.7) | 440 | (11.1) |
| Jordan | 1.50 | (0.10) | -0.22 | (0.11) | 1.10 | (0.04) | 1.84 | (0.04) | 3.27 | (0.06) | **448** | (6.1) | 413 | (6.1) | 412 | (6.5) | **414** | (5.0) |
| Kyrgyzstan | 1.49 | (0.11) | -0.38 | (0.10) | 1.15 | (0.03) | 1.94 | (0.05) | 3.26 | (0.06) | 313 | (5.4) | 312 | (6.9) | 341 | (7.1) | 317 | (7.9) |
| Latvia | 0.03 | (0.07) | -1.05 | (0.00) | -0.21 | (0.01) | 0.29 | (0.02) | 1.08 | (0.10) | 487 | (6.2) | 484 | (5.8) | 492 | (6.8) | 495 | (5.7) |
| Liechtenstein | c | c | c | c | c | c | c | c | c | c | c | c | c | c | c | c | c | c |
| Lithuania | 0.03 | (0.07) | -1.06 | (0.00) | -0.33 | (0.02) | 0.25 | (0.02) | 1.27 | (0.11) | 486 | (5.9) | 497 | (8.3) | 486 | (7.1) | 484 | (7.3) |
| Macao-China | 0.07 | (0.00) | -1.06 | (0.00) | -0.70 | (0.02) | 0.32 | (0.00) | 1.70 | (0.00) | 520 | (2.3) | 516 | (2.9) | 499 | (3.2) | 508 | (2.1) |
| Montenegro | -0.51 | (0.00) | c | c | c | c | c | c | c | c | c | c | c | c | c | c | c | c |
| Qatar | 0.36 | (0.00) | -1.06 | (0.00) | -0.41 | (0.01) | 0.43 | (0.00) | 2.48 | (0.01) | **372** | (2.3) | 347 | (2.6) | 340 | (2.8) | **351** | (1.8) |
| Romania | -0.61 | (0.06) | c | c | c | c | c | c | c | c | c | c | c | c | c | c | c | c |
| Russian Federation | 0.52 | (0.09) | -1.03 | (0.01) | 0.09 | (0.03) | 0.85 | (0.03) | 2.17 | (0.14) | 480 | (6.0) | 489 | (6.5) | 477 | (6.0) | 466 | (8.7) |
| Serbia | -0.61 | (0.05) | c | c | c | c | c | c | c | c | c | c | c | c | c | c | c | c |
| Slovenia | -0.66 | (0.01) | c | c | c | c | c | c | c | c | c | c | c | c | c | c | c | c |
| Chinese Taipei | -0.31 | (0.10) | c | c | c | c | c | c | c | c | c | c | c | c | c | c | c | c |
| Thailand | 0.65 | (0.06) | -0.44 | (0.07) | 0.46 | (0.03) | 0.96 | (0.02) | 1.62 | (0.07) | **441** | (7.1) | 427 | (4.9) | 412 | (4.6) | **404** | (4.8) |
| Tunisia | 0.14 | (0.07) | -1.04 | (0.01) | -0.05 | (0.04) | 0.58 | (0.02) | 1.07 | (0.05) | 370 | (8.6) | 392 | (9.4) | 392 | (6.8) | 388 | (8.6) |
| Uruguay | 0.19 | (0.06) | -1.06 | (0.00) | -0.34 | (0.05) | 0.63 | (0.02) | 1.54 | (0.04) | **445** | (9.2) | 424 | (7.2) | 428 | (6.6) | **416** | (6.6) |

Note: Values that are statistically significant are indicated in bold (see Annex A3).
1. Results based on reports from school principals and reported proportionate to the number of 15-year-olds enrolled in the school.
*StatLink* ⌐⌐⌐ http://dx.doi.org/10.1787/142127877152

Pour consulter la version française intégrale de ce tableau, suivre ce lien :
*StatLink* ⌐⌐⌐ http://dx.doi.org/10.1787/152751048643

[Part 2/2]

**Table 5.14** Index of teacher shortage and student performance on the science scale, by quarters of the index[1] and student/teacher ratio

Tableau 5.14 Indice de pénurie d'enseignants et performance des élèves sur l'échelle de culture scientifique, par quartile de l'indice, et nombre d'élèves par enseignant

| | | Change in the science score per unit of the index of teacher shortage | | Increased likelihood of students in the top quarter of this index scoring in the bottom quarter of the science performance distribution | | Explained variance in student performance (r-squared X 100) | | Student/teacher ratio | | | |
|---|---|---|---|---|---|---|---|---|---|---|---|
| | | Effect | S.E. | Ratio | S.E. | % | S.E. | Mean | S.E. | S.D. | S.E. |
| *OECD* | Australia | **-15.2** | (2.64) | **0.7** | (0.06) | 2.3 | (0.81) | 13.4 | (0.14) | 2.5 | (0.35) |
| | Austria | -10.4 | (6.12) | 0.9 | (0.12) | 0.7 | (0.90) | 11.3 | (0.39) | 6.7 | (0.53) |
| | Belgium | **-23.6** | (3.59) | **0.5** | (0.08) | 6.4 | (1.99) | 9.1 | (0.12) | 3.0 | (0.12) |
| | Canada | **-4.3** | (1.81) | 1.0 | (0.08) | 0.2 | (0.20) | 16.7 | (0.13) | 3.0 | (0.14) |
| | Czech Republic | **-43.7** | (6.98) | **0.5** | (0.10) | 9.5 | (3.18) | 13.6 | (0.28) | 3.8 | (0.20) |
| | Denmark | -4.3 | (4.06) | 0.9 | (0.09) | 0.1 | (0.23) | 11.7 | (0.17) | 2.5 | (0.15) |
| | Finland | **-7.6** | (3.50) | 0.8 | (0.08) | 0.3 | (0.29) | 11.3 | (0.16) | 2.2 | (0.15) |
| | France | w | w | w | w | w | w | w | w | w | w |
| | Germany | **-21.9** | (5.38) | **0.7** | (0.12) | 4.1 | (1.96) | 17.2 | (0.27) | 4.9 | (0.31) |
| | Greece | c | c | c | c | c | c | 8.9 | (0.19) | 2.7 | (0.19) |
| | Hungary | c | c | c | c | c | c | 12.1 | (0.35) | 4.7 | (0.36) |
| | Iceland | **-4.0** | (1.54) | 0.9 | (0.08) | 0.1 | (0.11) | 10.9 | (0.01) | 2.1 | (0.01) |
| | Ireland | 0.8 | (4.23) | 0.9 | (0.11) | 0.0 | (0.14) | 13.3 | (0.14) | 2.1 | (0.12) |
| | Italy | 7.5 | (4.16) | 1.3 | (0.15) | 0.6 | (0.70) | 9.2 | (0.12) | 2.7 | (0.10) |
| | Japan | c | c | c | c | c | c | 12.8 | (0.30) | 4.6 | (0.25) |
| | Korea | c | c | c | c | c | c | 16.3 | (0.16) | 2.5 | (0.27) |
| | Luxembourg | **5.4** | (1.25) | 1.0 | (0.07) | 0.2 | (0.11) | 9.5 | (0.00) | 1.4 | (0.00) |
| | Mexico | **-13.0** | (2.69) | **0.7** | (0.08) | 2.6 | (1.00) | 27.1 | (0.63) | 11.4 | (0.43) |
| | Netherlands | **-12.3** | (5.23) | 0.8 | (0.14) | 1.4 | (1.22) | 16.0 | (0.33) | 4.4 | (0.60) |
| | New Zealand | **-15.2** | (3.69) | **0.7** | (0.10) | 1.3 | (0.63) | 15.8 | (0.21) | 3.0 | (0.33) |
| | Norway | 3.8 | (5.07) | 1.2 | (0.15) | 0.1 | (0.28) | 10.7 | (0.14) | 2.0 | (0.11) |
| | Poland | c | c | c | c | c | c | 11.3 | (0.14) | 2.3 | (0.13) |
| | Portugal | c | c | c | c | c | c | 8.9 | (0.19) | 2.6 | (0.17) |
| | Slovak Republic | **-18.1** | (4.87) | **0.7** | (0.11) | 2.6 | (1.41) | 15.0 | (0.28) | 3.7 | (0.21) |
| | Spain | c | c | c | c | c | c | 12.4 | (0.16) | 4.3 | (0.16) |
| | Sweden | -6.0 | (3.46) | 1.0 | (0.10) | 0.2 | (0.27) | 12.3 | (0.20) | 2.5 | (0.19) |
| | Switzerland | **-9.8** | (4.89) | 0.8 | (0.09) | 0.6 | (0.55) | 11.9 | (0.16) | 3.1 | (0.28) |
| | Turkey | 2.8 | (2.98) | 1.3 | (0.18) | 0.2 | (0.37) | 18.5 | (0.63) | 8.4 | (0.58) |
| | United Kingdom | **-11.7** | (3.65) | 0.9 | (0.10) | 1.1 | (0.72) | 15.3 | (0.14) | 2.7 | (0.21) |
| | United States | -2.8 | (5.26) | 1.0 | (0.14) | 0.1 | (0.25) | 15.3 | (0.41) | 4.7 | (0.24) |
| | **OECD total** | **-16.6** | (1.61) | **0.8** | (0.04) | 2.8 | (0.52) | 15.5 | (0.16) | 6.9 | (0.14) |
| | **OECD average** | **-9.3** | (0.90) | **0.9** | (0.02) | 1.6 | (0.23) | 13.4 | (0.05) | 3.7 | (0.05) |
| *Partners* | Argentina | **-25.1** | (7.17) | 0.7 | (0.16) | 5.1 | (2.82) | 11.4 | (0.63) | 6.5 | (0.49) |
| | Azerbaijan | 0.8 | (2.56) | 1.3 | (0.18) | 0.0 | (0.22) | 9.9 | (0.24) | 3.2 | (0.30) |
| | Brazil | **-19.7** | (2.91) | **0.7** | (0.08) | 6.4 | (1.68) | 31.4 | (0.95) | 15.5 | (0.94) |
| | Bulgaria | 17.1 | (12.22) | 1.2 | (0.16) | 1.0 | (1.48) | 11.7 | (0.23) | 2.4 | (0.30) |
| | Chile | -6.3 | (5.40) | 0.9 | (0.15) | 0.5 | (0.81) | 24.9 | (0.68) | 7.0 | (0.42) |
| | Colombia | **-8.2** | (2.76) | 0.8 | (0.13) | 1.2 | (0.82) | 23.9 | (1.30) | 11.1 | (1.02) |
| | Croatia | **-17.5** | (4.49) | **0.7** | (0.09) | 2.5 | (1.32) | 13.9 | (0.23) | 3.2 | (0.20) |
| | Estonia | 4.0 | (3.24) | **1.3** | (0.16) | 0.2 | (0.33) | 15.3 | (0.16) | 3.4 | (0.09) |
| | Hong Kong-China | -9.6 | (4.99) | 0.9 | (0.14) | 1.0 | (1.05) | 17.9 | (0.14) | 2.1 | (0.15) |
| | Indonesia | **-13.6** | (3.59) | **0.6** | (0.12) | 3.9 | (1.93) | 18.5 | (0.51) | 7.6 | (0.54) |
| | Israel | -13.0 | (7.66) | 0.8 | (0.11) | 1.2 | (1.43) | 12.7 | (0.42) | 5.7 | (0.45) |
| | Jordan | **-9.6** | (2.22) | **0.6** | (0.08) | 2.1 | (0.99) | 18.3 | (0.35) | 6.2 | (0.26) |
| | Kyrgyzstan | 1.2 | (2.60) | 1.1 | (0.13) | 0.0 | (0.19) | 16.4 | (0.36) | 5.2 | (0.33) |
| | Latvia | 5.6 | (3.32) | 1.0 | (0.14) | 0.3 | (0.37) | 11.7 | (0.36) | 3.9 | (0.71) |
| | Liechtenstein | c | c | c | c | c | c | c | c | c | c |
| | Lithuania | -3.9 | (3.64) | 1.0 | (0.12) | 0.2 | (0.36) | 12.1 | (0.18) | 2.7 | (0.09) |
| | Macao-China | **-8.5** | (0.67) | **0.8** | (0.07) | 1.7 | (0.26) | 21.4 | (0.01) | 4.4 | (0.01) |
| | Montenegro | c | c | c | c | c | c | 16.6 | (0.01) | 4.0 | (0.01) |
| | Qatar | **-3.6** | (0.60) | **0.8** | (0.05) | 0.4 | (0.13) | 10.7 | (0.02) | 3.0 | (0.03) |
| | Romania | c | c | c | c | c | c | 16.6 | (0.36) | 5.3 | (0.45) |
| | Russian Federation | -6.0 | (3.75) | 1.0 | (0.14) | 0.7 | (0.91) | 13.0 | (0.37) | 5.8 | (0.53) |
| | Serbia | c | c | c | c | c | c | 13.3 | (0.23) | 2.8 | (0.23) |
| | Slovenia | c | c | c | c | c | c | 14.3 | (0.02) | 4.9 | (0.02) |
| | Chinese Taipei | c | c | c | c | c | c | 17.7 | (0.38) | 5.6 | (0.31) |
| | Thailand | **-18.2** | (4.19) | **0.7** | (0.12) | 3.9 | (1.77) | 23.0 | (0.46) | 5.4 | (0.31) |
| | Tunisia | 8.6 | (5.52) | **1.4** | (0.21) | 0.7 | (0.93) | 15.6 | (0.20) | 2.8 | (0.19) |
| | Uruguay | **-10.5** | (3.97) | **0.7** | (0.16) | 1.4 | (1.12) | 15.9 | (0.31) | 5.5 | (0.16) |

Note: Values that are statistically significant are indicated in bold (see Annex A3).
1. Results based on reports from school principals and reported proportionate to the number of 15-year-olds enrolled in the school.
StatLink http://dx.doi.org/10.1787/142127877152

Pour consulter la version française intégrale de ce tableau, suivre ce lien :
StatLink http://dx.doi.org/10.1787/152751048643

[Part 1/2]

**Table 5.15** **School principals' perceptions of the quality of the schools' educational resources and student performance on the science scale, by quarters of the index[1] and number of computers for instruction per student**

Tableau 5.15  Qualité des moyens éducatifs des établissements, selon l'avis du chef d'établissement, et performance des élèves sur l'échelle de culture scientifique, par quartile de l'indice, et nombre d'ordinateur utilisés aux fins d'instruction par chaque élève

| | Index of the quality of the schools' educational resources | | | | | | | | | | Performance on the science scale by quarters of this index | | | | | | | |
|---|---|---|---|---|---|---|---|---|---|---|---|---|---|---|---|---|---|---|
| | All students | | Bottom quarter | | Second quarter | | Third quarter | | Top quarter | | Bottom quarter | | Second quarter | | Third quarter | | Top quarter | |
| | Mean index | S.E. | Mean index | S.E. | Mean index | S.E. | Mean index | S.E. | Mean index | S.E. | Mean score | S.E. | Mean score | S.E. | Mean score | S.E. | Mean score | S.E. |
| Australia | 0.40 | (0.05) | -0.84 | (0.06) | -0.08 | (0.02) | 0.58 | (0.03) | 1.95 | (0.04) | **515** | (4.4) | 514 | (4.7) | 528 | (4.1) | **550** | (5.3) |
| Austria | 0.36 | (0.08) | -0.85 | (0.07) | -0.09 | (0.02) | 0.60 | (0.03) | 1.79 | (0.07) | 503 | (12.1) | 511 | (9.1) | 523 | (7.1) | 507 | (10.4) |
| Belgium | -0.03 | (0.06) | -1.05 | (0.04) | -0.42 | (0.02) | 0.12 | (0.02) | 1.22 | (0.08) | 507 | (7.8) | 508 | (8.6) | 526 | (8.7) | 502 | (8.2) |
| Canada | 0.09 | (0.06) | -1.02 | (0.06) | -0.30 | (0.01) | 0.18 | (0.02) | 1.50 | (0.07) | 531 | (4.6) | 538 | (3.7) | 535 | (3.7) | 537 | (4.6) |
| Czech Republic | -0.08 | (0.06) | -0.95 | (0.06) | -0.34 | (0.02) | 0.07 | (0.02) | 0.91 | (0.09) | 514 | (7.4) | 513 | (9.7) | 510 | (8.2) | 520 | (10.8) |
| Denmark | -0.09 | (0.06) | -0.96 | (0.08) | -0.40 | (0.02) | -0.01 | (0.02) | 1.00 | (0.10) | 493 | (6.2) | 486 | (7.5) | 506 | (5.1) | 499 | (5.3) |
| Finland | -0.23 | (0.06) | -1.22 | (0.06) | -0.45 | (0.02) | -0.01 | (0.01) | 0.77 | (0.10) | 570 | (4.2) | 559 | (3.5) | 561 | (3.7) | 564 | (4.8) |
| France | w | w | w | w | w | w | w | w | w | w | w | w | w | w | w | w | w | w |
| Germany | 0.11 | (0.07) | -1.09 | (0.06) | -0.26 | (0.02) | 0.32 | (0.03) | 1.46 | (0.07) | 513 | (10.5) | 506 | (8.6) | 518 | (9.3) | 529 | (9.6) |
| Greece | -0.03 | (0.08) | -1.17 | (0.10) | -0.23 | (0.02) | 0.17 | (0.01) | 1.12 | (0.10) | **442** | (10.1) | 478 | (7.2) | 482 | (7.1) | **491** | (6.3) |
| Hungary | 0.20 | (0.07) | -0.81 | (0.07) | -0.11 | (0.02) | 0.35 | (0.02) | 1.37 | (0.08) | 490 | (9.2) | 505 | (9.0) | 511 | (8.1) | 511 | (8.1) |
| Iceland | 0.20 | (0.00) | -0.71 | (0.00) | -0.27 | (0.00) | 0.21 | (0.00) | 1.56 | (0.01) | **477** | (2.7) | 493 | (3.1) | 495 | (3.4) | **496** | (3.2) |
| Ireland | -0.32 | (0.07) | -1.33 | (0.06) | -0.70 | (0.02) | -0.13 | (0.03) | 0.89 | (0.10) | 508 | (5.4) | 509 | (7.4) | 505 | (6.0) | 512 | (7.6) |
| Italy | 0.18 | (0.05) | -0.98 | (0.04) | -0.20 | (0.01) | 0.35 | (0.01) | 1.55 | (0.04) | **460** | (6.7) | 473 | (6.1) | 481 | (6.0) | **487** | (6.7) |
| Japan | 0.45 | (0.07) | -0.75 | (0.07) | 0.02 | (0.02) | 0.65 | (0.03) | 1.87 | (0.05) | 517 | (7.6) | 528 | (8.6) | 530 | (11.5) | 551 | (8.2) |
| Korea | -0.19 | (0.06) | -1.12 | (0.08) | -0.44 | (0.02) | -0.05 | (0.01) | 0.85 | (0.10) | 513 | (9.5) | 514 | (8.4) | 532 | (5.1) | 530 | (8.7) |
| Luxembourg | 0.26 | (0.00) | -0.87 | (0.00) | -0.07 | (0.00) | 0.50 | (0.00) | 1.49 | (0.00) | 481 | (2.2) | 493 | (3.0) | 491 | (3.0) | 480 | (2.5) |
| Mexico | -0.86 | (0.06) | -2.20 | (0.05) | -1.25 | (0.02) | -0.61 | (0.02) | 0.63 | (0.10) | 389 | (4.7) | 389 | (4.0) | 420 | (5.5) | 439 | (5.6) |
| Netherlands | 0.26 | (0.07) | -0.73 | (0.04) | -0.17 | (0.02) | 0.37 | (0.02) | 1.57 | (0.08) | 512 | (10.8) | 522 | (11.4) | 533 | (8.2) | 532 | (9.3) |
| New Zealand | 0.30 | (0.06) | -0.75 | (0.03) | -0.14 | (0.02) | 0.40 | (0.02) | 1.72 | (0.06) | 525 | (6.7) | 525 | (5.3) | 529 | (5.6) | **549** | (8.1) |
| Norway | -0.43 | (0.05) | -1.15 | (0.04) | -0.65 | (0.02) | -0.31 | (0.01) | 0.37 | (0.07) | 486 | (4.8) | 486 | (8.9) | 489 | (5.0) | 483 | (4.7) |
| Poland | -0.09 | (0.07) | -1.08 | (0.05) | -0.48 | (0.02) | 0.11 | (0.02) | 1.10 | (0.10) | 503 | (4.7) | 495 | (5.4) | 491 | (4.4) | 502 | (4.4) |
| Portugal | -0.38 | (0.06) | -1.21 | (0.05) | -0.68 | (0.02) | -0.26 | (0.02) | 0.63 | (0.13) | 475 | (7.7) | 467 | (7.2) | 476 | (7.0) | 480 | (7.4) |
| Slovak Republic | -0.54 | (0.05) | -1.41 | (0.05) | -0.78 | (0.01) | -0.38 | (0.01) | 0.39 | (0.07) | 487 | (9.1) | 502 | (6.9) | 481 | (8.5) | 484 | (8.5) |
| Spain | -0.02 | (0.06) | -1.19 | (0.05) | -0.41 | (0.02) | 0.19 | (0.02) | 1.32 | (0.08) | **481** | (4.9) | 482 | (5.5) | 491 | (4.7) | **500** | (5.4) |
| Sweden | 0.05 | (0.06) | -0.91 | (0.04) | -0.35 | (0.02) | 0.17 | (0.03) | 1.28 | (0.08) | 493 | (3.8) | 504 | (5.1) | 510 | (4.2) | 506 | (4.8) |
| Switzerland | 0.67 | (0.06) | -0.53 | (0.04) | 0.14 | (0.02) | 0.94 | (0.03) | 2.13 | (0.06) | 495 | (6.0) | 513 | (7.6) | 501 | (5.9) | 535 | (7.1) |
| Turkey | -0.84 | (0.08) | -1.94 | (0.09) | -1.11 | (0.03) | -0.62 | (0.04) | 0.32 | (0.10) | 407 | (8.9) | 433 | (9.4) | 427 | (9.8) | 434 | (10.7) |
| United Kingdom | 0.27 | (0.08) | -0.96 | (0.05) | -0.22 | (0.02) | 0.52 | (0.03) | 1.74 | (0.05) | **506** | (5.4) | 512 | (4.6) | 517 | (5.9) | **532** | (7.4) |
| United States | 0.29 | (0.08) | -0.80 | (0.04) | -0.14 | (0.02) | 0.41 | (0.04) | 1.68 | (0.08) | 483 | (11.0) | 477 | (9.4) | 498 | (7.0) | 500 | (8.5) |
| **OECD total** | 0.03 | (0.03) | -1.23 | (0.02) | -0.35 | (0.01) | 0.21 | (0.01) | 1.47 | (0.04) | **462** | (3.5) | 489 | (3.1) | 499 | (3.0) | **514** | (2.9) |
| **OECD average** | 0.00 | (0.01) | -1.05 | (0.01) | -0.36 | (0.00) | 0.17 | (0.00) | 1.25 | (0.01) | 492 | (1.4) | 498 | (1.3) | 503 | (1.2) | 508 | (1.4) |
| Argentina | -0.55 | (0.08) | -2.18 | (0.10) | -0.86 | (0.03) | -0.27 | (0.04) | 1.10 | (0.11) | **349** | (9.3) | 379 | (14.5) | 408 | (11.1) | **432** | (8.3) |
| Azerbaijan | -1.37 | (0.05) | -2.36 | (0.06) | -1.62 | (0.02) | -1.14 | (0.03) | -0.35 | (0.06) | **374** | (5.7) | 381 | (5.6) | 385 | (4.9) | **391** | (6.3) |
| Brazil | -0.98 | (0.06) | -2.40 | (0.06) | -1.42 | (0.02) | -0.87 | (0.02) | 0.79 | (0.09) | 351 | (4.3) | 375 | (5.0) | 394 | (5.7) | 442 | (6.8) |
| Bulgaria | -0.58 | (0.05) | -1.41 | (0.05) | -0.80 | (0.02) | -0.39 | (0.01) | 0.26 | (0.08) | 423 | (12.1) | 428 | (12.6) | 447 | (14.3) | 438 | (12.8) |
| Chile | -0.63 | (0.09) | -2.01 | (0.12) | -0.85 | (0.02) | -0.27 | (0.02) | 0.61 | (0.08) | **412** | (9.4) | 432 | (7.8) | 444 | (8.0) | **467** | (8.5) |
| Colombia | -1.17 | (0.07) | -2.45 | (0.11) | -1.51 | (0.02) | -0.95 | (0.03) | 0.22 | (0.09) | 373 | (5.1) | 386 | (6.6) | 374 | (8.0) | 421 | (7.2) |
| Croatia | -0.55 | (0.06) | -1.44 | (0.04) | -0.84 | (0.02) | -0.38 | (0.02) | 0.44 | (0.09) | 492 | (7.0) | 483 | (7.8) | 500 | (6.0) | 499 | (7.9) |
| Estonia | -0.28 | (0.05) | -1.04 | (0.04) | -0.54 | (0.02) | -0.18 | (0.01) | 0.63 | (0.09) | 528 | (5.0) | 528 | (6.4) | 537 | (5.3) | 533 | (5.6) |
| Hong Kong-China | 0.35 | (0.08) | -0.76 | (0.09) | 0.02 | (0.02) | 0.52 | (0.02) | 1.61 | (0.07) | 539 | (8.8) | 544 | (7.4) | 539 | (9.5) | 547 | (9.0) |
| Indonesia | -1.63 | (0.09) | -3.33 | (0.03) | -2.09 | (0.03) | -1.14 | (0.06) | 0.06 | (0.13) | 373 | (7.4) | 381 | (6.0) | 404 | (10.4) | 413 | (11.7) |
| Israel | 0.07 | (0.09) | -1.29 | (0.07) | -0.32 | (0.03) | 0.27 | (0.03) | 1.61 | (0.09) | 444 | (9.2) | 443 | (9.6) | 466 | (9.5) | 464 | (10.3) |
| Jordan | -0.74 | (0.08) | -1.88 | (0.08) | -1.05 | (0.02) | -0.52 | (0.03) | 0.51 | (0.09) | **411** | (6.8) | 412 | (4.7) | 425 | (6.6) | **439** | (8.9) |
| Kyrgyzstan | -2.31 | (0.06) | -3.44 | (0.00) | -2.78 | (0.04) | -1.98 | (0.03) | -1.07 | (0.08) | **309** | (7.2) | 321 | (6.3) | 322 | (6.3) | **333** | (6.7) |
| Latvia | -0.54 | (0.04) | -1.40 | (0.06) | -0.71 | (0.01) | -0.32 | (0.02) | 0.29 | (0.05) | 493 | (6.7) | 491 | (7.7) | 484 | (5.8) | 490 | (6.0) |
| Liechtenstein | c | c | c | c | c | c | c | c | c | c | c | c | c | c | c | c | c | c |
| Lithuania | -0.39 | (0.05) | -1.17 | (0.06) | -0.60 | (0.01) | -0.23 | (0.02) | 0.45 | (0.07) | 475 | (6.8) | 491 | (8.6) | 494 | (6.8) | 492 | (6.1) |
| Macao-China | 0.06 | (0.00) | -0.97 | (0.00) | -0.10 | (0.00) | 0.45 | (0.00) | 0.87 | (0.00) | **510** | (1.8) | 510 | (2.0) | 499 | (3.2) | **524** | (1.7) |
| Montenegro | -1.26 | (0.00) | -2.35 | (0.01) | -1.49 | (0.00) | -1.12 | (0.00) | -0.08 | (0.01) | 404 | (2.0) | 411 | (3.5) | 426 | (3.3) | 406 | (1.9) |
| Qatar | -0.08 | (0.00) | -1.42 | (0.00) | -0.58 | (0.00) | 0.18 | (0.00) | 1.49 | (0.00) | **338** | (2.3) | 343 | (1.8) | 360 | (2.1) | **374** | (1.7) |
| Romania | -0.74 | (0.07) | -1.76 | (0.09) | -0.91 | (0.02) | -0.58 | (0.03) | 0.27 | (0.09) | 398 | (9.7) | 420 | (9.0) | 415 | (13.1) | 441 | (7.1) |
| Russian Federation | -1.18 | (0.04) | -2.15 | (0.05) | -1.36 | (0.02) | -0.98 | (0.02) | -0.22 | (0.07) | **467** | (5.5) | 482 | (7.9) | 480 | (6.1) | **489** | (5.9) |
| Serbia | -0.69 | (0.05) | -1.60 | (0.07) | -0.89 | (0.02) | -0.44 | (0.02) | 0.16 | (0.04) | 441 | (8.0) | 422 | (7.7) | 441 | (8.0) | 438 | (6.9) |
| Slovenia | 0.22 | (0.01) | -0.61 | (0.01) | -0.08 | (0.00) | 0.28 | (0.00) | 1.27 | (0.01) | **501** | (2.3) | 521 | (3.2) | 526 | (3.3) | **528** | (3.0) |
| Chinese Taipei | 0.59 | (0.12) | -1.34 | (0.18) | 0.35 | (0.02) | 1.23 | (0.03) | 2.14 | (0.00) | 522 | (11.3) | 540 | (7.4) | 534 | (5.7) | 537 | (7.9) |
| Thailand | -0.67 | (0.07) | -2.06 | (0.09) | -0.95 | (0.02) | -0.30 | (0.02) | 0.64 | (0.12) | **400** | (5.5) | 405 | (4.0) | 428 | (7.0) | **451** | (6.4) |
| Tunisia | -0.69 | (0.05) | -1.53 | (0.05) | -0.97 | (0.02) | -0.52 | (0.02) | 0.26 | (0.08) | 386 | (7.5) | 386 | (9.4) | 379 | (7.4) | 390 | (8.6) |
| Uruguay | -0.72 | (0.07) | -2.43 | (0.07) | -1.15 | (0.04) | -0.35 | (0.03) | 1.07 | (0.10) | **406** | (4.9) | 415 | (6.5) | 430 | (6.2) | **460** | (11.1) |

Note: Values that are statistically significant are indicated in bold (see Annex A3).
1. Results based on reports from school principals and reported proportionate to the number of 15-year-olds enrolled in the school.
*StatLink* http://dx.doi.org/10.1787/142127877152

Pour consulter la version française intégrale de ce tableau, suivre ce lien :
*StatLink* http://dx.doi.org/10.1787/152751048643

[Part 1/2]

**Table 5.15** School principals' perceptions of the quality of the schools' educational resources and student performance on the science scale, by quarters of the index[1] and number of computers for instruction per student

**Tableau 5.15** Qualité des moyens éducatifs des établissements, selon l'avis du chef d'établissement, et performance des élèves sur l'échelle de culture scientifique, par quartile de l'indice, et nombre d'ordinateur utilisés aux fins d'instruction par chaque élève

| | Change in the science score per unit of this index | | Increased likelihood of students in the top quarter of this index scoring in the bottom quarter of the science performance distribution | | Explained variance in student performance (r-squared X 100) | | Computers for instruction per student | | | |
|---|---|---|---|---|---|---|---|---|---|---|
| | Effect | S.E. | Ratio | S.E. | % | S.E. | Mean | S.E. | S.D. | S.E. |
| Australia | **13.4** | (2.16) | **1.2** | (0.09) | 2.1 | (0.62) | 0.26 | (0.01) | 0.16 | (0.02) |
| Austria | 1.9 | (5.97) | 1.2 | (0.24) | 0.0 | (0.45) | 0.23 | (0.01) | 0.18 | (0.02) |
| Belgium | -0.6 | (4.53) | 1.0 | (0.14) | 0.0 | (0.18) | 0.14 | (0.01) | 0.13 | (0.02) |
| Canada | 2.4 | (2.21) | 1.1 | (0.09) | 0.1 | (0.14) | 0.19 | (0.01) | 0.12 | (0.01) |
| Czech Republic | 3.0 | (6.42) | 1.0 | (0.15) | 0.1 | (0.29) | 0.12 | (0.01) | 0.14 | (0.04) |
| Denmark | 3.1 | (3.11) | 1.1 | (0.12) | 0.1 | (0.16) | 0.18 | (0.01) | 0.08 | (0.01) |
| Finland | -1.4 | (3.19) | **0.8** | (0.08) | 0.0 | (0.10) | 0.15 | (0.01) | 0.08 | (0.01) |
| France | w | w | w | w | w | w | w | w | w | w |
| Germany | 6.6 | (4.92) | 1.0 | (0.19) | 0.4 | (0.75) | 0.09 | (0.00) | 0.07 | (0.01) |
| Greece | **17.3** | (5.58) | **1.9** | (0.29) | 3.2 | (1.88) | 0.08 | (0.00) | 0.07 | (0.01) |
| Hungary | 7.5 | (5.98) | 1.3 | (0.22) | 0.6 | (0.93) | 0.19 | (0.01) | 0.18 | (0.02) |
| Iceland | **5.5** | (1.57) | **1.3** | (0.09) | 0.3 | (0.16) | 0.15 | (0.00) | 0.09 | (0.00) |
| Ireland | 1.7 | (4.98) | 1.0 | (0.12) | 0.0 | (0.24) | 0.10 | (0.00) | 0.06 | (0.00) |
| Italy | **9.7** | (3.64) | **1.4** | (0.16) | 1.0 | (0.77) | 0.12 | (0.01) | 0.13 | (0.01) |
| Japan | **11.9** | (3.91) | 1.2 | (0.16) | 1.4 | (1.00) | 0.20 | (0.02) | 0.20 | (0.03) |
| Korea | 5.5 | (6.55) | 1.2 | (0.19) | 0.3 | (0.64) | 0.18 | (0.01) | 0.18 | (0.01) |
| Luxembourg | -0.6 | (1.18) | 1.1 | (0.06) | 0.0 | (0.02) | 0.24 | (0.00) | 0.23 | (0.00) |
| Mexico | **18.3** | (2.29) | **1.5** | (0.17) | 6.8 | (1.56) | 0.07 | (0.01) | 0.09 | (0.01) |
| Netherlands | 8.9 | (6.27) | 1.3 | (0.23) | 0.7 | (1.05) | 0.15 | (0.01) | 0.08 | (0.01) |
| New Zealand | **12.5** | (3.81) | 1.1 | (0.13) | 1.3 | (0.78) | 0.19 | (0.01) | 0.10 | (0.02) |
| Norway | -1.4 | (4.11) | 1.0 | (0.10) | 0.0 | (0.07) | 0.22 | (0.01) | 0.10 | (0.01) |
| Poland | 1.3 | (2.52) | 0.9 | (0.10) | 0.0 | (0.09) | 0.07 | (0.00) | 0.07 | (0.01) |
| Portugal | 6.9 | (4.95) | 1.0 | (0.15) | 0.4 | (0.70) | 0.07 | (0.00) | 0.04 | (0.00) |
| Slovak Republic | -6.9 | (5.83) | 1.0 | (0.19) | 0.3 | (0.59) | 0.08 | (0.00) | 0.06 | (0.01) |
| Spain | 7.5 | (2.87) | 1.2 | (0.10) | 0.7 | (0.53) | 0.10 | (0.00) | 0.09 | (0.00) |
| Sweden | 4.5 | (3.09) | 1.2 | (0.09) | 0.2 | (0.26) | 0.12 | (0.01) | 0.09 | (0.01) |
| Switzerland | **12.8** | (3.39) | **1.2** | (0.11) | 1.7 | (0.93) | 0.17 | (0.01) | 0.13 | (0.02) |
| Turkey | 5.3 | (5.05) | 1.4 | (0.23) | 0.3 | (0.70) | 0.05 | (0.00) | 0.05 | (0.01) |
| United Kingdom | **9.3** | (3.59) | 1.2 | (0.11) | 0.8 | (0.68) | 0.28 | (0.01) | 0.12 | (0.02) |
| United States | **10.4** | (5.24) | 1.1 | (0.22) | 0.9 | (0.98) | 0.23 | (0.01) | 0.13 | (0.01) |
| **OECD total** | **19.1** | (1.49) | **1.6** | (0.09) | 3.8 | (0.59) | 0.16 | (0.00) | 0.14 | (0.01) |
| **OECD average** | **6.1** | (0.81) | **1.2** | (0.03) | 0.8 | (0.14) | 0.15 | (0.00) | 0.11 | (0.00) |
| Argentina | **27.2** | (3.39) | **1.9** | (0.37) | 12.1 | (3.09) | 0.04 | (0.00) | 0.04 | (0.01) |
| Azerbaijan | 6.0 | (4.13) | 1.3 | (0.19) | 0.8 | (1.07) | 0.01 | (0.00) | 0.01 | (0.00) |
| Brazil | **30.2** | (2.14) | **1.9** | (0.18) | 19.0 | (2.46) | 0.02 | (0.00) | 0.05 | (0.02) |
| Bulgaria | 11.8 | (10.08) | 1.2 | (0.19) | 0.6 | (1.04) | 0.05 | (0.00) | 0.03 | (0.00) |
| Chile | **22.2** | (3.39) | **1.7** | (0.21) | 6.6 | (2.25) | 0.04 | (0.00) | 0.03 | (0.00) |
| Colombia | **16.8** | (3.19) | **1.3** | (0.14) | 4.6 | (1.62) | 0.10 | (0.02) | 0.21 | (0.04) |
| Croatia | 3.8 | (5.37) | 1.0 | (0.15) | 0.1 | (0.37) | 0.06 | (0.00) | 0.04 | (0.00) |
| Estonia | -1.2 | (5.01) | 1.0 | (0.13) | 0.0 | (0.17) | 0.07 | (0.00) | 0.04 | (0.00) |
| Hong Kong-China | 5.0 | (4.98) | 1.1 | (0.17) | 0.3 | (0.58) | 0.20 | (0.01) | 0.08 | (0.01) |
| Indonesia | **12.3** | (3.78) | 1.4 | (0.24) | 5.5 | (3.11) | 0.03 | (0.00) | 0.04 | (0.01) |
| Israel | 6.7 | (4.03) | 1.1 | (0.15) | 0.5 | (0.56) | 0.10 | (0.01) | 0.07 | (0.01) |
| Jordan | **12.5** | (3.00) | 1.2 | (0.15) | 1.8 | (0.91) | 0.05 | (0.00) | 0.03 | (0.00) |
| Kyrgyzstan | **10.7** | (3.68) | 1.3 | (0.16) | 1.6 | (1.12) | 0.01 | (0.00) | 0.02 | (0.01) |
| Latvia | -0.8 | (4.83) | 0.9 | (0.13) | 0.0 | (0.12) | 0.06 | (0.00) | 0.04 | (0.00) |
| Liechtenstein | c | c | c | c | c | c | c | c | c | c |
| Lithuania | **12.4** | (4.81) | 1.2 | (0.15) | 0.9 | (0.69) | 0.06 | (0.00) | 0.03 | (0.00) |
| Macao-China | **4.8** | (1.29) | 1.1 | (0.05) | 0.2 | (0.11) | 0.13 | (0.00) | 0.05 | (0.00) |
| Montenegro | **3.6** | (0.91) | 1.0 | (0.07) | 0.2 | (0.09) | 0.03 | (0.00) | 0.04 | (0.00) |
| Qatar | **15.1** | (0.80) | **1.2** | (0.07) | 4.0 | (0.43) | 0.12 | (0.00) | 0.10 | (0.00) |
| Romania | 16.6 | (6.17) | 1.8 | (0.42) | 3.0 | (2.13) | 0.06 | (0.00) | 0.06 | (0.01) |
| Russian Federation | **10.7** | (3.59) | 1.2 | (0.12) | 0.9 | (0.58) | 0.03 | (0.00) | 0.02 | (0.00) |
| Serbia | 1.7 | (6.32) | 0.9 | (0.15) | 0.0 | (0.25) | 0.05 | (0.00) | 0.04 | (0.01) |
| Slovenia | **4.5** | (2.15) | **1.2** | (0.07) | 0.1 | (0.12) | 0.14 | (0.00) | 0.16 | (0.00) |
| Chinese Taipei | 5.8 | (4.17) | 1.3 | (0.23) | 0.7 | (1.10) | 0.14 | (0.01) | 0.12 | (0.02) |
| Thailand | **18.5** | (2.80) | **1.5** | (0.16) | 6.9 | (1.82) | 0.08 | (0.00) | 0.07 | (0.01) |
| Tunisia | -0.8 | (5.49) | 1.0 | (0.16) | 0.0 | (0.22) | 0.02 | (0.00) | 0.01 | (0.00) |
| Uruguay | **17.2** | (2.62) | **1.4** | (0.18) | 6.2 | (1.97) | 0.05 | (0.00) | 0.05 | (0.00) |

Note: Values that are statistically significant are indicated in bold (see Annex A3).
1. Results based on reports from school principals and reported proportionate to the number of 15-year-olds enrolled in the school.
*StatLink* ᴍᴤᴸ http://dx.doi.org/10.1787/142127877152

Pour consulter la version française intégrale de ce tableau, suivre ce lien :
*StatLink* ᴍᴤᴸ http://dx.doi.org/10.1787/152751048643

[Part 1/2]
**Table 5.16 Percentage of students taking various science courses[1]**

Tableau 5.16  Pourcentage d'élèves par matière scientifique

| | General science courses | | | | Biology courses | | | | Physics courses | | | |
| | Compulsory | | Optional | | Compulsory | | Optional | | Compulsory | | Optional | |
| | % | S.E. | % | S.E. | % | S.E. | % | S.E. | % | S.E. | % | S.E. |
|---|---|---|---|---|---|---|---|---|---|---|---|---|
| Australia | 64.0 | (1.1) | 27.3 | (1.0) | 26.0 | (0.9) | 15.4 | (0.6) | 26.7 | (1.0) | 12.5 | (0.6) |
| Austria | a | a | a | a | 55.4 | (1.6) | 11.1 | (0.8) | 48.8 | (1.8) | 5.6 | (0.5) |
| Belgium | 55.0 | (1.2) | 12.4 | (0.5) | 46.5 | (1.3) | 8.0 | (0.6) | 55.1 | (1.4) | 11.9 | (0.6) |
| Canada | 84.4 | (0.4) | 17.8 | (0.5) | 31.1 | (0.7) | 11.9 | (0.4) | 32.8 | (0.6) | 8.2 | (0.3) |
| Czech Republic | 47.9 | (1.3) | 11.2 | (0.9) | 65.8 | (2.8) | 7.6 | (0.8) | 80.7 | (2.3) | 5.7 | (0.7) |
| Denmark | 15.9 | (0.8) | 7.1 | (0.5) | 85.9 | (0.8) | 9.2 | (0.7) | 89.3 | (0.7) | 10.6 | (0.7) |
| Finland | 86.2 | (0.8) | 7.1 | (0.7) | 95.1 | (0.5) | 4.6 | (0.5) | 94.7 | (0.5) | 4.5 | (0.5) |
| France | a | a | a | a | 82.1 | (1.3) | 5.2 | (0.5) | 92.9 | (0.4) | 5.2 | (0.4) |
| Germany | 68.9 | (1.1) | 20.5 | (1.1) | 73.5 | (1.2) | 11.2 | (0.8) | 81.0 | (0.9) | 8.9 | (0.6) |
| Greece | a | a | a | a | 22.1 | (0.7) | 11.5 | (0.6) | 83.5 | (0.8) | 29.1 | (0.8) |
| Hungary | a | a | a | a | 61.5 | (2.1) | 7.6 | (0.6) | 78.4 | (1.7) | 8.3 | (0.6) |
| Iceland | 86.2 | (0.5) | 31.9 | (0.7) | 71.0 | (0.7) | 21.0 | (0.6) | 72.3 | (0.6) | 22.7 | (0.5) |
| Ireland | 50.3 | (2.1) | 31.7 | (1.5) | a | a | 23.1 | (0.9) | a | a | 10.5 | (0.7) |
| Italy | 54.5 | (1.3) | a | a | 65.5 | (1.7) | a | a | 49.9 | (1.3) | a | a |
| Japan | 87.7 | (1.2) | 13.0 | (1.0) | 45.6 | (2.0) | 9.3 | (0.7) | 42.9 | (2.0) | 7.3 | (0.5) |
| Korea | 89.9 | (1.1) | 45.6 | (1.8) | a | a | 41.9 | (1.8) | a | a | 45.7 | (1.8) |
| Luxembourg | a | a | a | a | 78.7 | (0.5) | 16.1 | (0.5) | 65.8 | (0.5) | 12.0 | (0.5) |
| Mexico | 21.9 | (0.7) | 18.1 | (0.8) | 22.6 | (0.9) | 19.8 | (0.9) | 39.7 | (1.0) | 28.1 | (0.9) |
| Netherlands | 54.2 | (1.3) | 21.3 | (0.7) | 47.4 | (1.4) | 24.7 | (1.0) | 48.8 | (1.1) | 19.4 | (0.7) |
| New Zealand | 70.0 | (1.5) | 32.1 | (1.3) | 30.4 | (1.2) | 18.2 | (0.9) | 31.3 | (1.1) | 17.0 | (0.8) |
| Norway | 100.0 | (0.0) | a | a | a | a | a | a | a | a | a | a |
| Poland | a | a | a | a | 100.0 | (0.0) | a | a | 100.0 | (0.0) | a | a |
| Portugal | 72.9 | (1.1) | 30.8 | (0.9) | 23.8 | (1.2) | 15.7 | (0.6) | 48.6 | (1.1) | 20.1 | (0.8) |
| Slovak Republic | a | a | a | a | 65.9 | (2.1) | 9.7 | (0.6) | 80.1 | (2.2) | 8.1 | (0.6) |
| Spain | 58.4 | (0.9) | 29.3 | (0.8) | 56.6 | (1.0) | 33.2 | (1.0) | 64.4 | (0.7) | 35.4 | (0.9) |
| Sweden | 57.1 | (1.2) | 5.1 | (0.4) | 58.8 | (1.2) | 4.6 | (0.3) | 60.2 | (1.2) | 4.7 | (0.3) |
| Switzerland | 73.0 | (1.0) | 14.0 | (0.7) | 54.9 | (1.3) | 6.6 | (0.4) | 58.4 | (1.2) | 8.1 | (0.4) |
| Turkey | 44.9 | (1.6) | 20.3 | (0.8) | 49.7 | (1.8) | 21.2 | (1.0) | 54.5 | (1.9) | 22.8 | (1.0) |
| United Kingdom | m | m | m | m | m | m | m | m | m | m | m | m |
| United States | 64.5 | (1.0) | 25.9 | (0.7) | 52.2 | (1.9) | 15.2 | (0.7) | 16.9 | (0.9) | 11.0 | (0.7) |
| **OECD total** | 60.4 | (0.4) | 22.4 | (0.3) | 52.1 | (0.7) | 15.8 | (0.3) | 45.4 | (0.4) | 15.3 | (0.3) |
| **OECD average** | 64.0 | (0.2) | 21.1 | (0.2) | 56.5 | (0.3) | 14.8 | (0.2) | 61.4 | (0.2) | 14.7 | (0.1) |
| Argentina | 16.4 | (0.9) | 10.1 | (0.8) | 17.2 | (1.1) | 11.1 | (0.9) | 21.3 | (1.1) | 12.7 | (0.9) |
| Azerbaijan | a | a | a | a | 70.3 | (1.0) | 43.1 | (1.5) | 69.2 | (1.1) | 43.8 | (1.5) |
| Brazil | 8.0 | (0.5) | 5.5 | (0.4) | 9.6 | (0.7) | 5.8 | (0.4) | 11.2 | (0.7) | 7.3 | (0.4) |
| Bulgaria | a | a | a | a | 90.0 | (0.8) | 27.4 | (1.3) | 88.2 | (0.7) | 22.8 | (1.1) |
| Chile | 51.4 | (1.2) | 15.9 | (1.1) | 67.4 | (1.4) | 17.3 | (0.8) | 67.1 | (1.4) | 15.7 | (0.7) |
| Colombia | 12.8 | (0.9) | 14.9 | (2.2) | 12.7 | (0.9) | 15.0 | (2.1) | 15.6 | (0.9) | 18.3 | (2.2) |
| Croatia | a | a | a | a | 63.1 | (1.4) | 3.6 | (0.4) | 58.6 | (2.6) | 2.7 | (0.3) |
| Estonia | 41.6 | (0.9) | 9.9 | (0.5) | 78.5 | (1.0) | 14.2 | (0.8) | 76.8 | (1.0) | 10.3 | (0.5) |
| Hong Kong-China | 22.7 | (0.8) | 11.0 | (0.7) | 44.5 | (1.0) | 15.5 | (0.8) | 46.4 | (0.9) | 13.9 | (0.7) |
| Indonesia | 80.9 | (1.0) | 48.6 | (1.0) | 73.6 | (2.9) | 43.2 | (1.4) | 77.3 | (1.1) | 43.8 | (0.9) |
| Israel | 49.1 | (1.3) | 27.3 | (1.1) | 47.3 | (1.5) | 23.3 | (0.8) | 39.2 | (1.5) | 22.2 | (0.9) |
| Jordan | 51.5 | (1.9) | 28.4 | (1.3) | 71.8 | (1.3) | 28.3 | (1.2) | 71.9 | (1.3) | 27.4 | (1.2) |
| Kyrgyzstan | 64.6 | (1.0) | 43.0 | (1.2) | 72.5 | (0.9) | 46.3 | (1.1) | 67.6 | (1.1) | 42.3 | (1.1) |
| Latvia | 73.5 | (0.9) | 22.7 | (0.9) | 90.0 | (0.6) | 17.3 | (0.9) | 91.7 | (0.7) | 17.4 | (0.9) |
| Liechtenstein | 78.2 | (2.3) | 22.5 | (2.1) | 79.7 | (2.2) | 15.2 | (1.8) | 74.1 | (2.2) | 15.0 | (1.9) |
| Lithuania | a | a | a | a | 78.8 | (0.8) | 11.6 | (0.6) | 81.0 | (0.7) | 11.7 | (0.6) |
| Macao-China | 33.1 | (0.7) | 17.7 | (0.6) | 35.0 | (0.5) | 16.1 | (0.6) | 47.4 | (0.8) | 19.0 | (0.7) |
| Montenegro | 76.6 | (0.8) | 31.9 | (0.8) | 78.8 | (0.6) | 22.6 | (0.7) | 80.8 | (0.6) | 20.8 | (0.7) |
| Qatar | 60.4 | (0.7) | 36.6 | (0.7) | 56.2 | (0.7) | 32.6 | (0.6) | 56.5 | (0.7) | 33.1 | (0.7) |
| Romania | 29.3 | (1.4) | 21.5 | (1.0) | 41.1 | (1.5) | 20.2 | (1.1) | 44.4 | (1.8) | 20.0 | (1.0) |
| Russian Federation | 2.9 | (0.8) | 1.3 | (0.3) | 98.7 | (0.3) | 1.4 | (0.4) | 98.4 | (0.4) | 1.4 | (0.4) |
| Serbia | a | a | a | a | 72.1 | (1.4) | a | a | 78.9 | (1.1) | a | a |
| Slovenia | 55.9 | (0.8) | 5.8 | (0.4) | 77.3 | (0.3) | 7.2 | (0.4) | 65.8 | (0.4) | 5.4 | (0.4) |
| Chinese Taipei | 33.8 | (0.9) | 15.0 | (0.6) | 34.9 | (1.3) | 14.7 | (0.6) | 72.8 | (1.5) | 15.9 | (0.7) |
| Thailand | 81.0 | (1.0) | 50.5 | (1.0) | 61.5 | (1.4) | 41.4 | (1.0) | 55.7 | (1.2) | 37.9 | (1.0) |
| Tunisia | 64.6 | (1.0) | 44.8 | (1.2) | 47.9 | (1.0) | 34.2 | (0.9) | 66.9 | (0.9) | 43.8 | (1.0) |
| Uruguay | 37.8 | (1.1) | 7.4 | (0.5) | 54.0 | (1.1) | 9.8 | (0.7) | 56.9 | (1.0) | 9.8 | (0.7) |

1. Results based on students' self-reports.

StatLink ⟜ http://dx.doi.org/10.1787/142127877152

Pour consulter la version française intégrale de ce tableau, suivre ce lien :

StatLink ⟜ http://dx.doi.org/10.1787/152751048643

**Table 5.16**  **Percentage of students taking various science courses**[1]
[Part 2/2]

Tableau 5.16   Pourcentage d'élèves par matière scientifique

| | | Students taking various science courses | | | | Students taking any science courses that are | | | | | |
|---|---|---|---|---|---|---|---|---|---|---|---|
| | | Chemistry courses | | | | | | | | | |
| | | Compulsory | | Optional | | Compulsory | | Optional | | Compulsory or optional | |
| | | % | S.E. | % | S.E. | % | S.E. | % | S.E. | % | S.E. |
| OECD | Australia | 28.2 | (0.9) | 13.7 | (0.6) | 66.3 | (1.0) | 33.3 | (1.1) | 81.3 | (0.6) |
| | Austria | 38.8 | (2.0) | 6.2 | (0.5) | 83.0 | (1.0) | 15.9 | (0.9) | 84.3 | (1.0) |
| | Belgium | 47.9 | (1.2) | 9.7 | (0.5) | 86.2 | (0.7) | 23.5 | (0.8) | 87.7 | (0.6) |
| | Canada | 26.8 | (0.6) | 8.4 | (0.4) | 91.3 | (0.3) | 24.9 | (0.6) | 94.2 | (0.3) |
| | Czech Republic | 76.3 | (2.3) | 5.5 | (0.8) | 88.3 | (1.8) | 18.0 | (1.2) | 89.4 | (1.7) |
| | Denmark | 89.3 | (0.7) | 13.0 | (0.6) | 90.4 | (0.7) | 20.6 | (0.8) | 91.1 | (0.6) |
| | Finland | 73.3 | (1.6) | 3.8 | (0.6) | 97.8 | (0.4) | 11.9 | (0.9) | 97.9 | (0.4) |
| | France | 92.9 | (0.4) | 5.2 | (0.4) | 94.7 | (0.3) | 8.4 | (0.6) | 95.0 | (0.3) |
| | Germany | 78.7 | (1.1) | 9.6 | (0.8) | 91.2 | (0.5) | 26.8 | (1.2) | 93.9 | (0.5) |
| | Greece | 81.4 | (0.8) | 25.2 | (0.8) | 87.6 | (0.6) | 36.3 | (1.0) | 90.2 | (0.5) |
| | Hungary | 77.9 | (1.5) | 7.9 | (0.5) | 87.5 | (1.1) | 14.2 | (0.7) | 88.4 | (1.1) |
| | Iceland | 63.5 | (0.7) | 21.3 | (0.6) | 91.7 | (0.4) | 35.6 | (0.7) | 95.1 | (0.3) |
| | Ireland | a | a | 10.0 | (0.6) | 50.3 | (2.1) | 46.3 | (1.4) | 84.9 | (1.0) |
| | Italy | 47.3 | (1.4) | a | a | 90.1 | (1.3) | a | a | 90.1 | (1.3) |
| | Japan | 66.3 | (2.0) | 9.6 | (0.6) | 91.1 | (1.1) | 19.8 | (1.1) | 92.0 | (1.1) |
| | Korea | a | a | 43.9 | (1.8) | 89.9 | (1.1) | 64.5 | (1.8) | 91.9 | (1.0) |
| | Luxembourg | 64.9 | (0.5) | 12.2 | (0.5) | 84.7 | (0.4) | 21.7 | (0.5) | 87.7 | (0.4) |
| | Mexico | 51.0 | (1.0) | 35.0 | (1.0) | 59.8 | (0.9) | 45.6 | (0.9) | 69.8 | (0.9) |
| | Netherlands | 44.8 | (1.2) | 17.1 | (0.7) | 80.2 | (0.9) | 38.8 | (1.1) | 86.9 | (0.8) |
| | New Zealand | 31.6 | (1.1) | 17.0 | (0.8) | 73.7 | (1.4) | 43.3 | (1.5) | 90.4 | (0.7) |
| | Norway | a | a | a | a | 100.0 | (0.0) | a | a | 100.0 | (0.0) |
| | Poland | 100.0 | (0.0) | a | a | 100.0 | (0.0) | a | a | 100.0 | (0.0) |
| | Portugal | 45.8 | (1.1) | 18.1 | (0.7) | 78.0 | (1.0) | 37.8 | (1.0) | 82.2 | (0.8) |
| | Slovak Republic | 78.0 | (1.8) | 7.2 | (0.6) | 94.5 | (0.5) | 15.9 | (0.8) | 95.3 | (0.5) |
| | Spain | 61.8 | (0.7) | 34.3 | (0.9) | 79.6 | (0.8) | 49.5 | (1.0) | 91.6 | (0.5) |
| | Sweden | 58.8 | (1.1) | 5.0 | (0.4) | 65.3 | (1.1) | 8.7 | (0.5) | 66.2 | (1.1) |
| | Switzerland | 52.3 | (1.3) | 7.6 | (0.4) | 88.3 | (0.7) | 20.3 | (0.7) | 89.7 | (0.7) |
| | Turkey | 49.4 | (1.8) | 20.7 | (0.8) | 60.8 | (1.9) | 30.2 | (1.2) | 64.8 | (1.9) |
| | United Kingdom | m | m | m | m | m | m | m | m | m | m |
| | United States | 27.3 | (1.5) | 12.7 | (0.7) | 85.7 | (0.8) | 38.8 | (0.9) | 91.7 | (0.6) |
| | **OECD total** | 50.1 | (0.6) | 16.4 | (0.3) | | | | | | |
| | **OECD average** | 59.8 | (0.3) | 14.6 | (0.1) | 83.7 | (0.2) | 28.9 | (0.2) | 87.4 | (0.2) |
| Partners | Argentina | 15.6 | (1.0) | 10.4 | (0.8) | 30.5 | (1.4) | 21.8 | (1.2) | 36.7 | (1.4) |
| | Azerbaijan | 68.5 | (1.1) | 41.9 | (1.6) | 78.3 | (0.9) | 56.2 | (1.6) | 86.9 | (0.7) |
| | Brazil | 10.9 | (0.7) | 6.5 | (0.4) | 16.6 | (0.7) | 13.1 | (0.6) | 20.3 | (0.8) |
| | Bulgaria | 88.4 | (0.8) | 24.2 | (1.3) | 93.4 | (0.5) | 35.2 | (1.4) | 94.7 | (0.5) |
| | Chile | 67.7 | (1.3) | 16.4 | (0.9) | 75.1 | (1.3) | 28.8 | (1.1) | 78.7 | (1.1) |
| | Colombia | 15.8 | (0.8) | 19.2 | (2.9) | 24.8 | (1.2) | 30.4 | (2.4) | 39.5 | (2.2) |
| | Croatia | 64.2 | (1.6) | 3.3 | (0.3) | 76.8 | (1.4) | 6.8 | (0.4) | 77.5 | (1.4) |
| | Estonia | 76.8 | (1.0) | 11.6 | (0.6) | 83.8 | (0.9) | 23.6 | (0.9) | 87.2 | (0.8) |
| | Hong Kong-China | 46.4 | (0.9) | 14.1 | (0.7) | 55.7 | (0.9) | 22.0 | (0.9) | 61.0 | (0.9) |
| | Indonesia | 59.4 | (1.8) | 37.0 | (1.2) | 88.9 | (0.9) | 64.4 | (1.0) | 92.7 | (0.9) |
| | Israel | 36.7 | (1.5) | 20.1 | (0.8) | 68.6 | (1.2) | 44.2 | (1.1) | 74.7 | (1.1) |
| | Jordan | 72.3 | (1.3) | 29.2 | (1.4) | 82.8 | (1.3) | 42.9 | (1.5) | 88.7 | (1.1) |
| | Kyrgyzstan | 69.4 | (1.1) | 44.3 | (1.1) | 85.9 | (0.7) | 66.7 | (1.1) | 89.1 | (0.6) |
| | Latvia | 91.8 | (0.6) | 16.5 | (0.8) | 97.4 | (0.3) | 35.3 | (1.0) | 98.1 | (0.2) |
| | Liechtenstein | 59.0 | (2.6) | 15.0 | (1.9) | 92.1 | (1.5) | 28.2 | (2.0) | 92.4 | (1.5) |
| | Lithuania | 80.9 | (0.8) | 12.0 | (0.6) | 84.0 | (0.7) | 18.4 | (0.9) | 85.4 | (0.7) |
| | Macao-China | 44.8 | (0.7) | 18.2 | (0.7) | 56.6 | (0.7) | 31.4 | (0.7) | 63.0 | (0.7) |
| | Montenegro | 78.8 | (0.7) | 21.0 | (0.6) | 93.8 | (0.4) | 43.8 | (0.8) | 95.5 | (0.3) |
| | Qatar | 56.8 | (0.7) | 33.1 | (0.7) | 74.8 | (0.6) | 52.0 | (0.6) | 80.8 | (0.5) |
| | Romania | 45.9 | (2.0) | 21.0 | (1.0) | 59.6 | (1.4) | 42.7 | (1.2) | 66.9 | (1.4) |
| | Russian Federation | 98.4 | (0.3) | 0.9 | (0.3) | 99.1 | (0.2) | 2.4 | (0.7) | 99.9 | (0.1) |
| | Serbia | 84.3 | (0.8) | a | a | 88.0 | (0.8) | a | a | 88.0 | (0.8) |
| | Slovenia | 85.8 | (0.3) | 7.7 | (0.4) | 96.5 | (0.2) | 14.4 | (0.5) | 97.0 | (0.2) |
| | Chinese Taipei | 69.4 | (1.4) | 14.9 | (0.6) | 84.9 | (1.1) | 23.5 | (0.7) | 87.6 | (1.1) |
| | Thailand | 57.6 | (1.4) | 39.5 | (1.0) | 88.0 | (0.9) | 62.8 | (1.0) | 91.7 | (0.8) |
| | Tunisia | 44.6 | (1.1) | 31.8 | (1.0) | 79.9 | (0.8) | 66.9 | (1.1) | 88.8 | (0.6) |
| | Uruguay | 53.7 | (1.0) | 9.6 | (0.6) | 63.3 | (1.0) | 17.8 | (0.9) | 66.5 | (1.0) |

1. Results based on students' self-reports.
StatLink ⬛⬛ http://dx.doi.org/10.1787/142127877152

Pour consulter la version française intégrale de ce tableau, suivre ce lien :
StatLink ⬛⬛ http://dx.doi.org/10.1787/152751048643

[Part 1/3]
**Table 5.17 Percentage of students, by time spent on learning[1]**

Tableau 5.17 Pourcentage d'élèves par nombre hebdomadaire d'heures d'apprentissage

| | | Science | | | | | | | | | | |
|---|---|---|---|---|---|---|---|---|---|---|---|---|
| | | Regular lessons in school[2] | | | | Out-of-school lessons[2] | | | | Self-study or homework[2] | | | |
| | | Less than two hours a week | | Four hours a week or more | | Less than two hours a week | | Four hours a week or more | | Less than two hours a week | | Four hours a week or more | |
| | | % | S.E. | % | S.E. | % | S.E. | % | S.E. | % | S.E. | % | S.E. |
| *OECD* | Australia | 24.3 | (0.7) | 37.1 | (0.8) | 94.7 | (0.2) | 1.0 | (0.1) | 81.0 | (0.6) | 4.0 | (0.2) |
| | Austria | 44.6 | (1.3) | 20.4 | (1.3) | 96.3 | (0.3) | 0.9 | (0.2) | 78.6 | (0.9) | 6.5 | (0.4) |
| | Belgium | 42.2 | (1.0) | 23.8 | (0.8) | 95.0 | (0.3) | 1.1 | (0.2) | 79.2 | (0.7) | 3.7 | (0.3) |
| | Canada | 23.6 | (0.7) | 56.8 | (1.0) | 91.3 | (0.3) | 1.8 | (0.2) | 70.6 | (0.7) | 7.6 | (0.4) |
| | Czech Republic | 40.5 | (1.5) | 27.9 | (1.2) | 91.5 | (0.5) | 1.7 | (0.2) | 84.2 | (0.8) | 3.3 | (0.3) |
| | Denmark | 17.5 | (1.0) | 27.3 | (1.0) | 90.1 | (0.6) | 1.8 | (0.2) | 86.7 | (0.7) | 2.1 | (0.2) |
| | Finland | 23.0 | (0.8) | 27.1 | (1.4) | 96.0 | (0.3) | 0.5 | (0.1) | 87.6 | (0.7) | 1.6 | (0.2) |
| | France | 37.9 | (1.0) | 25.8 | (1.1) | 92.3 | (0.5) | 1.1 | (0.2) | 78.4 | (0.9) | 4.5 | (0.4) |
| | Germany | 34.6 | (1.1) | 32.3 | (1.0) | 91.4 | (0.5) | 1.6 | (0.2) | 68.5 | (0.8) | 8.2 | (0.4) |
| | Greece | 28.0 | (1.2) | 33.5 | (1.1) | 55.8 | (1.1) | 14.8 | (0.7) | 61.9 | (0.9) | 11.8 | (0.6) |
| | Hungary | 42.1 | (1.2) | 18.4 | (0.8) | 81.7 | (0.8) | 3.8 | (0.3) | 69.7 | (1.0) | 7.3 | (0.4) |
| | Iceland | 23.3 | (0.7) | 21.5 | (0.7) | 95.5 | (0.4) | 0.6 | (0.1) | 83.7 | (0.6) | 2.5 | (0.3) |
| | Ireland | 33.5 | (1.1) | 15.7 | (0.7) | 95.5 | (0.4) | 0.8 | (0.1) | 80.2 | (0.8) | 4.3 | (0.3) |
| | Italy | 34.3 | (1.2) | 24.9 | (1.0) | 89.5 | (0.3) | 2.8 | (0.2) | 56.0 | (1.0) | 14.9 | (0.6) |
| | Japan | 26.6 | (1.5) | 12.2 | (1.2) | 96.2 | (0.3) | 0.4 | (0.1) | 93.6 | (0.4) | 1.0 | (0.1) |
| | Korea | 9.3 | (1.2) | 35.7 | (1.6) | 77.9 | (0.9) | 3.3 | (0.5) | 80.6 | (1.2) | 4.5 | (0.9) |
| | Luxembourg | 50.6 | (0.6) | 17.8 | (0.6) | 91.6 | (0.4) | 1.7 | (0.2) | 80.6 | (0.6) | 4.9 | (0.3) |
| | Mexico | 41.0 | (0.7) | 36.7 | (0.7) | 81.4 | (0.7) | 5.3 | (0.4) | 58.3 | (0.7) | 15.3 | (0.5) |
| | Netherlands | 51.5 | (1.0) | 16.4 | (0.6) | 91.8 | (0.4) | 1.5 | (0.2) | 79.4 | (0.7) | 4.2 | (0.4) |
| | New Zealand | 16.5 | (0.8) | 64.8 | (1.1) | 94.0 | (0.4) | 1.3 | (0.2) | 78.7 | (0.7) | 4.2 | (0.3) |
| | Norway | 24.7 | (1.1) | 6.9 | (0.5) | m | m | m | m | m | m | m | m |
| | Poland | 36.7 | (1.0) | 20.8 | (0.8) | 91.0 | (0.5) | 1.5 | (0.2) | 58.9 | (0.8) | 11.8 | (0.5) |
| | Portugal | 37.6 | (1.1) | 35.4 | (0.9) | 88.4 | (0.5) | 3.0 | (0.3) | 56.9 | (1.0) | 14.7 | (0.6) |
| | Slovak Republic | 55.8 | (1.5) | 24.6 | (1.4) | 90.3 | (0.6) | 2.5 | (0.2) | 73.5 | (1.1) | 6.6 | (0.5) |
| | Spain | 27.7 | (0.8) | 26.9 | (0.9) | 86.1 | (0.6) | 4.1 | (0.3) | 65.2 | (0.8) | 9.7 | (0.4) |
| | Sweden | 20.0 | (0.9) | 10.7 | (0.6) | 93.6 | (0.3) | 0.8 | (0.2) | 86.0 | (0.7) | 2.7 | (0.3) |
| | Switzerland | 48.6 | (1.0) | 18.7 | (0.8) | 93.9 | (0.3) | 1.1 | (0.1) | 84.8 | (0.6) | 3.2 | (0.2) |
| | Turkey | 43.0 | (1.6) | 31.0 | (1.5) | 73.4 | (1.2) | 11.3 | (0.8) | 66.3 | (1.1) | 12.0 | (0.8) |
| | United Kingdom | 10.1 | (0.6) | 61.9 | (1.0) | 93.5 | (0.4) | 1.0 | (0.1) | 75.0 | (0.8) | 3.7 | (0.3) |
| | United States | 33.0 | (1.1) | 49.1 | (1.2) | 86.9 | (0.5) | 3.4 | (0.3) | 67.9 | (0.8) | 8.8 | (0.4) |
| | **OECD total** | 31.8 | (0.4) | 35.8 | (0.4) | 87.9 | (0.2) | 3.0 | (0.1) | 71.3 | (0.3) | 8.0 | (0.2) |
| | **OECD average** | 32.7 | (0.2) | 28.7 | (0.2) | 89.2 | (0.1) | 2.6 | (0.1) | 74.9 | (0.2) | 6.5 | (0.1) |
| *Partners* | Argentina | 51.3 | (1.6) | 16.4 | (1.1) | 91.5 | (0.5) | 1.8 | (0.2) | 70.9 | (1.1) | 8.2 | (0.6) |
| | Azerbaijan | 38.5 | (1.3) | 24.0 | (1.2) | 73.5 | (0.9) | 8.0 | (0.4) | 47.3 | (1.0) | 24.4 | (1.0) |
| | Brazil | 49.9 | (0.8) | 11.3 | (0.6) | 86.6 | (0.6) | 2.5 | (0.3) | 68.3 | (0.8) | 8.5 | (0.4) |
| | Bulgaria | 46.5 | (1.8) | 24.2 | (1.4) | 81.4 | (0.7) | 4.4 | (0.3) | 59.4 | (1.4) | 15.4 | (0.9) |
| | Chile | 52.8 | (1.1) | 19.8 | (1.0) | 86.5 | (0.5) | 2.6 | (0.2) | 72.0 | (0.8) | 6.7 | (0.4) |
| | Colombia | 23.9 | (1.7) | 42.3 | (2.7) | 83.4 | (0.9) | 4.9 | (0.5) | 65.4 | (1.1) | 12.1 | (0.7) |
| | Croatia | 49.9 | (1.2) | 10.3 | (0.6) | 92.5 | (0.4) | 1.5 | (0.2) | 69.4 | (1.0) | 7.9 | (0.5) |
| | Estonia | 28.2 | (0.9) | 31.6 | (0.9) | 87.1 | (0.6) | 2.3 | (0.3) | 70.9 | (0.8) | 7.1 | (0.4) |
| | Hong Kong-China | 42.8 | (1.0) | 40.2 | (0.9) | 82.2 | (0.8) | 5.4 | (0.4) | 71.4 | (0.8) | 10.3 | (0.5) |
| | Indonesia | 26.7 | (1.6) | 28.9 | (1.7) | 81.5 | (1.1) | 4.2 | (0.3) | 67.3 | (1.0) | 8.9 | (0.5) |
| | Israel | 48.5 | (1.2) | 23.3 | (1.0) | 81.9 | (0.8) | 5.0 | (0.4) | 72.7 | (1.0) | 7.8 | (0.5) |
| | Jordan | 36.4 | (1.1) | 38.3 | (1.4) | 68.0 | (0.9) | 9.7 | (0.5) | 44.9 | (0.9) | 23.8 | (0.8) |
| | Kyrgyzstan | 61.4 | (1.2) | 18.0 | (1.1) | 74.7 | (0.8) | 7.0 | (0.4) | 59.3 | (0.8) | 18.8 | (0.6) |
| | Latvia | 35.8 | (1.2) | 24.3 | (1.4) | 89.6 | (0.5) | 2.0 | (0.2) | 64.4 | (1.0) | 9.0 | (0.5) |
| | Liechtenstein | 39.2 | (2.3) | 15.5 | (1.8) | 91.1 | (1.6) | 1.5 | (0.7) | 85.4 | (1.7) | 3.9 | (1.0) |
| | Lithuania | 41.1 | (1.1) | 22.9 | (0.7) | 91.4 | (0.4) | 1.7 | (0.2) | 67.9 | (0.9) | 8.1 | (0.5) |
| | Macao-China | 26.0 | (0.6) | 45.6 | (0.7) | 82.9 | (0.6) | 6.3 | (0.4) | 75.5 | (0.8) | 7.2 | (0.4) |
| | Montenegro | 43.3 | (0.9) | 28.0 | (0.7) | 80.4 | (0.6) | 5.8 | (0.4) | 57.2 | (0.8) | 17.4 | (0.6) |
| | Qatar | 47.3 | (0.6) | 27.1 | (0.6) | 70.2 | (0.6) | 8.2 | (0.4) | 56.4 | (0.7) | 12.9 | (0.4) |
| | Romania | 54.4 | (2.2) | 17.8 | (1.0) | 82.1 | (0.6) | 4.5 | (0.4) | 70.1 | (1.2) | 10.4 | (0.7) |
| | Russian Federation | 29.3 | (1.2) | 45.1 | (1.6) | 80.2 | (0.8) | 5.3 | (0.4) | 40.0 | (1.3) | 27.5 | (1.0) |
| | Serbia | 38.0 | (1.3) | 25.5 | (1.0) | 86.0 | (0.6) | 3.0 | (0.3) | 65.3 | (1.0) | 11.1 | (0.6) |
| | Slovenia | 42.9 | (0.7) | 27.3 | (0.8) | 89.0 | (0.5) | 1.9 | (0.2) | 71.9 | (0.6) | 6.2 | (0.4) |
| | Chinese Taipei | 35.0 | (1.3) | 27.0 | (0.9) | 82.7 | (0.6) | 3.3 | (0.3) | 77.6 | (0.7) | 4.8 | (0.3) |
| | Thailand | 6.7 | (0.6) | 32.0 | (1.1) | 81.2 | (0.9) | 5.2 | (0.4) | 66.1 | (0.9) | 8.6 | (0.5) |
| | Tunisia | 45.4 | (1.1) | 21.5 | (0.8) | 60.2 | (0.8) | 13.0 | (0.6) | 46.0 | (0.9) | 23.3 | (0.8) |
| | Uruguay | 49.6 | (1.2) | 20.1 | (0.8) | 89.5 | (0.4) | 2.6 | (0.3) | 77.5 | (0.8) | 5.4 | (0.4) |

Note: Values that are statistically significant are indicated in bold (see Annex A3).
1. Results based on students' self-reports.
2. Percentages for the middle category can be obtained by subtracting the sum of the other two categories from 100%.
StatLink ⇒ http://dx.doi.org/10.1787/142127877152

Pour consulter la version française intégrale de ce tableau, suivre ce lien :
StatLink ⇒ http://dx.doi.org/10.1787/152751048643

[Part 2/3]

**Table 5.17  Percentage of students, by time spent on learning[1]**

Tableau 5.17  Pourcentage d'élèves par nombre hebdomadaire d'heures d'apprentissage

| | Reading | | | | | | | | | | | |
|---|---|---|---|---|---|---|---|---|---|---|---|---|
| | Regular lessons in school[2] | | | | Out-of-school lessons[2] | | | | Self-study or homework[2] | | | |
| | Less than two hours a week | | Four hours a week or more | | Less than two hours a week | | Four hours a week or more | | Less than two hours a week | | Four hours a week or more | |
| | % | S.E. | % | S.E. | % | S.E. | % | S.E. | % | S.E. | % | S.E. |
| **OECD** | | | | | | | | | | | | |
| Australia | 8.7 | (0.3) | 53.2 | (0.9) | 88.0 | (0.4) | 3.2 | (0.2) | 67.9 | (0.6) | 8.1 | (0.3) |
| Austria | 22.0 | (0.9) | 16.0 | (1.0) | 96.0 | (0.4) | 1.2 | (0.2) | 74.1 | (1.0) | 7.7 | (0.5) |
| Belgium | 21.8 | (0.7) | 46.0 | (0.9) | 92.2 | (0.3) | 2.0 | (0.2) | 79.0 | (0.6) | 3.6 | (0.2) |
| Canada | 16.6 | (0.5) | 65.3 | (0.9) | 84.4 | (0.4) | 5.4 | (0.3) | 67.0 | (0.7) | 10.8 | (0.5) |
| Czech Republic | 9.8 | (0.5) | 43.2 | (1.2) | 90.4 | (0.4) | 1.6 | (0.2) | 83.6 | (0.7) | 3.1 | (0.3) |
| Denmark | 2.9 | (0.3) | 85.5 | (0.7) | 63.4 | (0.8) | 9.8 | (0.5) | 52.9 | (0.9) | 11.5 | (0.5) |
| Finland | 14.7 | (0.9) | 20.4 | (1.8) | 95.3 | (0.3) | 0.8 | (0.1) | 87.0 | (0.7) | 2.1 | (0.2) |
| France | 9.9 | (0.6) | 58.6 | (0.9) | 87.1 | (0.5) | 2.2 | (0.2) | 72.5 | (0.7) | 5.4 | (0.4) |
| Germany | 13.8 | (0.7) | 43.3 | (1.0) | 88.7 | (0.6) | 3.2 | (0.3) | 62.7 | (0.9) | 10.1 | (0.5) |
| Greece | 26.2 | (1.0) | 28.3 | (0.8) | 64.8 | (0.8) | 10.4 | (0.6) | 60.2 | (0.8) | 12.7 | (0.6) |
| Hungary | 24.2 | (0.9) | 31.1 | (1.2) | 74.8 | (0.7) | 7.0 | (0.4) | 63.6 | (1.0) | 9.5 | (0.5) |
| Iceland | 5.8 | (0.4) | 67.4 | (0.7) | 92.9 | (0.5) | 1.9 | (0.2) | 72.3 | (0.6) | 5.3 | (0.3) |
| Ireland | 15.1 | (0.7) | 36.5 | (1.0) | 88.7 | (0.6) | 4.0 | (0.3) | 67.2 | (0.9) | 9.5 | (0.5) |
| Italy | 12.7 | (0.4) | 67.1 | (0.7) | 84.1 | (0.4) | 6.1 | (0.3) | 36.3 | (0.8) | 27.8 | (0.8) |
| Japan | 7.5 | (0.7) | 43.1 | (1.2) | 93.2 | (0.4) | 1.3 | (0.2) | 87.3 | (0.8) | 2.3 | (0.3) |
| Korea | 4.8 | (0.5) | 67.8 | (1.3) | 66.6 | (1.2) | 6.9 | (0.4) | 75.7 | (0.7) | 6.0 | (0.4) |
| Luxembourg | 16.3 | (0.5) | 40.4 | (0.8) | 90.0 | (0.4) | 3.1 | (0.2) | 78.4 | (0.6) | 5.5 | (0.3) |
| Mexico | 28.1 | (0.7) | 48.7 | (0.7) | 78.6 | (0.8) | 6.1 | (0.4) | 61.0 | (0.9) | 13.5 | (0.6) |
| Netherlands | 19.8 | (0.7) | 15.9 | (0.8) | 90.2 | (0.5) | 1.7 | (0.2) | 80.6 | (0.7) | 3.1 | (0.3) |
| New Zealand | 8.5 | (0.6) | 72.1 | (0.9) | 88.7 | (0.5) | 3.3 | (0.4) | 71.7 | (0.8) | 6.9 | (0.4) |
| Norway | 12.9 | (0.7) | 38.6 | (1.3) | m | m | m | m | m | m | m | m |
| Poland | 10.9 | (0.5) | 75.5 | (0.7) | 90.0 | (0.6) | 2.6 | (0.2) | 53.5 | (0.8) | 14.9 | (0.5) |
| Portugal | 16.6 | (0.8) | 26.0 | (0.8) | 90.9 | (0.5) | 1.8 | (0.2) | 66.7 | (0.9) | 8.6 | (0.4) |
| Slovak Republic | 22.4 | (1.5) | 27.7 | (1.4) | 85.8 | (0.7) | 2.8 | (0.2) | 64.6 | (1.0) | 8.3 | (0.5) |
| Spain | 13.3 | (0.6) | 41.5 | (0.9) | 88.7 | (0.5) | 3.6 | (0.2) | 62.0 | (0.8) | 10.4 | (0.5) |
| Sweden | 12.6 | (0.9) | 16.6 | (0.9) | 89.9 | (0.5) | 2.7 | (0.3) | 82.5 | (0.7) | 4.0 | (0.4) |
| Switzerland | 15.5 | (0.8) | 43.9 | (1.0) | 92.3 | (0.4) | 2.1 | (0.2) | 78.9 | (0.5) | 3.6 | (0.2) |
| Turkey | 13.8 | (0.9) | 53.6 | (1.5) | 62.3 | (1.1) | 13.6 | (0.9) | 56.0 | (1.2) | 16.0 | (0.8) |
| United Kingdom | 7.4 | (0.4) | 47.4 | (1.4) | 90.3 | (0.5) | 2.2 | (0.2) | 71.3 | (0.9) | 5.4 | (0.3) |
| United States | 30.5 | (1.2) | 50.8 | (1.2) | 78.6 | (0.7) | 6.1 | (0.4) | 63.3 | (1.0) | 11.5 | (0.5) |
| **OECD total** | 18.3 | (0.3) | 50.5 | (0.4) | 82.5 | (0.2) | 4.9 | (0.1) | 66.2 | (0.3) | 10.2 | (0.2) |
| **OECD average** | 14.8 | (0.1) | 45.7 | (0.2) | 85.1 | (0.1) | 4.1 | (0.1) | 69.0 | (0.2) | 8.5 | (0.1) |
| **Partners** | | | | | | | | | | | | |
| Argentina | 44.9 | (1.4) | 15.0 | (1.1) | 92.6 | (0.6) | 1.5 | (0.2) | 71.8 | (1.1) | 7.7 | (0.7) |
| Azerbaijan | 24.2 | (1.2) | 44.8 | (1.2) | 64.0 | (1.1) | 15.8 | (0.7) | 39.4 | (1.0) | 32.5 | (1.0) |
| Brazil | 32.1 | (1.1) | 31.4 | (0.8) | 77.5 | (0.7) | 5.9 | (0.4) | 68.2 | (0.7) | 9.7 | (0.5) |
| Bulgaria | 32.5 | (1.3) | 23.7 | (0.9) | 78.9 | (0.9) | 6.5 | (0.5) | 58.4 | (1.3) | 15.1 | (0.8) |
| Chile | 31.9 | (1.1) | 42.8 | (1.2) | 81.9 | (0.9) | 4.6 | (0.3) | 72.9 | (0.9) | 7.8 | (0.5) |
| Colombia | 14.6 | (1.0) | 54.8 | (1.9) | 77.9 | (0.9) | 5.9 | (0.4) | 65.3 | (1.0) | 11.3 | (0.7) |
| Croatia | 14.6 | (0.6) | 30.8 | (1.1) | 92.5 | (0.5) | 1.4 | (0.2) | 69.5 | (1.0) | 7.1 | (0.4) |
| Estonia | 16.5 | (0.9) | 37.9 | (1.1) | 84.1 | (0.7) | 3.4 | (0.3) | 69.5 | (0.9) | 7.1 | (0.3) |
| Hong Kong-China | 7.9 | (0.5) | 78.2 | (0.9) | 86.2 | (0.7) | 4.1 | (0.4) | 69.4 | (0.8) | 8.4 | (0.6) |
| Indonesia | 18.4 | (1.4) | 39.4 | (1.4) | 77.2 | (1.1) | 5.1 | (0.4) | 68.5 | (0.9) | 8.2 | (0.5) |
| Israel | 33.7 | (0.9) | 33.0 | (1.0) | 73.2 | (0.9) | 8.8 | (0.5) | 68.4 | (1.0) | 11.6 | (0.6) |
| Jordan | 33.4 | (1.0) | 45.3 | (1.1) | 62.1 | (1.0) | 13.5 | (0.6) | 46.7 | (1.0) | 22.9 | (0.8) |
| Kyrgyzstan | 44.1 | (1.2) | 27.4 | (1.1) | 67.4 | (0.8) | 11.6 | (0.5) | 54.8 | (0.8) | 21.3 | (0.7) |
| Latvia | 12.6 | (0.8) | 42.8 | (1.0) | 85.0 | (0.7) | 3.3 | (0.3) | 58.5 | (1.1) | 10.1 | (0.5) |
| Liechtenstein | 16.6 | (1.7) | 47.5 | (2.4) | 95.6 | (1.1) | 0.6 | (0.4) | 85.6 | (1.8) | 3.0 | (1.0) |
| Lithuania | 22.1 | (0.8) | 47.2 | (1.0) | 89.7 | (0.5) | 2.6 | (0.2) | 64.2 | (0.8) | 9.8 | (0.5) |
| Macao-China | 6.9 | (0.4) | 79.8 | (0.6) | 81.8 | (0.7) | 7.6 | (0.5) | 75.1 | (0.8) | 7.4 | (0.4) |
| Montenegro | 37.8 | (0.8) | 30.3 | (0.8) | 86.3 | (0.5) | 4.6 | (0.3) | 62.7 | (0.8) | 14.0 | (0.5) |
| Qatar | 41.8 | (0.6) | 29.8 | (0.6) | 68.1 | (0.7) | 10.8 | (0.4) | 59.5 | (0.6) | 14.7 | (0.5) |
| Romania | 23.6 | (1.5) | 34.7 | (1.4) | 69.2 | (1.0) | 8.7 | (0.5) | 56.1 | (1.0) | 15.4 | (0.7) |
| Russian Federation | 56.9 | (1.4) | 9.1 | (0.5) | 88.6 | (0.6) | 2.3 | (0.3) | 74.7 | (1.1) | 6.1 | (0.5) |
| Serbia | 20.4 | (1.0) | 26.6 | (0.9) | 82.6 | (0.6) | 4.8 | (0.3) | 67.3 | (0.9) | 9.8 | (0.5) |
| Slovenia | 26.0 | (0.7) | 38.2 | (0.7) | 87.7 | (0.5) | 2.0 | (0.2) | 74.8 | (0.7) | 5.3 | (0.3) |
| Chinese Taipei | 13.5 | (0.7) | 61.2 | (1.2) | 85.9 | (0.5) | 3.2 | (0.2) | 64.7 | (0.9) | 8.0 | (0.4) |
| Thailand | 13.4 | (0.6) | 16.9 | (0.8) | 89.9 | (0.6) | 2.3 | (0.3) | 70.3 | (0.9) | 7.7 | (0.5) |
| Tunisia | 33.9 | (1.1) | 39.5 | (1.1) | 64.5 | (1.1) | 12.5 | (0.6) | 58.2 | (1.1) | 15.0 | (0.7) |
| Uruguay | 32.8 | (1.0) | 20.8 | (0.9) | 88.9 | (0.6) | 2.8 | (0.3) | 78.0 | (0.7) | 5.1 | (0.3) |

Note: Values that are statistically significant are indicated in bold (see Annex A3).
1. Results based on students' self-reports.
2. Percentages for the middle category can be obtained by subtracting the sum of the other two categories from 100%.
StatLink ᴍᴤᴤ http://dx.doi.org/10.1787/142127877152

Pour consulter la version française intégrale de ce tableau, suivre ce lien :
StatLink ᴍᴤᴤ http://dx.doi.org/10.1787/152751048643

[Part 3/3]

**Table 5.17** **Percentage of students, by time spent on learning[1]**

Tableau 5.17 Pourcentage d'élèves par nombre hebdomadaire d'heures d'apprentissage

| | | Mathematics | | | | | | | | | | |
|---|---|---|---|---|---|---|---|---|---|---|---|---|
| | | Regular lessons in school[2] | | | | Out-of-school lessons[2] | | | | Self-study or homework[2] | | | |
| | | Less than two hours a week | | Four hours a week or more | | Less than two hours a week | | Four hours a week or more | | Less than two hours a week | | Four hours a week or more | |
| | | % | S.E. | % | S.E. | % | S.E. | % | S.E. | % | S.E. | % | S.E. |
| OECD | Australia | 8.8 | (0.3) | 54.4 | (1.0) | 86.4 | (0.5) | 3.2 | (0.2) | 64.9 | (0.7) | 9.1 | (0.4) |
| | Austria | 17.9 | (1.0) | 27.2 | (1.3) | 91.1 | (0.5) | 2.5 | (0.2) | 56.4 | (1.0) | 13.6 | (0.6) |
| | Belgium | 22.1 | (0.7) | 48.9 | (1.0) | 90.6 | (0.3) | 2.3 | (0.2) | 63.6 | (0.9) | 8.2 | (0.4) |
| | Canada | 15.2 | (0.5) | 66.9 | (0.9) | 82.7 | (0.5) | 4.7 | (0.2) | 60.2 | (0.7) | 13.0 | (0.5) |
| | Czech Republic | 10.0 | (0.7) | 54.0 | (1.6) | 87.3 | (0.6) | 2.9 | (0.2) | 79.8 | (0.8) | 5.3 | (0.4) |
| | Denmark | 4.0 | (0.3) | 66.2 | (1.2) | 72.3 | (0.8) | 5.0 | (0.4) | 65.2 | (0.8) | 5.9 | (0.4) |
| | Finland | 10.7 | (0.6) | 31.3 | (1.6) | 95.3 | (0.4) | 0.9 | (0.2) | 84.2 | (0.8) | 1.8 | (0.2) |
| | France | 10.9 | (0.6) | 51.7 | (1.0) | 83.7 | (0.5) | 2.6 | (0.3) | 66.0 | (0.9) | 7.4 | (0.5) |
| | Germany | 11.1 | (0.8) | 49.4 | (1.0) | 84.6 | (0.7) | 4.1 | (0.3) | 51.1 | (1.0) | 14.4 | (0.7) |
| | Greece | 18.6 | (0.9) | 37.0 | (1.3) | 49.7 | (1.2) | 19.4 | (1.0) | 58.4 | (1.0) | 14.1 | (0.6) |
| | Hungary | 22.1 | (0.8) | 33.4 | (1.4) | 76.2 | (0.8) | 6.1 | (0.4) | 64.3 | (1.0) | 9.6 | (0.6) |
| | Iceland | 4.8 | (0.3) | 73.7 | (0.7) | 87.1 | (0.6) | 2.7 | (0.2) | 67.0 | (0.7) | 7.6 | (0.4) |
| | Ireland | 13.5 | (0.7) | 39.7 | (0.9) | 87.5 | (0.6) | 2.9 | (0.3) | 65.6 | (0.9) | 8.7 | (0.5) |
| | Italy | 17.3 | (0.6) | 48.9 | (1.0) | 82.7 | (0.5) | 4.5 | (0.2) | 46.5 | (0.9) | 19.2 | (0.7) |
| | Japan | 8.3 | (1.0) | 56.3 | (1.9) | 86.7 | (0.8) | 2.8 | (0.3) | 73.6 | (1.4) | 7.6 | (0.8) |
| | Korea | 4.5 | (0.5) | 74.2 | (1.1) | 48.5 | (0.9) | 19.9 | (0.8) | 53.7 | (1.2) | 18.8 | (1.1) |
| | Luxembourg | 13.5 | (0.5) | 52.3 | (0.8) | 84.8 | (0.6) | 3.7 | (0.3) | 68.0 | (0.7) | 7.9 | (0.3) |
| | Mexico | 26.0 | (0.7) | 54.3 | (0.7) | 77.6 | (0.7) | 7.4 | (0.5) | 56.2 | (0.8) | 16.5 | (0.7) |
| | Netherlands | 23.6 | (1.1) | 19.8 | (0.8) | 89.4 | (0.6) | 2.0 | (0.2) | 73.5 | (1.1) | 4.5 | (0.4) |
| | New Zealand | 8.8 | (0.5) | 71.8 | (0.9) | 88.4 | (0.5) | 3.1 | (0.3) | 71.3 | (0.8) | 6.8 | (0.5) |
| | Norway | 12.9 | (0.6) | 30.8 | (1.0) | m | m | m | m | m | m | m | m |
| | Poland | 13.1 | (0.6) | 69.3 | (0.9) | 89.6 | (0.5) | 2.6 | (0.2) | 57.5 | (0.8) | 13.4 | (0.5) |
| | Portugal | 19.6 | (1.0) | 44.1 | (1.1) | 86.0 | (0.6) | 2.8 | (0.3) | 59.9 | (0.9) | 11.8 | (0.6) |
| | Slovak Republic | 20.6 | (1.3) | 33.9 | (1.7) | 86.4 | (0.6) | 2.8 | (0.3) | 66.3 | (1.0) | 8.0 | (0.5) |
| | Spain | 12.9 | (0.5) | 31.8 | (1.0) | 79.1 | (0.5) | 6.2 | (0.4) | 59.5 | (0.9) | 11.5 | (0.6) |
| | Sweden | 11.6 | (0.6) | 15.2 | (0.8) | 91.5 | (0.4) | 1.6 | (0.2) | 84.9 | (0.6) | 3.2 | (0.3) |
| | Switzerland | 13.6 | (0.7) | 50.3 | (1.0) | 88.4 | (0.5) | 2.6 | (0.2) | 68.4 | (0.7) | 5.8 | (0.3) |
| | Turkey | 19.7 | (1.2) | 54.8 | (1.4) | 56.0 | (1.1) | 18.8 | (0.8) | 51.8 | (1.1) | 19.3 | (0.8) |
| | United Kingdom | 7.7 | (0.4) | 42.4 | (1.3) | 90.4 | (0.4) | 1.8 | (0.2) | 74.9 | (0.7) | 4.0 | (0.3) |
| | United States | 27.4 | (1.0) | 53.0 | (1.3) | 78.2 | (0.7) | 6.3 | (0.4) | 58.5 | (0.8) | 13.9 | (0.5) |
| | **OECD total** | **17.7** | **(0.3)** | **52.2** | **(0.4)** | **79.5** | **(0.2)** | **6.1** | **(0.1)** | **60.8** | **(0.3)** | **12.5** | **(0.2)** |
| | **OECD average** | **14.4** | **(0.1)** | **47.9** | **(0.2)** | **82.0** | **(0.1)** | **5.1** | **(0.1)** | **64.5** | **(0.2)** | **10.0** | **(0.1)** |
| Partners | Argentina | 34.7 | (1.4) | 30.2 | (1.4) | 86.3 | (0.8) | 4.1 | (0.4) | 66.3 | (1.2) | 11.3 | (0.7) |
| | Azerbaijan | 26.9 | (1.0) | 47.9 | (1.2) | 66.4 | (1.1) | 14.9 | (0.9) | 43.5 | (1.3) | 31.0 | (1.2) |
| | Brazil | 30.0 | (0.9) | 32.5 | (0.8) | 76.9 | (0.7) | 6.2 | (0.4) | 66.6 | (0.8) | 10.5 | (0.5) |
| | Bulgaria | 33.5 | (1.4) | 26.3 | (1.5) | 78.3 | (0.8) | 6.4 | (0.6) | 58.9 | (1.5) | 16.4 | (1.0) |
| | Chile | 32.0 | (1.1) | 44.2 | (1.3) | 82.6 | (0.7) | 4.2 | (0.3) | 70.8 | (1.0) | 7.3 | (0.4) |
| | Colombia | 13.8 | (1.0) | 61.1 | (1.7) | 76.2 | (0.8) | 7.0 | (0.5) | 62.9 | (0.9) | 12.9 | (0.7) |
| | Croatia | 21.5 | (0.9) | 24.2 | (1.1) | 85.4 | (0.6) | 3.3 | (0.3) | 63.2 | (0.8) | 9.9 | (0.5) |
| | Estonia | 13.4 | (0.8) | 64.8 | (1.1) | 82.3 | (0.8) | 4.5 | (0.4) | 60.2 | (0.9) | 12.5 | (0.6) |
| | Hong Kong-China | 7.7 | (0.5) | 78.3 | (1.0) | 72.5 | (0.9) | 8.7 | (0.5) | 54.4 | (1.0) | 16.8 | (0.7) |
| | Indonesia | 14.4 | (1.2) | 52.0 | (1.7) | 73.7 | (1.3) | 6.7 | (0.5) | 61.5 | (0.8) | 10.9 | (0.6) |
| | Israel | 16.7 | (0.7) | 58.6 | (1.0) | 54.7 | (1.1) | 17.8 | (0.7) | 51.9 | (1.3) | 20.4 | (0.9) |
| | Jordan | 33.4 | (1.1) | 43.3 | (1.1) | 60.8 | (0.9) | 14.1 | (0.6) | 45.1 | (0.9) | 25.0 | (0.8) |
| | Kyrgyzstan | 44.2 | (1.0) | 32.1 | (1.0) | 71.2 | (0.8) | 10.7 | (0.6) | 58.6 | (0.8) | 20.3 | (0.7) |
| | Latvia | 8.1 | (0.6) | 66.2 | (1.1) | 77.4 | (1.1) | 4.8 | (0.4) | 47.8 | (1.1) | 18.3 | (0.8) |
| | Liechtenstein | 14.2 | (1.7) | 54.9 | (2.4) | 90.8 | (1.5) | 1.5 | (0.7) | 74.8 | (2.4) | 3.6 | (0.9) |
| | Lithuania | 23.1 | (1.0) | 42.3 | (1.0) | 89.3 | (0.5) | 2.4 | (0.2) | 65.2 | (0.7) | 9.4 | (0.4) |
| | Macao-China | 6.8 | (0.4) | 82.4 | (0.6) | 78.5 | (0.7) | 9.0 | (0.5) | 59.3 | (0.8) | 15.0 | (0.5) |
| | Montenegro | 35.4 | (0.8) | 32.1 | (0.8) | 82.8 | (0.6) | 6.1 | (0.4) | 62.9 | (0.8) | 14.7 | (0.6) |
| | Qatar | 38.2 | (0.7) | 35.3 | (0.6) | 61.6 | (0.6) | 13.9 | (0.5) | 53.8 | (0.7) | 17.5 | (0.5) |
| | Romania | 32.0 | (1.3) | 28.4 | (2.1) | 70.3 | (0.9) | 9.4 | (0.7) | 58.7 | (1.0) | 17.2 | (0.9) |
| | Russian Federation | 19.0 | (1.3) | 42.9 | (1.4) | 81.8 | (0.8) | 3.9 | (0.4) | 54.4 | (1.2) | 15.1 | (0.7) |
| | Serbia | 19.9 | (0.9) | 30.4 | (1.1) | 82.5 | (0.6) | 5.4 | (0.4) | 63.9 | (0.8) | 10.8 | (0.5) |
| | Slovenia | 22.1 | (0.6) | 36.4 | (0.7) | 81.5 | (0.5) | 4.5 | (0.3) | 61.9 | (0.7) | 10.9 | (0.4) |
| | Chinese Taipei | 17.3 | (0.8) | 59.2 | (1.3) | 62.2 | (1.0) | 8.7 | (0.4) | 61.0 | (1.0) | 10.9 | (0.4) |
| | Thailand | 5.4 | (0.3) | 35.8 | (1.2) | 81.1 | (0.8) | 4.4 | (0.4) | 66.3 | (0.9) | 8.8 | (0.4) |
| | Tunisia | 29.3 | (1.0) | 44.4 | (0.9) | 49.7 | (0.9) | 22.3 | (0.6) | 49.1 | (0.9) | 24.1 | (0.7) |
| | Uruguay | 23.7 | (0.2) | 35.0 | (1.2) | 84.5 | (0.7) | 4.2 | (0.4) | 73.4 | (0.9) | 7.7 | (0.5) |

Note: Values that are statistically significant are indicated in bold (see Annex A3).
1. Results based on students' self-reports.
2. Percentages for the middle category can be obtained by subtracting the sum of the other two categories from 100%.
*StatLink* http://dx.doi.org/10.1787/142127877152

Pour consulter la version française intégrale de ce tableau, suivre ce lien :
*StatLink* http://dx.doi.org/10.1787/152751048643

[Part 1/2]

**Table 5.18** Index of school activities to promote the learning of science and student performance on the science scale, by quarters of the index[1]

Tableau 5.18 Indice d'activités scolaires visant à promouvoir l'apprentissage des sciences et performance des élèves sur l'échelle de culture scientifique, par quartile de l'indice

| | | Index of school activities to promote the learning of science | | | | | | | | |
|---|---|---|---|---|---|---|---|---|---|---|
| | | All students | | Bottom quarter | | Second quarter | | Third quarter | | Top quarter | |
| | | Mean index | S.E. | Mean index | S.E. | Mean index | S.E. | Mean index | S.E. | Mean index | S.E. |
| OECD | Australia | 0.41 | (0.04) | -0.29 | (0.03) | 0.21 | (0.00) | 0.53 | (0.02) | 1.16 | (0.04) |
| | Austria | -0.38 | (0.07) | -1.48 | (0.07) | -0.84 | (0.03) | -0.06 | (0.04) | 0.85 | (0.08) |
| | Belgium | -0.23 | (0.05) | -1.31 | (0.06) | -0.37 | (0.01) | 0.14 | (0.01) | 0.65 | (0.06) |
| | Canada | 0.42 | (0.04) | -0.77 | (0.04) | 0.06 | (0.02) | 0.76 | (0.03) | 1.64 | (0.00) |
| | Czech Republic | 0.45 | (0.06) | -0.75 | (0.08) | 0.13 | (0.03) | 0.80 | (0.01) | 1.64 | (0.00) |
| | Denmark | -0.83 | (0.07) | -1.61 | (0.08) | -1.07 | (0.00) | -0.68 | (0.04) | 0.05 | (0.07) |
| | Finland | -0.60 | (0.06) | -1.36 | (0.08) | -0.85 | (0.03) | -0.33 | (0.00) | 0.14 | (0.04) |
| | France | w | w | w | w | w | w | w | w | w | w |
| | Germany | -0.11 | (0.05) | -1.25 | (0.06) | -0.51 | (0.03) | 0.17 | (0.01) | 1.15 | (0.06) |
| | Greece | -0.42 | (0.06) | -1.34 | (0.08) | -0.60 | (0.03) | -0.33 | (0.00) | 0.59 | (0.09) |
| | Hungary | 0.62 | (0.06) | -0.36 | (0.07) | 0.39 | (0.02) | 0.80 | (0.01) | 1.64 | (0.00) |
| | Iceland | -0.71 | (0.00) | c | c | c | c | c | c | c | c |
| | Ireland | 0.12 | (0.08) | -1.12 | (0.08) | -0.12 | (0.03) | 0.48 | (0.03) | 1.25 | (0.05) |
| | Italy | 0.01 | (0.04) | -1.03 | (0.04) | -0.25 | (0.01) | 0.26 | (0.02) | 1.06 | (0.05) |
| | Japan | -1.16 | (0.07) | -2.27 | (0.00) | -1.76 | (0.06) | -0.81 | (0.04) | 0.20 | (0.08) |
| | Korea | 0.54 | (0.07) | -0.59 | (0.08) | 0.26 | (0.01) | 0.87 | (0.03) | 1.64 | (0.00) |
| | Luxembourg | 0.15 | (0.00) | -1.12 | (0.01) | -0.19 | (0.01) | 0.53 | (0.00) | 1.38 | (0.01) |
| | Mexico | -0.02 | (0.04) | -1.28 | (0.05) | -0.28 | (0.01) | 0.32 | (0.02) | 1.14 | (0.03) |
| | Netherlands | -0.51 | (0.08) | -1.54 | (0.09) | -0.92 | (0.03) | -0.20 | (0.02) | 0.63 | (0.06) |
| | New Zealand | 0.51 | (0.06) | -0.56 | (0.09) | 0.34 | (0.02) | 0.76 | (0.00) | 1.49 | (0.02) |
| | Norway | -0.49 | (0.05) | -1.34 | (0.07) | -0.71 | (0.04) | -0.28 | (0.01) | 0.36 | (0.04) |
| | Poland | 0.58 | (0.04) | -0.07 | (0.05) | 0.26 | (0.01) | 0.76 | (0.00) | 1.36 | (0.04) |
| | Portugal | 0.66 | (0.06) | -0.28 | (0.08) | 0.45 | (0.03) | 0.83 | (0.03) | 1.64 | (0.00) |
| | Slovak Republic | 0.70 | (0.05) | -0.39 | (0.08) | 0.45 | (0.03) | 1.08 | (0.04) | 1.64 | (0.00) |
| | Spain | 0.19 | (0.06) | -0.83 | (0.05) | -0.15 | (0.02) | 0.48 | (0.03) | 1.28 | (0.05) |
| | Sweden | -0.49 | (0.07) | -1.75 | (0.10) | -0.63 | (0.03) | -0.11 | (0.03) | 0.54 | (0.06) |
| | Switzerland | -0.25 | (0.04) | -1.19 | (0.03) | -0.49 | (0.02) | 0.03 | (0.02) | 0.65 | (0.03) |
| | Turkey | -0.16 | (0.08) | -1.60 | (0.09) | -0.57 | (0.05) | 0.35 | (0.03) | 1.20 | (0.06) |
| | United Kingdom | 0.42 | (0.06) | -0.80 | (0.07) | 0.13 | (0.02) | 0.77 | (0.01) | 1.58 | (0.02) |
| | United States | 0.47 | (0.08) | -0.83 | (0.10) | 0.25 | (0.02) | 0.83 | (0.03) | 1.64 | (0.00) |
| | **OECD total** | 0.10 | (0.03) | -1.32 | (0.03) | -0.14 | (0.01) | 0.50 | (0.01) | 1.37 | (0.02) |
| | **OECD average** | 0.00 | (0.01) | -1.04 | (0.01) | -0.26 | (0.01) | 0.31 | (0.00) | 1.08 | (0.01) |
| Partners | Argentina | 0.11 | (0.07) | -1.10 | (0.10) | -0.16 | (0.03) | 0.48 | (0.03) | 1.21 | (0.06) |
| | Azerbaijan | 0.27 | (0.07) | -0.81 | (0.08) | -0.07 | (0.03) | 0.63 | (0.02) | 1.33 | (0.04) |
| | Brazil | 0.24 | (0.04) | -0.66 | (0.06) | 0.16 | (0.01) | 0.44 | (0.02) | 1.03 | (0.03) |
| | Bulgaria | 0.03 | (0.07) | -1.06 | (0.10) | -0.19 | (0.00) | 0.38 | (0.02) | 0.98 | (0.04) |
| | Chile | -0.26 | (0.12) | -2.02 | (0.07) | -0.55 | (0.05) | 0.33 | (0.03) | 1.20 | (0.06) |
| | Colombia | 0.82 | (0.08) | -0.15 | (0.07) | 0.62 | (0.03) | 1.19 | (0.05) | 1.64 | (0.00) |
| | Croatia | 0.15 | (0.08) | -1.23 | (0.09) | -0.06 | (0.04) | 0.58 | (0.03) | 1.32 | (0.05) |
| | Estonia | 0.90 | (0.04) | 0.14 | (0.03) | 0.76 | (0.00) | 1.05 | (0.03) | 1.64 | (0.00) |
| | Hong Kong-China | 0.92 | (0.06) | 0.06 | (0.06) | 0.76 | (0.00) | 1.22 | (0.04) | 1.64 | (0.00) |
| | Indonesia | -0.04 | (0.09) | -1.63 | (0.07) | -0.33 | (0.04) | 0.46 | (0.03) | 1.33 | (0.06) |
| | Israel | 0.21 | (0.09) | -1.25 | (0.08) | -0.10 | (0.04) | 0.68 | (0.02) | 1.50 | (0.03) |
| | Jordan | 0.87 | (0.07) | -0.33 | (0.11) | 0.61 | (0.03) | 1.57 | (0.01) | 1.64 | (0.00) |
| | Kyrgyzstan | 0.76 | (0.05) | -0.14 | (0.06) | 0.57 | (0.02) | 0.96 | (0.04) | 1.64 | (0.00) |
| | Latvia | 0.19 | (0.03) | c | c | c | c | c | c | c | c |
| | Liechtenstein | c | c | c | c | c | c | c | c | c | c |
| | Lithuania | 1.19 | (0.04) | c | c | c | c | c | c | c | c |
| | Macao-China | 0.45 | (0.00) | -0.35 | (0.01) | 0.21 | (0.00) | 0.69 | (0.00) | 1.24 | (0.01) |
| | Montenegro | 0.34 | (0.00) | -1.06 | (0.01) | 0.19 | (0.00) | 0.73 | (0.00) | 1.50 | (0.01) |
| | Qatar | 0.59 | (0.00) | -0.61 | (0.01) | 0.40 | (0.00) | 0.94 | (0.00) | 1.63 | (0.00) |
| | Romania | 0.77 | (0.08) | -0.33 | (0.05) | 0.52 | (0.03) | 1.27 | (0.05) | 1.64 | (0.00) |
| | Russian Federation | 1.19 | (0.05) | c | c | c | c | c | c | c | c |
| | Serbia | 0.31 | (0.07) | -1.10 | (0.11) | 0.14 | (0.01) | 0.65 | (0.02) | 1.56 | (0.02) |
| | Slovenia | 1.15 | (0.00) | c | c | c | c | c | c | c | c |
| | Chinese Taipei | 0.76 | (0.06) | c | c | c | c | c | c | c | c |
| | Thailand | 1.34 | (0.06) | c | c | c | c | c | c | c | c |
| | Tunisia | 0.36 | (0.08) | -0.94 | (0.10) | 0.06 | (0.04) | 0.82 | (0.02) | 1.51 | (0.03) |
| | Uruguay | -0.01 | (0.05) | -1.37 | (0.06) | -0.34 | (0.02) | 0.41 | (0.03) | 1.24 | (0.03) |

Note: Values that are statistically significant are indicated in bold (see Annex A3).
1. Results based on reports from school principals and reported proportionate to the number of 15-year-olds enrolled in the school.
*StatLink* http://dx.doi.org/10.1787/142127877152

Pour consulter la version française intégrale de ce tableau, suivre ce lien :
*StatLink* http://dx.doi.org/10.1787/152751048643

[Part 2/2]

**Table 5.18** **Index of school activities to promote the learning of science and student performance on the science scale, by quarters of the index[1]**

Tableau 5.18  Indice d'activités scolaires visant à promouvoir l'apprentissage des sciences et performance des élèves sur l'échelle de culture scientifique, par quartile de l'indice

| | Performance on the science scale by quarters of this index | | | | | | | | Change in the science score per unit of this index | | Increased likelihood of students in the bottom quarter of this index scoring in the bottom quarter of the science performance distribution | | Explained variance in student performance (r-squared x 100) | |
| | Bottom quarter | | Second quarter | | Third quarter | | Top quarter | | | | | | | |
| | Mean score | S.E. | Mean score | S.E. | Mean score | S.E. | Mean score | S.E. | Effect | S.E. | Ratio | S.E. | % | S.E. |
|---|---|---|---|---|---|---|---|---|---|---|---|---|---|---|
| Australia | **516** | (3.8) | 517 | (4.2) | 535 | (4.4) | **539** | (4.7) | **15.6** | (4.68) | **1.2** | (0.08) | 0.9 | (0.53) |
| Austria | **472** | (7.9) | 488 | (6.5) | 530 | (6.5) | **559** | (7.9) | **35.6** | (4.23) | **2.0** | (0.20) | 12.7 | (2.99) |
| Belgium | **481** | (9.8) | 516 | (7.3) | 530 | (5.8) | **518** | (6.6) | **19.3** | (5.87) | **1.7** | (0.24) | 2.5 | (1.40) |
| Canada | **530** | (3.8) | 532 | (4.0) | 535 | (3.7) | **544** | (4.0) | **5.4** | (2.13) | 1.1 | (0.08) | 0.3 | (0.25) |
| Czech Republic | **489** | (10.1) | 508 | (8.1) | 526 | (6.3) | **528** | (8.2) | **18.5** | (5.42) | **1.4** | (0.22) | 3.0 | (1.63) |
| Denmark | **491** | (6.0) | 490 | (5.4) | 495 | (4.6) | **508** | (5.1) | **10.7** | (3.89) | 1.0 | (0.13) | 0.7 | (0.51) |
| Finland | 563 | (3.6) | 566 | (4.4) | 566 | (4.8) | 557 | (4.4) | -2.5 | (3.23) | 1.0 | (0.08) | 0.0 | (0.10) |
| France | w | w | w | w | w | w | w | w | w | w | w | w | w | w |
| Germany | **465** | (8.4) | 499 | (7.1) | 534 | (8.8) | **568** | (6.5) | **40.5** | (3.85) | **2.2** | (0.25) | 14.7 | (2.63) |
| Greece | **441** | (9.0) | 472 | (4.8) | 486 | (4.9) | **493** | (6.5) | **27.6** | (5.02) | **2.0** | (0.26) | 5.7 | (1.99) |
| Hungary | **482** | (7.7) | 499 | (6.1) | 495 | (8.0) | **541** | (7.0) | **27.6** | (5.58) | **1.5** | (0.24) | 5.9 | (2.29) |
| Iceland | c | c | c | c | c | c | c | c | c | c | c | c | c | c |
| Ireland | **503** | (7.2) | 497 | (4.7) | 509 | (5.6) | **523** | (4.9) | **7.6** | (3.63) | 1.1 | (0.14) | 0.6 | (0.58) |
| Italy | **457** | (4.4) | 480 | (4.4) | 478 | (7.1) | **490** | (6.3) | **14.7** | (3.71) | **1.4** | (0.12) | 1.7 | (0.82) |
| Japan | **509** | (7.9) | 521 | (6.3) | 530 | (7.9) | **565** | (6.9) | **21.7** | (4.45) | **1.4** | (0.19) | 5.1 | (2.12) |
| Korea | **504** | (8.3) | 521 | (8.4) | 517 | (8.3) | **546** | (7.0) | **19.3** | (4.57) | **1.5** | (0.22) | 3.5 | (1.62) |
| Luxembourg | **458** | (3.2) | 479 | (4.3) | 502 | (2.7) | **505** | (2.6) | **19.4** | (0.99) | **1.5** | (0.15) | 4.3 | (0.42) |
| Mexico | **383** | (5.4) | 394 | (6.0) | 425 | (4.6) | **443** | (5.8) | **24.2** | (2.78) | **1.8** | (0.20) | 8.3 | (1.76) |
| Netherlands | **492** | (9.2) | 493 | (7.8) | 546 | (8.7) | **569** | (7.4) | **32.8** | (6.46) | **1.7** | (0.24) | 9.7 | (3.34) |
| New Zealand | **524** | (6.5) | 534 | (5.3) | 525 | (5.5) | **543** | (5.0) | 6.8 | (4.06) | 1.2 | (0.12) | 0.3 | (0.36) |
| Norway | 489 | (4.9) | 485 | (4.6) | 484 | (7.0) | 485 | (6.1) | 0.1 | (4.67) | 0.9 | (0.10) | 0.0 | (0.09) |
| Poland | **485** | (4.7) | 492 | (3.6) | 504 | (5.0) | **511** | (5.9) | **18.1** | (4.98) | **1.3** | (0.10) | 1.5 | (0.82) |
| Portugal | 459 | (8.5) | 478 | (5.2) | 483 | (6.3) | 477 | (6.9) | 10.5 | (5.23) | 1.4 | (0.21) | 0.8 | (0.84) |
| Slovak Republic | **469** | (5.7) | 481 | (6.3) | 496 | (6.0) | **504** | (6.1) | **16.9** | (4.36) | **1.3** | (0.15) | 2.3 | (1.18) |
| Spain | 479 | (4.3) | 487 | (3.8) | 496 | (4.5) | 492 | (6.3) | 5.9 | (3.80) | 1.2 | (0.11) | 0.3 | (0.42) |
| Sweden | 497 | (4.2) | 506 | (3.9) | 506 | (4.1) | 504 | (5.1) | 3.6 | (2.11) | 1.1 | (0.08) | 0.1 | (0.15) |
| Switzerland | **488** | (5.7) | 498 | (5.6) | 513 | (5.4) | **546** | (6.9) | **32.2** | (4.54) | **1.3** | (0.12) | 6.0 | (1.58) |
| Turkey | **395** | (5.7) | 414 | (6.6) | 429 | (7.4) | **458** | (10.9) | **22.1** | (4.22) | **1.5** | (0.18) | 8.9 | (3.14) |
| United Kingdom | 511 | (5.9) | 516 | (5.9) | 512 | (6.3) | 527 | (6.6) | 4.0 | (3.33) | 1.1 | (0.11) | 0.1 | (0.20) |
| United States | 504 | (7.7) | 485 | (5.5) | 487 | (7.8) | 493 | (9.1) | -4.6 | (4.78) | **0.8** | (0.10) | 0.2 | (0.32) |
| **OECD total** | **480** | (2.7) | **489** | (2.0) | **495** | (2.4) | **503** | (3.0) | **8.0** | (1.57) | **1.2** | (0.05) | 0.7 | (0.27) |
| **OECD average** | **484** | (1.3) | **495** | (1.1) | **506** | (1.2) | **519** | (1.2) | **16.2** | (0.82) | **1.4** | (0.03) | 3.6 | (0.30) |
| Argentina | 388 | (14.2) | 380 | (14.8) | 403 | (8.5) | 398 | (8.6) | 7.4 | (5.78) | 1.1 | (0.21) | 0.5 | (0.83) |
| Azerbaijan | **368** | (4.2) | 381 | (5.3) | 387 | (4.6) | **394** | (5.8) | **12.0** | (3.04) | **1.4** | (0.17) | 3.5 | (1.78) |
| Brazil | **370** | (6.7) | 396 | (4.6) | 399 | (4.4) | **397** | (6.0) | **18.1** | (4.99) | **1.4** | (0.16) | 2.0 | (1.14) |
| Bulgaria | **402** | (11.1) | 414 | (10.9) | 459 | (8.8) | **483** | (10.6) | **38.9** | (6.92) | **1.8** | (0.27) | 9.7 | (3.48) |
| Chile | **418** | (8.7) | 429 | (7.1) | 458 | (7.7) | **466** | (9.9) | **15.4** | (3.49) | **1.4** | (0.18) | 4.6 | (2.08) |
| Colombia | **372** | (6.7) | 387 | (6.6) | 391 | (6.8) | **404** | (6.6) | **14.3** | (4.55) | 1.4 | (0.19) | 1.6 | (0.91) |
| Croatia | **461** | (6.3) | 494 | (6.2) | 509 | (6.7) | **509** | (5.5) | **17.1** | (3.52) | **1.7** | (0.19) | 4.1 | (1.64) |
| Estonia | 521 | (7.0) | 538 | (4.1) | 535 | (5.6) | 531 | (5.6) | 5.6 | (5.97) | 1.2 | (0.17) | 0.2 | (0.35) |
| Hong Kong-China | 532 | (8.7) | 545 | (8.1) | 545 | (5.4) | 547 | (7.3) | 7.0 | (7.42) | 1.2 | (0.21) | 0.2 | (0.55) |
| Indonesia | **364** | (5.0) | 381 | (6.9) | 401 | (7.9) | **429** | (11.9) | **19.9** | (4.84) | **1.8** | (0.25) | 10.8 | (4.95) |
| Israel | 442 | (8.6) | 454 | (10.3) | 468 | (8.3) | 453 | (10.0) | 5.6 | (4.64) | 1.1 | (0.15) | 0.3 | (0.51) |
| Jordan | **406** | (5.3) | 412 | (6.0) | 436 | (5.6) | **435** | (5.2) | **12.6** | (3.99) | **1.3** | (0.13) | 1.6 | (0.99) |
| Kyrgyzstan | **314** | (6.1) | 313 | (4.6) | 317 | (5.3) | **344** | (6.8) | **15.8** | (4.74) | 1.2 | (0.13) | 1.9 | (1.07) |
| Latvia | c | c | c | c | c | c | c | c | c | c | c | c | c | c |
| Liechtenstein | c | c | c | c | c | c | c | c | c | c | c | c | c | c |
| Lithuania | c | c | c | c | c | c | c | c | c | c | c | c | c | c |
| Macao-China | **506** | (2.3) | 520 | (2.1) | 501 | (3.1) | **516** | (3.4) | **7.0** | (1.52) | **1.2** | (0.08) | 0.4 | (0.16) |
| Montenegro | **431** | (2.6) | 396 | (2.4) | 412 | (2.5) | **408** | (2.5) | **-7.0** | (1.15) | **0.7** | (0.05) | 0.8 | (0.26) |
| Qatar | 347 | (2.5) | 354 | (2.9) | 362 | (2.7) | 351 | (1.8) | 4.8 | (1.00) | 1.1 | (0.08) | 0.3 | (0.11) |
| Romania | **386** | (8.9) | 418 | (8.3) | 432 | (7.0) | **438** | (9.6) | **25.4** | (6.97) | **2.1** | (0.33) | 6.6 | (3.55) |
| Russian Federation | c | c | c | c | c | c | c | c | c | c | c | c | c | c |
| Serbia | **419** | (7.0) | 419 | (6.7) | 429 | (6.2) | **478** | (4.8) | **18.8** | (4.06) | 1.3 | (0.17) | 5.3 | (2.03) |
| Slovenia | c | c | c | c | c | c | c | c | c | c | c | c | c | c |
| Chinese Taipei | c | c | c | c | c | c | c | c | c | c | c | c | c | c |
| Thailand | c | c | c | c | c | c | c | c | c | c | c | c | c | c |
| Tunisia | 366 | (7.2) | 384 | (6.7) | 391 | (8.0) | 402 | (10.4) | 14.8 | (4.11) | 1.5 | (0.20) | 3.1 | (1.79) |
| Uruguay | **417** | (6.2) | 427 | (10.3) | 429 | (7.3) | **440** | (6.2) | 7.2 | (3.16) | 1.2 | (0.18) | 0.6 | (0.62) |

*OECD* — rows Australia through OECD average. *Partners* — rows Argentina through Uruguay.

Note: Values that are statistically significant are indicated in bold (see Annex A3).
1. Results based on reports from school principals and reported proportionate to the number of 15-year-olds enrolled in the school.
StatLink ⏎ http://dx.doi.org/10.1787/142127877152

Pour consulter la version française intégrale de ce tableau, suivre ce lien :
StatLink ⏎ http://dx.doi.org/10.1787/152751048643

[Part 1/1]

**Table 5.19a  Admitting, grouping and selecting and student performance in science**

Tableau 5.19a  Politiques d'admission, regroupement par aptitude et sélection des élèves, et performance des élèves en sciences

| | | Gross | | | Net | | |
|---|---|---|---|---|---|---|---|
| | | Change in score | S.E. | P-value | Change in score | S.E. | P-value |
| Intercept | | 464.4 | (7.8) | (0.000) | 468.4 | (5.6) | (0.000) |
| School with ability grouping for all subjects within school | 1 = yes; 0 = no | -10.2 | (2.3) | (0.000) | -4.5 | (1.5) | (0.002) |
| School with high academic selectivity of school admittance | 1 = yes; 0 = no | 30.4 | (4.5) | (0.000) | 18.1 | (2.7) | (0.000) |
| School with low academic selectivity of school admittance | 1 = yes; 0 = no | -14.5 | (3.0) | (0.000) | -1.6 | (1.4) | (0.264) |
| System with early selection (difference between the first age of selection and the age of 15) | 1 additional year | -4.2 | (4.2) | (0.331) | -0.4 | (3.9) | (0.927) |
| System-level number of school types or distinct educational programmes available to 15-year-olds | 1 additional programme | 6.9 | (7.4) | (0.357) | 3.3 | (6.3) | (0.607) |

*Background variables*

| | | Gross | | | Net | | |
|---|---|---|---|---|---|---|---|
| Student's PISA index of economic, social and cultural status | 1 = OECD S.D. | | | | 16.8 | (1.2) | (0.000) |
| Student's PISA index of economic, social and cultural status squared | | | | | 1.9 | (0.4) | (0.000) |
| Student is female | 1 = yes; 0 = no | | | | -5.9 | (1.1) | (0.000) |
| Student has no immigration background (student and parents were born in the country of assessment) | 1 = yes; 0 = no | | | | 10.4 | (3.3) | (0.002) |
| Student speaks the test language or other national language most of the time or always at home | 1 = yes; 0 = no | | | | 25.0 | (2.8) | (0.000) |
| School located in a small town or village (fewer than 15 000 people) | 1 = yes; 0 = no | | | | 7.1 | (1.6) | (0.000) |
| School located in a city (with over 100 000 people) | 1 = yes; 0 = no | | | | -6.2 | (1.4) | (0.000) |
| School size | 100 additional students | | | | 1.7 | (0.3) | (0.000) |
| School size squared | | | | | 0.0 | (0.0) | (0.000) |
| School average PISA index of economic, social and cultural status | 1 = OECD S.D. | | | | 50.4 | (3.6) | (0.000) |
| System average PISA index of economic, social and cultural status | 1 = OECD S.D. | | | | 12.0 | (10.7) | (0.266) |

| Variance explained (expressed as % of total variance) | | Gross | Net |
|---|---|---|---|
| | Student level | 0.0 | 2.4 |
| | School level | 1.7 | 15.3 |
| | System level | 0.8 | 13.0 |
| | Total | 2.5 | 30.7 |

| Variance explained (expressed as % of variance at each level) | | Gross | Net |
|---|---|---|---|
| | Student level | 0.0 | 5.0 |
| | School level | 6.5 | 57.4 |
| | System level | 2.9 | 49.7 |

Note: All slopes are fixed. All variables are grand-centred (a linear transformation of variables by subtracting the overall mean from the value proper). Intercept is random at all levels. The analysis is based on 55 countries. See Annex A8 for the detailed model specification.
**StatLink** http://dx.doi.org/10.1787/142127877152

Pour consulter la version française intégrale de ce tableau, suivre ce lien :
**StatLink** http://dx.doi.org/10.1787/152751048643

[Part 1/1]
**Table 5.19b   School management and funding and student performance in science**

Tableau 5.19b   Relation entre les modalités de gestion et de financement des établissements et la performance des élèves en sciences

| | | Gross | | | Net | | |
|---|---|---|---|---|---|---|---|
| | | Change in score | S.E. | P-value | Change in score | S.E. | P-value |
| Intercept | | 466.1 | (8.4) | (0.000) | 469.0 | (5.8) | (0.000) |
| School being privately managed | 1 = private; 0 = public | 20.0 | (6.4) | (0.002) | -2.6 | (2.8) | (0.353) |
| School with high proportion of school funding from government sources | Each additional 10% | -3.2 | (0.8) | (0.000) | 0.3 | (0.4) | (0.436) |

*Background variables*

| | | | | | | | |
|---|---|---|---|---|---|---|---|
| Student's PISA index of economic, social and cultural status | 1 = OECD S.D. | | | | 16.8 | (1.2) | (0.000) |
| Student's PISA index of economic, social and cultural status squared | | | | | 1.9 | (0.4) | (0.000) |
| Student is female | 1 = yes; 0 = no | | | | -5.9 | (1.1) | (0.000) |
| Student has no immigration background (student and parents were born in the country of assessment) | 1 = yes; 0 = no | | | | 10.4 | (3.3) | (0.002) |
| Student speaks the test language or other national language most of the time or always at home | 1 = yes; 0 = no | | | | 25.0 | (2.8) | (0.000) |
| School located in a small town or village (fewer than 15 000 people) | 1 = yes; 0 = no | | | | 6.4 | (1.7) | (0.000) |
| School located in a city (with over 100 000 people) | 1 = yes; 0 = no | | | | -6.0 | (1.4) | (0.000) |
| School size | 100 additional students | | | | 1.6 | (0.3) | (0.000) |
| School size squared | | | | | 0.0 | (0.0) | (0.001) |
| School average PISA index of economic, social and cultural status | 1 = OECD S.D. | | | | 53.2 | (4.1) | (0.000) |
| System average PISA index of economic, social and cultural status | 1 = OECD S.D. | | | | 9.3 | (11.8) | (0.430) |

| | | | |
|---|---|---|---|
| Variance explained (expressed as % of total variance) | Student level | 0.0 | 2.4 |
| | School level | 1.1 | 15.0 |
| | System level | -2.0 | 12.6 |
| | Total | -1.0 | 29.9 |

| | | | |
|---|---|---|---|
| Variance explained (expressed as % of variance at each level) | Student level | 0.0 | 5.0 |
| | School level | 3.9 | 56.0 |
| | System level | -7.7 | 48.1 |

Note: All slopes are fixed. All variables are grand-centred (a linear transformation of variables by subtracting the overall mean from the value proper). Intercept is random at all levels. The analysis is based on 55 countries. See Annex A8 for the detailed model specification.
StatLink ☜☞ http://dx.doi.org/10.1787/142127877152

Pour consulter la version française intégrale de ce tableau, suivre ce lien :
StatLink ☜☞ http://dx.doi.org/10.1787/152751048643

**[Part 1/1]**

**Table 5.19c**  **Parental pressure and choice and student performance in science**

Tableau 5.19c   Relation entre la liberté de choix de l'établissement et la pression parentale et la performance des élèves en sciences

| | | Gross | | | Net | | |
|---|---|---|---|---|---|---|---|
| | | Change in score | S.E. | P-value | Change in score | S.E. | P-value |
| Intercept | | 466.1 | (7.9) | (0.000) | 468.9 | (5.5) | (0.000) |
| School with high level of competition | 1 = yes; 0 = no | 17.9 | (2.5) | (0.000) | 1.9 | (1.6) | (0.245) |
| School with high levels of perceived parental pressure | 1 = yes; 0 = no | 11.2 | (2.5) | (0.000) | 2.0 | (1.6) | (0.228) |
| System with high proportion of competitive schools | Each additional 10% | 3.1 | (4.9) | (0.525) | 6.7 | (3.7) | (0.076) |

*Background variables*

| | | | | | | | |
|---|---|---|---|---|---|---|---|
| Student's PISA index of economic, social and cultural status | 1 = OECD S.D. | | | | 16.8 | (1.2) | (0.000) |
| Student's PISA index of economic, social and cultural status squared | | | | | 1.9 | (0.4) | (0.000) |
| Student is female | 1 = yes; 0 = no | | | | -5.9 | (1.1) | (0.000) |
| Student has no immigration background (student and parents were born in the country of assessment) | 1 = yes; 0 = no | | | | 10.4 | (3.3) | (0.002) |
| Student speaks the test language or other national language most of the time or always at home | 1 = yes; 0 = no | | | | 25.0 | (2.8) | (0.000) |
| School located in a small town or village (fewer than 15 000 people) | 1 = yes; 0 = no | | | | 6.8 | (1.7) | (0.000) |
| School located in a city (with over 100 000 people) | 1 = yes; 0 = no | | | | -6.1 | (1.4) | (0.000) |
| School size | 100 additional students | | | | 1.7 | (0.3) | (0.000) |
| School size squared | | | | | 0.0 | (0.0) | (0.001) |
| School average PISA index of economic, social and cultural status | 1 = OECD S.D. | | | | 52.0 | (3.8) | (0.000) |
| System average PISA index of economic, social and cultural status | 1 = OECD S.D. | | | | 13.6 | (10.7) | (0.209) |

| Variance explained (expressed as % of total variance) | | | |
|---|---|---|---|
| | Student level | 0.0 | 2.4 |
| | School level | 0.7 | 15.0 |
| | System level | 0.7 | 13.6 |
| | Total | 1.4 | 30.9 |

| Variance explained (expressed as % of variance at each level) | | | |
|---|---|---|---|
| | Student level | 0.0 | 5.0 |
| | School level | 2.7 | 56.0 |
| | System level | 2.6 | 51.9 |

Note: All slopes are fixed. All variables are grand-centred (a linear transformation of variables by subtracting the overall mean from the value proper). Intercept is random at all levels. The analysis is based on 55 countries. See Annex A8 for the detailed model specification.
StatLink ᵐˢᵖ http://dx.doi.org/10.1787/142127877152

Pour consulter la version française intégrale de ce tableau, suivre ce lien :
StatLink ᵐˢᵖ http://dx.doi.org/10.1787/152751048643

[Part 1/1]
**Table 5.19d** **Accountability policies and student performance in science**

Tableau 5.19d   Relation entre les politiques de responsabilisation et la performance des élèves en sciences

| | | Gross | | | Net | | |
|---|---|---|---|---|---|---|---|
| | | Change in score | S.E. | P-value | Change in score | S.E. | P-value |
| Intercept | | 464.3 | (7.7) | (0.000) | 468.2 | (5.5) | (0.000) |
| School informing parents of children's performance relative to other students in the school | 1 = yes; 0 = no | 4.7 | (3.2) | (0.140) | 2.8 | (1.9) | (0.139) |
| School informing parents of children's performance relative to national benchmarks | 1 = yes; 0 = no | 4.2 | (2.6) | (0.100) | 1.8 | (1.5) | (0.228) |
| School informing parents of students' performance relative to other schools | 1 = yes; 0 = no | -5.0 | (2.0) | (0.013) | -1.4 | (1.5) | (0.352) |
| School posting achievement data publicly | 1 = yes; 0 = no | 14.7 | (2.2) | (0.000) | 6.6 | (1.4) | (0.000) |
| School using achievement data for evaluating principals | 1 = yes; 0 = no | -2.3 | (2.4) | (0.354) | 0.0 | (1.4) | (0.993) |
| School using achievement data for evaluating teachers | 1 = yes; 0 = no | 4.3 | (2.4) | (0.076) | -0.5 | (1.4) | (0.711) |
| School using achievement data for allocating resources to schools | 1 = yes; 0 = no | -4.8 | (2.3) | (0.034) | -4.3 | (1.6) | (0.007) |
| School with achievement data tracked over time | 1 = yes; 0 = no | -2.4 | (2.5) | (0.327) | -1.2 | (1.6) | (0.443) |
| System with standards-based external examinations | ratio of existence | 36.1 | (16.0) | (0.028) | 17.0 | (13.9) | (0.226) |

*Background variables*

| | | | | | | | |
|---|---|---|---|---|---|---|---|
| Student's PISA index of economic, social and cultural status | 1 = OECD S.D. | | | | 16.8 | (1.2) | (0.000) |
| Student's PISA index of economic, social and cultural status squared | | | | | 1.9 | (0.4) | (0.000) |
| Student is female | 1 = yes; 0 = no | | | | -5.9 | (1.1) | (0.000) |
| Student has no immigration background (student and parents were born in the country of assessment) | 1 = yes; 0 = no | | | | 10.4 | (3.3) | (0.002) |
| Student speaks the test language or other national language most of the time or always at home | 1 = yes; 0 = no | | | | 25.0 | (2.8) | (0.000) |
| School located in a small town or village (fewer than 15 000 people) | 1 = yes; 0 = no | | | | 6.5 | (1.6) | (0.000) |
| School located in a city (with over 100 000 people) | 1 = yes; 0 = no | | | | -5.9 | (1.4) | (0.000) |
| School size | 100 additional students | | | | 1.6 | (0.3) | (0.000) |
| School size squared | | | | | 0.0 | (0.0) | (0.001) |
| School average PISA index of economic, social and cultural status | 1 = OECD S.D. | | | | 51.8 | (3.8) | (0.000) |
| System average PISA index of economic, social and cultural status | 1 = OECD S.D. | | | | 6.8 | (12.6) | (0.589) |

| | | | | |
|---|---|---|---|---|
| Variance explained (expressed as % of total variance) | Student level | | 0.0 | 2.4 |
| | School level | | 0.5 | 15.0 |
| | System level | | 2.1 | 13.0 |
| | Total | | 2.6 | 30.4 |

| | | | | |
|---|---|---|---|---|
| Variance explained (expressed as % of variance at each level) | Student level | | 0.0 | 5.0 |
| | School level | | 2.0 | 56.3 |
| | System level | | 7.9 | 49.5 |

Note: All slopes are fixed. All variables are grand-centred (a linear transformation of variables by subtracting the overall mean from the value proper). Intercept is random at all levels. The analysis is based on 55 countries. See Annex A8 for the detailed model specification.
**StatLink** http://dx.doi.org/10.1787/142127877152

Pour consulter la version française intégrale de ce tableau, suivre ce lien :
**StatLink** http://dx.doi.org/10.1787/152751048643

[Part 1/1]

**Table 5.19e   School autonomy and student performance in science**

Tableau 5.19e   Relation entre l'autonomie des établissements et la performance des élèves en sciences

| | | Gross | | | Net | | |
|---|---|---|---|---|---|---|---|
| | | Change in score | S.E. | P-value | Change in score | S.E. | P-value |
| Intercept | | 465.1 | (6.5) | (0.000) | 469.4 | (4.7) | (0.000) |
| School autonomy index in staffing | 1 = S.D. across 55 countries | 9.5 | (2.6) | (0.000) | -3.4 | (1.2) | (0.005) |
| School autonomy index in budgeting | 1 = S.D. across 55 countries | 1.1 | (1.5) | (0.457) | 1.5 | (0.7) | (0.045) |
| School autonomy index in educational content | 1 = S.D. across 55 countries | 0.9 | (1.6) | (0.573) | -0.8 | (0.9) | (0.368) |
| System average school autonomy index in staffing | 1 = S.D. across 55 countries | 0.7 | (9.2) | (0.936) | 1.5 | (6.8) | (0.829) |
| System average school autonomy index in budgeting | 1 = S.D. across 55 countries | 27.2 | (13.9) | (0.056) | 22.5 | (11.1) | (0.048) |
| System average school autonomy index in educational content | 1 = S.D. across 55 countries | 22.1 | (9.2) | (0.019) | 20.3 | (6.5) | (0.004) |

*Background variables*

| | | | | | | | |
|---|---|---|---|---|---|---|---|
| Student's PISA index of economic, social and cultural status | 1 = OECD S.D. | | | | 16.8 | (1.2) | (0.000) |
| Student's PISA index of economic, social and cultural status squared | | | | | 1.9 | (0.4) | (0.000) |
| Student is female | 1 = yes; 0 = no | | | | -5.9 | (1.1) | (0.000) |
| Student has no immigration background (student and parents were born in the country of assessment) | 1 = yes; 0 = no | | | | 10.4 | (3.3) | (0.002) |
| Student speaks the test language or other national language most of the time or always at home | 1 = yes; 0 = no | | | | 24.9 | (2.8) | (0.000) |
| School located in a small town or village (fewer than 15 000 people) | 1 = yes; 0 = no | | | | 6.5 | (1.7) | (0.000) |
| School located in a city (with over 100 000 people) | 1 = yes; 0 = no | | | | -5.8 | (1.4) | (0.000) |
| School size | 100 additional students | | | | 1.6 | (0.3) | (0.000) |
| School size squared | | | | | 0.0 | (0.0) | (0.001) |
| School average PISA index of economic, social and cultural status | 1 = OECD S.D. | | | | 53.3 | (3.9) | (0.000) |
| System average PISA index of economic, social and cultural status | 1 = OECD S.D. | | | | 2.9 | (10.8) | (0.790) |

| | | | | |
|---|---|---|---|---|
| Variance explained (expressed as % of total variance) | Student level | | 0.0 | 2.4 |
| | School level | | 0.5 | 15.0 |
| | System level | | 8.7 | 17.3 |
| | Total | | 9.2 | 34.6 |

| | | | | |
|---|---|---|---|---|
| Variance explained (expressed as % of variance at each level) | Student level | | 0.0 | 5.0 |
| | School level | | 1.8 | 56.1 |
| | System level | | 33.3 | 66.0 |

Note: All slopes are fixed. All variables are grand-centred (a linear transformation of variables by subtracting the overall mean from the value proper). Intercept is random at all levels. The analysis is based on 55 countries. See Annex A8 for the detailed model specification.
*StatLink* http://dx.doi.org/10.1787/142127877152

Pour consulter la version française intégrale de ce tableau, suivre ce lien :
*StatLink* http://dx.doi.org/10.1787/152751048643

[Part 1/1]

**Table 5.19f   School resources and student performance in science**

Tableau 5.19f   Relation entre la dotation des établissements et la performance des élèves en sciences

| | | Gross | | | Net | | |
|---|---|---|---|---|---|---|---|
| | | Change in score | S.E. | P-value | Change in score | S.E. | P-value |
| Intercept | | 470.7 | (6.2) | (0.000) | 471.0 | (4.7) | (0.000) |
| School average number of students per teacher | 1 additional student per teacher | 0.3 | (0.2) | (0.121) | -0.2 | (0.2) | (0.304) |
| School-level index of teacher shortage | 1 = OECD S.D. | -4.1 | (1.1) | (0.000) | -1.5 | (0.9) | (0.073) |
| School average number of computers for instruction per student | 1 additional computer per student | -12.5 | (13.6) | (0.359) | 2.5 | (10.8) | (0.817) |
| School-level index of quality of school educational resources | 1 = OECD S.D. | 5.1 | (1.2) | (0.000) | 0.2 | (0.7) | (0.798) |
| School average students' learning time for regular lessons in school | 1 additional hour per week | 14.3 | (1.0) | (0.000) | 8.7 | (0.7) | (0.000) |
| School average students' learning time for out-of-school lessons | 1 additional hour per week | -12.9 | (2.4) | (0.000) | -9.0 | (1.6) | (0.000) |
| School average students' learning time for self-study or homework | 1 additional hour per week | 3.8 | (1.3) | (0.004) | 3.1 | (0.9) | (0.001) |
| School providing opportunity of learning science | Each additional 10% | 1.7 | (1.0) | (0.080) | 1.4 | (0.6) | (0.016) |
| School average index of school activities to promote students' learning of science | 1 = OECD S.D. | 7.1 | (1.0) | (0.000) | 2.9 | (0.6) | (0.000) |

*Background variables*

| | | | | | | | |
|---|---|---|---|---|---|---|---|
| Student's PISA index of economic, social and cultural status | 1 = OECD S.D. | | | | 16.7 | (1.2) | (0.000) |
| Student's PISA index of economic, social and cultural status squared | | | | | 1.8 | (0.4) | (0.000) |
| Student is female | 1 = yes; 0 = no | | | | -6.2 | (1.1) | (0.000) |
| Student has no immigration background (student and parents were born in the country of assessment) | 1 = yes; 0 = no | | | | 10.5 | (3.3) | (0.002) |
| Student speaks the test language or other national language most of the time or always at home | 1 = yes; 0 = no | | | | 25.0 | (2.8) | (0.000) |
| School located in a small town or village (fewer than 15 000 people) | 1 = yes; 0 = no | | | | 3.5 | (1.4) | (0.016) |
| School located in a city (with over 100 000 people) | 1 = yes; 0 = no | | | | -4.3 | (1.1) | (0.000) |
| School size | 100 additional students | | | | 1.3 | (0.3) | (0.000) |
| School size squared | | | | | 0.0 | (0.0) | (0.001) |
| School average PISA index of economic, social and cultural status | 1 = OECD S.D. | | | | 34.2 | (2.9) | (0.000) |
| System average PISA index of economic, social and cultural status | 1 = OECD S.D. | | | | 18.1 | (10.5) | (0.089) |

| | | | | |
|---|---|---|---|---|
| Variance explained (expressed as % of total variance) | Student level | 0.0 | | 2.3 |
| | School level | 12.3 | | 18.2 |
| | System level | 11.2 | | 17.1 |
| | Total | 23.5 | | 37.7 |

| | | | | |
|---|---|---|---|---|
| Variance explained (expressed as % of variance at each level) | Student level | -0.1 | | 5.0 |
| | School level | 46.0 | | 68.0 |
| | System level | 42.9 | | 65.4 |

Note: All slopes are fixed. All variables are grand-centred (a linear transformation of variables by subtracting the overall mean from the value proper). Intercept is random at all levels. The analysis is based on 55 countries. See Annex A8 for the detailed model specification.
*StatLink*  http://dx.doi.org/10.1787/142127877152

Pour consulter la version française intégrale de ce tableau, suivre ce lien :
*StatLink* http://dx.doi.org/10.1787/152751048643

[Part 1/3]

**Table 5.19g    School and system factors and student performance in science, all significant factors combined**

Tableau 5.19g    Facteurs scolaires et systémiques et performances des élèves en sciences, tous facteurs significatifs combinés

| | | Model 0a Empty | | | Model 0b Background | | |
|---|---|---|---|---|---|---|---|
| | | Change in score | S.E. | P-value | Change in score | S.E. | P-value |
| Intercept | | 466.1 | (8.0) | (0.000) | 469.1 | (5.7) | (0.000) |
| **Admitting, grouping and selecting** | | | | | | | |
| School with ability grouping for all subjects within school | 1 = yes; 0 = no | | | | | | |
| School with high academic selectivity of school admittance | 1 = yes; 0 = no | | | | | | |
| School with low academic selectivity of school admittance | 1 = yes; 0 = no | | | | | | |
| **School management and funding** | | | | | | | |
| School being privately managed | 1 = private; 0 = public | | | | | | |
| School with high proportion of school funding from government sources | Each additional 10% | | | | | | |
| **Parental pressure and choice** | | | | | | | |
| School with high level of competition | 1 = yes; 0 = no | | | | | | |
| School with high levels of perceived parental pressure | 1 = yes; 0 = no | | | | | | |
| System with high proportion of competitive schools | Each additional 10% | | | | | | |
| **Accountability policies** | | | | | | | |
| School posting achievement data publicly | 1 = yes; 0 = no | | | | | | |
| System with standards-based external examinations | ratio of existence | | | | | | |
| **School autonomy** | | | | | | | |
| School autonomy index in staffing | 1 = S.D. across 55 countries | | | | | | |
| School autonomy index in budgeting | 1 = S.D. across 55 countries | | | | | | |
| School autonomy index in educational content | 1 = S.D. across 55 countries | | | | | | |
| System average school autonomy index in staffing | 1 = S.D. across 55 countries | | | | | | |
| System average school autonomy index in budgeting | 1 = S.D. across 55 countries | | | | | | |
| System average school autonomy index in educational content | 1 = S.D. across 55 countries | | | | | | |
| **School resources** | | | | | | | |
| School-level index of teacher shortage | 1 = OECD S.D. | | | | | | |
| School-level index of quality of school educational resources | 1 = OECD S.D. | | | | | | |
| School average students' learning time for regular lessons in school | 1 additional hour per week | | | | | | |
| School average students' learning time for out-of-school lessons | 1 additional hour per week | | | | | | |
| School average students' learning time for self-study or homework | 1 additional hour per week | | | | | | |
| School average index of school activities to promote students' learning of science | 1 = OECD S.D. | | | | | | |
| *Background variables* | | | | | | | |
| Student's PISA index of economic, social and cultural status | 1 = OECD S.D. | | | | 16.8 | (1.2) | (0.000) |
| Student's PISA index of economic, social and cultural status squared | | | | | 1.9 | (0.4) | (0.000) |
| Student is female | 1 = yes; 0 = no | | | | -5.9 | (1.1) | (0.000) |
| Student has no immigration background (student and parents were born in the country of assessment) | 1 = yes; 0 = no | | | | 10.4 | (3.3) | (0.002) |
| Student speaks the test language or other national language most of the time or always at home | 1 = yes; 0 = no | | | | 25.0 | (2.8) | (0.000) |
| School located in a small town or village (fewer than 15 000 people) | 1 = yes; 0 = no | | | | 6.5 | (1.7) | (0.000) |
| School located in a city (with over 100 000 people) | 1 = yes; 0 = no | | | | -6.2 | (1.4) | (0.000) |
| School size | 100 additional students | | | | 1.7 | (0.3) | (0.000) |
| School size squared | | | | | 0.0 | (0.0) | (0.001) |
| School average index of economic, social and cultural status | 1 = OECD S.D. | | | | 52.3 | (3.8) | (0.000) |
| System average index of economic, social and cultural status | 1 = OECD S.D. | | | | 11.5 | (11.4) | (0.320) |
| Variance explained (expressed as % of total variance)[1] | Student level | 47.1 | | | 2.4 | | |
| | School level | 26.7 | | | 14.9 | | |
| | System level | 26.2 | | | 12.6 | | |
| | Total | 100.0 | | | 29.9 | | |
| Variance explained (expressed as % of variance at each level) | Student level | | | | 5.0 | | |
| | School level | | | | 55.9 | | |
| | System level | | | | 48.1 | | |

Note: All slopes are fixed. All variables are grand-centred (a linear transformation of variables by subtracting the overall mean from the value proper). Intercept is random at all levels. The analysis is based on 55 countries. See Annex A8 for the detailed model specification.
1. For the Model 0a (empty model), variance decomposition among the three levels is presented.
*StatLink* http://dx.doi.org/10.1787/142127877152

Pour consulter la version française intégrale de ce tableau, suivre ce lien :
*StatLink* http://dx.doi.org/10.1787/152751048643

[Part 2/3]

**Table 5.19g  School and system factors and student performance in science, all significant factors combined**

Tableau 5.19g  Facteurs scolaires et systémiques et performances des élèves en sciences, tous facteurs significatifs combinés

| | | Model 1G First gross combined | | | Model 2G Second gross combined | | |
|---|---|---|---|---|---|---|---|
| | | Change in score | S.E. | P-value | Change in score | S.E. | P-value |
| Intercept | | 469.6 | (5.6) | (0.000) | 470.2 | (6.1) | (0.000) |
| ***Admitting, grouping and selecting*** | | | | | | | |
| School with ability grouping for all subjects within school | 1 = yes; 0 = no | -7.6 | (1.3) | (0.000) | -7.6 | (1.3) | (0.000) |
| School with high academic selectivity of school admittance | 1 = yes; 0 = no | 18.7 | (3.2) | (0.000) | 18.5 | (3.2) | (0.000) |
| School with low academic selectivity of school admittance | 1 = yes; 0 = no | -6.4 | (2.2) | (0.004) | -7.0 | (2.2) | (0.002) |
| ***School management and funding*** | | | | | | | |
| School being privately managed | 1 = private; 0 = public | 8.6 | (3.1) | (0.006) | | | |
| School with high proportion of school funding from government sources | Each additional 10% | -1.7 | (0.6) | (0.003) | -2.1 | (0.5) | (0.000) |
| ***Parental pressure and choice*** | | | | | | | |
| School with high level of competition | 1 = yes; 0 = no | 5.4 | (1.9) | (0.005) | 6.0 | (1.9) | (0.002) |
| School with high levels of preceived parental pressure | 1 = yes; 0 = no | 3.3 | (1.5) | (0.026) | | | |
| System with high proportion of competitive schools | Each additional 10% | -8.5 | (3.1) | (0.008) | -4.6 | (3.3) | (0.178) |
| ***Accountability policies*** | | | | | | | |
| School posting achievement data publicly | 1 = yes; 0 = no | 5.4 | (1.1) | (0.000) | 5.3 | (1.1) | (0.000) |
| System with standards-based external examinations | ratio of existence | 22.7 | (14.2) | (0.115) | | | |
| ***School autonomy*** | | | | | | | |
| School autonomy index in staffing | 1 = S.D. across 55 countries | -0.3 | (1.3) | (0.847) | | | |
| School autonomy index in budgeting | 1 = S.D. across 55 countries | 0.9 | (0.9) | (0.287) | 1.4 | (1.0) | (0.155) |
| School autonomy index in educational content | 1 = S.D. across 55 countries | -0.2 | (1.0) | (0.857) | | | |
| System average school autonomy index in staffing | 1 = S.D. across 55 countries | 10.9 | (8.5) | (0.203) | | | |
| System average school autonomy index in budgeting | 1 = S.D. across 55 countries | 24.4 | (11.1) | (0.032) | 28.6 | (12.2) | (0.023) |
| System average school autonomy index in educational content | 1 = S.D. across 55 countries | 3.9 | (9.8) | (0.689) | | | |
| ***School resources*** | | | | | | | |
| School-level index of teacher shortage | 1 = OECD S.D. | -3.6 | (1.0) | (0.000) | -3.5 | (1.0) | (0.000) |
| School-level index of quality of school educational resources | 1 = OECD S.D. | 3.8 | (1.0) | (0.000) | 3.9 | (1.1) | (0.000) |
| School average students' learning time for regular lessons in school | 1 additional hour per week | 13.9 | (0.8) | (0.000) | 14.0 | (0.8) | (0.000) |
| School average students' learning time for out-of-school lessons | 1 additional hour per week | -11.6 | (2.5) | (0.000) | -11.7 | (2.5) | (0.000) |
| School average students' learning time for self-study or homework | 1 additional hour per week | 3.7 | (1.2) | (0.002) | 3.8 | (1.2) | (0.002) |
| School average index of school activities to promote students' learning of science | 1 = OECD S.D. | 6.7 | (1.0) | (0.000) | 6.7 | (0.9) | (0.000) |
| | | | | | | | |
| *Background variables* | | | | | | | |
| Student's PISA index of economic, social and cultural status | 1 = OECD S.D. | | | | | | |
| Student's PISA index of economic, social and cultural status squared | | | | | | | |
| Student is female | 1 = yes; 0 = no | | | | | | |
| Student has no immigration background (student and parents were born in the country of assessment) | 1 = yes; 0 = no | | | | | | |
| Student speaks the test language or other national language most of the time or always at home | 1 = yes; 0 = no | | | | | | |
| School located in a small town or village (fewer than 15 000 people) | 1 = yes; 0 = no | | | | | | |
| School located in a city (with over 100 000 people) | 1 = yes; 0 = no | | | | | | |
| School size | 100 additional students | | | | | | |
| School size squared | | | | | | | |
| School average index of economic, social and cultural status | 1 = OECD S.D. | | | | | | |
| System average index of economic, social and cultural status | 1 = OECD S.D. | | | | | | |
| | | | | | | | |
| Variance explained (expressed as % of total variance) | Student level | 0.0 | | | 0.0 | | |
| | School level | 13.1 | | | 13.0 | | |
| | System level | 13.5 | | | 11.4 | | |
| | Total | 26.6 | | | 24.4 | | |
| | | | | | | | |
| Variance explained (expressed as % of variance at each level) | Student level | -0.1 | | | -0.1 | | |
| | School level | 49.0 | | | 48.8 | | |
| | System level | 51.7 | | | 43.6 | | |

Note: All slopes are fixed. All variables are grand-centred (a linear transformation of variables by subtracting the overall mean from the value proper). Intercept is random at all levels. The analysis is based on 55 countries. See Annex A8 for the detailed model specification.
*StatLink*  http://dx.doi.org/10.1787/142127877152

Pour consulter la version française intégrale de ce tableau, suivre ce lien :
*StatLink* http://dx.doi.org/10.1787/152751048643

[Part 3/3]

**Table 5.19g** School and system factors and student performance in science, all significant factors combined

*Tableau 5.19g* Facteurs scolaires et systémiques et performances des élèves en sciences, tous facteurs significatifs combinés

| | | Model 1N First net combined | | | Model 2N Second net combined | | |
|---|---|---|---|---|---|---|---|
| | | Change in score | S.E. | P-value | Change in score | S.E. | P-value |
| Intercept | | 471.1 | (4.1) | (0.000) | 471.0 | (4.2) | (0.000) |
| **Admitting, grouping and selecting** | | | | | | | |
| School with ability grouping for all subjects within school | 1 = yes; 0 = no | -4.5 | (1.2) | (0.000) | -4.5 | (1.2) | (0.000) |
| School with high academic selectivity of school admittance | 1 = yes; 0 = no | 14.3 | (2.5) | (0.000) | 14.4 | (2.5) | (0.000) |
| School with low academic selectivity of school admittance | 1 = yes; 0 = no | -1.3 | (1.4) | (0.359) | -1.3 | (1.4) | (0.378) |
| **School management and funding** | | | | | | | |
| School being privately managed | 1 = private; 0 = public | | | | | | |
| School with high proportion of school funding from government sources | Each additional 10% | | | | | | |
| **Parental pressure and choice** | | | | | | | |
| School with high level of competition | 1 = yes; 0 = no | -0.1 | (1.5) | (0.946) | | | |
| School with high levels of perceived parental pressure | 1 = yes; 0 = no | | | | | | |
| System with high proportion of competitive schools | Each additional 10% | -0.8 | (3.5) | (0.808) | | | |
| **Accountability policies** | | | | | | | |
| School posting achievement data publicly | 1 = yes; 0 = no | 3.6 | (1.1) | (0.001) | 3.5 | (1.1) | (0.001) |
| System with standards-based external examinations | ratio of existence | | | | | | |
| **School autonomy** | | | | | | | |
| School autonomy index in staffing | 1 = S.D. across 55 countries | | | | | | |
| School autonomy index in budgeting | 1 = S.D. across 55 countries | 1.1 | (0.7) | (0.110) | 0.9 | (0.7) | (0.188) |
| School autonomy index in educational content | 1 = S.D. across 55 countries | -1.3 | (0.9) | (0.134) | | | |
| System average school autonomy index in staffing | 1 = S.D. across 55 countries | | | | | | |
| System average school autonomy index in budgeting | 1 = S.D. across 55 countries | 20.8 | (8.7) | (0.021) | 25.7 | (9.3) | (0.008) |
| System average school autonomy index in educational content | 1 = S.D. across 55 countries | 10.5 | (6.8) | (0.128) | | | |
| **School resources** | | | | | | | |
| School-level index of teacher shortage | 1 = OECD S.D. | | | | | | |
| School-level index of quality of school educational resources | 1 = OECD S.D. | | | | | | |
| School average students' learning time for regular lessons in school | 1 additional hour per week | 8.7 | (0.6) | (0.000) | 8.8 | (0.6) | (0.000) |
| School average students' learning time for out-of-school lessons | 1 additional hour per week | -8.6 | (1.7) | (0.000) | -8.6 | (1.7) | (0.000) |
| School average students' learning time for self-study or homework | 1 additional hour per week | 3.1 | (0.8) | (0.000) | 3.1 | (0.8) | (0.000) |
| School average index of school activities to promote students' learning of science | 1 = OECD S.D. | 2.9 | (0.6) | (0.000) | 2.9 | (0.6) | (0.000) |
| *Background variables* | | | | | | | |
| Student's PISA index of economic, social and cultural status | 1 = OECD S.D. | 16.7 | (1.2) | (0.000) | 16.7 | (1.2) | (0.000) |
| Student's PISA index of economic, social and cultural status squared | | 1.8 | (0.4) | (0.000) | 1.8 | (0.4) | (0.000) |
| Student is female | 1 = yes; 0 = no | -6.2 | (1.1) | (0.000) | -6.2 | (1.1) | (0.000) |
| Student has no immigration background (student and parents were born in the country of assessment) | 1 = yes; 0 = no | 10.5 | (3.3) | (0.002) | 10.5 | (3.3) | (0.002) |
| Student speaks the test language or other national language most of the time or always at home | 1 = yes; 0 = no | 25.1 | (2.8) | (0.000) | 25.1 | (2.8) | (0.000) |
| School located in a small town or village (fewer than 15 000 people) | 1 = yes; 0 = no | 4.2 | (1.4) | (0.004) | 4.2 | (1.4) | (0.003) |
| School located in a city (with over 100 000 people) | 1 = yes; 0 = no | -4.0 | (1.0) | (0.000) | -4.1 | (1.0) | (0.000) |
| School size | 100 additional students | 1.2 | (0.2) | (0.000) | 1.2 | (0.2) | (0.000) |
| School size squared | | 0.0 | (0.0) | (0.001) | 0.0 | (0.0) | (0.000) |
| School average index of economic, social and cultural status | 1 = OECD S.D. | 33.5 | (2.8) | (0.000) | 33.3 | (2.8) | (0.000) |
| System average index of economic, social and cultural status | 1 = OECD S.D. | 16.5 | (11.2) | (0.148) | 18.5 | (10.7) | (0.089) |
| Variance explained (expressed as % of total variance) | Student level | 2.3 | | | 2.3 | | |
| | School level | 18.4 | | | 18.3 | | |
| | System level | 19.1 | | | 18.8 | | |
| | Total | 39.8 | | | 39.5 | | |
| Variance explained (expressed as % of variance at each level) | Student level | 5.0 | | | 5.0 | | |
| | School level | 6.9 | | | 68.7 | | |
| | System level | 73.1 | | | 71.8 | | |

Note: All slopes are fixed. All variables are grand-centred (a linear transformation of variables by subtracting the overall mean from the value proper). Intercept is random at all levels. The analysis is based on 55 countries. See Annex A8 for the detailed model specification.
*StatLink* http://dx.doi.org/10.1787/142127877152

Pour consulter la version française intégrale de ce tableau, suivre ce lien :
*StatLink* http://dx.doi.org/10.1787/152751048643

[Part 1/1]

**Table 5.20a  Admitting, grouping and selecting and the impact of socio-economic background on student performance in science**

Tableau 5.20a  Relation entre les politiques d'admission, le regroupement par aptitude, la sélection des élèves et l'impact du milieu socioéconomique sur la performance des élèves en sciences

| | | Variable name | Change in relationship | S.E. | P-value |
|---|---|---|---|---|---|
| **Estimates of within-school effect of the PISA index of economic, social and cultural status on performance (ESCS slope)** | | | | | |
| Intercept | | ESCS | 16.3 | (1.2) | (0.000) |
| School with ability grouping for all subjects within school | 1 = yes; 0 = no | ESCS*XABGR | 0.6 | (0.6) | (0.311) |
| School with high academic selectivity of school admittance | 1 = yes; 0 = no | ESCS*XHISELE | -1.2 | (0.8) | (0.139) |
| School with low academic selectivity of school admittance | 1 = yes; 0 = no | ESCS*XLOSELE | 1.1 | (0.6) | (0.084) |
| System with early selection (difference between the first age of selection and the age of 15) | 1 additional year | ESCS*YYRSSEP | -1.3 | (0.7) | (0.056) |
| System-level number of school types or distinct educational programmes available to 15-year-olds | 1 additional programme | ESCS*YNRTRACK | -1.3 | (1.2) | (0.294) |
| **Estimates of compositional effect of the school average PISA index of economic, social and cultural status on performance (XESCS slope)** | | | | | |
| Intercept | | XESCS | 56.7 | (3.3) | (0.000) |
| System with early selection (difference between the first age of selection and the age of 15) | 1 additional year | XESCS*YYRSSEP | 6.6 | (2.4) | (0.009) |
| System-level number of school types or distinct educational programmes available to 15-year-olds | 1 additional programme | XESCS*YNRTRACK | 6.2 | (3.1) | (0.049) |

| | | Variable name | Change in score | S.E. | P-value |
|---|---|---|---|---|---|
| **Estimates of the performance level in science (Intercept)** | | | | | |
| Intercept | | | 462.3 | (6.0) | (0.000) |
| School with ability grouping for all subjects within school | 1 = yes; 0 = no | XABGR | -3.5 | (1.2) | (0.005) |
| School with high academic selectivity of school admittance | 1 = yes; 0 = no | XHISELE | 16.2 | (2.5) | (0.000) |
| School with low academic selectivity of school admittance | 1 = yes; 0 = no | XLOSELE | -1.3 | (1.3) | (0.320) |
| System with early selection (difference between the first age of selection and the age of 15) | 1 additional year | YYRSSEP | -1.9 | (3.6) | (0.608) |
| System-level number of school types or distinct educational programmes available to 15-year-olds | 1 additional programme | YNRTRACK | 2.3 | (6.2) | (0.709) |

*Background variables*

| | | | | | |
|---|---|---|---|---|---|
| Student's PISA index of economic, social and cultural status squared | | ESCS$^2$ | 0.1 | (0.3) | (0.584) |
| Student is female | 1 = yes; 0 = no | FEMALE | -6.0 | (1.1) | (0.000) |
| Student has no immigration background (student and parents were born in the country of assessment) | 1 = yes; 0 = no | NATIVE | 10.2 | (3.1) | (0.002) |
| Student speaks the test language or other national language most of the time or always at home | 1 = yes; 0 = no | SAMELANG | 23.0 | (2.8) | (0.000) |
| School located in a small town or village (fewer than 15 000 people) | 1 = yes; 0 = no | XRURAL | 4.7 | (1.4) | (0.001) |
| School located in a city (with over 100 000 people) | 1 = yes; 0 = no | XCITY | -5.3 | (1.3) | (0.000) |
| School size | 100 additional students | XSCHSIZE | 1.5 | (0.3) | (0.000) |
| School size squared | | XSCHSIZ$^2$ | 0.0 | (0.0) | (0.001) |
| System average PISA index of economic, social and cultural status | 1 = OECD S.D. | YESCS | -2.3 | (10.1) | (0.821) |

Note: All slopes are fixed except ESCS and XESCS. All variables are grand-centred (a linear transformation of variables by subtracting the overall mean from the value proper). Intercept is random at all levels. The analysis is based on 55 countries. See Annex A8 for the detailed model specification.

StatLink 🖼 http://dx.doi.org/10.1787/142127877152

Pour consulter la version française intégrale de ce tableau, suivre ce lien :
StatLink 🖼 http://dx.doi.org/10.1787/152751048643

[Part 1/1]

**Table 5.20b** **School management and funding and the impact of socio-economic background on student performance in science**

Tableau 5.20b Relation entre les modalités de gestion et de financement des établissements et l'impact du milieu socioéconomique sur la performance des élèves en sciences

| | | Variable name | Change in relationship | S.E. | P-value |
|---|---|---|---|---|---|
| **Estimates of within-school effect of the PISA index of economic, social and cultural status on performance (ESCS slope)** | | | | | |
| Intercept | | ESCS | 16.3 | (1.3) | (0.000) |
| School being privately managed | 1 = private; 0 = public | ESCS*XPRIVMAN | -0.7 | (0.8) | (0.382) |
| School with high proportion of school funding from government sources | Each additional 10% | ESCS*XGOVFUND | 0.2 | (0.1) | (0.174) |
| **Estimates of compositional effect of the school average PISA index of economic, social and cultural status on performance (XESCS slope)** | | | | | |
| Intercept | | XESCS | 58.2 | (4.3) | (0.000) |

| | | Variable name | Change in score | S.E. | P-value |
|---|---|---|---|---|---|
| **Estimates of the performance level in science (Intercept)** | | | | | |
| Intercept | | | 462.9 | (5.8) | (0.000) |
| School being privately managed | 1 = private; 0 = public | XPRIVMAN | -1.1 | (3.1) | (0.714) |
| School with high proportion of school funding from government sources | Each additional 10% | XGOVFUND | 0.0 | (0.4) | (0.916) |

*Background variables*

| | | Variable name | Change in score | S.E. | P-value |
|---|---|---|---|---|---|
| Student's PISA index of economic, social and cultural status squared | | ESCS$^2$ | 0.2 | (0.3) | (0.556) |
| Student is female | 1 = yes; 0 = no | FEMALE | -6.0 | (1.1) | (0.000) |
| Student has no immigration background (student and parents were born in the country of assessment) | 1 = yes; 0 = no | NATIVE | 10.2 | (3.1) | (0.002) |
| Student speaks the test language or other national language most of the time or always at home | 1 = yes; 0 = no | SAMELANG | 23.0 | (2.8) | (0.000) |
| School located in a small town or village (fewer than 15 000 people) | 1 = yes; 0 = no | XRURAL | 4.1 | (1.5) | (0.007) |
| School located in a city (with over 100 000 people) | 1 = yes; 0 = no | XCITY | -5.3 | (1.4) | (0.000) |
| School size | 100 additional students | XSCHSIZE | 1.4 | (0.3) | (0.000) |
| School size squared | | XSCHSIZ$^2$ | 0.0 | (0.0) | (0.002) |
| System average PISA index of economic, social and cultural status | 1 = OECD S.D. | YESCS | -1.1 | (10.4) | (0.915) |

Note: All slopes are fixed except ESCS and XESCS. All variables are grand-centred (a linear transformation of variables by subtracting the overall mean from the value proper). Intercept is random at all levels. The analysis is based on 55 countries. See Annex A8 for the detailed model specification.
*StatLink* http://dx.doi.org/10.1787/142127877152

Pour consulter la version française intégrale de ce tableau, suivre ce lien :
*StatLink* http://dx.doi.org/10.1787/152751048643

[Part 1/1]

**Table 5.20c   Parental pressure and choice and the impact of socio-economic background on student performance in science**

Tableau 5.20c   Relation entre la liberté de choix de l'établissement, la pression parentale et l'impact du milieu socioéconomique sur la performance des élèves en sciences

| | | Variable name | Change in relationship | S.E. | P-value |
|---|---|---|---|---|---|
| **Estimates of within-school effect of the PISA index of economic, social and cultural status on performance (ESCS slope)** | | | | | |
| Intercept | | ESCS | 16.3 | (1.3) | (0.000) |
| School with high level of competition | 1 = yes; 0 = no | ESCS*XSCHLCOM | 1.0 | (0.6) | (0.083) |
| School with high levels of peceived parental pressure | 1 = yes; 0 = no | ESCS*XPRESSPA | 1.0 | (0.5) | (0.058) |
| System with high proportion of competitive schools | Each additional 10% | ESCS*YSCHLCOM | -0.8 | (0.8) | (0.291) |

| | | Variable name | Change in relationship | S.E. | P-value |
|---|---|---|---|---|---|
| **Estimates of compositional effect of the school average PISA index of economic, social and cultural status on performance (XESCS slope)** | | | | | |
| Intercept | | XESCS | 57.5 | (4.0) | (0.000) |
| System with high proportion of competitive schools | Each additional 10% | XESCS*YSCHLCOM | 3.5 | (2.8) | (0.211) |

| | | Variable name | Change in score | S.E. | P-value |
|---|---|---|---|---|---|
| **Estimates of  the performance level in science (Intercept)** | | | | | |
| Intercept | | | 462.7 | (5.6) | (0.000) |
| School with high level of competition | 1 = yes; 0 = no | XSCHLCOM | -0.3 | (1.3) | (0.797) |
| School with high levels of peceived parental pressure | 1 = yes; 0 = no | XPRESSPA | 1.5 | (1.4) | (0.261) |
| System with high proportion of competitive schools | Each additional 10% | YSCHLCOM | 4.3 | (3.7) | (0.250) |

*Background variables*

| | | Variable name | Change in score | S.E. | P-value |
|---|---|---|---|---|---|
| Student's PISA index of economic, social and cultural status squared | | ESCS$^2$ | 0.0 | (0.3) | (0.862) |
| Student is female | 1 = yes; 0 = no | FEMALE | -6.0 | (1.1) | (0.000) |
| Student has no immigration background (student and parents were born in the country of assessment) | 1 = yes; 0 = no | NATIVE | 10.2 | (3.1) | (0.002) |
| Student speaks the test language or other national language most of the time or always at home | 1 = yes; 0 = no | SAMELANG | 23.0 | (2.8) | (0.000) |
| School located in a small town or village (fewer than 15 000 people) | 1 = yes; 0 = no | XRURAL | 4.0 | (1.5) | (0.009) |
| School located in a city (with over 100 000 people) | 1 = yes; 0 = no | XCITY | -5.3 | (1.4) | (0.000) |
| School size | 100 additional students | XSCHSIZE | 1.5 | (0.3) | (0.000) |
| School size squared | | XSCHSIZ$^2$ | 0.0 | (0.0) | (0.002) |
| System average PISA index of economic, social and cultural status | 1 = OECD S.D. | YESCS | 2.8 | (10.2) | (0.786) |

Note: All slopes are fixed except ESCS and XESCS. All variables are grand-centred (a linear transformation of variables by subtracting the overall mean from the value proper). Intercept is random at all levels. The analysis is based on 55 countries. See Annex A8 for the detailed model specification.
StatLink ⟐ http://dx.doi.org/10.1787/142127877152

Pour consulter la version française intégrale de ce tableau, suivre ce lien :
StatLink ⟐ http://dx.doi.org/10.1787/152751048643

[Part 1/1]

**Table 5.20d Accountability policies and the impact of socio-economic background on student performance in science**

*Tableau 5.20d Relation entre les politiques de responsabilisation et l'impact du milieu socioéconomique sur la performance des élèves en sciences*

| | | Variable name | Change in relationship | S.E. | P-value |
|---|---|---|---|---|---|
| **Estimates of within-school effect of the PISA index of economic, social and cultural status on performance (ESCS slope)** | | | | | |
| Intercept | | ESCS | 16.1 | (1.2) | (0.000) |
| School informing parents of children's performance relative to other students in the school | 1 = yes; 0 = no | ESCS*XACC1 | -0.5 | (0.5) | (0.327) |
| School informing parents of children's performance relative to national benchmarks | 1 = yes; 0 = no | ESCS*XACC2 | 1.1 | (0.6) | (0.058) |
| School informing parents of students' performance relative to other schools | 1 = yes; 0 = no | ESCS*XACC3 | -0.4 | (0.6) | (0.557) |
| School posting achievement data publicly | 1 = yes; 0 = no | ESCS*XACC4 | 1.3 | (0.5) | (0.012) |
| School using achievement data for evaluating principals | 1 = yes; 0 = no | ESCS*XACC5 | 0.2 | (0.6) | (0.789) |
| School using achievement data for evaluating teachers | 1 = yes; 0 = no | ESCS*XACC6 | 0.4 | (0.6) | (0.566) |
| School using achievement data for allocating resources to schools | 1 = yes; 0 = no | ESCS*XACC7 | -0.3 | (0.6) | (0.599) |
| School with achievement data tracked over time | 1 = yes; 0 = no | ESCS*XACC8 | -0.4 | (0.6) | (0.514) |
| System with standards-based external examinations | ratio of existence | ESCS*YSCENTEX | 2.8 | (2.6) | (0.290) |
| **Estimates of compositional effect of the school average PISA index of economic, social and cultural status on performance (XESCS slope)** | | | | | |
| Intercept | | XESCS | 56.9 | (3.8) | (0.000) |
| System with standards-based external examinations | ratio of existence | XESCS*YSCENTEX | 12.7 | (8.0) | (0.120) |

| | | Variable name | Change in score | S.E. | P-value |
|---|---|---|---|---|---|
| **Estimates of the performance level in science (Intercept)** | | | | | |
| Intercept | | | 461.9 | (5.6) | (0.000) |
| School informing parents of children's performance relative to other students in school | 1 = yes; 0 = no | XACC1 | 1.7 | (1.4) | (0.231) |
| School informing parents of children's performance relative to national benchmarks | 1 = yes; 0 = no | XACC2 | 1.3 | (1.2) | (0.298) |
| School informing parents of students' performance relative to other schools | 1 = yes; 0 = no | XACC3 | -1.7 | (1.4) | (0.235) |
| School posting achievement data publicly | 1 = yes; 0 = no | XACC4 | 6.6 | (1.3) | (0.000) |
| School using achievement data for evaluating principals | 1 = yes; 0 = no | XACC5 | -0.1 | (1.4) | (0.948) |
| School using achievement data for evaluating teachers | 1 = yes; 0 = no | XACC6 | -0.5 | (1.3) | (0.716) |
| School using achievement data for allocating resources to schools | 1 = yes; 0 = no | XACC7 | -2.9 | (1.5) | (0.045) |
| School with achievement data tracked over time | 1 = yes; 0 = no | XACC8 | -1.3 | (1.4) | (0.344) |
| System with standards-based external examinations | ratio of existence | YSCENTEX | 21.5 | (13.6) | (0.118) |

*Background variables*

| | | Variable name | Change in score | S.E. | P-value |
|---|---|---|---|---|---|
| Student's PISA index of economic, social and cultural status squared | | ESCS$^2$ | 0.1 | (0.3) | (0.784) |
| Student is female | 1 = yes; 0 = no | FEMALE | -6.0 | (1.1) | (0.000) |
| Student has no immigration background (student and parents were born in the country of assessment) | 1 = yes; 0 = no | NATIVE | 10.2 | (3.1) | (0.002) |
| Student speaks the test language or other national language most of the time or always at home | 1 = yes; 0 = no | SAMELANG | 23.0 | (2.8) | (0.000) |
| School located in a small town or village (fewer than 15 000 people) | 1 = yes; 0 = no | XRURAL | 4.1 | (1.5) | (0.006) |
| School located in a city (with over 100 000 people) | 1 = yes; 0 = no | XCITY | -5.1 | (1.3) | (0.000) |
| School size | 100 additional students | XSCHSIZE | 1.4 | (0.3) | (0.000) |
| School size squared | | XSCHSIZ$^2$ | 0.0 | (0.0) | (0.002) |
| System average PISA index of economic, social and cultural status | 1 = OECD S.D. | YESCS | -3.8 | (11.4) | (0.741) |

Note: All slopes are fixed except ESCS and XESCS. All variables are grand-centred (a linear transformation of variables by subtracting the overall mean from the value proper). Intercept is random at all levels. The analysis is based on 55 countries. See Annex A8 for the detailed model specification.
*StatLink* http://dx.doi.org/10.1787/142127877152

Pour consulter la version française intégrale de ce tableau, suivre ce lien :
*StatLink* http://dx.doi.org/10.1787/152751048643

[Part 1/1]
**Table 5.20e  School autonomy and the impact of socio-economic background on student performance in science**

Tableau 5.20e  Relation entre l'autonomie des établissements et l'impact du milieu socioéconomique sur la performance des élèves en sciences

| | | Variable name | Change in relationship | S.E. | P-value |
|---|---|---|---|---|---|
| **Estimates of within-school effect of the PISA index of economic, social and cultural status on performance (ESCS slope)** | | | | | |
| Intercept | | ESCS | 16.3 | (1.3) | (0.000) |
| School autonomy index in staffing | 1 = S.D. across 55 countries | ESCS*XFACS | 0.0 | (0.4) | (0.943) |
| School autonomy index in budgeting | 1 = S.D. across 55 countries | ESCS*XFACB | 0.1 | (0.3) | (0.675) |
| School autonomy index in educational content | 1 = S.D. across 55 countries | ESCS*XFACC | 0.4 | (0.4) | (0.394) |
| System average school autonomy index in staffing | 1 = S.D. across 55 countries | ESCS*YFACS | 1.8 | (1.8) | (0.311) |
| System average school autonomy index in budgeting | 1 = S.D. across 55 countries | ESCS*YFACB | 1.0 | (3.3) | (0.765) |
| System average school autonomy index in educational contents | 1 = S.D. across 55 countries | ESCS*YFACC | 1.3 | (1.9) | (0.495) |
| **Estimates of compositional effect of the school average PISA index of economic, social and cultural status on performance (XESCS slope)** | | | | | |
| Intercept | | XESCS | 58.1 | (4.1) | (0.000) |
| System average school autonomy index in staffing | 1 = S.D. across 55 countries | XESCS*YFACS | 2.8 | (6.8) | (0.683) |
| System average school autonomy index in budgeting | 1 = S.D. across 55 countries | XESCS*YFACB | 6.6 | (8.4) | (0.436) |
| System average school autonomy index in educational content | 1 = S.D. across 55 countries | XESCS*YFACC | -1.3 | (5.3) | (0.806) |

| | | Variable name | Change in score | S.E. | P-value |
|---|---|---|---|---|---|
| **Estimates of the performance level in science (Intercept)** | | | | | |
| Intercept | | | 463.2 | (4.9) | (0.000) |
| School autonomy index in staffing | 1 = S.D. across 55 countries | XFACS | -1.5 | (1.3) | (0.255) |
| School autonomy index in budgeting | 1 = S.D. across 55 countries | XFACB | 1.0 | (0.7) | (0.125) |
| School autonomy index in educational content | 1 = S.D. across 55 countries | XFACC | -0.4 | (0.9) | (0.671) |
| System average school autonomy index in staffing | 1 = S.D. across 55 countries | YFACS | -0.8 | (7.4) | (0.915) |
| System average school autonomy index in budgeting | 1 = S.D. across 55 countries | YFACB | 17.0 | (11.6) | (0.149) |
| System average school autonomy index in educational content | 1 = S.D. across 55 countries | YFACC | 20.0 | (6.9) | (0.006) |

*Background variables*

| | | | | | |
|---|---|---|---|---|---|
| Student's PISA index of economic, social and cultural status squared | | ESCS$^2$ | 0.1 | (0.3) | (0.738) |
| Student is female | 1 = yes; 0 = no | FEMALE | -6.0 | (1.1) | (0.000) |
| Student has no immigration background (student and parents were born in the country of assessment) | 1 = yes; 0 = no | NATIVE | 10.2 | (3.1) | (0.002) |
| Student speaks the test language or other national language most of the time or always at home | 1 = yes; 0 = no | SAMELANG | 23.0 | (2.8) | (0.000) |
| School located in a small town or village (fewer than 15 000 people) | 1 = yes; 0 = no | XRURAL | 4.1 | (1.5) | (0.007) |
| School located in a city (with over 100 000 people) | 1 = yes; 0 = no | XCITY | -5.2 | (1.4) | (0.000) |
| School size | 100 additional students | XSCHSIZE | 1.4 | (0.3) | (0.000) |
| School size squared | | XSCHSIZ$^2$ | 0.0 | (0.0) | (0.002) |
| System average PISA index of economic, social and cultural status | 1 = OECD S.D. | YESCS | 4.6 | (10.8) | (0.674) |

Note: All slopes are fixed except ESCS and XESCS. All variables are grand-centred (a linear transformation of variables by subtracting the overall mean from the value proper). Intercept is random at all levels. The analysis is based on 55 countries. See Annex A8 for the detailed model specification.
StatLink http://dx.doi.org/10.1787/142127877152

Pour consulter la version française intégrale de ce tableau, suivre ce lien :
StatLink http://dx.doi.org/10.1787/152751048643

[Part 1/1]

**Table 5.20f** **School resources and the impact of socio-economic background on student performance in science**

Tableau 5.20f  Relation entre la dotation des établissements et l'impact du milieu socioéconomique sur la performance des élèves en sciences

| | | Variable name | Change in relationship | S.E. | P-value |
|---|---|---|---|---|---|
| **Estimates of within-school effect of the PISA index of economic, social and cultural status on performance (ESCS slope)** | | | | | |
| Intercept | | ESCS | 16.1 | (1.2) | (0.000) |
| School average number of students per teacher | 1 additional student per teacher | ESCS*XSTRATIO | 0.0 | (0.0) | (0.909) |
| School-level index of teacher shortage | 1 = OECD S.D. | ESCS*XTCSHORT | 0.0 | (0.2) | (0.865) |
| School average number of computers for instruction per student | 1 additional computer per student | ESCS*XIRATCOMP | -6.6 | (2.3) | (0.004) |
| School-level index of quality of school educational resources | 1 = OECD S.D. | ESCS*XSCMATED | 0.3 | (0.2) | (0.141) |
| School average students' learning time for regular lessons in school | 1 additional hour per week | ESCS*XLTSCTOT | 0.6 | (0.2) | (0.003) |
| School average students' learning time for out-of-school lessons | 1 additional hour per week | ESCS*XLTOSTOT | -0.8 | (0.4) | (0.020) |
| School average students' learning time for self-study or homework | 1 additional hour per week | ESCS*XLTSTTOT | -0.1 | (0.3) | (0.850) |
| School providing opportunity of learning science | Each additional 10% | ESCS*XANYSCIE | 0.1 | (0.2) | (0.438) |
| School average index of school activities to promote students' learning o science | 1 = OECD S.D. | ESCS*XSCIPROM | 0.5 | (0.3) | (0.117) |

| | | Variable name | Change in relationship | S.E. | P-value |
|---|---|---|---|---|---|
| **Estimates of compositional effect of the school average PISA index of economic, social and cultural status on performance (XESCS slope)** | | | | | |
| Intercept | | XESCS | 39.6 | (3.1) | (0.000) |

| | | Variable name | Change in score | S.E. | P-value |
|---|---|---|---|---|---|
| **Estimates of  the performance level in science (Intercept)** | | | | | |
| Intercept | | | 465.8 | (4.7) | (0.000) |
| School average number of students per teacher | 1 additional student per teacher | XSTRATIO | -0.2 | (0.1) | (0.143) |
| School-level index of teacher shortage | 1 = OECD S.D. | XTCSHORT | -1.4 | (0.8) | (0.096) |
| School average number of computers for instruction per student | 1 additional computer per student | XIRATCOMP | 12.8 | (8.4) | (0.126) |
| School-level index of quality of school educational resources | 1 = OECD S.D. | XSCMATED | 1.0 | (0.6) | (0.093) |
| School average students' learning time for regular lessons in school | 1 additional hour per week | XLTSCTOT | 8.4 | (0.7) | (0.000) |
| School average students' learning time for out-of-school lessons | 1 additional hour per week | XLTOSTOT | -8.8 | (1.4) | (0.000) |
| School average students' learning time for self-study or homework | 1 additional hour per week | XLTSTTOT | 2.6 | (0.8) | (0.001) |
| School providing opportunity of learning science | Each additional 10% | XANYSCIE | 1.2 | (0.6) | (0.050) |
| School average index of school activities to promote students' learning of science | 1 = OECD S.D. | XSCIPROM | 2.3 | (0.6) | (0.000) |

*Background variables*

| | | Variable name | Change in score | S.E. | P-value |
|---|---|---|---|---|---|
| Student's PISA index of economic, social and cultural status squared | | $ESCS^2$ | -0.3 | (0.3) | (0.292) |
| Student is female | 1 = yes; 0 = no | FEMALE | -6.3 | (1.1) | (0.000) |
| Student has no immigration background (student and parents were born in the country of assessment) | 1 = yes; 0 = no | NATIVE | 10.2 | (3.1) | (0.002) |
| Student speaks the test language or other national language most of the time or always at home | 1 = yes; 0 = no | SAMELANG | 23.0 | (2.8) | (0.000) |
| School located in a small town or village (fewer than 15 000 people) | 1 = yes; 0 = no | XRURAL | 2.1 | (1.4) | (0.135) |
| School located in a city (with over 100 000 people) | 1 = yes; 0 = no | XCITY | -4.0 | (1.1) | (0.001) |
| School size | 100 additional students | XSCHSIZE | 1.3 | (0.2) | (0.000) |
| School size squared | | $XSCHSIZ^2$ | 0.0 | (0.0) | (0.001) |
| System average PISA index of economic, social and cultural status | 1 = OECD S.D. | YESCS | 5.1 | (9.8) | (0.604) |

Note: All slopes are fixed except ESCS and XESCS. All variables are grand-centred (a linear transformation of variables by subtracting the overall mean from the value proper). Intercept is random at all levels. The analysis is based on 55 countries. See Annex A8 for the detailed model specification.
StatLink ᴀᴍᴨ http://dx.doi.org/10.1787/142127877152

Pour consulter la version française intégrale de ce tableau, suivre ce lien :
StatLink ᴀᴍᴨ http://dx.doi.org/10.1787/152751048643

[Part 1/3]

**Table 5.20g** **School and system factors and the impact of socio-economic background on student performance in science, all significant factors combined**

Tableau 5.20g Facteurs scolaires et systémiques et impact du milieu socioéconomique sur la performance des élèves en sciences, tous facteurs significatifs combinés

|  | | Variable name | Model 0b Background Model | | |
|---|---|---|---|---|---|
|  | | | Change in relationship | S.E. | P-value |
| **Estimates of within-school effect of the PISA index of economic, social and cultural status on performance (ESCS slope)** | | | | | |
| Intercept | | ESCS | 16.3 | (1.32) | (0.000) |
| *Admitting, grouping and selecting* | | | | | |
| System with early selection (difference between the first age of selection and the age of 15) | 1 additional year | ESCS*YYRSSEP | | | |
| *School resources* | | | | | |
| School average students' learning time for regular lessons in school | 1 additional hour per week | ESCS*XLTSCTOT | | | |
| School average number of computers for instruction per student | 1 additional computer per student | ESCS*XIRATCOM | | | |
| **Estimates of compositional effect of the school average PISA index of economic, social and cultural status on performance (XESCS slope)** | | | | | |
| Intercept | | XESCS | 57.7 | (4.01) | (0.000) |
| *Admitting, grouping and selecting* | | | | | |
| System with early selection (difference between the first age of selection and the age of 15) | 1 additional year | XESCS*YYRSSEP | | | |
| System-level number of school types or distinct educational programmes available to 15-year-olds | 1 additional programme | XESCS*YNRTRACKS | | | |

|  | | Variable name | Change in score | S.E. | P-value |
|---|---|---|---|---|---|
| **Estimates of the performance level in science (Intercept)** | | | | | |
| Intercept | | | 462.9 | (6.16) | (0.000) |
| *Admitting, grouping and selecting* | | | | | |
| System with early selection (difference between the first age of selection and the age of 15) | 1 additional year | YYRSSEP | | | |
| System-level number of school types or distinct educational programmes available to 15-year-olds | 1 additional programme | YNRTRACKS | | | |
| *School resources* | | | | | |
| School average students' learning time for regular lessons in school | 1 additional hour per week | XLTSCTOT | | | |
| School average number of computers for instruction per student | 1 additional computer per student | XIRATCOMP | | | |
| *Background variables* | | | | | |
| Student's PISA index of economic, social and cultural status squared | | $ESCS^2$ | 0.1 | (0.28) | (0.721) |
| Student is female | 1 = yes; 0 = no | FEMALE | -6.0 | (1.11) | (0.000) |
| Student has no immigration background (student and parents were born in the country of assessment) | 1 = yes; 0 = no | NATIVE | 10.2 | (3.14) | (0.002) |
| Student speaks the test language or other national language most of the time or always at home | 1 = yes; 0 = no | SAMELANG | 23.0 | (2.76) | (0.000) |
| School located in a small town or village (fewer than 15 000 people) | 1 = yes; 0 = no | XRURAL | 4.1 | (1.51) | (0.007) |
| School located in a city (with over 100 000 people) | 1 = yes; 0 = no | XCITY | -5.3 | (1.38) | (0.000) |
| School size | 100 additional students | XSCHSIZE | 1.5 | (0.29) | (0.000) |
| School size squared | | $XSCHSIZ^2$ | 0.0 | (0.01) | (0.002) |
| System average PISA index of economic, social and cultural status | 1 = OECD S.D. | YESCS | -0.7 | (11.18) | (0.951) |

Note: All slopes are fixed except ESCS and XESCS. All variables are grand-centred (a linear transformation of variables by subtracting the overall mean from the value proper). Intercept is random at all levels. The analysis is based on 55 countries. See Annex A8 for the detailed model specification.
StatLink ⬛📲 http://dx.doi.org/10.1787/142127877152

Pour consulter la version française intégrale de ce tableau, suivre ce lien :
StatLink ⬛📲 http://dx.doi.org/10.1787/152751048643

[Part 2/3]

**Table 5.20g** School and system factors and the impact of socio-economic background on student performance in science, all significant factors combined

Tableau 5.20g Facteurs scolaires et systémiques et impact du milieu socioéconomique sur la performance des élèves en sciences, tous facteurs significatifs combinés

| | | Variable name | Model 1 First combined | | |
|---|---|---|---|---|---|
| | | | Change in relationship | S.E. | P-value |
| **Estimates of within-school effect of the PISA index of economic, social and cultural status on performance (ESCS slope)** | | | | | |
| Intercept | | ESCS | 15.9 | (1.17) | (0.000) |
| *Admitting, grouping and selecting* | | | | | |
| System with early selection (difference between the first age of selection and the age of 15) | 1 additional year | ESCS*YYRSSEP | -1.9 | (0.64) | (0.005) |
| *School resources* | | | | | |
| School average students' learning time for regular lessons in school | 1 additional hour per week | ESCS*XLTSCTOT | 0.7 | (0.16) | (0.000) |
| School average number of computers for instruction per student | 1 additional computer per student | ESCS*XIRATCOM | -5.5 | (2.2) | (0.015) |
| **Estimates of compositional effect of the school average PISA index of economic, social and cultural status on performance (XESCS slope)** | | | | | |
| Intercept | | XESCS | 44.2 | (2.79) | (0.000) |
| *Admitting, grouping and selecting* | | | | | |
| System with early selection (difference between the first age of selection and the age of 15) | 1 additional year | XESCS*YYRSSEP | 7.1 | (2.21) | (0.003) |
| System-level number of school types or distinct educational programmes available to 15-year-olds | 1 additional programme | XESCS*YNRTRACKS | 4.0 | (2.49) | (0.111) |

| | | Variable name | Change in score | S.E. | P-value |
|---|---|---|---|---|---|
| **Estimates of the performance level in science (Intercept)** | | | | | |
| Intercept | | | 464.1 | (4.78) | (0.000) |
| *Admitting, grouping and selecting* | | | | | |
| System with early selection (difference between the first age of selection and the age of 15) | 1 additional year | YYRSSEP | -0.3 | (3.00) | (0.911) |
| System-level number of school types or distinct educational programmes available to 15-year-olds | 1 additional programme | YNRTRACKS | 6.4 | (4.71) | (0.177) |
| *School resources* | | | | | |
| School average students' learning time for regular lessons in school | 1 additional hour per week | XLTSCTOT | 8.9 | (0.56) | (0.000) |
| School average number of computers for instruction per student | 1 additional computer per student | XIRATCOMP | 20.6 | (8.36) | (0.014) |

*Background variables*

| | | Variable name | Change in score | S.E. | P-value |
|---|---|---|---|---|---|
| Student's PISA index of economic, social and cultural status squared | | ESCS$^2$ | -0.2 | (0.27) | (0.442) |
| Student is female | 1= yes; 0 = no | FEMALE | -6.2 | (1.10) | (0.000) |
| Student has no immigration background (student and parents were born in the country of assessment) | 1= yes; 0 = no | NATIVE | 10.2 | (3.14) | (0.002) |
| Student speaks the test language or other national language most of the time or always at home | 1= yes; 0 = no | SAMELANG | 23.1 | (2.76) | (0.000) |
| School located in a small town or village (fewer than 15 000 people) | 1= yes; 0 = no | XRURAL | 2.0 | (1.49) | (0.176) |
| School located in a city (with over 100 000 people) | 1= yes; 0 = no | XCITY | -4.1 | (1.24) | (0.001) |
| School size | 100 additional students | XSCHSIZE | 1.4 | (0.23) | (0.000) |
| School size squared | | XSCHSIZ$^2$ | 0.0 | (0.00) | (0.001) |
| System average PISA index of economic, social and cultural status | 1= OECD S.D. | YESCS | 9.8 | (8.95) | (0.279) |

Note: All slopes are fixed except ESCS and XESCS. All variables are grand-centred (a linear transformation of variables by subtracting the overall mean from the value proper). Intercept is random at all levels. The analysis is based on 55 countries. See Annex A8 for the detailed model specification.
*StatLink* http://dx.doi.org/10.1787/142127877152

Pour consulter la version française intégrale de ce tableau, suivre ce lien :
*StatLink* http://dx.doi.org/10.1787/152751048643

[Part 3/3]

**Table 5.20g** **School and system factors and the impact of socio-economic background on student performance in science, all significant factors combined**

Tableau 5.20g  Facteurs scolaires et systémiques et impact du milieu socioéconomique sur la performance des élèves en sciences, tous facteurs significatifs combinés

| | | Variable name | Model 2 Second combined | | |
|---|---|---|---|---|---|
| | | | Change in relationship | S.E. | P-value |
| **Estimates of within-school effect of the PISA index of economic, social and cultural status on performance (ESCS slope)** | | | | | |
| Intercept | | ESCS | 16.0 | (1.15) | (0.000) |
| *Admitting, grouping and selecting* | | | | | |
| System with early selection (difference between the first age of selection and the age of 15) | 1 additional year | ESCS*YYRSSEP | -1.9 | (0.62) | (0.004) |
| *School resources* | | | | | |
| School average students' learning time for regular lessons in school | 1 additional hour per week | ESCS*XLTSCTOT | 0.7 | (0.16) | (0.000) |
| School average number of computers for instruction per student | 1 additional computer per student | ESCS*XIRATCOM | | | |

| | | | Change in relationship | S.E. | P-value |
|---|---|---|---|---|---|
| **Estimates of compositional effect of the school average PISA index of economic, social and cultural status on performance (XESCS slope)** | | | | | |
| Intercept | | XESCS | 44.4 | (2.79) | (0.000) |
| *Admitting, grouping and selecting* | | | | | |
| System with early selection (difference between the first age of selection and the age of 15) | 1 additional year | XESCS*YYRSSEP | 8.9 | (1.88) | (0.000) |
| System-level number of school types or distinct educational programmes available to 15-year-olds | 1 additional programme | XESCS*YNRTRACKS | | | |

| | | Variable name | Change in score | S.E. | P-value |
|---|---|---|---|---|---|
| **Estimates of the performance level in science (Intercept)** | | | | | |
| Intercept | | | 464.5 | (4.76) | (0.000) |
| *Admitting, grouping and selecting* | | | | | |
| System with early selection (difference between the first age of selection and the age of 15) | 1 additional year | YYRSSEP | 2.7 | (2.32) | (0.256) |
| System-level number of school types or distinct educational programmes available to 15-year-olds | 1 additional programme | YNRTRACKS | | | |
| *School resources* | | | | | |
| School average students' learning time for regular lessons in school | 1 additional hour per week | XLTSCTOT | 8.9 | (0.56) | (0.000) |
| School average number of computers for instruction per student | 1 additional computer per student | XIRATCOMP | | | |

*Background variables*

| | | | | | |
|---|---|---|---|---|---|
| Student's PISA index of economic, social and cultural status squared | | ESCS$^2$ | -0.2 | (0.27) | (0.453) |
| Student is female | 1 = yes; 0 = no | FEMALE | -6.2 | (1.11) | (0.000) |
| Student has no immigration background (student and parents were born in the country of assessment) | 1 = yes; 0 = no | NATIVE | 10.2 | (3.14) | (0.002) |
| Student speaks the test language or other national language most of the time or always at home | 1 = yes; 0 = no | SAMELANG | 23.1 | (2.76) | (0.000) |
| School located in a small town or village (fewer than 15 000 people) | 1 = yes; 0 = no | XRURAL | 2.0 | (1.50) | (0.186) |
| School located in a city (with over 100 000 people) | 1 = yes; 0 = no | XCITY | -4.0 | (1.24) | (0.002) |
| School size | 100 additional students | XSCHSIZE | 1.2 | (0.24) | (0.000) |
| School size squared | | XSCHSIZ$^2$ | 0.0 | (0.00) | (0.003) |
| System average PISA index of economic, social and cultural status | 1 = OECD S.D. | YESCS | 15.5 | (9.15) | (0.095) |

Note: All slopes are fixed except ESCS and XESCS. All variables are grand-centred (a linear transformation of variables by subtracting the overall mean from the value proper). Intercept is random at all levels. The analysis is based on 55 countries. See Annex A8 for the detailed model specification.
StatLink http://dx.doi.org/10.1787/142127877152

Pour consulter la version française intégrale de ce tableau, suivre ce lien :
StatLink http://dx.doi.org/10.1787/152751048643

213

[Part 1/2]

**Table 5.21a** **Impact of demographic and socio-economic factors and of school factors on variance in student performance in science, by country**

Tableau 5.21a Impact des facteurs démographiques et socioéconomiques ainsi que des facteurs scolaires sur la variance de la performance des élèves en sciences, par pays

| | | Variance | | Remaining variance | | | | | |
| --- | --- | --- | --- | --- | --- | --- | --- | --- | --- |
| | | Empty (or fully unconditional) model[1] | | Model with demographic and socio-economic factors[2] | | Model with school factors[3] | | Model with demographic and socio-economic factors and school factors[4] | |
| | | Within-school | Between-school | Within-school | Between-school | Within-school | Between-school | Within-school | Between-school |
| OECD | Australia | 8 242 | 1 839 | 7 637 | 646 | 8 227 | 829 | 7 627 | 511 |
| | Austria | 4 552 | 5 464 | 4 184 | 1 512 | 4 550 | 1 864 | 4 186 | 834 |
| | Belgium | 4 803 | 5 182 | 4 419 | 1 242 | 4 800 | 1 403 | 4 415 | 678 |
| | Canada | 7 162 | 1 668 | 6 704 | 895 | 7 149 | 1 021 | 6 698 | 711 |
| | Czech Republic | 5 007 | 5 617 | 4 740 | 1 597 | 4 998 | 1 617 | 4 737 | 984 |
| | Denmark | 7 390 | 1 393 | 6 411 | 527 | 7 389 | 968 | 6 408 | 436 |
| | Finland | 6 910 | 433 | 6 244 | 268 | 6 904 | 286 | 6 236 | 174 |
| | Germany | 4 530 | 5 944 | 4 156 | 1 159 | 4 530 | 1 268 | 4 154 | 514 |
| | Greece | 4 985 | 4 369 | 4 775 | 1 630 | 4 997 | 1 368 | 4 784 | 813 |
| | Hungary | 3 459 | 5 453 | 3 287 | 1 161 | 3 465 | 1 334 | 3 289 | 647 |
| | Iceland | 8 632 | 898 | 7 761 | 537 | 8 604 | 561 | 7 768 | 281 |
| | Ireland | 7 419 | 1 539 | 6 887 | 390 | 7 420 | 883 | 6 888 | 251 |
| | Italy | 4 664 | 4 758 | 4 446 | 2 001 | 4 658 | 1 917 | 4 440 | 1 049 |
| | Japan | 5 407 | 4 867 | 5 332 | 1 969 | 5 405 | 1 768 | 5 332 | 1 295 |
| | Korea | 5 325 | 2 869 | 5 232 | 1 275 | 5 327 | 581 | 5 232 | 486 |
| | Luxembourg | 6 528 | 2 738 | 5 474 | 187 | 6 530 | 443 | 5 478 | 15 |
| | Mexico | 3 444 | 2 293 | 3 269 | 988 | 3 441 | 1 285 | 3 266 | 764 |
| | Netherlands | 3 583 | 5 359 | 3 359 | 1 479 | 3 583 | 1 192 | 3 359 | 744 |
| | New Zealand | 9 649 | 1 930 | 8 360 | 320 | 9 647 | 548 | 8 354 | 139 |
| | Norway | 8 186 | 964 | 7 367 | 452 | 8 175 | 724 | 7 361 | 393 |
| | Poland | 7 091 | 1 108 | 6 236 | 530 | 7 052 | 550 | 6 228 | 371 |
| | Portugal | 5 262 | 2 502 | 4 833 | 878 | 5 261 | 946 | 4 830 | 428 |
| | Slovak Republic | 4 995 | 3 690 | 4 660 | 1 664 | 4 993 | 1 704 | 4 655 | 1 009 |
| | Spain | 6 686 | 1 151 | 6 014 | 503 | 6 672 | 695 | 6 005 | 391 |
| | Sweden | 7 886 | 1 091 | 6 892 | 395 | 7 887 | 714 | 6 892 | 271 |
| | Switzerland | 6 012 | 3 375 | 5 024 | 1 421 | 6 017 | 1 366 | 5 026 | 692 |
| | Turkey | 3 213 | 3 653 | 3 108 | 1 414 | 3 213 | 949 | 3 108 | 646 |
| | United Kingdom | 8 856 | 2 200 | 8 141 | 786 | 8 825 | 750 | 8 120 | 452 |
| | United States | 8 467 | 2 626 | 7 650 | 776 | 8 463 | 610 | 7 647 | 392 |
| | **OECD average** | 6 150 | 2 999 | 5 607 | 986 | 6 144 | 1 039 | 5 604 | 564 |
| Partners | Argentina | 5 237 | 4 794 | 5 073 | 1 732 | 5 239 | 1 820 | 5 073 | 976 |
| | Azerbaijan | 1 619 | 1 612 | 1 555 | 1 351 | 1 619 | 1 184 | 1 555 | 1 112 |
| | Brazil | 4 186 | 3 711 | 4 055 | 1 466 | 4 176 | 2 099 | 4 043 | 1 148 |
| | Bulgaria | 5 334 | 6 226 | 5 219 | 1 750 | 5 341 | 1 895 | 5 224 | 1 055 |
| | Chile | 4 661 | 4 740 | 4 510 | 1 122 | 4 667 | 931 | 4 510 | 492 |
| | Colombia | 5 119 | 2 244 | 4 880 | 879 | 5 118 | 1 089 | 4 881 | 621 |
| | Croatia | 4 481 | 3 036 | 4 272 | 1 040 | 4 485 | 1 264 | 4 276 | 540 |
| | Estonia | 5 525 | 1 437 | 5 170 | 608 | 5 526 | 756 | 5 172 | 353 |
| | Hong Kong-China | 5 241 | 3 072 | 5 040 | 1 273 | 5 240 | 1 116 | 5 040 | 727 |
| | Indonesia | 2 276 | 1 745 | 2 241 | 965 | 2 276 | 1 126 | 2 240 | 715 |
| | Israel | 8 797 | 3 926 | 8 116 | 2 041 | 8 797 | 2 045 | 8 116 | 1 300 |
| | Jordan | 6 107 | 1 792 | 5 411 | 766 | 6 105 | 993 | 5 402 | 627 |
| | Kyrgyzstan | 4 367 | 2 763 | 4 222 | 1 029 | 4 366 | 1 476 | 4 222 | 781 |
| | Latvia | 5 790 | 1 316 | 5 384 | 658 | 5 790 | 713 | 5 383 | 448 |
| | Lithuania | 5 878 | 2 308 | 5 443 | 807 | 5 870 | 940 | 5 440 | 524 |
| | Macao-China | 4 942 | 1 739 | 4 704 | 1 026 | 4 940 | 494 | 4 702 | 411 |
| | Montenegro | 4 554 | 1 812 | 4 442 | 640 | 4 554 | 463 | 4 443 | 270 |
| | Romania | 3 379 | 3 182 | 3 243 | 1 437 | 3 379 | 1 184 | 3 243 | 793 |
| | Russian Federation | 5 999 | 2 166 | 5 740 | 1 306 | 6 002 | 1 319 | 5 738 | 837 |
| | Serbia | 4 378 | 3 086 | 4 224 | 1 026 | 4 381 | 1 057 | 4 226 | 691 |
| | Slovenia | 3 844 | 5 811 | 3 612 | 1 496 | 3 839 | 1 689 | 3 609 | 823 |
| | Chinese Taipei | 4 652 | 4 120 | 4 451 | 1 635 | 4 653 | 1 373 | 4 452 | 1 037 |
| | Thailand | 3 920 | 2 294 | 3 789 | 586 | 3 913 | 1 531 | 3 788 | 393 |
| | Tunisia | 3 951 | 2 904 | 3 886 | 1 488 | 3 951 | 962 | 3 886 | 635 |
| | Uruguay | 5 214 | 3 525 | 4 966 | 1 280 | 5 220 | 2 294 | 4 969 | 1 018 |

1. See Model 0a in Table 5.19g.
2. See Model 0b in Table 5.19g.
3. See Model 2G in Table 5.19g.
4. See Model 2N in Table 5.19g.
*StatLink* http://dx.doi.org/10.1787/142127877152

Pour consulter la version française intégrale de ce tableau, suivre ce lien :
*StatLink* http://dx.doi.org/10.1787/152751048643

[Part 2/2]

**Table 5.21a** **Impact of demographic and socio-economic factors and of school factors on variance in student performance in science, by country**

Tableau 5.21a Impact des facteurs démographiques et socioéconomiques ainsi que des facteurs scolaires sur la variance de la performance des élèves en sciences, par pays

| | | Between-school variance expressed as a percentage of the average of between-school variance in student performance in science across OECD countries | | | |
|---|---|---|---|---|---|
| | | Uniquely accounted for by demographic and socio-economic factors | Uniquely accounted for by school factors | Jointly accounted for by demographic and socio-economic factors and school factors | Remaining between-school variance |
| | | % | % | % | % |
| OECD | Australia | 10.6 | 4.5 | 29.1 | 17.0 |
| | Austria | 34.3 | 22.6 | 97.4 | 27.8 |
| | Belgium | 24.2 | 18.8 | 107.2 | 22.6 |
| | Canada | 10.3 | 6.1 | 15.4 | 23.7 |
| | Czech Republic | 21.1 | 20.4 | 112.9 | 32.8 |
| | Denmark | 17.7 | 3.0 | 11.2 | 14.5 |
| | Finland | 3.8 | 3.1 | 1.8 | 5.8 |
| | Germany | 25.2 | 21.5 | 134.4 | 17.1 |
| | Greece | 18.5 | 27.2 | 72.8 | 27.1 |
| | Hungary | 22.9 | 17.1 | 120.2 | 21.6 |
| | Iceland | 9.4 | 8.6 | 2.7 | 9.4 |
| | Ireland | 21.1 | 4.6 | 17.2 | 8.4 |
| | Italy | 29.0 | 31.7 | 63.0 | 35.0 |
| | Japan | 15.8 | 22.5 | 80.9 | 43.2 |
| | Korea | 3.1 | 26.3 | 50.0 | 16.2 |
| | Luxembourg | 14.3 | 5.7 | 70.8 | 0.5 |
| | Mexico | 17.4 | 7.5 | 26.2 | 25.5 |
| | Netherlands | 14.9 | 24.5 | 114.5 | 24.8 |
| | New Zealand | 13.7 | 6.0 | 40.0 | 4.6 |
| | Norway | 11.0 | 2.0 | 6.0 | 13.1 |
| | Poland | 6.0 | 5.3 | 13.3 | 12.4 |
| | Portugal | 17.3 | 15.0 | 36.9 | 14.3 |
| | Slovak Republic | 23.2 | 21.8 | 44.4 | 33.6 |
| | Spain | 10.1 | 3.8 | 11.5 | 13.0 |
| | Sweden | 14.8 | 4.1 | 8.4 | 9.0 |
| | Switzerland | 22.5 | 24.3 | 42.7 | 23.1 |
| | Turkey | 10.1 | 25.6 | 64.6 | 21.6 |
| | United Kingdom | 9.9 | 11.1 | 37.2 | 15.1 |
| | United States | 7.3 | 12.8 | 54.4 | 13.1 |
| | **OECD average** | **15.8** | **14.1** | **51.3** | **18.8** |
| Partners | Argentina | 28.1 | 25.2 | 74.0 | 32.5 |
| | Azerbaijan | 2.4 | 8.0 | 6.3 | 37.1 |
| | Brazil | 31.7 | 10.6 | 43.1 | 38.3 |
| | Bulgaria | 28.0 | 23.2 | 121.3 | 35.2 |
| | Chile | 14.7 | 21.0 | 106.0 | 16.4 |
| | Colombia | 15.6 | 8.6 | 29.9 | 20.7 |
| | Croatia | 24.1 | 16.7 | 42.4 | 18.0 |
| | Estonia | 13.4 | 8.5 | 14.2 | 11.8 |
| | Hong Kong-China | 13.0 | 18.2 | 47.0 | 24.2 |
| | Indonesia | 13.7 | 8.4 | 12.3 | 23.8 |
| | Israel | 24.8 | 24.7 | 38.0 | 43.4 |
| | Jordan | 12.2 | 4.6 | 22.0 | 20.9 |
| | Kyrgyzstan | 23.2 | 8.3 | 34.6 | 26.1 |
| | Latvia | 8.9 | 7.0 | 13.1 | 14.9 |
| | Lithuania | 13.9 | 9.4 | 36.2 | 17.5 |
| | Macao-China | 2.8 | 20.5 | 21.0 | 13.7 |
| | Montenegro | 6.4 | 12.4 | 32.6 | 9.0 |
| | Romania | 13.0 | 21.5 | 45.1 | 26.4 |
| | Russian Federation | 16.1 | 15.6 | 12.6 | 27.9 |
| | Serbia | 12.2 | 11.2 | 56.5 | 23.0 |
| | Slovenia | 28.9 | 22.4 | 115.0 | 27.4 |
| | Chinese Taipei | 11.2 | 19.9 | 71.7 | 34.6 |
| | Thailand | 37.9 | 6.4 | 19.0 | 13.1 |
| | Tunisia | 10.9 | 28.4 | 36.3 | 21.2 |
| | Uruguay | 42.5 | 8.7 | 32.3 | 33.9 |

StatLink ▅▅▅ http://dx.doi.org/10.1787/142127877152

Pour consulter la version française intégrale de ce tableau, suivre ce lien :
StatLink ▅▅▅ http://dx.doi.org/10.1787/152751048643

215

[Part 1/4]

**Table 5.21b** Effects of significant school factors[1] and demographic and socio-economic factors on student performance in science, by country

Tableau 5.21b  Effets des facteurs scolaires significatifs et des facteurs démographiques et socioéconomiques sur la performance des élèves en sciences, par pays

| | | Student socio-economic factors | | | | | | | | |
|---|---|---|---|---|---|---|---|---|---|---|
| | | Student is a female | | Student has no immigration background | | Student's language at home is the same as language that the test was taken in | | PISA index of economic, social and cultural status of student (1 unit increase) | | PISA index of economic, social and cultural status of student (squared) | |
| | | Change in score | S.E. | Change in score | S.E. | Change in score | S.E. | Change in score | S.E. | Change in score | S.E. |
| OECD | Australia | 0.5 | (2.1) | 0.5 | (2.7) | **16.2** | (4.4) | **28.7** | (1.4) | **-3.2** | (1.1) |
| | Austria | **-16.1** | (2.9) | **35.6** | (6.2) | **23.0** | (8.6) | **6.8** | (1.7) | **-3.2** | (1.0) |
| | Belgium | **-13.6** | (1.8) | **21.6** | (3.5) | **20.2** | (4.8) | **15.0** | (1.1) | -0.8 | (0.8) |
| | Canada | **-7.2** | (2.0) | **8.0** | (3.2) | **13.0** | (4.9) | **23.0** | (1.6) | -2.3 | (1.2) |
| | Czech Republic | **-16.8** | (2.8) | c | c | c | c | **17.7** | (1.7) | -1.8 | (1.3) |
| | Denmark | **-9.2** | (2.7) | **31.2** | (6.9) | **32.0** | (8.7) | **28.0** | (2.0) | 1.6 | (1.3) |
| | Finland | 2.1 | (2.8) | c | c | c | c | **27.0** | (1.6) | 2.8 | (1.5) |
| | Germany | **-15.4** | (2.3) | **28.3** | (5.0) | **19.0** | (5.4) | **10.0** | (1.5) | 0.6 | (0.8) |
| | Greece | -4.3 | (3.0) | -2.6 | (6.3) | **27.7** | (7.8) | **14.6** | (1.5) | -2.3 | (1.2) |
| | Hungary | **-25.8** | (2.4) | c | c | c | c | **4.5** | (1.3) | -0.5 | (0.9) |
| | Iceland | **6.4** | (3.0) | c | c | c | c | **29.3** | (3.0) | -1.2 | (1.6) |
| | Ireland | -2.0 | (3.1) | -10.1 | (8.1) | c | c | **27.9** | (2.0) | -0.8 | (1.4) |
| | Italy | **-13.1** | (1.9) | **38.1** | (6.6) | c | c | **5.8** | (1.0) | **-1.6** | (0.6) |
| | Japan | -2.8 | (2.5) | c | c | c | c | **5.1** | (2.2) | -2.2 | (2.0) |
| | Korea | -1.2 | (3.2) | c | c | c | c | **9.0** | (1.9) | 2.3 | (1.3) |
| | Luxembourg | **-8.5** | (2.5) | **22.7** | (4.3) | **22.6** | (4.3) | **15.4** | (1.7) | -1.1 | (0.8) |
| | Mexico | **-13.2** | (1.5) | c | c | c | c | **7.4** | (0.9) | 1.1 | (0.4) |
| | Netherlands | **-14.6** | (2.1) | **23.5** | (6.3) | **19.7** | (5.6) | **6.9** | (1.2) | 1.0 | (1.0) |
| | New Zealand | -4.1 | (3.4) | 7.6 | (4.0) | **28.7** | (6.4) | **39.4** | (1.9) | **3.2** | (1.5) |
| | Norway | 4.2 | (3.2) | 25.7 | (8.2) | 12.0 | (8.2) | **29.6** | (2.2) | -2.6 | (1.5) |
| | Poland | -1.6 | (2.4) | c | c | c | c | **34.9** | (1.6) | -0.8 | (1.1) |
| | Portugal | **-7.5** | (2.6) | **33.2** | (6.8) | c | c | **17.0** | (1.4) | 0.3 | (0.7) |
| | Slovak Republic | **-14.3** | (2.7) | c | c | c | c | **20.1** | (1.8) | **-4.8** | (1.2) |
| | Spain | **-5.2** | (2.0) | **41.6** | (5.5) | c | c | **21.8** | (1.3) | **-3.4** | (0.8) |
| | Sweden | -1.7 | (2.6) | **28.4** | (7.6) | **28.8** | (8.0) | **29.3** | (2.6) | -0.7 | (1.4) |
| | Switzerland | **-13.7** | (2.1) | **36.2** | (3.6) | **25.2** | (3.9) | **19.1** | (1.4) | -0.5 | (1.0) |
| | Turkey | 2.5 | (2.4) | c | c | c | c | **12.9** | (2.6) | **2.0** | (1.0) |
| | United Kingdom | **-10.2** | (2.4) | 1.8 | (4.6) | 11.8 | (9.1) | **32.4** | (2.1) | -2.3 | (1.5) |
| | United States | -4.7 | (2.5) | 7.4 | (5.0) | **21.6** | (6.1) | **31.2** | (1.9) | **3.4** | (1.2) |
| Partners | Argentina | 1.9 | (3.5) | c | c | c | c | **14.7** | (2.2) | 0.9 | (1.2) |
| | Azerbaijan | **7.6** | (1.5) | c | c | c | c | **7.4** | (1.0) | 0.9 | (0.6) |
| | Brazil | **-9.4** | (2.3) | c | c | c | c | **9.3** | (1.7) | 0.8 | (0.7) |
| | Bulgaria | -3.2 | (3.2) | c | c | **21.1** | (6.2) | **11.8** | (1.7) | -1.1 | (1.1) |
| | Chile | **-17.3** | (2.9) | c | c | c | c | **10.5** | (1.5) | 0.4 | (0.6) |
| | Colombia | **-12.3** | (3.5) | c | c | c | c | **10.9** | (2.9) | 0.0 | (1.0) |
| | Croatia | **-14.4** | (2.1) | **8.1** | (3.2) | c | c | **12.5** | (1.4) | **-2.4** | (1.1) |
| | Estonia | 1.6 | (2.4) | **9.0** | (4.2) | c | c | **21.7** | (1.8) | 2.1 | (1.9) |
| | Hong Kong-China | **-20.1** | (2.5) | **-6.6** | (2.9) | c | c | **7.4** | (2.3) | -1.8 | (1.1) |
| | Indonesia | **-8.4** | (1.6) | c | c | c | c | 2.8 | (2.0) | 0.6 | (0.7) |
| | Israel | -4.8 | (4.1) | 2.3 | (4.6) | -5.4 | (7.1) | **25.7** | (2.3) | **4.4** | (1.4) |
| | Jordan | 5.6 | (4.4) | **-7.4** | (3.3) | c | c | **23.4** | (1.7) | **2.4** | (0.6) |
| | Kyrgyzstan | **5.7** | (2.3) | c | c | c | c | **7.0** | (1.9) | 0.7 | (0.9) |
| | Latvia | 4.8 | (2.7) | 2.1 | (4.8) | c | c | **20.9** | (2.1) | -1.6 | (2.0) |
| | Lithuania | 3.8 | (2.6) | c | c | c | c | **24.5** | (1.5) | **-4.0** | (1.5) |
| | Macao-China | **-16.1** | (3.0) | **-19.8** | (2.7) | **31.0** | (8.8) | 5.7 | (2.6) | -1.1 | (1.1) |
| | Montenegro | **-7.8** | (2.4) | **-14.5** | (4.7) | c | c | **9.7** | (1.5) | -1.2 | (1.4) |
| | Romania | **-13.0** | (2.6) | c | c | c | c | **10.7** | (3.3) | -0.8 | (1.1) |
| | Russian Federation | **-7.2** | (2.4) | **11.2** | (4.2) | **23.5** | (6.7) | **19.6** | (1.8) | 0.0 | (1.9) |
| | Serbia | **-13.3** | (2.1) | 2.8 | (3.1) | c | c | **10.5** | (1.3) | **-2.4** | (1.0) |
| | Slovenia | **-22.7** | (2.4) | **22.4** | (4.4) | **20.8** | (5.7) | 1.9 | (1.3) | 1.3 | (1.2) |
| | Chinese Taipei | **-9.1** | (2.1) | c | c | c | c | **13.9** | (1.4) | 1.5 | (1.4) |
| | Thailand | **8.9** | (2.4) | c | c | c | c | **15.2** | (1.9) | **3.2** | (0.7) |
| | Tunisia | **-7.3** | (2.5) | c | c | 9.2 | (6.0) | **7.5** | (1.7) | **1.4** | (0.6) |
| | Uruguay | **-6.7** | (2.9) | c | c | c | c | **15.8** | (1.6) | **1.5** | (0.8) |

Note: Values that are statistically significant are indicated in bold (see Annex A3).
1. Significant school factors show effects even after accounting for other school and system-level factors and demographic and socio-economic factors (with statistical significance tested at the 0.5% level [p<0.005]). See Model 2N in Table 5.19g.
StatLink ⏷⏷ http://dx.doi.org/10.1787/142127877152

Pour consulter la version française intégrale de ce tableau, suivre ce lien :
StatLink ⏷⏷ http://dx.doi.org/10.1787/152751048643

[Part 2/4]

**Table 5.21b** **Effects of significant school factors[1] and demographic and socio-economic factors on student performance in science, by country**

Tableau 5.21b  Effets des facteurs scolaires significatifs et des facteurs démographiques et socioéconomiques sur la performance des élèves en sciences, par pays

| | School socio-economic factors | | | | | | | | | |
|---|---|---|---|---|---|---|---|---|---|---|
| | School average PISA index of economic, social and cultural status (1 unit increase) | | School size (per 100 students) | | School size (per 100 students) (squared) | | School in a small town or village (15 000 or less people) | | School in city (100 000 or more people) | |
| | Change in score | S.E. | Change in score | S.E. | Change in score | S.E. | Change in score | S.E. | Change in score | S.E. |
| **OECD** | | | | | | | | | | |
| Australia | 35.2 | (2.7) | -1.4 | (0.6) | 0.1 | (0.0) | -2.2 | (2.0) | -3.9 | (1.3) |
| Austria | 57.6 | (2.9) | 4.6 | (0.5) | -0.1 | (0.0) | 8.9 | (2.5) | 8.0 | (2.3) |
| Belgium | 50.6 | (1.7) | -2.6 | (0.9) | 0.2 | (0.1) | 2.7 | (1.0) | -15.0 | (1.3) |
| Canada | 27.2 | (2.2) | 2.6 | (0.4) | -0.1 | (0.0) | 4.7 | (1.7) | -4.6 | (1.4) |
| Czech Republic | 72.3 | (3.8) | -1.9 | (1.3) | 0.2 | (0.1) | -1.3 | (1.9) | -13.7 | (1.6) |
| Denmark | 32.2 | (4.5) | 4.6 | (2.4) | -0.4 | (0.2) | 3.1 | (2.4) | 1.9 | (3.8) |
| Finland | 7.3 | (4.4) | -0.1 | (2.5) | 0.3 | (0.2) | 9.3 | (2.7) | 3.7 | (3.0) |
| Germany | 49.3 | (3.2) | 7.8 | (0.8) | -0.4 | (0.0) | -1.6 | (1.8) | 1.6 | (1.9) |
| Greece | 32.4 | (3.3) | 0.8 | (2.3) | 0.2 | (0.2) | 13.3 | (3.7) | 5.6 | (2.8) |
| Hungary | 57.3 | (3.6) | -1.9 | (0.8) | 0.1 | (0.0) | -7.1 | (2.9) | -14.4 | (2.5) |
| Iceland | 29.0 | (8.1) | -7.4 | (4.3) | 0.1 | (0.5) | 0.0 | (5.0) | -11.3 | (5.1) |
| Ireland | 38.2 | (3.7) | 2.8 | (2.3) | -0.2 | (0.1) | 20.6 | (2.8) | 4.3 | (2.8) |
| Italy | 59.4 | (1.6) | 1.0 | (0.4) | 0.0 | (0.0) | 3.7 | (1.0) | -5.4 | (0.9) |
| Japan | 70.2 | (4.0) | 1.9 | (0.3) | 0.0 | (0.0) | 4.0 | (2.4) | -13.8 | (1.7) |
| Korea | 13.7 | (3.9) | 5.2 | (1.2) | -0.2 | (0.0) | 1.1 | (4.6) | -9.0 | (3.2) |
| Luxembourg | 44.3 | (5.7) | 3.7 | (1.5) | -0.1 | (0.0) | 8.5 | (3.8) | 1.7 | (5.0) |
| Mexico | 23.6 | (0.9) | 0.7 | (0.1) | 0.0 | (0.0) | -1.9 | (1.0) | -1.0 | (0.7) |
| Netherlands | 49.7 | (2.9) | 2.6 | (0.5) | -0.1 | (0.0) | 3.0 | (2.2) | -3.4 | (1.5) |
| New Zealand | 26.5 | (5.0) | 1.1 | (0.8) | 0.0 | (0.0) | 4.9 | (3.7) | -4.8 | (3.4) |
| Norway | 32.1 | (5.9) | -16.6 | (4.4) | 2.0 | (0.7) | 5.8 | (2.6) | 1.2 | (4.3) |
| Poland | 10.5 | (4.7) | 1.3 | (2.1) | -0.1 | (0.2) | 11.0 | (2.7) | -2.1 | (3.6) |
| Portugal | 18.4 | (2.4) | 4.2 | (0.9) | -0.1 | (0.0) | 9.8 | (1.9) | 3.3 | (2.6) |
| Slovak Republic | 51.7 | (3.0) | 2.8 | (1.1) | -0.1 | (0.1) | 7.2 | (1.8) | -12.5 | (2.1) |
| Spain | 13.8 | (1.8) | 0.3 | (0.6) | 0.0 | (0.0) | 9.8 | (1.3) | 4.8 | (1.3) |
| Sweden | 20.5 | (7.3) | -4.6 | (2.5) | 0.5 | (0.2) | 4.0 | (3.4) | 8.3 | (3.4) |
| Switzerland | 30.9 | (2.4) | 3.5 | (0.3) | 0.0 | (0.0) | 7.4 | (1.7) | -8.7 | (2.4) |
| Turkey | 28.4 | (2.1) | 1.2 | (0.2) | 0.0 | (0.0) | -7.5 | (1.8) | -4.6 | (1.3) |
| United Kingdom | 29.3 | (3.1) | 2.1 | (0.6) | -0.1 | (0.0) | 1.5 | (1.8) | -0.7 | (1.9) |
| United States | 2.6 | (3.4) | -0.9 | (0.3) | 0.0 | (0.0) | -5.4 | (2.3) | -9.4 | (2.7) |
| **Partners** | | | | | | | | | | |
| Argentina | 30.0 | (2.5) | 3.7 | (1.0) | -0.1 | (0.1) | -18.0 | (2.6) | -15.1 | (2.5) |
| Azerbaijan | 6.0 | (1.3) | -0.6 | (0.2) | 0.0 | (0.0) | 13.0 | (1.3) | 10.8 | (1.7) |
| Brazil | 37.1 | (1.7) | 1.5 | (0.2) | 0.0 | (0.0) | 10.3 | (1.7) | -3.4 | (1.5) |
| Bulgaria | 39.8 | (6.9) | -1.8 | (1.4) | 0.2 | (0.1) | 5.6 | (3.7) | -4.4 | (3.2) |
| Chile | 26.8 | (2.4) | -0.8 | (0.6) | 0.0 | (0.0) | 5.0 | (3.1) | -0.9 | (2.2) |
| Colombia | 25.3 | (2.7) | -0.2 | (0.3) | 0.0 | (0.0) | -4.2 | (3.5) | -11.3 | (2.8) |
| Croatia | 65.3 | (4.7) | 8.0 | (1.0) | -0.3 | (0.1) | 0.7 | (2.3) | -8.8 | (2.7) |
| Estonia | 35.4 | (4.5) | -3.6 | (1.3) | 0.3 | (0.1) | 20.5 | (2.5) | 2.0 | (2.4) |
| Hong Kong-China | 25.5 | (3.0) | 7.6 | (2.9) | 0.0 | (0.1) | c | c | c | c |
| Indonesia | 30.4 | (1.4) | 1.5 | (0.1) | 0.0 | (0.0) | 0.1 | (1.4) | -0.6 | (1.8) |
| Israel | 33.9 | (4.1) | 2.8 | (0.8) | -0.1 | (0.0) | 12.4 | (2.6) | -2.1 | (1.8) |
| Jordan | 8.3 | (2.0) | -2.0 | (0.6) | 0.1 | (0.0) | -8.1 | (2.5) | 0.0 | (2.2) |
| Kyrgyzstan | 43.7 | (3.1) | 2.6 | (0.6) | -0.1 | (0.0) | -12.0 | (2.8) | 12.1 | (2.4) |
| Latvia | 19.5 | (4.0) | 1.4 | (0.8) | -0.1 | (0.0) | 9.0 | (2.6) | 6.2 | (1.7) |
| Lithuania | 42.2 | (4.0) | -5.1 | (0.9) | 0.2 | (0.0) | 2.9 | (2.7) | -13.7 | (2.3) |
| Macao-China | 15.5 | (4.6) | 0.9 | (0.6) | 0.0 | (0.0) | 8.7 | (5.9) | 3.9 | (4.4) |
| Montenegro | 35.4 | (5.0) | -1.3 | (2.2) | 0.2 | (0.1) | -0.4 | (4.6) | -11.6 | (4.4) |
| Romania | 30.6 | (3.5) | 0.8 | (0.5) | 0.0 | (0.0) | -3.1 | (2.5) | 4.9 | (1.3) |
| Russian Federation | 14.9 | (4.3) | -1.9 | (0.9) | 0.1 | (0.0) | -14.8 | (3.0) | 5.6 | (2.4) |
| Serbia | 44.9 | (2.7) | -1.2 | (0.8) | 0.1 | (0.0) | -11.9 | (3.7) | -9.2 | (1.7) |
| Slovenia | 68.4 | (3.2) | 5.5 | (1.2) | -0.2 | (0.1) | 1.1 | (3.3) | -8.1 | (2.1) |
| Chinese Taipei | 40.5 | (2.1) | 0.8 | (0.1) | 0.0 | (0.0) | -6.1 | (2.1) | 4.8 | (1.4) |
| Thailand | 37.9 | (1.8) | 0.4 | (0.2) | 0.0 | (0.0) | -4.4 | (2.3) | -3.3 | (2.1) |
| Tunisia | 19.1 | (1.6) | 2.9 | (0.9) | -0.1 | (0.0) | 3.6 | (1.7) | -3.6 | (3.3) |
| Uruguay | 38.9 | (2.2) | 3.7 | (0.7) | -0.1 | (0.0) | 12.2 | (2.7) | -2.5 | (2.7) |

Note: Values that are statistically significant are indicated in bold (see Annex A3).
1. Significant school factors show effects even after accounting for other school and system-level factors and demographic and socio-economic factors (with statistical significance tested at the 0.5% level [p<0.005]). See Model 2N in Table 5.19g.
StatLink ⏷⏷ http://dx.doi.org/10.1787/142127877152

Pour consulter la version française intégrale de ce tableau, suivre ce lien :
StatLink ⏷⏷ http://dx.doi.org/10.1787/152751048643

[Part 3/4]

**Table 5.21b**   Effects of significant school factors[1] and demographic and socio-economic factors on student performance in science, by country

Tableau 5.21b   Effets des facteurs scolaires significatifs et des facteurs démographiques et socioéconomiques sur la performance des élèves en sciences, par pays

| | | School factors | | | | | | | |
|---|---|---|---|---|---|---|---|---|---|
| | | School with high academic selectivity of school admittance | | School with low academic selectivity of school admittance | | School with ability grouping for all subjects within school | | School posting achievement data publicly | |
| | | Change in score | S.E. | Change in score | S.E. | Change in score | S.E. | Change in score | S.E. |
| *OECD* | Australia | 24.6 | (4.2) | 6.7 | (1.3) | -10.1 | (3.0) | 4.6 | (1.2) |
| | Austria | 4.8 | (1.8) | -30.4 | (3.4) | -2.6 | (4.9) | 23.9 | (2.4) |
| | Belgium | -0.7 | (1.6) | -8.9 | (1.0) | -8.0 | (1.1) | -9.9 | (2.0) |
| | Canada | 8.8 | (1.8) | 0.1 | (1.0) | -1.5 | (1.4) | 6.1 | (1.1) |
| | Czech Republic | 37.8 | (2.1) | -7.7 | (2.6) | -4.7 | (2.9) | 6.6 | (1.8) |
| | Denmark | c | c | 4.6 | (1.9) | -11.6 | (3.4) | -5.3 | (2.2) |
| | Finland | c | c | 0.0 | (3.0) | c | c | 4.4 | (6.4) |
| | Germany | 15.9 | (2.1) | -2.8 | (1.8) | -10.5 | (3.1) | 5.8 | (1.9) |
| | Greece | c | c | 7.5 | (2.1) | c | c | 6.8 | (1.7) |
| | Hungary | 8.9 | (1.7) | -23.6 | (5.2) | c | c | 8.2 | (2.8) |
| | Iceland | c | c | -1.2 | (3.7) | 2.8 | (9.3) | -2.7 | (4.5) |
| | Ireland | c | c | -4.8 | (2.1) | 7.0 | (4.3) | -2.3 | (2.4) |
| | Italy | 1.7 | (2.1) | 0.3 | (0.8) | -4.4 | (1.0) | 3.7 | (0.8) |
| | Japan | 11.6 | (1.1) | c | c | -6.4 | (1.9) | 5.4 | (2.4) |
| | Korea | 11.3 | (1.9) | -6.0 | (2.2) | 14.5 | (3.6) | 9.6 | (1.8) |
| | Luxembourg | 3.0 | (3.4) | -1.6 | (4.7) | 0.1 | (3.2) | 6.9 | (3.4) |
| | Mexico | 4.0 | (0.8) | -4.4 | (0.7) | -1.0 | (1.0) | 2.4 | (0.6) |
| | Netherlands | 7.1 | (1.3) | c | c | -6.1 | (1.1) | 8.0 | (1.9) |
| | New Zealand | c | c | 3.7 | (2.7) | 4.3 | (6.5) | 5.8 | (2.9) |
| | Norway | c | c | 7.2 | (3.6) | c | c | 1.1 | (2.2) |
| | Poland | 7.3 | (4.1) | -7.0 | (2.4) | 14.1 | (5.9) | 9.8 | (2.0) |
| | Portugal | -21.6 | (4.6) | 8.8 | (2.2) | -16.8 | (2.5) | 2.9 | (2.0) |
| | Slovak Republic | 18.7 | (1.9) | -21.0 | (2.8) | -3.0 | (3.0) | 8.6 | (1.5) |
| | Spain | c | c | 4.5 | (1.6) | 5.0 | (1.4) | -0.2 | (1.8) |
| | Sweden | c | c | 10.2 | (4.0) | -13.3 | (4.8) | -0.4 | (2.8) |
| | Switzerland | 15.9 | (1.7) | -3.6 | (2.2) | -10.7 | (1.4) | 6.6 | (2.4) |
| | Turkey | 35.2 | (1.9) | 0.6 | (1.5) | 2.0 | (1.6) | 2.5 | (1.6) |
| | United Kingdom | 35.4 | (3.3) | -0.9 | (1.9) | -22.2 | (3.6) | 1.1 | (2.3) |
| | United States | 3.8 | (3.3) | 5.1 | (2.0) | 13.6 | (3.5) | 4.1 | (2.8) |
| *Partners* | Argentina | -7.7 | (3.6) | -6.0 | (2.1) | 0.8 | (1.9) | -3.3 | (3.6) |
| | Azerbaijan | 10.2 | (1.2) | -10.6 | (1.5) | 7.2 | (1.0) | 2.0 | (1.5) |
| | Brazil | -2.0 | (2.7) | -3.8 | (1.6) | -6.8 | (1.3) | 5.3 | (1.3) |
| | Bulgaria | 17.2 | (2.6) | -13.3 | (7.0) | 6.0 | (2.2) | 14.1 | (1.8) |
| | Chile | 6.9 | (2.2) | -7.5 | (2.5) | 9.9 | (2.1) | -0.7 | (2.3) |
| | Colombia | 17.4 | (2.7) | 13.8 | (1.8) | -9.8 | (2.1) | 4.3 | (2.0) |
| | Croatia | 10.4 | (2.3) | c | c | -5.0 | (1.4) | 1.8 | (1.1) |
| | Estonia | -0.8 | (2.1) | 3.9 | (4.0) | 4.0 | (2.0) | 0.4 | (2.0) |
| | Hong Kong-China | -0.8 | (1.2) | c | c | 0.8 | (2.0) | 6.4 | (1.5) |
| | Indonesia | 1.1 | (1.2) | 1.5 | (1.6) | -7.9 | (0.9) | 2.8 | (1.3) |
| | Israel | 19.6 | (3.2) | -8.7 | (3.1) | -6.2 | (2.6) | -7.3 | (2.0) |
| | Jordan | -0.6 | (2.0) | -7.8 | (2.0) | -6.8 | (1.5) | 6.9 | (1.7) |
| | Kyrgyzstan | -6.7 | (1.5) | 3.3 | (2.3) | -1.4 | (2.2) | 4.5 | (1.5) |
| | Latvia | 12.7 | (4.6) | -2.6 | (2.1) | -3.1 | (2.4) | 3.9 | (2.1) |
| | Lithuania | 33.2 | (3.4) | -3.5 | (2.1) | -14.6 | (2.9) | -3.6 | (2.6) |
| | Macao-China | 16.9 | (2.4) | c | c | -8.1 | (13.6) | 16.7 | (5.5) |
| | Montenegro | 8.1 | (4.5) | -8.8 | (7.1) | -9.8 | (3.5) | 1.4 | (4.0) |
| | Romania | 8.7 | (1.9) | -1.7 | (3.0) | 6.8 | (1.2) | 15.2 | (1.9) |
| | Russian Federation | -3.7 | (4.4) | 2.0 | (1.9) | -0.5 | (1.8) | 5.6 | (2.3) |
| | Serbia | 22.5 | (2.6) | c | c | 2.5 | (1.7) | -7.8 | (2.0) |
| | Slovenia | 5.4 | (3.0) | 4.1 | (2.0) | -8.2 | (4.1) | 1.3 | (2.1) |
| | Chinese Taipei | 17.9 | (1.4) | -0.5 | (1.2) | -12.4 | (2.0) | 2.6 | (1.3) |
| | Thailand | -8.7 | (1.7) | 11.6 | (2.5) | -2.9 | (1.6) | 10.0 | (1.7) |
| | Tunisia | 5.6 | (1.9) | -4.0 | (2.2) | 0.7 | (1.8) | -4.6 | (2.1) |
| | Uruguay | 19.8 | (3.5) | 17.7 | (2.6) | -3.8 | (2.8) | 6.1 | (3.6) |

Note: Values that are statistically significant are indicated in bold (see Annex A3).
1. Significant school factors show effects even after accounting for other school and system-level factors and demographic and socio-economic factors (with statistical significance tested at the 0.5% level [p< 0.005]). See Model 2N in Table 5.19g.
*StatLink* 🔗 http://dx.doi.org/10.1787/142127877152

Pour consulter la version française intégrale de ce tableau, suivre ce lien :
*StatLink* 🔗 http://dx.doi.org/10.1787/152751048643

[Part 4/4]

**Table 5.21b** Effects of significant school factors[1] and demographic and socio-economic factors on student performance in science, by country

Tableau 5.21b Effets des facteurs scolaires significatifs et des facteurs démographiques et socioéconomiques sur la performance des élèves en sciences, par pays

| | | School factors | | | | | | |
|---|---|---|---|---|---|---|---|---|
| | | School average students' learning time for regular lessons in school (hours per week) | | School average students' learning time for out-of-school lessons (hours per week) | | School average students' learning time for self-study or homework (hours per week) | | School average index of school activities to promote the learning of science (1 unit increase) | |
| | | Change in score | S.E. | Change in score | S.E. | Change in score | S.E. | Change in score | S.E. |
| OECD | Australia | 3.5 | (0.4) | -12.9 | (1.3) | 6.5 | (0.7) | 4.3 | (0.9) |
| | Austria | 6.9 | (0.6) | -17.7 | (2.0) | -4.1 | (1.0) | 4.2 | (1.2) |
| | Belgium | 3.2 | (0.4) | -29.9 | (0.7) | 14.7 | (0.6) | 2.5 | (0.6) |
| | Canada | 3.7 | (0.4) | -13.7 | (0.7) | 3.8 | (0.5) | 4.4 | (0.5) |
| | Czech Republic | 10.9 | (0.7) | -10.1 | (1.4) | 6.2 | (1.7) | 0.1 | (0.9) |
| | Denmark | 2.5 | (0.9) | -8.4 | (1.7) | 4.9 | (1.5) | 5.1 | (1.4) |
| | Finland | 2.4 | (1.2) | -19.5 | (3.9) | 6.7 | (2.4) | -4.5 | (1.5) |
| | Germany | 6.4 | (0.6) | -21.0 | (1.2) | -0.1 | (0.9) | 7.5 | (1.1) |
| | Greece | 14.2 | (1.2) | 4.5 | (0.9) | -3.9 | (1.5) | 3.9 | (1.9) |
| | Hungary | 11.0 | (1.2) | -9.5 | (1.5) | 3.9 | (1.9) | 1.0 | (1.2) |
| | Iceland | 0.0 | (2.2) | -20.6 | (2.4) | 3.9 | (2.6) | -6.5 | (3.0) |
| | Ireland | 4.2 | (1.0) | -16.0 | (2.0) | 8.5 | (1.3) | 0.5 | (1.3) |
| | Italy | 9.4 | (0.2) | -25.4 | (0.7) | 0.4 | (0.3) | -0.5 | (0.6) |
| | Japan | 7.5 | (0.4) | -22.7 | (1.1) | 11.8 | (0.6) | 3.9 | (0.8) |
| | Korea | 4.5 | (0.6) | -0.1 | (0.5) | 17.5 | (0.8) | 0.7 | (0.9) |
| | Luxembourg | 9.4 | (2.1) | -27.5 | (4.6) | 0.2 | (3.4) | -6.3 | (2.0) |
| | Mexico | 6.2 | (0.3) | -7.6 | (0.5) | 2.1 | (0.3) | 4.2 | (0.4) |
| | Netherlands | 9.0 | (0.9) | -30.5 | (0.8) | 19.2 | (0.9) | 3.4 | (1.0) |
| | New Zealand | 6.5 | (1.2) | -15.1 | (2.4) | 8.0 | (1.8) | -0.8 | (1.8) |
| | Norway | 4.1 | (1.0) | m | m | m | m | -2.3 | (1.6) |
| | Poland | 6.3 | (1.1) | -11.4 | (1.6) | 3.2 | (1.2) | 9.3 | (2.0) |
| | Portugal | 11.3 | (0.6) | -8.6 | (1.5) | 1.8 | (1.1) | 2.6 | (1.0) |
| | Slovak Republic | 3.7 | (0.6) | 0.6 | (1.0) | 6.0 | (1.1) | 0.5 | (1.1) |
| | Spain | 7.7 | (0.4) | -5.1 | (0.6) | 1.3 | (0.5) | 0.0 | (0.6) |
| | Sweden | 1.9 | (1.8) | -12.1 | (3.3) | 10.4 | (2.6) | 2.6 | (1.2) |
| | Switzerland | 4.7 | (0.5) | -24.8 | (1.1) | 10.2 | (0.9) | 8.3 | (0.9) |
| | Turkey | 12.1 | (0.6) | 0.7 | (1.1) | -4.9 | (1.1) | 0.8 | (0.8) |
| | United Kingdom | 2.1 | (0.7) | -20.2 | (1.2) | 9.1 | (1.0) | 2.5 | (0.8) |
| | United States | 6.0 | (0.9) | -17.2 | (1.5) | 12.1 | (1.6) | -2.2 | (1.0) |
| Partners | Argentina | 16.2 | (0.9) | -9.7 | (2.1) | -0.3 | (2.0) | 1.0 | (1.5) |
| | Azerbaijan | 6.2 | (0.4) | 1.1 | (0.6) | 0.0 | (0.6) | 8.2 | (0.3) |
| | Brazil | 10.0 | (0.5) | -6.3 | (0.7) | 0.1 | (0.6) | 4.6 | (1.1) |
| | Bulgaria | 5.8 | (1.3) | -16.9 | (2.0) | 6.6 | (1.4) | 8.6 | (1.5) |
| | Chile | 10.3 | (0.7) | -4.8 | (2.2) | -2.7 | (2.1) | 1.0 | (0.7) |
| | Colombia | 7.1 | (0.7) | 1.3 | (1.4) | -0.5 | (1.1) | 1.5 | (1.2) |
| | Croatia | 4.1 | (1.1) | -17.4 | (2.4) | 9.4 | (1.7) | 0.3 | (0.8) |
| | Estonia | 7.7 | (0.8) | -12.4 | (1.6) | -2.3 | (1.3) | 2.3 | (1.5) |
| | Hong Kong-China | 10.8 | (0.6) | -9.0 | (0.7) | 10.2 | (0.7) | -1.1 | (1.1) |
| | Indonesia | 6.3 | (0.2) | -4.0 | (0.6) | 0.0 | (0.5) | 6.0 | (0.5) |
| | Israel | 11.6 | (1.2) | -15.4 | (1.7) | 3.0 | (1.3) | 4.1 | (1.0) |
| | Jordan | 6.6 | (0.7) | -2.2 | (0.8) | 2.0 | (0.8) | 1.3 | (1.0) |
| | Kyrgyzstan | 6.2 | (0.5) | -8.1 | (0.7) | 2.1 | (0.6) | 4.3 | (1.1) |
| | Latvia | 10.3 | (1.0) | -6.7 | (1.5) | -2.3 | (1.8) | 3.4 | (1.7) |
| | Lithuania | 7.3 | (1.3) | -6.5 | (1.5) | 3.7 | (2.1) | 5.2 | (1.7) |
| | Macao-China | 11.3 | (2.8) | -14.9 | (2.3) | 5.8 | (2.6) | 11.5 | (2.1) |
| | Montenegro | 10.8 | (3.3) | -17.4 | (4.1) | -3.2 | (4.6) | -2.6 | (1.6) |
| | Romania | 12.9 | (0.8) | -7.1 | (1.3) | 0.9 | (1.3) | 3.3 | (0.7) |
| | Russian Federation | 11.3 | (0.8) | -1.8 | (1.1) | 0.0 | (0.9) | 2.4 | (1.8) |
| | Serbia | 6.7 | (0.8) | -12.8 | (2.1) | 4.3 | (2.2) | 3.7 | (0.9) |
| | Slovenia | 9.2 | (0.8) | -15.1 | (1.7) | 6.0 | (1.4) | 2.3 | (1.3) |
| | Chinese Taipei | 2.2 | (0.4) | -3.8 | (0.7) | 15.6 | (0.8) | 3.6 | (0.6) |
| | Thailand | 6.2 | (0.8) | -8.0 | (1.1) | -0.6 | (0.7) | 2.4 | (1.6) |
| | Tunisia | 17.0 | (0.5) | 4.2 | (1.4) | -2.9 | (1.4) | 4.6 | (0.6) |
| | Uruguay | 6.1 | (0.8) | -9.1 | (1.3) | 4.8 | (2.1) | -0.3 | (1.0) |

Note: Values that are statistically significant are indicated in bold (see Annex A3).
1. Significant school factors show effects even after accounting for other school and system-level factors and demographic and socio-economic factors (with statistical significance tested at the 0.5% level [p<0.005]). See Model 2N in Table 5.19g.
*StatLink* http://dx.doi.org/10.1787/142127877152

Pour consulter la version française intégrale de ce tableau, suivre ce lien :
*StatLink* http://dx.doi.org/10.1787/152751048643

[Part 1/2]

**Table 5.22** School and system characteristics of five OECD countries with above-average student performance in science and below-average impact of socio-economic background on student performance

Tableau 5.22 Caractéristiques scolaires et systémiques de cinq pays de l'OCDE dont la performance des élèves en sciences est supérieure à la moyenne et dont l'impact socioéconomique sur la performance des élèves est inférieur à la moyenne

| | Student achievement in science | | Impact of socio-economic background on science performance | | Admittance, selection and grouping policies | | | | | | | |
|---|---|---|---|---|---|---|---|---|---|---|---|---|
| | | | | | Percentage of students in | | | | | | Number of years between the age of first selection and the age of 15 | Number of school types or distinct educational programmes available to 15-year-olds |
| | | | | | Schools with ability grouping for all subjects within school[1] | | Schools with high academic selectivity of school admittance[1] | | Schools with low academic selectivity of school admittance[1] | | | |
| | Mean score | S.E. | Percentage of explained variance in student performance | S.E. | % | S.E. | % | S.E. | % | S.E. | Years | Programmes |
| **OECD** Australia | 527 | (2.30) | 11.3 | (0.78) | 5 | (1.31) | 4 | (1.16) | 25 | (2.60) | 0.0 | 1 |
| Canada | 534 | (2.00) | 8.2 | (0.68) | 15 | (1.69) | 9 | (1.16) | 34 | (2.28) | 0.0 | 1 |
| Finland | 563 | (2.00) | 8.3 | (0.87) | 2 | (1.09) | 3 | (1.60) | 79 | (3.49) | 0.0 | 1 |
| Japan | 531 | (3.40) | 7.4 | (0.95) | 10 | (2.46) | 72 | (3.03) | 1 | (0.74) | 0.0 | 2 |
| Korea | 522 | (3.40) | 8.1 | (1.49) | 7 | (2.52) | 46 | (4.22) | 27 | (3.30) | 1.0 | 3 |
| **5 countries average** | 535 | (1.21) | 8.7 | (0.45) | 8 | (0.85) | 26 | (1.14) | 33 | (1.19) | 0.2 | 1.6 |
| **OECD average** | 500 | (0.54) | 14.2 | (0.26) | 14 | (0.41) | 19 | (0.41) | 42 | (0.51) | 1.4 | 2.5 |
| **Participating countries average** | 475 | (0.43) | 13.6 | (0.22) | 20 | (0.35) | 24 | (0.34) | 33 | (0.37) | 1.2 | 2.3 |

| | School management and funding | | | | Parental pressure and choice | | | | Accountability practices | | | |
|---|---|---|---|---|---|---|---|---|---|---|---|---|
| | | | | | Percentage of students in | | | | Percentage of students in | | | |
| | Percentage of students in schools being privately managed[1] | | Proportion of school funding from government sources[1] | | Schools with high level of competition[1] | | Schools with high levels of perceived parental pressure[1] | | Schools informing parents of children's performance relative to other students in the school[1] | | Schools informing parents of children's performance relative to national benchmarks[1] | |
| | % | S.E. | % | S.E. | % | S.E. | % | S.E. | % | S.E. | % | S.E. |
| **OECD** Australia | w | w | 70 | (1.06) | 94 | (1.14) | 90 | (1.78) | 59 | (2.49) | 50 | (2.63) |
| Canada | 7 | (0.64) | 89 | (0.65) | 77 | (2.24) | 82 | (1.99) | 79 | (1.54) | 61 | (2.42) |
| Finland | 3 | (1.22) | 100 | (0.10) | 56 | (3.70) | 21 | (3.45) | 15 | (3.04) | 47 | (4.25) |
| Japan | 31 | (1.28) | 71 | (1.35) | 90 | (2.21) | 89 | (2.57) | 40 | (3.39) | 80 | (3.31) |
| Korea | 46 | (3.90) | 47 | (1.69) | 84 | (2.95) | 82 | (2.92) | 84 | (3.14) | 78 | (3.27) |
| **5 countries average** | 22 | (1.08) | 75 | (0.50) | 80 | (1.16) | 73 | (1.17) | 56 | (1.25) | 63 | (1.45) |
| **OECD average** | 17 | (0.35) | 85 | (0.23) | 74 | (0.51) | 68 | (0.54) | 54 | (0.57) | 47 | (0.55) |
| **Participating countries average** | 19 | (0.24) | 83 | (0.20) | 75 | (0.39) | 67 | (0.42) | 62 | (0.40) | 46 | (0.41) |

| | Accountability practices | | | | | | | | | | | |
|---|---|---|---|---|---|---|---|---|---|---|---|---|
| | Percentage of students in | | | | | | | | | | | |
| | Schools informing parents of students' performance relative to other schools[1] | | Schools posting achievement data publicly[1] | | Schools using achievement data for evaluating principals[1] | | Schools using achievement data for evaluating teachers[1] | | Schools using achievement data for allocating resources to schools[1] | | School with achievement data tracked over time[1] | |
| | % | S.E. | % | S.E. | % | S.E. | % | S.E. | % | S.E. | % | S.E. |
| **OECD** Australia | 20 | (2.15) | 60 | (2.55) | 48 | (3.07) | 43 | (3.00) | 58 | (2.96) | 88 | (2.09) |
| Canada | 34 | (2.56) | 64 | (2.74) | 22 | (2.31) | 19 | (1.99) | 57 | (2.50) | 91 | (1.14) |
| Finland | 16 | (3.01) | 4 | (1.44) | 3 | (1.32) | 14 | (2.89) | 7 | (2.14) | 54 | (4.13) |
| Japan | 0 | (0.00) | 11 | (2.68) | 10 | (2.34) | 26 | (3.68) | 6 | (1.86) | 16 | (2.53) |
| Korea | 42 | (4.09) | 17 | (3.26) | 23 | (3.15) | 34 | (3.65) | 30 | (4.06) | 52 | (4.06) |
| **5 countries average** | 22 | (1.22) | 31 | (1.16) | 21 | (1.13) | 27 | (1.39) | 32 | (1.26) | 60 | (1.35) |
| **OECD average** | 26 | (0.52) | 38 | (0.53) | 31 | (0.53) | 43 | (0.55) | 30 | (0.54) | 65 | (0.56) |
| **Participating countries average** | 29 | (0.41) | 38 | (0.42) | 38 | (0.41) | 56 | (0.39) | 37 | (0.41) | 68 | (0.42) |

Note: OECD average does not include France. Participating countries average does not include France and Qatar.
1. Results based on reports from school principals.
*StatLink* http://dx.doi.org/10.1787/142127877152

Pour consulter la version française intégrale de ce tableau, suivre ce lien :
*StatLink* http://dx.doi.org/10.1787/152751048643

[Part 2/2]

**Table 5.22** — School and system characteristics of five OECD countries with above-average student performance in science and below-average impact of socio-economic background on student performance

Tableau 5.22 — Caractéristiques scolaires et systémiques de cinq pays de l'OCDE dont la performance des élèves en sciences est supérieure à la moyenne et dont l'impact socioéconomique sur la performance des élèves est inférieur à la moyenne

| | Accountability practices | School autonomy | | | | | School resources | | | |
|---|---|---|---|---|---|---|---|---|---|---|
| | Standards-based external examinations | School autonomy index in staffing[1] | | School autonomy index in budgeting[1] | | School autonomy index in educational content[1] | | School average number of students per teacher[1] | | School-level index of teacher shortage[1] | |
| | Ratio | Mean | S.E. | Mean | S.E. | Mean | S.E. | Mean | S.E. | Mean | S.E. |
| Australia | 0.81 | -0.23 | (0.03) | 0.52 | (0.03) | 0.46 | (0.03) | 13.4 | (0.14) | 0.33 | (0.05) |
| Canada | 0.51 | -0.28 | (0.03) | -0.12 | (0.04) | -0.29 | (0.03) | 16.7 | (0.13) | 0.17 | (0.05) |
| Finland | 1.00 | -0.62 | (0.05) | 0.02 | (0.06) | 0.42 | (0.05) | 11.3 | (0.16) | -0.28 | (0.05) |
| Japan | 1.00 | -0.29 | (0.04) | -0.12 | (0.05) | 0.91 | (0.04) | 12.8 | (0.30) | -0.51 | (0.05) |
| Korea | 1.00 | -0.54 | (0.07) | 0.37 | (0.06) | 0.91 | (0.03) | 16.3 | (0.16) | -0.51 | (0.07) |
| **5 countries average** | 0.86 | -0.39 | (0.02) | 0.14 | (0.02) | 0.48 | (0.02) | 14.1 | (0.08) | -0.16 | (0.02) |
| **OECD average** | 0.59 | -0.02 | (0.01) | 0.19 | (0.01) | 0.15 | (0.01) | 13.4 | (0.05) | 0.01 | (0.01) |
| **Participating countries average** | 0.56 | 0.00 | (0.01) | 0.00 | (0.01) | 0.00 | (0.01) | 14.7 | (0.05) | 0.05 | (0.01) |

*OECD*

| | School resources | | | | | | | | | | | | |
|---|---|---|---|---|---|---|---|---|---|---|---|---|---|
| | School average number of computers for instruction per student[1] | | School-level index of quality of school educational resources[1] | | School average students' learning time for regular lessons in school | | School average students' learning time for out-of-school lessons | | School average students' learning time for self-study or homework | | School providing opportunity of learning science | | School average index of school activities to promote students' learning of science[1] | |
| | Mean | S.E. | Mean | S.E. | Hours per week | S.E. | Hours per week | S.E. | Hours per week | S.E. | % | S.E. | Mean | S.E. |
| Australia | 0.26 | (0.01) | 0.40 | (0.05) | 11.4 | (0.07) | 1.76 | (0.04) | 4.67 | (0.06) | 81 | (0.59) | 0.41 | (0.04) |
| Canada | 0.19 | (0.01) | 0.09 | (0.06) | 12.9 | (0.11) | 2.35 | (0.05) | 5.27 | (0.07) | 94 | (0.30) | 0.42 | (0.04) |
| Finland | 0.15 | (0.01) | -0.23 | (0.06) | 9.7 | (0.11) | 1.06 | (0.04) | 3.41 | (0.05) | 98 | (0.37) | -0.60 | (0.06) |
| Japan | 0.20 | (0.02) | 0.45 | (0.07) | 10.7 | (0.13) | 1.40 | (0.05) | 3.11 | (0.10) | 92 | (1.09) | -1.16 | (0.07) |
| Korea | 0.18 | (0.01) | -0.19 | (0.06) | 12.7 | (0.11) | 4.75 | (0.08) | 4.94 | (0.12) | 91 | (1.04) | 0.54 | (0.07) |
| **5 countries average** | 0.20 | (0.00) | 0.10 | (0.03) | 11.5 | (0.05) | 2.26 | (0.02) | 4.28 | (0.04) | 91 | (0.34) | -0.08 | (0.03) |
| **OECD average** | 0.15 | (0.00) | 0.00 | (0.01) | 10.6 | (0.02) | 2.42 | (0.01) | 4.92 | (0.01) | 85 | (0.17) | 0.00 | (0.01) |
| **Participating countries average** | 0.12 | (0.00) | -0.28 | (0.01) | 10.2 | (0.01) | 2.77 | (0.01) | 5.27 | (0.01) | 82 | (0.12) | 0.23 | (0.01) |

*OECD*

Note: OECD average does not include France. Participating countries average does not include France and Qatar.
1. Results based on reports from school principals.
**StatLink** http://dx.doi.org/10.1787/142127877152

Pour consulter la version française intégrale de ce tableau, suivre ce lien :
**StatLink** http://dx.doi.org/10.1787/152751048643

[Part 1/1]

**Table 6.1a** Percentage of students at each proficiency level on the reading scale

Tableau 6.1a   Pourcentage d'élèves à chaque niveau de compétence sur l'échelle de compréhension de l'écrit

| | | Proficiency levels | | | | | | | | | | |
|---|---|---|---|---|---|---|---|---|---|---|---|---|
| | | Below Level 1 (below 334.75 score points) | | Level 1 (from 334.75 to 407.47 score points) | | Level 2 (from 407.47 to 480.18 score points) | | Level 3 (from 480.18 to 552.89 score points) | | Level 4 (from 552.89 to 625.61 score points) | | Level 5 (above 625.61 score points) | |
| | | % | S.E. | % | S.E. | % | S.E. | % | S.E. | % | S.E. | % | S.E. |
| OECD | Australia | 3.8 | (0.3) | 9.6 | (0.5) | 21.0 | (0.7) | 30.1 | (0.6) | 24.9 | (0.7) | 10.6 | (0.6) |
| | Austria | 8.4 | (1.1) | 13.1 | (0.8) | 22.0 | (1.2) | 26.2 | (1.0) | 21.3 | (1.0) | 9.0 | (0.7) |
| | Belgium | 8.6 | (0.9) | 10.8 | (0.6) | 18.9 | (0.7) | 26.0 | (0.8) | 24.4 | (0.9) | 11.3 | (0.6) |
| | Canada | 3.4 | (0.4) | 7.6 | (0.4) | 18.0 | (0.8) | 29.4 | (1.0) | 27.2 | (0.8) | 14.5 | (0.7) |
| | Czech Republic | 9.9 | (1.1) | 14.9 | (0.9) | 22.3 | (1.0) | 24.5 | (0.9) | 19.3 | (1.0) | 9.2 | (0.8) |
| | Denmark | 4.5 | (0.6) | 11.5 | (0.7) | 25.7 | (0.9) | 31.8 | (1.0) | 20.7 | (0.9) | 5.9 | (0.6) |
| | Finland | 0.8 | (0.2) | 4.0 | (0.4) | 15.5 | (0.8) | 31.2 | (0.8) | 31.8 | (0.9) | 16.7 | (0.8) |
| | France | 8.5 | (1.0) | 13.3 | (1.0) | 21.3 | (1.0) | 27.9 | (1.3) | 21.8 | (1.2) | 7.3 | (0.7) |
| | Germany | 8.3 | (0.9) | 11.8 | (0.8) | 20.3 | (1.0) | 27.3 | (0.9) | 22.5 | (1.1) | 9.9 | (0.7) |
| | Greece | 11.9 | (1.2) | 15.8 | (0.8) | 26.6 | (1.2) | 27.9 | (1.1) | 14.3 | (0.9) | 3.5 | (0.4) |
| | Hungary | 6.6 | (0.8) | 14.0 | (0.9) | 25.3 | (1.1) | 30.6 | (1.1) | 18.8 | (1.0) | 4.7 | (0.6) |
| | Iceland | 7.1 | (0.6) | 13.4 | (0.7) | 25.1 | (1.0) | 29.6 | (0.8) | 18.9 | (1.0) | 6.0 | (0.5) |
| | Ireland | 3.2 | (0.6) | 9.0 | (0.8) | 20.9 | (0.9) | 30.2 | (0.8) | 25.1 | (1.0) | 11.7 | (0.8) |
| | Italy | 11.4 | (0.7) | 15.0 | (0.6) | 24.5 | (0.8) | 26.4 | (0.7) | 17.5 | (0.6) | 5.2 | (0.4) |
| | Japan | 6.7 | (0.7) | 11.7 | (1.0) | 22.0 | (0.9) | 28.7 | (1.0) | 21.5 | (0.9) | 9.4 | (0.7) |
| | Korea | 1.4 | (0.3) | 4.3 | (0.7) | 12.5 | (0.8) | 27.2 | (1.1) | 32.7 | (1.3) | 21.7 | (1.4) |
| | Luxembourg | 8.6 | (0.4) | 14.2 | (0.6) | 24.6 | (0.7) | 27.9 | (0.7) | 19.0 | (0.7) | 5.6 | (0.4) |
| | Mexico | 21.0 | (1.3) | 26.0 | (1.0) | 28.9 | (1.0) | 18.2 | (0.8) | 5.3 | (0.4) | 0.6 | (0.1) |
| | Netherlands | 5.2 | (0.7) | 9.9 | (0.9) | 21.3 | (0.9) | 28.9 | (1.0) | 25.6 | (1.0) | 9.1 | (0.6) |
| | New Zealand | 4.7 | (0.5) | 9.9 | (0.7) | 18.7 | (0.8) | 26.4 | (0.8) | 24.5 | (0.8) | 15.9 | (0.8) |
| | Norway | 8.4 | (0.7) | 14.0 | (0.7) | 23.3 | (0.8) | 27.6 | (0.9) | 19.0 | (0.8) | 7.7 | (0.6) |
| | Poland | 5.0 | (0.5) | 11.2 | (0.7) | 21.5 | (0.9) | 27.5 | (0.9) | 23.1 | (0.8) | 11.6 | (0.8) |
| | Portugal | 9.3 | (1.0) | 15.6 | (1.0) | 25.5 | (1.0) | 28.2 | (1.1) | 16.8 | (0.9) | 4.6 | (0.5) |
| | Slovak Republic | 11.2 | (0.9) | 16.6 | (0.9) | 25.1 | (1.0) | 25.9 | (1.2) | 15.8 | (0.8) | 5.4 | (0.5) |
| | Spain | 8.7 | (0.6) | 17.0 | (0.6) | 30.2 | (0.7) | 29.7 | (0.7) | 12.6 | (0.6) | 1.8 | (0.2) |
| | Sweden | 5.0 | (0.7) | 10.3 | (0.9) | 21.9 | (0.9) | 28.9 | (1.1) | 23.3 | (1.3) | 10.6 | (0.8) |
| | Switzerland | 5.3 | (0.6) | 11.1 | (0.6) | 22.9 | (1.0) | 30.4 | (0.9) | 22.6 | (0.9) | 7.7 | (0.7) |
| | Turkey | 10.8 | (1.0) | 21.4 | (1.4) | 31.0 | (1.3) | 24.5 | (1.2) | 10.3 | (1.1) | 2.1 | (0.6) |
| | United Kingdom | 6.8 | (0.5) | 12.2 | (0.6) | 22.7 | (0.7) | 28.7 | (0.7) | 20.5 | (0.7) | 9.0 | (0.6) |
| | United States | m | m | m | m | m | m | m | m | m | m | m | m |
| | **OECD total** | 8.9 | (0.2) | 14.2 | (0.2) | 23.1 | (0.2) | 26.6 | (0.2) | 19.2 | (0.3) | 8.1 | (0.2) |
| | **OECD average** | 7.4 | (0.1) | 12.7 | (0.1) | 22.7 | (0.2) | 27.8 | (0.2) | 20.7 | (0.2) | 8.6 | (0.1) |
| Partners | Argentina | 35.8 | (2.4) | 22.1 | (1.6) | 21.8 | (1.3) | 14.3 | (1.3) | 5.1 | (0.7) | 0.9 | (0.2) |
| | Azerbaijan | 41.2 | (2.0) | 38.3 | (1.5) | 16.5 | (1.0) | 3.4 | (0.5) | 0.6 | (0.2) | 0.1 | (0.1) |
| | Brazil | 27.8 | (1.2) | 27.7 | (0.9) | 25.3 | (1.1) | 13.4 | (0.8) | 4.7 | (0.5) | 1.1 | (0.3) |
| | Bulgaria | 28.8 | (2.2) | 22.3 | (1.3) | 22.4 | (1.3) | 16.4 | (1.3) | 8.1 | (1.1) | 2.1 | (0.5) |
| | Chile | 14.8 | (1.2) | 21.5 | (1.3) | 28.0 | (1.1) | 21.1 | (1.1) | 11.0 | (0.9) | 3.5 | (0.6) |
| | Colombia | 30.4 | (2.0) | 25.3 | (1.2) | 25.2 | (1.3) | 14.5 | (1.2) | 4.0 | (0.6) | 0.6 | (0.2) |
| | Croatia | 6.2 | (0.8) | 15.3 | (0.9) | 27.6 | (1.0) | 30.6 | (1.1) | 16.5 | (0.9) | 3.7 | (0.4) |
| | Estonia | 3.4 | (0.6) | 10.3 | (0.7) | 24.5 | (0.8) | 33.9 | (1.0) | 21.9 | (1.0) | 6.0 | (0.6) |
| | Hong Kong-China | 1.3 | (0.3) | 5.9 | (0.6) | 16.5 | (0.8) | 31.5 | (1.1) | 32.0 | (0.9) | 12.8 | (0.8) |
| | Indonesia | 21.8 | (2.1) | 36.5 | (2.1) | 29.1 | (1.6) | 11.1 | (2.1) | 1.5 | (0.4) | 0.1 | (0.0) |
| | Israel | 20.3 | (1.4) | 18.6 | (0.8) | 22.5 | (1.0) | 21.0 | (0.8) | 12.7 | (0.8) | 5.0 | (0.5) |
| | Jordan | 22.7 | (1.1) | 26.9 | (1.1) | 30.6 | (1.2) | 16.4 | (1.1) | 3.2 | (0.5) | 0.2 | (0.1) |
| | Kyrgyzstan | 70.5 | (1.3) | 17.8 | (0.8) | 8.1 | (0.6) | 3.0 | (0.4) | 0.6 | (0.2) | 0.1 | (0.1) |
| | Latvia | 6.0 | (0.7) | 15.2 | (1.1) | 27.6 | (1.2) | 29.9 | (1.4) | 16.7 | (1.2) | 4.5 | (0.5) |
| | Liechtenstein | 4.9 | (1.2) | 9.4 | (2.0) | 20.0 | (2.4) | 31.3 | (2.6) | 24.6 | (2.8) | 9.8 | (1.8) |
| | Lithuania | 8.7 | (0.6) | 17.0 | (0.9) | 26.9 | (1.1) | 27.4 | (1.0) | 15.6 | (1.0) | 4.4 | (0.5) |
| | Macao-China | 2.9 | (0.3) | 10.1 | (0.6) | 28.9 | (0.9) | 36.6 | (1.2) | 18.5 | (0.8) | 3.0 | (0.3) |
| | Montenegro | 26.3 | (0.7) | 30.0 | (0.8) | 27.2 | (0.9) | 13.1 | (0.9) | 2.9 | (0.3) | 0.4 | (0.2) |
| | Qatar | 61.1 | (0.7) | 20.4 | (0.6) | 11.2 | (0.4) | 4.9 | (0.3) | 1.7 | (0.2) | 0.6 | (0.1) |
| | Romania | 25.6 | (2.2) | 27.9 | (1.3) | 27.9 | (1.5) | 15.1 | (1.4) | 3.2 | (0.6) | 0.3 | (0.1) |
| | Russian Federation | 13.6 | (1.4) | 21.7 | (1.0) | 30.0 | (0.9) | 24.0 | (1.3) | 9.0 | (0.7) | 1.7 | (0.3) |
| | Serbia | 23.6 | (1.4) | 28.1 | (1.0) | 28.1 | (1.1) | 16.0 | (0.9) | 3.9 | (0.4) | 0.3 | (0.1) |
| | Slovenia | 4.4 | (0.4) | 12.1 | (0.6) | 24.7 | (0.8) | 31.6 | (1.0) | 21.9 | (0.8) | 5.3 | (0.5) |
| | Chinese Taipei | 3.8 | (0.6) | 11.5 | (0.9) | 24.4 | (0.9) | 34.0 | (1.1) | 21.6 | (1.0) | 4.7 | (0.6) |
| | Thailand | 15.6 | (1.1) | 29.0 | (1.2) | 33.4 | (1.1) | 17.4 | (0.9) | 4.2 | (0.4) | 0.3 | (0.1) |
| | Tunisia | 31.5 | (1.5) | 27.5 | (1.1) | 25.6 | (1.2) | 12.6 | (1.0) | 2.6 | (0.6) | 0.2 | (0.1) |
| | Uruguay | 25.3 | (1.2) | 21.3 | (0.8) | 23.4 | (1.0) | 18.0 | (0.8) | 8.9 | (0.6) | 3.1 | (0.4) |

*StatLink* 🔗 http://dx.doi.org/10.1787/142183565744

Pour consulter la version française intégrale de ce tableau, suivre ce lien :
*StatLink* 🔗 http://dx.doi.org/10.1787/152754053448

[Part 1/2]

**Table 6.1b  Percentage of students at each proficiency level on the reading scale, by gender**

Tableau 6.1b  Pourcentage d'élèves à chaque niveau de compétence sur l'échelle de compréhension de l'écrit, selon le sexe

| | Males – Proficiency levels | | | | | | | | | | | |
|---|---|---|---|---|---|---|---|---|---|---|---|---|
| | Below Level 1 (below 334.75 score points) | | Level 1 (from 334.75 to 407.47 score points) | | Level 2 (from 407.47 to 480.18 score points) | | Level 3 (from 480.18 to 552.89 score points) | | Level 4 (from 552.89 to 625.61 score points) | | Level 5 (above 625.61 score points) | |
| | % | S.E. | % | S.E. | % | S.E. | % | S.E. | % | S.E. | % | S.E. |
| Australia | 5.7 | (0.5) | 12.7 | (0.6) | 23.6 | (0.7) | 29.1 | (0.7) | 21.0 | (0.8) | 7.9 | (0.8) |
| Austria | 11.5 | (1.5) | 15.9 | (1.1) | 24.2 | (1.4) | 25.2 | (1.2) | 17.5 | (1.2) | 5.7 | (0.6) |
| Belgium | 11.6 | (1.2) | 13.3 | (0.8) | 20.5 | (1.0) | 25.1 | (1.0) | 20.8 | (0.9) | 8.7 | (0.6) |
| Canada | 4.7 | (0.6) | 9.8 | (0.6) | 20.6 | (1.0) | 29.3 | (1.4) | 24.3 | (0.9) | 11.3 | (0.8) |
| Czech Republic | 12.9 | (1.4) | 17.9 | (1.3) | 24.0 | (1.2) | 23.0 | (1.2) | 15.9 | (1.4) | 6.3 | (0.7) |
| Denmark | 6.3 | (0.8) | 14.4 | (1.2) | 27.5 | (1.4) | 30.3 | (1.4) | 17.3 | (1.0) | 4.1 | (0.7) |
| Finland | 1.5 | (0.3) | 6.6 | (0.7) | 21.7 | (1.1) | 34.5 | (1.2) | 26.0 | (1.3) | 9.6 | (0.8) |
| France | 11.7 | (1.5) | 15.6 | (1.2) | 22.7 | (1.4) | 26.2 | (1.7) | 18.3 | (1.6) | 5.5 | (0.8) |
| Germany | 11.0 | (1.3) | 14.5 | (1.3) | 22.3 | (1.3) | 26.3 | (1.2) | 18.9 | (1.4) | 7.0 | (0.8) |
| Greece | 18.9 | (2.0) | 19.7 | (1.1) | 26.2 | (1.5) | 22.8 | (1.4) | 10.1 | (0.9) | 2.3 | (0.4) |
| Hungary | 9.3 | (1.2) | 18.0 | (1.2) | 27.0 | (1.3) | 27.4 | (1.4) | 15.2 | (1.1) | 3.1 | (0.5) |
| Iceland | 11.1 | (0.8) | 17.2 | (1.1) | 27.3 | (1.5) | 26.6 | (1.2) | 14.3 | (1.0) | 3.6 | (0.6) |
| Ireland | 4.7 | (0.9) | 11.9 | (1.3) | 23.1 | (1.4) | 30.1 | (1.4) | 21.4 | (1.2) | 8.7 | (1.0) |
| Italy | 15.9 | (1.0) | 17.1 | (0.8) | 25.6 | (0.9) | 23.8 | (0.8) | 13.9 | (0.7) | 3.7 | (0.4) |
| Japan | 9.3 | (1.1) | 14.2 | (1.1) | 22.8 | (1.1) | 27.0 | (1.4) | 18.6 | (1.2) | 8.1 | (1.0) |
| Korea | 2.4 | (0.6) | 5.8 | (0.9) | 15.4 | (1.0) | 29.4 | (1.4) | 30.7 | (1.6) | 16.3 | (1.3) |
| Luxembourg | 11.5 | (0.6) | 16.7 | (0.9) | 25.5 | (1.1) | 26.2 | (1.1) | 15.9 | (0.7) | 4.2 | (0.5) |
| Mexico | 26.7 | (1.7) | 27.5 | (1.3) | 27.3 | (1.1) | 14.4 | (0.8) | 3.8 | (0.4) | 0.3 | (0.2) |
| Netherlands | 6.8 | (1.0) | 11.7 | (1.4) | 21.8 | (1.2) | 29.7 | (1.4) | 22.9 | (1.4) | 7.2 | (0.8) |
| New Zealand | 7.0 | (0.8) | 12.6 | (1.1) | 20.6 | (1.3) | 25.9 | (1.3) | 21.5 | (1.2) | 12.4 | (0.9) |
| Norway | 12.2 | (1.1) | 17.2 | (0.9) | 25.0 | (1.0) | 24.6 | (1.3) | 15.9 | (1.0) | 5.2 | (0.7) |
| Poland | 7.8 | (0.9) | 14.6 | (1.1) | 23.6 | (1.3) | 25.8 | (1.2) | 19.6 | (1.0) | 8.7 | (0.8) |
| Portugal | 12.3 | (1.4) | 18.4 | (1.5) | 27.1 | (1.6) | 25.5 | (1.3) | 13.2 | (1.0) | 3.5 | (0.6) |
| Slovak Republic | 15.6 | (1.4) | 19.4 | (1.3) | 25.4 | (1.2) | 23.3 | (1.4) | 12.7 | (0.9) | 3.6 | (0.5) |
| Spain | 12.5 | (1.0) | 19.8 | (0.8) | 31.1 | (1.0) | 26.0 | (1.0) | 9.5 | (0.8) | 1.1 | (0.3) |
| Sweden | 7.3 | (1.1) | 13.4 | (1.2) | 24.3 | (1.3) | 28.0 | (1.6) | 20.1 | (1.4) | 7.0 | (0.8) |
| Switzerland | 7.1 | (0.8) | 13.3 | (0.8) | 24.7 | (1.3) | 30.3 | (1.0) | 19.5 | (1.0) | 5.1 | (0.6) |
| Turkey | 15.5 | (1.4) | 25.5 | (1.6) | 29.8 | (1.6) | 20.1 | (1.7) | 7.7 | (1.2) | 1.4 | (0.5) |
| United Kingdom | 9.6 | (0.9) | 14.4 | (0.9) | 23.1 | (0.9) | 27.1 | (1.4) | 18.2 | (1.1) | 7.5 | (0.6) |
| United States | m | m | m | m | m | m | m | m | m | m | m | m |
| **OECD total** | 12.1 | (0.4) | 16.6 | (0.3) | 24.1 | (0.3) | 24.8 | (0.4) | 16.3 | (0.3) | 6.1 | (0.2) |
| **OECD average** | 10.4 | (0.2) | 15.5 | (0.2) | 24.3 | (0.2) | 26.3 | (0.2) | 17.4 | (0.2) | 6.2 | (0.1) |
| Argentina | 44.4 | (2.7) | 22.5 | (2.0) | 19.2 | (1.9) | 10.2 | (1.4) | 3.1 | (0.9) | 0.6 | (0.3) |
| Azerbaijan | 47.1 | (2.1) | 36.3 | (1.9) | 12.9 | (1.3) | 3.0 | (0.6) | 0.6 | (0.2) | 0.2 | (0.1) |
| Brazil | 34.4 | (1.6) | 27.6 | (1.3) | 22.7 | (1.2) | 10.6 | (0.9) | 3.8 | (0.6) | 0.9 | (0.3) |
| Bulgaria | 38.3 | (2.7) | 22.6 | (1.5) | 19.6 | (1.8) | 12.4 | (1.4) | 5.8 | (1.1) | 1.3 | (0.4) |
| Chile | 17.2 | (1.4) | 22.7 | (1.4) | 26.9 | (1.2) | 19.5 | (1.3) | 10.4 | (1.3) | 3.4 | (0.8) |
| Colombia | 33.6 | (2.4) | 24.7 | (1.8) | 24.9 | (1.6) | 13.3 | (1.3) | 3.2 | (0.6) | 0.4 | (0.2) |
| Croatia | 10.0 | (1.2) | 20.5 | (1.3) | 30.1 | (1.3) | 26.6 | (1.6) | 11.0 | (0.9) | 1.9 | (0.4) |
| Estonia | 5.5 | (1.0) | 14.4 | (1.1) | 27.7 | (1.0) | 32.9 | (1.2) | 16.4 | (1.0) | 3.0 | (0.4) |
| Hong Kong-China | 2.1 | (0.5) | 8.0 | (1.0) | 19.7 | (1.2) | 32.8 | (1.5) | 28.6 | (1.5) | 8.8 | (1.1) |
| Indonesia | 26.6 | (3.1) | 35.9 | (2.8) | 25.7 | (2.4) | 10.6 | (3.2) | 1.1 | (0.4) | 0.0 | a |
| Israel | 27.4 | (2.0) | 19.4 | (1.2) | 20.6 | (1.4) | 17.7 | (1.0) | 10.4 | (1.0) | 4.6 | (0.7) |
| Jordan | 33.4 | (2.1) | 28.0 | (1.5) | 24.9 | (1.6) | 11.6 | (1.6) | 2.0 | (0.6) | 0.1 | (0.1) |
| Kyrgyzstan | 78.5 | (1.4) | 13.1 | (1.0) | 5.9 | (0.7) | 2.0 | (0.5) | 0.4 | (0.3) | 0.1 | a |
| Latvia | 9.4 | (1.1) | 20.7 | (1.6) | 30.4 | (1.5) | 26.5 | (1.9) | 10.5 | (1.3) | 2.5 | (0.5) |
| Liechtenstein | 6.4 | (2.0) | 11.6 | (2.8) | 25.6 | (4.1) | 33.7 | (4.3) | 18.1 | (3.9) | 4.6 | (2.1) |
| Lithuania | 12.9 | (0.9) | 21.6 | (1.3) | 29.0 | (1.3) | 24.0 | (1.4) | 10.3 | (1.1) | 2.3 | (0.4) |
| Macao-China | 4.5 | (0.6) | 13.2 | (0.9) | 30.4 | (1.5) | 34.1 | (1.9) | 15.3 | (1.2) | 2.4 | (0.4) |
| Montenegro | 34.9 | (1.0) | 30.9 | (1.3) | 22.9 | (1.3) | 9.5 | (1.0) | 1.6 | (0.5) | 0.2 | (0.1) |
| Qatar | 74.4 | (1.0) | 13.4 | (0.9) | 6.6 | (0.6) | 3.5 | (0.6) | 1.6 | (0.3) | 0.5 | (0.2) |
| Romania | 34.0 | (2.2) | 29.5 | (1.7) | 24.0 | (1.7) | 10.4 | (1.2) | 1.9 | (0.4) | 0.1 | (0.1) |
| Russian Federation | 18.9 | (1.7) | 24.6 | (1.2) | 29.3 | (1.5) | 19.4 | (1.8) | 6.7 | (0.8) | 1.1 | (0.3) |
| Serbia | 30.8 | (1.7) | 30.5 | (1.2) | 24.5 | (1.4) | 11.8 | (1.0) | 2.3 | (0.4) | 0.2 | (0.1) |
| Slovenia | 7.4 | (0.7) | 17.8 | (1.0) | 28.6 | (1.1) | 28.3 | (1.3) | 15.0 | (0.9) | 2.7 | (0.5) |
| Chinese Taipei | 5.2 | (0.8) | 13.2 | (1.1) | 25.4 | (1.2) | 33.3 | (1.3) | 19.3 | (1.2) | 3.5 | (0.6) |
| Thailand | 27.1 | (2.1) | 33.9 | (1.8) | 25.6 | (1.4) | 11.2 | (0.9) | 2.1 | (0.5) | 0.1 | (0.1) |
| Tunisia | 39.6 | (1.9) | 27.1 | (1.7) | 22.0 | (1.6) | 9.1 | (1.0) | 2.1 | (0.6) | 0.1 | (0.1) |
| Uruguay | 32.2 | (1.8) | 22.5 | (1.3) | 21.8 | (1.3) | 14.5 | (1.0) | 6.5 | (0.7) | 2.4 | (0.5) |

StatLink ᏋᏌᏨ http://dx.doi.org/10.1787/142183565744

Pour consulter la version française intégrale de ce tableau, suivre ce lien :
StatLink ᏋᏌᏨ http://dx.doi.org/10.1787/152754053448

223

[Part 2/2]
**Table 6.1b** **Percentage of students at each proficiency level on the reading scale, by gender**

Tableau 6.1b Pourcentage d'élèves à chaque niveau de compétence sur l'échelle de compréhension de l'écrit, selon le sexe

| | | Females – Proficiency levels | | | | | | | | | | |
|---|---|---|---|---|---|---|---|---|---|---|---|---|
| | | Below Level 1 (below 334.75 score points) | | Level 1 (from 334.75 to 407.47 score points) | | Level 2 (from 407.47 to 480.18 score points) | | Level 3 (from 480.18 to 552.89 score points) | | Level 4 (from 552.89 to 625.61 score points) | | Level 5 (above 625.61 score points) | |
| | | % | S.E. | % | S.E. | % | S.E. | % | S.E. | % | S.E. | % | S.E. |
| OECD | Australia | 1.8 | (0.3) | 6.4 | (0.5) | 18.3 | (0.9) | 31.1 | (0.9) | 28.9 | (0.8) | 13.4 | (0.8) |
| | Austria | 5.2 | (1.5) | 10.2 | (1.0) | 19.7 | (1.6) | 27.1 | (1.4) | 25.3 | (1.4) | 12.4 | (1.2) |
| | Belgium | 5.2 | (0.8) | 8.1 | (0.8) | 17.1 | (1.0) | 27.0 | (1.2) | 28.4 | (1.5) | 14.1 | (1.0) |
| | Canada | 2.0 | (0.3) | 5.4 | (0.5) | 15.3 | (0.8) | 29.5 | (0.9) | 30.0 | (1.1) | 17.7 | (1.0) |
| | Czech Republic | 5.9 | (1.2) | 11.0 | (1.1) | 20.0 | (1.4) | 26.5 | (1.6) | 23.8 | (1.3) | 12.9 | (1.3) |
| | Denmark | 2.8 | (0.6) | 8.6 | (1.1) | 23.9 | (1.3) | 33.2 | (1.2) | 23.9 | (1.3) | 7.6 | (0.8) |
| | Finland | 0.1 | (0.1) | 1.5 | (0.4) | 9.4 | (0.8) | 27.9 | (1.2) | 37.4 | (1.1) | 23.7 | (1.3) |
| | France | 5.4 | (0.9) | 11.1 | (1.2) | 20.1 | (1.2) | 29.4 | (1.5) | 25.1 | (1.4) | 8.9 | (0.9) |
| | Germany | 5.3 | (0.9) | 8.9 | (0.9) | 18.2 | (1.2) | 28.3 | (1.2) | 26.4 | (1.3) | 12.9 | (1.0) |
| | Greece | 4.9 | (0.7) | 11.8 | (1.1) | 27.0 | (1.6) | 33.1 | (1.5) | 18.5 | (1.3) | 4.7 | (0.7) |
| | Hungary | 3.6 | (0.6) | 9.6 | (1.1) | 23.5 | (1.5) | 34.0 | (1.4) | 22.8 | (1.4) | 6.5 | (0.8) |
| | Iceland | 3.0 | (0.5) | 9.5 | (1.2) | 23.0 | (1.5) | 32.6 | (1.2) | 23.5 | (1.5) | 8.3 | (0.8) |
| | Ireland | 1.6 | (0.5) | 6.1 | (0.7) | 18.7 | (1.3) | 30.3 | (1.1) | 28.6 | (1.6) | 14.6 | (1.1) |
| | Italy | 7.0 | (0.6) | 12.9 | (0.8) | 23.5 | (1.1) | 28.9 | (0.9) | 21.0 | (0.9) | 6.7 | (0.6) |
| | Japan | 4.1 | (0.9) | 9.2 | (1.3) | 21.2 | (1.3) | 30.4 | (1.3) | 24.5 | (1.4) | 10.7 | (1.2) |
| | Korea | 0.4 | (0.2) | 2.8 | (0.6) | 9.5 | (1.1) | 25.0 | (1.4) | 34.9 | (1.8) | 27.3 | (2.0) |
| | Luxembourg | 5.7 | (0.6) | 11.7 | (0.9) | 23.8 | (1.0) | 29.7 | (1.0) | 22.1 | (1.2) | 7.1 | (0.7) |
| | Mexico | 15.7 | (1.1) | 24.7 | (1.1) | 30.4 | (1.3) | 21.8 | (1.1) | 6.7 | (0.6) | 0.8 | (0.2) |
| | Netherlands | 3.6 | (0.7) | 8.0 | (1.0) | 20.7 | (1.2) | 28.0 | (1.2) | 28.5 | (1.2) | 11.1 | (0.8) |
| | New Zealand | 2.5 | (0.5) | 7.3 | (0.8) | 16.9 | (1.1) | 26.9 | (1.1) | 27.3 | (1.2) | 19.1 | (1.2) |
| | Norway | 4.4 | (0.7) | 10.5 | (1.0) | 21.5 | (1.1) | 30.8 | (1.1) | 22.5 | (1.2) | 10.4 | (1.0) |
| | Poland | 2.3 | (0.4) | 7.9 | (0.7) | 19.4 | (1.1) | 29.3 | (1.3) | 26.6 | (1.0) | 14.5 | (1.1) |
| | Portugal | 6.5 | (0.9) | 13.1 | (1.2) | 23.9 | (1.2) | 30.7 | (1.4) | 20.1 | (1.1) | 5.7 | (0.7) |
| | Slovak Republic | 6.5 | (1.0) | 13.6 | (1.2) | 24.9 | (1.3) | 28.7 | (1.7) | 19.0 | (1.2) | 7.3 | (0.8) |
| | Spain | 4.8 | (0.6) | 14.1 | (0.8) | 29.2 | (0.9) | 33.6 | (0.9) | 15.9 | (0.8) | 2.4 | (0.4) |
| | Sweden | 2.5 | (0.5) | 7.1 | (0.9) | 19.4 | (1.4) | 29.7 | (1.3) | 26.7 | (1.5) | 14.5 | (1.1) |
| | Switzerland | 3.5 | (0.6) | 8.7 | (0.9) | 21.0 | (1.1) | 30.5 | (1.2) | 25.8 | (1.2) | 10.4 | (1.0) |
| | Turkey | 5.1 | (0.8) | 16.4 | (1.8) | 32.5 | (2.1) | 29.6 | (1.8) | 13.4 | (1.2) | 2.9 | (0.8) |
| | United Kingdom | 4.0 | (0.5) | 10.1 | (0.7) | 22.3 | (0.9) | 30.3 | (1.0) | 22.8 | (0.9) | 10.6 | (0.8) |
| | United States | m | m | m | m | m | m | m | m | m | m | m | m |
| | **OECD total** | 5.6 | (0.2) | 11.6 | (0.3) | 22.1 | (0.3) | 28.4 | (0.3) | 22.2 | (0.4) | 10.0 | (0.3) |
| | **OECD average** | 4.3 | (0.1) | 9.9 | (0.2) | 21.2 | (0.2) | 29.5 | (0.2) | 24.2 | (0.2) | 11.0 | (0.2) |
| Partners | Argentina | 28.1 | (2.5) | 21.7 | (1.7) | 24.1 | (1.5) | 17.9 | (1.6) | 6.9 | (1.1) | 1.3 | (0.4) |
| | Azerbaijan | 34.7 | (2.3) | 40.4 | (1.8) | 20.3 | (1.4) | 3.9 | (0.6) | 0.6 | (0.2) | 0.0 | a |
| | Brazil | 22.2 | (1.3) | 27.7 | (1.4) | 27.4 | (1.6) | 15.8 | (1.1) | 5.5 | (0.6) | 1.3 | (0.4) |
| | Bulgaria | 18.6 | (2.1) | 21.8 | (1.8) | 25.4 | (1.3) | 20.6 | (1.6) | 10.6 | (1.4) | 2.9 | (0.7) |
| | Chile | 12.0 | (1.3) | 20.0 | (1.6) | 29.4 | (1.9) | 23.0 | (1.5) | 11.8 | (1.3) | 3.7 | (0.7) |
| | Colombia | 27.8 | (2.0) | 25.7 | (1.4) | 25.4 | (1.5) | 15.5 | (1.6) | 4.8 | (0.9) | 0.8 | (0.4) |
| | Croatia | 2.4 | (0.5) | 10.2 | (1.2) | 25.0 | (1.5) | 34.7 | (1.3) | 22.1 | (1.4) | 5.6 | (0.8) |
| | Estonia | 1.1 | (0.3) | 5.9 | (0.8) | 21.1 | (1.2) | 35.0 | (1.5) | 27.8 | (1.4) | 9.2 | (1.1) |
| | Hong Kong-China | 0.5 | (0.2) | 3.8 | (0.5) | 13.5 | (1.2) | 30.2 | (1.9) | 35.2 | (1.6) | 16.8 | (1.4) |
| | Indonesia | 16.6 | (1.6) | 37.2 | (1.8) | 32.6 | (1.7) | 11.6 | (1.5) | 2.0 | (0.5) | 0.1 | a |
| | Israel | 13.3 | (1.3) | 17.9 | (1.0) | 24.4 | (1.4) | 24.1 | (1.1) | 14.9 | (1.0) | 5.4 | (0.7) |
| | Jordan | 12.2 | (1.1) | 25.7 | (1.5) | 36.2 | (1.3) | 21.2 | (1.4) | 4.5 | (0.7) | 0.3 | (0.1) |
| | Kyrgyzstan | 63.5 | (1.5) | 21.8 | (1.1) | 10.0 | (0.8) | 3.8 | (0.6) | 0.7 | (0.2) | 0.1 | (0.1) |
| | Latvia | 2.7 | (0.6) | 10.1 | (1.0) | 25.0 | (1.5) | 33.1 | (1.6) | 22.6 | (1.4) | 6.5 | (0.8) |
| | Liechtenstein | 3.6 | (1.6) | 7.5 | (2.8) | 15.1 | (2.8) | 29.1 | (3.5) | 30.3 | (4.5) | 14.4 | (3.3) |
| | Lithuania | 4.4 | (0.7) | 12.2 | (1.0) | 24.8 | (1.4) | 31.1 | (1.2) | 21.0 | (1.2) | 6.5 | (0.8) |
| | Macao-China | 1.3 | (0.3) | 6.8 | (0.7) | 27.4 | (1.1) | 39.1 | (1.3) | 21.8 | (1.0) | 3.7 | (0.5) |
| | Montenegro | 17.1 | (1.0) | 29.2 | (1.5) | 31.7 | (1.2) | 17.0 | (1.3) | 4.4 | (0.5) | 0.7 | (0.3) |
| | Qatar | 47.6 | (0.9) | 27.6 | (0.9) | 15.8 | (0.8) | 6.4 | (0.5) | 1.9 | (0.3) | 0.6 | (0.1) |
| | Romania | 17.2 | (2.4) | 26.3 | (1.9) | 31.8 | (1.9) | 19.7 | (1.8) | 4.5 | (1.0) | 0.5 | (0.2) |
| | Russian Federation | 8.7 | (1.3) | 19.0 | (1.3) | 30.7 | (1.1) | 28.2 | (1.3) | 11.2 | (1.0) | 2.3 | (0.4) |
| | Serbia | 16.1 | (1.6) | 25.7 | (1.6) | 31.8 | (1.4) | 20.4 | (1.3) | 5.5 | (0.8) | 0.4 | (0.2) |
| | Slovenia | 1.5 | (0.3) | 6.4 | (0.6) | 20.8 | (0.9) | 34.8 | (1.4) | 28.8 | (1.3) | 7.8 | (0.9) |
| | Chinese Taipei | 2.2 | (0.5) | 9.7 | (1.3) | 23.2 | (1.4) | 34.7 | (1.4) | 24.1 | (1.4) | 6.1 | (1.0) |
| | Thailand | 7.1 | (0.8) | 25.4 | (1.5) | 39.3 | (1.7) | 22.0 | (1.3) | 5.8 | (0.6) | 0.4 | (0.2) |
| | Tunisia | 24.1 | (1.5) | 27.9 | (1.3) | 28.8 | (1.5) | 15.8 | (1.2) | 3.2 | (0.7) | 0.2 | (0.1) |
| | Uruguay | 18.7 | (1.2) | 20.2 | (1.2) | 24.9 | (1.4) | 21.4 | (1.3) | 11.1 | (0.9) | 3.7 | (0.5) |

*StatLink* http://dx.doi.org/10.1787/142183565744

Pour consulter la version française intégrale de ce tableau, suivre ce lien :
*StatLink* http://dx.doi.org/10.1787/152754053448

[Part 1/2]

**Table 6.1c** **Mean score, variation and gender differences in student performance on the reading scale**

Tableau 6.1c  Score moyen, différences de score selon le sexe et répartition des scores sur l'échelle de compréhension de l'écrit

| | | All students | | | | Gender differences | | | | | |
|---|---|---|---|---|---|---|---|---|---|---|---|
| | | Mean score | | Standard deviation | | Males | | Females | | Difference (M - F) | |
| | | Mean | S.E. | S.D. | S.E. | Mean score | S.E. | Mean score | S.E. | Score dif. | S.E. |
| *OECD* | Australia | 513 | (2.1) | 94 | (1.0) | 495 | (3.0) | 532 | (2.2) | **-37** | (3.6) |
| | Austria | 490 | (4.1) | 108 | (3.2) | 468 | (4.9) | 513 | (5.5) | **-45** | (6.0) |
| | Belgium | 501 | (3.0) | 110 | (2.8) | 482 | (4.1) | 522 | (3.5) | **-40** | (4.8) |
| | Canada | 527 | (2.4) | 96 | (1.4) | 511 | (2.8) | 543 | (2.5) | **-32** | (2.3) |
| | Czech Republic | 483 | (4.2) | 111 | (2.9) | 463 | (5.0) | 509 | (5.4) | **-46** | (6.2) |
| | Denmark | 494 | (3.2) | 89 | (1.6) | 480 | (3.6) | 509 | (3.5) | **-30** | (3.2) |
| | Finland | 547 | (2.1) | 81 | (1.1) | 521 | (2.7) | 572 | (2.3) | **-51** | (2.8) |
| | France | 488 | (4.1) | 104 | (2.8) | 470 | (5.2) | 505 | (3.9) | **-35** | (4.4) |
| | Germany | 495 | (4.4) | 112 | (2.7) | 475 | (5.3) | 517 | (4.4) | **-42** | (3.9) |
| | Greece | 460 | (4.0) | 103 | (2.9) | 432 | (5.7) | 488 | (3.5) | **-57** | (5.6) |
| | Hungary | 482 | (3.3) | 94 | (2.4) | 463 | (3.7) | 503 | (3.9) | **-40** | (4.1) |
| | Iceland | 484 | (1.9) | 97 | (1.4) | 460 | (2.8) | 509 | (2.3) | **-48** | (3.3) |
| | Ireland | 517 | (3.5) | 92 | (1.9) | 500 | (4.5) | 534 | (3.8) | **-34** | (4.9) |
| | Italy | 469 | (2.4) | 109 | (1.8) | 448 | (3.4) | 489 | (2.8) | **-41** | (4.0) |
| | Japan | 498 | (3.6) | 102 | (2.4) | 483 | (5.4) | 513 | (5.2) | **-31** | (7.7) |
| | Korea | 556 | (3.8) | 88 | (2.7) | 539 | (4.6) | 574 | (4.5) | **-35** | (5.9) |
| | Luxembourg | 479 | (1.3) | 100 | (1.1) | 464 | (2.0) | 495 | (2.1) | **-32** | (3.2) |
| | Mexico | 410 | (3.1) | 96 | (2.3) | 393 | (3.5) | 427 | (3.0) | **-34** | (2.5) |
| | Netherlands | 507 | (2.9) | 97 | (2.5) | 495 | (3.7) | 519 | (3.0) | **-24** | (3.4) |
| | New Zealand | 521 | (3.0) | 105 | (1.6) | 502 | (3.6) | 539 | (3.6) | **-37** | (4.6) |
| | Norway | 484 | (3.2) | 105 | (1.9) | 462 | (3.8) | 508 | (3.3) | **-46** | (3.3) |
| | Poland | 508 | (2.8) | 100 | (1.5) | 487 | (3.4) | 528 | (2.8) | **-40** | (2.9) |
| | Portugal | 472 | (3.6) | 99 | (2.3) | 455 | (4.4) | 488 | (3.5) | **-33** | (3.7) |
| | Slovak Republic | 466 | (3.1) | 105 | (2.5) | 446 | (4.2) | 488 | (3.8) | **-42** | (5.4) |
| | Spain | 461 | (2.2) | 89 | (1.2) | 443 | (2.6) | 479 | (2.3) | **-35** | (2.1) |
| | Sweden | 507 | (3.4) | 98 | (1.8) | 488 | (4.0) | 528 | (3.5) | **-40** | (3.2) |
| | Switzerland | 499 | (3.1) | 94 | (1.8) | 484 | (3.2) | 515 | (3.3) | **-31** | (2.6) |
| | Turkey | 447 | (4.2) | 93 | (2.8) | 427 | (5.1) | 471 | (4.3) | **-44** | (4.3) |
| | United Kingdom | 495 | (2.3) | 102 | (1.7) | 480 | (3.0) | 510 | (2.6) | **-29** | (3.5) |
| | United States | m | m | m | m | m | m | m | m | m | m |
| | **OECD total** | 484 | (1.0) | 107 | (0.7) | 466 | (1.2) | 502 | (1.3) | **-36** | (1.4) |
| | **OECD average** | 492 | (0.6) | 99 | (0.4) | 473 | (0.7) | 511 | (0.7) | **-38** | (0.8) |
| *Partners* | Argentina | 374 | (7.2) | 124 | (3.7) | 345 | (8.3) | 399 | (7.4) | **-54** | (7.3) |
| | Azerbaijan | 353 | (3.1) | 70 | (2.1) | 343 | (3.5) | 363 | (3.3) | **-20** | (2.6) |
| | Brazil | 393 | (3.7) | 102 | (3.4) | 376 | (4.3) | 408 | (3.7) | **-32** | (3.0) |
| | Bulgaria | 402 | (6.9) | 118 | (4.0) | 374 | (7.7) | 432 | (6.9) | **-58** | (6.3) |
| | Chile | 442 | (5.0) | 103 | (2.5) | 434 | (6.0) | 451 | (5.4) | **-17** | (5.7) |
| | Colombia | 385 | (5.1) | 108 | (2.4) | 375 | (5.6) | 394 | (5.6) | **-19** | (5.3) |
| | Croatia | 477 | (2.8) | 89 | (2.1) | 452 | (3.8) | 502 | (3.3) | **-50** | (4.7) |
| | Estonia | 501 | (2.9) | 85 | (2.0) | 478 | (3.2) | 524 | (3.1) | **-46** | (2.7) |
| | Hong Kong-China | 536 | (2.4) | 82 | (1.9) | 520 | (3.5) | 551 | (3.0) | **-31** | (4.5) |
| | Indonesia | 393 | (5.9) | 75 | (2.4) | 384 | (8.7) | 402 | (4.2) | **-18** | (6.3) |
| | Israel | 439 | (4.6) | 119 | (2.8) | 417 | (6.5) | 460 | (4.6) | **-42** | (6.8) |
| | Jordan | 401 | (3.3) | 94 | (2.3) | 373 | (5.6) | 428 | (3.4) | **-55** | (6.5) |
| | Kyrgyzstan | 285 | (3.5) | 102 | (2.5) | 257 | (4.4) | 308 | (3.3) | **-51** | (3.4) |
| | Latvia | 479 | (3.7) | 91 | (1.8) | 454 | (4.3) | 504 | (3.5) | **-50** | (3.2) |
| | Liechtenstein | 510 | (3.9) | 95 | (4.0) | 486 | (7.7) | 531 | (6.3) | **-45** | (11.7) |
| | Lithuania | 470 | (3.0) | 96 | (1.5) | 445 | (3.5) | 496 | (3.2) | **-51** | (3.0) |
| | Macao-China | 492 | (1.1) | 77 | (0.9) | 479 | (1.8) | 505 | (1.5) | **-26** | (2.4) |
| | Montenegro | 392 | (1.2) | 90 | (1.1) | 370 | (2.0) | 415 | (1.8) | **-45** | (2.9) |
| | Qatar | 312 | (1.2) | 109 | (1.1) | 280 | (1.9) | 346 | (1.6) | **-66** | (2.6) |
| | Romania | 396 | (4.7) | 92 | (2.9) | 374 | (4.5) | 418 | (5.2) | **-44** | (3.4) |
| | Russian Federation | 440 | (4.3) | 93 | (1.9) | 420 | (4.8) | 458 | (4.3) | **-38** | (3.2) |
| | Serbia | 401 | (3.5) | 92 | (1.7) | 381 | (3.4) | 422 | (4.2) | **-42** | (4.0) |
| | Slovenia | 494 | (1.0) | 88 | (0.9) | 467 | (1.9) | 521 | (1.4) | **-54** | (2.7) |
| | Chinese Taipei | 496 | (3.4) | 84 | (1.8) | 486 | (4.4) | 507 | (4.2) | **-21** | (5.4) |
| | Thailand | 417 | (2.6) | 82 | (1.8) | 386 | (4.0) | 440 | (3.0) | **-54** | (4.7) |
| | Tunisia | 380 | (4.0) | 97 | (2.5) | 361 | (4.6) | 398 | (3.9) | **-38** | (3.6) |
| | Uruguay | 413 | (3.4) | 121 | (2.0) | 389 | (4.4) | 435 | (3.8) | **-45** | (4.9) |

Note: Values that are statistically significant are indicated in bold (see Annex A3).
StatLink ━━ http://dx.doi.org/10.1787/142183565744

Pour consulter la version française intégrale de ce tableau, suivre ce lien :
StatLink ━━ http://dx.doi.org/10.1787/152754053448

225

[Part 2/2]

**Table 6.1c  Mean score, variation and gender differences in student performance on the reading scale**

Tableau 6.1c  Score moyen, différences de score selon le sexe et répartition des scores sur l'échelle de compréhension de l'écrit

| | | **Percentiles** | | | | | | | | | | |
|---|---|---|---|---|---|---|---|---|---|---|---|---|
| | | **5th** | | **10th** | | **25th** | | **75th** | | **90th** | | **95th** | |
| | | Score | S.E. | Score | S.E. | Score | S.E. | Score | S.E. | Score | S.E. | Score | S.E. |
| **OECD** | Australia | 349 | (3.4) | 388 | (3.4) | 453 | (2.4) | 579 | (2.3) | 628 | (2.9) | 656 | (2.6) |
| | Austria | 298 | (11.9) | 348 | (9.4) | 421 | (5.5) | 568 | (3.7) | 621 | (3.1) | 651 | (3.7) |
| | Belgium | 297 | (10.1) | 347 | (8.3) | 433 | (4.7) | 581 | (2.3) | 631 | (2.2) | 657 | (2.8) |
| | Canada | 357 | (4.8) | 402 | (3.9) | 468 | (3.0) | 593 | (2.6) | 644 | (2.7) | 674 | (3.9) |
| | Czech Republic | 290 | (10.5) | 335 | (7.0) | 408 | (6.2) | 564 | (3.8) | 621 | (4.2) | 653 | (4.3) |
| | Denmark | 339 | (6.4) | 378 | (5.0) | 437 | (3.9) | 557 | (2.9) | 604 | (3.7) | 633 | (5.1) |
| | Finland | 410 | (4.8) | 441 | (3.8) | 494 | (2.9) | 603 | (2.2) | 649 | (2.5) | 675 | (2.8) |
| | France | 298 | (9.7) | 346 | (7.5) | 421 | (6.1) | 564 | (3.8) | 614 | (4.0) | 639 | (4.1) |
| | Germany | 299 | (9.7) | 350 | (8.0) | 429 | (5.9) | 573 | (3.4) | 625 | (3.7) | 657 | (3.7) |
| | Greece | 272 | (11.6) | 321 | (8.5) | 398 | (5.2) | 531 | (3.8) | 583 | (4.2) | 613 | (4.5) |
| | Hungary | 318 | (9.1) | 359 | (5.0) | 422 | (4.8) | 549 | (3.6) | 595 | (4.4) | 623 | (4.6) |
| | Iceland | 314 | (4.7) | 356 | (4.1) | 423 | (3.0) | 552 | (2.8) | 603 | (3.2) | 633 | (3.9) |
| | Ireland | 358 | (6.3) | 395 | (5.5) | 457 | (4.7) | 582 | (3.9) | 633 | (3.5) | 661 | (4.3) |
| | Italy | 276 | (5.9) | 325 | (4.8) | 402 | (3.6) | 546 | (2.3) | 599 | (2.9) | 627 | (2.8) |
| | Japan | 317 | (6.8) | 361 | (6.6) | 433 | (6.1) | 569 | (3.4) | 623 | (3.5) | 654 | (3.8) |
| | Korea | 399 | (9.7) | 440 | (7.9) | 503 | (4.8) | 617 | (3.4) | 663 | (4.3) | 688 | (5.0) |
| | Luxembourg | 302 | (5.1) | 344 | (3.3) | 415 | (2.3) | 552 | (1.8) | 602 | (2.5) | 630 | (2.8) |
| | Mexico | 247 | (7.5) | 285 | (6.2) | 348 | (4.2) | 478 | (2.8) | 530 | (3.1) | 559 | (3.0) |
| | Netherlands | 332 | (10.0) | 379 | (6.4) | 446 | (4.3) | 578 | (2.5) | 622 | (2.4) | 649 | (3.5) |
| | New Zealand | 339 | (5.8) | 381 | (4.6) | 453 | (4.5) | 595 | (2.9) | 651 | (2.8) | 683 | (4.5) |
| | Norway | 301 | (7.3) | 346 | (5.5) | 416 | (4.6) | 558 | (3.0) | 613 | (4.1) | 643 | (3.6) |
| | Poland | 335 | (4.8) | 374 | (4.6) | 441 | (3.5) | 579 | (3.2) | 633 | (3.4) | 663 | (4.0) |
| | Portugal | 299 | (7.6) | 339 | (6.3) | 408 | (5.3) | 543 | (3.6) | 594 | (3.7) | 622 | (4.5) |
| | Slovak Republic | 281 | (7.1) | 326 | (6.6) | 398 | (4.3) | 542 | (3.4) | 597 | (3.8) | 628 | (3.3) |
| | Spain | 304 | (4.6) | 343 | (4.1) | 405 | (2.9) | 523 | (2.3) | 569 | (2.7) | 594 | (2.8) |
| | Sweden | 335 | (7.7) | 378 | (5.6) | 445 | (3.8) | 575 | (3.3) | 629 | (4.0) | 658 | (4.9) |
| | Switzerland | 331 | (6.5) | 373 | (5.1) | 440 | (3.5) | 566 | (3.1) | 615 | (3.6) | 642 | (4.3) |
| | Turkey | 291 | (5.9) | 330 | (6.4) | 388 | (4.4) | 510 | (5.2) | 564 | (6.5) | 594 | (7.8) |
| | United Kingdom | 318 | (5.2) | 359 | (4.0) | 431 | (2.8) | 566 | (2.5) | 621 | (3.1) | 653 | (3.6) |
| | United States | m | m | m | m | m | m | m | m | m | m | m | m |
| | **OECD total** | 298 | (2.5) | 343 | (1.8) | 415 | (1.5) | 560 | (1.0) | 615 | (1.0) | 647 | (1.2) |
| | **OECD average** | 317 | (1.4) | 360 | (1.1) | 429 | (0.8) | 562 | (0.6) | 613 | (0.7) | 642 | (0.8) |
| **Partners** | Argentina | 155 | (14.8) | 209 | (10.7) | 291 | (9.0) | 464 | (7.1) | 527 | (7.0) | 560 | (5.9) |
| | Azerbaijan | 243 | (4.4) | 266 | (3.9) | 305 | (3.6) | 397 | (3.7) | 441 | (5.0) | 472 | (6.0) |
| | Brazil | 224 | (10.1) | 264 | (6.0) | 326 | (4.2) | 460 | (4.0) | 523 | (5.3) | 562 | (6.8) |
| | Bulgaria | 210 | (11.4) | 251 | (9.0) | 321 | (8.5) | 486 | (7.6) | 554 | (7.8) | 589 | (8.5) |
| | Chile | 271 | (7.5) | 310 | (5.8) | 373 | (5.4) | 513 | (6.4) | 575 | (6.7) | 609 | (6.6) |
| | Colombia | 200 | (9.1) | 243 | (7.0) | 316 | (7.2) | 462 | (5.6) | 518 | (5.2) | 550 | (5.9) |
| | Croatia | 324 | (6.6) | 359 | (5.4) | 418 | (4.1) | 540 | (3.0) | 589 | (3.4) | 615 | (3.3) |
| | Estonia | 353 | (7.2) | 389 | (5.4) | 448 | (3.8) | 560 | (2.8) | 606 | (3.2) | 632 | (3.8) |
| | Hong Kong-China | 390 | (6.2) | 426 | (5.8) | 484 | (3.7) | 594 | (2.4) | 636 | (2.9) | 660 | (2.7) |
| | Indonesia | 270 | (5.3) | 298 | (5.0) | 342 | (5.3) | 444 | (8.4) | 490 | (8.6) | 517 | (8.6) |
| | Israel | 237 | (10.1) | 280 | (8.0) | 356 | (6.2) | 526 | (4.8) | 588 | (4.9) | 626 | (5.0) |
| | Jordan | 233 | (7.3) | 277 | (6.1) | 342 | (3.7) | 467 | (3.8) | 514 | (4.5) | 541 | (4.9) |
| | Kyrgyzstan | 123 | (7.2) | 159 | (5.3) | 216 | (3.8) | 349 | (4.1) | 419 | (5.9) | 462 | (7.6) |
| | Latvia | 325 | (6.7) | 361 | (5.4) | 419 | (4.9) | 543 | (4.2) | 593 | (4.0) | 622 | (4.8) |
| | Liechtenstein | 337 | (14.0) | 379 | (10.6) | 452 | (9.9) | 578 | (6.5) | 623 | (10.5) | 658 | (11.5) |
| | Lithuania | 309 | (4.4) | 343 | (3.9) | 405 | (4.0) | 538 | (3.9) | 591 | (3.9) | 621 | (4.0) |
| | Macao-China | 359 | (4.3) | 394 | (2.5) | 445 | (1.9) | 545 | (1.6) | 587 | (1.8) | 610 | (2.4) |
| | Montenegro | 243 | (3.7) | 276 | (3.2) | 331 | (2.1) | 454 | (1.9) | 506 | (2.6) | 536 | (3.7) |
| | Qatar | 148 | (3.7) | 181 | (2.7) | 237 | (1.8) | 380 | (1.9) | 456 | (3.6) | 506 | (3.7) |
| | Romania | 243 | (6.6) | 274 | (7.2) | 333 | (7.3) | 461 | (5.2) | 512 | (5.6) | 541 | (6.1) |
| | Russian Federation | 281 | (7.3) | 316 | (6.0) | 377 | (5.7) | 505 | (4.2) | 556 | (3.6) | 586 | (4.9) |
| | Serbia | 246 | (5.7) | 282 | (4.6) | 339 | (4.5) | 466 | (3.9) | 518 | (3.7) | 546 | (3.9) |
| | Slovenia | 340 | (4.2) | 377 | (2.6) | 437 | (1.8) | 558 | (2.2) | 603 | (2.1) | 627 | (2.7) |
| | Chinese Taipei | 346 | (5.8) | 381 | (5.9) | 442 | (4.9) | 556 | (3.0) | 598 | (3.0) | 624 | (4.0) |
| | Thailand | 280 | (5.9) | 312 | (3.9) | 363 | (3.3) | 472 | (2.9) | 522 | (3.7) | 549 | (3.6) |
| | Tunisia | 217 | (7.3) | 252 | (5.3) | 315 | (4.4) | 450 | (5.0) | 502 | (5.3) | 532 | (6.8) |
| | Uruguay | 204 | (7.8) | 253 | (5.8) | 333 | (5.0) | 497 | (3.8) | 565 | (4.3) | 604 | (5.7) |

Note: Values that are statistically significant are indicated in bold (see Annex A3).
StatLink 🔗 http://dx.doi.org/10.1787/142183565744

Pour consulter la version française intégrale de ce tableau, suivre ce lien :
StatLink 🔗 http://dx.doi.org/10.1787/152754053448

[Part 1/1]

### Table 6.2a  Percentage of students at each proficiency level on the mathematics scale

Tableau 6.2a  Pourcentage d'élèves à chaque niveau de compétence sur l'échelle de culture mathématique

| | | Proficiency levels | | | | | | | | | | | | |
|---|---|---|---|---|---|---|---|---|---|---|---|---|---|---|
| | | Below Level 1 (below 357.77 score points) | | Level 1 (from 357.77 to 420.07 score points) | | Level 2 (from 420.07 to 482.38 score points) | | Level 3 (from 482.38 to 544.68 score points) | | Level 4 (from 544.68 to 606.99 score points) | | Level 5 (from 606.99 to 669.30 score points) | | Level 6 (above 669.30 score points) | |
| | | % | S.E. | % | S.E. | % | S.E. | % | S.E. | % | S.E. | % | S.E. | % | S.E. |
| *OECD* | Australia | 3.3 | (0.3) | 9.7 | (0.4) | 20.5 | (0.6) | 26.9 | (0.6) | 23.2 | (0.5) | 12.1 | (0.5) | 4.3 | (0.5) |
| | Austria | 7.5 | (0.9) | 12.5 | (1.1) | 19.5 | (1.1) | 23.3 | (0.9) | 21.3 | (1.1) | 12.3 | (0.8) | 3.5 | (0.5) |
| | Belgium | 7.1 | (0.9) | 10.2 | (0.7) | 17.0 | (0.7) | 21.4 | (0.7) | 21.9 | (0.8) | 16.0 | (0.7) | 6.4 | (0.4) |
| | Canada | 2.8 | (0.3) | 8.0 | (0.5) | 18.6 | (0.6) | 27.5 | (0.7) | 25.1 | (0.7) | 13.6 | (0.6) | 4.4 | (0.4) |
| | Czech Republic | 7.2 | (0.7) | 11.9 | (0.8) | 20.5 | (1.0) | 23.0 | (0.9) | 19.1 | (1.1) | 12.3 | (0.8) | 6.0 | (0.7) |
| | Denmark | 3.6 | (0.5) | 10.0 | (0.7) | 21.4 | (0.8) | 28.8 | (0.9) | 22.5 | (0.8) | 10.9 | (0.6) | 2.8 | (0.4) |
| | Finland | 1.1 | (0.2) | 4.8 | (0.5) | 14.4 | (0.7) | 27.2 | (0.7) | 28.1 | (0.8) | 18.1 | (0.8) | 6.3 | (0.5) |
| | France | 8.4 | (0.8) | 13.9 | (1.0) | 21.4 | (1.2) | 24.2 | (1.0) | 19.6 | (1.0) | 9.9 | (0.7) | 2.6 | (0.5) |
| | Germany | 7.3 | (1.0) | 12.5 | (0.8) | 21.2 | (1.1) | 24.0 | (1.1) | 19.4 | (0.9) | 11.0 | (0.8) | 4.5 | (0.5) |
| | Greece | 13.3 | (1.1) | 19.0 | (1.2) | 26.8 | (0.9) | 23.2 | (1.1) | 12.6 | (1.0) | 4.2 | (0.5) | 0.9 | (0.2) |
| | Hungary | 6.7 | (0.6) | 14.5 | (0.8) | 25.1 | (1.0) | 26.5 | (0.9) | 16.9 | (1.1) | 7.7 | (0.7) | 2.6 | (0.5) |
| | Iceland | 5.1 | (0.4) | 11.7 | (0.7) | 22.3 | (0.9) | 26.6 | (1.0) | 21.7 | (0.9) | 10.1 | (0.7) | 2.5 | (0.3) |
| | Ireland | 4.1 | (0.5) | 12.3 | (0.9) | 24.1 | (1.0) | 28.6 | (0.9) | 20.6 | (0.9) | 8.6 | (0.7) | 1.6 | (0.2) |
| | Italy | 13.5 | (0.7) | 19.3 | (0.7) | 25.5 | (0.7) | 22.1 | (0.7) | 13.3 | (0.6) | 5.0 | (0.4) | 1.3 | (0.3) |
| | Japan | 3.9 | (0.6) | 9.1 | (0.7) | 18.9 | (0.9) | 26.1 | (1.0) | 23.7 | (1.0) | 13.5 | (0.8) | 4.8 | (0.5) |
| | Korea | 2.3 | (0.5) | 6.5 | (0.7) | 15.2 | (0.7) | 23.5 | (1.1) | 25.5 | (1.0) | 18.0 | (0.8) | 9.1 | (1.3) |
| | Luxembourg | 8.3 | (0.5) | 14.5 | (0.7) | 23.2 | (0.7) | 25.2 | (0.8) | 18.2 | (1.0) | 8.2 | (0.5) | 2.3 | (0.3) |
| | Mexico | 28.4 | (1.4) | 28.1 | (0.9) | 25.2 | (0.8) | 13.1 | (0.6) | 4.3 | (0.4) | 0.8 | (0.2) | 0.1 | (0.0) |
| | Netherlands | 2.4 | (0.6) | 9.1 | (0.8) | 18.9 | (0.9) | 24.3 | (0.9) | 24.1 | (1.1) | 15.8 | (0.8) | 5.4 | (0.6) |
| | New Zealand | 4.0 | (0.3) | 10.0 | (0.8) | 19.5 | (1.0) | 25.5 | (1.1) | 22.1 | (1.0) | 13.2 | (0.7) | 5.7 | (0.5) |
| | Norway | 7.3 | (0.7) | 14.9 | (1.0) | 24.3 | (0.8) | 25.6 | (1.0) | 17.4 | (0.8) | 8.3 | (0.7) | 2.1 | (0.3) |
| | Poland | 5.7 | (0.4) | 14.2 | (0.7) | 24.7 | (0.8) | 26.2 | (0.7) | 18.6 | (0.8) | 8.6 | (0.7) | 2.0 | (0.3) |
| | Portugal | 12.0 | (1.0) | 18.7 | (0.9) | 25.1 | (0.9) | 24.0 | (0.9) | 14.4 | (0.8) | 4.9 | (0.4) | 0.8 | (0.2) |
| | Slovak Republic | 8.1 | (0.7) | 12.8 | (0.9) | 24.1 | (1.0) | 25.3 | (1.0) | 18.8 | (0.9) | 8.6 | (0.7) | 2.4 | (0.4) |
| | Spain | 8.6 | (0.5) | 16.1 | (0.8) | 25.2 | (0.9) | 26.2 | (0.6) | 16.8 | (0.5) | 6.1 | (0.4) | 1.2 | (0.2) |
| | Sweden | 5.4 | (0.6) | 12.9 | (0.8) | 23.0 | (0.8) | 26.0 | (1.0) | 20.1 | (0.9) | 9.7 | (0.6) | 2.9 | (0.4) |
| | Switzerland | 4.6 | (0.5) | 9.0 | (0.6) | 17.4 | (1.0) | 23.2 | (0.8) | 23.2 | (0.9) | 15.9 | (0.7) | 6.8 | (0.6) |
| | Turkey | 24.0 | (1.4) | 28.1 | (1.4) | 24.3 | (1.3) | 12.8 | (0.8) | 6.7 | (0.9) | 3.0 | (0.8) | 1.2 | (0.5) |
| | United Kingdom | 5.9 | (0.6) | 13.8 | (0.7) | 24.7 | (0.8) | 26.3 | (0.7) | 18.1 | (0.6) | 8.7 | (0.5) | 2.5 | (0.3) |
| | United States | 9.9 | (1.2) | 18.2 | (0.9) | 26.1 | (1.2) | 23.1 | (1.1) | 15.1 | (1.0) | 6.4 | (0.7) | 1.3 | (0.2) |
| | **OECD total** | 10.2 | (0.3) | 16.2 | (0.3) | 23.2 | (0.4) | 22.8 | (0.4) | 16.7 | (0.3) | 8.3 | (0.2) | 2.6 | (0.1) |
| | **OECD average** | 7.7 | (0.1) | 13.6 | (0.2) | 21.9 | (0.2) | 24.3 | (0.2) | 19.1 | (0.2) | 10.0 | (0.1) | 3.3 | (0.1) |
| *Partners* | Argentina | 39.4 | (2.7) | 24.7 | (1.5) | 20.4 | (1.7) | 10.6 | (1.1) | 3.8 | (0.6) | 0.9 | (0.3) | 0.1 | (0.1) |
| | Azerbaijan | 0.2 | (0.1) | 10.4 | (1.0) | 47.6 | (1.6) | 34.4 | (1.6) | 6.6 | (0.9) | 0.6 | (0.3) | 0.2 | (0.1) |
| | Brazil | 46.6 | (1.4) | 25.9 | (1.2) | 16.6 | (0.9) | 7.1 | (0.6) | 2.8 | (0.4) | 0.8 | (0.3) | 0.2 | (0.1) |
| | Bulgaria | 29.4 | (2.2) | 23.9 | (1.1) | 22.0 | (1.0) | 14.9 | (1.1) | 6.7 | (0.8) | 2.5 | (0.6) | 0.6 | (0.3) |
| | Chile | 28.2 | (1.9) | 26.9 | (1.2) | 23.9 | (1.1) | 13.9 | (1.0) | 5.6 | (0.7) | 1.3 | (0.3) | 0.1 | (0.1) |
| | Colombia | 44.6 | (1.8) | 27.3 | (1.1) | 18.2 | (1.3) | 7.6 | (0.7) | 1.9 | (0.4) | 0.4 | (0.2) | 0.0 | (0.0) |
| | Croatia | 9.3 | (0.7) | 19.3 | (0.9) | 28.9 | (1.1) | 24.3 | (0.9) | 13.6 | (0.7) | 4.0 | (0.5) | 0.8 | (0.2) |
| | Estonia | 2.7 | (0.5) | 9.4 | (0.8) | 21.9 | (0.9) | 30.2 | (1.0) | 23.3 | (1.1) | 10.0 | (0.6) | 2.6 | (0.4) |
| | Hong Kong-China | 2.9 | (0.5) | 6.6 | (0.6) | 14.4 | (0.8) | 22.7 | (1.1) | 25.6 | (0.9) | 18.7 | (0.8) | 9.0 | (0.8) |
| | Indonesia | 35.2 | (2.2) | 30.5 | (1.6) | 20.4 | (1.0) | 10.6 | (2.0) | 2.8 | (0.7) | 0.4 | (0.2) | 0.0 | a |
| | Israel | 22.2 | (1.5) | 19.8 | (1.0) | 21.8 | (1.0) | 18.4 | (0.9) | 11.8 | (0.8) | 4.8 | (0.5) | 1.3 | (0.2) |
| | Jordan | 36.9 | (1.4) | 29.4 | (1.0) | 21.9 | (0.9) | 9.3 | (0.8) | 2.2 | (0.4) | 0.2 | (0.1) | 0.0 | a |
| | Kyrgyzstan | 72.9 | (1.5) | 16.5 | (1.0) | 7.1 | (0.7) | 2.8 | (0.5) | 0.7 | (0.2) | 0.0 | (0.1) | 0.0 | a |
| | Latvia | 6.4 | (0.6) | 14.3 | (0.9) | 26.3 | (0.9) | 29.0 | (1.0) | 17.4 | (1.1) | 5.5 | (0.5) | 1.1 | (0.3) |
| | Liechtenstein | 4.0 | (1.1) | 9.2 | (2.0) | 18.2 | (3.0) | 26.4 | (3.8) | 23.7 | (2.9) | 12.6 | (2.1) | 5.8 | (1.2) |
| | Lithuania | 7.8 | (0.6) | 15.2 | (0.8) | 25.1 | (1.0) | 25.1 | (1.1) | 17.8 | (0.9) | 7.3 | (0.8) | 1.8 | (0.4) |
| | Macao-China | 2.6 | (0.3) | 8.3 | (0.6) | 20.0 | (0.9) | 27.3 | (0.9) | 24.4 | (0.8) | 13.6 | (0.6) | 3.8 | (0.4) |
| | Montenegro | 31.6 | (0.9) | 28.4 | (0.8) | 23.3 | (0.9) | 11.8 | (0.6) | 4.0 | (0.4) | 0.8 | (0.2) | 0.1 | (0.1) |
| | Qatar | 71.7 | (0.5) | 15.5 | (0.5) | 7.5 | (0.6) | 3.3 | (0.3) | 1.4 | (0.2) | 0.5 | (0.1) | 0.1 | (0.0) |
| | Romania | 24.7 | (2.2) | 28.0 | (1.9) | 26.5 | (1.8) | 14.1 | (1.1) | 5.4 | (0.8) | 1.1 | (0.3) | 0.1 | (0.1) |
| | Russian Federation | 9.1 | (0.9) | 17.6 | (1.1) | 27.0 | (1.4) | 24.2 | (0.9) | 14.7 | (1.0) | 5.7 | (0.6) | 1.7 | (0.3) |
| | Serbia | 19.6 | (1.3) | 23.0 | (1.1) | 26.8 | (1.0) | 18.7 | (1.0) | 9.1 | (0.7) | 2.4 | (0.4) | 0.4 | (0.1) |
| | Slovenia | 4.6 | (0.3) | 13.1 | (0.8) | 23.5 | (0.8) | 26.0 | (0.8) | 19.2 | (0.8) | 10.3 | (0.8) | 3.4 | (0.4) |
| | Chinese Taipei | 3.6 | (0.6) | 8.3 | (0.7) | 14.3 | (0.9) | 19.4 | (0.7) | 22.4 | (0.8) | 20.1 | (0.9) | 11.8 | (0.8) |
| | Thailand | 23.3 | (1.3) | 29.7 | (1.4) | 26.4 | (0.9) | 14.0 | (0.7) | 5.3 | (0.4) | 1.1 | (0.2) | 0.2 | (0.1) |
| | Tunisia | 48.5 | (1.8) | 24.0 | (1.1) | 16.5 | (1.1) | 8.1 | (0.9) | 2.4 | (0.6) | 0.5 | (0.2) | 0.0 | a |
| | Uruguay | 24.4 | (1.1) | 21.7 | (1.0) | 24.3 | (0.8) | 18.3 | (1.1) | 8.2 | (0.7) | 2.6 | (0.4) | 0.6 | (0.2) |

StatLink ᴪᴺᴾ http://dx.doi.org/10.1787/142183565744

Pour consulter la version française intégrale de ce tableau, suivre ce lien :
StatLink ᴪᴺᴾ http://dx.doi.org/10.1787/152754053448

[Part 1/2]

**Table 6.2b** **Percentage of students at each proficiency level on the mathematics scale, by gender**

*Tableau 6.2b* Pourcentage d'élèves à chaque niveau de compétence sur l'échelle de culture mathématique, selon le sexe

| | | Males – Proficiency levels | | | | | | | | | | | | | | | |
|---|---|---|---|---|---|---|---|---|---|---|---|---|---|---|---|---|---|
| | | Below Level 1 (below 357.77 score points) | | Level 1 (from 357.77 to 420.07 score points) | | Level 2 (from 420.07 to 482.38 score points) | | Level 3 (from 482.38 to 544.68 score points) | | Level 4 (from 544.68 to 606.99 score points) | | Level 5 (from 606.99 to 669.30 score points) | | Level 6 (above 669.30 score points) | |
| | | % | S.E. | % | S.E. | % | S.E. | % | S.E. | % | S.E. | % | S.E. | % | S.E. |
| OECD | Australia | 3.3 | (0.4) | 9.1 | (0.6) | 19.0 | (0.7) | 25.6 | (0.9) | 23.5 | (0.8) | 13.8 | (0.8) | 5.7 | (0.8) |
| | Austria | 5.8 | (1.0) | 11.6 | (1.3) | 18.4 | (1.3) | 23.2 | (1.2) | 21.6 | (1.3) | 14.5 | (1.0) | 4.9 | (0.6) |
| | Belgium | 7.3 | (1.1) | 10.4 | (1.2) | 16.3 | (0.8) | 20.1 | (1.1) | 21.0 | (1.1) | 17.0 | (0.8) | 7.9 | (0.6) |
| | Canada | 2.7 | (0.4) | 7.6 | (0.7) | 16.8 | (0.9) | 26.0 | (0.9) | 25.9 | (0.9) | 15.5 | (0.9) | 5.5 | (0.5) |
| | Czech Republic | 6.0 | (0.8) | 11.6 | (1.1) | 20.9 | (1.2) | 22.9 | (1.3) | 19.4 | (1.5) | 12.7 | (1.0) | 6.5 | (0.7) |
| | Denmark | 3.3 | (0.6) | 8.8 | (1.0) | 20.8 | (1.3) | 28.4 | (1.2) | 23.7 | (1.2) | 11.9 | (0.8) | 3.2 | (0.5) |
| | Finland | 1.2 | (0.3) | 4.7 | (0.7) | 13.3 | (0.9) | 25.1 | (1.1) | 27.8 | (1.0) | 19.8 | (1.1) | 8.0 | (0.7) |
| | France | 8.7 | (1.1) | 13.5 | (1.4) | 20.7 | (1.5) | 22.9 | (1.3) | 19.8 | (1.4) | 11.3 | (1.0) | 3.2 | (0.4) |
| | Germany | 6.2 | (1.1) | 11.6 | (1.0) | 20.4 | (1.4) | 23.4 | (1.4) | 19.8 | (1.4) | 12.9 | (1.1) | 5.8 | (0.7) |
| | Greece | 14.1 | (1.5) | 18.6 | (1.1) | 24.8 | (1.6) | 22.6 | (1.4) | 13.4 | (1.1) | 5.2 | (0.7) | 1.2 | (0.3) |
| | Hungary | 6.9 | (0.7) | 14.0 | (1.0) | 23.6 | (1.2) | 25.3 | (1.2) | 17.7 | (1.4) | 9.1 | (0.9) | 3.5 | (0.7) |
| | Iceland | 6.2 | (0.6) | 12.1 | (1.1) | 22.4 | (1.1) | 25.1 | (1.1) | 20.7 | (1.1) | 10.7 | (0.9) | 2.7 | (0.5) |
| | Ireland | 4.1 | (0.7) | 11.4 | (1.3) | 23.1 | (1.5) | 27.3 | (1.3) | 21.9 | (1.1) | 9.9 | (0.9) | 2.4 | (0.4) |
| | Italy | 13.0 | (0.9) | 17.0 | (0.9) | 24.1 | (0.8) | 22.7 | (0.8) | 14.8 | (0.7) | 6.6 | (0.6) | 1.8 | (0.3) |
| | Japan | 3.7 | (0.7) | 8.1 | (0.9) | 17.1 | (1.2) | 24.1 | (1.2) | 24.4 | (1.3) | 16.2 | (1.1) | 6.5 | (0.8) |
| | Korea | 2.7 | (0.7) | 6.4 | (0.9) | 14.3 | (1.0) | 22.1 | (1.3) | 24.7 | (1.4) | 19.0 | (1.2) | 10.9 | (1.6) |
| | Luxembourg | 7.7 | (0.6) | 13.4 | (0.8) | 21.6 | (1.2) | 25.1 | (1.1) | 19.0 | (1.0) | 10.0 | (0.8) | 3.2 | (0.4) |
| | Mexico | 27.1 | (1.7) | 26.9 | (1.1) | 25.7 | (1.0) | 14.1 | (0.7) | 5.0 | (0.5) | 1.1 | (0.3) | 0.1 | (0.1) |
| | Netherlands | 2.0 | (0.6) | 8.0 | (0.9) | 18.1 | (1.3) | 24.5 | (1.2) | 23.7 | (1.2) | 16.9 | (1.2) | 6.8 | (0.8) |
| | New Zealand | 4.0 | (0.5) | 9.9 | (1.0) | 18.6 | (1.3) | 23.7 | (1.4) | 21.8 | (1.3) | 14.8 | (1.1) | 7.1 | (0.8) |
| | Norway | 7.8 | (1.0) | 14.3 | (1.1) | 22.8 | (1.1) | 25.2 | (1.5) | 17.8 | (1.1) | 9.4 | (0.9) | 2.6 | (0.4) |
| | Poland | 5.5 | (0.5) | 13.6 | (0.8) | 23.9 | (1.2) | 25.8 | (1.0) | 18.6 | (1.0) | 9.9 | (1.0) | 2.7 | (0.5) |
| | Portugal | 11.1 | (1.2) | 17.5 | (1.1) | 24.2 | (1.2) | 23.9 | (1.4) | 15.5 | (1.1) | 6.6 | (0.8) | 1.3 | (0.4) |
| | Slovak Republic | 7.3 | (0.9) | 11.7 | (0.8) | 23.3 | (1.3) | 25.2 | (1.4) | 19.6 | (1.1) | 9.8 | (0.9) | 3.2 | (0.7) |
| | Spain | 8.4 | (0.6) | 16.0 | (1.1) | 23.7 | (1.1) | 25.5 | (1.1) | 17.5 | (0.9) | 7.3 | (0.6) | 1.7 | (0.3) |
| | Sweden | 5.4 | (0.8) | 12.5 | (1.0) | 22.5 | (1.3) | 22.9 | (1.7) | 20.3 | (1.3) | 10.3 | (0.9) | 3.3 | (0.5) |
| | Switzerland | 4.3 | (0.6) | 8.1 | (0.6) | 16.1 | (0.9) | 22.9 | (0.9) | 23.9 | (1.0) | 17.2 | (1.0) | 7.6 | (0.6) |
| | Turkey | 23.5 | (1.7) | 27.5 | (1.5) | 24.4 | (1.4) | 12.8 | (0.9) | 6.9 | (1.1) | 3.5 | (0.9) | 1.4 | (0.7) |
| | United Kingdom | 5.7 | (0.8) | 12.6 | (0.9) | 22.7 | (1.0) | 25.4 | (1.0) | 19.7 | (0.8) | 10.5 | (0.7) | 3.4 | (0.4) |
| | United States | 9.8 | (1.4) | 17.6 | (1.2) | 24.9 | (1.4) | 23.0 | (1.2) | 16.2 | (1.1) | 7.1 | (0.8) | 1.5 | (0.3) |
| | **OECD total** | 9.9 | (0.4) | 15.4 | (0.4) | 22.2 | (0.5) | 22.3 | (0.5) | 17.4 | (0.4) | 9.6 | (0.3) | 3.4 | (0.1) |
| | **OECD average** | 7.5 | (0.2) | 12.9 | (0.2) | 20.9 | (0.2) | 23.6 | (0.2) | 19.5 | (0.2) | 11.3 | (0.2) | 4.2 | (0.1) |
| Partners | Argentina | 37.3 | (2.9) | 24.8 | (1.5) | 21.0 | (1.7) | 11.6 | (1.5) | 4.3 | (0.7) | 0.9 | (0.3) | 0.1 | (0.1) |
| | Azerbaijan | 0.2 | (0.2) | 10.6 | (1.2) | 47.7 | (2.0) | 33.6 | (1.8) | 7.0 | (1.0) | 0.9 | (0.4) | 0.0 | a |
| | Brazil | 42.5 | (1.8) | 26.4 | (1.6) | 18.0 | (1.2) | 8.3 | (0.8) | 3.4 | (0.5) | 1.1 | (0.4) | 0.3 | (0.2) |
| | Bulgaria | 30.9 | (2.5) | 24.0 | (1.6) | 20.3 | (1.4) | 14.2 | (1.1) | 7.0 | (0.9) | 2.9 | (0.7) | 0.8 | (0.4) |
| | Chile | 23.2 | (2.0) | 26.3 | (1.5) | 25.7 | (1.4) | 15.5 | (1.2) | 7.1 | (1.0) | 2.0 | (0.6) | 0.2 | (0.1) |
| | Colombia | 38.4 | (2.1) | 28.1 | (2.0) | 20.7 | (1.6) | 9.6 | (1.0) | 2.7 | (0.5) | 0.5 | (0.3) | 0.1 | (0.1) |
| | Croatia | 9.4 | (0.9) | 17.4 | (1.1) | 27.1 | (1.2) | 24.5 | (1.1) | 15.2 | (1.0) | 5.2 | (0.7) | 1.2 | (0.3) |
| | Estonia | 3.3 | (0.7) | 9.5 | (1.3) | 21.5 | (1.2) | 28.8 | (1.3) | 22.9 | (1.6) | 10.8 | (0.9) | 3.2 | (0.5) |
| | Hong Kong-China | 2.7 | (0.7) | 6.0 | (0.8) | 13.1 | (1.2) | 21.3 | (1.5) | 25.9 | (1.5) | 19.6 | (1.0) | 11.4 | (1.3) |
| | Indonesia | 31.9 | (2.8) | 29.5 | (2.3) | 21.3 | (1.2) | 13.2 | (3.3) | 3.5 | (1.1) | 0.5 | (0.3) | 0.0 | a |
| | Israel | 22.2 | (2.1) | 18.0 | (1.4) | 20.1 | (1.3) | 18.5 | (1.3) | 13.3 | (1.2) | 6.0 | (0.8) | 1.9 | (0.4) |
| | Jordan | 39.3 | (2.2) | 26.9 | (1.7) | 20.9 | (1.3) | 9.9 | (1.3) | 2.6 | (0.7) | 0.3 | (0.2) | 0.0 | a |
| | Kyrgyzstan | 72.2 | (1.9) | 16.2 | (1.4) | 7.3 | (0.9) | 3.3 | (0.6) | 0.9 | (0.3) | 0.1 | a | 0.0 | a |
| | Latvia | 6.4 | (0.9) | 13.7 | (1.2) | 26.4 | (1.3) | 28.2 | (1.2) | 17.8 | (1.2) | 6.2 | (0.8) | 1.4 | (0.4) |
| | Liechtenstein | 3.8 | (1.9) | 7.8 | (3.2) | 18.9 | (5.8) | 29.2 | (7.2) | 22.8 | (4.7) | 12.4 | (2.9) | 5.3 | (2.2) |
| | Lithuania | 7.7 | (0.9) | 15.2 | (1.0) | 25.1 | (1.3) | 24.6 | (1.3) | 17.6 | (1.0) | 7.7 | (1.3) | 2.1 | (0.5) |
| | Macao-China | 2.9 | (0.4) | 8.0 | (1.0) | 18.5 | (1.2) | 25.8 | (1.5) | 24.3 | (1.3) | 15.8 | (0.9) | 4.8 | (0.6) |
| | Montenegro | 29.4 | (1.3) | 28.0 | (1.3) | 24.0 | (1.3) | 13.1 | (0.9) | 4.6 | (0.5) | 0.9 | (0.3) | 0.1 | a |
| | Qatar | 73.4 | (0.7) | 13.5 | (0.7) | 7.0 | (0.6) | 3.5 | (0.5) | 1.6 | (0.3) | 0.8 | (0.2) | 0.1 | (0.1) |
| | Romania | 24.5 | (2.1) | 26.6 | (2.1) | 26.7 | (2.2) | 14.2 | (1.1) | 6.3 | (0.9) | 1.6 | (0.4) | 0.2 | (0.1) |
| | Russian Federation | 9.3 | (1.4) | 17.0 | (1.3) | 26.4 | (1.7) | 23.2 | (1.0) | 15.6 | (1.3) | 6.6 | (0.8) | 2.0 | (0.3) |
| | Serbia | 19.0 | (1.4) | 23.8 | (1.3) | 25.7 | (1.1) | 18.3 | (1.2) | 9.5 | (1.4) | 3.0 | (0.6) | 0.6 | (0.2) |
| | Slovenia | 4.5 | (0.6) | 12.5 | (1.0) | 23.9 | (1.2) | 25.4 | (1.0) | 18.8 | (1.3) | 10.5 | (1.1) | 4.3 | (0.6) |
| | Chinese Taipei | 3.7 | (0.7) | 7.8 | (0.9) | 13.0 | (0.8) | 18.5 | (1.2) | 22.3 | (1.0) | 21.5 | (1.0) | 13.2 | (1.3) |
| | Thailand | 25.7 | (1.9) | 29.6 | (1.8) | 24.3 | (1.6) | 13.5 | (1.0) | 5.3 | (0.7) | 1.3 | (0.3) | 0.3 | (0.1) |
| | Tunisia | 45.0 | (1.9) | 24.5 | (1.2) | 17.9 | (1.4) | 8.8 | (1.1) | 3.1 | (0.7) | 0.7 | (0.4) | 0.0 | a |
| | Uruguay | 22.7 | (1.2) | 21.4 | (1.3) | 24.2 | (1.2) | 18.3 | (1.7) | 9.1 | (1.0) | 3.5 | (0.5) | 0.8 | (0.3) |

*StatLink* ᴴᴷᴸ http://dx.doi.org/10.1787/142183565744

Pour consulter la version française intégrale de ce tableau, suivre ce lien :
*StatLink* ᴴᴷᴸ http://dx.doi.org/10.1787/152754053448

[Part 2/2]

**Table 6.2b  Percentage of students at each proficiency level on the mathematics scale, by gender**

Tableau 6.2b  Pourcentage d'élèves à chaque niveau de compétence sur l'échelle de culture mathématique, selon le sexe

| | Females – Proficiency levels | | | | | | | | | | | | |
| | Below Level 1 (below 357.77 score points) | | Level 1 (from 357.77 to 420.07 score points) | | Level 2 (from 420.07 to 482.38 score points) | | Level 3 (from 482.38 to 544.68 score points) | | Level 4 (from 544.68 to 606.99 score points) | | Level 5 (from 606.99 to 669.30 score points) | | Level 6 (above 669.30 score points) | |
| | % | S.E. | % | S.E. | % | S.E. | % | S.E. | % | S.E. | % | S.E. | % | S.E. |
|---|---|---|---|---|---|---|---|---|---|---|---|---|---|---|
| Australia | 3.3 | (0.3) | 10.3 | (0.6) | 22.1 | (0.9) | 28.3 | (0.8) | 22.8 | (0.8) | 10.4 | (0.6) | 2.8 | (0.4) |
| Austria | 9.2 | (1.3) | 13.5 | (1.2) | 20.6 | (1.4) | 23.5 | (1.4) | 21.1 | (1.5) | 10.0 | (0.9) | 2.0 | (0.5) |
| Belgium | 6.9 | (0.8) | 10.1 | (0.8) | 17.8 | (1.0) | 22.9 | (1.1) | 22.8 | (1.0) | 14.7 | (1.0) | 4.8 | (0.5) |
| Canada | 2.9 | (0.3) | 8.4 | (0.6) | 20.4 | (0.9) | 29.1 | (0.9) | 24.4 | (1.0) | 11.6 | (0.7) | 3.2 | (0.3) |
| Czech Republic | 8.8 | (1.1) | 12.5 | (1.2) | 19.9 | (1.6) | 23.1 | (1.8) | 18.7 | (1.4) | 11.8 | (1.3) | 5.3 | (0.9) |
| Denmark | 3.9 | (0.7) | 11.3 | (0.8) | 22.1 | (1.0) | 29.2 | (1.3) | 21.3 | (1.1) | 9.9 | (0.8) | 2.5 | (0.4) |
| Finland | 1.1 | (0.3) | 4.9 | (0.8) | 15.4 | (1.2) | 29.2 | (1.1) | 28.3 | (1.2) | 16.5 | (0.9) | 4.6 | (0.6) |
| France | 8.1 | (0.8) | 14.3 | (1.3) | 22.0 | (1.3) | 25.5 | (1.3) | 19.5 | (1.3) | 8.7 | (0.8) | 1.9 | (0.5) |
| Germany | 8.5 | (1.1) | 13.5 | (0.9) | 22.1 | (1.4) | 24.7 | (1.2) | 19.1 | (1.1) | 9.0 | (0.8) | 3.0 | (0.5) |
| Greece | 12.5 | (1.5) | 19.5 | (1.8) | 28.7 | (1.6) | 23.9 | (1.7) | 11.8 | (1.5) | 3.1 | (0.6) | 0.5 | (0.2) |
| Hungary | 6.5 | (0.9) | 15.0 | (1.2) | 26.8 | (1.4) | 27.8 | (1.4) | 16.0 | (1.3) | 6.2 | (0.8) | 1.8 | (0.4) |
| Iceland | 4.0 | (0.5) | 11.3 | (0.8) | 22.1 | (1.2) | 28.0 | (1.5) | 22.7 | (1.2) | 9.6 | (1.0) | 2.3 | (0.4) |
| Ireland | 4.1 | (0.6) | 13.2 | (1.1) | 25.2 | (1.1) | 29.7 | (1.4) | 19.4 | (1.4) | 7.4 | (0.9) | 0.9 | (0.3) |
| Italy | 14.0 | (0.9) | 21.6 | (1.6) | 26.8 | (1.0) | 21.6 | (0.9) | 11.9 | (0.8) | 3.3 | (0.4) | 0.8 | (0.3) |
| Japan | 4.2 | (0.9) | 10.2 | (1.1) | 20.7 | (1.3) | 28.1 | (1.5) | 23.1 | (1.4) | 10.7 | (1.1) | 3.1 | (0.5) |
| Korea | 1.9 | (0.5) | 6.7 | (1.0) | 16.1 | (1.2) | 24.9 | (1.6) | 26.2 | (1.6) | 17.0 | (1.3) | 7.2 | (1.4) |
| Luxembourg | 8.9 | (0.9) | 15.6 | (1.3) | 24.9 | (1.0) | 25.3 | (1.3) | 17.4 | (1.3) | 6.5 | (0.7) | 1.4 | (0.4) |
| Mexico | 29.5 | (1.5) | 29.3 | (1.0) | 24.8 | (1.1) | 12.2 | (0.8) | 3.6 | (0.5) | 0.5 | (0.2) | 0.0 | (0.0) |
| Netherlands | 2.9 | (0.7) | 10.2 | (1.1) | 19.6 | (1.3) | 24.1 | (1.5) | 24.6 | (1.4) | 14.6 | (1.0) | 3.9 | (0.8) |
| New Zealand | 4.0 | (0.5) | 10.1 | (0.9) | 20.3 | (1.3) | 27.1 | (1.3) | 22.3 | (1.3) | 11.8 | (0.9) | 4.3 | (0.6) |
| Norway | 6.8 | (0.7) | 15.6 | (1.2) | 25.9 | (1.1) | 26.1 | (1.1) | 17.0 | (1.2) | 7.1 | (1.0) | 1.6 | (0.4) |
| Poland | 5.8 | (0.5) | 14.7 | (1.0) | 25.5 | (1.0) | 26.7 | (1.1) | 18.6 | (1.1) | 7.4 | (0.7) | 1.3 | (0.3) |
| Portugal | 12.8 | (1.2) | 19.9 | (1.2) | 26.0 | (1.2) | 24.2 | (1.2) | 13.4 | (0.8) | 3.3 | (0.5) | 0.3 | (0.1) |
| Slovak Republic | 9.0 | (1.1) | 13.9 | (1.3) | 24.9 | (1.4) | 25.4 | (1.4) | 18.0 | (1.2) | 7.3 | (1.1) | 1.5 | (0.3) |
| Spain | 8.7 | (0.7) | 16.3 | (1.0) | 26.7 | (1.3) | 26.9 | (1.0) | 16.1 | (0.8) | 4.7 | (0.5) | 0.6 | (0.1) |
| Sweden | 5.4 | (0.8) | 13.3 | (1.0) | 23.5 | (1.2) | 26.3 | (1.1) | 19.8 | (1.6) | 9.1 | (0.8) | 2.5 | (0.5) |
| Switzerland | 4.8 | (0.6) | 9.9 | (0.9) | 18.9 | (1.4) | 23.5 | (1.5) | 22.5 | (1.4) | 14.5 | (0.9) | 5.8 | (0.8) |
| Turkey | 24.6 | (1.9) | 28.8 | (1.9) | 24.1 | (1.9) | 12.8 | (1.2) | 6.4 | (1.1) | 2.3 | (0.7) | 0.9 | (0.4) |
| United Kingdom | 6.2 | (0.6) | 15.1 | (1.0) | 26.7 | (1.3) | 27.2 | (1.1) | 16.5 | (0.8) | 6.9 | (0.6) | 1.5 | (0.3) |
| United States | 10.1 | (1.1) | 18.8 | (1.1) | 27.3 | (1.4) | 23.2 | (1.3) | 13.9 | (1.2) | 5.6 | (0.8) | 1.0 | (0.3) |
| **OECD total** | 10.6 | (0.4) | 16.9 | (0.3) | 24.2 | (0.5) | 23.3 | (0.5) | 16.0 | (0.4) | 7.1 | (0.3) | 1.9 | (0.1) |
| **OECD average** | 8.0 | (0.2) | 14.3 | (0.2) | 22.9 | (0.2) | 25.0 | (0.2) | 18.6 | (0.2) | 8.7 | (0.2) | 2.5 | (0.1) |
| Argentina | 41.3 | (3.0) | 24.7 | (2.0) | 19.9 | (2.1) | 9.7 | (1.1) | 3.3 | (0.7) | 0.9 | (0.5) | 0.2 | a |
| Azerbaijan | 0.1 | (0.1) | 10.1 | (1.2) | 47.5 | (1.8) | 35.2 | (1.9) | 6.2 | (0.9) | 0.4 | (0.2) | 0.5 | (0.3) |
| Brazil | 50.1 | (1.5) | 25.6 | (1.2) | 15.3 | (1.1) | 6.1 | (0.6) | 2.3 | (0.5) | 0.6 | (0.3) | 0.1 | (0.1) |
| Bulgaria | 27.7 | (2.4) | 23.9 | (1.6) | 23.9 | (1.5) | 15.7 | (1.6) | 6.4 | (1.0) | 2.0 | (0.6) | 0.4 | (0.3) |
| Chile | 34.1 | (2.5) | 27.7 | (1.8) | 21.9 | (1.4) | 11.9 | (1.2) | 3.9 | (0.6) | 0.5 | (0.2) | 0.0 | a |
| Colombia | 49.9 | (2.4) | 26.7 | (1.7) | 16.0 | (1.6) | 5.9 | (0.9) | 1.3 | (0.6) | 0.3 | (0.1) | 0.0 | a |
| Croatia | 9.3 | (0.9) | 21.1 | (1.3) | 30.6 | (1.5) | 24.1 | (1.3) | 11.9 | (0.9) | 2.7 | (0.4) | 0.3 | (0.2) |
| Estonia | 2.1 | (0.4) | 9.2 | (1.0) | 22.3 | (1.4) | 31.7 | (1.6) | 23.6 | (1.5) | 9.1 | (0.8) | 2.0 | (0.4) |
| Hong Kong-China | 3.1 | (0.5) | 7.1 | (0.8) | 15.7 | (1.1) | 24.1 | (1.4) | 25.4 | (1.2) | 17.9 | (1.3) | 6.7 | (0.9) |
| Indonesia | 38.8 | (2.2) | 31.6 | (1.5) | 19.4 | (1.3) | 7.9 | (1.3) | 2.1 | (0.6) | 0.2 | (0.1) | a | a |
| Israel | 22.2 | (1.8) | 21.6 | (1.2) | 23.4 | (1.6) | 18.3 | (1.1) | 10.3 | (0.8) | 3.6 | (0.5) | 0.7 | (0.3) |
| Jordan | 34.5 | (2.1) | 31.9 | (1.1) | 23.0 | (1.3) | 8.8 | (0.8) | 1.7 | (0.4) | 0.1 | (0.1) | a | a |
| Kyrgyzstan | 73.6 | (1.6) | 16.7 | (1.1) | 6.8 | (0.8) | 2.3 | (0.5) | 0.6 | (0.2) | 0.0 | a | 0.0 | a |
| Latvia | 6.5 | (0.7) | 14.8 | (1.2) | 26.3 | (1.3) | 29.8 | (1.4) | 16.9 | (1.2) | 4.8 | (0.6) | 0.8 | (0.4) |
| Liechtenstein | 4.1 | (1.6) | 10.5 | (2.8) | 17.7 | (3.7) | 24.0 | (4.2) | 24.6 | (3.4) | 12.8 | (2.9) | 6.3 | (2.2) |
| Lithuania | 7.9 | (0.7) | 15.1 | (1.0) | 25.0 | (1.4) | 25.6 | (1.4) | 18.1 | (1.1) | 6.9 | (1.0) | 1.4 | (0.4) |
| Macao-China | 2.4 | (0.4) | 8.6 | (1.0) | 21.5 | (1.2) | 28.8 | (1.3) | 24.5 | (1.2) | 11.5 | (0.8) | 2.7 | (0.5) |
| Montenegro | 34.1 | (1.1) | 28.8 | (1.1) | 22.6 | (1.2) | 10.5 | (0.9) | 3.3 | (0.6) | 0.7 | (0.3) | 0.0 | a |
| Qatar | 70.0 | (0.8) | 17.5 | (0.8) | 7.9 | (0.8) | 3.2 | (0.3) | 1.1 | (0.2) | 0.3 | (0.1) | 0.0 | a |
| Romania | 25.0 | (2.6) | 29.5 | (2.4) | 26.4 | (2.0) | 14.0 | (1.6) | 4.5 | (1.0) | 0.7 | (0.3) | 0.0 | a |
| Russian Federation | 8.8 | (0.9) | 18.1 | (1.4) | 27.6 | (1.7) | 25.1 | (1.3) | 14.0 | (1.2) | 4.9 | (0.6) | 1.4 | (0.4) |
| Serbia | 20.3 | (1.8) | 22.2 | (1.4) | 28.0 | (1.5) | 19.0 | (1.3) | 8.7 | (0.9) | 1.8 | (0.5) | 0.2 | (0.1) |
| Slovenia | 4.6 | (0.5) | 13.6 | (1.0) | 23.1 | (1.1) | 26.6 | (1.2) | 19.5 | (1.0) | 10.1 | (0.9) | 2.4 | (0.5) |
| Chinese Taipei | 3.6 | (0.7) | 8.9 | (1.0) | 15.7 | (1.4) | 20.4 | (1.3) | 22.5 | (1.4) | 18.6 | (1.3) | 10.2 | (1.3) |
| Thailand | 21.6 | (1.4) | 29.8 | (1.5) | 27.9 | (1.0) | 14.3 | (0.9) | 5.3 | (0.5) | 1.0 | (0.3) | 0.1 | (0.1) |
| Tunisia | 51.7 | (2.1) | 23.5 | (1.6) | 15.3 | (1.4) | 7.4 | (1.2) | 1.8 | (0.6) | 0.3 | (0.2) | 0.0 | a |
| Uruguay | 26.1 | (1.2) | 21.9 | (1.1) | 24.3 | (1.2) | 18.3 | (1.2) | 7.2 | (0.7) | 1.8 | (0.4) | 0.3 | (0.1) |

StatLink ⊞ http://dx.doi.org/10.1787/142183565744

Pour consulter la version française intégrale de ce tableau, suivre ce lien :
StatLink ⊞ http://dx.doi.org/10.1787/152754053448

[Part 1/2]

**Table 6.2c** Mean score, variation and gender differences in student performance on the mathematics scale

Tableau 6.2c Score moyen, différences de score selon le sexe et répartition des scores sur l'échelle de culture mathématique

| | | All students | | | | Gender differences | | | | | |
|---|---|---|---|---|---|---|---|---|---|---|---|
| | | Mean score | | Standard deviation | | Males | | Females | | Difference (M - F) | |
| | | Mean | S.E. | S.D. | S.E. | Mean score | S.E. | Mean score | S.E. | Score dif. | S.E. |
| OECD | Australia | 520 | (2.2) | 88 | (1.1) | 527 | (3.2) | 513 | (2.4) | 14 | (3.4) |
| | Austria | 505 | (3.7) | 98 | (2.3) | 517 | (4.4) | 494 | (4.1) | 23 | (4.7) |
| | Belgium | 520 | (3.0) | 106 | (3.3) | 524 | (4.1) | 517 | (3.4) | 7 | (4.8) |
| | Canada | 527 | (2.0) | 86 | (1.1) | 534 | (2.4) | 520 | (2.0) | 14 | (1.9) |
| | Czech Republic | 510 | (3.6) | 103 | (2.1) | 514 | (4.2) | 504 | (4.8) | 11 | (5.6) |
| | Denmark | 513 | (2.6) | 85 | (1.5) | 518 | (2.9) | 508 | (3.0) | 10 | (2.8) |
| | Finland | 548 | (2.3) | 81 | (1.0) | 554 | (2.7) | 543 | (2.6) | 12 | (2.6) |
| | France | 496 | (3.2) | 96 | (2.0) | 499 | (4.0) | 492 | (3.3) | 6 | (3.7) |
| | Germany | 504 | (3.9) | 99 | (2.6) | 513 | (4.6) | 494 | (3.9) | 20 | (3.7) |
| | Greece | 459 | (3.0) | 92 | (2.4) | 462 | (4.3) | 457 | (3.0) | 5 | (4.5) |
| | Hungary | 491 | (2.9) | 91 | (2.0) | 496 | (3.5) | 486 | (3.7) | 10 | (4.3) |
| | Iceland | 506 | (1.8) | 88 | (1.1) | 503 | (2.6) | 508 | (2.2) | -4 | (3.2) |
| | Ireland | 501 | (2.8) | 82 | (1.5) | 507 | (3.7) | 496 | (3.2) | 11 | (4.1) |
| | Italy | 462 | (2.3) | 96 | (1.7) | 470 | (2.9) | 453 | (2.7) | 17 | (3.4) |
| | Japan | 523 | (3.3) | 91 | (2.1) | 533 | (4.8) | 513 | (4.9) | 20 | (7.2) |
| | Korea | 547 | (3.8) | 93 | (3.1) | 552 | (5.3) | 543 | (4.5) | 9 | (6.3) |
| | Luxembourg | 490 | (1.1) | 93 | (1.0) | 498 | (1.7) | 482 | (1.8) | 17 | (2.8) |
| | Mexico | 406 | (2.9) | 85 | (2.2) | 410 | (3.4) | 401 | (3.1) | 9 | (2.6) |
| | Netherlands | 531 | (2.6) | 89 | (2.2) | 537 | (3.1) | 524 | (2.8) | 13 | (2.8) |
| | New Zealand | 522 | (2.4) | 93 | (1.2) | 527 | (3.1) | 517 | (3.6) | 11 | (4.7) |
| | Norway | 490 | (2.6) | 92 | (1.4) | 493 | (3.3) | 487 | (2.8) | 6 | (3.1) |
| | Poland | 495 | (2.4) | 87 | (1.2) | 500 | (2.8) | 491 | (2.7) | 9 | (2.6) |
| | Portugal | 466 | (3.1) | 91 | (2.0) | 474 | (3.7) | 459 | (3.2) | 15 | (3.3) |
| | Slovak Republic | 492 | (2.8) | 95 | (2.5) | 499 | (3.7) | 485 | (3.5) | 14 | (4.6) |
| | Spain | 480 | (2.3) | 89 | (1.1) | 484 | (2.6) | 476 | (2.6) | 9 | (2.2) |
| | Sweden | 502 | (2.4) | 90 | (1.4) | 505 | (2.7) | 500 | (3.0) | 5 | (2.9) |
| | Switzerland | 530 | (3.2) | 97 | (1.6) | 536 | (3.3) | 523 | (3.6) | 13 | (2.7) |
| | Turkey | 424 | (4.9) | 93 | (4.3) | 427 | (5.6) | 421 | (5.1) | 6 | (4.6) |
| | United Kingdom | 495 | (2.1) | 89 | (1.3) | 504 | (2.6) | 487 | (2.6) | 17 | (2.9) |
| | United States | 474 | (4.0) | 90 | (1.9) | 479 | (4.6) | 470 | (3.9) | 9 | (2.9) |
| | **OECD total** | 484 | (1.2) | 98 | (0.7) | 489 | (1.3) | 478 | (1.3) | 12 | (1.2) |
| | **OECD average** | 498 | (0.5) | 92 | (0.4) | 503 | (0.7) | 492 | (0.6) | 11 | (0.7) |
| Partners | Argentina | 381 | (6.2) | 101 | (3.5) | 388 | (6.5) | 375 | (7.2) | 13 | (5.6) |
| | Azerbaijan | 476 | (2.3) | 48 | (1.7) | 475 | (2.4) | 477 | (2.6) | -1 | (2.0) |
| | Brazil | 370 | (2.9) | 92 | (2.7) | 380 | (3.4) | 361 | (3.0) | 19 | (2.8) |
| | Bulgaria | 413 | (6.1) | 101 | (3.6) | 412 | (6.7) | 415 | (6.5) | -4 | (4.9) |
| | Chile | 411 | (4.6) | 87 | (2.2) | 424 | (5.5) | 396 | (4.7) | 28 | (4.8) |
| | Colombia | 370 | (3.8) | 88 | (2.5) | 382 | (4.1) | 360 | (5.0) | 22 | (4.6) |
| | Croatia | 467 | (2.4) | 83 | (1.5) | 474 | (3.2) | 461 | (2.8) | 13 | (3.8) |
| | Estonia | 515 | (2.7) | 80 | (1.5) | 515 | (3.3) | 514 | (3.0) | 1 | (3.2) |
| | Hong Kong-China | 547 | (2.7) | 93 | (2.4) | 555 | (3.9) | 540 | (3.7) | 16 | (5.5) |
| | Indonesia | 391 | (5.6) | 80 | (3.2) | 399 | (8.3) | 382 | (4.0) | 17 | (7.3) |
| | Israel | 442 | (4.3) | 107 | (3.3) | 448 | (6.6) | 436 | (4.3) | 12 | (6.9) |
| | Jordan | 384 | (3.3) | 84 | (2.0) | 381 | (5.3) | 388 | (3.9) | -7 | (6.5) |
| | Kyrgyzstan | 311 | (3.4) | 87 | (2.1) | 311 | (4.0) | 310 | (3.4) | 1 | (2.9) |
| | Latvia | 486 | (3.0) | 83 | (1.6) | 489 | (3.5) | 484 | (3.2) | 5 | (3.0) |
| | Liechtenstein | 525 | (4.2) | 93 | (3.2) | 525 | (7.4) | 525 | (7.0) | 0 | (11.7) |
| | Lithuania | 486 | (2.9) | 90 | (1.8) | 487 | (3.3) | 485 | (3.3) | 2 | (3.0) |
| | Macao-China | 525 | (1.3) | 84 | (0.9) | 530 | (2.1) | 520 | (1.7) | 11 | (2.9) |
| | Montenegro | 399 | (1.4) | 85 | (1.0) | 405 | (2.3) | 393 | (1.9) | 12 | (3.3) |
| | Qatar | 318 | (1.0) | 91 | (0.8) | 311 | (1.6) | 325 | (1.3) | -14 | (2.1) |
| | Romania | 415 | (4.2) | 84 | (2.9) | 418 | (4.2) | 412 | (4.9) | 7 | (3.3) |
| | Russian Federation | 476 | (3.9) | 90 | (1.7) | 479 | (4.6) | 473 | (3.9) | 6 | (3.3) |
| | Serbia | 435 | (3.5) | 92 | (1.8) | 438 | (4.0) | 433 | (4.4) | 5 | (4.5) |
| | Slovenia | 504 | (1.0) | 89 | (0.9) | 507 | (1.8) | 502 | (1.8) | 5 | (2.9) |
| | Chinese Taipei | 549 | (4.1) | 103 | (2.2) | 556 | (4.7) | 543 | (5.9) | 13 | (6.7) |
| | Thailand | 417 | (2.3) | 81 | (1.6) | 413 | (3.8) | 420 | (2.6) | -7 | (4.2) |
| | Tunisia | 365 | (4.0) | 92 | (2.3) | 373 | (4.4) | 358 | (4.4) | 15 | (3.6) |
| | Uruguay | 427 | (2.6) | 99 | (1.8) | 433 | (3.6) | 420 | (3.1) | 13 | (4.2) |

Note: Values that are statistically significant are indicated in bold (see Annex A3).
StatLink ￼ http://dx.doi.org/10.1787/142183565744

Pour consulter la version française intégrale de ce tableau, suivre ce lien :
StatLink ￼ http://dx.doi.org/10.1787/152754053448

[Part 2/2]
**Table 6.2c   Mean score, variation and gender differences in student performance on the mathematics scale**

Tableau 6.2c   Score moyen, différences de score selon le sexe et répartition des scores sur l'échelle de culture mathématique

| | | Percentiles | | | | | | | | | | |
|---|---|---|---|---|---|---|---|---|---|---|---|---|
| | | 5th | | 10th | | 25th | | 75th | | 90th | | 95th | |
| | | Score | S.E. | Score | S.E. | Score | S.E. | Score | S.E. | Score | S.E. | Score | S.E. |
| OECD | Australia | 375 | (3.2) | 406 | (2.7) | 460 | (2.3) | 581 | (2.5) | 633 | (3.3) | 663 | (4.0) |
| | Austria | 338 | (6.8) | 373 | (6.3) | 438 | (5.5) | 577 | (4.0) | 630 | (3.8) | 657 | (4.0) |
| | Belgium | 337 | (8.9) | 381 | (6.6) | 451 | (4.0) | 598 | (2.5) | 650 | (2.4) | 678 | (2.7) |
| | Canada | 383 | (4.0) | 416 | (3.3) | 470 | (2.4) | 587 | (2.3) | 635 | (2.3) | 664 | (3.3) |
| | Czech Republic | 340 | (5.2) | 376 | (4.7) | 441 | (4.3) | 582 | (4.7) | 644 | (4.8) | 677 | (6.0) |
| | Denmark | 371 | (5.0) | 404 | (4.3) | 456 | (3.4) | 572 | (2.8) | 621 | (3.4) | 649 | (4.3) |
| | Finland | 411 | (5.0) | 444 | (3.4) | 494 | (2.6) | 605 | (2.6) | 652 | (2.8) | 678 | (3.0) |
| | France | 334 | (5.5) | 369 | (5.4) | 429 | (4.7) | 565 | (3.8) | 617 | (3.8) | 646 | (4.0) |
| | Germany | 339 | (8.5) | 375 | (6.8) | 437 | (4.9) | 574 | (3.9) | 632 | (3.8) | 664 | (4.6) |
| | Greece | 304 | (7.3) | 341 | (5.6) | 399 | (3.9) | 522 | (4.0) | 575 | (4.1) | 607 | (4.5) |
| | Hungary | 343 | (5.6) | 377 | (3.9) | 431 | (2.9) | 551 | (4.1) | 609 | (5.0) | 643 | (5.8) |
| | Iceland | 357 | (3.5) | 391 | (3.6) | 446 | (2.4) | 567 | (2.4) | 618 | (3.2) | 646 | (4.4) |
| | Ireland | 366 | (4.6) | 396 | (4.4) | 445 | (4.1) | 559 | (3.1) | 608 | (3.2) | 634 | (2.9) |
| | Italy | 305 | (4.4) | 341 | (3.3) | 398 | (2.7) | 527 | (2.8) | 584 | (4.2) | 616 | (3.8) |
| | Japan | 370 | (6.4) | 404 | (5.5) | 463 | (4.6) | 587 | (3.0) | 638 | (3.6) | 668 | (4.2) |
| | Korea | 392 | (7.1) | 426 | (6.1) | 485 | (4.3) | 612 | (4.4) | 664 | (6.9) | 694 | (8.2) |
| | Luxembourg | 332 | (4.4) | 368 | (3.5) | 426 | (1.9) | 555 | (1.9) | 610 | (2.7) | 641 | (3.6) |
| | Mexico | 268 | (6.6) | 299 | (4.9) | 349 | (3.7) | 463 | (2.8) | 514 | (3.3) | 546 | (4.2) |
| | Netherlands | 382 | (6.0) | 412 | (5.0) | 467 | (4.6) | 596 | (2.7) | 645 | (3.3) | 672 | (4.3) |
| | New Zealand | 368 | (3.6) | 401 | (4.1) | 458 | (3.2) | 587 | (3.0) | 643 | (4.0) | 674 | (3.6) |
| | Norway | 339 | (6.0) | 373 | (3.8) | 428 | (3.9) | 552 | (2.8) | 609 | (3.3) | 638 | (2.8) |
| | Poland | 353 | (3.3) | 384 | (3.4) | 435 | (2.8) | 557 | (3.3) | 610 | (3.7) | 638 | (3.5) |
| | Portugal | 315 | (6.5) | 348 | (5.2) | 404 | (4.2) | 530 | (3.0) | 583 | (2.8) | 612 | (3.8) |
| | Slovak Republic | 333 | (7.0) | 370 | (5.1) | 433 | (3.6) | 558 | (3.5) | 611 | (4.4) | 640 | (4.8) |
| | Spain | 332 | (4.4) | 366 | (2.8) | 421 | (3.2) | 542 | (2.5) | 593 | (2.9) | 622 | (3.3) |
| | Sweden | 354 | (5.6) | 387 | (4.2) | 442 | (3.5) | 565 | (3.2) | 617 | (2.8) | 649 | (4.2) |
| | Switzerland | 362 | (5.5) | 401 | (4.7) | 464 | (4.1) | 600 | (3.7) | 652 | (3.7) | 682 | (4.2) |
| | Turkey | 287 | (6.1) | 316 | (4.0) | 360 | (3.3) | 477 | (7.2) | 550 | (12.4) | 595 | (15.8) |
| | United Kingdom | 351 | (5.0) | 381 | (3.3) | 434 | (2.7) | 557 | (2.5) | 612 | (3.2) | 643 | (3.8) |
| | United States | 328 | (7.6) | 358 | (5.8) | 411 | (4.8) | 537 | (5.0) | 593 | (4.8) | 625 | (4.8) |
| | **OECD total** | 323 | (2.3) | 357 | (1.9) | 416 | (1.7) | 553 | (1.3) | 612 | (1.4) | 644 | (1.3) |
| | **OECD average** | 346 | (1.1) | 379 | (0.9) | 436 | (0.7) | 561 | (0.6) | 615 | (0.8) | 645 | (0.9) |
| Partners | Argentina | 209 | (11.2) | 249 | (9.8) | 316 | (7.9) | 451 | (6.9) | 508 | (7.6) | 543 | (9.2) |
| | Azerbaijan | 403 | (2.4) | 419 | (2.2) | 443 | (2.5) | 505 | (3.0) | 536 | (3.6) | 556 | (5.2) |
| | Brazil | 225 | (6.4) | 255 | (4.5) | 308 | (3.0) | 427 | (3.7) | 487 | (5.8) | 530 | (8.3) |
| | Bulgaria | 251 | (8.3) | 287 | (7.2) | 345 | (6.1) | 481 | (6.8) | 543 | (8.4) | 583 | (11.0) |
| | Chile | 273 | (5.6) | 302 | (4.3) | 350 | (4.4) | 470 | (5.1) | 527 | (6.6) | 561 | (7.7) |
| | Colombia | 226 | (8.4) | 258 | (5.6) | 311 | (4.9) | 428 | (4.6) | 482 | (3.8) | 515 | (6.1) |
| | Croatia | 332 | (4.3) | 361 | (3.3) | 410 | (3.0) | 524 | (3.3) | 576 | (3.6) | 605 | (3.8) |
| | Estonia | 381 | (5.9) | 411 | (4.3) | 461 | (3.5) | 570 | (3.3) | 618 | (3.2) | 646 | (4.1) |
| | Hong Kong-China | 386 | (6.1) | 423 | (6.4) | 486 | (4.5) | 614 | (3.1) | 665 | (3.5) | 692 | (4.8) |
| | Indonesia | 265 | (5.6) | 293 | (3.9) | 336 | (4.2) | 444 | (9.3) | 498 | (9.4) | 528 | (10.3) |
| | Israel | 266 | (11.2) | 304 | (6.9) | 368 | (5.4) | 518 | (4.7) | 581 | (5.0) | 615 | (4.7) |
| | Jordan | 244 | (5.7) | 279 | (4.3) | 330 | (3.4) | 441 | (3.9) | 489 | (5.0) | 519 | (5.8) |
| | Kyrgyzstan | 175 | (5.1) | 204 | (5.0) | 253 | (3.6) | 363 | (4.2) | 423 | (5.9) | 465 | (7.6) |
| | Latvia | 347 | (5.6) | 378 | (5.2) | 432 | (3.6) | 542 | (3.2) | 590 | (3.4) | 619 | (4.2) |
| | Liechtenstein | 367 | (9.7) | 402 | (11.1) | 464 | (10.0) | 588 | (5.2) | 643 | (9.5) | 677 | (10.6) |
| | Lithuania | 338 | (4.9) | 369 | (4.3) | 426 | (3.3) | 549 | (3.6) | 602 | (4.9) | 632 | (4.6) |
| | Macao-China | 384 | (3.6) | 416 | (3.1) | 467 | (2.1) | 585 | (2.0) | 632 | (2.4) | 660 | (3.3) |
| | Montenegro | 261 | (3.3) | 291 | (3.0) | 342 | (2.0) | 456 | (2.4) | 510 | (2.4) | 543 | (3.6) |
| | Qatar | 187 | (2.9) | 212 | (2.2) | 257 | (1.3) | 368 | (1.7) | 438 | (2.7) | 486 | (3.0) |
| | Romania | 278 | (6.5) | 307 | (7.4) | 358 | (5.5) | 470 | (4.9) | 523 | (7.1) | 557 | (7.7) |
| | Russian Federation | 331 | (5.4) | 363 | (4.8) | 416 | (4.2) | 535 | (5.1) | 592 | (5.3) | 625 | (5.5) |
| | Serbia | 282 | (6.2) | 318 | (5.0) | 375 | (4.4) | 498 | (3.8) | 553 | (3.9) | 584 | (4.4) |
| | Slovenia | 361 | (2.7) | 390 | (2.1) | 441 | (2.4) | 566 | (2.1) | 623 | (2.7) | 654 | (3.8) |
| | Chinese Taipei | 373 | (7.2) | 409 | (6.2) | 477 | (6.1) | 625 | (3.3) | 677 | (3.4) | 707 | (3.9) |
| | Thailand | 289 | (4.8) | 317 | (3.5) | 362 | (3.3) | 470 | (2.9) | 524 | (3.7) | 558 | (4.6) |
| | Tunisia | 219 | (4.9) | 250 | (3.9) | 301 | (3.7) | 427 | (5.5) | 488 | (7.8) | 522 | (7.7) |
| | Uruguay | 261 | (4.1) | 296 | (4.4) | 360 | (3.5) | 495 | (3.5) | 551 | (5.5) | 587 | (5.6) |

Note: Values that are statistically significant are indicated in bold (see Annex A3).
StatLink ⟐ http://dx.doi.org/10.1787/142183565744

Pour consulter la version française intégrale de ce tableau, suivre ce lien :
StatLink ⟐ http://dx.doi.org/10.1787/152754053448

[Part 1/3]

**Table 6.3a** Trends in reading since PISA 2000

Tableau 6.3a Évolution des performances en compréhension de l'écrit depuis PISA 2000

| | | Reading score in PISA 2006 | Differences in reading performance between PISA 2003 and PISA 2000 (PISA 2003 – PISA 2000) | | | | | | | |
|---|---|---|---|---|---|---|---|---|---|---|
| | | | All students | | Males | | Females | | Gender difference (M – F) | |
| | | | Dif. | S.E. | Dif. | S.E. | Dif. | S.E. | Dif. | S.E. |
| OECD | Australia | 513 | -3 | (6.7) | -7 | (7.2) | -1 | (7.6) | -6 | (6.5) |
| | Austria | 490 | -1 | (7.0) | -9 | (7.9) | 5 | (7.8) | *-14* | (7.8) |
| | Belgium | 501 | 0 | (6.9) | -3 | (7.8) | 1 | (8.0) | -4 | (7.9) |
| | Canada | 527 | -6 | (5.8) | -5 | (6.0) | -6 | (5.9) | 1 | (2.6) |
| | Czech Republic | 483 | -3 | (6.8) | 0 | (7.9) | -6 | (7.4) | 6 | (6.8) |
| | Denmark | 494 | -5 | (6.5) | -6 | (6.9) | -5 | (6.7) | -1 | (4.4) |
| | Finland | 547 | -3 | (6.1) | 1 | (6.5) | -6 | (6.3) | *7* | (3.7) |
| | France | 488 | -9 | (6.5) | *-14* | (7.4) | -5 | (6.8) | *-9* | (5.6) |
| | Germany | 495 | 7 | (6.8) | 3 | (7.5) | 11 | (7.6) | -7 | (7.0) |
| | Greece | 460 | -2 | (8.3) | -3 | (9.5) | -2 | (8.1) | 0 | (6.5) |
| | Hungary | 482 | 2 | (7.1) | 3 | (8.2) | 2 | (7.5) | 1 | (6.9) |
| | Iceland | 484 | **-15** | (5.7) | **-25** | (6.2) | -7 | (6.1) | **-18** | (4.7) |
| | Ireland | 517 | *-11* | (6.7) | -12 | (7.5) | -11 | (7.4) | 0 | (6.4) |
| | Italy | 469 | *-12* | (6.8) | -14 | (9.0) | *-13* | (7.2) | -1 | (9.3) |
| | Japan | 498 | **-24** | (8.4) | **-21** | (10.2) | **-28** | (8.6) | 7 | (8.4) |
| | Korea | 556 | 9 | (6.6) | 7 | (7.5) | *14* | (7.8) | -7 | (8.2) |
| | Luxembourg | 479 | m | m | m | m | m | m | m | m |
| | Mexico | 410 | **-22** | (7.5) | **-23** | (8.1) | **-22** | (8.0) | -1 | (6.2) |
| | Netherlands | 507 | m | m | m | m | m | m | m | m |
| | New Zealand | 521 | -7 | (6.5) | 1 | (7.4) | **-17** | (7.3) | **18** | (7.7) |
| | Norway | 484 | -6 | (6.6) | -10 | (7.3) | -4 | (6.9) | -6 | (5.5) |
| | Poland | 508 | **17** | (7.5) | **15** | (8.8) | **19** | (8.3) | -3 | (7.9) |
| | Portugal | 472 | 7 | (7.9) | 1 | (8.4) | 12 | (8.0) | **-12** | (5.0) |
| | Slovak Republic | 466 | m | m | m | m | m | m | m | m |
| | Spain | 461 | *-12* | (6.5) | **-21** | (7.3) | -6 | (6.5) | **-15** | (5.0) |
| | Sweden | 507 | -2 | (6.2) | -3 | (6.5) | -3 | (6.5) | 0 | (4.2) |
| | Switzerland | 499 | 5 | (7.5) | 2 | (8.4) | 7 | (7.6) | -6 | (6.3) |
| | Turkey | 447 | m | m | m | m | m | m | m | m |
| | United Kingdom | 495 | m | m | m | m | m | m | m | m |
| | United States | m | -9 | (9.4) | -10 | (10.6) | -7 | (8.9) | -3 | (5.3) |
| | **OECD average** | 492 | -4 | (5.4) | -6 | (5.4) | -3 | (5.4) | -3 | (5.4) |
| Partners | Argentina | 374 | m | m | m | m | m | m | m | m |
| | Brazil | 393 | 7 | (7.7) | -3 | (8.8) | *15* | (7.5) | **-18** | (5.5) |
| | Bulgaria | 402 | m | m | m | m | m | m | m | m |
| | Chile | 442 | m | m | m | m | m | m | m | m |
| | Hong Kong-China | 536 | **-16** | (7.1) | **-24** | (8.9) | -8 | (7.3) | *-16* | (8.2) |
| | Indonesia | 393 | 11 | (7.5) | 9 | (7.3) | 13 | (8.1) | -4 | (4.4) |
| | Israel | 439 | m | m | m | m | m | m | m | m |
| | Latvia | 479 | **32** | (8.3) | **38** | (8.9) | **24** | (8.4) | 14 | (6.0) |
| | Liechtenstein | 510 | **42** | (7.6) | **48** | (11.6) | **34** | (10.8) | 14 | (16.6) |
| | Macao-China | 492 | m | m | m | m | m | m | m | m |
| | Romania | 396 | m | m | m | m | m | m | m | m |
| | Russian Federation | 440 | **-20** | (7.8) | *-15* | (8.4) | **-25** | (7.6) | 10 | (4.9) |
| | Thailand | 417 | -11 | (6.8) | -10 | (7.6) | -8 | (6.8) | -2 | (5.5) |
| | Tunisia | 380 | m | m | m | m | m | m | m | m |
| | Uruguay | 413 | m | m | m | m | m | m | m | m |

Note: Differences that are statistically significant at the 95% confidence level are indicated in bold and at the 90% confidence level are indicated in bold italic (see Annex A3).

*StatLink* ᴬᴿˢᴬ http://dx.doi.org/10.1787/142183565744

Pour consulter la version française intégrale de ce tableau, suivre ce lien :
*StatLink* ᴬᴿˢᴬ http://dx.doi.org/10.1787/152754053448

[Part 2/3]
**Table 6.3a  Trends in reading since PISA 2000**

Tableau 6.3a  Évolution des performances en compréhension de l'écrit depuis PISA 2000

| | | Differences in reading performance between PISA 2006 and PISA 2000 (PISA 2006 – PISA 2000) | | | | | | | |
| | | All students | | Males | | Females | | Gender difference (M – F) | |
| | | Dif. | S.E. | Dif. | S.E. | Dif. | S.E. | Dif. | S.E. |
|---|---|---|---|---|---|---|---|---|---|
| OECD | Australia | -15 | (6.4) | -18 | (7.1) | -14 | (7.2) | -3 | (6.5) |
| | Austria | -2 | (7.0) | -7 | (7.9) | 4 | (8.4) | -11 | (8.3) |
| | Belgium | -6 | (6.8) | -10 | (7.7) | -3 | (7.8) | -7 | (7.7) |
| | Canada | -7 | (5.8) | -8 | (6.0) | -8 | (5.8) | 0 | (2.8) |
| | Czech Republic | -9 | (6.9) | -10 | (8.2) | -1 | (7.7) | -8 | (7.8) |
| | Denmark | -2 | (6.4) | -6 | (6.8) | -1 | (6.7) | -5 | (4.6) |
| | Finland | 0 | (6.0) | 1 | (6.4) | 1 | (6.2) | 1 | (3.9) |
| | France | -17 | (7.0) | -21 | (8.0) | -14 | (6.9) | -6 | (5.6) |
| | Germany | 11 | (7.1) | 7 | (7.9) | *14* | (7.7) | -7 | (6.5) |
| | Greece | *-14* | (8.1) | -24 | (9.7) | -5 | (7.6) | -20 | (7.5) |
| | Hungary | 2 | (7.2) | -1 | (8.2) | 7 | (7.7) | -8 | (7.1) |
| | Iceland | -22 | (5.5) | -28 | (6.1) | -19 | (5.9) | *-9* | (4.6) |
| | Ireland | -9 | (6.9) | -13 | (7.9) | -8 | (7.2) | -5 | (6.7) |
| | Italy | -19 | (6.3) | -22 | (7.9) | -18 | (6.7) | -3 | (8.1) |
| | Japan | -24 | (8.1) | -25 | (10.0) | -24 | (9.0) | -1 | (10.0) |
| | Korea | 31 | (6.7) | 20 | (7.8) | 41 | (7.7) | -21 | (8.4) |
| | Luxembourg | m | m | m | m | m | m | m | m |
| | Mexico | *-11* | (6.7) | -18 | (7.4) | -5 | (6.9) | -13 | (5.0) |
| | Netherlands | m | m | m | m | m | m | m | m |
| | New Zealand | -8 | (6.4) | -5 | (7.4) | *-14* | (7.2) | 8 | (7.8) |
| | Norway | -21 | (6.5) | -24 | (7.3) | -21 | (6.6) | -3 | (5.2) |
| | Poland | 29 | (7.2) | 26 | (8.5) | 30 | (7.9) | -4 | (7.6) |
| | Portugal | 2 | (7.6) | -2 | (8.3) | 6 | (7.7) | -8 | (5.3) |
| | Slovak Republic | m | m | m | m | m | m | m | m |
| | Spain | -32 | (6.1) | -38 | (6.5) | -27 | (6.1) | -11 | (3.8) |
| | Sweden | -9 | (6.4) | -11 | (6.9) | -8 | (6.6) | -4 | (4.2) |
| | Switzerland | 5 | (7.2) | 4 | (7.7) | 5 | (7.5) | -1 | (4.9) |
| | Turkey | m | m | m | m | m | m | m | m |
| | United Kingdom | m | m | m | m | m | m | m | m |
| | United States | m | m | m | m | m | m | m | m |
| | **OECD average** | -6 | (5.1) | *-10* | (5.1) | -3 | (5.1) | -6 | (5.0) |
| Partners | Argentina | -45 | (13.2) | -48 | (12.4) | -38 | (15.2) | -10 | (12.9) |
| | Brazil | -3 | (7.0) | -12 | (7.7) | 3 | (7.1) | -15 | (5.0) |
| | Bulgaria | -28 | (9.8) | -34 | (10.3) | -23 | (10.6) | -11 | (8.4) |
| | Chile | 33 | (7.9) | 38 | (8.9) | 30 | (8.7) | 8 | (8.0) |
| | Hong Kong-China | *11* | (6.3) | 3 | (7.7) | 18 | (6.8) | -16 | (7.6) |
| | Indonesia | 22 | (8.7) | 24 | (10.7) | 22 | (8.0) | 2 | (7.2) |
| | Israel | -14 | (10.8) | -26 | (13.6) | 0 | (10.5) | -26 | (11.4) |
| | Latvia | 21 | (8.2) | 22 | (8.6) | 19 | (8.1) | 3 | (5.3) |
| | Liechtenstein | 28 | (7.6) | 18 | (11.7) | 31 | (10.6) | -14 | (16.5) |
| | Macao-China | m | m | m | m | m | m | m | m |
| | Romania | -32 | (7.7) | -47 | (8.0) | -17 | (8.3) | -30 | (5.9) |
| | Russian Federation | -22 | (7.8) | -23 | (8.3) | -23 | (7.7) | 0 | (4.3) |
| | Thailand | -14 | (6.5) | -21 | (7.5) | -8 | (6.6) | -13 | (6.0) |
| | Tunisia | m | m | m | m | m | m | m | m |
| | Uruguay | m | m | m | m | m | m | m | m |

Note: Differences that are statistically significant at the 95% confidence level are indicated in bold and at the 90% confidence level are indicated in bold italic (see Annex A3).
*StatLink* http://dx.doi.org/10.1787/142183565744

Pour consulter la version française intégrale de ce tableau, suivre ce lien :
*StatLink* http://dx.doi.org/10.1787/152754053448

[Part 3/3]

**Table 6.3a** Trends in reading since PISA 2000

Tableau 6.3a  Évolution des performances en compréhension de l'écrit depuis PISA 2000

| | | Differences in reading performance between PISA 2006 and PISA 2003 (PISA 2006 – PISA 2003) | | | | | | | |
|---|---|---|---|---|---|---|---|---|---|
| | | All students | | Males | | Females | | Gender difference (M – F) | |
| | | Dif. | S.E. | Dif. | S.E. | Dif. | S.E. | Dif. | S.E. |
| *OECD* | Australia | **-13** | (5.4) | *-11* | (6.1) | **-14** | (5.6) | 2 | (5.1) |
| | Austria | 0 | (7.1) | 1 | (8.0) | -1 | (8.3) | 3 | (7.9) |
| | Belgium | -6 | (6.0) | -7 | (7.1) | -4 | (6.6) | -3 | (7.0) |
| | Canada | -1 | (5.4) | -3 | (5.7) | -2 | (5.4) | 0 | (3.1) |
| | Czech Republic | -6 | (7.0) | -10 | (7.9) | 4 | (8.3) | *-14* | (7.9) |
| | Denmark | 2 | (6.2) | 0 | (6.6) | 5 | (6.4) | -4 | (4.3) |
| | Finland | 3 | (5.2) | 0 | (5.7) | 7 | (5.4) | *-7* | (3.9) |
| | France | -8 | (6.6) | -6 | (7.8) | -10 | (6.7) | 3 | (6.3) |
| | Germany | 4 | (7.1) | 4 | (8.1) | 4 | (7.4) | 0 | (6.0) |
| | Greece | *-13* | (7.3) | **-21** | (8.8) | -2 | (6.9) | **-19** | (7.0) |
| | Hungary | 1 | (6.1) | -4 | (6.6) | 5 | (6.7) | -9 | (5.6) |
| | Iceland | -7 | (5.1) | -3 | (5.8) | **-13** | (5.5) | *9* | (4.8) |
| | Ireland | 2 | (6.3) | -1 | (7.2) | 4 | (6.9) | -5 | (6.7) |
| | Italy | -7 | (5.9) | -8 | (7.6) | -6 | (6.3) | -2 | (7.2) |
| | Japan | 0 | (7.0) | -4 | (8.9) | 4 | (8.0) | -8 | (9.4) |
| | Korea | **22** | (6.6) | *13* | (7.4) | **27** | (7.6) | *-14* | (8.1) |
| | Luxembourg | 0 | (4.9) | 1 | (5.6) | 0 | (5.3) | 1 | (4.6) |
| | Mexico | 11 | (6.8) | 4 | (7.3) | 17 | (7.0) | **-12** | (5.0) |
| | Netherlands | -6 | (6.1) | -8 | (6.9) | -5 | (6.3) | -3 | (5.2) |
| | New Zealand | -1 | (5.9) | -6 | (6.5) | 4 | (6.6) | -10 | (6.3) |
| | Norway | **-15** | (6.2) | *-13* | (6.8) | **-17** | (6.5) | 3 | (5.0) |
| | Poland | *11* | (6.0) | 11 | (6.6) | *11* | (6.2) | -1 | (4.7) |
| | Portugal | -5 | (6.8) | -3 | (7.6) | -7 | (6.8) | 4 | (5.0) |
| | Slovak Republic | -3 | (6.3) | -7 | (7.2) | 2 | (6.8) | -9 | (6.4) |
| | Spain | **-20** | (5.6) | **-17** | (6.4) | **-21** | (5.6) | 4 | (4.4) |
| | Sweden | -7 | (6.1) | -8 | (6.6) | -5 | (6.4) | -4 | (4.5) |
| | Switzerland | 0 | (6.3) | 2 | (7.0) | -2 | (6.4) | 5 | (5.4) |
| | Turkey | 6 | (8.4) | 1 | (9.6) | 12 | (8.7) | -10 | (7.3) |
| | United Kingdom | m | m | m | m | m | m | m | m |
| | United States | m | m | m | m | m | m | m | m |
| | **OECD average** | **-2** | **(4.6)** | **-4** | **(4.6)** | **0** | **(4.6)** | **-4** | **(4.5)** |
| *Partners* | Argentina | m | m | m | m | m | m | m | m |
| | Brazil | -10 | (7.4) | -8 | (8.5) | -11 | (7.1) | 3 | (4.9) |
| | Bulgaria | m | m | m | m | m | m | m | m |
| | Chile | m | m | m | m | m | m | m | m |
| | Hong Kong-China | **27** | (6.3) | **26** | (7.8) | **26** | (6.4) | 0 | (7.1) |
| | Indonesia | 11 | (8.2) | 15 | (10.4) | 9 | (7.3) | 6 | (6.9) |
| | Israel | m | m | m | m | m | m | m | m |
| | Latvia | -11 | (6.9) | **-17** | (7.7) | -5 | (6.7) | **-11** | (5.3) |
| | Liechtenstein | **-15** | (6.9) | **-30** | (11.5) | -3 | (10.1) | -27 | (16.7) |
| | Macao-China | -5 | (5.1) | *-11* | (6.0) | 1 | (5.5) | **-13** | (5.3) |
| | Romania | m | m | m | m | m | m | m | m |
| | Russian Federation | -2 | (7.4) | -8 | (8.1) | 2 | (7.2) | *-9* | (5.0) |
| | Thailand | -3 | (5.9) | -11 | (7.0) | 1 | (6.2) | **-12** | (6.2) |
| | Tunisia | 6 | (6.6) | -1 | (7.2) | *11* | (6.8) | **-12** | (5.1) |
| | Uruguay | **-22** | (6.6) | **-25** | (7.7) | **-19** | (6.9) | -6 | (6.8) |

Note: Differences that are statistically significant at the 95% confidence level are indicated in bold and at the 90% confidence level are indicated in bold italic (see Annex A3).
StatLink ⟐ http://dx.doi.org/10.1787/142183565744

Pour consulter la version française intégrale de ce tableau, suivre ce lien :
StatLink ⟐ http://dx.doi.org/10.1787/152754053448

[Part 1/1]
**Table 6.3b** **Trends in mathematics since PISA 2003**

Tableau 6.3b  Évolution des performances en mathématiques depuis PISA 2003

| | Mathematics score in PISA 2006 | Differences in mathematics performance between PISA 2006 and PISA 2003 (PISA 2006 – PISA 2003) | | | | | | | |
| | | All students | | Males | | Females | | Gender difference (M – F) | |
| | | Dif. | S.E. | Dif. | S.E. | Dif. | S.E. | Dif. | S.E. |
|---|---|---|---|---|---|---|---|---|---|
| Australia | 520 | -4 | (3.4) | 0 | (4.6) | **-9** | (3.9) | **9** | (5.1) |
| Austria | 505 | 0 | (5.2) | 7 | (6.1) | -8 | (5.9) | **15** | (6.4) |
| Belgium | 520 | **-9** | (4.0) | *-9* | (5.5) | **-9** | (4.9) | -1 | (6.8) |
| Canada | 527 | *-5* | (3.0) | *-7* | (3.4) | **-10** | (3.1) | 3 | (2.9) |
| Czech Republic | 510 | -7 | (5.2) | -9 | (6.1) | -5 | (6.7) | -4 | (7.5) |
| Denmark | 513 | -1 | (4.0) | -5 | (4.7) | 2 | (4.4) | -6 | (4.2) |
| Finland | 548 | 4 | (3.3) | 6 | (3.9) | 2 | (3.6) | 4 | (3.7) |
| France | 496 | **-15** | (4.3) | **-16** | (5.5) | **-14** | (4.6) | -2 | (5.6) |
| Germany | 504 | 1 | (5.3) | 5 | (6.2) | -5 | (5.7) | *11* | (5.7) |
| Greece | 459 | **14** | (5.1) | 7 | (6.6) | **21** | (5.1) | **-15** | (5.8) |
| Hungary | 491 | 1 | (4.3) | 2 | (5.0) | 0 | (5.1) | 2 | (5.6) |
| Iceland | 506 | **-10** | (2.7) | -4 | (3.7) | **-15** | (3.4) | **11** | (4.7) |
| Ireland | 501 | -1 | (4.0) | -3 | (5.0) | 0 | (4.9) | -3 | (5.9) |
| Italy | 462 | -4 | (4.1) | -5 | (5.6) | -4 | (4.9) | -1 | (6.8) |
| Japan | 523 | **-11** | (5.4) | -6 | (7.6) | **-17** | (6.5) | 11 | (9.3) |
| Korea | 547 | 5 | (5.2) | 0 | (7.0) | **14** | (7.2) | -14 | (9.3) |
| Luxembourg | 490 | -3 | (2.0) | -4 | (2.9) | -3 | (2.8) | -1 | (4.0) |
| Mexico | 406 | **20** | (4.9) | **19** | (5.6) | **21** | (5.3) | -2 | (4.7) |
| Netherlands | 531 | *-7* | (4.3) | -3 | (5.3) | **-11** | (4.7) | 8 | (5.1) |
| New Zealand | 522 | -1 | (3.6) | -3 | (4.4) | 1 | (5.0) | -4 | (6.1) |
| Norway | 490 | -5 | (3.8) | -5 | (4.5) | -5 | (4.3) | 0 | (4.5) |
| Poland | 495 | 5 | (3.8) | 7 | (4.3) | 3 | (4.2) | 3 | (4.1) |
| Portugal | 466 | 0 | (4.8) | 1 | (5.8) | -1 | (4.9) | 3 | (4.6) |
| Slovak Republic | 492 | -6 | (4.6) | -8 | (5.6) | -4 | (5.2) | -4 | (5.9) |
| Spain | 480 | -5 | (3.6) | -5 | (4.5) | -5 | (3.7) | 0 | (3.7) |
| Sweden | 502 | *-7* | (3.8) | *-7* | (4.2) | -6 | (4.5) | -1 | (4.4) |
| Switzerland | 530 | 3 | (4.8) | 2 | (6.0) | 5 | (5.3) | -3 | (5.6) |
| Turkey | 424 | 1 | (8.4) | -4 | (9.8) | 6 | (8.5) | -9 | (7.7) |
| United Kingdom | 495 | m | m | m | m | m | m | m | m |
| United States | 474 | **-9** | (5.2) | -7 | (5.9) | **-10** | (5.2) | 2 | (4.1) |
| **OECD average** | **498** | -2 | (1.6) | -2 | (1.7) | -2 | (1.7) | 0 | (1.7) |
| Brazil | 370 | **13** | (5.8) | **15** | (7.1) | **12** | (5.5) | 2 | (4.9) |
| Hong Kong-China | 547 | -3 | (5.4) | 3 | (7.7) | -9 | (6.1) | 12 | (8.6) |
| Indonesia | 391 | **31** | (7.0) | **38** | (9.3) | **24** | (6.2) | *14* | (8.0) |
| Latvia | 486 | 3 | (5.0) | 4 | (6.1) | 2 | (5.0) | 2 | (5.0) |
| Liechtenstein | 525 | *-11* | (6.1) | **-25** | (10.4) | 4 | (9.5) | *-29* | (16.0) |
| Macao-China | 525 | -2 | (3.5) | -8 | (5.4) | 3 | (3.9) | -10 | (6.5) |
| Russian Federation | 476 | 7 | (5.9) | 5 | (7.1) | 10 | (5.9) | -5 | (5.5) |
| Thailand | 417 | 0 | (4.0) | -1 | (5.7) | 1 | (4.5) | -3 | (6.0) |
| Tunisia | 365 | 7 | (4.9) | 9 | (5.3) | 5 | (5.5) | 3 | (4.4) |
| Uruguay | 427 | 5 | (4.4) | 5 | (5.5) | 4 | (5.1) | 1 | (5.9) |

*OECD*

*Partners*

Note: Differences that are statistically significant at the 95% confidence level are indicated in bold and at the 90% confidence level are indicated in bold italic (see Annex A3).
*StatLink* ◼◼▣◼ http://dx.doi.org/10.1787/142183565744

Pour consulter la version française intégrale de ce tableau, suivre ce lien :
*StatLink* ◼◼▣◼ http://dx.doi.org/10.1787/152754053448

[Part 1/3]

**Table 6.3c** Differences in percentiles in reading between PISA 2000, PISA 2003 and PISA 2006

Tableau 6.3c  Différences observées en compréhension de l'écrit entre centiles de PISA 2000, PISA 2003 et PISA 2006

| | | Differences observed in the percentiles in reading between PISA 2003 and PISA 2000 (PISA 2003 – PISA 2000) | | | | | | | | | | |
|---|---|---|---|---|---|---|---|---|---|---|---|---|
| | | 5th | | 10th | | 25th | | 75th | | 90th | | 95th | |
| | | Dif. | S.E. | Dif. | S.E. | Dif. | S.E. | Dif. | S.E. | Dif. | S.E. | Dif. | S.E. |
| OECD | Australia | -2 | (8.7) | 1 | (7.8) | 6 | (7.5) | -8 | (7.5) | -12 | (7.3) | *-13* | (7.6) |
| | Austria | -4 | (11.0) | -5 | (10.1) | -5 | (8.0) | 2 | (7.6) | 4 | (7.5) | 4 | (8.2) |
| | Belgium | -8 | (14.3) | 1 | (12.3) | 3 | (9.5) | 0 | (6.2) | 2 | (6.3) | 3 | (6.4) |
| | Canada | 2 | (7.2) | 0 | (6.6) | 0 | (6.1) | *-11* | (5.9) | **-16** | (6.0) | **-18** | (6.5) |
| | Czech Republic | 0 | (13.4) | -6 | (10.0) | -6 | (7.6) | -2 | (7.2) | -3 | (7.3) | -2 | (7.5) |
| | Denmark | 12 | (10.5) | 9 | (8.6) | 4 | (7.4) | *-13* | (6.7) | **-16** | (6.6) | **-18** | (7.5) |
| | Finland | 9 | (9.3) | 8 | (8.0) | 2 | (6.5) | -9 | (6.1) | *-12* | (6.4) | **-15** | (6.8) |
| | France | **-24** | (11.3) | -14 | (10.2) | -8 | (8.0) | -5 | (6.5) | -5 | (6.6) | -5 | (7.2) |
| | Germany | 11 | (12.3) | 5 | (10.7) | 2 | (9.0) | 9 | (7.0) | 4 | (6.8) | 2 | (7.3) |
| | Greece | -17 | (11.5) | -9 | (11.7) | -3 | (10.5) | 3 | (8.2) | 5 | (8.6) | 6 | (9.6) |
| | Hungary | 3 | (9.8) | 7 | (8.7) | 8 | (8.2) | -2 | (7.7) | -1 | (7.7) | -1 | (9.1) |
| | Iceland | **-29** | (9.7) | **-21** | (8.0) | **-17** | (6.5) | **-12** | (6.1) | -9 | (7.0) | -8 | (7.4) |
| | Ireland | 3 | (11.0) | 0 | (9.5) | -8 | (7.8) | **-16** | (7.0) | **-19** | (7.3) | **-22** | (7.1) |
| | Italy | **-36** | (13.2) | **-26** | (10.4) | **-17** | (8.0) | -5 | (6.7) | -3 | (6.3) | -1 | (6.7) |
| | Japan | **-56** | (14.6) | **-52** | (12.9) | **-40** | (10.3) | -8 | (7.8) | -1 | (8.5) | 3 | (8.3) |
| | Korea | -9 | (9.6) | -5 | (8.7) | 3 | (7.3) | **16** | (6.6) | **26** | (7.3) | **30** | (8.0) |
| | Luxembourg | m | m | m | m | m | m | m | m | m | m | m | m |
| | Mexico | **-46** | (9.2) | **-37** | (8.4) | **-25** | (8.1) | *-15* | (8.4) | -14 | (9.7) | -14 | (9.9) |
| | Netherlands | m | m | m | m | m | m | m | m | m | m | m | m |
| | New Zealand | 1 | (11.0) | -1 | (8.7) | -7 | (7.6) | -10 | (6.7) | -9 | (7.5) | -11 | (8.8) |
| | Norway | 1 | (10.0) | 0 | (8.9) | -6 | (7.9) | -9 | (6.9) | -6 | (7.3) | -4 | (8.0) |
| | Poland | **26** | (12.0) | **31** | (10.0) | **22** | (8.6) | 12 | (8.6) | 13 | (9.1) | 15 | (9.1) |
| | Portugal | 11 | (10.5) | 14 | (10.8) | 15 | (9.8) | 2 | (7.8) | 0 | (7.6) | -3 | (7.7) |
| | Slovak Republic | m | m | m | m | m | m | m | m | m | m | m | m |
| | Spain | **-31** | (9.8) | **-25** | (8.8) | **-16** | (7.8) | -5 | (6.5) | 0 | (6.5) | 5 | (6.8) |
| | Sweden | -5 | (9.2) | -2 | (7.9) | -3 | (7.0) | 0 | (6.8) | 1 | (6.7) | 3 | (7.1) |
| | Switzerland | 14 | (9.6) | *18* | (9.7) | 12 | (8.9) | -2 | (8.0) | -6 | (8.6) | -8 | (9.1) |
| | Turkey | m | m | m | m | m | m | m | m | m | m | m | m |
| | United Kingdom | m | m | m | m | m | m | m | m | m | m | m | m |
| | United States | -1 | (14.4) | -2 | (13.6) | -7 | (11.1) | -9 | (9.4) | -14 | (9.1) | *-18* | (9.8) |
| | **OECD average** | -7 | (5.7) | -5 | (5.6) | -4 | (5.5) | -4 | (5.4) | -4 | (5.4) | -4 | (5.4) |
| Partners | Argentina | m | m | m | m | m | m | m | m | m | m | m | m |
| | Brazil | **-42** | (10.3) | **-32** | (10.2) | -11 | (8.4) | **27** | (8.1) | **35** | (8.5) | **41** | (10.3) |
| | Bulgaria | m | m | m | m | m | m | m | m | m | m | m | m |
| | Chile | m | m | m | m | m | m | m | m | m | m | m | m |
| | Hong Kong-China | -14 | (14.4) | -17 | (11.2) | *-16* | (8.3) | **-15** | (6.6) | **-16** | (6.7) | **-17** | (7.2) |
| | Indonesia | 4 | (9.0) | 5 | (8.3) | 11 | (7.8) | 11 | (8.7) | 14 | (9.9) | 17 | (10.8) |
| | Israel | m | m | m | m | m | m | m | m | m | m | m | m |
| | Latvia | **52** | (12.7) | **50** | (11.1) | **41** | (10.0) | **24** | (8.2) | *16* | (9.1) | 15 | (9.6) |
| | Liechtenstein | **55** | (22.5) | **55** | (17.4) | **48** | (14.1) | **37** | (9.7) | **35** | (14.8) | **35** | (17.3) |
| | Macao-China | m | m | m | m | m | m | m | m | m | m | m | m |
| | Romania | m | m | m | m | m | m | m | m | m | m | m | m |
| | Russian Federation | **-24** | (11.1) | **-22** | (9.8) | **-19** | (9.1) | **-20** | (8.0) | **-21** | (8.2) | **-20** | (8.8) |
| | Thailand | -8 | (8.7) | -11 | (8.0) | **-15** | (7.3) | -11 | (7.2) | -6 | (8.4) | -5 | (9.3) |
| | Tunisia | m | m | m | m | m | m | m | m | m | m | m | m |
| | Uruguay | m | m | m | m | m | m | m | m | m | m | m | m |

Note: Differences that are statistically significant at the 95% confidence level are indicated in bold and at the 90% confidence level are indicated in bold italic (see Annex A3).

StatLink ᴹˢᴾ http://dx.doi.org/10.1787/142183565744

Pour consulter la version française intégrale de ce tableau, suivre ce lien :
StatLink ᴹˢᴾ http://dx.doi.org/10.1787/152754053448

[Part 2/3]

**Table 6.3c** **Differences in percentiles in reading between PISA 2000, PISA 2003 and PISA 2006**

Tableau 6.3c  Différences observées en compréhension de l'écrit entre centiles de PISA 2000, PISA 2003 et PISA 2006

| | | Differences observed in the percentiles in reading between PISA 2006 and PISA 2000 (PISA 2006 – PISA 2000) | | | | | | | | | | |
|---|---|---|---|---|---|---|---|---|---|---|---|---|
| | | 5th | | 10th | | 25th | | 75th | | 90th | | 95th | |
| | | Dif. | S.E. | Dif. | S.E. | Dif. | S.E. | Dif. | S.E. | Dif. | S.E. | Dif. | S.E. |
| *OECD* | Australia | -5 | (7.7) | -6 | (7.4) | -5 | (7.1) | **-23** | (7.2) | **-27** | (7.1) | **-29** | (7.2) |
| | Austria | -19 | (14.3) | -11 | (12.1) | -8 | (8.2) | 6 | (7.1) | 8 | (7.0) | 10 | (7.5) |
| | Belgium | -11 | (15.2) | -7 | (13.1) | -4 | (9.5) | -6 | (6.0) | -3 | (6.0) | -2 | (6.2) |
| | Canada | *-13* | (7.9) | -8 | (6.8) | -4 | (6.2) | -7 | (5.8) | -8 | (6.0) | -7 | (6.8) |
| | Czech Republic | **-30** | (14.0) | **-32** | (9.9) | **-25** | (8.4) | 6 | (6.9) | 12 | (7.2) | *15* | (7.5) |
| | Denmark | 13 | (10.2) | 11 | (8.7) | 4 | (7.2) | -9 | (6.4) | *-12* | (6.8) | -12 | (8.0) |
| | Finland | 19 | (9.0) | 12 | (8.1) | 2 | (6.5) | -5 | (6.0) | -5 | (6.2) | -6 | (6.7) |
| | France | **-47** | (12.6) | **-35** | (10.3) | **-23** | (9.1) | -7 | (6.7) | -5 | (7.0) | -7 | (7.4) |
| | Germany | 15 | (14.4) | 14 | (11.4) | 12 | (9.0) | 10 | (6.8) | 5 | (6.8) | 7 | (7.0) |
| | Greece | **-33** | (15.0) | -21 | (13.0) | -11 | (10.3) | -12 | (7.7) | -12 | (8.3) | -12 | (9.0) |
| | Hungary | -2 | (11.8) | 5 | (8.9) | 8 | (8.7) | 0 | (7.6) | -3 | (8.0) | -3 | (8.8) |
| | Iceland | **-31** | (8.4) | **-28** | (7.4) | **-24** | (6.6) | **-20** | (6.1) | **-18** | (6.9) | **-15** | (7.3) |
| | Ireland | -3 | (10.2) | -6 | (9.8) | -11 | (8.1) | -11 | (7.3) | -8 | (7.3) | -8 | (7.4) |
| | Italy | **-55** | (11.5) | **-43** | (9.0) | **-26** | (7.4) | -6 | (6.4) | -2 | (6.4) | 0 | (6.5) |
| | Japan | **-49** | (14.2) | **-46** | (12.8) | **-38** | (10.5) | *-13* | (7.5) | -2 | (7.6) | 4 | (7.6) |
| | Korea | -3 | (12.1) | 7 | (10.4) | 21 | (7.5) | 44 | (6.6) | 55 | (7.2) | 59 | (7.7) |
| | Luxembourg | m | m | m | m | m | m | m | m | m | m | m | m |
| | Mexico | **-37** | (10.0) | **-26** | (8.6) | *-12* | (7.5) | -4 | (7.4) | -5 | (8.0) | -6 | (8.5) |
| | Netherlands | m | m | m | m | m | m | m | m | m | m | m | m |
| | New Zealand | 2 | (10.6) | -1 | (8.5) | -6 | (7.8) | *-11* | (6.5) | -10 | (7.2) | -10 | (9.1) |
| | Norway | *-19* | (10.6) | **-18** | (9.2) | **-24** | (8.1) | **-21** | (6.4) | **-18** | (7.1) | **-17** | (7.7) |
| | Poland | 31 | (11.1) | 31 | (9.6) | 27 | (8.4) | 28 | (8.4) | 30 | (8.9) | 32 | (8.7) |
| | Portugal | -1 | (11.0) | 2 | (10.2) | 5 | (9.7) | 2 | (7.6) | 2 | (7.5) | 3 | (7.8) |
| | Slovak Republic | m | m | m | m | m | m | m | m | m | m | m | m |
| | Spain | **-40** | (8.9) | **-36** | (8.2) | **-31** | (7.4) | **-30** | (6.1) | **-28** | (6.2) | **-26** | (6.4) |
| | Sweden | *-19* | (10.2) | -13 | (8.5) | -11 | (7.0) | -6 | (6.7) | -2 | (7.0) | 1 | (7.6) |
| | Switzerland | 15 | (9.8) | **18** | (9.1) | 13 | (8.2) | -1 | (7.5) | -6 | (8.2) | -9 | (8.5) |
| | Turkey | m | m | m | m | m | m | m | m | m | m | m | m |
| | United Kingdom | m | m | m | m | m | m | m | m | m | m | m | m |
| | United States | m | m | m | m | m | m | m | m | m | m | m | m |
| | **OECD average** | **-13** | (5.4) | *-10* | (5.3) | -7 | (5.1) | -4 | (5.1) | -3 | (5.1) | -2 | (5.1) |
| *Partners* | Argentina | **-78** | (19.2) | **-61** | (16.5) | **-53** | (16.7) | **-31** | (12.4) | **-27** | (12.9) | **-28** | (12.7) |
| | Brazil | **-31** | (12.3) | **-24** | (9.0) | *-13* | (7.4) | 8 | (7.2) | *16* | (8.4) | **23** | (10.1) |
| | Bulgaria | **-48** | (14.6) | **-44** | (12.2) | **-40** | (11.4) | -16 | (11.2) | -6 | (11.8) | -5 | (13.3) |
| | Chile | 15 | (11.3) | 18 | (9.3) | 23 | (8.5) | 41 | (9.0) | 51 | (9.2) | 54 | (9.5) |
| | Hong Kong-China | *21* | (12.1) | 13 | (10.6) | 8 | (7.2) | 10 | (6.2) | *12* | (6.4) | 14 | (6.9) |
| | Indonesia | 20 | (8.7) | 21 | (8.1) | 21 | (8.5) | 22 | (11.3) | 26 | (12.1) | 29 | (12.3) |
| | Israel | -22 | (19.5) | -25 | (16.1) | *-23* | (13.6) | -7 | (10.6) | 1 | (10.0) | 8 | (10.6) |
| | Latvia | 43 | (12.8) | 39 | (11.0) | 29 | (9.8) | 13 | (8.4) | 7 | (8.6) | 5 | (9.5) |
| | Liechtenstein | 27 | (21.7) | *30* | (16.6) | 33 | (14.5) | **26** | (10.0) | 22 | (13.6) | *32* | (15.0) |
| | Macao-China | m | m | m | m | m | m | m | m | m | m | m | m |
| | Romania | -17 | (11.9) | *-21* | (10.7) | -24 | (11.3) | **-37** | (8.0) | **-47** | (8.3) | **-51** | (8.8) |
| | Russian Federation | -25 | (11.2) | -24 | (9.5) | -23 | (9.1) | -21 | (7.9) | -23 | (7.5) | -23 | (8.8) |
| | Thailand | **-21** | (9.1) | **-20** | (7.9) | -18 | (7.2) | -10 | (6.6) | -4 | (7.7) | -5 | (8.3) |
| | Tunisia | m | m | m | m | m | m | m | m | m | m | m | m |
| | Uruguay | m | m | m | m | m | m | m | m | m | m | m | m |

Note: Differences that are statistically significant at the 95% confidence level are indicated in bold and at the 90% confidence level are indicated in bold italic (see Annex A3).

*StatLink* ᵐˢ¹ http://dx.doi.org/10.1787/142183565744

Pour consulter la version française intégrale de ce tableau, suivre ce lien :
*StatLink* ᵐˢ¹ http://dx.doi.org/10.1787/152754053448

[Part 3/3]

**Table 6.3c** Differences in percentiles in reading between PISA 2000, PISA 2003 and PISA 2006

Tableau 6.3c Différences observées en compréhension de l'écrit entre centiles de PISA 2000, PISA 2003 et PISA 2006

| | | 5th | | 10th | | 25th | | 75th | | 90th | | 95th | |
|---|---|---|---|---|---|---|---|---|---|---|---|---|---|
| | | Dif. | S.E. | Dif. | S.E. | Dif. | S.E. | Dif. | S.E. | Dif. | S.E. | Dif. | S.E. |
| OECD | Australia | -3 | (7.4) | -6 | (6.7) | *-11* | (5.9) | -15 | (5.6) | -16 | (6.0) | -17 | (6.0) |
| | Austria | -15 | (14.8) | -6 | (12.2) | -3 | (8.7) | 3 | (7.2) | 4 | (6.6) | 5 | (7.5) |
| | Belgium | -3 | (13.9) | -7 | (11.5) | -7 | (7.7) | -6 | (5.5) | -4 | (5.4) | -5 | (5.9) |
| | Canada | **-15** | (7.2) | -8 | (6.7) | -4 | (5.9) | 3 | (5.6) | 8 | (5.6) | *11* | (6.4) |
| | Czech Republic | **-31** | (14.8) | **-26** | (10.8) | **-20** | (9.0) | 8 | (7.1) | **15** | (7.2) | **17** | (7.4) |
| | Denmark | 1 | (10.2) | 2 | (8.1) | 0 | (7.2) | 3 | (6.1) | 4 | (6.4) | 6 | (7.8) |
| | Finland | 10 | (8.1) | 4 | (6.7) | 0 | (5.9) | 4 | (5.3) | 7 | (5.6) | 9 | (5.8) |
| | France | *-23* | (13.2) | *-21* | (11.2) | *-15* | (8.6) | -2 | (6.5) | 0 | (6.6) | -2 | (6.9) |
| | Germany | 4 | (12.2) | 9 | (11.4) | 10 | (9.3) | 1 | (6.6) | 1 | (6.6) | 5 | (7.0) |
| | Greece | -16 | (13.9) | -12 | (11.5) | -8 | (8.6) | **-15** | (7.3) | **-17** | (7.5) | **-18** | (8.4) |
| | Hungary | -6 | (11.8) | -2 | (7.9) | 0 | (7.3) | 3 | (6.6) | -2 | (7.1) | -1 | (8.1) |
| | Iceland | -2 | (9.1) | -7 | (7.7) | -7 | (5.9) | -8 | (5.7) | -9 | (6.2) | -7 | (6.9) |
| | Ireland | -6 | (10.7) | -6 | (8.5) | -3 | (7.5) | 5 | (6.6) | 11 | (6.4) | *14* | (7.0) |
| | Italy | *-19* | (11.4) | *-17* | (9.4) | -9 | (7.2) | -1 | (5.6) | 1 | (5.7) | 0 | (5.9) |
| | Japan | 7 | (10.9) | 6 | (10.3) | 2 | (9.3) | -5 | (6.7) | -1 | (7.4) | 2 | (7.5) |
| | Korea | 6 | (12.3) | 12 | (10.5) | **19** | (7.7) | **27** | (6.3) | **29** | (7.5) | **28** | (8.4) |
| | Luxembourg | 0 | (7.8) | 1 | (6.3) | 0 | (5.7) | 0 | (5.2) | 1 | (5.5) | 3 | (5.9) |
| | Mexico | 9 | (10.6) | 11 | (9.4) | 13 | (7.9) | *11* | (6.8) | 9 | (8.2) | 7 | (7.7) |
| | Netherlands | **-37** | (12.7) | **-22** | (9.4) | -8 | (7.7) | 2 | (6.0) | 2 | (5.8) | 4 | (7.0) |
| | New Zealand | 1 | (9.6) | 0 | (7.8) | 0 | (7.3) | -1 | (6.0) | -1 | (6.0) | 1 | (7.2) |
| | Norway | *-20* | (10.5) | **-18** | (8.5) | **-18** | (7.5) | *-12* | (6.5) | -12 | (7.2) | *-13* | (7.0) |
| | Poland | 4 | (9.1) | 0 | (8.1) | 5 | (6.7) | **16** | (6.3) | **17** | (6.6) | **18** | (7.5) |
| | Portugal | -12 | (11.0) | -12 | (10.5) | -10 | (8.7) | -1 | (6.7) | 2 | (6.8) | 6 | (7.5) |
| | Slovak Republic | **-29** | (10.1) | **-21** | (9.9) | -10 | (7.7) | 6 | (6.5) | 10 | (6.6) | **15** | (6.5) |
| | Spain | -9 | (8.6) | -10 | (7.8) | **-15** | (6.3) | **-25** | (5.8) | **-28** | (5.9) | **-31** | (6.1) |
| | Sweden | -14 | (10.7) | -11 | (8.3) | -8 | (6.8) | -6 | (6.3) | -3 | (6.7) | -2 | (7.6) |
| | Switzerland | 1 | (9.8) | 0 | (8.8) | 1 | (7.2) | 1 | (6.6) | 0 | (7.0) | -1 | (8.0) |
| | Turkey | 0 | (9.7) | 6 | (9.4) | 11 | (8.5) | 10 | (9.5) | 2 | (13.9) | -14 | (21.4) |
| | United Kingdom | m | m | m | m | m | m | m | m | m | m | m | m |
| | United States | m | m | m | m | m | m | m | m | m | m | m | m |
| | **OECD average** | *-8* | (4.8) | -6 | (4.7) | -4 | (4.6) | 0 | (4.6) | 1 | (4.6) | 1 | (4.6) |
| Partners | Argentina | m | m | m | m | m | m | m | m | m | m | m | m |
| | Brazil | 11 | (13.2) | 8 | (10.6) | -2 | (8.3) | **-19** | (7.9) | **-20** | (8.7) | *-19* | (10.7) |
| | Bulgaria | m | m | m | m | m | m | m | m | m | m | m | m |
| | Chile | m | m | m | m | m | m | m | m | m | m | m | m |
| | Hong Kong-China | **35** | (12.5) | **30** | (9.9) | **23** | (7.7) | **25** | (5.8) | **28** | (6.1) | **30** | (4.1) |
| | Indonesia | *16* | (8.7) | **16** | (8.3) | 10 | (7.9) | 11 | (10.3) | 13 | (10.7) | 12 | (10.5) |
| | Israel | m | m | m | m | m | m | m | m | m | m | m | m |
| | Latvia | -9 | (10.3) | -11 | (8.8) | -12 | (8.2) | -11 | (7.1) | -10 | (7.6) | -10 | (6.7) |
| | Liechtenstein | -28 | (21.0) | -25 | (16.4) | -15 | (14.2) | -11 | (9.8) | -13 | (16.4) | -3 | (18.3) |
| | Macao-China | **-22** | (8.8) | **-15** | (7.2) | -10 | (6.0) | 1 | (6.5) | 4 | (6.1) | *8* | (4.9) |
| | Romania | m | m | m | m | m | m | m | m | m | m | m | m |
| | Russian Federation | 0 | (11.0) | -2 | (9.6) | -4 | (9.1) | -1 | (7.2) | -2 | (7.3) | -2 | (6.8) |
| | Thailand | -13 | (8.9) | -10 | (6.8) | -3 | (6.4) | 1 | (6.4) | 2 | (7.4) | 0 | (6.4) |
| | Tunisia | 1 | (9.8) | 2 | (8.0) | 5 | (7.0) | 9 | (7.6) | 6 | (8.1) | 2 | (8.8) |
| | Uruguay | *-20* | (10.7) | **-19** | (9.4) | **-22** | (8.1) | **-21** | (7.3) | **-23** | (7.7) | **-25** | (8.3) |

Note: Differences that are statistically significant at the 95% confidence level are indicated in bold and at the 90% confidence level are indicated in bold italic (see Annex A3).

StatLink http://dx.doi.org/10.1787/142183565744

Pour consulter la version française intégrale de ce tableau, suivre ce lien :
StatLink http://dx.doi.org/10.1787/152754053448

[Part 1/1]

**Table 6.3d Differences in percentiles in mathematics between PISA 2003 and PISA 2006**

Tableau 6.3d Différences observées en culture mathématique entre centiles de PISA 2003 et PISA 2006

| | | 5th | | 10th | | 25th | | 75th | | 90th | | 95th | |
|---|---|---|---|---|---|---|---|---|---|---|---|---|---|
| | | Dif. | S.E. | Dif. | S.E. | Dif. | S.E. | Dif. | S.E. | Dif. | S.E. | Dif. | S.E. |
| **OECD** | Australia | *11* | (5.7) | *8* | (4.6) | 0 | (3.8) | **-11** | (3.8) | **-12** | (4.7) | **-12** | (5.5) |
| | Austria | -15 | (9.6) | -12 | (7.8) | -2 | (6.9) | 5 | (5.9) | 3 | (5.6) | -1 | (6.5) |
| | Belgium | 3 | (11.2) | 0 | (8.2) | -6 | (5.4) | **-13** | (3.8) | **-14** | (3.6) | **-16** | (3.8) |
| | Canada | -3 | (5.2) | -4 | (4.4) | -4 | (3.6) | **-7** | (3.4) | **-9** | (3.7) | **-8** | (4.9) |
| | Czech Republic | **-18** | (8.2) | **-15** | (7.5) | -9 | (6.4) | -2 | (6.3) | 3 | (6.6) | 5 | (7.8) |
| | Denmark | 10 | (6.8) | 8 | (6.4) | 3 | (5.2) | -7 | (4.4) | *-10* | (5.2) | **-13.1** | (6.5) |
| | Finland | 5 | (6.4) | 6 | (4.6) | 6 | (3.6) | 3 | (3.7) | 0 | (4.2) | -2 | (4.6) |
| | France | **-19** | (8.2) | **-20** | (7.9) | **-20** | (6.1) | **-10** | (5.0) | *-10* | (5.4) | *-10* | (5.5) |
| | Germany | 15 | (10.5) | 12 | (8.9) | 5 | (6.9) | -5 | (5.4) | 0 | (5.4) | 2 | (6.1) |
| | Greece | *16* | (9.2) | 17 | (7.7) | 17 | (6.2) | 14 | (6.0) | 9 | (6.8) | 9 | (7.0) |
| | Hungary | 8 | (8.1) | 7 | (5.9) | 5 | (4.4) | -5 | (5.8) | -2 | (7.0) | -1 | (7.5) |
| | Iceland | -5 | (5.5) | -5 | (4.7) | **-8** | (4.0) | **-11** | (3.4) | **-11** | (4.6) | **-12** | (6.0) |
| | Ireland | 6 | (6.7) | 3 | (5.6) | 0 | (5.5) | -3 | (4.5) | -6 | (5.0) | -7 | (4.6) |
| | Italy | -2 | (7.9) | -1 | (6.9) | -2 | (5.3) | -3 | (4.4) | -5 | (5.7) | -7 | (5.5) |
| | Japan | 9 | (10.5) | 2 | (8.5) | -5 | (7.2) | **-18** | (5.5) | **-22** | (7.2) | **-23** | (7.9) |
| | Korea | 5 | (8.5) | 4 | (7.7) | 6 | (5.8) | 6 | (6.2) | 5 | (8.9) | 4 | (10.7) |
| | Luxembourg | -7 | (6.0) | -4 | (4.6) | -4 | (3.2) | -2 | (3.0) | -2 | (4.4) | -1 | (4.7) |
| | Mexico | 20 | (8.6) | 23 | (7.0) | 22 | (5.9) | 19 | (5.5) | 17 | (5.9) | 19 | (7.1) |
| | Netherlands | -3 | (9.2) | -3 | (7.8) | -4 | (7.3) | **-12** | (4.9) | **-12** | (4.8) | **-12** | (5.7) |
| | New Zealand | 9 | (5.6) | 6 | (5.8) | 3 | (4.6) | -6 | (4.0) | -7 | (5.3) | *-9* | (4.8) |
| | Norway | -4 | (7.3) | -3 | (5.3) | -5 | (5.0) | *-8* | (4.6) | -5 | (5.0) | -6 | (5.0) |
| | Poland | 9 | (6.8) | 8 | (5.1) | 7 | (4.4) | 4 | (4.6) | 2 | (5.2) | -2 | (5.2) |
| | Portugal | -6 | (9.1) | -3 | (7.5) | -2 | (6.6) | 4 | (4.8) | 3 | (4.5) | 2 | (5.5) |
| | Slovak Republic | -10 | (9.9) | -8 | (7.9) | -3 | (6.0) | -7 | (5.3) | -8 | (5.8) | -8 | (6.4) |
| | Spain | -3 | (6.9) | -3 | (4.7) | -5 | (4.6) | -5 | (4.3) | -5 | (4.7) | -4 | (5.2) |
| | Sweden | 1 | (7.8) | 0 | (6.2) | -4 | (4.8) | **-11** | (4.7) | **-13** | (4.9) | **-13** | (6.5) |
| | Switzerland | 3 | (7.5) | 5 | (6.4) | 4 | (5.6) | 5 | (6.3) | -1 | (6.6) | -2 | (8.1) |
| | Turkey | 17 | (8.5) | 16 | (6.6) | 9 | (6.3) | -8 | (11.2) | -10 | (19.0) | -19 | (27.7) |
| | United Kingdom | m | m | m | m | m | m | m | m | m | m | m | m |
| | United States | 5 | (9.1) | 2 | (7.5) | -7 | (6.2) | **-12** | (6.2) | **-15** | (6.3) | *-13* | (7.2) |
| | **OECD average** | 2 | (2.0) | 2 | (1.8) | 0 | (1.7) | **-4** | (1.7) | **-5** | (1.8) | **-5** | (2.0) |
| **Partners** | Brazil | **23** | (8.8) | **22** | (7.1) | **22** | (5.7) | 8 | (7.4) | -1 | (11.2) | 2 | (14.1) |
| | Hong Kong-China | 12 | (12.7) | 6 | (10.4) | 1 | (8.4) | -8 | (5.0) | -7 | (5.5) | -8 | (6.4) |
| | Indonesia | **32** | (7.8) | **32** | (6.4) | **30** | (5.6) | **32** | (10.5) | **32** | (11.5) | **29** | (12.9) |
| | Latvia | 8 | (8.2) | 8 | (7.4) | 8 | (5.5) | -2 | (5.9) | -6 | (5.7) | -7 | (6.7) |
| | Liechtenstein | 5 | (22.0) | -6 | (14.9) | -5 | (12.6) | **-20** | (9.6) | -12 | (13.5) | -10 | (19.6) |
| | Macao-China | 2 | (9.6) | 1 | (6.9) | 0 | (5.1) | -2 | (4.7) | -7 | (6.2) | -8 | (9.0) |
| | Russian Federation | *13* | (7.8) | *12* | (7.0) | 10 | (6.6) | 5 | (7.2) | 4 | (7.6) | 3 | (8.3) |
| | Thailand | -1 | (6.4) | 1 | (4.9) | 2 | (4.6) | 0 | (4.9) | -2 | (6.1) | -2 | (8.0) |
| | Tunisia | -9 | (6.3) | -6 | (5.4) | -2 | (4.7) | **16** | (6.7) | **22** | (9.2) | **21** | (10.3) |
| | Uruguay | 6 | (6.1) | 5 | (6.0) | 7 | (5.5) | 5 | (5.3) | 1 | (7.1) | 4 | (7.4) |

*Multi-row spanning header:* Differences observed in the percentiles in mathematics between PISA 2006 and PISA 2003 (PISA 2006 – PISA 2003)

Note: Differences that are statistically significant at the 95% confidence level are indicated in bold and at the 90% confidence level are indicated in bold italic (see Annex A3).
StatLink http://dx.doi.org/10.1787/142183565744

Pour consulter la version française intégrale de ce tableau, suivre ce lien :
StatLink http://dx.doi.org/10.1787/152754053448

[Part 1/1]

**Table 6.4a** **Effect of the highest level of parents' education on student performance in science since PISA 2000**

Tableau 6.4a  Évolution de l'effet du niveau de formation le plus élevé des deux parents sur la performance des élèves en sciences depuis PISA 2000

| | | PISA 2000 | | | | | | PISA 2003 | | | | | | PISA 2006 | | | | | |
|---|---|---|---|---|---|---|---|---|---|---|---|---|---|---|---|---|---|---|---|
| | | Intercept | | Standardised regression coefficient | | Variance explained | | Intercept | | Standardised regression coefficient | | Variance explained | | Intercept | | Standardised regression coefficient | | Variance explained | |
| | | Score | S.E. | Score | S.E. | % | S.E. | Score | S.E. | Score | S.E. | % | S.E. | Score | S.E. | Score | S.E. | % | S.E. |
| OECD | Australia | 529 | (3.1) | 23 | (2.6) | 6 | (1.13) | 527 | (1.9) | 22 | (2.1) | 5 | (0.74) | 529 | (1.9) | 24 | (1.2) | 6 | (0.57) |
| | Austria | 507 | (3.0) | 27 | (2.6) | 8 | (1.47) | 493 | (2.9) | 24 | (2.3) | 6 | (1.19) | 512 | (3.6) | 24 | (3.0) | 6 | (1.71) |
| | Belgium | 501 | (3.7) | 24 | (2.1) | 5 | (1.04) | 518 | (2.1) | 30 | (1.7) | 8 | (0.92) | 515 | (2.2) | 30 | (1.6) | 9 | (1.03) |
| | Canada | 531 | (1.4) | 19 | (1.0) | 5 | (0.46) | 524 | (1.7) | 19 | (1.2) | 4 | (0.43) | 537 | (1.8) | 19 | (1.2) | 4 | (0.49) |
| | Czech Republic | 513 | (2.1) | 32 | (2.3) | 11 | (1.90) | 529 | (2.7) | 32 | (2.0) | 10 | (1.28) | 514 | (3.4) | 21 | (2.0) | 5 | (0.86) |
| | Denmark | 484 | (2.5) | 36 | (2.4) | 12 | (1.54) | 478 | (2.5) | 26 | (2.0) | 7 | (0.98) | 498 | (2.7) | 25 | (1.9) | 7 | (1.16) |
| | Finland | 539 | (2.5) | 15 | (2.1) | 3 | (0.85) | 549 | (1.9) | 15 | (1.5) | 3 | (0.55) | 564 | (1.9) | 17 | (1.4) | 4 | (0.62) |
| | France | 504 | (2.9) | 27 | (2.6) | 7 | (1.40) | 515 | (2.7) | 31 | (2.5) | 8 | (1.22) | 500 | (2.9) | 30 | (2.4) | 9 | (1.35) |
| | Germany | 494 | (2.4) | 37 | (2.5) | 13 | (2.04) | 516 | (3.2) | 39 | (2.1) | 14 | (1.35) | 520 | (3.2) | 30 | (1.8) | 9 | (1.07) |
| | Greece | 461 | (4.7) | 21 | (2.9) | 5 | (1.21) | 481 | (3.3) | 23 | (2.4) | 5 | (0.99) | 474 | (2.9) | 28 | (2.1) | 10 | (1.35) |
| | Hungary | 497 | (3.4) | 43 | (3.0) | 18 | (2.03) | 504 | (2.4) | 37 | (2.1) | 15 | (1.43) | 505 | (2.3) | 36 | (1.7) | 17 | (1.53) |
| | Iceland | 498 | (2.2) | 17 | (2.2) | 4 | (0.94) | 496 | (1.4) | 18 | (1.7) | 4 | (0.72) | 493 | (1.7) | 23 | (1.6) | 6 | (0.78) |
| | Ireland | 514 | (2.9) | 20 | (2.5) | 5 | (1.18) | 506 | (2.3) | 23 | (2.0) | 6 | (1.10) | 510 | (2.8) | 25 | (1.8) | 7 | (0.99) |
| | Italy | 479 | (2.9) | 23 | (2.8) | 6 | (1.27) | 487 | (2.9) | 28 | (2.4) | 7 | (1.04) | 476 | (1.9) | 21 | (1.4) | 5 | (0.62) |
| | Japan | m | m | m | m | m | m | 548 | (4.0) | 25 | (3.9) | 5 | (1.36) | 533 | (3.1) | 28 | (2.0) | 8 | (1.06) |
| | Korea | 552 | (2.5) | 17 | (2.2) | 4 | (1.12) | 539 | (3.5) | 22 | (2.4) | 5 | (0.98) | 523 | (3.1) | 19 | (2.5) | 4 | (1.04) |
| | Luxembourg | m | m | m | m | m | m | 488 | (1.7) | 29 | (1.7) | 8 | (0.92) | 489 | (1.2) | 35 | (1.4) | 13 | (0.96) |
| | Mexico | 422 | (2.7) | 26 | (2.8) | 12 | (2.27) | 405 | (2.9) | 25 | (2.3) | 8 | (1.28) | 410 | (2.3) | 27 | (1.8) | 11 | (1.39) |
| | Netherlands | m | m | m | m | m | m | 531 | (3.0) | 24 | (2.1) | 6 | (1.14) | 526 | (2.5) | 25 | (2.0) | 7 | (1.08) |
| | New Zealand | 534 | (2.5) | 21 | (2.3) | 5 | (0.97) | 528 | (2.2) | 24 | (1.8) | 5 | (0.82) | 537 | (2.5) | 26 | (1.6) | 6 | (0.72) |
| | Norway | 503 | (2.8) | 20 | (2.3) | 5 | (1.18) | 487 | (2.8) | 19 | (1.6) | 3 | (0.60) | 490 | (2.7) | 15 | (1.8) | 3 | (0.63) |
| | Poland | 487 | (4.6) | 29 | (3.4) | 10 | (2.00) | 498 | (2.5) | 32 | (2.0) | 10 | (1.05) | 499 | (2.0) | 31 | (1.5) | 12 | (1.06) |
| | Portugal | 461 | (3.6) | 22 | (3.0) | 6 | (1.64) | 469 | (3.0) | 25 | (2.0) | 7 | (1.08) | 475 | (2.7) | 27 | (1.8) | 9 | (1.18) |
| | Slovak Republic | m | m | m | m | m | m | 495 | (3.0) | 34 | (3.6) | 11 | (1.91) | 489 | (2.3) | 32 | (2.2) | 12 | (1.54) |
| | Spain | 493 | (2.4) | 31 | (2.4) | 11 | (1.55) | 489 | (2.2) | 27 | (2.0) | 7 | (0.99) | 490 | (2.1) | 27 | (1.5) | 9 | (0.97) |
| | Sweden | 514 | (2.4) | 14 | (1.9) | 2 | (0.62) | 509 | (2.5) | 21 | (1.7) | 4 | (0.66) | 506 | (2.3) | 17 | (1.4) | 3 | (0.56) |
| | Switzerland | 497 | (3.9) | 35 | (2.5) | 12 | (1.55) | 515 | (3.2) | 34 | (1.9) | 10 | (1.00) | 513 | (2.8) | 31 | (1.5) | 10 | (0.82) |
| | Turkey | m | m | m | m | m | m | 435 | (4.6) | 36 | (4.7) | 14 | (2.80) | 424 | (3.3) | 26 | (3.7) | 10 | (2.40) |
| | United Kingdom | m | m | m | m | m | m | m | m | m | m | m | m | 523 | (2.0) | 21 | (1.6) | 4 | (0.70) |
| | United States | 504 | (5.5) | 33 | (3.4) | 11 | (2.48) | 493 | (2.7) | 23 | (1.8) | 5 | (0.90) | 490 | (3.7) | 32 | (2.2) | 9 | (1.16) |
| | **OECD average** | 501 | (0.6) | 25 | (0.5) | 8 | (0.31) | 502 | (0.5) | 26 | (0.4) | 7 | (0.22) | 502 | (0.5) | 26 | (0.4) | 8 | (0.20) |
| Partners | Argentina | 398 | (6.4) | 31 | (4.1) | 8 | (2.13) | m | m | m | m | m | m | 392 | (5.1) | 33 | (2.6) | 10 | (1.48) |
| | Azerbaijan | m | m | m | m | m | m | m | m | m | m | m | m | 383 | (2.8) | 11 | (1.6) | 4 | (1.14) |
| | Brazil | 376 | (3.1) | 26 | (3.0) | 8 | (1.75) | 391 | (4.0) | 17 | (2.5) | 3 | (0.86) | 391 | (2.6) | 25 | (2.2) | 8 | (1.15) |
| | Bulgaria | 451 | (3.9) | 31 | (3.0) | 11 | (2.03) | m | m | m | m | m | m | 435 | (5.1) | 38 | (3.5) | 12 | (2.02) |
| | Chile | 415 | (3.0) | 29 | (2.2) | 10 | (1.34) | m | m | m | m | m | m | 439 | (3.1) | 36 | (2.0) | 15 | (1.49) |
| | Colombia | m | m | m | m | m | m | m | m | m | m | m | m | 388 | (3.2) | 20 | (2.0) | 6 | (1.13) |
| | Croatia | m | m | m | m | m | m | m | m | m | m | m | m | 493 | (2.4) | 18 | (1.5) | 5 | (0.73) |
| | Estonia | m | m | m | m | m | m | m | m | m | m | m | m | 532 | (2.4) | 13 | (1.7) | 2 | (0.62) |
| | Hong Kong-China | 541 | (2.8) | 21 | (2.3) | 6 | (1.36) | 541 | (4.1) | 13 | (2.0) | 2 | (0.61) | 542 | (2.4) | 19 | (1.8) | 5 | (0.88) |
| | Indonesia | 395 | (3.5) | 13 | (2.9) | 3 | (1.41) | 395 | (3.1) | 11 | (2.1) | 3 | (0.89) | 393 | (5.2) | 17 | (2.4) | 6 | (1.42) |
| | Israel | 441 | (8.2) | 39 | (4.2) | 10 | (2.01) | m | m | m | m | m | m | 458 | (3.6) | 24 | (2.0) | 5 | (0.60) |
| | Jordan | m | m | m | m | m | m | m | m | m | m | m | m | 423 | (2.5) | 25 | (1.9) | 8 | (1.07) |
| | Kyrgyzstan | m | m | m | m | m | m | m | m | m | m | m | m | 323 | (2.8) | 12 | (2.0) | 2 | (0.63) |
| | Latvia | 462 | (5.4) | 18 | (3.3) | 3 | (1.24) | 490 | (3.9) | 10 | (2.2) | 1 | (0.54) | 490 | (2.8) | 14 | (1.8) | 3 | (0.69) |
| | Liechtenstein | 478 | (7.2) | 27 | (7.6) | 8 | (5.20) | 527 | (4.5) | 33 | (5.2) | 10 | (3.26) | 525 | (4.0) | 35 | (5.3) | 14 | (4.03) |
| | Lithuania | m | m | m | m | m | m | m | m | m | m | m | m | 489 | (2.5) | 23 | (2.0) | 6 | (0.96) |
| | Macao-China | m | m | m | m | m | m | 525 | (3.0) | 8 | (3.0) | 1 | (0.65) | 511 | (1.1) | 9 | (1.4) | 1 | (0.44) |
| | Montenegro | m | m | m | m | m | m | m | m | m | m | m | m | 412 | (1.1) | 15 | (1.3) | 4 | (0.63) |
| | Qatar | m | m | m | m | m | m | m | m | m | m | m | m | 351 | (0.8) | 13 | (1.0) | 2 | (0.35) |
| | Romania | 443 | (3.5) | 15 | (3.3) | 3 | (1.12) | m | m | m | m | m | m | 418 | (4.1) | 17 | (3.2) | 4 | (1.71) |
| | Russian Federation | 461 | (4.6) | 16 | (2.3) | 3 | (0.73) | 490 | (3.8) | 20 | (2.0) | 4 | (0.79) | 480 | (3.5) | 16 | (2.0) | 3 | (0.72) |
| | Serbia | m | m | m | m | m | m | m | m | m | m | m | m | 436 | (2.8) | 19 | (1.7) | 5 | (0.81) |
| | Slovenia | m | m | m | m | m | m | m | m | m | m | m | m | 519 | (1.1) | 32 | (1.5) | 11 | (1.08) |
| | Chinese Taipei | m | m | m | m | m | m | m | m | m | m | m | m | 533 | (3.1) | 29 | (1.6) | 9 | (1.00) |
| | Thailand | 437 | (2.8) | 19 | (2.7) | 6 | (1.69) | 429 | (2.5) | 24 | (2.2) | 8 | (1.46) | 421 | (1.9) | 24 | (2.1) | 10 | (1.74) |
| | Tunisia | m | m | m | m | m | m | 385 | (2.5) | 15 | (2.8) | 3 | (1.06) | 386 | (2.7) | 16 | (2.8) | 4 | (1.26) |
| | Uruguay | m | m | m | m | m | m | 439 | (2.7) | 27 | (2.2) | 6 | (0.90) | 429 | (2.6) | 31 | (1.6) | 11 | (0.99) |

StatLink ⧉ http://dx.doi.org/10.1787/142183565744

Pour consulter la version française intégrale de ce tableau, suivre ce lien :
StatLink ⧉ http://dx.doi.org/10.1787/152754053448

[Part 1/1]

**Table 6.4b   Effect of the highest level of parents' education on student performance in reading since PISA 2000**

Tableau 6.4b   Évolution de l'effet du niveau de formation le plus élevé des deux parents sur la performance des élèves en compréhension de l'écrit depuis PISA 2000

| | PISA 2000 Intercept Score | S.E. | Std reg coef Score | S.E. | Var % | S.E. | PISA 2003 Intercept Score | S.E. | Std reg coef Score | S.E. | Var % | S.E. | PISA 2006 Intercept Score | S.E. | Std reg coef Score | S.E. | Var % | S.E. |
|---|---|---|---|---|---|---|---|---|---|---|---|---|---|---|---|---|---|---|
| Australia | 530 | (3.1) | 27 | (2.3) | 7 | (1.04) | 528 | (1.9) | 20 | (1.9) | 4 | (0.67) | 515 | (1.8) | 23 | (1.1) | 6 | (0.54) |
| Austria | 496 | (2.8) | 30 | (2.0) | 9 | (1.13) | 494 | (3.1) | 26 | (2.3) | 7 | (1.23) | 491 | (3.8) | 21 | (3.8) | 4 | (1.48) |
| Belgium | 512 | (3.2) | 24 | (2.2) | 5 | (1.15) | 518 | (2.3) | 28 | (1.8) | 7 | (0.92) | 506 | (2.9) | 29 | (2.0) | 7 | (0.97) |
| Canada | 536 | (1.4) | 20 | (1.0) | 5 | (0.39) | 532 | (1.5) | 14 | (1.0) | 3 | (0.35) | 529 | (2.2) | 19 | (1.3) | 4 | (0.53) |
| Czech Republic | 493 | (1.9) | 35 | (2.6) | 14 | (2.39) | 497 | (2.4) | 26 | (1.9) | 9 | (1.23) | 484 | (4.0) | 18 | (2.8) | 3 | (0.81) |
| Denmark | 500 | (2.0) | 35 | (1.6) | 13 | (1.19) | 495 | (2.4) | 24 | (1.8) | 7 | (1.01) | 496 | (2.9) | 21 | (1.9) | 6 | (0.98) |
| Finland | 548 | (2.5) | 17 | (1.5) | 3 | (0.59) | 544 | (1.6) | 15 | (1.3) | 4 | (0.58) | 548 | (2.0) | 16 | (1.4) | 4 | (0.63) |
| France | 508 | (2.4) | 22 | (1.6) | 6 | (0.90) | 500 | (2.3) | 26 | (2.4) | 8 | (1.31) | 493 | (3.7) | 25 | (2.5) | 6 | (1.20) |
| Germany | 492 | (2.2) | 37 | (3.3) | 12 | (1.95) | 506 | (3.0) | 34 | (2.1) | 11 | (1.31) | 501 | (3.8) | 30 | (2.0) | 8 | (1.05) |
| Greece | 475 | (4.7) | 23 | (2.6) | 6 | (1.17) | 472 | (3.6) | 22 | (2.4) | 4 | (0.91) | 460 | (3.7) | 25 | (2.6) | 6 | (1.16) |
| Hungary | 481 | (3.1) | 40 | (2.3) | 18 | (1.89) | 482 | (2.1) | 34 | (2.0) | 14 | (1.50) | 483 | (2.9) | 35 | (2.0) | 14 | (1.40) |
| Iceland | 510 | (1.5) | 19 | (1.6) | 4 | (0.72) | 493 | (1.6) | 13 | (1.8) | 2 | (0.54) | 487 | (2.0) | 21 | (1.8) | 5 | (0.77) |
| Ireland | 528 | (2.9) | 17 | (2.0) | 3 | (0.78) | 516 | (2.3) | 20 | (1.8) | 5 | (1.03) | 520 | (3.2) | 23 | (1.9) | 6 | (1.00) |
| Italy | 488 | (2.8) | 23 | (2.3) | 6 | (1.15) | 476 | (2.9) | 25 | (2.0) | 6 | (0.93) | 469 | (2.4) | 20 | (1.8) | 3 | (0.57) |
| Japan | m | m | m | m | m | m | 499 | (3.8) | 23 | (4.0) | 5 | (1.45) | 500 | (3.4) | 27 | (2.4) | 7 | (1.13) |
| Korea | 525 | (2.3) | 16 | (1.6) | 5 | (0.99) | 535 | (3.1) | 17 | (2.1) | 4 | (0.92) | 556 | (3.7) | 15 | (2.3) | 3 | (0.80) |
| Luxembourg | m | m | m | m | m | m | 485 | (1.5) | 28 | (1.5) | 8 | (0.89) | 482 | (1.4) | 33 | (1.5) | 11 | (0.93) |
| Mexico | 423 | (2.7) | 34 | (2.7) | 15 | (2.20) | 401 | (3.4) | 28 | (2.6) | 9 | (1.51) | 411 | (2.6) | 31 | (2.4) | 10 | (1.50) |
| Netherlands | m | m | m | m | m | m | 520 | (2.6) | 17 | (1.9) | 5 | (1.02) | 508 | (2.7) | 22 | (2.0) | 5 | (0.98) |
| New Zealand | 537 | (2.7) | 20 | (2.0) | 4 | (0.68) | 529 | (2.2) | 23 | (1.8) | 5 | (0.82) | 528 | (2.8) | 23 | (1.8) | 5 | (0.79) |
| Norway | 509 | (2.8) | 18 | (2.0) | 3 | (0.75) | 503 | (2.7) | 17 | (1.5) | 3 | (0.55) | 489 | (2.9) | 13 | (1.9) | 2 | (0.50) |
| Poland | 484 | (4.1) | 30 | (2.8) | 10 | (1.56) | 497 | (2.6) | 26 | (2.2) | 7 | (1.03) | 509 | (2.5) | 30 | (1.7) | 9 | (0.98) |
| Portugal | 472 | (4.0) | 25 | (2.7) | 7 | (1.41) | 479 | (3.4) | 21 | (2.4) | 5 | (1.12) | 474 | (3.2) | 30 | (2.2) | 9 | (1.25) |
| Slovak Republic | m | m | m | m | m | m | 470 | (2.6) | 27 | (2.4) | 9 | (1.45) | 467 | (2.9) | 31 | (2.9) | 9 | (1.58) |
| Spain | 495 | (2.1) | 28 | (1.5) | 11 | (1.15) | 483 | (2.3) | 21 | (2.1) | 5 | (0.90) | 463 | (1.9) | 23 | (1.6) | 7 | (0.92) |
| Sweden | 519 | (2.0) | 15 | (1.6) | 3 | (0.57) | 518 | (2.1) | 18 | (1.7) | 4 | (0.67) | 511 | (3.3) | 16 | (1.6) | 3 | (0.53) |
| Switzerland | 497 | (3.7) | 32 | (2.1) | 10 | (1.16) | 501 | (2.9) | 27 | (1.8) | 9 | (1.07) | 501 | (2.7) | 27 | (1.5) | 8 | (0.85) |
| Turkey | m | m | m | m | m | m | 441 | (4.6) | 33 | (4.5) | 12 | (2.69) | 447 | (3.8) | 23 | (3.5) | 6 | (1.82) |
| United Kingdom | m | m | m | m | m | m | m | m | m | m | m | m | 503 | (2.1) | 19 | (1.6) | 4 | (0.63) |
| United States | 509 | (5.1) | 30 | (2.7) | 8 | (1.68) | 497 | (2.9) | 22 | (1.7) | 5 | (0.83) | m | m | m | m | m | m |
| OECD average | 503 | (0.6) | 26 | (0.4) | 8 | (0.3) | 497 | (0.5) | 23 | (0.4) | 6 | (0.2) | 494 | (0.5) | 24 | (0.4) | 6 | (0.2) |
| Argentina | 419 | (8.0) | 34 | (3.8) | 10 | (2.05) | m | m | m | m | m | m | 375 | (6.3) | 30 | (3.1) | 6 | (1.22) |
| Azerbaijan | m | m | m | m | m | m | m | m | m | m | m | m | 353 | (3.1) | 14 | (2.2) | 4 | (1.11) |
| Brazil | 397 | (2.8) | 25 | (2.2) | 9 | (1.43) | 404 | (4.3) | 16 | (2.6) | 2 | (0.65) | 393 | (3.6) | 25 | (2.7) | 6 | (1.02) |
| Bulgaria | 433 | (4.1) | 35 | (3.1) | 12 | (1.96) | m | m | m | m | m | m | 404 | (5.8) | 40 | (4.1) | 12 | (2.10) |
| Chile | 410 | (3.1) | 33 | (2.0) | 14 | (1.60) | m | m | m | m | m | m | 443 | (3.9) | 36 | (2.8) | 12 | (1.59) |
| Colombia | m | m | m | m | m | m | m | m | m | m | m | m | 385 | (4.7) | 24 | (2.9) | 5 | (1.23) |
| Croatia | m | m | m | m | m | m | m | m | m | m | m | m | 478 | (2.8) | 16 | (1.6) | 3 | (0.63) |
| Estonia | m | m | m | m | m | m | m | m | m | m | m | m | 501 | (2.8) | 10 | (1.9) | 1 | (0.56) |
| Hong Kong-China | 526 | (2.7) | 19 | (2.2) | 5 | (1.14) | 511 | (3.5) | 10 | (2.0) | 1 | (0.58) | 536 | (2.3) | 15 | (1.9) | 3 | (0.87) |
| Indonesia | 373 | (3.4) | 17 | (2.6) | 5 | (1.60) | 382 | (3.2) | 11 | (2.1) | 2 | (0.77) | 393 | (5.4) | 17 | (2.5) | 5 | (1.40) |
| Israel | 460 | (7.9) | 34 | (3.4) | 10 | (1.89) | m | m | m | m | m | m | 444 | (4.5) | 21 | (2.2) | 3 | (0.56) |
| Jordan | m | m | m | m | m | m | m | m | m | m | m | m | 401 | (3.0) | 25 | (2.2) | 7 | (1.26) |
| Kyrgyzstan | m | m | m | m | m | m | m | m | m | m | m | m | 285 | (3.4) | 16 | (2.4) | 3 | (0.68) |
| Latvia | 460 | (5.2) | 16 | (2.5) | 3 | (0.76) | 491 | (3.7) | 7 | (2.1) | 1 | (0.37) | 480 | (3.5) | 15 | (2.3) | 3 | (0.76) |
| Liechtenstein | 488 | (4.8) | 28 | (5.3) | 9 | (3.71) | 527 | (3.7) | 24 | (5.1) | 7 | (3.14) | 514 | (3.9) | 30 | (5.2) | 10 | (3.79) |
| Lithuania | m | m | m | m | m | m | m | m | m | m | m | m | 471 | (2.8) | 22 | (2.1) | 5 | (0.96) |
| Macao-China | m | m | m | m | m | m | 497 | (2.2) | 4 | (2.2) | 0 | (0.38) | 493 | (1.1) | 7 | (1.7) | 1 | (0.42) |
| Montenegro | m | m | m | m | m | m | m | m | m | m | m | m | 392 | (1.3) | 16 | (1.5) | 3 | (0.61) |
| Qatar | m | m | m | m | m | m | m | m | m | m | m | m | 315 | (1.2) | 15 | (1.4) | 2 | (0.36) |
| Romania | 430 | (3.5) | 22 | (2.3) | 5 | (0.98) | m | m | m | m | m | m | 396 | (4.6) | 13 | (3.8) | 2 | (1.19) |
| Russian Federation | 463 | (3.9) | 14 | (1.8) | 2 | (0.59) | 443 | (3.6) | 19 | (1.8) | 4 | (0.80) | 440 | (4.2) | 15 | (2.1) | 3 | (0.69) |
| Serbia | m | m | m | m | m | m | m | m | m | m | m | m | 401 | (3.3) | 20 | (1.9) | 5 | (0.82) |
| Slovenia | m | m | m | m | m | m | m | m | m | m | m | m | 495 | (1.0) | 27 | (1.6) | 9 | (1.08) |
| Chinese Taipei | m | m | m | m | m | m | m | m | m | m | m | m | 497 | (3.0) | 25 | (1.5) | 9 | (1.03) |
| Thailand | 432 | (3.0) | 17 | (2.6) | 5 | (1.44) | 420 | (2.6) | 19 | (2.2) | 6 | (1.31) | 417 | (2.5) | 23 | (2.2) | 8 | (1.57) |
| Tunisia | m | m | m | m | m | m | 375 | (2.7) | 15 | (3.0) | 3 | (0.99) | 381 | (3.7) | 16 | (3.2) | 3 | (1.07) |
| Uruguay | m | m | m | m | m | m | 435 | (3.2) | 30 | (2.6) | 6 | (0.97) | 414 | (3.4) | 33 | (2.8) | 8 | (1.16) |

StatLink http://dx.doi.org/10.1787/142183565744

Pour consulter la version française intégrale de ce tableau, suivre ce lien :
StatLink http://dx.doi.org/10.1787/152754053448

[Part 1/1]

**Table 6.4c** **Effect of the highest level of parents' education on student performance in mathematics since PISA 2000**

Tableau 6.4c Évolution de l'effet du niveau de formation le plus élevé des deux parents sur la performance des élèves en mathématiques depuis PISA 2000

| | | PISA 2000 | | | | | | PISA 2003 | | | | | | PISA 2006 | | | | | |
|---|---|---|---|---|---|---|---|---|---|---|---|---|---|---|---|---|---|---|---|
| | | Intercept | | Standardised regression coefficient | | Variance explained | | Intercept | | Standardised regression coefficient | | Variance explained | | Intercept | | Standardised regression coefficient | | Variance explained | |
| | | Score | S.E. | Score | S.E. | % | S.E. | Score | S.E. | Score | S.E. | % | S.E. | Score | S.E. | Score | S.E. | % | S.E. |
| OECD | Australia | 535 | (3.1) | 27 | (2.6) | 9 | (1.5) | 526 | (2.0) | 19 | (2.1) | 4 | (0.8) | 522 | (2.0) | 21 | (1.2) | 6 | (0.6) |
| | Austria | 505 | (2.7) | 29 | (2.8) | 9 | (1.7) | 508 | (2.9) | 20 | (2.1) | 5 | (1.0) | 506 | (3.5) | 21 | (2.9) | 4 | (1.4) |
| | Belgium | 525 | (3.4) | 25 | (2.5) | 6 | (1.3) | 539 | (1.9) | 30 | (1.6) | 8 | (0.9) | 525 | (2.5) | 30 | (2.3) | 8 | (1.2) |
| | Canada | 535 | (1.3) | 18 | (1.0) | 4 | (0.5) | 537 | (1.5) | 17 | (1.1) | 4 | (0.5) | 529 | (1.8) | 15 | (1.1) | 3 | (0.4) |
| | Czech Republic | 498 | (2.3) | 35 | (2.1) | 13 | (1.9) | 523 | (2.8) | 32 | (2.0) | 12 | (1.4) | 511 | (3.4) | 24 | (2.1) | 6 | (1.0) |
| | Denmark | 517 | (2.2) | 28 | (2.4) | 11 | (1.5) | 517 | (2.3) | 24 | (1.8) | 7 | (1.0) | 515 | (2.4) | 21 | (1.8) | 6 | (1.1) |
| | Finland | 537 | (2.1) | 16 | (1.7) | 4 | (0.8) | 545 | (1.8) | 15 | (1.3) | 3 | (0.6) | 549 | (2.2) | 16 | (1.4) | 4 | (0.7) |
| | France | 520 | (2.4) | 20 | (2.2) | 5 | (1.1) | 514 | (2.2) | 26 | (1.8) | 8 | (1.1) | 500 | (2.7) | 28 | (2.2) | 9 | (1.3) |
| | Germany | 496 | (2.3) | 36 | (3.3) | 13 | (2.4) | 515 | (3.0) | 33 | (2.0) | 11 | (1.3) | 509 | (3.4) | 28 | (2.0) | 8 | (1.1) |
| | Greece | 448 | (5.3) | 27 | (4.0) | 6 | (1.7) | 445 | (3.3) | 23 | (2.3) | 6 | (1.1) | 459 | (2.6) | 29 | (2.2) | 10 | (1.4) |
| | Hungary | 490 | (3.0) | 44 | (2.6) | 21 | (2.1) | 490 | (2.4) | 40 | (2.1) | 19 | (1.6) | 492 | (2.4) | 40 | (1.9) | 19 | (1.6) |
| | Iceland | 517 | (2.2) | 17 | (2.7) | 4 | (1.3) | 516 | (1.4) | 17 | (1.4) | 3 | (0.6) | 507 | (1.8) | 23 | (1.6) | 7 | (0.9) |
| | Ireland | 504 | (2.5) | 17 | (2.1) | 4 | (1.0) | 504 | (2.1) | 23 | (1.6) | 7 | (1.0) | 503 | (2.5) | 22 | (1.7) | 7 | (1.1) |
| | Italy | 459 | (3.0) | 18 | (2.3) | 4 | (1.0) | 466 | (3.0) | 23 | (1.9) | 6 | (0.9) | 462 | (2.1) | 19 | (1.3) | 4 | (0.5) |
| | Japan | m | m | m | m | m | m | 535 | (3.9) | 24 | (3.9) | 6 | (1.6) | 525 | (3.0) | 28 | (2.1) | 10 | (1.2) |
| | Korea | 547 | (2.5) | 23 | (2.0) | 7 | (1.2) | 543 | (3.2) | 24 | (2.4) | 7 | (1.2) | 548 | (3.6) | 22 | (2.9) | 5 | (1.2) |
| | Luxembourg | m | m | m | m | m | m | 498 | (1.2) | 25 | (1.4) | 8 | (0.8) | 493 | (1.2) | 27 | (1.2) | 9 | (0.8) |
| | Mexico | 388 | (2.9) | 31 | (2.7) | 14 | (2.2) | 386 | (3.0) | 25 | (2.3) | 9 | (1.4) | 406 | (2.4) | 28 | (2.1) | 11 | (1.5) |
| | Netherlands | m | m | m | m | m | m | 546 | (2.7) | 22 | (2.0) | 6 | (1.2) | 532 | (2.4) | 21 | (1.8) | 6 | (1.0) |
| | New Zealand | 545 | (3.0) | 20 | (2.5) | 4 | (1.0) | 530 | (2.1) | 23 | (1.7) | 6 | (0.9) | 527 | (2.2) | 21 | (1.4) | 5 | (0.7) |
| | Norway | 502 | (2.8) | 14 | (2.6) | 2 | (0.9) | 498 | (2.3) | 17 | (1.4) | 4 | (0.6) | 493 | (2.5) | 13 | (1.5) | 2 | (0.5) |
| | Poland | 476 | (5.0) | 30 | (2.9) | 9 | (1.6) | 490 | (2.2) | 26 | (1.8) | 8 | (1.0) | 496 | (2.2) | 28 | (1.4) | 11 | (1.0) |
| | Portugal | 455 | (3.5) | 23 | (2.7) | 6 | (1.5) | 468 | (3.0) | 24 | (1.8) | 8 | (1.2) | 467 | (2.8) | 27 | (1.9) | 9 | (1.2) |
| | Slovak Republic | m | m | m | m | m | m | 499 | (2.7) | 31 | (2.5) | 11 | (1.5) | 492 | (2.5) | 32 | (2.9) | 12 | (1.9) |
| | Spain | 478 | (2.6) | 27 | (2.1) | 9 | (1.4) | 487 | (2.4) | 23 | (1.8) | 7 | (0.9) | 481 | (2.0) | 25 | (1.6) | 8 | (1.0) |
| | Sweden | 512 | (2.3) | 11 | (2.4) | 2 | (0.6) | 512 | (2.3) | 19 | (1.6) | 4 | (0.7) | 505 | (2.3) | 15 | (1.4) | 3 | (0.6) |
| | Switzerland | 532 | (3.9) | 31 | (2.5) | 10 | (1.5) | 528 | (3.0) | 29 | (1.6) | 9 | (0.9) | 531 | (2.8) | 28 | (1.5) | 8 | (0.8) |
| | Turkey | m | m | m | m | m | m | 424 | (5.3) | 39 | (5.3) | 14 | (2.8) | 424 | (4.2) | 30 | (4.4) | 10 | (2.4) |
| | United Kingdom | m | m | m | m | m | m | m | m | m | m | m | m | 501 | (2.0) | 17 | (1.3) | 4 | (0.6) |
| | United States | 498 | (5.9) | 31 | (2.6) | 10 | (2.1) | 484 | (2.6) | 23 | (1.4) | 6 | (0.8) | 475 | (3.6) | 27 | (2.0) | 9 | (1.2) |
| | **OECD average** | 501 | (0.6) | 25 | (0.5) | 8 | (0.3) | 502 | (0.5) | 25 | (0.4) | 7 | (0.2) | 500 | (0.5) | 24 | (0.4) | 7 | (0.2) |
| Partners | Argentina | 388 | (7.7) | 39 | (5.4) | 10 | (2.7) | m | m | m | m | m | m | 382 | (5.3) | 32 | (2.9) | 10 | (1.5) |
| | Azerbaijan | m | m | m | m | m | m | m | m | m | m | m | m | 476 | (2.3) | 2 | (1.3) | 0 | (0.3) |
| | Brazil | 335 | (3.3) | 30 | (3.6) | 10 | (2.1) | 358 | (4.5) | 20 | (2.8) | 4 | (1.0) | 370 | (2.7) | 28 | (2.6) | 9 | (1.3) |
| | Bulgaria | 433 | (4.9) | 34 | (3.7) | 10 | (2.0) | m | m | m | m | m | m | 414 | (5.2) | 35 | (3.6) | 12 | (2.0) |
| | Chile | 384 | (3.2) | 33 | (2.0) | 13 | (1.5) | m | m | m | m | m | m | 412 | (3.4) | 36 | (2.2) | 17 | (1.7) |
| | Colombia | m | m | m | m | m | m | m | m | m | m | m | m | 370 | (3.5) | 23 | (2.5) | 7 | (1.4) |
| | Croatia | m | m | m | m | m | m | m | m | m | m | m | m | 467 | (2.3) | 17 | (1.4) | 4 | (0.7) |
| | Estonia | m | m | m | m | m | m | m | m | m | m | m | m | 515 | (2.6) | 14 | (1.8) | 3 | (0.8) |
| | Hong Kong-China | 561 | (3.1) | 18 | (2.6) | 4 | (1.1) | 552 | (4.4) | 13 | (2.5) | 2 | (0.6) | 547 | (2.5) | 19 | (2.1) | 4 | (0.9) |
| | Indonesia | 369 | (3.9) | 17 | (3.6) | 4 | (1.6) | 361 | (3.8) | 12 | (2.5) | 2 | (0.8) | 391 | (5.1) | 18 | (2.8) | 5 | (1.4) |
| | Israel | 440 | (9.1) | 42 | (4.2) | 10 | (2.0) | m | m | m | m | m | m | 446 | (4.2) | 24 | (1.9) | 5 | (0.7) |
| | Jordan | m | m | m | m | m | m | m | m | m | m | m | m | 385 | (2.9) | 26 | (1.9) | 9 | (1.2) |
| | Kyrgyzstan | m | m | m | m | m | m | m | m | m | m | m | m | 311 | (3.3) | 15 | (1.9) | 3 | (0.7) |
| | Latvia | 464 | (4.4) | 14 | (3.0) | 2 | (0.8) | 484 | (3.8) | 11 | (1.9) | 2 | (0.5) | 487 | (2.9) | 17 | (1.9) | 4 | (0.9) |
| | Liechtenstein | 520 | (7.1) | 25 | (7.7) | 7 | (4.1) | 537 | (4.3) | 30 | (4.6) | 9 | (3.2) | 527 | (4.2) | 29 | (5.9) | 10 | (4.1) |
| | Lithuania | m | m | m | m | m | m | m | m | m | m | m | m | 487 | (2.7) | 26 | (1.9) | 8 | (1.1) |
| | Macao-China | m | m | m | m | m | m | 527 | (2.9) | 7 | (3.1) | 1 | (0.6) | 525 | (1.3) | 9 | (1.6) | 1 | (0.4) |
| | Montenegro | m | m | m | m | m | m | m | m | m | m | m | m | 400 | (1.4) | 17 | (1.7) | 4 | (0.8) |
| | Qatar | m | m | m | m | m | m | m | m | m | m | m | m | 319 | (1.1) | 18 | (1.1) | 4 | (0.5) |
| | Romania | 428 | (4.3) | 22 | (4.7) | 4 | (1.5) | m | m | m | m | m | m | 415 | (4.1) | 16 | (3.4) | 4 | (1.6) |
| | Russian Federation | 480 | (5.3) | 14 | (2.6) | 2 | (0.7) | 469 | (3.9) | 19 | (1.7) | 4 | (0.7) | 476 | (3.7) | 15 | (2.3) | 3 | (0.8) |
| | Serbia | m | m | m | m | m | m | m | m | m | m | m | m | 436 | (3.3) | 20 | (1.8) | 5 | (0.8) |
| | Slovenia | m | m | m | m | m | m | m | m | m | m | m | m | 505 | (1.1) | 30 | (1.6) | 12 | (1.3) |
| | Chinese Taipei | m | m | m | m | m | m | m | m | m | m | m | m | 550 | (3.5) | 30 | (2.0) | 9 | (1.1) |
| | Thailand | 433 | (3.3) | 21 | (2.9) | 7 | (1.6) | 417 | (2.9) | 22 | (2.5) | 7 | (1.5) | 417 | (2.2) | 25 | (2.0) | 9 | (1.5) |
| | Tunisia | m | m | m | m | m | m | 359 | (2.4) | 19 | (2.8) | 5 | (1.4) | 366 | (3.5) | 25 | (3.4) | 7 | (1.8) |
| | Uruguay | m | m | m | m | m | m | 423 | (3.0) | 27 | (2.4) | 7 | (1.2) | 428 | (2.5) | 33 | (1.8) | 11 | (1.1) |

StatLink http://dx.doi.org/10.1787/142183565744

Pour consulter la version française intégrale de ce tableau, suivre ce lien :
StatLink http://dx.doi.org/10.1787/152754053448

[Part 1/1]

**Table 6.5a** **Effect of the highest occupational status of parents on student performance in science since PISA 2000**

Tableau 6.5a Évolution de l'effet du statut professionnel le plus élevé des deux parents sur la performance des élèves en sciences depuis PISA 2000

| | | PISA 2000 | | | | | | PISA 2003 | | | | | | PISA 2006 | | | | |
|---|---|---|---|---|---|---|---|---|---|---|---|---|---|---|---|---|---|---|
| | | Intercept | | Standardised regression coefficient | | Variance explained | | Intercept | | Standardised regression coefficient | | Variance explained | | Intercept | | Standardised regression coefficient | | Variance explained |
| | Score | S.E. | Score | S.E. | % | S.E. | Score | S.E. | Score | S.E. | % | S.E. | Score | S.E. | Score | S.E. | % | S.E. |
| **OECD** | | | | | | | | | | | | | | | | | | |
| Australia | 530 | (3.1) | 26 | (2.4) | 8 | (1.47) | 529 | (1.8) | 31 | (1.4) | 9 | (0.75) | 530 | (1.9) | 29 | (1.1) | 9 | (0.63) |
| Austria | 506 | (2.5) | 33 | (2.3) | 12 | (1.56) | 493 | (2.7) | 34 | (1.7) | 13 | (1.14) | 512 | (3.6) | 33 | (2.4) | 12 | (1.42) |
| Belgium | 502 | (3.5) | 41 | (2.9) | 14 | (1.54) | 518 | (2.0) | 41 | (1.7) | 16 | (1.12) | 515 | (2.0) | 37 | (1.6) | 15 | (1.24) |
| Canada | 532 | (1.4) | 23 | (1.3) | 7 | (0.72) | 524 | (1.6) | 27 | (1.3) | 7 | (0.67) | 537 | (1.8) | 25 | (1.2) | 7 | (0.63) |
| Czech Republic | 513 | (2.1) | 36 | (2.1) | 15 | (1.49) | 529 | (2.7) | 31 | (1.8) | 10 | (1.11) | 516 | (3.2) | 37 | (1.9) | 14 | (1.13) |
| Denmark | 486 | (2.6) | 32 | (2.5) | 10 | (1.55) | 477 | (2.5) | 29 | (2.3) | 8 | (1.18) | 499 | (2.5) | 28 | (1.9) | 9 | (1.22) |
| Finland | 539 | (2.3) | 18 | (2.2) | 5 | (1.02) | 549 | (1.8) | 20 | (1.4) | 5 | (0.68) | 564 | (1.9) | 20 | (1.4) | 6 | (0.78) |
| France | 506 | (2.8) | 35 | (2.3) | 12 | (1.47) | 515 | (2.5) | 39 | (2.8) | 13 | (1.67) | 501 | (2.6) | 41 | (2.2) | 17 | (1.63) |
| Germany | 490 | (2.3) | 39 | (2.4) | 15 | (1.57) | 516 | (2.9) | 44 | (2.2) | 18 | (1.59) | 522 | (2.8) | 36 | (1.8) | 14 | (1.17) |
| Greece | 462 | (4.4) | 28 | (3.3) | 8 | (1.86) | 483 | (3.0) | 29 | (2.0) | 8 | (1.23) | 475 | (2.6) | 32 | (2.1) | 12 | (1.41) |
| Hungary | 499 | (3.3) | 41 | (3.1) | 17 | (2.16) | 507 | (2.5) | 35 | (2.2) | 13 | (1.46) | 507 | (2.3) | 32 | (1.9) | 13 | (1.41) |
| Iceland | 497 | (2.2) | 14 | (2.3) | 2 | (0.81) | 496 | (1.5) | 14 | (1.8) | 2 | (0.56) | 493 | (1.6) | 22 | (1.5) | 6 | (0.73) |
| Ireland | 515 | (2.8) | 28 | (2.1) | 9 | (1.30) | 508 | (2.2) | 31 | (2.1) | 11 | (1.48) | 512 | (2.6) | 27 | (1.7) | 8 | (1.02) |
| Italy | 479 | (2.9) | 24 | (2.1) | 6 | (1.06) | 488 | (2.9) | 32 | (2.1) | 9 | (1.00) | 477 | (1.8) | 27 | (1.5) | 8 | (0.84) |
| Japan | 565 | (7.2) | 8 | (2.8) | 1 | (0.55) | 552 | (3.9) | 20 | (2.8) | 4 | (0.87) | 535 | (3.3) | 16 | (1.8) | 3 | (0.58) |
| Korea | 554 | (2.4) | 17 | (2.5) | 5 | (1.31) | 540 | (3.4) | 20 | (2.8) | 4 | (1.08) | 523 | (3.2) | 15 | (2.1) | 3 | (0.74) |
| Luxembourg | m | m | m | m | m | m | 485 | (1.5) | 38 | (1.8) | 14 | (1.23) | 488 | (1.1) | 41 | (1.4) | 18 | (1.14) |
| Mexico | 423 | (2.7) | 27 | (2.6) | 12 | (2.26) | 407 | (2.8) | 24 | (2.1) | 8 | (1.28) | 412 | (2.2) | 28 | (1.8) | 12 | (1.40) |
| Netherlands | m | m | m | m | m | m | 531 | (2.8) | 33 | (2.0) | 12 | (1.25) | 529 | (2.1) | 35 | (1.8) | 14 | (1.28) |
| New Zealand | 532 | (2.2) | 32 | (2.5) | 11 | (1.53) | 522 | (2.2) | 33 | (1.7) | 10 | (0.99) | 535 | (2.4) | 35 | (1.7) | 11 | (1.01) |
| Norway | 503 | (2.6) | 24 | (2.3) | 7 | (1.29) | 487 | (2.6) | 31 | (1.9) | 9 | (1.02) | 491 | (2.6) | 26 | (1.7) | 8 | (1.01) |
| Poland | 489 | (4.5) | 32 | (2.8) | 11 | (1.87) | 499 | (2.4) | 36 | (1.8) | 12 | (1.21) | 499 | (2.1) | 29 | (1.5) | 11 | (0.96) |
| Portugal | 462 | (3.3) | 31 | (2.2) | 13 | (1.89) | 469 | (2.9) | 32 | (2.1) | 12 | (1.46) | 476 | (2.4) | 34 | (1.8) | 15 | (1.43) |
| Slovak Republic | m | m | m | m | m | m | 499 | (2.7) | 34 | (2.1) | 12 | (1.29) | 492 | (2.3) | 34 | (2.1) | 14 | (1.50) |
| Spain | 493 | (2.4) | 31 | (2.3) | 10 | (1.55) | 488 | (2.0) | 27 | (1.9) | 8 | (1.02) | 490 | (2.0) | 28 | (1.5) | 10 | (1.07) |
| Sweden | 514 | (2.3) | 25 | (1.8) | 8 | (1.05) | 509 | (2.3) | 30 | (2.0) | 8 | (1.03) | 506 | (2.2) | 29 | (1.5) | 10 | (0.90) |
| Switzerland | 498 | (3.6) | 40 | (2.5) | 16 | (1.83) | 516 | (3.2) | 34 | (1.9) | 10 | (0.99) | 513 | (2.7) | 34 | (1.6) | 12 | (1.03) |
| Turkey | m | m | m | m | m | m | 437 | (4.9) | 33 | (5.0) | 12 | (3.03) | 425 | (3.4) | 26 | (3.3) | 10 | (2.21) |
| United Kingdom | m | m | m | m | m | m | m | m | m | m | m | m | 520 | (1.9) | 36 | (1.6) | 12 | (1.09) |
| United States | 509 | (5.7) | 34 | (3.4) | 12 | (1.87) | 496 | (2.5) | 32 | (1.6) | 10 | (0.96) | 495 | (3.2) | 35 | (2.2) | 11 | (1.26) |
| **OECD average** | 504 | (0.7) | 29 | (0.5) | 10 | (0.30) | 502 | (0.5) | 31 | (0.4) | 10 | (0.23) | 503 | (0.5) | 30 | (0.3) | 11 | (0.22) |
| **Partners** | | | | | | | | | | | | | | | | | | |
| Argentina | 401 | (5.9) | 37 | (3.9) | 12 | (2.37) | m | m | m | m | m | m | 397 | (4.9) | 34 | (3.5) | 11 | (2.46) |
| Azerbaijan | m | m | m | m | m | m | m | m | m | m | m | m | 386 | (2.7) | 11 | (1.7) | 4 | (1.26) |
| Brazil | 378 | (3.1) | 27 | (3.4) | 9 | (2.07) | 394 | (3.5) | 34 | (3.0) | 12 | (2.01) | 393 | (2.4) | 32 | (2.3) | 13 | (1.63) |
| Bulgaria | 453 | (3.7) | 30 | (3.6) | 11 | (2.32) | m | m | m | m | m | m | 441 | (4.5) | 44 | (3.4) | 17 | (2.23) |
| Chile | 417 | (2.9) | 36 | (2.2) | 15 | (1.52) | m | m | m | m | m | m | 439 | (4.5) | 39 | (2.0) | 18 | (1.80) |
| Colombia | m | m | m | m | m | m | m | m | m | m | m | m | 390 | (3.2) | 23 | (2.0) | 7 | (1.29) |
| Croatia | m | m | m | m | m | m | m | m | m | m | m | m | 496 | (2.2) | 29 | (1.7) | 11 | (1.19) |
| Estonia | m | m | m | m | m | m | m | m | m | m | m | m | 532 | (2.3) | 26 | (1.5) | 10 | (1.04) |
| Hong Kong-China | 544 | (2.8) | 19 | (2.5) | 5 | (1.42) | 544 | (3.6) | 17 | (2.0) | 3 | (0.80) | 545 | (2.3) | 17 | (2.0) | 4 | (0.86) |
| Indonesia | 395 | (3.5) | 19 | (3.4) | 7 | (2.12) | 397 | (2.9) | 20 | (2.1) | 8 | (1.56) | 395 | (5.5) | 18 | (2.9) | 6 | (1.63) |
| Israel | 449 | (7.4) | 33 | (3.6) | 7 | (1.58) | m | m | m | m | m | m | 466 | (3.5) | 31 | (2.2) | 8 | (1.02) |
| Jordan | m | m | m | m | m | m | m | m | m | m | m | m | 433 | (2.5) | 26 | (1.9) | 9 | (1.19) |
| Kyrgyzstan | m | m | m | m | m | m | m | m | m | m | m | m | 326 | (2.7) | 21 | (2.3) | 6 | (1.16) |
| Latvia | 464 | (4.9) | 22 | (3.3) | 5 | (1.52) | 491 | (3.5) | 22 | (2.2) | 6 | (1.13) | 492 | (2.7) | 24 | (2.2) | 8 | (1.33) |
| Liechtenstein | 482 | (7.2) | 33 | (7.2) | 14 | (5.51) | 527 | (4.8) | 42 | (6.0) | 16 | (4.07) | 523 | (4.3) | 34 | (5.7) | 12 | (3.98) |
| Lithuania | m | m | m | m | m | m | m | m | m | m | m | m | 491 | (2.4) | 29 | (2.0) | 10 | (1.25) |
| Macao-China | m | m | m | m | m | m | 526 | (3.2) | 2 | (3.1) | 0 | (0.24) | 512 | (1.1) | 7 | (1.3) | 1 | (0.29) |
| Montenegro | m | m | m | m | m | m | m | m | m | m | m | m | 417 | (1.2) | 23 | (1.4) | 8 | (0.98) |
| Qatar | m | m | m | m | m | m | m | m | m | m | m | m | m | m | m | m | m | m |
| Romania | 443 | (3.4) | 17 | (2.6) | 3 | (0.94) | m | m | m | m | m | m | 422 | (3.8) | 32 | (3.2) | 16 | (3.03) |
| Russian Federation | 462 | (4.3) | 25 | (2.3) | 7 | (1.11) | 490 | (3.8) | 23 | (1.9) | 5 | (0.82) | 481 | (3.2) | 22 | (1.7) | 6 | (0.93) |
| Serbia | m | m | m | m | m | m | m | m | m | m | m | m | 437 | (2.5) | 29 | (1.6) | 12 | (1.11) |
| Slovenia | m | m | m | m | m | m | m | m | m | m | m | m | 521 | (1.2) | 37 | (1.4) | 14 | (1.11) |
| Chinese Taipei | m | m | m | m | m | m | m | m | m | m | m | m | 537 | (3.1) | 24 | (1.6) | 7 | (0.83) |
| Thailand | 440 | (2.9) | 20 | (2.1) | 6 | (1.37) | 431 | (2.4) | 25 | (2.1) | 9 | (1.43) | 424 | (2.0) | 26 | (1.8) | 12 | (1.58) |
| Tunisia | m | m | m | m | m | m | 386 | (2.5) | 24 | (2.8) | 8 | (1.74) | 387 | (2.3) | 26 | (2.9) | 10 | (2.12) |
| Uruguay | m | m | m | m | m | m | 444 | (2.6) | 34 | (2.4) | 10 | (1.39) | 430 | (2.6) | 35 | (1.5) | 13 | (1.06) |

StatLink ᵐˢᵖ http://dx.doi.org/10.1787/142183565744

Pour consulter la version française intégrale de ce tableau, suivre ce lien :
StatLink ᵐˢᵖ http://dx.doi.org/10.1787/152754053448

[Part 1/1]

**Table 6.5b** **Effect of the highest occupational status of parents on student performance in reading since PISA 2000**

Tableau 6.5b  Évolution de l'effet du statut professionnel le plus élevé des deux parents sur la performance des élèves en compréhension de l'écrit depuis PISA 2000

| | PISA 2000 | | | | | | PISA 2003 | | | | | | PISA 2006 | | | | | |
|---|---|---|---|---|---|---|---|---|---|---|---|---|---|---|---|---|---|---|
| | Intercept | | Standardised regression coefficient | | Variance explained | | Intercept | | Standardised regression coefficient | | Variance explained | | Intercept | | Standardised regression coefficient | | Variance explained | |
| | Score | S.E. | Score | S.E. | % | S.E. | Score | S.E. | Score | S.E. | % | S.E. | Score | S.E. | Score | S.E. | % | S.E. |
| Australia | 532 | (2.9) | 32 | (2.1) | 10 | (1.34) | 531 | (1.7) | 29 | (1.5) | 9 | (0.81) | a | a | a | a | a | a |
| Austria | 494 | (2.5) | 34 | (2.0) | 13 | (1.26) | 494 | (2.8) | 39 | (2.0) | 15 | (1.32) | 516 | (1.7) | 28 | (1.0) | 9 | (0.64) |
| Belgium | 513 | (2.9) | 39 | (2.3) | 14 | (1.38) | 517 | (2.2) | 38 | (1.9) | 14 | (1.10) | 492 | (3.7) | 36 | (2.6) | 11 | (1.37) |
| Canada | 537 | (1.3) | 25 | (1.0) | 7 | (0.53) | 533 | (1.4) | 21 | (1.2) | 6 | (0.62) | 506 | (2.6) | 37 | (1.8) | 12 | (1.12) |
| Czech Republic | 494 | (1.8) | 37 | (1.4) | 15 | (1.15) | 497 | (2.4) | 28 | (1.7) | 10 | (1.16) | 530 | (2.2) | 24 | (1.3) | 7 | (0.65) |
| Denmark | 503 | (1.9) | 29 | (1.9) | 9 | (1.20) | 494 | (2.5) | 23 | (1.6) | 7 | (0.90) | 487 | (3.7) | 39 | (2.3) | 13 | (1.16) |
| Finland | 548 | (2.4) | 21 | (1.8) | 6 | (0.79) | 544 | (1.5) | 18 | (1.3) | 5 | (0.71) | 498 | (2.7) | 24 | (1.8) | 8 | (1.09) |
| France | 510 | (2.2) | 32 | (2.0) | 13 | (1.45) | 500 | (2.2) | 33 | (2.3) | 12 | (1.50) | 548 | (2.0) | 19 | (1.4) | 6 | (0.78) |
| Germany | 488 | (2.1) | 43 | (2.0) | 16 | (1.47) | 505 | (2.8) | 37 | (2.0) | 14 | (1.26) | 493 | (3.5) | 37 | (2.4) | 13 | (1.44) |
| Greece | 476 | (4.3) | 31 | (2.8) | 10 | (1.58) | 475 | (3.3) | 30 | (2.0) | 8 | (1.20) | 503 | (3.4) | 35 | (2.0) | 11 | (1.05) |
| Hungary | 483 | (2.3) | 38 | (2.3) | 17 | (1.78) | 485 | (2.1) | 33 | (2.0) | 13 | (1.45) | 462 | (3.4) | 33 | (2.6) | 11 | (1.41) |
| Iceland | 509 | (1.4) | 20 | (1.5) | 5 | (0.66) | 494 | (1.6) | 12 | (1.8) | 1 | (0.46) | 486 | (3.0) | 33 | (2.1) | 13 | (1.37) |
| Ireland | 529 | (2.8) | 29 | (1.7) | 10 | (1.06) | 518 | (2.2) | 28 | (2.0) | 11 | (1.49) | 487 | (2.0) | 19 | (1.6) | 4 | (0.66) |
| Italy | 489 | (2.6) | 26 | (1.8) | 8 | (1.11) | 478 | (2.8) | 30 | (1.9) | 9 | (1.05) | 521 | (2.9) | 26 | (1.6) | 8 | (0.95) |
| Japan | 539 | (6.2) | 6 | (2.4) | 1 | (0.50) | 504 | (3.6) | 19 | (2.6) | 3 | (0.86) | 470 | (2.3) | 27 | (1.7) | 6 | (0.75) |
| Korea | 526 | (2.3) | 13 | (1.9) | 4 | (0.99) | 536 | (2.9) | 15 | (2.3) | 4 | (1.02) | 503 | (3.3) | 18 | (1.9) | 3 | (0.62) |
| Luxembourg | m | m | m | m | m | m | 483 | (1.5) | 34 | (1.8) | 12 | (1.20) | 557 | (3.7) | 14 | (2.0) | 2 | (0.67) |
| Mexico | 425 | (2.7) | 33 | (2.4) | 15 | (2.05) | 402 | (3.4) | 28 | (2.8) | 9 | (1.65) | 482 | (1.4) | 42 | (1.5) | 18 | (1.08) |
| Netherlands | m | m | m | m | m | m | 519 | (2.4) | 27 | (1.8) | 11 | (1.30) | 413 | (2.4) | 30 | (2.3) | 10 | (1.32) |
| New Zealand | 534 | (2.4) | 33 | (2.2) | 10 | (1.13) | 523 | (2.4) | 33 | (1.9) | 10 | (1.15) | 511 | (2.5) | 33 | (2.0) | 12 | (1.25) |
| Norway | 508 | (2.5) | 28 | (1.9) | 8 | (1.02) | 503 | (2.5) | 27 | (1.8) | 7 | (0.94) | 526 | (2.7) | 33 | (1.8) | 11 | (0.99) |
| Poland | 486 | (3.9) | 34 | (2.6) | 12 | (1.63) | 499 | (2.4) | 33 | (1.9) | 12 | (1.21) | 490 | (2.7) | 29 | (1.9) | 8 | (0.98) |
| Portugal | 474 | (3.5) | 38 | (2.1) | 15 | (1.75) | 479 | (3.2) | 31 | (2.1) | 11 | (1.28) | 510 | (2.6) | 31 | (1.6) | 10 | (0.89) |
| Slovak Republic | m | m | m | m | m | m | 473 | (2.4) | 32 | (1.9) | 12 | (1.23) | 474 | (2.9) | 39 | (2.3) | 15 | (1.51) |
| Spain | 495 | (2.1) | 27 | (1.6) | 10 | (1.21) | 482 | (2.1) | 25 | (1.8) | 7 | (0.95) | 471 | (2.9) | 34 | (2.7) | 11 | (1.50) |
| Sweden | 518 | (1.8) | 27 | (1.5) | 9 | (0.97) | 517 | (2.0) | 26 | (1.8) | 8 | (0.94) | 463 | (1.9) | 24 | (1.6) | 8 | (0.93) |
| Switzerland | 497 | (3.4) | 40 | (2.2) | 16 | (1.56) | 502 | (2.8) | 29 | (1.7) | 10 | (1.00) | 510 | (3.3) | 27 | (1.8) | 8 | (1.01) |
| Turkey | m | m | m | m | m | m | 443 | (4.9) | 30 | (4.6) | 10 | (2.70) | 501 | (2.6) | 31 | (1.4) | 11 | (0.90) |
| United Kingdom | m | m | m | m | m | m | m | m | m | m | m | m | 448 | (3.8) | 27 | (3.2) | 9 | (1.92) |
| United States | 514 | (5.0) | 34 | (2.7) | 11 | (1.47) | 501 | (2.6) | 29 | (1.6) | 9 | (0.88) | m | m | m | m | m | m |
| **OECD average** | 505 | (0.6) | 30 | (0.4) | 11 | (0.26) | 498 | (0.5) | 28 | (0.4) | 9 | (0.23) | 488 | (0.8) | 35 | (0.7) | 11 | (0.36) |
| Argentina | 424 | (6.6) | 41 | (2.8) | 16 | (1.99) | m | m | m | m | m | m | 381 | (5.9) | 37 | (4.3) | 9 | (2.22) |
| Azerbaijan | m | m | m | m | m | m | m | m | m | m | m | m | 357 | (3.2) | 18 | (2.4) | 6 | (1.56) |
| Brazil | 401 | (2.6) | 27 | (2.0) | 10 | (1.43) | 408 | (3.8) | 34 | (3.2) | 9 | (1.67) | 396 | (3.5) | 34 | (2.9) | 11 | (1.51) |
| Bulgaria | 436 | (3.8) | 37 | (3.7) | 14 | (2.14) | m | m | m | m | m | m | 410 | (5.0) | 46 | (3.6) | 16 | (2.12) |
| Chile | 412 | (2.8) | 37 | (1.8) | 18 | (1.34) | m | m | m | m | m | m | 444 | (3.9) | 40 | (2.8) | 15 | (1.91) |
| Colombia | m | m | m | m | m | m | m | m | m | m | m | m | 388 | (4.7) | 26 | (2.5) | 6 | (1.09) |
| Croatia | m | m | m | m | m | m | m | m | m | m | m | m | 480 | (2.5) | 27 | (1.8) | 10 | (1.09) |
| Estonia | m | m | m | m | m | m | m | m | m | m | m | m | 502 | (2.8) | 26 | (1.9) | 10 | (1.16) |
| Hong Kong-China | 529 | (2.7) | 15 | (2.4) | 4 | (1.12) | 514 | (3.1) | 13 | (2.0) | 3 | (0.77) | 539 | (2.3) | 14 | (1.9) | 3 | (0.86) |
| Indonesia | 373 | (3.5) | 24 | (3.0) | 11 | (2.28) | 383 | (3.0) | 22 | (2.2) | 8 | (1.50) | 395 | (5.6) | 19 | (2.8) | 7 | (1.62) |
| Israel | 468 | (6.8) | 33 | (2.3) | 11 | (1.60) | m | m | m | m | m | m | 452 | (4.2) | 31 | (2.7) | 7 | (1.13) |
| Jordan | m | m | m | m | m | m | m | m | m | m | m | m | 414 | (3.0) | 25 | (2.1) | 8 | (1.23) |
| Kyrgyzstan | m | m | m | m | m | m | m | m | m | m | m | m | 291 | (3.1) | 27 | (2.6) | 7 | (1.18) |
| Latvia | 462 | (4.8) | 24 | (2.5) | 6 | (1.13) | 492 | (3.4) | 20 | (2.3) | 5 | (1.17) | 483 | (3.2) | 25 | (2.2) | 8 | (1.19) |
| Liechtenstein | 486 | (4.7) | 31 | (4.9) | 11 | (3.40) | 528 | (3.9) | 35 | (5.2) | 16 | (4.43) | 512 | (4.2) | 33 | (5.3) | 12 | (3.70) |
| Lithuania | m | m | m | m | m | m | m | m | m | m | m | m | 473 | (2.7) | 29 | (2.1) | 9 | (1.30) |
| Macao-China | m | m | m | m | m | m | 498 | (2.2) | 3 | (2.4) | 0 | (0.33) | 493 | (1.2) | 6 | (1.4) | 1 | (0.29) |
| Montenegro | m | m | m | m | m | m | m | m | m | m | m | m | 398 | (1.4) | 23 | (1.6) | 7 | (0.98) |
| Qatar | m | m | m | m | m | m | m | m | m | m | m | m | 337 | (1.7) | 18 | (1.7) | 3 | (0.50) |
| Romania | 432 | (3.5) | 25 | (2.4) | 6 | (1.16) | m | m | m | m | m | m | 400 | (4.4) | 31 | (3.2) | 11 | (2.30) |
| Russian Federation | 463 | (3.6) | 28 | (1.9) | 9 | (1.17) | 443 | (3.6) | 23 | (1.8) | 6 | (0.86) | 442 | (3.9) | 22 | (1.9) | 6 | (0.93) |
| Serbia | m | m | m | m | m | m | m | m | m | m | m | m | 403 | (2.9) | 32 | (1.9) | 12 | (1.23) |
| Chinese Taipei | m | m | m | m | m | m | m | m | m | m | m | m | 501 | (2.9) | 22 | (1.4) | 7 | (0.85) |
| Slovenia | m | m | m | m | m | m | m | m | m | m | m | m | 496 | (1.0) | 31 | (1.5) | 13 | (1.20) |
| Thailand | 433 | (3.3) | 20 | (2.4) | 6 | (1.48) | 422 | (2.6) | 22 | (2.0) | 8 | (1.38) | 420 | (2.3) | 26 | (1.9) | 11 | (1.54) |
| Tunisia | m | m | m | m | m | m | 377 | (2.8) | 29 | (2.7) | 9 | (1.76) | 382 | (3.2) | 29 | (3.2) | 9 | (2.09) |
| Uruguay | m | m | m | m | m | m | 440 | (3.1) | 36 | (2.5) | 9 | (1.19) | 415 | (3.3) | 39 | (2.5) | 11 | (1.27) |

StatLink ᴴᴴᴴ http://dx.doi.org/10.1787/142183565744

Pour consulter la version française intégrale de ce tableau, suivre ce lien :
StatLink ᴴᴴᴴ http://dx.doi.org/10.1787/152754053448

[Part 1/1]

**Table 6.5c** **Effect of the highest occupational status of parents on student performance in mathematics since PISA 2000**

Tableau 6.5c Évolution de l'effet du statut professionnel le plus élevé des deux parents sur la performance des élèves en mathématiques depuis PISA 2000

| | PISA 2000 | | | | | | PISA 2003 | | | | | | PISA 2006 | | | | | |
|---|---|---|---|---|---|---|---|---|---|---|---|---|---|---|---|---|---|---|
| | Intercept | | Standardised regression coefficient | | Variance explained | | Intercept | | Standardised regression coefficient | | Variance explained | | Intercept | | Standardised regression coefficient | | Variance explained | |
| | Score | S.E. | Score | S.E. | % | S.E. | Score | S.E. | Score | S.E. | % | S.E. | Score | S.E. | Score | S.E. | % | S.E. |
| **OECD** | | | | | | | | | | | | | | | | | | |
| Australia | 536 | (2.9) | 30 | (2.3) | 12 | (1.68) | 528 | (1.8) | 29 | (1.3) | 10 | (0.73) | 523 | (1.9) | 26 | (1.0) | 9 | (0.66) |
| Austria | 504 | (2.6) | 30 | (2.5) | 10 | (1.63) | 508 | (2.7) | 30 | (1.9) | 11 | (1.22) | 506 | (3.5) | 31 | (2.7) | 10 | (1.57) |
| Belgium | 525 | (3.2) | 39 | (2.8) | 14 | (1.70) | 539 | (1.9) | 41 | (1.7) | 15 | (1.16) | 525 | (2.5) | 38 | (1.7) | 13 | (1.32) |
| Canada | 535 | (1.2) | 21 | (1.0) | 6 | (0.58) | 537 | (1.4) | 24 | (1.1) | 7 | (0.66) | 529 | (1.8) | 22 | (1.1) | 7 | (0.65) |
| Czech Republic | 499 | (2.4) | 35 | (2.0) | 13 | (1.33) | 523 | (2.8) | 33 | (1.7) | 13 | (1.19) | 513 | (3.2) | 38 | (2.1) | 14 | (1.27) |
| Denmark | 519 | (2.1) | 24 | (2.0) | 9 | (1.42) | 516 | (2.3) | 27 | (1.6) | 9 | (1.02) | 516 | (2.3) | 24 | (1.7) | 8 | (1.10) |
| Finland | 537 | (2.0) | 19 | (1.6) | 6 | (1.00) | 545 | (1.7) | 22 | (1.3) | 7 | (0.83) | 549 | (2.2) | 21 | (1.3) | 7 | (0.85) |
| France | 522 | (2.3) | 28 | (2.3) | 10 | (1.60) | 514 | (2.1) | 32 | (2.0) | 13 | (1.39) | 501 | (2.5) | 38 | (2.3) | 17 | (1.71) |
| Germany | 493 | (2.4) | 39 | (2.4) | 15 | (1.78) | 515 | (2.8) | 38 | (1.9) | 15 | (1.38) | 510 | (2.9) | 37 | (2.0) | 15 | (1.18) |
| Greece | 449 | (4.9) | 34 | (3.6) | 10 | (1.90) | 447 | (3.0) | 30 | (2.2) | 11 | (1.52) | 461 | (2.4) | 31 | (2.1) | 12 | (1.34) |
| Hungary | 491 | (3.2) | 41 | (2.9) | 17 | (2.12) | 493 | (2.4) | 38 | (2.0) | 17 | (1.51) | 494 | (2.4) | 35 | (1.9) | 16 | (1.45) |
| Iceland | 516 | (2.3) | 17 | (2.1) | 4 | (0.96) | 516 | (1.5) | 15 | (1.5) | 3 | (0.57) | 507 | (1.8) | 22 | (1.4) | 6 | (0.80) |
| Ireland | 505 | (2.3) | 24 | (2.1) | 9 | (1.41) | 505 | (1.9) | 26 | (1.8) | 10 | (1.30) | 505 | (2.2) | 25 | (1.6) | 9 | (1.20) |
| Italy | 459 | (2.9) | 21 | (2.4) | 5 | (1.26) | 467 | (3.0) | 28 | (1.9) | 8 | (1.03) | 463 | (2.1) | 26 | (1.6) | 7 | (0.84) |
| Japan | 573 | (7.4) | 9 | (3.3) | 1 | (0.88) | 538 | (3.8) | 21 | (2.8) | 4 | (1.00) | 526 | (3.3) | 18 | (1.6) | 4 | (0.64) |
| Korea | 550 | (2.4) | 19 | (2.0) | 5 | (1.14) | 544 | (3.0) | 22 | (2.7) | 5 | (1.27) | 548 | (3.6) | 17 | (2.3) | 3 | (0.83) |
| Luxembourg | m | m | m | m | m | m | 495 | (1.0) | 34 | (1.6) | 14 | (1.15) | 492 | (1.2) | 38 | (1.3) | 17 | (1.11) |
| Mexico | 390 | (2.7) | 31 | (2.6) | 14 | (2.30) | 387 | (3.0) | 26 | (2.1) | 9 | (1.38) | 408 | (2.4) | 27 | (1.9) | 11 | (1.29) |
| Netherlands | m | m | m | m | m | m | 545 | (2.6) | 31 | (2.0) | 13 | (1.32) | 534 | (2.2) | 31 | (2.0) | 12 | (1.38) |
| New Zealand | 542 | (2.8) | 32 | (2.7) | 11 | (1.66) | 524 | (2.1) | 29 | (1.6) | 9 | (1.01) | 526 | (2.1) | 29 | (1.5) | 10 | (0.95) |
| Norway | 501 | (2.8) | 24 | (2.3) | 7 | (1.25) | 497 | (2.2) | 27 | (1.5) | 9 | (0.93) | 494 | (2.3) | 26 | (1.8) | 8 | (1.10) |
| Poland | 477 | (4.7) | 33 | (2.8) | 12 | (1.77) | 492 | (2.1) | 32 | (1.6) | 13 | (1.19) | 497 | (2.2) | 28 | (1.3) | 10 | (0.88) |
| Portugal | 458 | (3.1) | 33 | (2.3) | 14 | (2.08) | 468 | (2.8) | 34 | (1.7) | 15 | (1.47) | 468 | (2.5) | 35 | (1.9) | 15 | (1.47) |
| Slovak Republic | m | m | m | m | m | m | 502 | (2.6) | 33 | (1.8) | 13 | (1.20) | 496 | (2.5) | 33 | (2.4) | 13 | (1.57) |
| Spain | 478 | (2.6) | 28 | (2.4) | 10 | (1.56) | 486 | (1.9) | 25 | (1.4) | 8 | (0.90) | 482 | (1.9) | 26 | (1.5) | 9 | (0.98) |
| Sweden | 512 | (2.1) | 30 | (2.0) | 11 | (1.38) | 512 | (2.1) | 28 | (1.8) | 9 | (1.03) | 505 | (2.2) | 28 | (1.4) | 10 | (0.94) |
| Switzerland | 532 | (3.7) | 34 | (2.0) | 12 | (1.53) | 529 | (2.9) | 30 | (1.7) | 9 | (0.96) | 531 | (2.8) | 30 | (1.6) | 10 | (0.93) |
| Turkey | m | m | m | m | m | m | 426 | (5.7) | 36 | (5.6) | 12 | (2.98) | 426 | (4.3) | 30 | (4.0) | 10 | (2.24) |
| United Kingdom | m | m | m | m | m | m | m | m | m | m | m | m | 499 | (1.8) | 31 | (1.4) | 12 | (1.10) |
| United States | 503 | (5.5) | 36 | (3.2) | 14 | (2.19) | 488 | (2.3) | 30 | (1.4) | 10 | (0.88) | 479 | (3.2) | 30 | (1.9) | 11 | (1.18) |
| **OECD total** | | | | | | | | | | | | | 487 | (0.9) | 33 | (0.7) | 12 | (0.46) |
| **OECD average** | 504 | (0.7) | 29 | (0.5) | 10 | (0.32) | 503 | (0.5) | 29 | (0.4) | 10 | (0.23) | 500 | (0.5) | 29 | (0.3) | 11 | (0.22) |
| **Partners** | | | | | | | | | | | | | | | | | | |
| Argentina | 394 | (6.3) | 49 | (4.1) | 17 | (2.72) | m | m | m | m | m | m | 387 | (5.0) | 33 | (3.6) | 11 | (2.19) |
| Azerbaijan | m | m | m | m | m | m | m | m | m | m | m | m | 477 | (2.2) | 3 | (1.2) | 0 | (0.32) |
| Brazil | 338 | (3.2) | 35 | (3.4) | 13 | (2.31) | 361 | (3.8) | 39 | (3.6) | 15 | (2.55) | 372 | (2.6) | 33 | (2.8) | 13 | (1.81) |
| Bulgaria | 437 | (4.7) | 38 | (4.4) | 13 | (2.52) | m | m | m | m | m | m | 419 | (4.7) | 40 | (3.3) | 16 | (2.13) |
| Chile | 386 | (2.9) | 37 | (2.2) | 16 | (1.60) | m | m | m | m | m | m | 412 | (3.4) | 39 | (2.4) | 20 | (2.09) |
| Colombia | m | m | m | m | m | m | m | m | m | m | m | m | 372 | (3.4) | 26 | (2.6) | 9 | (1.57) |
| Croatia | m | m | m | m | m | m | m | m | m | m | m | m | 470 | (2.2) | 27 | (1.6) | 11 | (1.16) |
| Estonia | m | m | m | m | m | m | m | m | m | m | m | m | 516 | (2.5) | 28 | (1.7) | 12 | (1.20) |
| Hong Kong-China | 564 | (3.1) | 13 | (3.1) | 2 | (1.04) | 554 | (3.9) | 18 | (2.2) | 4 | (0.82) | 550 | (2.4) | 19 | (2.2) | 4 | (0.96) |
| Indonesia | 369 | (4.2) | 22 | (4.0) | 6 | (2.12) | 362 | (3.5) | 23 | (2.5) | 8 | (1.68) | 393 | (5.3) | 21 | (2.9) | 7 | (1.53) |
| Israel | 449 | (7.5) | 45 | (3.5) | 13 | (1.98) | m | m | m | m | m | m | 454 | (3.8) | 32 | (2.2) | 10 | (1.08) |
| Jordan | m | m | m | m | m | m | m | m | m | m | m | m | 395 | (2.9) | 25 | (2.0) | 9 | (1.29) |
| Kyrgyzstan | m | m | m | m | m | m | m | m | m | m | m | m | 316 | (3.1) | 24 | (2.3) | 8 | (1.36) |
| Latvia | 466 | (4.5) | 16 | (2.7) | 2 | (0.83) | 485 | (3.4) | 21 | (1.7) | 6 | (0.98) | 488 | (2.8) | 23 | (2.1) | 8 | (1.28) |
| Liechtenstein | 519 | (7.1) | 22 | (7.7) | 5 | (3.47) | 538 | (4.5) | 38 | (5.4) | 15 | (3.40) | 526 | (4.4) | 31 | (5.3) | 11 | (3.74) |
| Lithuania | m | m | m | m | m | m | m | m | m | m | m | m | 489 | (2.7) | 30 | (1.8) | 11 | (1.24) |
| Macao-China | m | m | m | m | m | m | 528 | (3.0) | 9 | (2.9) | 1 | (0.68) | 526 | (1.3) | 7 | (1.4) | 1 | (0.29) |
| Montenegro | m | m | m | m | m | m | m | m | m | m | m | m | 405 | (1.5) | 22 | (1.7) | 7 | (1.04) |
| Qatar | m | m | m | m | m | m | m | m | m | m | m | m | m | m | m | m | m | m |
| Romania | 429 | (3.8) | 28 | (3.6) | 6 | (1.47) | m | m | m | m | m | m | 418 | (3.7) | 33 | (3.1) | 16 | (2.67) |
| Russian Federation | 480 | (5.1) | 25 | (2.5) | 6 | (1.15) | 469 | (3.9) | 22 | (1.8) | 6 | (0.85) | 477 | (3.5) | 22 | (1.9) | 6 | (1.01) |
| Serbia | m | m | m | m | m | m | m | m | m | m | m | m | 438 | (2.9) | 30 | (1.9) | 11 | (1.17) |
| Slovenia | m | m | m | m | m | m | m | m | m | m | m | m | 506 | (1.2) | 34 | (1.6) | 14 | (1.38) |
| Chinese Taipei | m | m | m | m | m | m | m | m | m | m | m | m | 554 | (3.4) | 26 | (1.9) | 6 | (0.92) |
| Thailand | 435 | (3.6) | 23 | (3.1) | 8 | (1.89) | 419 | (2.8) | 25 | (2.2) | 9 | (1.47) | 420 | (2.2) | 27 | (2.0) | 11 | (1.53) |
| Tunisia | m | m | m | m | m | m | 360 | (2.3) | 31 | (2.8) | 14 | (2.36) | 367 | (2.9) | 38 | (3.0) | 17 | (2.68) |
| Uruguay | m | m | m | m | m | m | 428 | (2.9) | 34 | (2.0) | 12 | (1.28) | 430 | (2.4) | 34 | (1.9) | 12 | (1.25) |

StatLink ⟨⟩ http://dx.doi.org/10.1787/142183565744

Pour consulter la version française intégrale de ce tableau, suivre ce lien :
StatLink ⟨⟩ http://dx.doi.org/10.1787/152754053448

# 11. Results for regions within countries/

*Résultats des régions au sein des pays*

### DEFINITION

**Adjudicated regions**

Data for which adherence to the PISA sampling standards and international comparability was internationally adjudicated.

**Non-adjudicated regions**

Data for which adherence to the PISA sampling standards at sub-national levels was assessed by the countries concerned.

In these countries, adherence to the PISA sampling standards and international comparability was internationally adjudicated only for the combined set of all sub-national entities.

### *DÉFINITIONS*

**Régions adjugées**

*Les normes d'échantillonnage et de comparabilité internationale PISA ont été respectées, les données de ces régions ont été adjugées au niveau international.*

**Régions non adjugées**

*Les normes d'échantillonnage PISA au niveau régional ont été évaluées par les pays concernés.*

*Dans ces pays, le respect des normes d'échantillonnage et de comparabilité internationale PISA a été évalué et adjugé au niveau international uniquement pour les données de l'ensemble des régions du pays concerné.*

[Part 1/1]

**Table S2a   Percentage of students at each proficiency level on the science scale**

Tableau S2a   Pourcentage d'élèves à chaque niveau de compétence sur l'échelle de culture scientifique

| | Proficiency levels | | | | | | | | | | | | |
|---|---|---|---|---|---|---|---|---|---|---|---|---|---|
| | Below Level 1 (below 334.94 score points) | | Level 1 (from 334.94 to 409.54 score points) | | Level 2 (from 409.54 to 484.14 score points) | | Level 3 (from 484.14 to 558.73 score points) | | Level 4 (from 558.73 to 633.33 score points) | | Level 5 (from 633.33 to 707.93 score points) | | Level 6 (above 707.93 score points) | |
| | % | S.E. | % | S.E. | % | S.E. | % | S.E. | % | S.E. | % | S.E. | % | S.E. |
| **Adjudicated** | | | | | | | | | | | | | | |
| Belgium (Flemish Community) | 2.7 | (0.8) | 8.9 | (0.6) | 18.4 | (0.9) | 28.8 | (1.1) | 28.9 | (1.1) | 11.2 | (0.7) | 1.1 | (0.3) |
| Italy (Provincia Autonoma of Bolzano) | 1.9 | (0.5) | 7.9 | (0.7) | 21.5 | (1.4) | 31.8 | (1.7) | 26.4 | (1.3) | 9.5 | (0.7) | 1.1 | (0.3) |
| Italy (Provincia Campania) | 9.7 | (1.4) | 26.0 | (2.3) | 32.9 | (2.1) | 23.4 | (1.9) | 7.0 | (1.3) | 1.1 | (0.5) | 0.0 | a |
| Italy (Provincia Basilicata) | 8.7 | (1.6) | 24.0 | (1.8) | 33.1 | (2.2) | 23.1 | (2.0) | 9.7 | (1.0) | 1.3 | (0.4) | 0.1 | (0.1) |
| Italy (Provincia Emilia Romagna) | 3.8 | (0.8) | 11.8 | (1.0) | 22.5 | (1.5) | 29.9 | (1.7) | 23.4 | (1.4) | 7.8 | (1.1) | 1.0 | (0.3) |
| Italy (Provincia Friuli Venezia Giulia) | 1.6 | (0.5) | 6.2 | (0.7) | 18.8 | (1.4) | 34.3 | (1.6) | 28.0 | (1.5) | 9.7 | (1.2) | 1.4 | (0.4) |
| Italy (Provincia Sicilia) | 16.1 | (2.0) | 25.5 | (2.0) | 27.1 | (2.1) | 21.1 | (2.1) | 8.6 | (1.2) | 1.7 | (0.6) | 0.0 | a |
| Italy (Provincia Liguria) | 6.4 | (1.5) | 14.9 | (1.8) | 24.8 | (2.0) | 29.8 | (1.5) | 18.5 | (1.7) | 5.1 | (0.9) | 0.5 | (0.3) |
| Italy (Provincia Lombardia) | 5.3 | (1.4) | 12.7 | (1.5) | 23.2 | (1.8) | 31.2 | (1.7) | 20.9 | (1.8) | 6.2 | (1.0) | 0.6 | (0.3) |
| Italy (Provincia Piemonte) | 3.6 | (0.7) | 10.8 | (1.2) | 22.9 | (1.6) | 32.5 | (1.7) | 22.7 | (2.0) | 6.9 | (1.1) | 0.5 | (0.3) |
| Italy (Provincia Trento) | 2.7 | (0.4) | 10.1 | (0.7) | 19.8 | (1.2) | 30.7 | (1.4) | 26.0 | (1.8) | 9.6 | (1.2) | 1.2 | (0.3) |
| Italy (Provincia Sardegna) | 11.6 | (1.9) | 23.0 | (2.1) | 29.4 | (2.3) | 23.8 | (1.9) | 10.5 | (1.6) | 1.7 | (0.7) | 0.1 | a |
| Italy (Provincia Puglia) | 8.3 | (1.3) | 24.9 | (1.9) | 34.0 | (2.0) | 23.2 | (1.5) | 8.3 | (1.1) | 1.3 | (0.4) | 0.0 | a |
| Italy (Provincia Veneto) | 2.0 | (0.5) | 8.7 | (1.0) | 21.6 | (1.9) | 30.8 | (1.6) | 26.4 | (2.0) | 9.2 | (1.2) | 1.3 | (0.3) |
| Spain (Andalusia) | 5.9 | (1.0) | 17.4 | (1.2) | 30.2 | (1.6) | 29.0 | (1.5) | 14.6 | (1.1) | 2.8 | (0.6) | 0.1 | (0.1) |
| Spain (Basque Country) | 3.2 | (0.6) | 12.5 | (1.0) | 27.9 | (1.1) | 33.5 | (1.2) | 18.5 | (1.1) | 4.0 | (0.6) | 0.3 | (0.1) |
| Spain (Cantabria) | 2.9 | (0.6) | 9.6 | (1.2) | 24.8 | (1.5) | 33.1 | (1.6) | 22.8 | (1.5) | 6.4 | (0.7) | 0.4 | (0.2) |
| Spain (Galicia) | 2.8 | (0.5) | 11.4 | (0.9) | 26.9 | (1.3) | 30.8 | (1.4) | 21.4 | (1.4) | 6.0 | (0.7) | 0.7 | (0.3) |
| Spain (La Rioja) | 2.0 | (0.4) | 8.3 | (1.0) | 23.3 | (1.9) | 32.4 | (1.7) | 25.1 | (1.4) | 8.0 | (0.9) | 0.8 | (0.3) |
| Spain (Castile and Leon) | 0.9 | (0.5) | 7.9 | (1.1) | 24.4 | (1.8) | 34.0 | (1.6) | 25.1 | (1.6) | 7.1 | (0.8) | 0.6 | (0.3) |
| Spain (Navarre) | 2.0 | (0.5) | 11.6 | (1.0) | 24.9 | (1.4) | 30.6 | (1.4) | 22.5 | (1.4) | 7.6 | (0.8) | 0.9 | (0.4) |
| Spain (Aragon) | 2.4 | (0.6) | 9.9 | (1.3) | 24.3 | (1.8) | 31.0 | (1.7) | 24.5 | (1.7) | 7.2 | (0.8) | 0.8 | (0.2) |
| Spain (Catalonia) | 4.7 | (0.9) | 13.9 | (1.3) | 26.2 | (1.8) | 31.7 | (1.7) | 18.9 | (1.8) | 4.2 | (0.7) | 0.4 | (0.2) |
| Spain (Asturias) | 2.3 | (0.7) | 10.0 | (1.3) | 24.8 | (1.6) | 35.0 | (1.5) | 22.1 | (1.6) | 5.2 | (0.9) | 0.5 | (0.2) |
| United Kingdom (Scotland) | 3.6 | (0.6) | 11.0 | (1.0) | 24.1 | (1.2) | 27.9 | (1.1) | 20.7 | (1.1) | 10.1 | (0.9) | 2.4 | (0.5) |
| **Non-adjudicated** | | | | | | | | | | | | | | |
| Belgium (French Community) | 7.7 | (1.2) | 16.5 | (1.2) | 23.9 | (1.6) | 26.1 | (1.5) | 18.7 | (1.0) | 6.3 | (0.8) | 0.8 | (0.2) |
| Belgium (German-Speaking Community) | 3.1 | (0.7) | 12.4 | (1.1) | 21.2 | (1.4) | 28.1 | (1.8) | 23.4 | (1.6) | 10.5 | (1.1) | 1.4 | (0.5) |
| Finland (Finnish Speaking) | 0.5 | (0.1) | 3.4 | (0.5) | 13.3 | (0.7) | 29.0 | (1.2) | 32.4 | (1.0) | 17.3 | (0.8) | 4.1 | (0.4) |
| Finland (Swedish Speaking) | 2.0 | (1.2) | 7.4 | (2.2) | 19.2 | (2.6) | 31.2 | (3.6) | 28.7 | (3.5) | 10.3 | (2.6) | 1.1 | (0.8) |
| United Kingdom (England) | 4.9 | (0.6) | 11.8 | (0.7) | 21.5 | (0.9) | 25.7 | (0.8) | 22.1 | (0.7) | 11.0 | (0.6) | 3.0 | (0.4) |
| United Kingdom (Northern Ireland) | 6.6 | (0.7) | 13.7 | (0.7) | 20.6 | (1.1) | 24.3 | (1.5) | 20.9 | (1.4) | 11.2 | (1.1) | 2.7 | (0.4) |
| United Kingdom (Wales) | 4.5 | (0.7) | 13.6 | (0.8) | 24.3 | (1.0) | 26.9 | (1.0) | 19.8 | (1.0) | 9.0 | (0.8) | 1.9 | (0.4) |

Note: See Table 2.1a for national data.
*StatLink* http://dx.doi.org/10.1787/142184405135

Pour consulter la version française intégrale de ce tableau, suivre ce lien :
*StatLink* http://dx.doi.org/10.1787/152830402855

[Part 1/1]

**Table S2b  Percentage of students at each proficiency level on the science scale, by gender**

Tableau S2b  Pourcentage d'élèves à chaque niveau de compétence sur l'échelle de culture scientifique, selon le sexe

### Males – Proficiency levels

| | Below Level 1 (below 334.94 score points) | | Level 1 (from 334.94 to 409.54 score points) | | Level 2 (from 409.54 to 484.14 score points) | | Level 3 (from 484.14 to 558.73 score points) | | Level 4 (from 558.73 to 633.33 score points) | | Level 5 (from 633.33 to 707.93 score points) | | Level 6 (above 707.93 score points) | |
|---|---|---|---|---|---|---|---|---|---|---|---|---|---|---|
| | % | S.E. | % | S.E. | % | S.E. | % | S.E. | % | S.E. | % | S.E. | % | S.E. |
| **Adjudicated** | | | | | | | | | | | | | | |
| Belgium (Flemish Community) | 2.6 | (1.2) | 9.4 | (0.6) | 19.4 | (1.1) | 26.1 | (1.3) | 28.9 | (1.3) | 12.2 | (1.0) | 1.5 | (0.3) |
| Italy (Provincia Autonoma of Bolzano) | 1.9 | (0.6) | 7.9 | (1.2) | 18.5 | (2.2) | 31.8 | (2.3) | 27.7 | (1.9) | 10.9 | (1.1) | 1.4 | (0.4) |
| Italy (Provincia Campania) | 8.1 | (1.3) | 22.2 | (2.4) | 27.4 | (2.4) | 27.4 | (2.5) | 8.2 | (1.4) | 1.3 | (0.8) | 0.0 | a |
| Italy (Provincia Basilicata) | 10.5 | (2.5) | 24.3 | (2.4) | 30.8 | (2.4) | 22.4 | (2.6) | 10.2 | (1.5) | 1.5 | (0.6) | 0.3 | (0.2) |
| Italy (Provincia Emilia Romagna) | 3.0 | (0.8) | 10.2 | (1.5) | 22.0 | (1.7) | 31.8 | (2.1) | 23.3 | (1.9) | 8.3 | (1.3) | 1.4 | (0.5) |
| Italy (Provincia Friuli Venezia Giulia) | 1.7 | (0.9) | 5.5 | (1.3) | 18.9 | (2.3) | 33.0 | (2.3) | 28.1 | (2.0) | 11.1 | (1.7) | 1.6 | (0.6) |
| Italy (Provincia Sicilia) | 18.8 | (3.1) | 24.1 | (3.2) | 23.1 | (2.2) | 21.0 | (2.6) | 10.5 | (1.8) | 2.5 | (1.0) | a | a |
| Italy (Provincia Liguria) | 8.4 | (2.3) | 16.8 | (2.5) | 24.1 | (2.4) | 27.1 | (2.3) | 16.6 | (1.7) | 6.2 | (1.3) | 0.7 | (0.4) |
| Italy (Provincia Lombardia) | 5.9 | (2.4) | 13.9 | (2.4) | 23.5 | (2.4) | 29.3 | (2.4) | 19.7 | (2.7) | 6.8 | (1.4) | 0.8 | (0.4) |
| Italy (Provincia Piemonte) | 5.1 | (1.4) | 11.6 | (2.0) | 23.6 | (2.0) | 30.3 | (2.2) | 21.9 | (2.5) | 6.9 | (1.3) | 0.7 | (0.4) |
| Italy (Provincia Trento) | 3.4 | (0.5) | 11.2 | (1.1) | 19.5 | (1.5) | 27.8 | (2.5) | 24.4 | (3.1) | 11.6 | (2.2) | 2.1 | (0.7) |
| Italy (Provincia Sardegna) | 13.9 | (2.8) | 24.5 | (2.8) | 26.1 | (3.1) | 21.3 | (2.7) | 11.5 | (2.1) | 2.5 | (1.2) | 0.2 | a |
| Italy (Provincia Puglia) | 9.0 | (1.5) | 27.0 | (2.2) | 30.8 | (2.4) | 22.8 | (1.8) | 8.8 | (1.6) | 1.6 | (0.7) | 0.0 | a |
| Italy (Provincia Veneto) | 1.4 | (0.6) | 7.7 | (1.9) | 20.6 | (2.3) | 30.0 | (2.4) | 28.0 | (2.4) | 10.7 | (1.5) | 1.6 | (0.4) |
| Spain (Andalusia) | 5.9 | (1.2) | 16.0 | (1.5) | 28.7 | (2.5) | 29.0 | (2.7) | 16.8 | (1.7) | 3.4 | (0.9) | 0.2 | (0.2) |
| Spain (Basque Country) | 4.1 | (0.8) | 13.5 | (1.1) | 26.6 | (1.3) | 31.8 | (1.3) | 19.0 | (1.3) | 4.6 | (0.7) | 0.3 | (0.2) |
| Spain (Cantabria) | 3.4 | (0.8) | 10.0 | (1.3) | 24.5 | (1.9) | 30.0 | (1.9) | 24.2 | (2.4) | 7.4 | (1.1) | 0.5 | (0.3) |
| Spain (Galicia) | 3.4 | (0.8) | 11.6 | (1.3) | 26.1 | (1.6) | 28.4 | (1.8) | 22.2 | (1.5) | 7.3 | (0.9) | 1.0 | (0.4) |
| Spain (La Rioja) | 2.3 | (0.7) | 8.6 | (1.4) | 22.5 | (2.3) | 30.9 | (2.6) | 26.1 | (2.1) | 8.8 | (1.4) | 0.9 | (0.4) |
| Spain (Castile and Leon) | 0.9 | (0.6) | 8.6 | (1.3) | 22.9 | (2.1) | 34.4 | (2.3) | 25.2 | (2.0) | 7.6 | (1.1) | 0.4 | (0.3) |
| Spain (Navarre) | 2.2 | (0.6) | 12.5 | (1.5) | 23.3 | (2.2) | 28.4 | (2.0) | 23.3 | (2.0) | 9.0 | (1.1) | 1.2 | (0.5) |
| Spain (Aragon) | 2.3 | (0.8) | 11.5 | (1.7) | 24.4 | (2.1) | 29.6 | (2.3) | 23.7 | (2.3) | 7.3 | (1.1) | 1.1 | (0.5) |
| Spain (Catalonia) | 4.4 | (1.1) | 13.4 | (1.4) | 24.8 | (2.0) | 32.6 | (2.4) | 19.5 | (2.2) | 4.5 | (1.0) | 0.7 | (0.4) |
| Spain (Asturias) | 2.6 | (1.1) | 10.1 | (1.7) | 23.7 | (2.4) | 34.2 | (2.0) | 22.3 | (1.8) | 6.3 | (1.3) | 0.8 | (0.4) |
| United Kingdom (Scotland) | 4.2 | (0.9) | 10.7 | (1.3) | 22.6 | (1.5) | 27.2 | (1.7) | 22.1 | (1.7) | 10.6 | (1.4) | 2.5 | (0.6) |
| **Non-adjudicated** | | | | | | | | | | | | | | |
| Belgium (French Community) | 8.4 | (1.8) | 17.7 | (2.1) | 22.6 | (2.0) | 25.0 | (1.9) | 18.6 | (1.4) | 6.8 | (1.0) | 0.9 | (0.3) |
| Belgium (German-Speaking Community) | 3.6 | (1.0) | 12.5 | (2.2) | 20.4 | (2.0) | 25.0 | (2.4) | 23.8 | (2.3) | 12.4 | (1.9) | 2.4 | (0.8) |
| Finland (Finnish Speaking) | 0.5 | (0.2) | 4.3 | (0.7) | 14.5 | (0.9) | 27.8 | (1.4) | 30.8 | (1.2) | 17.3 | (1.0) | 4.8 | (0.5) |
| Finland (Swedish Speaking) | 2.6 | (1.6) | 5.4 | (1.5) | 17.1 | (5.0) | 33.0 | (3.5) | 30.2 | (4.0) | 10.2 | (3.2) | 1.6 | (1.3) |
| United Kingdom (England) | 5.4 | (0.9) | 11.3 | (1.0) | 20.2 | (1.0) | 23.8 | (1.0) | 22.7 | (1.0) | 12.6 | (0.9) | 3.9 | (0.6) |
| United Kingdom (Northern Ireland) | 7.0 | (1.1) | 13.9 | (1.4) | 20.1 | (1.5) | 23.3 | (1.5) | 20.2 | (1.9) | 12.3 | (1.5) | 3.2 | (0.7) |
| United Kingdom (Wales) | 4.4 | (0.9) | 13.4 | (1.1) | 22.7 | (1.3) | 26.1 | (1.2) | 21.5 | (1.3) | 9.5 | (1.0) | 2.4 | (0.6) |

### Females – Proficiency levels

| | Below Level 1 (below 334.94 score points) | | Level 1 (from 334.94 to 409.54 score points) | | Level 2 (from 409.54 to 484.14 score points) | | Level 3 (from 484.14 to 558.73 score points) | | Level 4 (from 558.73 to 633.33 score points) | | Level 5 (from 633.33 to 707.93 score points) | | Level 6 (above 707.93 score points) | |
|---|---|---|---|---|---|---|---|---|---|---|---|---|---|---|
| | % | S.E. | % | S.E. | % | S.E. | % | S.E. | % | S.E. | % | S.E. | % | S.E. |
| **Adjudicated** | | | | | | | | | | | | | | |
| Belgium (Flemish Community) | 2.8 | (0.6) | 8.5 | (1.0) | 17.2 | (1.3) | 31.9 | (1.6) | 28.9 | (1.6) | 10.1 | (0.9) | 0.6 | (0.3) |
| Italy (Provincia Autonoma of Bolzano) | 1.9 | (0.7) | 7.9 | (1.1) | 24.4 | (1.6) | 31.8 | (2.0) | 25.0 | (1.6) | 8.2 | (1.0) | 0.9 | (0.3) |
| Italy (Provincia Campania) | 11.3 | (2.1) | 29.7 | (3.1) | 33.1 | (3.1) | 19.4 | (2.4) | 5.7 | (1.5) | 0.9 | (0.5) | a | a |
| Italy (Provincia Basilicata) | 6.6 | (1.2) | 23.6 | (2.3) | 35.6 | (3.0) | 23.9 | (2.6) | 9.1 | (1.5) | 1.0 | (0.7) | 0.0 | a |
| Italy (Provincia Emilia Romagna) | 4.5 | (1.3) | 13.4 | (1.6) | 23.1 | (2.1) | 27.9 | (2.2) | 23.4 | (1.8) | 7.2 | (1.5) | 0.5 | (0.4) |
| Italy (Provincia Friuli Venezia Giulia) | 1.5 | (0.8) | 6.8 | (1.2) | 18.7 | (2.0) | 35.5 | (2.3) | 28.0 | (2.3) | 8.4 | (1.5) | 1.1 | (0.5) |
| Italy (Provincia Sicilia) | 13.4 | (2.4) | 26.8 | (2.4) | 30.8 | (3.1) | 21.2 | (2.0) | 6.7 | (1.4) | 1.0 | (0.6) | 0.0 | a |
| Italy (Provincia Liguria) | 4.4 | (1.1) | 12.8 | (2.0) | 25.4 | (2.6) | 32.6 | (2.1) | 20.5 | (2.4) | 4.0 | (1.0) | 0.2 | (0.2) |
| Italy (Provincia Lombardia) | 4.7 | (1.1) | 11.5 | (1.6) | 22.9 | (2.3) | 33.0 | (2.3) | 22.0 | (1.9) | 5.6 | (1.2) | 0.4 | (0.3) |
| Italy (Provincia Piemonte) | 2.3 | (0.9) | 10.2 | (1.2) | 22.4 | (2.2) | 34.4 | (2.1) | 23.4 | (2.4) | 6.9 | (1.4) | 0.4 | (0.4) |
| Italy (Provincia Trento) | 1.9 | (0.6) | 8.9 | (1.2) | 20.1 | (1.8) | 33.6 | (2.2) | 27.6 | (2.5) | 7.6 | (1.5) | 0.2 | (0.2) |
| Italy (Provincia Sardegna) | 9.1 | (1.7) | 21.4 | (2.7) | 32.7 | (2.4) | 26.4 | (2.4) | 9.4 | (2.0) | 1.0 | (0.5) | a | a |
| Italy (Provincia Puglia) | 7.6 | (1.5) | 22.8 | (2.2) | 37.1 | (3.0) | 23.7 | (1.9) | 7.8 | (1.1) | 0.9 | (0.5) | a | a |
| Italy (Provincia Veneto) | 2.7 | (0.8) | 9.8 | (1.6) | 22.7 | (2.6) | 31.7 | (2.6) | 24.7 | (3.1) | 7.6 | (1.7) | 0.9 | (0.5) |
| Spain (Andalusia) | 6.0 | (1.2) | 18.7 | (1.4) | 31.6 | (2.1) | 29.0 | (2.4) | 12.5 | (1.3) | 2.2 | (0.7) | 0.1 | a |
| Spain (Basque Country) | 2.3 | (0.6) | 11.5 | (1.1) | 29.3 | (1.3) | 35.2 | (1.8) | 18.0 | (1.3) | 3.5 | (0.8) | 0.3 | (0.2) |
| Spain (Cantabria) | 2.5 | (0.7) | 9.2 | (1.6) | 25.2 | (2.0) | 36.3 | (2.5) | 21.4 | (2.0) | 5.3 | (0.9) | 0.2 | a |
| Spain (Galicia) | 2.2 | (0.6) | 11.2 | (1.3) | 27.7 | (2.2) | 33.5 | (2.2) | 20.4 | (2.0) | 4.6 | (1.1) | 0.4 | (0.3) |
| Spain (La Rioja) | 1.8 | (0.5) | 8.0 | (1.5) | 24.3 | (3.1) | 33.9 | (2.4) | 24.1 | (1.9) | 7.3 | (1.2) | 0.7 | (0.4) |
| Spain (Castile and Leon) | 0.8 | (0.5) | 7.2 | (1.3) | 26.1 | (2.8) | 33.7 | (2.9) | 25.0 | (2.4) | 6.5 | (1.1) | 0.7 | (0.5) |
| Spain (Navarre) | 1.8 | (0.6) | 10.6 | (1.3) | 26.5 | (1.9) | 32.7 | (2.2) | 21.7 | (1.8) | 6.1 | (1.1) | 0.5 | (0.4) |
| Spain (Aragon) | 2.6 | (0.7) | 8.2 | (1.5) | 24.2 | (2.5) | 32.3 | (2.1) | 25.2 | (2.3) | 7.0 | (1.4) | 0.5 | (0.4) |
| Spain (Catalonia) | 5.0 | (1.1) | 14.5 | (1.4) | 27.5 | (2.3) | 30.8 | (2.0) | 18.2 | (2.2) | 3.8 | (1.0) | 0.1 | a |
| Spain (Asturias) | 2.0 | (0.8) | 10.0 | (1.6) | 25.9 | (2.8) | 35.9 | (2.8) | 21.9 | (2.0) | 4.1 | (1.0) | 0.2 | a |
| United Kingdom (Scotland) | 3.0 | (0.7) | 11.4 | (1.5) | 25.7 | (2.1) | 28.7 | (1.6) | 19.3 | (1.4) | 9.6 | (1.1) | 2.4 | (0.7) |
| **Non-adjudicated** | | | | | | | | | | | | | | |
| Belgium (French Community) | 7.0 | (1.3) | 15.2 | (1.6) | 25.2 | (2.0) | 27.4 | (1.9) | 18.8 | (1.6) | 5.9 | (1.2) | 0.6 | (0.3) |
| Belgium (German-Speaking Community) | 2.6 | (0.9) | 12.3 | (2.0) | 22.0 | (2.5) | 31.2 | (2.7) | 23.1 | (2.2) | 8.5 | (1.6) | 0.4 | (0.5) |
| Finland (Finnish Speaking) | 0.4 | (0.2) | 2.5 | (0.5) | 12.2 | (0.9) | 30.3 | (1.3) | 34.0 | (1.3) | 17.2 | (1.0) | 3.4 | (0.5) |
| Finland (Swedish Speaking) | 1.4 | a | 9.5 | (3.7) | 21.3 | (4.0) | 29.5 | (6.3) | 27.2 | (5.7) | 10.4 | (3.6) | 0.7 | a |
| United Kingdom (England) | 4.3 | (0.6) | 12.4 | (1.0) | 22.7 | (1.2) | 27.7 | (1.2) | 21.4 | (1.1) | 9.5 | (0.8) | 2.1 | (0.5) |
| United Kingdom (Northern Ireland) | 6.2 | (1.1) | 13.6 | (1.3) | 21.0 | (1.8) | 25.2 | (2.2) | 21.7 | (1.8) | 10.0 | (1.4) | 2.3 | (0.5) |
| United Kingdom (Wales) | 4.7 | (0.8) | 13.7 | (1.5) | 25.9 | (1.5) | 27.8 | (1.5) | 18.1 | (1.4) | 8.4 | (1.2) | 1.4 | (0.5) |

Note: See Table 2.1b for national data.

StatLink ᓚᔕᒃ http://dx.doi.org/10.1787/142184405135

Pour consulter la version française intégrale de ce tableau, suivre ce lien :
StatLink ᓚᔕᒃ http://dx.doi.org/10.1787/152830402855

[Part 1/1]

**Table S2c   Mean score, variation and gender differences in student performance on the science scale**

Tableau S2c   Score moyen, différences de score selon le sexe et répartition des scores sur l'échelle de culture scientifique

| | All students | | | | Gender differences | | | | | |
|---|---|---|---|---|---|---|---|---|---|---|
| | Mean score | | Standard deviation | | Males | | Females | | Difference (M – F) | |
| | Mean | S.E. | S.D. | S.E. | Mean score | S.E. | Mean score | S.E. | Score dif. | S.E. |
| **Adjudicated** | | | | | | | | | | |
| Belgium (Flemish Community) | 529 | (3.2) | 93 | (2.8) | 530 | (4.0) | 528 | (3.7) | 3 | (4.5) |
| Italy (Provincia Autonoma of Bolzano) | 526 | (2.0) | 88 | (1.6) | 532 | (3.1) | 520 | (2.6) | **12** | (4.1) |
| Italy (Provincia Campania) | 442 | (5.9) | 83 | (3.3) | 453 | (5.6) | 432 | (7.3) | **20** | (6.3) |
| Italy (Provincia Basilicata) | 451 | (5.0) | 85 | (2.8) | 449 | (6.8) | 453 | (5.3) | -4 | (7.2) |
| Italy (Provincia Emilia Romagna) | 510 | (3.7) | 94 | (2.8) | 516 | (4.9) | 503 | (4.5) | **13** | (5.6) |
| Italy (Provincia Friuli Venezia Giulia) | 534 | (3.3) | 85 | (2.6) | 536 | (5.4) | 531 | (4.9) | 6 | (7.9) |
| Italy (Provincia Sicilia) | 433 | (7.2) | 98 | (4.3) | 432 | (9.8) | 434 | (7.8) | -2 | (10.0) |
| Italy (Provincia Liguria) | 488 | (6.7) | 96 | (3.0) | 482 | (9.1) | 495 | (6.1) | -13 | (8.0) |
| Italy (Provincia Lombardia) | 499 | (6.2) | 95 | (3.8) | 496 | (10.4) | 503 | (5.5) | -7 | (10.9) |
| Italy (Provincia Piemonte) | 508 | (4.7) | 90 | (3.0) | 503 | (6.8) | 513 | (5.3) | -10 | (7.5) |
| Italy (Provincia Trento) | 521 | (2.0) | 93 | (1.7) | 522 | (3.9) | 520 | (2.8) | 2 | (5.4) |
| Italy (Provincia Sardegna) | 449 | (6.1) | 92 | (3.6) | 446 | (8.9) | 452 | (5.9) | -6 | (8.7) |
| Italy (Provincia Puglia) | 447 | (4.3) | 83 | (2.3) | 446 | (5.6) | 449 | (4.3) | -4 | (4.8) |
| Italy (Provincia Veneto) | 524 | (5.4) | 89 | (2.3) | 532 | (6.9) | 515 | (8.0) | 17 | (10.8) |
| Spain (Andalusia) | 474 | (4.0) | 88 | (2.4) | 480 | (5.0) | 468 | (4.1) | **11** | (4.5) |
| Spain (Basque Country) | 495 | (3.5) | 84 | (1.9) | 493 | (4.1) | 496 | (3.5) | -3 | (3.2) |
| Spain (Cantabria) | 509 | (3.6) | 86 | (1.8) | 511 | (5.1) | 508 | (3.3) | 3 | (4.7) |
| Spain (Galicia) | 505 | (3.4) | 87 | (1.6) | 507 | (3.8) | 502 | (3.9) | 4 | (3.4) |
| Spain (La Rioja) | 520 | (2.5) | 87 | (2.1) | 521 | (3.5) | 518 | (3.7) | 3 | (5.1) |
| Spain (Castile and Leon) | 520 | (3.9) | 79 | (1.6) | 521 | (4.3) | 519 | (4.4) | 2 | (3.8) |
| Spain (Navarre) | 511 | (2.9) | 88 | (2.0) | 514 | (3.5) | 509 | (3.7) | 5 | (4.2) |
| Spain (Aragon) | 513 | (3.9) | 88 | (1.9) | 512 | (5.4) | 515 | (4.4) | -4 | (5.9) |
| Spain (Catalonia) | 491 | (5.1) | 90 | (2.3) | 496 | (6.5) | 487 | (4.9) | 9 | (5.2) |
| Spain (Asturias) | 508 | (4.9) | 83 | (2.4) | 511 | (6.3) | 506 | (4.8) | 5 | (5.1) |
| United Kingdom (Scotland) | 515 | (4.0) | 100 | (2.0) | 517 | (5.0) | 512 | (4.0) | 4 | (4.4) |
| **Non-adjudicated** | | | | | | | | | | |
| Belgium (French Community) | 486 | (4.3) | 103 | (3.0) | 484 | (5.6) | 487 | (5.4) | -3 | (6.8) |
| Belgium (German-Speaking Community) | 516 | (2.9) | 97 | (2.5) | 521 | (4.2) | 511 | (4.8) | 10 | (7.0) |
| Finland (Finnish Speaking) | 565 | (2.1) | 85 | (1.0) | 563 | (2.7) | 567 | (2.4) | -4 | (3.1) |
| Finland (Swedish Speaking) | 531 | (6.2) | 86 | (4.1) | 536 | (6.9) | 526 | (9.2) | 10 | (10.5) |
| United Kingdom (England) | 516 | (2.7) | 107 | (1.8) | 521 | (3.5) | 510 | (3.2) | **11** | (4.1) |
| United Kingdom (Northern Ireland) | 508 | (3.3) | 113 | (2.3) | 509 | (6.0) | 507 | (5.8) | 2 | (9.7) |
| United Kingdom (Wales) | 505 | (3.5) | 102 | (1.9) | 510 | (4.0) | 500 | (4.2) | **10** | (4.3) |

| | Percentiles | | | | | | | | | | | |
|---|---|---|---|---|---|---|---|---|---|---|---|---|
| | 5th | | 10th | | 25th | | 75th | | 90th | | 95th | |
| | Score | S.E. | Score | S.E. | Score | S.E. | Score | S.E. | Score | S.E. | Score | S.E. |
| **Adjudicated** | | | | | | | | | | | | |
| Belgium (Flemish Community) | 363 | (10.1) | 400 | (6.7) | 468 | (4.5) | 598 | (2.6) | 642 | (2.7) | 665 | (2.9) |
| Italy (Provincia Autonoma of Bolzano) | 374 | (8.2) | 411 | (5.2) | 468 | (4.4) | 589 | (2.4) | 636 | (2.8) | 664 | (4.3) |
| Italy (Provincia Campania) | 311 | (7.0) | 336 | (5.3) | 383 | (5.8) | 501 | (7.5) | 549 | (7.9) | 577 | (10.2) |
| Italy (Provincia Basilicata) | 312 | (9.0) | 341 | (7.9) | 393 | (7.0) | 509 | (5.9) | 565 | (5.7) | 593 | (5.7) |
| Italy (Provincia Emilia Romagna) | 348 | (10.0) | 381 | (7.9) | 448 | (6.1) | 579 | (4.4) | 627 | (6.0) | 656 | (7.5) |
| Italy (Provincia Friuli Venezia Giulia) | 390 | (9.2) | 423 | (5.4) | 480 | (3.9) | 591 | (4.6) | 638 | (6.4) | 668 | (7.9) |
| Italy (Provincia Sicilia) | 276 | (7.7) | 307 | (7.3) | 363 | (8.0) | 503 | (8.6) | 560 | (6.9) | 592 | (9.4) |
| Italy (Provincia Liguria) | 323 | (13.7) | 356 | (11.3) | 423 | (9.8) | 556 | (6.7) | 610 | (6.7) | 639 | (9.3) |
| Italy (Provincia Lombardia) | 332 | (15.1) | 371 | (12.7) | 438 | (9.9) | 566 | (6.6) | 616 | (6.0) | 643 | (6.6) |
| Italy (Provincia Piemonte) | 354 | (9.4) | 390 | (6.9) | 449 | (6.9) | 572 | (7.0) | 621 | (5.8) | 650 | (7.3) |
| Italy (Provincia Trento) | 361 | (3.6) | 395 | (3.9) | 460 | (3.0) | 588 | (3.5) | 636 | (5.5) | 662 | (4.6) |
| Italy (Provincia Sardegna) | 298 | (9.7) | 327 | (8.9) | 383 | (7.8) | 515 | (7.7) | 571 | (9.8) | 598 | (9.4) |
| Italy (Provincia Puglia) | 316 | (6.7) | 342 | (6.2) | 390 | (5.9) | 503 | (5.6) | 557 | (6.5) | 588 | (8.1) |
| Italy (Provincia Veneto) | 372 | (8.3) | 405 | (8.0) | 463 | (7.5) | 588 | (5.9) | 635 | (5.4) | 663 | (7.7) |
| Spain (Andalusia) | 327 | (9.2) | 359 | (7.6) | 414 | (5.6) | 536 | (3.9) | 586 | (4.5) | 614 | (5.7) |
| Spain (Basque Country) | 354 | (5.5) | 386 | (4.7) | 439 | (4.2) | 554 | (3.9) | 601 | (3.9) | 628 | (4.9) |
| Spain (Cantabria) | 363 | (7.7) | 399 | (6.4) | 454 | (4.2) | 570 | (3.9) | 618 | (4.6) | 644 | (5.6) |
| Spain (Galicia) | 359 | (6.4) | 389 | (5.2) | 445 | (4.4) | 567 | (4.6) | 617 | (4.1) | 644 | (5.2) |
| Spain (La Rioja) | 377 | (8.9) | 408 | (4.9) | 461 | (5.4) | 582 | (3.7) | 628 | (4.6) | 655 | (5.8) |
| Spain (Castile and Leon) | 386 | (7.8) | 417 | (6.9) | 464 | (5.0) | 576 | (4.1) | 623 | (4.8) | 649 | (6.1) |
| Spain (Navarre) | 365 | (5.6) | 394 | (3.9) | 448 | (5.0) | 576 | (4.1) | 627 | (5.1) | 655 | (7.2) |
| Spain (Aragon) | 366 | (7.5) | 398 | (6.3) | 454 | (4.9) | 576 | (5.2) | 625 | (5.2) | 652 | (6.0) |
| Spain (Catalonia) | 338 | (8.2) | 370 | (6.5) | 432 | (6.6) | 555 | (6.4) | 603 | (5.6) | 631 | (6.7) |
| Spain (Asturias) | 365 | (10.8) | 399 | (8.0) | 454 | (6.4) | 566 | (5.3) | 613 | (4.8) | 639 | (5.6) |
| United Kingdom (Scotland) | 350 | (7.5) | 387 | (6.4) | 446 | (4.7) | 585 | (5.2) | 646 | (5.8) | 679 | (6.7) |
| **Non-adjudicated** | | | | | | | | | | | | |
| Belgium (French Community) | 312 | (9.4) | 349 | (8.4) | 413 | (6.5) | 561 | (5.1) | 618 | (5.1) | 648 | (5.9) |
| Belgium (German-Speaking Community) | 354 | (8.1) | 387 | (5.4) | 446 | (4.7) | 588 | (4.3) | 641 | (5.0) | 667 | (7.7) |
| Finland (Finnish Speaking) | 421 | (4.6) | 454 | (3.0) | 508 | (2.9) | 623 | (2.4) | 674 | (2.8) | 701 | (3.0) |
| Finland (Swedish Speaking) | 374 | (21.4) | 415 | (21.0) | 474 | (9.4) | 590 | (7.7) | 639 | (9.3) | 663 | (12.5) |
| United Kingdom (England) | 336 | (6.8) | 375 | (5.1) | 442 | (3.6) | 592 | (3.3) | 653 | (3.5) | 686 | (3.8) |
| United Kingdom (Northern Ireland) | 320 | (6.4) | 359 | (4.9) | 428 | (4.8) | 590 | (4.9) | 652 | (3.3) | 686 | (4.5) |
| United Kingdom (Wales) | 339 | (5.9) | 373 | (5.6) | 433 | (4.2) | 577 | (4.3) | 638 | (5.2) | 673 | (5.7) |

Note: Values that are statistically significant are indicated in bold (see Annex A3). See Table 2.1c for national data.
StatLink ᴓᴴᴸ http://dx.doi.org/10.1787/142184405135

Pour consulter la version française intégrale de ce tableau, suivre ce lien :
StatLink ᴓᴴᴸ http://dx.doi.org/10.1787/152830402855

[Part 1/1]

**Table S2d** **Percentage of students at each proficiency level on the *identifying scientific issues* scale**

Tableau S2d   Pourcentage d'élèves à chaque niveau de compétence sur l'échelle d'*identification des questions d'ordre scientifique*

| | Proficiency levels | | | | | | | | | | | | |
|---|---|---|---|---|---|---|---|---|---|---|---|---|---|
| | Below Level 1 (below 334.94 score points) | | Level 1 (from 334.94 to 409.54 score points) | | Level 2 (from 409.54 to 484.14 score points) | | Level 3 (from 484.14 to 558.73 score points) | | Level 4 (from 558.73 to 633.33 score points) | | Level 5 (from 633.33 to 707.93 score points) | | Level 6 (above 707.93 score points) | |
| | % | S.E. | % | S.E. | % | S.E. | % | S.E. | % | S.E. | % | S.E. | % | S.E. |
| **Adjudicated** | | | | | | | | | | | | | | |
| Belgium (Flemish Community) | 2.3 | (0.8) | 8.4 | (0.7) | 19.3 | (0.8) | 30.5 | (1.1) | 26.9 | (1.0) | 11.1 | (0.8) | 1.5 | (0.3) |
| Italy (Provincia Autonoma of Bolzano) | 2.2 | (0.4) | 9.0 | (0.9) | 22.6 | (1.4) | 33.8 | (1.6) | 24.6 | (1.3) | 7.4 | (0.8) | 0.5 | (0.2) |
| Italy (Provincia Campania) | 11.2 | (1.9) | 23.9 | (2.0) | 31.7 | (2.2) | 22.9 | (2.2) | 8.9 | (1.5) | 1.4 | (0.5) | 0.1 | a |
| Italy (Provincia Basilicata) | 10.3 | (1.2) | 21.8 | (1.6) | 31.3 | (1.7) | 24.2 | (1.6) | 10.3 | (1.1) | 2.0 | (0.5) | 0.2 | (0.2) |
| Italy (Provincia Emilia Romagna) | 4.1 | (0.8) | 11.6 | (1.2) | 23.8 | (1.5) | 28.0 | (1.5) | 23.0 | (1.3) | 8.6 | (1.3) | 1.0 | (0.3) |
| Italy (Provincia Friuli Venezia Giulia) | 1.9 | (0.6) | 7.6 | (1.0) | 18.6 | (1.4) | 30.5 | (1.7) | 28.3 | (1.7) | 11.3 | (1.3) | 1.7 | (0.6) |
| Italy (Provincia Sicilia) | 16.2 | (2.3) | 22.9 | (2.1) | 28.8 | (1.8) | 21.1 | (2.3) | 9.2 | (1.5) | 1.7 | (0.5) | 0.1 | a |
| Italy (Provincia Liguria) | 6.8 | (1.0) | 14.6 | (1.6) | 25.5 | (1.8) | 29.6 | (1.7) | 18.2 | (1.7) | 4.9 | (0.8) | 0.3 | (0.2) |
| Italy (Provincia Lombardia) | 6.4 | (1.4) | 12.1 | (1.4) | 24.4 | (1.5) | 29.8 | (1.9) | 20.6 | (2.1) | 6.1 | (1.2) | 0.6 | (0.3) |
| Italy (Provincia Piemonte) | 3.7 | (0.7) | 11.1 | (1.2) | 23.8 | (1.8) | 32.2 | (2.2) | 21.6 | (1.9) | 6.8 | (1.0) | 0.8 | (0.3) |
| Italy (Provincia Trento) | 3.6 | (0.4) | 9.6 | (0.8) | 19.0 | (1.0) | 29.0 | (1.8) | 25.2 | (2.3) | 11.0 | (1.3) | 2.5 | (0.6) |
| Italy (Provincia Sardegna) | 11.0 | (1.7) | 21.1 | (2.0) | 29.2 | (2.1) | 25.9 | (1.9) | 10.9 | (1.8) | 1.6 | (0.7) | 0.2 | (0.1) |
| Italy (Provincia Puglia) | 10.0 | (1.7) | 22.5 | (1.4) | 34.5 | (1.4) | 21.9 | (1.6) | 9.2 | (1.0) | 1.8 | (0.4) | 0.1 | (0.1) |
| Italy (Provincia Veneto) | 2.1 | (0.6) | 9.6 | (1.5) | 22.3 | (1.7) | 30.6 | (1.5) | 25.1 | (1.8) | 8.8 | (1.2) | 1.4 | (0.5) |
| Spain (Andalusia) | 5.3 | (0.9) | 16.3 | (1.3) | 31.0 | (1.3) | 29.9 | (1.3) | 14.6 | (1.0) | 2.7 | (0.5) | 0.2 | (0.1) |
| Spain (Basque Country) | 4.2 | (0.6) | 13.6 | (1.0) | 29.4 | (1.0) | 33.2 | (1.1) | 16.4 | (1.0) | 3.0 | (0.5) | 0.2 | (0.1) |
| Spain (Cantabria) | 3.3 | (0.7) | 9.7 | (1.1) | 26.2 | (1.5) | 34.6 | (1.6) | 20.9 | (1.3) | 4.8 | (0.7) | 0.6 | (0.2) |
| Spain (Galicia) | 3.4 | (0.7) | 10.3 | (1.1) | 26.6 | (1.2) | 32.0 | (1.7) | 21.8 | (1.5) | 5.3 | (0.8) | 0.6 | (0.2) |
| Spain (La Rioja) | 2.7 | (0.6) | 9.0 | (1.1) | 23.9 | (1.7) | 34.9 | (2.2) | 23.2 | (1.6) | 6.0 | (0.8) | 0.4 | (0.2) |
| Spain (Castile and Leon) | 1.4 | (0.5) | 8.4 | (1.4) | 26.2 | (2.0) | 35.1 | (1.5) | 22.3 | (1.9) | 5.8 | (1.2) | 0.7 | (0.3) |
| Spain (Navarre) | 2.8 | (0.6) | 12.5 | (1.1) | 25.7 | (1.5) | 32.0 | (1.7) | 21.1 | (1.3) | 5.6 | (0.8) | 0.3 | (0.2) |
| Spain (Aragon) | 3.2 | (0.6) | 11.1 | (1.4) | 24.7 | (2.6) | 31.7 | (1.7) | 22.6 | (1.9) | 6.2 | (1.0) | 0.5 | (0.3) |
| Spain (Catalonia) | 4.6 | (0.9) | 12.7 | (1.5) | 25.6 | (1.7) | 34.6 | (1.8) | 18.7 | (1.3) | 3.6 | (0.6) | 0.2 | (0.1) |
| Spain (Asturias) | 2.4 | (0.7) | 10.0 | (1.2) | 23.5 | (1.4) | 35.5 | (1.4) | 22.5 | (1.6) | 5.6 | (0.8) | 0.4 | (0.2) |
| United Kingdom (Scotland) | 3.5 | (0.6) | 10.7 | (1.0) | 23.9 | (1.3) | 28.4 | (1.3) | 20.9 | (0.9) | 9.8 | (0.8) | 2.8 | (0.5) |
| **Non-adjudicated** | | | | | | | | | | | | | | |
| Belgium (French Community) | 7.5 | (1.4) | 13.4 | (1.2) | 23.5 | (1.4) | 25.9 | (1.5) | 20.2 | (1.0) | 7.9 | (0.8) | 1.5 | (0.4) |
| Belgium (German-Speaking Community) | 2.3 | (0.8) | 11.1 | (1.6) | 25.6 | (2.0) | 28.7 | (2.5) | 22.8 | (1.8) | 8.4 | (1.1) | 1.1 | (0.5) |
| Finland (Finnish Speaking) | 0.8 | (0.2) | 3.8 | (0.4) | 14.2 | (0.7) | 30.4 | (1.0) | 33.1 | (1.1) | 14.9 | (0.8) | 2.7 | (0.3) |
| Finland (Swedish Speaking) | 2.5 | (1.2) | 7.2 | (2.4) | 20.9 | (3.0) | 32.7 | (3.2) | 27.7 | (3.7) | 8.1 | (2.5) | 0.9 | (0.9) |
| United Kingdom (England) | 4.9 | (0.6) | 11.1 | (0.7) | 22.3 | (0.7) | 26.5 | (0.9) | 22.2 | (0.8) | 10.3 | (0.6) | 2.7 | (0.3) |
| United Kingdom (Northern Ireland) | 6.5 | (0.8) | 13.4 | (0.9) | 21.9 | (0.9) | 25.1 | (1.2) | 21.6 | (1.0) | 9.4 | (0.7) | 2.1 | (0.4) |
| United Kingdom (Wales) | 4.9 | (0.6) | 14.2 | (0.9) | 24.8 | (1.3) | 26.7 | (1.2) | 20.0 | (1.0) | 7.7 | (0.7) | 1.7 | (0.5) |

Note: See Table 2.2a for national data.
*StatLink* 🛢🖼 http://dx.doi.org/10.1787/142184405135

Pour consulter la version française intégrale de ce tableau, suivre ce lien :
*StatLink* 🛢🖼 http://dx.doi.org/10.1787/152830402855

[Part 1/1]

**Table S2e** Percentage of students at each proficiency level on the *identifying scientific issues* scale, by gender

Tableau S2e Pourcentage d'élèves à chaque niveau de compétence sur l'échelle d'*identification des questions d'ordre scientifique*, selon le sexe

### Males – Proficiency levels

| | Below Level 1 (below 334.94 score points) | | Level 1 (from 334.94 to 409.54 score points) | | Level 2 (from 409.54 to 484.14 score points) | | Level 3 (from 484.14 to 558.73 score points) | | Level 4 (from 558.73 to 633.33 score points) | | Level 5 (from 633.33 to 707.93 score points) | | Level 6 (above 707.93 score points) | |
|---|---|---|---|---|---|---|---|---|---|---|---|---|---|---|
| | % | S.E. | % | S.E. | % | S.E. | % | S.E. | % | S.E. | % | S.E. | % | S.E. |
| **Adjudicated** | | | | | | | | | | | | | | |
| Belgium (Flemish Community) | 2.6 | (1.2) | 9.7 | (0.9) | 20.5 | (1.2) | 29.1 | (1.7) | 26.6 | (1.4) | 10.0 | (1.0) | 1.5 | (0.3) |
| Italy (Provincia Autonoma of Bolzano) | 3.1 | (0.7) | 10.8 | (1.6) | 21.8 | (2.3) | 32.7 | (2.4) | 24.5 | (1.8) | 6.6 | (0.9) | 0.5 | (0.3) |
| Italy (Provincia Campania) | 12.1 | (2.2) | 24.2 | (2.4) | 30.8 | (2.8) | 23.6 | (3.2) | 7.8 | (1.8) | 1.4 | (0.6) | a | a |
| Italy (Provincia Basilicata) | 13.8 | (2.1) | 25.3 | (2.1) | 28.1 | (2.6) | 21.7 | (2.1) | 9.0 | (1.4) | 2.0 | (0.6) | 0.3 | (0.2) |
| Italy (Provincia Emilia Romagna) | 4.4 | (1.1) | 11.4 | (1.8) | 24.7 | (1.7) | 29.4 | (2.2) | 20.9 | (2.4) | 7.9 | (1.6) | 1.3 | (0.5) |
| Italy (Provincia Friuli Venezia Giulia) | 2.5 | (1.0) | 8.1 | (1.7) | 20.7 | (2.3) | 30.0 | (2.7) | 27.7 | (2.2) | 9.5 | (1.9) | 1.4 | (0.7) |
| Italy (Provincia Sicilia) | 21.3 | (3.4) | 21.8 | (2.9) | 25.2 | (2.3) | 18.3 | (2.6) | 11.4 | (2.3) | 2.0 | (0.8) | a | a |
| Italy (Provincia Liguria) | 10.0 | (1.9) | 18.6 | (2.4) | 25.3 | (2.7) | 26.4 | (2.6) | 14.6 | (2.1) | 4.6 | (1.1) | 0.5 | (0.3) |
| Italy (Provincia Lombardia) | 8.6 | (2.3) | 13.9 | (2.3) | 25.5 | (2.4) | 28.3 | (2.8) | 17.5 | (2.8) | 5.6 | (1.3) | 0.6 | (0.3) |
| Italy (Provincia Piemonte) | 5.6 | (1.5) | 14.0 | (1.8) | 25.1 | (3.1) | 29.7 | (3.4) | 18.2 | (2.1) | 6.6 | (1.4) | 0.9 | (0.4) |
| Italy (Provincia Trento) | 5.0 | (0.8) | 12.1 | (1.2) | 20.4 | (1.6) | 26.0 | (2.2) | 21.3 | (2.3) | 11.3 | (1.7) | 3.9 | (1.1) |
| Italy (Provincia Sardegna) | 15.2 | (2.9) | 23.2 | (2.9) | 27.8 | (3.0) | 21.2 | (2.5) | 10.5 | (2.1) | 1.8 | (0.9) | 0.3 | (0.2) |
| Italy (Provincia Puglia) | 13.1 | (2.5) | 24.8 | (2.0) | 31.0 | (2.1) | 20.9 | (1.8) | 8.5 | (1.3) | 1.6 | (0.4) | 0.0 | a |
| Italy (Provincia Veneto) | 2.3 | (0.8) | 9.8 | (2.2) | 23.3 | (2.5) | 30.2 | (2.4) | 24.1 | (2.8) | 8.8 | (1.9) | 1.5 | (0.6) |
| Spain (Andalusia) | 7.1 | (1.4) | 17.1 | (1.8) | 30.7 | (1.9) | 27.6 | (2.3) | 14.9 | (1.6) | 2.4 | (0.8) | 0.1 | (0.2) |
| Spain (Basque Country) | 6.6 | (0.9) | 16.3 | (1.4) | 30.1 | (1.4) | 29.8 | (1.4) | 14.7 | (1.2) | 2.4 | (0.5) | 0.1 | (0.1) |
| Spain (Cantabria) | 4.5 | (0.9) | 11.2 | (1.6) | 27.3 | (2.5) | 31.0 | (2.6) | 20.2 | (1.8) | 4.9 | (0.8) | 0.8 | (0.3) |
| Spain (Galicia) | 4.2 | (0.9) | 12.8 | (1.4) | 28.4 | (1.7) | 29.2 | (2.3) | 19.4 | (1.7) | 5.3 | (1.1) | 0.6 | (0.3) |
| Spain (La Rioja) | 3.4 | (0.9) | 10.2 | (1.7) | 26.3 | (2.3) | 32.7 | (2.7) | 21.6 | (2.1) | 5.3 | (0.9) | 0.5 | (0.3) |
| Spain (Castile and Leon) | 2.1 | (0.7) | 10.3 | (1.7) | 28.1 | (2.6) | 33.2 | (2.0) | 21.2 | (2.3) | 4.7 | (1.2) | 0.4 | (0.3) |
| Spain (Navarre) | 3.6 | (0.9) | 14.5 | (1.6) | 24.1 | (1.9) | 30.5 | (2.2) | 20.1 | (2.1) | 6.9 | (1.2) | 0.4 | (0.3) |
| Spain (Aragon) | 3.1 | (0.9) | 13.4 | (1.6) | 24.8 | (2.8) | 30.8 | (2.6) | 21.6 | (2.3) | 6.0 | (1.1) | 0.5 | (0.3) |
| Spain (Catalonia) | 5.5 | (1.5) | 13.3 | (2.1) | 27.5 | (2.4) | 33.1 | (2.1) | 17.2 | (1.8) | 3.0 | (0.9) | 0.3 | (0.2) |
| Spain (Asturias) | 3.4 | (1.0) | 11.2 | (1.7) | 24.8 | (2.3) | 33.1 | (2.1) | 21.3 | (2.0) | 5.6 | (1.1) | 0.6 | (0.3) |
| United Kingdom (Scotland) | 4.9 | (0.9) | 11.4 | (1.3) | 24.0 | (1.9) | 27.8 | (2.0) | 19.8 | (1.3) | 9.9 | (1.1) | 2.1 | (0.5) |
| **Non-adjudicated** | | | | | | | | | | | | | | |
| Belgium (French Community) | 9.5 | (2.3) | 15.0 | (1.8) | 23.7 | (2.1) | 24.1 | (2.0) | 18.9 | (1.9) | 7.2 | (1.0) | 1.6 | (0.5) |
| Belgium (German-Speaking Community) | 3.7 | (1.0) | 12.1 | (1.9) | 24.0 | (2.5) | 26.7 | (2.8) | 22.7 | (2.4) | 9.3 | (1.7) | 1.6 | (0.9) |
| Finland (Finnish Speaking) | 1.2 | (0.3) | 5.7 | (0.6) | 17.0 | (1.0) | 31.5 | (1.0) | 30.0 | (1.2) | 12.4 | (0.9) | 2.2 | (0.3) |
| Finland (Swedish Speaking) | 4.2 | (2.2) | 7.6 | (2.5) | 21.4 | (6.0) | 35.9 | (4.6) | 24.3 | (4.7) | 6.1 | (2.5) | 0.4 | a |
| United Kingdom (England) | 5.8 | (0.8) | 12.1 | (0.9) | 21.5 | (1.0) | 25.7 | (1.3) | 21.4 | (1.5) | 10.6 | (0.9) | 2.9 | (0.5) |
| United Kingdom (Northern Ireland) | 7.9 | (1.2) | 14.4 | (1.3) | 22.7 | (1.6) | 24.1 | (1.5) | 20.0 | (1.6) | 8.7 | (1.0) | 2.1 | (0.5) |
| United Kingdom (Wales) | 5.4 | (0.7) | 15.6 | (1.2) | 24.1 | (1.7) | 25.9 | (1.6) | 19.8 | (1.4) | 7.7 | (0.8) | 1.5 | (0.5) |

### Females – Proficiency levels

| | Below Level 1 (below 334.94 score points) | | Level 1 (from 334.94 to 409.54 score points) | | Level 2 (from 409.54 to 484.14 score points) | | Level 3 (from 484.14 to 558.73 score points) | | Level 4 (from 558.73 to 633.33 score points) | | Level 5 (from 633.33 to 707.93 score points) | | Level 6 (above 707.93 score points) | |
|---|---|---|---|---|---|---|---|---|---|---|---|---|---|---|
| | % | S.E. | % | S.E. | % | S.E. | % | S.E. | % | S.E. | % | S.E. | % | S.E. |
| **Adjudicated** | | | | | | | | | | | | | | |
| Belgium (Flemish Community) | 2.0 | (0.5) | 6.9 | (0.9) | 17.9 | (1.3) | 32.1 | (1.3) | 27.1 | (1.4) | 12.4 | (1.2) | 1.6 | (0.4) |
| Italy (Provincia Autonoma of Bolzano) | 1.2 | (0.4) | 7.2 | (1.5) | 23.3 | (1.7) | 34.9 | (1.8) | 24.6 | (1.9) | 8.3 | (1.1) | 0.5 | (0.3) |
| Italy (Provincia Campania) | 10.2 | (2.2) | 23.6 | (2.5) | 32.6 | (2.5) | 22.1 | (2.5) | 10.0 | (1.9) | 1.5 | (0.6) | 0.1 | a |
| Italy (Provincia Basilicata) | 6.6 | (1.0) | 18.0 | (2.3) | 34.7 | (2.2) | 26.9 | (2.0) | 11.7 | (1.7) | 2.0 | (0.8) | 0.2 | (0.2) |
| Italy (Provincia Emilia Romagna) | 3.8 | (1.1) | 11.8 | (1.5) | 22.8 | (2.0) | 26.5 | (2.5) | 25.1 | (2.1) | 9.2 | (1.9) | 0.7 | (0.3) |
| Italy (Provincia Friuli Venezia Giulia) | 1.2 | (0.8) | 7.2 | (1.5) | 16.5 | (1.8) | 31.0 | (2.4) | 28.9 | (2.8) | 13.1 | (2.0) | 2.1 | (0.9) |
| Italy (Provincia Sicilia) | 11.4 | (2.7) | 24.0 | (2.9) | 32.2 | (2.8) | 23.7 | (3.1) | 7.1 | (1.6) | 1.5 | (0.5) | 0.1 | a |
| Italy (Provincia Liguria) | 3.5 | (0.8) | 10.4 | (1.7) | 25.8 | (2.5) | 33.0 | (1.9) | 21.9 | (2.2) | 5.2 | (1.2) | 0.2 | (0.2) |
| Italy (Provincia Lombardia) | 4.3 | (1.0) | 10.2 | (1.3) | 23.4 | (2.4) | 31.3 | (3.1) | 23.6 | (2.6) | 6.6 | (1.8) | 0.6 | (0.5) |
| Italy (Provincia Piemonte) | 2.1 | (0.8) | 8.6 | (1.2) | 22.6 | (1.8) | 34.4 | (2.0) | 24.5 | (2.6) | 7.0 | (1.5) | 0.7 | (0.3) |
| Italy (Provincia Trento) | 2.2 | (0.6) | 7.1 | (0.9) | 17.7 | (1.4) | 32.0 | (2.6) | 29.2 | (3.4) | 10.7 | (2.0) | 1.1 | (0.6) |
| Italy (Provincia Sardegna) | 6.6 | (1.3) | 19.1 | (2.5) | 30.7 | (2.5) | 30.8 | (2.3) | 11.4 | (2.2) | 1.4 | (0.8) | a | a |
| Italy (Provincia Puglia) | 6.9 | (1.5) | 20.3 | (2.1) | 37.9 | (2.1) | 22.7 | (2.3) | 9.9 | (1.2) | 2.0 | (0.6) | 0.3 | (0.2) |
| Italy (Provincia Veneto) | 2.0 | (0.7) | 9.5 | (2.2) | 21.2 | (2.3) | 31.0 | (2.6) | 26.1 | (3.0) | 8.9 | (1.6) | 1.3 | (0.7) |
| Spain (Andalusia) | 3.6 | (1.0) | 15.5 | (1.7) | 31.3 | (2.1) | 32.2 | (1.9) | 14.3 | (1.6) | 3.0 | (0.6) | 0.2 | (0.2) |
| Spain (Basque Country) | 1.8 | (0.4) | 10.9 | (1.1) | 28.7 | (1.4) | 36.7 | (1.5) | 18.1 | (1.4) | 3.6 | (0.8) | 0.3 | (0.2) |
| Spain (Cantabria) | 2.1 | (0.7) | 8.1 | (1.3) | 25.0 | (2.0) | 38.2 | (2.4) | 21.5 | (2.3) | 4.8 | (1.1) | 0.3 | (0.2) |
| Spain (Galicia) | 2.4 | (0.8) | 7.5 | (1.3) | 24.6 | (1.9) | 35.1 | (1.9) | 24.4 | (1.9) | 5.3 | (1.1) | 0.7 | (0.3) |
| Spain (La Rioja) | 2.0 | (0.7) | 7.7 | (1.3) | 21.4 | (2.0) | 37.1 | (3.1) | 24.8 | (2.5) | 6.7 | (1.2) | 0.2 | a |
| Spain (Castile and Leon) | 0.7 | (0.4) | 6.3 | (1.4) | 24.1 | (2.4) | 37.2 | (2.1) | 23.6 | (2.1) | 7.1 | (1.7) | 0.9 | (0.4) |
| Spain (Navarre) | 2.0 | (0.8) | 10.5 | (1.3) | 27.3 | (2.5) | 33.5 | (2.2) | 22.1 | (1.7) | 4.3 | (0.9) | 0.2 | (0.1) |
| Spain (Aragon) | 3.2 | (0.8) | 8.8 | (1.4) | 24.6 | (3.0) | 32.7 | (2.1) | 23.8 | (2.3) | 6.4 | (1.6) | 0.6 | (0.5) |
| Spain (Catalonia) | 3.7 | (0.9) | 12.1 | (1.6) | 23.7 | (1.9) | 36.0 | (2.4) | 20.1 | (1.8) | 4.2 | (0.9) | 0.1 | a |
| Spain (Asturias) | 1.3 | (0.6) | 8.8 | (1.6) | 22.1 | (1.7) | 38.1 | (1.8) | 23.9 | (2.2) | 5.6 | (1.0) | 0.3 | (0.2) |
| United Kingdom (Scotland) | 2.1 | (0.5) | 9.9 | (1.2) | 23.7 | (1.3) | 29.0 | (1.5) | 21.9 | (1.4) | 9.8 | (1.1) | 3.6 | (0.9) |
| **Non-adjudicated** | | | | | | | | | | | | | | |
| Belgium (French Community) | 5.4 | (1.1) | 11.7 | (1.3) | 23.4 | (1.4) | 27.9 | (2.0) | 21.5 | (1.9) | 8.7 | (1.2) | 1.4 | (0.4) |
| Belgium (German-Speaking Community) | 1.0 | (0.9) | 10.1 | (2.1) | 27.2 | (2.9) | 30.6 | (3.5) | 22.9 | (2.8) | 7.5 | (1.5) | 0.7 | (0.5) |
| Finland (Finnish Speaking) | 0.4 | (0.1) | 2.0 | (0.4) | 11.5 | (1.1) | 29.4 | (1.8) | 36.2 | (1.6) | 17.3 | (1.4) | 3.2 | (0.4) |
| Finland (Swedish Speaking) | 0.8 | (1.0) | 6.8 | (3.2) | 20.3 | (3.9) | 29.4 | (5.6) | 31.2 | (5.6) | 10.1 | (3.8) | 1.5 | a |
| United Kingdom (England) | 3.9 | (0.7) | 10.1 | (0.9) | 23.0 | (1.1) | 27.4 | (1.2) | 23.0 | (1.1) | 10.1 | (0.9) | 2.5 | (0.4) |
| United Kingdom (Northern Ireland) | 4.9 | (1.0) | 12.4 | (1.3) | 21.1 | (1.6) | 26.0 | (2.0) | 23.2 | (1.8) | 10.0 | (1.1) | 2.2 | (0.6) |
| United Kingdom (Wales) | 4.5 | (0.8) | 12.8 | (1.4) | 25.5 | (1.8) | 27.4 | (2.2) | 20.3 | (1.9) | 7.6 | (1.0) | 2.0 | (0.8) |

Note: See Table 2.2b for national data.

StatLink 🔗 http://dx.doi.org/10.1787/142184405135
Pour consulter la version française intégrale de ce tableau, suivre ce lien :
StatLink 🔗 http://dx.doi.org/10.1787/152830402855

[Part 1/1]

**Table S2f** Mean score, variation and gender differences in student performance on the *identifying scientific issues* scale

Tableau S2f Score moyen, différences de score selon le sexe et répartition des scores sur l'échelle d'*identification des questions d'ordre scientifique*

| | All students | | | | Gender differences | | | | | |
|---|---|---|---|---|---|---|---|---|---|---|
| | Mean score | | Standard deviation | | Males | | Females | | Difference (M – F) | |
| | Mean | S.E. | S.D. | S.E. | Mean score | S.E. | Mean score | S.E. | Score dif. | S.E. |
| **Adjudicated** | | | | | | | | | | |
| Belgium (Flemish Community) | 529 | (3.4) | 92 | (3.1) | 524 | (4.4) | 536 | (3.6) | **-12** | (4.4) |
| Italy (Provincia Autonoma of Bolzano) | 517 | (2.0) | 85 | (1.6) | 512 | (2.9) | 522 | (2.9) | **-10** | (4.1) |
| Italy (Provincia Campania) | 444 | (6.2) | 90 | (3.4) | 441 | (6.4) | 448 | (7.6) | -7 | (6.4) |
| Italy (Provincia Basilicata) | 453 | (4.9) | 91 | (2.7) | 440 | (6.8) | 466 | (4.8) | **-26** | (6.9) |
| Italy (Provincia Emilia Romagna) | 508 | (4.8) | 97 | (2.9) | 506 | (6.3) | 511 | (4.7) | -6 | (5.7) |
| Italy (Provincia Friuli Venezia Giulia) | 534 | (3.6) | 91 | (2.7) | 526 | (6.0) | 541 | (5.9) | -15 | (9.4) |
| Italy (Provincia Sicilia) | 435 | (7.9) | 101 | (5.0) | 427 | (10.7) | 442 | (8.7) | **-16** | (11.2) |
| Italy (Provincia Liguria) | 486 | (5.5) | 96 | (2.0) | 471 | (7.7) | 503 | (5.6) | **-32** | (8.3) |
| Italy (Provincia Lombardia) | 495 | (6.6) | 99 | (4.3) | 483 | (10.7) | 507 | (4.9) | **-24** | (10.0) |
| Italy (Provincia Piemonte) | 506 | (4.3) | 92 | (2.8) | 493 | (6.6) | 517 | (4.5) | **-23** | (7.1) |
| Italy (Provincia Trento) | 525 | (2.3) | 101 | (2.1) | 518 | (4.1) | 532 | (3.4) | **-14** | (6.0) |
| Italy (Provincia Sardegna) | 452 | (6.8) | 95 | (3.7) | 440 | (9.7) | 465 | (6.4) | **-25** | (9.3) |
| Italy (Provincia Puglia) | 448 | (4.9) | 89 | (2.8) | 439 | (6.0) | 457 | (4.8) | **-19** | (3.7) |
| Italy (Provincia Veneto) | 521 | (5.0) | 91 | (2.5) | 518 | (6.9) | 523 | (7.8) | -4 | (10.8) |
| Spain (Andalusia) | 477 | (3.7) | 87 | (2.3) | 470 | (4.7) | 482 | (4.3) | **-12** | (5.2) |
| Spain (Basque Country) | 487 | (3.5) | 84 | (1.6) | 474 | (4.0) | 500 | (3.6) | **-26** | (2.9) |
| Spain (Cantabria) | 504 | (3.8) | 85 | (1.9) | 499 | (5.0) | 510 | (3.7) | **-11** | (4.5) |
| Spain (Galicia) | 504 | (4.1) | 88 | (2.0) | 495 | (4.8) | 514 | (4.6) | **-19** | (4.5) |
| Spain (La Rioja) | 511 | (2.6) | 85 | (2.3) | 503 | (3.8) | 519 | (3.2) | **-15** | (5.0) |
| Spain (Castile and Leon) | 513 | (5.5) | 81 | (2.1) | 504 | (5.9) | 524 | (5.6) | **-19** | (4.0) |
| Spain (Navarre) | 502 | (3.0) | 86 | (2.3) | 500 | (4.0) | 505 | (3.5) | -4 | (4.6) |
| Spain (Aragon) | 507 | (4.6) | 89 | (1.9) | 502 | (5.5) | 512 | (5.3) | -10 | (5.8) |
| Spain (Catalonia) | 492 | (4.5) | 87 | (2.4) | 486 | (5.8) | 498 | (4.6) | **-12** | (5.3) |
| Spain (Asturias) | 510 | (4.3) | 84 | (2.2) | 504 | (5.5) | 516 | (4.4) | **-12** | (5.2) |
| United Kingdom (Scotland) | 516 | (4.1) | 101 | (2.2) | 509 | (4.8) | 523 | (4.4) | **-15** | (4.0) |
| **Non-adjudicated** | | | | | | | | | | |
| Belgium (French Community) | 496 | (4.6) | 107 | (3.5) | 487 | (6.3) | 506 | (5.5) | **-19** | (7.6) |
| Belgium (German-Speaking Community) | 512 | (2.7) | 91 | (2.1) | 511 | (4.2) | 513 | (4.6) | -2 | (6.9) |
| Finland (Finnish Speaking) | 556 | (2.3) | 84 | (1.1) | 543 | (2.7) | 569 | (2.7) | **-26** | (2.9) |
| Finland (Swedish Speaking) | 525 | (6.5) | 85 | (4.1) | 513 | (8.4) | 537 | (8.2) | **-23** | (10.8) |
| United Kingdom (England) | 515 | (2.8) | 106 | (1.8) | 512 | (3.4) | 518 | (3.3) | -6 | (3.9) |
| United Kingdom (Northern Ireland) | 504 | (3.8) | 109 | (2.7) | 496 | (6.0) | 512 | (5.6) | -16 | (8.8) |
| United Kingdom (Wales) | 500 | (3.3) | 101 | (1.7) | 497 | (3.4) | 504 | (4.3) | -7 | (4.3) |

| | Percentiles | | | | | | | | | | | |
|---|---|---|---|---|---|---|---|---|---|---|---|---|
| | 5th | | 10th | | 25th | | 75th | | 90th | | 95th | |
| | Score | S.E. | Score | S.E. | Score | S.E. | Score | S.E. | Score | S.E. | Score | S.E. |
| **Adjudicated** | | | | | | | | | | | | |
| Belgium (Flemish Community) | 369 | (11.1) | 406 | (6.8) | 469 | (4.2) | 595 | (3.3) | 644 | (3.8) | 671 | (3.9) |
| Italy (Provincia Autonoma of Bolzano) | 369 | (6.3) | 404 | (6.5) | 461 | (4.1) | 577 | (2.9) | 624 | (3.2) | 649 | (3.9) |
| Italy (Provincia Campania) | 299 | (9.7) | 330 | (8.8) | 384 | (7.8) | 507 | (8.1) | 560 | (6.8) | 592 | (8.4) |
| Italy (Provincia Basilicata) | 306 | (7.7) | 333 | (5.9) | 390 | (7.0) | 515 | (5.9) | 571 | (6.4) | 603 | (8.5) |
| Italy (Provincia Emilia Romagna) | 345 | (9.0) | 380 | (7.4) | 442 | (6.0) | 580 | (5.2) | 632 | (7.0) | 659 | (4.7) |
| Italy (Provincia Friuli Venezia Giulia) | 374 | (9.4) | 414 | (7.9) | 475 | (5.0) | 597 | (4.2) | 646 | (4.9) | 675 | (5.9) |
| Italy (Provincia Sicilia) | 264 | (24.3) | 304 | (12.9) | 368 | (8.5) | 505 | (8.6) | 564 | (8.6) | 596 | (8.0) |
| Italy (Provincia Liguria) | 320 | (8.4) | 359 | (6.8) | 423 | (8.3) | 554 | (5.6) | 607 | (6.5) | 636 | (7.1) |
| Italy (Provincia Lombardia) | 320 | (14.8) | 364 | (11.9) | 435 | (9.6) | 565 | (6.2) | 615 | (6.3) | 646 | (7.8) |
| Italy (Provincia Piemonte) | 350 | (8.4) | 385 | (8.2) | 446 | (6.5) | 571 | (6.4) | 619 | (6.5) | 650 | (5.9) |
| Italy (Provincia Trento) | 351 | (6.5) | 391 | (4.9) | 460 | (4.3) | 595 | (4.1) | 651 | (7.4) | 685 | (8.4) |
| Italy (Provincia Sardegna) | 287 | (11.4) | 330 | (10.7) | 390 | (7.9) | 520 | (8.2) | 571 | (9.9) | 602 | (12.3) |
| Italy (Provincia Puglia) | 303 | (10.6) | 335 | (10.1) | 391 | (7.4) | 506 | (4.8) | 565 | (5.8) | 599 | (5.1) |
| Italy (Provincia Veneto) | 366 | (9.9) | 401 | (7.8) | 458 | (7.3) | 586 | (4.8) | 635 | (6.2) | 665 | (6.5) |
| Spain (Andalusia) | 332 | (9.1) | 366 | (6.2) | 420 | (5.2) | 537 | (4.0) | 586 | (5.2) | 612 | (5.6) |
| Spain (Basque Country) | 345 | (6.5) | 376 | (4.4) | 433 | (4.9) | 545 | (3.6) | 591 | (3.8) | 618 | (4.5) |
| Spain (Cantabria) | 359 | (8.6) | 398 | (5.9) | 449 | (5.2) | 562 | (4.2) | 610 | (5.0) | 636 | (5.4) |
| Spain (Galicia) | 355 | (10.4) | 393 | (6.4) | 447 | (4.2) | 565 | (4.8) | 613 | (4.7) | 640 | (6.0) |
| Spain (La Rioja) | 368 | (7.0) | 402 | (5.7) | 460 | (4.4) | 570 | (3.9) | 616 | (4.5) | 641 | (5.0) |
| Spain (Castile and Leon) | 380 | (9.1) | 411 | (6.9) | 461 | (6.2) | 569 | (5.6) | 617 | (6.9) | 643 | (7.9) |
| Spain (Navarre) | 359 | (6.1) | 388 | (5.4) | 443 | (5.3) | 563 | (3.5) | 612 | (4.0) | 638 | (6.0) |
| Spain (Aragon) | 353 | (7.1) | 390 | (5.6) | 447 | (6.0) | 570 | (5.0) | 619 | (5.2) | 644 | (6.8) |
| Spain (Catalonia) | 338 | (9.4) | 373 | (7.0) | 436 | (6.6) | 553 | (3.7) | 598 | (4.3) | 623 | (5.3) |
| Spain (Asturias) | 362 | (9.1) | 399 | (7.4) | 456 | (6.3) | 567 | (4.1) | 614 | (4.4) | 640 | (4.7) |
| United Kingdom (Scotland) | 351 | (6.2) | 388 | (6.5) | 448 | (5.0) | 583 | (4.5) | 648 | (5.8) | 682 | (7.5) |
| **Non-adjudicated** | | | | | | | | | | | | |
| Belgium (French Community) | 311 | (11.8) | 354 | (11.2) | 425 | (6.9) | 573 | (4.6) | 630 | (5.0) | 662 | (6.7) |
| Belgium (German-Speaking Community) | 362 | (8.5) | 396 | (4.8) | 447 | (4.0) | 579 | (5.1) | 631 | (5.1) | 659 | (6.3) |
| Finland (Finnish Speaking) | 413 | (4.0) | 448 | (3.4) | 503 | (3.1) | 614 | (2.9) | 660 | (2.9) | 687 | (3.2) |
| Finland (Swedish Speaking) | 375 | (23.4) | 411 | (18.0) | 473 | (6.8) | 584 | (8.6) | 631 | (13.6) | 687 | (15.5) |
| United Kingdom (England) | 337 | (7.3) | 377 | (5.3) | 444 | (3.5) | 588 | (3.1) | 649 | (3.4) | 683 | (3.7) |
| United Kingdom (Northern Ireland) | 320 | (7.1) | 361 | (6.9) | 430 | (5.1) | 583 | (4.5) | 641 | (4.3) | 674 | (6.4) |
| United Kingdom (Wales) | 336 | (6.2) | 370 | (4.8) | 430 | (4.0) | 572 | (4.0) | 631 | (4.1) | 665 | (5.4) |

Note: Values that are statistically significant are indicated in bold (see Annex A3). See Table 2.2c for national data.
*StatLink* http://dx.doi.org/10.1787/142184405135

Pour consulter la version française intégrale de ce tableau, suivre ce lien :
*StatLink* http://dx.doi.org/10.1787/152830402855

253

[Part 1/1]

**Table S2g** Percentage of students at each proficiency level on the *explaining phenomena scientifically* scale

Tableau S2g Pourcentage d'élèves à chaque niveau de compétence sur l'échelle d'*explication scientifique de phénomènes*

| | Proficiency levels | | | | | | | | | | | | |
|---|---|---|---|---|---|---|---|---|---|---|---|---|---|
| | Below Level 1 (below 334.94 score points) | | Level 1 (from 334.94 to 409.54 score points) | | Level 2 (from 409.54 to 484.14 score points) | | Level 3 (from 484.14 to 558.73 score points) | | Level 4 (from 558.73 to 633.33 score points) | | Level 5 (from 633.33 to 707.93 score points) | | Level 6 (above 707.93 score points) | |
| | % | S.E. | % | S.E. | % | S.E. | % | S.E. | % | S.E. | % | S.E. | % | S.E. |
| **Adjudicated** | | | | | | | | | | | | | | |
| Belgium (Flemish Community) | 3.2 | (1.0) | 9.6 | (0.8) | 19.6 | (0.9) | 28.8 | (0.9) | 26.3 | (1.0) | 11.0 | (0.7) | 1.5 | (0.2) |
| Italy (Provincia Autonoma of Bolzano) | 2.2 | (0.5) | 7.9 | (1.1) | 20.8 | (1.4) | 29.5 | (1.3) | 25.5 | (1.4) | 11.8 | (0.8) | 2.3 | (0.4) |
| Italy (Provincia Campania) | 10.4 | (1.6) | 23.2 | (1.9) | 32.8 | (1.9) | 24.3 | (2.0) | 7.5 | (1.3) | 1.5 | (0.6) | 0.3 | (0.3) |
| Italy (Provincia Basilicata) | 8.7 | (1.4) | 23.3 | (2.1) | 32.9 | (2.4) | 23.1 | (1.6) | 9.9 | (1.2) | 2.0 | (0.7) | 0.0 | a |
| Italy (Provincia Emilia Romagna) | 4.2 | (0.9) | 11.4 | (1.1) | 21.9 | (1.5) | 28.7 | (1.7) | 22.7 | (1.4) | 9.2 | (0.8) | 2.0 | (0.4) |
| Italy (Provincia Friuli Venezia Giulia) | 2.0 | (0.5) | 5.6 | (0.8) | 18.7 | (1.3) | 32.6 | (1.6) | 27.2 | (1.6) | 11.0 | (1.3) | 2.9 | (0.6) |
| Italy (Provincia Sicilia) | 15.7 | (2.1) | 24.1 | (2.4) | 26.4 | (2.0) | 21.3 | (2.1) | 9.5 | (1.4) | 2.8 | (0.8) | 0.1 | (0.1) |
| Italy (Provincia Liguria) | 6.2 | (1.2) | 14.5 | (1.9) | 24.3 | (1.9) | 28.5 | (2.0) | 19.3 | (1.7) | 6.3 | (1.2) | 0.9 | (0.4) |
| Italy (Provincia Lombardia) | 6.2 | (1.4) | 11.1 | (1.6) | 22.4 | (1.9) | 29.8 | (2.2) | 21.6 | (1.7) | 7.8 | (1.1) | 1.2 | (0.4) |
| Italy (Provincia Piemonte) | 3.6 | (0.8) | 10.4 | (1.4) | 22.6 | (1.7) | 31.8 | (2.1) | 22.1 | (2.0) | 8.3 | (1.1) | 1.1 | (0.3) |
| Italy (Provincia Trento) | 3.2 | (0.4) | 9.9 | (0.8) | 19.8 | (1.1) | 28.6 | (1.7) | 25.3 | (1.8) | 10.5 | (1.2) | 2.7 | (0.5) |
| Italy (Provincia Sardegna) | 11.7 | (2.0) | 21.0 | (1.9) | 29.0 | (1.7) | 24.5 | (1.6) | 11.3 | (1.3) | 2.4 | (0.7) | 0.1 | (0.1) |
| Italy (Provincia Puglia) | 8.8 | (1.2) | 24.2 | (1.5) | 31.2 | (1.7) | 25.3 | (1.7) | 8.3 | (1.2) | 2.1 | (0.7) | 0.1 | (0.1) |
| Italy (Provincia Veneto) | 2.0 | (0.5) | 8.9 | (1.3) | 20.5 | (1.7) | 29.7 | (1.9) | 25.9 | (1.9) | 10.9 | (1.2) | 2.1 | (0.6) |
| Spain (Andalusia) | 7.6 | (1.0) | 17.8 | (1.3) | 27.4 | (1.7) | 27.6 | (2.0) | 14.9 | (1.5) | 4.1 | (0.5) | 0.6 | (0.2) |
| Spain (Basque Country) | 4.4 | (0.6) | 13.8 | (1.1) | 27.3 | (1.0) | 30.7 | (1.0) | 18.0 | (0.9) | 5.1 | (0.6) | 0.7 | (0.2) |
| Spain (Cantabria) | 3.1 | (0.6) | 9.8 | (1.1) | 23.8 | (1.4) | 29.9 | (1.4) | 22.1 | (1.7) | 9.8 | (0.8) | 1.5 | (0.4) |
| Spain (Galicia) | 3.1 | (0.6) | 12.3 | (1.2) | 25.5 | (1.3) | 29.8 | (1.4) | 20.7 | (1.3) | 7.4 | (0.6) | 1.3 | (0.3) |
| Spain (La Rioja) | 2.4 | (0.5) | 7.5 | (0.9) | 21.1 | (1.5) | 30.0 | (1.6) | 25.5 | (1.7) | 11.4 | (1.3) | 2.1 | (0.4) |
| Spain (Castile and Leon) | 1.6 | (0.5) | 8.3 | (0.9) | 22.0 | (1.5) | 30.0 | (1.5) | 25.6 | (1.5) | 10.7 | (1.0) | 1.8 | (0.6) |
| Spain (Navarre) | 2.4 | (0.5) | 11.5 | (1.2) | 24.2 | (1.5) | 27.6 | (1.2) | 22.6 | (1.3) | 10.1 | (1.1) | 1.6 | (0.4) |
| Spain (Aragon) | 2.8 | (0.5) | 9.2 | (0.9) | 22.8 | (2.0) | 29.1 | (1.8) | 23.4 | (1.5) | 10.3 | (1.2) | 2.3 | (0.7) |
| Spain (Catalonia) | 6.1 | (1.0) | 14.9 | (1.4) | 25.5 | (1.6) | 28.4 | (1.7) | 18.4 | (1.9) | 5.9 | (1.1) | 0.9 | (0.3) |
| Spain (Asturias) | 2.1 | (0.5) | 10.9 | (1.3) | 23.6 | (1.7) | 32.1 | (1.8) | 22.6 | (1.4) | 7.3 | (1.1) | 1.4 | (0.4) |
| United Kingdom (Scotland) | 4.0 | (0.7) | 13.1 | (1.1) | 25.4 | (1.2) | 26.5 | (1.1) | 18.8 | (1.1) | 9.5 | (0.9) | 2.7 | (0.5) |
| **Non-adjudicated** | | | | | | | | | | | | | | |
| Belgium (French Community) | 9.3 | (1.3) | 18.8 | (1.1) | 25.2 | (1.3) | 25.1 | (1.1) | 15.8 | (1.2) | 5.0 | (0.7) | 0.7 | (0.2) |
| Belgium (German-Speaking Community) | 2.6 | (0.6) | 12.4 | (1.1) | 23.6 | (1.5) | 28.0 | (2.1) | 22.4 | (1.8) | 8.9 | (1.1) | 2.0 | (0.6) |
| Finland (Finnish Speaking) | 0.5 | (0.1) | 3.3 | (0.3) | 13.7 | (0.6) | 28.1 | (0.9) | 31.5 | (0.9) | 17.7 | (0.8) | 5.2 | (0.5) |
| Finland (Swedish Speaking) | 1.3 | (0.8) | 8.0 | (2.0) | 17.6 | (2.5) | 28.5 | (4.1) | 30.9 | (3.6) | 11.5 | (2.9) | 2.2 | (1.5) |
| United Kingdom (England) | 4.6 | (0.5) | 12.5 | (0.7) | 21.2 | (0.8) | 25.0 | (0.8) | 21.0 | (0.7) | 11.7 | (0.7) | 3.9 | (0.3) |
| United Kingdom (Northern Ireland) | 6.2 | (0.7) | 13.6 | (0.9) | 20.8 | (1.2) | 24.6 | (1.1) | 20.8 | (1.1) | 10.2 | (0.8) | 3.7 | (0.5) |
| United Kingdom (Wales) | 4.6 | (0.6) | 13.5 | (1.3) | 23.9 | (1.6) | 26.1 | (1.1) | 19.3 | (1.1) | 9.8 | (0.8) | 2.8 | (0.5) |

Note: See Table 2.3a for national data.
StatLink ﹏ http://dx.doi.org/10.1787/142184405135

Pour consulter la version française intégrale de ce tableau, suivre ce lien :
StatLink ﹏ http://dx.doi.org/10.1787/152830402855

[Part 1/1]

**Table S2h** **Percentage of students at each proficiency level on the *explaining phenomena scientifically* scale, by gender**

Tableau S2h  Pourcentage d'élèves à chaque niveau de compétence sur l'échelle d'*explication scientifique de phénomènes*, selon le sexe

### Males – Proficiency levels

| | Below Level 1 (below 334.94 score points) | | Level 1 (from 334.94 to 409.54 score points) | | Level 2 (from 409.54 to 484.14 score points) | | Level 3 (from 484.14 to 558.73 score points) | | Level 4 (from 558.73 to 633.33 score points) | | Level 5 (from 633.33 to 707.93 score points) | | Level 6 (above 707.93 score points) | |
|---|---|---|---|---|---|---|---|---|---|---|---|---|---|---|
| | % | S.E. | % | S.E. | % | S.E. | % | S.E. | % | S.E. | % | S.E. | % | S.E. |
| **Adjudicated** | | | | | | | | | | | | | | |
| Belgium (Flemish Community) | 2.7 | (1.2) | 9.3 | (0.9) | 18.6 | (1.0) | 26.8 | (1.2) | 26.9 | (1.3) | 13.4 | (1.0) | 2.4 | (0.4) |
| Italy (Provincia Autonoma of Bolzano) | 2.2 | (0.7) | 6.0 | (1.3) | 17.2 | (2.1) | 28.4 | (2.0) | 28.4 | (2.3) | 14.8 | (1.5) | 3.1 | (0.5) |
| Italy (Provincia Campania) | 6.3 | (0.9) | 20.0 | (2.3) | 32.9 | (2.7) | 28.5 | (2.5) | 10.0 | (1.6) | 1.9 | (0.8) | 0.4 | (0.4) |
| Italy (Provincia Basilicata) | 9.5 | (2.1) | 21.2 | (2.5) | 30.8 | (3.4) | 24.1 | (2.1) | 11.5 | (1.4) | 2.8 | (0.8) | 0.1 | a |
| Italy (Provincia Emilia Romagna) | 2.5 | (0.6) | 8.9 | (1.3) | 20.7 | (2.1) | 30.3 | (2.3) | 23.8 | (2.0) | 10.8 | (1.0) | 3.0 | (0.7) |
| Italy (Provincia Friuli Venezia Giulia) | 1.6 | (0.6) | 4.7 | (1.5) | 16.4 | (1.8) | 31.2 | (2.0) | 29.1 | (2.3) | 12.8 | (1.8) | 4.2 | (1.0) |
| Italy (Provincia Sicilia) | 16.6 | (3.0) | 22.3 | (3.0) | 23.7 | (2.4) | 21.0 | (2.7) | 12.1 | (2.0) | 4.1 | (1.2) | 0.1 | a |
| Italy (Provincia Liguria) | 7.6 | (1.9) | 14.7 | (2.6) | 22.5 | (2.3) | 27.5 | (3.1) | 18.5 | (2.0) | 7.9 | (1.5) | 1.3 | (0.6) |
| Italy (Provincia Lombardia) | 6.0 | (2.2) | 11.3 | (2.4) | 22.1 | (2.4) | 28.2 | (2.8) | 21.5 | (2.7) | 9.3 | (1.7) | 1.5 | (0.5) |
| Italy (Provincia Piemonte) | 4.2 | (1.2) | 10.4 | (1.8) | 21.9 | (2.1) | 29.5 | (3.1) | 22.5 | (2.7) | 9.9 | (1.4) | 1.5 | (0.5) |
| Italy (Provincia Trento) | 3.5 | (0.7) | 10.3 | (1.1) | 18.3 | (1.5) | 25.4 | (2.0) | 24.5 | (1.9) | 13.2 | (1.6) | 4.8 | (1.0) |
| Italy (Provincia Sardegna) | 12.7 | (2.8) | 21.5 | (3.0) | 26.9 | (2.8) | 22.1 | (2.4) | 13.3 | (2.0) | 3.3 | (1.3) | 0.2 | (0.2) |
| Italy (Provincia Puglia) | 8.4 | (1.3) | 24.8 | (2.5) | 28.8 | (2.8) | 26.1 | (2.3) | 8.9 | (1.9) | 2.9 | (0.9) | 0.2 | (0.2) |
| Italy (Provincia Veneto) | 1.1 | (0.6) | 6.3 | (1.3) | 18.8 | (2.3) | 27.8 | (2.4) | 29.3 | (2.4) | 13.9 | (1.7) | 2.9 | (0.9) |
| Spain (Andalusia) | 6.1 | (1.5) | 15.9 | (1.8) | 25.3 | (2.3) | 28.3 | (3.0) | 17.9 | (2.1) | 5.5 | (0.8) | 1.0 | (0.4) |
| Spain (Basque Country) | 4.9 | (0.8) | 13.2 | (1.4) | 25.1 | (1.3) | 30.3 | (1.3) | 19.3 | (1.2) | 6.2 | (1.0) | 0.9 | (0.3) |
| Spain (Cantabria) | 3.0 | (0.8) | 9.1 | (1.2) | 22.0 | (1.8) | 29.0 | (2.2) | 23.3 | (2.8) | 11.6 | (1.3) | 2.1 | (0.7) |
| Spain (Galicia) | 2.8 | (0.9) | 10.6 | (1.5) | 23.4 | (1.5) | 28.0 | (2.1) | 23.5 | (1.8) | 9.5 | (0.8) | 2.2 | (0.6) |
| Spain (La Rioja) | 2.3 | (0.6) | 6.0 | (1.3) | 19.9 | (2.1) | 27.9 | (2.2) | 27.7 | (2.4) | 13.6 | (1.9) | 2.7 | (0.7) |
| Spain (Castile and Leon) | 1.6 | (0.7) | 6.9 | (1.3) | 19.8 | (2.5) | 30.2 | (2.0) | 26.6 | (2.0) | 12.5 | (1.3) | 2.5 | (0.8) |
| Spain (Navarre) | 2.0 | (0.7) | 10.9 | (1.6) | 22.6 | (2.0) | 24.8 | (2.0) | 24.5 | (2.2) | 12.9 | (1.5) | 2.2 | (0.6) |
| Spain (Aragon) | 2.7 | (0.7) | 9.2 | (1.4) | 22.9 | (3.0) | 27.3 | (3.0) | 23.6 | (2.4) | 11.4 | (1.9) | 2.9 | (1.0) |
| Spain (Catalonia) | 4.4 | (1.1) | 13.7 | (2.0) | 24.1 | (2.1) | 28.2 | (2.7) | 21.2 | (2.3) | 7.1 | (1.6) | 1.3 | (0.6) |
| Spain (Asturias) | 2.3 | (0.8) | 9.9 | (1.7) | 21.7 | (1.8) | 31.5 | (1.7) | 23.4 | (1.7) | 9.1 | (1.3) | 2.2 | (0.6) |
| United Kingdom (Scotland) | 3.9 | (0.8) | 11.9 | (1.3) | 24.2 | (1.8) | 25.8 | (1.6) | 20.0 | (1.5) | 10.8 | (1.2) | 3.4 | (0.7) |
| **Non-adjudicated** | | | | | | | | | | | | | | |
| Belgium (French Community) | 9.3 | (1.7) | 18.8 | (1.5) | 23.5 | (1.8) | 24.1 | (1.9) | 17.1 | (1.9) | 6.0 | (0.9) | 1.2 | (0.3) |
| Belgium (German-Speaking Community) | 2.6 | (1.0) | 10.7 | (1.6) | 20.0 | (2.4) | 27.4 | (3.5) | 23.8 | (2.6) | 12.1 | (2.3) | 3.5 | (1.2) |
| Finland  (Finnish Speaking) | 0.5 | (0.2) | 3.7 | (0.5) | 13.3 | (0.9) | 26.1 | (1.2) | 30.7 | (1.2) | 18.9 | (1.0) | 6.8 | (0.7) |
| Finland  (Swedish Speaking) | 1.1 | (1.0) | 5.4 | (2.5) | 16.3 | (4.0) | 26.8 | (5.7) | 34.4 | (5.5) | 12.9 | (3.9) | 3.2 | (2.0) |
| United Kingdom (England) | 4.5 | (0.7) | 11.1 | (0.8) | 19.5 | (1.0) | 23.6 | (1.1) | 21.5 | (1.1) | 14.3 | (0.9) | 5.5 | (0.6) |
| United Kingdom (Northern Ireland) | 6.1 | (1.1) | 13.1 | (1.6) | 19.3 | (1.7) | 23.6 | (1.4) | 21.9 | (1.5) | 11.3 | (1.2) | 4.7 | (0.7) |
| United Kingdom (Wales) | 3.9 | (0.6) | 12.6 | (1.7) | 21.7 | (2.1) | 25.3 | (1.7) | 21.5 | (1.7) | 11.6 | (1.1) | 3.4 | (0.7) |

### Females – Proficiency levels

| | Below Level 1 (below 334.94 score points) | | Level 1 (from 334.94 to 409.54 score points) | | Level 2 (from 409.54 to 484.14 score points) | | Level 3 (from 484.14 to 558.73 score points) | | Level 4 (from 558.73 to 633.33 score points) | | Level 5 (from 633.33 to 707.93 score points) | | Level 6 (above 707.93 score points) | |
|---|---|---|---|---|---|---|---|---|---|---|---|---|---|---|
| | % | S.E. | % | S.E. | % | S.E. | % | S.E. | % | S.E. | % | S.E. | % | S.E. |
| **Adjudicated** | | | | | | | | | | | | | | |
| Belgium (Flemish Community) | 3.9 | (0.8) | 10.0 | (1.1) | 20.7 | (1.3) | 31.0 | (1.4) | 25.7 | (1.3) | 8.2 | (0.8) | 0.6 | (0.2) |
| Italy (Provincia Autonoma of Bolzano) | 2.2 | (0.6) | 9.8 | (1.3) | 24.4 | (2.2) | 30.6 | (2.3) | 22.7 | (1.6) | 8.7 | (1.0) | 1.6 | (0.5) |
| Italy (Provincia Campania) | 14.4 | (2.6) | 26.3 | (2.9) | 32.7 | (2.9) | 20.2 | (2.6) | 5.1 | (1.4) | 1.1 | (0.8) | 0.1 | a |
| Italy (Provincia Basilicata) | 7.7 | (1.4) | 25.6 | (2.8) | 35.2 | (2.4) | 22.1 | (2.2) | 8.1 | (1.6) | 1.3 | (0.7) | a | a |
| Italy (Provincia Emilia Romagna) | 5.9 | (1.6) | 13.9 | (1.9) | 23.2 | (2.6) | 27.1 | (2.2) | 21.5 | (1.6) | 7.6 | (1.2) | 1.0 | (0.4) |
| Italy (Provincia Friuli Venezia Giulia) | 2.4 | (1.0) | 6.5 | (1.2) | 21.0 | (1.8) | 33.9 | (2.3) | 25.3 | (2.0) | 9.3 | (1.4) | 1.6 | (0.6) |
| Italy (Provincia Sicilia) | 14.8 | (2.4) | 25.8 | (3.1) | 28.9 | (2.8) | 21.7 | (2.8) | 7.1 | (1.9) | 1.6 | (0.8) | 0.1 | a |
| Italy (Provincia Liguria) | 4.8 | (1.1) | 14.3 | (2.5) | 26.2 | (2.7) | 29.5 | (2.1) | 20.2 | (2.5) | 4.6 | (1.2) | 0.4 | (0.3) |
| Italy (Provincia Lombardia) | 6.4 | (1.4) | 10.8 | (1.9) | 22.6 | (2.8) | 31.4 | (3.2) | 21.6 | (1.8) | 6.3 | (1.2) | 0.8 | (0.5) |
| Italy (Provincia Piemonte) | 3.1 | (1.0) | 10.4 | (1.7) | 23.3 | (2.3) | 33.8 | (2.2) | 21.7 | (2.2) | 6.9 | (1.2) | 0.8 | (0.4) |
| Italy (Provincia Trento) | 2.9 | (0.6) | 9.5 | (1.1) | 21.4 | (2.0) | 31.7 | (3.1) | 26.0 | (3.0) | 7.9 | (1.7) | 0.6 | (0.5) |
| Italy (Provincia Sardegna) | 10.7 | (2.2) | 20.4 | (2.2) | 32.2 | (1.9) | 27.0 | (2.5) | 9.2 | (1.6) | 1.5 | (0.6) | 0.0 | a |
| Italy (Provincia Puglia) | 9.3 | (1.6) | 23.5 | (2.0) | 33.5 | (2.2) | 24.6 | (2.0) | 7.6 | (1.2) | 1.4 | (0.6) | 0.0 | a |
| Italy (Provincia Veneto) | 3.0 | (0.9) | 11.5 | (2.2) | 22.3 | (2.7) | 31.8 | (2.8) | 22.3 | (2.8) | 7.8 | (1.4) | 1.2 | (0.7) |
| Spain (Andalusia) | 9.0 | (1.6) | 19.6 | (2.3) | 29.3 | (2.4) | 27.0 | (2.5) | 12.0 | (1.5) | 2.7 | (0.9) | 0.3 | a |
| Spain (Basque Country) | 4.0 | (0.6) | 14.5 | (1.3) | 29.4 | (1.6) | 31.1 | (1.8) | 16.7 | (1.2) | 3.9 | (0.6) | 0.5 | (0.2) |
| Spain (Cantabria) | 3.3 | (1.0) | 10.4 | (1.8) | 25.7 | (1.9) | 30.9 | (2.1) | 20.9 | (1.9) | 7.9 | (1.0) | 0.9 | (0.3) |
| Spain (Galicia) | 3.4 | (1.0) | 14.2 | (1.8) | 27.8 | (2.1) | 31.8 | (2.4) | 17.5 | (2.1) | 5.1 | (1.1) | 0.3 | (0.3) |
| Spain (La Rioja) | 2.5 | (0.8) | 9.0 | (1.3) | 22.3 | (2.1) | 32.2 | (2.2) | 23.4 | (1.7) | 9.2 | (1.5) | 1.5 | (0.5) |
| Spain (Castile and Leon) | 1.5 | (0.6) | 9.8 | (1.4) | 24.5 | (2.2) | 29.8 | (2.2) | 24.4 | (2.1) | 8.8 | (1.4) | 1.1 | (0.5) |
| Spain (Navarre) | 2.7 | (0.7) | 12.2 | (1.5) | 25.8 | (2.0) | 30.3 | (1.9) | 20.8 | (1.8) | 7.3 | (1.2) | 1.0 | (0.6) |
| Spain (Aragon) | 3.0 | (0.6) | 9.2 | (1.3) | 22.8 | (2.1) | 30.9 | (2.3) | 23.3 | (1.8) | 9.2 | (1.7) | 1.6 | (0.7) |
| Spain (Catalonia) | 7.7 | (1.6) | 16.0 | (2.0) | 27.0 | (2.5) | 28.5 | (2.6) | 15.7 | (2.2) | 4.7 | (1.0) | 0.4 | (0.3) |
| Spain (Asturias) | 1.9 | (0.7) | 11.9 | (1.9) | 25.7 | (2.3) | 32.7 | (3.2) | 21.8 | (2.2) | 5.4 | (1.3) | 0.6 | (0.4) |
| United Kingdom (Scotland) | 4.0 | (0.8) | 14.3 | (1.4) | 26.6 | (1.7) | 27.2 | (2.0) | 17.6 | (1.4) | 8.2 | (1.2) | 2.1 | (0.6) |
| **Non-adjudicated** | | | | | | | | | | | | | | |
| Belgium (French Community) | 9.2 | (1.5) | 18.8 | (1.5) | 27.1 | (1.7) | 26.2 | (1.6) | 14.4 | (1.8) | 4.0 | (0.8) | 0.2 | (0.2) |
| Belgium (German-Speaking Community) | 2.7 | (0.9) | 14.0 | (2.0) | 27.2 | (2.8) | 28.7 | (2.8) | 21.0 | (2.6) | 5.8 | (1.4) | 0.6 | (0.5) |
| Finland  (Finnish Speaking) | 0.4 | (0.2) | 2.8 | (0.5) | 14.1 | (0.9) | 30.1 | (1.3) | 32.2 | (1.6) | 16.6 | (1.1) | 3.7 | (0.6) |
| Finland  (Swedish Speaking) | 1.4 | (1.4) | 10.7 | (3.6) | 18.9 | (5.2) | 30.2 | (4.7) | 27.3 | (4.8) | 10.1 | (3.2) | 1.2 | a |
| United Kingdom (England) | 4.7 | (0.5) | 13.9 | (1.0) | 22.9 | (1.4) | 26.5 | (1.0) | 20.4 | (0.9) | 9.2 | (0.9) | 2.4 | (0.4) |
| United Kingdom (Northern Ireland) | 6.3 | (1.1) | 14.2 | (1.3) | 22.4 | (1.5) | 25.6 | (1.9) | 19.7 | (1.8) | 9.1 | (1.3) | 2.7 | (0.7) |
| United Kingdom (Wales) | 5.2 | (0.9) | 14.5 | (1.5) | 26.1 | (1.7) | 26.9 | (1.6) | 17.1 | (1.4) | 8.0 | (0.9) | 2.1 | (0.6) |

Note: See Table 2.3b for national data.

*StatLink* http://dx.doi.org/10.1787/142184405135

Pour consulter la version française intégrale de ce tableau, suivre ce lien :
*StatLink* http://dx.doi.org/10.1787/152830402855

[Part 1/1]

**Table S2i** Mean score, variation and gender differences in student performance on the *explaining phenomena scientifically* scale

**Tableau S2i** Score moyen, différences de score selon le sexe et répartition des scores sur l'*échelle d'explication scientifique de phénomènes*

| | All students | | | | Gender differences | | | | | |
|---|---|---|---|---|---|---|---|---|---|---|
| | Mean score | | Standard deviation | | Males | | Females | | Difference (M – F) | |
| | Mean | S.E. | S.D. | S.E. | Mean score | S.E. | Mean score | S.E. | Score dif. | S.E. |
| **Adjudicated** | | | | | | | | | | |
| Belgium (Flemish Community) | 525 | (3.3) | 96 | (2.7) | 533 | (4.0) | 515 | (3.7) | **18** | (4.2) |
| Italy (Provincia Autonoma of Bolzano) | 531 | (2.1) | 94 | (1.7) | 544 | (3.0) | 517 | (2.8) | **27** | (4.0) |
| Italy (Provincia Campania) | 447 | (6.4) | 87 | (4.1) | 464 | (5.4) | 430 | (7.9) | **34** | (6.2) |
| Italy (Provincia Basilicata) | 452 | (4.6) | 88 | (2.5) | 457 | (6.4) | 447 | (5.4) | 10 | (7.4) |
| Italy (Provincia Emilia Romagna) | 513 | (3.9) | 100 | (2.8) | 527 | (4.8) | 499 | (5.1) | **28** | (6.3) |
| Italy (Provincia Friuli Venezia Giulia) | 539 | (4.0) | 91 | (2.9) | 550 | (5.8) | 527 | (5.3) | **22** | (8.0) |
| Italy (Provincia Sicilia) | 439 | (7.9) | 103 | (5.1) | 444 | (10.2) | 434 | (8.6) | 10 | (10.2) |
| Italy (Provincia Liguria) | 493 | (7.2) | 99 | (2.8) | 493 | (9.2) | 492 | (6.9) | 1 | (7.7) |
| Italy (Provincia Lombardia) | 504 | (6.2) | 100 | (3.2) | 507 | (10.4) | 502 | (6.3) | 5 | (11.7) |
| Italy (Provincia Piemonte) | 512 | (5.1) | 94 | (3.1) | 514 | (7.2) | 510 | (5.3) | 4 | (7.5) |
| Italy (Provincia Trento) | 525 | (2.1) | 99 | (1.9) | 533 | (3.6) | 517 | (3.1) | **16** | (5.2) |
| Italy (Provincia Sardegna) | 453 | (6.2) | 95 | (3.3) | 455 | (8.9) | 452 | (6.0) | 3 | (8.8) |
| Italy (Provincia Puglia) | 451 | (4.3) | 88 | (2.5) | 454 | (5.6) | 448 | (4.4) | 6 | (5.4) |
| Italy (Provincia Veneto) | 529 | (5.8) | 93 | (2.7) | 545 | (5.9) | 512 | (8.5) | **33** | (10.3) |
| Spain (Andalusia) | 475 | (4.2) | 97 | (2.0) | 489 | (5.2) | 462 | (5.0) | **26** | (5.8) |
| Spain (Basque Country) | 493 | (3.4) | 91 | (1.7) | 498 | (4.3) | 488 | (3.4) | **10** | (3.5) |
| Spain (Cantabria) | 516 | (3.3) | 95 | (1.9) | 523 | (4.6) | 508 | (4.2) | **15** | (5.8) |
| Spain (Galicia) | 507 | (3.8) | 93 | (2.1) | 519 | (4.2) | 493 | (4.1) | **25** | (3.6) |
| Spain (La Rioja) | 529 | (2.5) | 94 | (2.2) | 539 | (3.6) | 520 | (3.6) | **19** | (5.2) |
| Spain (Castile and Leon) | 528 | (3.7) | 90 | (2.0) | 537 | (3.9) | 519 | (4.5) | **18** | (3.7) |
| Spain (Navarre) | 516 | (3.6) | 95 | (1.8) | 526 | (4.1) | 506 | (4.3) | **20** | (4.6) |
| Spain (Aragon) | 522 | (3.5) | 95 | (2.2) | 526 | (5.4) | 519 | (4.0) | 7 | (6.5) |
| Spain (Catalonia) | 490 | (5.3) | 97 | (2.4) | 501 | (7.0) | 479 | (5.0) | **22** | (6.0) |
| Spain (Asturias) | 514 | (5.0) | 90 | (2.2) | 522 | (6.0) | 506 | (5.4) | **16** | (5.4) |
| United Kingdom (Scotland) | 508 | (4.3) | 103 | (2.1) | 516 | (5.2) | 501 | (4.2) | **15** | (4.4) |
| **Non-adjudicated** | | | | | | | | | | |
| Belgium (French Community) | 473 | (4.3) | 103 | (2.8) | 478 | (5.5) | 468 | (5.3) | 10 | (6.6) |
| Belgium (German-Speaking Community) | 515 | (2.9) | 97 | (2.3) | 530 | (4.3) | 500 | (4.6) | **30** | (6.7) |
| Finland (Finnish Speaking) | 567 | (2.1) | 88 | (1.1) | 572 | (2.6) | 563 | (2.7) | **9** | (3.1) |
| Finland (Swedish Speaking) | 539 | (6.2) | 89 | (3.7) | 551 | (6.0) | 528 | (9.5) | **23** | (10.0) |
| United Kingdom (England) | 518 | (2.7) | 110 | (1.6) | 529 | (3.5) | 507 | (3.3) | **22** | (4.2) |
| United Kingdom (Northern Ireland) | 510 | (3.2) | 113 | (2.3) | 517 | (6.0) | 502 | (5.8) | 15 | (9.9) |
| United Kingdom (Wales) | 508 | (3.7) | 106 | (1.9) | 519 | (4.1) | 498 | (4.3) | **21** | (4.1) |

| | Percentiles | | | | | | | | | | | |
|---|---|---|---|---|---|---|---|---|---|---|---|---|
| | 5th | | 10th | | 25th | | 75th | | 90th | | 95th | |
| | Score | S.E. | Score | S.E. | Score | S.E. | Score | S.E. | Score | S.E. | Score | S.E. |
| **Adjudicated** | | | | | | | | | | | | |
| Belgium (Flemish Community) | 357 | (11.5) | 394 | (7.5) | 461 | (4.4) | 595 | (2.9) | 644 | (3.1) | 671 | (3.3) |
| Italy (Provincia Autonoma of Bolzano) | 373 | (5.1) | 408 | (5.5) | 466 | (3.3) | 597 | (3.7) | 650 | (3.9) | 680 | (5.1) |
| Italy (Provincia Campania) | 304 | (8.4) | 334 | (7.4) | 388 | (7.4) | 505 | (7.4) | 556 | (9.5) | 589 | (14.9) |
| Italy (Provincia Basilicata) | 311 | (8.5) | 341 | (7.2) | 393 | (6.5) | 513 | (5.7) | 570 | (5.4) | 601 | (6.6) |
| Italy (Provincia Emilia Romagna) | 343 | (9.0) | 381 | (7.5) | 449 | (5.6) | 582 | (3.9) | 639 | (5.8) | 670 | (6.1) |
| Italy (Provincia Friuli Venezia Giulia) | 386 | (11.1) | 424 | (6.2) | 481 | (3.8) | 599 | (5.5) | 654 | (8.2) | 689 | (6.7) |
| Italy (Provincia Sicilia) | 277 | (11.8) | 309 | (8.7) | 366 | (8.2) | 512 | (10.1) | 572 | (9.2) | 607 | (10.2) |
| Italy (Provincia Liguria) | 324 | (12.1) | 360 | (10.4) | 424 | (10.1) | 563 | (6.7) | 617 | (7.9) | 649 | (8.8) |
| Italy (Provincia Lombardia) | 322 | (11.8) | 366 | (12.1) | 442 | (9.9) | 575 | (6.0) | 628 | (6.5) | 659 | (5.8) |
| Italy (Provincia Piemonte) | 350 | (10.8) | 389 | (8.8) | 451 | (6.8) | 578 | (7.4) | 631 | (6.3) | 660 | (7.1) |
| Italy (Provincia Trento) | 359 | (6.3) | 395 | (3.7) | 459 | (3.7) | 594 | (3.9) | 649 | (5.6) | 683 | (7.6) |
| Italy (Provincia Sardegna) | 299 | (9.3) | 326 | (8.7) | 387 | (8.2) | 521 | (7.8) | 576 | (8.3) | 606 | (10.1) |
| Italy (Provincia Puglia) | 313 | (6.9) | 340 | (5.8) | 390 | (5.0) | 510 | (4.9) | 562 | (9.1) | 599 | (10.6) |
| Italy (Provincia Veneto) | 370 | (11.2) | 405 | (8.0) | 466 | (7.5) | 596 | (7.3) | 646 | (6.2) | 677 | (6.9) |
| Spain (Andalusia) | 316 | (7.2) | 349 | (6.6) | 409 | (5.8) | 541 | (5.5) | 597 | (4.6) | 631 | (4.8) |
| Spain (Basque Country) | 341 | (6.5) | 376 | (4.5) | 431 | (4.0) | 555 | (3.7) | 609 | (4.2) | 639 | (5.3) |
| Spain (Cantabria) | 356 | (7.5) | 392 | (7.3) | 452 | (5.0) | 583 | (4.6) | 640 | (4.7) | 670 | (5.7) |
| Spain (Galicia) | 353 | (6.6) | 388 | (6.2) | 444 | (5.0) | 572 | (5.1) | 626 | (4.8) | 659 | (7.2) |
| Spain (La Rioja) | 372 | (8.1) | 410 | (6.5) | 466 | (4.9) | 595 | (3.3) | 648 | (6.2) | 677 | (5.5) |
| Spain (Castile and Leon) | 380 | (8.0) | 411 | (5.8) | 465 | (5.0) | 593 | (4.1) | 645 | (4.9) | 674 | (7.5) |
| Spain (Navarre) | 362 | (7.7) | 393 | (6.3) | 447 | (4.6) | 586 | (4.5) | 641 | (4.7) | 672 | (5.9) |
| Spain (Aragon) | 366 | (6.9) | 399 | (6.7) | 458 | (5.4) | 590 | (4.9) | 645 | (4.6) | 678 | (7.1) |
| Spain (Catalonia) | 327 | (8.2) | 363 | (6.8) | 425 | (5.9) | 559 | (5.6) | 613 | (8.4) | 646 | (7.6) |
| Spain (Asturias) | 365 | (9.6) | 397 | (7.1) | 454 | (5.9) | 576 | (5.5) | 627 | (5.8) | 658 | (7.1) |
| United Kingdom (Scotland) | 345 | (6.4) | 378 | (6.2) | 435 | (5.0) | 579 | (5.6) | 645 | (5.7) | 683 | (6.0) |
| **Non-adjudicated** | | | | | | | | | | | | |
| Belgium (French Community) | 306 | (8.6) | 339 | (7.0) | 400 | (5.8) | 548 | (5.1) | 607 | (5.2) | 640 | (5.7) |
| Belgium (German-Speaking Community) | 354 | (8.6) | 387 | (5.9) | 445 | (5.5) | 583 | (4.8) | 638 | (5.7) | 670 | (8.5) |
| Finland (Finnish Speaking) | 423 | (4.8) | 454 | (3.5) | 507 | (2.8) | 627 | (2.6) | 680 | (2.7) | 710 | (4.3) |
| Finland (Swedish Speaking) | 379 | (14.2) | 415 | (16.7) | 479 | (11.5) | 603 | (7.4) | 647 | (13.0) | 678 | (17.1) |
| United Kingdom (England) | 340 | (5.4) | 376 | (4.0) | 441 | (3.6) | 596 | (3.5) | 662 | (4.1) | 698 | (4.2) |
| United Kingdom (Northern Ireland) | 324 | (6.7) | 361 | (5.6) | 430 | (4.6) | 590 | (4.3) | 654 | (4.6) | 691 | (6.6) |
| United Kingdom (Wales) | 339 | (6.1) | 373 | (5.1) | 433 | (4.2) | 582 | (4.5) | 648 | (5.4) | 684 | (6.7) |

Note: Values that are statistically significant are indicated in bold (see Annex A3). See Table 2.3c for national data.
StatLink http://dx.doi.org/10.1787/142184405135

Pour consulter la version française intégrale de ce tableau, suivre ce lien :
StatLink http://dx.doi.org/10.1787/152830402855

[Part 1/1]

**Table S2j** **Percentage of students at each proficiency level on the *using scientific evidence* scale**

Tableau S2j   Pourcentage d'élèves à chaque niveau de compétence sur l'échelle d'*utilisation de faits scientifiques*

| | Proficiency levels | | | | | | | | | | | | |
|---|---|---|---|---|---|---|---|---|---|---|---|---|---|
| | Below Level 1 (below 334.94 score points) | | Level 1 (from 334.94 to 409.54 score points) | | Level 2 (from 409.54 to 484.14 score points) | | Level 3 (from 484.14 to 558.73 score points) | | Level 4 (from 558.73 to 633.33 score points) | | Level 5 (from 633.33 to 707.93 score points) | | Level 6 (above 707.93 score points) | |
| | % | S.E. | % | S.E. | % | S.E. | % | S.E. | % | S.E. | % | S.E. | % | S.E. |
| **Adjudicated** | | | | | | | | | | | | | | |
| Belgium (Flemish Community) | 4.8 | (1.1) | 8.6 | (0.7) | 16.2 | (0.9) | 24.8 | (0.9) | 28.3 | (0.9) | 15.1 | (0.9) | 2.3 | (0.3) |
| Italy (Provincia Autonoma of Bolzano) | 2.8 | (0.4) | 9.9 | (1.1) | 17.6 | (1.3) | 29.0 | (1.6) | 27.0 | (1.2) | 11.7 | (0.9) | 2.1 | (0.5) |
| Italy (Provincia Campania) | 17.4 | (2.0) | 24.4 | (1.9) | 28.0 | (1.9) | 20.8 | (2.1) | 7.8 | (1.2) | 1.4 | (0.6) | 0.1 | (0.1) |
| Italy (Provincia Basilicata) | 15.3 | (2.1) | 21.1 | (1.8) | 29.1 | (1.7) | 21.8 | (1.7) | 10.0 | (1.2) | 2.6 | (0.6) | 0.1 | a |
| Italy (Provincia Emilia Romagna) | 5.7 | (1.1) | 11.8 | (1.0) | 21.0 | (1.7) | 29.2 | (1.8) | 21.4 | (1.4) | 9.5 | (1.3) | 1.6 | (0.4) |
| Italy (Provincia Friuli Venezia Giulia) | 2.8 | (0.7) | 8.5 | (1.0) | 19.2 | (1.3) | 29.4 | (1.3) | 26.5 | (1.3) | 11.1 | (1.3) | 2.5 | (0.6) |
| Italy (Provincia Sicilia) | 22.0 | (2.7) | 23.6 | (2.4) | 25.7 | (1.7) | 18.1 | (1.6) | 8.4 | (1.3) | 2.0 | (0.7) | 0.1 | (0.2) |
| Italy (Provincia Liguria) | 10.8 | (2.1) | 14.4 | (1.5) | 22.5 | (1.7) | 27.1 | (1.7) | 17.7 | (1.8) | 6.9 | (1.1) | 0.7 | (0.3) |
| Italy (Provincia Lombardia) | 7.7 | (2.1) | 13.0 | (1.7) | 21.9 | (1.6) | 28.5 | (1.6) | 19.9 | (1.8) | 7.8 | (1.0) | 1.3 | (0.5) |
| Italy (Provincia Piemonte) | 6.2 | (0.9) | 12.0 | (1.4) | 21.4 | (1.5) | 28.9 | (1.6) | 21.4 | (1.4) | 9.0 | (1.1) | 1.2 | (0.4) |
| Italy (Provincia Trento) | 4.7 | (0.4) | 10.7 | (0.9) | 19.5 | (1.2) | 28.7 | (1.5) | 25.6 | (1.4) | 9.8 | (1.2) | 1.0 | (0.4) |
| Italy (Provincia Sardegna) | 19.4 | (2.6) | 20.6 | (1.8) | 25.5 | (1.9) | 21.3 | (1.3) | 10.1 | (1.6) | 2.8 | (0.8) | 0.3 | (0.2) |
| Italy (Provincia Puglia) | 14.0 | (1.6) | 24.6 | (1.6) | 30.8 | (1.8) | 19.8 | (1.7) | 8.3 | (1.1) | 2.3 | (0.8) | 0.2 | (0.2) |
| Italy (Provincia Veneto) | 3.3 | (0.7) | 10.2 | (1.3) | 21.7 | (1.8) | 27.9 | (1.5) | 24.9 | (1.8) | 10.0 | (1.3) | 2.1 | (0.5) |
| Spain (Andalusia) | 9.5 | (1.1) | 17.2 | (1.2) | 27.5 | (1.6) | 26.8 | (1.2) | 15.3 | (1.4) | 3.3 | (0.7) | 0.4 | (0.2) |
| Spain (Basque Country) | 5.3 | (0.7) | 12.1 | (0.8) | 25.0 | (1.1) | 30.4 | (0.9) | 20.0 | (1.0) | 6.3 | (0.7) | 0.8 | (0.2) |
| Spain (Cantabria) | 4.7 | (0.8) | 11.7 | (1.0) | 24.5 | (1.2) | 31.5 | (1.6) | 20.3 | (1.2) | 6.7 | (0.8) | 0.7 | (0.2) |
| Spain (Galicia) | 4.7 | (0.6) | 13.0 | (1.0) | 24.2 | (1.3) | 28.6 | (1.7) | 21.2 | (1.5) | 7.2 | (0.9) | 1.1 | (0.4) |
| Spain (La Rioja) | 3.1 | (0.5) | 9.8 | (1.1) | 22.8 | (1.4) | 28.6 | (1.5) | 24.5 | (1.5) | 9.9 | (1.0) | 1.2 | (0.3) |
| Spain (Castile and Leon) | 2.5 | (0.7) | 10.2 | (1.2) | 23.9 | (1.5) | 33.5 | (1.2) | 22.3 | (2.0) | 6.9 | (1.0) | 0.8 | (0.4) |
| Spain (Navarre) | 3.5 | (0.8) | 11.9 | (1.4) | 23.1 | (1.4) | 29.3 | (1.9) | 21.4 | (1.6) | 9.2 | (1.0) | 1.6 | (0.4) |
| Spain (Aragon) | 4.6 | (0.8) | 11.4 | (1.3) | 23.5 | (1.5) | 28.1 | (1.4) | 22.5 | (1.7) | 9.0 | (1.2) | 0.9 | (0.4) |
| Spain (Catalonia) | 6.5 | (1.1) | 13.3 | (1.6) | 24.2 | (1.5) | 30.0 | (1.4) | 19.5 | (1.4) | 5.6 | (0.9) | 1.0 | (0.4) |
| Spain (Asturias) | 4.9 | (1.1) | 11.7 | (1.3) | 22.9 | (2.1) | 32.6 | (2.3) | 20.7 | (1.9) | 6.3 | (1.0) | 0.9 | (0.4) |
| United Kingdom (Scotland) | 5.1 | (0.7) | 11.6 | (0.9) | 20.7 | (1.1) | 24.4 | (1.5) | 21.6 | (1.6) | 11.9 | (1.0) | 4.7 | (0.6) |
| **Non-adjudicated** | | | | | | | | | | | | | | |
| Belgium (French Community) | 10.1 | (1.2) | 13.7 | (1.0) | 20.6 | (1.1) | 24.5 | (1.3) | 20.0 | (1.2) | 9.2 | (1.0) | 1.9 | (0.5) |
| Belgium (German-Speaking Community) | 6.5 | (0.7) | 11.7 | (1.3) | 16.5 | (1.5) | 25.9 | (2.4) | 23.9 | (1.6) | 12.7 | (1.2) | 2.8 | (0.7) |
| Finland  (Finnish Speaking) | 0.9 | (0.2) | 4.3 | (0.4) | 13.5 | (0.7) | 25.9 | (0.7) | 29.8 | (0.8) | 18.7 | (0.8) | 7.0 | (0.5) |
| Finland  (Swedish Speaking) | 2.7 | (1.0) | 7.3 | (1.8) | 23.1 | (3.0) | 28.6 | (3.6) | 26.6 | (3.4) | 9.8 | (1.8) | 1.9 | (1.1) |
| United Kingdom (England) | 6.8 | (0.7) | 12.4 | (0.7) | 20.0 | (0.8) | 23.8 | (0.9) | 21.1 | (1.0) | 11.8 | (0.6) | 4.0 | (0.4) |
| United Kingdom (Northern Ireland) | 9.1 | (0.9) | 13.5 | (0.9) | 18.6 | (1.1) | 22.3 | (1.2) | 20.3 | (1.0) | 11.8 | (0.9) | 4.4 | (0.6) |
| United Kingdom (Wales) | 6.6 | (0.8) | 13.8 | (0.8) | 22.3 | (1.0) | 24.7 | (0.9) | 20.0 | (1.1) | 9.8 | (0.8) | 2.8 | (0.5) |

Note: See Table 2.4a for national data.
*StatLink* http://dx.doi.org/10.1787/142184405135

Pour consulter la version française intégrale de ce tableau, suivre ce lien :
*StatLink* http://dx.doi.org/10.1787/152830402855

257

[Part 1/1]

**Table S2k** Percentage of students at each proficiency level on the *using scientific evidence* scale, by gender

Tableau S2k Pourcentage d'élèves à chaque niveau de compétence sur l'échelle d'*utilisation de faits scientifiques*, selon le sexe

| | Males – Proficiency levels | | | | | | | | | | | | | |
|---|---|---|---|---|---|---|---|---|---|---|---|---|---|---|
| | Below Level 1 (below 334.94 score points) | | Level 1 (from 334.94 to 409.54 score points) | | Level 2 (from 409.54 to 484.14 score points) | | Level 3 (from 484.14 to 558.73 score points) | | Level 4 (from 558.73 to 633.33 score points) | | Level 5 (from 633.33 to 707.93 score points) | | Level 6 (above 707.93 score points) | |
| | % | S.E. | % | S.E. | % | S.E. | % | S.E. | % | S.E. | % | S.E. | % | S.E. |
| **Adjudicated** | | | | | | | | | | | | | | |
| Belgium (Flemish Community) | 5.3 | (1.5) | 9.6 | (1.0) | 17.2 | (1.1) | 23.2 | (1.0) | 27.2 | (1.1) | 14.9 | (1.1) | 2.6 | (0.5) |
| Italy (Provincia Autonoma of Bolzano) | 3.1 | (0.6) | 10.2 | (1.4) | 16.6 | (1.8) | 30.0 | (2.1) | 26.3 | (1.7) | 11.7 | (1.1) | 2.3 | (0.6) |
| Italy (Provincia Campania) | 16.0 | (2.2) | 21.7 | (2.5) | 28.4 | (2.5) | 23.8 | (2.9) | 8.2 | (1.4) | 1.7 | (0.8) | 0.2 | a |
| Italy (Provincia Basilicata) | 18.8 | (3.4) | 20.1 | (2.2) | 27.1 | (2.3) | 21.3 | (2.4) | 9.7 | (1.5) | 2.8 | (0.7) | 0.1 | a |
| Italy (Provincia Emilia Romagna) | 5.1 | (1.1) | 10.7 | (1.3) | 21.0 | (1.7) | 30.7 | (2.3) | 21.3 | (1.7) | 9.1 | (1.7) | 2.1 | (0.7) |
| Italy (Provincia Friuli Venezia Giulia) | 3.4 | (1.2) | 8.8 | (1.9) | 20.6 | (2.2) | 27.0 | (1.9) | 24.9 | (2.3) | 12.5 | (1.9) | 2.8 | (0.9) |
| Italy (Provincia Sicilia) | 25.0 | (3.3) | 21.7 | (2.7) | 23.0 | (1.9) | 17.6 | (2.1) | 10.2 | (2.0) | 2.3 | (0.9) | 0.1 | a |
| Italy (Provincia Liguria) | 14.5 | (3.4) | 15.7 | (2.5) | 21.8 | (2.8) | 24.6 | (2.4) | 15.2 | (1.9) | 7.3 | (1.5) | 0.8 | (0.4) |
| Italy (Provincia Lombardia) | 9.3 | (3.9) | 13.5 | (2.3) | 22.8 | (2.3) | 27.0 | (1.9) | 18.5 | (2.4) | 7.5 | (1.3) | 1.3 | (0.5) |
| Italy (Provincia Piemonte) | 8.5 | (1.5) | 13.1 | (1.9) | 22.0 | (2.2) | 27.4 | (2.3) | 19.1 | (2.4) | 8.6 | (1.7) | 1.4 | (0.5) |
| Italy (Provincia Trento) | 5.7 | (0.7) | 12.1 | (1.1) | 19.3 | (1.7) | 26.4 | (2.2) | 24.4 | (2.4) | 10.7 | (2.0) | 1.5 | (0.7) |
| Italy (Provincia Sardegna) | 21.9 | (3.9) | 20.5 | (2.4) | 24.4 | (2.7) | 18.8 | (1.9) | 10.3 | (2.2) | 3.6 | (1.5) | 0.6 | (0.4) |
| Italy (Provincia Puglia) | 14.4 | (2.2) | 26.7 | (2.3) | 28.6 | (2.1) | 19.1 | (1.6) | 8.5 | (1.5) | 2.4 | (0.9) | 0.2 | a |
| Italy (Provincia Veneto) | 2.9 | (0.9) | 9.7 | (1.8) | 21.3 | (2.4) | 27.5 | (2.1) | 25.4 | (2.5) | 10.7 | (1.5) | 2.5 | (0.6) |
| Spain (Andalusia) | 9.7 | (1.5) | 16.4 | (1.6) | 25.4 | (2.1) | 27.6 | (2.1) | 16.4 | (1.9) | 4.1 | (1.0) | 0.4 | (0.3) |
| Spain (Basque Country) | 7.1 | (1.0) | 12.9 | (1.0) | 23.8 | (1.2) | 28.6 | (1.3) | 19.8 | (1.3) | 7.0 | (0.8) | 1.0 | (0.4) |
| Spain (Cantabria) | 6.2 | (1.2) | 13.1 | (1.4) | 24.9 | (1.7) | 28.0 | (1.7) | 20.2 | (1.9) | 6.8 | (1.0) | 0.8 | (0.3) |
| Spain (Galicia) | 5.9 | (0.9) | 14.1 | (1.4) | 23.6 | (2.0) | 26.3 | (2.2) | 20.4 | (1.9) | 8.3 | (1.2) | 1.4 | (0.5) |
| Spain (La Rioja) | 3.5 | (0.8) | 10.3 | (1.5) | 24.1 | (1.9) | 26.7 | (2.0) | 24.0 | (1.9) | 10.1 | (1.3) | 1.3 | (0.5) |
| Spain (Castile and Leon) | 2.8 | (0.8) | 11.9 | (1.5) | 21.3 | (1.8) | 33.7 | (1.7) | 22.2 | (2.9) | 7.4 | (1.3) | 0.8 | (0.5) |
| Spain (Navarre) | 4.5 | (1.2) | 12.9 | (1.9) | 22.8 | (1.6) | 26.9 | (2.2) | 20.9 | (1.7) | 9.8 | (1.3) | 2.1 | (0.6) |
| Spain (Aragon) | 5.3 | (1.4) | 12.4 | (1.7) | 24.8 | (2.0) | 27.4 | (2.0) | 20.3 | (1.9) | 8.9 | (1.6) | 0.9 | (0.5) |
| Spain (Catalonia) | 7.0 | (1.5) | 12.0 | (2.1) | 23.7 | (2.2) | 31.0 | (1.9) | 18.9 | (1.9) | 6.1 | (1.2) | 1.3 | (0.7) |
| Spain (Asturias) | 5.9 | (1.7) | 12.3 | (1.8) | 22.5 | (2.7) | 30.4 | (2.7) | 21.0 | (2.3) | 6.5 | (1.1) | 1.4 | (0.6) |
| United Kingdom (Scotland) | 6.0 | (1.0) | 10.8 | (1.2) | 19.2 | (1.4) | 24.6 | (1.8) | 22.0 | (1.9) | 12.7 | (1.2) | 4.7 | (0.7) |
| **Non-adjudicated** | | | | | | | | | | | | | | |
| Belgium (French Community) | 11.6 | (1.5) | 14.5 | (1.4) | 20.0 | (1.8) | 24.3 | (1.8) | 18.8 | (1.7) | 8.8 | (1.3) | 2.0 | (0.5) |
| Belgium (German-Speaking Community) | 8.1 | (1.4) | 13.0 | (3.0) | 16.6 | (2.8) | 22.1 | (3.1) | 23.0 | (2.1) | 13.6 | (1.6) | 3.7 | (1.0) |
| Finland (Finnish Speaking) | 1.1 | (0.3) | 5.2 | (0.6) | 14.6 | (1.0) | 25.1 | (1.1) | 28.2 | (1.1) | 18.3 | (1.0) | 7.4 | (0.7) |
| Finland (Swedish Speaking) | 2.7 | (1.3) | 5.5 | (2.3) | 21.8 | (4.7) | 32.0 | (7.2) | 28.8 | (4.0) | 7.6 | (2.0) | 1.7 | (1.3) |
| United Kingdom (England) | 7.5 | (0.9) | 11.9 | (0.9) | 19.1 | (1.0) | 22.7 | (1.3) | 20.8 | (1.4) | 13.3 | (0.9) | 4.8 | (0.7) |
| United Kingdom (Northern Ireland) | 9.7 | (1.3) | 14.3 | (1.3) | 18.3 | (1.5) | 20.9 | (1.5) | 19.5 | (1.4) | 12.4 | (1.3) | 4.7 | (0.8) |
| United Kingdom (Wales) | 6.5 | (1.0) | 14.0 | (1.1) | 20.7 | (1.2) | 24.8 | (1.3) | 20.2 | (1.3) | 10.6 | (1.1) | 3.2 | (0.6) |

| | Females – Proficiency levels | | | | | | | | | | | | | |
|---|---|---|---|---|---|---|---|---|---|---|---|---|---|---|
| | Below Level 1 (below 334.94 score points) | | Level 1 (from 334.94 to 409.54 score points) | | Level 2 (from 409.54 to 484.14 score points) | | Level 3 (from 484.14 to 558.73 score points) | | Level 4 (from 558.73 to 633.33 score points) | | Level 5 (from 633.33 to 707.93 score points) | | Level 6 (above 707.93 score points) | |
| | % | S.E. | % | S.E. | % | S.E. | % | S.E. | % | S.E. | % | S.E. | % | S.E. |
| **Adjudicated** | | | | | | | | | | | | | | |
| Belgium (Flemish Community) | 4.1 | (0.9) | 7.5 | (1.0) | 15.1 | (1.1) | 26.6 | (1.4) | 29.5 | (1.4) | 15.4 | (1.2) | 1.8 | (0.4) |
| Italy (Provincia Autonoma of Bolzano) | 2.5 | (0.6) | 9.5 | (1.8) | 18.7 | (2.0) | 28.0 | (2.1) | 27.7 | (1.7) | 11.7 | (1.4) | 2.0 | (0.8) |
| Italy (Provincia Campania) | 18.8 | (3.1) | 27.1 | (2.1) | 27.6 | (2.5) | 17.9 | (2.4) | 7.4 | (1.6) | 1.1 | (0.7) | 0.0 | a |
| Italy (Provincia Basilicata) | 11.5 | (1.4) | 22.2 | (2.4) | 31.2 | (2.4) | 22.4 | (2.5) | 10.3 | (1.8) | 2.4 | (0.8) | 0.1 | a |
| Italy (Provincia Emilia Romagna) | 6.3 | (1.6) | 12.9 | (1.8) | 20.9 | (2.5) | 27.6 | (2.2) | 21.4 | (1.7) | 9.8 | (1.5) | 1.1 | (0.6) |
| Italy (Provincia Friuli Venezia Giulia) | 2.2 | (0.7) | 8.2 | (1.2) | 17.8 | (1.8) | 31.8 | (1.8) | 28.1 | (1.8) | 9.7 | (1.5) | 2.2 | (0.8) |
| Italy (Provincia Sicilia) | 19.3 | (3.3) | 25.3 | (3.0) | 28.3 | (2.8) | 18.5 | (2.3) | 6.7 | (1.3) | 1.8 | (0.8) | 0.1 | a |
| Italy (Provincia Liguria) | 6.8 | (1.3) | 13.0 | (2.0) | 23.2 | (2.1) | 29.7 | (1.9) | 20.4 | (2.4) | 6.4 | (1.3) | 0.5 | (0.3) |
| Italy (Provincia Lombardia) | 6.0 | (1.5) | 12.6 | (1.9) | 21.0 | (2.4) | 29.9 | (2.6) | 21.2 | (2.1) | 8.1 | (1.5) | 1.3 | (0.7) |
| Italy (Provincia Piemonte) | 4.3 | (0.8) | 11.1 | (1.7) | 20.8 | (2.0) | 30.1 | (2.0) | 23.4 | (2.3) | 9.3 | (1.7) | 1.0 | (0.4) |
| Italy (Provincia Trento) | 3.7 | (0.7) | 9.3 | (1.3) | 19.8 | (1.6) | 31.0 | (1.9) | 26.8 | (2.0) | 9.0 | (1.6) | 0.4 | (0.4) |
| Italy (Provincia Sardegna) | 16.8 | (2.1) | 20.7 | (2.6) | 26.6 | (2.4) | 23.9 | (1.9) | 9.9 | (1.7) | 2.0 | (0.7) | 0.0 | a |
| Italy (Provincia Puglia) | 13.6 | (2.1) | 22.6 | (1.7) | 32.8 | (2.8) | 20.5 | (2.7) | 8.1 | (1.5) | 2.2 | (0.9) | 0.2 | (0.2) |
| Italy (Provincia Veneto) | 3.7 | (1.1) | 10.7 | (2.2) | 22.2 | (2.4) | 28.3 | (2.5) | 24.4 | (2.5) | 9.2 | (1.6) | 1.6 | (0.6) |
| Spain (Andalusia) | 9.3 | (1.3) | 17.9 | (1.6) | 29.5 | (2.5) | 26.0 | (1.7) | 14.2 | (1.6) | 2.6 | (0.7) | 0.4 | (0.3) |
| Spain (Basque Country) | 3.5 | (0.7) | 11.4 | (1.1) | 26.2 | (1.6) | 32.3 | (1.5) | 20.3 | (1.4) | 5.6 | (0.8) | 0.7 | (0.2) |
| Spain (Cantabria) | 3.2 | (0.8) | 10.4 | (1.4) | 24.0 | (2.0) | 35.0 | (2.3) | 20.3 | (1.7) | 6.5 | (1.1) | 0.5 | (0.4) |
| Spain (Galicia) | 3.3 | (0.7) | 11.8 | (1.4) | 24.8 | (1.9) | 31.2 | (2.1) | 22.1 | (2.1) | 6.0 | (1.3) | 0.8 | (0.5) |
| Spain (La Rioja) | 2.7 | (0.9) | 9.3 | (1.7) | 21.6 | (1.9) | 30.4 | (2.3) | 25.1 | (2.4) | 9.7 | (1.3) | 1.1 | (0.4) |
| Spain (Castile and Leon) | 2.1 | (0.8) | 8.3 | (1.5) | 26.7 | (2.3) | 33.3 | (1.9) | 22.5 | (2.6) | 6.2 | (1.3) | 0.7 | (0.5) |
| Spain (Navarre) | 2.5 | (0.8) | 10.8 | (1.5) | 23.3 | (1.9) | 31.6 | (2.6) | 21.9 | (2.4) | 8.7 | (1.3) | 1.1 | (0.5) |
| Spain (Aragon) | 3.9 | (0.9) | 10.3 | (1.5) | 22.2 | (2.0) | 28.8 | (1.9) | 24.7 | (2.3) | 9.1 | (1.3) | 1.0 | (0.5) |
| Spain (Catalonia) | 6.1 | (1.3) | 14.6 | (1.9) | 24.7 | (2.3) | 29.0 | (2.0) | 20.0 | (2.0) | 5.1 | (1.0) | 0.6 | (0.4) |
| Spain (Asturias) | 3.8 | (0.9) | 11.1 | (1.6) | 23.3 | (2.0) | 34.9 | (2.6) | 20.3 | (2.2) | 6.1 | (1.2) | 0.4 | (0.4) |
| United Kingdom (Scotland) | 4.1 | (0.7) | 12.4 | (1.2) | 22.2 | (1.4) | 24.2 | (1.9) | 21.2 | (2.3) | 11.1 | (1.3) | 4.7 | (0.9) |
| **Non-adjudicated** | | | | | | | | | | | | | | |
| Belgium (French Community) | 8.6 | (1.4) | 12.9 | (1.4) | 21.2 | (1.7) | 24.7 | (1.5) | 21.3 | (1.6) | 9.6 | (1.2) | 1.7 | (0.7) |
| Belgium (German-Speaking Community) | 5.0 | (1.5) | 10.5 | (2.6) | 16.3 | (2.5) | 29.6 | (2.9) | 24.8 | (2.5) | 11.9 | (2.1) | 1.9 | (0.8) |
| Finland (Finnish Speaking) | 0.7 | (0.2) | 3.3 | (0.6) | 12.4 | (0.9) | 26.7 | (1.0) | 31.4 | (1.2) | 19.1 | (1.0) | 6.5 | (0.7) |
| Finland (Swedish Speaking) | 2.6 | (2.2) | 9.2 | (3.2) | 24.5 | (4.3) | 25.1 | (4.3) | 24.3 | (5.0) | 12.1 | (3.2) | 2.2 | (1.6) |
| United Kingdom (England) | 6.2 | (0.7) | 12.9 | (1.1) | 20.9 | (1.2) | 24.9 | (1.3) | 21.4 | (1.1) | 10.4 | (0.8) | 3.2 | (0.5) |
| United Kingdom (Northern Ireland) | 8.4 | (1.3) | 12.7 | (1.4) | 18.9 | (1.6) | 23.7 | (1.7) | 21.0 | (1.5) | 11.2 | (1.3) | 4.1 | (0.7) |
| United Kingdom (Wales) | 6.7 | (0.9) | 13.5 | (1.2) | 23.8 | (1.5) | 24.7 | (1.5) | 19.7 | (1.5) | 9.0 | (1.0) | 2.5 | (0.6) |

Note: See Table 2.4b for national data.

StatLink http://dx.doi.org/10.1787/142184405135

Pour consulter la version française intégrale de ce tableau, suivre ce lien :
StatLink http://dx.doi.org/10.1787/152830402855

[Part 1/1]

**Table S2l** Mean score, variation and gender differences in student performance on the *using scientific evidence* scale

Tableau S2l Score moyen, différences de score selon le sexe et répartition des scores sur l'échelle d'*utilisation de faits scientifiques*

| | All students | | | | Gender differences | | | | | |
| --- | --- | --- | --- | --- | --- | --- | --- | --- | --- | --- |
| | Mean score | | Standard deviation | | Males | | Females | | Difference (M – F) | |
| | Mean | S.E. | S.D. | S.E. | Mean score | S.E. | Mean score | S.E. | Score dif. | S.E. |
| **Adjudicated** | | | | | | | | | | |
| Belgium (Flemish Community) | 534 | (4.1) | 106 | (3.8) | 530 | (5.0) | 538 | (4.6) | -8 | (5.2) |
| Italy (Provincia Autonoma of Bolzano) | 529 | (2.2) | 98 | (1.8) | 529 | (3.3) | 530 | (3.0) | -1 | (4.4) |
| Italy (Provincia Campania) | 429 | (6.9) | 98 | (3.8) | 437 | (7.3) | 422 | (8.9) | 15 | (8.8) |
| Italy (Provincia Basilicata) | 441 | (6.1) | 102 | (3.4) | 436 | (8.6) | 448 | (6.2) | -12 | (8.9) |
| Italy (Provincia Emilia Romagna) | 508 | (4.6) | 104 | (3.7) | 512 | (6.1) | 504 | (5.2) | 8 | (6.5) |
| Italy (Provincia Friuli Venezia Giulia) | 530 | (3.7) | 97 | (2.7) | 528 | (6.5) | 532 | (4.9) | -3 | (8.9) |
| Italy (Provincia Sicilia) | 419 | (8.3) | 111 | (4.5) | 417 | (10.1) | 421 | (9.6) | -4 | (10.6) |
| Italy (Provincia Liguria) | 482 | (8.1) | 110 | (3.6) | 470 | (11.3) | 494 | (7.0) | **-24** | (9.9) |
| Italy (Provincia Lombardia) | 496 | (7.5) | 108 | (6.3) | 489 | (12.4) | 503 | (6.3) | -15 | (12.2) |
| Italy (Provincia Piemonte) | 505 | (5.1) | 105 | (3.6) | 494 | (7.8) | 514 | (5.1) | **-20** | (8.2) |
| Italy (Provincia Trento) | 516 | (2.0) | 99 | (1.6) | 513 | (3.4) | 519 | (3.1) | -6 | (5.2) |
| Italy (Provincia Sardegna) | 434 | (8.0) | 112 | (4.6) | 430 | (11.3) | 438 | (7.4) | -8 | (10.3) |
| Italy (Provincia Puglia) | 437 | (5.3) | 98 | (2.8) | 435 | (6.4) | 440 | (6.1) | -5 | (6.4) |
| Italy (Provincia Veneto) | 521 | (5.8) | 98 | (2.8) | 525 | (7.6) | 517 | (8.2) | 9 | (11.0) |
| Spain (Andalusia) | 469 | (4.8) | 101 | (2.3) | 473 | (5.7) | 466 | (5.2) | 7 | (5.2) |
| Spain (Basque Country) | 498 | (3.9) | 96 | (2.4) | 495 | (4.8) | 502 | (3.8) | -7 | (3.8) |
| Spain (Cantabria) | 500 | (3.8) | 94 | (2.6) | 495 | (5.7) | 506 | (3.2) | **-12** | (5.2) |
| Spain (Galicia) | 502 | (3.7) | 99 | (1.9) | 499 | (4.2) | 505 | (4.1) | -6 | (3.7) |
| Spain (La Rioja) | 518 | (2.5) | 95 | (2.0) | 515 | (3.6) | 522 | (3.6) | -6 | (5.1) |
| Spain (Castile and Leon) | 511 | (4.8) | 87 | (2.1) | 511 | (5.3) | 511 | (5.4) | -1 | (4.5) |
| Spain (Navarre) | 512 | (3.6) | 98 | (2.0) | 509 | (3.9) | 514 | (4.7) | -5 | (4.8) |
| Spain (Aragon) | 508 | (5.0) | 99 | (2.5) | 502 | (6.4) | 514 | (5.4) | -12 | (6.6) |
| Spain (Catalonia) | 493 | (5.9) | 99 | (2.8) | 496 | (7.1) | 491 | (6.1) | 5 | (5.9) |
| Spain (Asturias) | 502 | (6.1) | 95 | (3.3) | 501 | (8.1) | 503 | (5.5) | -2 | (6.6) |
| United Kingdom (Scotland) | 521 | (4.1) | 113 | (2.2) | 523 | (5.3) | 520 | (4.1) | 3 | (4.8) |
| **Non-adjudicated** | | | | | | | | | | |
| Belgium (French Community) | 493 | (4.9) | 117 | (3.3) | 487 | (6.3) | 499 | (6.2) | -11 | (7.8) |
| Belgium (German-Speaking Community) | 519 | (2.9) | 113 | (2.5) | 515 | (4.5) | 523 | (5.0) | -8 | (7.5) |
| Finland (Finnish Speaking) | 569 | (2.4) | 96 | (1.2) | 566 | (3.1) | 573 | (2.8) | **-7** | (3.4) |
| Finland (Swedish Speaking) | 527 | (6.1) | 93 | (4.0) | 528 | (5.8) | 525 | (9.2) | 3 | (9.4) |
| United Kingdom (England) | 514 | (2.9) | 117 | (2.1) | 517 | (3.7) | 510 | (3.7) | 7 | (4.6) |
| United Kingdom (Northern Ireland) | 508 | (3.7) | 125 | (2.5) | 507 | (6.7) | 509 | (6.4) | -2 | (10.7) |
| United Kingdom (Wales) | 504 | (4.1) | 112 | (2.1) | 507 | (4.6) | 501 | (4.8) | 6 | (4.6) |

| | Percentiles | | | | | | | | | | | |
| --- | --- | --- | --- | --- | --- | --- | --- | --- | --- | --- | --- | --- |
| | 5th | | 10th | | 25th | | 75th | | 90th | | 95th | |
| | Score | S.E. | Score | S.E. | Score | S.E. | Score | S.E. | Score | S.E. | Score | S.E. |
| **Adjudicated** | | | | | | | | | | | | |
| Belgium (Flemish Community) | 338 | (13.9) | 385 | (9.9) | 466 | (5.6) | 612 | (3.2) | 659 | (2.8) | 684 | (3.2) |
| Italy (Provincia Autonoma of Bolzano) | 361 | (6.4) | 398 | (6.1) | 465 | (5.6) | 598 | (3.3) | 651 | (3.9) | 679 | (4.2) |
| Italy (Provincia Campania) | 268 | (7.6) | 302 | (7.7) | 362 | (8.1) | 498 | (7.4) | 555 | (8.8) | 589 | (11.7) |
| Italy (Provincia Basilicata) | 268 | (13.1) | 305 | (13.5) | 374 | (9.2) | 514 | (7.7) | 572 | (6.3) | 609 | (6.5) |
| Italy (Provincia Emilia Romagna) | 329 | (9.7) | 366 | (8.2) | 442 | (6.6) | 581 | (5.7) | 639 | (7.0) | 668 | (7.7) |
| Italy (Provincia Friuli Venezia Giulia) | 366 | (9.3) | 404 | (5.3) | 468 | (4.5) | 596 | (5.1) | 650 | (6.4) | 682 | (7.1) |
| Italy (Provincia Sicilia) | 231 | (16.6) | 274 | (13.3) | 346 | (10.5) | 497 | (8.9) | 562 | (9.2) | 598 | (12.9) |
| Italy (Provincia Liguria) | 287 | (14.6) | 330 | (16.0) | 409 | (12.2) | 560 | (7.7) | 621 | (8.0) | 651 | (7.0) |
| Italy (Provincia Lombardia) | 308 | (25.0) | 355 | (16.2) | 429 | (11.0) | 571 | (7.2) | 629 | (7.3) | 660 | (7.7) |
| Italy (Provincia Piemonte) | 322 | (9.6) | 366 | (8.7) | 437 | (8.6) | 578 | (7.2) | 634 | (7.1) | 664 | (8.2) |
| Italy (Provincia Trento) | 338 | (6.8) | 381 | (3.8) | 449 | (4.0) | 587 | (4.9) | 636 | (4.3) | 661 | (5.8) |
| Italy (Provincia Sardegna) | 238 | (12.9) | 282 | (13.6) | 359 | (10.5) | 514 | (9.3) | 574 | (8.8) | 612 | (12.6) |
| Italy (Provincia Puglia) | 284 | (9.5) | 318 | (6.5) | 374 | (7.0) | 502 | (6.0) | 563 | (8.6) | 600 | (10.8) |
| Italy (Provincia Veneto) | 354 | (9.7) | 391 | (7.5) | 454 | (7.1) | 590 | (6.6) | 643 | (7.6) | 676 | (8.4) |
| Spain (Andalusia) | 296 | (9.9) | 338 | (9.0) | 405 | (5.8) | 540 | (5.2) | 594 | (5.6) | 624 | (6.5) |
| Spain (Basque Country) | 332 | (7.5) | 375 | (5.9) | 437 | (4.9) | 565 | (4.2) | 618 | (4.7) | 650 | (5.5) |
| Spain (Cantabria) | 339 | (8.5) | 376 | (7.7) | 440 | (5.2) | 565 | (3.6) | 619 | (4.7) | 651 | (5.7) |
| Spain (Galicia) | 339 | (6.0) | 374 | (6.0) | 436 | (4.5) | 571 | (4.2) | 624 | (6.0) | 656 | (5.7) |
| Spain (La Rioja) | 358 | (8.9) | 393 | (6.1) | 455 | (4.7) | 586 | (4.1) | 639 | (4.6) | 665 | (5.4) |
| Spain (Castile and Leon) | 367 | (8.4) | 397 | (7.4) | 452 | (5.1) | 571 | (4.7) | 622 | (5.7) | 649 | (7.5) |
| Spain (Navarre) | 349 | (6.8) | 385 | (5.5) | 447 | (4.5) | 579 | (4.5) | 638 | (5.6) | 668 | (7.0) |
| Spain (Aragon) | 340 | (10.9) | 379 | (7.2) | 443 | (6.5) | 580 | (6.6) | 634 | (6.0) | 661 | (5.9) |
| Spain (Catalonia) | 323 | (8.6) | 363 | (9.3) | 429 | (7.2) | 562 | (6.2) | 615 | (7.5) | 645 | (7.8) |
| Spain (Asturias) | 336 | (13.1) | 375 | (9.3) | 441 | (8.0) | 566 | (5.7) | 618 | (6.1) | 647 | (6.9) |
| United Kingdom (Scotland) | 335 | (10.1) | 375 | (5.6) | 443 | (5.0) | 601 | (4.4) | 666 | (5.3) | 705 | (5.2) |
| **Non-adjudicated** | | | | | | | | | | | | |
| Belgium (French Community) | 286 | (11.5) | 334 | (9.0) | 415 | (7.1) | 577 | (5.4) | 639 | (6.1) | 671 | (7.5) |
| Belgium (German-Speaking Community) | 318 | (10.6) | 363 | (7.5) | 441 | (6.4) | 601 | (4.7) | 657 | (6.4) | 688 | (8.0) |
| Finland (Finnish Speaking) | 408 | (5.6) | 445 | (3.9) | 506 | (3.3) | 635 | (2.8) | 691 | (2.8) | 723 | (4.0) |
| Finland (Swedish Speaking) | 370 | (17.6) | 410 | (12.4) | 463 | (12.5) | 596 | (11.4) | 641 | (9.8) | 675 | (16.1) |
| United Kingdom (England) | 315 | (7.3) | 360 | (5.0) | 434 | (4.2) | 598 | (3.6) | 662 | (3.7) | 699 | (4.1) |
| United Kingdom (Northern Ireland) | 297 | (9.1) | 342 | (6.7) | 420 | (5.3) | 599 | (4.7) | 665 | (6.0) | 702 | (6.4) |
| United Kingdom (Wales) | 321 | (7.1) | 360 | (7.0) | 426 | (5.4) | 585 | (4.4) | 647 | (4.7) | 684 | (5.6) |

Note: Values that are statistically significant are indicated in bold (see Annex A3). See Table 2.4c for national data.
*StatLink* http://dx.doi.org/10.1787/142184405135

Pour consulter la version française intégrale de ce tableau, suivre ce lien :
*StatLink* http://dx.doi.org/10.1787/152830402855

[Part 1/1]

**Table S2m** Mean score, variation and gender differences in student performance on the *knowledge about science* scale[1]

Tableau S2m   Score moyen, différences de score selon le sexe et répartition des scores sur l'échelle *connaissances à propos des sciences*

| | All students | | | | Gender differences | | | | | |
|---|---|---|---|---|---|---|---|---|---|---|
| | Mean score | | Standard deviation | | Males | | Females | | Difference (M – F) | |
| | Mean | S.E. | S.D. | S.E. | Mean score | S.E. | Mean score | S.E. | Score dif. | S.E. |
| **Adjudicated** | | | | | | | | | | |
| Belgium (Flemish Community) | 535 | (2.9) | 95 | (2.2) | 531 | (3.7) | 540 | (3.3) | **-10** | (4.2) |
| Italy (Provincia Autonoma of Bolzano) | 519 | (2.1) | 88 | (1.6) | 518 | (3.1) | 520 | (2.8) | -2 | (4.3) |
| Italy (Provincia Campania) | 438 | (5.2) | 89 | (2.3) | 441 | (5.1) | 435 | (6.7) | 6 | (6.0) |
| Italy (Provincia Basilicata) | 445 | (4.5) | 91 | (2.4) | 438 | (6.1) | 452 | (5.2) | **-15** | (6.9) |
| Italy (Provincia Emilia Romagna) | 508 | (3.4) | 96 | (2.5) | 508 | (4.6) | 509 | (4.1) | 0 | (5.4) |
| Italy (Provincia Friuli Venezia Giulia) | 531 | (3.1) | 90 | (2.0) | 526 | (5.1) | 536 | (5.0) | -10 | (7.8) |
| Italy (Provincia Sicilia) | 435 | (6.5) | 100 | (3.5) | 433 | (8.3) | 437 | (7.9) | -4 | (9.5) |
| Italy (Provincia Liguria) | 481 | (6.4) | 102 | (2.7) | 471 | (8.4) | 491 | (6.2) | **-19** | (7.7) |
| Italy (Provincia Lombardia) | 496 | (5.3) | 97 | (3.2) | 486 | (8.8) | 506 | (5.1) | **-20** | (9.6) |
| Italy (Provincia Piemonte) | 506 | (4.0) | 92 | (2.4) | 496 | (6.0) | 514 | (4.5) | **-17** | (6.6) |
| Italy (Provincia Trento) | 512 | (2.6) | 103 | (2.3) | 506 | (4.3) | 517 | (3.6) | -11 | (6.0) |
| Italy (Provincia Sardegna) | 446 | (5.4) | 93 | (2.9) | 438 | (7.6) | 454 | (5.5) | **-16** | (7.5) |
| Italy (Provincia Puglia) | 446 | (3.4) | 88 | (1.9) | 439 | (5.2) | 453 | (4.3) | **-14** | (6.1) |
| Italy (Provincia Veneto) | 512 | (4.8) | 94 | (2.6) | 513 | (6.3) | 511 | (7.5) | 2 | (10.0) |
| Spain (Andalusia) | 477 | (3.2) | 87 | (1.9) | 477 | (4.2) | 476 | (3.9) | 1 | (4.9) |
| Spain (Basque Country) | 492 | (3.1) | 86 | (1.3) | 485 | (3.9) | 498 | (3.0) | **-13** | (3.5) |
| Spain (Cantabria) | 507 | (3.0) | 81 | (2.0) | 501 | (4.5) | 512 | (3.3) | **-11** | (4.9) |
| Spain (Galicia) | 503 | (3.0) | 90 | (2.1) | 498 | (3.3) | 509 | (3.7) | **-11** | (3.6) |
| Spain (La Rioja) | 517 | (3.2) | 89 | (2.2) | 512 | (4.0) | 523 | (4.5) | **-12** | (5.6) |
| Spain (Castile and Leon) | 513 | (3.2) | 78 | (1.4) | 509 | (3.9) | 518 | (3.8) | **-9** | (4.2) |
| Spain (Navarre) | 510 | (2.7) | 87 | (2.0) | 505 | (3.4) | 514 | (4.0) | -9 | (5.0) |
| Spain (Aragon) | 508 | (3.3) | 89 | (2.1) | 503 | (4.7) | 512 | (4.3) | -9 | (6.2) |
| Spain (Catalonia) | 493 | (4.3) | 89 | (2.0) | 491 | (5.4) | 495 | (4.8) | -4 | (5.4) |
| Spain (Asturias) | 505 | (4.4) | 86 | (1.9) | 504 | (6.0) | 507 | (4.1) | -3 | (5.6) |
| United Kingdom (Scotland) | 520 | (3.4) | 99 | (2.3) | 520 | (4.6) | 521 | (3.8) | -1 | (5.0) |

| | Percentiles | | | | | | | | | | | |
|---|---|---|---|---|---|---|---|---|---|---|---|---|
| | 5th | | 10th | | 25th | | 75th | | 90th | | 95th | |
| | Score | S.E. | Score | S.E. | Score | S.E. | Score | S.E. | Score | S.E. | Score | S.E. |
| **Adjudicated** | | | | | | | | | | | | |
| Belgium (Flemish Community) | 369 | (6.6) | 405 | (6.4) | 473 | (2.8) | 602 | (2.9) | 655 | (3.9) | 685 | (4.9) |
| Italy (Provincia Autonoma of Bolzano) | 370 | (7.6) | 400 | (5.1) | 460 | (3.3) | 582 | (2.6) | 630 | (4.5) | 661 | (5.1) |
| Italy (Provincia Campania) | 295 | (7.2) | 320 | (6.8) | 377 | (5.3) | 501 | (6.5) | 552 | (7.7) | 583 | (9.4) |
| Italy (Provincia Basilicata) | 293 | (8.1) | 323 | (5.7) | 382 | (6.3) | 509 | (5.8) | 565 | (5.3) | 595 | (8.1) |
| Italy (Provincia Emilia Romagna) | 343 | (8.7) | 379 | (5.1) | 444 | (5.6) | 573 | (3.8) | 632 | (4.3) | 663 | (9.2) |
| Italy (Provincia Friuli Venezia Giulia) | 378 | (8.3) | 414 | (5.2) | 472 | (5.1) | 592 | (5.0) | 642 | (4.9) | 671 | (7.6) |
| Italy (Provincia Sicilia) | 277 | (11.5) | 309 | (6.9) | 364 | (7.9) | 505 | (9.5) | 563 | (7.6) | 604 | (8.9) |
| Italy (Provincia Liguria) | 311 | (10.2) | 345 | (9.1) | 410 | (8.2) | 552 | (6.0) | 610 | (6.4) | 644 | (9.0) |
| Italy (Provincia Lombardia) | 336 | (14.1) | 371 | (7.7) | 429 | (6.9) | 564 | (6.9) | 620 | (4.2) | 651 | (7.8) |
| Italy (Provincia Piemonte) | 353 | (10.2) | 385 | (7.3) | 443 | (5.4) | 570 | (5.4) | 621 | (5.9) | 651 | (5.6) |
| Italy (Provincia Trento) | 336 | (7.5) | 375 | (4.2) | 443 | (5.0) | 583 | (5.6) | 644 | (7.5) | 677 | (7.4) |
| Italy (Provincia Sardegna) | 292 | (9.2) | 323 | (8.4) | 382 | (5.8) | 511 | (8.4) | 569 | (7.1) | 600 | (6.8) |
| Italy (Provincia Puglia) | 302 | (6.2) | 334 | (6.2) | 388 | (5.0) | 506 | (4.3) | 563 | (5.1) | 595 | (6.8) |
| Italy (Provincia Veneto) | 352 | (9.5) | 385 | (6.9) | 449 | (5.2) | 577 | (6.8) | 633 | (4.8) | 660 | (7.9) |
| Spain (Andalusia) | 336 | (7.0) | 361 | (6.6) | 417 | (4.2) | 536 | (5.1) | 592 | (5.9) | 619 | (4.9) |
| Spain (Basque Country) | 350 | (5.1) | 380 | (3.2) | 435 | (3.4) | 550 | (4.6) | 603 | (3.6) | 631 | (4.2) |
| Spain (Cantabria) | 371 | (8.9) | 399 | (6.8) | 454 | (3.8) | 562 | (3.0) | 609 | (5.0) | 636 | (5.6) |
| Spain (Galicia) | 356 | (5.9) | 384 | (4.9) | 440 | (4.3) | 566 | (4.9) | 618 | (4.4) | 648 | (6.0) |
| Spain (La Rioja) | 367 | (9.0) | 404 | (5.6) | 457 | (3.9) | 579 | (5.0) | 631 | (5.5) | 660 | (7.8) |
| Spain (Castile and Leon) | 382 | (8.0) | 410 | (4.3) | 459 | (5.0) | 567 | (3.7) | 610 | (3.7) | 637 | (3.9) |
| Spain (Navarre) | 366 | (4.9) | 392 | (3.7) | 450 | (4.5) | 570 | (4.5) | 624 | (3.4) | 651 | (5.2) |
| Spain (Aragon) | 361 | (5.4) | 388 | (4.6) | 447 | (3.7) | 571 | (5.3) | 621 | (5.4) | 651 | (7.4) |
| Spain (Catalonia) | 339 | (7.4) | 374 | (7.2) | 434 | (5.5) | 556 | (5.0) | 607 | (6.7) | 637 | (4.4) |
| Spain (Asturias) | 356 | (9.2) | 388 | (7.8) | 451 | (5.2) | 564 | (4.2) | 616 | (5.7) | 641 | (5.1) |
| United Kingdom (Scotland) | 356 | (6.6) | 388 | (6.5) | 452 | (5.0) | 588 | (5.2) | 647 | (6.2) | 687 | (5.8) |

Note: Values that are statistically significant are indicated in bold (see Annex A3). See Table 2.7 for national data.
1. The scaling model for this scale does not allow analysis by subgroup other than adjudicated regions.
StatLink ⬛️➪ http://dx.doi.org/10.1787/142184405135

Pour consulter la version française intégrale de ce tableau, suivre ce lien :
StatLink ⬛️➪ http://dx.doi.org/10.1787/152830402855

[Part 1/1]

**Table S2n** Mean score, variation and gender differences in student performance on the "Earth and space systems" scale[1]

Tableau S2n  Score moyen, différences de score selon le sexe et répartition des scores sur l'échelle « systèmes de la Terre et de l'univers »

| | All students | | | | Gender differences | | | | | |
| | Mean score | | Standard deviation | | Males | | Females | | Difference (M – F) | |
| | Mean | S.E. | S.D. | S.E. | Mean score | S.E. | Mean score | S.E. | Score dif. | S.E. |
|---|---|---|---|---|---|---|---|---|---|---|
| **Adjudicated** | | | | | | | | | | |
| Belgium (Flemish Community) | 520 | (3.1) | 107 | (2.3) | 532 | (4.0) | 505 | (3.6) | **27** | (4.6) |
| Italy (Provincia Autonoma of Bolzano) | 533 | (2.6) | 111 | (2.0) | 552 | (4.2) | 514 | (3.7) | **38** | (6.1) |
| Italy (Provincia Campania) | 437 | (5.8) | 99 | (2.8) | 454 | (5.9) | 420 | (7.1) | **34** | (6.8) |
| Italy (Provincia Basilicata) | 444 | (4.8) | 101 | (3.2) | 451 | (6.3) | 437 | (5.8) | 14 | (7.4) |
| Italy (Provincia Emilia Romagna) | 510 | (3.7) | 114 | (3.0) | 527 | (5.3) | 493 | (4.7) | **34** | (6.8) |
| Italy (Provincia Friuli Venezia Giulia) | 549 | (3.3) | 95 | (2.8) | 558 | (5.1) | 540 | (5.0) | 18 | (7.9) |
| Italy (Provincia Sicilia) | 435 | (7.8) | 122 | (3.7) | 445 | (10.6) | 427 | (9.2) | 18 | (12.3) |
| Italy (Provincia Liguria) | 489 | (7.7) | 124 | (3.7) | 489 | (10.6) | 489 | (7.3) | 0 | (9.9) |
| Italy (Provincia Lombardia) | 506 | (6.3) | 119 | (4.2) | 509 | (10.6) | 503 | (6.2) | 6 | (11.8) |
| Italy (Provincia Piemonte) | 515 | (4.4) | 100 | (2.6) | 522 | (6.2) | 509 | (5.0) | 13 | (7.0) |
| Italy (Provincia Trento) | 530 | (3.6) | 112 | (2.1) | 527 | (5.3) | 533 | (5.0) | -7 | (7.5) |
| Italy (Provincia Sardegna) | 443 | (6.0) | 107 | (3.3) | 447 | (8.6) | 440 | (5.9) | 7 | (8.6) |
| Italy (Provincia Puglia) | 436 | (4.1) | 96 | (2.2) | 439 | (5.8) | 432 | (4.6) | 7 | (6.8) |
| Italy (Provincia Veneto) | 528 | (6.2) | 114 | (3.0) | 541 | (7.7) | 514 | (9.1) | 26 | (12.2) |
| Spain (Andalusia) | 474 | (3.7) | 101 | (2.0) | 488 | (4.5) | 461 | (4.6) | **27** | (5.4) |
| Spain (Basque Country) | 492 | (3.3) | 97 | (1.4) | 498 | (4.2) | 486 | (3.3) | **12** | (3.7) |
| Spain (Cantabria) | 518 | (4.1) | 100 | (1.9) | 531 | (6.7) | 505 | (3.8) | **27** | (7.3) |
| Spain (Galicia) | 505 | (4.0) | 102 | (2.8) | 519 | (4.3) | 490 | (5.0) | **29** | (4.9) |
| Spain (La Rioja) | 524 | (3.9) | 107 | (3.3) | 531 | (5.9) | 518 | (5.2) | 13 | (8.0) |
| Spain (Castile and Leon) | 532 | (3.8) | 101 | (2.1) | 541 | (4.5) | 523 | (4.7) | **19** | (5.1) |
| Spain (Navarre) | 522 | (3.1) | 95 | (2.3) | 533 | (3.6) | 511 | (4.8) | **22** | (6.1) |
| Spain (Aragon) | 527 | (3.4) | 99 | (2.6) | 534 | (5.3) | 521 | (4.6) | 13 | (7.2) |
| Spain (Catalonia) | 502 | (5.3) | 113 | (2.2) | 517 | (7.0) | 488 | (5.3) | **29** | (6.4) |
| Spain (Asturias) | 518 | (5.0) | 109 | (2.4) | 532 | (7.4) | 504 | (5.6) | **29** | (8.4) |
| United Kingdom (Scotland) | 497 | (3.7) | 110 | (2.8) | 512 | (5.2) | 482 | (3.9) | **30** | (5.6) |

| | Percentiles | | | | | | | | | | | |
| | 5th | | 10th | | 25th | | 75th | | 90th | | 95th | |
| | Score | S.E. | Score | S.E. | Score | S.E. | Score | S.E. | Score | S.E. | Score | S.E. |
|---|---|---|---|---|---|---|---|---|---|---|---|---|
| **Adjudicated** | | | | | | | | | | | | |
| Belgium (Flemish Community) | 336 | (7.8) | 380 | (6.0) | 449 | (3.7) | 595 | (3.0) | 656 | (4.5) | 691 | (3.7) |
| Italy (Provincia Autonoma of Bolzano) | 351 | (7.5) | 387 | (5.9) | 457 | (5.1) | 606 | (4.5) | 674 | (6.3) | 717 | (8.9) |
| Italy (Provincia Campania) | 277 | (8.3) | 308 | (7.3) | 371 | (8.3) | 505 | (7.1) | 568 | (6.1) | 601 | (6.8) |
| Italy (Provincia Basilicata) | 276 | (9.7) | 313 | (8.2) | 376 | (7.5) | 514 | (8.1) | 579 | (8.4) | 613 | (9.2) |
| Italy (Provincia Emilia Romagna) | 316 | (10.0) | 357 | (7.4) | 435 | (6.1) | 591 | (4.4) | 657 | (7.0) | 691 | (7.1) |
| Italy (Provincia Friuli Venezia Giulia) | 384 | (7.8) | 423 | (6.3) | 489 | (5.3) | 613 | (5.3) | 669 | (5.9) | 700 | (8.9) |
| Italy (Provincia Sicilia) | 247 | (11.8) | 286 | (9.7) | 349 | (9.0) | 519 | (11.0) | 595 | (10.9) | 639 | (13.6) |
| Italy (Provincia Liguria) | 285 | (12.4) | 326 | (12.2) | 404 | (10.1) | 578 | (8.0) | 649 | (8.8) | 695 | (11.4) |
| Italy (Provincia Lombardia) | 310 | (13.4) | 351 | (11.4) | 426 | (8.7) | 588 | (7.7) | 656 | (7.9) | 696 | (8.0) |
| Italy (Provincia Piemonte) | 344 | (5.9) | 386 | (10.4) | 450 | (6.5) | 586 | (6.0) | 640 | (4.8) | 672 | (8.6) |
| Italy (Provincia Trento) | 342 | (9.3) | 384 | (5.2) | 455 | (2.9) | 605 | (5.7) | 674 | (7.1) | 707 | (9.1) |
| Italy (Provincia Sardegna) | 268 | (10.8) | 308 | (7.5) | 370 | (9.0) | 515 | (8.4) | 587 | (8.7) | 624 | (11.9) |
| Italy (Provincia Puglia) | 282 | (7.7) | 314 | (7.0) | 369 | (6.3) | 499 | (4.9) | 565 | (6.6) | 601 | (10.2) |
| Italy (Provincia Veneto) | 330 | (10.1) | 376 | (7.6) | 452 | (8.8) | 608 | (7.5) | 674 | (9.8) | 714 | (6.4) |
| Spain (Andalusia) | 309 | (12.9) | 344 | (7.8) | 407 | (4.5) | 544 | (5.1) | 603 | (7.3) | 639 | (8.1) |
| Spain (Basque Country) | 329 | (6.1) | 367 | (3.6) | 427 | (3.7) | 558 | (3.5) | 620 | (4.9) | 652 | (4.3) |
| Spain (Cantabria) | 348 | (10.1) | 387 | (6.7) | 452 | (4.6) | 589 | (5.2) | 647 | (5.8) | 682 | (6.8) |
| Spain (Galicia) | 332 | (8.1) | 373 | (7.1) | 437 | (5.4) | 577 | (7.6) | 638 | (6.0) | 673 | (5.7) |
| Spain (La Rioja) | 345 | (11.1) | 384 | (7.2) | 454 | (6.1) | 596 | (6.4) | 664 | (5.0) | 699 | (5.9) |
| Spain (Castile and Leon) | 366 | (6.1) | 399 | (5.5) | 462 | (5.0) | 603 | (5.4) | 664 | (7.5) | 698 | (5.8) |
| Spain (Navarre) | 363 | (6.5) | 397 | (5.7) | 459 | (5.7) | 589 | (4.7) | 647 | (4.5) | 677 | (4.4) |
| Spain (Aragon) | 357 | (7.7) | 395 | (5.4) | 460 | (6.7) | 598 | (5.6) | 656 | (6.8) | 686 | (7.7) |
| Spain (Catalonia) | 316 | (8.2) | 359 | (6.2) | 425 | (6.3) | 580 | (6.7) | 650 | (8.4) | 692 | (8.2) |
| Spain (Asturias) | 333 | (9.0) | 373 | (7.8) | 446 | (7.0) | 592 | (6.6) | 659 | (6.2) | 699 | (10.3) |
| United Kingdom (Scotland) | 315 | (8.7) | 353 | (6.2) | 423 | (4.3) | 574 | (5.0) | 645 | (7.3) | 680 | (5.6) |

Note: Values that are statistically significant are indicated in bold (see Annex A3). See Table 2.8 for national data.
1. The scaling model for this scale does not allow analysis by subgroup other than adjudicated regions.
StatLink ⟴ http://dx.doi.org/10.1787/142184405135

Pour consulter la version française intégrale de ce tableau, suivre ce lien :
StatLink ⟴ http://dx.doi.org/10.1787/152830402855

[Part 1/1]

**Table S2o** **Mean score, variation and gender differences in student performance on the "Living systems" scale[1]**

Tableau S2o   Score moyen, différences de score selon le sexe et répartition des scores sur l'échelle « systèmes vivants »

| | All students | | | | Gender differences | | | | | |
| --- | --- | --- | --- | --- | --- | --- | --- | --- | --- | --- |
| | Mean score | | Standard deviation | | Males | | Females | | Difference (M – F) | |
| | Mean | S.E. | S.D. | S.E. | Mean score | S.E. | Mean score | S.E. | Score dif. | S.E. |
| **Adjudicated** | | | | | | | | | | |
| Belgium (Flemish Community) | 519 | (2.8) | 96 | (2.0) | 520 | (3.5) | 518 | (3.4) | 2 | (4.1) |
| Italy (Provincia Autonoma of Bolzano) | 543 | (2.2) | 90 | (1.6) | 547 | (3.2) | 540 | (3.3) | 8 | (4.8) |
| Italy (Provincia Campania) | 457 | (4.9) | 86 | (2.4) | 464 | (4.9) | 449 | (6.0) | **15** | (5.5) |
| Italy (Provincia Basilicata) | 463 | (4.3) | 90 | (2.2) | 460 | (5.6) | 465 | (5.0) | -5 | (6.5) |
| Italy (Provincia Emilia Romagna) | 519 | (3.8) | 104 | (3.0) | 522 | (5.0) | 515 | (4.9) | 7 | (6.3) |
| Italy (Provincia Friuli Venezia Giulia) | 543 | (3.5) | 90 | (2.3) | 551 | (5.3) | 534 | (5.3) | **17** | (8.1) |
| Italy (Provincia Sicilia) | 450 | (6.9) | 104 | (3.4) | 457 | (8.7) | 444 | (8.2) | 13 | (9.8) |
| Italy (Provincia Liguria) | 498 | (6.7) | 107 | (2.9) | 496 | (8.9) | 500 | (6.5) | -4 | (8.3) |
| Italy (Provincia Lombardia) | 509 | (5.4) | 100 | (3.0) | 502 | (9.0) | 517 | (5.3) | -15 | (10.2) |
| Italy (Provincia Piemonte) | 516 | (4.5) | 97 | (2.6) | 510 | (6.4) | 522 | (5.0) | -12 | (6.9) |
| Italy (Provincia Trento) | 525 | (2.6) | 91 | (2.3) | 525 | (4.5) | 526 | (3.2) | -1 | (5.7) |
| Italy (Provincia Sardegna) | 464 | (5.8) | 99 | (3.1) | 461 | (8.4) | 466 | (5.5) | -6 | (8.1) |
| Italy (Provincia Puglia) | 461 | (3.5) | 87 | (2.2) | 460 | (4.9) | 462 | (4.3) | -2 | (5.7) |
| Italy (Provincia Veneto) | 530 | (5.2) | 99 | (2.6) | 540 | (6.4) | 521 | (8.0) | 19 | (10.6) |
| Spain (Andalusia) | 483 | (3.7) | 102 | (2.1) | 493 | (4.6) | 473 | (4.5) | **19** | (5.4) |
| Spain (Basque Country) | 500 | (3.4) | 99 | (1.5) | 502 | (4.4) | 498 | (3.3) | 4 | (3.9) |
| Spain (Cantabria) | 528 | (3.6) | 99 | (2.4) | 526 | (5.2) | 530 | (4.1) | -5 | (6.1) |
| Spain (Galicia) | 514 | (3.4) | 101 | (2.9) | 521 | (3.6) | 506 | (4.3) | **15** | (4.2) |
| Spain (La Rioja) | 531 | (3.1) | 99 | (2.7) | 532 | (4.3) | 530 | (4.5) | 2 | (6.2) |
| Spain (Castile and Leon) | 543 | (3.6) | 96 | (2.4) | 544 | (4.2) | 541 | (4.4) | 4 | (4.4) |
| Spain (Navarre) | 522 | (3.4) | 104 | (3.2) | 526 | (4.2) | 518 | (4.7) | 8 | (5.8) |
| Spain (Aragon) | 533 | (3.5) | 98 | (2.2) | 532 | (5.3) | 534 | (4.6) | -2 | (7.2) |
| Spain (Catalonia) | 490 | (4.5) | 98 | (2.3) | 495 | (5.9) | 485 | (4.7) | 10 | (5.7) |
| Spain (Asturias) | 507 | (4.5) | 95 | (2.1) | 512 | (6.4) | 502 | (4.3) | 10 | (6.2) |
| United Kingdom (Scotland) | 515 | (3.5) | 104 | (2.7) | 515 | (4.7) | 515 | (4.1) | -1 | (5.4) |

| | Percentiles | | | | | | | | | | | |
| --- | --- | --- | --- | --- | --- | --- | --- | --- | --- | --- | --- | --- |
| | 5th | | 10th | | 25th | | 75th | | 90th | | 95th | |
| | Score | S.E. | Score | S.E. | Score | S.E. | Score | S.E. | Score | S.E. | Score | S.E. |
| **Adjudicated** | | | | | | | | | | | | |
| Belgium (Flemish Community) | 355 | (7.5) | 388 | (5.5) | 456 | (3.5) | 587 | (3.0) | 638 | (5.3) | 670 | (3.2) |
| Italy (Provincia Autonoma of Bolzano) | 391 | (4.2) | 421 | (4.9) | 484 | (4.3) | 605 | (4.0) | 655 | (5.1) | 689 | (5.3) |
| Italy (Provincia Campania) | 316 | (5.9) | 343 | (5.2) | 397 | (7.3) | 516 | (6.4) | 568 | (7.9) | 600 | (8.3) |
| Italy (Provincia Basilicata) | 315 | (6.7) | 347 | (6.0) | 399 | (5.4) | 525 | (4.9) | 579 | (5.3) | 609 | (6.2) |
| Italy (Provincia Emilia Romagna) | 341 | (5.8) | 381 | (8.1) | 450 | (5.4) | 590 | (4.6) | 653 | (6.9) | 686 | (8.7) |
| Italy (Provincia Friuli Venezia Giulia) | 387 | (10.1) | 428 | (6.7) | 483 | (5.7) | 604 | (4.5) | 654 | (5.1) | 686 | (7.7) |
| Italy (Provincia Sicilia) | 288 | (12.6) | 322 | (9.4) | 377 | (8.8) | 525 | (9.5) | 586 | (9.9) | 628 | (12.3) |
| Italy (Provincia Liguria) | 322 | (9.6) | 358 | (11.8) | 423 | (9.9) | 571 | (5.6) | 638 | (7.5) | 668 | (9.1) |
| Italy (Provincia Lombardia) | 340 | (12.9) | 377 | (10.2) | 440 | (8.8) | 581 | (6.7) | 634 | (5.5) | 672 | (7.0) |
| Italy (Provincia Piemonte) | 354 | (8.0) | 388 | (7.3) | 451 | (6.7) | 585 | (4.4) | 639 | (7.0) | 670 | (6.5) |
| Italy (Provincia Trento) | 375 | (8.0) | 410 | (4.4) | 464 | (4.5) | 587 | (4.7) | 641 | (7.2) | 673 | (10.4) |
| Italy (Provincia Sardegna) | 300 | (7.8) | 333 | (8.6) | 396 | (8.0) | 530 | (6.3) | 594 | (10.8) | 629 | (11.1) |
| Italy (Provincia Puglia) | 321 | (4.9) | 350 | (5.2) | 401 | (3.9) | 520 | (5.4) | 576 | (6.2) | 606 | (7.9) |
| Italy (Provincia Veneto) | 363 | (10.3) | 400 | (8.5) | 464 | (6.8) | 598 | (7.1) | 658 | (6.1) | 685 | (5.4) |
| Spain (Andalusia) | 318 | (8.5) | 355 | (7.7) | 414 | (4.0) | 551 | (5.3) | 617 | (7.1) | 651 | (7.3) |
| Spain (Basque Country) | 341 | (5.6) | 377 | (4.6) | 430 | (3.6) | 566 | (4.6) | 628 | (4.6) | 662 | (4.5) |
| Spain (Cantabria) | 364 | (8.4) | 399 | (6.3) | 461 | (5.8) | 595 | (5.8) | 655 | (4.8) | 687 | (4.5) |
| Spain (Galicia) | 349 | (9.7) | 383 | (6.0) | 444 | (4.5) | 583 | (6.9) | 645 | (5.9) | 680 | (7.6) |
| Spain (La Rioja) | 362 | (8.2) | 401 | (9.6) | 464 | (6.6) | 599 | (5.0) | 656 | (5.8) | 692 | (6.6) |
| Spain (Castile and Leon) | 379 | (9.9) | 417 | (7.1) | 480 | (4.1) | 611 | (5.2) | 668 | (5.5) | 700 | (4.7) |
| Spain (Navarre) | 348 | (11.6) | 386 | (7.7) | 451 | (6.5) | 592 | (5.5) | 659 | (5.7) | 689 | (9.5) |
| Spain (Aragon) | 371 | (6.1) | 403 | (6.8) | 466 | (4.7) | 600 | (5.7) | 661 | (4.0) | 690 | (7.5) |
| Spain (Catalonia) | 326 | (7.3) | 359 | (6.5) | 423 | (5.9) | 559 | (5.5) | 613 | (7.5) | 648 | (6.2) |
| Spain (Asturias) | 345 | (9.0) | 379 | (7.1) | 445 | (6.3) | 569 | (5.1) | 628 | (7.4) | 660 | (7.6) |
| United Kingdom (Scotland) | 345 | (6.6) | 379 | (5.7) | 444 | (5.3) | 585 | (6.0) | 648 | (4.8) | 685 | (8.1) |

Note: Values that are statistically significant are indicated in bold (see Annex A3). See Table 2.9 for national data.
1. The scaling model for this scale does not allow analysis by subgroup other than adjudicated regions.
*StatLink* http://dx.doi.org/10.1787/142184405135

Pour consulter la version française intégrale de ce tableau, suivre ce lien :
*StatLink* http://dx.doi.org/10.1787/152830402855

[Part 1/1]

**Table S2p**   Mean score, variation and gender differences in student performance on the "Physical systems" scale[1]

Tableau S2p   Score moyen, différences de score selon le sexe et répartition des scores sur l'échelle « systèmes physiques »

| | All students | | | | Gender differences | | | | | |
| | Mean score | | Standard deviation | | Males | | Females | | Difference (M – F) | |
| | Mean | S.E. | S.D. | S.E. | Mean score | S.E. | Mean score | S.E. | Score dif. | S.E. |
|---|---|---|---|---|---|---|---|---|---|---|
| **Adjudicated** | | | | | | | | | | |
| Belgium (Flemish Community) | 532 | (2.7) | 98 | (2.1) | 543 | (3.4) | 518 | (3.2) | **25** | (3.9) |
| Italy (Provincia Autonoma of Bolzano) | 515 | (2.3) | 94 | (1.9) | 542 | (3.7) | 489 | (3.1) | **53** | (5.2) |
| Italy (Provincia Campania) | 442 | (5.6) | 88 | (2.5) | 462 | (5.3) | 423 | (6.9) | **40** | (6.2) |
| Italy (Provincia Basilicata) | 447 | (4.3) | 89 | (2.3) | 458 | (5.7) | 436 | (4.8) | 22 | (6.0) |
| Italy (Provincia Emilia Romagna) | 506 | (3.3) | 97 | (2.6) | 528 | (4.6) | 483 | (4.5) | **44** | (6.4) |
| Italy (Provincia Friuli Venezia Giulia) | 524 | (3.6) | 96 | (2.3) | 542 | (5.0) | 508 | (5.3) | **34** | (8.1) |
| Italy (Provincia Sicilia) | 440 | (6.5) | 101 | (3.3) | 453 | (8.4) | 428 | (7.8) | **25** | (9.9) |
| Italy (Provincia Liguria) | 484 | (6.6) | 104 | (3.1) | 490 | (9.2) | 478 | (6.1) | 12 | (8.6) |
| Italy (Provincia Lombardia) | 493 | (5.5) | 100 | (2.8) | 501 | (8.9) | 484 | (5.2) | 17 | (9.6) |
| Italy (Provincia Piemonte) | 500 | (4.5) | 95 | (2.5) | 511 | (5.9) | 490 | (5.4) | 21 | (7.1) |
| Italy (Provincia Trento) | 520 | (2.8) | 93 | (2.0) | 523 | (4.5) | 517 | (3.9) | 6 | (6.4) |
| Italy (Provincia Sardegna) | 444 | (5.5) | 94 | (3.0) | 452 | (7.9) | 436 | (5.1) | **16** | (7.9) |
| Italy (Provincia Puglia) | 445 | (3.8) | 94 | (2.3) | 454 | (5.7) | 437 | (4.1) | **16** | (6.9) |
| Italy (Provincia Veneto) | 516 | (5.2) | 97 | (2.5) | 532 | (6.3) | 500 | (7.4) | **32** | (10.2) |
| Spain (Andalusia) | 463 | (3.4) | 90 | (1.9) | 480 | (3.8) | 448 | (4.5) | **32** | (4.9) |
| Spain (Basque Country) | 479 | (2.9) | 88 | (1.3) | 488 | (3.9) | 469 | (3.0) | **19** | (3.6) |
| Spain (Cantabria) | 494 | (3.2) | 92 | (2.2) | 506 | (5.0) | 482 | (4.1) | **24** | (6.7) |
| Spain (Galicia) | 493 | (2.8) | 94 | (2.3) | 507 | (3.2) | 478 | (3.7) | **29** | (3.9) |
| Spain (La Rioja) | 501 | (3.1) | 85 | (2.4) | 510 | (4.1) | 493 | (4.4) | 17 | (5.9) |
| Spain (Castile and Leon) | 505 | (3.2) | 87 | (1.8) | 520 | (4.0) | 489 | (3.9) | **30** | (4.6) |
| Spain (Navarre) | 499 | (3.2) | 92 | (2.2) | 511 | (4.1) | 487 | (4.2) | **24** | (5.6) |
| Spain (Aragon) | 500 | (3.1) | 92 | (2.0) | 508 | (4.8) | 491 | (3.8) | 17 | (6.0) |
| Spain (Catalonia) | 483 | (4.1) | 93 | (1.7) | 498 | (5.3) | 468 | (4.5) | **30** | (5.2) |
| Spain (Asturias) | 495 | (4.3) | 90 | (1.9) | 509 | (6.0) | 481 | (4.2) | **28** | (5.7) |
| United Kingdom (Scotland) | 508 | (3.5) | 106 | (2.4) | 522 | (4.8) | 493 | (3.9) | **29** | (5.3) |

| | Percentiles | | | | | | | | | | | |
| | 5th | | 10th | | 25th | | 75th | | 90th | | 95th | |
| | Score | S.E. | Score | S.E. | Score | S.E. | Score | S.E. | Score | S.E. | Score | S.E. |
|---|---|---|---|---|---|---|---|---|---|---|---|---|
| **Adjudicated** | | | | | | | | | | | | |
| Belgium (Flemish Community) | 367 | (5.8) | 401 | (4.5) | 464 | (4.2) | 600 | (3.1) | 657 | (3.6) | 691 | (2.5) |
| Italy (Provincia Autonoma of Bolzano) | 355 | (5.2) | 392 | (4.9) | 451 | (3.3) | 579 | (3.7) | 634 | (4.7) | 670 | (5.8) |
| Italy (Provincia Campania) | 299 | (9.4) | 328 | (6.9) | 379 | (7.9) | 503 | (7.5) | 558 | (8.2) | 591 | (9.3) |
| Italy (Provincia Basilicata) | 303 | (7.3) | 332 | (6.3) | 385 | (6.3) | 509 | (4.5) | 564 | (6.8) | 596 | (6.7) |
| Italy (Provincia Emilia Romagna) | 340 | (8.6) | 376 | (4.9) | 442 | (4.4) | 573 | (4.8) | 628 | (4.4) | 659 | (8.0) |
| Italy (Provincia Friuli Venezia Giulia) | 364 | (7.2) | 400 | (7.9) | 461 | (4.5) | 590 | (4.6) | 647 | (5.6) | 680 | (5.0) |
| Italy (Provincia Sicilia) | 281 | (13.6) | 314 | (8.3) | 367 | (5.9) | 511 | (9.3) | 574 | (9.0) | 608 | (9.9) |
| Italy (Provincia Liguria) | 314 | (9.0) | 348 | (8.8) | 410 | (9.8) | 555 | (6.0) | 615 | (8.7) | 648 | (12.0) |
| Italy (Provincia Lombardia) | 327 | (9.2) | 362 | (9.5) | 425 | (8.6) | 564 | (8.3) | 624 | (5.8) | 654 | (5.3) |
| Italy (Provincia Piemonte) | 336 | (8.5) | 377 | (7.8) | 437 | (6.3) | 565 | (4.9) | 620 | (8.1) | 649 | (6.9) |
| Italy (Provincia Trento) | 368 | (4.7) | 403 | (5.4) | 455 | (4.2) | 586 | (3.8) | 640 | (7.7) | 675 | (5.9) |
| Italy (Provincia Sardegna) | 294 | (6.8) | 323 | (7.0) | 377 | (8.4) | 509 | (7.6) | 568 | (7.7) | 602 | (8.3) |
| Italy (Provincia Puglia) | 294 | (7.1) | 327 | (5.9) | 379 | (4.9) | 508 | (6.1) | 571 | (6.5) | 606 | (6.7) |
| Italy (Provincia Veneto) | 353 | (8.5) | 389 | (7.1) | 452 | (8.0) | 582 | (6.3) | 637 | (6.4) | 672 | (8.1) |
| Spain (Andalusia) | 316 | (9.3) | 350 | (6.5) | 402 | (4.4) | 525 | (3.9) | 579 | (4.8) | 616 | (6.5) |
| Spain (Basque Country) | 333 | (4.6) | 366 | (5.4) | 419 | (4.0) | 538 | (3.1) | 593 | (4.8) | 626 | (4.3) |
| Spain (Cantabria) | 343 | (6.6) | 374 | (5.4) | 431 | (5.2) | 556 | (5.0) | 615 | (5.4) | 645 | (5.9) |
| Spain (Galicia) | 342 | (6.2) | 371 | (4.6) | 427 | (5.1) | 558 | (4.0) | 614 | (4.4) | 651 | (6.4) |
| Spain (La Rioja) | 359 | (9.5) | 388 | (7.1) | 446 | (4.4) | 559 | (4.8) | 614 | (5.8) | 642 | (5.2) |
| Spain (Castile and Leon) | 361 | (8.0) | 392 | (6.0) | 445 | (5.5) | 564 | (4.1) | 616 | (4.9) | 645 | (7.8) |
| Spain (Navarre) | 352 | (4.7) | 378 | (4.8) | 433 | (5.5) | 562 | (3.6) | 621 | (6.2) | 654 | (5.4) |
| Spain (Aragon) | 353 | (5.5) | 379 | (4.3) | 435 | (6.0) | 564 | (5.8) | 622 | (7.1) | 654 | (6.4) |
| Spain (Catalonia) | 331 | (5.6) | 361 | (6.5) | 418 | (4.8) | 547 | (5.1) | 604 | (5.8) | 638 | (7.8) |
| Spain (Asturias) | 342 | (8.4) | 377 | (7.8) | 435 | (6.2) | 556 | (4.6) | 609 | (6.5) | 643 | (5.3) |
| United Kingdom (Scotland) | 336 | (8.0) | 371 | (5.9) | 433 | (5.7) | 580 | (4.1) | 649 | (6.7) | 685 | (5.8) |

Note: Values that are statistically significant are indicated in bold (see Annex A3). See Table 2.10 for national data.
1. The scaling model for this scale does not allow analysis by subgroup other than adjudicated regions.
StatLink ⬛🔗 http://dx.doi.org/10.1787/142184405135

Pour consulter la version française intégrale de ce tableau, suivre ce lien :
StatLink ⬛🔗 http://dx.doi.org/10.1787/152830402855

263

[Part 1/2]

**Table S3a  Index of self-efficacy in science and performance on the science scale, by quarters of the index[1]**

Tableau S3a  Indice de perception des capacités personnelles en sciences et scores sur l'échelle de culture scientifique, par quartile de l'indice

| | Index of self-efficacy in science | | | | | | | | | | | | | | | |
|---|---|---|---|---|---|---|---|---|---|---|---|---|---|---|---|---|
| | All students | | Males | | Females | | Gender difference (M - F) | | Bottom quarter | | Second quarter | | Third quarter | | Top quarter | |
| | Mean index | S.E. | Mean index | S.E. | Mean index | S.E. | Dif. | S.E. | Mean index | S.E. | Mean index | S.E. | Mean index | S.E. | Mean index | S.E. |
| **Adjudicated** | | | | | | | | | | | | | | | | |
| Belgium (Flemish Community) | -0.06 | (0.03) | -0.02 | (0.04) | -0.11 | (0.03) | **0.09** | (0.04) | -1.36 | (0.03) | -0.33 | (0.00) | 0.25 | (0.01) | 1.20 | (0.02) |
| Italy (Provincia Autonoma of Bolzano) | -0.27 | (0.02) | -0.17 | (0.03) | -0.37 | (0.03) | **0.21** | (0.03) | -1.24 | (0.03) | -0.50 | (0.01) | -0.07 | (0.01) | 0.73 | (0.03) |
| Italy (Provincia Campania) | -0.16 | (0.03) | -0.06 | (0.03) | -0.26 | (0.04) | **0.20** | (0.04) | -1.09 | (0.03) | -0.40 | (0.01) | 0.03 | (0.01) | 0.83 | (0.04) |
| Italy (Provincia Basilicata) | -0.14 | (0.02) | -0.09 | (0.03) | -0.20 | (0.04) | **0.11** | (0.05) | -1.06 | (0.03) | -0.38 | (0.01) | 0.02 | (0.01) | 0.83 | (0.02) |
| Italy (Provincia Emilia Romagna) | -0.22 | (0.02) | -0.12 | (0.02) | -0.31 | (0.04) | **0.18** | (0.05) | -1.15 | (0.02) | -0.43 | (0.01) | 0.00 | (0.01) | 0.73 | (0.02) |
| Italy (Provincia Friuli Venezia Giulia) | -0.16 | (0.03) | -0.15 | (0.04) | -0.18 | (0.04) | 0.03 | (0.06) | -1.07 | (0.04) | -0.38 | (0.01) | 0.04 | (0.01) | 0.76 | (0.03) |
| Italy (Provincia Sicilia) | -0.21 | (0.04) | -0.15 | (0.06) | -0.27 | (0.03) | 0.11 | (0.07) | -1.13 | (0.04) | -0.41 | (0.01) | -0.04 | (0.01) | 0.74 | (0.04) |
| Italy (Provincia Liguria) | -0.24 | (0.03) | -0.16 | (0.05) | -0.32 | (0.04) | **0.16** | (0.04) | -1.25 | (0.04) | -0.45 | (0.01) | -0.03 | (0.01) | 0.79 | (0.03) |
| Italy (Provincia Lombardia) | -0.26 | (0.02) | -0.23 | (0.04) | -0.29 | (0.03) | 0.06 | (0.05) | -1.17 | (0.04) | -0.44 | (0.01) | -0.06 | (0.01) | 0.63 | (0.03) |
| Italy (Provincia Piemonte) | -0.21 | (0.04) | -0.16 | (0.05) | -0.26 | (0.04) | **0.10** | (0.04) | -1.14 | (0.03) | -0.41 | (0.01) | -0.03 | (0.01) | 0.73 | (0.06) |
| Italy (Provincia Trento) | -0.25 | (0.02) | -0.15 | (0.03) | -0.34 | (0.03) | **0.18** | (0.04) | -1.18 | (0.03) | -0.44 | (0.01) | -0.06 | (0.01) | 0.70 | (0.04) |
| Italy (Provincia Sardegna) | -0.22 | (0.04) | -0.16 | (0.05) | -0.28 | (0.05) | 0.12 | (0.07) | -1.32 | (0.07) | -0.44 | (0.01) | 0.05 | (0.01) | 0.83 | (0.03) |
| Italy (Provincia Puglia) | -0.10 | (0.03) | -0.03 | (0.03) | -0.17 | (0.03) | **0.14** | (0.04) | -1.00 | (0.03) | -0.36 | (0.01) | 0.09 | (0.01) | 0.86 | (0.02) |
| Italy (Provincia Veneto) | -0.19 | (0.03) | -0.14 | (0.03) | -0.25 | (0.04) | **0.11** | (0.04) | -1.07 | (0.04) | -0.39 | (0.01) | 0.00 | (0.01) | 0.70 | (0.02) |
| Spain (Andalusia) | -0.18 | (0.03) | -0.17 | (0.03) | -0.19 | (0.04) | 0.02 | (0.05) | -1.49 | (0.03) | -0.49 | (0.01) | 0.16 | (0.01) | 1.10 | (0.00) |
| Spain (Basque Country) | -0.22 | (0.03) | -0.17 | (0.04) | -0.26 | (0.03) | **0.09** | (0.04) | -1.52 | (0.03) | -0.49 | (0.01) | 0.09 | (0.01) | 1.06 | (0.02) |
| Spain (Cantabria) | -0.03 | (0.04) | -0.04 | (0.05) | -0.02 | (0.04) | -0.01 | (0.05) | -1.36 | (0.03) | -0.34 | (0.01) | 0.31 | (0.01) | 1.28 | (0.04) |
| Spain (Galicia) | 0.02 | (0.05) | 0.08 | (0.06) | -0.05 | (0.05) | **0.13** | (0.06) | -1.33 | (0.03) | -0.31 | (0.01) | 0.34 | (0.01) | 1.38 | (0.04) |
| Spain (La Rioja) | 0.18 | (0.03) | 0.28 | (0.05) | 0.08 | (0.04) | **0.21** | (0.06) | -1.17 | (0.04) | -0.16 | (0.01) | 0.49 | (0.01) | 1.57 | (0.04) |
| Spain (Castile and Leon) | 0.10 | (0.03) | 0.14 | (0.04) | 0.06 | (0.05) | 0.09 | (0.06) | -1.16 | (0.04) | -0.21 | (0.01) | 0.44 | (0.01) | 1.35 | (0.03) |
| Spain (Navarre) | -0.18 | (0.02) | -0.11 | (0.04) | -0.25 | (0.03) | **0.14** | (0.05) | -1.53 | (0.03) | -0.50 | (0.01) | 0.15 | (0.01) | 1.17 | (0.04) |
| Spain (Aragon) | 0.05 | (0.03) | 0.07 | (0.04) | 0.03 | (0.05) | 0.04 | (0.06) | -1.21 | (0.04) | -0.29 | (0.01) | 0.34 | (0.01) | 1.36 | (0.03) |
| Spain (Catalonia) | -0.01 | (0.04) | 0.06 | (0.05) | -0.08 | (0.05) | **0.14** | (0.06) | -1.28 | (0.03) | -0.31 | (0.01) | 0.31 | (0.01) | 1.25 | (0.02) |
| Spain (Asturias) | 0.02 | (0.04) | 0.11 | (0.05) | -0.07 | (0.05) | **0.18** | (0.06) | -1.35 | (0.05) | -0.34 | (0.01) | 0.33 | (0.01) | 1.45 | (0.04) |
| United Kingdom (Scotland) | -0.05 | (0.03) | 0.07 | (0.04) | -0.16 | (0.04) | **0.23** | (0.06) | -1.37 | (0.04) | -0.37 | (0.01) | 0.22 | (0.01) | 1.33 | (0.03) |
| **Non-adjudicated** | | | | | | | | | | | | | | | | |
| Belgium (French Community) | -0.08 | (0.03) | -0.01 | (0.04) | -0.15 | (0.03) | **0.14** | (0.04) | -1.19 | (0.03) | -0.34 | (0.01) | 0.18 | (0.01) | 1.04 | (0.02) |
| Belgium (German-Speaking Community) | -0.30 | (0.03) | -0.19 | (0.05) | -0.40 | (0.04) | **0.21** | (0.07) | -1.46 | (0.05) | -0.55 | (0.01) | -0.02 | (0.01) | 0.83 | (0.03) |
| Finland (Finnish Speaking) | 0.03 | (0.02) | 0.08 | (0.02) | -0.01 | (0.02) | **0.10** | (0.03) | -1.06 | (0.02) | -0.27 | (0.00) | 0.27 | (0.01) | 1.19 | (0.02) |
| Finland (Swedish Speaking) | -0.20 | (0.05) | -0.09 | (0.08) | -0.31 | (0.06) | **0.23** | (0.11) | -1.25 | (0.06) | -0.42 | (0.02) | 0.04 | (0.02) | 0.85 | (0.07) |
| United Kingdom (England) | 0.22 | (0.02) | 0.36 | (0.03) | 0.08 | (0.02) | **0.28** | (0.03) | -0.99 | (0.02) | -0.14 | (0.01) | 0.45 | (0.01) | 1.56 | (0.02) |
| United Kingdom (Northern Ireland) | 0.05 | (0.02) | 0.13 | (0.03) | -0.04 | (0.04) | **0.18** | (0.06) | -1.22 | (0.03) | -0.24 | (0.01) | 0.33 | (0.01) | 1.33 | (0.02) |
| United Kingdom (Wales) | 0.10 | (0.02) | 0.21 | (0.03) | 0.00 | (0.03) | **0.21** | (0.04) | -1.03 | (0.02) | -0.23 | (0.01) | 0.33 | (0.01) | 1.35 | (0.03) |

Note: Values that are statistically significant are indicated in bold (see Annex A3). See Table 3.3 for national data.
1. Results based on students' self-reports.
*StatLink* http://dx.doi.org/10.1787/142184405135

Pour consulter la version française intégrale de ce tableau, suivre ce lien :
*StatLink* http://dx.doi.org/10.1787/152830402855

[Part 2/2]

**Table S3a    Index of self-efficacy in science and performance on the science scale, by quarters of the index[1]**

Tableau S3a    Indice de perception des capacités personnelles en sciences et scores sur l'échelle de culture scientifique, par quartile de l'indice

| | Performance on the science scale, by quarters of this index | | | | | | | | Change in the science score per unit of this index | | Increased likelihood of students in the bottom quarter of this index scoring in the bottom quarter of the science performance distribution | | Explained variance in student performance (r-squared x 100) | |
| | Bottom quarter | | Second quarter | | Third quarter | | Top quarter | | | | | | | |
| | Mean score | S.E. | Mean score | S.E. | Mean score | S.E. | Mean score | S.E | Effect | S.E. | Ratio | S.E. | % | S.E. |
|---|---|---|---|---|---|---|---|---|---|---|---|---|---|---|
| **Adjudicated** | | | | | | | | | | | | | | |
| Belgium (Flemish Community) | **479** | (5.8) | 524 | (2.6) | 547 | (3.3) | **587** | (3.1) | **38.8** | (1.41) | **2.6** | (0.15) | 21.1 | (1.36) |
| Italy (Provincia Autonoma of Bolzano) | **480** | (4.6) | 511 | (4.3) | 545 | (4.0) | **572** | (4.1) | **44.0** | (2.80) | **2.2** | (0.20) | 17.4 | (1.77) |
| Italy (Provincia Campania) | **412** | (6.4) | 433 | (7.4) | 456 | (7.0) | **471** | (7.3) | **28.9** | (3.38) | **1.8** | (0.21) | 8.0 | (1.74) |
| Italy (Provincia Basilicata) | **420** | (7.1) | 446 | (5.8) | 458 | (6.4) | **481** | (6.8) | **28.3** | (3.24) | **1.8** | (0.22) | 7.0 | (1.38) |
| Italy (Provincia Emilia Romagna) | **463** | (6.5) | 503 | (4.6) | 528 | (4.5) | **548** | (6.6) | **41.2** | (4.03) | **2.3** | (0.23) | 12.1 | (1.93) |
| Italy (Provincia Friuli Venezia Giulia) | **492** | (5.9) | 525 | (4.5) | 548 | (4.6) | **572** | (6.5) | **40.7** | (4.20) | **2.3** | (0.29) | 13.8 | (2.85) |
| Italy (Provincia Sicilia) | **393** | (7.7) | 422 | (9.3) | 446 | (9.0) | **473** | (9.8) | **43.6** | (5.31) | **1.9** | (0.32) | 11.8 | (3.89) |
| Italy (Provincia Liguria) | **445** | (7.1) | 484 | (7.2) | 501 | (7.2) | **523** | (10.1) | **35.1** | (3.60) | **1.9** | (0.26) | 10.0 | (2.07) |
| Italy (Provincia Lombardia) | **457** | (8.6) | 491 | (7.6) | 516 | (8.1) | **534** | (8.8) | **43.5** | (5.03) | **2.0** | (0.25) | 12.2 | (2.82) |
| Italy (Provincia Piemonte) | **465** | (5.4) | 503 | (6.8) | 521 | (4.3) | **545** | (6.8) | **41.3** | (3.42) | **2.1** | (0.22) | 12.9 | (1.81) |
| Italy (Provincia Trento) | **476** | (4.2) | 511 | (5.0) | 536 | (6.4) | **564** | (4.4) | **40.4** | (3.25) | **2.2** | (0.20) | 12.1 | (1.73) |
| Italy (Provincia Sardegna) | **403** | (7.5) | 441 | (7.6) | 468 | (6.6) | **487** | (9.4) | **37.1** | (3.17) | **2.3** | (0.28) | 13.5 | (2.00) |
| Italy (Provincia Puglia) | **417** | (5.4) | 442 | (6.4) | 462 | (4.9) | **471** | (6.3) | **26.9** | (2.94) | **1.8** | (0.20) | 6.4 | (1.53) |
| Italy (Provincia Veneto) | **481** | (7.1) | 516 | (5.8) | 543 | (5.8) | **556** | (6.8) | **42.5** | (3.15) | **2.2** | (0.25) | 12.2 | (1.53) |
| Spain (Andalusia) | **428** | (5.6) | 462 | (6.6) | 483 | (5.1) | **526** | (4.6) | **35.8** | (2.51) | **2.2** | (0.30) | 18.3 | (1.92) |
| Spain (Basque Country) | **459** | (3.9) | 486 | (4.2) | 502 | (4.6) | **534** | (4.9) | **27.3** | (1.72) | **1.9** | (0.15) | 12.0 | (1.32) |
| Spain (Cantabria) | **458** | (5.2) | 502 | (5.0) | 529 | (5.6) | **552** | (4.3) | **34.8** | (2.24) | **2.7** | (0.27) | 19.2 | (1.86) |
| Spain (Galicia) | **453** | (4.1) | 499 | (4.9) | 518 | (5.4) | **549** | (5.4) | **32.7** | (2.28) | **2.5** | (0.21) | 17.0 | (2.11) |
| Spain (La Rioja) | **470** | (5.2) | 511 | (5.1) | 540 | (5.1) | **559** | (5.1) | **31.8** | (2.53) | **2.4** | (0.29) | 16.3 | (2.36) |
| Spain (Castile and Leon) | **484** | (4.7) | 506 | (4.3) | 532 | (5.4) | **558** | (5.6) | **28.8** | (2.07) | **2.0** | (0.16) | 13.5 | (1.73) |
| Spain (Navarre) | **463** | (4.2) | 499 | (4.8) | 521 | (4.9) | **563** | (5.0) | **33.2** | (1.73) | **2.3** | (0.17) | 16.7 | (1.42) |
| Spain (Aragon) | **469** | (5.3) | 502 | (4.6) | 530 | (5.3) | **554** | (5.8) | **31.5** | (2.41) | **2.2** | (0.23) | 14.1 | (1.72) |
| Spain (Catalonia) | **443** | (6.1) | 484 | (6.1) | 502 | (6.3) | **538** | (5.9) | **35.6** | (2.02) | **2.2** | (0.23) | 16.8 | (1.67) |
| Spain (Asturias) | **465** | (5.6) | 498 | (5.5) | 520 | (6.2) | **553** | (4.8) | **30.0** | (1.69) | **2.4** | (0.26) | 17.1 | (1.83) |
| United Kingdom (Scotland) | **456** | (3.3) | 496 | (4.8) | 526 | (5.9) | **583** | (6.2) | **43.3** | (2.23) | **2.4** | (0.20) | 22.8 | (2.01) |
| **Non-adjudicated** | | | | | | | | | | | | | | |
| Belgium (French Community) | **439** | (5.0) | 486 | (5.3) | 499 | (5.8) | **537** | (5.8) | **39.4** | (2.57) | **2.1** | (0.18) | 12.7 | (1.58) |
| Belgium (German-Speaking Community) | **465** | (6.1) | 509 | (6.1) | 531 | (6.5) | **570** | (7.5) | **41.3** | (3.86) | **2.3** | (0.31) | 16.9 | (2.79) |
| Finland (Finnish Speaking) | **516** | (2.6) | 549 | (2.8) | 581 | (3.4) | **614** | (3.2) | **40.6** | (1.63) | **2.5** | (0.16) | 19.5 | (1.51) |
| Finland (Swedish Speaking) | **479** | (14.0) | 521 | (10.3) | 548 | (8.6) | **576** | (11.0) | **41.2** | (4.78) | **2.5** | (0.55) | 17.6 | (3.23) |
| United Kingdom (England) | **443** | (3.8) | 498 | (2.9) | 533 | (3.7) | **593** | (3.1) | **53.8** | (1.44) | **2.9** | (0.16) | 27.4 | (1.26) |
| United Kingdom (Northern Ireland) | **438** | (5.4) | 494 | (5.2) | 528 | (4.5) | **579** | (4.3) | **49.8** | (1.91) | **2.7** | (0.23) | 22.2 | (1.41) |
| United Kingdom (Wales) | **439** | (4.2) | 481 | (4.0) | 517 | (4.4) | **583** | (4.8) | **55.3** | (2.07) | **2.6** | (0.17) | 28.1 | (1.70) |

Note: Values that are statistically significant are indicated in bold (see Annex A3). See Table 3.3 for national data.
1. Results based on students' self-reports.
*StatLink* http://dx.doi.org/10.1787/142184405135

Pour consulter la version française intégrale de ce tableau, suivre ce lien :
*StatLink* http://dx.doi.org/10.1787/152830402855

[Part 1/2]

**Table S3b**  Index of self-concept in science and performance on the science scale, by quarters of the index[1]

Tableau S3b  Indice de perception de soi en sciences et scores sur l'échelle de culture scientifique, par quartile de l'indice

| | Index of self-concept in science | | | | | | | | | | | | | | |
|---|---|---|---|---|---|---|---|---|---|---|---|---|---|---|---|
| | All students | | Males | | Females | | Gender difference (M - F) | | Bottom quarter | | Second quarter | | Third quarter | | Top quarter | |
| | Mean index | S.E. | Mean index | S.E. | Mean index | S.E. | Dif. | S.E. | Mean index | S.E. | Mean index | S.E. | Mean index | S.E. | Mean index | S.E. |
| **Adjudicated** | | | | | | | | | | | | | | | | |
| Belgium (Flemish Community) | -0.27 | (0.02) | -0.15 | (0.03) | -0.41 | (0.02) | **0.26** | (0.04) | -1.49 | (0.03) | -0.50 | (0.01) | 0.03 | (0.00) | 0.88 | (0.02) |
| Italy (Provincia Autonoma of Bolzano) | 0.13 | (0.02) | 0.19 | (0.03) | 0.08 | (0.03) | **0.11** | (0.05) | -1.12 | (0.03) | -0.13 | (0.01) | 0.42 | (0.01) | 1.37 | (0.02) |
| Italy (Provincia Campania) | 0.32 | (0.03) | 0.46 | (0.03) | 0.17 | (0.04) | **0.29** | (0.05) | -0.68 | (0.03) | 0.03 | (0.01) | 0.56 | (0.01) | 1.37 | (0.02) |
| Italy (Provincia Basilicata) | 0.27 | (0.03) | 0.36 | (0.03) | 0.16 | (0.05) | **0.20** | (0.06) | -0.74 | (0.03) | -0.03 | (0.01) | 0.51 | (0.01) | 1.32 | (0.02) |
| Italy (Provincia Emilia Romagna) | 0.01 | (0.03) | 0.14 | (0.04) | -0.13 | (0.05) | **0.28** | (0.05) | -1.07 | (0.03) | -0.32 | (0.01) | 0.27 | (0.01) | 1.18 | (0.03) |
| Italy (Provincia Friuli Venezia Giulia) | 0.03 | (0.03) | 0.15 | (0.03) | -0.09 | (0.03) | **0.24** | (0.04) | -0.98 | (0.04) | -0.27 | (0.01) | 0.26 | (0.01) | 1.11 | (0.03) |
| Italy (Provincia Sicilia) | 0.34 | (0.03) | 0.43 | (0.06) | 0.25 | (0.04) | **0.18** | (0.08) | -0.63 | (0.04) | 0.05 | (0.01) | 0.55 | (0.01) | 1.40 | (0.03) |
| Italy (Provincia Liguria) | 0.06 | (0.04) | 0.20 | (0.05) | -0.09 | (0.04) | **0.29** | (0.06) | -1.06 | (0.03) | -0.23 | (0.01) | 0.35 | (0.02) | 1.20 | (0.03) |
| Italy (Provincia Lombardia) | -0.03 | (0.03) | 0.07 | (0.03) | -0.14 | (0.05) | **0.21** | (0.05) | -1.10 | (0.03) | -0.33 | (0.01) | 0.23 | (0.01) | 1.08 | (0.02) |
| Italy (Provincia Piemonte) | 0.09 | (0.05) | 0.15 | (0.04) | 0.03 | (0.06) | **0.13** | (0.06) | -0.96 | (0.03) | -0.24 | (0.01) | 0.33 | (0.01) | 1.22 | (0.06) |
| Italy (Provincia Trento) | 0.00 | (0.02) | 0.17 | (0.03) | -0.16 | (0.03) | **0.34** | (0.05) | -1.05 | (0.03) | -0.30 | (0.01) | 0.27 | (0.01) | 1.09 | (0.03) |
| Italy (Provincia Sardegna) | 0.18 | (0.05) | 0.29 | (0.06) | 0.05 | (0.06) | **0.24** | (0.08) | -1.01 | (0.05) | -0.14 | (0.01) | 0.49 | (0.01) | 1.38 | (0.02) |
| Italy (Provincia Puglia) | 0.25 | (0.04) | 0.35 | (0.04) | 0.14 | (0.05) | **0.20** | (0.06) | -0.84 | (0.03) | -0.06 | (0.01) | 0.52 | (0.01) | 1.38 | (0.02) |
| Italy (Provincia Veneto) | 0.05 | (0.04) | 0.16 | (0.04) | -0.08 | (0.04) | **0.25** | (0.05) | -1.00 | (0.03) | -0.27 | (0.01) | 0.29 | (0.01) | 1.16 | (0.02) |
| Spain (Andalusia) | -0.13 | (0.03) | 0.00 | (0.04) | -0.24 | (0.05) | **0.24** | (0.06) | -1.34 | (0.03) | -0.43 | (0.01) | 0.16 | (0.01) | 1.11 | (0.03) |
| Spain (Basque Country) | -0.09 | (0.02) | 0.04 | (0.03) | -0.22 | (0.03) | **0.26** | (0.04) | -1.44 | (0.02) | -0.37 | (0.01) | 0.26 | (0.01) | 1.18 | (0.02) |
| Spain (Cantabria) | 0.06 | (0.03) | 0.13 | (0.04) | -0.02 | (0.03) | **0.15** | (0.04) | -1.11 | (0.03) | -0.28 | (0.01) | 0.37 | (0.02) | 1.26 | (0.03) |
| Spain (Galicia) | 0.11 | (0.04) | 0.23 | (0.04) | -0.01 | (0.04) | **0.24** | (0.05) | -1.15 | (0.03) | -0.23 | (0.01) | 0.43 | (0.01) | 1.41 | (0.03) |
| Spain (La Rioja) | 0.12 | (0.03) | 0.18 | (0.05) | 0.05 | (0.04) | **0.13** | (0.06) | -1.14 | (0.04) | -0.20 | (0.01) | 0.42 | (0.01) | 1.40 | (0.03) |
| Spain (Castile and Leon) | 0.08 | (0.03) | 0.16 | (0.04) | -0.02 | (0.04) | **0.18** | (0.06) | -1.13 | (0.03) | -0.24 | (0.01) | 0.40 | (0.01) | 1.28 | (0.03) |
| Spain (Navarre) | -0.15 | (0.04) | -0.06 | (0.05) | -0.24 | (0.04) | **0.18** | (0.07) | -1.57 | (0.03) | -0.43 | (0.01) | 0.24 | (0.01) | 1.16 | (0.03) |
| Spain (Aragon) | 0.03 | (0.03) | 0.15 | (0.04) | -0.10 | (0.04) | **0.25** | (0.06) | -1.26 | (0.03) | -0.27 | (0.01) | 0.40 | (0.01) | 1.24 | (0.03) |
| Spain (Catalonia) | -0.03 | (0.04) | 0.12 | (0.05) | -0.17 | (0.05) | **0.29** | (0.06) | -1.28 | (0.02) | -0.34 | (0.01) | 0.30 | (0.01) | 1.22 | (0.03) |
| Spain (Asturias) | 0.09 | (0.03) | 0.20 | (0.03) | -0.04 | (0.06) | **0.24** | (0.07) | -1.22 | (0.04) | -0.23 | (0.01) | 0.43 | (0.01) | 1.37 | (0.03) |
| United Kingdom (Scotland) | -0.07 | (0.02) | 0.05 | (0.04) | -0.19 | (0.03) | **0.24** | (0.05) | -1.34 | (0.03) | -0.35 | (0.01) | 0.23 | (0.01) | 1.17 | (0.02) |
| **Non-adjudicated** | | | | | | | | | | | | | | | | |
| Belgium (French Community) | 0.03 | (0.03) | 0.18 | (0.04) | -0.11 | (0.03) | **0.29** | (0.05) | -1.21 | (0.03) | -0.21 | (0.01) | 0.34 | (0.01) | 1.21 | (0.02) |
| Belgium (German-Speaking Community) | -0.02 | (0.05) | 0.15 | (0.07) | -0.18 | (0.06) | **0.33** | (0.09) | -1.44 | (0.05) | -0.31 | (0.02) | 0.33 | (0.02) | 1.35 | (0.04) |
| Finland (Finnish Speaking) | 0.07 | (0.02) | 0.17 | (0.02) | -0.03 | (0.02) | **0.20** | (0.03) | -0.96 | (0.02) | -0.22 | (0.01) | 0.37 | (0.01) | 1.07 | (0.02) |
| Finland (Swedish Speaking) | 0.05 | (0.08) | 0.15 | (0.06) | -0.06 | (0.13) | 0.21 | (0.13) | -1.15 | (0.12) | -0.22 | (0.03) | 0.42 | (0.03) | 1.16 | (0.08) |
| United Kingdom (England) | 0.03 | (0.01) | 0.22 | (0.02) | -0.15 | (0.02) | **0.36** | (0.03) | -1.05 | (0.02) | -0.22 | (0.00) | 0.28 | (0.01) | 1.12 | (0.02) |
| United Kingdom (Northern Ireland) | -0.06 | (0.02) | 0.07 | (0.03) | -0.18 | (0.03) | **0.25** | (0.04) | -1.24 | (0.03) | -0.32 | (0.01) | 0.18 | (0.01) | 1.15 | (0.02) |
| United Kingdom (Wales) | 0.03 | (0.02) | 0.19 | (0.02) | -0.14 | (0.02) | **0.32** | (0.03) | -1.01 | (0.02) | -0.20 | (0.00) | 0.27 | (0.01) | 1.05 | (0.02) |

Note: Values that are statistically significant are indicated in bold (see Annex A3). See Table 3.4 for national data.
1. Results based on students' self-reports.
StatLink ⊠ http://dx.doi.org/10.1787/142184405135

Pour consulter la version française intégrale de ce tableau, suivre ce lien :
StatLink ⊠ http://dx.doi.org/10.1787/152830402855

[Part 2/2]

**Table S3b** **Index of self-concept in science and performance on the science scale, by quarters of the index[1]**

Tableau S3b  Indice de perception de soi en sciences et scores sur l'échelle de culture scientifique, par quartile de l'indice

| | Performance on the science scale, by quarters of this index | | | | | | | | Change in the science score per unit of this index | | Increased likelihood of students in the bottom quarter of this index scoring in the bottom quarter of the science performance distribution | | Explained variance in student performance (r-squared x 100) | |
| | Bottom quarter | | Second quarter | | Third quarter | | Top quarter | | | | | | | |
| | Mean score | S.E. | Mean score | S.E. | Mean score | S.E. | Mean score | S.E | Effect | S.E. | Ratio | S.E. | % | S.E. |
|---|---|---|---|---|---|---|---|---|---|---|---|---|---|---|
| **Adjudicated** | | | | | | | | | | | | | | |
| Belgium (Flemish Community) | **502** | (5.4) | 532 | (4.0) | 555 | (4.4) | **582** | (4.2) | **34.8** | (2.26) | **1.9** | (0.14) | 14.0 | (1.34) |
| Italy (Provincia Autonoma of Bolzano) | **491** | (5.3) | 524 | (4.7) | 543 | (5.0) | **562** | (4.7) | 29.6 | (2.63) | 1.9 | (0.20) | 10.8 | (1.89) |
| Italy (Provincia Campania) | **423** | (8.4) | 429 | (7.3) | 450 | (7.2) | **458** | (8.1) | 18.7 | (5.03) | 1.4 | (0.20) | 3.5 | (1.82) |
| Italy (Provincia Basilicata) | **426** | (5.1) | 443 | (6.0) | 455 | (7.3) | **462** | (7.5) | 18.1 | (3.66) | 1.3 | (0.16) | 3.3 | (1.36) |
| Italy (Provincia Emilia Romagna) | **479** | (6.5) | 507 | (6.2) | 507 | (4.9) | **540** | (7.8) | 24.8 | (3.84) | 1.5 | (0.21) | 6.0 | (1.79) |
| Italy (Provincia Friuli Venezia Giulia) | **511** | (5.9) | 517 | (5.5) | 549 | (6.0) | **559** | (5.5) | 24.4 | (3.46) | 1.4 | (0.20) | 6.1 | (1.69) |
| Italy (Provincia Sicilia) | **416** | (9.0) | 428 | (10.8) | 440 | (9.9) | **450** | (10.6) | 16.4 | (7.05) | 1.3 | (0.22) | 1.8 | (1.71) |
| Italy (Provincia Liguria) | **460** | (7.4) | 474 | (9.8) | 484 | (9.9) | **511** | (12.8) | 23.7 | (4.31) | 1.2 | (0.21) | 5.1 | (1.95) |
| Italy (Provincia Lombardia) | **474** | (7.2) | 497 | (5.9) | 504 | (8.5) | **522** | (12.2) | 21.1 | (4.27) | 1.4 | (0.19) | 4.0 | (1.69) |
| Italy (Provincia Piemonte) | **480** | (5.6) | 494 | (6.3) | 509 | (7.6) | **539** | (8.7) | 28.5 | (3.40) | 1.5 | (0.18) | 8.1 | (2.29) |
| Italy (Provincia Trento) | **494** | (4.7) | 515 | (4.5) | 534 | (5.5) | **552** | (6.5) | 26.0 | (3.32) | 1.6 | (0.17) | 6.2 | (1.57) |
| Italy (Provincia Sardegna) | **408** | (7.9) | 438 | (6.9) | 446 | (7.7) | **470** | (10.9) | 23.1 | (3.91) | 1.6 | (0.23) | 5.8 | (1.77) |
| Italy (Provincia Puglia) | **432** | (5.7) | 442 | (4.8) | 453 | (6.2) | **462** | (6.8) | 14.9 | (2.49) | 1.3 | (0.15) | 2.7 | (0.92) |
| Italy (Provincia Veneto) | **493** | (6.7) | 510 | (7.8) | 541 | (6.7) | **557** | (7.3) | 31.3 | (3.02) | 1.7 | (0.24) | 9.5 | (1.67) |
| Spain (Andalusia) | **449** | (5.6) | 456 | (4.2) | 485 | (5.8) | **514** | (6.6) | 28.4 | (2.70) | 1.5 | (0.20) | 10.2 | (1.67) |
| Spain (Basque Country) | **459** | (3.5) | 481 | (4.0) | 508 | (4.3) | **534** | (5.2) | 28.1 | (1.81) | 1.8 | (0.14) | 12.5 | (1.36) |
| Spain (Cantabria) | **473** | (5.6) | 497 | (4.3) | 524 | (5.3) | **549** | (5.3) | 31.0 | (2.72) | 1.9 | (0.21) | 12.3 | (1.99) |
| Spain (Galicia) | **476** | (4.8) | 487 | (5.8) | 521 | (5.0) | **540** | (6.1) | 25.3 | (1.88) | 1.6 | (0.21) | 9.0 | (1.48) |
| Spain (La Rioja) | **481** | (5.2) | 506 | (4.6) | 533 | (5.4) | **562** | (5.7) | 32.1 | (2.47) | 2.0 | (0.28) | 14.6 | (2.14) |
| Spain (Castile and Leon) | **487** | (5.0) | 513 | (5.4) | 531 | (5.4) | **551** | (5.0) | 26.0 | (2.49) | 1.8 | (0.17) | 10.2 | (1.86) |
| Spain (Navarre) | **478** | (4.3) | 498 | (5.0) | 522 | (6.7) | **553** | (6.6) | 26.0 | (1.99) | 1.7 | (0.17) | 10.3 | (1.54) |
| Spain (Aragon) | **477** | (4.7) | 500 | (6.1) | 528 | (6.0) | **552** | (6.3) | 28.7 | (2.58) | 1.8 | (0.19) | 11.0 | (1.68) |
| Spain (Catalonia) | **460** | (5.9) | 484 | (6.1) | 500 | (6.9) | **528** | (7.8) | 27.2 | (2.99) | 1.5 | (0.24) | 9.3 | (2.10) |
| Spain (Asturias) | **476** | (4.8) | 502 | (5.9) | 521 | (7.0) | **540** | (6.7) | 23.3 | (2.38) | 1.8 | (0.22) | 8.6 | (1.68) |
| United Kingdom (Scotland) | **478** | (4.4) | 506 | (5.0) | 525 | (5.0) | **562** | (6.7) | **31.2** | (2.13) | **1.6** | (0.14) | 9.9 | (1.34) |
| **Non-adjudicated** | | | | | | | | | | | | | | |
| Belgium (French Community) | **469** | (5.5) | 495 | (6.0) | 508 | (7.2) | **524** | (7.4) | 23.5 | (2.61) | 1.7 | (0.14) | 5.2 | (1.17) |
| Belgium (German-Speaking Community) | **487** | (7.6) | 524 | (6.7) | 540 | (7.9) | **573** | (8.0) | 32.3 | (3.34) | 1.8 | (0.28) | 13.2 | (2.60) |
| Finland (Finnish Speaking) | **526** | (3.1) | 549 | (3.1) | 580 | (3.4) | **608** | (3.5) | 41.5 | (1.68) | 2.0 | (0.12) | 16.7 | (1.36) |
| Finland (Swedish Speaking) | **495** | (7.8) | 508 | (9.9) | 552 | (15.8) | **578** | (12.5) | 37.2 | (7.07) | 2.0 | (0.39) | 18.0 | (6.47) |
| United Kingdom (England) | **476** | (3.4) | 503 | (4.2) | 529 | (4.0) | **565** | (4.2) | 39.8 | (2.05) | 1.6 | (0.11) | 11.0 | (1.10) |
| United Kingdom (Northern Ireland) | **475** | (5.1) | 495 | (4.9) | 522 | (5.1) | **553** | (5.6) | 31.5 | (2.62) | 1.5 | (0.12) | 7.4 | (1.24) |
| United Kingdom (Wales) | **460** | (5.0) | 488 | (3.7) | 519 | (4.6) | **557** | (5.7) | 45.5 | (2.77) | 1.8 | (0.16) | 13.9 | (1.56) |

Note: Values that are statistically significant are indicated in bold (see Annex A3). See Table 3.4 for national data.
1. Results based on students' self-reports.
StatLink ⌨📊 http://dx.doi.org/10.1787/142184405135

Pour consulter la version française intégrale de ce tableau, suivre ce lien :
StatLink ⌨📊 http://dx.doi.org/10.1787/152830402855

267

[Part 1/2]

**Table S3c** Index of personal value of science and performance on the science scale, by quarters of the index[1]

Tableau S3c Indice de valorisation personnelle des sciences et scores sur l'échelle de culture scientifique, par quartile de l'indice

| | All students | | Males | | Females | | Gender difference (M - F) | | Bottom quarter | | Second quarter | | Third quarter | | Top quarter | |
|---|---|---|---|---|---|---|---|---|---|---|---|---|---|---|---|---|
| | Mean index | S.E. | Mean index | S.E. | Mean index | S.E. | Dif. | S.E. | Mean index | S.E. | Mean index | S.E. | Mean index | S.E. | Mean index | S.E. |
| **Adjudicated** | | | | | | | | | | | | | | | | |
| Belgium (Flemish Community) | -0.20 | (0.02) | -0.12 | (0.03) | -0.28 | (0.02) | **0.16** | (0.03) | -1.24 | (0.02) | -0.47 | (0.01) | 0.07 | (0.01) | 0.86 | (0.02) |
| Italy (Provincia Autonoma of Bolzano) | -0.16 | (0.03) | -0.09 | (0.04) | -0.22 | (0.03) | **0.13** | (0.05) | -1.39 | (0.04) | -0.46 | (0.01) | 0.15 | (0.01) | 1.07 | (0.03) |
| Italy (Provincia Campania) | 0.27 | (0.03) | 0.35 | (0.03) | 0.20 | (0.03) | **0.15** | (0.04) | -0.62 | (0.03) | 0.02 | (0.01) | 0.46 | (0.01) | 1.24 | (0.03) |
| Italy (Provincia Basilicata) | 0.16 | (0.02) | 0.21 | (0.03) | 0.11 | (0.03) | **0.10** | (0.04) | -0.86 | (0.02) | -0.09 | (0.01) | 0.42 | (0.01) | 1.18 | (0.02) |
| Italy (Provincia Emilia Romagna) | 0.05 | (0.02) | 0.13 | (0.03) | -0.03 | (0.03) | **0.16** | (0.05) | -0.93 | (0.03) | -0.22 | (0.01) | 0.26 | (0.01) | 1.08 | (0.02) |
| Italy (Provincia Friuli Venezia Giulia) | 0.03 | (0.03) | 0.14 | (0.04) | -0.07 | (0.05) | **0.21** | (0.06) | -0.95 | (0.03) | -0.22 | (0.01) | 0.24 | (0.01) | 1.06 | (0.03) |
| Italy (Provincia Sicilia) | 0.34 | (0.03) | 0.37 | (0.05) | 0.30 | (0.03) | 0.07 | (0.06) | -0.63 | (0.03) | 0.10 | (0.01) | 0.54 | (0.01) | 1.33 | (0.02) |
| Italy (Provincia Liguria) | 0.06 | (0.04) | 0.10 | (0.05) | 0.03 | (0.04) | 0.07 | (0.04) | -1.00 | (0.03) | -0.20 | (0.01) | 0.26 | (0.01) | 1.19 | (0.02) |
| Italy (Provincia Lombardia) | 0.00 | (0.03) | 0.04 | (0.03) | -0.04 | (0.03) | **0.08** | (0.04) | -1.01 | (0.04) | -0.24 | (0.01) | 0.23 | (0.01) | 1.01 | (0.03) |
| Italy (Provincia Piemonte) | 0.07 | (0.04) | 0.12 | (0.03) | 0.04 | (0.05) | 0.08 | (0.06) | -0.91 | (0.03) | -0.15 | (0.01) | 0.28 | (0.01) | 1.09 | (0.02) |
| Italy (Provincia Trento) | 0.06 | (0.02) | 0.18 | (0.03) | -0.06 | (0.03) | **0.24** | (0.04) | -0.93 | (0.02) | -0.18 | (0.01) | 0.28 | (0.01) | 1.07 | (0.03) |
| Italy (Provincia Sardegna) | 0.14 | (0.03) | 0.20 | (0.04) | 0.07 | (0.04) | **0.13** | (0.06) | -0.96 | (0.03) | -0.10 | (0.01) | 0.37 | (0.01) | 1.26 | (0.03) |
| Italy (Provincia Puglia) | 0.27 | (0.03) | 0.31 | (0.03) | 0.24 | (0.04) | 0.06 | (0.05) | -0.74 | (0.02) | -0.01 | (0.01) | 0.53 | (0.01) | 1.32 | (0.02) |
| Italy (Provincia Veneto) | 0.10 | (0.03) | 0.17 | (0.03) | 0.03 | (0.04) | **0.14** | (0.05) | -0.88 | (0.02) | -0.12 | (0.01) | 0.30 | (0.01) | 1.11 | (0.02) |
| Spain (Andalusia) | 0.02 | (0.03) | 0.10 | (0.04) | -0.05 | (0.04) | **0.15** | (0.05) | -1.12 | (0.03) | -0.26 | (0.01) | 0.28 | (0.01) | 1.19 | (0.03) |
| Spain (Basque Country) | -0.01 | (0.02) | 0.04 | (0.03) | -0.07 | (0.03) | **0.10** | (0.03) | -1.23 | (0.02) | -0.31 | (0.01) | 0.26 | (0.01) | 1.22 | (0.02) |
| Spain (Cantabria) | 0.08 | (0.02) | 0.09 | (0.03) | 0.07 | (0.03) | 0.02 | (0.04) | -1.07 | (0.02) | -0.19 | (0.01) | 0.34 | (0.01) | 1.25 | (0.03) |
| Spain (Galicia) | 0.07 | (0.03) | 0.12 | (0.05) | 0.00 | (0.05) | 0.12 | (0.07) | -1.14 | (0.03) | -0.22 | (0.01) | 0.33 | (0.01) | 1.31 | (0.03) |
| Spain (La Rioja) | 0.15 | (0.03) | 0.21 | (0.04) | 0.08 | (0.04) | **0.13** | (0.06) | -1.04 | (0.03) | -0.15 | (0.01) | 0.42 | (0.01) | 1.36 | (0.03) |
| Spain (Castile and Leon) | 0.13 | (0.03) | 0.16 | (0.03) | 0.10 | (0.04) | 0.06 | (0.04) | -1.01 | (0.03) | -0.16 | (0.01) | 0.38 | (0.01) | 1.32 | (0.03) |
| Spain (Navarre) | -0.08 | (0.03) | -0.06 | (0.04) | -0.10 | (0.04) | 0.04 | (0.04) | -1.34 | (0.03) | -0.41 | (0.01) | 0.24 | (0.01) | 1.19 | (0.03) |
| Spain (Aragon) | 0.03 | (0.03) | 0.07 | (0.04) | -0.01 | (0.04) | 0.08 | (0.05) | -1.15 | (0.03) | -0.25 | (0.01) | 0.30 | (0.01) | 1.23 | (0.03) |
| Spain (Catalonia) | -0.04 | (0.03) | 0.00 | (0.05) | -0.07 | (0.05) | 0.07 | (0.08) | -1.20 | (0.03) | -0.36 | (0.01) | 0.23 | (0.01) | 1.19 | (0.02) |
| Spain (Asturias) | 0.06 | (0.03) | 0.06 | (0.04) | 0.07 | (0.05) | 0.00 | (0.06) | -1.15 | (0.04) | -0.23 | (0.01) | 0.33 | (0.01) | 1.32 | (0.02) |
| United Kingdom (Scotland) | 0.03 | (0.03) | 0.13 | (0.04) | -0.07 | (0.03) | **0.20** | (0.05) | -1.25 | (0.03) | -0.32 | (0.01) | 0.31 | (0.01) | 1.38 | (0.02) |
| **Non-adjudicated** | | | | | | | | | | | | | | | | |
| Belgium (French Community) | -0.08 | (0.02) | -0.01 | (0.03) | -0.16 | (0.03) | **0.15** | (0.05) | -1.29 | (0.03) | -0.40 | (0.01) | 0.21 | (0.01) | 1.16 | (0.02) |
| Belgium (German-Speaking Community) | -0.37 | (0.04) | -0.26 | (0.05) | -0.48 | (0.05) | **0.22** | (0.07) | -1.64 | (0.04) | -0.70 | (0.01) | -0.10 | (0.02) | 0.97 | (0.04) |
| Finland (Finnish Speaking) | -0.09 | (0.02) | -0.14 | (0.02) | -0.04 | (0.02) | **-0.10** | (0.02) | -1.14 | (0.02) | -0.40 | (0.01) | 0.19 | (0.01) | 0.99 | (0.02) |
| Finland (Swedish Speaking) | -0.15 | (0.07) | -0.08 | (0.12) | -0.23 | (0.06) | 0.15 | (0.14) | -1.18 | (0.09) | -0.52 | (0.02) | 0.12 | (0.03) | 0.99 | (0.09) |
| United Kingdom (England) | 0.03 | (0.03) | 0.12 | (0.02) | -0.06 | (0.02) | **0.18** | (0.03) | -1.13 | (0.01) | -0.32 | (0.01) | 0.26 | (0.00) | 1.32 | (0.02) |
| United Kingdom (Northern Ireland) | 0.03 | (0.02) | 0.08 | (0.03) | -0.03 | (0.04) | **0.11** | (0.04) | -1.22 | (0.02) | -0.30 | (0.01) | 0.31 | (0.01) | 1.33 | (0.02) |
| United Kingdom (Wales) | 0.13 | (0.02) | 0.22 | (0.03) | 0.04 | (0.03) | **0.18** | (0.04) | -1.00 | (0.02) | -0.22 | (0.01) | 0.34 | (0.01) | 1.41 | (0.02) |

Note: Values that are statistically significant are indicated in bold (see Annex A3). See Table 3.6 for national data.
1. Results based on students' self-reports.
*StatLink* http://dx.doi.org/10.1787/142184405135

Pour consulter la version française intégrale de ce tableau, suivre ce lien :
*StatLink* http://dx.doi.org/10.1787/152830402855

[Part 2/2]

**Table S3c** Index of personal value of science and performance on the science scale, by quarters of the index[1]

Tableau S3c Indice de valorisation personnelle des sciences et scores sur l'échelle de culture scientifique, par quartile de l'indice

| | Performance on the science scale, by quarters of this index | | | | | | | | Change in the science score per unit of this index | | Increased likelihood of students in the bottom quarter of this index scoring in the bottom quarter of the science performance distribution | | Explained variance in student performance (r-squared x 100) | |
| | Bottom quarter | | Second quarter | | Third quarter | | Top quarter | | | | | | | |
| | Mean score | S.E. | Mean score | S.E. | Mean score | S.E. | Mean score | S.E | Effect | S.E. | Ratio | S.E. | % | S.E. |
|---|---|---|---|---|---|---|---|---|---|---|---|---|---|---|
| **Adjudicated** | | | | | | | | | | | | | | |
| Belgium (Flemish Community) | 505 | (5.4) | 530 | (3.4) | 543 | (3.8) | 559 | (4.0) | 24.9 | (2.75) | 1.6 | (0.11) | 5.8 | (1.15) |
| Italy (Provincia Autonoma of Bolzano) | 507 | (5.8) | 524 | (4.9) | 529 | (4.5) | 547 | (4.7) | 16.7 | (2.51) | 1.3 | (0.18) | 3.6 | (1.14) |
| Italy (Provincia Campania) | 432 | (7.7) | 441 | (6.7) | 448 | (7.1) | 449 | (7.5) | 10.8 | (4.30) | 1.3 | (0.16) | 1.0 | (0.78) |
| Italy (Provincia Basilicata) | 430 | (6.3) | 453 | (5.9) | 456 | (6.6) | 465 | (7.1) | 15.6 | (2.92) | 1.4 | (0.16) | 2.3 | (0.84) |
| Italy (Provincia Emilia Romagna) | 484 | (6.3) | 509 | (5.0) | 515 | (5.4) | 532 | (5.3) | 22.4 | (3.05) | 1.5 | (0.18) | 3.8 | (0.95) |
| Italy (Provincia Friuli Venezia Giulia) | 504 | (5.3) | 534 | (5.7) | 549 | (4.8) | 551 | (5.8) | 25.8 | (3.31) | 1.7 | (0.18) | 6.4 | (1.53) |
| Italy (Provincia Sicilia) | 418 | (10.9) | 426 | (9.9) | 435 | (12.9) | 456 | (9.1) | 22.4 | (6.45) | 1.2 | (0.27) | 3.2 | (2.13) |
| Italy (Provincia Liguria) | 465 | (8.9) | 485 | (7.9) | 497 | (8.1) | 506 | (10.3) | 19.8 | (4.18) | 1.4 | (0.19) | 3.3 | (1.37) |
| Italy (Provincia Lombardia) | 468 | (7.7) | 504 | (6.4) | 511 | (7.2) | 516 | (10.5) | 24.9 | (3.87) | 1.5 | (0.15) | 4.6 | (1.45) |
| Italy (Provincia Piemonte) | 480 | (6.5) | 510 | (7.3) | 512 | (6.7) | 535 | (6.4) | 24.7 | (3.98) | 1.6 | (0.21) | 4.8 | (1.44) |
| Italy (Provincia Trento) | 492 | (4.5) | 519 | (4.8) | 524 | (5.5) | 552 | (5.5) | 27.9 | (3.04) | 1.5 | (0.17) | 6.0 | (1.28) |
| Italy (Provincia Sardegna) | 420 | (8.8) | 451 | (6.1) | 451 | (9.3) | 476 | (8.9) | 22.3 | (4.10) | 1.7 | (0.19) | 4.7 | (1.66) |
| Italy (Provincia Puglia) | 430 | (5.7) | 446 | (6.3) | 450 | (5.7) | 466 | (6.9) | 14.8 | (3.39) | 1.3 | (0.18) | 2.2 | (0.97) |
| Italy (Provincia Veneto) | 495 | (6.3) | 523 | (6.9) | 530 | (5.9) | 550 | (8.6) | 26.9 | (3.66) | 1.6 | (0.19) | 5.8 | (1.49) |
| Spain (Andalusia) | 444 | (5.7) | 467 | (5.6) | 483 | (5.5) | 504 | (5.0) | 25.7 | (2.90) | 1.6 | (0.17) | 7.4 | (1.41) |
| Spain (Basque Country) | 461 | (3.8) | 487 | (4.0) | 504 | (4.2) | 528 | (4.7) | 26.1 | (1.50) | 1.8 | (0.13) | 9.4 | (1.00) |
| Spain (Cantabria) | 477 | (4.6) | 503 | (5.0) | 520 | (5.6) | 541 | (4.6) | 25.3 | (2.02) | 1.8 | (0.21) | 7.9 | (1.16) |
| Spain (Galicia) | 476 | (5.4) | 503 | (5.5) | 513 | (5.3) | 526 | (4.9) | 19.2 | (1.65) | 1.5 | (0.16) | 4.8 | (0.85) |
| Spain (La Rioja) | 487 | (4.6) | 519 | (4.8) | 528 | (6.4) | 545 | (5.5) | 21.4 | (2.88) | 1.7 | (0.21) | 5.7 | (1.44) |
| Spain (Castile and Leon) | 491 | (5.6) | 517 | (5.6) | 530 | (5.0) | 542 | (5.9) | 21.7 | (2.09) | 1.7 | (0.15) | 6.5 | (1.24) |
| Spain (Navarre) | 469 | (4.9) | 509 | (5.5) | 526 | (4.4) | 542 | (5.4) | 28.4 | (2.36) | 2.1 | (0.23) | 10.5 | (1.71) |
| Spain (Aragon) | 481 | (6.2) | 510 | (6.8) | 522 | (5.4) | 541 | (5.1) | 22.0 | (2.54) | 1.7 | (0.25) | 5.9 | (1.29) |
| Spain (Catalonia) | 465 | (7.1) | 485 | (6.3) | 497 | (6.8) | 520 | (8.4) | 22.7 | (3.54) | 1.5 | (0.21) | 5.9 | (1.88) |
| Spain (Asturias) | 477 | (6.4) | 508 | (4.8) | 517 | (6.6) | 536 | (5.6) | 21.2 | (2.47) | 1.8 | (0.19) | 6.5 | (1.40) |
| United Kingdom (Scotland) | 474 | (4.8) | 499 | (4.8) | 526 | (6.1) | 563 | (5.6) | 32.6 | (2.04) | 1.8 | (0.14) | 11.8 | (1.38) |
| | | | | | | | | | | | | | | |
| **Non-adjudicated** | | | | | | | | | | | | | | |
| Belgium (French Community) | 458 | (6.3) | 485 | (4.6) | 498 | (5.3) | 519 | (6.0) | 24.5 | (2.29) | 1.6 | (0.13) | 5.5 | (0.96) |
| Belgium (German-Speaking Community) | 497 | (6.4) | 510 | (7.8) | 521 | (7.0) | 549 | (7.4) | 20.4 | (3.26) | 1.4 | (0.18) | 4.9 | (1.52) |
| Finland (Finnish Speaking) | 534 | (3.1) | 557 | (3.0) | 572 | (3.4) | 597 | (2.5) | 29.1 | (1.45) | 1.8 | (0.12) | 9.0 | (0.89) |
| Finland (Swedish Speaking) | 508 | (10.9) | 511 | (13.9) | 541 | (12.7) | 564 | (10.9) | 25.5 | (5.56) | 1.3 | (0.36) | 7.5 | (3.57) |
| United Kingdom (England) | 482 | (4.3) | 500 | (3.7) | 522 | (3.5) | 564 | (3.9) | 32.7 | (1.71) | 1.6 | (0.09) | 9.0 | (0.90) |
| United Kingdom (Northern Ireland) | 477 | (5.7) | 498 | (4.8) | 513 | (5.1) | 551 | (4.7) | 27.4 | (2.45) | 1.5 | (0.13) | 6.3 | (1.06) |
| United Kingdom (Wales) | 471 | (4.4) | 491 | (5.3) | 505 | (5.2) | 554 | (5.7) | 33.3 | (2.14) | 1.5 | (0.11) | 10.0 | (1.21) |

Note: Values that are statistically significant are indicated in bold (see Annex A3). See Table 3.6 for national data.
1. Results based on students' self-reports.
*StatLink* ᴍᴤᴸ http://dx.doi.org/10.1787/142184405135

Pour consulter la version française intégrale de ce tableau, suivre ce lien :
*StatLink* ᴍᴤᴸ http://dx.doi.org/10.1787/152830402855

269

[Part 1/2]

**Table S3d** Index of general interest in science and performance on the science scale, by quarters of the index[1]

Tableau S3d  Indice d'intérêt général pour les sciences et scores sur l'échelle de culture scientifique, par quartile de l'indice

| | Index of general interest in science | | | | | | | | | | | | | | | |
|---|---|---|---|---|---|---|---|---|---|---|---|---|---|---|---|---|
| | All students | | Males | | Females | | Gender difference (M - F) | | Bottom quarter | | Second quarter | | Third quarter | | Top quarter | |
| | Mean index | S.E. | Mean index | S.E. | Mean index | S.E. | Dif. | S.E. | Mean index | S.E. | Mean index | S.E. | Mean index | S.E. | Mean index | S.E. |
| **Adjudicated** | | | | | | | | | | | | | | | | |
| Belgium (Flemish Community) | -0.10 | (0.03) | -0.15 | (0.04) | -0.05 | (0.03) | **-0.09** | (0.04) | -1.50 | (0.04) | -0.24 | (0.00) | 0.29 | (0.00) | 1.05 | (0.01) |
| Italy (Provincia Autonoma of Bolzano) | 0.06 | (0.02) | 0.03 | (0.04) | 0.10 | (0.03) | -0.07 | (0.05) | -1.07 | (0.05) | -0.08 | (0.01) | 0.36 | (0.01) | 1.04 | (0.02) |
| Italy (Provincia Campania) | 0.31 | (0.02) | 0.34 | (0.04) | 0.29 | (0.04) | 0.04 | (0.05) | -0.57 | (0.03) | 0.07 | (0.01) | 0.51 | (0.01) | 1.25 | (0.03) |
| Italy (Provincia Basilicata) | 0.24 | (0.03) | 0.24 | (0.04) | 0.25 | (0.04) | -0.02 | (0.05) | -0.70 | (0.04) | 0.05 | (0.01) | 0.45 | (0.01) | 1.17 | (0.03) |
| Italy (Provincia Emilia Romagna) | 0.07 | (0.03) | 0.10 | (0.04) | 0.04 | (0.04) | 0.06 | (0.05) | -0.95 | (0.04) | -0.09 | (0.01) | 0.31 | (0.01) | 1.03 | (0.02) |
| Italy (Provincia Friuli Venezia Giulia) | 0.03 | (0.04) | 0.01 | (0.05) | 0.06 | (0.05) | -0.05 | (0.07) | -1.03 | (0.06) | -0.10 | (0.01) | 0.30 | (0.01) | 0.98 | (0.02) |
| Italy (Provincia Sicilia) | 0.33 | (0.04) | 0.34 | (0.06) | 0.33 | (0.03) | 0.01 | (0.06) | -0.59 | (0.05) | 0.09 | (0.01) | 0.52 | (0.01) | 1.30 | (0.05) |
| Italy (Provincia Liguria) | 0.10 | (0.04) | 0.05 | (0.06) | 0.14 | (0.04) | -0.09 | (0.05) | -1.00 | (0.06) | -0.05 | (0.01) | 0.36 | (0.01) | 1.08 | (0.03) |
| Italy (Provincia Lombardia) | 0.00 | (0.03) | -0.04 | (0.05) | 0.05 | (0.03) | -0.09 | (0.05) | -1.07 | (0.05) | -0.14 | (0.01) | 0.27 | (0.01) | 0.95 | (0.02) |
| Italy (Provincia Piemonte) | 0.11 | (0.03) | 0.07 | (0.04) | 0.15 | (0.04) | -0.08 | (0.05) | -0.87 | (0.03) | -0.05 | (0.01) | 0.36 | (0.01) | 1.02 | (0.03) |
| Italy (Provincia Trento) | 0.11 | (0.02) | 0.15 | (0.03) | 0.06 | (0.03) | **0.09** | (0.04) | -0.93 | (0.04) | -0.08 | (0.01) | 0.33 | (0.01) | 1.10 | (0.03) |
| Italy (Provincia Sardegna) | 0.11 | (0.04) | 0.09 | (0.06) | 0.12 | (0.04) | -0.02 | (0.07) | -0.99 | (0.05) | -0.09 | (0.01) | 0.35 | (0.01) | 1.16 | (0.04) |
| Italy (Provincia Puglia) | 0.23 | (0.03) | 0.23 | (0.04) | 0.22 | (0.03) | 0.01 | (0.05) | -0.71 | (0.03) | 0.01 | (0.01) | 0.45 | (0.01) | 1.17 | (0.03) |
| Italy (Provincia Veneto) | 0.11 | (0.03) | 0.11 | (0.03) | 0.11 | (0.04) | 0.00 | (0.05) | -0.89 | (0.03) | -0.06 | (0.01) | 0.37 | (0.01) | 1.04 | (0.03) |
| Spain (Andalusia) | -0.17 | (0.03) | -0.15 | (0.04) | -0.19 | (0.04) | 0.04 | (0.05) | -1.30 | (0.04) | -0.31 | (0.01) | 0.11 | (0.01) | 0.81 | (0.03) |
| Spain (Basque Country) | -0.12 | (0.03) | -0.13 | (0.04) | -0.12 | (0.03) | -0.02 | (0.04) | -1.51 | (0.04) | -0.29 | (0.00) | 0.25 | (0.01) | 1.06 | (0.02) |
| Spain (Cantabria) | -0.22 | (0.03) | -0.29 | (0.04) | -0.14 | (0.04) | **-0.14** | (0.04) | -1.49 | (0.05) | -0.35 | (0.01) | 0.12 | (0.01) | 0.86 | (0.03) |
| Spain (Galicia) | -0.17 | (0.03) | -0.19 | (0.05) | -0.15 | (0.04) | -0.05 | (0.06) | -1.47 | (0.04) | -0.32 | (0.01) | 0.14 | (0.01) | 0.96 | (0.03) |
| Spain (La Rioja) | -0.18 | (0.03) | -0.22 | (0.04) | -0.13 | (0.04) | -0.10 | (0.06) | -1.43 | (0.05) | -0.31 | (0.01) | 0.14 | (0.01) | 0.90 | (0.02) |
| Spain (Castile and Leon) | -0.10 | (0.03) | -0.15 | (0.03) | -0.05 | (0.04) | **-0.10** | (0.05) | -1.21 | (0.05) | -0.25 | (0.01) | 0.18 | (0.01) | 0.87 | (0.03) |
| Spain (Navarre) | -0.30 | (0.03) | -0.31 | (0.03) | -0.29 | (0.04) | -0.02 | (0.05) | -1.74 | (0.04) | -0.43 | (0.01) | 0.11 | (0.01) | 0.87 | (0.02) |
| Spain (Aragon) | -0.35 | (0.04) | -0.40 | (0.05) | -0.30 | (0.04) | -0.10 | (0.06) | -1.67 | (0.05) | -0.45 | (0.01) | -0.03 | (0.01) | 0.73 | (0.02) |
| Spain (Catalonia) | -0.14 | (0.04) | -0.18 | (0.05) | -0.11 | (0.04) | -0.07 | (0.04) | -1.29 | (0.05) | -0.31 | (0.01) | 0.10 | (0.01) | 0.94 | (0.03) |
| Spain (Asturias) | -0.24 | (0.04) | -0.30 | (0.05) | -0.17 | (0.05) | **-0.13** | (0.06) | -1.58 | (0.05) | -0.34 | (0.01) | 0.10 | (0.01) | 0.87 | (0.03) |
| United Kingdom (Scotland) | -0.29 | (0.02) | -0.22 | (0.04) | -0.36 | (0.03) | **0.14** | (0.05) | -1.66 | (0.03) | -0.43 | (0.01) | 0.07 | (0.01) | 0.86 | (0.02) |
| **Non-adjudicated** | | | | | | | | | | | | | | | | |
| Belgium (French Community) | 0.19 | (0.03) | 0.19 | (0.05) | 0.20 | (0.03) | 0.00 | (0.05) | -1.03 | (0.03) | -0.01 | (0.01) | 0.52 | (0.01) | 1.30 | (0.02) |
| Belgium (German-Speaking Community) | -0.12 | (0.03) | -0.15 | (0.04) | -0.09 | (0.04) | -0.06 | (0.07) | -1.55 | (0.06) | -0.25 | (0.01) | 0.25 | (0.01) | 1.08 | (0.03) |
| Finland (Finnish Speaking) | -0.25 | (0.02) | -0.25 | (0.03) | -0.25 | (0.02) | 0.00 | (0.03) | -1.46 | (0.02) | -0.45 | (0.00) | 0.05 | (0.00) | 0.86 | (0.02) |
| Finland (Swedish Speaking) | -0.18 | (0.09) | -0.12 | (0.13) | -0.25 | (0.08) | 0.12 | (0.11) | -1.34 | (0.11) | -0.36 | (0.01) | 0.09 | (0.02) | 0.89 | (0.07) |
| United Kingdom (England) | 0.01 | (0.02) | 0.08 | (0.02) | -0.06 | (0.02) | **0.14** | (0.03) | -1.14 | (0.03) | -0.16 | (0.00) | 0.31 | (0.00) | 1.03 | (0.01) |
| United Kingdom (Northern Ireland) | -0.08 | (0.02) | -0.05 | (0.04) | -0.11 | (0.04) | 0.06 | (0.06) | -1.45 | (0.04) | -0.20 | (0.01) | 0.29 | (0.01) | 1.05 | (0.02) |
| United Kingdom (Wales) | 0.11 | (0.02) | 0.19 | (0.02) | 0.03 | (0.03) | **0.16** | (0.03) | -1.02 | (0.03) | -0.05 | (0.01) | 0.43 | (0.01) | 1.09 | (0.02) |

Note: Values that are statistically significant are indicated in bold (see Annex A3). See Table 3.8 for national data.
1. Results based on students' self-reports.
*StatLink* ᴍ㎖ http://dx.doi.org/10.1787/142184405135

Pour consulter la version française intégrale de ce tableau, suivre ce lien :
*StatLink* ᴍ㎖ http://dx.doi.org/10.1787/152830402855

[Part 2/2]

**Table S3d** Index of general interest in science and performance on the science scale, by quarters of the index[1]

Tableau S3d  Indice d'intérêt général pour les sciences et scores sur l'échelle de culture scientifique, par quartile de l'indice

| | Performance on the science scale, by quarters of this index | | | | | | | | Change in the science score per unit of this index | | Increased likelihood of students in the bottom quarter of this index scoring in the bottom quarter of the science performance distribution | | Explained variance in student performance (r-squared x 100) | |
| | Bottom quarter | | Second quarter | | Third quarter | | Top quarter | | | | | | | |
| | Mean score | S.E. | Mean score | S.E. | Mean score | S.E. | Mean score | S.E | Effect | S.E. | Ratio | S.E. | % | S.E. |
|---|---|---|---|---|---|---|---|---|---|---|---|---|---|---|
| **Adjudicated** | | | | | | | | | | | | | | |
| Belgium (Flemish Community) | 477 | (6.3) | 519 | (3.1) | 549 | (3.0) | 573 | (3.7) | 35.9 | (2.43) | 2.4 | (0.16) | 17.0 | (2.10) |
| Italy (Provincia Autonoma of Bolzano) | 493 | (4.6) | 528 | (4.3) | 538 | (4.2) | 548 | (4.3) | 26.0 | (2.82) | 1.8 | (0.19) | 7.2 | (1.61) |
| Italy (Provincia Campania) | 418 | (6.1) | 435 | (7.6) | 449 | (9.0) | 468 | (6.7) | 22.3 | (3.32) | 1.7 | (0.17) | 4.5 | (1.32) |
| Italy (Provincia Basilicata) | 417 | (7.1) | 446 | (6.9) | 459 | (6.8) | 482 | (7.6) | 29.3 | (3.96) | 1.8 | (0.22) | 7.6 | (1.89) |
| Italy (Provincia Emilia Romagna) | 479 | (5.3) | 502 | (4.9) | 520 | (5.4) | 539 | (6.3) | 28.6 | (3.44) | 1.7 | (0.17) | 6.6 | (1.43) |
| Italy (Provincia Friuli Venezia Giulia) | 500 | (5.2) | 525 | (5.3) | 549 | (4.8) | 564 | (6.7) | 31.0 | (3.72) | 2.1 | (0.23) | 10.1 | (2.30) |
| Italy (Provincia Sicilia) | 405 | (11.3) | 420 | (11.6) | 446 | (8.5) | 463 | (8.2) | 26.6 | (5.04) | 1.7 | (0.34) | 4.7 | (2.04) |
| Italy (Provincia Liguria) | 444 | (8.0) | 485 | (8.2) | 503 | (7.6) | 520 | (8.7) | 32.2 | (3.14) | 2.1 | (0.21) | 9.2 | (1.81) |
| Italy (Provincia Lombardia) | 464 | (8.6) | 497 | (6.4) | 511 | (8.0) | 526 | (10.1) | 29.8 | (3.94) | 1.9 | (0.24) | 7.2 | (1.65) |
| Italy (Provincia Piemonte) | 478 | (5.1) | 496 | (7.2) | 522 | (5.9) | 539 | (7.3) | 30.0 | (3.20) | 1.8 | (0.22) | 7.2 | (1.44) |
| Italy (Provincia Trento) | 481 | (4.7) | 505 | (4.5) | 544 | (5.4) | 556 | (5.4) | 34.2 | (2.96) | 2.1 | (0.18) | 10.4 | (1.76) |
| Italy (Provincia Sardegna) | 412 | (8.3) | 439 | (6.7) | 464 | (8.3) | 484 | (9.5) | 28.8 | (3.61) | 2.1 | (0.25) | 8.6 | (1.90) |
| Italy (Provincia Puglia) | 419 | (4.8) | 442 | (5.1) | 457 | (5.6) | 475 | (7.4) | 22.5 | (3.28) | 1.6 | (0.17) | 4.8 | (1.30) |
| Italy (Provincia Veneto) | 482 | (5.8) | 518 | (7.9) | 537 | (6.8) | 560 | (6.9) | 34.7 | (3.12) | 2.1 | (0.23) | 10.0 | (1.70) |
| Spain (Andalusia) | 435 | (7.5) | 469 | (6.0) | 486 | (5.0) | 507 | (5.8) | 31.5 | (3.40) | 2.0 | (0.27) | 10.3 | (1.80) |
| Spain (Basque Country) | 459 | (4.2) | 486 | (4.6) | 507 | (4.5) | 527 | (4.0) | 24.2 | (1.54) | 2.0 | (0.15) | 9.6 | (1.16) |
| Spain (Cantabria) | 475 | (5.9) | 492 | (6.0) | 526 | (4.2) | 549 | (4.9) | 29.8 | (2.18) | 2.0 | (0.19) | 12.1 | (1.47) |
| Spain (Galicia) | 471 | (5.1) | 493 | (5.4) | 518 | (4.7) | 536 | (4.8) | 24.7 | (2.06) | 1.8 | (0.19) | 8.4 | (1.42) |
| Spain (La Rioja) | 489 | (5.3) | 510 | (5.0) | 524 | (5.2) | 558 | (5.5) | 25.2 | (3.25) | 1.9 | (0.30) | 8.0 | (1.98) |
| Spain (Castile and Leon) | 490 | (5.6) | 503 | (5.5) | 533 | (5.5) | 554 | (4.9) | 27.0 | (2.53) | 1.7 | (0.20) | 9.1 | (1.54) |
| Spain (Navarre) | 477 | (4.8) | 502 | (5.1) | 523 | (5.9) | 545 | (5.3) | 23.3 | (2.05) | 1.8 | (0.18) | 8.0 | (1.29) |
| Spain (Aragon) | 478 | (6.3) | 505 | (5.1) | 527 | (5.4) | 545 | (5.1) | 27.2 | (1.93) | 1.8 | (0.19) | 9.6 | (1.34) |
| Spain (Catalonia) | 468 | (6.5) | 480 | (7.1) | 496 | (6.7) | 524 | (7.4) | 22.2 | (2.95) | 1.5 | (0.19) | 5.4 | (1.44) |
| Spain (Asturias) | 481 | (5.8) | 501 | (6.0) | 520 | (6.5) | 535 | (5.6) | 19.5 | (2.08) | 1.8 | (0.23) | 6.0 | (1.29) |
| United Kingdom (Scotland) | 468 | (4.6) | 497 | (5.0) | 530 | (5.1) | 566 | (5.6) | 36.3 | (2.02) | 2.0 | (0.15) | 13.8 | (1.39) |
| **Non-adjudicated** | | | | | | | | | | | | | | |
| Belgium (French Community) | 443 | (5.9) | 489 | (4.8) | 502 | (5.4) | 514 | (6.7) | 27.1 | (2.50) | 2.0 | (0.18) | 6.8 | (1.09) |
| Belgium (German-Speaking Community) | 475 | (5.7) | 509 | (5.9) | 524 | (6.1) | 558 | (7.3) | 29.1 | (3.40) | 1.9 | (0.24) | 10.6 | (2.37) |
| Finland  (Finnish Speaking) | 526 | (3.3) | 557 | (3.0) | 575 | (2.5) | 603 | (3.6) | 31.9 | (1.78) | 2.1 | (0.12) | 12.5 | (1.24) |
| Finland  (Swedish Speaking) | 496 | (14.0) | 514 | (9.9) | 546 | (13.8) | 567 | (15.7) | 25.1 | (9.58) | 2.1 | (0.74) | 7.6 | (5.15) |
| United Kingdom (England) | 480 | (4.2) | 510 | (3.6) | 536 | (3.6) | 541 | (4.3) | 26.8 | (1.79) | 1.7 | (0.12) | 5.6 | (0.74) |
| United Kingdom (Northern Ireland) | 464 | (5.4) | 501 | (4.8) | 534 | (5.6) | 538 | (5.0) | 30.2 | (1.94) | 1.8 | (0.13) | 8.4 | (1.03) |
| United Kingdom (Wales) | 463 | (4.4) | 499 | (6.2) | 518 | (5.8) | 541 | (5.6) | 33.0 | (2.14) | 1.8 | (0.13) | 8.6 | (1.02) |

Note: Values that are statistically significant are indicated in bold (see Annex A3). See Table 3.8 for national data.
1. Results based on students' self-reports.
*StatLink* ᵉᵖᵐ http://dx.doi.org/10.1787/142184405135

Pour consulter la version française intégrale de ce tableau, suivre ce lien :
*StatLink* ᵉᵖᵐ http://dx.doi.org/10.1787/152830402855

[Part 1/2]

**Table S3e**  **Index of enjoyment of science and performance on the science scale, by quarters of the index[1]**

Tableau S3e  Indice du plaisir apporté par les sciences et scores sur l'échelle de culture scientifique, par quartile de l'indice

| | Index of enjoyment of science | | | | | | | | | | | | | | | |
|---|---|---|---|---|---|---|---|---|---|---|---|---|---|---|---|---|
| | All students | | Males | | Females | | Gender difference (M - F) | | Bottom quarter | | Second quarter | | Third quarter | | Top quarter | |
| | Mean index | S.E. | Mean index | S.E. | Mean index | S.E. | Dif. | S.E. | Mean index | S.E. | Mean index | S.E. | Mean index | S.E. | Mean index | S.E. |
| **Adjudicated** | | | | | | | | | | | | | | | | |
| Belgium (Flemish Community) | -0.13 | (0.03) | -0.09 | (0.04) | -0.17 | (0.03) | 0.08 | (0.04) | -1.33 | (0.03) | -0.42 | (0.01) | 0.20 | (0.01) | 1.05 | (0.01) |
| Italy (Provincia Autonoma of Bolzano) | -0.01 | (0.03) | 0.00 | (0.04) | -0.03 | (0.03) | 0.03 | (0.05) | -1.31 | (0.03) | -0.39 | (0.01) | 0.33 | (0.01) | 1.32 | (0.02) |
| Italy (Provincia Campania) | 0.13 | (0.03) | 0.19 | (0.03) | 0.07 | (0.03) | **0.13** | (0.05) | -0.88 | (0.02) | -0.10 | (0.01) | 0.39 | (0.01) | 1.11 | (0.03) |
| Italy (Provincia Basilicata) | 0.09 | (0.03) | 0.12 | (0.04) | 0.06 | (0.03) | 0.06 | (0.05) | -0.97 | (0.02) | -0.15 | (0.01) | 0.38 | (0.01) | 1.11 | (0.02) |
| Italy (Provincia Emilia Romagna) | 0.01 | (0.03) | 0.05 | (0.04) | -0.03 | (0.04) | 0.08 | (0.05) | -1.10 | (0.03) | -0.25 | (0.01) | 0.31 | (0.01) | 1.10 | (0.03) |
| Italy (Provincia Friuli Venezia Giulia) | 0.05 | (0.03) | 0.08 | (0.04) | 0.01 | (0.04) | 0.07 | (0.06) | -1.06 | (0.03) | -0.23 | (0.01) | 0.35 | (0.01) | 1.12 | (0.03) |
| Italy (Provincia Sicilia) | 0.30 | (0.03) | 0.33 | (0.06) | 0.27 | (0.04) | 0.07 | (0.08) | -0.72 | (0.03) | 0.06 | (0.01) | 0.59 | (0.01) | 1.27 | (0.02) |
| Italy (Provincia Liguria) | 0.00 | (0.04) | 0.00 | (0.06) | 0.01 | (0.04) | -0.01 | (0.05) | -1.16 | (0.03) | -0.27 | (0.01) | 0.33 | (0.01) | 1.11 | (0.02) |
| Italy (Provincia Lombardia) | -0.06 | (0.04) | -0.03 | (0.04) | -0.08 | (0.04) | 0.05 | (0.04) | -1.16 | (0.03) | -0.29 | (0.01) | 0.24 | (0.01) | 0.99 | (0.03) |
| Italy (Provincia Piemonte) | 0.08 | (0.04) | 0.09 | (0.05) | 0.08 | (0.05) | 0.01 | (0.06) | -0.99 | (0.03) | -0.18 | (0.01) | 0.36 | (0.01) | 1.14 | (0.03) |
| Italy (Provincia Trento) | 0.04 | (0.02) | 0.15 | (0.03) | -0.07 | (0.03) | **0.22** | (0.04) | -1.05 | (0.02) | -0.22 | (0.01) | 0.34 | (0.01) | 1.10 | (0.03) |
| Italy (Provincia Sardegna) | 0.03 | (0.03) | 0.07 | (0.05) | -0.01 | (0.04) | 0.09 | (0.06) | -1.14 | (0.05) | -0.26 | (0.01) | 0.37 | (0.01) | 1.15 | (0.03) |
| Italy (Provincia Puglia) | 0.16 | (0.03) | 0.18 | (0.04) | 0.14 | (0.05) | 0.04 | (0.06) | -0.99 | (0.03) | -0.09 | (0.01) | 0.45 | (0.01) | 1.25 | (0.02) |
| Italy (Provincia Veneto) | 0.09 | (0.04) | 0.12 | (0.04) | 0.07 | (0.05) | 0.05 | (0.06) | -1.01 | (0.02) | -0.19 | (0.01) | 0.37 | (0.01) | 1.20 | (0.03) |
| Spain (Andalusia) | -0.13 | (0.04) | -0.09 | (0.04) | -0.18 | (0.05) | **0.09** | (0.04) | -1.34 | (0.02) | -0.41 | (0.01) | 0.15 | (0.01) | 1.07 | (0.02) |
| Spain (Basque Country) | -0.31 | (0.03) | -0.33 | (0.03) | -0.30 | (0.03) | -0.03 | (0.03) | -1.62 | (0.02) | -0.64 | (0.01) | 0.00 | (0.01) | 1.02 | (0.02) |
| Spain (Cantabria) | -0.14 | (0.03) | -0.22 | (0.04) | -0.05 | (0.03) | **-0.17** | (0.04) | -1.33 | (0.02) | -0.40 | (0.01) | 0.14 | (0.01) | 1.05 | (0.03) |
| Spain (Galicia) | -0.11 | (0.03) | -0.13 | (0.04) | -0.09 | (0.04) | -0.04 | (0.04) | -1.38 | (0.02) | -0.40 | (0.01) | 0.18 | (0.01) | 1.15 | (0.02) |
| Spain (La Rioja) | -0.05 | (0.03) | -0.09 | (0.05) | 0.00 | (0.03) | -0.08 | (0.05) | -1.30 | (0.03) | -0.31 | (0.01) | 0.26 | (0.01) | 1.17 | (0.03) |
| Spain (Castile and Leon) | -0.06 | (0.03) | -0.09 | (0.04) | -0.02 | (0.04) | -0.08 | (0.05) | -1.28 | (0.03) | -0.33 | (0.01) | 0.23 | (0.01) | 1.14 | (0.02) |
| Spain (Navarre) | -0.24 | (0.04) | -0.29 | (0.05) | -0.20 | (0.05) | **-0.10** | (0.05) | -1.56 | (0.03) | -0.55 | (0.01) | 0.09 | (0.01) | 1.05 | (0.03) |
| Spain (Aragon) | -0.24 | (0.03) | -0.26 | (0.05) | -0.22 | (0.04) | -0.04 | (0.06) | -1.51 | (0.03) | -0.56 | (0.01) | 0.07 | (0.01) | 1.05 | (0.02) |
| Spain (Catalonia) | -0.15 | (0.04) | -0.19 | (0.05) | -0.11 | (0.06) | -0.08 | (0.06) | -1.30 | (0.04) | -0.47 | (0.01) | 0.08 | (0.01) | 1.09 | (0.03) |
| Spain (Asturias) | -0.23 | (0.04) | -0.24 | (0.05) | -0.22 | (0.06) | -0.02 | (0.06) | -1.50 | (0.03) | -0.54 | (0.01) | 0.09 | (0.01) | 1.03 | (0.03) |
| United Kingdom (Scotland) | -0.13 | (0.02) | -0.03 | (0.04) | -0.24 | (0.03) | **0.21** | (0.05) | -1.35 | (0.02) | -0.43 | (0.01) | 0.21 | (0.01) | 1.03 | (0.02) |
| **Non-adjudicated** | | | | | | | | | | | | | | | | |
| Belgium (French Community) | 0.14 | (0.03) | 0.19 | (0.05) | 0.09 | (0.03) | **0.10** | (0.05) | -1.10 | (0.03) | -0.14 | (0.01) | 0.41 | (0.01) | 1.41 | (0.02) |
| Belgium (German-Speaking Community) | -0.30 | (0.03) | -0.27 | (0.06) | -0.32 | (0.04) | 0.05 | (0.08) | -1.69 | (0.02) | -0.74 | (0.01) | -0.01 | (0.02) | 1.25 | (0.03) |
| Finland (Finnish Speaking) | 0.12 | (0.02) | 0.02 | (0.02) | 0.21 | (0.02) | **-0.20** | (0.03) | -1.03 | (0.01) | -0.12 | (0.01) | 0.46 | (0.01) | 1.16 | (0.02) |
| Finland (Swedish Speaking) | 0.01 | (0.08) | 0.06 | (0.11) | -0.04 | (0.10) | 0.10 | (0.12) | -1.06 | (0.06) | -0.29 | (0.02) | 0.24 | (0.02) | 1.18 | (0.07) |
| United Kingdom (England) | -0.08 | (0.02) | 0.04 | (0.02) | -0.19 | (0.03) | **0.23** | (0.03) | -1.22 | (0.02) | -0.33 | (0.01) | 0.22 | (0.01) | 1.02 | (0.02) |
| United Kingdom (Northern Ireland) | -0.17 | (0.02) | -0.11 | (0.03) | -0.24 | (0.03) | **0.13** | (0.04) | -1.42 | (0.02) | -0.46 | (0.01) | 0.17 | (0.01) | 1.03 | (0.02) |
| United Kingdom (Wales) | -0.02 | (0.02) | 0.07 | (0.03) | -0.11 | (0.03) | **0.18** | (0.04) | -1.15 | (0.02) | -0.31 | (0.01) | 0.28 | (0.01) | 1.09 | (0.02) |

Note: Values that are statistically significant are indicated in bold (see Annex A3). See Table 3.9 for national data.
1. Results based on students' self-reports.
*StatLink* http://dx.doi.org/10.1787/142184405135

Pour consulter la version française intégrale de ce tableau, suivre ce lien :
*StatLink* http://dx.doi.org/10.1787/152830402855

[Part 2/2]

**Table S3e** Index of enjoyment of science and performance on the science scale, by quarters of the index[1]

Tableau S3e Indice du plaisir apporté par les sciences et scores sur l'échelle de culture scientifique, par quartile de l'indice

| | Performance on the science scale, by quarters of this index | | | | | | | | Change in the science score per unit of this index | | Increased likelihood of students in the bottom quarter of this index scoring in the bottom quarter of the science performance distribution | | Explained variance in student performance (r-squared x 100) | |
| | Bottom quarter | | Second quarter | | Third quarter | | Top quarter | | | | | | | |
| | Mean score | S.E. | Mean score | S.E. | Mean score | S.E. | Mean score | S.E | Effect | S.E. | Ratio | S.E. | % | S.E. |
|---|---|---|---|---|---|---|---|---|---|---|---|---|---|---|
| **Adjudicated** | | | | | | | | | | | | | | |
| Belgium (Flemish Community) | 483 | (6.2) | 512 | (3.7) | 548 | (3.7) | 574 | (3.8) | 38.4 | (3.14) | 2.1 | (0.15) | 15.5 | (2.12) |
| Italy (Provincia Autonoma of Bolzano) | 493 | (5.1) | 521 | (4.6) | 534 | (3.7) | 559 | (4.8) | 25.7 | (2.11) | 1.8 | (0.24) | 9.1 | (1.47) |
| Italy (Provincia Campania) | 421 | (7.8) | 432 | (7.0) | 447 | (8.0) | 470 | (6.9) | 26.0 | (3.07) | 1.6 | (0.16) | 6.5 | (1.41) |
| Italy (Provincia Basilicata) | 425 | (6.6) | 444 | (7.3) | 465 | (7.4) | 470 | (7.7) | 22.5 | (3.66) | 1.5 | (0.19) | 4.8 | (1.50) |
| Italy (Provincia Emilia Romagna) | 477 | (6.1) | 504 | (5.4) | 521 | (6.4) | 538 | (6.8) | 27.2 | (3.37) | 1.7 | (0.16) | 6.6 | (1.53) |
| Italy (Provincia Friuli Venezia Giulia) | 500 | (5.5) | 522 | (4.2) | 550 | (5.9) | 565 | (5.8) | 31.0 | (2.92) | 1.8 | (0.24) | 10.5 | (1.80) |
| Italy (Provincia Sicilia) | 410 | (9.7) | 421 | (9.6) | 451 | (7.7) | 454 | (12.4) | 28.4 | (7.10) | 1.5 | (0.29) | 5.4 | (2.92) |
| Italy (Provincia Liguria) | 448 | (9.4) | 482 | (6.4) | 504 | (6.3) | 518 | (10.9) | 29.7 | (3.87) | 1.9 | (0.17) | 8.0 | (1.99) |
| Italy (Provincia Lombardia) | 466 | (8.0) | 485 | (7.0) | 514 | (8.1) | 534 | (10.7) | 32.6 | (4.87) | 1.7 | (0.23) | 8.8 | (2.85) |
| Italy (Provincia Piemonte) | 480 | (5.0) | 493 | (7.2) | 523 | (5.3) | 540 | (7.5) | 28.0 | (3.11) | 1.8 | (0.19) | 7.1 | (1.57) |
| Italy (Provincia Trento) | 485 | (5.2) | 507 | (4.6) | 532 | (5.2) | 561 | (5.8) | 34.6 | (2.85) | 1.9 | (0.17) | 10.7 | (1.63) |
| Italy (Provincia Sardegna) | 417 | (6.1) | 434 | (7.4) | 466 | (8.4) | 481 | (9.8) | 28.6 | (3.44) | 1.7 | (0.18) | 8.2 | (1.90) |
| Italy (Provincia Puglia) | 417 | (5.0) | 446 | (6.5) | 458 | (5.0) | 472 | (6.8) | 22.9 | (2.78) | 1.8 | (0.22) | 6.1 | (1.36) |
| Italy (Provincia Veneto) | 484 | (7.2) | 519 | (6.4) | 533 | (6.0) | 561 | (7.5) | 35.4 | (3.07) | 2.0 | (0.26) | 12.1 | (2.11) |
| Spain (Andalusia) | 438 | (6.5) | 460 | (4.0) | 483 | (5.4) | 517 | (5.5) | 33.1 | (2.99) | 1.9 | (0.18) | 12.8 | (2.06) |
| Spain (Basque Country) | 451 | (3.5) | 480 | (4.3) | 507 | (4.5) | 543 | (4.0) | 34.2 | (1.67) | 2.3 | (0.18) | 17.8 | (1.47) |
| Spain (Cantabria) | 471 | (4.6) | 491 | (4.7) | 522 | (5.9) | 557 | (3.7) | 36.3 | (1.83) | 2.0 | (0.21) | 16.3 | (1.50) |
| Spain (Galicia) | 467 | (6.0) | 490 | (4.3) | 519 | (5.3) | 542 | (5.3) | 29.5 | (1.57) | 2.0 | (0.21) | 11.2 | (1.22) |
| Spain (La Rioja) | 483 | (4.5) | 508 | (5.1) | 527 | (5.6) | 562 | (6.7) | 33.0 | (2.62) | 2.0 | (0.20) | 13.6 | (2.00) |
| Spain (Castile and Leon) | 485 | (5.8) | 504 | (5.0) | 531 | (5.1) | 560 | (4.9) | 31.0 | (1.94) | 1.9 | (0.20) | 14.0 | (1.89) |
| Spain (Navarre) | 468 | (4.6) | 493 | (5.3) | 530 | (4.8) | 554 | (5.4) | 33.8 | (2.12) | 2.1 | (0.19) | 15.4 | (1.76) |
| Spain (Aragon) | 473 | (5.9) | 495 | (4.9) | 525 | (4.7) | 561 | (5.1) | 33.4 | (2.33) | 2.0 | (0.19) | 14.8 | (1.78) |
| Spain (Catalonia) | 459 | (6.9) | 477 | (5.8) | 498 | (5.9) | 534 | (7.7) | 32.3 | (3.29) | 1.7 | (0.21) | 11.5 | (2.33) |
| Spain (Asturias) | 475 | (5.7) | 497 | (6.3) | 519 | (5.0) | 545 | (6.1) | 26.9 | (2.28) | 1.8 | (0.19) | 10.5 | (1.78) |
| United Kingdom (Scotland) | 464 | (4.9) | 496 | (5.3) | 527 | (6.7) | 574 | (5.9) | 43.6 | (2.19) | 2.2 | (0.17) | 17.6 | (1.60) |
| **Non-adjudicated** | | | | | | | | | | | | | | |
| Belgium (French Community) | 447 | (5.0) | 477 | (5.8) | 495 | (5.7) | 526 | (6.1) | 30.5 | (2.51) | 1.8 | (0.19) | 8.5 | (1.48) |
| Belgium (German-Speaking Community) | 475 | (5.4) | 493 | (6.7) | 533 | (6.1) | 564 | (6.7) | 32.8 | (2.57) | 1.9 | (0.24) | 14.6 | (2.22) |
| Finland (Finnish Speaking) | 527 | (3.1) | 560 | (3.5) | 575 | (3.2) | 598 | (3.4) | 32.1 | (1.62) | 2.0 | (0.13) | 11.3 | (1.08) |
| Finland (Swedish Speaking) | 493 | (12.1) | 527 | (10.4) | 541 | (13.5) | 562 | (12.7) | 29.6 | (7.01) | 1.9 | (0.58) | 9.8 | (5.03) |
| United Kingdom (England) | 472 | (4.4) | 499 | (3.6) | 527 | (3.6) | 568 | (4.5) | 42.9 | (2.10) | 1.8 | (0.13) | 13.1 | (1.20) |
| United Kingdom (Northern Ireland) | 462 | (5.4) | 489 | (5.9) | 529 | (5.9) | 557 | (4.9) | 40.0 | (2.44) | 1.8 | (0.16) | 12.3 | (1.35) |
| United Kingdom (Wales) | 456 | (4.6) | 486 | (5.7) | 518 | (4.6) | 559 | (5.0) | 44.2 | (2.14) | 2.0 | (0.13) | 15.3 | (1.32) |

Note: Values that are statistically significant are indicated in bold (see Annex A3). See Table 3.9 for national data.
1. Results based on students' self-reports.
*StatLink* http://dx.doi.org/10.1787/142184405135

Pour consulter la version française intégrale de ce tableau, suivre ce lien :
*StatLink* http://dx.doi.org/10.1787/152830402855

*273*

[Part 1/2]

**Table S3f  Index of future-oriented motivation to learn science and performance on the science scale, by quarters of the index[1]**

Tableau S3f  Indice de motivation prospective pour l'apprentissage des sciences et scores sur l'échelle de culture scientifique, par quartile de l'indice

| | Index of future-oriented motivation to learn science | | | | | | | | | | | | | | |
|---|---|---|---|---|---|---|---|---|---|---|---|---|---|---|---|
| | All students | | Males | | Females | | Gender difference (M - F) | | Bottom quarter | | Second quarter | | Third quarter | | Top quarter | |
| | Mean index | S.E. | Mean index | S.E. | Mean index | S.E. | Dif. | S.E. | Mean index | S.E. | Mean index | S.E. | Mean index | S.E. | Mean index | S.E. |
| **Adjudicated** | | | | | | | | | | | | | | | | |
| Belgium (Flemish Community) | -0.02 | (0.02) | 0.07 | (0.03) | -0.11 | (0.02) | **0.18** | (0.04) | -1.27 | (0.01) | -0.23 | (0.01) | 0.22 | (0.01) | 1.21 | (0.01) |
| Italy (Provincia Autonoma of Bolzano) | -0.16 | (0.02) | -0.12 | (0.04) | -0.20 | (0.03) | 0.08 | (0.05) | -1.34 | (0.01) | -0.55 | (0.02) | 0.12 | (0.01) | 1.13 | (0.03) |
| Italy (Provincia Campania) | 0.30 | (0.04) | 0.40 | (0.04) | 0.21 | (0.06) | **0.19** | (0.06) | -0.80 | (0.03) | 0.02 | (0.01) | 0.57 | (0.01) | 1.43 | (0.03) |
| Italy (Provincia Basilicata) | 0.20 | (0.04) | 0.29 | (0.04) | 0.10 | (0.05) | **0.18** | (0.05) | -0.95 | (0.03) | -0.05 | (0.00) | 0.45 | (0.01) | 1.35 | (0.03) |
| Italy (Provincia Emilia Romagna) | 0.07 | (0.03) | 0.17 | (0.04) | -0.04 | (0.04) | **0.20** | (0.05) | -1.17 | (0.02) | -0.14 | (0.01) | 0.30 | (0.01) | 1.29 | (0.03) |
| Italy (Provincia Friuli Venezia Giulia) | 0.03 | (0.04) | 0.11 | (0.05) | -0.05 | (0.04) | **0.16** | (0.06) | -1.17 | (0.02) | -0.17 | (0.01) | 0.26 | (0.01) | 1.20 | (0.03) |
| Italy (Provincia Sicilia) | 0.42 | (0.04) | 0.49 | (0.05) | 0.35 | (0.04) | **0.14** | (0.06) | -0.60 | (0.03) | 0.12 | (0.01) | 0.70 | (0.01) | 1.46 | (0.03) |
| Italy (Provincia Liguria) | 0.11 | (0.04) | 0.20 | (0.06) | 0.02 | (0.04) | **0.18** | (0.06) | -1.11 | (0.02) | -0.11 | (0.01) | 0.38 | (0.01) | 1.28 | (0.03) |
| Italy (Provincia Lombardia) | 0.01 | (0.04) | 0.09 | (0.05) | -0.07 | (0.05) | **0.16** | (0.05) | -1.20 | (0.02) | -0.20 | (0.01) | 0.25 | (0.01) | 1.19 | (0.04) |
| Italy (Provincia Piemonte) | 0.10 | (0.04) | 0.16 | (0.05) | 0.05 | (0.06) | 0.11 | (0.06) | -1.12 | (0.02) | -0.12 | (0.01) | 0.36 | (0.01) | 1.29 | (0.02) |
| Italy (Provincia Trento) | 0.07 | (0.02) | 0.18 | (0.04) | -0.05 | (0.04) | **0.23** | (0.05) | -1.14 | (0.02) | -0.14 | (0.01) | 0.33 | (0.01) | 1.23 | (0.03) |
| Italy (Provincia Sardegna) | 0.12 | (0.05) | 0.18 | (0.06) | 0.05 | (0.05) | **0.13** | (0.06) | -1.10 | (0.02) | -0.10 | (0.01) | 0.35 | (0.01) | 1.31 | (0.03) |
| Italy (Provincia Puglia) | 0.19 | (0.04) | 0.27 | (0.05) | 0.13 | (0.05) | **0.14** | (0.05) | -0.98 | (0.02) | -0.05 | (0.00) | 0.41 | (0.01) | 1.40 | (0.02) |
| Italy (Provincia Veneto) | 0.13 | (0.05) | 0.21 | (0.04) | 0.04 | (0.07) | **0.17** | (0.06) | -1.05 | (0.02) | -0.11 | (0.01) | 0.36 | (0.01) | 1.30 | (0.02) |
| Spain (Andalusia) | 0.05 | (0.03) | 0.15 | (0.03) | -0.04 | (0.05) | **0.19** | (0.05) | -1.27 | (0.01) | -0.24 | (0.02) | 0.33 | (0.01) | 1.40 | (0.02) |
| Spain (Basque Country) | 0.10 | (0.02) | 0.17 | (0.03) | 0.03 | (0.03) | **0.14** | (0.04) | -1.34 | (0.01) | -0.23 | (0.01) | 0.52 | (0.01) | 1.45 | (0.01) |
| Spain (Cantabria) | 0.10 | (0.04) | 0.08 | (0.04) | 0.11 | (0.04) | -0.03 | (0.05) | -1.29 | (0.01) | -0.21 | (0.01) | 0.41 | (0.02) | 1.48 | (0.03) |
| Spain (Galicia) | 0.11 | (0.03) | 0.17 | (0.03) | 0.04 | (0.04) | **0.13** | (0.05) | -1.26 | (0.01) | -0.19 | (0.01) | 0.42 | (0.01) | 1.48 | (0.02) |
| Spain (La Rioja) | 0.10 | (0.03) | 0.13 | (0.05) | 0.07 | (0.04) | 0.06 | (0.06) | -1.28 | (0.01) | -0.21 | (0.01) | 0.41 | (0.02) | 1.47 | (0.03) |
| Spain (Castile and Leon) | 0.16 | (0.03) | 0.15 | (0.04) | 0.17 | (0.04) | -0.02 | (0.05) | -1.21 | (0.02) | -0.18 | (0.01) | 0.53 | (0.01) | 1.51 | (0.02) |
| Spain (Navarre) | 0.08 | (0.03) | 0.10 | (0.04) | 0.06 | (0.05) | 0.04 | (0.05) | -1.37 | (0.01) | -0.30 | (0.02) | 0.46 | (0.02) | 1.54 | (0.02) |
| Spain (Aragon) | 0.09 | (0.03) | 0.14 | (0.03) | 0.04 | (0.04) | 0.10 | (0.05) | -1.31 | (0.01) | -0.24 | (0.02) | 0.44 | (0.02) | 1.47 | (0.02) |
| Spain (Catalonia) | -0.03 | (0.05) | 0.02 | (0.05) | -0.08 | (0.06) | 0.10 | (0.06) | -1.42 | (0.00) | -0.47 | (0.02) | 0.26 | (0.02) | 1.51 | (0.02) |
| Spain (Asturias) | 0.14 | (0.04) | 0.20 | (0.04) | 0.08 | (0.06) | 0.11 | (0.07) | -1.30 | (0.01) | -0.21 | (0.01) | 0.53 | (0.02) | 1.55 | (0.02) |
| United Kingdom (Scotland) | -0.09 | (0.02) | 0.01 | (0.04) | -0.19 | (0.03) | **0.20** | (0.05) | -1.38 | (0.01) | -0.38 | (0.01) | 0.19 | (0.01) | 1.22 | (0.02) |
| **Non-adjudicated** | | | | | | | | | | | | | | | | |
| Belgium (French Community) | -0.05 | (0.03) | 0.04 | (0.05) | -0.13 | (0.03) | **0.17** | (0.05) | -1.37 | (0.01) | -0.38 | (0.02) | 0.22 | (0.01) | 1.34 | (0.02) |
| Belgium (German-Speaking Community) | -0.32 | (0.03) | -0.17 | (0.05) | -0.47 | (0.05) | **0.30** | (0.07) | -1.42 | (0.00) | -1.02 | (0.02) | -0.02 | (0.02) | 1.19 | (0.03) |
| Finland  (Finnish Speaking) | -0.18 | (0.02) | -0.23 | (0.02) | -0.12 | (0.02) | **-0.12** | (0.03) | -1.33 | (0.00) | -0.33 | (0.01) | 0.04 | (0.00) | 0.92 | (0.01) |
| Finland  (Swedish Speaking) | -0.07 | (0.08) | 0.00 | (0.09) | -0.13 | (0.08) | **0.13** | (0.05) | -1.26 | (0.03) | -0.24 | (0.03) | 0.14 | (0.02) | 1.10 | (0.06) |
| United Kingdom (England) | -0.13 | (0.02) | -0.04 | (0.02) | -0.21 | (0.03) | **0.18** | (0.03) | -1.37 | (0.00) | -0.43 | (0.01) | 0.14 | (0.01) | 1.16 | (0.02) |
| United Kingdom (Northern Ireland) | -0.09 | (0.02) | -0.04 | (0.03) | -0.13 | (0.04) | **0.09** | (0.04) | -1.38 | (0.01) | -0.39 | (0.01) | 0.22 | (0.01) | 1.20 | (0.02) |
| United Kingdom (Wales) | 0.01 | (0.02) | 0.08 | (0.03) | -0.06 | (0.03) | **0.14** | (0.04) | -1.25 | (0.01) | -0.21 | (0.01) | 0.26 | (0.01) | 1.24 | (0.02) |

Note: Values that are statistically significant are indicated in bold (see Annex A3). See Table 3.11 for national data.
1. Results based on students' self-reports.
*StatLink* ᐧᒐ http://dx.doi.org/10.1787/142184405135

Pour consulter la version française intégrale de ce tableau, suivre ce lien :
*StatLink* ᐧᒐ http://dx.doi.org/10.1787/152830402855

[Part 2/2]

**Table S3f** **Index of future-oriented motivation to learn science and performance on the science scale, by quarters of the index[1]**

Tableau S3f Indice de motivation prospective pour l'apprentissage des sciences et scores sur l'échelle de culture scientifique, par quartile de l'indice

| | Performance on the science scale, by quarters of this index | | | | | | | | Change in the science score per unit of this index | | Increased likelihood of students in the bottom quarter of this index scoring in the bottom quarter of the science performance distribution | | Explained variance in student performance (r-squared x 100) | |
| | Bottom quarter | | Second quarter | | Third quarter | | Top quarter | | | | | | | |
| | Mean score | S.E. | Mean score | S.E. | Mean score | S.E. | Mean score | S.E | Effect | S.E. | Ratio | S.E. | % | S.E. |
| **Adjudicated** | | | | | | | | | | | | | | |
| Belgium (Flemish Community) | **506** | (5.0) | 518 | (3.2) | 530 | (4.1) | **582** | (3.8) | **29.9** | (1.91) | **1.6** | (0.09) | 10.1 | (1.03) |
| Italy (Provincia Autonoma of Bolzano) | **505** | (4.4) | 527 | (4.9) | 526 | (5.4) | **549** | (4.2) | **17.3** | (2.43) | **1.5** | (0.14) | 3.6 | (1.01) |
| Italy (Provincia Campania) | **432** | (6.5) | 436 | (6.4) | 440 | (8.1) | **460** | (8.3) | **11.7** | (3.57) | 1.2 | (0.17) | 1.6 | (0.95) |
| Italy (Provincia Basilicata) | **440** | (4.7) | 446 | (6.6) | 451 | (7.2) | **468** | (8.3) | **12.5** | (3.94) | 1.1 | (0.14) | 1.7 | (1.15) |
| Italy (Provincia Emilia Romagna) | **488** | (5.0) | 499 | (5.8) | 510 | (7.2) | **545** | (6.5) | **21.6** | (2.99) | **1.4** | (0.15) | 4.8 | (1.30) |
| Italy (Provincia Friuli Venezia Giulia) | **511** | (5.7) | 524 | (5.3) | 532 | (5.3) | **570** | (6.1) | **25.3** | (3.63) | **1.5** | (0.18) | 7.5 | (1.99) |
| Italy (Provincia Sicilia) | **420** | (9.6) | 433 | (8.6) | 432 | (14.1) | **452** | (9.7) | **14.9** | (6.09) | 1.2 | (0.21) | 1.6 | (1.38) |
| Italy (Provincia Liguria) | **469** | (9.3) | 483 | (7.0) | 486 | (7.4) | **516** | (9.8) | **19.4** | (4.00) | 1.3 | (0.15) | 3.4 | (1.38) |
| Italy (Provincia Lombardia) | **485** | (6.8) | 492 | (7.0) | 503 | (7.6) | **521** | (14.3) | **15.5** | (5.70) | 1.2 | (0.20) | 2.3 | (1.75) |
| Italy (Provincia Piemonte) | **492** | (8.1) | 495 | (6.2) | 511 | (6.4) | **538** | (6.7) | **21.8** | (3.74) | 1.3 | (0.20) | 5.1 | (1.63) |
| Italy (Provincia Trento) | **501** | (4.4) | 507 | (4.4) | 530 | (5.3) | **551** | (5.7) | **23.7** | (2.96) | **1.5** | (0.16) | 5.6 | (1.37) |
| Italy (Provincia Sardegna) | **436** | (7.1) | 437 | (8.5) | 452 | (8.7) | **475** | (9.8) | **17.0** | (4.61) | 1.2 | (0.18) | 3.0 | (1.50) |
| Italy (Provincia Puglia) | **445** | (5.5) | 433 | (5.5) | 453 | (4.7) | **465** | (8.9) | **11.3** | (3.39) | 0.9 | (0.12) | 1.6 | (0.92) |
| Italy (Provincia Veneto) | **499** | (6.5) | 502 | (5.8) | 532 | (6.9) | **565** | (6.9) | **29.3** | (3.60) | **1.5** | (0.19) | 9.0 | (2.10) |
| Spain (Andalusia) | **456** | (5.1) | 460 | (4.9) | 473 | (5.9) | **510** | (5.7) | **22.0** | (2.47) | **1.3** | (0.15) | 6.6 | (1.42) |
| Spain (Basque Country) | **467** | (3.7) | 475 | (3.5) | 504 | (4.6) | **535** | (4.6) | **25.0** | (1.50) | **1.7** | (0.12) | 10.1 | (1.14) |
| Spain (Cantabria) | **482** | (5.8) | 491 | (4.8) | 515 | (6.1) | **554** | (4.2) | **27.3** | (1.86) | **1.6** | (0.16) | 11.5 | (1.39) |
| Spain (Galicia) | **488** | (5.4) | 488 | (4.9) | 504 | (6.8) | **541** | (5.3) | **19.1** | (2.18) | 1.2 | (0.15) | 5.3 | (1.22) |
| Spain (La Rioja) | **493** | (4.7) | 507 | (5.6) | 519 | (5.8) | **564** | (6.2) | **26.9** | (2.57) | **1.6** | (0.20) | 10.8 | (1.94) |
| Spain (Castile and Leon) | **493** | (5.1) | 502 | (6.4) | 526 | (5.6) | **559** | (4.9) | **25.4** | (1.89) | **1.6** | (0.19) | 11.1 | (1.75) |
| Spain (Navarre) | **482** | (4.8) | 490 | (3.8) | 515 | (5.4) | **561** | (5.4) | **27.9** | (2.09) | **1.6** | (0.15) | 12.3 | (1.73) |
| Spain (Aragon) | **482** | (5.2) | 495 | (6.4) | 520 | (5.5) | **559** | (5.4) | **28.8** | (2.22) | **1.6** | (0.14) | 12.1 | (1.60) |
| Spain (Catalonia) | **477** | (6.6) | 479 | (5.3) | 489 | (7.5) | **525** | (8.1) | **17.8** | (2.84) | 1.2 | (0.17) | 5.0 | (1.65) |
| Spain (Asturias) | **483** | (4.3) | 501 | (6.1) | 510 | (6.0) | **543** | (7.6) | **20.2** | (2.33) | **1.6** | (0.19) | 7.0 | (1.70) |
| United Kingdom (Scotland) | **479** | (4.9) | 501 | (5.0) | 515 | (5.0) | **568** | (6.1) | **33.6** | (1.99) | **1.7** | (0.13) | 11.4 | (1.36) |
| **Non-adjudicated** | | | | | | | | | | | | | | |
| Belgium (French Community) | **469** | (4.7) | 484 | (5.6) | 490 | (6.4) | **523** | (6.3) | **19.3** | (2.25) | **1.3** | (0.09) | 3.9 | (0.96) |
| Belgium (German-Speaking Community) | **500** | (6.1) | 511 | (5.9) | 516 | (7.1) | **551** | (6.8) | **19.8** | (3.18) | 1.2 | (0.19) | 4.7 | (1.52) |
| Finland (Finnish Speaking) | **532** | (2.9) | 558 | (3.6) | 563 | (3.0) | **608** | (3.0) | **32.7** | (1.47) | **1.8** | (0.13) | 10.9 | (0.97) |
| Finland (Swedish Speaking) | **501** | (10.9) | 521 | (12.0) | 537 | (11.1) | **568** | (17.5) | **30.4** | (6.49) | 1.7 | (0.45) | 10.3 | (4.19) |
| United Kingdom (England) | **487** | (3.8) | 511 | (4.2) | 509 | (3.7) | **564** | (4.9) | **28.5** | (1.93) | **1.4** | (0.10) | 6.9 | (0.98) |
| United Kingdom (Northern Ireland) | **472** | (5.4) | 503 | (5.0) | 508 | (4.4) | **560** | (5.6) | **32.4** | (2.53) | **1.6** | (0.13) | 8.4 | (1.30) |
| United Kingdom (Wales) | **474** | (4.8) | 490 | (4.5) | 498 | (5.1) | **559** | (5.7) | **33.9** | (2.31) | **1.5** | (0.12) | 10.1 | (1.25) |

Note: Values that are statistically significant are indicated in bold (see Annex A3). See Table 3.11 for national data.
1. Results based on students' self-reports.
*StatLink* ▄▄▄ http://dx.doi.org/10.1787/142184405135

Pour consulter la version française intégrale de ce tableau, suivre ce lien :
*StatLink* ▄▄▄ http://dx.doi.org/10.1787/152830402855

275

[Part 1/2]

**Table S4a** Between-school and within-school variance in student performance on the science scale in PISA 2006

Tableau S4a  Variance intra- et inter-établissements du score des élèves sur l'échelle de culture scientifique du cycle PISA 2006

| | Total variance in SP[2] | Variance expressed as a percentage of the average variance in student performance (SP) across OECD countries[1] | | | | |
|---|---|---|---|---|---|---|
| | | Total variance in SP expressed as a percentage of the average variance in student performance across OECD countries[3] | Total variance in SP between schools[4] | Total variance in SP within schools | Variance explained by the PISA index of economic, social and cultural status of students | |
| | | | | | Between-school variance explained | Within-school variance explained |
| **Adjudicated** | | | | | | |
| Belgium (Flemish Community) | 8 528 | 94.7 | 51.5 | 46.2 | 10.9 | 1.9 |
| Italy (Provincia Autonoma of Bolzano) | 7 698 | 85.4 | 36.9 | 51.6 | 3.3 | 0.4 |
| Italy (Provincia Campania) | 6 842 | 75.9 | 29.9 | 49.0 | 2.9 | 0.2 |
| Italy (Provincia Basilicata) | 7 290 | 80.9 | 37.6 | 45.6 | 5.3 | 0.5 |
| Italy (Provincia Emilia Romagna) | 8 877 | 98.5 | 42.5 | 60.4 | 5.9 | 0.7 |
| Italy (Provincia Friuli Venezia Giulia) | 7 079 | 78.6 | 30.4 | 51.5 | 2.7 | 0.3 |
| Italy (Provincia Sicilia) | 9 675 | 107.4 | 54.8 | 54.5 | 7.8 | 1.6 |
| Italy (Provincia Liguria) | 9 255 | 102.7 | 55.7 | 56.4 | 9.6 | 1.4 |
| Italy (Provincia Lombardia) | 8 865 | 98.4 | 57.4 | 51.5 | 4.9 | 0.4 |
| Italy (Provincia Piemonte) | 8 136 | 90.3 | 39.0 | 53.5 | 5.7 | 0.6 |
| Italy (Provincia Trento) | 8 538 | 94.8 | 50.3 | 49.1 | 1.5 | 0.0 |
| Italy (Provincia Sardegna) | 8 434 | 93.6 | 42.4 | 50.4 | 4.0 | 0.1 |
| Italy (Provincia Puglia) | 6 708 | 74.5 | 27.8 | 49.5 | 3.4 | 0.3 |
| Italy (Provincia Veneto) | 7 937 | 88.1 | 44.8 | 48.0 | 3.8 | 0.3 |
| Spain (Andalusia) | 7 797 | 86.6 | 7.5 | 79.0 | 4.8 | 8.4 |
| Spain (Basque Country) | 6 968 | 77.3 | 17.7 | 60.3 | 5.4 | 2.5 |
| Spain (Cantabria) | 7 200 | 79.9 | 7.1 | 72.9 | 3.9 | 6.6 |
| Spain (Galicia) | 7 551 | 83.8 | 6.0 | 77.7 | 3.6 | 3.9 |
| Spain (La Rioja) | 7 582 | 84.2 | 9.0 | 77.4 | 1.4 | 6.5 |
| Spain (Castile and Leon) | 6 331 | 70.3 | 6.8 | 63.4 | 2.0 | 3.9 |
| Spain (Navarre) | 7 827 | 86.9 | 11.3 | 75.8 | 4.1 | 6.0 |
| Spain (Aragon) | 7 686 | 85.3 | 9.1 | 76.2 | 4.9 | 7.4 |
| Spain (Catalonia) | 8 048 | 89.3 | 16.1 | 72.2 | 7.2 | 3.5 |
| Spain (Asturias) | 6 895 | 76.5 | 11.9 | 64.7 | 5.5 | 6.2 |
| United Kingdom (Scotland) | 9 921 | 110.1 | 18.7 | 91.4 | 8.1 | 8.9 |
| **Non-adjudicated** | | | | | | |
| Belgium (French Community) | 10 446 | 115.9 | 53.9 | 61.4 | 12.7 | 2.2 |
| Belgium (German-Speaking Community) | 9 453 | 104.9 | 52.5 | 66.9 | 6.2 | 1.1 |
| Finland (Finnish Speaking) | 7 258 | 80.6 | 4.4 | 76.3 | 1.3 | 5.5 |
| Finland (Swedish Speaking) | 7 157 | 79.4 | 0.2 | 79.0 | -0.4 | 5.4 |
| United Kingdom (England) | 11 261 | 125.0 | 26.6 | 98.6 | 9.9 | 5.6 |
| United Kingdom (Northern Ireland) | 12 474 | 138.5 | 68.7 | 73.1 | 11.9 | 2.2 |
| United Kingdom (Wales) | 10 306 | 114.4 | 15.6 | 99.2 | 6.3 | 10.1 |

Note: See Table 4.1a for national data.
1. The variance components were estimated for all students in participating countries with data on socio-economic background and study programmes. Students in special education programmes were excluded from these analyses.
2. The total variance in student performance is obtained as the square of the standard deviation shown in Chapter 2. The statistical variance in student performance and not the standard deviation is used for this comparison to allow for the decomposition.
3. The sum of the between- and within-school variance components, as an estimate from a sample, does not necessarily add up to the total.
4. In some countries, sub-units within schools were sampled instead of schools and this may effect the estimation of the between-school variance components (see Annex A2).
StatLink 🔗 http://dx.doi.org/10.1787/142184405135

Pour consulter la version française intégrale de ce tableau, suivre ce lien :
StatLink 🔗 http://dx.doi.org/10.1787/152830402855

[Part 2/2]

**Table S4a    Between-school and within-school variance in student performance on the science scale in PISA 2006**

Tableau S4a    Variance intra- et inter-établissements du score des élèves sur l'échelle de culture scientifique du cycle PISA 2006

| | Variance expressed as a percentage of the average variance in student performance (SP) across OECD countries[1] | | | | | | Total variance between schools expressed as a percentage of the total variance within the country[5] |
|---|---|---|---|---|---|---|---|
| | Variance explained by the PISA index of economic, social and cultural status of students and schools | | Variance explained by students' study programmes | | Variance explained by students' study programmes and the PISA index of economic, social and cultural status of students and schools | | |
| | Between-school variance explained | Within-school variance explained | Between-school variance explained | Within-school variance explained | Between-school variance explained | Within-school variance explained | |
| **Adjudicated** | | | | | | | |
| Belgium (Flemish Community) | 38.6 | 1.9 | 44.2 | 12.7 | 46.0 | 13.2 | 54.4 |
| Italy (Provincia Autonoma of Bolzano) | 17.8 | 0.4 | 19.9 | 0.0 | 21.6 | 0.4 | 43.2 |
| Italy (Provincia Campania) | 18.9 | 0.2 | 16.8 | 0.1 | 21.4 | 0.3 | 39.3 |
| Italy (Provincia Basilicata) | 29.3 | 0.4 | 26.5 | 0.1 | 31.4 | 0.5 | 46.4 |
| Italy (Provincia Emilia Romagna) | 24.8 | 0.7 | 33.1 | 0.0 | 33.2 | 0.7 | 43.2 |
| Italy (Provincia Friuli Venezia Giulia) | 10.7 | 0.2 | 19.5 | -0.1 | 19.7 | 0.2 | 38.7 |
| Italy (Provincia Sicilia) | 26.5 | 1.6 | 34.9 | 0.0 | 38.2 | 1.6 | 51.0 |
| Italy (Provincia Liguria) | 28.7 | 1.6 | 42.0 | 0.3 | 42.0 | 1.7 | 54.3 |
| Italy (Provincia Lombardia) | 28.3 | 0.3 | 42.6 | -0.1 | 42.6 | 0.3 | 58.4 |
| Italy (Provincia Piemonte) | 24.2 | 0.6 | 31.1 | 0.0 | 32.0 | 0.6 | 43.2 |
| Italy (Provincia Trento) | 31.2 | 0.0 | 42.5 | 0.0 | 43.6 | 0.0 | 53.0 |
| Italy (Provincia Sardegna) | 25.4 | 0.2 | 29.8 | 0.1 | 30.7 | 0.2 | 45.3 |
| Italy (Provincia Puglia) | 19.3 | 0.4 | 22.3 | 0.1 | 23.9 | 0.4 | 37.4 |
| Italy (Provincia Veneto) | 23.0 | 0.3 | 30.6 | 0.0 | 32.0 | 0.3 | 50.9 |
| Spain (Andalusia) | 5.1 | 8.4 | 0.2 | 0.4 | 5.2 | 8.8 | 8.7 |
| Spain (Basque Country) | 9.0 | 2.5 | 0.0 | 0.1 | 9.0 | 2.6 | 22.9 |
| Spain (Cantabria) | 4.5 | 6.7 | 0.0 | 0.0 | 4.5 | 6.7 | 8.9 |
| Spain (Galicia) | 3.9 | 3.9 | 0.0 | 0.0 | 3.9 | 3.9 | 7.1 |
| Spain (La Rioja) | 1.3 | 6.5 | 0.0 | 0.0 | 1.3 | 6.5 | 10.7 |
| Spain (Castile and Leon) | 2.3 | 3.9 | 0.0 | 0.0 | 2.3 | 3.9 | 9.7 |
| Spain (Navarre) | 4.6 | 6.0 | -0.1 | 0.1 | 4.5 | 6.1 | 13.0 |
| Spain (Aragon) | 5.7 | 7.4 | -0.1 | 0.4 | 5.6 | 7.6 | 10.7 |
| Spain (Catalonia) | 10.8 | 3.6 | 0.2 | 0.3 | 10.9 | 4.0 | 18.0 |
| Spain (Asturias) | 6.4 | 6.2 | 0.1 | 0.9 | 6.6 | 7.0 | 15.6 |
| United Kingdom (Scotland) | 11.7 | 9.0 | 0.8 | 4.7 | 11.5 | 13.0 | 17.0 |
| **Non-adjudicated** | | | | | | | |
| Belgium (French Community) | 40.6 | 2.2 | 34.7 | 13.0 | 47.2 | 13.8 | 46.5 |
| Belgium (German-Speaking Community) | 30.4 | 1.1 | 41.8 | 15.3 | 42.0 | 15.6 | 50.0 |
| Finland (Finnish Speaking) | 1.4 | 5.5 | 0.0 | 0.0 | 1.4 | 5.5 | 5.4 |
| Finland (Swedish Speaking) | -0.1 | 5.3 | 0.0 | 0.0 | -0.1 | 5.3 | 0.2 |
| United Kingdom (England) | 17.5 | 5.6 | 0.2 | 0.6 | 17.5 | 6.1 | 21.3 |
| United Kingdom (Northern Ireland) | 47.2 | 2.3 | 4.2 | 3.0 | 46.4 | 5.1 | 49.6 |
| United Kingdom (Wales) | 8.6 | 10.2 | -0.1 | 3.9 | 8.6 | 13.0 | 13.6 |

Note: See Table 4.1a for national data.
1. The variance components were estimated for all students in participating countries with data on socio-economic background and study programmes. Students in special education programmes were excluded from these analyses.
5. This index is often referred to as the intra-class correlation (rho).
*StatLink* ▅▅▅ http://dx.doi.org/10.1787/142184405135

Pour consulter la version française intégrale de ce tableau, suivre ce lien :
*StatLink* ▅▅▅ http://dx.doi.org/10.1787/152830402855

277

[Part 1/1]

**Table S4b** **Differences in student performance in science by immigrant status**

Tableau S4b   Variation de la performance des élèves en sciences selon l'ascendance autochtone ou allochtone

| | Performance on the science scale | | | | | | Difference in science performance | | | | | |
|---|---|---|---|---|---|---|---|---|---|---|---|---|
| | Native students | | Second-generation students | | First-generation students | | Second-generation students minus native students | | First-generation students minus native students | | First-generation students minus second-generation students | |
| | Mean score | S.E. | Mean score | S.E. | Mean score | S.E. | Dif. | S.E. | Dif. | S.E. | Dif. | S.E. |
| **Adjudicated** | | | | | | | | | | | | |
| Belgium (Flemish Community) | 536 | (3.1) | 440 | (11.1) | 459 | (12.3) | **-96** | (10.6) | **-77** | (12.0) | 19 | (14.7) |
| Italy (Provincia Autonoma of Bolzano) | 529 | (2.1) | c | c | 443 | (15.9) | c | c | **-87** | (16.1) | c | c |
| Italy (Provincia Campania) | 444 | (5.6) | c | c | c | c | c | c | c | c | c | c |
| Italy (Provincia Basilicata) | 453 | (4.7) | c | c | c | c | c | c | c | c | c | c |
| Italy (Provincia Emilia Romagna) | 516 | (3.5) | c | c | 426 | (11.6) | c | c | **-90** | (11.3) | c | c |
| Italy (Provincia Friuli Venezia Giulia) | 539 | (3.1) | c | c | 458 | (13.5) | c | c | **-81** | (13.2) | c | c |
| Italy (Provincia Sicilia) | 438 | (7.0) | c | c | c | c | c | c | c | c | c | c |
| Italy (Provincia Liguria) | 498 | (6.9) | c | c | 387 | (11.0) | c | c | **-111** | (11.7) | c | c |
| Italy (Provincia Lombardia) | 507 | (5.7) | c | c | 409 | (18.7) | c | c | **-99** | (18.3) | c | c |
| Italy (Provincia Piemonte) | 513 | (4.4) | c | c | 446 | (11.1) | c | c | **-67** | (10.5) | c | c |
| Italy (Provincia Trento) | 527 | (2.2) | c | c | 458 | (11.3) | c | c | **-69** | (11.8) | c | c |
| Italy (Provincia Sardegna) | 451 | (6.1) | c | c | c | c | c | c | c | c | c | c |
| Italy (Provincia Puglia) | 449 | (4.1) | c | c | c | c | c | c | c | c | c | c |
| Italy (Provincia Veneto) | 530 | (4.9) | c | c | 431 | (11.6) | c | c | **-99** | (10.8) | c | c |
| Spain (Andalusia) | 475 | (3.7) | c | c | c | c | c | c | c | c | c | c |
| Spain (Basque Country) | 499 | (3.4) | c | c | 424 | (9.9) | c | c | **-74** | (10.4) | c | c |
| Spain (Cantabria) | 513 | (3.5) | c | c | 447 | (13.8) | c | c | **-66** | (13.6) | c | c |
| Spain (Galicia) | 506 | (3.5) | c | c | c | c | c | c | c | c | c | c |
| Spain (La Rioja) | 526 | (2.5) | c | c | 445 | (11.7) | c | c | **-80** | (11.8) | c | c |
| Spain (Castile and Leon) | 522 | (3.8) | c | c | c | c | c | c | c | c | c | c |
| Spain (Navarre) | 515 | (3.2) | c | c | 468 | (10.4) | c | c | **-47** | (11.4) | c | c |
| Spain (Aragon) | 518 | (3.9) | c | c | 433 | (11.3) | c | c | **-85** | (12.1) | c | c |
| Spain (Catalonia) | 499 | (5.0) | c | c | 421 | (9.7) | c | c | **-78** | (8.6) | c | c |
| Spain (Asturias) | 511 | (4.8) | c | c | c | c | c | c | c | c | c | c |
| United Kingdom (Scotland) | 516 | (3.8) | c | c | c | c | c | c | c | c | c | c |
| **Non-adjudicated** | | | | | | | | | | | | |
| Belgium (French Community) | 503 | (4.3) | 444 | (10.0) | 415 | (9.7) | **-59** | (9.8) | **-88** | (9.6) | **-28** | (9.6) |
| Belgium (German-Speaking Community) | 529 | (3.2) | c | c | 468 | (8.6) | c | c | **-61** | (9.4) | c | c |
| Finland  (Finnish Speaking) | 567 | (2.0) | c | c | c | c | c | c | c | c | c | c |
| Finland  (Swedish Speaking) | 533 | (6.3) | c | c | c | c | c | c | c | c | c | c |
| United Kingdom (England) | 521 | (2.4) | 493 | (9.3) | 478 | (15.5) | **-28** | (9.3) | **-43** | (15.2) | -15 | (16.1) |
| United Kingdom (Northern Ireland) | 512 | (3.2) | c | c | c | c | c | c | c | c | c | c |
| United Kingdom (Wales) | 507 | (3.4) | c | c | c | c | c | c | c | c | c | c |

Notes: Values that are statistically significant are indicated in bold (see Annex A3). See Table 4.2a and Table 4.2c for national data.
*StatLink* http://dx.doi.org/10.1787/142184405135

Pour consulter la version française intégrale de ce tableau, suivre ce lien :
*StatLink* http://dx.doi.org/10.1787/152830402855

[Part 1/2]

**Table S4c** Relationship between student performance in science and the PISA index of economic, social and cultural status (ESCS)

Tableau S4c Relation entre la performance des élèves en sciences et l'indice PISA de statut économique, social et culturel (SESC)

| | Unadjusted mean score | | Mean score if the mean ESCS would be equal in all OECD countries | | Strength of the relationship between student performance and the ESCS | | Slope of the socio-economic gradient[1] | | Length of the projection of the gradient line | | | | | |
| | | | | | | | | | 5th percentile of the ESCS | | 95th percentile of the ESCS | | Difference between 95th and 5th percentile of the ESCS | |
| | Mean score | S.E. | Mean score | S.E. | Percentage of explained variance in student performance | S.E. | Score point difference associated with one unit on the ESCS | S.E. | Index | S.E. | Index | S.E. | Dif. | S.E. |
| **Adjudicated** | | | | | | | | | | | | | | |
| Belgium (Flemish Community) | 529 | (3.2) | 521 | (3.2) | 19.3 | (1.46) | 45 | (2.0) | -1.19 | (0.04) | 1.59 | (0.02) | 2.78 | (0.05) |
| Italy (Provincia Autonoma of Bolzano) | 526 | (2.0) | 529 | (2.0) | 7.3 | (1.46) | 29 | (3.1) | -1.40 | (0.05) | 1.38 | (0.06) | 2.79 | (0.07) |
| Italy (Provincia Campania) | 442 | (5.9) | 445 | (5.2) | 7.6 | (2.14) | 22 | (3.5) | -1.65 | (0.02) | 1.72 | (0.06) | 3.37 | (0.06) |
| Italy (Provincia Basilicata) | 451 | (5.0) | 459 | (4.2) | 12.6 | (2.25) | 32 | (3.3) | -1.69 | (0.03) | 1.49 | (0.08) | 3.18 | (0.08) |
| Italy (Provincia Emilia Romagna) | 510 | (3.7) | 505 | (3.5) | 10.2 | (2.26) | 31 | (3.6) | -1.38 | (0.05) | 1.78 | (0.06) | 3.16 | (0.09) |
| Italy (Provincia Friuli Venezia Giulia) | 534 | (3.3) | 532 | (3.3) | 6.3 | (2.03) | 23 | (3.9) | -1.36 | (0.03) | 1.78 | (0.09) | 3.13 | (0.09) |
| Italy (Provincia Sicilia) | 433 | (7.2) | 439 | (6.2) | 12.7 | (2.29) | 34 | (3.4) | -1.72 | (0.04) | 1.70 | (0.08) | 3.43 | (0.08) |
| Italy (Provincia Liguria) | 488 | (6.7) | 484 | (6.6) | 7.6 | (4.29) | 27 | (7.6) | -1.49 | (0.05) | 1.85 | (0.09) | 3.34 | (0.08) |
| Italy (Provincia Lombardia) | 499 | (6.2) | 504 | (5.6) | 9.9 | (2.63) | 33 | (4.2) | -1.54 | (0.03) | 1.46 | (0.03) | 3.00 | (0.05) |
| Italy (Provincia Piemonte) | 508 | (4.7) | 506 | (3.9) | 12.0 | (2.41) | 32 | (3.6) | -1.51 | (0.07) | 1.77 | (0.11) | 3.29 | (0.10) |
| Italy (Provincia Trento) | 521 | (2.0) | 523 | (2.1) | 8.5 | (1.52) | 30 | (2.8) | -1.43 | (0.04) | 1.51 | (0.09) | 2.95 | (0.10) |
| Italy (Provincia Sardegna) | 449 | (6.1) | 455 | (5.2) | 12.3 | (2.86) | 32 | (3.8) | -1.62 | (0.05) | 1.73 | (0.10) | 3.35 | (0.10) |
| Italy (Provincia Puglia) | 447 | (4.3) | 456 | (3.9) | 7.6 | (2.07) | 23 | (3.3) | -1.72 | (0.04) | 1.49 | (0.12) | 3.21 | (0.12) |
| Italy (Provincia Veneto) | 524 | (5.4) | 524 | (4.7) | 9.4 | (1.97) | 29 | (3.6) | -1.46 | (0.02) | 1.67 | (0.07) | 3.13 | (0.06) |
| Spain (Andalusia) | 474 | (4.0) | 495 | (3.1) | 15.2 | (2.19) | 32 | (2.8) | -2.14 | (0.05) | 1.33 | (0.08) | 3.46 | (0.08) |
| Spain (Basque Country) | 495 | (3.5) | 497 | (2.8) | 10.8 | (1.57) | 28 | (2.0) | -1.63 | (0.05) | 1.56 | (0.04) | 3.19 | (0.06) |
| Spain (Cantabria) | 509 | (3.6) | 515 | (3.0) | 13.1 | (1.74) | 32 | (2.1) | -1.69 | (0.05) | 1.55 | (0.06) | 3.24 | (0.06) |
| Spain (Galicia) | 505 | (3.4) | 514 | (3.1) | 9.0 | (1.96) | 25 | (2.6) | -1.93 | (0.05) | 1.55 | (0.10) | 3.48 | (0.10) |
| Spain (La Rioja) | 520 | (2.5) | 523 | (2.4) | 8.2 | (1.79) | 25 | (2.7) | -1.66 | (0.05) | 1.61 | (0.06) | 3.27 | (0.08) |
| Spain (Castile and Leon) | 520 | (3.9) | 525 | (3.6) | 8.5 | (2.05) | 23 | (3.0) | -1.70 | (0.04) | 1.48 | (0.09) | 3.18 | (0.09) |
| Spain (Navarre) | 511 | (2.9) | 516 | (3.1) | 11.9 | (1.66) | 30 | (2.2) | -1.79 | (0.08) | 1.56 | (0.04) | 3.34 | (0.08) |
| Spain (Aragon) | 513 | (3.9) | 518 | (3.3) | 14.6 | (1.78) | 33 | (2.4) | -1.73 | (0.04) | 1.56 | (0.06) | 3.29 | (0.07) |
| Spain (Catalonia) | 491 | (5.1) | 496 | (4.1) | 13.6 | (2.91) | 31 | (3.1) | -1.77 | (0.06) | 1.61 | (0.14) | 3.38 | (0.14) |
| Spain (Asturias) | 508 | (4.9) | 514 | (3.6) | 15.5 | (2.40) | 32 | (2.5) | -1.74 | (0.06) | 1.64 | (0.14) | 3.38 | (0.14) |
| United Kingdom (Scotland) | 515 | (4.0) | 503 | (3.4) | 15.7 | (2.15) | 50 | (3.7) | -0.98 | (0.04) | 1.55 | (0.03) | 2.53 | (0.05) |
| **Non-adjudicated** | | | | | | | | | | | | | | |
| Belgium (French Community) | 486 | (4.3) | 481 | (3.4) | 20.1 | (2.32) | 49 | (3.3) | -1.41 | (0.07) | 1.57 | (0.05) | 2.98 | (0.09) |
| Belgium (German-Speaking Community) | 516 | (2.9) | 513 | (3.0) | 6.5 | (1.59) | 29 | (3.6) | -1.23 | (0.11) | 1.57 | (0.07) | 2.80 | (0.14) |
| Finland (Finnish Speaking) | 565 | (2.1) | 557 | (1.9) | 8.4 | (0.91) | 31 | (1.6) | -1.06 | (0.04) | 1.48 | (0.02) | 2.54 | (0.04) |
| Finland (Swedish Speaking) | 531 | (6.2) | 524 | (6.8) | 6.3 | (3.05) | 29 | (7.5) | -0.93 | (0.11) | 1.50 | (0.12) | 2.43 | (0.16) |
| United Kingdom (England) | 516 | (2.7) | 509 | (2.3) | 13.7 | (1.26) | 48 | (2.1) | -1.13 | (0.03) | 1.50 | (0.01) | 2.63 | (0.03) |
| United Kingdom (Northern Ireland) | 508 | (3.3) | 508 | (3.2) | 14.8 | (1.82) | 55 | (3.5) | -1.13 | (0.03) | 1.36 | (0.05) | 2.50 | (0.07) |
| United Kingdom (Wales) | 505 | (3.5) | 500 | (3.1) | 14.2 | (1.54) | 48 | (2.8) | -1.12 | (0.04) | 1.47 | (0.04) | 2.58 | (0.05) |

Notes: Values that are statistically significant are indicated in bold (see Annex A3). See Table 4.4a for national data.
1. Single-level bivariate regression of science performance on the ESCS, the slope is the regression coefficient for the ESCS.
2. Student-level regression of science performance on the ESCS and the squared term of the ESCS, the index of curvelinearity is the regression coefficient for the squared term.
StatLink http://dx.doi.org/10.1787/142184405135

Pour consulter la version française intégrale de ce tableau, suivre ce lien :
StatLink http://dx.doi.org/10.1787/152830402855

[Part 2/2]

**Table S4c** Relationship between student performance in science and the PISA index of economic, social and cultural status (ESCS)

Tableau S4c Relation entre la performance des élèves en sciences et l'indice PISA de statut économique, social et culturel (SESC)

| | ESCS mean | | Variability in the ESCS | | Index of curvelinearity[2] | | Index of skewness in the distribution of the ESCS | | Percentage of students that fall within the lowest 15 per cent of the international distribution on the ESCS | |
|---|---|---|---|---|---|---|---|---|---|---|
| | Mean index | S.E. | Standard deviation | S.E. | Score point difference associated with one unit on the ESCS squared | S.E. | Index | S.E. | Approximated by the percentage of students with a value on the PISA index of economic, social and cultural status smaller than -1 | S.E. |
| **Adjudicated** | | | | | | | | | | |
| Belgium (Flemish Community) | 0.21 | (0.02) | 0.90 | (0.01) | **-4.35** | (1.02) | -0.28 | (0.07) | 7.7 | (0.5) |
| Italy (Provincia Autonoma of Bolzano) | -0.08 | (0.02) | 0.82 | (0.01) | -3.91 | (2.70) | 0.17 | (0.07) | 12.7 | (0.9) |
| Italy (Provincia Campania) | -0.12 | (0.04) | 1.02 | (0.02) | -1.10 | (2.23) | 0.31 | (0.05) | 21.0 | (1.5) |
| Italy (Provincia Basilicata) | -0.26 | (0.04) | 0.95 | (0.02) | -1.19 | (1.92) | 0.34 | (0.05) | 24.9 | (1.6) |
| Italy (Provincia Emilia Romagna) | 0.17 | (0.04) | 0.97 | (0.02) | **-5.14** | (1.86) | 0.00 | (0.07) | 13.0 | (1.1) |
| Italy (Provincia Friuli Venezia Giulia) | 0.08 | (0.05) | 0.93 | (0.02) | -2.39 | (2.12) | 0.27 | (0.05) | 12.8 | (1.2) |
| Italy (Provincia Sicilia) | -0.18 | (0.05) | 1.03 | (0.02) | 1.05 | (2.03) | 0.23 | (0.05) | 23.7 | (2.1) |
| Italy (Provincia Liguria) | 0.17 | (0.07) | 0.98 | (0.02) | -9.76 | (2.58) | 0.03 | (0.05) | 13.0 | (1.3) |
| Italy (Provincia Lombardia) | -0.13 | (0.05) | 0.91 | (0.03) | -4.61 | (3.05) | 0.15 | (0.07) | 19.2 | (1.6) |
| Italy (Provincia Piemonte) | 0.09 | (0.07) | 0.99 | (0.03) | **-3.98** | (2.00) | 0.09 | (0.06) | 14.8 | (1.2) |
| Italy (Provincia Trento) | -0.04 | (0.02) | 0.89 | (0.02) | **-6.04** | (2.66) | 0.24 | (0.07) | 14.5 | (0.9) |
| Italy (Provincia Sardegna) | -0.17 | (0.09) | 1.02 | (0.04) | -3.37 | (1.98) | 0.34 | (0.07) | 23.7 | (2.4) |
| Italy (Provincia Puglia) | -0.32 | (0.05) | 0.97 | (0.02) | 2.00 | (2.03) | 0.37 | (0.05) | 28.0 | (2.0) |
| Italy (Provincia Veneto) | 0.00 | (0.05) | 0.92 | (0.02) | **-6.22** | (2.57) | 0.21 | (0.06) | 14.5 | (1.3) |
| Spain (Andalusia) | -0.64 | (0.06) | 1.06 | (0.02) | -1.45 | (1.80) | 0.38 | (0.06) | 41.9 | (2.2) |
| Spain (Basque Country) | -0.04 | (0.04) | 0.99 | (0.01) | -1.59 | (1.09) | 0.01 | (0.04) | 18.4 | (0.9) |
| Spain (Cantabria) | -0.16 | (0.05) | 0.97 | (0.02) | 0.46 | (2.17) | 0.15 | (0.05) | 21.1 | (1.5) |
| Spain (Galicia) | -0.34 | (0.07) | 1.04 | (0.03) | -1.63 | (1.86) | 0.30 | (0.06) | 27.6 | (1.8) |
| Spain (La Rioja) | -0.12 | (0.03) | 1.00 | (0.02) | **-9.78** | (2.15) | 0.23 | (0.05) | 20.7 | (1.2) |
| Spain (Castile and Leon) | -0.21 | (0.05) | 1.01 | (0.02) | -1.19 | (1.95) | 0.20 | (0.05) | 23.7 | (1.5) |
| Spain (Navarre) | -0.14 | (0.04) | 1.02 | (0.02) | 1.75 | (2.25) | 0.10 | (0.05) | 20.6 | (1.1) |
| Spain (Aragon) | -0.14 | (0.05) | 1.02 | (0.02) | **-5.59** | (1.88) | 0.09 | (0.05) | 22.2 | (1.5) |
| Spain (Catalonia) | -0.15 | (0.08) | 1.05 | (0.04) | -0.42 | (3.19) | 0.09 | (0.06) | 23.0 | (1.7) |
| Spain (Asturias) | -0.15 | (0.07) | 1.02 | (0.03) | 0.09 | (1.52) | 0.16 | (0.05) | 20.4 | (1.5) |
| United Kingdom (Scotland) | 0.26 | (0.03) | 0.78 | (0.01) | 2.32 | (2.29) | -0.03 | (0.05) | 4.9 | (0.5) |
| **Non-adjudicated** | | | | | | | | | | |
| Belgium (French Community) | 0.13 | (0.04) | 0.93 | (0.02) | 1.64 | (1.75) | -0.22 | (0.06) | 9.8 | (0.9) |
| Belgium (German-Speaking Community) | 0.14 | (0.03) | 0.86 | (0.02) | -1.78 | (3.30) | 0.07 | (0.08) | 7.7 | (0.9) |
| Finland (Finnish Speaking) | 0.26 | (0.02) | 0.79 | (0.01) | 1.61 | (1.62) | -0.18 | (0.04) | 5.7 | (0.4) |
| Finland (Swedish Speaking) | 0.27 | (0.04) | 0.72 | (0.03) | 4.35 | (7.43) | 0.09 | (0.17) | 3.4 | (1.5) |
| United Kingdom (England) | 0.19 | (0.02) | 0.82 | (0.01) | -0.73 | (1.84) | -0.15 | (0.05) | 6.7 | (0.5) |
| United Kingdom (Northern Ireland) | 0.06 | (0.02) | 0.79 | (0.01) | -2.10 | (2.76) | 0.13 | (0.05) | 7.5 | (0.6) |
| United Kingdom (Wales) | 0.14 | (0.03) | 0.80 | (0.02) | 3.39 | (1.87) | 0.00 | (0.06) | 6.6 | (0.6) |

Notes: Values that are statistically significant are indicated in bold (see Annex A3). See Table 4.4a for national data.
1. Single-level bivariate regression of science performance on the ESCS, the slope is the regression coefficient for the ESCS.
2. Student-level regression of science performance on the ESCS and the squared term of the ESCS, the index of curvelinearity is the regression coefficient for the squared term.

StatLink http://dx.doi.org/10.1787/142184405135

Pour consulter la version française intégrale de ce tableau, suivre ce lien :
StatLink http://dx.doi.org/10.1787/152830402855

[Part 1/1]

**Table S4d** Relationship between science motivational indices and the PISA index of economic, social and cultural status (ESCS)

Tableau S4d   Relation entre les indices de motivation et l'indice PISA de statut économique, social et culturel (SESC)

| | Percentage of variance for the following indices explained by ESCS | | | | | | | | | |
|---|---|---|---|---|---|---|---|---|---|---|
| | Interest in learning science topics | | General interest in science | | Enjoyment of science | | Instrumental motivation to learn science | | Future-oriented motivation to learn science | |
| | % | S.E. | % | S.E. | % | S.E. | % | S.E. | % | S.E. |
| **Adjudicated** | | | | | | | | | | |
| Belgium (Flemish Community) | 0.0 | (0.05) | 5.1 | (0.83) | 3.6 | (0.73) | 1.6 | (0.50) | 2.5 | (0.51) |
| Italy (Provincia Autonoma of Bolzano) | 0.6 | (0.41) | 1.9 | (0.78) | 2.2 | (0.80) | 0.6 | (0.39) | 1.0 | (0.44) |
| Italy (Provincia Campania) | 0.2 | (0.30) | 1.7 | (0.92) | 0.9 | (0.65) | 0.9 | (0.74) | 0.4 | (0.50) |
| Italy (Provincia Basilicata) | 0.3 | (0.37) | 4.2 | (1.32) | 1.8 | (0.82) | 1.4 | (0.71) | 1.1 | (0.65) |
| Italy (Provincia Emilia Romagna) | 0.2 | (0.45) | 1.4 | (1.01) | 1.1 | (0.80) | 2.2 | (1.30) | 1.0 | (0.84) |
| Italy (Provincia Friuli Venezia Giulia) | 0.2 | (0.28) | 1.0 | (0.64) | 1.1 | (0.55) | 1.9 | (0.92) | 1.1 | (0.60) |
| Italy (Provincia Sicilia) | 0.1 | (0.36) | 1.6 | (1.19) | 1.2 | (0.69) | 2.8 | (1.21) | 1.8 | (1.10) |
| Italy (Provincia Liguria) | 0.2 | (0.41) | 1.8 | (1.05) | 0.9 | (0.84) | 2.3 | (1.53) | 0.7 | (0.70) |
| Italy (Provincia Lombardia) | 0.3 | (0.29) | 3.8 | (1.41) | 3.6 | (1.51) | 2.6 | (0.99) | 2.9 | (1.29) |
| Italy (Provincia Piemonte) | 0.0 | (0.19) | 1.9 | (0.93) | 1.9 | (0.65) | 2.0 | (0.80) | 1.4 | (0.56) |
| Italy (Provincia Trento) | 1.0 | (0.59) | 5.8 | (1.31) | 2.8 | (0.97) | 2.8 | (0.97) | 2.4 | (0.84) |
| Italy (Provincia Sardegna) | 0.2 | (0.26) | 3.3 | (1.11) | 1.5 | (0.84) | 1.3 | (1.04) | 0.4 | (0.65) |
| Italy (Provincia Puglia) | 0.0 | (0.20) | 0.9 | (0.62) | 1.4 | (0.63) | 1.3 | (0.71) | 1.7 | (0.59) |
| Italy (Provincia Veneto) | 0.4 | (0.38) | 3.3 | (0.76) | 3.7 | (1.28) | 3.2 | (1.34) | 3.2 | (1.26) |
| Spain (Andalusia) | 0.0 | (0.15) | 3.4 | (0.86) | 2.8 | (1.04) | 3.6 | (0.97) | 2.8 | (0.82) |
| Spain (Basque Country) | 0.5 | (0.26) | 3.3 | (0.59) | 4.3 | (0.83) | 3.0 | (0.66) | 2.8 | (0.60) |
| Spain (Cantabria) | 0.0 | (0.11) | 4.0 | (0.82) | 4.0 | (0.80) | 3.2 | (0.98) | 4.8 | (1.04) |
| Spain (Galicia) | 0.2 | (0.34) | 3.8 | (1.04) | 3.8 | (1.26) | 4.8 | (1.31) | 3.9 | (1.10) |
| Spain (La Rioja) | 0.4 | (0.45) | 1.8 | (0.86) | 2.1 | (0.85) | 2.6 | (0.86) | 2.3 | (0.77) |
| Spain (Castile and Leon) | 0.0 | (0.14) | 0.9 | (0.52) | 2.1 | (0.83) | 1.9 | (0.78) | 1.6 | (0.64) |
| Spain (Navarre) | 0.0 | (0.10) | 1.6 | (0.56) | 2.5 | (1.01) | 3.1 | (1.07) | 3.3 | (0.92) |
| Spain (Aragon) | 0.4 | (0.40) | 2.8 | (0.89) | 4.0 | (0.80) | 3.0 | (0.84) | 4.9 | (0.96) |
| Spain (Catalonia) | 0.0 | (0.16) | 1.9 | (0.83) | 3.5 | (1.48) | 2.3 | (1.31) | 2.6 | (1.29) |
| Spain (Asturias) | 0.0 | (0.16) | 3.0 | (1.13) | 3.0 | (0.93) | 3.2 | (0.83) | 3.7 | (1.08) |
| United Kingdom (Scotland) | 1.9 | (0.64) | 5.5 | (0.95) | 5.9 | (1.02) | 3.3 | (0.94) | 3.3 | (0.87) |
| **Non-adjudicated** | | | | | | | | | | |
| Belgium (French Community) | 0.3 | (0.26) | 3.0 | (1.00) | 2.8 | (0.82) | 0.9 | (0.41) | 1.4 | (0.60) |
| Belgium (German-Speaking Community) | 1.3 | (0.75) | 5.2 | (1.33) | 3.1 | (1.23) | 2.8 | (1.31) | 3.1 | (1.17) |
| Finland  (Finnish Speaking) | 1.5 | (0.46) | 2.7 | (0.55) | 2.2 | (0.51) | 3.3 | (0.57) | 3.2 | (0.59) |
| Finland  (Swedish Speaking) | 0.7 | (1.27) | 2.4 | (2.59) | 2.0 | (1.83) | 1.3 | (1.46) | 2.4 | (2.49) |
| United Kingdom (England) | 0.6 | (0.28) | 1.6 | (0.44) | 2.7 | (0.59) | 1.3 | (0.37) | 1.0 | (0.35) |
| United Kingdom (Northern Ireland) | 1.0 | (0.49) | 2.2 | (0.60) | 2.4 | (0.65) | 1.6 | (0.61) | 1.5 | (0.56) |
| United Kingdom (Wales) | 1.0 | (0.45) | 2.5 | (0.66) | 3.0 | (0.69) | 2.5 | (0.66) | 2.4 | (0.69) |

Note: See Table 4.5 for national data.
*StatLink* ⛭ http://dx.doi.org/10.1787/142184405135

Pour consulter la version française intégrale de ce tableau, suivre ce lien :
*StatLink* ⛭ http://dx.doi.org/10.1787/152830402855

[Part 1/1]

**Table S4e** **Relationship between student perceptions of science and the PISA index of economic, social and cultural status (ESCS)**

Tableau S4e  Relation entre les indices d'attitude à l'égard des sciences et l'indice PISA de statut économique, social et culturel (SESC)

| | Percentage of variance for the following indices explained by ESCS | | | | | | | | | |
| --- | --- | --- | --- | --- | --- | --- | --- | --- | --- | --- |
| | Support for scientific enquiry | | General value of science | | Personal value of science | | Self-efficacy in science | | Self-concept in science | |
| | % | S.E. | % | S.E. | % | S.E. | % | S.E. | % | S.E. |
| **Adjudicated** | | | | | | | | | | |
| Belgium (Flemish Community) | 3.1 | (0.66) | 2.2 | (0.52) | 2.5 | (0.59) | 4.6 | (0.66) | 2.4 | (0.59) |
| Italy (Provincia Autonoma of Bolzano) | 1.9 | (0.70) | 1.5 | (0.65) | 0.9 | (0.49) | 4.7 | (1.17) | 2.2 | (0.85) |
| Italy (Provincia Campania) | 1.1 | (0.67) | 1.7 | (0.67) | 0.2 | (0.36) | 4.1 | (0.94) | 1.7 | (0.92) |
| Italy (Provincia Basilicata) | 3.8 | (1.27) | 3.3 | (1.01) | 1.2 | (0.70) | 4.7 | (1.29) | 1.9 | (0.75) |
| Italy (Provincia Emilia Romagna) | 3.3 | (1.49) | 3.9 | (1.15) | 1.2 | (0.95) | 2.9 | (1.55) | 0.5 | (0.65) |
| Italy (Provincia Friuli Venezia Giulia) | 2.4 | (0.96) | 2.4 | (0.92) | 1.2 | (0.66) | 3.7 | (0.94) | 0.5 | (0.30) |
| Italy (Provincia Sicilia) | 3.4 | (1.13) | 4.7 | (1.29) | 1.7 | (0.75) | 4.7 | (1.57) | 1.1 | (0.59) |
| Italy (Provincia Liguria) | 3.2 | (1.70) | 2.9 | (1.17) | 1.8 | (1.07) | 3.9 | (1.47) | 2.7 | (0.97) |
| Italy (Provincia Lombardia) | 2.9 | (1.04) | 3.2 | (1.14) | 2.7 | (1.07) | 5.7 | (1.47) | 1.7 | (0.88) |
| Italy (Provincia Piemonte) | 2.6 | (1.06) | 3.2 | (0.97) | 2.0 | (0.69) | 5.9 | (1.46) | 2.5 | (1.10) |
| Italy (Provincia Trento) | 6.0 | (1.30) | 5.3 | (1.37) | 3.8 | (1.19) | 4.5 | (1.42) | 1.8 | (0.81) |
| Italy (Provincia Sardegna) | 4.4 | (1.35) | 4.5 | (1.12) | 0.9 | (0.93) | 6.1 | (1.25) | 1.9 | (0.93) |
| Italy (Provincia Puglia) | 2.4 | (1.18) | 1.8 | (0.97) | 1.7 | (0.76) | 1.5 | (0.66) | 0.2 | (0.23) |
| Italy (Provincia Veneto) | 4.3 | (0.99) | 6.1 | (1.51) | 3.4 | (0.99) | 4.4 | (1.05) | 1.9 | (0.73) |
| Spain (Andalusia) | 2.0 | (1.11) | 3.1 | (0.85) | 4.1 | (0.96) | 6.4 | (1.16) | 5.5 | (1.22) |
| Spain (Basque Country) | 2.6 | (0.68) | 3.1 | (0.64) | 3.2 | (0.54) | 3.8 | (0.75) | 4.4 | (0.82) |
| Spain (Cantabria) | 2.0 | (0.89) | 1.9 | (0.78) | 2.7 | (0.72) | 4.8 | (0.96) | 3.8 | (1.07) |
| Spain (Galicia) | 3.2 | (1.13) | 3.4 | (0.92) | 5.4 | (1.49) | 8.4 | (1.51) | 5.7 | (1.14) |
| Spain (La Rioja) | 1.8 | (1.03) | 3.2 | (1.17) | 4.0 | (1.17) | 6.2 | (1.64) | 4.7 | (1.19) |
| Spain (Castile and Leon) | 0.8 | (0.67) | 1.8 | (0.60) | 1.7 | (0.50) | 3.4 | (1.15) | 2.3 | (0.83) |
| Spain (Navarre) | 2.8 | (0.92) | 3.5 | (0.98) | 3.8 | (1.05) | 5.2 | (0.88) | 3.4 | (1.20) |
| Spain (Aragon) | 2.4 | (0.91) | 2.9 | (0.83) | 3.3 | (0.90) | 3.8 | (1.25) | 3.7 | (1.01) |
| Spain (Catalonia) | 2.2 | (1.17) | 3.3 | (1.12) | 3.4 | (1.21) | 5.5 | (1.37) | 2.8 | (1.11) |
| Spain (Asturias) | 0.6 | (0.58) | 2.8 | (0.94) | 3.5 | (0.89) | 7.2 | (1.27) | 3.8 | (1.31) |
| United Kingdom (Scotland) | 6.0 | (1.27) | 7.3 | (1.36) | 6.5 | (1.21) | 10.3 | (1.43) | 3.8 | (0.85) |
| **Non-adjudicated** | | | | | | | | | | |
| Belgium (French Community) | 2.6 | (0.84) | 2.4 | (0.70) | 3.0 | (0.80) | 5.3 | (0.97) | 1.9 | (0.67) |
| Belgium (German-Speaking Community) | 2.9 | (1.17) | 3.0 | (1.24) | 2.9 | (1.14) | 5.3 | (1.39) | 3.4 | (1.40) |
| Finland (Finnish Speaking) | 2.6 | (0.59) | 4.0 | (0.58) | 3.6 | (0.57) | 5.4 | (0.83) | 3.7 | (0.69) |
| Finland (Swedish Speaking) | 2.0 | (2.54) | 3.3 | (2.00) | 3.0 | (3.26) | 4.8 | (2.73) | 5.0 | (2.47) |
| United Kingdom (England) | 2.8 | (0.64) | 3.8 | (0.53) | 2.6 | (0.44) | 8.0 | (0.80) | 2.1 | (0.46) |
| United Kingdom (Northern Ireland) | 3.8 | (0.94) | 3.8 | (0.77) | 2.8 | (0.72) | 7.7 | (1.32) | 1.9 | (0.57) |
| United Kingdom (Wales) | 3.2 | (0.71) | 3.8 | (0.70) | 3.8 | (0.78) | 9.3 | (1.08) | 3.2 | (0.73) |

Note: See Table 4.6 for national data.
*StatLink* http://dx.doi.org/10.1787/142184405135

Pour consulter la version française intégrale de ce tableau, suivre ce lien :
*StatLink* http://dx.doi.org/10.1787/152830402855

[Part 1/1]

**Table S5a** **School admittance policies**[1]

Tableau S5a   Politiques d'admission des établissements

| | Percentage of students in schools where the principal reported the following statements as a "prerequisite" or a "high priority" for admittance at their school | | | | | | | | | | | |
|---|---|---|---|---|---|---|---|---|---|---|---|---|
| | Residence in a particular area | | Students' academic records | | Recommendations of feeder schools | | Parents' endorsement of the instructional or religious philosophy of the school | | Students' needs or desires for a special programme | | Attendance of other family members at the school | |
| | % | S.E. | % | S.E. | % | S.E. | % | S.E. | % | S.E. | % | S.E. |
| **Adjudicated** | | | | | | | | | | | | |
| Belgium (Flemish Community) | 0.5 | (0.3) | 34.9 | (3.9) | 9.4 | (2.7) | 37.2 | (3.9) | 8.0 | (2.3) | 7.4 | (2.2) |
| Italy (Provincia Autonoma of Bolzano) | 8.4 | (0.4) | 5.9 | (0.1) | 1.0 | (0.1) | 10.5 | (0.2) | 25.4 | (0.3) | 2.8 | (0.5) |
| Italy (Provincia Campania) | 22.0 | (7.2) | 8.7 | (4.4) | 7.2 | (3.7) | 5.5 | (3.2) | 22.6 | (5.7) | 28.1 | (6.1) |
| Italy (Provincia Basilicata) | 0.4 | (0.1) | 4.6 | (2.7) | 2.2 | (2.5) | 9.1 | (2.9) | 24.3 | (5.3) | 4.6 | (2.2) |
| Italy (Provincia Emilia Romagna) | 2.5 | (2.2) | 2.7 | (1.6) | 7.9 | (4.0) | 6.9 | (3.7) | 46.6 | (6.4) | 10.1 | (4.4) |
| Italy (Provincia Friuli Venezia Giulia) | 2.1 | (2.1) | 6.9 | (2.6) | 8.2 | (2.9) | 6.5 | (2.5) | 34.1 | (5.0) | 5.1 | (3.0) |
| Italy (Provincia Sicilia) | 2.5 | (2.4) | 5.6 | (3.5) | 14.6 | (7.7) | 23.1 | (8.0) | 43.9 | (8.4) | 11.7 | (4.8) |
| Italy (Provincia Liguria) | 2.7 | (0.7) | 4.9 | (3.4) | 3.8 | (3.0) | 13.3 | (4.5) | 39.0 | (7.4) | 10.5 | (4.1) |
| Italy (Provincia Lombardia) | 7.9 | (4.2) | 4.4 | (3.7) | 2.3 | (2.3) | 12.1 | (4.2) | 48.8 | (7.0) | 2.7 | (2.7) |
| Italy (Provincia Piemonte) | 6.1 | (3.2) | 8.9 | (4.3) | 6.1 | (3.1) | 14.2 | (6.2) | 37.0 | (7.8) | 6.3 | (3.7) |
| Italy (Provincia Trento) | 2.2 | (0.1) | 6.7 | (1.1) | 6.9 | (0.2) | 3.9 | (0.1) | 36.2 | (0.8) | 7.2 | (0.1) |
| Italy (Provincia Sardegna) | 6.2 | (3.8) | 7.0 | (3.9) | 7.4 | (3.7) | 8.7 | (4.1) | 37.6 | (8.6) | 7.3 | (3.9) |
| Italy (Provincia Puglia) | 2.2 | (2.0) | 10.4 | (4.7) | 6.5 | (3.2) | 14.8 | (5.8) | 34.1 | (7.2) | 8.3 | (3.8) |
| Italy (Provincia Veneto) | 0.6 | (0.6) | 5.5 | (3.2) | 5.8 | (3.4) | 9.1 | (3.5) | 25.0 | (6.5) | 2.3 | (2.3) |
| Spain (Andalusia) | 66.3 | (6.4) | 1.5 | (1.6) | 1.4 | (1.4) | 9.3 | (4.2) | 18.0 | (6.2) | 38.3 | (6.8) |
| Spain (Basque Country) | 53.4 | (3.8) | a | a | 0.8 | (0.8) | 19.0 | (3.1) | 12.4 | (2.3) | 28.2 | (3.6) |
| Spain (Cantabria) | 67.4 | (5.7) | a | a | 0.4 | (0.3) | 13.0 | (4.8) | 10.9 | (4.8) | 31.6 | (7.1) |
| Spain (Galicia) | 73.5 | (6.3) | a | a | 2.0 | (2.0) | 17.1 | (3.9) | 15.1 | (4.1) | 18.3 | (5.3) |
| Spain (La Rioja) | 65.4 | (0.4) | a | a | 2.5 | (0.3) | 17.2 | (0.2) | 11.7 | (0.4) | 35.7 | (0.5) |
| Spain (Castile and Leon) | 52.6 | (6.0) | a | a | a | a | 12.2 | (4.3) | 9.8 | (4.4) | 38.3 | (6.2) |
| Spain (Navarre) | 67.1 | (4.8) | 1.8 | (1.9) | 3.3 | (2.3) | 17.1 | (4.7) | 9.8 | (4.3) | 35.8 | (3.6) |
| Spain (Aragon) | 75.1 | (4.5) | 1.5 | (1.5) | a | a | 7.4 | (3.7) | 15.0 | (5.7) | 26.5 | (6.1) |
| Spain (Catalonia) | 67.9 | (8.1) | 4.3 | (3.1) | 8.2 | (3.2) | 13.2 | (3.3) | 14.6 | (6.1) | 69.9 | (6.6) |
| Spain (Asturias) | 75.1 | (6.2) | a | a | a | a | 14.3 | (5.1) | 8.4 | (3.4) | 36.4 | (6.6) |
| United Kingdom (Scotland) | 73.2 | (4.8) | 5.4 | (2.6) | 8.5 | (3.0) | 8.3 | (2.7) | 17.2 | (4.2) | 25.1 | (3.9) |
| **Non-adjudicated** | | | | | | | | | | | | |
| Belgium (French Community) | 5.0 | (2.5) | 13.2 | (3.7) | 4.8 | (2.4) | 44.7 | (5.4) | 19.4 | (4.6) | 13.4 | (3.6) |
| Belgium (German-Speaking Community) | 1.6 | (0.2) | 13.1 | (0.2) | a | a | 32.5 | (0.2) | 36.0 | (0.2) | a | a |
| Finland  (Finnish Speaking) | 77.4 | (3.8) | 4.4 | (1.9) | 2.2 | (1.2) | 10.3 | (2.8) | 17.0 | (3.6) | 12.5 | (3.0) |
| Finland  (Swedish Speaking) | 21.2 | (16.8) | a | a | a | a | a | a | 6.9 | (7.5) | 18.2 | (16.7) |
| United Kingdom (England) | 60.3 | (3.8) | 9.6 | (1.6) | 6.3 | (1.9) | 12.4 | (2.3) | 9.5 | (2.2) | 33.0 | (3.5) |
| United Kingdom (Northern Ireland) | 34.5 | (3.7) | 38.4 | (1.8) | 7.3 | (2.2) | 17.4 | (3.8) | 3.1 | (1.8) | 42.9 | (4.2) |
| United Kingdom (Wales) | 64.4 | (4.5) | 1.8 | (0.9) | 16.3 | (3.4) | 14.8 | (3.6) | 5.4 | (2.1) | 29.9 | (4.0) |

Note: See Table 5.1 for national data.
1. Results based on reports from school principals and reported proportionate to the number of 15-year-olds enrolled in the school.
*StatLink* http://dx.doi.org/10.1787/142184405135

Pour consulter la version française intégrale de ce tableau, suivre ce lien :
*StatLink* http://dx.doi.org/10.1787/152830402855

283

[Part 1/3]

**Table S5b** **Percentage of students and student performance on the science, reading and mathematics scales, by type of school[1]**

Tableau S5b Pourcentage d'élèves et scores des élèves sur les échelles de culture scientifique, de compréhension de l'écrit et de culture mathématique, selon le type d'établissement

| | Government or public schools[2] | | | | | | | | Government-dependent private schools[3] | | | | | | | |
|---|---|---|---|---|---|---|---|---|---|---|---|---|---|---|---|---|
| | % of students | S.E. | Performance on the science scale Mean score | S.E. | Performance on the reading scale Mean score | S.E. | Performance on the mathematics scale Mean score | S.E. | % of students | S.E. | Performance on the science scale Mean score | S.E. | Performance on the reading scale Mean score | S.E. | Performance on the mathematics scale Mean score | S.E. |
| **Adjudicated** | | | | | | | | | | | | | | | | |
| Belgium (Flemish Community) | w | w | w | w | w | w | w | w | w | w | w | w | w | w | w | w |
| Italy (Provincia Autonoma of Bolzano) | 96.6 | (0.1) | 526 | (2.1) | 502 | (2.3) | 513 | (1.9) | 3.1 | (0.1) | 537 | (7.4) | 515 | (7.6) | 529 | (7.4) |
| Italy (Provincia Campania) | 99.2 | (0.7) | 443 | (5.9) | 439 | (5.9) | 437 | (9.1) | c | c | c | c | c | c | c | c |
| Italy (Provincia Basilicata) | 100.0 | (0.0) | 451 | (5.0) | 446 | (6.3) | 443 | (5.1) | c | c | c | c | c | c | c | c |
| Italy (Provincia Emilia Romagna) | 96.3 | (2.3) | 510 | (3.8) | 495 | (4.8) | 494 | (3.6) | 2.1 | (2.1) | c | c | c | c | c | c |
| Italy (Provincia Friuli Venezia Giulia) | 96.8 | (2.4) | 535 | (3.8) | 518 | (4.4) | 513 | (4.0) | c | c | c | c | c | c | c | c |
| Italy (Provincia Sicilia) | 96.9 | (2.8) | 435 | (6.6) | 425 | (8.5) | 427 | (4.9) | 1.2 | (0.9) | c | c | c | c | c | c |
| Italy (Provincia Liguria) | 91.5 | (4.7) | 495 | (5.0) | 490 | (6.1) | 478 | (5.8) | 1.9 | (0.1) | c | c | c | c | c | c |
| Italy (Provincia Lombardia) | 92.8 | (2.8) | 505 | (6.2) | 495 | (7.4) | 491 | (6.9) | 2.1 | (2.0) | c | c | c | c | c | c |
| Italy (Provincia Piemonte) | 89.2 | (5.8) | 507 | (5.4) | 504 | (6.0) | 491 | (4.9) | c | c | c | c | c | c | c | c |
| Italy (Provincia Trento) | 84.7 | (0.3) | 537 | (2.3) | 528 | (2.9) | 523 | (2.6) | 15.3 | (0.3) | 431 | (3.6) | 400 | (3.7) | 423 | (3.8) |
| Italy (Provincia Sardegna) | 97.6 | (2.4) | 451 | (6.4) | 436 | (8.6) | 432 | (7.3) | c | c | c | c | c | c | c | c |
| Italy (Provincia Puglia) | 97.7 | (2.3) | 447 | (4.4) | 440 | (6.7) | 434 | (4.8) | 2.3 | (2.3) | c | c | c | c | c | c |
| Italy (Provincia Veneto) | 91.2 | (3.6) | 531 | (5.6) | 519 | (6.0) | 517 | (6.8) | 4.1 | (3.0) | 421 | (7.9) | 431 | (36.3) | 412 | (12.9) |
| Spain (Andalusia) | 74.7 | (1.6) | 471 | (4.6) | 439 | (4.1) | 459 | (4.9) | 24.1 | (2.5) | 480 | (8.5) | 459 | (11.0) | 473 | (8.5) |
| Spain (Basque Country) | 41.7 | (0.8) | 478 | (4.7) | 469 | (6.9) | 483 | (4.9) | 58.3 | (0.8) | 506 | (5.0) | 500 | (5.3) | 513 | (5.0) |
| Spain (Cantabria) | 65.6 | (2.3) | 504 | (4.1) | 469 | (4.3) | 498 | (3.5) | 32.3 | (3.2) | 516 | (8.9) | 483 | (10.1) | 505 | (6.4) |
| Spain (Galicia) | 70.7 | (0.8) | 497 | (4.1) | 469 | (4.0) | 487 | (3.9) | 18.4 | (3.3) | 523 | (10.5) | 503 | (9.3) | 506 | (13.7) |
| Spain (La Rioja) | 61.1 | (0.2) | 515 | (3.4) | 484 | (3.3) | 523 | (2.9) | 33.5 | (0.3) | 526 | (3.9) | 502 | (3.6) | 531 | (3.5) |
| Spain (Castile and Leon) | 63.5 | (1.8) | 515 | (5.4) | 469 | (4.4) | 507 | (4.6) | 30.7 | (3.7) | 530 | (6.7) | 498 | (6.4) | 526 | (4.5) |
| Spain (Navarre) | 59.4 | (1.5) | 498 | (3.6) | 469 | (3.7) | 500 | (4.4) | 37.7 | (2.5) | 529 | (4.9) | 495 | (4.6) | 536 | (6.6) |
| Spain (Aragon) | 64.3 | (3.7) | 503 | (5.1) | 474 | (6.2) | 504 | (5.8) | 33.5 | (3.5) | 522 | (9.5) | 491 | (11.0) | 518 | (10.8) |
| Spain (Catalonia) | 55.5 | (2.4) | 471 | (6.7) | 458 | (6.3) | 468 | (5.8) | 21.5 | (4.2) | 503 | (10.6) | 486 | (14.0) | 492 | (10.2) |
| Spain (Asturias) | 63.5 | (1.5) | 499 | (6.2) | 467 | (6.2) | 490 | (5.6) | 23.2 | (4.3) | 512 | (9.7) | 486 | (9.1) | 494 | (9.1) |
| United Kingdom (Scotland) | 94.7 | (2.5) | 510 | (3.7) | 498 | (4.1) | 502 | (3.6) | 1.2 | (1.1) | c | c | c | c | c | c |
| **Non-adjudicated** | | | | | | | | | | | | | | | | |
| Belgium (French Community) | w | w | w | w | w | w | w | w | w | w | w | w | w | w | w | w |
| Belgium (German-Speaking Community) | w | w | w | w | w | w | w | w | w | w | w | w | w | w | w | w |
| Finland (Finnish Speaking) | 97.7 | (1.1) | 565 | (2.0) | 548 | (2.3) | 550 | (2.3) | 2.3 | (1.1) | c | c | c | c | c | c |
| Finland (Swedish Speaking) | 95.7 | (3.7) | 533 | (6.1) | 528 | (5.9) | 534 | (7.7) | 4.3 | (3.7) | 482 | (11.4) | 453 | (15.4) | 504 | (11.4) |
| United Kingdom (England) | 93.2 | (1.1) | 511 | (2.8) | 491 | (2.9) | 491 | (2.6) | c | c | c | c | c | c | c | c |
| United Kingdom (Northern Ireland) | 97.4 | (1.5) | 510 | (4.2) | 498 | (4.1) | 495 | (3.5) | 2.6 | (1.5) | c | c | c | c | c | c |
| United Kingdom (Wales) | 98.9 | (0.6) | 504 | (3.3) | 480 | (3.5) | 484 | (2.9) | c | c | c | c | c | c | c | c |

Note: See Table 5.4 for national data.
1. Results based on reports from school principals and reported proportionate to the number of 15-year-olds enrolled in the school.
2. Schools which are directly controlled or managed by: i) a public education authority or agency, or ii) a government agency directly or a governing body, most of whose members are either appointed by a public authority or elected by public franchise.
3. Schools which receive 50% or more of their core funding – funding that supports the basic educational services of the institution – from government agencies.
StatLink http://dx.doi.org/10.1787/142184405135

Pour consulter la version française intégrale de ce tableau, suivre ce lien :
StatLink http://dx.doi.org/10.1787/152830402855

[Part 2/3]

**Table S5b** **Percentage of students and student performance on the science, reading and mathematics scales, by type of school[1]**

Tableau S5b Pourcentage d'élèves et scores des élèves sur les échelles de culture scientifique, de compréhension de l'écrit et de culture mathématique, selon le type d'établissement

| | Government-independent private schools[4] | | | | | | | | Difference in performance on the science scale between public and private schools (government-dependent and government-independent schools combined) | |
| | | | Performance on the science scale | | Performance on the reading scale | | Performance on the mathematics scale | | | |
| | % of students | S.E. | Mean score | S.E. | Mean score | S.E. | Mean score | S.E. | Dif. (Pub. - Priv.) | S.E. |
|---|---|---|---|---|---|---|---|---|---|---|
| **Adjudicated** | | | | | | | | | | |
| Belgium (Flemish Community) | w | w | w | w | w | w | w | w | w | w |
| Italy (Provincia Autonoma of Bolzano) | 0.3 | (0.0) | c | c | c | c | c | c | -8 | (7.4) |
| Italy (Provincia Campania) | 0.8 | (0.7) | c | c | c | c | c | c | c | c |
| Italy (Provincia Basilicata) | c | c | c | c | c | c | c | c | c | c |
| Italy (Provincia Emilia Romagna) | 1.5 | (1.1) | c | c | c | c | c | c | -13 | (6.2) |
| Italy (Provincia Friuli Venezia Giulia) | 3.2 | (2.4) | 496 | (35.3) | 534 | (23.2) | 497 | (43.5) | 39 | (37.3) |
| Italy (Provincia Sicilia) | 1.8 | (2.4) | c | c | c | c | c | c | 72 | (22.1) |
| Italy (Provincia Liguria) | 6.5 | (4.7) | 422 | (34.2) | 429 | (41.1) | 430 | (30.3) | 82 | (21.8) |
| Italy (Provincia Lombardia) | 5.1 | (2.1) | 461 | (58.8) | 466 | (47.7) | 459 | (46.5) | 57 | (43.1) |
| Italy (Provincia Piemonte) | 10.8 | (5.8) | 515 | (37.8) | 517 | (39.5) | 502 | (43.0) | -8 | (40.6) |
| Italy (Provincia Trento) | c | c | c | c | c | c | c | c | 106 | (4.5) |
| Italy (Provincia Sardegna) | 2.4 | (2.4) | c | c | c | c | c | c | c | c |
| Italy (Provincia Puglia) | c | c | c | c | c | c | c | c | c | c |
| Italy (Provincia Veneto) | 4.7 | (2.3) | 508 | (22.0) | 474 | (37.0) | 490 | (20.7) | 64 | (21.8) |
| Spain (Andalusia) | 1.2 | (1.2) | c | c | c | c | c | c | -12 | (8.8) |
| Spain (Basque Country) | c | c | c | c | c | c | c | c | -28 | (6.9) |
| Spain (Cantabria) | 2.0 | (2.0) | c | c | c | c | c | c | -14 | (9.0) |
| Spain (Galicia) | 10.9 | (3.4) | 525 | (4.1) | 503 | (11.9) | 520 | (9.3) | -27 | (8.0) |
| Spain (La Rioja) | 5.4 | (0.2) | 533 | (8.1) | 514 | (8.4) | 531 | (9.2) | -12 | (4.9) |
| Spain (Castile and Leon) | 5.8 | (3.9) | 526 | (9.8) | 479 | (16.5) | 543 | (23.5) | -15 | (7.2) |
| Spain (Navarre) | 2.8 | (2.4) | c | c | c | c | c | c | -32 | (5.3) |
| Spain (Aragon) | 2.2 | (2.1) | c | c | c | c | c | c | -20 | (10.6) |
| Spain (Catalonia) | 23.0 | (4.7) | 528 | (15.4) | 513 | (16.1) | 529 | (18.5) | -46 | (9.5) |
| Spain (Asturias) | 13.3 | (4.2) | 546 | (10.6) | 509 | (6.4) | 534 | (8.2) | -26 | (10.4) |
| United Kingdom (Scotland) | 4.1 | (2.3) | 629 | (5.7) | 581 | (10.5) | 606 | (14.3) | -102 | (15.6) |
| **Non-adjudicated** | | | | | | | | | | |
| Belgium (French Community) | w | w | w | w | w | w | w | w | w | w |
| Belgium (German-Speaking Community) | w | w | w | w | w | w | w | w | w | w |
| Finland (Finnish Speaking) | c | c | c | c | c | c | c | c | c | c |
| Finland (Swedish Speaking) | c | c | c | c | c | c | c | c | 51 | (11.8) |
| United Kingdom (England) | 6.8 | (1.1) | 595 | (9.1) | 576 | (9.9) | 569 | (7.9) | -84 | (9.6) |
| United Kingdom (Northern Ireland) | c | c | c | c | c | c | c | c | c | c |
| United Kingdom (Wales) | 1.1 | (0.6) | c | c | c | c | c | c | c | c |

Note: Values that are statistically significant are indicated in bold (see Annex A3). See Table 5.4 for national data.
1. Results based on reports from school principals and reported proportionate to the number of 15-year-olds enrolled in the school.
4. Schools which receive less than 50% of their core funding – funding that supports the basic educational services of the institution – from government agencies.
*StatLink* http://dx.doi.org/10.1787/142184405135

Pour consulter la version française intégrale de ce tableau, suivre ce lien :
*StatLink* http://dx.doi.org/10.1787/152830402855

285

[Part 3/3]

**Table S5b**  **Percentage of students and student performance on the science, reading and mathematics scales, by type of school[1]**

Tableau S5b   Pourcentage d'élèves et scores des élèves sur les échelles de culture scientifique, de compréhension de l'écrit et de culture mathématique, selon le type d'établissement

| | PISA index of economic, social and cultural status | | | | | | Difference in performance on the science scales between public and private schools after accounting for the PISA index of economic, social and cultural status of: | | | |
| | Public schools | | Private schools (Government-dependent and government-independent) | | Difference | | Students | | Students and schools | |
| | Mean index | S.E | Mean index | S.E. | Dif. (Pub. – Priv.) | S.E | Dif. (Pub. – Priv.) | S.E | Dif. (Pub. – Priv.) | S.E |
|---|---|---|---|---|---|---|---|---|---|---|
| **Adjudicated** | | | | | | | | | | |
| Belgium (Flemish Community) | w | w | w | w | w | w | w | w | w | w |
| Italy (Provincia Autonoma of Bolzano) | -0.10 | (0.02) | 0.32 | (0.08) | **-0.42** | (0.09) | -4 | (7.7) | **31** | (6.5) |
| Italy (Provincia Campania) | -0.13 | (0.04) | c | c | c | c | c | c | c | c |
| Italy (Provincia Basilicata) | -0.26 | (0.04) | c | c | c | c | c | c | c | c |
| Italy (Provincia Emilia Romagna) | 0.14 | (0.04) | 0.62 | (0.34) | -0.49 | (0.34) | 3 | (9.9) | 36 | (32.1) |
| Italy (Provincia Friuli Venezia Giulia) | 0.05 | (0.03) | 1.12 | (0.06) | **-1.07** | (0.08) | 67 | (35.0) | **124** | (31.5) |
| Italy (Provincia Sicilia) | -0.17 | (0.05) | -0.36 | (0.11) | 0.18 | (0.11) | **67** | (19.0) | **55** | (15.2) |
| Italy (Provincia Liguria) | 0.13 | (0.03) | 0.61 | (0.40) | -0.48 | (0.39) | **94** | (29.8) | **114** | (41.3) |
| Italy (Provincia Lombardia) | -0.13 | (0.05) | -0.04 | (0.22) | -0.08 | (0.23) | 59 | (36.9) | **64** | (30.7) |
| Italy (Provincia Piemonte) | 0.01 | (0.05) | 0.79 | (0.37) | **-0.78** | (0.38) | 18 | (30.4) | **65** | (13.7) |
| Italy (Provincia Trento) | 0.04 | (0.02) | -0.49 | (0.04) | **0.53** | (0.04) | **93** | (4.9) | **59** | (5.0) |
| Italy (Provincia Sardegna) | -0.18 | (0.09) | c | c | c | c | c | c | c | c |
| Italy (Provincia Puglia) | -0.31 | (0.05) | c | c | c | c | c | c | c | c |
| Italy (Provincia Veneto) | 0.00 | (0.05) | 0.04 | (0.37) | -0.04 | (0.37) | **65** | (12.7) | **68** | (15.3) |
| Spain (Andalusia) | -0.78 | (0.05) | -0.21 | (0.16) | **-0.57** | (0.16) | 7 | (7.0) | 15 | (9.8) |
| Spain (Basque Country) | -0.24 | (0.04) | 0.10 | (0.07) | **-0.34** | (0.08) | -18 | (5.5) | -9 | (5.4) |
| Spain (Cantabria) | -0.31 | (0.05) | 0.05 | (0.10) | **-0.36** | (0.11) | -2 | (6.9) | 4 | (6.6) |
| Spain (Galicia) | -0.57 | (0.07) | 0.21 | (0.15) | **-0.77** | (0.16) | -9 | (6.4) | -4 | (7.6) |
| Spain (La Rioja) | -0.37 | (0.04) | 0.26 | (0.04) | **-0.62** | (0.06) | 4 | (4.9) | 0 | (6.6) |
| Spain (Castile and Leon) | -0.42 | (0.04) | 0.12 | (0.11) | **-0.53** | (0.11) | -2 | (6.5) | 4 | (7.0) |
| Spain (Navarre) | -0.40 | (0.04) | 0.20 | (0.08) | **-0.60** | (0.10) | -16 | (6.0) | **-11** | (8.1) |
| Spain (Aragon) | -0.32 | (0.08) | 0.11 | (0.12) | **-0.44** | (0.16) | -7 | (8.5) | -2 | (8.8) |
| Spain (Catalonia) | -0.46 | (0.06) | 0.23 | (0.16) | **-0.69** | (0.17) | -27 | (8.2) | -12 | (10.0) |
| Spain (Asturias) | -0.36 | (0.05) | 0.17 | (0.15) | **-0.54** | (0.16) | -9 | (7.2) | -1 | (7.0) |
| United Kingdom (Scotland) | 0.24 | (0.03) | 1.10 | (0.08) | **-0.86** | (0.08) | **-61** | (12.5) | **-29** | (14.5) |
| **Non-adjudicated** | | | | | | | | | | |
| Belgium (French Community) | w | w | w | w | w | w | w | w | w | w |
| Belgium (German-Speaking Community) | w | w | w | w | w | w | w | w | w | w |
| Finland (Finnish Speaking) | 0.25 | (0.02) | c | c | c | c | c | c | c | c |
| Finland (Swedish Speaking) | 0.27 | (0.04) | 0.26 | (0.01) | 0.01 | (0.04) | **32** | (12.4) | **32** | (12.1) |
| United Kingdom (England) | 0.15 | (0.02) | 0.84 | (0.11) | **-0.69** | (0.11) | **-50** | (8.2) | -15 | (10.8) |
| United Kingdom (Northern Ireland) | 0.07 | (0.02) | c | c | c | c | c | c | c | c |
| United Kingdom (Wales) | 0.13 | (0.02) | c | c | c | c | c | c | c | c |

Note: Values that are statistically significant are indicated in bold (see Annex A3). See Table 5.4 for national data.
1. Results based on reports from school principals and reported proportionate to the number of 15-year-olds enrolled in the school.
*StatLink* http://dx.doi.org/10.1787/142184405135

Pour consulter la version française intégrale de ce tableau, suivre ce lien :
*StatLink* http://dx.doi.org/10.1787/152830402855

[Part 1/1]

**Table S5c** **School choice[1]**

Tableau S5c Choix de l'établissement

| | Number of schools competing for students in the same area | | | | | |
| | Two or more other schools | | One other school | | No other schools | |
| | % | S.E. | % | S.E. | % | S.E. |
|---|---|---|---|---|---|---|
| **Adjudicated** | | | | | | |
| Belgium (Flemish Community) | 79.1 | (3.0) | 14.2 | (2.6) | 6.7 | (1.9) |
| Italy (Provincia Autonoma of Bolzano) | 38.1 | (0.4) | 27.2 | (0.3) | 34.7 | (0.4) |
| Italy (Provincia Campania) | 77.6 | (7.2) | 14.2 | (5.6) | 8.2 | (4.8) |
| Italy (Provincia Basilicata) | 69.5 | (5.7) | 4.8 | (3.0) | 25.8 | (5.0) |
| Italy (Provincia Emilia Romagna) | 67.7 | (7.9) | 7.8 | (3.7) | 24.4 | (7.3) |
| Italy (Provincia Friuli Venezia Giulia) | 63.4 | (5.7) | 14.0 | (4.4) | 22.6 | (5.4) |
| Italy (Provincia Sicilia) | 75.1 | (6.5) | 1.5 | (1.5) | 23.4 | (6.3) |
| Italy (Provincia Liguria) | 68.0 | (5.8) | 9.8 | (4.3) | 22.3 | (4.1) |
| Italy (Provincia Lombardia) | 59.7 | (7.0) | 21.8 | (6.9) | 18.5 | (6.5) |
| Italy (Provincia Piemonte) | 71.8 | (6.4) | 8.6 | (4.3) | 19.5 | (4.8) |
| Italy (Provincia Trento) | 62.2 | (0.8) | 17.9 | (0.3) | 19.9 | (0.9) |
| Italy (Provincia Sardegna) | 68.4 | (7.0) | 12.1 | (4.2) | 19.5 | (6.2) |
| Italy (Provincia Puglia) | 70.0 | (7.3) | 16.4 | (5.4) | 13.6 | (5.4) |
| Italy (Provincia Veneto) | 77.3 | (5.1) | 10.3 | (3.9) | 12.4 | (5.3) |
| Spain (Andalusia) | 58.0 | (6.6) | 14.5 | (5.1) | 27.5 | (6.9) |
| Spain (Basque Country) | 81.5 | (3.0) | 15.7 | (2.9) | 2.7 | (1.3) |
| Spain (Cantabria) | 68.0 | (7.2) | 24.9 | (6.7) | 7.1 | (3.1) |
| Spain (Galicia) | 56.0 | (5.6) | 21.1 | (5.7) | 22.9 | (6.2) |
| Spain (La Rioja) | 74.3 | (0.4) | 20.9 | (0.3) | 4.8 | (0.2) |
| Spain (Castile and Leon) | 69.8 | (6.7) | 15.9 | (5.2) | 14.4 | (5.1) |
| Spain (Navarre) | 69.7 | (4.7) | 10.1 | (2.7) | 20.2 | (4.2) |
| Spain (Aragon) | 66.4 | (7.5) | 19.3 | (6.5) | 14.3 | (4.9) |
| Spain (Catalonia) | 63.8 | (5.8) | 22.1 | (6.0) | 14.1 | (5.2) |
| Spain (Asturias) | 57.6 | (5.8) | 30.6 | (5.8) | 11.8 | (4.5) |
| United Kingdom (Scotland) | 45.5 | (5.6) | 18.4 | (4.3) | 36.1 | (5.1) |
| **Non-adjudicated** | | | | | | |
| Belgium (French Community) | 62.4 | (5.3) | 24.9 | (5.0) | 12.8 | (3.9) |
| Belgium (German-Speaking Community) | 73.1 | (0.2) | a | a | 26.9 | (0.2) |
| Finland (Finnish Speaking) | 42.4 | (4.4) | 15.6 | (2.9) | 42.0 | (3.9) |
| Finland (Swedish Speaking) | 1.5 | (0.6) | 14.0 | (14.2) | 84.5 | (14.3) |
| United Kingdom (England) | 87.7 | (2.8) | 7.7 | (2.2) | 4.6 | (1.7) |
| United Kingdom (Northern Ireland) | 90.4 | (2.5) | 3.6 | (1.8) | 6.0 | (1.8) |
| United Kingdom (Wales) | 69.8 | (4.0) | 14.1 | (3.1) | 16.1 | (2.9) |

Note: See Table 5.5 for national data.
1. Results based on reports from school principals and reported proportionate to the number of 15-year-olds enrolled in the school.
*StatLink* http://dx.doi.org/10.1787/142184405135

Pour consulter la version française intégrale de ce tableau, suivre ce lien :
*StatLink* http://dx.doi.org/10.1787/152830402855

[Part 1/1]

**Table S5d** **School accountability to parents and parental expectation for high academic standards[1]**

Tableau S5d  Responsabilité des établissements à l'égard des parents et pressions parentales en faveur de performances scolaires élevées

| | Percentage of students in schools where the principal reported that the school provided information to parents on student performance relative to | | | | | | Parental expectations are characterised by pressure on the school to achieve high academic standards among students from | | | | | |
|---|---|---|---|---|---|---|---|---|---|---|---|---|
| | Other students in the same school | | Other students in other schools | | National or regional benchmarks | | Many parents | | A minority of parents | | Very few parents | |
| | % | S.E. | % | S.E. | % | S.E. | % | S.E. | % | S.E. | % | S.E. |
| **Adjudicated** | | | | | | | | | | | | |
| Belgium (Flemish Community) | 54.1 | (4.2) | 0.4 | (0.3) | 0.3 | (0.3) | 9.1 | (2.1) | 36.2 | (3.6) | 54.6 | (3.8) |
| Italy (Provincia Autonoma of Bolzano) | 30.9 | (0.3) | 22.5 | (0.3) | 21.2 | (0.3) | 13.4 | (0.2) | 54.2 | (0.6) | 32.4 | (0.5) |
| Italy (Provincia Campania) | 29.5 | (7.3) | 15.8 | (6.5) | 16.6 | (5.7) | 34.1 | (5.7) | 47.3 | (6.7) | 18.5 | (5.6) |
| Italy (Provincia Basilicata) | 18.7 | (4.9) | 2.9 | (0.1) | 21.8 | (4.2) | 15.7 | (3.9) | 59.0 | (6.2) | 25.3 | (4.8) |
| Italy (Provincia Emilia Romagna) | 15.4 | (5.2) | 2.9 | (1.8) | 19.2 | (6.6) | 36.3 | (5.6) | 48.7 | (6.6) | 15.1 | (5.1) |
| Italy (Provincia Friuli Venezia Giulia) | 8.8 | (3.3) | 4.9 | (2.0) | 11.7 | (3.0) | 15.1 | (3.7) | 62.3 | (6.0) | 22.6 | (5.0) |
| Italy (Provincia Sicilia) | 16.3 | (6.5) | 14.1 | (5.3) | 16.4 | (5.8) | 26.1 | (7.1) | 58.9 | (7.4) | 15.0 | (4.7) |
| Italy (Provincia Liguria) | 24.6 | (6.6) | 8.8 | (4.2) | 16.7 | (5.6) | 23.2 | (3.0) | 63.0 | (4.5) | 13.8 | (4.4) |
| Italy (Provincia Lombardia) | 11.6 | (5.1) | 8.1 | (4.1) | 25.6 | (6.9) | 13.1 | (3.9) | 57.2 | (6.9) | 29.7 | (6.7) |
| Italy (Provincia Piemonte) | 13.4 | (5.7) | 4.8 | (3.5) | 17.5 | (5.9) | 18.5 | (5.9) | 69.9 | (7.8) | 11.6 | (4.9) |
| Italy (Provincia Trento) | 10.7 | (1.1) | 6.7 | (1.1) | 40.6 | (0.7) | 7.8 | (0.2) | 64.8 | (0.8) | 27.4 | (0.9) |
| Italy (Provincia Sardegna) | 5.8 | (3.1) | 4.9 | (3.1) | 8.0 | (3.6) | 28.4 | (6.5) | 39.6 | (6.3) | 32.0 | (5.8) |
| Italy (Provincia Puglia) | 29.3 | (6.1) | 6.5 | (3.1) | 14.1 | (4.6) | 20.8 | (6.2) | 55.7 | (7.5) | 23.5 | (6.2) |
| Italy (Provincia Veneto) | 19.1 | (6.1) | 18.5 | (5.7) | 25.3 | (6.8) | 22.2 | (4.8) | 57.6 | (8.0) | 20.2 | (7.0) |
| Spain (Andalusia) | 58.8 | (6.9) | 6.4 | (3.8) | 6.2 | (3.4) | 4.7 | (2.7) | 28.4 | (5.9) | 66.9 | (6.0) |
| Spain (Basque Country) | 38.6 | (3.9) | 14.7 | (2.9) | 14.8 | (3.1) | 12.3 | (2.5) | 33.8 | (3.8) | 53.9 | (4.0) |
| Spain (Cantabria) | 47.1 | (7.7) | 18.9 | (5.7) | 18.1 | (5.5) | 2.1 | (2.0) | 21.8 | (4.8) | 76.1 | (5.2) |
| Spain (Galicia) | 41.8 | (5.9) | 7.2 | (3.4) | 5.9 | (3.2) | 3.2 | (2.2) | 22.0 | (6.2) | 74.8 | (6.6) |
| Spain (La Rioja) | 38.0 | (0.4) | 4.1 | (0.1) | 4.3 | (0.1) | 4.2 | (0.2) | 31.8 | (0.6) | 64.0 | (0.6) |
| Spain (Castile and Leon) | 57.3 | (8.6) | 6.6 | (3.7) | 9.3 | (4.1) | a | a | 24.2 | (4.4) | 75.8 | (4.4) |
| Spain (Navarre) | 42.2 | (4.1) | 14.0 | (2.9) | 18.2 | (3.3) | 12.3 | (3.1) | 34.8 | (4.1) | 52.9 | (4.4) |
| Spain (Aragon) | 44.0 | (7.2) | 3.7 | (0.4) | 6.0 | (3.5) | 5.5 | (3.9) | 34.9 | (6.4) | 59.6 | (5.5) |
| Spain (Catalonia) | 23.3 | (6.1) | 5.0 | (3.0) | 2.7 | (2.0) | 16.8 | (4.5) | 37.8 | (5.3) | 45.4 | (6.3) |
| Spain (Asturias) | 32.1 | (6.4) | 2.7 | (1.6) | 8.7 | (3.9) | 5.7 | (3.3) | 31.4 | (6.9) | 63.0 | (7.6) |
| United Kingdom (Scotland) | 33.3 | (4.8) | 37.2 | (5.5) | 79.8 | (4.4) | 30.3 | (4.6) | 55.4 | (5.6) | 14.4 | (4.2) |
| | | | | | | | | | | | | |
| **Non-adjudicated** | | | | | | | | | | | | |
| Belgium (French Community) | 10.0 | (3.1) | 1.4 | (1.4) | 32.6 | (4.8) | 7.7 | (2.9) | 28.9 | (5.0) | 63.4 | (5.3) |
| Belgium (German-Speaking Community) | 28.5 | (0.2) | a | a | a | a | a | a | 28.5 | (0.2) | 71.5 | (0.2) |
| Finland (Finnish Speaking) | 15.0 | (3.2) | 16.0 | (3.1) | 46.0 | (4.5) | 1.4 | (1.0) | 16.6 | (3.4) | 82.0 | (3.5) |
| Finland (Swedish Speaking) | 22.6 | (14.7) | 21.6 | (14.7) | 69.7 | (18.2) | 1.5 | (0.6) | 85.2 | (13.3) | 13.3 | (13.3) |
| United Kingdom (England) | 54.9 | (3.7) | 36.9 | (3.7) | 81.5 | (3.0) | 38.8 | (3.4) | 50.2 | (3.3) | 11.0 | (2.0) |
| United Kingdom (Northern Ireland) | 78.0 | (3.7) | 23.4 | (3.2) | 56.1 | (4.3) | 43.9 | (4.5) | 38.7 | (4.4) | 17.5 | (3.7) |
| United Kingdom (Wales) | 66.4 | (4.2) | 32.5 | (4.2) | 75.8 | (3.6) | 26.6 | (3.8) | 57.9 | (4.8) | 15.5 | (3.4) |

Note: See Tables 5.6 and 5.9 for national data.
1. Results based on reports from school principals and reported proportionate to the number of 15-year-olds enrolled in the school.
*StatLink* ᐧᑎᐧ http://dx.doi.org/10.1787/142184405135

Pour consulter la version française intégrale de ce tableau, suivre ce lien :
*StatLink* ᐧᑎᐧ http://dx.doi.org/10.1787/152830402855

[Part 1/1]

**Table S5e**  Use of achievement data for accountability purposes[1]

Tableau S5e  Usage des résultats scolaires aux fins de responsabilisation

| | Percentage of students in schools where the principal reported that achievement data are | | | | | | | | | |
|---|---|---|---|---|---|---|---|---|---|---|
| | Posted publicly | | Used in evaluation of the principal's performance | | Used in evaluation of teachers' performance | | Used in decisions about instructional resource allocation to the school | | Tracked over time by an administrative authority | |
| | % | S.E. | % | S.E. | % | S.E. | % | S.E. | % | S.E. |
| **Adjudicated** | | | | | | | | | | |
| Belgium (Flemish Community) | 4.3 | (1.3) | 7.2 | (2.3) | 15.2 | (3.0) | 4.5 | (1.7) | 72.2 | (3.5) |
| Italy (Provincia Autonoma of Bolzano) | 11.3 | (0.5) | 20.1 | (0.7) | 8.0 | (0.1) | 21.3 | (0.5) | 52.5 | (0.6) |
| Italy (Provincia Campania) | 28.0 | (6.6) | 36.7 | (6.4) | 27.6 | (4.3) | 58.9 | (6.6) | 25.5 | (6.7) |
| Italy (Provincia Basilicata) | 21.4 | (3.6) | 25.9 | (6.8) | 29.4 | (6.5) | 60.4 | (5.9) | 19.4 | (4.7) |
| Italy (Provincia Emilia Romagna) | 56.8 | (8.3) | 18.0 | (6.0) | 15.3 | (6.1) | 48.8 | (7.6) | 29.3 | (6.0) |
| Italy (Provincia Friuli Venezia Giulia) | 49.4 | (5.0) | 9.3 | (4.1) | 12.4 | (4.1) | 48.6 | (5.6) | 19.9 | (5.0) |
| Italy (Provincia Sicilia) | 19.3 | (6.4) | 24.4 | (5.0) | 20.1 | (5.8) | 65.9 | (7.0) | 14.3 | (5.6) |
| Italy (Provincia Liguria) | 47.6 | (6.1) | 17.2 | (5.0) | 22.8 | (7.0) | 62.8 | (6.4) | 26.2 | (5.6) |
| Italy (Provincia Lombardia) | 36.1 | (6.1) | 28.3 | (7.1) | 34.7 | (6.9) | 52.7 | (7.7) | 26.3 | (6.3) |
| Italy (Provincia Piemonte) | 37.2 | (7.5) | 14.8 | (5.2) | 24.6 | (6.5) | 44.1 | (7.8) | 19.7 | (5.8) |
| Italy (Provincia Trento) | 41.3 | (0.8) | 51.5 | (0.6) | 15.0 | (0.3) | 46.2 | (0.6) | 50.6 | (0.6) |
| Italy (Provincia Sardegna) | 23.9 | (6.0) | 21.7 | (6.9) | 17.8 | (5.6) | 43.7 | (8.2) | 23.2 | (6.3) |
| Italy (Provincia Puglia) | 22.7 | (6.8) | 10.1 | (3.9) | 20.2 | (5.4) | 51.9 | (7.1) | 31.7 | (6.6) |
| Italy (Provincia Veneto) | 43.5 | (7.9) | 18.1 | (5.9) | 22.8 | (5.4) | 67.8 | (8.7) | 17.1 | (6.3) |
| Spain (Andalusia) | 5.8 | (3.0) | 6.5 | (3.4) | 42.3 | (7.9) | 31.5 | (7.1) | 49.1 | (5.9) |
| Spain (Basque Country) | 13.8 | (2.5) | 11.2 | (2.5) | 48.1 | (2.9) | 61.9 | (3.9) | 75.3 | (3.6) |
| Spain (Cantabria) | 9.9 | (2.6) | 9.1 | (3.6) | 47.6 | (8.0) | 44.7 | (6.1) | 77.6 | (5.6) |
| Spain (Galicia) | 5.7 | (3.4) | 7.0 | (3.5) | 31.7 | (6.3) | 27.6 | (4.6) | 54.0 | (6.9) |
| Spain (La Rioja) | 10.0 | (0.3) | 1.2 | (0.1) | 26.2 | (0.5) | 32.4 | (0.4) | 40.5 | (0.5) |
| Spain (Castile and Leon) | 7.9 | (4.5) | 3.8 | (2.8) | 34.3 | (6.4) | 17.1 | (4.5) | 67.9 | (5.6) |
| Spain (Navarre) | 12.4 | (3.4) | 6.1 | (2.7) | 24.1 | (5.7) | 38.3 | (3.6) | 80.4 | (3.9) |
| Spain (Aragon) | 1.6 | (1.7) | 4.5 | (3.2) | 29.2 | (4.8) | 40.6 | (6.7) | 68.7 | (6.3) |
| Spain (Catalonia) | 7.9 | (4.0) | 25.3 | (6.8) | 57.9 | (5.9) | 58.4 | (7.0) | 80.0 | (5.0) |
| Spain (Asturias) | 5.9 | (3.1) | 15.5 | (2.9) | 41.8 | (5.0) | 29.8 | (6.7) | 73.9 | (5.2) |
| United Kingdom (Scotland) | 82.2 | (4.5) | 65.4 | (5.6) | 72.9 | (5.2) | 41.4 | (5.4) | 98.6 | (1.5) |
| **Non-adjudicated** | | | | | | | | | | |
| Belgium (French Community) | 5.9 | (2.8) | 6.0 | (2.7) | 13.9 | (3.7) | 49.4 | (5.2) | 35.8 | (5.8) |
| Belgium (German-Speaking Community) | a | a | 3.7 | (0.0) | a | a | 9.0 | (0.1) | 8.6 | (0.0) |
| Finland  (Finnish Speaking) | 4.4 | (1.5) | 3.1 | (1.4) | 13.9 | (2.9) | 7.3 | (2.2) | 56.6 | (4.2) |
| Finland  (Swedish Speaking) | 5.8 | (6.3) | a | a | 12.7 | (12.5) | 5.8 | (6.3) | 5.8 | (6.3) |
| United Kingdom (England) | 95.2 | (1.8) | 94.3 | (1.6) | 96.7 | (1.5) | 66.8 | (4.4) | 91.9 | (1.8) |
| United Kingdom (Northern Ireland) | 80.9 | (3.5) | 63.8 | (4.5) | 63.0 | (4.3) | 41.1 | (3.9) | 81.8 | (3.6) |
| United Kingdom (Wales) | 74.5 | (3.5) | 93.5 | (2.3) | 93.8 | (2.3) | 53.7 | (4.1) | 98.3 | (1.3) |

Note: See Table 5.8 for national data.
1. Results based on reports from school principals and reported proportionate to the number of 15-year-olds enrolled in the school.
*StatLink* http://dx.doi.org/10.1787/142184405135

Pour consulter la version française intégrale de ce tableau, suivre ce lien :
*StatLink* http://dx.doi.org/10.1787/152830402855

[Part 1/2]

**Table S5f  Index of teacher shortage and student performance on the science scale, by quarters of the index[1]**

Tableau S5f  Indice de pénurie d'enseignants et performance des élèves sur l'échelle de culture scientifique, par quartile de l'indice

| | Index of teacher shortage | | | | | | | | | |
|---|---|---|---|---|---|---|---|---|---|---|
| | All students | | Bottom quarter | | Second quarter | | Third quarter | | Top quarter | |
| | Mean index | S.E. | Mean index | S.E. | Mean index | S.E. | Mean index | S.E. | Mean index | S.E. |
| **Adjudicated** | | | | | | | | | | |
| Belgium (Flemish Community) | 0.00 | (0.07) | -1.06 | (0.00) | -0.44 | (0.05) | 0.40 | (0.03) | 1.11 | (0.05) |
| Italy (Provincia Autonoma of Bolzano) | 0.48 | (0.01) | -0.60 | (0.02) | 0.42 | (0.01) | 0.79 | (0.00) | 1.32 | (0.01) |
| Italy (Provincia Campania) | c | c | c | c | c | c | c | c | c | c |
| Italy (Provincia Basilicata) | c | c | c | c | c | c | c | c | c | c |
| Italy (Provincia Emilia Romagna) | 0.24 | (0.13) | -1.06 | (0.00) | 0.02 | (0.06) | 0.69 | (0.04) | 1.32 | (0.05) |
| Italy (Provincia Friuli Venezia Giulia) | 0.00 | (0.11) | -1.06 | (0.00) | -0.60 | (0.08) | 0.41 | (0.06) | 1.27 | (0.08) |
| Italy (Provincia Sicilia) | 0.02 | (0.16) | -1.06 | (0.00) | -0.67 | (0.13) | 0.62 | (0.05) | 1.18 | (0.10) |
| Italy (Provincia Liguria) | -0.13 | (0.13) | -1.06 | (0.00) | -0.79 | (0.09) | 0.34 | (0.05) | 1.00 | (0.09) |
| Italy (Provincia Lombardia) | 0.26 | (0.17) | -1.01 | (0.02) | 0.01 | (0.08) | 0.74 | (0.02) | 1.30 | (0.10) |
| Italy (Provincia Piemonte) | 0.22 | (0.12) | -1.06 | (0.00) | -0.04 | (0.06) | 0.67 | (0.03) | 1.30 | (0.11) |
| Italy (Provincia Trento) | 0.57 | (0.02) | -0.53 | (0.03) | 0.55 | (0.01) | 0.86 | (0.00) | 1.42 | (0.01) |
| Italy (Provincia Sardegna) | 0.07 | (0.15) | -1.06 | (0.00) | -0.40 | (0.09) | 0.54 | (0.04) | 1.20 | (0.09) |
| Italy (Provincia Puglia) | -0.10 | (0.14) | -1.06 | (0.00) | -0.70 | (0.07) | 0.40 | (0.05) | 0.98 | (0.10) |
| Italy (Provincia Veneto) | 0.33 | (0.13) | -0.73 | (0.11) | 0.21 | (0.04) | 0.69 | (0.02) | 1.15 | (0.07) |
| Spain (Andalusia) | c | c | c | c | c | c | c | c | c | c |
| Spain (Basque Country) | c | c | c | c | c | c | c | c | c | c |
| Spain (Cantabria) | c | c | c | c | c | c | c | c | c | c |
| Spain (Galicia) | c | c | c | c | c | c | c | c | c | c |
| Spain (La Rioja) | c | c | c | c | c | c | c | c | c | c |
| Spain (Castile and Leon) | c | c | c | c | c | c | c | c | c | c |
| Spain (Navarre) | c | c | c | c | c | c | c | c | c | c |
| Spain (Aragon) | c | c | c | c | c | c | c | c | c | c |
| Spain (Catalonia) | c | c | c | c | c | c | c | c | c | c |
| Spain (Asturias) | c | c | c | c | c | c | c | c | c | c |
| United Kingdom (Scotland) | 0.29 | (0.11) | -1.04 | (0.01) | -0.06 | (0.05) | 0.65 | (0.04) | 1.62 | (0.09) |
| **Non-adjudicated** | | | | | | | | | | |
| Belgium (French Community) | 1.14 | (0.10) | -0.01 | (0.10) | 0.82 | (0.03) | 1.50 | (0.03) | 2.24 | (0.11) |
| Belgium (German-Speaking Community) | 0.92 | (0.00) | 0.05 | (0.00) | 0.77 | (0.02) | 1.23 | (0.00) | 1.62 | (0.00) |
| Finland (Finnish Speaking) | -0.31 | (0.05) | -1.06 | (0.00) | -0.48 | (0.03) | -0.15 | (0.02) | 0.45 | (0.05) |
| Finland (Swedish Speaking) | 0.29 | (0.19) | -0.42 | (0.16) | 0.05 | (0.10) | 0.53 | (0.08) | 1.02 | (0.11) |
| United Kingdom (England) | 0.11 | (0.06) | -1.06 | (0.00) | -0.31 | (0.04) | 0.46 | (0.02) | 1.36 | (0.08) |
| United Kingdom (Northern Ireland) | c | c | c | c | c | c | c | c | c | c |
| United Kingdom (Wales) | c | c | c | c | c | c | c | c | c | c |

| | Performance on the science scale by quarters of the index of teacher shortage | | | | | | | |
|---|---|---|---|---|---|---|---|---|
| | Bottom quarter | | Second quarter | | Third quarter | | Top quarter | |
| | Mean score | S.E. | Mean score | S.E. | Mean score | S.E. | Mean score | S.E. |
| **Adjudicated** | | | | | | | | |
| Belgium (Flemish Community) | **550** | (7.8) | 530 | (7.4) | 522 | (11.3) | **519** | (8.2) |
| Italy (Provincia Autonoma of Bolzano) | 519 | (4.2) | 517 | (4.2) | 549 | (3.4) | 520 | (4.9) |
| Italy (Provincia Campania) | c | c | c | c | c | c | c | c |
| Italy (Provincia Basilicata) | c | c | c | c | c | c | c | c |
| Italy (Provincia Emilia Romagna) | 519 | (16.3) | 491 | (17.0) | 519 | (16.2) | 512 | (15.0) |
| Italy (Provincia Friuli Venezia Giulia) | **514** | (8.2) | 521 | (6.9) | 556 | (11.7) | **550** | (8.2) |
| Italy (Provincia Sicilia) | 401 | (14.7) | 413 | (15.1) | 473 | (17.9) | 446 | (18.7) |
| Italy (Provincia Liguria) | 496 | (10.7) | 490 | (12.4) | 480 | (16.1) | 486 | (11.9) |
| Italy (Provincia Lombardia) | 507 | (19.9) | 485 | (16.2) | 505 | (11.7) | 486 | (23.9) |
| Italy (Provincia Piemonte) | 506 | (12.7) | 493 | (18.4) | 535 | (15.2) | 501 | (17.9) |
| Italy (Provincia Trento) | **487** | (5.5) | 532 | (5.1) | 539 | (4.3) | **529** | (3.9) |
| Italy (Provincia Sardegna) | 439 | (12.7) | 458 | (17.7) | 455 | (9.3) | 443 | (15.7) |
| Italy (Provincia Puglia) | 433 | (9.5) | 437 | (11.8) | 474 | (7.5) | 448 | (13.7) |
| Italy (Provincia Veneto) | 509 | (14.8) | 522 | (12.9) | 522 | (15.2) | 547 | (17.5) |
| Spain (Andalusia) | c | c | c | c | c | c | c | c |
| Spain (Basque Country) | c | c | c | c | c | c | c | c |
| Spain (Cantabria) | c | c | c | c | c | c | c | c |
| Spain (Galicia) | c | c | c | c | c | c | c | c |
| Spain (La Rioja) | c | c | c | c | c | c | c | c |
| Spain (Castile and Leon) | c | c | c | c | c | c | c | c |
| Spain (Navarre) | c | c | c | c | c | c | c | c |
| Spain (Aragon) | c | c | c | c | c | c | c | c |
| Spain (Catalonia) | c | c | c | c | c | c | c | c |
| Spain (Asturias) | c | c | c | c | c | c | c | c |
| United Kingdom (Scotland) | **529** | (10.0) | 519 | (7.9) | 516 | (9.2) | **500** | (8.7) |
| **Non-adjudicated** | | | | | | | | |
| Belgium (French Community) | **505** | (12.6) | 499 | (13.3) | 486 | (11.0) | **461** | (13.6) |
| Belgium (German-Speaking Community) | 554 | (5.8) | 523 | (6.0) | 444 | (6.2) | 543 | (6.0) |
| Finland (Finnish Speaking) | 571 | (3.6) | 561 | (4.3) | 563 | (3.9) | 564 | (4.3) |
| Finland (Swedish Speaking) | 524 | (13.5) | 530 | (18.4) | 531 | (7.6) | 537 | (9.7) |
| United Kingdom (England) | **528** | (10.1) | 529 | (6.7) | 513 | (7.3) | **502** | (6.6) |
| United Kingdom (Northern Ireland) | c | c | c | c | c | c | c | c |
| United Kingdom (Wales) | c | c | c | c | c | c | c | c |

Note: Values that are statistically significant are indicated in bold (see Annex A3). See Table 5.14 for national data.
1. Results based on reports from school principals and reported proportionate to the number of 15-year-olds enrolled in the school.
*StatLink* http://dx.doi.org/10.1787/142184405135

Pour consulter la version française intégrale de ce tableau, suivre ce lien :
*StatLink* http://dx.doi.org/10.1787/152830402855

[Part 2/2]

**Table S5f** **Index of teacher shortage and student performance on the science scale, by quarters of the index[1]**

Tableau S5f  Indice de pénurie d'enseignants et performance des élèves sur l'échelle de culture scientifique, par quartile de l'indice

| | Change in the science score per unit of the index of teacher shortage | | Increased likelihood of students in the top quarter of this index scoring in the bottom quarter of the science performance distribution | | Explained variance in student performance (r-squared X 100) | |
|---|---|---|---|---|---|---|
| | Effect | S.E. | Ratio | S.E. | % | S.E. |
| **Adjudicated** | | | | | | |
| Belgium (Flemish Community) | **-14.1** | (5.95) | **0.7** | (0.15) | 1.8 | (1.52) |
| Italy (Provincia Autonoma of Bolzano) | -1.0 | (2.60) | 1.1 | (0.13) | 0.0 | (0.06) |
| Italy (Provincia Campania) | c | c | c | c | c | c |
| Italy (Provincia Basilicata) | c | c | c | c | c | c |
| Italy (Provincia Emilia Romagna) | 1.1 | (10.16) | 0.8 | (0.27) | 0.0 | (0.76) |
| Italy (Provincia Friuli Venezia Giulia) | **16.2** | (4.52) | 1.4 | (0.30) | 3.4 | (1.84) |
| Italy (Provincia Sicilia) | **26.7** | (10.28) | 1.6 | (0.40) | 6.8 | (4.84) |
| Italy (Provincia Liguria) | -6.5 | (8.31) | 0.9 | (0.22) | 0.4 | (0.98) |
| Italy (Provincia Lombardia) | -8.0 | (14.06) | 0.9 | (0.36) | 0.6 | (2.27) |
| Italy (Provincia Piemonte) | 2.4 | (8.73) | 1.0 | (0.28) | 0.1 | (0.70) |
| Italy (Provincia Trento) | **23.8** | (3.90) | **2.1** | (0.15) | 4.1 | (1.20) |
| Italy (Provincia Sardegna) | 1.7 | (10.09) | 1.3 | (0.33) | 0.0 | (0.93) |
| Italy (Provincia Puglia) | 9.2 | (8.84) | 1.3 | (0.26) | 0.9 | (1.82) |
| Italy (Provincia Veneto) | 19.5 | (13.11) | 1.3 | (0.40) | 2.7 | (3.73) |
| Spain (Andalusia) | c | c | c | c | c | c |
| Spain (Basque Country) | c | c | c | c | c | c |
| Spain (Cantabria) | c | c | c | c | c | c |
| Spain (Galicia) | c | c | c | c | c | c |
| Spain (La Rioja) | c | c | c | c | c | c |
| Spain (Castile and Leon) | c | c | c | c | c | c |
| Spain (Navarre) | c | c | c | c | c | c |
| Spain (Aragon) | c | c | c | c | c | c |
| Spain (Catalonia) | c | c | c | c | c | c |
| Spain (Asturias) | c | c | c | c | c | c |
| United Kingdom (Scotland) | **-11.5** | (5.17) | 0.8 | (0.13) | 1.4 | (1.24) |
| **Non-adjudicated** | | | | | | |
| Belgium (French Community) | **-23.5** | (7.03) | 0.7 | (0.19) | 4.6 | (2.82) |
| Belgium (German-Speaking Community) | **-26.7** | (4.80) | **0.5** | (0.09) | 2.9 | (0.97) |
| Finland (Finnish Speaking) | **-6.1** | (3.57) | 0.9 | (0.08) | 0.2 | (0.23) |
| Finland (Swedish Speaking) | 9.4 | (8.65) | 1.2 | (0.31) | 0.4 | (0.91) |
| United Kingdom (England) | **-12.4** | (4.39) | 0.9 | (0.13) | 1.3 | (0.90) |
| United Kingdom (Northern Ireland) | c | c | c | c | c | c |
| United Kingdom (Wales) | c | c | c | c | c | c |

Note: Values that are statistically significant are indicated in bold (see Annex A3). See Table 5.14 for national data.
1. Results based on reports from school principals and reported proportionate to the number of 15-year-olds enrolled in the school.
*StatLink* ▨▨▨ http://dx.doi.org/10.1787/142184405135

Pour consulter la version française intégrale de ce tableau, suivre ce lien :
*StatLink* ▨▨▨ http://dx.doi.org/10.1787/152830402855

[Part 1/2]

**Table S5g**

**School principals' perceptions of the quality of the schools' educational resources and student performance on the science scale, by quarters of the index[1]**

Tableau S5g  Qualité des moyens éducatifs selon l'avis du chef d'établissement et performance des élèves sur l'échelle de culture scientifique, par quartile de l'indice

| | Index of the quality of the schools' educational resources | | | | | | | | | |
| | All students | | Bottom quarter | | Second quarter | | Third quarter | | Top quarter | |
| | Mean index | S.E. | Mean index | S.E. | Mean index | S.E. | Mean index | S.E. | Mean index | S.E. |
|---|---|---|---|---|---|---|---|---|---|---|
| **Adjudicated** | | | | | | | | | | |
| Belgium (Flemish Community) | 0.07 | (0.06) | -0.91 | (0.05) | -0.23 | (0.02) | 0.24 | (0.02) | 1.18 | (0.09) |
| Italy (Provincia Autonoma of Bolzano) | 0.50 | (0.01) | -0.68 | (0.01) | 0.08 | (0.00) | 0.67 | (0.01) | 1.95 | (0.01) |
| Italy (Provincia Campania) | -0.01 | (0.16) | -1.30 | (0.09) | -0.49 | (0.06) | 0.19 | (0.04) | 1.57 | (0.18) |
| Italy (Provincia Basilicata) | -0.08 | (0.10) | -1.22 | (0.07) | -0.40 | (0.07) | 0.14 | (0.04) | 1.17 | (0.08) |
| Italy (Provincia Emilia Romagna) | 0.23 | (0.10) | -0.76 | (0.03) | -0.23 | (0.04) | 0.31 | (0.04) | 1.62 | (0.14) |
| Italy (Provincia Friuli Venezia Giulia) | 0.12 | (0.15) | -1.10 | (0.08) | -0.39 | (0.02) | 0.23 | (0.05) | 1.75 | (0.09) |
| Italy (Provincia Sicilia) | 0.01 | (0.14) | -1.05 | (0.14) | -0.36 | (0.05) | 0.10 | (0.04) | 1.35 | (0.21) |
| Italy (Provincia Liguria) | 0.25 | (0.14) | -0.66 | (0.07) | -0.16 | (0.02) | 0.25 | (0.03) | 1.56 | (0.11) |
| Italy (Provincia Lombardia) | 0.44 | (0.11) | -0.54 | (0.10) | 0.19 | (0.03) | 0.56 | (0.04) | 1.55 | (0.14) |
| Italy (Provincia Piemonte) | 0.17 | (0.12) | -0.83 | (0.09) | -0.25 | (0.05) | 0.58 | (0.04) | 1.21 | (0.10) |
| Italy (Provincia Trento) | 0.53 | (0.01) | -0.48 | (0.02) | 0.13 | (0.00) | 0.77 | (0.01) | 1.70 | (0.01) |
| Italy (Provincia Sardegna) | -0.24 | (0.09) | -1.29 | (0.07) | -0.57 | (0.03) | 0.04 | (0.04) | 0.84 | (0.14) |
| Italy (Provincia Puglia) | 0.13 | (0.17) | -1.01 | (0.16) | -0.37 | (0.03) | 0.22 | (0.07) | 1.66 | (0.19) |
| Italy (Provincia Veneto) | 0.23 | (0.12) | -0.80 | (0.09) | -0.12 | (0.04) | 0.40 | (0.05) | 1.45 | (0.18) |
| Spain (Andalusia) | -0.39 | (0.12) | -1.65 | (0.14) | -0.61 | (0.04) | -0.10 | (0.04) | 0.81 | (0.21) |
| Spain (Basque Country) | 0.09 | (0.07) | -1.04 | (0.06) | -0.20 | (0.03) | 0.35 | (0.02) | 1.24 | (0.09) |
| Spain (Cantabria) | 0.00 | (0.11) | -0.83 | (0.07) | -0.26 | (0.04) | -0.02 | (0.02) | 1.14 | (0.15) |
| Spain (Galicia) | -0.21 | (0.14) | -1.22 | (0.11) | -0.53 | (0.03) | -0.09 | (0.03) | 1.01 | (0.20) |
| Spain (La Rioja) | 0.17 | (0.01) | -0.81 | (0.01) | -0.22 | (0.01) | 0.40 | (0.01) | 1.34 | (0.02) |
| Spain (Castile and Leon) | 0.21 | (0.13) | -0.83 | (0.13) | -0.22 | (0.02) | 0.32 | (0.05) | 1.57 | (0.19) |
| Spain (Navarre) | 0.24 | (0.10) | -0.83 | (0.09) | -0.03 | (0.02) | 0.36 | (0.02) | 1.45 | (0.12) |
| Spain (Aragon) | 0.22 | (0.11) | -0.82 | (0.09) | -0.12 | (0.04) | 0.42 | (0.06) | 1.40 | (0.17) |
| Spain (Catalonia) | 0.23 | (0.16) | -0.89 | (0.08) | -0.30 | (0.06) | 0.45 | (0.04) | 1.68 | (0.18) |
| Spain (Asturias) | 0.15 | (0.12) | -0.89 | (0.14) | -0.21 | (0.04) | 0.32 | (0.04) | 1.38 | (0.14) |
| United Kingdom (Scotland) | 0.58 | (0.11) | -0.62 | (0.08) | 0.08 | (0.03) | 0.92 | (0.06) | 1.94 | (0.06) |
| **Non-adjudicated** | | | | | | | | | | |
| Belgium (French Community) | -0.16 | (0.10) | -1.19 | (0.06) | -0.60 | (0.02) | -0.12 | (0.04) | 1.28 | (0.14) |
| Belgium (German-Speaking Community) | -0.53 | (0.00) | -1.12 | (0.01) | -0.62 | (0.00) | -0.34 | (0.01) | -0.06 | (0.01) |
| Finland (Finnish Speaking) | -0.23 | (0.06) | -1.22 | (0.07) | -0.46 | (0.03) | -0.01 | (0.01) | 0.78 | (0.11) |
| Finland (Swedish Speaking) | -0.17 | (0.26) | -1.07 | (0.33) | -0.33 | (0.06) | 0.23 | (0.12) | 0.49 | (0.02) |
| United Kingdom (England) | 0.26 | (0.09) | -0.97 | (0.06) | -0.22 | (0.03) | 0.52 | (0.03) | 1.73 | (0.06) |
| United Kingdom (Northern Ireland) | 0.38 | (0.09) | -0.77 | (0.04) | -0.19 | (0.02) | 0.47 | (0.05) | 2.01 | (0.04) |
| United Kingdom (Wales) | -0.12 | (0.08) | -1.17 | (0.06) | -0.53 | (0.03) | 0.01 | (0.03) | 1.20 | (0.11) |

Note: See Table 5.15 for national data.
1. Results based on reports from school principals and reported proportionate to the number of 15-year-olds enrolled in the school.
StatLink http://dx.doi.org/10.1787/142184405135

Pour consulter la version française intégrale de ce tableau, suivre ce lien :
StatLink http://dx.doi.org/10.1787/152830402855

[Part 2/2]

**Table S5g** School principals' perception of the quality of the schools' educational resources and student performance on the science scale, by quarters of the index[1]

Tableau S5g Qualité des moyens éducatifs selon l'avis du chef d'établissement et performance des élèves sur l'échelle de culture scientifique, par quartile de l'indice

| | Performance on the science scale by quarters of this index | | | | | | | Change in the science score per unit of this index | | Increased likelihood of students in the top quarter of this index scoring in the bottom quarter of the science performance distribution | | Explained variance in student performance (r-squared X 100) | |
| | Bottom quarter | | Second quarter | | Third quarter | | Top quarter | | | | | | | |
| | Mean score | S.E. | Mean score | S.E. | Mean score | S.E. | Mean score | S.E. | Effect | S.E. | Ratio | S.E. | % | S.E. |
|---|---|---|---|---|---|---|---|---|---|---|---|---|---|---|
| **Adjudicated** | | | | | | | | | | | | | | |
| Belgium (Flemish Community) | 532 | (8.8) | 542 | (9.1) | 536 | (13.1) | 508 | (9.7) | **-11.4** | (5.65) | 0.9 | (0.19) | 1.1 | (1.10) |
| Italy (Provincia Autonoma of Bolzano) | 516 | (5.0) | 534 | (4.0) | 529 | (3.6) | 524 | (4.5) | -1.3 | (2.13) | 1.2 | (0.13) | 0.0 | (0.09) |
| Italy (Provincia Campania) | **403** | (9.9) | 445 | (14.0) | 460 | (8.5) | **462** | (15.1) | **18.6** | (6.24) | **2.0** | (0.43) | 6.4 | (4.16) |
| Italy (Provincia Basilicata) | 451 | (13.1) | 427 | (12.1) | 479 | (13.8) | 448 | (10.8) | 3.1 | (5.97) | 1.0 | (0.43) | 0.1 | (0.62) |
| Italy (Provincia Emilia Romagna) | 487 | (19.4) | 492 | (13.2) | 531 | (10.6) | 528 | (9.2) | **18.6** | (5.77) | 1.8 | (0.49) | 3.3 | (1.95) |
| Italy (Provincia Friuli Venezia Giulia) | 533 | (14.1) | 512 | (6.0) | 537 | (9.9) | 559 | (9.9) | 10.2 | (5.70) | 1.0 | (0.32) | 1.8 | (2.05) |
| Italy (Provincia Sicilia) | **455** | (15.0) | 435 | (20.0) | 428 | (18.6) | **416** | (11.8) | -9.7 | (6.43) | 0.7 | (0.19) | 0.9 | (1.10) |
| Italy (Provincia Liguria) | 467 | (15.9) | 517 | (12.3) | 492 | (7.2) | 476 | (13.8) | 0.6 | (8.98) | 1.7 | (0.36) | 0.0 | (0.55) |
| Italy (Provincia Lombardia) | 498 | (16.6) | 486 | (18.0) | 475 | (16.8) | 524 | (13.8) | 15.2 | (9.32) | 1.0 | (0.34) | 1.7 | (2.11) |
| Italy (Provincia Piemonte) | 493 | (18.0) | 519 | (16.6) | 511 | (15.1) | 511 | (11.9) | 4.9 | (11.75) | 1.5 | (0.51) | 0.2 | (1.34) |
| Italy (Provincia Trento) | 508 | (5.8) | 543 | (3.9) | 516 | (3.6) | 520 | (3.8) | 1.3 | (2.28) | **1.6** | (0.13) | 0.0 | (0.08) |
| Italy (Provincia Sardegna) | 422 | (19.4) | 472 | (16.1) | 447 | (15.6) | 447 | (13.6) | 7.9 | (9.55) | 1.7 | (0.57) | 0.5 | (1.24) |
| Italy (Provincia Puglia) | 450 | (13.4) | 444 | (12.2) | 449 | (12.7) | 447 | (12.5) | 0.8 | (7.11) | 1.0 | (0.33) | 0.0 | (0.67) |
| Italy (Provincia Veneto) | 526 | (17.0) | 539 | (13.5) | 514 | (17.6) | 520 | (16.8) | 1.9 | (10.28) | 1.0 | (0.30) | 0.1 | (0.77) |
| Spain (Andalusia) | 487 | (8.7) | 452 | (7.5) | 480 | (6.8) | 476 | (8.0) | 1.7 | (3.41) | 0.8 | (0.17) | 0.0 | (0.20) |
| Spain (Basque Country) | 486 | (7.2) | 500 | (5.4) | 504 | (8.9) | 488 | (6.2) | 0.4 | (3.72) | 1.2 | (0.17) | 0.0 | (0.13) |
| Spain (Cantabria) | 515 | (8.1) | 513 | (7.8) | 502 | (7.5) | 508 | (7.4) | -2.2 | (4.47) | 0.9 | (0.16) | 0.0 | (0.19) |
| Spain (Galicia) | 501 | (5.6) | 506 | (7.3) | 503 | (7.8) | 509 | (10.5) | -0.7 | (5.27) | 1.1 | (0.12) | 0.0 | (0.27) |
| Spain (La Rioja) | 527 | (6.2) | 521 | (6.1) | 517 | (5.2) | 513 | (5.0) | -6.1 | (3.17) | 0.9 | (0.15) | 0.4 | (0.37) |
| Spain (Castile and Leon) | 526 | (6.2) | 525 | (10.4) | 520 | (7.8) | 509 | (6.4) | **-6.8** | (3.31) | 0.8 | (0.16) | 0.7 | (0.70) |
| Spain (Navarre) | 499 | (9.1) | 524 | (9.1) | 508 | (7.5) | 514 | (7.2) | 3.5 | (4.32) | 1.3 | (0.25) | 0.1 | (0.36) |
| Spain (Aragon) | 509 | (10.5) | 514 | (8.0) | 515 | (8.1) | 520 | (8.7) | 6.4 | (5.26) | 1.1 | (0.24) | 0.4 | (0.68) |
| Spain (Catalonia) | **470** | (9.8) | 487 | (10.7) | 492 | (11.6) | **515** | (13.6) | **13.0** | (5.91) | 1.4 | (0.30) | 2.2 | (1.96) |
| Spain (Asturias) | 495 | (12.2) | 506 | (7.6) | 516 | (8.8) | 518 | (8.8) | 6.7 | (6.23) | 1.3 | (0.29) | 0.5 | (0.98) |
| United Kingdom (Scotland) | 510 | (6.8) | 514 | (9.6) | 511 | (10.1) | 529 | (9.7) | 5.7 | (4.59) | 1.1 | (0.15) | 0.3 | (0.52) |
| **Non-adjudicated** | | | | | | | | | | | | | | |
| Belgium (French Community) | 490 | (11.3) | 472 | (15.2) | 485 | (12.1) | 495 | (13.3) | 4.4 | (6.18) | 0.8 | (0.16) | 0.2 | (0.57) |
| Belgium (German-Speaking Community) | **530** | (6.0) | 553 | (6.2) | 539 | (5.9) | 442 | (6.7) | **-74.2** | (5.74) | **0.6** | (0.12) | 10.8 | (1.54) |
| Finland (Finnish Speaking) | 571 | (4.2) | 560 | (3.6) | 562 | (3.7) | 566 | (4.8) | -1.4 | (3.15) | 0.8 | (0.08) | 0.0 | (0.10) |
| Finland (Swedish Speaking) | 532 | (11.4) | 523 | (13.8) | 530 | (14.0) | 538 | (10.3) | 2.9 | (7.66) | 0.9 | (0.29) | 0.1 | (0.41) |
| United Kingdom (England) | **507** | (6.5) | 514 | (5.7) | 518 | (6.6) | **533** | (9.0) | **9.6** | (4.27) | 1.2 | (0.13) | 0.9 | (0.83) |
| United Kingdom (Northern Ireland) | **480** | (12.0) | 500 | (13.0) | 532 | (12.5) | **534** | (10.2) | **19.4** | (5.72) | 1.6 | (0.29) | 3.4 | (1.89) |
| United Kingdom (Wales) | 502 | (7.3) | 507 | (5.7) | 508 | (7.2) | 506 | (8.1) | 1.8 | (4.58) | 1.1 | (0.14) | 0.0 | (0.23) |

Note: Values that are statistically significant are indicated in bold (see Annex A3). See Table 5.15 for national data.
1. Results based on reports from school principals and reported proportionate to the number of 15-year-olds enrolled in the school.
*StatLink* http://dx.doi.org/10.1787/142184405135

Pour consulter la version française intégrale de ce tableau, suivre ce lien :
*StatLink* http://dx.doi.org/10.1787/152830402855

[Part 1/1]

**Table S5h** **Percentage of students taking various science courses[1]**

*Tableau S5h* Pourcentage d'élèves par matière scientifique

| | All students | | | | | | | | | | | | | | | |
|---|---|---|---|---|---|---|---|---|---|---|---|---|---|---|---|---|
| | General science courses | | | | Biology courses | | | | Physics courses | | | | Chemistry courses | | | |
| | Compulsory | | Optional | | Compulsory | | Optional | | Compulsory | | Optional | | Compulsory | | Optional | |
| | % | S.E. | % | S.E. | % | S.E. | % | S.E. | % | S.E. | % | S.E. | % | S.E. | % | S.E. |
| **Adjudicated** | | | | | | | | | | | | | | | | |
| Belgium (Flemish Community) | 45.4 | (1.4) | 8.3 | (0.5) | 63.1 | (1.7) | 9.6 | (0.5) | 74.2 | (1.0) | 11.5 | (0.5) | 68.9 | (1.2) | 10.1 | (0.5) |
| Italy (Provincia Autonoma of Bolzano) | 58.6 | (1.1) | m | m | 66.4 | (0.9) | m | m | 49.5 | (0.8) | m | m | 45.4 | (1.0) | m | m |
| Italy (Provincia Campania) | 48.1 | (3.3) | m | m | 68.5 | (4.9) | m | m | 49.7 | (3.8) | m | m | 43.0 | (3.6) | m | m |
| Italy (Provincia Basilicata) | 56.0 | (2.4) | m | m | 62.3 | (3.7) | m | m | 51.2 | (3.8) | m | m | 46.9 | (2.7) | m | m |
| Italy (Provincia Emilia Romagna) | 47.9 | (3.2) | m | m | 68.4 | (3.3) | m | m | 55.1 | (3.8) | m | m | 55.4 | (2.9) | m | m |
| Italy (Provincia Friuli Venezia Giulia) | 60.4 | (3.5) | m | m | 65.7 | (2.7) | m | m | 48.1 | (4.0) | m | m | 45.5 | (2.8) | m | m |
| Italy (Provincia Sicilia) | 57.9 | (3.0) | m | m | 69.7 | (3.5) | m | m | 50.3 | (4.6) | m | m | 40.9 | (3.7) | m | m |
| Italy (Provincia Liguria) | 54.1 | (3.9) | m | m | 53.1 | (4.0) | m | m | 46.3 | (4.0) | m | m | 44.4 | (3.4) | m | m |
| Italy (Provincia Lombardia) | 57.5 | (3.6) | m | m | 62.9 | (3.3) | m | m | 53.4 | (3.3) | m | m | 52.8 | (3.4) | m | m |
| Italy (Provincia Piemonte) | 61.3 | (4.1) | m | m | 65.8 | (4.3) | m | m | 47.6 | (3.2) | m | m | 50.6 | (3.5) | m | m |
| Italy (Provincia Trento) | 51.2 | (1.1) | m | m | 62.7 | (1.1) | m | m | 48.2 | (1.1) | m | m | 44.5 | (0.9) | m | m |
| Italy (Provincia Sardegna) | 51.7 | (3.2) | m | m | 52.7 | (4.8) | m | m | 45.6 | (4.2) | m | m | 42.0 | (3.9) | m | m |
| Italy (Provincia Puglia) | 53.7 | (2.9) | m | m | 62.6 | (2.6) | m | m | 50.9 | (3.1) | m | m | 48.5 | (2.7) | m | m |
| Italy (Provincia Veneto) | 55.6 | (2.6) | m | m | 70.5 | (3.2) | m | m | 46.5 | (3.0) | m | m | 50.0 | (3.5) | m | m |
| Spain (Andalusia) | 59.4 | (2.2) | 29.1 | (2.0) | 63.8 | (2.2) | 32.3 | (1.8) | 63.7 | (1.5) | 32.3 | (2.0) | 60.7 | (1.5) | 30.5 | (1.9) |
| Spain (Basque Country) | 49.2 | (1.9) | 33.6 | (1.6) | 37.5 | (2.3) | 38.4 | (1.8) | 51.0 | (2.2) | 46.1 | (1.6) | 49.2 | (2.2) | 44.2 | (1.7) |
| Spain (Cantabria) | 56.9 | (1.5) | 30.1 | (1.3) | 64.8 | (2.0) | 38.4 | (1.3) | 62.9 | (2.2) | 41.5 | (1.7) | 60.9 | (2.2) | 40.4 | (1.6) |
| Spain (Galicia) | 53.6 | (1.9) | 29.8 | (1.5) | 60.0 | (2.0) | 38.5 | (2.1) | 65.6 | (2.3) | 36.8 | (1.8) | 62.5 | (2.4) | 35.5 | (1.8) |
| Spain (La Rioja) | 51.8 | (1.3) | 34.8 | (1.4) | 55.9 | (1.2) | 42.2 | (1.5) | 60.3 | (1.2) | 45.0 | (1.5) | 58.2 | (1.4) | 42.6 | (1.4) |
| Spain (Castile and Leon) | 52.9 | (2.1) | 35.9 | (1.6) | 60.5 | (2.6) | 45.4 | (2.1) | 63.9 | (1.8) | 45.5 | (1.4) | 62.3 | (1.9) | 44.6 | (1.4) |
| Spain (Navarre) | 35.3 | (1.5) | 12.5 | (2.1) | 37.4 | (2.3) | 16.5 | (2.0) | 37.4 | (2.4) | 17.3 | (2.3) | 36.6 | (2.3) | 16.9 | (2.2) |
| Spain (Aragon) | 51.9 | (2.4) | 38.7 | (2.1) | 53.0 | (2.4) | 42.9 | (1.7) | 57.9 | (2.4) | 44.4 | (2.1) | 56.1 | (2.3) | 43.4 | (2.0) |
| Spain (Catalonia) | 82.8 | (1.5) | 27.9 | (1.5) | 40.3 | (3.1) | 12.8 | (2.0) | 80.8 | (1.5) | 23.5 | (1.4) | 75.0 | (2.3) | 22.4 | (2.3) |
| Spain (Asturias) | 53.2 | (1.7) | 39.9 | (2.2) | 56.9 | (1.8) | 45.7 | (2.0) | 59.5 | (1.6) | 51.0 | (2.0) | 58.3 | (1.8) | 49.6 | (2.2) |
| United Kingdom (Scotland) | 35.6 | (1.5) | 43.6 | (1.5) | 17.3 | (1.1) | 37.8 | (1.4) | 14.9 | (0.7) | 32.0 | (1.2) | 15.1 | (0.9) | 37.1 | (1.3) |
| **Non-adjudicated** | | | | | | | | | | | | | | | | |
| Belgium (French Community) | 67.9 | (2.3) | 17.7 | (1.1) | 25.1 | (2.0) | 5.9 | (1.1) | 30.5 | (2.6) | 12.4 | (1.3) | 20.8 | (2.1) | 9.1 | (1.0) |
| Belgium (German-Speaking Community) | 41.2 | (1.2) | 13.8 | (1.2) | 33.6 | (0.9) | 3.8 | (0.6) | 36.2 | (1.1) | 10.7 | (0.8) | 29.0 | (0.8) | 8.8 | (0.9) |
| Finland (Finnish Speaking) | 87.1 | (0.8) | 7.1 | (0.7) | 95.8 | (0.4) | 4.5 | (0.5) | 95.6 | (0.4) | 4.6 | (0.5) | 74.0 | (1.7) | 3.3 | (0.4) |
| Finland (Swedish Speaking) | 66.6 | (6.2) | 8.8 | (6.1) | 80.5 | (5.6) | 7.5 | (3.2) | 75.4 | (5.0) | 2.6 | (0.9) | 57.6 | (5.0) | 13.6 | (9.1) |
| United Kingdom (England) | 15.6 | (1.0) | 13.1 | (0.7) | 11.9 | (0.8) | 11.7 | (0.8) | 18.6 | (1.2) | 15.3 | (0.9) | 13.9 | (0.9) | 13.7 | (0.9) |
| United Kingdom (Northern Ireland) | 21.8 | (1.1) | 18.0 | (1.1) | 17.8 | (1.1) | 18.1 | (1.1) | 27.7 | (1.3) | 23.3 | (1.2) | 23.4 | (1.3) | 23.6 | (1.2) |
| United Kingdom (Wales) | 29.0 | (1.9) | 18.7 | (1.1) | 27.1 | (1.9) | 19.1 | (1.0) | 32.3 | (2.0) | 22.0 | (1.2) | 29.3 | (1.8) | 21.1 | (1.2) |

Note: See Table 5.16 for national data.
1. Results based on students' self-reports.
*StatLink* http://dx.doi.org/10.1787/142184405135

Pour consulter la version française intégrale de ce tableau, suivre ce lien :
*StatLink* http://dx.doi.org/10.1787/152830402855

[Part 1/3]

**Table S5i** **Percentage of students, by time spent on learning**[1]

Tableau S5i  Pourcentage d'élèves par nombre hebdomadaire d'heures d'apprentissage

| | Science | | | | | | | | | | | |
| --- | --- | --- | --- | --- | --- | --- | --- | --- | --- | --- | --- | --- |
| | Regular lessons in school[2] | | | | Out-of-school lessons[2] | | | | Self-study or homework[2] | | | |
| | Less than two hours a week | | Four hours a week or more | | Less than two hours a week | | Four hours a week or more | | Less than two hours a week | | Four hours a week or more | |
| | % | S.E. | % | S.E. | % | S.E. | % | S.E. | % | S.E. | % | S.E. |
| **Adjudicated** | | | | | | | | | | | | |
| Belgium (Flemish Community) | 48.6 | (1.1) | 20.7 | (0.8) | 96.4 | (0.4) | 0.6 | (0.2) | 79.8 | (0.8) | 3.4 | (0.3) |
| Italy (Provincia Autonoma of Bolzano) | 37.0 | (1.1) | 25.6 | (0.9) | 95.4 | (0.5) | 1.0 | (0.2) | 78.4 | (1.0) | 5.1 | (0.6) |
| Italy (Provincia Campania) | 40.8 | (2.9) | 20.2 | (1.9) | 86.5 | (1.0) | 3.3 | (0.6) | 54.8 | (2.5) | 15.9 | (1.3) |
| Italy (Provincia Basilicata) | 37.0 | (2.2) | 25.6 | (2.0) | 85.3 | (1.0) | 4.3 | (0.6) | 55.5 | (2.0) | 15.4 | (1.2) |
| Italy (Provincia Emilia Romagna) | 31.7 | (2.6) | 27.1 | (1.6) | 92.5 | (0.8) | 1.5 | (0.3) | 56.8 | (2.5) | 13.5 | (1.4) |
| Italy (Provincia Friuli Venezia Giulia) | 30.9 | (2.2) | 26.0 | (1.9) | 93.3 | (0.8) | 1.6 | (0.4) | 59.5 | (2.3) | 11.1 | (1.1) |
| Italy (Provincia Sicilia) | 35.8 | (2.5) | 25.9 | (3.0) | 85.2 | (1.1) | 4.3 | (0.6) | 50.3 | (2.4) | 20.1 | (2.1) |
| Italy (Provincia Liguria) | 43.1 | (3.0) | 18.8 | (1.6) | 91.5 | (0.6) | 2.2 | (0.4) | 66.4 | (2.3) | 10.2 | (0.9) |
| Italy (Provincia Lombardia) | 29.4 | (2.6) | 27.7 | (2.3) | 93.2 | (0.7) | 1.2 | (0.3) | 59.8 | (2.3) | 10.3 | (1.0) |
| Italy (Provincia Piemonte) | 32.1 | (3.4) | 27.3 | (2.6) | 92.7 | (0.7) | 2.2 | (0.3) | 61.0 | (2.3) | 12.1 | (1.5) |
| Italy (Provincia Trento) | 35.5 | (1.4) | 25.3 | (1.2) | 93.6 | (0.7) | 1.4 | (0.3) | 62.1 | (1.4) | 12.5 | (1.0) |
| Italy (Provincia Sardegna) | 50.4 | (2.9) | 15.8 | (1.7) | 89.7 | (0.8) | 2.2 | (0.4) | 68.7 | (2.0) | 10.5 | (1.1) |
| Italy (Provincia Puglia) | 34.5 | (2.1) | 24.8 | (1.7) | 87.1 | (1.1) | 4.3 | (0.6) | 50.5 | (2.1) | 16.0 | (1.4) |
| Italy (Provincia Veneto) | 30.5 | (2.4) | 27.8 | (1.9) | 91.4 | (0.8) | 1.5 | (0.2) | 54.8 | (2.5) | 14.9 | (1.5) |
| Spain (Andalusia) | 29.7 | (1.9) | 26.7 | (1.6) | 85.9 | (1.2) | 4.1 | (0.6) | 64.4 | (1.6) | 9.8 | (0.8) |
| Spain (Basque Country) | 26.4 | (1.1) | 25.2 | (1.2) | 87.4 | (0.7) | 3.1 | (0.3) | 72.2 | (1.1) | 5.7 | (0.4) |
| Spain (Cantabria) | 25.8 | (1.4) | 30.6 | (1.3) | 78.0 | (1.2) | 8.1 | (0.8) | 63.7 | (1.2) | 9.8 | (0.9) |
| Spain (Galicia) | 30.1 | (1.8) | 24.8 | (1.6) | 82.2 | (1.4) | 6.6 | (0.9) | 68.5 | (1.5) | 8.1 | (0.6) |
| Spain (La Rioja) | 23.5 | (1.1) | 28.9 | (1.4) | 84.5 | (1.0) | 3.8 | (0.5) | 63.5 | (1.4) | 9.4 | (0.9) |
| Spain (Castile and Leon) | 24.5 | (1.3) | 31.2 | (1.7) | 86.4 | (1.0) | 2.6 | (0.5) | 59.7 | (1.5) | 11.3 | (1.0) |
| Spain (Navarre) | 30.8 | (1.2) | 43.6 | (1.8) | 88.6 | (0.8) | 3.0 | (0.5) | 64.5 | (1.2) | 10.8 | (1.0) |
| Spain (Aragon) | 26.1 | (2.0) | 29.9 | (1.6) | 88.2 | (0.7) | 3.2 | (0.5) | 62.4 | (1.9) | 13.0 | (0.9) |
| Spain (Catalonia) | 15.8 | (1.3) | 19.7 | (2.8) | 89.4 | (0.7) | 1.6 | (0.3) | 69.1 | (1.8) | 6.9 | (0.7) |
| Spain (Asturias) | 29.3 | (1.8) | 28.6 | (1.7) | 78.6 | (0.8) | 9.3 | (0.8) | 62.7 | (1.4) | 11.4 | (0.8) |
| United Kingdom (Scotland) | 17.5 | (1.2) | 32.0 | (1.6) | 92.5 | (0.5) | 0.8 | (0.2) | 75.7 | (1.2) | 5.0 | (0.6) |
| **Non-adjudicated** | | | | | | | | | | | | |
| Belgium (French Community) | 33.6 | (1.9) | 28.1 | (1.6) | 93.1 | (0.5) | 1.8 | (0.3) | 78.3 | (1.1) | 4.2 | (0.5) |
| Belgium (German-Speaking Community) | 46.1 | (1.5) | 22.4 | (1.3) | 95.7 | (0.7) | 0.6 | (0.3) | 79.9 | (1.5) | 4.7 | (0.7) |
| Finland (Finnish Speaking) | 22.8 | (0.9) | 27.5 | (1.4) | 96.1 | (0.3) | 0.5 | (0.1) | 87.4 | (0.7) | 1.7 | (0.2) |
| Finland (Swedish Speaking) | 26.3 | (3.3) | 19.1 | (2.5) | 93.8 | (2.0) | 0.2 | (0.2) | 91.5 | (1.6) | 0.7 | (0.4) |
| United Kingdom (England) | 9.2 | (0.7) | 64.6 | (1.2) | 93.5 | (0.5) | 1.0 | (0.1) | 75.3 | (1.0) | 3.5 | (0.3) |
| United Kingdom (Northern Ireland) | 13.8 | (0.7) | 55.9 | (1.0) | 92.8 | (0.6) | 1.9 | (0.3) | 68.9 | (1.1) | 5.7 | (0.5) |
| United Kingdom (Wales) | 9.7 | (0.6) | 68.2 | (1.2) | 93.9 | (0.5) | 0.8 | (0.1) | 74.2 | (1.1) | 4.2 | (0.4) |

Note: See Table 5.17 for national data.
1. Results based on students' self-reports.
2. Percentages for the middle category can be obtained by subtracting the sum of the other two categories from 100%.
*StatLink* http://dx.doi.org/10.1787/142184405135

Pour consulter la version française intégrale de ce tableau, suivre ce lien :
*StatLink* http://dx.doi.org/10.1787/152830402855

[Part 2/3]

**Table S5i** **Percentage of students, by time spent on learning**[1]

Tableau S5i Pourcentage d'élèves par nombre hebdomadaire d'heures d'apprentissage

| | Reading | | | | | | | | | | | |
|---|---|---|---|---|---|---|---|---|---|---|---|---|
| | Regular lessons in school[2] | | | | Out-of-school lessons[2] | | | | Self-study or homework[2] | | | |
| | Less than two hours a week | | Four hours a week or more | | Less than two hours a week | | Four hours a week or more | | Less than two hours a week | | Four hours a week or more | |
| | % | S.E. | % | S.E. | % | S.E. | % | S.E. | % | S.E. | % | S.E. |
| **Adjudicated** | | | | | | | | | | | | |
| Belgium (Flemish Community) | 27.5 | (1.0) | 31.2 | (1.0) | 94.5 | (0.4) | 1.6 | (0.3) | 82.2 | (0.6) | 3.0 | (0.3) |
| Italy (Provincia Autonoma of Bolzano) | 13.3 | (0.9) | 55.1 | (1.0) | 93.9 | (0.5) | 1.5 | (0.3) | 74.9 | (1.1) | 5.9 | (0.6) |
| Italy (Provincia Campania) | 11.9 | (0.9) | 67.6 | (2.0) | 77.4 | (1.2) | 10.2 | (1.1) | 27.8 | (1.8) | 39.8 | (2.4) |
| Italy (Provincia Basilicata) | 12.5 | (1.0) | 67.3 | (1.3) | 77.9 | (1.1) | 8.1 | (1.0) | 29.6 | (1.8) | 33.7 | (2.0) |
| Italy (Provincia Emilia Romagna) | 12.2 | (1.0) | 70.3 | (1.5) | 89.6 | (0.9) | 3.4 | (0.5) | 41.4 | (1.6) | 23.1 | (1.2) |
| Italy (Provincia Friuli Venezia Giulia) | 11.3 | (0.9) | 69.1 | (1.5) | 91.1 | (0.7) | 3.3 | (0.5) | 43.1 | (2.0) | 19.3 | (1.3) |
| Italy (Provincia Sicilia) | 14.3 | (1.4) | 65.4 | (2.4) | 78.3 | (2.0) | 8.1 | (0.8) | 31.3 | (2.0) | 31.7 | (2.4) |
| Italy (Provincia Liguria) | 13.7 | (1.0) | 62.9 | (1.7) | 88.3 | (1.0) | 3.9 | (0.6) | 46.5 | (1.7) | 20.9 | (1.7) |
| Italy (Provincia Lombardia) | 13.2 | (1.3) | 66.5 | (2.3) | 90.0 | (1.0) | 3.2 | (0.4) | 45.7 | (2.4) | 19.9 | (1.4) |
| Italy (Provincia Piemonte) | 11.1 | (1.1) | 69.7 | (2.0) | 89.1 | (0.7) | 4.0 | (0.5) | 45.0 | (2.0) | 19.5 | (2.0) |
| Italy (Provincia Trento) | 15.1 | (0.8) | 62.2 | (1.4) | 91.6 | (0.8) | 2.8 | (0.4) | 47.4 | (1.4) | 20.4 | (1.2) |
| Italy (Provincia Sardegna) | 16.2 | (1.3) | 60.9 | (2.8) | 81.7 | (1.3) | 6.8 | (0.9) | 39.6 | (2.5) | 24.8 | (2.3) |
| Italy (Provincia Puglia) | 13.4 | (1.1) | 66.4 | (1.5) | 79.8 | (1.3) | 8.3 | (0.7) | 29.2 | (1.6) | 36.6 | (1.5) |
| Italy (Provincia Veneto) | 12.6 | (1.0) | 64.8 | (1.8) | 90.4 | (0.9) | 3.0 | (0.4) | 44.2 | (1.8) | 19.9 | (1.4) |
| Spain (Andalusia) | 13.8 | (1.4) | 58.2 | (1.6) | 86.0 | (0.9) | 4.6 | (0.6) | 57.2 | (1.9) | 12.8 | (1.3) |
| Spain (Basque Country) | 12.0 | (0.6) | 26.3 | (1.6) | 91.5 | (0.6) | 2.4 | (0.3) | 72.8 | (1.2) | 6.4 | (0.5) |
| Spain (Cantabria) | 10.3 | (0.7) | 62.2 | (1.4) | 84.1 | (1.2) | 5.9 | (0.8) | 56.2 | (2.0) | 10.3 | (1.1) |
| Spain (Galicia) | 15.9 | (1.1) | 16.8 | (1.4) | 87.2 | (1.1) | 4.5 | (0.7) | 67.4 | (1.8) | 7.7 | (0.7) |
| Spain (La Rioja) | 10.8 | (0.9) | 59.6 | (1.5) | 90.0 | (0.8) | 2.7 | (0.5) | 59.3 | (1.5) | 8.3 | (0.9) |
| Spain (Castile and Leon) | 12.0 | (1.2) | 57.9 | (1.8) | 92.2 | (0.9) | 2.5 | (0.5) | 59.1 | (1.6) | 11.3 | (0.9) |
| Spain (Navarre) | 5.5 | (0.7) | 47.3 | (3.0) | 90.4 | (1.1) | 2.6 | (0.4) | 57.9 | (1.6) | 10.9 | (0.9) |
| Spain (Aragon) | 11.0 | (1.1) | 55.1 | (1.9) | 90.7 | (0.8) | 2.5 | (0.3) | 59.0 | (1.7) | 11.9 | (1.0) |
| Spain (Catalonia) | 11.8 | (1.2) | 11.4 | (2.4) | 91.3 | (0.7) | 2.0 | (0.4) | 71.5 | (1.3) | 7.1 | (0.6) |
| Spain (Asturias) | 11.7 | (1.3) | 57.8 | (2.3) | 85.2 | (1.2) | 6.3 | (0.7) | 57.6 | (1.5) | 10.3 | (0.8) |
| United Kingdom (Scotland) | 8.5 | (0.7) | 56.2 | (1.6) | 86.9 | (0.8) | 3.1 | (0.4) | 70.6 | (1.4) | 7.2 | (0.8) |
| **Non-adjudicated** | | | | | | | | | | | | |
| Belgium (French Community) | 14.3 | (1.1) | 65.5 | (1.7) | 89.1 | (0.6) | 2.6 | (0.3) | 74.9 | (1.1) | 4.3 | (0.4) |
| Belgium (German-Speaking Community) | 11.0 | (1.1) | 68.4 | (1.4) | 95.5 | (0.7) | 2.2 | (0.5) | 77.6 | (1.5) | 4.9 | (0.8) |
| Finland (Finnish Speaking) | 14.6 | (1.0) | 21.1 | (1.8) | 95.3 | (0.4) | 0.8 | (0.1) | 86.8 | (0.7) | 2.2 | (0.4) |
| Finland  (Swedish Speaking) | 15.9 | (1.9) | 6.5 | (2.1) | 94.4 | (1.1) | 1.0 | (0.5) | 91.8 | (2.2) | 0.0 | (0.0) |
| United Kingdom (England) | 7.3 | (0.5) | 46.6 | (1.6) | 90.5 | (0.5) | 2.2 | (0.2) | 71.6 | (1.0) | 5.0 | (0.4) |
| United Kingdom (Northern Ireland) | 9.6 | (0.7) | 46.4 | (1.4) | 90.9 | (0.5) | 2.4 | (0.3) | 65.3 | (1.4) | 7.9 | (0.6) |
| United Kingdom (Wales) | 6.9 | (0.5) | 47.7 | (1.5) | 91.4 | (0.6) | 1.6 | (0.3) | 71.5 | (1.0) | 6.3 | (0.5) |

Note: See Table 5.17 for national data.
1. Results based on students' self-reports.
2. Percentages for the middle category can be obtained by subtracting the sum of the other two categories from 100%.
*StatLink* ᠁᠊᠊᠊ http://dx.doi.org/10.1787/142184405135

Pour consulter la version française intégrale de ce tableau, suivre ce lien :
*StatLink* ᠁᠊᠊᠊ http://dx.doi.org/10.1787/152830402855

[Part 3/3]

**Table S5i**   **Percentage of students, by time spent on learning[1]**

Tableau S5i   Pourcentages d'élèves par nombre hebdomadaire d'heures d'apprentissage

| | Mathematics | | | | | | | | | | | |
| --- | --- | --- | --- | --- | --- | --- | --- | --- | --- | --- | --- | --- |
| | Regular lessons in school[2] | | | | Out-of-school lessons[2] | | | | Self-study or homework[2] | | | |
| | Less than two hours a week | | Four hours a week or more | | Less than two hours a week | | Four hours a week or more | | Less than two hours a week | | Four hours a week or more | |
| | % | S.E. | % | S.E. | % | S.E. | % | S.E. | % | S.E. | % | S.E. |
| **Adjudicated** | | | | | | | | | | | | |
| Belgium (Flemish Community) | 25.6 | (0.9) | 40.1 | (1.1) | 93.7 | (0.4) | 1.6 | (0.2) | 63.7 | (1.0) | 8.0 | (0.5) |
| Italy (Provincia Autonoma of Bolzano) | 16.6 | (0.9) | 42.9 | (1.1) | 91.1 | (0.8) | 2.1 | (0.5) | 73.8 | (1.3) | 5.2 | (0.6) |
| Italy (Provincia Campania) | 21.7 | (1.8) | 44.4 | (3.0) | 76.4 | (1.3) | 6.8 | (0.7) | 42.8 | (2.1) | 24.0 | (1.6) |
| Italy (Provincia Basilicata) | 18.9 | (1.3) | 47.0 | (1.8) | 80.2 | (1.6) | 6.3 | (0.7) | 45.5 | (2.0) | 20.5 | (1.2) |
| Italy (Provincia Emilia Romagna) | 15.8 | (1.0) | 52.2 | (2.1) | 86.1 | (0.9) | 3.0 | (0.4) | 49.1 | (2.1) | 16.7 | (1.4) |
| Italy (Provincia Friuli Venezia Giulia) | 13.9 | (1.3) | 52.5 | (2.5) | 87.6 | (1.0) | 2.3 | (0.3) | 49.1 | (1.9) | 14.5 | (1.5) |
| Italy (Provincia Sicilia) | 17.8 | (2.2) | 50.9 | (3.2) | 78.4 | (1.6) | 6.7 | (0.7) | 40.6 | (2.6) | 23.5 | (1.6) |
| Italy (Provincia Liguria) | 19.6 | (1.4) | 43.3 | (2.5) | 86.0 | (0.9) | 3.2 | (0.6) | 55.6 | (1.8) | 13.4 | (1.2) |
| Italy (Provincia Lombardia) | 15.3 | (1.4) | 51.9 | (2.3) | 87.3 | (1.0) | 3.2 | (0.4) | 52.5 | (2.3) | 13.8 | (1.2) |
| Italy (Provincia Piemonte) | 16.0 | (1.9) | 46.9 | (3.1) | 87.0 | (0.9) | 2.8 | (0.5) | 51.9 | (2.4) | 14.6 | (1.4) |
| Italy (Provincia Trento) | 16.7 | (0.9) | 43.3 | (1.3) | 89.5 | (0.9) | 2.2 | (0.4) | 52.8 | (1.3) | 16.2 | (1.0) |
| Italy (Provincia Sardegna) | 23.8 | (1.7) | 37.8 | (3.0) | 84.4 | (1.5) | 3.2 | (0.4) | 57.4 | (1.7) | 12.6 | (0.9) |
| Italy (Provincia Puglia) | 19.4 | (1.4) | 48.3 | (2.0) | 80.9 | (1.2) | 6.5 | (0.7) | 42.9 | (1.9) | 22.5 | (1.3) |
| Italy (Provincia Veneto) | 16.4 | (1.5) | 51.9 | (2.8) | 86.7 | (0.9) | 2.2 | (0.4) | 47.3 | (2.7) | 18.0 | (1.7) |
| Spain (Andalusia) | 13.7 | (1.4) | 26.8 | (1.6) | 76.6 | (1.2) | 7.3 | (1.1) | 57.3 | (1.9) | 13.0 | (1.2) |
| Spain (Basque Country) | 10.6 | (0.8) | 32.3 | (2.1) | 80.1 | (0.9) | 4.6 | (0.4) | 66.3 | (1.3) | 7.2 | (0.5) |
| Spain (Cantabria) | 10.6 | (0.8) | 54.6 | (1.4) | 65.6 | (1.2) | 14.3 | (1.5) | 57.3 | (1.7) | 10.7 | (0.9) |
| Spain (Galicia) | 14.0 | (1.1) | 22.4 | (1.6) | 71.9 | (1.7) | 10.6 | (1.1) | 61.3 | (1.7) | 11.2 | (0.9) |
| Spain (La Rioja) | 9.6 | (1.0) | 63.4 | (1.5) | 71.5 | (1.5) | 6.2 | (0.8) | 53.5 | (1.6) | 12.1 | (0.9) |
| Spain (Castile and Leon) | 9.7 | (1.2) | 53.4 | (1.6) | 77.7 | (1.4) | 5.0 | (0.6) | 51.8 | (1.9) | 13.5 | (1.0) |
| Spain (Navarre) | 5.7 | (0.7) | 46.3 | (2.6) | 79.4 | (1.1) | 4.5 | (0.5) | 53.0 | (1.4) | 12.1 | (1.1) |
| Spain (Aragon) | 11.5 | (1.1) | 24.5 | (2.0) | 80.2 | (1.2) | 5.5 | (0.8) | 56.8 | (1.9) | 12.4 | (1.1) |
| Spain (Catalonia) | 10.8 | (1.0) | 20.7 | (3.9) | 88.2 | (0.9) | 2.9 | (0.6) | 68.4 | (1.7) | 7.8 | (0.9) |
| Spain (Asturias) | 12.0 | (1.5) | 24.9 | (2.0) | 64.7 | (1.6) | 15.5 | (1.3) | 57.4 | (1.7) | 12.8 | (1.0) |
| United Kingdom (Scotland) | 8.8 | (0.7) | 55.2 | (1.7) | 86.3 | (0.7) | 2.3 | (0.3) | 67.4 | (1.3) | 7.0 | (0.6) |
| **Non-adjudicated** | | | | | | | | | | | | |
| Belgium (French Community) | 17.6 | (1.2) | 60.6 | (1.9) | 86.3 | (0.6) | 3.2 | (0.3) | 63.5 | (1.5) | 8.4 | (0.5) |
| Belgium (German-Speaking Community) | 13.8 | (1.2) | 56.7 | (1.4) | 94.1 | (0.8) | 1.6 | (0.4) | 65.2 | (1.8) | 8.0 | (0.9) |
| Finland (Finnish Speaking) | 10.6 | (0.6) | 32.1 | (1.7) | 95.2 | (0.4) | 0.9 | (0.2) | 84.1 | (0.8) | 1.9 | (0.2) |
| Finland (Swedish Speaking) | 11.8 | (2.1) | 14.7 | (3.6) | 95.9 | (1.1) | 0.0 | (0.0) | 86.6 | (2.5) | 1.5 | (0.6) |
| United Kingdom (England) | 7.6 | (0.5) | 41.0 | (1.5) | 90.8 | (0.5) | 1.8 | (0.2) | 76.0 | (0.8) | 3.6 | (0.3) |
| United Kingdom (Northern Ireland) | 9.6 | (0.7) | 45.6 | (1.4) | 90.5 | (0.6) | 1.9 | (0.3) | 63.3 | (1.3) | 6.7 | (0.5) |
| United Kingdom (Wales) | 6.9 | (0.6) | 44.7 | (1.6) | 91.1 | (0.5) | 1.2 | (0.2) | 75.0 | (0.8) | 4.1 | (0.3) |

Note: See Table 5.17 for national data.
1. Results based on students' self-reports.
2. Percentages for the middle category can be obtained by subtracting the sum of the other two categories from 100%.
*StatLink* http://dx.doi.org/10.1787/142184405135

Pour consulter la version française intégrale de ce tableau, suivre ce lien :
*StatLink* http://dx.doi.org/10.1787/152830402855

[Part 1/1]

**Table S5j** **Percentage of students participating in school activities to promote the learning of science[1]**

*Tableau S5j* Pourcentage d'élèves participant à des activités scolaires visant à promouvoir l'apprentissage des sciences

| | Percentage of students whose principals report the following school activities to promote the learning of science | | | | | | | | | |
|---|---|---|---|---|---|---|---|---|---|---|
| | Science clubs | | Science fairs | | Science competitions | | Extracurricular science projects | | Excursions and field trips | |
| | % | S.E. | % | S.E. | % | S.E. | % | S.E. | % | S.E. |
| **Adjudicated** | | | | | | | | | | |
| Belgium (Flemish Community) | 4.5 | (1.7) | 22.6 | (3.6) | 57.8 | (3.8) | 50.7 | (4.3) | 87.9 | (2.8) |
| Italy (Provincia Autonoma of Bolzano) | 31.0 | (0.7) | 0.5 | (0.0) | 29.5 | (0.5) | 61.2 | (0.5) | 96.5 | (0.1) |
| Italy (Provincia Campania) | 44.8 | (7.4) | 17.4 | (5.6) | 44.5 | (8.3) | 79.9 | (6.3) | 100.0 | (0.0) |
| Italy (Provincia Basilicata) | 24.2 | (3.6) | 5.4 | (2.2) | 20.4 | (4.1) | 70.9 | (6.7) | 92.2 | (2.8) |
| Italy (Provincia Emilia Romagna) | 38.8 | (6.8) | 12.8 | (5.0) | 27.8 | (6.2) | 80.4 | (6.1) | 95.2 | (3.4) |
| Italy (Provincia Friuli Venezia Giulia) | 37.0 | (4.6) | 12.5 | (2.6) | 35.3 | (5.4) | 75.8 | (3.7) | 95.5 | (3.1) |
| Italy (Provincia Sicilia) | 40.2 | (6.7) | 13.0 | (5.6) | 47.4 | (9.3) | 74.9 | (7.2) | 92.6 | (4.0) |
| Italy (Provincia Liguria) | 37.0 | (6.5) | 32.4 | (6.1) | 31.4 | (4.9) | 82.6 | (5.2) | 94.4 | (2.3) |
| Italy (Provincia Lombardia) | 33.2 | (6.8) | 12.0 | (5.2) | 24.1 | (7.0) | 69.7 | (6.9) | 96.8 | (2.4) |
| Italy (Provincia Piemonte) | 31.1 | (7.6) | 9.6 | (4.7) | 29.3 | (6.1) | 71.1 | (6.2) | 95.8 | (3.0) |
| Italy (Provincia Trento) | 37.7 | (0.5) | 6.9 | (0.1) | 39.9 | (0.6) | 76.6 | (0.2) | 98.5 | (0.1) |
| Italy (Provincia Sardegna) | 27.7 | (6.7) | 17.5 | (5.7) | 26.2 | (7.3) | 79.1 | (6.1) | 87.0 | (6.2) |
| Italy (Provincia Puglia) | 31.7 | (6.8) | 20.3 | (5.9) | 33.3 | (7.9) | 83.6 | (5.1) | 92.1 | (3.0) |
| Italy (Provincia Veneto) | 32.6 | (7.5) | 0.9 | (0.9) | 31.9 | (5.2) | 65.0 | (6.7) | 99.0 | (1.1) |
| Spain (Andalusia) | 73.3 | (5.9) | 61.1 | (6.6) | 25.4 | (5.3) | 26.0 | (6.4) | 99.1 | (0.9) |
| Spain (Basque Country) | 64.7 | (3.7) | 53.5 | (3.6) | 19.6 | (3.3) | 26.9 | (4.0) | 94.4 | (1.8) |
| Spain (Cantabria) | 68.6 | (6.3) | 60.2 | (6.2) | 32.2 | (6.2) | 27.9 | (6.3) | 98.1 | (1.9) |
| Spain (Galicia) | 58.1 | (7.8) | 67.1 | (7.3) | 31.8 | (5.5) | 40.7 | (8.3) | 94.9 | (2.5) |
| Spain (La Rioja) | 58.3 | (0.4) | 48.3 | (0.5) | 54.7 | (0.5) | 53.6 | (0.6) | 98.2 | (0.1) |
| Spain (Castile and Leon) | 68.9 | (5.7) | 56.4 | (6.6) | 49.5 | (6.4) | 48.3 | (8.5) | 98.4 | (1.6) |
| Spain (Navarre) | 39.6 | (5.1) | 31.9 | (5.4) | 29.4 | (3.2) | 18.6 | (5.0) | 100.0 | (0.0) |
| Spain (Aragon) | 62.8 | (7.3) | 70.1 | (7.0) | 37.2 | (7.6) | 41.5 | (7.6) | 94.1 | (3.7) |
| Spain (Catalonia) | 50.9 | (7.4) | 50.0 | (8.0) | 36.7 | (7.8) | 40.3 | (6.8) | 83.1 | (5.1) |
| Spain (Asturias) | 66.1 | (5.7) | 54.2 | (6.7) | 30.5 | (6.8) | 33.1 | (7.6) | 97.9 | (2.0) |
| United Kingdom (Scotland) | 47.8 | (5.2) | 46.2 | (5.1) | 78.1 | (4.7) | 47.4 | (6.2) | 94.6 | (2.7) |
| **Non-adjudicated** | | | | | | | | | | |
| Belgium (French Community) | 6.3 | (2.7) | 51.2 | (5.5) | 45.3 | (4.6) | 43.0 | (5.5) | 94.8 | (2.4) |
| Belgium (German-Speaking Community) | a | a | 70.4 | (0.3) | 19.3 | (0.1) | 64.0 | (0.2) | 100.0 | (0.0) |
| Finland (Finnish Speaking) | 7.8 | (2.2) | 7.0 | (2.2) | 36.6 | (4.5) | 23.1 | (3.7) | 93.7 | (2.1) |
| Finland (Swedish Speaking) | 34.0 | (18.1) | 52.2 | (19.0) | 49.1 | (19.1) | 14.3 | (13.6) | 99.2 | (0.9) |
| United Kingdom (England) | 76.4 | (2.9) | 34.2 | (3.7) | 71.0 | (3.2) | 61.6 | (3.9) | 85.8 | (2.8) |
| United Kingdom (Northern Ireland) | 54.3 | (5.0) | 45.2 | (4.7) | 66.6 | (3.7) | 53.3 | (4.7) | 92.5 | (2.3) |
| United Kingdom (Wales) | 68.6 | (3.6) | 33.5 | (4.1) | 75.9 | (4.1) | 56.4 | (4.7) | 93.7 | (2.3) |

Note: See Figure 5.18 for national data.
1. Results based on reports from school principals and reported proportionate to the number of 15-year-olds enrolled in the school.
*StatLink* ▄▄▄ http://dx.doi.org/10.1787/142184405135

Pour consulter la version française intégrale de ce tableau, suivre ce lien :
*StatLink* ▄▄▄ http://dx.doi.org/10.1787/152830402855

[Part 1/2]

**Table S5k** Index of school activities to promote the learning of science and student performance on the science scale, by quarters of the index[1]

Tableau S5k Indice de participation à des activités scolaires visant à promouvoir l'apprentissage des sciences et performances des élèves sur l'échelle de culture scientifique, par quartile de l'indice

| | Index of school activities to promote the learning of science | | | | | | | | | |
|---|---|---|---|---|---|---|---|---|---|---|
| | All students | | Bottom quarter | | Second quarter | | Third quarter | | Top quarter | |
| | Mean index | S.E. | Mean index | S.E. | Mean index | S.E. | Mean index | S.E. | Mean index | S.E. |
| **Adjudicated** | | | | | | | | | | |
| Belgium (Flemish Community) | -0.29 | (0.07) | -1.43 | (0.09) | -0.40 | (0.02) | 0.09 | (0.02) | 0.58 | (0.08) |
| Italy (Provincia Autonoma of Bolzano) | -0.23 | (0.01) | -1.24 | (0.01) | -0.47 | (0.01) | -0.02 | (0.01) | 0.82 | (0.02) |
| Italy (Provincia Campania) | 0.19 | (0.12) | -0.71 | (0.09) | -0.24 | (0.03) | 0.46 | (0.07) | 1.23 | (0.11) |
| Italy (Provincia Basilicata) | -0.26 | (0.09) | -1.19 | (0.08) | -0.43 | (0.03) | -0.05 | (0.05) | 0.64 | (0.04) |
| Italy (Provincia Emilia Romagna) | -0.07 | (0.11) | -1.01 | (0.18) | -0.33 | (0.00) | 0.11 | (0.03) | 0.94 | (0.15) |
| Italy (Provincia Friuli Venezia Giulia) | -0.04 | (0.07) | -1.09 | (0.15) | -0.33 | (0.00) | 0.14 | (0.03) | 1.10 | (0.04) |
| Italy (Provincia Sicilia) | 0.00 | (0.15) | -1.28 | (0.18) | -0.06 | (0.06) | 0.26 | (0.02) | 1.07 | (0.10) |
| Italy (Provincia Liguria) | 0.10 | (0.09) | -0.89 | (0.14) | -0.18 | (0.04) | 0.31 | (0.05) | 1.15 | (0.09) |
| Italy (Provincia Lombardia) | -0.16 | (0.09) | -0.89 | (0.07) | -0.33 | (0.00) | -0.01 | (0.05) | 0.62 | (0.12) |
| Italy (Provincia Piemonte) | -0.16 | (0.12) | -1.15 | (0.10) | -0.35 | (0.01) | -0.01 | (0.06) | 0.90 | (0.17) |
| Italy (Provincia Trento) | 0.04 | (0.01) | -0.88 | (0.01) | -0.30 | (0.00) | 0.31 | (0.01) | 1.03 | (0.00) |
| Italy (Provincia Sardegna) | -0.14 | (0.16) | -1.41 | (0.21) | -0.34 | (0.00) | 0.25 | (0.04) | 0.96 | (0.10) |
| Italy (Provincia Puglia) | -0.07 | (0.12) | -1.24 | (0.14) | -0.19 | (0.04) | 0.22 | (0.00) | 0.95 | (0.10) |
| Italy (Provincia Veneto) | -0.20 | (0.08) | -1.06 | (0.05) | -0.33 | (0.00) | 0.09 | (0.03) | 0.50 | (0.08) |
| Spain (Andalusia) | 0.16 | (0.10) | -0.76 | (0.10) | -0.12 | (0.04) | 0.34 | (0.04) | 1.18 | (0.10) |
| Spain (Basque Country) | -0.03 | (0.06) | -1.14 | (0.07) | -0.27 | (0.01) | 0.24 | (0.01) | 1.04 | (0.07) |
| Spain (Cantabria) | 0.19 | (0.10) | -0.78 | (0.09) | -0.09 | (0.05) | 0.34 | (0.04) | 1.31 | (0.09) |
| Spain (Galicia) | 0.18 | (0.11) | -0.69 | (0.12) | -0.12 | (0.04) | 0.42 | (0.05) | 1.11 | (0.12) |
| Spain (La Rioja) | 0.33 | (0.01) | -0.69 | (0.01) | 0.11 | (0.01) | 0.48 | (0.01) | 1.43 | (0.02) |
| Spain (Castile and Leon) | 0.37 | (0.11) | -0.61 | (0.10) | 0.06 | (0.05) | 0.57 | (0.05) | 1.45 | (0.06) |
| Spain (Navarre) | -0.29 | (0.06) | -1.06 | (0.00) | -0.44 | (0.05) | -0.15 | (0.03) | 0.51 | (0.06) |
| Spain (Aragon) | 0.28 | (0.13) | -0.92 | (0.09) | -0.10 | (0.07) | 0.54 | (0.07) | 1.62 | (0.02) |
| Spain (Catalonia) | -0.04 | (0.17) | -1.40 | (0.16) | -0.39 | (0.03) | 0.29 | (0.06) | 1.33 | (0.12) |
| Spain (Asturias) | 0.09 | (0.12) | -1.04 | (0.11) | 0.06 | (0.06) | 0.34 | (0.04) | 1.00 | (0.09) |
| United Kingdom (Scotland) | 0.33 | (0.09) | -0.60 | (0.09) | 0.06 | (0.03) | 0.55 | (0.04) | 1.34 | (0.07) |
| **Non-adjudicated** | | | | | | | | | | |
| Belgium (French Community) | -0.14 | (0.08) | -1.16 | (0.06) | -0.34 | (0.00) | 0.19 | (0.01) | 0.74 | (0.09) |
| Belgium (German-Speaking Community) | -0.08 | (0.00) | -0.90 | (0.02) | -0.15 | (0.01) | 0.21 | (0.00) | 0.53 | (0.01) |
| Finland (Finnish Speaking) | -0.62 | (0.06) | -1.37 | (0.09) | -0.89 | (0.03) | -0.33 | (0.00) | 0.09 | (0.04) |
| Finland (Swedish Speaking) | -0.11 | (0.22) | -0.91 | (0.16) | -0.28 | (0.06) | 0.21 | (0.00) | 0.56 | (0.16) |
| United Kingdom (England) | 0.43 | (0.06) | -0.82 | (0.08) | 0.15 | (0.02) | 0.79 | (0.01) | 1.59 | (0.02) |
| United Kingdom (Northern Ireland) | 0.30 | (0.10) | -1.20 | (0.11) | -0.01 | (0.04) | 0.82 | (0.02) | 1.61 | (0.02) |
| United Kingdom (Wales) | 0.42 | (0.08) | -0.65 | (0.06) | 0.15 | (0.02) | 0.71 | (0.01) | 1.49 | (0.03) |

Note: See Table 5.18 for national data.
1. Results based on reports from school principals and reported proportionate to the number of 15-year-olds enrolled in the school.
*StatLink* ▒▒▒ http://dx.doi.org/10.1787/142184405135

Pour consulter la version française intégrale de ce tableau, suivre ce lien :
*StatLink* ▒▒▒ http://dx.doi.org/10.1787/152830402855

[Part 2/2]

**Table S5k** Index of school activities to promote the learning of science and student performance on the science scale, by quarters of the index[1]

Tableau S5k  Indice de participation à des activités scolaires visant à promouvoir l'apprentissage des sciences et performances des élèves sur l'échelle de culture scientifique, par quartile de l'indice

| | Performance on the science scale by quarters of this index | | | | | | | | Change in the science score per unit of this index | | Increased likelihood of students in the bottom quarter of this index scoring in the bottom quarter of the science performance distribution | | Explained variance in student performance (r-squared x 100) | |
| | Bottom quarter | | Second quarter | | Third quarter | | Top quarter | | | | | | | |
| | Mean score | S.E. | Mean score | S.E. | Mean score | S.E. | Mean score | S.E | Effect | S.E. | Ratio | S.E. | % | S.E. |
|---|---|---|---|---|---|---|---|---|---|---|---|---|---|---|
| **Adjudicated** | | | | | | | | | | | | | | |
| Belgium (Flemish Community) | **496** | (12.6) | 534 | (6.6) | 545 | (5.6) | **544** | (6.5) | **26.2** | (6.58) | **1.9** | (0.31) | 5.6 | (2.68) |
| Italy (Provincia Autonoma of Bolzano) | **498** | (6.1) | 512 | (7.5) | 533 | (5.0) | **565** | (5.4) | **28.1** | (3.29) | **1.6** | (0.26) | 6.7 | (1.50) |
| Italy (Provincia Campania) | 433 | (11.3) | 435 | (12.3) | 454 | (12.0) | 449 | (9.8) | 9.7 | (7.80) | 1.3 | (0.24) | 0.9 | (1.40) |
| Italy (Provincia Basilicata) | **431** | (9.6) | 444 | (13.1) | 463 | (11.8) | **469** | (8.7) | **21.8** | (6.38) | 1.5 | (0.43) | 3.5 | (2.12) |
| Italy (Provincia Emilia Romagna) | **499** | (12.6) | 483 | (10.9) | 518 | (7.8) | **538** | (10.8) | 13.8 | (9.25) | 1.4 | (0.25) | 1.5 | (1.89) |
| Italy (Provincia Friuli Venezia Giulia) | **518** | (9.9) | 527 | (10.0) | 523 | (12.6) | **564** | (7.3) | **19.2** | (5.38) | 1.3 | (0.22) | 4.0 | (2.20) |
| Italy (Provincia Sicilia) | 406 | (19.0) | 438 | (14.3) | 451 | (16.5) | 438 | (18.7) | 14.2 | (10.17) | 1.7 | (0.60) | 1.9 | (2.76) |
| Italy (Provincia Liguria) | **453** | (16.1) | 467 | (15.8) | 508 | (12.7) | **518** | (7.3) | 25.0 | (14.09) | **2.0** | (0.43) | 4.6 | (4.43) |
| Italy (Provincia Lombardia) | 484 | (13.1) | 509 | (9.2) | 489 | (16.7) | 510 | (16.6) | 18.3 | (15.25) | 1.4 | (0.35) | 1.5 | (2.57) |
| Italy (Provincia Piemonte) | **461** | (13.3) | 517 | (12.9) | 523 | (10.0) | **536** | (8.9) | **30.6** | (5.33) | **2.4** | (0.46) | 7.9 | (2.92) |
| Italy (Provincia Trento) | **477** | (6.8) | 523 | (4.1) | 552 | (4.2) | **537** | (4.5) | **31.0** | (3.07) | **2.6** | (0.24) | 6.5 | (1.25) |
| Italy (Provincia Sardegna) | 458 | (22.0) | 425 | (16.6) | 446 | (17.4) | 468 | (15.4) | 3.0 | (13.24) | 0.9 | (0.39) | 0.1 | (1.50) |
| Italy (Provincia Puglia) | 449 | (11.8) | 442 | (6.6) | 435 | (10.8) | 464 | (16.6) | 11.0 | (8.46) | 1.0 | (0.34) | 1.4 | (2.39) |
| Italy (Provincia Veneto) | **489** | (17.4) | 534 | (11.6) | 535 | (10.8) | **542** | (11.4) | **33.0** | (12.63) | **2.1** | (0.54) | 5.3 | (3.96) |
| Spain (Andalusia) | 466 | (9.1) | 470 | (7.1) | 470 | (7.5) | 489 | (9.4) | 9.6 | (6.15) | 1.1 | (0.18) | 0.7 | (0.89) |
| Spain (Basque Country) | 498 | (7.7) | 490 | (7.3) | 495 | (6.8) | 496 | (6.4) | -1.1 | (3.84) | 0.9 | (0.16) | 0.0 | (0.15) |
| Spain (Cantabria) | 516 | (6.7) | 508 | (7.9) | 505 | (7.1) | 508 | (9.8) | -3.7 | (5.92) | 0.9 | (0.15) | 0.1 | (0.59) |
| Spain (Galicia) | 505 | (7.1) | 505 | (7.0) | 503 | (6.1) | 505 | (7.3) | -1.7 | (4.80) | 1.0 | (0.15) | 0.0 | (0.19) |
| Spain (La Rioja) | 527 | (5.2) | 517 | (5.2) | 523 | (5.7) | 514 | (6.8) | -3.1 | (3.31) | 0.8 | (0.13) | 0.1 | (0.22) |
| Spain (Castile and Leon) | 515 | (7.3) | 524 | (5.4) | 524 | (5.5) | 517 | (9.2) | 0.1 | (5.07) | 1.1 | (0.18) | 0.0 | (0.20) |
| Spain (Navarre) | 514 | (6.4) | 514 | (6.8) | 507 | (5.9) | 511 | (8.2) | -4.0 | (6.41) | 0.9 | (0.12) | 0.1 | (0.26) |
| Spain (Aragon) | 512 | (8.8) | 513 | (9.4) | 514 | (7.5) | 514 | (10.6) | 1.0 | (5.12) | 0.9 | (0.20) | 0.0 | (0.30) |
| Spain (Catalonia) | 483 | (11.0) | 485 | (8.7) | 491 | (7.8) | 508 | (15.2) | 12.0 | (6.33) | 1.1 | (0.24) | 2.0 | (2.36) |
| Spain (Asturias) | 493 | (13.0) | 519 | (8.8) | 517 | (7.4) | 506 | (7.4) | 5.1 | (7.91) | 1.4 | (0.28) | 0.2 | (0.87) |
| United Kingdom (Scotland) | 516 | (8.2) | 527 | (9.2) | 511 | (7.8) | 508 | (6.2) | -3.9 | (5.19) | 0.9 | (0.14) | 0.1 | (0.27) |
| **Non-adjudicated** | | | | | | | | | | | | | | |
| Belgium (French Community) | 459 | (15.8) | 490 | (14.9) | 505 | (12.2) | 490 | (9.7) | 15.1 | (9.55) | 1.6 | (0.34) | 1.2 | (1.62) |
| Belgium (German-Speaking Community) | 507 | (5.6) | 516 | (6.1) | 512 | (8.5) | 529 | (9.0) | **12.4** | (4.55) | 1.1 | (0.15) | 0.6 | (0.41) |
| Finland  (Finnish Speaking) | 564 | (3.3) | 566 | (3.4) | 569 | (4.5) | 561 | (4.8) | 0.0 | (3.21) | 1.0 | (0.09) | 0.0 | (0.06) |
| Finland  (Swedish Speaking) | **548** | (9.1) | 527 | (15.1) | 533 | (11.7) | **515** | (11.1) | **-19.6** | (4.55) | 0.7 | (0.21) | 1.9 | (1.36) |
| United Kingdom (England) | 515 | (7.0) | 514 | (6.9) | 515 | (7.7) | 528 | (7.8) | 3.2 | (3.80) | 1.0 | (0.13) | 0.1 | (0.19) |
| United Kingdom (Northern Ireland) | **479** | (14.2) | 502 | (11.3) | 515 | (11.5) | **548** | (13.8) | **20.4** | (8.01) | 1.5 | (0.30) | 4.0 | (3.04) |
| United Kingdom (Wales) | **491** | (7.3) | 509 | (8.2) | 503 | (7.4) | **520** | (6.9) | **10.3** | (4.60) | **1.3** | (0.16) | 0.7 | (0.66) |

Note: Values that are statistically significant are indicated in bold (see Annex A3). See Table 5.18 for national data.
1. Results based on reports from school principals and reported proportionate to the number of 15-year-olds enrolled in the school.
*StatLink* http://dx.doi.org/10.1787/142184405135

Pour consulter la version française intégrale de ce tableau, suivre ce lien :
*StatLink* http://dx.doi.org/10.1787/152830402855

[Part 1/1]

**Table S6a** **Percentage of students at each proficiency level on the reading scale**

Tableau S6a  Pourcentage d'élèves à chaque niveau de compétence sur l'échelle de compréhension de l'écrit

| | Proficiency levels | | | | | | | | | | |
|---|---|---|---|---|---|---|---|---|---|---|---|
| | Below Level 1 (below 334.75 score points) | | Level 1 (from 334.75 to 407.47 score points) | | Level 2 (from 407.47 to 480.18 score points) | | Level 3 (from 480.18 to 552.89 score points) | | Level 4 (from 552.89 to 625.61 score points) | | Level 5 (above 625.61 score points) | |
| | % | S.E. | % | S.E. | % | S.E. | % | S.E. | % | S.E. | % | S.E. |
| **Adjudicated** | | | | | | | | | | | | |
| Belgium (Flemish Community) | 6.0 | (1.1) | 8.1 | (0.6) | 15.8 | (0.8) | 26.5 | (1.0) | 28.8 | (1.1) | 14.7 | (0.8) |
| Italy (Provincia Autonoma of Bolzano) | 5.8 | (1.0) | 11.0 | (1.2) | 21.3 | (1.6) | 29.5 | (1.5) | 23.1 | (1.2) | 9.4 | (0.8) |
| Italy (Provincia Campania) | 13.8 | (1.6) | 22.3 | (2.0) | 29.9 | (1.7) | 22.4 | (1.8) | 9.4 | (1.1) | 2.1 | (0.6) |
| Italy (Provincia Basilicata) | 14.7 | (2.1) | 19.2 | (1.6) | 27.6 | (1.9) | 23.5 | (1.8) | 11.8 | (1.5) | 3.1 | (0.6) |
| Italy (Provincia Emilia Romagna) | 6.1 | (1.1) | 12.3 | (1.1) | 22.8 | (1.3) | 27.6 | (1.7) | 23.1 | (1.4) | 8.1 | (0.9) |
| Italy (Provincia Friuli Venezia Giulia) | 3.0 | (0.9) | 7.3 | (1.0) | 19.7 | (1.3) | 33.3 | (1.7) | 27.4 | (1.7) | 9.3 | (1.0) |
| Italy (Provincia Sicilia) | 20.3 | (2.9) | 20.5 | (2.2) | 26.9 | (2.1) | 21.0 | (2.0) | 9.9 | (1.5) | 1.4 | (0.4) |
| Italy (Provincia Liguria) | 9.4 | (1.7) | 13.5 | (1.7) | 22.8 | (1.6) | 27.2 | (2.0) | 19.6 | (1.8) | 7.6 | (1.2) |
| Italy (Provincia Lombardia) | 8.4 | (2.0) | 11.1 | (1.4) | 22.0 | (1.8) | 29.1 | (2.1) | 22.4 | (1.9) | 7.0 | (1.4) |
| Italy (Provincia Piemonte) | 5.0 | (1.1) | 9.8 | (1.0) | 21.1 | (1.6) | 30.5 | (1.7) | 25.0 | (1.7) | 8.6 | (1.0) |
| Italy (Provincia Trento) | 5.7 | (0.5) | 10.3 | (0.8) | 18.3 | (1.3) | 30.1 | (1.6) | 25.7 | (1.4) | 9.8 | (1.3) |
| Italy (Provincia Sardegna) | 19.5 | (2.6) | 17.7 | (1.6) | 24.3 | (1.7) | 22.8 | (1.6) | 12.7 | (1.4) | 3.1 | (0.5) |
| Italy (Provincia Puglia) | 14.3 | (1.8) | 22.0 | (1.8) | 28.4 | (2.0) | 22.8 | (2.0) | 9.9 | (1.5) | 2.7 | (0.6) |
| Italy (Provincia Veneto) | 4.5 | (1.2) | 10.3 | (1.5) | 19.9 | (2.0) | 29.1 | (2.1) | 26.1 | (2.0) | 10.1 | (1.0) |
| Spain (Andalusia) | 11.0 | (1.4) | 20.3 | (1.4) | 32.3 | (1.7) | 26.9 | (1.7) | 8.8 | (0.9) | 0.7 | (0.3) |
| Spain (Basque Country) | 5.2 | (0.8) | 12.5 | (1.0) | 25.9 | (1.2) | 33.0 | (1.2) | 19.3 | (1.3) | 4.2 | (0.6) |
| Spain (Cantabria) | 5.6 | (0.8) | 14.1 | (1.3) | 30.5 | (1.6) | 32.0 | (1.6) | 15.3 | (1.3) | 2.5 | (0.6) |
| Spain (Galicia) | 6.1 | (0.7) | 14.0 | (1.4) | 27.5 | (1.8) | 32.8 | (1.5) | 16.4 | (1.2) | 3.3 | (0.5) |
| Spain (La Rioja) | 3.3 | (0.7) | 12.3 | (1.1) | 26.2 | (1.5) | 34.7 | (1.9) | 19.9 | (1.3) | 3.7 | (0.8) |
| Spain (Castile and Leon) | 3.6 | (0.7) | 13.9 | (1.4) | 32.3 | (2.0) | 33.5 | (2.1) | 15.1 | (1.2) | 1.6 | (0.4) |
| Spain (Navarre) | 4.4 | (0.6) | 13.2 | (1.1) | 29.6 | (1.8) | 35.2 | (1.5) | 15.5 | (1.1) | 2.1 | (0.4) |
| Spain (Aragon) | 5.4 | (1.0) | 12.6 | (1.5) | 27.1 | (2.0) | 34.2 | (1.6) | 17.5 | (1.8) | 3.2 | (0.6) |
| Spain (Catalonia) | 6.6 | (1.2) | 14.6 | (1.4) | 27.1 | (2.0) | 31.6 | (1.3) | 17.1 | (1.7) | 3.1 | (0.8) |
| Spain (Asturias) | 5.7 | (1.2) | 12.5 | (1.5) | 29.9 | (1.5) | 33.9 | (1.6) | 15.6 | (1.3) | 2.4 | (0.5) |
| United Kingdom (Scotland) | 5.2 | (0.7) | 11.5 | (1.0) | 23.5 | (1.1) | 30.9 | (1.3) | 20.6 | (1.1) | 8.5 | (0.9) |
| **Non-adjudicated** | | | | | | | | | | | | |
| Belgium (French Community) | 11.9 | (1.4) | 14.4 | (1.1) | 22.9 | (1.2) | 25.3 | (1.4) | 18.7 | (1.2) | 6.7 | (0.9) |
| Belgium (German-Speaking Community) | 6.7 | (0.9) | 12.6 | (1.4) | 20.5 | (1.6) | 27.2 | (1.8) | 23.3 | (2.0) | 9.7 | (1.2) |
| Finland  (Finnish Speaking) | 0.7 | (0.2) | 4.0 | (0.4) | 15.3 | (0.8) | 30.9 | (0.9) | 32.0 | (0.9) | 17.0 | (0.9) |
| Finland  (Swedish Speaking) | 1.9 | (1.0) | 5.1 | (1.4) | 19.9 | (3.0) | 36.9 | (3.8) | 26.2 | (3.8) | 9.9 | (2.3) |
| United Kingdom (England) | 6.8 | (0.6) | 12.1 | (0.7) | 22.5 | (0.8) | 28.7 | (0.8) | 20.6 | (0.9) | 9.2 | (0.7) |
| United Kingdom (Northern Ireland) | 7.7 | (1.0) | 13.2 | (1.0) | 21.8 | (1.3) | 25.5 | (1.1) | 21.4 | (1.2) | 10.4 | (1.0) |
| United Kingdom (Wales) | 7.6 | (0.9) | 14.4 | (0.8) | 26.5 | (1.1) | 27.7 | (1.1) | 17.4 | (1.2) | 6.4 | (0.9) |

Note: See Table 6.1a for national data.
*StatLink* ◼◼◼ http://dx.doi.org/10.1787/142184405135

Pour consulter la version française intégrale de ce tableau, suivre ce lien :
*StatLink* ◼◼◼ http://dx.doi.org/10.1787/152830402855

[Part 1/2]

**Table S6b** Percentage of students at each proficiency level on the reading scale, by gender

Tableau S6b Pourcentage d'élèves à chaque niveau de compétence sur l'échelle de compréhension de l'écrit, selon le sexe

| | Males – Proficiency levels | | | | | | | | | | | |
|---|---|---|---|---|---|---|---|---|---|---|---|---|
| | Below Level 1 (below 334.75 score points) | | Level 1 (from 334.75 to 407.47 score points) | | Level 2 (from 407.47 to 480.18 score points) | | Level 3 (from 480.18 to 552.89 score points) | | Level 4 (from 552.89 to 625.61 score points) | | Level 5 (above 625.61 score points) | |
| | % | S.E. | % | S.E. | % | S.E. | % | S.E. | % | S.E. | % | S.E. |
| **Adjudicated** | | | | | | | | | | | | |
| Belgium (Flemish Community) | 7.6 | (1.4) | 10.4 | (1.0) | 18.2 | (1.3) | 27.0 | (1.1) | 25.1 | (1.3) | 11.7 | (0.9) |
| Italy (Provincia Autonoma of Bolzano) | 8.6 | (1.4) | 14.3 | (2.1) | 23.9 | (2.7) | 29.6 | (2.2) | 18.4 | (1.5) | 5.1 | (0.9) |
| Italy (Provincia Campania) | 17.3 | (2.5) | 22.4 | (2.8) | 30.1 | (2.3) | 20.7 | (2.9) | 7.5 | (1.7) | 2.0 | (0.7) |
| Italy (Provincia Basilicata) | 21.8 | (3.2) | 22.5 | (2.4) | 26.2 | (2.4) | 18.9 | (2.0) | 8.7 | (1.6) | 1.8 | (0.7) |
| Italy (Provincia Emilia Romagna) | 8.2 | (1.7) | 13.7 | (2.1) | 26.1 | (2.1) | 29.5 | (2.8) | 17.8 | (1.9) | 4.8 | (0.7) |
| Italy (Provincia Friuli Venezia Giulia) | 5.4 | (1.5) | 9.9 | (1.5) | 24.1 | (1.8) | 32.4 | (2.6) | 20.8 | (2.3) | 7.5 | (1.1) |
| Italy (Provincia Sicilia) | 29.0 | (4.2) | 22.4 | (3.1) | 23.9 | (3.3) | 15.8 | (2.8) | 7.8 | (1.8) | 1.2 | (0.6) |
| Italy (Provincia Liguria) | 15.1 | (3.1) | 17.2 | (2.2) | 25.8 | (3.1) | 23.7 | (3.3) | 13.8 | (1.9) | 4.5 | (1.2) |
| Italy (Provincia Lombardia) | 11.9 | (3.3) | 14.3 | (2.1) | 25.0 | (2.3) | 27.5 | (2.4) | 16.7 | (2.4) | 4.5 | (1.2) |
| Italy (Provincia Piemonte) | 8.4 | (1.9) | 13.7 | (1.8) | 24.8 | (2.4) | 28.6 | (2.9) | 18.8 | (2.6) | 5.7 | (1.3) |
| Italy (Provincia Trento) | 9.0 | (0.8) | 12.8 | (1.2) | 20.9 | (1.9) | 30.2 | (2.2) | 21.1 | (1.9) | 6.0 | (1.3) |
| Italy (Provincia Sardegna) | 29.2 | (4.0) | 21.9 | (2.3) | 22.5 | (2.2) | 17.6 | (2.3) | 7.2 | (1.6) | 1.7 | (0.6) |
| Italy (Provincia Puglia) | 19.0 | (2.6) | 25.9 | (2.6) | 26.4 | (2.5) | 18.5 | (2.0) | 8.4 | (1.3) | 1.7 | (0.7) |
| Italy (Provincia Veneto) | 6.4 | (2.0) | 13.2 | (2.3) | 22.1 | (2.3) | 28.3 | (2.9) | 22.0 | (2.8) | 8.0 | (1.3) |
| Spain (Andalusia) | 13.9 | (2.1) | 23.0 | (2.4) | 31.9 | (2.7) | 23.3 | (2.2) | 7.6 | (1.3) | 0.4 | (0.4) |
| Spain (Basque Country) | 8.2 | (1.2) | 15.5 | (1.3) | 28.4 | (1.6) | 29.5 | (1.6) | 15.0 | (1.3) | 3.2 | (0.5) |
| Spain (Cantabria) | 9.2 | (1.4) | 17.4 | (2.1) | 31.9 | (3.1) | 27.4 | (2.6) | 12.2 | (1.3) | 2.0 | (0.5) |
| Spain (Galicia) | 9.3 | (1.4) | 18.4 | (1.9) | 29.4 | (2.1) | 28.3 | (2.1) | 11.8 | (1.6) | 2.8 | (0.6) |
| Spain (La Rioja) | 4.5 | (1.2) | 15.1 | (1.6) | 29.9 | (2.1) | 34.3 | (2.4) | 14.6 | (1.6) | 1.6 | (0.5) |
| Spain (Castile and Leon) | 5.1 | (1.1) | 17.5 | (2.0) | 32.1 | (1.4) | 31.5 | (2.5) | 12.9 | (1.7) | 1.0 | (0.4) |
| Spain (Navarre) | 6.9 | (1.1) | 16.6 | (1.9) | 31.7 | (3.0) | 31.6 | (2.6) | 12.0 | (1.7) | 1.2 | (0.5) |
| Spain (Aragon) | 8.5 | (1.5) | 16.6 | (2.3) | 30.5 | (2.7) | 30.5 | (2.7) | 12.6 | (2.1) | 1.3 | (0.6) |
| Spain (Catalonia) | 8.8 | (2.0) | 16.2 | (1.7) | 29.9 | (2.5) | 29.2 | (2.3) | 13.6 | (1.9) | 2.3 | (0.8) |
| Spain (Asturias) | 8.8 | (2.1) | 14.9 | (1.8) | 32.4 | (2.2) | 30.3 | (2.3) | 12.0 | (1.6) | 1.7 | (0.5) |
| United Kingdom (Scotland) | 7.5 | (1.4) | 13.2 | (1.7) | 24.4 | (1.4) | 29.8 | (1.8) | 18.1 | (1.5) | 7.0 | (1.1) |
| **Non-adjudicated** | | | | | | | | | | | | |
| Belgium (French Community) | 17.0 | (2.1) | 17.2 | (1.4) | 23.6 | (1.6) | 22.5 | (1.8) | 15.0 | (1.4) | 4.7 | (0.8) |
| Belgium (German-Speaking Community) | 9.8 | (1.4) | 16.3 | (1.9) | 21.0 | (2.3) | 24.7 | (2.7) | 19.9 | (2.5) | 8.3 | (1.6) |
| Finland (Finnish Speaking) | 1.4 | (0.3) | 6.6 | (0.8) | 21.7 | (1.2) | 34.2 | (1.3) | 26.2 | (1.4) | 9.9 | (0.9) |
| Finland (Swedish Speaking) | 3.4 | (1.7) | 7.1 | (2.6) | 22.6 | (5.5) | 40.1 | (6.2) | 23.1 | (4.8) | 3.6 | (2.1) |
| United Kingdom (England) | 9.8 | (1.0) | 14.4 | (1.0) | 22.8 | (1.0) | 27.0 | (1.6) | 18.4 | (1.3) | 7.7 | (0.7) |
| United Kingdom (Northern Ireland) | 10.9 | (1.3) | 15.0 | (1.5) | 22.2 | (1.8) | 24.6 | (1.6) | 19.3 | (1.4) | 8.1 | (1.2) |
| United Kingdom (Wales) | 10.4 | (1.2) | 17.1 | (1.0) | 27.2 | (1.4) | 25.9 | (1.7) | 14.7 | (1.3) | 4.7 | (0.8) |

Note: See Table 6.1b for national data.
*StatLink* http://dx.doi.org/10.1787/142184405135

Pour consulter la version française intégrale de ce tableau, suivre ce lien :
*StatLink* http://dx.doi.org/10.1787/152830402855

[Part 2/2]

**Table S6b** **Percentage of students at each proficiency level on the reading scale, by gender**

Tableau S6b   Pourcentage d'élèves à chaque niveau de compétence sur l'échelle de compréhension de l'écrit, selon le sexe

| | Females – Proficiency levels | | | | | | | | | | | |
|---|---|---|---|---|---|---|---|---|---|---|---|---|
| | Below Level 1 (below 334.75 score points) | | Level 1 (from 334.75 to 407.47 score points) | | Level 2 (from 407.47 to 480.18 score points) | | Level 3 (from 480.18 to 552.89 score points) | | Level 4 (from 552.89 to 625.61 score points) | | Level 5 (above 625.61 score points) | |
| | % | S.E. | % | S.E. | % | S.E. | % | S.E. | % | S.E. | % | S.E. |
| **Adjudicated** | | | | | | | | | | | | |
| Belgium (Flemish Community) | 4.3 | (1.0) | 5.5 | (0.7) | 13.0 | (1.1) | 26.0 | (1.7) | 32.9 | (1.6) | 18.2 | (1.4) |
| Italy (Provincia Autonoma of Bolzano) | 3.1 | (1.0) | 7.6 | (1.1) | 18.7 | (1.6) | 29.3 | (2.2) | 27.7 | (2.1) | 13.7 | (1.4) |
| Italy (Provincia Campania) | 10.4 | (1.5) | 22.2 | (2.5) | 29.7 | (2.5) | 24.1 | (2.4) | 11.4 | (1.6) | 2.2 | (0.8) |
| Italy (Provincia Basilicata) | 7.1 | (1.4) | 15.7 | (1.8) | 29.1 | (3.0) | 28.5 | (2.8) | 15.2 | (2.1) | 4.5 | (1.2) |
| Italy (Provincia Emilia Romagna) | 3.8 | (1.0) | 11.0 | (1.2) | 19.4 | (1.5) | 25.8 | (2.2) | 28.6 | (1.8) | 11.4 | (1.7) |
| Italy (Provincia Friuli Venezia Giulia) | 0.7 | (0.4) | 4.6 | (1.0) | 15.4 | (1.8) | 34.2 | (2.4) | 34.0 | (2.3) | 11.2 | (1.7) |
| Italy (Provincia Sicilia) | 12.0 | (3.1) | 18.8 | (3.3) | 29.7 | (2.4) | 26.0 | (2.8) | 12.0 | (2.0) | 1.5 | (0.6) |
| Italy (Provincia Liguria) | 3.4 | (0.9) | 9.6 | (1.8) | 19.6 | (2.7) | 30.8 | (2.0) | 25.6 | (2.6) | 10.8 | (1.5) |
| Italy (Provincia Lombardia) | 4.9 | (1.4) | 8.0 | (1.5) | 18.9 | (2.6) | 30.6 | (3.4) | 28.0 | (2.8) | 9.6 | (2.2) |
| Italy (Provincia Piemonte) | 2.0 | (0.8) | 6.5 | (0.9) | 17.9 | (1.8) | 32.1 | (2.2) | 30.4 | (1.9) | 11.1 | (1.4) |
| Italy (Provincia Trento) | 2.5 | (0.8) | 7.8 | (1.2) | 15.8 | (1.4) | 30.1 | (2.3) | 30.3 | (2.2) | 13.6 | (2.0) |
| Italy (Provincia Sardegna) | 9.5 | (1.7) | 13.4 | (2.1) | 26.2 | (2.7) | 28.2 | (2.5) | 18.3 | (2.1) | 4.5 | (0.9) |
| Italy (Provincia Puglia) | 9.8 | (1.8) | 18.3 | (2.5) | 30.3 | (2.7) | 26.9 | (2.7) | 11.3 | (2.1) | 3.6 | (0.8) |
| Italy (Provincia Veneto) | 2.6 | (0.9) | 7.2 | (1.7) | 17.5 | (2.5) | 29.9 | (2.3) | 30.4 | (2.7) | 12.4 | (1.7) |
| Spain (Andalusia) | 8.2 | (1.3) | 17.8 | (1.6) | 32.6 | (2.0) | 30.3 | (2.0) | 10.0 | (1.1) | 1.1 | (0.4) |
| Spain (Basque Country) | 2.1 | (0.6) | 9.5 | (1.2) | 23.3 | (1.3) | 36.4 | (1.7) | 23.5 | (1.6) | 5.2 | (1.0) |
| Spain (Cantabria) | 2.0 | (0.7) | 10.9 | (1.5) | 29.0 | (2.1) | 36.6 | (2.1) | 18.4 | (1.8) | 3.0 | (0.9) |
| Spain (Galicia) | 2.5 | (0.7) | 9.0 | (1.5) | 25.4 | (2.4) | 37.8 | (3.0) | 21.5 | (1.9) | 3.8 | (0.8) |
| Spain (La Rioja) | 2.0 | (0.6) | 9.4 | (1.5) | 22.5 | (2.2) | 35.1 | (3.4) | 25.2 | (2.6) | 5.8 | (1.3) |
| Spain (Castile and Leon) | 2.0 | (0.5) | 9.9 | (1.4) | 32.4 | (2.8) | 35.8 | (2.7) | 17.6 | (1.8) | 2.3 | (0.7) |
| Spain (Navarre) | 1.9 | (0.7) | 9.7 | (1.4) | 27.5 | (2.0) | 38.9 | (2.5) | 19.0 | (1.9) | 3.0 | (0.6) |
| Spain (Aragon) | 2.3 | (0.7) | 8.5 | (1.3) | 23.6 | (2.0) | 38.0 | (1.8) | 22.5 | (2.3) | 5.2 | (1.0) |
| Spain (Catalonia) | 4.4 | (0.9) | 13.1 | (1.8) | 24.3 | (2.3) | 33.9 | (2.0) | 20.5 | (2.8) | 3.8 | (1.0) |
| Spain (Asturias) | 2.5 | (0.8) | 9.9 | (2.1) | 27.4 | (1.9) | 37.7 | (2.5) | 19.5 | (1.8) | 3.1 | (0.7) |
| United Kingdom (Scotland) | 2.8 | (0.8) | 9.7 | (1.1) | 22.6 | (1.7) | 31.9 | (1.6) | 23.0 | (1.5) | 9.9 | (1.3) |
| **Non-adjudicated** | | | | | | | | | | | | |
| Belgium (French Community) | 6.5 | (1.2) | 11.4 | (1.4) | 22.2 | (1.8) | 28.4 | (1.7) | 22.6 | (2.1) | 8.9 | (1.5) |
| Belgium (German-Speaking Community) | 3.7 | (1.1) | 8.9 | (1.9) | 20.1 | (2.0) | 29.6 | (2.7) | 26.7 | (3.1) | 11.1 | (1.9) |
| Finland  (Finnish Speaking) | 0.1 | (0.1) | 1.4 | (0.5) | 9.1 | (0.8) | 27.7 | (1.3) | 37.8 | (1.1) | 24.0 | (1.3) |
| Finland  (Swedish Speaking) | 0.3 | (0.6) | 3.1 | (2.2) | 17.1 | (3.7) | 33.7 | (5.0) | 29.5 | (6.0) | 16.3 | (3.6) |
| United Kingdom (England) | 4.0 | (0.6) | 10.0 | (0.8) | 22.2 | (1.1) | 30.3 | (1.2) | 22.9 | (1.0) | 10.7 | (0.9) |
| United Kingdom (Northern Ireland) | 4.4 | (1.1) | 11.4 | (1.5) | 21.3 | (2.2) | 26.5 | (1.5) | 23.6 | (1.8) | 12.8 | (1.4) |
| United Kingdom (Wales) | 4.9 | (1.0) | 11.7 | (1.1) | 25.7 | (1.6) | 29.5 | (1.5) | 20.2 | (1.5) | 8.0 | (1.2) |

Note: See Table 6.1b for national data.
*StatLink* ☜☞ http://dx.doi.org/10.1787/142184405135

Pour consulter la version française intégrale de ce tableau, suivre ce lien :
*StatLink* ☜☞ http://dx.doi.org/10.1787/152830402855

303

[Part 1/1]

**Table S6c** Mean score, variation and gender differences in student performance on the reading scale

Tableau S6c Score moyen, différences de score selon le sexe et répartition des scores sur l'échelle de compréhension de l'écrit

| | All students | | | | Gender differences | | | | | |
| | Mean score | | Standard deviation | | Males | | Females | | Difference (M - F) | |
| | Mean | S.E. | S.D. | S.E. | Mean score | S.E. | Mean score | S.E. | Score dif. | S.E. |
|---|---|---|---|---|---|---|---|---|---|---|
| **Adjudicated** | | | | | | | | | | |
| Belgium (Flemish Community) | 522 | (4.1) | 105 | (4.5) | 506 | (5.2) | 540 | (4.5) | -35 | (5.3) |
| Italy (Provincia Autonoma of Bolzano) | 502 | (2.2) | 100 | (2.6) | 479 | (3.5) | 525 | (3.1) | -46 | (5.0) |
| Italy (Provincia Campania) | 438 | (5.8) | 97 | (3.2) | 428 | (8.2) | 449 | (6.1) | -21 | (8.5) |
| Italy (Provincia Basilicata) | 446 | (6.3) | 103 | (3.2) | 420 | (7.8) | 473 | (6.4) | -53 | (7.5) |
| Italy (Provincia Emilia Romagna) | 496 | (4.5) | 99 | (3.0) | 477 | (6.9) | 516 | (4.6) | -38 | (7.9) |
| Italy (Provincia Friuli Venezia Giulia) | 519 | (4.2) | 88 | (3.8) | 499 | (7.1) | 539 | (4.5) | -40 | (9.4) |
| Italy (Provincia Sicilia) | 424 | (8.4) | 108 | (5.6) | 399 | (10.8) | 447 | (9.3) | -49 | (11.5) |
| Italy (Provincia Liguria) | 483 | (6.9) | 105 | (3.3) | 452 | (9.5) | 516 | (6.1) | -64 | (9.4) |
| Italy (Provincia Lombardia) | 491 | (7.1) | 106 | (5.9) | 465 | (10.6) | 515 | (6.4) | -50 | (11.0) |
| Italy (Provincia Piemonte) | 506 | (5.1) | 95 | (3.8) | 481 | (7.4) | 528 | (4.5) | -47 | (7.1) |
| Italy (Provincia Trento) | 508 | (2.5) | 100 | (1.9) | 486 | (3.6) | 531 | (3.8) | -45 | (5.3) |
| Italy (Provincia Sardegna) | 435 | (8.2) | 118 | (5.4) | 399 | (11.9) | 473 | (6.4) | -75 | (11.7) |
| Italy (Provincia Puglia) | 440 | (6.7) | 104 | (4.0) | 421 | (8.0) | 458 | (7.3) | -37 | (5.6) |
| Italy (Provincia Veneto) | 511 | (5.9) | 96 | (4.2) | 494 | (9.8) | 529 | (6.2) | -35 | (11.7) |
| Spain (Andalusia) | 445 | (4.1) | 87 | (2.5) | 431 | (5.7) | 457 | (3.8) | -26 | (5.0) |
| Spain (Basque Country) | 487 | (4.2) | 89 | (2.4) | 469 | (4.9) | 506 | (4.0) | -37 | (3.4) |
| Spain (Cantabria) | 475 | (4.0) | 86 | (2.0) | 457 | (4.7) | 493 | (4.2) | -36 | (3.8) |
| Spain (Galicia) | 479 | (3.4) | 90 | (1.9) | 459 | (4.5) | 501 | (3.1) | -42 | (4.0) |
| Spain (La Rioja) | 492 | (2.6) | 82 | (2.2) | 475 | (3.4) | 509 | (3.6) | -34 | (5.1) |
| Spain (Castile and Leon) | 478 | (3.4) | 76 | (1.9) | 467 | (4.1) | 491 | (3.7) | -24 | (4.0) |
| Spain (Navarre) | 481 | (2.7) | 79 | (1.8) | 464 | (3.7) | 497 | (3.3) | -34 | (4.2) |
| Spain (Aragon) | 483 | (5.2) | 86 | (2.4) | 461 | (6.5) | 506 | (4.5) | -45 | (5.1) |
| Spain (Catalonia) | 477 | (5.1) | 90 | (3.2) | 463 | (6.0) | 490 | (5.3) | -27 | (5.3) |
| Spain (Asturias) | 477 | (4.7) | 84 | (3.0) | 461 | (6.4) | 494 | (4.1) | -34 | (5.3) |
| United Kingdom (Scotland) | 499 | (4.0) | 96 | (1.8) | 486 | (5.0) | 512 | (4.1) | -26 | (4.4) |
| | | | | | | | | | | |
| **Non-adjudicated** | | | | | | | | | | |
| Belgium (French Community) | 473 | (5.0) | 110 | (3.3) | 450 | (6.6) | 498 | (5.5) | -48 | (7.6) |
| Belgium (German-Speaking Community) | 499 | (3.0) | 103 | (3.0) | 481 | (4.6) | 517 | (4.9) | -36 | (7.5) |
| Finland (Finnish Speaking) | 548 | (2.3) | 81 | (1.2) | 522 | (2.9) | 573 | (2.5) | -51 | (3.0) |
| Finland (Swedish Speaking) | 525 | (6.5) | 80 | (4.8) | 504 | (7.4) | 546 | (8.3) | -42 | (8.5) |
| United Kingdom (England) | 496 | (2.7) | 102 | (2.0) | 481 | (3.6) | 510 | (3.1) | -29 | (4.1) |
| United Kingdom (Northern Ireland) | 495 | (3.5) | 106 | (2.8) | 479 | (5.5) | 512 | (5.1) | -33 | (8.0) |
| United Kingdom (Wales) | 481 | (3.7) | 98 | (2.3) | 465 | (4.2) | 496 | (4.2) | -31 | (4.0) |

| | Percentiles | | | | | | | | | | | |
| | 5th | | 10th | | 25th | | 75th | | 90th | | 95th | |
| | Score | S.E. | Score | S.E. | Score | S.E. | Score | S.E. | Score | S.E. | Score | S.E. |
|---|---|---|---|---|---|---|---|---|---|---|---|---|
| **Adjudicated** | | | | | | | | | | | | |
| Belgium (Flemish Community) | 322 | (14.0) | 377 | (11.0) | 462 | (5.4) | 597 | (2.6) | 642 | (2.9) | 667 | (3.3) |
| Italy (Provincia Autonoma of Bolzano) | 326 | (10.9) | 369 | (7.5) | 439 | (3.6) | 573 | (2.9) | 623 | (3.8) | 652 | (5.5) |
| Italy (Provincia Campania) | 277 | (12.3) | 314 | (8.3) | 377 | (6.8) | 504 | (5.5) | 559 | (6.9) | 592 | (8.8) |
| Italy (Provincia Basilicata) | 273 | (8.8) | 309 | (12.4) | 379 | (10.0) | 518 | (7.1) | 575 | (6.2) | 607 | (5.7) |
| Italy (Provincia Emilia Romagna) | 321 | (11.1) | 361 | (8.2) | 431 | (7.2) | 568 | (4.3) | 616 | (4.8) | 645 | (5.8) |
| Italy (Provincia Friuli Venezia Giulia) | 368 | (10.9) | 406 | (9.1) | 466 | (6.3) | 578 | (3.8) | 623 | (4.6) | 651 | (6.9) |
| Italy (Provincia Sicilia) | 233 | (22.4) | 277 | (17.1) | 355 | (11.1) | 500 | (6.5) | 558 | (7.3) | 586 | (8.1) |
| Italy (Provincia Liguria) | 298 | (11.6) | 340 | (13.8) | 415 | (10.3) | 559 | (5.6) | 612 | (7.4) | 643 | (7.5) |
| Italy (Provincia Lombardia) | 297 | (19.9) | 349 | (16.2) | 431 | (10.7) | 564 | (6.1) | 611 | (7.9) | 638 | (8.2) |
| Italy (Provincia Piemonte) | 336 | (18.2) | 382 | (10.4) | 447 | (7.9) | 574 | (5.2) | 620 | (4.6) | 645 | (5.4) |
| Italy (Provincia Trento) | 327 | (4.5) | 369 | (5.3) | 448 | (4.0) | 578 | (5.6) | 624 | (6.7) | 652 | (8.9) |
| Italy (Provincia Sardegna) | 221 | (17.6) | 278 | (16.9) | 361 | (12.4) | 520 | (7.2) | 578 | (6.8) | 609 | (6.7) |
| Italy (Provincia Puglia) | 272 | (13.5) | 311 | (10.2) | 374 | (7.2) | 509 | (7.6) | 567 | (7.9) | 599 | (7.6) |
| Italy (Provincia Veneto) | 340 | (14.5) | 383 | (12.1) | 447 | (9.6) | 580 | (4.8) | 626 | (4.7) | 654 | (6.2) |
| Spain (Andalusia) | 290 | (9.4) | 330 | (8.1) | 390 | (6.2) | 506 | (3.1) | 551 | (4.0) | 573 | (5.4) |
| Spain (Basque Country) | 333 | (8.1) | 372 | (7.1) | 432 | (5.4) | 549 | (3.8) | 594 | (4.5) | 620 | (4.5) |
| Spain (Cantabria) | 330 | (6.6) | 366 | (7.8) | 422 | (5.4) | 533 | (4.1) | 579 | (3.3) | 605 | (4.5) |
| Spain (Galicia) | 324 | (6.4) | 363 | (6.6) | 424 | (5.1) | 540 | (3.7) | 586 | (5.7) | 613 | (5.9) |
| Spain (La Rioja) | 353 | (6.8) | 383 | (6.8) | 439 | (5.1) | 550 | (3.3) | 591 | (4.4) | 616 | (5.3) |
| Spain (Castile and Leon) | 347 | (7.7) | 379 | (5.8) | 428 | (5.3) | 531 | (2.9) | 573 | (2.7) | 598 | (4.7) |
| Spain (Navarre) | 342 | (6.5) | 375 | (5.6) | 430 | (4.3) | 536 | (3.9) | 578 | (3.5) | 601 | (4.8) |
| Spain (Aragon) | 330 | (10.5) | 370 | (7.8) | 431 | (7.0) | 543 | (5.5) | 585 | (5.6) | 611 | (7.2) |
| Spain (Catalonia) | 319 | (11.4) | 360 | (9.3) | 420 | (6.7) | 540 | (6.5) | 586 | (5.9) | 610 | (7.0) |
| Spain (Asturias) | 327 | (15.7) | 367 | (10.5) | 427 | (7.0) | 535 | (4.4) | 578 | (3.9) | 601 | (5.1) |
| United Kingdom (Scotland) | 334 | (7.8) | 371 | (6.2) | 439 | (4.3) | 564 | (4.1) | 617 | (4.7) | 650 | (7.3) |
| | | | | | | | | | | | | |
| **Non-adjudicated** | | | | | | | | | | | | |
| Belgium (French Community) | 275 | (11.3) | 322 | (9.5) | 401 | (7.7) | 554 | (5.1) | 608 | (4.9) | 637 | (5.5) |
| Belgium (German-Speaking Community) | 312 | (13.8) | 362 | (6.9) | 433 | (5.1) | 575 | (3.6) | 625 | (4.9) | 649 | (7.3) |
| Finland (Finnish Speaking) | 410 | (4.6) | 441 | (4.0) | 495 | (3.0) | 604 | (2.4) | 649 | (2.5) | 676 | (3.1) |
| Finland (Swedish Speaking) | 387 | (22.9) | 429 | (15.7) | 476 | (10.0) | 577 | (10.8) | 626 | (7.2) | 649 | (12.7) |
| United Kingdom (England) | 317 | (6.5) | 358 | (4.8) | 431 | (3.3) | 567 | (3.0) | 622 | (3.6) | 654 | (4.0) |
| United Kingdom (Northern Ireland) | 311 | (8.3) | 352 | (8.7) | 424 | (5.5) | 572 | (3.2) | 627 | (4.8) | 659 | (6.0) |
| United Kingdom (Wales) | 312 | (8.1) | 352 | (7.7) | 417 | (4.7) | 550 | (3.7) | 603 | (5.2) | 635 | (6.4) |

Note: Values that are statistically significant are indicated in bold (see Annex A3). See Table 6.1c for national data.
StatLink ⟐ http://dx.doi.org/10.1787/142184405135

Pour consulter la version française intégrale de ce tableau, suivre ce lien :
StatLink ⟐ http://dx.doi.org/10.1787/152830402855

[Part 1/1]

**Table S6d** **Percentage of students at each proficiency level on the mathematics scale**

Tableau S6d  Pourcentage d'élèves à chaque niveau de compétence sur l'échelle de culture mathématique

| | Proficiency levels | | | | | | | | | | | | | |
| | Below Level 1 (below 357.77 score points) | | Level 1 (from 357.77 to 420.07 score points) | | Level 2 (from 420.07 to 482.38 score points) | | Level 3 (from 482.38 to 544.68 score points) | | Level 4 (from 544.68 to 606.99 score points) | | Level 5 (from 606.99 to 669.30 score points) | | Level 6 (above 669.30 score points) | |
| | % | S.E. | % | S.E. | % | S.E. | % | S.E. | % | S.E. | % | S.E. | % | S.E. |
|---|---|---|---|---|---|---|---|---|---|---|---|---|---|---|
| **Adjudicated** | | | | | | | | | | | | | | |
| Belgium (Flemish Community) | 4.2 | (1.0) | 7.7 | (0.7) | 14.0 | (0.8) | 20.8 | (1.0) | 24.7 | (1.1) | 19.9 | (0.8) | 8.7 | (0.7) |
| Italy (Provincia Autonoma of Bolzano) | 4.1 | (0.5) | 10.1 | (1.3) | 21.6 | (1.6) | 27.2 | (1.6) | 22.3 | (1.4) | 11.4 | (0.9) | 3.3 | (0.7) |
| Italy (Provincia Campania) | 18.6 | (2.4) | 25.7 | (2.1) | 28.1 | (2.2) | 17.6 | (1.6) | 6.2 | (1.2) | 1.8 | (0.6) | 1.9 | (1.8) |
| Italy (Provincia Basilicata) | 15.3 | (1.9) | 23.1 | (1.6) | 29.4 | (1.5) | 20.8 | (1.6) | 8.9 | (1.1) | 2.3 | (0.5) | 0.2 | (0.3) |
| Italy (Provincia Emilia Romagna) | 8.7 | (1.0) | 14.0 | (1.2) | 20.5 | (1.5) | 25.0 | (1.6) | 20.2 | (1.2) | 9.1 | (0.9) | 2.6 | (0.6) |
| Italy (Provincia Friuli Venezia Giulia) | 3.6 | (0.7) | 10.0 | (0.9) | 20.9 | (1.4) | 29.9 | (1.6) | 22.4 | (1.3) | 10.2 | (1.1) | 3.1 | (0.7) |
| Italy (Provincia Sicilia) | 23.5 | (2.7) | 25.4 | (1.6) | 25.4 | (1.9) | 16.1 | (1.9) | 7.5 | (1.0) | 1.9 | (0.5) | 0.2 | (0.2) |
| Italy (Provincia Liguria) | 10.4 | (1.6) | 16.8 | (1.7) | 25.7 | (2.1) | 26.0 | (1.8) | 15.3 | (1.9) | 4.7 | (1.1) | 1.1 | (0.6) |
| Italy (Provincia Lombardia) | 8.5 | (2.1) | 14.6 | (1.2) | 22.8 | (1.7) | 26.8 | (2.0) | 18.3 | (1.7) | 7.7 | (1.2) | 1.4 | (0.5) |
| Italy (Provincia Piemonte) | 6.0 | (1.3) | 12.8 | (1.5) | 26.0 | (2.1) | 28.5 | (1.9) | 18.5 | (1.4) | 6.8 | (1.1) | 1.5 | (0.5) |
| Italy (Provincia Trento) | 6.4 | (0.6) | 11.4 | (0.7) | 19.2 | (1.0) | 25.7 | (1.5) | 22.5 | (1.6) | 11.3 | (1.5) | 3.5 | (0.9) |
| Italy (Provincia Sardegna) | 23.2 | (2.6) | 22.1 | (1.9) | 24.6 | (1.6) | 18.1 | (1.8) | 8.5 | (1.4) | 3.0 | (0.8) | 0.4 | (0.2) |
| Italy (Provincia Puglia) | 16.7 | (1.6) | 26.3 | (2.2) | 28.2 | (2.2) | 18.8 | (1.9) | 8.1 | (1.1) | 1.8 | (0.5) | 0.2 | (0.2) |
| Italy (Provincia Veneto) | 4.4 | (0.7) | 12.3 | (1.6) | 21.5 | (2.5) | 25.1 | (2.0) | 22.4 | (2.3) | 11.0 | (1.3) | 3.4 | (0.8) |
| Spain (Andalusia) | 10.9 | (1.3) | 19.0 | (1.4) | 28.0 | (1.4) | 25.0 | (1.7) | 13.0 | (1.2) | 3.6 | (0.7) | 0.5 | (0.2) |
| Spain (Basque Country) | 5.1 | (0.7) | 11.8 | (1.0) | 23.0 | (1.0) | 28.2 | (1.0) | 21.7 | (1.1) | 8.5 | (0.7) | 1.6 | (0.3) |
| Spain (Cantabria) | 5.7 | (0.7) | 11.2 | (1.1) | 22.6 | (1.7) | 27.9 | (1.4) | 22.2 | (1.5) | 8.6 | (1.1) | 1.8 | (0.5) |
| Spain (Galicia) | 5.3 | (0.7) | 13.0 | (1.1) | 25.4 | (1.6) | 28.8 | (1.2) | 18.9 | (1.7) | 7.0 | (1.1) | 1.6 | (0.5) |
| Spain (La Rioja) | 3.1 | (0.5) | 8.0 | (1.1) | 18.8 | (1.3) | 27.0 | (1.6) | 24.8 | (1.5) | 13.8 | (1.3) | 4.5 | (0.8) |
| Spain (Castile and Leon) | 2.6 | (0.5) | 9.8 | (1.1) | 22.4 | (1.3) | 28.9 | (1.2) | 22.4 | (1.4) | 11.0 | (0.9) | 2.8 | (0.5) |
| Spain (Navarre) | 4.4 | (0.9) | 11.0 | (1.1) | 20.7 | (1.5) | 24.2 | (1.5) | 23.1 | (1.3) | 13.3 | (1.2) | 3.2 | (0.8) |
| Spain (Aragon) | 5.9 | (0.8) | 10.7 | (1.2) | 20.8 | (1.4) | 23.8 | (1.2) | 21.9 | (1.3) | 12.1 | (1.3) | 4.7 | (0.8) |
| Spain (Catalonia) | 7.6 | (1.1) | 13.4 | (1.2) | 22.5 | (1.7) | 27.4 | (1.7) | 18.3 | (1.7) | 6.8 | (1.3) | 1.3 | (0.5) |
| Spain (Asturias) | 4.8 | (1.0) | 11.7 | (1.8) | 24.8 | (1.9) | 30.3 | (1.6) | 19.9 | (1.6) | 7.2 | (1.1) | 1.3 | (0.4) |
| United Kingdom (Scotland) | 3.8 | (0.7) | 11.7 | (0.9) | 24.1 | (1.1) | 28.2 | (1.2) | 20.0 | (1.2) | 9.4 | (0.9) | 2.7 | (0.5) |
| | | | | | | | | | | | | | | |
| **Non-adjudicated** | | | | | | | | | | | | | | |
| Belgium (French Community) | 11.0 | (1.5) | 13.5 | (1.2) | 20.8 | (1.1) | 22.2 | (1.0) | 18.2 | (1.0) | 10.8 | (1.0) | 3.4 | (0.5) |
| Belgium (German-Speaking Community) | 6.2 | (0.8) | 10.7 | (1.2) | 19.0 | (1.6) | 24.1 | (2.1) | 22.6 | (1.6) | 13.1 | (1.3) | 4.3 | (0.8) |
| Finland (Finnish Speaking) | 1.1 | (0.2) | 4.7 | (0.5) | 14.2 | (0.7) | 27.1 | (0.7) | 28.2 | (0.8) | 18.3 | (0.8) | 6.4 | (0.5) |
| Finland (Swedish Speaking) | 1.5 | (0.9) | 6.8 | (1.8) | 17.7 | (3.7) | 29.2 | (4.2) | 26.4 | (4.4) | 14.4 | (2.8) | 4.0 | (1.7) |
| United Kingdom (England) | 6.0 | (0.7) | 13.9 | (0.8) | 24.7 | (1.0) | 26.2 | (0.8) | 18.0 | (0.7) | 8.7 | (0.6) | 2.5 | (0.3) |
| United Kingdom (Northern Ireland) | 7.3 | (0.9) | 15.3 | (1.0) | 23.2 | (1.1) | 23.3 | (1.3) | 18.8 | (1.0) | 9.6 | (0.8) | 2.6 | (0.3) |
| United Kingdom (Wales) | 6.0 | (0.5) | 16.1 | (0.9) | 27.0 | (1.1) | 27.5 | (1.1) | 16.1 | (1.1) | 6.0 | (0.6) | 1.2 | (0.3) |

Note: See Table 6.2a for national data.
*StatLink* ⟳ http://dx.doi.org/10.1787/142184405135

Pour consulter la version française intégrale de ce tableau, suivre ce lien :
*StatLink* ⟳ http://dx.doi.org/10.1787/152830402855

[Part 1/2]

**Table S6e** **Percentage of students at each proficiency level on the mathematics scale, by gender**

Tableau S6e   Pourcentage d'élèves à chaque niveau de compétence sur l'échelle de culture mathématique, selon le sexe

| | Males – Proficiency levels | | | | | | | | | | | | |
|---|---|---|---|---|---|---|---|---|---|---|---|---|---|
| | Below Level 1 (below 357.77 score points) | | Level 1 (from 357.77 to 420.07 score points) | | Level 2 (from 420.07 to 482.38 score points) | | Level 3 (from 482.38 to 544.68 score points) | | Level 4 (from 544.68 to 606.99 score points) | | Level 5 (from 606.99 to 669.30 score points) | | Level 6 (above 669.30 score points) | |
| | % | S.E. | % | S.E. | % | S.E. | % | S.E. | % | S.E. | % | S.E. | % | S.E. |
| **Adjudicated** | | | | | | | | | | | | | | |
| Belgium (Flemish Community) | 3.5 | (1.2) | 7.9 | (1.0) | 14.1 | (1.0) | 19.6 | (1.5) | 23.6 | (1.3) | 20.9 | (1.1) | 10.4 | (0.9) |
| Italy (Provincia Autonoma of Bolzano) | 4.2 | (0.8) | 9.3 | (1.5) | 18.2 | (1.9) | 26.3 | (2.0) | 23.5 | (1.7) | 13.6 | (1.4) | 5.0 | (0.9) |
| Italy (Provincia Campania) | 14.6 | (1.9) | 21.4 | (2.7) | 28.4 | (2.7) | 22.0 | (2.1) | 9.0 | (1.8) | 2.7 | (0.9) | 1.9 | (1.8) |
| Italy (Provincia Basilicata) | 16.4 | (2.7) | 22.6 | (2.0) | 26.5 | (2.0) | 21.1 | (2.2) | 10.6 | (1.3) | 2.6 | (0.6) | 0.3 | a |
| Italy (Provincia Emilia Romagna) | 5.6 | (1.5) | 11.3 | (1.8) | 19.2 | (1.9) | 27.4 | (2.9) | 22.5 | (2.2) | 10.3 | (1.3) | 3.7 | (0.9) |
| Italy (Provincia Friuli Venezia Giulia) | 3.2 | (0.9) | 8.9 | (1.4) | 19.6 | (2.2) | 28.3 | (2.2) | 23.8 | (2.0) | 12.0 | (1.7) | 4.2 | (1.0) |
| Italy (Provincia Sicilia) | 23.0 | (2.9) | 23.9 | (2.8) | 23.3 | (2.6) | 16.4 | (2.7) | 9.7 | (1.5) | 3.4 | (1.1) | 0.3 | (0.3) |
| Italy (Provincia Liguria) | 11.4 | (2.5) | 16.0 | (2.3) | 23.8 | (2.9) | 24.6 | (2.4) | 16.5 | (2.3) | 6.0 | (1.3) | 1.6 | (1.0) |
| Italy (Provincia Lombardia) | 9.9 | (3.8) | 14.8 | (2.5) | 21.8 | (2.5) | 23.7 | (2.1) | 17.7 | (2.5) | 9.9 | (2.2) | 2.2 | (0.9) |
| Italy (Provincia Piemonte) | 6.9 | (1.8) | 12.2 | (2.3) | 24.8 | (3.2) | 28.2 | (2.7) | 18.2 | (2.0) | 7.9 | (1.4) | 1.8 | (0.7) |
| Italy (Provincia Trento) | 6.5 | (1.0) | 10.5 | (1.1) | 17.3 | (1.7) | 22.5 | (2.0) | 22.3 | (1.9) | 14.8 | (2.1) | 6.0 | (1.6) |
| Italy (Provincia Sardegna) | 21.8 | (3.5) | 19.1 | (2.0) | 24.6 | (2.6) | 18.4 | (2.3) | 10.7 | (1.9) | 4.7 | (1.3) | 0.8 | (0.4) |
| Italy (Provincia Puglia) | 16.2 | (2.2) | 24.4 | (2.3) | 27.6 | (2.1) | 19.7 | (2.3) | 9.5 | (1.3) | 2.3 | (0.6) | 0.3 | (0.3) |
| Italy (Provincia Veneto) | 2.8 | (0.7) | 10.2 | (2.5) | 20.1 | (3.7) | 24.5 | (2.6) | 23.2 | (2.6) | 13.9 | (1.7) | 5.2 | (1.2) |
| Spain (Andalusia) | 9.9 | (1.5) | 19.0 | (2.3) | 25.9 | (2.6) | 25.5 | (3.1) | 14.6 | (2.0) | 4.5 | (1.1) | 0.6 | (0.3) |
| Spain (Basque Country) | 5.9 | (0.9) | 12.4 | (1.3) | 21.4 | (1.5) | 26.4 | (1.6) | 21.8 | (1.3) | 10.0 | (1.1) | 2.1 | (0.5) |
| Spain (Cantabria) | 6.2 | (1.0) | 11.2 | (1.6) | 20.5 | (2.4) | 26.1 | (1.9) | 22.5 | (2.1) | 10.9 | (1.7) | 2.6 | (0.8) |
| Spain (Galicia) | 6.0 | (1.1) | 12.3 | (1.3) | 23.6 | (1.6) | 26.8 | (1.7) | 20.4 | (2.3) | 8.4 | (1.6) | 2.5 | (0.7) |
| Spain (La Rioja) | 2.7 | (0.8) | 7.9 | (1.4) | 16.8 | (1.8) | 25.7 | (2.2) | 26.2 | (2.1) | 15.3 | (2.2) | 5.3 | (1.3) |
| Spain (Castile and Leon) | 2.6 | (0.6) | 9.8 | (1.6) | 20.2 | (1.9) | 28.2 | (2.2) | 23.1 | (2.1) | 12.4 | (1.7) | 3.7 | (0.9) |
| Spain (Navarre) | 4.2 | (1.0) | 11.9 | (1.8) | 19.0 | (2.3) | 22.3 | (2.0) | 23.2 | (1.6) | 15.0 | (1.7) | 4.5 | (1.1) |
| Spain (Aragon) | 4.8 | (1.0) | 10.0 | (1.4) | 20.0 | (1.9) | 22.9 | (1.7) | 23.1 | (1.9) | 13.2 | (1.6) | 6.0 | (1.4) |
| Spain (Catalonia) | 7.6 | (1.6) | 12.6 | (2.1) | 23.7 | (1.9) | 26.9 | (2.5) | 18.6 | (1.9) | 8.6 | (1.8) | 1.9 | (0.9) |
| Spain (Asturias) | 5.2 | (1.3) | 11.2 | (2.0) | 22.3 | (1.8) | 30.1 | (2.3) | 20.4 | (2.1) | 9.0 | (1.6) | 1.8 | (0.6) |
| United Kingdom (Scotland) | 3.9 | (0.8) | 10.5 | (1.2) | 21.3 | (1.5) | 27.9 | (1.9) | 22.0 | (1.5) | 10.9 | (1.2) | 3.5 | (0.7) |
| **Non-adjudicated** | | | | | | | | | | | | | | |
| Belgium (French Community) | 12.5 | (2.1) | 13.7 | (2.2) | 19.2 | (1.7) | 20.8 | (1.3) | 17.4 | (1.5) | 11.8 | (1.3) | 4.5 | (0.7) |
| Belgium (German-Speaking Community) | 6.8 | (1.2) | 10.5 | (1.7) | 17.7 | (2.1) | 21.4 | (2.3) | 22.2 | (2.3) | 15.5 | (1.8) | 6.0 | (1.5) |
| Finland  (Finnish Speaking) | 1.2 | (0.3) | 4.7 | (0.8) | 13.4 | (1.0) | 24.9 | (1.1) | 27.7 | (1.1) | 19.9 | (1.1) | 8.2 | (0.7) |
| Finland  (Swedish Speaking) | 2.7 | (1.7) | 4.5 | (2.2) | 12.2 | (4.1) | 29.5 | (3.7) | 30.2 | (4.5) | 16.9 | (3.1) | 4.1 | (3.2) |
| United Kingdom (England) | 5.8 | (0.9) | 12.6 | (1.0) | 22.7 | (1.2) | 25.2 | (1.2) | 19.6 | (1.0) | 10.7 | (0.8) | 3.5 | (0.4) |
| United Kingdom (Northern Ireland) | 7.5 | (1.2) | 15.1 | (1.4) | 22.0 | (1.7) | 22.5 | (1.6) | 19.0 | (1.6) | 10.8 | (1.1) | 3.1 | (0.5) |
| United Kingdom (Wales) | 5.4 | (0.7) | 14.7 | (1.3) | 25.0 | (1.4) | 27.8 | (1.6) | 18.3 | (1.5) | 7.2 | (1.1) | 1.6 | (0.5) |

Note: See Table 6.2b for national data.
*StatLink* http://dx.doi.org/10.1787/142184405135

Pour consulter la version française intégrale de ce tableau, suivre ce lien :
*StatLink* http://dx.doi.org/10.1787/152830402855

[Part 2/2]

**Table S6e** **Percentage of students at each proficiency level on the mathematics scale, by gender**

Tableau S6e   Pourcentage d'élèves à chaque niveau de compétence sur l'échelle de culture mathématique, selon le sexe

| | Females – Proficiency levels | | | | | | | | | | | | |
|---|---|---|---|---|---|---|---|---|---|---|---|---|---|
| | Below Level 1 (below 357.77 score points) | | Level 1 (from 357.77 to 420.07 score points) | | Level 2 (from 420.07 to 482.38 score points) | | Level 3 (from 482.38 to 544.68 score points) | | Level 4 (from 544.68 to 606.99 score points) | | Level 5 (from 606.99 to 669.30 score points) | | Level 6 (above 669.30 score points) | |
| | % | S.E. | % | S.E. | % | S.E. | % | S.E. | % | S.E. | % | S.E. | % | S.E. |
| **Adjudicated** | | | | | | | | | | | | | | |
| Belgium (Flemish Community) | 5.1 | (0.9) | 7.4 | (0.9) | 13.9 | (1.1) | 22.3 | (1.3) | 25.8 | (1.3) | 18.8 | (1.4) | 6.7 | (0.9) |
| Italy (Provincia Autonoma of Bolzano) | 4.0 | (0.9) | 10.9 | (1.8) | 24.9 | (2.7) | 28.2 | (2.4) | 21.1 | (1.8) | 9.2 | (1.4) | 1.6 | (0.6) |
| Italy (Provincia Campania) | 22.5 | (3.5) | 30.0 | (2.6) | 27.8 | (2.9) | 13.3 | (2.3) | 3.5 | (1.0) | 1.0 | (0.6) | 1.9 | (1.8) |
| Italy (Provincia Basilicata) | 14.1 | (1.8) | 23.7 | (2.4) | 32.6 | (2.4) | 20.5 | (2.7) | 7.0 | (1.6) | 1.9 | (0.8) | 0.1 | a |
| Italy (Provincia Emilia Romagna) | 11.8 | (1.6) | 16.7 | (1.2) | 21.9 | (1.9) | 22.6 | (1.7) | 17.8 | (1.8) | 7.8 | (1.5) | 1.5 | (0.7) |
| Italy (Provincia Friuli Venezia Giulia) | 3.9 | (1.1) | 11.1 | (1.9) | 22.2 | (1.9) | 31.5 | (1.9) | 21.1 | (1.9) | 8.3 | (1.3) | 2.0 | (0.8) |
| Italy (Provincia Sicilia) | 24.0 | (3.3) | 26.7 | (2.5) | 27.5 | (2.4) | 15.9 | (2.4) | 5.4 | (1.0) | 0.5 | a | 0.0 | a |
| Italy (Provincia Liguria) | 9.3 | (1.4) | 17.6 | (2.1) | 27.8 | (2.4) | 27.5 | (2.3) | 14.0 | (2.2) | 3.3 | (1.2) | 0.6 | (0.3) |
| Italy (Provincia Lombardia) | 7.1 | (1.3) | 14.4 | (2.0) | 23.7 | (2.2) | 29.8 | (3.0) | 18.8 | (2.5) | 5.6 | (1.2) | 0.5 | (0.4) |
| Italy (Provincia Piemonte) | 5.2 | (1.4) | 13.4 | (1.6) | 27.0 | (2.9) | 28.8 | (2.8) | 18.7 | (2.0) | 5.8 | (1.3) | 1.2 | (0.6) |
| Italy (Provincia Trento) | 6.3 | (0.9) | 12.2 | (1.4) | 21.1 | (1.9) | 28.9 | (2.1) | 22.6 | (2.3) | 7.9 | (1.7) | 0.9 | (0.5) |
| Italy (Provincia Sardegna) | 24.7 | (3.2) | 25.1 | (2.9) | 24.6 | (2.5) | 17.9 | (2.1) | 6.3 | (1.4) | 1.2 | (0.6) | 0.1 | a |
| Italy (Provincia Puglia) | 17.2 | (1.7) | 28.2 | (2.7) | 28.7 | (3.2) | 17.8 | (2.2) | 6.7 | (1.3) | 1.4 | (0.5) | 0.1 | a |
| Italy (Provincia Veneto) | 6.0 | (1.1) | 14.6 | (2.2) | 23.0 | (2.6) | 25.6 | (2.6) | 21.5 | (3.7) | 7.9 | (1.9) | 1.4 | (0.7) |
| Spain (Andalusia) | 11.9 | (1.6) | 19.1 | (1.8) | 29.9 | (1.9) | 24.6 | (2.3) | 11.5 | (1.4) | 2.7 | (0.7) | 0.3 | (0.2) |
| Spain (Basque Country) | 4.3 | (0.7) | 11.2 | (1.2) | 24.6 | (1.4) | 30.0 | (1.4) | 21.6 | (1.6) | 7.1 | (0.8) | 1.1 | (0.3) |
| Spain (Cantabria) | 5.2 | (1.0) | 11.2 | (1.4) | 24.6 | (2.0) | 29.8 | (2.0) | 22.0 | (1.9) | 6.2 | (1.1) | 1.0 | (0.3) |
| Spain (Galicia) | 4.5 | (0.8) | 13.9 | (1.7) | 27.3 | (2.6) | 31.1 | (1.5) | 17.2 | (1.8) | 5.4 | (1.2) | 0.6 | (0.4) |
| Spain (La Rioja) | 3.4 | (0.8) | 8.2 | (1.5) | 20.9 | (1.8) | 28.4 | (2.1) | 23.3 | (1.9) | 12.2 | (1.5) | 3.6 | (1.0) |
| Spain (Castile and Leon) | 2.6 | (0.9) | 9.8 | (1.4) | 24.7 | (2.3) | 29.7 | (1.9) | 21.7 | (1.7) | 9.5 | (1.4) | 1.9 | (0.6) |
| Spain (Navarre) | 4.7 | (1.3) | 10.1 | (1.4) | 22.4 | (2.6) | 26.2 | (2.3) | 23.0 | (2.0) | 11.7 | (1.5) | 1.9 | (0.7) |
| Spain (Aragon) | 7.1 | (1.0) | 11.4 | (1.6) | 21.6 | (1.8) | 24.7 | (1.9) | 20.8 | (2.2) | 10.9 | (1.7) | 3.4 | (0.7) |
| Spain (Catalonia) | 7.6 | (1.1) | 14.2 | (1.4) | 26.6 | (2.2) | 27.9 | (2.0) | 18.0 | (2.1) | 5.1 | (1.4) | 0.6 | (0.3) |
| Spain (Asturias) | 4.4 | (1.3) | 12.2 | (2.2) | 27.3 | (2.9) | 30.5 | (2.2) | 19.3 | (2.1) | 5.3 | (1.3) | 0.9 | (0.5) |
| United Kingdom (Scotland) | 3.7 | (0.9) | 13.0 | (1.2) | 27.0 | (1.7) | 28.5 | (1.6) | 18.0 | (1.5) | 7.9 | (1.1) | 1.9 | (0.6) |
| **Non-adjudicated** | | | | | | | | | | | | | | |
| Belgium (French Community) | 9.3 | (1.4) | 13.4 | (1.2) | 22.5 | (1.5) | 23.7 | (1.6) | 19.0 | (1.4) | 9.7 | (1.3) | 2.3 | (0.6) |
| Belgium (German-Speaking Community) | 5.6 | (1.3) | 10.9 | (2.0) | 20.3 | (2.2) | 26.8 | (3.6) | 23.1 | (2.3) | 10.7 | (2.1) | 2.6 | (0.9) |
| Finland  (Finnish Speaking) | 1.1 | (0.3) | 4.7 | (0.8) | 15.0 | (1.1) | 29.2 | (1.1) | 28.6 | (1.2) | 16.7 | (0.9) | 4.7 | (0.6) |
| Finland  (Swedish Speaking) | 0.3 | (0.4) | 9.1 | (2.9) | 23.4 | (5.5) | 29.0 | (6.5) | 22.5 | (6.0) | 11.9 | (4.8) | 3.9 | (1.8) |
| United Kingdom (England) | 6.3 | (0.7) | 15.1 | (1.1) | 26.7 | (1.5) | 27.2 | (1.3) | 16.4 | (0.9) | 6.8 | (0.7) | 1.5 | (0.4) |
| United Kingdom (Northern Ireland) | 7.1 | (1.1) | 15.5 | (1.6) | 24.3 | (1.5) | 24.1 | (1.8) | 18.5 | (1.4) | 8.3 | (1.1) | 2.1 | (0.5) |
| United Kingdom (Wales) | 6.7 | (0.8) | 17.6 | (1.7) | 29.0 | (1.5) | 27.2 | (1.4) | 14.0 | (1.4) | 4.9 | (0.8) | 0.8 | (0.3) |

Note: See Table 6.2b for national data.
*StatLink* ⛁ http://dx.doi.org/10.1787/142184405135

Pour consulter la version française intégrale de ce tableau, suivre ce lien :
*StatLink* ⛁ http://dx.doi.org/10.1787/152830402855

[Part 1/1]

**Table S6f**  **Mean score, variation and gender differences in student performance on the mathematics scale**

*Tableau S6f*  *Score moyen, différences de score selon le sexe et répartition des scores sur l'échelle de culture mathématique*

| | All students | | | | Gender differences | | | | | |
| --- | --- | --- | --- | --- | --- | --- | --- | --- | --- | --- |
| | Mean score | | Standard deviation | | Males | | Females | | Difference (M - F) | |
| | Mean | S.E. | S.D. | S.E. | Mean score | S.E. | Mean score | S.E. | Score dif. | S.E. |
| **Adjudicated** | | | | | | | | | | |
| Belgium (Flemish Community) | 543 | (3.7) | 98 | (3.0) | 549 | (4.4) | 537 | (4.5) | **12** | (5.0) |
| Italy (Provincia Autonoma of Bolzano) | 513 | (1.8) | 88 | (1.6) | 523 | (3.0) | 503 | (2.5) | **20** | (4.1) |
| Italy (Provincia Campania) | 436 | (9.0) | 92 | (10.3) | 453 | (8.8) | 420 | (9.9) | **33** | (6.9) |
| Italy (Provincia Basilicata) | 443 | (5.0) | 84 | (3.3) | 445 | (6.8) | 442 | (5.4) | 3 | (7.2) |
| Italy (Provincia Emilia Romagna) | 494 | (3.4) | 96 | (2.2) | 510 | (4.8) | 478 | (4.3) | **32** | (6.3) |
| Italy (Provincia Friuli Venezia Giulia) | 513 | (3.6) | 84 | (2.5) | 521 | (5.7) | 505 | (4.7) | **16** | (7.8) |
| Italy (Provincia Sicilia) | 423 | (6.5) | 90 | (4.2) | 431 | (7.9) | 415 | (7.6) | 16 | (8.5) |
| Italy (Provincia Liguria) | 473 | (6.4) | 89 | (3.5) | 476 | (8.7) | 469 | (5.9) | 7 | (7.7) |
| Italy (Provincia Lombardia) | 487 | (6.6) | 92 | (4.9) | 488 | (11.2) | 486 | (5.6) | 2 | (11.8) |
| Italy (Provincia Piemonte) | 492 | (4.8) | 85 | (3.7) | 493 | (6.6) | 490 | (5.2) | 3 | (6.8) |
| Italy (Provincia Trento) | 508 | (2.3) | 95 | (1.6) | 520 | (3.8) | 497 | (3.0) | **22** | (5.1) |
| Italy (Provincia Sardegna) | 429 | (6.9) | 99 | (3.6) | 440 | (9.0) | 419 | (7.5) | **21** | (10.0) |
| Italy (Provincia Puglia) | 435 | (4.8) | 88 | (4.7) | 440 | (5.5) | 430 | (5.0) | **10** | (4.7) |
| Italy (Provincia Veneto) | 510 | (6.2) | 90 | (2.7) | 525 | (7.8) | 495 | (7.8) | **29** | (10.3) |
| Spain (Andalusia) | 463 | (4.2) | 85 | (2.2) | 468 | (5.3) | 457 | (4.3) | **11** | (4.7) |
| Spain (Basque Country) | 501 | (3.4) | 85 | (1.8) | 502 | (4.2) | 500 | (3.4) | 3 | (3.3) |
| Spain (Cantabria) | 502 | (2.6) | 86 | (2.0) | 506 | (4.0) | 497 | (3.5) | 9 | (5.2) |
| Spain (Galicia) | 494 | (4.1) | 83 | (1.9) | 499 | (4.8) | 488 | (4.3) | **10** | (4.4) |
| Spain (La Rioja) | 526 | (2.2) | 87 | (2.4) | 533 | (3.5) | 519 | (3.5) | **13** | (5.5) |
| Spain (Castile and Leon) | 515 | (3.3) | 82 | (1.3) | 520 | (3.9) | 509 | (3.9) | **11** | (4.0) |
| Spain (Navarre) | 515 | (3.5) | 90 | (2.2) | 520 | (4.4) | 510 | (4.6) | 10 | (5.8) |
| Spain (Aragon) | 513 | (4.5) | 97 | (2.2) | 521 | (5.7) | 504 | (5.2) | **18** | (6.1) |
| Spain (Catalonia) | 488 | (5.2) | 87 | (2.5) | 493 | (6.3) | 482 | (5.2) | **11** | (5.1) |
| Spain (Asturias) | 497 | (4.9) | 82 | (2.2) | 502 | (6.1) | 493 | (4.9) | 9 | (5.4) |
| United Kingdom (Scotland) | 506 | (3.6) | 85 | (1.9) | 514 | (4.2) | 498 | (4.0) | **16** | (4.0) |
| **Non-adjudicated** | | | | | | | | | | |
| Belgium (French Community) | 490 | (5.2) | 109 | (5.8) | 490 | (7.3) | 491 | (5.5) | -1 | (7.9) |
| Belgium (German-Speaking Community) | 514 | (3.1) | 97 | (2.4) | 520 | (4.4) | 509 | (4.9) | 12 | (7.1) |
| Finland (Finnish Speaking) | 549 | (2.3) | 81 | (1.1) | 555 | (2.8) | 543 | (2.6) | **11** | (2.7) |
| Finland (Swedish Speaking) | 533 | (7.5) | 81 | (3.9) | 542 | (7.5) | 524 | (9.4) | **18** | (8.5) |
| United Kingdom (England) | 495 | (2.5) | 89 | (1.6) | 504 | (3.0) | 487 | (3.1) | **17** | (3.5) |
| United Kingdom (Northern Ireland) | 494 | (2.8) | 93 | (1.9) | 497 | (5.3) | 491 | (4.4) | 7 | (8.1) |
| United Kingdom (Wales) | 484 | (2.9) | 83 | (1.2) | 492 | (3.1) | 476 | (3.5) | **16** | (3.3) |

| | Percentiles | | | | | | | | | | | |
| --- | --- | --- | --- | --- | --- | --- | --- | --- | --- | --- | --- | --- |
| | 5th | | 10th | | 25th | | 75th | | 90th | | 95th | |
| | Score | S.E. | Score | S.E. | Score | S.E. | Score | S.E. | Score | S.E. | Score | S.E. |
| **Adjudicated** | | | | | | | | | | | | |
| Belgium (Flemish Community) | 366 | (10.8) | 409 | (8.8) | 479 | (5.0) | 616 | (3.0) | 663 | (3.3) | 688 | (3.4) |
| Italy (Provincia Autonoma of Bolzano) | 367 | (5.4) | 401 | (5.3) | 453 | (3.8) | 575 | (2.8) | 627 | (4.4) | 654 | (4.2) |
| Italy (Provincia Campania) | 298 | (10.3) | 327 | (8.2) | 376 | (7.6) | 489 | (8.8) | 545 | (15.7) | 586 | (30.3) |
| Italy (Provincia Basilicata) | 305 | (8.7) | 335 | (7.6) | 388 | (7.1) | 501 | (5.6) | 551 | (5.7) | 580 | (7.4) |
| Italy (Provincia Emilia Romagna) | 332 | (7.0) | 366 | (7.1) | 429 | (5.4) | 563 | (4.4) | 614 | (4.8) | 644 | (6.7) |
| Italy (Provincia Friuli Venezia Giulia) | 373 | (6.6) | 403 | (5.0) | 458 | (4.3) | 569 | (4.4) | 619 | (6.0) | 651 | (9.6) |
| Italy (Provincia Sicilia) | 278 | (15.9) | 310 | (11.7) | 362 | (8.1) | 484 | (6.6) | 542 | (7.8) | 570 | (7.7) |
| Italy (Provincia Liguria) | 324 | (8.3) | 356 | (7.9) | 413 | (8.2) | 533 | (7.3) | 584 | (7.8) | 612 | (10.9) |
| Italy (Provincia Lombardia) | 329 | (19.7) | 367 | (13.3) | 426 | (8.0) | 551 | (7.1) | 603 | (5.7) | 631 | (6.5) |
| Italy (Provincia Piemonte) | 349 | (11.3) | 384 | (8.8) | 437 | (5.5) | 549 | (6.0) | 599 | (7.0) | 627 | (7.7) |
| Italy (Provincia Trento) | 346 | (5.1) | 383 | (3.9) | 444 | (3.0) | 574 | (3.1) | 628 | (5.5) | 657 | (6.5) |
| Italy (Provincia Sardegna) | 260 | (11.7) | 298 | (11.1) | 364 | (9.6) | 498 | (8.3) | 555 | (9.2) | 591 | (9.3) |
| Italy (Provincia Puglia) | 303 | (8.3) | 334 | (3.9) | 381 | (4.7) | 492 | (7.0) | 545 | (7.0) | 572 | (7.2) |
| Italy (Provincia Veneto) | 364 | (6.1) | 394 | (6.0) | 447 | (7.0) | 574 | (7.8) | 624 | (7.7) | 654 | (8.5) |
| Spain (Andalusia) | 321 | (9.1) | 353 | (7.1) | 406 | (6.1) | 521 | (4.4) | 571 | (5.7) | 599 | (5.3) |
| Spain (Basque Country) | 357 | (7.0) | 390 | (4.6) | 445 | (4.3) | 562 | (3.5) | 607 | (3.8) | 634 | (4.0) |
| Spain (Cantabria) | 351 | (7.5) | 386 | (6.3) | 445 | (4.8) | 562 | (4.0) | 609 | (5.3) | 636 | (5.9) |
| Spain (Galicia) | 356 | (5.6) | 389 | (6.0) | 439 | (4.8) | 551 | (5.5) | 600 | (6.3) | 629 | (7.8) |
| Spain (La Rioja) | 381 | (9.2) | 415 | (4.9) | 468 | (3.5) | 588 | (3.8) | 638 | (4.5) | 664 | (7.3) |
| Spain (Castile and Leon) | 382 | (6.5) | 410 | (5.5) | 459 | (4.2) | 572 | (4.2) | 623 | (4.2) | 650 | (5.9) |
| Spain (Navarre) | 363 | (8.3) | 395 | (5.5) | 449 | (5.1) | 582 | (4.0) | 630 | (5.1) | 656 | (5.8) |
| Spain (Aragon) | 349 | (7.6) | 387 | (7.3) | 448 | (4.7) | 580 | (5.9) | 634 | (5.6) | 667 | (7.6) |
| Spain (Catalonia) | 336 | (8.3) | 372 | (7.3) | 432 | (5.0) | 547 | (5.8) | 597 | (7.8) | 626 | (6.8) |
| Spain (Asturias) | 359 | (10.5) | 393 | (7.5) | 444 | (6.4) | 553 | (5.7) | 600 | (6.1) | 628 | (8.5) |
| United Kingdom (Scotland) | 367 | (6.2) | 398 | (4.6) | 447 | (4.2) | 564 | (4.7) | 616 | (5.1) | 647 | (6.5) |
| **Non-adjudicated** | | | | | | | | | | | | |
| Belgium (French Community) | 302 | (16.1) | 352 | (10.2) | 421 | (5.2) | 568 | (5.3) | 626 | (5.6) | 655 | (5.3) |
| Belgium (German-Speaking Community) | 346 | (8.4) | 385 | (8.1) | 451 | (5.9) | 584 | (5.3) | 636 | (5.6) | 664 | (6.1) |
| Finland (Finnish Speaking) | 413 | (5.4) | 445 | (3.4) | 495 | (2.7) | 606 | (2.7) | 652 | (2.9) | 678 | (3.1) |
| Finland (Swedish Speaking) | 399 | (14.8) | 431 | (13.4) | 478 | (12.1) | 591 | (10.6) | 639 | (14.0) | 662 | (10.5) |
| United Kingdom (England) | 350 | (6.1) | 380 | (3.7) | 434 | (3.1) | 557 | (3.0) | 613 | (3.6) | 643 | (4.3) |
| United Kingdom (Northern Ireland) | 341 | (6.8) | 373 | (4.9) | 427 | (4.3) | 561 | (3.5) | 616 | (3.4) | 647 | (4.8) |
| United Kingdom (Wales) | 351 | (4.0) | 378 | (3.7) | 428 | (3.0) | 541 | (3.4) | 592 | (4.4) | 621 | (4.9) |

Note: Values that are statistically significant are indicated in bold (see Annex A3). See Table 6.2c for national data.
*StatLink* http://dx.doi.org/10.1787/142184405135

Pour consulter la version française intégrale de ce tableau, suivre ce lien :
*StatLink* http://dx.doi.org/10.1787/152830402855

[Part 1/1]

**Table S6g**  **Trends in reading since PISA 2000**

Tableau S6g  Évolution des performances en compréhension de l'écrit depuis PISA 2000

| | Differences in reading performance between PISA 2003 and PISA 2000 (PISA 2003 – PISA 2000) | | | | | | | |
| --- | --- | --- | --- | --- | --- | --- | --- | --- |
| | All students | | Males | | Females | | Gender difference (M – F) | |
| | Dif. | S.E. | Dif. | S.E. | Dif. | S.E. | Dif. | S.E. |
| **Adjudicated** | | | | | | | | |
| Belgium (Flemish Community) | -2 | (7.1) | 0 | (8.8) | -7 | (8.2) | 7 | (9.5) |
| United Kingdom (Scotland) | -10 | (7.0) | -7 | (7.6) | *-14* | (7.6) | 7 | (6.3) |
| **Non-adjudicated** | | | | | | | | |
| Belgium (French Community) | 1 | (10.3) | -4 | (12.6) | 6 | (11.2) | -11 | (13.2) |

| | Differences in reading performance between PISA 2006 and PISA 2000 (PISA 2006 – PISA 2000) | | | | | | | |
| --- | --- | --- | --- | --- | --- | --- | --- | --- |
| | All students | | Males | | Females | | Gender difference (M – F) | |
| | Dif. | S.E. | Dif. | S.E. | Dif. | S.E. | Dif. | S.E. |
| **Adjudicated** | | | | | | | | |
| Belgium (Flemish Community) | -10 | (7.7) | -11 | (9.4) | -11 | (8.5) | 0 | (9.2) |
| United Kingdom (Scotland) | **-27** | (7.4) | **-25** | (8.3) | **-29** | (7.8) | 4 | (6.3) |
| **Non-adjudicated** | | | | | | | | |
| Belgium (French Community) | -2 | (10.1) | -10 | (12.2) | 3 | (10.9) | -14 | (12.3) |
| Belgium (German-Speaking Community) | m | m | m | m | m | m | m | m |

| | Differences in reading performance between PISA 2006 and PISA 2003 (PISA 2006 – PISA 2003) | | | | | | | |
| --- | --- | --- | --- | --- | --- | --- | --- | --- |
| | All students | | Males | | Females | | Gender difference (M – F) | |
| | Dif. | S.E. | Dif. | S.E. | Dif. | S.E. | Dif. | S.E. |
| **Adjudicated** | | | | | | | | |
| Belgium (Flemish Community) | -8 | (6.4) | -11 | (7.7) | -4 | (7.3) | -7 | (7.9) |
| Italy (Provincia Autonoma of Bolzano) | **-42** | (7.4) | **-45** | (9.0) | **-36** | (7.4) | -9 | (7.3) |
| Italy (Provincia Lombardia) | **-24** | (10.9) | -24 | (16.6) | **-25** | (9.4) | 1 | (18.0) |
| Italy (Provincia Piemonte) | 4 | (7.9) | 3 | (11.0) | 6 | (8.4) | -3 | (11.1) |
| Italy (Provincia Trento) | **-34** | (5.6) | **-46** | (6.8) | **-20** | (6.7) | **-26** | (7.6) |
| Italy (Provincia Veneto) | -3 | (9.7) | 0 | (14.6) | -6 | (10.3) | 6 | (17.1) |
| Spain (Basque Country) | **-10** | (6.8) | -6 | (7.9) | *-13* | (6.7) | 7 | (5.6) |
| Spain (Castile and Leon) | **-21** | (6.9) | -13 | (8.1) | **-26** | (7.4) | *13* | (7.1) |
| Spain (Catalonia) | -6 | (8.1) | 2 | (9.0) | -12 | (9.1) | 14 | (9.1) |
| United Kingdom (Scotland) | **-17** | (6.5) | **-18** | (7.4) | **-15** | (6.9) | -3 | (6.2) |
| **Non-adjudicated** | | | | | | | | |
| Belgium (French Community) | -3 | (8.4) | -6 | (10.5) | -3 | (9.3) | -3 | (11.7) |
| Belgium (German-Speaking Community) | 1 | (6.0) | 10 | (8.0) | -8 | (8.2) | *18* | (11.0) |

Note: Differences that are statistically significant at the 95% confidence level are indicated in bold and at the 90% confidence level are indicated in bold italic (see Annex A3). See Table 6.3a for national data.
*StatLink* ᴍᴪ⋙ http://dx.doi.org/10.1787/142184405135

Pour consulter la version française intégrale de ce tableau, suivre ce lien :
*StatLink* ᴍᴪ⋙ http://dx.doi.org/10.1787/152830402855

309

[Part 1/1]

**Table S6h** Trends in mathematics since PISA 2003

Tableau S6h Évolution des performances en mathématiques depuis PISA 2003

| | Differences in mathematics performance between PISA 2006 and PISA 2003 (PISA 2006 – PISA 2003) | | | | | | | |
|---|---|---|---|---|---|---|---|---|
| | All students | | Males | | Females | | Gender difference (M – F) | |
| | Dif. | S.E. | Dif. | S.E. | Dif. | S.E. | Dif. | S.E. |
| **Adjudicated** | | | | | | | | |
| Belgium (Flemish Community) | **-10** | (4.5) | **-12** | (5.9) | -8 | (5.9) | -4 | (7.6) |
| Italy (Provincia Autonoma of Bolzano) | **-23** | (5.3) | **-29** | (6.6) | **-19** | (5.4) | *-11* | (6.1) |
| Italy (Provincia Lombardia) | **-33** | (10.0) | *-35* | (18.1) | **-30** | (8.6) | -5 | (20.1) |
| Italy (Provincia Piemonte) | -2 | (7.0) | -9 | (9.3) | 4 | (8.1) | -12 | (10.7) |
| Italy (Provincia Trento) | **-39** | (4.0) | **-51** | (5.6) | **-31** | (5.1) | **-20** | (7.3) |
| Italy (Provincia Veneto) | -1 | (8.4) | 10 | (12.4) | -12 | (10.3) | 21 | (16.1) |
| Spain (Basque Country) | -1 | (4.7) | 0 | (5.9) | -1 | (4.8) | 1 | (5.3) |
| Spain (Castile and Leon) | **12** | (5.4) | *11* | (6.9) | *11* | (6.3) | 0 | (7.5) |
| Spain (Catalonia) | -7 | (7.1) | -11 | (8.5) | -4 | (7.9) | -7 | (8.0) |
| United Kingdom (Scotland) | **-18** | (4.5) | **-14** | (5.5) | **-23** | (5.2) | 9 | (5.7) |
| **Non-adjudicated** | | | | | | | | |
| Belgium (French Community) | -7 | (6.9) | -8 | (9.7) | -7 | (7.8) | -2 | (11.1) |
| Belgium (German-Speaking Community) | -1 | (4.5) | 8 | (6.7) | -9 | (6.6) | *18* | (9.9) |

Note: Differences that are statistically significant at the 95% confidence level are indicated in bold and at the 90% confidence level are indicated in bold italic (see Annex A3). See Table 6.3b for national data.

*StatLink* ᴹᴸ http://dx.doi.org/10.1787/142184405135

Pour consulter la version française intégrale de ce tableau, suivre ce lien :
*StatLink* ᴹᴸ http://dx.doi.org/10.1787/152830402855

# This book has...

# StatLinks

## A service that delivers Excel® files from the printed page!

Look for the *StatLinks* at the bottom right-hand corner of the tables or graphs in this book. To download the matching Excel® spreadsheet, just type the link into your Internet browser, starting with the *http://dx.doi.org* prefix.
If you're reading the PDF e-book edition, and your PC is connected to the Internet, simply click on the link.
You'll find *StatLinks* appearing in more OECD books.

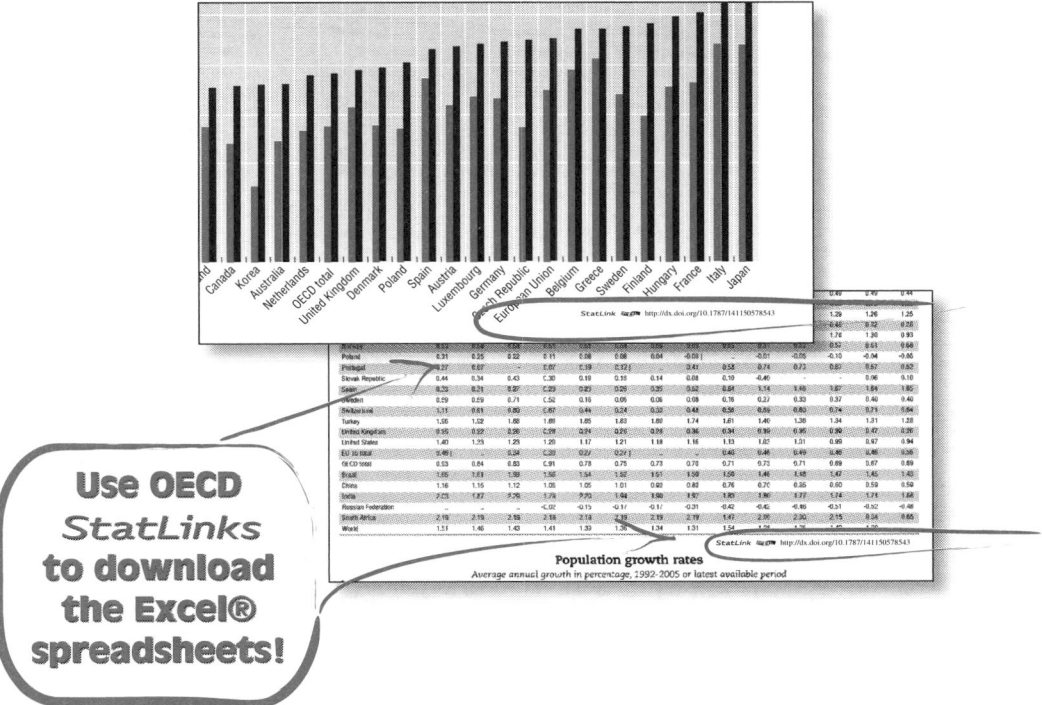

**Use OECD StatLinks to download the Excel® spreadsheets!**

*StatLinks* 🔳🄢🄻 : another innovation from OECD Publishing.

Learn more at *www.oecd.org/statistics/statlink*

We'd like to hear what you think about our publications and services like *StatLinks*: e-mail us at oecdpublishing@oecd.org

OECD PUBLICATIONS, 2, rue André-Pascal, 75775 PARIS CEDEX 16
PRINTED IN FRANCE
(98 2007 02 3 P) ISBN 978-92-64-04014-4 – No. 55884 2007

*Imprimé en France.* - JOUVE, 11, bd de Sébastopol, 75001 PARIS
N° 444349G - Dépôt légal : novembre 2007